Lecture Notes in Computer Science 8692

Commenced Publication in 1973
Founding and Former Series Editors:
Gerhard Goos, Juris Hartmanis, and Jan van Leeuwen

David Fleet   Tomas Pajdla   Bernt Schiele
Tinne Tuytelaars (Eds.)

Computer Vision – ECCV 2014

13th European Conference
Zurich, Switzerland, September 6-12, 2014
Proceedings, Part IV

 Springer

Preface

Welcome to the proceedings of the 2014 European Conference on Computer Vision (ECCV 2014) that was in Zurich, Switzerland. We are delighted to present this volume reflecting a strong and exciting program, the result of an extensive review process. In total, we received 1,444 paper submissions. Of these, 85 violated the ECCV submission guidelines and were rejected without review. Of the remainder, 363 were accepted (26,7%): 325 as posters (23,9%) and 38 as oral presentations (2,8%). This selection process was a combined effort of four program co-chairs (PCs), 53 area chairs (ACs), 803 Program Committee members and 247 additional reviewers.

As PCs we were primarily responsible for the design and execution of the review process. Beyond administrative rejections, we were not directly involved in acceptance decisions. Because the general co-chairs were permitted to submit papers, they played no role in the review process and were treated as any other author.

Acceptance decisions were made by the AC Committee. There were 53 ACs in total, selected by the PCs to provide sufficient technical expertise, geographical diversity (21 from Europe, 7 from Asia, and 25 from North America) and a mix of AC experience (7 had no previous AC experience, 18 had served as AC of a major international vision conference once since 2010, 8 had served twice, 13 had served three times, and 7 had served 4 times).

ACs were aided by 803 Program Committee members to whom papers were assigned for reviewing. There were 247 additional reviewers, each supervised by a Program Committee member. The Program Committee was based on suggestions from ACs, and committees from previous conferences. Google Scholar profiles were collected for all candidate Program Committee members and vetted by PCs. Having a large pool of Program Committee members for reviewing allowed us to match expertise while bounding reviewer loads. No more than nine papers were assigned to any one Program Committee member, with a maximum of six to graduate students.

The ECCV 2014 review process was double blind. Authors did not know the reviewers' identities, nor the ACs handling their paper(s). We did our utmost to ensure that ACs and reviewers did not know authors' identities, even though anonymity becomes difficult to maintain as more and more submissions appear concurrently on arXiv.org.

Particular attention was paid to minimizing potential conflicts of interest. Conflicts of interest between ACs, Program Committee members, and papers were based on authorship of ECCV 2014 submissions, on their home institutions, and on previous collaborations. To find institutional conflicts, all authors,

Program Committee members, and ACs were asked to list the Internet domains of their current institutions. To find collaborators, the DBLP (www.dblp.org) database was used to find any co-authored papers in the period 2010–2014.

We initially assigned approximately 100 papers to each AC, based on affinity scores from the Toronto Paper Matching System and authors' AC suggestions. ACs then bid on these, indicating their level of expertise. Based on these bids, and conflicts of interest, approximately 27 papers were assigned to each AC, for which they would act as the primary AC. The primary AC then suggested seven reviewers from the pool of Program Committee members (in rank order) for each paper, from which three were chosen per paper, taking load balancing and conflicts of interest into account.

Many papers were also assigned a secondary AC, either directly by the PCs, or as a consequence of the primary AC requesting the aid of an AC with complementary expertise. Secondary ACs could be assigned at any stage in the process, but in most cases this occurred about two weeks before the final AC meeting. Hence, in addition to their initial load of approximately 27 papers, each AC was asked to handle three to five more papers as a secondary AC; they were expected to read and write a short assessment of such papers. In addition, two of the 53 ACs were not directly assigned papers. Rather, they were available throughout the process to aid other ACs at any stage (e.g., with decisions, evaluating technical issues, additional reviews, etc.).

The initial reviewing period was three weeks long, after which reviewers provided reviews with preliminary recommendations. Three weeks is somewhat shorter than normal, but this did not seem to cause any unusual problems. With the generous help of several last-minute reviewers, each paper received three reviews.

Authors were then given the opportunity to rebut the reviews, primarily to identify any factual errors. Following this, reviewers and ACs discussed papers at length, after which reviewers finalized their reviews and gave a final recommendation to the ACs. Many ACs requested help from secondary ACs at this time.

Papers, for which rejection was clear and certain, based on the reviews and the AC's assessment, were identified by their primary ACs and vetted by a shadow AC prior to rejection. (These shadow ACs were assigned by the PCs.) All papers with any chance of acceptance were further discussed at the AC meeting. Those deemed "strong" by primary ACs (about 140 in total) were also assigned a secondary AC.

The AC meeting, with all but two of the primary ACs present, took place in Zurich. ACs were divided into 17 triplets for each morning, and a different set of triplets for each afternoon. Given the content of the three (or more) reviews along with reviewer recommendations, rebuttals, online discussions among reviewers and primary ACs, written input from and discussions with secondary ACs, the

AC triplets then worked together to resolve questions, calibrate assessments, and make acceptance decisions.

To select oral presentations, all strong papers, along with any others put forward by triplets (about 155 in total), were then discussed in four panels, each comprising four or five triplets. Each panel ranked these oral candidates, using four categories. Papers in the two top categories provided the final set of 38 oral presentations.

We want to thank everyone involved in making the ECCV 2014 Program possible. First and foremost, the success of ECCV 2014 depended on the quality of papers submitted by authors, and on the very hard work of the reviewers, the Program Committee members and the ACs. We are particularly grateful to Kyros Kutulakos for his enormous software support before and during the AC meeting, to Laurent Charlin for the use of the Toronto Paper Matching System, and Chaohui Wang for help optimizing the assignment of papers to ACs. We also owe a debt of gratitude for the great support of Zurich local organizers, especially Susanne Keller and her team.

September 2014

David Fleet
Tomas Pajdla
Bernt Schiele
Tinne Tuytelaars

Organization

General Chairs

Luc Van Gool   ETH Zurich, Switzerland
Marc Pollefeys   ETH Zurich, Switzerland

Program Chairs

Tinne Tuytelaars   KU Leuven, Belgium
Bernt Schiele   MPI Informatics, Saarbrücken, Germany
Tomas Pajdla   CTU Prague, Czech Republic
David Fleet   University of Toronto, Canada

Local Arrangements Chairs

Konrad Schindler   ETH Zurich, Switzerland
Vittorio Ferrari   University of Edinburgh, UK

Workshop Chairs

Lourdes Agapito   University College London, UK
Carsten Rother   TU Dresden, Germany
Michael Bronstein   University of Lugano, Switzerland

Tutorial Chairs

Bastian Leibe   RWTH Aachen, Germany
Paolo Favaro   University of Bern, Switzerland
Christoph Lampert   IST Austria

Poster Chair

Helmut Grabner   ETH Zurich, Switzerland

Publication Chairs

Mario Fritz   MPI Informatics, Saarbrücken, Germany
Michael Stark   MPI Informatics, Saarbrücken, Germany

Demo Chairs

Davide Scaramuzza   University of Zurich, Switzerland
Jan-Michael Frahm   University of North Carolina at Chapel Hill,
                           USA

Exhibition Chair

Tamar Tolcachier   University of Zurich, Switzerland

Industrial Liaison Chairs

Alexander Sorkine-Hornung Disney Research Zurich, Switzerland
Fatih Porikli   ANU, Australia

Student Grant Chair

Seon Joo Kim   Yonsei University, Korea

Air Shelters Accommodation Chair

Maros Blaha   ETH Zurich, Switzerland

Website Chairs

Lorenz Meier   ETH Zurich, Switzerland
Bastien Jacquet   ETH Zurich, Switzerland

Internet Chair

Thorsten Steenbock   ETH Zurich, Switzerland

Student Volunteer Chairs

Andrea Cohen   ETH Zurich, Switzerland
Ralf Dragon   ETH Zurich, Switzerland
Laura Leal-Taixé   ETH Zurich, Switzerland

Finance Chair

Amael Delaunoy   ETH Zurich, Switzerland

Conference Coordinator

Susanne H. Keller   ETH Zurich, Switzerland

Area Chairs

Lourdes Agapito	University College London, UK
Sameer Agarwal	Google Research, USA
Shai Avidan	Tel Aviv University, Israel
Alex Berg	UNC Chapel Hill, USA
Yuri Boykov	University of Western Ontario, Canada
Thomas Brox	University of Freiburg, Germany
Jason Corso	SUNY at Buffalo, USA
Trevor Darrell	UC Berkeley, USA
Fernando de la Torre	Carnegie Mellon University, USA
Frank Dellaert	Georgia Tech, USA
Alexei Efros	UC Berkeley, USA
Vittorio Ferrari	University of Edinburgh, UK
Andrew Fitzgibbon	Microsoft Research, Cambridge, UK
JanMichael Frahm	UNC Chapel Hill, USA
Bill Freeman	Massachusetts Institute of Technology, USA
Peter Gehler	Max Planck Institute for Intelligent Systems, Germany
Kristen Graumann	University of Texas at Austin, USA
Wolfgang Heidrich	University of British Columbia, Canada
Herve Jegou	Inria Rennes, France
Fredrik Kahl	Lund University, Sweden
Kyros Kutulakos	University of Toronto, Canada
Christoph Lampert	IST Austria
Ivan Laptev	Inria Paris, France
Kyuong Mu Lee	Seoul National University, South Korea
Bastian Leibe	RWTH Aachen, Germany
Vincent Lepetit	TU Graz, Austria
Hongdong Li	Australian National University
David Lowe	University of British Columbia, Canada
Greg Mori	Simon Fraser University, Canada
Srinivas Narasimhan	Carnegie Mellon University, PA, USA
Nassir Navab	TU Munich, Germany
Ko Nishino	Drexel University, USA
Maja Pantic	Imperial College London, UK
Patrick Perez	Technicolor Research, Rennes, France
Pietro Perona	California Institute of Technology, USA
Ian Reid	University of Adelaide, Australia
Stefan Roth	TU Darmstadt, Germany
Carsten Rother	TU Dresden, Germany
Sudeep Sarkar	University of South Florida, USA
Silvio Savarese	Stanford University, USA
Christoph Schnoerr	Heidelberg University, Germany
Jamie Shotton	Microsoft Research, Cambridge, UK

Kaleem Siddiqi	McGill, Canada
Leonid Sigal	Disney Research, Pittsburgh, PA, USA
Noah Snavely	Cornell, USA
Raquel Urtasun	University of Toronto, Canada
Andrea Vedaldi	University of Oxford, UK
Jakob Verbeek	Inria Rhone-Alpes, France
Xiaogang Wang	Chinese University of Hong Kong, SAR China
Ming-Hsuan Yang	UC Merced, CA, USA
Lihi Zelnik-Manor	Technion, Israel
Song-Chun Zhu	UCLA, USA
Todd Zickler	Harvard, USA

Program Committee

Gaurav Aggarwal	Joao Barreto	Kristin Branson
Amit Agrawal	Jonathan Barron	Steven Branson
Haizhou Ai	Adrien Bartoli	Francois Bremond
Ijaz Akhter	Arslan Basharat	Michael Bronstein
Karteek Alahari	Dhruv Batra	Gabriel Brostow
Alexandre Alahi	Luis Baumela	Michael Brown
Andrea Albarelli	Maximilian Baust	Matthew Brown
Saad Ali	Jean-Charles Bazin	Marcus Brubaker
Jose M. Alvarez	Loris Bazzani	Andres Bruhn
Juan Andrade-Cetto	Chris Beall	Joan Bruna
Bjoern Andres	Vasileios Belagiannis	Aurelie Bugeau
Mykhaylo Andriluka	Csaba Beleznai	Darius Burschka
Elli Angelopoulou	Moshe Ben-ezra	Ricardo Cabral
Roland Angst	Ohad Ben-Shahar	Jian-Feng Cai
Relja Arandjelovic	Ismail Ben Ayed	Neill D.F. Campbell
Ognjen Arandjelovic	Rodrigo Benenson	Yong Cao
Helder Araujo	Ryad Benosman	Barbara Caputo
Pablo Arbelez	Tamara Berg	Joao Carreira
Vasileios Argyriou	Margrit Betke	Jan Cech
Antonis Argyros	Ross Beveridge	Jinxiang Chai
Kalle Astroem	Bir Bhanu	Ayan Chakrabarti
Vassilis Athitsos	Horst Bischof	Tat-Jen Cham
Yannis Avrithis	Arijit Biswas	Antoni Chan
Yusuf Aytar	Andrew Blake	Manmohan Chandraker
Xiang Bai	Aaron Bobick	Vijay Chandrasekhar
Luca Ballan	Piotr Bojanowski	Hong Chang
Yingze Bao	Ali Borji	Ming-Ching Chang
Richard Baraniuk	Terrance Boult	Rama Chellappa
Adrian Barbu	Lubomir Bourdev	Chao-Yeh Chen
Kobus Barnard	Patrick Bouthemy	David Chen
Connelly Barnes	Edmond Boyer	Hwann-Tzong Chen

Tsuhan Chen
Xilin Chen
Chao Chen
Longbin Chen
Minhua Chen
Anoop Cherian
Liang-Tien Chia
Tat-Jun Chin
Sunghyun Cho
Minsu Cho
Nam Ik Cho
Wongun Choi
Mario Christoudias
Wen-Sheng Chu
Yung-Yu Chuang
Ondrej Chum
James Clark
Brian Clipp
Isaac Cohen
John Collomosse
Bob Collins
Tim Cootes
David Crandall
Antonio Criminisi
Naresh Cuntoor
Qieyun Dai
Jifeng Dai
Kristin Dana
Kostas Daniilidis
Larry Davis
Andrew Davison
Goksel Dedeoglu
Koichiro Deguchi
Alberto Del Bimbo
Alessio Del Bue
Hervé Delingette
Andrew Delong
Stefanie Demirci
David Demirdjian
Jia Deng
Joachim Denzler
Konstantinos Derpanis
Thomas Deselaers
Frederic Devernay
Michel Dhome

Anthony Dick
Ajay Divakaran
Santosh Kumar Divvala
Minh Do
Carl Doersch
Piotr Dollar
Bin Dong
Weisheng Dong
Michael Donoser
Gianfranco Doretto
Matthijs Douze
Bruce Draper
Mark Drew
Bertram Drost
Lixin Duan
Jean-Luc Dugelay
Enrique Dunn
Pinar Duygulu
Jan-Olof Eklundh
James H. Elder
Ian Endres
Olof Enqvist
Markus Enzweiler
Aykut Erdem
Anders Eriksson
Ali Eslami
Irfan Essa
Francisco Estrada
Bin Fan
Quanfu Fan
Jialue Fan
Sean Fanello
Ali Farhadi
Giovanni Farinella
Ryan Farrell
Alireza Fathi
Paolo Favaro
Michael Felsberg
Pedro Felzenszwalb
Rob Fergus
Basura Fernando
Frank Ferrie
Sanja Fidler
Boris Flach
Francois Fleuret

David Fofi
Wolfgang Foerstner
David Forsyth
Katerina Fragkiadaki
Jean-Sebastien Franco
Friedrich Fraundorfer
Mario Fritz
Yun Fu
Pascal Fua
Hironobu Fujiyoshi
Yasutaka Furukawa
Ryo Furukawa
Andrea Fusiello
Fabio Galasso
Juergen Gall
Andrew Gallagher
David Gallup
Arvind Ganesh
Dashan Gao
Shenghua Gao
James Gee
Andreas Geiger
Yakup Genc
Bogdan Georgescu
Guido Gerig
David Geronimo
Theo Gevers
Bernard Ghanem
Andrew Gilbert
Ross Girshick
Martin Godec
Guy Godin
Roland Goecke
Michael Goesele
Alvina Goh
Bastian Goldluecke
Boqing Gong
Yunchao Gong
Raghuraman Gopalan
Albert Gordo
Lena Gorelick
Paulo Gotardo
Stephen Gould
Venu Madhav Govindu
Helmut Grabner

Roger Grosse
Matthias Grundmann
Chunhui Gu
Xianfeng Gu
Jinwei Gu
Sergio Guadarrama
Matthieu Guillaumin
Jean-Yves Guillemaut
Hatice Gunes
Ruiqi Guo
Guodong Guo
Abhinav Gupta
Abner Guzman Rivera
Gregory Hager
Ghassan Hamarneh
Bohyung Han
Tony Han
Jari Hannuksela
Tatsuya Harada
Mehrtash Harandi
Bharath Hariharan
Stefan Harmeling
Tal Hassner
Daniel Hauagge
Søren Hauberg
Michal Havlena
James Hays
Kaiming He
Xuming He
Martial Hebert
Felix Heide
Jared Heinly
Hagit Hel-Or
Lionel Heng
Philipp Hennig
Carlos Hernandez
Aaron Hertzmann
Adrian Hilton
David Hogg
Derek Hoiem
Byung-Woo Hong
Anthony Hoogs
Joachim Hornegger
Timothy Hospedales
Wenze Hu

Zhe Hu
Gang Hua
Xian-Sheng Hua
Dong Huang
Gary Huang
Heng Huang
Sung Ju Hwang
Wonjun Hwang
Ivo Ihrke
Nazli Ikizler-Cinbis
Slobodan Ilic
Horace Ip
Michal Irani
Hiroshi Ishikawa
Laurent Itti
Nathan Jacobs
Max Jaderberg
Omar Javed
C.V. Jawahar
Bruno Jedynak
Hueihan Jhuang
Qiang Ji
Hui Ji
Kui Jia
Yangqing Jia
Jiaya Jia
Hao Jiang
Zhuolin Jiang
Sam Johnson
Neel Joshi
Armand Joulin
Frederic Jurie
Ioannis Kakadiaris
Zdenek Kalal
Amit Kale
Joni-Kristian
    Kamarainen
George Kamberov
Kenichi Kanatani
Sing Bing Kang
Vadim Kantorov
Jörg Hendrik Kappes
Leonid Karlinsky
Zoltan Kato
Hiroshi Kawasaki

Verena Kaynig
Cem Keskin
Margret Keuper
Daniel Keysers
Sameh Khamis
Fahad Khan
Saad Khan
Aditya Khosla
Martin Kiefel
Gunhee Kim
Jaechul Kim
Seon Joo Kim
Tae-Kyun Kim
Byungsoo Kim
Benjamin Kimia
Kris Kitani
Hedvig Kjellstrom
Laurent Kneip
Reinhard Koch
Kevin Koeser
Ullrich Koethe
Effrosyni Kokiopoulou
Iasonas Kokkinos
Kalin Kolev
Vladimir Kolmogorov
Vladlen Koltun
Nikos Komodakis
Piotr Koniusz
Peter Kontschieder
Ender Konukoglu
Sanjeev Koppal
Hema Koppula
Andreas Koschan
Jana Kosecka
Adriana Kovashka
Adarsh Kowdle
Josip Krapac
Dilip Krishnan
Zuzana Kukelova
Brian Kulis
Neeraj Kumar
M. Pawan Kumar
Cheng-Hao Kuo
In So Kweon
Junghyun Kwon

Junseok Kwon
Simon Lacoste-Julien
Shang-Hong Lai
Jean-François Lalonde
Tian Lan
Michael Langer
Doug Lanman
Diane Larlus
Longin Jan Latecki
Svetlana Lazebnik
Laura Leal-Taixé
Erik Learned-Miller
Honglak Lee
Yong Jae Lee
Ido Leichter
Victor Lempitsky
Frank Lenzen
Marius Leordeanu
Thomas Leung
Maxime Lhuillier
Chunming Li
Fei-Fei Li
Fuxin Li
Rui Li
Li-Jia Li
Chia-Kai Liang
Shengcai Liao
Joerg Liebelt
Jongwoo Lim
Joseph Lim
Ruei-Sung Lin
Yen-Yu Lin
Zhouchen Lin
Liang Lin
Haibin Ling
James Little
Baiyang Liu
Ce Liu
Feng Liu
Guangcan Liu
Jingen Liu
Wei Liu
Zicheng Liu
Zongyi Liu
Tyng-Luh Liu

Xiaoming Liu
Xiaobai Liu
Ming-Yu Liu
Marcus Liwicki
Stephen Lombardi
Roberto Lopez-Sastre
Manolis Lourakis
Brian Lovell
Chen Change Loy
Jiangbo Lu
Jiwen Lu
Simon Lucey
Jiebo Luo
Ping Luo
Marcus Magnor
Vijay Mahadevan
Julien Mairal
Michael Maire
Subhransu Maji
Atsuto Maki
Yasushi Makihara
Roberto Manduchi
Luca Marchesotti
Aleix Martinez
Bogdan Matei
Diana Mateus
Stefan Mathe
Yasuyuki Matsushita
Iain Matthews
Kevin Matzen
Bruce Maxwell
Stephen Maybank
Walterio Mayol-Cuevas
David McAllester
Gerard Medioni
Christopher Mei
Paulo Mendonca
Thomas Mensink
Domingo Mery
Ajmal Mian
Branislav Micusik
Ondrej Miksik
Anton Milan
Majid Mirmehdi
Anurag Mittal

Hossein Mobahi
Pranab Mohanty
Pascal Monasse
Vlad Morariu
Philippos Mordohai
Francesc Moreno-Noguer
Luce Morin
Nigel Morris
Bryan Morse
Eric Mortensen
Yasuhiro Mukaigawa
Lopamudra Mukherjee
Vittorio Murino
David Murray
Sobhan Naderi Parizi
Hajime Nagahara
Laurent Najman
Karthik Nandakumar
Fabian Nater
Jan Neumann
Lukas Neumann
Ram Nevatia
Richard Newcombe
Minh Hoai Nguyen
Bingbing Ni
Feiping Nie
Juan Carlos Niebles
Marc Niethammer
Claudia Nieuwenhuis
Mark Nixon
Mohammad Norouzi
Sebastian Nowozin
Matthew O'Toole
Peter Ochs
Jean-Marc Odobez
Francesca Odone
Eyal Ofek
Sangmin Oh
Takahiro Okabe
Takayuki Okatani
Aude Oliva
Carl Olsson
Bjorn Ommer
Magnus Oskarsson
Wanli Ouyang

Geoffrey Oxholm
Mustafa Ozuysal
Nicolas Padoy
Caroline Pantofaru
Nicolas Papadakis
George Papandreou
Nikolaos
   Papanikolopoulos
Nikos Paragios
Devi Parikh
Dennis Park
Vishal Patel
Ioannis Patras
Vladimir Pavlovic
Kim Pedersen
Marco Pedersoli
Shmuel Peleg
Marcello Pelillo
Tingying Peng
A.G. Amitha Perera
Alessandro Perina
Federico Pernici
Florent Perronnin
Vladimir Petrovic
Tomas Pfister
Jonathon Phillips
Justus Piater
Massimo Piccardi
Hamed Pirsiavash
Leonid Pishchulin
Robert Pless
Thomas Pock
Jean Ponce
Gerard Pons-Moll
Ronald Poppe
Andrea Prati
Victor Prisacariu
Kari Pulli
Yu Qiao
Lei Qin
Novi Quadrianto
Rahul Raguram
Varun Ramakrishna
Srikumar Ramalingam
Narayanan Ramanathan

Konstantinos
   Rapantzikos
Michalis Raptis
Nalini Ratha
Avinash Ravichandran
Michael Reale
Dikpal Reddy
James Rehg
Jan Reininghaus
Xiaofeng Ren
Jerome Revaud
Morteza Rezanejad
Hayko Riemenschneider
Tammy Riklin Raviv
Antonio Robles-Kelly
Erik Rodner
Emanuele Rodola
Mikel Rodriguez
Marcus Rohrbach
Javier Romero
Charles Rosenberg
Bodo Rosenhahn
Arun Ross
Samuel Rota Bul
Peter Roth
Volker Roth
Anastasios Roussos
Sebastien Roy
Michael Rubinstein
Olga Russakovsky
Bryan Russell
Michael S. Ryoo
Mohammad Amin
   Sadeghi
Kate Saenko
Albert Ali Salah
Imran Saleemi
Mathieu Salzmann
Conrad Sanderson
Aswin
   Sankaranarayanan
Benjamin Sapp
Radim Sara
Scott Satkin
Imari Sato

Yoichi Sato
Bogdan Savchynskyy
Hanno Scharr
Daniel Scharstein
Yoav Y. Schechner
Walter Scheirer
Kevin Schelten
Frank Schmidt
Uwe Schmidt
Julia Schnabel
Alexander Schwing
Nicu Sebe
Shishir Shah
Mubarak Shah
Shiguang Shan
Qi Shan
Ling Shao
Abhishek Sharma
Viktoriia Sharmanska
Eli Shechtman
Yaser Sheikh
Alexander Shekhovtsov
Chunhua Shen
Li Shen
Yonggang Shi
Qinfeng Shi
Ilan Shimshoni
Takaaki Shiratori
Abhinav Shrivastava
Behjat Siddiquie
Nathan Silberman
Karen Simonyan
Richa Singh
Vikas Singh
Sudipta Sinha
Josef Sivic
Dirk Smeets
Arnold Smeulders
William Smith
Cees Snoek
Eric Sommerlade
Alexander
   Sorkine-Hornung
Alvaro Soto
Richard Souvenir

Anuj Srivastava
Ioannis Stamos
Michael Stark
Chris Stauffer
Bjorn Stenger
Charles Stewart
Rainer Stiefelhagen
Juergen Sturm
Yusuke Sugano
Josephine Sullivan
Deqing Sun
Min Sun
Hari Sundar
Ganesh Sundaramoorthi
Kalyan Sunkavalli
Sabine Süsstrunk
David Suter
Tomas Svoboda
Rahul Swaminathan
Tanveer
  Syeda-Mahmood
Rick Szeliski
Raphael Sznitman
Yuichi Taguchi
Yu-Wing Tai
Jun Takamatsu
Hugues Talbot
Ping Tan
Robby Tan
Kevin Tang
Huixuan Tang
Danhang Tang
Marshall Tappen
Jean-Philippe Tarel
Danny Tarlow
Gabriel Taubin
Camillo Taylor
Demetri Terzopoulos
Christian Theobalt
Yuandong Tian
Joseph Tighe
Radu Timofte
Massimo Tistarelli
George Toderici
Sinisa Todorovic

Giorgos Tolias
Federico Tombari
Tatiana Tommasi
Yan Tong
Akihiko Torii
Antonio Torralba
Lorenzo Torresani
Andrea Torsello
Tali Treibitz
Rudolph Triebel
Bill Triggs
Roberto Tron
Tomasz Trzcinski
Ivor Tsang
Yanghai Tsin
Zhuowen Tu
Tony Tung
Pavan Turaga
Engin Türetken
Oncel Tuzel
Georgios Tzimiropoulos
Norimichi Ukita
Martin Urschler
Arash Vahdat
Julien Valentin
Michel Valstar
Koen van de Sande
Joost van de Weijer
Anton van den Hengel
Jan van Gemert
Daniel Vaquero
Kiran Varanasi
Mayank Vatsa
Ashok Veeraraghavan
Olga Veksler
Alexander Vezhnevets
Rene Vidal
Sudheendra
  Vijayanarasimhan
Jordi Vitria
Christian Vogler
Carl Vondrick
Sven Wachsmuth
Stefan Walk
Chaohui Wang

Jingdong Wang
Jue Wang
Ruiping Wang
Kai Wang
Liang Wang
Xinggang Wang
Xin-Jing Wang
Yang Wang
Heng Wang
Yu-Chiang Frank Wang
Simon Warfield
Yichen Wei
Yair Weiss
Gordon Wetzstein
Oliver Whyte
Richard Wildes
Christopher Williams
Lior Wolf
Kwan-Yee Kenneth
  Wong
Oliver Woodford
John Wright
Changchang Wu
Xinxiao Wu
Ying Wu
Tianfu Wu
Yang Wu
Yingnian Wu
Jonas Wulff
Yu Xiang
Tao Xiang
Jianxiong Xiao
Dong Xu
Li Xu
Yong Xu
Kota Yamaguchi
Takayoshi Yamashita
Shuicheng Yan
Jie Yang
Qingxiong Yang
Ruigang Yang
Meng Yang
Yi Yang
Chih-Yuan Yang
Jimei Yang

Bangpeng Yao	Stefanos Zafeiriou	Weishi Zheng
Angela Yao	Hongbin Zha	Bo Zheng
Dit-Yan Yeung	Lei Zhang	Changyin Zhou
Alper Yilmaz	Junping Zhang	Huiyu Zhou
Lijun Yin	Shaoting Zhang	Kevin Zhou
Xianghua Ying	Xiaoqin Zhang	Bolei Zhou
Kuk-Jin Yoon	Guofeng Zhang	Feng Zhou
Shiqi Yu	Tianzhu Zhang	Jun Zhu
Stella Yu	Ning Zhang	Xiangxin Zhu
Jingyi Yu	Lei Zhang	Henning Zimmer
Junsong Yuan	Li Zhang	Karel Zimmermann
Lu Yuan	Bin Zhao	Andrew Zisserman
Alan Yuille	Guoying Zhao	Larry Zitnick
Ramin Zabih	Ming Zhao	Daniel Zoran
Christopher Zach	Yibiao Zhao	

Additional Reviewers

Austin Abrams	Lukas Bossard	Victor Escorcia
Hanno Ackermann	Katie Bouman	Sandro Esquivel
Daniel Adler	Hilton Bristow	Nicola Fioraio
Muhammed Zeshan	Daniel Canelhas	Michael Firman
Afzal	Olivier Canevet	Alex Fix
Pulkit Agrawal	Spencer Cappallo	Oliver Fleischmann
Edilson de Aguiar	Ivan Huerta Casado	Marco Fornoni
Unaiza Ahsan	Daniel Castro	David Fouhey
Amit Aides	Ishani Chakraborty	Vojtech Franc
Zeynep Akata	Chenyi Chen	Jorge Martinez G.
Jon Almazan	Sheng Chen	Silvano Galliani
David Altamar	Xinlei Chen	Pablo Garrido
Marina Alterman	Wei-Chen Chiu	Efstratios Gavves
Mohamed Rabie Amer	Hang Chu	Timnit Gebru
Manuel Amthor	Yang Cong	Georgios Giannoulis
Shawn Andrews	Sam Corbett-Davies	Clement Godard
Oisin Mac Aodha	Zhen Cui	Ankur Gupta
Federica Arrigoni	Maria A. Davila	Saurabh Gupta
Yuval Bahat	Oliver Demetz	Amirhossein Habibian
Luis Barrios	Meltem Demirkus	David Hafner
John Bastian	Chaitanya Desai	Tom S.F. Haines
Florian Becker	Pengfei Dou	Vladimir Haltakov
C. Fabian	Ralf Dragon	Christopher Ham
Benitez-Quiroz	Liang Du	Xufeng Han
Vinay Bettadapura	David Eigen	Stefan Heber
Brian G. Booth	Jakob Engel	Yacov Hel-Or

David Held

Benjamin Hell

Jan Heller

Anton van den Hengel

Robert Henschel

Steven Hickson

Michael Hirsch

Jan Hosang

Shell Hu

Zhiwu Huang

Daniel Huber

Ahmad Humayun

Corneliu Ilisescu

Zahra Iman

Thanapong Intharah

Phillip Isola

Hamid Izadinia

Edward Johns

Justin Johnson

Andreas Jordt

Anne Jordt

Cijo Jose

Daniel Jung

Meina Kan

Ben Kandel

Vasiliy Karasev

Andrej Karpathy

Jan Kautz

Changil Kim

Hyeongwoo Kim

Rolf Koehler

Daniel Kohlsdorf

Svetlana Kordumova

Jonathan Krause

Till Kroeger

Malte Kuhlmann

Ilja Kuzborskij

Alina Kuznetsova

Sam Kwak

Peihua Li

Michael Lam

Maksim Lapin

Gil Levi

Aviad Levis

Yan Li

Wenbin Li

Yin Li

Zhenyang Li

Pengpeng Liang

Jinna Lie

Qiguang Liu

Tianliang Liu

Alexander Loktyushin

Steven Lovegrove

Feng Lu

Jake Lussier

Xutao Lv

Luca Magri

Behrooz Mahasseni

Aravindh Mahendran

Siddharth Mahendran

Francesco Malapelle

Mateusz Malinowski

Santiago Manen

Timo von Marcard

Ricardo Martin-Brualla

Iacopo Masi

Roberto Mecca

Tomer Michaeli

Hengameh Mirzaalian

Kylia Miskell

Ishan Misra

Javier Montoya

Roozbeh Mottaghi

Panagiotis Moutafis

Oliver Mueller

Daniel Munoz

Rajitha Navarathna

James Newling

Mohamed Omran

Vicente Ordonez

Sobhan Naderi Parizi

Omkar Parkhi

Novi Patricia

Kuan-Chuan Peng

Bojan Pepikj

Federico Perazzi

Loic Peter

Alioscia Petrelli

Sebastian Polsterl

Alison Pouch

Vittal Premanchandran

James Pritts

Luis Puig

Julian Quiroga

Vignesh Ramanathan

Rene Ranftl

Mohammad Rastegari

S. Hussain Raza

Michael Reale

Malcolm Reynolds

Alimoor Reza

Christian Richardt

Marko Ristin

Beatrice Rossi

Rasmus Rothe

Nasa Rouf

Anirban Roy

Fereshteh Sadeghi

Zahra Sadeghipoor

Faraz Saedaar

Tanner Schmidt

Anna Senina

Lee Seversky

Yachna Sharma

Chen Shen

Javen Shi

Tomas Simon

Gautam Singh

Brandon M. Smith

Shuran Song

Mohamed Souiai

Srinath Sridhar

Abhilash Srikantha

Michael Stoll

Aparna Taneja

Lisa Tang

Moria Tau

J. Rafael Tena

Roberto Toldo

Manolis Tsakiris

Dimitrios Tzionas

Vladyslav Usenko

Danny Veikherman

Fabio Viola

Minh Vo
Christoph Vogel
Sebastian Volz
Jacob Walker
Li Wan
Chen Wang
Jiang Wang
Oliver Wang
Peng Wang
Jan Dirk Wegner
Stephan Wenger
Scott Workman
Chenglei Wu

Yuhang Wu
Fan Yang
Mark Yatskar
Bulent Yener
Serena Yeung
Kwang M. Yi
Gokhan Yildirim
Ryo Yonetani
Stanislav Yotov
Chong You
Quanzeng You
Fisher Yu
Pei Yu

Kaan Yucer
Clausius Zelenka
Xing Zhang
Xinhua Zhang
Yinda Zhang
Jiejie Zhu
Shengqi Zhu
Yingying Zhu
Yuke Zhu
Andrew Ziegler

Table of Contents

Vision

Poster Session 5

Schwarps: Locally Projective Image Warps Based on 2D Schwarzian Derivatives

Rahat Khan, Daniel Pizarro, and Adrien Bartoli

ISIT, UMR 6284 CNRS-UdA, Clermont-Ferrand, France

Abstract. Image warps -or just warps- capture the geometric deformation existing between two images of a deforming surface. The current approach to enforce a warp's smoothness is to penalize its second order partial derivatives. Because this favors locally affine warps, this fails to capture the local projective component of the image deformation. This may have a negative impact on applications such as image registration and deformable 3D reconstruction. We propose a novel penalty designed to smooth the warp while capturing the deformation's local projective structure. Our penalty is based on equivalents to the Schwarzian derivatives, which are projective differential invariants exactly preserved by homographies. We propose a methodology to derive a set of Partial Differential Equations with homographies as solutions. We call this system the Schwarzian equations and we explicitly derive them for 2D functions using differential properties of homographies. We name as Schwarp a warp which is estimated by penalizing the residual of Schwarzian equations. Experimental evaluation shows that Schwarps outperform existing warps in modeling and extrapolation power, and lead to far better results in Shape-from-Template and camera calibration from a deformable surface.

Keywords: Schwarzian Penalizer, Bending Energy, Projective Differential Invariants, Image Warps.

1 Introduction

Projective geometry studies the geometric properties of projective transformations. During the last 30 years, projective geometry has successfully modeled important problems in computer vision, such as image stitching [28], image registration [29] and Structure-from-Motion (SfM) [10,9]. These problems assume the scene is rigid. However, if the scene geometry deforms over time, the current tools from projective geometry cannot model it. They are thus insufficient for problems like Non-Rigid Structure-from-Motion (NRSfM) [30], Shape-from-Template[1] (SfT) [25] and non-rigid image registration [3]. In a deformable environment, a fundamental problem is the modeling of the image warp -or just warp-, the function which maps points between images of a deforming surface. A

---

[1] In SfT, the 3D shape of a deformable surface is computed from the warp between a template and an input image. The shape of the template is known a priori.

D. Fleet et al. (Eds.): ECCV 2014, Part IV, LNCS 8692, pp. 1–15, 2014.

warp is generally represented by a linear basis expansion such as the Thin-Plate Spline (TPS) [6], the tensor-product B-Spline (BS) [24], finite elements [23] and finite differences (as in optical flow) [11]. A warp is also generally assumed to be smooth or piecewise smooth. This is modeled by existing approaches as a penalty on the warp's derivatives. For instance, penalizing second order derivatives leads to the popular bending energy, which forces the warp to be locally affine. A direct consequence is that the local projective information cannot be captured by the warp. Interestingly, it was attempted to solve that problem by modeling the warp with rational basis expansion. This led to the Generalized TPS [5] and the NURBS warp [7]. Theoretically, rational warps can be smooth and capture the local projective structure. However, their main problem is that they are non-convex and may be unstable due to their rational structure. We propose a novel penalty which is able to smooth a warp while allowing it to capture the local projective structure. This penalty may be used to estimate *any* type of warp model. Therefore, it may be applied to linear basis expansions, and does not require the use of a rational warp. Our penalty is based on the theory of Projective Differential Geometry (PDG), which we argue is a fundamental tool in warp modeling. PDG is a branch of mathematics that studies the properties of projective transformations at an infinitesimal scale. So far, PDG has been used to a much smaller extent than projective geometry in computer vision [13,26]. An important result of PDG is the Schwarzian derivative [22]. It originated from the study of projective differential invariants, but also appears in many other fields of mathematics such as the dynamical system theory and differential equation solving. The Schwarzian derivative models cross-ratio at a differential level [22]. The cross-ratio of points is well-known in computer vision [17,14] as it represents a projective invariant between two images related by a homography. In $\mathbb{RP}_1$, cross-ratio is defined for 4 colinear points. In the differential cross-ratio the distances among these points are infinitesimal. The Schwarzian derivative is a differential operator that vanishes for functions that preserve the differential cross-ratio. The Schwarzian derivative is well defined in the 1D case [22,27]. However, we are interested in images and thus in the 2D case. Several extensions of the Schwarzian derivative to higher dimensions were proposed [15,19,21]. Computing Schwarzian derivatives of an image warp requires one to find a system of PDEs that, as in the case of the 1D Schwarzian derivative, has homographies as solutions. Unfortunately, it is far from straightforward to arrive from the existing multidimensional Schwarzians to the sought system of PDEs (see section 2.3 for details).

We bring two core contributions. The first one is a new derivation framework for the 1D Schwarzian derivative which extends to higher dimensions. In particular, we use our framework to explicitly derive a system of PDEs that we call the *2D Schwarzian equations*. Our second core contribution is the *Schwarp*, which is defined as an image warp which was estimated while penalizing our 2D Schwarzian equations, preserving local projective properties. The intuition underlying this penalizer is that a warp with small residuals for our 2D Schwarzian equations behaves locally like a homography. A Schwarp may be constructed

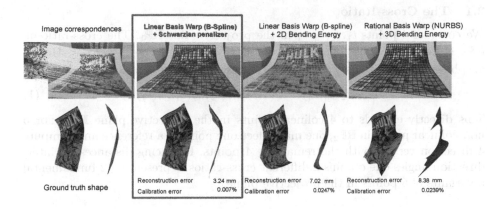

Fig. 1. Shape-from-Template (SfT) results for different warp models. The first column shows the input feature correspondences and the ground truth shape obtained by Structure-from-Motion for multiple images. In these examples, the BS-warp is used as the linear basis warp and the NURBS-warp as the rational basis warp. It is clear that the warp that uses Schwarzian equations as a penalizer improves accuracy over the other warps. SfT depends on the first derivative of the warp which is captured with our penalizer to a better extent.

with any warp representation and improves over classical approaches based on using the bending energy as a penalizer, favoring a locally affine behavior (see figure 1).

We report an extensive set of experimental results. Schwarps do better in two ways: *(i)* the warp's extrapolation power increases, especially in perspective imaging conditions, *(ii)* the accuracy of the warp's derivatives is improved by a large margin. We validated the impact of Schwarps on two applications: SfT [2] and camera calibration from a deformable surface [4].

2   Background on Projective Differential Invariants

Projective differential invariants have been studied in computer vision in a few previous papers [13,1]. In [13], the authors focus on qualitative local projective differential invariants whereas [1] focuses on non-algebraic planar curves. We now present one of the most fundamental projective differential invariants, the Schwarzian derivative which has rarely been studied in computer vision. We start our discussion with the cross-ratio of 4 points in the projective line and 5 points in the projective plane. We then give the differential version of the cross-ratio in the projective line, leading to the 1D Schwarzian derivative.

2.1   The Cross-Ratio

We consider 4 points t_1, t_2, t_3, t_4 in the projective line $\mathbb{RP}_1$. The cross-ratio on $\mathbb{RP}_1$ is defined by the following scalar $\Phi(t_1, t_2, t_3, t_4) = \frac{(t_1-t_3)(t_2-t_4)}{(t_2-t_3)(t_1-t_4)}$. Homographic transformations $\gamma : \mathbb{RP}_1 \to \mathbb{RP}_1$ preserve the cross-ratio:

$$\Phi(t_1, t_2, t_3, t_4) = \Phi(\gamma(t_1), \gamma(t_2), \gamma(t_3), \gamma(t_4)). \tag{1}$$

This directly extends to 4 colinear points in the projective plane $\mathbb{RP}_2$. For 5 non-colinear points in $\mathbb{RP}_2$, one may select one point as a reference and compute 4 direction vectors with the remaining 4 points. Replacing distances by inter-direction angles one obtains 2 different cross-ratios, representing 2 fundamental invariants of 5 points in the projective plane.

2.2   The 1D Schwarzian Derivative

The most popular projective differential invariant is the Schwarzian derivative [22]. We give its derivation as can be found in the literature. We consider a diffeomorphism γ which acts on 4 points $t_1, t_2, t_3, t_4 \in \mathbb{RP}_1$. We assume that the 4 points are spread so that t_2, t_3, t_4 can be defined by their distances to t_1 as a function of $\epsilon \in \mathbb{R}$: $t_2 = t_1 + \epsilon$, $t_3 = t_1 + 2\epsilon$ and $t_4 = t_1 + 3\epsilon$. So, the 4 points become $t_1, t_1 + \epsilon, t_1 + 2\epsilon, t_1 + 3\epsilon$ and they are related by the variable ϵ. The Schwarzian derivative measures the effect of γ on the cross-ratio as ϵ tends to zero. In other words, the Schwarzian derivative measures the cross-ratio of the points when they are infinitesimally close. To obtain the Schwarzian derivative one forms the Taylor expansion of Φ when ϵ goes to zero and keeps the first non-zero term of the expansion:

$$\Phi(\gamma(t_1), \gamma(t_2), \gamma(t_3), \gamma(t_4)) = \Phi(t_1, t_2, t_3, t_4) - \epsilon^2 S[\gamma](t_1) + O(\epsilon^3) \tag{2}$$

In the above equation $S[\gamma]$ is the Schwarzian derivative for $\mathbb{RP}_1$, defined by:

$$S[\gamma] = \frac{\gamma'''}{\gamma'} - \frac{3}{2}\left(\frac{\gamma''}{\gamma'}\right)^2 \tag{3}$$

The Schwarzian derivative $S[\gamma]$ has some remarkable properties. From equation (2) it is easy to see that if γ is a homography, $S[\gamma] = 0$ as the cross ratio is zero. Conversely, it can be proved that $S[\gamma] = 0$ implies that γ is a homography [21]. Therefore, homographies are the only solutions of the differential equation $S[\gamma] = 0$. With the Schwarzian derivative one can thus measure how close γ is to a homography. Unfortunately, this derivation of the Schwarzian derivative in $\mathbb{RP}_1$ does not readily extend to $\mathbb{RP}_2$.

2.3   Multidimensional Schwarzian Derivatives (MSDs)

The original Schwarzian derivative was only defined in 1D [12,8]. However, over the last few decades, mathematicians have extended it to higher dimensions. Ovsienko et al. [22] summarize a general two-step recipe to obtain MSDs for any group of diffeomorphisms:

1. Choose a group of diffeomorphisms and a subgroup G that has a 'nice' geometrical meaning (for instance, the projective group).
2. Find a G-invariant 1-cocycle on the group of diffeomorphisms.

Examples of MSDs can be found for different groups of diffeomorphisms. Oda [18] first defined an MSD for locally biholomorphic mappings. [19] proposed the conformal MSD whereas [20] proposed the 'Lagrangian Schwarzian' modeled on the group of symmetric matrices. The case of MSD for differential projective structures, which is the extension to higher dimensions of the 1D Schwarzian, has also been studied by several authors [15,16,21]. They provide as a general result for MSDs the 1-cocycle, that is a non-linear differential operator that vanishes for homographies. The 1-cocycle includes second order partial derivatives and rational terms. The 1-cocycle cannot be used to define the Schwarp as it also can vanish for other functions rather than homographies.

3 Schwarzian Equations in Two Dimensions

We propose to derive the Schwarzian equations, that is, a system of PDEs with homographies as solutions. Unlike MSDs that are described by the 1-cocycle, we define the multidimensional Schwarzian equations as a set of PDEs where each member of the set vanishes for homographies. Interestingly, our Schwarzian equations in 2D are quadratic second order PDEs. This allows us to optimize the Schwarp without using rational terms. We first show how to find the 1D Schwarzian derivative (3). We then use the same methodology to find the 2D Schwarzian equations.

3.1 The 1D Schwarzian Derivative

We define γ as a general projective function, formed by the ratio of two linear functions:

$$\gamma = \frac{\delta}{\zeta}, \quad \text{where} \quad \delta'' = 0, \quad \zeta'' = 0 \quad \text{and} \quad \zeta \neq 0. \tag{4}$$

By multiplying equation (4) with ζ and taking its third order derivatives we obtain the following PDE:

$$\gamma'''\zeta + 3\gamma''\zeta' = 0. \tag{5}$$

Differentiating equation (4) and multiplying by ζ^2 on both sides we obtain:

$$\gamma'\zeta^2 = \delta'\zeta - \delta\zeta'. \tag{6}$$

By differentiating equation (6) we obtain:

$$\gamma''\zeta^2 + 2\gamma'\zeta\zeta' = 0$$
$$\zeta' = -\frac{1}{2}\frac{\gamma''}{\gamma'}\zeta. \tag{7}$$

We substitute equation (7) in equation (5), and cancel ζ and ζ'

$$\gamma''' - \frac{3}{2}\frac{(\gamma'')^2}{\gamma'} = 0. \tag{8}$$

Dividing equation (8) by γ' gives the 1D Schwarzian derivative as can be verified by directly comparing it to equation (3). Multiplying equation (8) by γ', we arrive at the following third order quadratic PDE:

$$\gamma'\gamma''' - \frac{3}{2}(\gamma'')^2 = 0. \tag{9}$$

The main difference between equation (9) and the Schwarzian derivative is that equation (9) does not have the rational term. Despite that, both of them, have only homographies as solution.

3.2 2D Schwarzian Equations

We propose a system of PDEs that represent the 2D Schwarzian equations. This system has by construction homographies as solutions

We define function $\eta : (u,v)^\top \to (x,y)^\top$ as an homography:

$$\eta = \left(\eta^x \ \eta^y\right)^\top \quad \text{with} \quad \eta^x = \frac{\delta^x}{\zeta} \quad \eta^y = \frac{\delta^y}{\zeta} \quad \zeta \neq 0, \tag{10}$$

and where δ^x, δ^y and ζ are linear scalar functions whose second order partial derivatives vanish:

$$\delta^x_{uu} = \zeta_{uu} = \delta^y_{uu} = 0 \quad \delta^x_{vv} = \zeta_{vv} = \delta^y_{vv} = 0 \quad \delta^x_{uv} = \zeta_{uv} = \delta^y_{uv} = 0. \tag{11}$$

We first multiply η^x and η^y by ζ and differentiate them with respect to u:

$$\eta^x_u\zeta + \eta^x\zeta_u = \gamma_u \quad \eta^y_u\zeta + \eta^y\zeta_u = \delta_u. \tag{12}$$

We differentiate them again with respect to u using equations (11) to remove second order derivatives of δ^x, δ^y and ζ:

$$\eta^x_{uu}\zeta + 2\eta^x_u\zeta_u = 0 \quad \eta^y_{uu}\zeta + 2\eta^y_u\zeta_u = 0. \tag{13}$$

By solving for ζ_u in equation (13), we find the first 2D Schwarzian equation:

$$\frac{\eta^x_{uu}\zeta}{2\eta^x_u} = \frac{\eta^y_{uu}\zeta}{2\eta^y_u} \tag{14}$$

$$\boxed{\eta^x_{uu}\eta^y_u - \eta^y_{uu}\eta^x_u = 0.} \tag{15}$$

We now multiply η^x and η^y by ζ and we differentiate twice with respect to v:

$$\eta^x_{vv}\zeta + 2\eta^x_v\zeta_v = 0 \quad \eta^y_{vv}\zeta + 2\eta^y_v\zeta_v = 0. \tag{16}$$

Solving for ζ_v in equation (16) gives the second 2D Schwarzian equation:

$$\boxed{\eta_{vv}^x \eta_v^y - \eta_{vv}^y \eta_v^x = 0.}$$ (17)

We then take the partial derivatives of equations (12) with respect to v:

$$\eta_{uv}^x \zeta + \eta_u^x \zeta_v + \eta_v^x \zeta_u = 0 \qquad \eta_{uv}^y \zeta + \eta_u^y \zeta_v + \eta_v^y \zeta_u = 0.$$ (18)

Solving for ζ_v in equation (18) yields:

$$(\eta_{uv}^x \eta_u^y - \eta_{uv}^y \eta_u^x)\zeta + (\eta_v^x \eta_u^y - \eta_v^y \eta_u^x)\zeta_u = 0.$$ (19)

Multiplying the two equations in equation (13) by η_v^y and η_v^x respectively and subtracting them we obtain the following equation:

$$(\eta_{uu}^x \eta_v^y - \eta_{uu}^y \eta_v^x)\zeta - 2(\eta_v^x \eta_u^y - \eta_v^y \eta_u^x)\zeta_u = 0,$$ (20)

which we combine with equation (19) to remove ζ_u, giving the third 2D Schwarzian equation:

$$\boxed{(\eta_{uu}^x \eta_v^y - \eta_{uu}^y \eta_v^x) + 2(\eta_{uv}^x \eta_u^y - \eta_{uv}^y \eta_u^x) = 0.}$$ (21)

In a similar way we can obtain the fourth and last 2D Schwarzian equations by solving for ζ_v in equation (18) and combining the result with equation (16). The complete system of 4 2D Schwarzian equations is finally given by:

$$\text{2D-Schwarzian equations} \quad \begin{cases} S_1[\eta] = \eta_{uu}^x \eta_u^y - \eta_{uu}^y \eta_u^x = 0 \\ S_2[\eta] = \eta_{vv}^x \eta_v^y - \eta_{vv}^y \eta_v^x = 0 \\ S_3[\eta] = (\eta_{uu}^x \eta_v^y - \eta_{uu}^y \eta_v^x) + 2(\eta_{uv}^x \eta_u^y - \eta_{uv}^y \eta_u^x) = 0 \\ S_4[\eta] = (\eta_{vv}^x \eta_u^y - \eta_{vv}^y \eta_u^x) + 2(\eta_{uv}^x \eta_v^y - \eta_{uv}^y \eta_v^x) = 0. \end{cases}$$ (22)

In contrast with the third order 1D Schwarzian derivative, the 2D Schwarzian equations form a second order quadratic system of PDEs.

4 Modeling the Projection of Deforming Surfaces

The warp between two images of a plane is a homography. In that case, the 2D Schwarzian derivatives vanish, by definition. With a non-planar and possibly deforming surface, the image warp does not anymore satisfy the Schwarzian equations exactly. For a smooth surface deformation however, each small patch on the surface can be approximated by its tangent plane (see figure 2). The warp η can then be locally approximated by a homography between the projections of the tangent planes. The Schwarzian derivatives form differential invariants and we thus expect the system in equation (22) to have small residuals for the projection of infinitesimal planes.

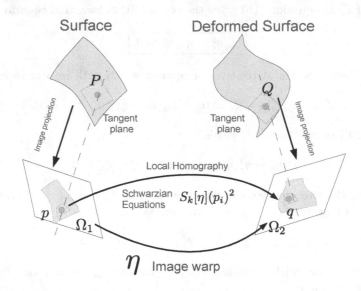

Fig. 2. The 2D Schwarzian derivatives have small residuals for the warp η between the images of a smooth deforming surface

4.1   The Schwarp

For an image warp $\eta : \Omega_1 \rightarrow \Omega_2$, the 2D Schwarzian derivatives measure how near is η from a homography infinitesimally at each point. We define the Schwarp as a warp whose 2D Schwarzian derivatives were penalized for its estimation. As a result the Schwarp can be smooth while preserving differential projective properties.

The Schwarp is defined as the solution of the following variational problem:

$$\min_{\eta} \epsilon_d[\eta] + \epsilon_s[\eta], \tag{23}$$

where $\epsilon_d[\eta]$ is a data term measuring registration error (for instance, transport error between point correspondences) and $\epsilon_s[\eta]$ is the Schwarzian penalizer:

$$\epsilon_s = \lambda \int_{\Omega} \left(S_1[\eta]^2 + S_2[\eta]^2 + S_3[\eta]^2 + S_4[\eta]^2 \right) d_{\Omega}, \tag{24}$$

where λ is a hyperparameter which weighs the influence of the Schwarzian derivatives over the data term. In practice we replace the integral in equation (24) with a sum over a discretization $\widetilde{\Omega}$ of the domain Ω:

$$\epsilon_s \approx \lambda \sum_{\mathbf{p}_i \in \widetilde{\Omega}} \sum_{k=1}^{4} S_k[\eta](\mathbf{p}_i)^2. \tag{25}$$

The Schwarzian penalty is quartic and non-convex. Solving the optimization problem (23) thus requires iterative optimization. We use the Levenberg-Marquardt algorithm.

5   Experimental Results

We compare Schwarp to state of the art warps, namely the BS-warp [24], TPS-warp [6], DP-warp [5] and NURBS-warp [7]. In table 1 we summarize the details of warps used in our experiments.

Table 1. Summary of warps used in our Experiments

Name	Warp Model	Penalizer
BS-warp	BS	Bending Energy
Schwarp	BS	Schwarzian Equations
TPS-warp	TPS	Bending Energy
DP-warp	DP	3D Bending Energy
NURBS-warp	NURBS	3D Bending Energy

5.1   Implementation Details

For the experiments with synthetic data, we generate a set of 100 images for each case while varying imaging conditions (pose and focal length) and present the average values for each of the criteria over the 100 images. We keep the resolution of the images at 640×480 pixels. We vary the focal length between 100 and 500 pixels. We fix the number of feature correspondences, control centers and a gaussian noise distribution (we vary the amount of noise for the same distribution). For all the other warps we use code publicly available from their authors.

5.2   Synthetic Data

We simulate images of rigid and deformable surfaces. In the rigid case, we use a plane and in the deformable case we wrap a surface around a longitudinal cut of a barrel. For both types of data, we examine the performance of all the warps against an increasing amount of noise, perspective and their sensitivity to the weight of the penalty. For the experiments with deformable surfaces, we add an additional experiment to compare them against an increasing amount of deformation. For all cases, we compare the warps based on three criteria: generalization error (ϵ_1), 1st derivative error (ϵ_2) and second derivative error (ϵ_3) compared to the ground truth. The generalization error is the transfer error measured in terms of RMSR (Root Mean Square Residual) between the warp and ground truth. This is computed over some points which were not used to estimate the warps. We give a relative error for the 1st and 2nd derivatives compared to ground truth.

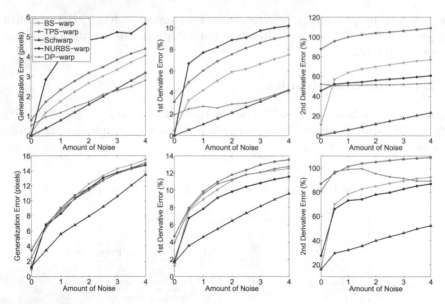

Fig. 3. Comparison of Schwarp with other warps against noise on synthetically generated images. The first and second rows are for the planar and deformable surfaces respectively.

Effect of Noise and Hyperparameter. We compute the warps with an increasing amount of noise and optimize the hyperparameter controlling smooothness in each case. Figure 3 presents the performance of all the warps against noise. In these experiments, Schwarp outperforms all the other warps in all criteria examined. This is true for both planar and deformable surfaces. As expected, the most significant improvement of Schwarp is in the case of 2nd derivatives. Schwarp does not penalize the bending energy and thus preserves the 2nd derivatives much better than any other warp that penalizes the bending energy.

To measure the sensitivities of the warps against the hyperparameter, we recompute all the warps as in the previous experiment. However, this time we do not optimize the hyperparameter in each case. Instead, we use the mean of the optimal hyperparameter of an image for all different noise level. This gives us 5 curves as in figure 3 but with larger errors since the hyperparameter is suboptimal for each case. For a given warp, the area between this new curve and the corresponding one in Figure 3 gives an estimate on a warp's sensitivity to the its hyperparameter. If this area is large, the warp is very sensitive to the hyperparameter. In table 2, we present the area between the two curves (with optimal and average hyperparameter) for all warps for planar and deformable case. It is clear from these results that Schwarp is the most stable against hyperparameter. In all cases, it undergoes the smallest deviation from the optimal curve.

Effect of Perspective. We compare the warps with a set of images with increasing perspective. To control the amount of perspective, we follow a single

Table 2. Sensitivities of the warps to their hyperparameter. The larger the number the more sensitive the warp to its hyperparameter.

Algorithms	Planar Case			Deformable Case		
	ϵ_1	ϵ_2	ϵ_3	ϵ_1	ϵ_2	ϵ_3
BS-warp	2.3948	0.0566	0.4630	10.2054	0.1172	0.4537
Schwarp	**0.0275**	**0.0006**	**0.0025**	**3.6637**	**0.0329**	**0.1098**
TPS-warp	2.0912	0.0470	0.1830	9.5280	0.0791	0.1895
DP-warp	10.1772	0.3194	1.2826	47.7706	0.1858	0.3079
NURBS-warp	0.4227	0.0216	0.3859	5.7904	0.1151	0.7170

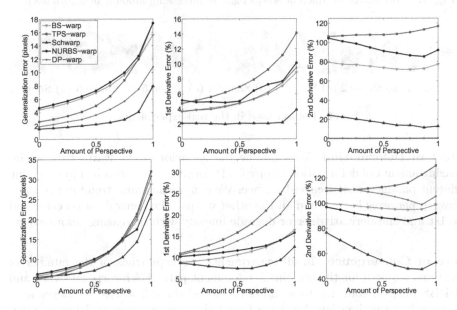

Fig. 4. Performance of the different warps against increasing amount of perspective. The first and second rows are for planar and deformable surfaces respectively.

parameter projection model that allows us to select the amount of perspective required. With this model, a point $P = [P_x, P_y, P_z]^\top$ is projected as:

$$\Pi_t(P) = \left((t+1)f\frac{P_x}{P_z + tf} \qquad (t+1)f\frac{P_y}{P_z + tf} \right)^\top. \qquad (26)$$

Equation (26) becomes orthographic projection when $t \to \infty$. Figure 4 shows that Schwarp outperforms all the other warps with a significant margin. The errors increase linearly first, and then quadratically, with increasing perspective. It is interesting to note that Schwarp models perspective better than the rational warps (DP-warp and NURBS-warp).

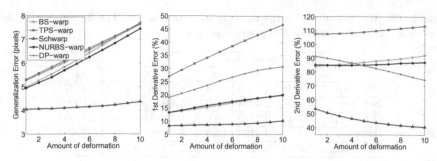

Fig. 5. Performance of different warps against increasing amount of deformation

(a) Shape 1 (b) Shape 2 (c) Shape 3 (d) Shape 4 (e) Shape 5 (f) Shape 6 (g) Shape 7

Fig. 6. Dataset used in the real experiments

Effect of Deformation. We examine the behavior of the warps with an increasing amount of deformation (figure 5). Deformation is controlled by changing different parameters of a curved surface. We can see a similar trend in this case: Schwarp performs better than all the other warps. The generalization error and the 1st and 2nd derivatives error degrade linearly with increasing deformation.

Rate of Convergence. In all experiments, we kept track of the number of iterations required for the non-linear refinement part of Schwarp, DP-warp and NURBS-warp to converge to a solution. Indeed these 3 warps use Levenberg-Marquardt for estimation. We have found that on an average Schwarp takes only 10-15 iterations to converge, whereas DP-warp and NURBS-warp require hundreds of iterations. This indicates that Schwarp is more stable numerically. This is due to the rational modeling of DP-warp and NURBS-warp.

5.3   Real Data

We compare the performance of the warps in different applications on real images. In Figure 6, we present the dataset used in the experiments. As a surface, we use a textured paper of size $210mm \times 297mm$. We deform the paper on several occasions and capture images of those deformations. The resolutions of these images are 3264×4928 pixels. The focal length used is 2534 pixels. For each deformation, we obtain the ground truth shape Ψ using Structure-from-Motion.

SfT. Here, we show the experimental results for SfT. In SfT, the shape of an image is inferred from the warp computed between a template and the image

Table 3. Reconstruction error (in mm) for SfT on the 7 images of Figure 6

	Shape 1	Shape 2	Shape 3	Shape 4	Shape 5	Shape 6	Shape 7
BS-warp	7.02	33.78	13.67	8.14	5.88	**10.42**	8.52
Schwarp	**3.24**	**30.02**	**10.49**	**8.08**	**2.06**	11.72	**7.99**
TPS-warp	21.08	46.20	18.81	10.41	17.19	15.46	11.88
DP-warp	16.95	43.74	14.05	10.26	6.82	13.62	11.28
NURBS-warp	8.38	45.69	15.56	10.10	6.70	15.78	12.46

Table 4. Relative calibration recovery error on the 7 images of Figure 6

	Shape 1	Shape 2	Shape 3	Shape 4	Shape 5	Shape 6	Shape 7
BS-warp	0.0247	0.0826	0.0475	**0.0267**	**0.0137**	0.0463	0.0063
Schwarp	**0.0071**	**0.0038**	0.0284	0.0275	**0.0137**	**0.0165**	**0.0055**
TPS-warp	0.0945	0.1793	0.0565	0.1287	0.2038	0.0712	0.0300
DP-warp	0.0577	0.1455	**0.0165**	0.1014	0.0512	0.0724	0.0263
NURBS-warp	0.0239	0.0985	0.0186	0.0798	0.0210	0.0561	0.0275

itself. In our implementation, we use a feature based approach to SfT. We use feature matching to find correspondences between the template and the target image and use those matches to compute the warp. Table 3 shows the reconstruction errors of SfT for each warp. The reconstruction error is computed between the reconstructed shape Ψ' and Ψ, using $\sum_{i,j\in\tilde{\Omega}}|\Psi'_{i,j} - \Psi_{i,j})|$, where $\tilde{\Omega}$ is the discretization of the domain. The errors are given in millimeters. In most cases, Schwarp outperforms the other warps. However, in one case, it gives the second best score after BS-warp.

Calibration in SfT. Calibration in SfT allows one to compute the focal length of the camera from the warp. We implemented the method proposed in [4]. We use all the computed warps for all the real images to recover the focal length($\hat{f}$). We compute the relative error from the true focal length f, using $\frac{|\hat{f}-f|}{f}$. The results are presented in Table 4. Here, our warp performs better than the other warps in 5 out of 7 cases.

6   Conclusion

In this paper, we have studied differential projective invariants and their application for modeling the projection of deforming surfaces. We have presented the 2D Schwarzian derivatives and we introduced a new type of penalty based on penalizing Schwarzian derivatives of the warp. Schwarzian derivatives model projective functions differentially. We have conducted experiments on real and simulated data. We have shown that Schwarps (Schwarzian penalized warps) notably improve accuracy in deformable surface reconstruction and camera calibration in SfT.

Acknowledgments. This research has received funding from the EU's FP7 ERC research grant 307483 FLEXABLE.

References

1. Astrom, K.: Fundamental limitations on projective invariants of planar curves. IEEE Transactions on Pattern Analysis and Machine Intelligence 17(1), 77–81 (1995)
2. Bartoli, A., Gérard, Y., Chadebecq, F., Collins, T.: On template-based reconstruction from a single view: Analytical solutions and proofs of well-posedness for developable, isometric and conformal surfaces. In: Computer Vision and Pattern Recognition (2012)
3. Bartoli, A., Zisserman, A.: Direct estimation of non-rigid registrations. In: British Machine Vision Conference (2004)
4. Bartoli, A., Collins, T.: Template-based isometric deformable 3D reconstruction with sampling-based focal length self-calibration. In: Computer Vision and Pattern Recognition (2013)
5. Bartoli, A., Perriollat, M., Chambon, S.: Generalized thin-plate spline warps. International Journal of Computer Vision 88(1), 85–110 (2010)
6. Bookstein, F.L.: Principal warps: Thin-plate splines and the decomposition of deformations. IEEE Transaction on Pattern Analysis Machine Intelligence 11(6), 567–585 (1989)
7. Brunet, F., Bartoli, A., Navab, N., Malgouyres, R.: NURBS warps. In: British Machine Vision Conference (2009)
8. Cayley, A.: On the Schwarzian derivatives and the polyhedral functions. Transaction of Cambridge Philosophical Society 13 (1880)
9. Faugeras, O.D., Luong, Q.T., Papadopoulo, T.: The Geometry of Multiple Images: The Laws that Govern the Formation of Multiple Images of a Scene and Some of Their Applications. MIT Press (2001)
10. Hartley, R.I., Zisserman, A.: Multiple View Geometry in Computer Vision. Cambridge University Press (2003) ISBN: 0521623049
11. Horn, B., Schunck, B.: Determining optical flow. Artificial Intelligence 17, 185–203 (1981)
12. Kummer, E.E.: Über die hypergeometrische reihe. Journal Fur Die Reine Und Angewandte Mathematik 1836(15), 39–83 (1836)
13. Lazebnik, S., Ponce, J.: The local projective shape of smooth surfaces and their outlines. International Journal of Computer Vision 63, 65–83 (2005)
14. Lei, G.: Recognition of planar objects in 3D space from single perspective views using cross ratio. IEEE Transactions on Robotics and Automation 6(4), 432–437 (1990)
15. Matsumoto, K., Sasaki, T., Yoshida, M.: Recent progress of gauss-schwartz theory and related geometric structures. Memoirs of the Faculty of Science 47(2), 283–381 (1993)
16. Molzon, R., Mortensen, K.P.: The Schwarzian derivative for maps between manifolds with complex projective connections. Transactions of the American Mathematical Society 348(8), 3015–3036 (1996)
17. Mundy, J.L., Zisserman, A.: Geometric invariance in computer vision. MIT Press (1992)

18. Oda, T.: On schwarzian derivatives in several variables. Kokyuroku Research Institute for Mathematical Sciences 226, 82–85 (1974) (in Japanese)
19. Osgood, B., Stowe, D.: The Schwarzian derivative and conformal mapping of Riemannian manifolds. Duke Mathematical Journal 67(1), 57–99 (1992)
20. Ovsienko, V.: Lagrange Schwarzian derivative. Moscow University Mechanics Bulletin 44(6), 8–13 (1989)
21. Ovsienko, V., Tabachnikov, S.: Projective Differential Geometry Old and New: From the Schwarzian Derivative to the Cohomology of Diffeomorphism Groups. Cambridge University Press (2005)
22. Ovsienko, V., Tabachnikov, S.: What is...the Schwarzian derivative? North American Mathematical Society 56, 34–36 (2009)
23. Pilet, J., Lepetit, V., Fua, P.: Fast non-rigid surface detection, registration and realistic augmentation. International Journal of Computer Vision 76(2), 109–122 (2007)
24. Rueckert, D., Sonoda, L.I., Hayes, C., Hill, D.L.G., Leach, M.O., Hawkes, D.J.: Nonrigid registration using free-form deformations: Application to breast MR images. IEEE Transactions on Medical Imaging 18, 712–721 (1999)
25. Salzmann, M., Pilet, J., Ilic, S., Fua, P.: Surface deformation models for nonrigid 3D shape recovery. Transactions on Pattern Analysis and Machine Intelligence 29(8), 1481–1487 (2007)
26. Schmid, C., Zisserman, A.: The geometry and matching of lines and curves over multiple views. International Journal of Computer Vision 40, 199–233 (2000)
27. Singer, D.: Stable orbits and bifurcation of maps of the interval. SIAM Journal of Applied Mathematics 35(2), 260–267 (1978)
28. Szeliski, R.: Image alignment and stitching: A tutorial. Foundations and Trends in Computer Graphics and Computer Vision 2(1), 1–104 (2006)
29. Torr, P.: MLESAC: A new robust estimator with application to estimating image geometry. Computer Vision and Image Understanding 78, 138–156 (2000)
30. Torresani, L., Hertzmann, A., Bregler, C.: Non-rigid structure-from-motion: Estimating shape and motion with hierarchical priors. IEEE Transactions on Pattern Analysis and Machine Intelligence 30(5), 878–892 (2008)

gDLS: A Scalable Solution
to the Generalized Pose and Scale Problem

Chris Sweeney, Victor Fragoso, Tobias Höllerer, and Matthew Turk

University of California, Santa Barbara, USA
{cmsweeney,vfragoso,holl,mturk}@cs.ucsb.edu

Abstract. In this work, we present a scalable least-squares solution for computing a seven degree-of-freedom similarity transform. Our method utilizes the generalized camera model to compute relative rotation, translation, and scale from four or more 2D-3D correspondences. In particular, structure and motion estimations from monocular cameras lack scale without specific calibration. As such, our methods have applications in loop closure in visual odometry and registering multiple structure from motion reconstructions where scale must be recovered. We formulate the generalized pose and scale problem as a minimization of a least squares cost function and solve this minimization without iterations or initialization. Additionally, we obtain all minima of the cost function. The order of the polynomial system that we solve is independent of the number of points, allowing our overall approach to scale favorably. We evaluate our method experimentally on synthetic and real datasets and demonstrate that our methods produce higher accuracy similarity transform solutions than existing methods.

1 Introduction

The problem of determining camera position and orientation given a set of correspondences between image observations and known 3D points is a fundamental problem in computer vision. This set of problems has a wide range of applications in computer vision, including camera calibration, object tracking, simultaneous localization and mapping (SLAM), structure-from-motion (SfM), and augmented reality. In the case of a calibrated camera, several minimal methods exist to determine the camera pose from three correspondences (P3P) [9, 13]. The Perspective-n-Point (PnP) problem determines the pose for a single calibrated camera from n 2D-3D observations [10,16]. These methods, however, are all designed for localization of a single perspective camera and there are few methods that are able to jointly utilize information from many cameras simultaneously. As illustrated in Figure 1a, multiple cameras (or multiple images from a single moving camera) can be described with the generalized camera model [20]. However, the internal scale of each generalized camera is not guaranteed to be consistent, so the relative scale between the generalized cameras must be recovered in addition to the rotation and translation.

In this paper, we propose a new solution for the seven degree-of-freedom (d.o.f.) generalized pose-and-scale problem for multiple cameras. The generalized

D. Fleet et al. (Eds.): ECCV 2014, Part IV, LNCS 8692, pp. 16–31, 2014.

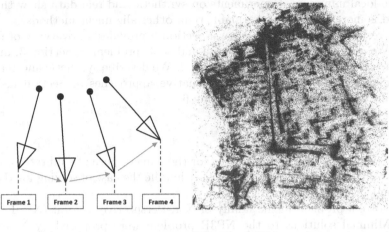

(a) SLAM motion.

(b) Two SfM reconstructions of Dubrovnik [17] (one red, one blue) are accurately aligned with our method.

Fig. 1. (a) The generalized camera model represents a set of image rays that do not need to share a common origin. This allows for multiple cameras, or multiple images from a single camera in motion to be modeled with the generalized camera model. We use the generalized camera model to solve the generalized pose-and-scale problem. (b) Our scalable method can be used to accurately align two SfM reconstructions containing millions of points.

pose-and-scale problem is equivalent to the problem of estimating a similarity transform between two coordinate systems. Our method is a generalization of the PnP problem to multiple cameras which are represented by a generalized camera; we recover the position and orientation as well as the internal scale of the generalized camera with respect to known 3D points.

The generalized pose-and-scale problem is one that frequently arises in SLAM and SfM. It is impossible to recover scale from images alone. Scale may be recovered in special cases, for instance, when observing an object with known metric dimensions or with the aid of sensor measurements, but these cases are not common. As a result, the relative scale must be reconciled, for example, during loop closure for SLAM or when registering multiple reconstructions from SfM (see Figure 1b). The generalized pose-and-scale problem aims to compute a similarity transform that will align two coordinate systems from 2D-3D correspondences.

The solution proposed in this paper solves the generalized pose-and-scale problem, estimating rotation, translation, and scale directly given n 2D-3D observations. Our approach is $O(n)$ in the number of observations, making it useful for real-time applications, and does not require initialization. Additionally, we solve for all minima of our least squares cost function simultaneously instead of a single local minimum. Experiments on synthetic and real data show that our method is more accurate and scalable than other alignment methods.

The rest of the paper is as follows: Section 2 provides an overview of related work. We present the generalized pose-and-scale problem in Section 3, and our approach is described in detail in Section 4. We describe synthetic and real data experiments with comparisons to alternative approaches in Section 5, before providing concluding remarks in Section 6.

2   Related Work

There is much recent work on solving for the camera pose of calibrated cameras [2,9,13–15]. However, these methods only handle the case of solving for the pose of a single calibrated camera.

We solve a problem in the family of Non-Perspective-n-Point (NPnP) problems. Minimal solutions to the NP3P problem were proposed by Níster and Stéwenius [19] and Chen and Chang [3] for generalized cameras. Níster and Stéwenius reduce the NP3P problem to the solution of an octic polynomial which can be solved efficiently with root finding schemes. Chen and Chang propose an iterative solution to the NPnP problem, deriving a solution to the NP3P problem as a special case. Other iterative solutions have been proposed [21,23], though they are computationally expensive and depend heavily on a good initialization. Ess *et al.* [8] presented a non-iterative method, however, the complexity is at least quadratic in the number of points. Lepetit *et al.* [16] propose the EPnP algorithm that is $O(n)$ by representing the 3D points as a sum of 4 virtual control points, reducing the problem to estimating the positions of the control points. This method, however, is only applicable for a single perspective camera. The gPnP algorithm of Kneip *et al.* [12] is an extension of the EPnP algorithm [16] to generalized cameras. By utilizing Gröbner basis computations, they solve the NPnP problem in $O(n)$. However, the gPnP algorithm does not estimate scale. Ventura *et al.* [26] presented the first minimal solution to the similarity transformation problem. They use the generalized camera model and employ Gröbner basis computations to efficiently solve for scale, rotation, and translation using 4 2D-3D correspondences. They call this minimal problem the gP+s or NP4P+s problem. We are solving for scale, rotation, and translation using $n \geq 4$ points and thus call our problem the gPnP+s, or NPnP+s problem.

Our work is closely related to the Direct Least Squares (DLS) PnP algorithm of Hesch and Roumeliotis [10]. In this work, a modified least squares cost function is used to first solve for the rotation estimation as the solution to a set of third-order polynomials, then solve for translation with back-substitution. We derive a generalization of the DLS PnP algorithm that allows for multiple cameras while additionally recovering scale. As such, we call our algorithm gDLS. The solution proposed in this paper requires solving a polynomial system of exactly the same scale as DLS PnP, despite the additional complexity of our problem. This allows our solution to remain $O(n)$ in the number of points.

The proposed algorithm is especially useful in applications like loop closure in visual odometry, SLAM, and SfM. Various strategies for loop closure exist [5–7, 11, 24, 27], most of which involve either computing the absolute orientation to align landmarks, or PnP algorithms used to localize each camera individually. Iterative Closest Point (ICP) [1, 28] methods may also be used to align two 3D point clouds, though they are extremely sensitive to initialization and are often slow to converge. In contrast, our method uses 2D-3D correspondences. Additionally, these methods do not directly estimate relative scale, but rather estimate it as a preprocessing step by, for instance, using the distance between cameras or the depth of 3D points to estimate relative scale [4, 27]. Estimating similarity transformations from 2D-2D correspondences is currently an open problem in computer vision. Our proposed algorithm is a replacement for the aforementioned loop-closing algorithms and can estimate the similarity transformation directly and efficiently even for a large number of correspondences.

3 Problem Statement

Our aim is to solve the generalized pose-and-scale problem given n 2D-3D correspondences. That is, we would like to determine the pose and internal scale of a generalized camera with respect to n known 3D points. This is equivalent to aligning the two coordinate systems that define the generalized camera and the 3D points. The generalized camera model jointly considers image observations from multiple cameras such that each observation i has a ray origin at point q_i and a unit direction $\bar{r}_i$. The corresponding world point is denoted r_i. We want to find a rotation R, translation t and scale s such that the image rays coincide with the world points:

$$sq_i + \alpha_i \bar{r}_i = Rr_i + t, \qquad i = 1, \ldots, n \tag{1}$$

where α_i is a scalar which stretches the image ray such that it meets the world point r_i such that $\alpha_i = ||Rr_i + t - sq_i||$. We use the Cayley-Gibbs-Rodriguez parameterization of the rotation matrix such that R can be formed with just three unknowns. When considering all n correspondences, there exists $7 + n$ unknown variables (3 for rotation, 3 for translation, 1 for scale, and 1 unknown depth per observation). The gPnP+s problem can be formulated from Eq. (1) as a non-linear least-squares minimization such that the sum of squared measurement errors is minimized. Thus, we aim to minimize the cost function:

$$C(R, t, s) = \sum_{i=1}^{n} ||\bar{r}_i - \frac{1}{\alpha_i}(Rr_i + t - sq_i)||^2. \tag{2}$$

This non-linear least squares problem can be solved with iterative methods such as Gauss-Newton, however, these techniques are sensitive to initialization and only converge to a single local minimum. In Section 4, we describe our method for directly solving for all minima of a slightly modified cost function without the need for initialization. We call our method the generalized Direct Least Squares (gDLS) solution, as it is a generalization of the DLS algorithm presented in [10].

4 Solution Method

The geometric constraint equation of Eq. (1) leads to a non-linear system of equations that can be minimized by a least squares solver that minimizes Eq. (2). We would instead like to rewrite this system of equations in terms of fewer unknowns. Specifically, we can rewrite this equation solely in terms of the unknown rotation, R. When we relax the constraint that $\alpha_i = ||Rr_i + t - sq_i||$ and treat each α_i as a free variable, α_i, s, and t appear linearly and can be easily reduced from Eq. (2). Note that this relaxation is reasonable since solving the optimality conditions results in $\alpha_i^* = z_i^\top (Rr_i + t - sq_i)$ where z_i is $\bar{r}_i$ corrupted by measurement noise.

We begin by rewriting our system of equations from Eq. (1) in matrix-vector form:

$$\underbrace{\begin{bmatrix} \bar{r}_1 & & q_1 & -I \\ & \ddots & \vdots & \vdots \\ & \bar{r}_n & q_n & -I \end{bmatrix}}_{A} \underbrace{\begin{bmatrix} \alpha_1 \\ \vdots \\ \alpha_n \\ s \\ t \end{bmatrix}}_{x} = \underbrace{\begin{bmatrix} R & & \\ & \ddots & \\ & & R \end{bmatrix}}_{W} \underbrace{\begin{bmatrix} r_1 \\ \vdots \\ r_n \end{bmatrix}}_{b} \tag{3}$$

$$\Leftrightarrow Ax = Wb, \tag{4}$$

where A and b consist of known and observed values, x is the vector of unknown variables we will eliminate from the system of equations, and W is the block-diagonal matrix of the unknown rotation matrix. From Eq. (3), we can create a simple expression for x:

$$x = (A^\top A)^{-1} A^\top W b = \begin{bmatrix} U \\ S \\ V \end{bmatrix} W b. \tag{5}$$

We have partitioned $(A^\top A)^{-1} A^\top$ into constant matrices U, S, and V such that the depth, scale, and translation parameters are functions of U, S, and V respectively. Matrices U, S, and V can be efficiently computed in closed form by exploiting the sparse structure of the block matrices (see Appendix A for the full derivation). Note that α_i, s, and t may now be written concisely as linear functions of the rotation:

$$\alpha_i = u_i^\top W b \tag{6}$$

$$s = SWb \tag{7}$$

$$t = VWb, \tag{8}$$

where $u_i^\top$ is the i-th row of U. Through substitution, the geometric constraint equation (1) can be rewritten as:

$$\underbrace{SWb}_{s} q_i + \underbrace{u_i^\top W b}_{\alpha_i} \bar{r}_i = Rr_i + \underbrace{VWb}_{t}. \tag{9}$$

This new constraint is quadratic in the three unknown rotation variables given by the Cayley-Gibbs-Rodriguez representation.

4.1 A New Least Squares Cost Function

The new geometric constraint equation (9) assumes noise-free observations. We assume that each observation is noisy, with a zero mean noise η_i. We can denote our noisy observations as $\bar{z}_i = \bar{r}_i + \eta_i$. We can rewrite our measurement constraint in terms of our noisy observation:

$$SWbq_i + u_i^\top Wb(\bar{z}_i - \eta_i) = Rr_i + VWb \tag{10}$$

$$\Rightarrow \eta_i' = SWbq_i + u_i^\top Wb\bar{z}_i - Rr_i - VWB, \tag{11}$$

where η_i' is a zero-mean noise term that is a function of η_i (but whose covariance depends on the system parameters, as noted by Hesch and Roumeliotis [10]). We evaluate u_i, S, and V at $\bar{r}_i = \bar{z}_i$ without loss of generality. Observe that u_i can be eliminated from Eq. 11 by noting that:

$$UWb = \begin{bmatrix} \bar{z}_i^\top & & \\ & \ddots & \\ & & \bar{z}_n^\top \end{bmatrix} Wb - \begin{bmatrix} \bar{z}_1^\top q_1 \\ \vdots \\ \bar{z}_n^\top 1_n \end{bmatrix} SWb + \begin{bmatrix} \bar{z}_1^\top \\ \vdots \\ \bar{z}_n^\top \end{bmatrix} VWb \tag{12}$$

$$\Rightarrow u_i^\top Wb = \bar{z}_i^\top Rr_i - \bar{z}_i^\top q_i SWbq_i + \bar{z}_i^\top VWb. \tag{13}$$

Through substitution, Eq. (11) can be refactored such that:

$$\eta_i' = (\bar{z}_i\bar{z}_i^\top - I_3)(Rr_i - SWbq_i + VWb). \tag{14}$$

Eq. (14) allows the gPnP+s problem to be formulated as an unconstrained least-squares minimization in 3 unknown rotation parameters. We formulate our new least squares cost function, C', as the sum of the squared constraint errors from Eq. (14):

$$C'(R) - \sum_{i=1}^{n} \|(\bar{z}_i\bar{z}_i^\top - I_3)(Rr_i - SWbq_i + VWb)\|^2 \tag{15}$$

$$= \sum_{i=1}^{n} \eta_i'^\top \eta_i'. \tag{16}$$

Thus, we have reduced the number of unknowns in our system from $7 + n$ to 3. This is an important part of our formulation, as it allows the size of the system we solve to be independent of the number of observations and thus scalable.

4.2 Macaulay Matrix Solution

We have reduced our original geometric constraint of Eq. (1) to a least-squares minimization as a function of only the three unknown rotation parameters in

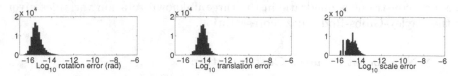

Fig. 2. Histograms of numerical errors in the computed similarity transforms based on 10^5 random trials with the minimal 4 correspondences

Eq. (15). That is, we wish to find unknown rotation parameters v_1, v_2, v_3 such that C' is minimized. This polynomial is of the same form and order as the DLS PnP algorithm [10], but with different coefficients. Thus, we can solve our least squares system of Eq. (15) with the same technique without modification. For a full explanation, see [10]. We will briefly summarize the technique in this section. The cost function of Eq. (15) may be minimized with the Gröbner basis technique; however, we found that the technique of [10] produced more accurate results at nearly the same efficiency.

We employ the Macaulay matrix [18] to determine the solution to our polynomial system. This matrix is formed from the partial derivatives of our cost function C' with respect to the three unknown rotation parameters. These three equations each equal zero when C' is minimal, so the roots of these polynomials produce the solution to our system. We consider one additional linear equation of the form $F_0 = u_0 + u_1v_1 + u_2v_2 + u_3v_3$ for random coefficients $u_0, \ldots, u_3$. This equation is generally non-zero at the roots of our polynomial system. The Macaulay matrix, M, formed from the three partial derivatives and the additional linear equation forms an extended polynomial system as a 120×120 matrix that contains coefficients to 120 monomials of the polynomial system.

Using the Schur complement trick, the Macaulay resultant matrix can be reduced to a 27×27 matrix whose eigenvectors correspond to the monomials of our cost function. The unknown rotation variables appear in these monomials, and can be directly extracted from the eigenvectors. This leads to 27 real and imaginary critical points, though the number of solutions can be reduced by considering only real solutions that place points in front of cameras. In practice, when using $n \geq 6$ points there exists only one valid minimum. After obtaining all minima, we evaluate the cost function Eq. (15) to determine the best orientation and compute the corresponding scale and translation through back substitution.

5 Experiments

5.1 Numerical Stability

We tested the numerical stability of our solution over 10^5 random trials. We generated random camera configurations that placed cameras (*i.e.*, ray origins) in the cube $[-1, 1] \times [-1, 1] \times [-1, 1]$ around the origin. 3D points were randomly placed in the volume $[-1, 1] \times [-1, 1] \times [2, 4]$. Ray directions were computed as unit vectors from camera origins to 3D points. An identity similarity transformation

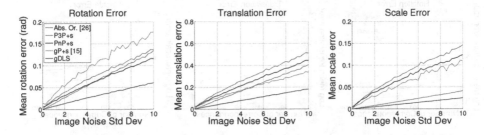

Fig. 3. We compared similarity transform algorithms with increasing levels of image noise to measure the pose error performance: the absolute orientation algorithm of [25], P3P+s, PnP+s, gP+s [26], and our algorithm, gDLS. Each algorithm was run with the same camera and point configuration for 1000 trials per noise level. Our algorithm has mean better rotation, translation, and scale errors for all levels of image noise.

was used (*i.e.*, $R = I$, $t = 0$, $s = 1$). For each trial, we computed solutions using the minimal 4 correspondences. We calculated the angular rotation error, the translation error, and the scale error for each trial, and plot the results in Figure 2. The errors are very stable, with 98% of all errors less than 10^{-12}.

5.2 Simulations with Noisy Synthetic Data

We performed two experiments with synthetic data to analyze the performance of our algorithm as the amount of image noise increases and as the number of correspondences increases. For both experiments we use a focal length of 800 and [640, 480] resolution. Two cameras are placed randomly in the cube $[-1, 1] \times [-1, 1] \times [-1, 1]$ around the origin with three 3D points randomly placed in the volume $[-1, 1] \times [-1, 1] \times [2, 4]$. Both cameras observe each 3D point, so there are six total 2D-3D observations. Using the known 2D-3D correspondences, we apply a similarity transformation with a random rotation in the range of $[-30, 30]$ degrees about each of the x, y, and z axes, a random translation with a distance between 0.5 and 10, and a random scale change between 0.1 and 10. We measure the performance of the following similarity transform algorithms:

- **Absolute Orientation:** The absolute orientation method of Umeyama [25] is used to align the known 3D points to 3D points triangulated from 2D correspondences. This algorithm is only an alignment method and does not utilize any 2D correspondences.
- **P3P+s:** The P3P algorithm of Kneip *et al.* [13] is used to localize the first camera and the corresponding rotation and translation is used for the similarity transformation. The scale is then estimated from the median estimate from triangulated point matches. This process is repeated for all cameras, and the camera localization and scale estimation that yields the largest number of inliers is used as the similarity transformation.
- **PnP+s:** The similarity transformation is computed the same way as P3P+s, but the DLS PnP algorithm of Hesch and Roumeliotis [10] is used to localize

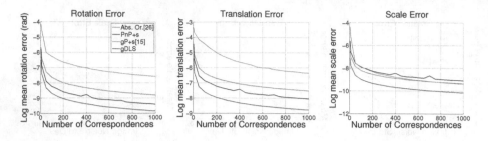

Fig. 4. We measured the accuracy of similarity transformation estimations as the number of correspondences increased. The mean of the log rotation, translation, and scale errors are plotted from 1000 trials at each level of correspondences used. A Gaussian image noise of 0.5 pixels was used for all trials. We did not use P3P+s in this experiment because P3P only uses 3 correspondences. Our algorithm has better accuracy for all number of correspondences used and a runtime complexity of $O(n)$, making it ideal for use at scale.

each camera instead of P3P[1]. PnP+s uses $n \geq 3$ 2D-3D correspondences, whereas P3P+s can only use 3.

- **gP+s:** The minimal solver of Ventura *et al.* [26] is used with 2D-3D correspondences from all cameras. While the algorithm is intended for the minimal case of $n = 4$ correspondences, it can compute an overdetermined solution for $n \geq 4$ correspondences.
- **gDLS:** The algorithm presented in this paper, which uses $n \geq 4$ 2D-3D correspondences from all cameras.

After running each algorithm on the same camera and point configuration, we calculate the rotation, translation, and scale errors with respect to the known similarity transformation.

Image Noise Experiment: For our first experiment, we evaluated the similarity transformation algorithms under increased levels of image noise. Using the configuration described above, we increased the image noise from 0 to 10 pixels standard deviation, and ran 1000 trials at each level. Our algorithm outperforms each of the other similarity transformation algorithms for all levels of image noise, as shown in Figure 3. The fact that our algorithm returns all minima of our modified cost function is advantageous under high levels of noise as we are not susceptible to getting stuck in a bad local minimum. This allows our algorithm to be very robust to image noise as compared to other algorithms.

Scalability Experiment: For the second experiment, we evaluate the rotation, translation, and scale error as the number of 2D-3D correspondences increases. We use the same camera configuration described above, but vary the number of 3D points used to compute the similarity transformation from 4 to 1000. Each

---

[1] We found that DLS [10] performed comparably to alternative algorithms such as OPnP [29] in the context of PnP+s.

Fig. 5. In our real data experiments we compute the similarity transformation that aligns cameras from a SLAM system (blue) to a preexisting SfM reconstruction using 2D-3D correspondences. The ground truth positions (green) were recorded with a high-accuracy ART-2 tracker.

3D point is observed by both cameras. We ran 1000 trials for each number of correspondences used with a Gaussian noise level of 0.5 pixels standard deviation for all trials. We did not use the P3P+s algorithm for this experiment since P3P is a minimal solver and cannot utilize the additional correspondences. Although gP+s is a minimal solver, it can utilize all n correspondences in an overdetermined solution. The accuracy of each similarity transformation algorithm as the number of correspondences increases is shown in Figure 4. Our algorithm performs very well as the number of correspondences increases, and is more accurate than alternative algorithms for all numbers of correspondences tested. Further, our algorithm is $O(n)$ so the performance cost of using additional correspondences is favorable compared to the alternative algorithms (see Section 5.4 for a full runtime analysis).

5.3   SLAM Registration with Real Images

We tested our solver for registration of a SLAM reconstruction with respect to an existing SfM reconstruction using a dataset from [26]. This dataset consists of an indoor reconstruction with precise 3D and camera position data obtained with an ART-2 optical tracker. Several image sequences in this environment were run through a real-time keyframe-based SLAM system to obtain a local tracking sequence that can be registered to the ground-truth environment via a similarity transform (see Figure 5). SIFT keypoints were used to establish 2D-3D correspondences using approximate nearest-neighbor techniques and a ratio test. We compare our method to several other techniques for registering SLAM maps to a global point cloud. We compare our algorithm to the absolute

Table 1. Average position error in centimeters for aligning a SLAM sequence to a pre-existing SfM reconstruction. An ART-2 tracker was used to provide highly accurate ground truth measurements for error analysis. Camera positions were computed using the respective similarity transformations and the mean camera position error of each sequence is listed below. Both the minimal version of our solver, gDLS4, and the nonminimal gDLS10 (both shown in bold below) outperform the alternative methods.

Sequence	# Images	Abs. Ori. [25]	P3P+s	PnP+s	gP+s [26]	gDLS4	gDLS10
office1	9	6.37	6.14	4.38	6.12	**3.97**	**3.04**
office2	9	8.09	7.81	6.90	9.32	**5.89**	**5.80**
office3	33	8.29	9.31	8.89	6.78	**6.08**	**4.69**
office4	9	4.76	4.48	3.98	4.00	**3.81**	**3.35**
office5	15	3.63	3.42	3.39	4.75	**3.39**	**3.09**
office6	24	5.15	5.23	5.01	5.91	**4.51**	**4.45**
office7	9	6.33	7.08	7.16	7.07	**4.65**	**3.21**
office8	11	4.72	4.85	3.62	4.59	**2.85**	**2.45**
office9	7	8.41	8.44	4.08	6.65	**3.19**	**2.33**
office10	23	5.88	6.60	5.73	5.88	**4.94**	**4.87**
office11	58	5.19	4.85	4.80	6.74	**4.77**	**4.65**
office12	67	5.53	5.20	4.97	4.86	**4.81**	**4.75**

orientation algorithm [25], P3P+s, PnP+s (using 10 correspondences), and gP+s [26] as described in Section 5.2. All algorithms are used in a PROSAC loop except for the absolute orientation algorithm which is used in a RANSAC loop. The absolute orientation algorithm does not use feature matches (it only aligns 3D point clouds) and thus cannot utilize matching scores in a PROSAC loop. We compare these algorithms to two versions of our solver: one using the minimal 4 correspondences (gDLS4) inside a PROSAC loop, and an over-determined solution using 10 correspondences (gDLS10) inside a PROSAC loop. No refinement is performed after RANSAC/PROSAC for any of the algorithms.

We compute the average position error of all keyframes with respect to the ground truth data. The position errors, reported in centimeters, are shown in Table 1. Both the minimal and non-minimal versions of our solver give higher accuracy results for every image sequence tested compared to alternative algorithms. By using the generalized camera model, we are able to exploit 2D-3D constraints from multiple cameras at the same time as opposed to considering only one camera (such as P3P+s and PnP+s). This allows the similarity transformation to be optimized for all cameras and observations simultaneously, leading to high-accuracy results.

5.4   Runtime Analysis

In this section we present a runtime analysis of each similarity transformation algorithm when registering n points and m cameras. The absolute orientation algorithm requires aligning sets of 3D points, making it $O(n)$. In theory, the covariance matrix used to compute the least-squares solution has a lower bound

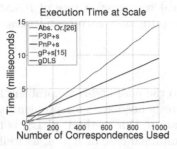
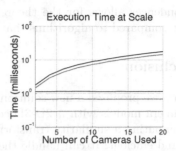

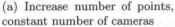

(a) Increase number of points, constant number of cameras

(b) Constant number of points, increasing number of cameras

Fig. 6. (a) We plot the mean execution time while increasing the number of 2D-3D correspondences used and keeping the number of cameras constant at 2. Our gDLS method is slightly slower than gP+s [26] though our method is much more accurate at scale (Figure 4). (b) The number of cameras was increased while using the 100 2D-3D correspondences (each point is seen in every camera). The runtimes of the absolute orientation method [25], gP+s [26], and our gDLS method are independent of the number of cameras.

of $O(n)$, however, in practice it is often slower. The P3P+s algorithm relies on the extremely efficient P3P algorithm (which can be considered to run in constant time), however, in order to recover scale it must triangulate points across all cameras, leading to $O(n)$ complexity. Further, P3P+s computes the similarity transformation by localizing each camera and estimating scale. Thus, for m cameras the expected runtime is $O(mn)$. The PnP+s algorithm operates the same way as P3P, though the PnP algorithm is at best $O(n)$, resulting in an overall runtime of $O(mn^2)$. In practice, the PnP+s algorithm outperforms the P3P+s algorithm as the number of points increases as shown in Figure 6. This is because the P3P algorithm returns 4 solutions, while the DLS PnP algorithm returns only 1 solution in most cases. All n points must be triangulated for each solution, leading to an increased runtime for P3P+s. The gP+s algorithm requires computing the null space of a matrix that is of size $2n$, which is $O(n)$ in theory though efficient in practice even for large n. The gP+s algorithm is roughly $2 - 8\times$ faster than our algorithm, however, as shown in Sections 5.2 and 5.3 it is less accurate than our algorithm.

As described in Section 4.1, our algorithm is $O(n)$ in the number of points, making the runtime favorable as the number of points increases. Additionally, our algorithm is independent of the number of cameras, as shown in Figure 6b. In our experiments conducted on a 2.26 GHz Quad-Core Mac Pro, we observed a mean runtime of roughly 0.842 milliseconds over 10^5 trials when using 4 points. When using 10 points, the mean runtime increased to roughly 0.863 milliseconds. The timing results as the number of correspondences and cameras increases is shown in Figure 6. This efficiency allows our method to be used in real-time within a RANSAC loop. Additionally, the fact that our method can be used with only

4 correspondences allows for the theoretical convergence rate of RANSAC to remain low compared to algorithms that require more correspondences.

6 Conclusion

In this work, we proposed a new solution to the pose-and-scale problem for generalized camera models with n 2D-3D correspondences. This problem is equivalent to computing a similarity transformation. Our method, gDLS, is flexible, accurate, and efficient. It can handle the minimal case of $n = 4$, as well as the overdetermined case of $n > 4$. We formulate a least squares cost function that can be solved efficiently as a system of third degree polynomials, resulting in a system that is $O(n)$ in the number of correspondences. This makes it applicable for real-time frameworks and is useful, for example, for loop closure with SLAM and visual odometry. We have evaluated our method on synthetic data to show the numerical stability, accuracy under image noise, and scalability of our method. We validated our method with experiments using real data which shows that our method is more accurate than other methods when computing the similarity transformation for registering reconstructions. Our gDLS algorithm has been made publicly available as part of the open source library Theia[2] [22].

Experiments have shown our method to be extremely accurate and efficient even at scale. Our method can be used on thousands of correspondences when the ground truth correspondences are known, or as a refinement step on inliers from a minimal estimation. However, as with all non-minimal pose solvers, it is difficult to make use of a large number of correspondences because of the likelihood of false features matches when using many correspondences. For future work, we plan to explore ways to increase robustness to false correspondences by incorporating feature distances into the similarity transform estimation process so that our method can be more readily used with thousands of correspondences.

Acknowledgments. The authors would like to thank Jonathan Ventura for his insights and for providing the SLAM datasets used in our real data experiments. This work was supported in part by UC MEXUS-CONACYT (Fellowships 212913), NSF Grant IIS-1219261, NSF Graduate Research Fellowship Grant DGE-1144085, NSF CAREER Grant IIS-0747520, and ONR Grant N00014-09-1-113.

Appendix

A Computing Matrices U, S, and V for Depth, Scale, and Translation

The constant matrices U, S, and V are used to recover depth, scale, and translation from the solution for the rotation matrix. These matrices are constructed

---

[2] http://cs.ucsb.edu/~cmsweeney/theia

as a function of known measurements from the matrix $(A^\top A)^{-1} A^\top$. Using the expression for A from Eq. (3), we have:

$$A^\top A = \left[\begin{array}{ccc|cc} 1 & & & \bar{r}_1{}^\top q_1 & -\bar{r}_1{}^\top \\ & \ddots & & \vdots & \vdots \\ & & 1 & \bar{r}_n{}^\top q_n & -\bar{r}_n{}^\top \\ \hline q_1^\top \bar{r}_1 & \cdots & q_n^\top \bar{r}_n & \sum_{i=1}^n q_i^\top q_i & \sum_{i=1}^n -q_i^\top \\ -\bar{r}_1 & \cdots & -\bar{r}_n & \sum_{i=1}^n -q_i & nI \end{array}\right] = \left[\begin{array}{c|c} \mathcal{A} & \mathcal{B} \\ \hline \mathcal{B}^\top & \mathcal{D} \end{array}\right], \quad (17)$$

where solid lines represent the block-matrix boundaries. Through block matrix inversion, we can conveniently solve for the inverse:

$$(A^\top A)^{-1} = \left[\begin{array}{c|c} \mathcal{E} & \mathcal{F} \\ \hline \mathcal{G} & \mathcal{H} \end{array}\right]$$

$$\mathcal{E} = I + \mathcal{B}\mathcal{H}\mathcal{B}^\top$$

$$\mathcal{F} = -\mathcal{B}\mathcal{H}$$

$$\mathcal{G} = -\mathcal{H}\mathcal{B}^\top$$

$$\mathcal{H} = \left(\begin{bmatrix} \sum_{i=1}^n q_i^\top q_i & \sum_{i=1}^n -q_i^\top \\ \sum_{i=1}^n -q_i & nI \end{bmatrix} - \begin{bmatrix} \sum_{i=1}^n q_i^\top \bar{r}_i \bar{r}_i{}^\top q_i & \sum_{i=1}^n -q_i^\top \bar{r}_i \bar{r}_i{}^\top \\ \sum_{i=1}^n -\bar{r}_i \bar{r}_i{}^\top q_i & \sum_{i=1}^n \bar{r}_i \bar{r}_i{}^\top \end{bmatrix}\right)^{-1}.$$

$$(18)$$

Finally, we can compute U, S, and V from Eq. (18). Many of the terms can be simplified because of multiplications involving $\bar{r}_i{}^\top \bar{r}_i = 1$. This leaves us with a greatly simplified expression for U, S, and V:

$$\begin{bmatrix} U \\ \hline S \\ \hline V \end{bmatrix} = (A^\top A)^{-1} A^\top$$

$$U = \begin{bmatrix} \bar{r}_i{}^\top & & \\ & \ddots & \\ & & \bar{r}_n{}^\top \end{bmatrix} + \mathcal{B}\begin{bmatrix} S \\ V \end{bmatrix} \quad (19)$$

$$\begin{bmatrix} S \\ \hline V \end{bmatrix} = -\mathcal{H}\mathcal{B}^\top \begin{bmatrix} \bar{r}_i{}^\top & & \\ & \ddots & \\ & & \bar{r}_n{}^\top \end{bmatrix} + \mathcal{H}\begin{bmatrix} q_1^\top & \cdots & q_n^\top \\ -I & \cdots & -I \end{bmatrix}$$

$$= \mathcal{H}\begin{bmatrix} q_1^\top - q_1^\top \bar{r}_1 \bar{r}_1{}^\top & \cdots & q_n^\top - q_n^\top \bar{r}_n \bar{r}_n{}^\top \\ \bar{r}_1 \bar{r}_1{}^\top - I & \cdots & \bar{r}_n \bar{r}_n{}^\top - I \end{bmatrix}.$$

References

1. Besl, P.J., McKay, N.D.: A method for registration of 3-d shapes. IEEE Transactions on Pattern Analysis and Machine Intelligence 4(2), 239–256 (1992)
2. Bujnak, M., Kukelova, Z., Pajdla, T.: A general solution to the p4p problem for camera with unknown focal length. In: Proc. IEEE Conference on Computer Vision and Pattern Recognition, pp. 1–8. IEEE (2008)
3. Chen, C.S., Chang, W.Y.: On pose recovery for generalized visual sensors. IEEE Transactions on Pattern Analysis and Machine Intelligence 26(7), 848–861 (2004)
4. Clemente, L.A., Davison, A.J., Reid, I.D., Neira, J., Tardós, J.D.: Mapping large loops with a single hand-held camera. In: Robotics: Science and Systems (2007)
5. Courchay, J., Dalalyan, A., Keriven, R., Sturm, P.: Exploiting loops in the graph of trifocal tensors for calibrating a network of cameras. In: Daniilidis, K., Maragos, P., Paragios, N. (eds.) ECCV 2010, Part II. LNCS, vol. 6312, pp. 85–99. Springer, Heidelberg (2010)
6. Davison, A.J., Reid, I.D., Molton, N.D., Stasse, O.: Monoslam: Real-time single camera slam. IEEE Transactions on Pattern Analysis and Machine Intelligence 29(6), 1052–1067 (2007)
7. Eade, E., Drummond, T.: Unified loop closing and recovery for real time monocular slam. In: Proc. British Machine Vision Conference, vol. 13, p. 136. Citeseer (2008)
8. Ess, A., Neubeck, A., Van Gool, L.J.: Generalised linear pose estimation. In: Proc. British Machine Vision Conference, pp. 1–10 (2007)
9. Fischler, M.A., Bolles, R.C.: Random sample consensus: a paradigm for model fitting with applications to image analysis and automated cartography. Communications of the ACM 24(6), 381–395 (1981)
10. Hesch, J., Roumeliotis, S.: A direct least-squares (dls) solution for pnp. In: Proc. of the International Conference on Computer Vision. IEEE (2011)
11. Klopschitz, M., Zach, C., Irschara, A., Schmalstieg, D.: Generalized detection and merging of loop closures for video sequences. In: Proc. 3D Data Processing, Visualization, and Transmission (2008)
12. Kneip, L., Furgale, P., Siegwart, R.: Using multi-camera systems in robotics: Efficient solutions to the npnp problem. In: Proc. International Conference on Robotics and Automation, pp. 3770–3776. IEEE (2013)
13. Kneip, L., Scaramuzza, D., Siegwart, R.: A novel parametrization of the perspective-three-point problem for a direct computation of absolute camera position and orientation. In: Proc. IEEE Conference on Computer Vision and Pattern Recognition, pp. 2969–2976. IEEE (2011)
14. Kukelova, Z., Bujnak, M., Pajdla, T.: Automatic generator of minimal problem solvers. In: Forsyth, D., Torr, P., Zisserman, A. (eds.) ECCV 2008, Part III. LNCS, vol. 5304, pp. 302–315. Springer, Heidelberg (2008)
15. Kukelova, Z., Bujnak, M., Pajdla, T.: Polynomial eigenvalue solutions to minimal problems in computer vision. IEEE Transactions on Pattern Analysis and Machine Intelligence 34(7), 1381–1393 (2012)
16. Lepetit, V., Moreno-Noguer, F., Fua, P.: Epnp: An accurate o (n) solution to the pnp problem. International Journal of Computer Vision 81(2), 155–166 (2009)
17. Li, Y., Snavely, N., Huttenlocher, D.: Location recognition using prioritized feature matching. In: Daniilidis, K., Maragos, P., Paragios, N. (eds.) ECCV 2010, Part II. LNCS, vol. 6312, pp. 791–804. Springer, Heidelberg (2010)
18. Macaulay, F.: Some formulae in elimination. In: Proc. London Mathematical Society, vol. 1(1), pp. 3–27 (1902)

19. Nistér, D., Stewénius, H.: A minimal solution to the generalised 3-point pose problem. Journal of Mathematical Imaging and Vision 27(1), 67–79 (2007)
20. Pless, R.: Using many cameras as one. In: Proc. IEEE Conference on Conference on Computer Vision and Pattern Recognition, vol. 2, pp. II–587. IEEE (2003)
21. Schweighofer, G., Pinz, A.: Globally optimal o(n) solution to the pnp problem for general camera models. In: Proc. British Machine Vision Conference, pp. 1–10 (2008)
22. Sweeney, C.: Theia Multiview Geometry Library: Tutorial & Reference. University of California, Santa Barbara, http://cs.ucsb.edu/~cmsweeney/theia
23. Tariq, S., Dellaert, F.: A multi-camera 6-dof pose tracker. In: Proc. International Symposium on Mixed and Augmented Reality, pp. 296–297. IEEE (2004)
24. Thrun, S., Montemerlo, M.: The graph slam algorithm with applications to large-scale mapping of urban structures. The International Journal of Robotics Research 25(5-6), 403–429 (2006)
25. Umeyama, S.: Least-squares estimation of transformation parameters between two point patterns. IEEE Transactions on Pattern Analysis and Machine Intelligence 13(4), 376–380 (1991)
26. Ventura, J., Arth, C., Reitmayr, G., Schmalstieg, D.: A minimal solution to the generalized pose-and-scale problem. Accepted to: IEEE Conference on Computer Vision and Pattern Recognition (2014)
27. Williams, B., Cummins, M., Neira, J., Newman, P., Reid, I., Tardós, J.: An image-to-map loop closing method for monocular slam. In: Proc. International Conference on Intelligent Robots and Systems, pp. 2053–2059. IEEE (2008)
28. Yang, J., Li, H., Jia, Y.: Go-icp: Solving 3d registration efficiently and globally optimally. In: Proc. The International Conference on Computer Vision. IEEE (2013)
29. Zheng, Y., Kuang, Y., Sugimoto, S., Astrom, K., Okutomi, M.: Revisiting the pnp problem: A fast, general and optimal solution. In: Proc. of the International Conference on Computer Vision. IEEE (December 2013)

Generalized Connectivity Constraints
for Spatio-temporal 3D Reconstruction

Martin Ralf Oswald, Jan Stühmer, and Daniel Cremers

Department of Computer Science, Technische Universität München*
Boltzmannstr. 3, 85748 Garching, Germany

Abstract. This paper introduces connectivity preserving constraints into spatio-temporal multi-view reconstruction. We efficiently model connectivity constraints by precomputing a geodesic shortest path tree on the occupancy likelihood. Connectivity of the final occupancy labeling is ensured with a set of linear constraints on the labeling function. In order to generalize the connectivity constraints from objects with genus 0 to an arbitrary genus, we detect loops by analyzing the visual hull of the scene. A modification of the constraints ensures connectivity in the presence of loops. The proposed efficient implementation adds little runtime and memory overhead to the reconstruction method. Several experiments show significant improvement over state-of-the-art methods and validate the practical use of this approach in scenes with fine structured details.

Keywords: connectivity constraints, spatio-temporal 3D reconstruction.

| 1 of 16 input images | No Connectivity Constraint [22] | With a Connectivity Constraint [25]+[22] | Generalized Connectivity Constraint |

Fig. 1. Embedding connectivity constraints into multi-view reconstruction clearly helps to recover fine structures like the rope. The tree-shaped connectivity prior [25] only works for objects without holes (genus 0), resulting in disconnected parts when the rope touches the head. The proposed generalized connectivity constraint works for objects with arbitrary genus. Dataset: 'jumping rope' sequence from the INRIA 4D repository [16].

* This work was supported by the ERC Starting Grant 'Convex Vision' and the Technische Universität München - Institute for Advanced Study, funded by the German Excellence Initiative.

D. Fleet et al. (Eds.): ECCV 2014, Part IV, LNCS 8692, pp. 32–46, 2014.
© Springer International Publishing Switzerland 2014

1 Introduction

Multi-view 3D reconstruction is a central research topic in computer vision that is driven in many different directions. Apart from a realistic physical modeling of the inverted imaging process, it is also of common interest to model learned and prior information (e.g. smoothness or shape priors), or imposing intuitive constraints on the solution, such as symmetry, connectedness or surface genus. In this work, we propose a method that is first: able to enforce connectedness of the computed solution, and second: able to preserve holes of the reconstructed scene within a multi-view reconstruction setup. We can guarantee that the solutions' surface genus is not smaller than the one of the visual hull.

Our approach is motivated by the spatio-temporal multi-view 3D reconstruction of scenes containing small object structures that we want to preserve in the reconstruction. Although fine object structures can also be preserved by incorporating exact silhouette information, such as in the work of Cremers and Kolev [6], this method is not applicable if the precomputed silhouettes are not accurate.

1.1 Contributions

- We embed the concept of connectivity constraints for image segmentation into a spatio temporal multi view reconstruction setup.
- Since the connectivity constraints proposed in [25] only work well for scenes and objects of genus zero, we propose a generalization of the connectivity constraints to an arbitrary genus.
- We suggest an efficient implementation of the generalized connectivity constraints with a small additional memory footprint and an almost unchanged computation runtime per optimization iteration. The necessary preprocessing only adds around one minute to the three minutes computation time per frame for the presented experiments.

1.2 Related Work

Spatio-temporal multi-view reconstruction on dense occupancy grids has been pioneered by Goldlücke et al. [12], [11] with a level set representation of the space-time surface. The drawback of this approach is its dependency on a good initialization due to the locally optimal optimization procedure. Aganj et al. [1] compute a spatio-temporal Delaunay mesh that automatically provides temporal correspondences of mesh vertices by using silhouettes. Starck and Hilton [24] proposed a spatio-temporal reconstruction pipeline which first estimates shapes from silhouettes and later refines the reconstruction with photometrically matched features and information about the reconstruction result from the previous time step. In [13], Guillemaut and Hilton propose a method that concurrently estimates a multi-layer segmentation and corresponding depth values of the scene based on confidence-weighted optical flow measures.

We use the spatio-temporal reconstruction method from Oswald and Cremers [22] as the basis of our work. This method is a generalization of the 3D reconstruction by Kolev et al. [19] to the temporal domain. Both approaches use a volumetric representation of the surface within an energy minimization framework which makes it easy to impose additional constraints on the solution.

To the best of our knowledge the only previous work on connectivity in 3D reconstruction is the work of Bleyer et al. [3], in which the authors propose to use connectivity information for joint stereo matching and object segmentation. In contrast to our work, this method is rather a 2.5D than a 3D or even a 4D reconstruction method. While the authors in [3] correctly define connectivity as the existence of a connecting path, they instead propose to determine the connectivity of a pair of points by testing along a straight line that connects both points, thus only favoring convexity of objects.

In the field of image segmentation, topology preserving extensions have been proposed in different algorithmic frameworks. For the graph cut [4] algorithm, Zeng et al. [27] proposed a topology preserving refinement scheme. Chen et al. [5] propose to alternatingly estimate a graph cut segmentation and alter the respective unaries based on a level-set representation in order to fulfill predefined topological constraints. In contrast to our approach, this method does not compute minimal geodesic connections with respect to the input data and its runtime is much higher due to the iterative optimization. For the level set method a topology preserving extension was proposed by Han et al. [15]. Vicente et al. [26] use connectivity priors for a Markov random field segmentation. The authors propose an approximation scheme to enforce connectivity of the segmented object with respect to user given seed points. The drawback of all methods on connectivity mentioned so far is that they only converge to a local minimum and therefore depend on the initialization. Moreover, apart from Bleyer et al. [3] all approaches are made for a 2D domain.

Recently, three different globally optimal approaches were proposed. One is the work of Nowozin and Lampert [21], in which the constrained image segmentation problem is formulated as a linear programming relaxation. The drawback of this method is that the complexity does not scale well with the image size and therefore prevents its use for 3D or 4D reconstruction methods where the problem size easily reaches thousands or even millions of variables.

A closely related work is that of Gulshan et al. [14]. The foreground segment is restricted to the shape of a geodesic star with respect to a geodesic distance measure that depends on the image gradient. By placing several input seeds, this constraint allows several geodesic star shaped objects, their union is called a geodesic forest. However, the authors only present results on 2D image data and because the method is formulated in a graph-cut segmentation framework the boundary length regularizer is affected by the discretization.

Another globally optimal segmentation method with connectivity constraints is the work of Stühmer et al. [25]. The authors propose a geodesic tree-shaped connectivity prior for image segmentation in an efficient convex optimization framework that allows the segmentation of large scale problems as they arise for example in 3D medical imaging data. In contrast to [14], this method is formulated using a continuous segmentation framework and does not suffer from discretization artifacts with respect to the boundary length regularizer. It is perfectly suited to accurately segment objects with a fine detailed tree-like structure, such as blood vessels in angiography, or the legs of insects in photographs. They first compute a single-source geodesic shortest path tree based on the image data. Then, the tree-connected segmentation is computed by imposing linear constraints on the solution, based on the precomputed shortest path tree. As such, these constraints only impose connectivity for objects without any holes or loops (genus 0).

We follow this idea in the context of spatio-temporal multi-view reconstruction and generalize the connectivity constraint to objects with arbitrary genus.

2   3D Reconstruction with Connectivity Constraints

First, we give an introduction to the spatio-temporal 3D reconstruction approach of [22] which allows 3D reconstructions of moving scenes by using video data from several viewpoints. Then we show how the connectivity constraint of [25] can be incorporated into the reconstruction. The combination of both methods allows image based globally optimal 3D reconstruction while preserving connectivity of the object. As shown later in the experiments, this constraint also helps to reconstruct fine scale details of the scene.

2.1   Spatio-temporal Multi-view Reconstruction

This section briefly repeats the spatio-temporal 3D reconstruction approach in [22], which forms the basis of the proposed approach. The temporally changing scene is represented by an hypersurface $\Sigma \subset V \times T$ that is embedded in the spatio-temporal product space of the three-dimensional space $V \subset \mathbb{R}^3$ that changes over time $T \subset \mathbb{R}_{\geq 0}$. At every time instant t, the scene is observed by N static cameras with known projection matrices $\{\pi_i\}_{i=1}^N$ and approximate silhouettes $\{S_i(t)\}_{i=1}^N$. We do not need exact silhouettes, which is a desirable property in a 4D setup, because it is not easy to automatically generate exact silhouettes for all cameras and all time steps. The silhouettes contain valuable information about the number of holes in the scene, that is, the genus of the scene. Bringing this information into space-time, we will later use the visual hull $\mathcal{VH}(t) = \bigcap_{i=1}^N \pi_i^{-1}(S_i(t))$ to analyze the scene structure and to impose constraints on the connectedness of the reconstructed surface.

For mathematical convenience with respect to the final optimization procedure, we represent the hypersurface Σ as the boundary between the interior and the exterior part of the scene. Thus, hypersurface Σ is expressed by the binary labeling function $u : V \times T \mapsto \{0, 1\}$, indicating either interior or exterior for every point in space-time. This automatically ensures a closed manifold without boundaries and easily deals with arbitrary topologies. Stated as an energy minimization, the 3D reconstruction problem is described as finding a surface with minimal area that best fits the input data, represented by a photoconsistency measure $\rho : V \times T \mapsto \mathbb{R}_{\geq 0}$ and a data term $f : V \times T \mapsto \mathbb{R}$:

$$E(u) = \int_{V \times T} \left(\rho|\nabla_{\boldsymbol{x}} u| + g_t|\nabla_t u| \right) \, d\boldsymbol{x}dt + \lambda \int_{V \times T} fu \, d\boldsymbol{x}dt \tag{1}$$

with $\lambda > 0$ steering the smoothness of reconstructed hypersurface. The data term $f : V \times T \mapsto \mathbb{R}$ locally expresses an affinity to an interior ($f < 0$) or an exterior ($f > 0$) labeling. Similar to [22], we restrict the solution space of the energy minimization in (1) to the visual hull. As a consequence, the approximate silhouettes can be 'larger', but not 'smaller' in order to ensure that the corresponding visual hull fully contains the true scene. The function $g_t(\boldsymbol{x}, t) = \exp\left(-|\nabla f(\boldsymbol{x}, t)|\right)$ weights the temporal smoothing based on f to account for fast motions.

The photoconsistency measure $\rho(\boldsymbol{x})$ resembles truncated normalized cross-correlation matching scores C_i between neighboring camera pairs and is defined as

$$\rho(\boldsymbol{x}) = \exp\left[-\mu \sum_{i \in \mathcal{C}} \underbrace{\delta\left(d_i^{\max} = \text{depth}_i(\boldsymbol{x})\right) \cdot C_i(\boldsymbol{x}, d_i^{\max})}_{\text{VOTE}_i(\boldsymbol{x})} \right] . \tag{2}$$

The delta function δ in combination with $d_i^{\max} = \arg\max_d C_i(\boldsymbol{x}, d)$ performs a ray-based denoising of these measures and represents the voting scheme proposed by Hernández and Schmitt [9] and μ is a scaling parameter. The data term f avoids trivial solutions of energy (1) by propagating the photometric information from Eq. (2) in a probabilistic manner into the volume.

$$f(\boldsymbol{x}, t) = -\ln\left(\frac{1 - P(\boldsymbol{x} \in int(\Sigma))}{P(\boldsymbol{x} \in int(\Sigma))} \right) . \tag{3}$$

The probability $P(\boldsymbol{x} \in int(\Sigma))$ that point $\boldsymbol{x}$ belongs to the interior of surface Σ is defined based on the voting locations and qualities of corresponding camera rays $r_i(\boldsymbol{x}, \cdot)$ through point $\boldsymbol{x}$

$$P(\boldsymbol{x} \in int(\Sigma)) = \prod_{i=1}^{N} \prod_{j=1}^{N} \prod_{\substack{\text{depth}_i(\boldsymbol{x}) < d \leq d_i^{\max}}} \frac{1}{Z_j} \exp\left[-\eta \cdot \text{VOTE}_j\left(r_i(\boldsymbol{x}, d)\right) \right] \tag{4}$$

As suggested in [22] we limit the memory consumption of the method by setting $|T| = 3$ and taking the center frame as a smooth solution. For each frame a mesh is extracted with the Marching Cubes algorithm [20] at an iso-level of 0.5.

2.2   Connectivity Constraints via Directed Graphs

Without loss of generality we assume that the visual hull is connected. For the case that is not connected, the same approach can be applied component-wise after identifying independent connected components of the visual hull. We define connectivity constraints independently for each time step to allow for topology changes between time steps. For better readability we drop the temporal dependency in the following notation.

Graph Structure. For every time step we define a geodesic shortest path tree $\mathcal{G}_s$ on the visual hull $\mathcal{VH}$ with respect to a given source node s that contains for each point $x \in \mathcal{VH}$ inside the visual hull the shortest geodesic path C_s^x from s to x that minimizes the cost function

$$\mathcal{D}_s(x) = \ell(C_s^x) = \int_0^1 e^{f(C_s^x(r))} dr ,$$ (5)

which is a positive geodesic measure that depends on the data term. Variable r parametrizes the path from s to x. $\mathcal{D}_s(x)$ is a shorthand for the distance map of the shortest geodesic path from the source node s to any point $x \in \mathcal{VH}$. The edges of the shortest paths form the edge set $\mathcal{E}$ of the shortest path tree $\mathcal{G}_s$.

Source Node Computation. It is desirable to center the source node for the geodesic shortest path computation within the data term. To this end, we compute the source node $s(t)$ as the point which minimizes a spatio-temporal convolution of the data term f with a sufficiently large Gaussian kernel $\mathcal{G}$.

$$s(t) = \arg\min_x \int_{t-1}^{t+1} (f * \mathcal{G})(x, \tau) \, d\tau$$ (6)

The minimization reflects the fact that negative data term values $f < 0$ indicate a favor for an interior label and thus ensures a position that has high probability of being interior. The position of the source node has not much influence on the result, but this choice favors a smoothly temporal change of its position within the data term while maximizing the distance to the surface. An example rendering of a shortest path from a leaf node to the source is shown in Fig. 4a.

Constrained Optimization. The connectivity constraint from [25] is included into the reconstruction process as a monotonicity constraint of the labeling function u with respect to the edges $\mathcal{E}$ in $\mathcal{G}_s$. This monotonicity can be ensured by including inequality constraints on the directional derivative $\delta_e\left(u(x,t)\right)$ of u along every edge $e \in \mathcal{E}$. Thus, computing a spatio-temporal 3D reconstruction with connectivity constraints can be achieved by computing a minimizer of the constrained optimization problem

$$\min_{u \in \mathcal{BV}(V \times T; \{0,1\})} E(u)$$ (7)

$$\text{s. t.} \quad \delta_e\left(u(x,t)\right) \leq 0, \quad e \in \mathcal{E}$$

with one constraint for each edge e in the edge set $\mathcal{E}$ of the shortest path tree $\mathcal{G}_s$. $\mathcal{BV}(\cdot)$ denotes the function space of bounded variations [2].

3   Generalized Connectivity Constraints for Objects of Arbitrary Genus

The key idea to generalize the connectivity constraint to objects with arbitrary genus is a modification of the constraints that are defined on the geodesic shortest path tree. The key ingredient to this modification is to detect loops in the object and to identify parts of these loops with a 'thin' geometry, called handles. This is described in the following.

3.1 Handle and Tunnel Loops

In [8], Dey et al. study arbitrary surfaces represented by a simplicial complex, that is, a hierarchy of p-simplices with different dimensions p (e.g. $p = 0, \ldots, 2$ corresponding to points, edges, and faces). The surface $\mathbb{M}$ separates the simplicial complex into an interior part $\mathbb{I}$ and an exterior part $\mathbb{E}$, both including the surface, i.e. $\mathbb{I} \cap \mathbb{E} = \mathbb{M}$. Since we want to analyze the topology of the visual hull, these sets will be shorthands for $\mathbb{M} = \partial \mathcal{VH}$, $\mathbb{I} = \mathcal{VH}$ and $\mathbb{E} = (V \setminus \mathcal{VH}) \cup \partial \mathcal{VH}$.

The authors in [8] define and study cycles of edges ('loops') on the surface which build equivalence classes with respect to contraction or translation of the cycle - like a rubber band which can be moved along the surface, but not above holes in the surface. In this paper will call this equivalence relation $\sim_{\mathrm{M}}$ 'contractible' on the set $\mathbb{M}$, for example, we denote the relation that a loop $l_1 \subset \mathbb{M}$ is contractible to a loop $l_2 \subset \mathbb{M}$ on the set $\mathbb{M}$ as $l_1 \sim_{\mathrm{M}} l_2$. For simplicity we try to define terms and notation on a more intuitive level which should be sufficient to follow the rest of the paper. For mathematically precise definitions based on persistent homology we refer to [8]. Following their work, we now consider loops on the surface with the following properties.

Definition 1 (Handle and tunnel loops). *A **handle loop** $h \subset \mathbb{M}$ is a cycle of edges on the surface that is contractible in the interior $(h \sim_{\mathrm{I}} 0)$ and not contractible on the surface $(h \nsim_{\mathrm{M}} 0)$. A **tunnel loop** $t \subset \mathbb{M}$ is a cycle of edges on the surface that is contractible in the exterior $(h \sim_{\mathrm{E}} 0)$ and not contractible on the surface $(h \nsim_{\mathrm{M}} 0)$.*

With respect to the above mentioned equivalence relation, a closed surface of genus g has exactly g classes of handle loops and g classes of tunnel loops induced by the surface embedding. We consider one representative loop with approximate minimal geometric length per class and denote them as the set of handle loops $\{h_i\}_{i=1}^{g}$ and the set of tunnel loops $\{t_i\}_{i=1}^{g}$. Hence, for each surface hole i we have a corresponding pair (h_i, t_i) of representative handle and tunnel loops.

Examples of handle and tunnel loops are shown in Figs. 2, 3, 4c. Dey et al. [8] also propose an algorithm which computes handle and tunnel loops with approximate minimal length that is perfectly suited to process volumetric data. However, this algorithm is considerably slower than a recently published algorithm by Dey et al. [7] which only works for meshes. To this end, we extract an iso-surface mesh of the visual hull to efficiently compute handle and tunnel loops. The speed advantage of the method in [7] stems from the fact that it does not need a 3D tessellation of the scene. In [7], the concept of Reeb graphs is used to estimate an initial set of handle and tunnel loops and their geometric length is shortened in a subsequent refinement step.

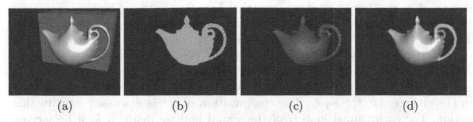

(a)   (b)   (c)   (d)

Fig. 2. Various sets defined in this section visualized on a teapot model of genus 2. (a) Exterior $\mathbb{E}$ (red), (b) Interior $\mathbb{I}$ (green), (c) Handle and tunnel loops $\{h_1, h_2\}, \{t_1, t_2\}$ (green+red), (d) Handle segments H_1, H_2 (yellow+blue).

Handle Segmentation. We aim to segment the 'thin' geometric parts around the holes of the surface, called handles. These handle segments will help to make the connectivity constraints adaptive to the data term. For this purpose we introduce the following definitions.

Definition 2 (Handle Segment Surface). *We define the handle segment surface as the connected subset of all points $x \in \mathbb{M}$ for which a handle loop h_x exists which is contractible to h_i subject to the additional constraint that the ratio of $\ell(h_x)$ and $\ell(h_i)$ does not exceed a user given threshold σ:*

$$\mathbb{M}_{H_i} = \left\{ x \in \mathbb{M} \ \middle| \ \exists h_x \subset \mathbb{M} : h_x \sim_{\mathbb{I}}^{\sigma} h_i \right\} \tag{8}$$

where $h_x \subseteq \mathbb{M}$ denotes a handle loop through the surface point x and $h_x \sim_{\mathbb{I}}^{\sigma} h_i$ means that handle loop h_x is contractible to h_i subject to the constraint $\ell(h_x) < \sigma \ell(h_i)$.

Definition 3 (Handle Segment). *Given the handle segment surface $\mathbb{M}_{H_i}$ from the previous definition, we define the corresponding volumetric handle segment $H_i \subseteq \mathbb{I}$ as the set of all points in the visual hull for which the closest point on the visual hull boundary is on the handle segment surface $\mathbb{M}_{H_i}$.*

$$H_i = \left\{ x \in \mathbb{I} \ \middle| \ \underset{y \in \mathbb{M}}{\arg\min} \operatorname{dist}(x, y) \in \mathbb{M}_{H_i} \right\} \tag{9}$$

where $\operatorname{dist}(x, y)$ denotes the Euclidean distance between point $x \in \mathbb{I}$ in the interior and point $y \in \mathbb{M}$ on the surface.

In practice, we compute H_i by a breadth first search algorithm on the visual hull. Starting from the handle loop h_i a wavefront is propagated in both directions. Independently for each wavefront, we stop the search if the ratio between the current length of the wavefront and the initial position exceeds the threshold σ.

3.2 Loop Connectivity Constraints

With the handle and tunnel loops of the visual hull we are now able to generalize the connectivity constraint in the presence of loops. By enforcing interior labels along each tunnel loop t_i we can assure that loops in the visual hull are preserved in the final segmentation. However, in order add a minimum amount of costs to the energy (7) when enforcing loop connectivity, we need to find corresponding loops that respect the costs of the data term. We approximate these geodesics shortest loops by computing corresponding loops $t_i^{\mathcal{G}_s} \subset \mathbb{I}$ on the precomputed geodesic shortest path tree $\mathcal{G}_s$ which are contractible to the original tunnel loop on the surface, i.e. $t_i^{\mathcal{G}_s} \sim_{\mathbb{I}} t_i$. The computation of $t_i^{\mathcal{G}_s}$ is discussed later in this section. For each tunnel loop t_i of the visual hull we define a *loop preserving constraint* as

$$\forall i \in [1, \ldots, g] : \quad \left\{ \forall \boldsymbol{x} \in t_i^{\mathcal{G}_s} : u(\boldsymbol{x}) = 1 \right\}. \tag{C0}$$

Proposition 1. *The constraint* (C0) *preserves the handle and tunnel loops and thus all holes of the visual hull in the reconstructed object. The topological genus of the reconstructed object is larger or equal to the one of the visual hull.*

Proof. Let us assume that the proposition does not hold. To let the genus of the reconstructed object decrease, either (i) at least one hole of the visual hull needs to be filled or (ii) at least one tunnel loop has to be disconnected in the reconstructed object. Because the domain of the reconstructed object is restricted to the visual hull, (i) cannot be fulfilled. By construction, (ii) is fulfilled if (C0) is fulfilled. Therefore the genus of the reconstructed object has to be larger or equal to the genus of the visual hull.

Note that, depending on the data term f the reconstructed object is allowed to have more holes than the visual hull. In some cases, it is not desirable to exactly preserve all holes and corresponding handles of the visual hull. A possible scenario is depicted in Fig. 3 where aliasing artifacts of the visual hull lead to spurious handle loops which should not be preserved in the final reconstruction. Therefore we propose to relax the loop preserving constraint (C0) such that either the connectivity of a handle is preserved in the final reconstruction or, in case the photometric support via f is not strong enough, the handle segment H_i is suppressed completely. We define the *generalized connectivity* constraint as

$$\forall i \in [1, \ldots, g] : \quad \left\{ \forall \boldsymbol{x} \in t_i^{\mathcal{G}_s} \cap H_i : \frac{d}{ds} u(\boldsymbol{x}) = 0 \right\} \tag{C1}$$

where $\frac{d}{ds}$ is the directional derivative along the loop $t_i^{\mathcal{G}_s}$.

Finding the optimal connected loop $t_i^{\mathcal{G}_s}$. For objects of genus 0, the use of the shortest path tree in the connectivity constraint is motivated by the optimal connecting path, that adds the minimum cost to the final segmentation result. In case of objects with higher genus, we wish to preserve the connectivity with respect to loops in the final segmentation. Therefore a loop through each handle needs to be found, which is optimal in the same way, i.e. that it also adds the minimum cost to the final segmentation. Using the already computed shortest path tree $\mathcal{G}_s$, we can find the shortest loop $t_i^{\mathcal{G}_s}$ with respect to $\mathcal{G}_s$ for each

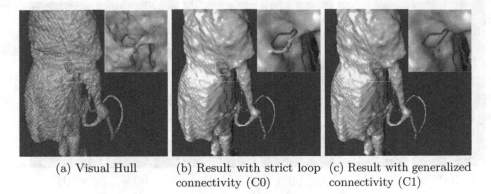

(a) Visual Hull   (b) Result with strict loop   (c) Result with generalized
                          connectivity (C0)   connectivity (C1)

Fig. 3. (a) In some cases artifacts of the visual hull can lead to spurious handle loops which should not be preserved in the final reconstruction. (b) The constraint C0 strictly preserves all loops in the solution. (c) Relaxing the topology preserving constraint to our generalized connectivity constraint allows to suppress handles where the photoconsistency is not strong enough. The rope, where the support of the photoconsistency is sufficient, is still completely preserved. Handle and tunnel loops are depicted in green and red, respectively.

handle i by the following steps: With a depth first search on $\mathcal{G}_s$, starting from the boundary of a handle segment H_i, we compute the partitions $H_i^1 \cup H_i^2 = H_i$, $H_i^1 \cap H_i^2 = \emptyset$ which are disconnected on the shortest path tree $\mathcal{G}_s$. These partitions are shown in Fig. 4d. If one of these partitions is empty, i.e. all points in the handle segment H_i are connected on $\mathcal{G}_s$, then no further constraints need to be added in order to preserve handle segment H_i. Otherwise, we compute an optimal pair of points

$$(\boldsymbol{p}, \boldsymbol{q}) = \underset{(\boldsymbol{x} \in H_i^1, \boldsymbol{y} \in H_i^2, \boldsymbol{y} \in \mathcal{N}(\boldsymbol{x}))}{\arg\min} \mathcal{D}_s(\boldsymbol{x}) + \mathcal{D}_s(\boldsymbol{y}) \tag{10}$$

which are leaf-nodes in $\mathcal{G}_s$. The set $\mathcal{N}(\boldsymbol{x})$ denotes the local spatial neighborhood of a point $\boldsymbol{x} \in V$. The optimal path through the handle is computed by tracing the path backwards along the predecessors of both nodes $\boldsymbol{p}, \boldsymbol{q}$ in $\mathcal{G}_s$, resulting in the path with minimum costs through the handle (Fig. 4e).

While the tree connectivity constraint resulted in an inequality constraint on the derivative of the label function, the loop connectivity is preserved by adding the equality constraints

$$\delta_e \left(u(\boldsymbol{x}, t) \right) = 0, \quad e \in \mathcal{E}_=. \tag{11}$$

to the optimization problem (7), where $\mathcal{E}_=$ is the set of edges of the optimal path through the handle.

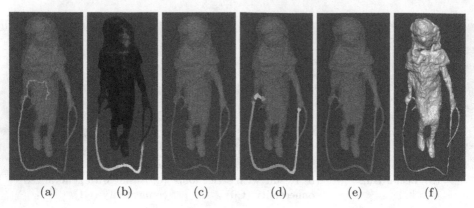

| (a) | (b) | (c) | (d) | (e) | (f) |

Fig. 4. Visualization of various properties that we compute based on the shape of the visual hull (genus 2 in this case) and the data term. (a) Example shortest path from a leaf node to the source node s (red); (b) color-coded geodesic distance map $\mathcal{D}_s$ with respect to the source node s; (c) handle (green) and tunnel (red) loops; (d) handle segmentations $H_i = H_i^1 \cup H_i^2$ (green+orange), the coloring shows disconnected parts within the handle with respect to the geodesic path tree $\mathcal{G}_s$. (e) shortest path through the handle for which the equality constraints (C1) are imposed; (f) final reconstruction result.

4   Numerical Optimization

To minimize energy (7) using convex optimization we first relax the discrete image function to the continuous interval $[0, 1]$. The constraints defined on the derivative of the image function remain the same as in the discrete setting.

Because the total variation norm is non-differentiable, we introduce a dual variable $p : V \times T \mapsto \mathbb{R}^4$ and reformulate the optimization problem Eq.(7) as the equivalent saddle-point problem

$$\min_{u} \max_{\|p\| \leq 1} \int_{V \times T} \langle u, -\operatorname{div}(p) \rangle \; d\boldsymbol{x}dt + \lambda \int_{V \times T} fu \; d\boldsymbol{x}dt \; . \tag{12}$$

$$\text{s. t.} \qquad \delta_e\left(u(\boldsymbol{x}, t)\right) \leq 0, \quad e \in \mathcal{E}$$
$$\delta_e\left(u(\boldsymbol{x}, t)\right) = 0, \quad e \in \mathcal{E}_=$$

The constraints on u over the edge sets $\mathcal{E}$ and $\mathcal{E}_=$ are included in the optimization using Lagrangian multipliers β and γ. The Lagrangian associated to problem (12) becomes

$$\min_{u} \max_{\substack{\|p\| \leq 1, \\ \beta \geq 0, \\ \gamma}} \int_{V \times T} \langle u, -\operatorname{div}(p) \rangle \; d\boldsymbol{x}dt + \lambda \int_{V \times T} fu \; d\boldsymbol{x}dt \tag{13}$$

$$+ \int_{T} \left\{ \sum_{e \in \mathcal{E}} \beta_e \, \delta_e\left(u\right) + \sum_{e \in \mathcal{E}_=} \gamma_e \, \delta_e\left(u\right) \right\} dt \; .$$

This saddle point problem is optimized using the preconditioned primal-dual algorithm by Pock and Chambolle [23]. The algorithm results in an iterative update scheme with a gradient ascent in the dual and a gradient descent in the primal variable

$$
\begin{aligned}
p^{n+1} &= \Pi_C \left[p^n + \sigma \nabla \bar{u}^n \right] \\
\beta_e^{n+1} &= \Pi_{\geq 0} (\beta_e^n + \mu \, \delta_e (\bar{u}^n)) \\
\gamma_e^{n+1} &= \gamma_e^n + \nu \, \delta_e (\bar{u}^n) \\
u^{n+1} &= \Pi_{[0,1]} \left[u^n + \tau \left(\operatorname{div} p^{n+1} + \operatorname{div} \beta^{n+1} + \operatorname{div} \gamma^{n+1} - \lambda f \right) \right] \\
\bar{u}^{n+1} &= 2u^{n+1} - u^n
\end{aligned}
\tag{14}
$$

where $\Pi_{[0,1]}$ is the projection of u onto the unit interval $[0,1]$ and $\Pi_{\geq 0}$ onto positive values. The projection onto the set $C = \{ q = (q_x, q_t)^T : V \times T \mapsto \mathbb{R}^4 | \, \|q_x\| \leq 1, |q_t| \leq 1 \}$ is a projection on a 4D hyperball and can be done as follows:

$$
\Pi_C(q) = \left(\frac{q_x}{\max(1, \frac{\|q_x\|}{\rho})}, \max \left(-g_t, \min(g_t, q_t) \right) \right)^T
\tag{15}
$$

The step sizes τ, σ, μ and ν are chosen as suggested in [23]. Because our energy model is convex and the linear constraints preserve convexity of the optimization problem, the update scheme (14) converges to a global minimum of the relaxed energy (7). An optimal binary labeling can be found by thresholding the relaxed solution [23].

Implementation. The proposed iterative scheme for minimal surface reconstruction with connectivity constraints (14) allows a high degree of parallelization and is implemented using the CUDA programming framework. The connectivity graph precomputation is more difficult to parallelize and therefore is implemented on the CPU.

5   Experiments

We evaluated our method on several spatio-temporal multi-view data sets provided by the INRIA 4D repository [16]. All scenes were synchronously recorded by 16 cameras in a green room environment.

In the experiments we mainly focus on comparing reconstruction results with and without connectivity constraints. Since no other 4D reconstruction methods are publicly available, we compare our results with the ones of the state-of-the-art 3D reconstruction methods by Jancosek and Pajdla [17] and the combination of Furukawa et al. (PMVS) [10] and Poisson surface reconstruction [18].

Approximate silhouette information was used for all methods except of the method by Jancosek and Pajdla [17] for which it cannot be used. We used the 6-neighborhood for the computation of the geodesic shortest path tree $\mathcal{G}_s$. In this setting, the generalization to arbitrary genus by using equality constraints does not increase the number of dual variables (Lagrange multipliers), because some inequality constraints are exchanged by equality constraints.

44   M.R. Oswald, J. Stühmer, and D. Cremers

1 of 16 Input Images

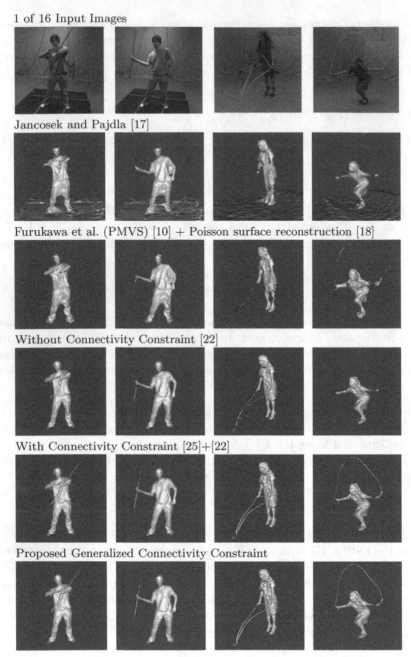

Jancosek and Pajdla [17]

Furukawa et al. (PMVS) [10] + Poisson surface reconstruction [18]

Without Connectivity Constraint [22]

With Connectivity Constraint [25]+[22]

Proposed Generalized Connectivity Constraint

Fig. 5. Comparison of different reconstruction methods: Existing state-of-the art approaches [17,10,18] fail to recover thin structures like the stick and the rope. The connectivity constraint allows to preserve the stick, but for the rope-jump scene with higher genus, it does not completely preserve the connection of the rope. Our proposed generalized connectivity constraint allows to correctly reconstruct both scenes (volume resolution $|V| = 384^3$).

Runtime and Memory Resource Evaluation. The memory footprint of the suggested implementation increases only by $|V \times T|$ bytes in comparison to the original approach. The numerical optimization runtime per iteration remains almost unchanged, but depending on the scene structure more iterations are needed for sufficient convergence. All experiments were run on a Linux-based Intel Xeon E5520 PC with 24GB RAM and NVidia GTX Titan graphics card. For the genus 0 connectivity [25] the precomputation time per frame was about 20 sec for computing the tree of the tree-shaped connectivity constraints. For the generalized connectivity constraints the precomputation time was about 1 min for handle and tunnel loop detection, handle segmentation and computation of the tree. The optimization needs about 3 min per frame resulting in a total runtime of about 4 minutes per frame when using the generalized connectivity constraints.

6   Conclusion

In this paper we introduced tree-shaped connectivity constraints into spatio-temporal multi-view 3D reconstruction. By detecting loops in the object we are able to generalize the connectivity constraint to objects with non-tree structure of arbitrary genus. In several experiments, we demonstrated that the proposed connectivity constraints significantly improve the reconstruction quality in the presence of fine elongated structures.

To the best of our knowledge, apart from the work in [3], which uses a strong simplification of a connectivity prior and essentially is a 2.5D method, this is the first work which imposes connectivity constraints in a multi-view 3D reconstruction setup.

The connectivity constraint is especially useful in 4D multi-view settings, for which exact silhouettes are usually not available and exact silhouette constraints are not applicable. Assuring temporal coherence of the connectivity constraints would need explicit modeling of the occupancy flow and remains for future work.

References

1. Aganj, E., Pons, J.P., Ségonne, F., Keriven, R.: Spatio-temporal shape from silhouette using four-dimensional delaunay meshing. In: ICCV, pp. 1–8 (2007)
2. Ambrosio, L., Fusco, N., Pallara, D.: Functions of bounded variation and free discontinuity problems. Oxford Mathematical Monographs. The Clarendon Press Oxford University Press, New York (2000)
3. Bleyer, M., Rother, C., Kohli, P., Scharstein, D., Sinha, S.: Object stereojoint stereo matching and object segmentation. In: CVPR, pp. 3081–3088. IEEE (2011)
4. Boykov, Y., Veksler, O., Zabih, R.: Fast approximate energy minimization via graph cuts. IEEE TPAMI 23(11), 1222–1239 (2001)
5. Chen, C., Freedman, D., Lampert, C.H.: Enforcing topological constraints in random field image segmentation. In: CVPR, pp. 2089–2096 (2011)
6. Cremers, D., Kolev, K.: Multiview stereo and silhouette consistency via convex functionals over convex domains. IEEE TPAMI 33, 1161–1174 (2011)

7. Dey, T.K., Fan, F., Wang, Y.: An efficient computation of handle and tunnel loops via reeb graphs. ACM Trans. Graph. 32(4), 32 (2013)
8. Dey, T.K., Li, K., Sun, J., Cohen-Steiner, D.: Computing geometry-aware handle and tunnel loops in 3d models. ACM Trans. Graph. 27(3) (2008)
9. Esteban, C.H., Schmitt, F.: Silhouette and stereo fusion for 3d object modeling. CVIU 96(3), 367–392 (2004)
10. Furukawa, Y., Ponce, J.: Accurate, dense, and robust multiview stereopsis. IEEE TPAMI 32(8), 1362–1376 (2010), http://dx.doi.org/10.1109/TPAMI.2009.161
11. Goldluecke, B., Ihrke, I., Linz, C., Magnor, M.: Weighted minimal hypersurface reconstruction. IEEE TPAMI 29(7), 1194–1208 (2007)
12. Goldluecke, B., Magnor, M.: Space-time isosurface evolution for temporally coherent 3D reconstruction. In: CVPR, vol. I, pp. 350–355 (July 2004)
13. Guillemaut, J.Y., Hilton, A.: Space-time joint multi-layer segmentation and depth estimation. In: 3DIMPVT, pp. 440–447 (2012)
14. Gulshan, V., Rother, C., Criminisi, A., Blake, A., Zisserman, A.: Geodesic star convexity for interactive image segmentation. In: CVPR, pp. 3129–3136. IEEE (2010)
15. Han, X., Xu, C., Prince, J.L.: A topology preserving level set method for geometric deformable models. IEEE TPAMI 25(6), 755–768 (2003)
16. Institut national de recherche en informatique et en automatique (INRIA) Rhône Alpes: 4d repository, http://4drepository.inrialpes.fr/
17. Jancosek, M., Pajdla, T.: Multi-view reconstruction preserving weakly-supported surfaces. In: CVPR, pp. 3121–3128 (2011)
18. Kazhdan, M.M., Bolitho, M., Hoppe, H.: Poisson surface reconstruction. In: Symposium on Geometry Processing, pp. 61–70 (2006)
19. Kolev, K., Klodt, M., Brox, T., Cremers, D.: Continuous global optimization in multiview 3d reconstruction. IJCV 84(1), 80–96 (2009)
20. Lorensen, W.E., Cline, H.E.: Marching cubes: A high resolution 3d surface construction algorithm. SIGGRAPH Comput. Graph. 21, 163–169 (1987)
21. Nowozin, S., Lampert, C.H.: Global connectivity potentials for random field models. In: CVPR, pp. 818–825. IEEE (2009)
22. Oswald, M.R., Cremers, D.: A convex relaxation approach to space time multi-view 3d reconstruction. In: ICCV - Workshop on Dynamic Shape Capture and Analysis (4DMOD) (2013)
23. Pock, T., Chambolle, A.: Diagonal preconditioning for first order primal-dual algorithms in convex optimization. In: ICCV, Washington, DC, USA, pp. 1762–1769 (2011)
24. Starck, J., Hilton, A.: Surface capture for performance-based animation. IEEE Computer Graphics and Applications 27(3), 21–31 (2007)
25. Stühmer, J., Schröder, P., Cremers, D.: Tree shape priors with connectivity constraints using convex relaxation on general graphs. In: ICCV, Sydney, Australia (December 2013)
26. Vicente, S., Kolmogorov, V., Rother, C.: Graph cut based image segmentation with connectivity priors. In: CVPR (2008)
27. Zeng, Y., Samaras, D., Chen, W., Peng, Q.: Topology cuts: A novel min-cut/max-flow algorithm for topology preserving segmentation in n–d images. Computer Vision and Image Understanding 112(1), 81–90 (2008)

Passive Tomography of Turbulence Strength

Marina Alterman[1], Yoav Y. Schechner[1],
Minh Vo[2], and Srinivasa G. Narasimhan[2]

[1] Dept. Electrical Eng., Technion - Israel Institute of Technology, Haifa, Israel
[2] Robotics Institute, Carnegie Mellon University, Pittsburgh, PA, USA

Abstract. Turbulence is studied extensively in remote sensing, astronomy, meteorology, aerodynamics and fluid dynamics. The strength of
turbulence is a statistical measure of local variations in the turbulent
medium. It influences engineering decisions made in these domains. Turbulence strength (TS) also affects safety of aircraft and tethered bal-
loons, and reliability of free-space electromagnetic relays. We show that
it is possible to estimate TS, without having to reconstruct instantaneous
fluid flow fields. Instead, the TS field can be directly recovered, passively,
using videos captured from different viewpoints. We formulate this as a
linear tomography problem with a structure unique to turbulence fields.
No tight synchronization between cameras is needed. Thus, realization is
very simple to deploy using consumer-grade cameras. We experimentally
demonstrate this both in a lab and in a large-scale uncontrolled complex
outdoor environment, which includes industrial, rural and urban areas.

1 The Need to Recover Turbulence Strength

Turbulence creates refractive perturbations to light passing through a scene.
This causes random distortions when imaging background objects. Hence, modeling and trying to compensate for random refractive distortions has long been
studied in remote sensing [40], astronomy [34] and increasingly in computer vision [2,4,10,14,18,35,38,41,52,55]. Nevertheless, these distortion are not necessarily a problem: they offer information about the medium and the scene itself [44].
This insight is analogous to imaging in scattering media (fog [29], haze [19,37],
water [11,30]), where visibility reduction yields ranging and characterizing of the
medium. Similar efforts are made to reconstruct refracting (transparent) solids
or water surfaces [3,16,28,43,46] from images of a distorted background or light
field [50,51]. In turbulence, refraction occurs continuously throughout a volume.

We *exploit* random image distortions as a means to estimate the spatial (volumetric) distribution of *turbulence strength* (TS). The strength of turbulence
is a statistical measure of local variations in the medium [20,21]. Often, it is
not necessary to estimate an instantaneous snapshot of air density or refraction
field [32,42]. Rather *local statistics* is relied upon heavily in many applications.
Meteorologists rely on TS to understand convection (which forms clouds), wind,
and atmospheric stability. This is measured using special Doppler lidars [9,31],
which are very expensive. Turbulence significantly affects the efficiency of wind

D. Fleet et al. (Eds.): ECCV 2014, Part IV, LNCS 8692, pp. 47–60, 2014.
© Springer International Publishing Switzerland 2014

turbine farms [31], hence optimizing turbines and farms involves measuring TS. Similarly, the design and performance of other aerodynamic objects (wings, winglets, jets engines etc.) is tied to the strength of the non-laminar flow around them. In such cases, the statistics of the flow field are important, as they convey transfer of energy, loads, correlations and spatiotemporal spectra. The TS is also an indicator for gliding birds who use convection for lift. Moreover, determining which areas have stronger or weaker turbulence can optimize free-space optical relay of communication and power [31].

One might estimate TS using many consecutively recovered instantaneous refractive fields [33,47,48]. These instantaneous fields may themselves be estimated by multiview tightly-synchronized image sequences. Indeed, several works recover time-varying 3D gas flows [6,7,52]. However, there are advantages for measuring the TS directly, without recovering instantaneous fields. Estimating an instantaneous refractive field may be ill-posed [7] or require more complex setups involving active light-field probes [17,39]. In addition, direct estimation of the TS avoids any propagation of errors stemming from inaccurate instantaneous fields. TS is passively estimated in [54] assuming a path-constant (uniform) TS rather than a spatially varying field. Another related work is [44]. There, spatially stationary turbulence is exploited to estimate object range.

In this paper, we describe how the TS field can be directly estimated using only passive multiview observations of a background. The variances in image projections of background features are computed by tracking those features over a few hundred frames. The variance at each pixel at each camera viewpoint is simply a weighted integral of the TS field along the respective pixels' line of sight (LOS). The LOSs of all pixels from all viewpoints crisscross the turbulence field. Estimating the TS's volumetric distribution is then equivalent to solving a linear tomography problem. While linear tomography is common in medical imaging, the specific structure here is different. Thus, our domain and model form a new addition to the set of tomographic problems, which recently raise interest in computational photography and vision [1,7,13,26,27,36,46,51].

We demonstrate our model and method using experiments indoors and outdoors, as well as simulations. Outdoors, we estimate the TS field in a large scale: a city, in a complex terrain including urban, industrial and rural areas. We believe this is the first attempt to reconstruct such a large field passively.

2   Theoretical Background

2.1   Turbulence Statistics and Refraction

The refractive index of air $n(\mathbf{X}, t)$ at spatial location $\mathbf{X} = (X, Y, Z)$ and time t is a function of various meteorological parameters (air pressure, temperature, humidity etc.). Due to random spatiotemporal fluctuations of these parameters, $n(\mathbf{X}, t)$ is random in space and time. Temporally stationary atmospheric turbulence is characterized by a *structure function* for refractive index fluctuations. The refractive index structure function [22,44] is

$$\mathcal{D}_n(\mathbf{X}_1, \mathbf{X}_2) = \langle [n(\mathbf{X}_1, t) - n(\mathbf{X}_2, t)]^2 \rangle_t. \tag{1}$$

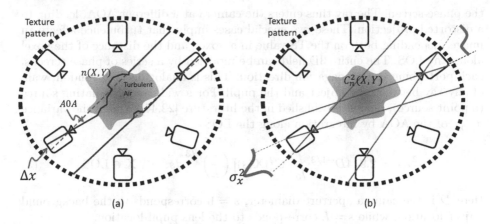

Fig. 1. Multiple cameras are placed around a chunk of turbulent air. (a) An object point of a textured pattern projects to a camera pixel through air having a spatially varying refractive index. (b) Temporal variance of pixel displacement of a textured object is associated to a pixel. This yields data for linear tomography of the statistical field C_n^2.

It represents the mean squared difference of refractive indices at different locations $\mathbf{X}_1$ and $\mathbf{X}_2$. When the structure function depends only on the distance $\rho = ||\mathbf{X}_1 - \mathbf{X}_2||$, Kolmogorov [20,21] showed that

$$\mathcal{D}_n(\rho) = C_n^2 \rho^{2/3}. \tag{2}$$

Here C_n^2 is the refractive index structure constant [22,44]. The parameter C_n^2 expresses TS. High values of C_n^2 imply strong turbulence, while $C_n^2 = 0$ means that the air is not turbulent.[1] The TS changes spatially, thus we denote it $C_n^2(\mathbf{X})$.

There is an LOS between a background object point and a camera at distance L away. Without turbulence, the LOS has an angle of arrival (AOA) relative to the optical axis. Fluctuations of the atmospheric refractive index lead to random refractions of propagating light (see Fig. 1a). Hence turbulence perturbs the LOS. To gain intuition, consider an object point that radiates to all directions, and an atmosphere which is not turbulent, other than a single thin phase screen. A phase screen represents a layer having spatiotemporal $n(\mathbf{X}, t)$. At any t the phase screen randomly deviates the direction of each incoming ray, once. Suppose the phase screen is just adjacent to the object point. In this case, the direction of rays emanating from the point are randomly permuted. Nevertheless, overall rays appear to radiate in all directions, just as a point source without turbulence. Hence, in this case, the turbulent layer does not affect the image.

On the other hand, suppose the phase screen is adjacent to the camera's exit pupil. A ray between the object and the pupil varies its direction as it passes

---

[1] The distance ρ is in units of m. Then, the units of C_n^2 are $m^{-2/3}$. Typical values of C_n^2 are in the range $10^{-17} - 10^{-13}$ $m^{-2/3}$.

the phase-screen. The ray thus enters the camera at a different AOA, leading to a distorted projection. These two special cases imply that turbulence affects an image, depending both on the TS value in a voxel, and the distance of the voxel along any LOS. The entire 3D field can be modeled by a series of phase screens, each perturbing the propagation direction. This is analogous to a random walk of any ray between the object and the pupil. For a wide-angle radiating source (a point source), models established in the literature [22,44] express the variance σ^2_{AOA} of the AOA by integration along the LOS

$$\sigma^2_{\text{AOA}} = 2.914 D^{-1/3} \int_0^L C_n^2[\mathbf{X}(s)] \left(\frac{s}{L}\right)^{5/3} ds, \qquad \mathbf{X} \in \text{LOS}. \tag{3}$$

Here D is the camera aperture diameter, $s = 0$ corresponds to the background object location, while $s = L$ corresponds to the lens pupil location.

2.2   Linear Tomography

A linear emission tomography model typically applies to independent emitters, e.g., fluorescent molecules and radioactive probes used in SPECT. A volumetric field $e(\mathbf{X})$ of emitters is projected by a camera at some pose. Pixel $\mathbf{p}$ then corresponds to a particular LOS, denoted $\text{LOS}_{\mathbf{p}}$. Parameterize a position on $\text{LOS}_{\mathbf{p}}$ by $s \in [0, L]$. Set $s = 0$ at a background point, while $s = L$ corresponds to the lens pupil. The measured intensity at $\mathbf{p}$ is then the line integral

$$I(\mathbf{p}) \propto \int_0^L e[\mathbf{X}(s)]ds, \qquad \mathbf{X} \in \text{LOS}_{\mathbf{p}}. \tag{4}$$

Different LOSs can provide independent linear equations as (4). Based on these equations, $e(\mathbf{X})$ can be estimated $\forall \mathbf{X}$. The line integral in Eq. (4) is insensitive to flipping of the coordinate system (counter propagation): if the pupil moves to $s = 0$ while the background point is at $s = L$, Eq. (4) yields the same value. Hence, in typical linear emission tomography, it suffices to measure $I(\mathbf{p})$ from half the directional domain.

3   Principle of C_n^2 Tomography

As seen in Eq. (3), a single LOS is perturbed by a path-averaged $C_n^2(\mathbf{X})$. By utilizing *several* viewpoints, it may be possible to recover the spatial distribution $C_n^2(\mathbf{X})$ based on Eq. (3). This is a new field for linear tomography. Data on σ^2_{AOA} can be obtained by analyzing either AOA fluctuations [54] for short exposures or image blur for long exposures, at scene features of known range. Here too, pixel $\mathbf{p}$ corresponds to $\text{LOS}_{\mathbf{p}}$. Using Eqs. (3,4), the measured AOA variance at $\mathbf{p}$ is

$$\sigma^2_{\text{AOA}}(\mathbf{p}) \propto \int_0^L C_n^2[\mathbf{X}(s)]s^{5/3}ds, \qquad \mathbf{X} \in \text{LOS}_{\mathbf{p}}. \tag{5}$$

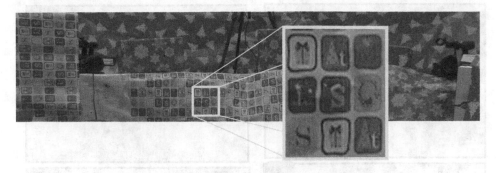

Fig. 2. An example of an image frame as seen through turbulent air. Notice the distorted edges in the magnified region.

Analogously to Sec. 2.2, different LOSs can provide independent linear equations as (5), relating the unknown field C_n^2, to the measured σ_{AOA}^2. Based on these equations, $C_n^2[\mathbf{X}(s)]$ can be estimated $\forall \mathbf{X}$. However, contrary to linear emission tomography, the line integral in Eq. (5) is *sensitive* to flipping the coordinate system (counter propagation): voxels closer to the camera have more weight in Eq. (5), than distant voxels (for which $s \to 0$). Thus, counter-directions yield independent measurements.

3.1 Numeric Tomographic Recovery of C_n^2

Consider the setup in Fig. 1(a). The background is a textured pattern. Multiple cameras are placed around a chunk of air. An object point projects to pixel

$$x = f \tan \mathrm{AOA}, \tag{6}$$

where f is the focal length of the camera. Due to turbulence, random image distortions are observed over time. Each temporal frame is spatially distorted (in Fig. 2, notice the distorted edges in the magnified region). The image pixel displacement has variance

$$\sigma_{\mathsf{x}}^2 \approx f^2 \left[\frac{d\tan(\mathrm{AOA})}{d\mathrm{AOA}}\right]^2 \sigma_{\mathrm{AOA}}^2 = f^2 \frac{1}{\cos^4(\mathrm{AOA})} \sigma_{\mathrm{AOA}}^2. \tag{7}$$

Later, in Sec. 5.1, we describe an experiment in which air is heated by electric griddles, creating turbulence that distorts a background texture. Fig. 3 shows displacement variance maps from different viewpoints. High variance in the map means that a LOS passes through more turbulence, than at pixels exhibiting low displacement variance.

As illustrated in Fig. 4, we discretize the volume domain into a 3D grid of voxels $\{V_k\}_{k=1}^{N_{\mathrm{voxels}}}$. Without turbulence, pixel $\mathbf{p}$ observes object point $\mathbf{O}$ through

Fig. 3. Sample variance images from an experiment corresponding to Fig. 6. A textured pattern which is placed behind the stove is shown aligned with its variance image, from one view. Sample variance images of pixel displacements, in various views, with corresponding camera indices. Red expresses high variance while blue represents low variance. High variance regions appear only behind hot stoves.

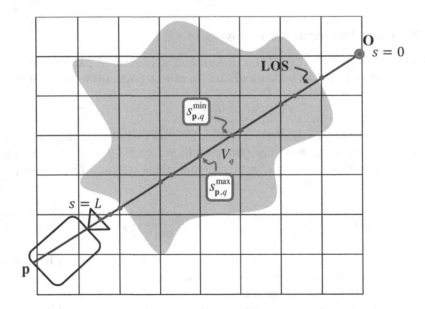

Fig. 4. The volume is discretized into voxels. The LOS intersects voxel V_q at points $s_{\mathbf{p},q}^{\min}$ and $s_{\mathbf{p},q}^{\max}$. The voxel intersection points $\Psi_{\mathbf{p},q} \equiv \mathrm{LOS}_{\mathbf{p}} \cap V_q$ are used as weights in the LOS integration (9).

$\text{LOS}_\mathbf{p}$. Let $\text{LOS}_\mathbf{p}$ intersect voxel V_q. The line intersection is $\Psi_{\mathbf{p},q} \equiv \text{LOS}_\mathbf{p} \cap V_q$. It is bounded by two points,[2] at corresponding distances from $\mathbf{O}$:

$$s_{\mathbf{p},q}^{\min} = \min_{\mathbf{X} \in \Psi_{\mathbf{p},q}} \|\mathbf{X} - \mathbf{O}\| \qquad s_{\mathbf{p},q}^{\max} = \max_{\mathbf{X} \in \Psi_{\mathbf{p},q}} \|\mathbf{X} - \mathbf{O}\|. \qquad (8)$$

Approximate C_n^2 as constant in each voxel. Based on Eqs. (3,7,8),

$$\sigma_\mathbf{x}^2(\mathbf{p}) = \alpha_\mathbf{p} \sum_{\Psi_{\mathbf{p},q} \neq \emptyset} C_n^2(q) \int_{s_{\mathbf{p},q}^{\min}}^{s_{\mathbf{p},q}^{\max}} s^{5/3} ds = \frac{3\alpha_\mathbf{p}}{8} \sum_{\Psi_{\mathbf{p},q} \neq \emptyset} C_n^2(q)[(s_{\mathbf{p},q}^{\max})^{8/3} - (s_{\mathbf{p},q}^{\min})^{8/3}]$$

$$(9)$$

where

$$\alpha_\mathbf{p} = \frac{2.914 f^2}{D^{1/3} L_\mathbf{p}^{5/3} \cos^4(\text{AOA}_\mathbf{p})}. \qquad (10)$$

Here $L_\mathbf{p}$ is the length of $\text{LOS}_\mathbf{p}$ and $\text{AOA}_\mathbf{p}$ is the AOA of pixel $\mathbf{p}$. Let N_{pixels} be the total number of pixels in all viewpoints. Define a $N_{\text{pixels}} \times N_{\text{voxels}}$ matrix $\mathbf{A}$, whose element (p, q) is

$$A(k, q) = \begin{cases} 0 & \text{if } \Psi_{\mathbf{p},q} = \emptyset \\ \frac{3\alpha_\mathbf{p}}{8}[(s_{\mathbf{p},q}^{\max})^{8/3} - (s_{\mathbf{p},q}^{\min})^{8/3}] & \text{otherwise} \end{cases}. \qquad (11)$$

Matrix $\mathbf{A}$ is sparse. Column-stack the measured $\sigma_\mathbf{x}^2(\mathbf{p})$ to vector $\mathbf{m}$. Column-stack the unknown $C_n^2(k)$ to vector $\mathbf{c}$. Then, Eqs. (9,11) can be posed in vector form as

$$\mathbf{m} = \mathbf{Ac}. \qquad (12)$$

This linear system of equations can be solved by any standard solver. For example, it may be possible to use constrained and/or regularized least-squares:

$$\hat{\mathbf{c}} = \arg \min_\mathbf{c} \left(\|\mathbf{m} - \mathbf{Ac}\|^2 + \lambda \|\nabla^2 \mathbf{c}\|^2 \right) \qquad \text{s.t. } \mathbf{c} \geq \mathbf{0}, \qquad (13)$$

where λ weights a spatial smoothness regularizing term. When $\mathbf{A}$ is large, we use the Simultaneous Algebraic Reconstruction Technique (SART) [12] as the solver. Other priors [19], such as sparsity or a parametric form of $\mathbf{c}$ can also be used.

4 Simulation

We simulated volumetric distributions of C_n^2 as mixtures of 3D spatial Gaussians surrounded by 14 cameras across $70 \times 20 \times 70$ voxels. The cameras captured simulated pixel displacement variances, to which white Gaussian noise of standard deviation 0.05 pixels was added. We examined the reconstruction as a function

---

[2] We used the ray tracing algorithm from [5].

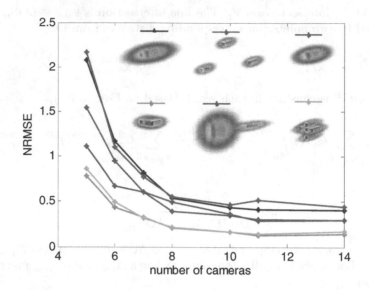

Fig. 5. Simulation results, for various simulated distributions of TS. NRMSE is plotted versus the number of cameras.

of the number of views considered, as shown in Fig. 5. The normalized root mean squared error (NRMSE)

$$\text{NRMSE} = \frac{\sqrt{\langle(\hat{C}_n^2 - C_n^2)^2\rangle_{\mathbf{x}}}}{\max_{\mathbf{x}}(C_n^2)} \qquad (14)$$

is plotted as a function of the number of cameras. Here $\hat{C}_n^2$ is the estimated TS while C_n^2 is the true simulated TS. We used the Laplacian operator with $0.01 \leq \lambda \leq 0.6$ with low values for large number of cameras and high values for small number of cameras. As the number of viewpoints increases, the recovery error drops. Errors are larger for large blobs and vice versa, as typical in tomography.

In addition, we compared two cases: a set of cameras forming a 360° circle versus 180° half circle. A 360° setting yields a smaller error, for the same number of cameras. This is expected, given the directional sensitivity described in Sec. 3.

5   Experiments

5.1   Laboratory

The experimental setup is shown in Fig. 6[Left]. Cooking stoves (Brentwood TS-322 1000W) produced heat, similarly to [44]. We used 11 stoves as shown in Fig. 6[Left]. Hot air from the stoves results in turbulence above the griddles.

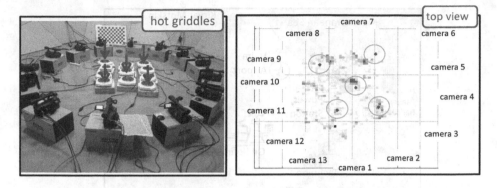

Fig. 6. [Left] Laboratory experimental setup. Multiple cameras encircle hot electric cooking stoves which create turbulence. Sample variance images from different viewpoints are shown in Fig. 3. [Right] Top view of an estimated C_n^2. Red dots indicate the true locations of hot operating stoves. Camera locations are also shown.

Various turbulence fields can be generated by individually controlling the power of each stove and its location. As background we placed a high frequency texture pattern [8], shown at the top of Fig. 3. Thirteen camcorders[3] observed the shimmering of the background through the turbulence field, at 30 fps. The cameras were calibrated using the method described in [49].

To use Eq. (12), $\mathbf{A}$ is derived by line integrals. We know the path length L from each camera to the pattern (Fig. 3[Top]). To compute the pixel displacement variance $\mathbf{m}$, we use dense optical flow [53] implemented in OpenCV. Sample variance images are shown in Fig. 3. Only voxels which are seen by most of the cameras are included in the reconstruction. Voxels that are not seen, or only seen by a few cameras, are excluded, similarly to the visual hull constraint as in [15]. The result of the estimated C_n^2 is shown in Fig. 6[Right]. Red dots indicate the true 3D location of stoves that were on during the experiment. Notice "hot-spots" of the estimated C_n^2 in the vicinity of the hot stoves.[4]

5.2 Outdoors

The outdoor experiment took place on a sunny day around noon, from 11:00AM until 2:30PM. Around noon, atmospheric turbulence should be the strongest and stationary over several hours [54]. The scene is Haifa Bay area. It is a valley with major industrial facilities interleaved by agricultural areas and some towns. Specifically, the area includes oil refineries with a lot of chimneys. In addition, Haifa Bay includes a port, an airport and a power station. Refer to Fig. 7 for a sketch map of the area. We used a Nikon D7100 DSLR camera with a telephoto

---

[3] The cameras are Canon HS-G1s high definition (HD), with F#=3.2 and exposure time 1/180 sec.

[4] The location of the hot stoves was estimated based on stereo triangulation using two cameras.

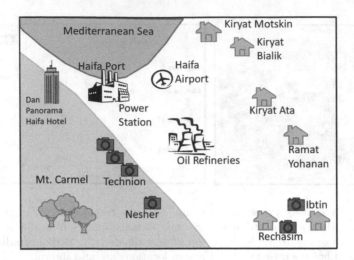

Fig. 7. Map of the Haifa Bay area. It has a valley which includes coastal suburbs (Kiryat Haim, Kiryat Motzkin and Kiryat Bialik), agricultural zones and heavy industry. The valley is surrounded by higher terrain, including Mt. Carmel (Technion, the cities of Haifa and Nesher) and hilly towns (Kfar Hasidim, Rechasim, Ibtin, Kiryat Ata). Red cameras mark locations from which we took image sequences during an experiment.

lens of $f = 300$mm, $F\# = 14$ and exposure time of 1/600sec. To gain a wide field of view (FOV), multiple narrow FOV videos were collected. We shot 30fps HD videos of ≈ 100 temporal frames for each narrow FOV. The scene was imaged from six viewpoints on the surrounding hills (see the red cameras in 7). The location of each view was recorded using GPS. Sample images of views and a stitched panorama are shown in Fig. 8.

To compute the line integrals in **A**, the locations of various scene objects in the images must be known. We used Google maps to locate the coordinates of multiple known landmarks in the valley landscape. We located, overall, 360 landmarks across all views. Fig. 9[Left] depicts the outdoor experimental setup. The rays to the known landmarks are shown by blue lines. The GPS Coordinates (latitude, longitude) were converted to local navigation coordinates (north, east, up) relative to the camera position in view 2. Our reconstruction area is essentially the area where rays cross.

Then, pixel displacement statistics (mean and variance) were computed for these landmarks in each temporal sequence of frames. The Kanade-Lucas-Tomasi (KLT) [25,45] algorithm implemented in Matlab was used for tracking corner points. The variance of each trajectory was computed to construct the vector **m**. The reconstruction area was divided into $20 \times 20 \times 1$ voxels. The estimated turbulence strength parameter (C_n^2) is shown in Fig. 9[Right] as a 2D map. We used the Laplacian regularization with $\lambda = 0.4$. The positions of the cameras are overlayed in green. Notice that a region with strong turbulence was estimated as the refineries plant ($C_n^2 = 1.7 \cdot 10^{-14} \ m^{-2/3}$). The second-strongest hot-spot

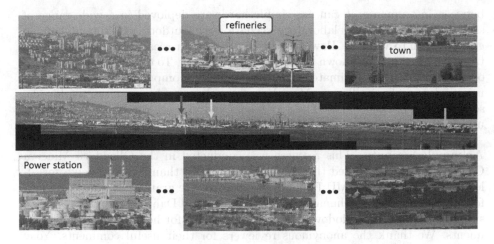

Fig. 8. Sample images from an outdoor experiment. Images of different views are shown. Places of interest are indicated on the images and also on the panorama. [Middle] The panorama image of view-2 was created using Microsoft image composite editor.

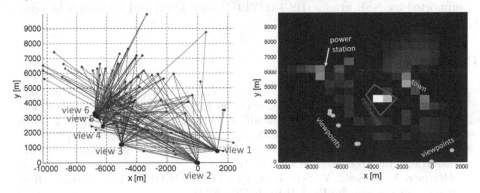

Fig. 9. [Left] Experimental setup of the outdoor experiment. Black dots indicate viewpoints. Any blue line represents a ray between a viewpoint and an object point. Figure axes are aligned to the compass cardinal directions in our region. [Right] The estimated TS parameter C_n^2 shown in a 2D map. Bright areas represent high values while dark areas represent low values. Regional places of interest are overlayed on the map. Notice the hottest spot is at the oil refineries.

was near the power station ($C_n^2 = 0.45 \cdot 10^{-14} \ m^{-2/3}$). A third, diffuse turbulent region was the town of Kiryat Ata. The agricultural fields around the refineries have weak turbulence. This agrees with our expectations.

6 Discussion

We describe a passive approach for estimating the volumetric spatially varying turbulence-strength field. As the approach does not require synchronization between instruments, it can use simple hardware deployed in a wide range of scales. In contrast to a laboratory scenario, the outdoor experiment had no ground truth to validate. However, the results appear reasonable, at least qualitatively, based on the known landmarks in the valley. To quantitatively validate outdoor results, the estimated TS field might be compared to measurements using lidars and scintillators. More broadly, webcams observe cities worldwide, some over long ranges [23]. Their locations and viewing directions [24] can be used with our framework for potentially large-scale turbulence measurements.

Acknowledgments. This research was conducted in the Ollendorff Minerva Center. Minerva is funded through the BMBF. We thank Yaser Sheikh for allowing the use of the CMU Panoptic Studio. We are grateful to Joseph Shamir for useful discussions; Johanan Erez, Ina Talmon and Dani Yagodin for technical support; and Vadim Holodovsky and Mark Sheinin for helping with the experiments. We thank the anonymous reviewers for their useful comments. Yoav Schechner is a Landau Fellow - supported by the Taub Foundation. The work in the Technion group is supported by the Israel Science Foundation (ISF Grant 1467/12), and the Asher Space Research Fund. The work in the CMU group is supported by NSF grants (IIS-1317749 ,IIS-0964562) and by Tonbo Imaging Gift.

References

1. Aides, A., Schechner, Y.Y., Holodovsky, V., Garay, M.J., Davis, A.B.: Multi sky-view 3D aerosol distribution recovery. Optics Express 21(22), 25820–25833 (2013)
2. Alterman, M., Schechner, Y.Y., Shamir, J., Perona, P.: Detecting motion through dynamic refraction. IEEE TPAMI 35, 245–251 (2013)
3. Alterman, M., Schechner, Y.Y., Swirski, Y.: Triangulation in random refractive distortions. In: Proc. IEEE ICCP (2013)
4. Alterman, M., Swirski, Y., Schechner, Y.: STELLA MARIS: Stellar marine refractive imaging sensor. In: Proc. IEEE ICCP (2014)
5. Amanatides, J., Woo, A.: A fast voxel traversal algorithm for ray tracing. Eurographics 87(3), 3–10 (1987)
6. Atcheson, B., Heidrich, W., Ihrke, I.: An evaluation of optical flow algorithms for background oriented Schlieren imaging. Experiments in Fluids 46(3), 467–476 (2009)
7. Atcheson, B., Ihrke, I., Heidrich, W., Tevs, A., Bradley, D., Magnor, M., Seidel, H.P.: Time-resolved 3D capture of non-stationary gas flows. ACM TOG 27(5), 132:1–132:9 (2008)
8. Couture, V., Martin, N., Roy, S.: Unstructured light scanning to overcome interreflections. In: Proc. IEEE ICCV, pp. 1895–1902 (2011)
9. Engelmann, R., Wandinger, U., Ansmann, A., Müller, D., Žeromskis, E., Althausen, D., Wehner, B.: Lidar observations of the vertical aerosol flux in the planetary boundary layer. J. Atmospheric & Oceanic Tech. 25(8), 1296–1306 (2008)
10. Gilles, J., Dagobert, T., De Franchis, C.: Atmospheric turbulence restoration by diffeomorphic image registration and blind deconvolution. In: Blanc-Talon, J., Bourennane, S., Philips, W., Popescu, D., Scheunders, P. (eds.) ACIVS 2008. LNCS, vol. 5259, pp. 400–409. Springer, Heidelberg (2008)

11. Gupta, M., Narasimhan, S.G., Schechner, Y.Y.: On controlling light transport in poor visibility environments. In: Proc. IEEE CVPR (2008)
12. Hansen, P.C., Saxild-Hansen, M.: AIR tools MATLAB package of algebraic iterative reconstruction methods. J. Computational and Applied Mathematics 236(8), 2167–2178 (2012)
13. Hargather, M.J., Settles, G.S.: Natural-background-oriented schlieren imaging. Experiments in Fluids 48(1), 59–68 (2010)
14. Harmeling, S., Hirsch, M., Sra, S., Schölkopf, B.: Online blind deconvolution for astronomy. In: Proc. IEEE ICCP (2009)
15. Ihrke, I., Magnor, M.: Image-based tomographic reconstruction of flames. In: Proc. ACM/EG Sympos. on Animation, pp. 367–375 (2004)
16. Ihrke, I., Goidluecke, B., Magnor, M.: Reconstructing the geometry of flowing water. In: Proc. IEEE ICCV, vol. 2, pp. 1055–1060 (2005)
17. Ji, Y., Ye, J., Yu, J.: Reconstructing gas flows using light-path approximation. In: Proc. IEEE CVPR (2013)
18. Joshi, N., Cohen, M.F.: Seeing Mt. Rainier: Lucky imaging for multi-image denoising, sharpening, and haze removal. In: Proc. IEEE ICCP (2010)
19. Kaftory, R., Schechner, Y.Y., Zeevi, Y.Y.: Variational distance-dependent image restoration. In: Proc. IEEE CVPR (2007)
20. Kolmogorov, A.N.: Dissipation of energy in locally isotropic turbulence. Dokl. Akad. Nauk. SSSR 32, 16–18 (1941)
21. Kolmogorov, A.N.: The local structure of turbulence in incompressible viscous fluid for very large reynolds numbers. Dokl. Akad. Nauk. SSSR 30, 299–303 (1941)
22. Kopeika, N.S.: A System Engineering Approach to Imaging. SPIE Press (1998)
23. Lalonde, J.F., Efros, A.A., Narasimhan, S.G.: Webcam clip art: Appearance and illuminant transfer from time-lapse sequences. ACM TOG 28(5), 131:1–131:10 (2009)
24. Lalonde, J.F., Narasimhan, S.G., Efros, A.A.: What do the sun and the sky tell us about the camera? IJCV 88(1), 24–51 (2010)
25. Lucas, B., Kanade, T.: An iterative image registration technique with an application to stereo vision. IJCAI 81, 674–679 (1981)
26. Ma, C., Lin, X., Suo, J., Dai, Q., Wetzstein, G.: Transparent object reconstruction via coded transport of intensity. In: Proc. IEEE CVPR (2014)
27. Messer, H., Zinevich, A., Alpert, P.: Environmental sensor networks using existing wireless communication systems for rainfall and wind velocity measurements. IEEE Instrum. Meas. Mag., 32–38 (2012)
28. Morris, N., Kutulakos, K.: Dynamic refraction stereo. In: Proc. IEEE ICCV, vol. 2, pp. 1573–1580 (2005)
29. Narasimhan, S., Nayar, S.: Vision and the atmosphere. IJCV 48(3) (2002)
30. Narasimhan, S.G., Nayar, S.K., Sun, B., Koppal, S.J.: Structured light in scattering media. In: IEEE ICCV, vol. 1, pp. 420–427 (2005)
31. Oberlack, M., Peinke, J., Talamelli, A., Castillo, L., Hölling, M.: Progress in Turbulence Wind Energy IV. In: Proc. iTi Conf. in Turbulence (2010)
32. Ramlau, R., Rosensteiner, M.: An efficient solution to the atmospheric turbulence tomography problem using Kaczmarz iteration. Inverse Problems 28(9), 095004 (2012)
33. Richard, H., Raffel, M., Rein, M., Kompenhans, J., Meier, G.: Demonstration of the applicability of a background oriented Schlieren (BOS) method. In: Intl. Symp. on Applications of Laser Techniques to Fluid Mechanics, pp. 145–156 (2000)
34. Roggemann, M.C., Welsh, B.: Imaging Through Turbulence. CRC Press (1996)

35. Schechner, Y.Y.: A view through the waves. Marine Technology Society Journal 47, 148–150 (2013)
36. Schechner, Y.Y., Diner, D.J., Martonchik, J.V.: Spaceborne underwater imaging. In: Proc. IEEE ICCP (2011)
37. Schechner, Y., Narasimhan, S., Nayar, S.: Polarization-based vision through haze. Applied Optics 42(3), 511–525 (2003)
38. Sedlazeck, A., Koser, K., Koch, R.: 3D reconstruction based on underwater video from ROV Kiel 6000 considering underwater imaging conditions. In: Proc. IEEE OCEANS EUROPE (2009)
39. Settles, G.S.: Schlieren and Shadowgraph Techniques: Visualizing Phenomena in Transparent Media. Springer (2001)
40. Shimizu, M., Yoshimura, S., Tanaka, M., Okutomi, M.: Super-resolution from image sequence under influence of hot-air optical turbulence. In: Proc. IEEE CVPR (2008)
41. Swirski, Y., Schechner, Y.Y.: 3Deflicker from motion. In: Proc. IEEE ICCP (2013)
42. Tatarskii, V.: Wave Propagation in a Turbulent Medium. McGraw-Hill Books (1961)
43. Tian, Y., Narasimhan, S.G.: Seeing through water: Image restoration using model-based tracking. In: Proc. IEEE ICCV, pp. 2303–2310 (2009)
44. Tian, Y., Narasimhan, S., Vannevel, A.: Depth from optical turbulence. In: Proc. IEEE CVPR (2012)
45. Tomasi, C., Kanade, T.: Detection and tracking of point features. Carnegie Mellon University Technical Report CMU-CS-91-132 (1991)
46. Trifonov, B., Bradley, D., Heidrich, W.: Tomographic reconstruction of transparent objects. In: Proc. Eurographics Symposium on Rendering, pp. 51–60 (2006)
47. Vasudeva, G., Honnery, D.R., Soria, J.: Non-intrusive measurement of a density field using the background oriented Schlieren (BOS) method. In: Proc. Australian Conf. Laser Diagnostic in Fluid Mechanics & Combustion (2005)
48. Venkatakrishnan, L., Meier, G.E.A.: Density measurements using the background oriented Schlieren technique. Experiments in Fluids 37, 237–247 (2004)
49. Vo, M., Wang, Z., Pan, B., Pan, T.: Hyper-accurate flexible calibration technique for fringe-projection-based three-dimensional imaging. Opt. Express 20(15), 16926–16941 (2012)
50. Wetzstein, G., Raskar, R., Heidrich, W.: Hand-held schlieren photography with light field probes. In: Proc. IEEE ICCP (2011)
51. Wetzstein, G., Roodnick, D., Raskar, R., Heidrich, W.: Refractive shape from light field distortion. In: Proc. IEEE ICCV (2011)
52. Xue, T., Rubinstein, M., Wadhwa, N., Levin, A., Durand, F., Freeman, W.T.: Refraction wiggles for measuring fluid depth and velocity from video. In: Proc. ECCV (2014)
53. Zach, C., Pock, T., Bischof, H.: A duality based approach for realtime TV-L1 optical flow. In: Hamprecht, F.A., Schnörr, C., Jähne, B. (eds.) DAGM 2007. LNCS, vol. 4713, pp. 214–223. Springer, Heidelberg (2007)
54. Zamek, S., Yitzhaky, Y.: Turbulence strength estimation from an arbitrary set of atmospherically degraded images. JOSA A 23(12), 3106–3113 (2006)
55. Zhu, X., Milanfar, P.: Stabilizing and deblurring atmospheric turbulence. In: Proc. IEEE ICCP (2011)

A Non-local Method
for Robust Noisy Image Completion

Wei Li, Lei Zhao, Duanqing Xu, and Dongming Lu

Zhejiang University, Hangzhou, China

Abstract. The problem of noisy image completion refers to recovering an image from a random subset of its noisy intensities. In this paper, we propose a non-local patch-based algorithm to settle the noisy image completion problem following the methodology "grouping and collaboratively filtering". The target of "grouping" is to form patch matrices by matching and stacking similar image patches. And the "collaboratively filtering" is achieved by transforming the tasks of simultaneously estimating missing values and removing noises for the stacked patch matrices into low-rank matrix completion problems, which can be efficiently solved by minimizing the nuclear norm of the matrix with linear constraints. The final output is produced by synthesizing all the restored patches. To improve the robustness of our algorithm, we employ an efficient and accurate patch matching method with adaptations including pre-completion and outliers removal, etc. Experiments demonstrate that our approach achieves state-of-the-art performance for the noisy image completion problem in terms of both PSNR and subjective visual quality.

1 Introduction

In this paper, we aim at recovering an image from a subset of its noisy entries, which means that the image not only suffers from information loss, but also is corrupted by an amount of additive noise. Actually, this problem arises from various practical applications. For example, the task of simultaneously removing impulsive noise and mixed additive noise as described in [29] can be regarded as a practical case of the proposed problem. Since the pixels damaged by impulsive noise contain no information about the true image, it's quite natural to treat them as empty values and thus the task is indeed transformed into a noisy image completion problem. As another case, the problem is involved in the restoration of archived photographs and films [17][16][25][26]. As detailed in [16], archived materials may be degraded due to physical problems or simply chemical decomposition, which typically lead to noise, Dirt and Sparkle, etc. So there is also a necessity to develop techniques to deal with noise and missing data jointly. Besides, in certain difficult imaging situations, e.g., capturing images with a faulted camera or a low-end webcam under low light conditions, it is also a possibility that the captured data contains both missing and noisy intensities.

Compared with traditional image completion and denoising problems, noisy image completion problem is obviously more challenging since both completion

D. Fleet et al. (Eds.): ECCV 2014, Part IV, LNCS 8692, pp. 61–74, 2014.

and denoising techniques cannot handle the problem trivially. Numerical methods are the simplest tools to solve the proposed problem, e.g., total variation [23] and wavelet [6]. However, those methods generally produce coarse recovered results with poor visual quality and noticeable artifacts. Another way to solve the noisy completion problem is to combine image completion and denoising techniques in a straightforward way: one first estimates the missing entries in a corrupted image without considering the noise and then applys a denoising algorithm to the intermediate completed result. This "completion + denoising" scheme is able to produce visually pleasant results in some situations, but the disadvantage is also obvious: estimated values for empty pixels by no matter straightforward interpolation methods or state-of-the-art example-based inpainting approaches are not sufficiently reliable due to the existence of noise, then the generated error will not be further corrected by directly applying denoising techniques. The scheme works even worse when the ratio of the missing pixels increases, which will be demonstrated in experiments.

Recent studies about non-local and patch-based image processing techniques following the idea of "grouping and collaboratively filtering" [4,8,14] provide us a novel way to think about our problem. In general, this kind of methods builds upon a patch-wise restoration for the corrupted image, where three steps are commonly involved. Initially, for a given reference patch in the image, an amount of similar patches are matched and grouped by testing the similarity between the reference patch and the candidate patch located at different spatial position. Then, redundant information among the stacked patches is utilized to perform a restoration, e.g., estimating missing values and removing noises simultaneously. At last, the final restored image is synthesized from all the restored patches. This is also the sketch of our approach proposed in this paper. However, considering the specific noisy image completion problem here, we make two major adaptations within the framework. Firstly, an efficient and robust patch matching algorithm is developed to collect similar patches for each reference patch in the image. Secondly, for each patch group, a patch matrix is formed by stacking the patches and the repair of the matrix is transformed into a problem of low-rank matrix completion from noisy entries, which can be efficiently solved by minimizing the nuclear norm of the matrix with linear constraints [5,15].

Contributions. We propose a robust and accurate noisy image completion algorithm which fills the missing values and removes the noise in an damaged image simultaneously. Our algorithm follows the methodology of "grouping and collaboratively filtering" and combines several recent powerful tools including total variation (TV) [23], adapted PatchMatch [2], and low rank matrix completion with ADMM solver [19] in an effective manner. Experiments demonstrate that our algorithm produces results with better visual quality than existing techniques.

2 Related Works

There are many available methods that can handle the noisy image completion problem. As a straightforward method, the total variation (TV) based image processing method was first proposed in [23] as an efficient tool for denoising. And TV was further extended to deal with more applications like debluring, inpainting and super-resolution [27,30,9]. Actually, a common TV inpainting method can be easily modified to handle an incomplete image with noisy entries by relaxing the constraints of the observed values. In a similar way, wavelet filtering methods [6,10] can also be adapted to solve the noisy completion problem. In [17], a MCMC sampling-based approach was proposed for joint noise reduction and missing data treatment. In [1], a PDE-based method was proposed to settle the problem: after filling the missing pixels by solving a PDE, it then employed the Mean Curvature Flow and a selective diffusion equation to smooth out the noise for the pixels inside and outside the empty regions respectively. However, the above mentioned methods generally produce coarse recovered results with poor visual quality and noticeable artifacts.

The proposed approach in this paper is inspired by the recent progress of the non-local patch-based techniques, which demonstrated impressive capability in solving inpainting [28,7,18,24,22] and denoising [4,8,14,11,20,21] problems. To list a few, in patch-based inpainting algorithms such as [7,24], one first filled the regions by searching and copying proper content from the observed part of the image and then synthesized the result in a visually acceptable way. In [22], the authors extended the traditional quadratic regularization used for inverse problems to non-smooth energies by defining graph-based TV on images. The regularized formalization was utilized to solve inverse problems including image completion. As a pioneer of the non-local based denoising algorithm, the NL-Means algorithm [4] estimated the value of each pixel in an image as an average of the values of all the pixels whose Gaussian neighborhood looked like the neighborhood of the current pixel. The K-SVD algorithm [11,21] utilized highly overcomplete dictionaries obtained via a preliminary training procedure to exploit the 2-D transform sparsity in image patches for the purpose of patch-wise denoising. BM3D proposed in [8] stacked similar image patches in a 3D array based on the similarity between patches and then applied a shrinkage operator in 3D transform domain on the 3D array. The denoised image is synthesized from denoised patches after inverse 3D transform.

3 The Proposed Algorithm

3.1 Overview

Let $I \in \mathbb{R}^{m \times n}$ be a damaged image which is represented as:

$$I = (G + N)_\Omega, \tag{1}$$

where $G \in \mathbb{R}^{m \times n}$ is the original image, N is an additive noise and Ω indexes a random subset of pixels which are observed. How to accurately recover original image G from its noisy and incomplete observation I is the main target.

Following the methodology of "grouping and collaboratively filtering", we propose a non-local and patch-based approach for the noisy image completion problem, where "grouping" and "collaboratively filtering" are the two major components. The purpose of "grouping" is to exploit the spatial redundancy in the corrupted image by matching and staking similar patches. Initially, let $p_{i,j}$ be an image patch in I of size $s \times s$ centered at pixel (i, j), and every pixel in the image corresponds to such a patch except for those whose $s \times s$ surrounding regions exceed the image bound. Then given a patch $p_{i,j}$, we search for several similar patches from all the candidates in terms of ℓ_2 distance and put all the matched patches into a patch group $\{p_{i,j}^0, p_{i,j}^1, \ldots, p_{i,j}^k\}$. Here $p_{i,j}^0$ refers to the given patch, or reference patch. By concatenating all columns of each patch in the group into a long vector and stacking all the vectors, a patch matrix $P_{i,j} \in \mathbb{R}^{s^2 \times (k+1)}$ is formed as:

$$P_{i,j} = (\mathbf{p}_{i,j}^0, \mathbf{p}_{i,j}^1, \ldots, \mathbf{p}_{i,j}^k). \tag{2}$$

Corresponding to Equ.(1), $P_{i,j}$ can be also represented as the following equation:

$$P_{i,j} = (Q_{i,j} + E_{i,j})_{\Omega_{i,j}}, \tag{3}$$

where $Q_{i,j}$ denote the patch matrix from the underlying groundtruth G, $E_{i,j}$ is the noise and $\Omega_{i,j}$ indexes the given entries in the patch matrix. Thus recovering G from its incomplete and noisy observation I equals to firstly decomposing Q from P for all of the patch matrices and then combining the results. This is what the "collaboratively filtering" does.

Assuming that I is complete and free of noise ($I = G$, $P_{i,j} = Q_{i,j}$) and the patch matching is still perfect, the grouped patches should exhibit high mutual similarity. Thus $Q_{i,j}$ should be low-rank and $E_{i,j} = 0$. Then in the existence of noise and missing values, if the patch matching is still perfect, $Q_{i,j}$ will also be low-rank and E will contain the noise. Therefore, calculating a low-rank matrix $Q_{i,j}$ from the noisy incomplete patch matrix $P_{i,j}$ is actually a problem of low-rank matrix completion from noisy entries [5,15].

However, as we only have the noisy and incomplete pixels, how to perfectly perform patch matching is a difficult problem. In our approach, several measures are taken to ensure the robustness of patch matching. First, we complete the empty pixels without considering the noise using TV [23]. Then an improved PatchMatch [2] algorithm is applied to the pre-completion result to efficiently search for similar patches for each reference patch. The patch matrix $P_{i,j}$ is formed by utilizing the patch matching result but taking values from the corrupted image I. A visualized description of the procedure is shown in Fig.1. Furthermore, in the formed patch matrix $P_{i,j}$, elements far away from the average of its corresponding row vector are considered as highly unreliable elements to be discarded. Details will be stated in the following sections.

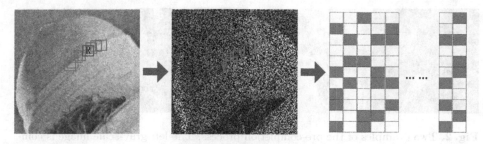

Fig. 1. The forming of a patch matrix. The patch matching is executed on the pre-completion result. Then a patch matrix is formed by taking values from the corrupted image according to the matching result. Reference patch (red box with a 'R') and matched patches (green boxes) are drawn in the two images. For all the patches including the reference patch, by concatenating all of its columns into a long vector and staking all the vectors, we get the right patch matrix. Each column in the patch matrix corresponds to a columns-concatenated patch. And in each column, we represent the missing pixels as the blue grids.

3.2 Robust Patch Matching and Grouping

In this section, we describe how we perform the efficient and robust patch matching and grouping process to search and stack similar patches for each reference patch, where three stages are involved.

Pre-completion. Before we really execute patch matching, we should firstly give proper values to the empty pixels. This is even more necessary in working over highly incomplete data because the captured entries may be insufficient to provide a reliable computation of the similarity between patches. Here we adopt a TV-based image completion algorithm for the pre-completion process which is described as the following equation:

$$\min_{X} \left\{ TV(X) = \sum_{i,j} \left(|D^h X_{i,j}| + |D^v X_{i,j}| \right) \right\}$$

$$s.t. \ X_{\Omega} = I_{\Omega}.$$

(4)

where $D^h X_{i,j}$ and $D^v X_{i,j}$ are the horizontal and vertical components of the gradient of element $X_{i,j}$ respectively. For colored images, vectorial total variation (VTV) [12] is a better choice than applying TV in a channel-by-channel manner, which is defined as:

$$VTV(X) = \sum_{i,j,k} \left(|D^h X_{i,j,k}| + |D^v X_{i,j,k}| \right),$$

(5)

where k represent channels. We refer interesting readers to [27,30,9,13,3] for details and efficient solvers for TV and VTV.

Actually, as we will further employ an improved PatchMatch method and an outlier remover in this robust patch matching stage, excessive computation involved in estimating the missing entries is unnecessary. Therefore, we adopt TV

Fig. 2. Two examples of the pre-completion process. The left gray-scale image is completed using TV formulation while the right colored image is processed using VTV.

in the pre-completion mainly for its computational efficiency and that the primary completed result is also accurate enough for the following patch matching process. Fig.2 gives two examples of the pre-completion, where the gray-scale image and the colored image are processed with TV and VTV respectively.

Improved PatchMatch. PatchMatch proposed in [2] is an efficient nearest neighbour searching algorithm, which is employed in our approach for the patch matching and grouping purpose. Applying the PatchMatch algorithm to the pre-completion result will help us find out a given number of similar patches in terms of ℓ_2 distance for all the reference patches. Then for each reference patch, all the matched patches are grouped by considering the reference patch as some sort of "centroid" for the group. Due to the space limitation, the PatchMatch algorithm is not detailed here, and we mainly discuss the two improvements we make for our specific application. At first, as there is not a built-in distance restriction in the PatchMatch algorithm, "diameter" of each group (the largest ℓ_2 distance between any two patches in the group) may be too large that may degrade the following collaborative filtering process. Therefore, the matched patches in each group should be pruned by setting a threshold for the distance between any two patches. Secondly, despite the existence of noise, original captured values are obviously more reliable than the estimated ones in the pre-completion result, thus higher importance should be attached to the observed entries in calculating similarities between two patches. Therefore, the ℓ_2 distance used in PatchMatch is indeed a weighted ℓ_2 distance. Specifically, let p_A and p_B be the two patches from a pre-completion result, and $\omega(\cdot) : \mathbb{R}^{s \times s} \to \mathbb{R}^{s \times s}$ to be a function that reads the weights of every elements in the patch, then the weighted ℓ_2 distance we use in our implementation is:

$$\mathrm{Dist}(p_A, p_B) = \|(p_A - p_B) \odot \omega(p_A) \odot \omega(p_B)\|_2,$$

where the symbol $\odot$ denotes the element-wise multiplication of two equal-sized matrices. The weight for the observed pixels must be no smaller than that of the missing ones, while the specific values should be adapted to the specific noise level and missing rate.

Outliers Removal. Since a low-rank matrix can be recovered from only a small fraction of its entries as proved in [5,15], we only keep those elements of high reliability and discard all the other elements. So detecting and discarding the outliers before solving the low-rank matrix completion problem is necessary. For each row in the formed patch matrix as described in Equ.(2), elements which deviate away from the mean value of the row vector by an amount larger than a pre-defined threshold will be treated as outliers to be discarded. Therefore, in the following low-rank matrix completion problem, the empty elements consist of two sources, one corresponds to the original missing pixels and the other indexes the abandoned outliers.

3.3 Collaborative Filtering Using Low-Rank Matrix Completion

For each grouping formed in the previous stage, a corresponding patch matrix is constructed by concatenating all columns of each patch into a long vector and staking all the vectors, which is a noisy and incomplete version of the underlying original patch matrix. As is discussed in **Section 3.1**, our goal here is to extract the matrix Q with a low rank from P. Mathematically, the task is generalized as the problem of low-rank matrix completion with noisy entries [5,15] in the following form:

$$\min_Q \|Q\|_n$$
$$s.t. \ \|(Q - P)_\Omega\|_F \leq \delta, \tag{6}$$

where $\delta \geq 0$ measures the noise level, $\|\cdot\|_n$ is the nuclear norm defined as the summation of all singular values which is shown to be the tightest convex approximation for the rank of matrices, and $\|\cdot\|_F$ denotes the Frobenious norm. Ω indexes all the given elements as discussed in previous sections.

We adopt alternating direction method of multipliers (ADMM) [19] in our approach for its implementation simplicity and computational efficiency. Initially, we reformulate Equ.(6) into the following nuclear-norm-regularized least squares problem which is the ADMM applicable form:

$$\min_Q \ \|Q\|_n$$
$$s.t. \ Q - T = 0, \tag{7}$$
$$T \in \mathbb{U} = \{\|(U - P)_\Omega\|_F \leq \delta\}.$$

Then the ADMM works by minimizing the augmented Lagrangian function of the above problem:

$$\mathcal{L}(Q, T, Z, \beta) = \|Q\|_n - \langle Z, Q - T \rangle + \frac{\beta}{2}\|Q - T\|_F^2, \tag{8}$$

with respect to the unknown variables Q, T one at a time. Here Z is the Lagrange multiplier of the linear constraint, $\beta > 0$ is the penalty parameter for the violation of the linear constraint and $\langle \cdot, \cdot \rangle$ denotes the standard trace inner produce. The ADMM iteratively updates all the variables as follows:

$$T^{k+1} = arg \min_{T \in \mathbb{U}} \mathcal{L}(Q^k, T, Z^k, \beta), \tag{9}$$

$$Q^{k+1} = arg \min_X \mathcal{L}(Q, T^{k+1}, Z^k, \beta), \tag{10}$$

$$Z^{k+1} = Z^k - \gamma\beta(Q^{k+1} - T^{k+1}), \tag{11}$$

where $\gamma \in (0, \frac{\sqrt{5}+1}{2})$ is a constant. In this iterative scheme, the computation of each iteration is dominated by solving the two subproblems Equ.(9) and Equ.(10). At first, the solution for the subproblem Equ.(9) is given by:

$$T^{k+1} = \left(\min\left\{ \frac{\delta}{\|(B^{k+1} - P)_\Omega\|_F}, 1 \right\} - 1 \right)(B^{k+1} - P)_\Omega + B^{k+1}, \tag{12}$$

where $B^{k+1} = Q^k - \frac{1}{\beta}Z^k$.

Secondly, let

$$A^{k+1} = T^{k+1} + \frac{1}{\beta}Z^k = U^{k+1}\Sigma^{k+1}(V^{k+1})^T, \tag{13}$$

be the singular value decomposition (SVD) for A^{k+1}, then we get the closed-form solution for subproblem Equ.(10):

$$Q^{k+1} = U^{k+1}\hat{\Sigma}^{k+1}(V^{k+1})^T, \tag{14}$$

where $\hat{\Sigma}^{k+1} = diag(\max(\sigma_i^{k+1} - \frac{1}{\beta}, 0))$ with $\sigma_i(X)$ denoting the i-th largest singular value.

Synthesizing the Final Output. With all the restored patch matrices, the generation of the final output is straightforward. Firstly, the recovered result of the reference patch in each patch matrix is attached to the corresponding position in the result image. Thus each pixel is covered by several patches with overlapping regions. Then, the final value for the pixel is computed as the average of all the covered patches at this position.

4   Implementation Details and Experiments

In this section, we first give implementation details and then show the advantage of our algorithm over three existing techniques for the noisy image completion problem.

4.1   Implementation Details

Firstly, the famous SplitBregman algorithm proposed in [13] is employed for solving the TV and VTV pre-completion problems. Secondly, in the improved PatchMatch, the size of each patch is set as 7×7 and reference patches are sampled with 3×3 interval. For each reference patch, 20 nearest neighbours are

Table 1. The PSNR values of the recovered results with respect to different missing rates (MR) and noise levels (σ). A simple observation is made that our approach is sensitive to the Gaussian noise but robust to the missing values.

PSNR＼MR σ	20%	30%	40%	50%
15	35.32	34.66	34.10	33.15
25	34.24	33.80	33.17	32.22
40	32.13	31.59	31.06	30.65
50	30.67	29.84	29.64	28.79

collected in terms of weighted ℓ_2 distance as described in **Section 3.2**. Then, the threshold used in detecting outlier pixels from the patch matrix is chosen to be $2\bar{\sigma}$, where $\bar{\sigma}$ is defined as the mean of the standard deviation of the given entries in each row vector. Besides, the noise level δ in the problem of noisy low-rank matrix completion described in Equ.(6) is evaluated as $\delta = \bar{\sigma}\|\Omega\|_0$, where $\|\cdot\|_0$ counts the amount of the observed entries indexed by Ω. And the ADMM solver for the low-rank matrix completion problem is terminated if the tolerance $RSE < 1 \times 10^{-5}$ is met.

4.2 Results and Comparisons

As stated before, the problem of noisy image completion arises from several applications, so images to be restored in the experiments are artificially trimmed-degraded images rather than real damaged data for the universality. For the same consideration, without loss of generality, the Gaussian noise is mainly tested here. Two set of experiments are conducted in this section: one is to demonstrate how our approach performs with respect to different noise levels and missing rates, the other is to show the advantage of our algorithm compared with other methods for the application. Accuracy of the recovered results is evaluated by PSNR.

Robustness Tests. Table 1 exhibits the performance of our method in dealing with input data of different noise levels and missing rates: the standard deviation σ of the Gaussian noise varies from 15 to 50 while the missing rate (MR) changes between 20% and 50%. It can be easily read from each column in the table that for a certain missing rate, the PSNR drops dramatically when σ increases. On the contrary, when we keep the noise level unchanged, the recovery quality is more stable as is shown in each row of Table 1. This merit is easily comprehended: the estimated value in the pre-completion result is only involved in the patch matching process but not used in collaborative filtering stage, thus the original missing entries can be exactly re-computed by low-rank matrix completion.

Comparisons. In the comparison experiments, we compare our algorithm with three methods, which are mainly derived from state-of-the-art approaches in the

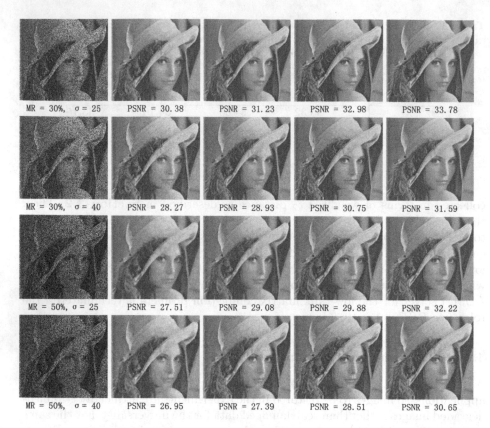

MR = 30%, σ = 25	PSNR = 30. 38	PSNR = 31. 23	PSNR = 32. 98	PSNR = 33. 78
MR = 30%, σ = 40	PSNR = 28. 27	PSNR = 28. 93	PSNR = 30. 75	PSNR = 31. 59
MR = 50%, σ = 25	PSNR = 27. 51	PSNR = 29. 08	PSNR = 29. 88	PSNR = 32. 22
MR = 50%, σ = 40	PSNR = 26. 95	PSNR = 27. 39	PSNR = 28. 51	PSNR = 30. 65

Fig. 3. From left to right: corrupted images, restored results of TV-based method, NL-Means, BM3D and our approach. Our approach outperforms the others for all the situations especially for the examples with high missing rates.

field of image denoising. The first method is similar to the TV pre-completion stage but with soft constraints, which equals to solving the following function:

$$\min_X \ TV(X) + \frac{\mu}{2}\|X_\Omega - I_\Omega\|_F^2, \tag{15}$$

where μ is a constant denoting the regularization parameter. The above equation is easily solvable using the gradient decent method. The other two approaches to be compared with are built upon the scheme of "completion + denoising", which means that we first fill the missing pixels using TV or VTV without considering the noise, which is the same to our pre-completion step, and then apply denoising methods to the intermediate result. The denoising methods adopted here are the former mentioned NL-Means [4] and BM3D [8].

Fig.3 shows the performance of our algorithm and three other methods in dealing with inputs with different missing rates and noise levels. In general, the primary TV-based method performs poorest among all the involved algorithms, which can only provide coarse outputs with noticeable visual artifacts. And

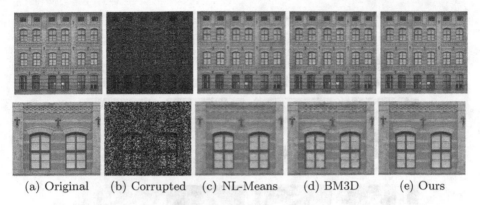

(a) Original   (b) Corrupted   (c) NL-Means   (d) BM3D   (e) Ours

Fig. 4. Details are better recovered by our approach than NL-Means and BM3D. And the PSNR values of the three results (c), (d) and (e) are, 24.28dB, 25.04dB and 27.25dB respectively.

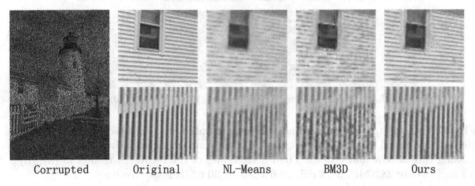

Corrupted   Original   NL-Means   BM3D   Ours

Fig. 5. The close-ups exhibit the extraordinary capability of our approach in recovering regular structures in a corrupted image

compared with the two "completion + denoising" methods using NL-Means and BM3D, our approach generates the best recovered images in terms of both PSNR and visual quality in all of the examples. Specifically, when we keep the missing rate of the input data fixed, all the methods are sensitive to the changes of standard deviation σ of the Gaussian noise, but our approach obviously has better capability of removing the noise. Things are different when we maintain σ but change the missing rate. As stated before, our algorithm is robust to the existence of missing pixels, so it can be seen from the visualized results in Fig.3 that the final synthesized images are not degraded noticeably when the missing rate increases. On the contrary, in the two methods based on NL-Means and BM3D, since denoising operation is directly applied to the completed result which is indeed not sufficiently reliable, errors produced in estimating the missing values won't be further corrected. As a consequence, visual artifacts are clearly observed in the final repaired results as displayed in Fig.3 especially the two examples with missing rate 50%.

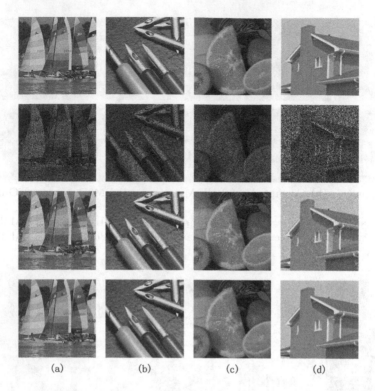

(a)   (b)   (c)   (d)

Fig. 6. From top to bottom: original images, corrupted images, pre-completion results and the recovered results of our approach. The damaged images here have a higher missing rate of 60% and $\sigma = 25$. The PSNR values of the recovered results in (a), (b), (c) and (d) are 28.37dB, 30.35dB, 28.64dB and 30.62dB respectively.

Another two comparison examples with close-ups are displayed in Fig.4 and Fig.5, where the original images have clear and repetitive structures. Here we leave out the TV-based method due to its poor performance in processing such sources. In both of the inputs, the missing rate is 50% and $\sigma = 25$. It can be clearly seen from the close-ups in the two figures that regular structures in the images are well reconstructed by our approach while the results of NL-Means and BM3D are quite unpleasant. In Fig.6, we further increase the missing rate of the images to 60% and apply our approach to these data. The visually pleasant results exhibit the brilliant applicability of our algorithm in working over such severely corrupted data. Please refer to the supplementary material for more results.

In summary, we argue that our algorithm has excellent ability of repairing noisy incomplete images. And compared with existing techniques, our approach works much better in processing examples with high missing rate and in recovering structures in images.

5 Conclusions and Future Works

In this paper, we propose a novel robust algorithm following the scheme "grouping and collaboratively filtering" for the problem of noisy image completion. There are two key steps in our approach: firstly, an efficient and robust patch matching method is developed for matching and grouping patches; secondly, the problem of estimating missing values and denoising is transformed to the problem of low-rank matrix completion from noisy entries. Experiments exhibit the extraordinary performance of our approach compared with existing techniques and recovered results will benefit much from multiple circulation of the process. There are also limitations. First, noticeable visual artifacts may exist in working over corrupted images with large missing regions, e.g., wrong completed content or overly smoothed regions. Second, like many other methods of this category, our algorithm also imposes high computational burden. Another limitation comes from the averaging in the last step which obviously blurs the result. So settling the remain problems is our future work.

Acknowledgements. This work was supported in part by the National projects: 2012BAH03F02, 2012BAH43F02, and 2012BAH43F05, the National Basic Research Program (973) project: 2012CB725305, and the Zhejiang Provincial projects: 2012C11010, 2010R50040, and 2012BAH03F03.

References

1. Barcelos, C.A.Z., Batista, M.A.: Image restoration using digital inpainting and noise removal. Image and Vision Computing 25(1), 61–69 (2007)
2. Barnes, C., Shechtman, E., Finkelstein, A., Goldman, D.B.: Patchmatch: a randomized correspondence algorithm for structural image editing. In: SIGGRAPH (2009)
3. Beck, A., Teboulle, M.: Fast gradient-based algorithms for constrained total variation image denoising and deblurring problems. IEEE TIP 18(11), 2419–2434 (2009)
4. Buades, A., Coll, B., Morel, J.M.: A review of image denoising algorithms, with a new one. Multiscale Modeling and Simulation 4(2), 490–530 (2005)
5. Candès, E.J., Plan, Y.: Matrix completion with noise. Proceedings of the IEEE 98(6), 925–936 (2010)
6. Coifman, R.R., Donoho, D.L.: Translation-invariant de-noising. Springer (1995)
7. Criminisi, A., Pérez, P., Toyama, K.: Region filling and object removal by exemplar-based image inpainting. IEEE TIP 13(9), 1200–1212 (2004)
8. Dabov, K., Foi, A., Katkovnik, V., Egiazarian, K.: Image denoising by sparse 3-D transform-domain collaborative filtering. IEEE TIP 16(8), 2080–2095 (2007)
9. Dahl, J., Hansen, P.C., Jensen, S.H., Jensen, T.L.: Algorithms and software for total variation image reconstruction via first-order methods. Numerical Algorithms 53(1), 67–92 (2010)
10. Donoho, D.L., Johnstone, J.M.: Ideal spatial adaptation by wavelet shrinkage. Biometrika 81(3), 425–455 (1994)
11. Elad, M., Aharon, M.: Image denoising via sparse and redundant representations over learned dictionaries. IEEE TIP 15(12), 3736–3745 (2006)

12. Goldluecke, B., Strekalovskiy, E., Cremers, D.: The natural vectorial total variation which arises from geometric measure theory. SIAM Journal on Imaging Sciences 5(2), 537–563 (2012)
13. Goldstein, T., Osher, S.: The split bregman method for l1-regularized problems. SIAM Journal on Imaging Sciences 2(2), 323–343 (2009)
14. Ji, H., Liu, C., Shen, Z., Xu, Y.: Robust video denoising using low rank matrix completion. In: CVPR (2010)
15. Keshavan, R.H., Montanari, A., Oh, S.: Matrix completion from noisy entries. Journal of Machine Learning Research 11(2057-2078), 1 (2010)
16. Kokaram, A.C.: On missing data treatment for degraded video and film archives: a survey and a new bayesian approach. IEEE TIP 13(3), 397–415 (2004)
17. Kokaram, A.C., Godsill, S.J.: Mcmc for joint noise reduction and missing data treatment in degraded video. IEEE TSP 50(2), 189–205 (2002)
18. Komodakis, N., Tziritas, G.: Image completion using efficient belief propagation via priority scheduling and dynamic pruning. IEEE TIP 16(11), 2649–2661 (2007)
19. Lin, Z., Chen, M., Ma, Y.: The augmented lagrange multiplier method for exact recovery of corrupted low-rank matrices. UIUC Technical Report UILUENG-09-2215 (2010)
20. Mairal, J., Bach, F., Ponce, J., Sapiro, G., Zisserman, A.: Non-local sparse models for image restoration. In: ICCV (2009)
21. Mairal, J., Elad, M., Sapiro, G.: Sparse representation for color image restoration. IEEE TIP 17(1), 53–69 (2008)
22. Peyré, G., Bougleux, S., Cohen, L.: Non-local regularization of inverse problems. In: Forsyth, D., Torr, P., Zisserman, A. (eds.) ECCV 2008, Part III. LNCS, vol. 5304, pp. 57–68. Springer, Heidelberg (2008)
23. Rudin, L.I., Osher, S., Fatemi, E.: Nonlinear total variation based noise removal algorithms. Physica D: Nonlinear Phenomena 60(1), 259–268 (1992)
24. Simakov, D., Caspi, Y., Shechtman, E., Irani, M.: Summarizing visual data using bidirectional similarity. In: CVPR (2008)
25. Subrahmanyam, G., Aravind, R.A., Recursive, R.: framework for joint inpainting and de-noising of photographic films. JOSA A 27(5), 1091–1099 (2010)
26. Wang, X., Mirmehdi, M.: Archive film restoration based on spatiotemporal random walks. In: Daniilidis, K., Maragos, P., Paragios, N. (eds.) ECCV 2010, Part V. LNCS, vol. 6315, pp. 478–491. Springer, Heidelberg (2010)
27. Wang, Y., Yang, J., Yin, W., Zhang, Y.: A new alternating minimization algorithm for total variation image reconstruction. SIAM Journal on Imaging Sciences 1(3), 248–272 (2008)
28. Wei, L.Y., Levoy, M.: Fast texture synthesis using tree-structured vector quantization. In: SIGGRAPH (2000)
29. Yan, M.: Restoration of images corrupted by impulse noise and mixed gaussian impulse noise using blind inpainting. SIAM Journal on Imaging Sciences 6(3), 1227–1245 (2013)
30. Zhu, M., Wright, S.J., Chan, T.F.: Duality-based algorithms for total-variation-regularized image restoration. Computational Optimization and Applications 47(3), 377–400 (2010)

Improved Motion Invariant Deblurring
through Motion Estimation

Scott McCloskey

Honeywell Labs, USA

Abstract. We address the capture of sharp images of fast-moving objects, and build on the Motion Invariant photographic technique. The key advantage of motion invariance is that, unlike other computational photographic techniques, it does not require pre-exposure velocity estimation in order to ensure numerically stable deblurring. Its disadvantage is that the invariance is only approximate - objects moving with non-zero velocity will exhibit artifacts in the deblurred image related to tail clipping in the motion Point Spread Function (PSF). We model these artifacts as a convolution of the desired latent image with an error PSF, and demonstrate that the spatial scale of these artifacts corresponds to the object velocity. Surprisingly, despite the use of parabolic motion to capture an image in which blur is invariant to motion, we demonstrate that the motion invariant image can be used to estimate object motion *post-capture*. With real camera images, we demonstrate significant reductions in the artifacts by using the estimated motion for deblurring. We also quantify a 96% reduction in reconstruction error, relative to a floor established by exact PSF deconvolution, via simulation with a large test set of photographic images.

1 Introduction

Motion deblurring is one of the longest standing problems in computational photography, and has been addressed in a number of ways. Classic blind deblurring - estimating blur and then applying deconvolution - has long been used on images captured with traditional cameras. However, it is well-known that deconvolving very common motions - such as vehicles moving at a constant velocity - is ill-conditioned under traditional capture methods. In order to address this, various computational cameras have been proposed to capture *invertible* motion blur. The flutter shutter [18] does this by capturing a multiple exposure image, but pre-exposure velocity estimation is required to ensure invertibility [13].

In order to avoid pre-exposure motion estimation, Levin et al. [12] proposed *motion invariant photography*, whereby the camera captures an image in which the blur PSF is both invertible and approximately invariant to subject velocity. This approximate invariance holds over a range of velocities, so a reasonably good image can be produced without the need for pre-exposure velocity estimation. However, the approximate nature of the invariance results in certain artifacts (see Fig. 1) which are aesthetically unpleasant.

D. Fleet et al. (Eds.): ECCV 2014, Part IV, LNCS 8692, pp. 75–89, 2014.

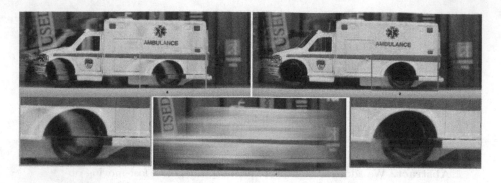

Fig. 1. (Top left) A motion invariant image, deblurred as in previous work. The invariance approximation results in artifacts, most notable in the wheel area. (Top right) Using our motion estimation algorithm, we avoid these artifacts and improve the quality of the reconstruction. (Bottom row) zoomed views of annotated regions, plus a traditional image of the moving object to convey the extent of motion.

We model motion invariant capture and deconvolution in order to demonstrate, for the first time, that these artifacts are indicators of the underlying velocity. Whereas the image captured by the camera is approximately motion invariant, we show that the artifacts in a processed version of that image are distinctive enough to estimate the object velocity. We propose a motion invariant motion estimation algorithm which determines velocity by matching edges to artifacts arising therefrom. This estimate is then be used to re-process the image, reducing artifacts and improving the final image quality. We demonstrate the qualitative improvements - as in Fig. 1 - using a real camera whose stabilizing lens is moved to implement motion invariance. By synthetically blurring and then processing images from a public dataset, we quantify an 96% reduction in reconstruction errors, relative to a floor established by exact PSF deconvolution, as a result of our blur estimation.

2   Previous Work

Our work builds on Levin et al. [12], who introduced motion invariance and later extend it to cases where the motion direction is not known [4], by capturing two images with orthogonal motion. A key step to 2D motion invariance is blur estimation *from a pair of images*; we estimate motion from a single parabolic exposure, and note that many of our results (e.g. Fig. 1) involve objects moving too fast to capture in multiple frames. Webster and Dorrel [21] argue for the inclusion of a variable opacity optical element in motion invariant cameras to reduce artifacts arising from PSF variance, but do not support their simulations with real images and do not model the effect of light loss through the additional optical element. More recently, other implementations of motion invariance have been described in the literature. In previous work, we [15] describe an implementation of motion invariance using the image stabilization hardware in a Canon

DSLR lens. The actual motion that the lens undergoes during exposure, combined with prior information about camera and/or subject motion, is shown to improve the quality of the deblurred image in [16]. Sonoda et al. [19] describe an implementation of motion invariance using a Liquid Crystal on Silicon (LCoS) element, though that implementation involves about three stops (90%) of light loss due to the combined effects of polarization, fill factor, reflectivity, and the reduction of the reflective region. All of the previous work in motion invariance deconvolves the PSF of a stationary object and, as we show, will introduce certain artifacts when objects are in motion. We introduce a post-capture motion estimation algorithm which greatly reduces these artifacts.

Besides motion invariance, several computational photographic techniques have been developed to address motion blur. Notably, coded exposure [18] addresses the lack of motion blur invertibility in traditional imaging, but its lack of invariance requires pre- and/or post-capture motion estimation. Coded exposure blur estimation has been developed using either edge priors [2] or natural image statistics [14]. Coded exposure and motion invariance have been compared with respect to noise performance and other criteria [1], though that analysis includes the artifacts which we reduce by motion estimation. Both coded exposure and motion invariance have analogous approaches for handling optical blur, as well. Coded aperture photography [11,20] selectively occludes light paths to the sensor, and has been used for extended depth of field imaging. Similar to motion invariance, flexible depth of field photography [17] captures a coded image using lens motion, as the lens moves along the optical axis to make defocus blur invariant over an depth range. More recently, Bando et al. [3] analyze these computational cameras in the framework of a time-varying light field, and come to the surprising conclusion that focal sweep is optimal for both defocus and motion blur. However, their motions are smaller than the ones considered here, and the analysis depends on the 'infinite exposure' assumption, and thus doesn't account for motion invariant artifacts.

Despite the associated invertibility problems, there is a large amount of research addressing both blur estimation and deblurring of images from traditional cameras. Recently, work in this area has addressed spatially variant blur arising from camera rotations [22,5]. Interestingly, experiments by Köhler et al. with a dataset of hand-held camera motions [8] have shown that these methods don't necessarily out-perform those based on a shift-invariant model of motion blur. In fact, the work of Xu and Jia [23] performed best despite assuming uniform blur. However, [8]'s evaluation results on blind deconvolution do not necessarily reflect performance on motion invariant deblurring, where the invariant PSF is known ahead of time. In our experiments, we use the method of Krishnan and Fergus [9] for the non-blind deconvolution of motion invariant images, and note that it performs well in the blind deconvolution evaluation.

3   Motion Invariant Capture

The objective of motion invariant image capture is to obviate PSF estimation, thus avoiding *blind* deconvolution, by capturing an image with a motion blur PSF

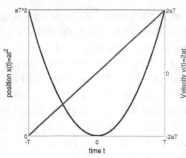

Fig. 2. Motion invariant capture: parabolic motion in position versus time (black curve/axis) capturing an image where velocities in a range are stabilized for the same period of time due to the linearity of velocity as a function of time (blue line/axis)

that does not depend on the velocity of a moving object. For an object with any particular velocity, of course, motion blur can be prevented by translating the lens/camera in the same direction and with the same speed as the object in order to stop motion, i.e. to ensure that its projection on the sensor does not move. The intuitive explanation of motion invariant capture is that, by translating the lens with constant acceleration along the object motion direction, all objects with velocities in a certain range will have the motion of their projections stopped momentarily, and these objects will have approximately the same PSF.

Motion invariance can be implemented by translating any of the camera body, sensor, or lens with constant acceleration. We use optical stabilization hardware to implement motion invariance by lens motion, as suggested by Levin et al. in [12,4]. In the 1D case, the lens moves along a line in the direction of expected motion; without loss of generality, we will discuss horizontal lens motion with initial rightward velocity. At the beginning of the image's exposure, the lens translates right with a given velocity, and constant (negative) acceleration a is applied. During an exposure duration of $2T$ milliseconds, with the time variable $t \in [-T, T]$ for mathematical convenience, the acceleration causes the lens to come to a stop at $t = 0$ and, at the end of the exposure period $(t = T)$, the lens has returned to its initial position with the same velocity magnitude (but in the opposite direction) as in the beginning. Though the motion of the lens is linear, this pattern is referred to as *parabolic motion* because the horizontal position x is a parabolic function of time t,

$$x(t) = at^2. \tag{1}$$

Figure 2 shows parabolic motion and lens velocity (the derivative of x), illustrating the range of object velocities which are stabilized during exposure.

As in other work, blur in a motion invariant image is modeled as the convolution of a latent image I with a PSF B, giving the blurred image

$$I_b = I * B + \eta, \tag{2}$$

where η represents noise. While deconvolution methods based on this model can perform quite well in practice, the model is mostly limited to subject motion. Because motion arising from unsteady hands holding the camera generally involves some rotation [8], this model is best suited to stationary camera scenarios. The 1D motion invariance considered here is also limited to constant velocity

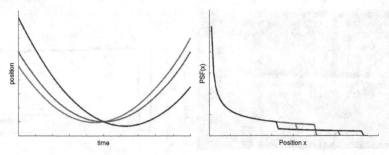

Fig. 3. (Left) Trajectories of points with different velocities as observed on the sensor of a lens undergoing parabolic motion. (Right) Using the PSF model of eq. 4, non-zero velocities result in clipped tails of the PSFs.

motion, which has been shown to hold approximately when the short exposure duration allows for good approximations of slight acceleration/deceleration [12].

As discussed in [12], there are tradeoffs in adopting motion invariant photography over traditional imaging. First, stationary objects in the scene will be blurred in the image due to the motion of the lens and, while deconvolving B is numerically stable, deblurring amplifies noise η everywhere. The second issue is that the convolution model of eq. 2 does not hold at occluding contours, so artifacts arise when both foreground and background are textured. Our experiments show that motion estimation reduces these artifacts. Finally, and most importantly for our purposes, the invariance of B to velocity is approximate, and fails entirely when the object's projection on the sensor moves too fast to be stabilized. For different object velocities which are stabilized, their PSFs have some variation which leads to artifacts when the wrong PSF is deblurred.

3.1 Motion Invariance Artifacts

In this section, we elaborate on the variation in the PSF induced by changing object velocity, and model the artifacts that arise therefrom. Consider the effect of subject motion of a point P on its PSF B, when that motion is linear with constant velocity s. During exposure, the motion of P on the sensor combines P's real-world motion and parabolic motion of the lens (eq. 1), as

$$x(t) = at^2 + st. \tag{3}$$

Fig. 3 shows these trajectories for three different values of s. Because the value of the PSF B_s at a particular sensor point is proportional to the amount of time P's reflected/emitted light lands there, we can derive the continuous PSF as in [12] (with slightly modified notation)

$$B_s(x) = \begin{cases} \left(a\left(x+\frac{s^2}{4a}\right)\right)^{-1/2} & \text{if } 0 \leq x + \frac{s^2}{4a} \leq a\left(T-\frac{s}{2a}\right)^2 \\ \frac{1}{2}\left(a\left(x+\frac{s^2}{4a}\right)\right)^{-1/2} & \text{if } a\left(T-\frac{s}{2a}\right)^2 < x + \frac{s^2}{4a} \leq a\left(T+\frac{s}{2a}\right)^2 \\ 0 & \text{otherwise} \end{cases} \tag{4}$$

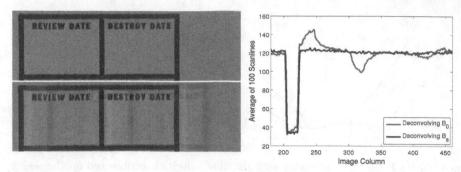

Fig. 4. Example of motion invariant artifacts. (Top left) Reference image of a cardboard box. (Bottom left) When the motion invariant image of the moving box is deblurred with B_0, printed regions 'echo' in the image. (Right) Plots of the average intensity over 100 rows of pixels covering the right-most printed edge and its echo, when the motion invariant image is deblurred with B_0 (red line) and the actual PSF B_s (blue line).

Note that, when $s \neq 0$, the change from the first to the second clauses results in a halving of the PSF, which is described as 'tail clipping'. This arises because, while the lens returns to its original position by the end of the exposure period, the light from P will be displaced by a distance of $2sT$. Fig. 3 illustrates this tail clipping effect on the PSFs corresponding to the three parabolas shown.

While eq. 4 indicates that B depends on velocity, motion invariant images in all previous work have been deblurred using the PSF B_0 of stationary objects. The differences between a moving object's actual PSF and the one used in deblurring will introduce certain artifacts, as illustrated in Fig. 4. In this example, the printed lines on the box appear reasonably sharp, but regions which should appear uniform brown instead have intensity changes which appear as 'echos' of the printed lines. First, there is a vertical band of brighter pixels immediately to the right of the printed edges. Next there is a darker band of pixels about 100 pixels to the right of the printed edges. Finally, there are adjacent dark and bright bands beginning about 200 pixels to the right of the printed edges. The plot shows the average intensity over 100 rows of pixels spanning the right-most printed edge and its echo, to give a better sense of the artifact's magnitude. We can avoid these artifacts by deconvolving the actual PSF B_s from the motion invariant image, as shown by the blue line in the plot.

What we will show in the remainder of this section is that - despite the objective of capturing an image which is invariant to object motion - the artifacts arising from deconvolving B_0 are, themselves, a cue to subject motion. This surprising result is due to the fact that the effect of deconvolving B_0 is the same as convolving the true latent image with an error PSF which has peaks at locations uniquely determined by the object velocity s. To show this, we express the convolution blur model of eq. 2 in the Fourier domain as

$$\widehat{I_b} = \hat{I} \cdot \hat{B_s} + \hat{\eta}, \tag{5}$$

where symbols under the ̂ are the Fourier representations of the image/PSF/noise and · represents multiplication. We use $\mathcal{F}$ to represent the Fourier transform, so $\hat{I} = \mathcal{F}(I)$. By deconvolving B_0 from I_b, we compute a latent image estimate

$$J_0 = \mathcal{F}^{-1}\left(\frac{\hat{I}_b}{\hat{B}_0}\right) = I * \mathcal{F}^{-1}\left(\frac{\hat{B}_s}{\hat{B}_0}\right) + \mathcal{F}^{-1}\left(\frac{\hat{\eta}}{\hat{B}_0}\right). \tag{6}$$

So the latent image estimated by deconvolving B_0 is itself a convolution of the true latent image with an error PSF

$$E_s = \mathcal{F}^{-1}\left(\frac{\hat{B}_s}{\hat{B}_0}\right), \tag{7}$$

plus the image noise amplified by deconvolution. Recall that B_0 satisfies the invertibility conditions discussed in [18], so the deconvolution is numerically stable (i.e., there is no division by 0). Obviously, for stationary objects $B_s = B_0$, the error PSF is the δ function, and the latent image estimate matches the true latent image (modulo amplified noise). When the object is moving ($s \neq 0$), $\hat{B}_s \neq \hat{B}_0$, and the error PSF introduces the artifacts illustrated above.

Example error PSFs are shown in Fig. 5, using the same colors/speeds as in Fig. 3. This figure illustrates how the error PSF - and thus the artifacts in the initial latent image estimate - relate to the ground truth PSF. The negative peaks in the error PSF occur in two places: first, at the location where the PSF B_s's tail clips

$$x + \frac{s^2}{4a} = a\left(T - \frac{s}{2a}\right)^2, \tag{8}$$

and, second, at the location where B_s goes to zero

$$x + \frac{s^2}{4a} = a\left(T + \frac{s}{2a}\right)^2. \tag{9}$$

The error PSF also has a positive peak at $x = aT^2$, where the B_0 goes to zero. The key to understanding our motion invariance motion estimation algorithm is that the distance between the two negative peaks in the error PSF E_s is exactly $2sT$. At a high level, then, our algorithm for motion estimation computes the initial latent image estimate J_0, localizes artifacts in this image, and uses the peak-to-peak distance to estimate s. We then deblur the original motion invariant image image again - this time with the exact PSF - to get an artifact-free latent image. The next section describes our method in greater detail.

4 Artifact-Based Motion Estimation

Having shown that deblurred motion invariant images contain artifacts which reflect the underlying object speed, it remains to be shown that these artifacts can be reliably detected. The box image shown in Fig 4 is a simple case, in that the background is a uniform intensity brown; a general solution must address

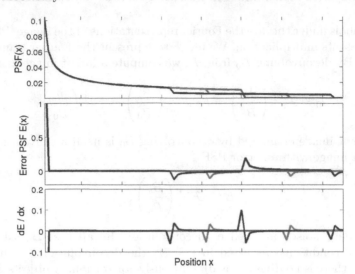

Fig. 5. (Top) Three motion invariant PSFs for velocities $s = 0$, $\frac{aT}{10}$, and $-\frac{aT}{5}$ in red, magenta, and blue, respectively. (Middle) The corresponding error PSFs E_s: the red curve is the delta function, whereas the blue and magenta curves have positive/negative peaks (and their positive peaks overlap). Comparing the top two plots, we see that the first negative peak in the error PSF coincides with the start of tail clipping, the second with the last non-zero entry, and the positive peak in between occurs at the length of the PSF B_0. (Bottom) The derivative of the error PSF introduces distinctive sign changes in the image's gradient magnitude at these same locations.

detection in regions of natural image texture. To handle this, we employ the well-known sparse gradient distribution used in [11] and elsewhere. One consequence of this prior is that, if we average the horizontal image gradient over a set of pixel locations *in a well-focused natural image*, the value will tend to 0 with an equal probability of negative and positive values. What happens when, instead of doing this to a well-focused natural image, we average horizontal gradient values in the initial latent image estimate J_0? Per eq. 6,

$$\frac{dJ_0}{dx} = \frac{d\left(I * \mathcal{F}^{-1}\left(\frac{\hat{B}_s}{\hat{B}_0}\right)\right)}{dx} + \frac{d\left(\mathcal{F}^{-1}\left(\frac{\hat{\eta}}{\hat{B}_0}\right)\right)}{dx}. \tag{10}$$

The noise term, even after deconvolving B_0, is still zero mean and does not bias the gradient to positive or negative values. However, the first term is equivalent to convolving the sharp latent image (with no bias for positive or negative gradients) with the horizontal derivative of the error PSF. As shown in Fig. 5, this kernel induces a sign change in the derivative image *at the same three locations as the error PSF has peaks.*

As with other work in PSF estimation [7], and following the intuition of Fig 4, we use edge points in the image to infer the scale of the PSF. Specifically, we look for pronounced sign changes in the average gradient magnitude of pixels over a range of horizontal distances from edges in the image. If the object attached to

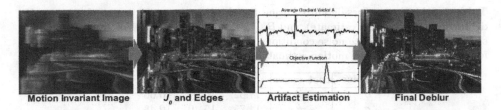

Fig. 6. An overview of our motion estimation method. The motion invariant image is deblurred using B_0. Edges are detected in the resulting image, and artifacts arising from them are used to estimate s. Finally, we deconvolve the exact PSF B_s from the original motion invariant image.

the edge was moving ($s \neq 0$), there will be a zero-crossing of the gradient at a distance of aT^2 from the edge, and additional zero-crossings separated by $2sT$.

The steps of our algorithm are as follows, and are illustrated in Fig. 6.

1. Compute the initial latent image estimate J_0 by deconvolving B_0.
2. Find vertical edges in J_0 using the Sobel detector. Discard edge points below the 80th percentile strength.
3. Compute $H = \frac{dJ_0}{dx}$.
4. Compute the average gradient sign vector A, weighted by the strength of edge points x, as

$$A(i) = \frac{\sum_x |H(x)| sign(H(x+i))}{\sum_x |H(x)|} \quad \forall i \in [0, 4aT^2]. \tag{11}$$

5. **If** $\sum_{x=aT^2-1}^{aT^2+1} A(x)^2 < \tau$, $\tilde{s} = 0$ and return; **else**

$$\tilde{s} = argmax_{s \in S} \sum A \cdot \frac{dE_s}{dx}. \tag{12}$$

The threshold $\tau = 5 * 10^{-10}$ is used to determine whether there is a zero-crossing at aT^2. The space of potential velocities is quantized to the set S such that consecutive values shift the peaks in the error PSF E by 1 pixel and $s \leq 2aT$, which is the maximum velocity that the lens stabilized.

5   Experiments

In order to validate our motion estimation algorithm, and to demonstrate the improvement in image quality, we describe two experiments. First, we apply uniform blur PSFs representing a range of velocities to images from the IM2GPS [6] dataset in order to quantify motion estimation performance and image quality improvement in the presence of a wide range of image texture. In the second, we capture motion invariant images using a Canon 60D camera with a 100mm image stabilizing lens which has been modified to execute parabolic motion during exposure. Note that, with the exception of data presented in Sec. 5.1, all images shown in this paper are real images from our Canon camera.

Table 1. RMSE of images deblurred using B_0 (showing the performance of existing MI deblurring), $B_{\tilde{s}}$ (i.e., our estimate), and B_s (i.e., the ground truth PSF and lower bound of RMSE). Rows separate noise conditions, and we show separate RMSE performance for those cases where our motion estimate is inaccurate.

noise	test cases	B_0	$B_{\tilde{s}}$	B_s
$\sigma = 1$	all	14.52	10.77	10.66
$\sigma = 1$	$\tilde{s} \neq s$	14.75	15.40	10.48
$\sigma = 2.5$	all	18.96	16.24	16.11
$\sigma = 2.5$	$\tilde{s} \neq s$	18.99	19.53	16.01

5.1   Synthetic Data

In order to avoid the small sample size issues associated with presenting only real camera results, we first present results on the 163 landscape-oriented images from the IM2GPS [6] test set. We synthetically blur the entire image using the PSF B_s (eq. 4), with $T = 50ms$ (i.e., a 100ms exposure time), $a = 0.04^1$, and s uniformly sampled in $[0, 2aT]$. We test 21 different values of s for each image. Blur is simulated using eq. 2, and we test two levels of Gaussian white noise η with $\sigma = 1$ and 2.5 relative to 8 bit intensity values.

Under the $\sigma = 1$ case, we estimate s to within the resolution of our quantization of S in 3,346 of 3,423 cases (98%). Under the $\sigma = 2.5$ condition, we do so in 3,299 of 3,423 cases (96%). Most of the errors come from two images, where the algorithm always estimates $\tilde{s} = 0$. In one, the 'latent image' contains motion blur - a clear violation of the natural image prior. The second has no strong edges from which to estimate motion.

Table 1 shows the computed Root Mean Squared Error (RMSE) between the reference latent image and motion invariant images deblurred using B_0 (showing the performance of existing MI deblurring), $B_{\tilde{s}}$ (i.e., our estimate), and B_s (i.e., the ground truth PSF and lower bound of RMSE). When averaged over all image/velocity combinations, the use of our estimate in deblurring eliminates 96% of the RMSE relative to the use of the ground truth s. In the very few cases where our velocity estimate is off by one or more quantization level ($\tilde{s} \neq s$), the resulting RMSE is only slightly worse than the state of the art.

5.2   Real Camera Images

Our motion invariant camera is made of a stock Canon 60D DSLR body with a modified Canon EF 100mm f/2.8L Macro IS lens. As described in [15], the standard mode of operation for image stabilization is a closed control loop where motion detected by sensors within the lens induces a compensating motion of the stabilizing element. Lens motion is achieved by modulating electromagnets,

---

[1] These values produce a PSF B_0 with 100 non-zero entries. We choose this so the ratio of PSF length to image width is consistent with our camera; they are about twice as wide as IM2GPS images, and our camera produces a PSF B_0 that's 200 pixels in length.

Fig. 7. Our prototype Motion Invariance camera, based on an unmodified Canon 60D with a modified 100mm Macro IS lens. The hot shoe triggers our Texas Instruments MSP430F2618 microprocessor (located inside the metal box) to start parabolic lens motion.

and its position is recorded using two embedded position sensors. In order to drive the lens to parabolic motion, we break the control loop and decouple the stabilizing element from the motion sensor. We then add an independent Texas Instruments MSP430F2618 microprocessor which controls motion through pulse width modulation, and monitors its progress by reading the position sensors through 12-bit ADCs. Control loops running on our added microcontroller execute the desired parabolic motion, which is synchronized with the camera's shutter via the hot shoe trigger. An image of the camera is shown in Figure 7, and additional detail about the hardware implementation is given in [16].

While the stabilizing lens accurately traces the desired parabolic trajectory, our real image PSFs differ from the analytic form due to a delay in the start of motion. The issue is that our motion starts based on the camera body's hot shoe, which is designed for flash triggering. In order to avoid flash synchronization issues - particularly a flash firing when the shutter is not completely open - the hot shoe's first signal occurs when the first curtain is completely open. On our 60D body, the transit of the shutter blade from bottom to top takes about 4ms, so the lens will be stationary for as much as the first 4ms of exposure. The example in Fig. 1 was a 100ms exposure, so the amount of time the lens is stationary is comparable to the amount of time that it stabilizes any moving object. When estimating blur using images from this camera, we add an additional delay term in B to model the correct error PSFs.

In addition to Fig. 1, the deblurred results in Fig. 8 show the improved image quality that we enable with our motion estimation algorithm. Images in the left column, which are generated by deconvolving B_0, have significant echo artifacts due to the use of the incorrect PSF. Our results, in the right column, have significantly reduced echo artifacts, based on deconvolution of the correct PSF as determined by our motion estimation algorithm.

6   Limitations

Like previous work in Motion Invariance, our method assumes that objects move in a linear direction which is known a priori. The linear motion assumption holds up well in practice as long as the camera is stationary, since moving objects have inertia which precludes rapid direction changes. A priori knowledge of the motion direction is available in many cases: vehicles drive within lanes on roads, people walk down hallways and along sidewalks, etc. The rear hubcap in the bottom row of Fig. 8, which is rotating rather than translating, violates this assumption and results in slight artifacts. As well, the limited dynamic range of the sensor

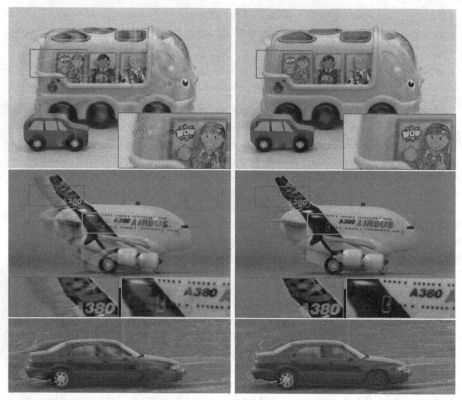

Fig. 8. Experimental results with our real camera. Left column shows the result of deconvolving B_0, as in previous motion invariant work. Right column shows the result of deconvolving $B_{\hat{s}}$, after applying our motion estimation algorithm. Echo artifacts are noticeably reduced when deconvolving $B_{\hat{s}}$. **Best viewed electronically.**

causes some artifacts in deblurred images; in our case, this is evident in the top row of Fig. 8, where the eye at the front of the bus has some artifact due to saturated pixels in the motion invariant image. In both cases, though, the severity of artifacts is reduced by our method relative to the existing approach.

As discussed above, motion invariance amplifies noise on stationary parts of the scene. By deconvolving a PSF B_s with $s \neq 0$, we may further exacerbate this issue (see the blue car in the top row of Fig. 8).

7   Multiple Moving Objects

While our algorithm is designed to estimate the velocity of a single, dominant object in the scene, we also note that the method performs well in cases where multiple objects have different velocities. This is partially due to the fact that the PSF depends only on the magnitude of object velocity, so $B_{-s} = B_s$. In the general case when there are two objects with velocities s_1 and s_2, our algorithm

Fig. 9. Multiple moving objects. Here, the green train moves faster than the red, and its image velocity is even higher due to motion parallax. Our motion estimation algorithm finds the velocity of the green train, and our result (right image) significantly reduces echos of the wheels compared to the existing method (left image). Though the red train is deblurred with the PSF of the green train, this is still a better approximation than B_0, so artifacts are also reduced on the red train (e.g., reduced echo of the numeral 5 at the left edge of the coal car and reduction of artificial highlight to the right of the 5). **Best viewed electronically.**

will estimate the velocity of the larger object (i.e., the one with the most edge points), say s_1, due to the use of $argmax$ in eq. 12. Because the point where the PSF's tail clips moves continuously with velocity, our method will also improve (in the sense of RMSE) the estimate of the smaller object in cases where $\|s_2\| > \|\frac{s_1}{2}\|$. An example of this is shown in Fig. 9, where two moving objects have different velocities and our method produces better latent image estimates for both, as compared to the existing method. In future work, we hope to extend the method to incorporate explicit motion segmentation, perhaps along the lines of Levin [10], though we note that this is more challenging from motion invariant images due to the blurring of stationary scene elements.

8   Conclusion

Surprisingly, despite the use of parabolic motion to capture an image in which blur is decoupled from an object's velocity, we have successfully demonstrated a motion estimation algorithm using motion invariant images. We further show that using our algorithm to determine which PSF should be deconvolved significantly reduces both quantitative RMSE and the severity of motion invariant artifacts, using both a large-scale synthetic experiment and validation with real camera images. Using this method, we get the benefit of deconvolving the exact PSF (in the 96+% of cases where we accurately estimate motion) *without* the need for pre-exposure velocity estimation, as in coded exposure. The key to enabling this is our modeling of the artifacts introduced by the traditional motion invariant approach, and quantifying the relationship between velocity and the spacing of these artifacts.

Relative to other work attempting to improve motion invariant image quality, notably [21], we achieve better image quality without the need for additional hardware elements or the associated light loss. Our prototype camera does not introduce additional elements in the optical path, and therefore maintains high light throughput.

Knowing that parabolic motion does not capture an image with strict motion invariance, and having shown that this can lead to significant artifacts, one may ask whether this approach is still worthwhile. We believe that it is, because the parabolic motion produces a PSF with a sharp peak which makes deconvolution well-posed without the need for pre-exposure motion estimation. When combined with our post-capture motion estimation, we can produce high-quality images that would not be possible with traditional camera hardware.

References

1. Agrawal, A., Raskar, R.: Optimal single image capture for motion deblurring. In: Computer Vision and Pattern Recognition, pp. 2560–2567 (2009)
2. Agrawal, A., Xu, Y.: Coded exposure deblurring: Optimized codes for PSF estimation and invertibility. In: Computer Vision and Pattern Recognition (2009)
3. Bando, Y., Holtzman, H., Raskar, R.: Near-invariant blur for depth and 2d motion via time-varying light field analysis. ACM Transactions on Graphics (Proceedings of SIGGRAPH), 13:1–13:15 (2013)
4. Cho, T.S., Levin, A., Durand, F., Freeman, W.T.: Motion blur removal with orthogonal parabolic exposures. In: Int'l Conf. on Computational Photography (2010)
5. Gupta, A., Joshi, N., Lawrence Zitnick, C., Cohen, M., Curless, B.: Single image deblurring using motion density functions. In: Daniilidis, K., Maragos, P., Paragios, N. (eds.) ECCV 2010, Part I. LNCS, vol. 6311, pp. 171–184. Springer, Heidelberg (2010)
6. Hays, J., Efros, A.A.: Im2gps: estimating geographic information from a single image. In: Computer Vision and Pattern Recognition (2008)
7. Joshi, N., Szeliski, R., Kriegman, D.: Psf estimation using sharp edge prediction. In: Computer Vision and Pattern Recognition (2008)
8. Köhler, R., Hirsch, M., Mohler, B., Schölkopf, B., Harmeling, S.: Recording and playback of camera shake: benchmarking blind deconvolution with a real-world database. In: Fitzgibbon, A., Lazebnik, S., Perona, P., Sato, Y., Schmid, C. (eds.) ECCV 2012, Part VII. LNCS, vol. 7578, pp. 27–40. Springer, Heidelberg (2012)
9. Krishnan, D., Fergus, R.: Fast image deconvolution using hyper-laplacian priors. In: NIPS (2009)
10. Levin, A.: Blind motion deblurring using image statistics. In: NIPS, pp. 841–848 (2006)
11. Levin, A., Fergus, R., Fergus, R., Durand, F., Freeman, W.T.: Image and depth from a conventional camera with a coded aperture. In: SIGGRAPH (2007)
12. Levin, A., Sand, P., Cho, T.S., Durand, F., Freeman, W.T.: Motion-invariant photography. In: SIGGRAPH (2008)
13. McCloskey, S.: Velocity-dependent shutter sequences for motion deblurring. In: Daniilidis, K., Maragos, P., Paragios, N. (eds.) ECCV 2010, Part VI. LNCS, vol. 6316, pp. 309–322. Springer, Heidelberg (2010)

14. McCloskey, S., Ding, Y., Yu, J.: Design and estimation of coded exposure point spread functions. IEEE Trans. Pattern Analysis and Machine Intelligence 34(10), 2071–2077 (2012)
15. McCloskey, S., Muldoon, K., Venkatesha, S.: Motion invariance and custom blur from lens motion. In: Int'l Conf. on Computational Photography (2011)
16. McCloskey, S., Muldoon, K., Venkatesha, S.: Motion aware motion invariance. In: Int'l Conf. on Computational Photography (2014)
17. Nagahara, H., Kuthirummal, S., Zhou, C.Y., Nayar, S.K.: Flexible Depth of Field Photography. In: Forsyth, D., Torr, P., Zisserman, A. (eds.) ECCV 2008, Part IV. LNCS, vol. 5305, pp. 60–73. Springer, Heidelberg (2008)
18. Raskar, R., Agrawal, A., Tumblin, J.: Coded exposure photography: motion deblurring using fluttered shutter. ACM Trans. on Graphics 25(3), 795–804 (2006)
19. Sonoda, T., Nagahara, H., Taniguchi, R.-I.: Motion-invariant coding using a programmable aperture camera. In: Lee, K.M., Matsushita, Y., Rehg, J.M., Hu, Z. (eds.) ACCV 2012, Part IV. LNCS, vol. 7727, pp. 379–391. Springer, Heidelberg (2013)
20. Veeraraghavan, A., Raskar, R., Agrawal, A., Mohan, A., Tumblin, J.: Dappled photography: Mask enhanced cameras for heterodyned light fields and coded aperture refocusing. In: SIGGRAPH (2007)
21. Webster, S., Dorrell, A.: Improved motion invariant imaging with time varying shutter functions. In: Proc. of SPIE-IS&T Electronic Imaging. SPIE, vol. 7876, pp. 787604–787604–8 (2011)
22. Whyte, O., Sivic, J., Zisserman, A., Ponce, J.: Non-uniform deblurring for shaken images. Int'l Journal of Computer Vision 98(2), 168–186 (2012)
23. Xu, L., Jia, J.: Two-phase kernel estimation for robust motion deblurring. In: Daniilidis, K., Maragos, P., Paragios, N. (eds.) ECCV 2010, Part I. LNCS, vol. 6311, pp. 157–170. Springer, Heidelberg (2010)

Consistent Matting for Light Field Images

Donghyeon Cho, Sunyeong Kim, and Yu-Wing Tai

Korea Advanced Institute of Science and Technology (KAIST)

Abstract. We present a new image matting algorithm to extract consistent alpha mattes across sub-images of a light field image. Instead of matting each sub-image individually, our approach utilizes the epipolar plane image (EPI) to construct comprehensive foreground and background sample sets across the sub-images without missing a true sample. The sample sets represent all color variation of foreground and background in a light field image, and the optimal alpha matte is obtained by choosing the best combination of foreground and background samples that minimizes the linear composite error subject to the EPI correspondence constraint. To further preserve consistency of the estimated alpha mattes across different sub-images, we impose a smoothness constraint along the EPI of alpha mattes. In experimental evaluations, we have created a dataset where the ground truth alpha mattes of light field images were obtained by using the blue screen technique. A variety of experiments show that our proposed algorithm produces both visually and quantitatively high-quality matting results for light field images.

Keywords: Image Matting, Light field image, EPI.

1 Introduction

Image Matting aims to extract a soft and accurate alpha matte of foreground given a trimap of an image. Generally, colors of an image can be expressed as a linear combination of foreground and background colors as follows:

$$I = \alpha F + (1 - \alpha)B, \tag{1}$$

where F, B and α represent the foreground, the background, and the mixing coefficients, respectively. Since most matting algorithms were developed for matting a single image, it is less effective when facing multiple input images, e.g. multiple sub-images of a light field image, where consistent alpha mattes across the multiple images are necessary. In this paper, we introduce a new image matting algorithm targeting for a light field image.

A light field image consists of $m \times n$ sub-images where each sub-image was captured from slightly different perspectives. The correlation among the sub-images are encoded in the epipolar plane image (EPI), and the estimated alpha mattes across sub-images also need to follow the EPI constraint. Otherwise flickering artifacts will appear when moving an interpolated view point from one sub-image to another sub-image.

D. Fleet et al. (Eds.): ECCV 2014, Part IV, LNCS 8692, pp. 90–104, 2014.

By Equation (1), image matting is an ill-posed problem because the number of unknowns is more than the number of equations that can be derived from a single image. State-of-the-art matting algorithms can be categorized into two groups: color sampling based, and alpha propagation based methods. The color sampling based methods [7,28,21,11,13,24,23] sample foreground and background colors from the known regions, *i.e.*the definite foreground and the definite background regions, to estimate alpha mattes within the unknown region. The alpha propagation based approaches [26,17,32,14,18,16,3,4] assumes local/nonlocal smoothness of alpha values and propagate alpha values from the known regions to the unknown regions.

In the light field image matting problem, although the number of input images have increased, the number of unknown have also increased which makes it also an ill-posed problem. However, because of the EPI correlation among the sub-images, we can sample foreground and background colors across sub-images. Even if a true color sample in a sub-image is missing, we can still reliably estimate the true color sample from another sub-image. This allows us to achieve better performance than existing color sampling matting techniques. In addition, using the EPI constraint, we can propagate alpha values not only from the known regions to the unknown regions within a sub-image, but also along EPI of alpha mattes across sub-images. This provides an accurate and consistent alpha estimation across sub-images. As demonstrated in our experimental results, our algorithm reduces weaknesses and maximize strengths of both kinds of image matting techniques.

We evaluate and compare performance of our proposed algorithm and state-of-the-art image matting algorithms. To quantitatively compare the performance, we created a new light field matting dataset where the ground truth alpha mattes are obtained by using the blue screen matting procedures introduced in [22]. Our evaluations show that our algorithm produces both visually and quantitatively high-quality matting results for light field images, and have outperformed existing matting algorithms in term of both accuracy and consistency.

2   Related Works

We review previous works that are the most relevant to our work. In particular, we discuss the works related to the two categories of image matting and the works related to light field image processing.

As aforementioned, most image matting techniques can be categorized into color sampling based and alpha propagation based methods. The color sampling based methods [7,28,21,11,13,24,23] solve the matting problem by finding color samples from the known foreground and background pixels to estimate alpha mattes in unknown regions. In [7], the Bayesian matting by Chuang *et al.* analyzes unknown pixels using local color distribution by statistical methods. Robust Matting [28] collects color samples with respect to the color composite equation and are spatially close to the unknown pixels. Shared matting [11] and weighted color and texture matting [24] find the best samples by combining spatial, photometric, and probabilistic information measured by color and texture, respectively. In [13], He *et al.* proposed the global sampling matting which uses all color samples in the known regions to find the best combination of foreground and background samples for matte estimation. Recently, Shahrian *et al.*[23] proposed the comprehensive sampling matting which uses Gaussian Mixture Model (GMM) to cover all color variations in the foreground and background regions of an image for accurate alpha matte estimation.

The alpha propagation based approaches [26,17,32,14,18,16,3,4] analyze statistical correlation among pixels to propagate alpha values from the known regions to the unknown regions. The Poisson Matting by Sun *et al.* [26] estimates an alpha matte by solving a Possion equation to reconstruct an alpha matte from gradients subject to the boundary condition of alpha matte in the known regions. Levin *et al.* [17] introduced the color line model and propose the matting Laplacian to solve the matte estimation problem in a closed form. This work is later extended by He *et al.* [14] who proposed the large kernel matting for matting high resolution images. Lin *et al.* [18] introduced motion regularization for matting motion blurred objects. Based on the nonlocal principle, Lee and Wu [16] introduced the nonlocal matting which propagate alpha values across nonlocal neighbor of a pixel. This work is later extended by Chen *et al.* [3] who proposed the KNN matting to propagate alpha across the k nearest nonlocal neighbors, and by Chen *et al.* [4] who combined local and nonlocal smoothness prior for alpha propagation.

In light field image processing, since Ng *et al.* [20] introduce the prototype of micro lens array light field camera, a lot of follow up works have been proposed. The work by Dansereau *et al.* [9] estimates a depth map of the corresponding elements in a scene using gradient vector. Bishop and Favaro [1] estimate depth map by evaluating aliasing across multiple views. Wanner *et al.* [29,31] use epipolar plane images to estimate depth map with consideration of global and local consistent. The work by Goldluecke and Wanner [12] computes depth maps by using the local derivative constraint with a convex prior derived from a 4d light-field image. Recently, Wanner and Goldluecke [30] suggested a depth map reconstruction method for reflective and transparent surfaces through 4D light-field image analysis.

Comparing our work with previous works, as far as we are aware, this is the first work to seriously address the matting problem in light-field images. Utilizing the additional EPI information, we introduce a method to construct color sample sets across multiple sub-image, and to encode the EPI smoothness constraint in the matting Laplacian by introducing nonlocal smoothness term across multiple sub-images. To facilitate future research in light field matting, we have also created a dataset to quantitatively evaluate performance of matting algorithms.

3 EPI in Light Field Images

3.1 The EPI Constraint

A light field image is typically represented as a 4D function, $L(x, y, s, t)$, which records the intensity of a light ray passing through two parallel planes, $x - y$

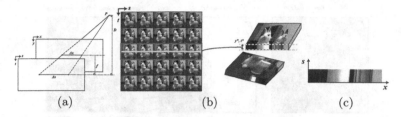

Fig. 1. (a) Parallel plane representation of a light field image. (b) The multiple sub-images of a light field image after decoding. (c) After stacking the images within the yellow line region in (b), we have an epipolar plane image in $x - s$ plane with fixed y,t.

and $s - t$ planes, in a 3D space as illustrated in Figure 1(a). To capture a light field image, one can use a camera array or a consumer level micro lens light field camera, e.g. Lytro [19]. After decoding [10,5], we can obtain multiple sub-images where each sub-image represents image captured from slightly different perspective as illustrated in Figure 1(b).

Since a light field image captures light rays in a 3D space, a light ray from an object at different distance from a camera would pass through the two parallel image planes at different angle. This relationship is captured in the EPI of a light field image. For instance, if we fixed the index of y and t in $L(x,y,s,t)$, we can plot the EPI of $x - s$ plane as illustrated in Figure 1(c). Mathematically, we can derive [2,8,29]:

$$\Delta x = \frac{f}{D}\Delta s, \tag{2}$$

where f is the distance between the two parallel image planes and D is the distance of a object from a camera as illustrated in Figure 1(a). Using Equation (2), we can obtain pixel correspondences across sub-images in x-direction by measuring the image gradients in the EPI of $x - s$ plane. Similarly, we can obtain pixel correspondences in y direction through measuring the image gradients in the EPI of $y - t$ plane. Since colors of correspondent pixels across sub-images come from the same light ray in 3D, the estimated foreground/background colors as well as the alpha values are expected to be the same across the same EPI correspondents. This defines the EPI constraint across the multiple sub-images of a light field image.

3.2 Color Sample Correspondences in EPI

Using the EPI constraint, we can define pixel correspondences across the multiple sub-images and expect the color values as well as the alpha mattes along the EPI correspondences to be identical. In practice, because of the mixing effect in matting areas, the EPI constraint may not hold along the matting boundary since the measured intensity is the result of alpha blending of two light rays from different direction as illustrated in Figure 2(a).

In order to utilize the EPI constraint, we assume the EPI of foreground and background are spatially smooth in the unknown region of a trimap. Intuitively,

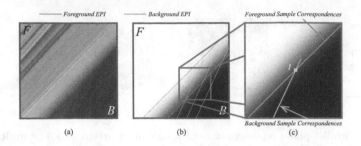

Fig. 2. (a) EPI of matting boundary. (b) Alpha matte of the EPI image. (c) Foreground and background color sample correspondences of a pixel in the matting area.

we assume the depth of foreground and background within the unknown region are similar to the depth of foreground and background in the known region. Thus, we can propagate the EPI constraint from the known region to the unknown region through extrapolation (details will be described in Section 4.2). Figure 2(c) illustrates the color sample correspondences of a pixel in a matting area using the propagated EPI constraint. Note that the foreground and the background color sample correspondences are defined differently since the foreground and background EPI have different light ray direction. In the next section, we will discuss how to use the EPI color sample correspondences to select color samples for better alpha matte estimation.

4   Consistent Matting for Light Field Images

4.1   Pre-processing: Color Samples Collection

In order to efficiently process color samples from the known regions, we follow the steps in [23] to construct a comprehensive color sample sets of foreground and background in a light field image. Specifically, we follow the two-level hierarchical clustering process by first using colors to estimate the global color distribution of foreground and background described by the Gaussian mixture models (GMM). In the second level, we include spatial index of pixels to estimate local color distribution of foreground and background. This provides us the comprehensive sample set which covering all possible foreground and background colors in a light field image. We have also followed the steps to expand trimap regions in color samples collection. This gives us a more accurate estimation of color distribution. We refer readers to [23] for further details of these steps in constructing the comprehensive sample set of foreground and background.

4.2   EPI Estimation and Propagation

Although EPI estimation is not the focus of this paper, the performance of our algorithm depends on the accuracy of estimated EPI since the EPI defines the pixel correspondences between sub-images of a light field image. In our implementation, we use the depth estimation method by [27] to estimate the EPI in the definite foreground and the definite background regions. A median filter is applied to reduce effects of noise in the estimated EPI. In the unknown regions, we propagate the EPI from definite foreground and definite background regions by assuming the EPI in the unknown regions are spatially smooth. The propagation is achieved by solving the Poisson equation by setting zero gradient of EPI in the unknown regions, subject to the boundary constraint of the estimated EPI along the trimap, to extrapolate the EPI in the unknown regions. The extrapolation of foreground and background EPI are performed independently. Thus, two different set of EPI correspondences will be defined within the unknown regions as illustrated in Figure 2. We note that there are better EPI estimation algorithms such as the works by [31,12,30]. In experiments, we found that our EPI estimation and propagation algorithm provides sufficient accuracy for our examples. In implementation, the center view trimap is provided by user manually, and we use it to estimate EPIs in definite foreground and definite background regions, and propagate the EPI propagation to unknown regions in the center view. After that, the center view trimap is propagated to other sub-images automatically using the estimated foreground EPI.

4.3   Color Sample Selection

In previous sampling based matting algorithms, color samples are selected to minimize the linear composite error defined by the matting equation in Equation (1). A major challenge in this process is that there are multiple pairs of foreground and background samples that can minimize the error but the estimated alpha values can be totally different. Researches in sampling based matting algorithm have extensively focused on how to resolve this ambiguity by using different cues or making different assumptions about the true color samples. In this section, we describe how to resolve this ambiguity by using the EPI correspondence defined in the previous section.

Assumption. *We assume foreground and background are located at different depth from camera such that the foreground and the background color sample correspondences are misaligned as illustrated in Figure 2(c). If foreground and background are located at the same (or very closed) depth, the observed intensity across multiple sub-images will be identical. In such case, we will apply the method in [23] to select the optimal color samples based on color similarity, spatial distance, and distribution of sample sets. We will also assume the EPI correspondences are accurate.*

In a practical scenario, we have two different cases as illustrated in Figure 3 in handling the color sample selection problem:

Case 1: Background Samples along EPI of Foreground Are Known
This case happens when a background sample is partially occluded in one sub-image, but is disoccluded in another sub-image. The disoccluded background samples can be detected using the background color sample correspondence defined by the background EPI where pixels along background EPI are not entirely included in the unknown regions.

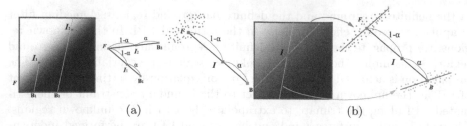

(a)   (b)

Fig. 3. (a) Case 1: If $B_1 \neq B_2$, we solve the alpha in a closed form. If $B_1 = B_2$, we solve the alpha using the comprehensive sample set. (b) Case 2: Foreground and Background samples are solved individually along its EPI, and the median F and B are selected to solve the alpha.

To estimate the color of a foreground sample with known background colors, we can derive multiple equations along the foreground color sample correspondence defined by the foreground EPI:

$$I_1 = \alpha F + (1 - \alpha)B_1,$$
$$\vdots$$
$$I_n = \alpha F + (1 - \alpha)B_n, \tag{3}$$

where $\{I_1, \ldots, I_n\}$ are the observed intensity along the foreground color sample correspondence, and $\{B_1, \ldots, B_n\}$ are the known background colors. Thus, we have number of equations more than or equal to the number of unknown when $n \geq 2$. When $n = 2$, we can obtain the alpha in a closed form:

$$\hat{\alpha} = 1 - \frac{I_1 - I_2}{B_1 - B_2}. \tag{4}$$

When $n > 2$, we solve the alpha using the least square error method by computing the weighted average α across the solution of all pairs of pixels in the foreground color sample correspondences with known background color. Weighting factors for each α are determined by the distance between two background color samples. Larger weight coefficient is given to α with longer distance between background color samples because it is more reliable to estimate α value than the inverse case when denominator is close to zero. With the estimated alpha, $\hat{\alpha}$ and the known background colors, B_i, the foreground color, F, can be computed accordingly. In order to avoid errors caused by image noise, we apply this method only when the number of disoccluded pixels is more than 4 along the EPI correspondence.

In a degenerated case when colors of all background samples are identical, e.g. homogeneous background color, we use the comprehensive sample set collected from the known foreground region to estimate the alpha. Specifically, the observed intensity I and the known background color B form a line constraint where the true foreground color F must be located along the line extrapolated from $I - B$. This line constraint guides the searching of true foreground color sample from the comprehensive sample set. In the case when there are multiple foreground color samples that satisfied the line constraint, we choose the solution which produces the minimum differences of alpha value around the solution within the local neighborhood of a pixel.

Case 2: Background Samples along EPI of Foreground Are Not Known.
When alpha matte area is large, background pixels closed to foreground region will be occluded/partially occluded in all sub-images. In this case, we apply the following method to estimate foreground and background samples. Again, we assume the foreground EPI and the background EPI are misaligned and they are accurately estimated.

For a pixel with different foreground and background color sample correspondence, we first compute the foreground and background sample pairs for each pixels along the foreground EPI and the background EPI independently. This process is done by using the method proposed in [23] to select the optimal color samples from the comprehensive sample set collected from the known foreground and background regions. Next, assuming that majority of the estimated color samples are correct, we apply a simple linear regression to fit a line to the estimated foreground and background samples. Note that when computing the foreground color, only the estimated foreground samples along the foreground EPI were used. This is the same case for the background color estimation. After fitting the color line, we sort the color samples along the estimated color line and choose the median foreground color and the median background color as the true foreground color and the true background color respectively. Once the true foreground and background colors are estimated, the alpha value can be computed as:

$$\hat{\alpha} = \frac{(I - B) \cdot (F - B)}{||F - B||^2}. \tag{5}$$

While this method is simple, we find that the method robust and reliable. In a degenerated case where all foreground and background colors along the two different EPIs are identical, this reduces the problem to the conventional setting of color sample estimation since the two EPIs do not provide additional information to assist the color sample selection.

Implementation: Solving Alpha in the Order to Reduce Ambiguity
Since pixels are interconnected by the foreground and the background EPI, and each pixel in the unknown region have two different set of correspondences, once the foreground color of a pixel with known background samples (Case 1) is estimated, the estimated foreground color can be used to estimate background color of a pixel where its background samples are unknown (Case 2). Using this strategy, we can significantly reduces the ambiguity in color sample selection by reducing the Case 2 scenario to the Case 1 scenario using the estimated color as the known color samples. In our implementation, we use a priority queue to rank the pixels in the unknown region according to the number of known color samples along the foreground or background EPI. The priority of a pixel in the priority queue will be updated once color of a pixel along the EPI correspondence is solved. Intuitively, using this strategy, alpha value of pixels

are solved progressively from the boundary of background region towards the boundary of foreground region.

Due to the small angular resolution of the light-field images, propagation method on the EPI image has ambiguity. In order to reduce this ambiguity, we take multiple directional EPI images, $0°$, $45°$, $90°$ and $135°$ and average the estimated alpha using following confident weighting factor:

$$W_i = \frac{w_i}{\sum w_i}, \quad w_i = exp(-\frac{\|I - \alpha_i F_i - (1 - \alpha_i)B_i\|_2^2}{2\sigma}),$$
$$i = (0°, 45°, 90°, 135°) \tag{6}$$

where α_i, F_i, B_i and W_i are estimated α, foreground, background samples and confidence weighting at each direction respectively. By using this weighting strategy, more reliable and accurate alpha and color samples can be estimated.

4.4 Consistent Matting with the EPI Smoothness Term

The previous color sampling step estimates alpha value of each pixel independently although the selected color samples is guided by the EPI constraint. In this section, we describe the process to further improve the alpha matte by considering smoothness among neighboring pixels. This is also a common post-processing step in many previous matting algorithms.

Using the results, $\hat{\alpha}$, from the Equation (4) or Equation (5) as a data term, and the smoothness term defined by the matting Laplacian matrix L [17], we can obtain the final alpha by:

$$\alpha = \arg\min \alpha^T L\alpha + \lambda(\alpha - \hat{\alpha})^T D(\alpha - \hat{\alpha}) \tag{7}$$

where λ is a weighting parameter, and D is a diagonal matrix. Its diagonal element is a large constant for the known pixel, and a confidence $c = \exp(\|I - (\hat{\alpha}F + (1 - \hat{\alpha})B\|^2/\sigma^2)$ for the unknown pixel.

In order to further consider the smoothness constraint along the EPI of the extracted foreground, we extend Equation (7) to include an additional nonlocal smoothness term in L, and solve the alpha matte of multiple sub-images simultaneously. In particular, we extend Equation (7) as follows:

$$\alpha = \arg\min \alpha^T \mathbf{L}\alpha + \lambda(\alpha - \hat{\alpha})^T \mathbf{D}(\alpha - \hat{\alpha}), \tag{8}$$

and

$$\alpha = \begin{bmatrix} \alpha_1 \\ \alpha_2 \\ \alpha_3 \end{bmatrix}, \mathbf{L} = \begin{bmatrix} L_{11} & L_{12} & L_{13} \\ L_{21} & L_{22} & L_{23} \\ L_{31} & L_{32} & L_{33} \end{bmatrix}, \mathbf{D} = \begin{bmatrix} D_1 & 0 & 0 \\ 0 & D_2 & 0 \\ 0 & 0 & D_3 \end{bmatrix} \tag{9}$$

where L_{ii}, $i = \{1, 2, 3\}$, are the matting Laplacian of the sub-image I_i, and L_{ij}, $i \neq j$, are the cross sub-images smoothness term with each entry defined as:

$$L_{ij}(x, x') = \exp(-\frac{\|I_i(x) - I_j(x')\|^2}{2\sigma_c^2}),$$

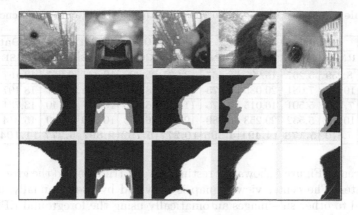

Fig. 4. Our dataset for testing

if x and x' are the foreground EPI correspondence between I_i and I_j, and $L_{ij}(x, x') = 0$ if otherwise. For a sub-image I_1, I_2 is the sub-image next to I_1 in horizontal direction, and I_3 is the sub-image next to I_1 in vertical direction. Thus, we can solve the alpha matte of three sub-images simultaneously with consideration of the EPI smoothness of alpha matte across the sub-images. Although we can solve the alpha matte of sub-images altogether by further extending Equation (9) to include more sub-images, the computation cost increases dramatically deal to the large linear system. In experiments, we found that using more adjacent sub-images does not improve much in accuracy. Thus, we only solve the alpha matte of three sub-images simultaneously.

5   Experimental Results

5.1   Light Field Matting Dataset

We follow the steps in [22] to create a new dataset to evaluate the performance of matting algorithms applied on light field images. In order to derive a high-quality ground truth alpha matte, we placed the matting objects in front of a monitor, and we displayed four different single-colored background (i.e. black, red, green, blue). The images are captured with a Lytro camera mounted on a tripod, and we use the method in [5] to decode the captured light field images from its RAW image data. This gives us 45 sub-images (7 × 7 without four corners) of a light field image. Each of the sub-image is of resolution 300 × 300 with 12-bits per color channel. With the different monochrome color background, we apply the blue screen matting [25] to get the ground truth alpha matte by triangulation. To capture the images for testing, we change the background on the monitor with natural background images. Finally, the images were cropped at a bounding box that was casually drawn around the foreground objects, resulting in the test scenes. Our dataset consists of 5 testing images, and the foreground objects were chosen to cover different properties with hard and soft boundaries, as well

Table 1. Quantitative Comparisons in term of RMSE and Consistency

	Data01		Data02		Data03		Data04		Data05	
	RMSE	CONS	RMSE	CONS	RMSE	CONS	RMSE	CONS	RMSE	CONS
GSM	8.259	5.267	15.997	8.567	13.967	5.900	10.341	6.057	13.167	7.498
KNN	10.508	7.681	20.085	5.575	12.822	8.315	13.605	8.597	18.197	11.855
COM	**7.776**	5.501	16.015	5.375	11.627	6.330	10.347	6.740	13.731	7.761
VIDEO	10.356	5.532	29.253	5.480	19.020	6.383	10.209	5.389	15.314	8.184
OUR	7.870	**5.178**	**14.491**	**4.595**	**10.277**	**5.792**	**9.897**	**5.277**	**11.194**	**6.929**

as translucency. Figure 4 shows our testing images, trimaps and the ground truth alpha mattes. The center view trimap is provided by user manually, and it is propagated to other sub-images automatically using the foreground EPI.

5.2 Evaluations

We evaluate the performance of our algorithm in term of RMSE and consistency. The RMSE is computed as follows:

$$RMSE(\alpha) = \sqrt{\frac{1}{N} \sum_i (\alpha_i^* - \alpha_i)^2}, \tag{10}$$

where α^* is the ground truth alpha and N is the total number of pixels. The consistency is evaluated as follows:

$$CONS(\alpha) = \sqrt{\frac{1}{N} \sum_i (\frac{1}{N_{EPI_i}} \sum_{j \in EPI_i} ||\alpha_i - \alpha_j||^2)}, \tag{11}$$

where α_i and α_j are the EPI correspondences defined by the foreground EPI in $x - s$ plane and $y - t$ plane respectively. The estimated alpha matte of the center view is used for evaluation.

5.3 Comparisons

We compare the performance of our algorithm with the state-of-the-art matting algorithms: global sampling matting [13], KNN matting [3], comprehensive matting [23], and video matting [6]. Table 1 summarizes the comparisons. In Figure 5, we also show the qualitative comparisons on the results of our dataset. As presented in the Table 1 and Figure 5, our algorithm achieves the minimum RMSE in most cases. Also, our results are more consistent across sub-images deal to the EPI smoothness term in our consistent matting algorithm.

Additionally, we also apply our algorithm to a real world example from UCSD in [15]. Figure 6 shows the comparisons using UCSD light field data [15] which are captured by cameras in a row. We use 20 sequential sub-images which include a pink gorilla as the foreground with the background. Since the sub-images are arranged horizontally, we have only the $x - s$ plane in EPI. As shown in Figure 6, our matting result is similar to the results from previous method, but the alpha matte in EPI is smoother which shows that our result is more consistent.

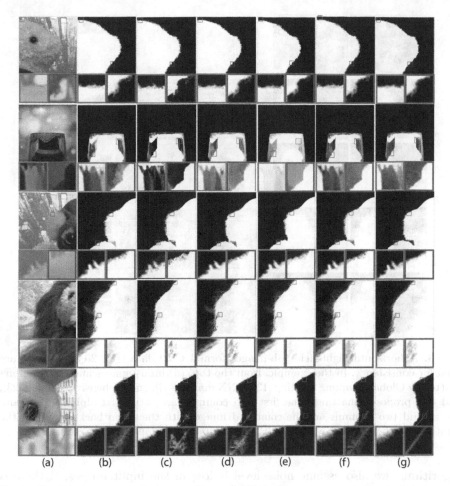

   (a)   (b)   (c)   (d)   (e)   (f)   (g)

Fig. 5. Qualitative comparisons on dataset. We compare our estimated alpha mattes with results from previous methods. (a) Inputs, (b) Results from global sampling matting [13], (c) Results from KNN matting [3], (d) Results from comprehensive matting [23], (e) Results from video matting [6], (f) Our results, (g) Ground truth.

6 Limitation and Discussion

In this paper, we assume foreground and background have sufficient distance such that the directions of foreground EPI and background EPI are very different from each other. If this assumption is violated, *i.e.*the foreground EPI and background EPI are parallel to each other, our approach is less effective since the EPI constraint cannot be used to resolve the ambiguity in color sample selection.

Our another assumption is that the EPIs in unknown regions can be smoothly extrapolated from known regions. If there is significant depth changes in matting area, the errors in extrapolated EPIs will be propagated to our matting results since the EPI correspondences are incorrect. Similar to previous matting

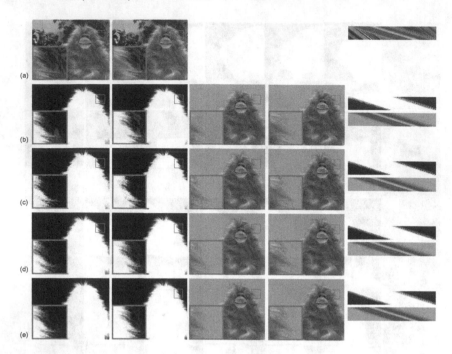

Fig. 6. A horizontal light field sub-images form UCSD data [15]. 20 sub-images are used for consistency. In the example, from the top, (a) input images and (b)-(e) alpha mattes by Global sampling matting [13], KNN matting [3], comprehensive matting [23], and our proposed matting. The first two columns are estimated alpha mattes and the second two columns are the combined image with the green background. In the righthand column, we provide the EPIs to compare the slopes for the consistency.

algorithms, we also assume noise level is low in the input images. If there is significant amount of noise, our EPI estimation method may be broken. In such case, better EPI estimation algorithm should be utilized.

7   Conclusion

In this paper, we have presented a method for light field image matting which estimates consistent alpha mattes of foreground across multiple sub-images in a light field image. By using the EPI constraint, we can define different sets of pixel correspondences for foreground and background. In the color sample selection, we have presented a method to estimate foreground samples alpha with known and unknown background samples. We have also introduced a method to include the EPI smoothness constraint and proposed to solve alpha matte of multiple sub-images simultaneously. In the experimental evaluations, we have created a new dataset with ground truth alpha mattes to quantitatively compare the performance of our algorithm with the performance of state-of-the-art image matting algorithms. Our algorithm outperforms previous work in term of both

RMSE and consistency. As for future work, we are interested in extending our work in other applications that utilize light field image data.

Acknowledgement. We thank the anonymous reviewers for their valuable comments. This research is supported by the MSIP, Korea, under the IT/SW Creative research program supervised by the NIPA (NIPA-2013-H0503-13-1011), and the Multi-ray camera System funded by the Samsung Electronics Co., Ltd (DMC R&D center) (IO130806-00717-01).

References

1. Bishop, T.E., Zanetti, S., Favaro, P.: Plenoptic depth estimation from multiple aliased views. In: IEEE ICCV Workshops (2009)
2. Bolles, R.C., Baker, H.H., Marimont, D.H.: Epipolar-plane image analysis: An approach to determining structure from motion. IJCV 1(1), 7–55 (1987)
3. Chen, Q., Li, D., Tang, C.K.: Knn matting. In: IEEE CVPR (2012)
4. Chen, X., Zou, D., Zhou, S.Z., Zhao, Q., Tan, P.: Image matting with local and nonlocal smooth priors. In: IEEE CVPR (2013)
5. Cho, D., Lee, M., Kim, S., Tai, Y.W.: Modeling the calibration pipeline of the lytro camera for high quality light-field image reconstruction. In: IEEE ICCV (2013)
6. Choi, I., Lee, M., Tai, Y.-W.: Video matting using multi-frame nonlocal matting laplacian. In: Fitzgibbon, A., Lazebnik, S., Perona, P., Sato, Y., Schmid, C. (eds.) ECCV 2012, Part VI. LNCS, vol. 7577, pp. 540–553. Springer, Heidelberg (2012)
7. Chuang, Y.Y., Curless, B., Salesin, D.H., Szeliski, R.: A bayesian approach to digital matting. In: IEEE CVPR (2001)
8. Criminisi, A., Kang, S.B., Swaminathan, R., Szeliski, R., Anandan, P.: Extracting layers and analyzing their specular properties using epipolar-plane-image analysis. Computer Vision and Image Understanding (CVIU) 97(1), 51–85 (2005)
9. Dansereau, D.G., Bruton, L.T.: Gradient-based depth estimation from 4d light fields. In: IEEE International Symposium on Circuits and Systems (ISCAS) (2004)
10. Dansereau, D.G., Pizarro, O., Williams, S.B.: Decoding, calibration and rectification for lenselet-based plenoptic cameras. In: IEEE CVPR (2013)
11. Gastal, E.S.L., Oliveira, M.M.: Shared sampling for real-time alpha matting. In: Eurographics (2010)
12. Goldluecke, B., Wanner, S.: The variational structure of disparity and regularization of 4d light fields. In: IEEE CVPR (2013)
13. He, K., Rhemann, C., Rother, C., Tang, X., Sun, J.: A global sampling method for alpha matting. In: IEEE CVPR (2011)
14. He, K., Sun, J., Tang, X.: Fast matting using large kernel matting laplacian matrices. In: IEEE CVPR (2010)
15. Joshi, N., Matusik, W., Avidan, S.: Natural video matting using camera arrays. In: ACM SIGGRAPH (2006)
16. Lee, P., Wu, Y.: Nonlocal matting. In: IEEE CVPR (2011)
17. Levin, A., Lischinski, D., Weiss, Y.: A closed-form solution to natural image matting. IEEE Trans. on PAMI 30(2), 162–8828 (2008)
18. Lin, H., Tai, Y.W., Brown, M.S.: Motion regularization for matting motion blurred objects. IEEE Trans. on PAMI 33(11), 2329–2336 (2011)
19. Lytro: The lytro camera, https://www.lytro.com

20. Ng, R., Levoy, M., Brédif, M., Duval, G., Horowitz, M., Hanrahan, P.: Light field photography with a hand-held plenoptic camera. Tech. rep. (2005)
21. Rhemann, C., Rother, C., Gelautz, M.: Improving color modeling for alpha matting. In: British Machine Vision Conference (BMVC) (2008)
22. Rhemann, C., Rother, C., Wang, J., Gelautz, M., Kohli, P., Rott, P.: A perceptually motivated online benchmark for image matting. In: IEEE CVPR (2009)
23. Shahrian, E., Rajan, D., Price, B., Cohen, S.: Improving image matting using comprehensive sampling sets. In: IEEE CVPR (2013)
24. Shahrian, E., Rajan, D.: Weighted color and texture sample selection for image matting. In: IEEE CVPR (2012)
25. Smith, A.R., Blinn, J.F.: Blue screen matting. In: ACM SIGGRAPH (1996)
26. Sun, J., Jia, J., Tang, C.K., Shum, H.Y.: Poisson matting. ACM TOG 23(3), 315–321 (2004)
27. Tao, M.W., Hadap, S., Malik, J., Ramamoorthi, R.: Depth from combining defocus and correspondence using light-field cameras. In: IEEE ICCV (2013)
28. Wang, J., Cohen, M.F.: Optimized color sampling for robust matting. In: IEEE CVPR (2007)
29. Wanner, S., Goldluecke, B.: Globally consistent depth labeling of 4D lightfields. In: IEEE CVPR (2012)
30. Wanner, S., Goldluecke, B.: Reconstructing reflective and transparent surfaces from epipolar plane images. In: Weickert, J., Hein, M., Schiele, B. (eds.) GCPR 2013. LNCS, vol. 8142, pp. 1–10. Springer, Heidelberg (2013)
31. Wanner, S., Straehle, C., Goldluecke, B.: Globally consistent multi-label assignment on the ray space of 4d light fields. In: IEEE CVPR (2013)
32. Zheng, Y., Kambhamettu, C.: Learning based digital matting. In: IEEE ICCV (2009)

Consensus of Regression for Occlusion-Robust Facial Feature Localization

Xiang Yu[1], Zhe Lin[2], Jonathan Brandt[2], and Dimitris N. Metaxas[1]

[1] Rutgers University, Piscataway, NJ 08854, USA
[2] Adobe Research, San Jose, CA 95110, USA

Abstract. We address the problem of robust facial feature localization in the presence of occlusions, which remains a lingering problem in facial analysis despite intensive long-term studies. Recently, regression-based approaches to localization have produced accurate results in many cases, yet are still subject to significant error when portions of the face are occluded. To overcome this weakness, we propose an occlusion-robust regression method by forming a consensus from estimates arising from a set of occlusion-specific regressors. That is, each regressor is trained to estimate facial feature locations under the precondition that a particular pre-defined region of the face is occluded. The predictions from each regressor are robustly merged using a Bayesian model that models each regressor's prediction correctness likelihood based on local appearance and consistency with other regressors with overlapping occlusion regions. After localization, the occlusion state for each landmark point is estimated using a Gaussian MRF semi-supervised learning method. Experiments on both non-occluded and occluded face databases demonstrate that our approach achieves consistently better results over state-of-the-art methods for facial landmark localization and occlusion detection.

Keywords: Facial feature localization, Consensus of Regression, Occlusion detection, Face alignment.

1 Introduction

Facial feature localization is a longstanding active research topic due to its wide applicability in computer vision and graphics [2,4,8,20,26,33]. Accurate localization is crucial for many applications, including automated face editing, face recognition, tracking, and expression analysis. Recent state-of-the-art methods such as [2,26] have achieved impressive results, not only on near-frontal faces but also faces in the wild. Despite these advances, the problem remains challenging due to large viewpoint variation, severe illumination conditions, various types of occlusions, etc.

Early successes in facial feature localization, epitomized by the Active Shape Model(ASM) [7] and Active Appearance Model(AAM) [6,17], are characterized by a parametric template that is fit to a given image by optimizing over the template's parameter space. Although effective for many cases, these parametric

D. Fleet et al. (Eds.): ECCV 2014, Part IV, LNCS 8692, pp. 105–118, 2014.

Fig. 1. Sample visual results from Helen, LFPW and COFW databases. Landmarks estimated by proposed method with occlusion detection (red: occluded, green: non-occluded).

approaches tend to break down under extreme pose, lighting and expression, due to lack of flexibility in the representation. Recently, regression-based methods [4,8,10,26] have been shown to overcome some of these difficulties, and have achieved high accuracy, largely due to their greater flexibility as compared to parametric methods, as well as effective sub-pixel localization capability. Despite these successes, a major weakness of the regression-based approach is occlusions, which occur often in faces in the wild (see, for example, Fig. 1). Regression-baded methods depend heavily on local appearance to obtain reliable feature location estimates. Occluded regions produce noisy features and result in erroneous location updates that not only affect the predicted locations of the occluded landmarks, but result in biased estimates of the visible landmarks as well.

In this paper, we propose to overcome the occlusion problem and improve the regression-based approach for facial feature localization. Our approach is based on the "consensus of experts" concept in machine learning. In our case, the "experts" are regressors that are each trained specifically to predict facial feature locations under the precondition that a particular region of the face is occluded. The occlusion region for each regressor is different from, yet overlapping with others. This enables a robust consensus to be formed using Bayesian inference. Note that regressor training requires no occlusion ground truth information because occlusion information is not used for each specific regressor. Once the landmark locations are determined, we employ a semi-supervised Gaussian MRF to smoothly propagate occlusion state labels from high-confident areas to the rest of the face.

Our contributions are as follows: 1) We propose a new regression-based facial feature localization method using a consensus of occlusion-specific regressors that effectively resists occlusions and achieves consistently better performance compared to state-of-the-art methods. The occlusion-specific regressors can be trained on standard landmark datasets without occlusion labels. 2) We propose a semi-supervised method using local occlusion detectors and a Gaussian MRF formulation to robustly identify coherent occluded regions. The resulting occlusion labels are shown to be competitive with the latest occlusion detection methods. 3) Extensive experiments on non-occlusion databases and occlusion databases are conducted to demonstrate the effectiveness of the proposed method.

2 Related Work

Facial landmark localization methods can be roughly divided into two major categories: parametric vs. non-parametric. Parametric methods are characterized by a model that attempts to capture facial appearance variations in terms of an underlying parameter space. Inference amounts to search in parameter space for the best-fitting model to the given image. In contrast, non-parametric methods learn to predict the face shape via training on a database, or by directly drawing exemplars in a data-driven manner.

The Active Shape Model (ASM) [7] and Active Appearance Model (AAM) [6] are both classical, seminal contributions to the parametric approach, with much follow-on work. Subsequently, the Constrained Local Model (CLM) [9,21] was introduced, which combines each local patch's alignment likelihood and predicts the optimal solution by maximizing the overall alignment likelihood. Component-wise ASM was proposed [13] to reduce the alignment error propagated among components. Le et al. [14] introduced a Viterbi process on facial contour fitting and user interaction model to improve the accuracy. Recently a fast AAM algorithm was presented for real time alignment [23], and an ensemble of AAM [5] was proposed to jointly register landmarks for image sequence. The combination of a part model and CLM [29] was proposed to alleviate pose variations, while other CLM frameworks focused on local patch expert learning [1].

In the category of non-parametric methods, Belhumeur et al. [2] proposed a data-driven method that employed RANSAC to robustly fit exemplar landmark configurations drawn from a database to a set of local landmark detections. Similar methods [22,31] either considered temporal feature similarity for joint face alignment or used graph matching to enhance the landmark localization. Notably, Zhu et al. [33] modeled the landmarks as a tree so that the positions could be efficiently optimized through dynamic programming.

Regression-based methods represent a significant sub-category of the non-parametric approach that have recently achieved high accuracy on standard benchmarks. An early contribution in this domain is Liang et al. [15], who proposed directional classifiers to predict the direction and step size of a landmark's update. Cristinacce and Cootes employed boosted regression [10] for local landmark alignment. Regression forest voting for accurate shape fitting was proposed by Cootes et al [8]. Valstar et al. [24] combined boosted regression with a graph model. Martinez et al. [16] proposed local evidence aggregation for regression based alignment. Dantone et al. [11] introduced conditional regression forests to treat faces with different poses separately. Dollar et al. [12] proposed cascaded pose regression to approximate 2D pose of objects. Rivera and Martinez [18] use kernel regression to handle low resolution images. Cao et al. [4] proposed a real-time explicit holistic shape regression method with robust shape indexed features. Xiong and De la Torre [26] proposed an efficient supervised descent method for regression training and inference. Yang et al. [28] employed dense interest points detection with sieving regression forests to obtain good results on faces in the wild.

In general, the regression-based approaches provide good accuracy with fast runtime. However, these methods suffer from the presence of occlusion due to the global nature of the regression which relies on the appearance around all the landmarks. To overcome this shortcoming, some researchers have proposed methods to cope with occlusion handling. For example, Roh et al. [19] used a large amount of facial feature detectors to provide over-sufficient landmark candidates and a RANSAC-based hypothesis and test method to robustly determine the whole shape. This method relies heavily on the facial feature detectors and is consequently computationally demanding. In [27], occlusion is modeled as a sparse outlier and the sparse constraint is applied during the optimization process. The sparse error could be from either occluded landmarks or perturbation of visible landmarks. Supervised occlusion detection methods are also proposed [25,30]. However, if a particular occlusion case is missing from the training set,these methods may fail. A recent work on face alignment with occlusion [3] attempts to use regression to predict the occlusion likelihood of landmarks. They divide the facial area into 3 by 3 blocks and use one non-occluded block each time to predict the landmark positions. The approach shows its positive effects but the statistical prior of each block's occlusion condition is fixed. In contrast, our approach uses all the features from the non-occluded regions. Though there is no occlusion prior, the proposed method applies Bayesian consensus over all the regressors to handle the occlusion.

3   Localization through Occlusion-Robust Regression

Linear regression has proven its effectiveness in facial landmark localization [4,26]. In order to tackle occlusion, we design a set of regressors which are designed specific to different occlusion conditions. For instance, a right eye regressor extracts features over all the landmarks except the landmarks of right eye, which we note as an occlusion-specific regressor. Then a Bayesian inference framework is introduced to predict the landmark positions by jointly considering all the regressor outputs and evidence of low-level appearance models. Encouraged by the regression results, we further apply SVM and Gaussian MRF regularization to identify the occluded landmarks.

3.1   Occlusion-Specific Regressors

As defined in [26], a linear regression based framework models the relationship between landmark displacement Δs and the local appearance Φ, shown in Eqn. 1.

$$\Delta s = A\Phi + b, R = (A, b) \tag{1}$$

where A is a regression matrix and b is the intercept. Φ is a feature vector concatenated by n feature vectors extracted at each fiducial point $(\tilde{x}_i, \tilde{y}_i)$, which indicates that each facial landmark's displacement is related to all other fiducial points' appearance.

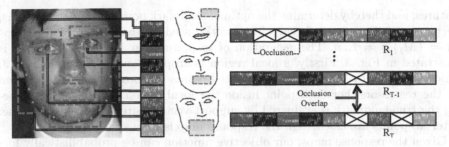

Fig. 2. Illustration of occlusion-specific regressors. Color blocks are regression weights for different components, i.e. left profile, mouth, etc. For different occlusion states, i.e. right eyebrow and right eye occlusion, the regressors are designed not to use the features from the occluded region. Those occlusion states are defined to have occlusion overlap with each other, e.g. mouth occlusion and mouth chin occlusion have overlap on the mouth area.

Based on this observation, we propose to train an ensemble of regressors, each of which handles one type of occlusions. The occlusions are combinations of different facial components, i.e. eyebrow, nose, left profile etc. The illustration is shown in Fig. 2. The training is almost the same as supervised descent method (SDM) [26]. The difference is that here we only extract features at those non-occluded landmarks, i.e. for training the mouth occlusion regressor, we only extract features at non-mouth landmarks. For robustness, the layouts of landmarks between different regressors overlap with each other. In this way, it is expected to be more than one regression result approaching optimal solution, which provides potential to conduct consensus of regressors.

Suppose there are T such regressors. (We define those T regressors as right-eyebrow-eye, right-eyebrow, right-eye, right-contour, left-eyebrow-eye, left-eye brow, left-eye, left-contour, chin, both-eyebrow, all-contour, both-eyes, chin-mouth, nose-mouth and mouth respectively). All of them are visually different because they are designed for different occlusions. In the training part, the goal is to minimize the regression error over all the training faces and all initialized landmark positions $s_t^k, t = 1, ..., T, k = 1, ..., K$. The superscript k means the kth iteration of regressor R_t in the training. Advantageous to other occlusion detection methods, our method needs no occlusion information because the occlusion-specific regressors do not take the occlusion region into consideration. For instance, to train left-eye occlusion regressor, based on general non-occluded facial images, we only consider the features from all other areas except left eye, no matter left eye is occluded or not. Thus the general face image database is sufficient for training our method. As in SDM, practically four to five linear regression steps are needed to reach the convergence. We learn T regressors $R_1, ..., R_T$, each of which consists of K cascaded single regressor $R_t = \{R_t^1, ..., R_t^K\}$.

3.2   Consensus of Regression on Local Response Maps

Given the multiple landmark predictions resulting from the T cascaded regressors, it is necessary to select which of these is uncorrupted by occluded features, and thereby determine the optimal landmark positions. To achieve this, we propose a Bayesian inference framework based on the local response maps $\mathcal{M} = \{M_j\}, j = 1...n$. The generation of response map M_j for a landmark is illustrated in Fig. 3. Firstly, a local region is cropped out as shown in Fig. 3, which is formed by bounding the estimated points (denoted as green dots) from all the regressors. For each point inside the local region, its likelihood of being the true landmark is evaluated by support vector regression trained off-line. After all points are calculated, the response map is formed as in Fig. 3.

Given the response maps, our objective function can be probabilistically formulated as Eqn. 2.

$$\arg\max_s p(s|\hat{s}_1, \hat{s}_2, ..., \hat{s}_T, \mathcal{M}), \tag{2}$$

where $\hat{s}_1, \hat{s}_2, ..., \hat{s}_T$ denote the shape predictions from the T regressors.

To handle occlusion, we introduce $v_i, i = 1,...,T$, which is a binary variable that is true if regressor R_i's landmarks are non-occluded. Thus, the probability that the regression result $\hat{s}_i$ approximates the true position can be represented as $p(v_i = 1|\hat{s}_1, \hat{s}_2, ..., \hat{s}_T)$. Suppose there are sufficient such regressors, weighted mean is a straight forward way to estimate the optimum. But this naive method ignores the cue from the response maps. Our Bayesian framework takes the response maps into consideration by computing $p(s|v_i, \mathcal{M})$. Consequently, Eqn. 2 can be rewritten as:

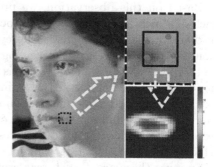

Fig. 3. Illustration of response map

$$p(s|\hat{s}_1, \hat{s}_2, ..., \hat{s}_t, \mathcal{M}) = \sum_{i=1}^{T} \sum_{v_i=\{0,1\}} p(s|v_i, \hat{s}_i, \mathcal{M})p(v_i|\hat{s}_1, \hat{s}_2, ..., \hat{s}_T), \tag{3}$$

where the second term models the deviation of regressor R_i's output from the majority, which can be expressed as:

$$p(v_i = 1|\hat{s}_1, \hat{s}_2, ..., \hat{s}_T) = exp(-\eta\|\hat{s}_i - \bar{s}\|_2^2). \tag{4}$$

In the above model, we define $\bar{s}$ as the reference shape, which is obtained by an iterative outlier removal and averaging algorithm based on the T observations. The goal is to compute a robust mean while excluding the effect of outliers caused by none-compatible regressors.

Given conditional independence assumption of individual landmarks, the shape alignment probability (the first term) in the objective function can be modeled as:

$$p(s|v_i, \hat{s}_i, \mathcal{M}) = \prod_{j=1}^{n} p(x_j|\hat{x}_j^i, \mathcal{M}) \tag{5}$$

where $s = (x_1, x_2, ..., x_n)$ and $\hat{s}_i = (\hat{x}_1^i, \hat{x}_2^i, ..., \hat{x}_n^i)$, x_j denotes a landmark prediction and $\hat{x}_j^i$ denotes a landmark observation.

Each landmark's alignment probability can be modeled as a response map update problem:

$$p(x_j | \hat{x}_j^i, \mathcal{M}) = \sum_{y \in \phi \subset \mathcal{M}} p(x_j | y) p(y | \hat{x}_j^i). \tag{6}$$

Given the current estimate $\hat{x}_j^i$, we consider all the neighboring points y which forms neighborhood $\phi \subset \mathcal{M}$ of $\hat{x}_j^i$ to indicate the alignment likelihood of the next update position x_j. The posterior $p(x_j | y)$ is assumed Gaussian distribution $p(x_j | y) \sim N(x_j; y, \sigma_j I)$.

The probability map $p(y | \hat{x}_j^i)$ is obtained from the response map which is modeled by SVM from training data. Consequently, the response map update can be achieved by fitting a Mixture of Gaussian (MoG) model:

$$p(x_j | \hat{x}_j^i, \mathcal{M}) = \sum_{y \in \phi \subset \mathcal{M}} \gamma_y^i N(x_j; y, \sigma_j I) \tag{7}$$

where $\gamma_y^i = p(y | \hat{x}_j^i)$. The overall objective function now becomes:

$$\arg\max_s \sum_{i=1}^{T} p(v_i | \hat{s}_1, \hat{s}_2, ..., \hat{s}_T) \prod_{j=1}^{n} \sum_{y \in \phi \subset \mathcal{M}} \gamma_y^i N(x_j; y, \sigma_j I) \tag{8}$$

For optimization, we take an alternating scheme: fixing $p(x_k | \hat{x}_k^i, \mathcal{M})$ for all landmarks $k \neq j$, and optimize for the jth landmark via the Expectation Maximization (EM) algorithm. We can iterate this alternating process multiple times until convergence.

3.3 Occlusion Inference

Compared to fully visible facial images, occluded faces are with one or several facial parts that are sheltered by obstacles. As we know, occlusion of landmarks is highly pose-dependent. The same landmark with different head poses may have different appearance. The head pose can be inferred by Procrustes Analysis over the predicted landmarks and the 3D reference face shape [29]. Then our inference process starts with classifying each landmark as occluded or non-occluded under different poses. By extracting pyramid SIFT descriptor $h(x)$, a standard linear SVM framework is applied to provide the detection score, $f(h(x)) = \omega^T h(x) + \beta$. In the training part, well-aligned landmark appearance and occluded appearance are collected with respect to three head poses, left head pose $(-45°, -15°)$, near-frontal head pose $(-15°, 15°)$ and right head pose $(15°, 45°)$. The testing examines the head pose first and apply the pose-dependent occlusion classifier.

Usually the classification might be sensitive and not consistent among landmarks. But we can obtain some detections with high confidence. These highly confident detections are labeled with occlusion state labels. We use a graph-based

Fig. 4. Visualization of weights for label propagation. The size of a landmark is proportional to its weight. Yellow triangle is the central landmark being processed. Red landmarks are with positive weights which are similar to the central landmark while green landmarks are with negative weights which are dissimilar to the central landmark.

method to jointly infer the occlusion status for all the landmarks. Motivated by the work from Zhu et al. [32], assuming there are m labeled points $x_1, ..., x_m$, and $n - m$ unlabeled points $x_{m+1}, ..., x_n$, which constitutes the node set V. All those points are fully connected, which forms the edge set E. The weights between edges are defined by Eqn. 9.

$$w_{ij} = exp\left(-\|x_i - x_j\|^2_{\Sigma_d^{-1}} - \lambda\|h(x_i) - h(x_j)\|^2_{\Sigma_h^{-1}}\right) \tag{9}$$

The first term in the exponential represents the spatial distance, Σ_d is the covariance matrix of all the landmark positions. The second term measures the similarity of feature vectors, h denotes the feature extractor and Σ_h is the covariance matrix of all the features. λ is a balancing factor between the two terms. The similarity between different landmarks is visualized in Fig. 4.

Given such graph $G = (V, E)$, with the edges defined by the weights w_{ij}, the task becomes a label propagation problem on Graph G. By assuming the joint probability of the graph nodes a Gaussian distribution, we can use the closed form solution in [32] to predict occlusion confidence for all the landmarks jointly.

4   Results and Discussions

Our method is mainly focused on facial landmark localization under both non-occluded and occluded conditions. We evaluate our method on two challenging benchmarks, non-occluded images in Labeled Facial Parts in the Wild (LFPW) [2] and Helen facial feature database [14]. Moreover, we evaluate occluded images from both LFPW and Helen databases, denoted as LFPW-O and Helen-O. Together with Caltech Occluded Faces in the Wild (COFW) [3], we evaluate our method on the three occlusion datasets and compare with several state-of-the-art algorithms. We also evaluate the occlusion detection performance on COFW and compare it to [3].

4.1   Experimental Setup

In the experiments, we use the 66 points annotation from 300 Faces in-the-Wild challenge [20] for both training and testing, omitting two inner mouth corner points. The annotation is consistent across different databases, e.g. LFPW and Helen. Since COFW uses the 29 points annotation same as the original annotation of LFPW, when evaluating on COFW, we use the overlapped 19 points which are defined by both 66 points annotation and 29 points annotation.

LFPW consists of face images under wild conditions. The images vary significantly in pose, illumination and occlusion. There are 811 training images and 224 testing images in this database. We selected all occluded images, which is 112 out of 224 testing images to form LFPW-O. Helen is another wild face database, consisting of faces under all kinds of natural conditions, both indoor and outdoor. Most of the images are of high resolution. The training set contains 2000 images and testing set contains 330 images. We randomly selected 290 occluded face images out of 2330 images to form Helen-O. In the training of our regressors, we select 402 Helen training images which are not included in Helen-O and 468 LFPW training images.

We compare our method Consensus of Regression (*CoR*) with 4 state-of-the-art methods, Supervised Descent Method (SDM) [26], Robust Cascaded Pose Regression (RCPR) [3], Discriminative Response Map Fitting (DRMF) [1] and Optimized Part Mixture with Cascaded Deformable Shape Model (CDSM) [29]. These methods report the top performance among the literature. SDM and RCPR are non-parametric methods while DRMF and CDSM are parametric methods. The codes used for this experiments are downloaded from internet provided by the authors. The DRMF and CDSM are 66 points annotation. RCPR's annotation is flexible since it provides the training code in which the annotation can be defined by users. To compare on Helen and LFPW, we re-trained RCPR model with the same training set which we used to train our occlusion-specific regressors. SDM only provides 49 points annotation, omitting 17 profile and jaw-line fiducial points. To make the comparison consistent, on LFPW and Helen, we adopt 49 points evaluation over all the methods. On COFW, we adopt the intersected 19 fiducial points which are defined by all the methods.

4.2   Evaluation on Facial Feature Localization

Non-occlusion Datasets: We compare the alignment accuracy on non-occluded images from LFPW and Helen databases with 4 state-of-the-art methods as shown in Fig. 5. The measurement is Cumulative Distribution Function (CDF).

Almost all methods encounter failure during testing. It may be from the failure of face detection, improper initialization and the algorithm itself. For fairness, we compare on the images that encounter no failure by all the methods. In Fig. 5 (a), SDM and *CoR* (the proposed method) perform almost the same, which significantly outperform other methods with at least 10% proportion gap. In Fig. 5 (b), the proposed *CoR* method achieves better results than all other methods. Nevertheless, considering the failure cases, besides the face detection failure, our method achieves 9.7% and 33.3% failure rate on LFPW and Helen while SDM achieves 10.2% and 36.6% respectively. The non-occlusion evaluation over LFPW and Helen demonstrates that *CoR* is among the top level while marginally better than those methods.

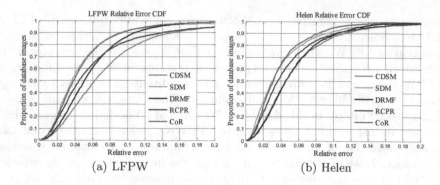

Fig. 5. Relative error Cumulative Distribution Function curves for landmark localization on LFPW and Helen (non-occlusion images), comparing the proposed method *CoR* in Red curve with other state-of-the-art methods. (a) Error cumulative distribution tested on LFPW database. (b) Error cumulative distribution tested on Helen database.

Occlusion Datasets: When evaluating on occluded faces, traditional methods may have problems, i.e. SDM extracts every landmark's local appearance information for regression. The occluded landmarks' appearance which brings in error degrades the regression results significantly. We compare all the methods on the LFPW-O, Helen-O and COFW in Fig. 6.

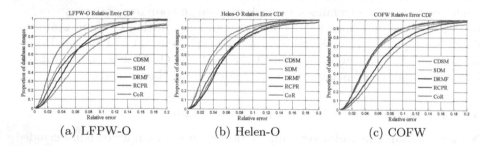

Fig. 6. Relative error Cumulative Distribution Function curves for landmark localization on LFPW-O, Helen-O and COFW, comparing the proposed method *CoR* in Red curve with other state-of-the-art methods. (a) Error cumulative distribution tested on all occluded images from LFPW database. (b) Error cumulative distribution tested on occluded images selected from Helen database. (c) Error cumulative distribution tested on COFW database.

From all the plots, our method accomplishes significantly better accuracy than the rest of the methods especially on LFPW-O and Helen-O. For the COFW dataset, our method approaches the performance of RCPR and is significantly better than other methods. The RCPR result on COFW is trained based on COFW. But our method is trained on part of LFPW and Helen images. When

RCPR is trained on the same training set part of LFPW and Helen, the performance of RCPR on Helen, LFPW as well as Helen-O and LFPW-O is not as good as our method. Compared to non-occlusion results, the margin between the proposed method and SDM is larger when evaluating on LFPW-O and Helen-O. It is because our method is particularly designed with occlusion-specific regressors which shows the effectiveness in handling occlusion.

Quantitative results are evaluated in terms of Average RMSE in Table 1. *CoR* provides the most consistent and accurate performance against other methods on Helen, Helen-O and LFPW-O. It is very competitive to the state-of-the-arts on LFPW and COFW. As we know, the profile and jawline parts suffer the largest variance in face shape. The 49-point annotation in SDM omits the profile and jawline, which imports less variance. While in our method, we consider the profile and jawline and simultaneously optimize all the facial components, which needs to overcome more regression variance than SDM. Even so, *CoR* achieves the same while sometimes better performance than SDM.

Table 1. Average Root Mean Square Error (in pixels) of CDSM, DRMF, RCPR, SDM and proposed method *CoR* on LFPW, Helen, LFPW-O, Helen-O and COFW databases

Method	LFPW	Helen	LFPW-O	Helen-O	COFW
CDSM	6.33	9.57	5.81	10.28	5.17
DRMF	4.90	9.59	5.40	10.23	4.50
RCPR	5.49	8.75	6.32	10.62	**3.38**
SDM	**3.84**	8.16	4.62	8.93	3.80
CoR	3.96	**7.23**	**3.49**	**7.18**	3.51

4.3 Evaluation on *CoR* Framework

In this section, we investigate the effectiveness of the proposed *CoR* framework. We look into the comparison of *CoR*, wm-agg and gm-agg. In Table 2, wm-agg represents the weighted mean aggregation over all T regressors and gm-agg represents geometric mean over all regressors. The table shows that *CoR* consistently outperforms wm-agg and gm-agg with a significant margin, which

Table 2. Average Root Mean Square Error (in pixels) of *CoR*, weighted mean aggregation (wm-agg) and geometric mean aggregation (gm-agg) methods on LFPW, Helen, LFPW-O, Helen-O and COFW databases.

Method	LFPW	Helen	LFPW-O	Helen-O	COFW
CoR	**3.96**	**7.23**	**3.49**	**7.18**	**3.51**
wm-agg	4.32	7.34	3.61	7.41	3.63
gm-agg	4.43	7.66	3.65	7.53	3.66

indicates that the Bayesian consensus of regression scheme is a more robust and effective way in optimizing the positions.

4.4   Evaluation on Occlusion Detection

Among the previous methods, only RCPR detects occlusion. Thus, we compare the performance of occlusion detection with RCPR. Since other databases do not provide occlusion ground truth, we only focus on COFW for evaluation. For RCPR, as the code published by the authors, we do not tune any parameter and simply use the default settings. In our method, we also fix the parameters for testing. The parameters are tuned via 3-fold cross validation. Fig. 7 shows some visual results on occlusion detection. Compared to ground truth, the RCPR results seem to miss out many occluded landmarks while our method hit more occluded ones.

Quantitatively, by holding the false alarm at the same level, our method achieves 41.44% accuracy while RCPR is with 34.16%. Since the annotations of the two methods are different, if we count the component occlusion condition in which the component is labeled occluded if at least one landmark in a component is occluded,(landmarks are categorized into 7 components, left/right eyebrow, left/right eye, nose, mouth and chin), our method is with 47.18% and

(a) Ground truth landmarks of COFW

(b) Localization and occlusion detection result by RCPR

(c) Localization and occlusion detection result by proposed *CoR*

Fig. 7. Occlusion detection comparison of *CoR* and RCPR on COFW database (Red dots: occlusion, green dots: non-occlusion). (a) The first row shows ground truth from COFW. (b) The second row shows the results of RCPR with default parameters. (c) The third row shows the results of proposed *CoR* method.

RCPR is with 37.43%, which reveals that our method improves the detection precision by about 10%.

5 Conclusions

We proposed a new consensus of regression based approach which trains an ensemble of occlusion-specific regressors to handle occluded faces in the wild. Due to the non-existence of occlusion priors, we conduct the consensus of the occlusion-specific regressors under a Bayesian framework to optimize the inference. A graph-based semi-supervised learning is also utilized to explicitly detect the occlusion. Our method shows consistent improvement of facial feature localization on both non-occlusion and occlusion face databases. Additionally, our method demonstrates improvement on occlusion detection compared to the state-of-the-art.

References

1. Asthana, A., Cheng, S., Zafeiriou, S., Pantic, M.: Robust discriminative response map fitting with constrained local models. In: CVPR (2013)
2. Belhumeur, P., Jacobs, D., Kriegman, D., Kumar, N.: Localizing parts of faces using a consensus of exemplars. In: CVPR (2011)
3. Burgos-Artizzu, X., Perona, P., Dollar, P.: Robust face landmark estimation under occlusion. In: ICCV (2013)
4. Cao, X., Wei, Y., Wen, F., Sun, J.: Face alignment by explicit shape regression. In: CVPR (2012)
5. Cheng, X., Sridharan, S., Saragih, J., Lucey, S.: Rank minimization across appearance and shape for aam ensemble fitting. In: ICCV (2013)
6. Cootes, T.F., Edwards, G.J., Taylor, C.J.: Active appearance models. In: Burkhardt, H., Neumann, B. (eds.) ECCV 1998. LNCS, vol. 1407, pp. 484–498. Springer, Heidelberg (1998)
7. Cootes, T., Taylor, C., Cooper, D., Graham, J.: Active shape models-their training and application. Computer Vision and Image Understanding 61(1), 38–59 (1995)
8. Cootes, T.F., Ionita, M.C., Lindner, C., Sauer, P.: Robust and accurate shape model fitting using random forest regression voting. In: Fitzgibbon, A., Lazebnik, S., Perona, P., Sato, Y., Schmid, C. (eds.) ECCV 2012, Part VII. LNCS, vol. 7578, pp. 278–291. Springer, Heidelberg (2012)
9. Cristinacce, D., Cootes, T.: Automatic feature localization with constrained local models. Pattern Recognition 41(10), 3054–3067 (2007)
10. Cristinacce, D., Cootes, T.: Boosted regression active shape models. In: BMVC (2007)
11. Dantone, M., Gall, J., Fanelli, G., Gool, L.: Real-time facial feature detection using conditional regression forests. In: CVPR (2012)
12. Dollar, P., Welinder, P., Perona, P.: Cascaded pose regression. In: CVPR (2010)
13. Huang, Y., Liu, Q., Metaxas, D.: A component based deformable model for generalized face alignment. In: ICCV (2007)
14. Le, V., Brandt, J., Lin, Z., Bourdev, L., Huang, T.S.: Interactive facial feature localization. In: Fitzgibbon, A., Lazebnik, S., Perona, P., Sato, Y., Schmid, C. (eds.) ECCV 2012, Part III. LNCS, vol. 7574, pp. 679–692. Springer, Heidelberg (2012)

15. Liang, L., Xiao, R., Wen, F., Sun, J.: Face alignment via component-based discriminative search. In: Forsyth, D., Torr, P., Zisserman, A. (eds.) ECCV 2008, Part II. LNCS, vol. 5303, pp. 72–85. Springer, Heidelberg (2008)

16. Martinez, B., Valstar, M., Binefa, X., Pantic, M.: Local evidence aggregation for regression-based faical point detection. IEEE Transactions on Pattern Analysis and Machine Intelligence 35(5), 1149–1163 (2013)

17. Matthews, I., Baker, S.: Active appearance models revisited. International Journal of Computer Vision 60(2), 135–164 (2004)

18. Rivera, S., Martinez, A.: Learning deformable shape manifolds. Pattern Recognition 45(4), 1792–1801 (2012)

19. Roh, M., Oguri, T., Kanade, T.: Face alignment robust to occlusion. In: Automatic Face and Gesture Recognition (2011)

20. Sagonas, C., Tzimiropoulos, G., Zafeiriou, S., Pantic, M.: 300 faces in-the-wild challenge: The first facial landmark localization challenge. In: ICCV Workshop (2013)

21. Saragih, J., Lucey, S., Cohn, J.: Deformable model fitting by regularized landmark mean-shift. International Journal of Computer Vision 91(2), 200–215 (2011)

22. Smith, B.M., Zhang, L.: Joint face alignment with non-parametric shape models. In: Fitzgibbon, A., Lazebnik, S., Perona, P., Sato, Y., Schmid, C. (eds.) ECCV 2012, Part III. LNCS, vol. 7574, pp. 43–56. Springer, Heidelberg (2012)

23. Tzimiropoulos, G., Pantic, M.: Optimization problems for fast aam fitting in-the-wild. In: ICCV (2013)

24. Valstar, M., Martinez, B., Binefa, X., Pantic, M.: Facial point detection using boosted regression and graph models. In: CVPR (2010)

25. Wang, X., Han, T., Yan, S.: An hog-lbp human detector with partial occlusion handling. In: ICCV (2011)

26. Xiong, X., De la Torre, F.: Supervised descent method and its applications to face alignment. In: CVPR (2013)

27. Yang, F., Huang, J., Metaxas, D.N.: Sparse shape registration for occluded facial feature localization. In: Automatic Face and Gesture Recognition (2011)

28. Yang, H., Patras, I.: Sieving regression forest votes for facial feature detection in the wild. In: ICCV (2013)

29. Yu, X., Huang, J., Zhang, S., Yan, W., Metaxas, D.N.: Pose-free facial landmark fitting via optimized part mixtures and cascaded deformable shape model. In: ICCV (2013)

30. Yu, X., Yang, F., Huang, J., Metaxas, D.N.: Explicit occlusion detection based deformable fitting for facial landmark localization. In: Automatic Face and Gesture Recognition (2013)

31. Zhou, F., Brandt, J., Lin, Z.: Exemplar-based graph matching for robust facial landmark localization. In: ICCV (2013)

32. Zhu, X., Ghahramani, Z., Lafferty, J.: Semi-supervised learning using gaussian fields and harmonic functions. In: ICML (2003)

33. Zhu, X., Ramanan, D.: Face detection, pose estimation and landmark localization in the wild. In: CVPR (2012)

Learning the Face Prior
for Bayesian Face Recognition

Chaochao Lu and Xiaoou Tang

Department of Information Engineering,
The Chinese University of Hong Kong, China

Abstract. For the traditional Bayesian face recognition methods, a simple prior on face representation cannot cover large variations in facial poses, illuminations, expressions, aging, and occlusions in the wild. In this paper, we propose a new approach to learn the face prior for Bayesian face recognition. First, we extend Manifold Relevance Determination to learn the identity subspace for each individual automatically. Based on the structure of the learned identity subspaces, we then propose to estimate Gaussian mixture densities in the observation space with Gaussian process regression. During the training of our approach, the leave-set-out algorithm is also developed for overfitting avoidance. On extensive experimental evaluations, the learned face prior can improve the performance of the traditional Bayesian face and other related methods significantly. It is also proved that the simple Bayesian face method with the learned face prior can handle the complex intra-personal variations such as large poses and large occlusions. Experiments on the challenging LFW benchmark shows that our algorithm outperforms most of the state-of-art methods.

1 Introduction

Face recognition is an active research field in computer vision, and has been studied extensively [36,1,23,21,38,7,27,15,4,2,8,31]. It mainly consists of two sub-problems: face verification (i.e., to verify whether a pair of face images are from the same person.) and face identification (i.e., to recognize the identity of a query face image given a gallery face set.). As the former is the foundation of the latter and has more applications, we focus on face verification in this paper.

Among the face verification methods, Bayesian face recognition [23] is a representative and successful one. It presents a probabilistic similarity measure based on the Bayesian belief that the difference $\Delta = x_1 - x_2$ of two faces x_1 and x_2 is characteristic of typical facial variations in appearance of an individual. It then formulates the face verification as a binary Bayesian decision problem. In other words, it classifies Δ as intra-personal variations Ω_I (i.e., the variations are from the same individual) or extra-personal variations Ω_E (i.e., the variations are from different individuals). Therefore, based on the MAP (Maximum a Posterior) rule, the similarity measure between x_1 and x_2 can be expressed by the logarithm likelihood ratio between $p(\Delta|\Omega_I)$ and $p(\Delta|\Omega_E)$, where both $p(\Delta|\Omega_I)$ and $p(\Delta|\Omega_E)$ are assumed to follow one multivariate Gaussian distribution [23].

D. Fleet et al. (Eds.): ECCV 2014, Part IV, LNCS 8692, pp. 119–134, 2014.
© Springer International Publishing Switzerland 2014

However, two limitations have restricted the performance of Bayesian face recognition. First, the above Bayesian face method, including several related methods [38,39,37], is based on the difference of a given face pair, which discards the discriminative information and reduce the separability [7]. Second, the distributions of $p(\Delta|\Omega_I)$ and $p(\Delta|\Omega_E)$ are oversimplified, assuming one multivariate Gaussian distribution can cover large variations in facial poses, illuminations, expressions, aging, occlusions, makeups and hair styles in the real world.

Recently, Chen et al. [7] proposed a joint formulation for Bayesian face, which has solved the first problem successfully, but the second problem still remains unsolved. In [19,27], a series of probabilistic models were developed to evaluate the probability that two faces have the same underlying identity cause. These parametric models are less flexible when dealing with complex data distributions. Therefore, it is difficult to capture the intrinsic features of the identity space by means of these existing Bayesian face methods.

To overcome the second problem in this paper, we propose a method to learn the two conditional distributions of $\{x_1, x_2\}$, denoted by $p(\{x_1, x_2\}|\Omega_I)$ and $p(\{x_1, x_2\}|\Omega_E)$. For brevity, we call the two conditional distributions as the *face prior*. Our method mainly consists of two steps.

In the first step, we exploit three properties of Manifold Relevance Determination (MRD) [9]: (1) It can learn a factorized latent variable representation of multiple observation spaces; (2) Each latent variable is either associated with a private space or a shared space; (3) It is a fully Bayesian model and allows estimation of both the dimensionality and the structure of the latent representation to be done automatically. We first extend MRD to learn an identity subspace for each individual automatically. As MRD is based on Gaussian Process latent variable models (GP-LVMs) [16], it is flexible enough to fit complex data. Then, we can obtain their corresponding latent representations z_1 and z_2 for x_1 and x_2 in the learned identity subspace. Therefore, two categories can be generated for training. One category includes K matched pairs, where each pair $\{z_1, z_2\}$ is from the same individual. The other category includes K mismatched pairs, where each pair is from different individuals.

In the second step, we propose to estimate Gaussian mixture densities for each category in the observed data space with Gaussian process regression (GPR) [30]. For each category, there is a clear one-to-one relationship between the latent input $[z_1, z_2]$ and the observed output $[x_1, x_2]$. We model this relationship with GPR, where the leave-set-out (LSO) technique is proposed for training in order to avoid overfitting. In fact, we interpret latent points as centers of a mixture of Gaussian distributions in the latent space that are projected forward by the Gaussian process to produce a high-dimensional Gaussian mixture in the observation space. Since the latent space only contains the identity information, the learned density can fully reflect the distribution of identities of face pairs $[x_1, x_2]$ in the observation space. The resulting distributions $p(\{x_1, x_2\}|\Omega_I)$ and $p(\{x_1, x_2\}|\Omega_E)$ can further improve the performance of Bayesian face recognition.

In summary, there are three contributions in this paper:

1) We introduce MRD and extend it to learn the identity subspace accurately, where the estimation of both the dimensionality and the structure of the subspace can be done automatically.
2) We propose to estimate Gaussian mixture densities with Gaussian process regression (GPR), which allows to estimate the densities in the high-dimensional observation space based on the structure of the low-dimensional latent space. Moreover, in order to avoid overfitting for training, the leave-set-out technique is also proposed.
3) We demonstrate that the learned face prior can improve the performance of Bayesian face recognition significantly, and the simple Bayesian face method with our face prior even outperforms the state-of-art methods.

2   Related Work

Our method is to learn the face prior for Bayesian face recognition. It consists of two steps: learn identity subspace and learn the distributions of identity. Therefore, we introduce some works of particular relevance to ours from the following two perspectives: learn subspace and learn the distributions of face images.

From the perspective of learning subspace, it has been extensively studied in recent face recognition [38,39,36,1,35,13,16]. The representative subspace methods are Principal Component Analysis (PCA) [36] and Linear Discriminant Analysis (LDA) [1]. The former produces the most expressive subspace for face representation, and the latter seeks the most discriminative subspace. Wang et al. [38] proposed a unified framework for subspace face recognition, where face difference is decomposed into three components: intrinsic difference, transformation difference, and noise. They only extracted the intrinsic difference for face recognition, and better performance can be achieved. In [39], a random mixture model was developed to handle complex intra-personal variations and the problem of high dimensions. As mentioned previously, most of these methods are based on the difference of a given face pair, which discards the discriminative information and reduce the separability. Besides, it is also unrealistic to accurately obtain the intra-personal subspace using the linear or simple parametric model in the complex real world. Besides, several probabilistic models, such as Probabilistic Principal Component Analysis (PPCA) [35], Probabilistic Linear Discriminant Analysis (PLDA) [13] and Gaussian Process Latent Variable Models (GP-LVMs) [16], were also proposed. However, these models assume that a single latent variable can represent general modalities, which is not realistic in the complex environment.

From the perspective of learning the distributions of face images, of particular relevance to our work is the Gaussian mixture model with GP-LVMs proposed by Nickisch et al. [25]. However, the problem in [25] is different from ours. In [25], in order to model the density for high dimensional data, GP-LVMs is firstly used to obtain a lower dimensional manifold that captures the main characteristics of the data, and then the density of high-dimensional data can be estimated based on the low-dimensional manifold, but the hyperparameters of the model and the low-dimensional manifold need to be estimated simultaneously. In our method, the low-dimensional manifold (i.e., identity subspace) has been obtained from the first step, and only the hyperparameters need to be estimated. Thus GP-LVMs is not applicable for our problem. Further, as the low-dimensional manifold is fixed, the leave-out technique for overfitting avoidance is not suitable for our problem. A series of probabilistic models for inference about identity were also given in [19,27]. These parametric models assume that there exists a parametric function between the observation space and the latent space, so they are not flexible enough to learn a valid latent space in the complex real world. This also restricts their ability to learn the valid distribution for the identity.

3   Learning Identity Subspace

In this section, we first present how to extend MRD [9] to automatically learn the identity subspace for each individual, and then introduce the construction of the identity subspace. Finally, the construction of the training set for Bayesian face is presented.

3.1   Notation

We assume that the training set consists of N face images from M individuals, where the i-th individual has N_i ($N_i \geq 2$) D-dimensional face images, denoted by $X_i \in \mathbb{R}^{N_i \times D}$, and $N = N_1 + \cdots + N_M$. For each individual, we assume that X_i is partitioned into c subsets of the same size n_i, denoted by $X_i = \{X_i^1, \cdots, X_i^j, \cdots, X_i^c\}$, where $X_i^j \in \mathbb{R}^{n_i \times D}$. We further assume that the single latent identity subspace $Z_i \in \mathbb{R}^{n_i \times Q}$ ($Q \ll D$) exists for each individual, which gives a low-dimensional latent representation of the observed data through the mappings $F^{i,j} = \{f_d^{i,j}\}_{d=1}^D : Z_i \mapsto X_i^j$. In detail, we have $x_{nd}^{i,j} = f_d^{i,j}(z_n^i) + \epsilon_{nd}^{i,j}$, where $x_{nd}^{i,j}$ represents dimension d of point n in the observation space X_i^j, z_n^i represents point n in the latent space Z_i, and ϵ is the additive Gaussian noise.

3.2   The Extended Model of MRD

Although the proposed MRD in [9] only gave the analysis on the case of two views of data, it is easy to extend the model to the case of multiple views of data, as shown in Figure 1. For each observation space X_i^j, D latent functions $f_d^{i,j}$ are selected to be independent draws of a zero-mean Gaussian processes (GPs) with an automatic relevance determination (ARD) [30] covariance function of the form as follows,

$$k^{i,j}(z_a^i, z_b^i) = (\sigma^{i,j})^2 \exp\left(-\frac{1}{2}\sum_{q=1}^Q w_q^{i,j}(z_{aq}^i - z_{bq}^i)^2\right),\tag{1}$$

where we define the ARD weights as $\mathbf{w}^{i,j} = \{w_q^{i,j}\}_{q=1}^Q$ that can automatically infer the responsibility of each latent dimension for each observation space X_i^j. Thus, we can obtain the following likelihood,

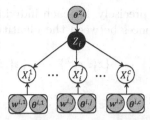

Fig. 1. The graphical model for multiple views of data in the extended model of MRD. In this figure, in order to emphasize the function of the ARD weights, $\mathbf{w}^{i,j}$ are separated from other hyperparameters $\boldsymbol{\theta}^{i,j}$ such as $\sigma^{i,j}$ and those in the addictive Gaussian noise. The ARD weights can encode the relevance of each dimension in the latent space Z_i for each observation space X_i^j. $\boldsymbol{\theta}^{Z_i}$ is the hyperparameters of prior knowledge about Z_i.

$$p(X_i^1, \cdots, X_i^c | Z_i, \boldsymbol{\theta}^{X_i}) = \prod_{j=1}^c \int p(X_i^j | F^{i,j}) p(F^{i,j} | Z_i, \mathbf{w}^{i,j}, \boldsymbol{\theta}^{i,j}) \mathrm{d}F^{i,j}, \quad (2)$$

where $\boldsymbol{\theta}^{X_i} = \{\mathbf{w}^{i,1}, \cdots, \mathbf{w}^{i,c}, \boldsymbol{\theta}^{i,1}, \cdots, \boldsymbol{\theta}^{i,c}\}$, and $p(F^{i,j} | Z_i, \mathbf{w}^{i,j}, \boldsymbol{\theta}^{i,j})$ can be modeled as a product of independent GPs parameterized by $k^{i,j}$. A fully Bayesian training procedure requires to maximize the joint marginal likelihood as follows,

$$p(X_i^1, \cdots, X_i^c | \boldsymbol{\theta}^{X_i}, \boldsymbol{\theta}^{Z_i}) = \int p(X_i^1, \cdots, X_i^c | Z_i, \boldsymbol{\theta}^{X_i}) p(Z_i | \boldsymbol{\theta}^{Z_i}) \mathrm{d}Z_i, \quad (3)$$

where $p(Z_i | \boldsymbol{\theta}^{Z_i})$ is a prior distribution placed on Z_i. We then use the approach proposed in [9] to obtain the final solution $\{Z_i, \boldsymbol{\theta}^{X_i}, \boldsymbol{\theta}^{Z_i}\}$.

3.3 The Construction of Identity Subspace

After the Bayesian training, we can acquire $\{Z_i, \boldsymbol{\theta}^{X_i}, \boldsymbol{\theta}^{Z_i}\}$ for each individual. Then, a segmentation of the latent space Z_i can be automatically determined as $Z_i = (Z_i^S, Z_i^1, \cdots, Z_i^j, \cdots, Z_i^c)$, where $Z_i^S \in \mathbb{R}^{n_i \times Q_S^i}$ ($Q_S^i \leq Q$) is the latent space shared by $\{X_i^j\}_{j=1}^c$, and $Z_i^j \in \mathbb{R}^{n_i \times Q_j^i}$ ($Q_j^i \leq Q$) is the private latent space for each X_i^j. Each dimension of Z_i^S, denoted by q, is selected from the set of dimensions $\{1, \cdots, Q\}$ with the constraint that $w_q^{i,1}, \cdots, w_q^{i,c} > \delta$, where δ is a threshold close to zero. Similarly, each dimension of Z_i^j is selected with the constraint that $w_q^{i,j} > \delta$ and $w_q^{i,1}, \cdots, w_q^{i,j-1}, w_q^{i,j+1}, \cdots, w_q^{i,c} < \delta$. Since Z_i^S only contains the information about the identity, we call it *identity subspace* for each individual.

Clearly, the model is independently trained for each individual. So the dimensions of their shared latent spaces may be different, meaning that the values of $\{Q_S^i\}_{i=1}^M$ are not consistent. To make each individual lie in the identity subspace with the same dimension Q_S, we let $Q_S = \min(Q_S^1, \cdots, Q_S^M)$. For $Q_S^i > Q_S$, we only select the dimensions with Q_S largest ARD weights.

3.4 The Construction of Training Set for Bayesian Face

Until now, each individual has two types of data: the identity subspace Z_i^S and the observation space X_i, where each z_n^i corresponds to the set $\{x_n^{i,j}\}_{j=1}^c$ through the mapping set $F^{i,j}$. More precisely, for each individual, we can construct the following $n_i \times c$ correspondences between the identity subspace and the observation space,

$$
\begin{bmatrix}
\{z_1^i, x_1^{i,1}\} & \cdots & \{z_1^i, x_1^{i,j}\} & \cdots & \{z_1^i, x_1^{i,c}\} \\
\vdots & & \vdots & & \vdots \\
\{z_n^i, x_n^{i,1}\} & \cdots & \{z_n^i, x_n^{i,j}\} & \cdots & \{z_n^i, x_n^{i,c}\} \\
\vdots & & \vdots & & \vdots \\
\{z_{n_i}^i, x_{n_i}^{i,1}\} & \cdots & \{z_{n_i}^i, x_{n_i}^{i,j}\} & \cdots & \{z_{n_i}^i, x_{n_i}^{i,c}\}
\end{bmatrix}.
\tag{4}
$$

Based on these correspondences from all individuals in the training set, two categories respectively consisting of K matched pairs and K mismatched pairs, denoted by Π_1 and Π_2, can be generated using the following criterion,

$$
\pi^k = \{[z_a^{i_a}, z_b^{i_b}], [x_a^{i_a, j_a}, x_b^{i_b, j_b}]\}, \quad k = 1, \ldots, K
\tag{5}
$$

where $\pi^k \in \Pi_1$ when $i_a = i_b$ and $\pi^k \in \Pi_2$ when $i_a \neq i_b$. For convenience in the following sections, let $\pi^k = \{\mathbf{z}^k, \mathbf{x}^k\}$, where $\mathbf{z}^k = [z_a^{i_a}, z_b^{i_b}]^\top \in \mathbb{R}^{2Q_s}$ and $\mathbf{x}^k = [x_a^{i_a, j_a}, x_b^{i_b, j_b}]^\top \in \mathbb{R}^{2D}$. The two categories can be regarded as the training set for Bayesian face.

As mentioned above, we learn the identity subspace for each individual independently, thus the Bayesian training procedure can be conducted in parallel. Also, each individual generally does not contain too many images. Therefore, the time of Bayesian training is short, and the usage of memory can be controlled adaptively and reasonably.

4   Learning the Distributions of Identity

In this section, we propose to utilize GPR to estimate the density in the high-dimensional observation space based on the structure in the low-dimensional identity subspace. As we know, Gaussian mixture models (GMMs) are hard to fit in high dimensions while working well in low dimensions, as each component is either diagonal or has in the order of D^2 parameters [3]. Therefore, we first fit GMMs in the low-dimensional identity subspace, and then map it to the density in the high-dimensional observation space using GPR. Moreover, the leave-set-out technique is also proposed to avoid overfitting for training. In addition, we also present how to use the face prior for Bayesian face recognition.

4.1   Review of GPs and GPR

Here, we give a brief review of Gaussian processes (GPs) and GPR [30]. GPs are the extension of multivariate Gaussian distributions to infinite dimensionality. It is a probability distribution over functions, which is parameterized by a mean function $m(\cdot)$ and a covariance function $k(\cdot, \cdot)$. Without loss of generality, we let $m(\cdot) = 0$ and $k(\cdot, \cdot)$ be the ARD covariance function with the similar form as Equation (1),

$$\hat{k}(\mathbf{z}^a, \mathbf{z}^b) = \sigma_f^2 \exp\Big(-\frac{1}{2}\sum_{q=1}^{2Q_S} w_q(z_q^a - z_q^b)^2\Big) + \sigma_\epsilon^2 \delta(\mathbf{z}^a, \mathbf{z}^b), \qquad (6)$$

where $\delta(\cdot, \cdot)$ is the Kronecker delta function, σ_f^2 and σ_ϵ^2 denote the signal and noise variances, respectively. For simplicity, these hyperparameters are collectively denoted by $\theta^{\mathcal{K}} = \{w_1, \dots, w_{2Q_S}, \sigma_f^2, \sigma_\epsilon^2\}$. Compared with Equation (1), the noise is folded into the covariance function for simplicity in the following. In GPR with vector-valued outputs, $2D$ independent GP priors with the same covariance and mean functions are placed on the latent functions $\mathbf{f} = \{f_i\}_{i=1}^{2D} : \mathcal{Z} \mapsto \mathcal{X}$. Given the training set $\{\mathbf{z}^k, \mathbf{x}^k\}_{k=1}^K$, if $\mathbf{z} \sim \mathcal{N}(\boldsymbol{\mu_z}, \boldsymbol{\Sigma_z})$, then the distribution of $\mathbf{x}$ can be approximated by the following Gaussian distribution,

$$\mathbf{x} \sim \mathcal{N}(\boldsymbol{\mu_x}, \boldsymbol{\Sigma_x}), \qquad (7)$$

with $\boldsymbol{\mu_x} = \mathbf{C}\bar{\mathbf{k}}$, and $\boldsymbol{\Sigma_x} = (\bar{k} - \mathrm{Tr}(\mathbf{K}^{-1}\bar{\mathbf{K}}))\mathbf{I} + \mathbf{C}(\bar{\mathbf{K}} - \bar{\mathbf{k}}\bar{\mathbf{k}}^\top)\mathbf{C}^\top$, where $\mathbf{C} = [\mathbf{x}^1, \dots, \mathbf{x}^K]\mathbf{K}^{-1}$, $\bar{\mathbf{k}} = \mathbb{E}[\mathbf{k}]$, $\bar{\mathbf{K}} = \mathbb{E}[\mathbf{k}\mathbf{k}^\top]$, $\mathbf{k} = [\hat{k}(\mathbf{z}^1, \mathbf{z}), \dots, \hat{k}(\mathbf{z}^K, \mathbf{z})]^\top$, $\mathbf{K} = [\hat{k}(\mathbf{z}^a, \mathbf{z}^b)]_{a,b=1..K}$ and $\bar{k} = \hat{k}(\boldsymbol{\mu_z}, \boldsymbol{\mu_z})$. The two expectations can be evaluated in closed form [25,29].

4.2   Gaussian Mixture Modeling with GPR

According to the relationship between the distributions of $\mathbf{z}$ and $\mathbf{x}$, firstly, it is natural to build a GMM model on the latent identity subspace $\mathcal{Z} = \{\mathbf{z}^k\}_{k=1}^K$ as follows,

$$p(\mathbf{z}) = \sum_{l=1}^{L} \lambda_l \mathcal{N}(\mathbf{z}|\boldsymbol{\mu_z^l}, \boldsymbol{\Sigma_z^l}), \qquad (8)$$

where L is the number of components, $\{\lambda_l\}_{l=1}^L$ are the mixture weights satisfying the constraint that $\sum_{l=1}^L \lambda_l = 1$, and each mixture component of the GMM is a $2Q_S$-variate Gaussian density with the mean $\boldsymbol{\mu_z^i}$ and the covariance $\boldsymbol{\Sigma_z^i}$. These parameters are collectively represented by the notation, $\theta^{\mathcal{G}} = \{\lambda_l, \boldsymbol{\mu_z^l}, \boldsymbol{\Sigma_z^l}\}_{l=1}^L$. We resort to the Expectation-Maximization (EM) algorithm to obtain an estimate of $\theta^{\mathcal{G}}$. Secondly, each point $\mathbf{z}^k$ in the identity subspace is assigned to certain mixture component with the highest probability $\mathcal{N}(\mathbf{z}^k|\boldsymbol{\mu_z^l}, \boldsymbol{\Sigma_z^l})$. In other words, each mixture component should contain a subset of points in the identity subspace, denoted by $\{\mathbf{z}^k\}_{k \in I_l}$, where I_l is the subset of indices of $\mathcal{Z}$ assigned to the l-th mixture component of the GMM. Thirdly, assuming that the parameters $\theta^{\mathcal{K}}$ of the covariance function in Equation (6) have been estimated, we can utilize Equation (7) to calculate $\boldsymbol{\mu_x^l}$ and $\boldsymbol{\Sigma_x^l}$ based on $\{\mathbf{z}^k, \mathbf{x}^k\}_{k \in I_l}$ and $\{\mathbf{z}^k\}_{k \in I_l} \sim \mathcal{N}(\boldsymbol{\mu_z^l}, \boldsymbol{\Sigma_z^l})$, and then obtain $\{\mathbf{x}^k\}_{k \in I_l} \sim \mathcal{N}(\boldsymbol{\mu_x^l}, \boldsymbol{\Sigma_x^l})$. Therefore, we can finally acquire the distribution of identity in the observation space as follows,

$$p(\mathbf{x}) = \sum_{l=1}^{L} \lambda_l \mathcal{N}(\mathbf{x}|\boldsymbol{\mu_x^l}, \boldsymbol{\Sigma_x^l}). \qquad (9)$$

4.3   The Leave-Set-Out Method

Now, the last question is how to estimate the parameters $\theta^{\mathcal{K}}$ of the covariance function in Equation (6) on the training set $\{\mathbf{z}^k, \mathbf{x}^k\}_{k=1}^K$. Intuitively, we can attain $\theta^{\mathcal{K}}$ by maximizing the following log likelihood of the data,

$$\mathcal{L}(\theta^{\mathcal{K}}) = \sum_{k=1}^{K} \ln p(\mathbf{x}^k) = \sum_{k=1}^{K} \ln \sum_{l=1}^{L} \lambda_l \mathcal{N}(\mathbf{x}^k | \boldsymbol{\mu}_{\mathbf{x}}^l, \boldsymbol{\Sigma}_{\mathbf{x}}^l). \tag{10}$$

However, the above logarithm likelihood easily leads to overfitting on the training set. Inspired by the leave-out techniques in [40,25], for our specific problem, we propose the leave-set-out (LSO) method to prevent overfitting,

$$\mathcal{L}_{LSO}(\theta^{\mathcal{K}}) = \sum_{l=1}^{L} \sum_{k \in I_l} \ln \sum_{l' \neq l} \lambda_{l'} \mathcal{N}(\mathbf{x}^k | \boldsymbol{\mu}_{\mathbf{x}}^{l'}, \boldsymbol{\Sigma}_{\mathbf{x}}^{l'}). \tag{11}$$

Compared with $\mathcal{L}(\theta^{\mathcal{K}})$ in the objective (10), $\mathcal{L}_{LSO}(\theta^{\mathcal{K}})$ enforces that the set of $\{\mathbf{x}^k\}_{k \in I_l}$ has the high density even though the set of the mixture components $\{\lambda_l \mathcal{N}(\mathbf{x}^k | \boldsymbol{\mu}_{\mathbf{x}}^l, \boldsymbol{\Sigma}_{\mathbf{x}}^l)\}_{k \in I_l}$ has been removed from the mixture, so we call it the *leave-set-out* method. Finally, we use the scaled conjugate gradients [24] to optimize $\mathcal{L}_{LSO}(\theta^{\mathcal{K}})$ with respect to $\theta^{\mathcal{K}}$.

4.4   Bayesian Face Recognition Using the Face Prior

When the probability (9) is obtained from Π_1, it describes the distribution of the identity information from the same individual in the observation space, thus we regard it as $p(\mathbf{x}|\Omega_I)$. Similarly, when the probability (9) is obtained from Π_2, it describes the distribution of the identity information from different individuals in the observation space, and we regard it as $p(\mathbf{x}|\Omega_E)$. At the testing step, given a pair of face images x_1 and x_2, so the similarity metric between them can be computed using the following logarithm likelihood ratio,

$$s(x_1, x_2) = \log \frac{p(\mathbf{x}|\Omega_I)}{p(\mathbf{x}|\Omega_E)}, \tag{12}$$

where $\mathbf{x} = [x_1, x_2]$. Since the above formulation is the traditional Bayesian face recognition based on the leaned face prior, for notational convenience in the following, we call it *the learned Bayesian*.

4.5   Discussion

It is worth noting that $\mathcal{L}_{LSO}$ proposed in this paper is different from the leave-out techniques such as $\mathcal{L}_{LOO}$ and $\mathcal{L}_{LPO}$ in [25]. There are four main differences as follows: (a) Only the hyperparameters need to be estimated in $\mathcal{L}_{LSO}$, whereas both $\mathcal{L}_{LOO}$ and $\mathcal{L}_{LPO}$ need to estimate the latent subspace and the hyperparameters; (b) Since we build a GMM in the latent identity subspace in advance, and all points have been partitioned into different disjoint subsets, therefore, removing the mixture component is enough to avoid overfitting. However, this is not the case in $\mathcal{L}_{LOO}$ and $\mathcal{L}_{LPO}$, because the latent points are still unknown and need to be computed; (c) It is easy to leave out the set of points in $\mathcal{L}_{LSO}$, but it is hard in $\mathcal{L}_{LOO}$ and $\mathcal{L}_{LPO}$ as the number of points left out cannot be determined accurately; (d) In $\mathcal{L}_{LSO}$, a set of points with I_l shares the same mixture component $\mathcal{N}(\mathbf{x}^k|\boldsymbol{\mu}_\mathbf{x}^l, \boldsymbol{\Sigma}_\mathbf{x}^l)$ rather than each point has one unique Gaussian density in $\mathcal{L}_{LOO}$ and $\mathcal{L}_{LPO}$. Therefore, our method is much faster than the methods in [25] during the training procedure.

5   Experimental Results

In this section, we first introduce several datasets used in our experiments, and then analyze the validity of our approach. Next, we compare our approach with conventional Bayesian face. Finally, our approach is also compared with other competitive face verification methods in different tasks.

5.1   Datasets

In our experiments, the following five datasets are used for different tasks,

- **Multi-PIE** [11] This dataset contains 755,370 face images from 337 individuals under 15 view points and 20 illumination conditions in four recording sessions. Each individual has hundreds of face images.
- **Label Face in the Wild (LFW)** [12] This dataset contains 13,233 uncontrolled face images of 5,749 public figures collected from the Web with large variations in poses, expressions, illuminations, aging, hair styles and occlusions. Of these, 4069 people have just a single image, and only 95 people have more than 15 images in the dataset.
- **AR** [22] This dataset consists of over 4,000 color images from 126 people (70 males and 56 females). All images correspond to frontal view faces with different facial expressions, different illumination conditions and with different occlusions (people wearing sun-glasses or scarf). The number of image per person is 26.
- **PubFig** [15] This dataset is a large, real-world face dataset consisting of 58,797 images of 200 people collected from the Internet. Although the number of persons is small, every person has more than 200 images on average.
- **Wide and Deep Reference (WDRef)** [7] This dataset contains 99,773 images of 2995 people. Of them, 2065 people have more than 15 images, and over 1000 people have more 40 images. It is worth emphasizing that there is no overlap between this dataset and LFW.

To perform the fair comparison with the recent face verification methods, each face image is cropped and resized to 150×120 pixels with the eyes, nose, and mouth corners aligned, and then LBP feature [26] is extracted in each rectified holistic face (if not otherwise specified).

5.2   Parameter Setting

According to the descriptions in the preceding sections, our approach involves two types of parameters: the hyperparameters $\{\theta^{\mathcal{G}}, \theta^{\mathcal{K}}\}$ and the general parameters $\{c, L\}$. Since the hyperparameters can be automatically learned from the data, so we only need to focus on how to select the values of the general parameters. In fact, the parameter c controls the number of conditions influencing intra-personal variations, and the parameter L implies the complexity of the distributions of identity. As the two general parameters play a very important role in our approach, we give a detailed description about how to determine them.

Given the training set and the validation set, we then can determine the values of $\{c, L\}$ using the following two methods based on the characteristics of each dataset:

Method 1. For the datasets under controlled conditions (e.g., Multi-PIE and AR), we directly let c be the number of controlled conditions, and then tune L. Each time we tune L, our approach can be trained on the training set, and then tested on the validation set. Finally, the value of L that leads to the best performance on the validation set is determined.

Method 2. For the datasets under uncontrolled conditions (e.g., LFW, PubFig, and WDRef), we first fix c, and then tune L in the same method as **Method 1**. After the optimal L is determined, we fix L, and then tune c in the same method again. Thus we can obtain the final c and L.

5.3   Performance Analysis of the Proposed Approach

In this section, we conduct three experiments to analyze the validity of our approach. All the experiments are performed by using the training set (PubFig), validation set (the testing set in View 1 of LFW) and testing set (View 2 of LFW). In the training set, all 200 different individuals are used, and 200 images are randomly selected for each individual. In the testing set, we strictly follow the standard 10 fold cross validation experimental setting of LFW under the unrestricted protocol.

For the first experiment, we demonstrate the validity of our method for learning identity subspace by comparing PCA [36], LDA [1], PPCA [35], PLDA [13] with our extension of MRD. In detail, since our approach consists of two steps, so we can replace our extension of MRD with the above conventional subspace methods in the first step to learn the identity subspace, while both the construction of training set in Section 3.4 and the method of learning the distributions of identity in Section 4 are kept unchanged. In the experiment, for PCA and PPCA, the original 10,620 ($15 \times 12 \times 59$) dimensional LBP feature can be directly reduced to the best dimension. However, for LDA and PLDA, the original LBP feature can be first reduced to the best dimension by PCA, and then is further reduced to lower dimensional subspace. For our extension of MRD, the dimension of identity subspace can be determined automatically. We vary the the number of individuals in the training set from 50 to 200 to study the performance of our approach w.r.t. the training data size. Each time the training data size changes, the best c and L is estimated using **Method 2** in Section 5.2 for

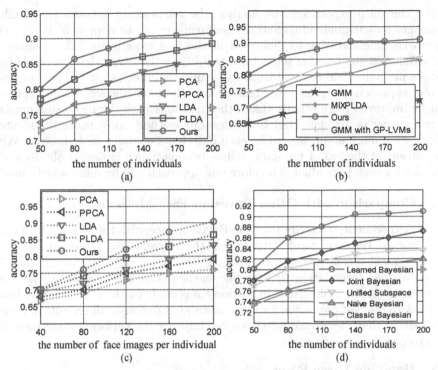

Fig. 2. Verification of the validity of our approach. (a) To verify the validity of learning identity subspace in our approach. (b) To verify the validity of learning the distributions of identity in our approach. (c) To verify the relationship between the number of images for each individual and the performance of our approach. (d) Comparison with other Bayesian face methods.

our approach, because PubFig is an uncontrolled dataset. Figure 2 (a) shows the performances of our approach with different subspace methods replaced in the first step, where the performance of our approach with the extension of MRD is better than others on various training data sizes. This has demonstrated the validity of our method for learning identity subspace.

For the second experiment, we prove the validity of our method for learning the distributions of identity. This step is to estimate the Gaussian mixture density in the observation space based on its corresponding known latent subspace. From the view of mixture models, we can compare our method with conventional GMMs, GMM with GP-LVMs [25] and Mixtures of PLDAs (MIXPLDA) [19]. For the fair comparison, the number of mixture components is set to the same L as ours for all methods. Similar to that in the first experiment, we also vary the number of individuals in the training set from 50 to 200 to study the performance of our approach. Each time we estimate the optimal c and L using **Method 2**. As shown in Figure 2 (b), our method for learning the distributions of identity outperforms other methods on the training set with different numbers of individuals.

For the third experiment, we analyze the relationship between the number of images for each individual and the performance of our approach. We use the same experiment setting as described in the first experiment. The number of individuals on the training set is fixed to 140, we then vary the number of face images per individual from 40 to 200 to study its influence on the performance of our approach. As shown in Figure 2 (c), the performance of our approach can be improved more rapidly than other methods with the increasing number of images per individual. That is because our method can capture the identity information more accurately when each individual contains more images. With the advent of the era of big data, it has become much easier to obtain many samples for each individual. Therefore our approach will be more widely used.

5.4   Comparison with Other Bayesian Face Methods

In this experiment, we verify that the Bayesian face with the learned face prior (the learned Bayesian face) outperforms the conventional Bayesian face [23]. Besides, we also compare unified subspace [38], naive Bayesian formulation [7], joint Bayesian formulation [7] with our learned Bayesian face. Here, the same experiment setting as described in Section 5.3 is used. The LBP feature is reduced by PCA to the best dimension for those methods. Obviously, the results in Figure 2 (d) shows that the learned face prior can improve the performance of Bayesian face recognition significantly.

5.5   Handling Large Poses

Face recognition with large pose variations is always a challenging problem. In this experiment, we demonstrate that our approach is also robust to large pose variations. Existing methods can be mainly divided into two categories: 2D methods and 3D methods (or their hybrids). Although 3D model based methods generally have higher precision than 2D methods, our approach is the 2D method, and therefore compared with several recent popular 2D pose robust methods: APEM [18], Eigen light-fields (ELF) [10], coupled bias-variance tradeoff (CBVT) [17], tied factor analysis (TFA) [28], Locally Linear Regression (LLR) [6], and multi-view discriminant analysis (MvDA) [14]. Of them, APEM, CBVT, TFA and MvDA are from authors' implementation, and the remaining is based on our own implementation. All methods are tested on the Multi-PIE dataset. As we only consider the pose variations in this experiment, so we choose a subset of individuals from MultiPIE, where each individual contains the images with all 15 poses, the neutral expression, and 6 similar illumination conditions (the indices of the selected illumination conditions are $\{07, 08, 09, 10, 11, 12\}$ in this experiment). Then, the subset is split into two mutually exclusive parts: 100 different individuals are used for testing, and the others are for training. At the training step, we let $c = 15$, meaning that all images of an individual is partitioned into 15 subsets, where each subset only contains the images with one pose. Then, L is estimated using **Method 1** on the training set and the validation set (View 1 of LFW), where 10,000 matched pairs and mismatched pairs are constructed respectively. At the testing step, to verify the performance

Table 1. Results (%) on the Multi-PIE dataset

Pose Pairs	APEM	ELF	CBVT	TFA	LLR	MvDA	Learned Bayesian
$\{0°, +60°\}$	65.3	77.4	86.7	89.1	85.4	86.4	**93.6**
$\{0°, +75°\}$	51.7	63.9	79.2	86.5	74.7	82.3	**91.2**
$\{0°, +90°\}$	40.1	38.9	70.1	82.4	64.2	73.6	**88.5**
$\{+15°, +75°\}$	60.2	75.1	81.6	86.5	82.3	75.4	**89.1**
$\{+15°, +90°\}$	45.8	55.2	75.2	81.2	78.6	79.3	**89.2**
$\{+30°, +90°\}$	41.2	57.3	73.2	84.4	79.1	77.2	**90.3**

of our approach on large poses, we split the testing set into different groups. Each group contains all images from one pose pair in the testing set. Similar to the protocol in LFW, all images in each group are also divided into 10 cross-validation sets and each set contains 300 intra-personal and extra-personal pairs. all the methods are tested on each group. Due to space limitation, we only present some results on the groups with over 45° pose differences. As shown in Table 2, our approach outperforms other methods on these groups. Further, we can observe that the performance of our approach becomes more noticeable with the increasing pose differences.

5.6   Handling Large Occlusions

In this experiment, we show that our approach can handle the face images with large occlusions. Our approach is compared with three representative methods: sparse representation classification (SRC) [41], the sparsity based algorithm using MRFs (SMRFs) [43], and Gabor-feature based SRC (GSRC) [42]. All methods are tested on the AR dataset. First, we chose a subset of AR dataset, where only the images with the neutral expression and the norm illumination are considered. Then, we partition the selected subset into two parts: 40 individuals are used for testing, and the remaining are used for training. During the training procedure, let c be the number of types of occlusions ($c = 3$ in this experiment, i.e., all images of each individual are split into three subsets: no wearing, wearing glasses, and wearing scarf), and then L is optimized using **Method 1** on the training set and the validation set (View 1 of LFW), where 400 matched pairs and mismatched pairs are constructed respectively. At the testing step, similar to the protocol in LFW, the testing images are divided into 10 cross-validation sets and each set contains 100 intra-personal and extra-personal pairs. As shown in Table 2, our approach is also robust to large occlusions, because our approach can accurately learn the identity subspace for each individual with occlusions.

Table 2. Results on the AR dataset

Method	SRC	SMRFs	GSRC	Learned Bayesian
Accuracy (%)	87.13	92.42	94.38	**96.23**

5.7 Comparison with the State-of-Art Methods

Finally, to compare with the state-of-art methods and better investigate our approach, we present our best verification result on the LFW benchmark with the outside training data (WDRef). LBP [26] and LE [5] features are extracted from these two datasets[1]. We combine the similar scores with a linear SVM classifier to make the final decision. In the experiment, we strictly follow the standard unrestricted protocol in LFW. First, to make better use of the strengths of our approach as indicated in the third experiment of Section 5.3, we choose a subset of WDRef with the individuals containing at least 30 images. Then, our approach is trained on WDRef and validated on the View 1 of LFW to estimate the optimal general parameters L and c. Finally, we test our approach on the View 2 of LFW under the standard unrestricted protocol. As shown in Figure 3, our approach, i.e., the learned Bayesian face, achieves **96.65%** accuracy. The previously published best Bayesian result on the LFW dataset (96.33%, unrestricted protocol) was achieved by the transfer learning algorithm [4] trained on the WDRef dataset based on the combined Joint Bayesian method [7] and the high-dimensional features [8], while our approach is trained on the same dataset using only the simple low-dimensional features. It is also shown that the accuracy of the simple Bayesian face method with our face prior can outperform most of the state-of-art methods [2,8,31,4,7], and is even comparable with the current best results [34,20,33,32].

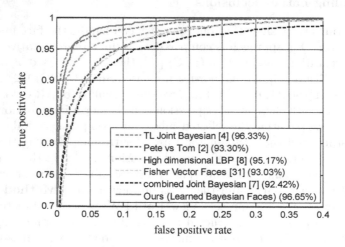

Fig. 3. Verification performance on LFW with the outside training data

6 Conclusions

In this paper, we have proposed a new approach to learn the face prior for the traditional Bayesian face recognition. Our approach consists of two steps. In

---

[1] These two kinds of extracted features of the LFW and WDRef datasets and annotations are provided by the authors [7], and can be downloaded from their project website.

the first step, MRD is extended to automatically learn the identity subspace for each individual. In the second step, GMM with GPR is proposed to estimate the density of identities in the observation space based on the structure of identity subspace. Moreover, we propose to use the leave-set-out technique to avoid overfitting. Extensive experiments shows that the learned face prior significantly improves the performance of the Bayesian face method, and the simple Bayesian face method with our face prior even outperforms most of the state-of-art methods.

References

1. Belhumeur, P.N., Hespanha, J.P., Kriegman, D.: Eigenfaces vs. fisherfaces: Recognition using class specific linear projection. TPAMI (1997)
2. Berg, T., Belhumeur, P.N.: Tom-vs-pete classifiers and identity-preserving alignment for face verification. In: BMVC (2012)
3. Bishop, C.M.: Pattern recognition and machine learning (2006)
4. Cao, X., Wipf, D., Wen, F., Duan, G., Sun, J.: A practical transfer learning algorithm for face verification. In: ICCV (2013)
5. Cao, Z., Yin, Q., Tang, X., Sun, J.: Face recognition with learning-based descriptor. In: CVPR (2010)
6. Chai, X., Shan, S., Chen, X., Gao, W.: Locally linear regression for pose-invariant face recognition. TIP (2007)
7. Chen, D., Cao, X., Wang, L., Wen, F., Sun, J.: Bayesian face revisited: A joint formulation. In: Fitzgibbon, A., Lazebnik, S., Perona, P., Sato, Y., Schmid, C. (eds.) ECCV 2012, Part III. LNCS, vol. 7574, pp. 566–579. Springer, Heidelberg (2012)
8. Chen, D., Cao, X., Wen, F., Sun, J.: Blessing of dimensionality: High-dimensional feature and its efficient compression for face verification. In: CVPR (2013)
9. Damianou, A., Ek, C., Titsias, M.K., Lawrence, N.D.: Manifold relevance determination. In: ICML (2012)
10. Gross, R., Matthews, I., Baker, S.: Appearance-based face recognition and lightfields. TPAMI (2004)
11. Gross, R., Matthews, I., Cohn, J., Kanade, T., Baker, S.: Multipie. Image and Vision Computing (2010)
12. Huang, G.B., Ramesh, M., Berg, T., Learned-Miller, E.: Labeled faces in the wild: A database for studying face recognition in unconstrained environments. Tech. rep., University of Massachusetts, Amherst (2007)
13. Ioffe, S.: Probabilistic linear discriminant analysis. In: Leonardis, A., Bischof, H., Pinz, A. (eds.) ECCV 2006, Part IV. LNCS, vol. 3954, pp. 531–542. Springer, Heidelberg (2006)
14. Kan, M., Shan, S., Zhang, H., Lao, S., Chen, X.: Multi-view discriminant analysis. In: Fitzgibbon, A., Lazebnik, S., Perona, P., Sato, Y., Schmid, C. (eds.) ECCV 2012, Part I. LNCS, vol. 7572, pp. 808–821. Springer, Heidelberg (2012)
15. Kumar, N., Berg, A.C., Belhumeur, P.N., Nayar, S.K.: Attribute and Simile Classifiers for Face Verification. In: ICCV (2009)
16. Lawrence, N.D.: Gaussian process latent variable models for visualisation of high dimensional data. In: NIPS (2003)
17. Li, A., Shan, S., Gao, W.: Coupled bias–variance tradeoff for cross-pose face recognition. TIP (2012)
18. Li, H., Hua, G., Lin, Z., Brandt, J., Yang, J.: Probabilistic elastic matching for pose variant face verification. In: CVPR (2013)

19. Li, P., Fu, Y., Mohammed, U., Elder, J.H., Prince, S.J.: Probabilistic models for inference about identity. TPAMI (2012)
20. Lu, C., Tang, X.: Surpassing human-level face verification performance on lfw with gaussianface. arXiv preprint arXiv:1404.3840 (2014)
21. Lu, C., Zhao, D., Tang, X.: Face recognition using face patch networks. In: ICCV (2013)
22. Martinez, A.M.: The ar face database. CVC Technical Report (1998)
23. Moghaddam, B., Jebara, T., Pentland, A.: Bayesian face recognition. Pattern Recognition (2000)
24. Nabney, I.: Netlab: algorithms for pattern recognition. Springer (2002)
25. Nickisch, H., Rasmussen, C.E.: Gaussian mixture modeling with gaussian process latent variable models. In: Goesele, M., Roth, S., Kuijper, A., Schiele, B., Schindler, K. (eds.) DAGM 2010. LNCS, vol. 6376, pp. 272–282. Springer, Heidelberg (2010)
26. Ojala, T., Pietikainen, M., Maenpaa, T.: Multiresolution gray-scale and rotation invariant texture classification with local binary patterns. TPAMI (2002)
27. Prince, S.J., Elder, J.H.: Probabilistic linear discriminant analysis for inferences about identity. In: ICCV (2007)
28. Prince, S.J., Warrell, J., Elder, J.H., Felisberti, F.M.: Tied factor analysis for face recognition across large pose differences. TPAMI (2008)
29. Quinonero-Candela, J., Girard, A., Rasmussen, C.E.: Prediction at an Uncertain Input for Gaussian Processes and Relevance Vector Machines Application to Multiple-Step Ahead Time-Series Forecasting. IMM, Informatik og Matematisk Modelling, DTU (2003)
30. Rasmussen, C.E., Williams, C.K.: Gaussian processes for machine learning (2006)
31. Simonyan, K., Parkhi, O.M., Vedaldi, A., Zisserman, A.: Fisher vector faces in the wild. In: BMVC (2013)
32. Sun, Y., Wang, X., Tang, X.: Deep learning face representation by joint identification-verification. arXiv preprint arXiv:1406.4773 (2014)
33. Sun, Y., Wang, X., Tang, X.: Deep learning face representation from predicting 10,000 classes. In: CVPR (2014)
34. Taigman, Y., Yang, M., Ranzato, M., Wolf, L.: Deepface: Closing the gap to human-level performance in face verification. In: CVPR (2014)
35. Tipping, M.E., Bishop, C.M.: Probabilistic principal component analysis. Journal of the Royal Statistical Society: Series B (Statistical Methodology) (1999)
36. Turk, M., Pentland, A.: Eigenfaces for recognition. Journal of cognitive neuroscience (1991)
37. Wang, X., Tang, X.: Bayesian face recognition using gabor features. In: ACM SIGMM Workshop on Biometrics Methods and Applications (2003)
38. Wang, X., Tang, X.: A unified framework for subspace face recognition. TPAMI (2004)
39. Wang, X., Tang, X.: Subspace analysis using random mixture models. In: CVPR (2005)
40. Wasserman, L.: All of nonparametric statistics. Springer (2006)
41. Wright, J., Yang, A., Ganesh, A., Sastry, S., Ma, Y.: Robust face recognition via sparse representation. TPAMI (2009)
42. Yang, M., Zhang, L.: Gabor feature based sparse representation for face recognition with gabor occlusion dictionary. In: Daniilidis, K., Maragos, P., Paragios, N. (eds.) ECCV 2010, Part VI. LNCS, vol. 6316, pp. 448–461. Springer, Heidelberg (2010)
43. Zhou, Z., Wagner, A., Mobahi, H., Wright, J., Ma, Y.: Face recognition with contiguous occlusion using markov random fields. In: ICCV (2009)

Spatio-temporal Event Classification Using Time-Series Kernel Based Structured Sparsity[*]

László A. Jeni[1], András Lőrincz[2], Zoltán Szabó[3],
Jeffrey F. Cohn[1,4], and Takeo Kanade[1]

[1] Robotics Institute, Carnegie Mellon University, Pittsburgh, PA, USA
[2] Faculty of Informatics, Eötvös Loránd University, Budapest, Hungary
[3] Gatsby Computational Neuroscience Unit, University College London, London, UK
[4] Department of Psychology, University of Pittsburgh, Pittsburgh, PA, USA
laszlo.jeni@ieee.org, andras.lorincz@elte.hu,
zoltan.szabo@gatsby.ucl.ac.uk, {jeffcohn,tk}@cs.cmu.edu

Abstract. In many behavioral domains, such as facial expression and gesture, sparse structure is prevalent. This sparsity would be well suited for event detection but for one problem. Features typically are confounded by alignment error in space and time. As a consequence, high-dimensional representations such as SIFT and Gabor features have been favored despite their much greater computational cost and potential loss of information. We propose a Kernel Structured Sparsity (KSS) method that can handle both the temporal alignment problem and the structured sparse reconstruction within a common framework, and it can rely on simple features. We characterize spatio-temporal events as time-series of motion patterns and by utilizing time-series kernels we apply standard structured-sparse coding techniques to tackle this important problem. We evaluated the KSS method using both gesture and facial expression datasets that include spontaneous behavior and differ in degree of difficulty and type of ground truth coding. KSS outperformed both sparse and non-sparse methods that utilize complex image features and their temporal extensions. In the case of early facial event classification KSS had 10% higher accuracy as measured by F_1 score over kernel SVM methods[1].

Keywords: structured sparsity, time-series kernels, facial expression classification, gesture recognition.

1 Introduction

The analysis and identification of spatio-temporal processes are of great importance in facial expression identification. The change of pixel intensities around 3D landmark points of the face, such as the corners of the mouth or eyes or the motion patterns of the 3D landmark points themselves, are the natural descriptors of the phenomena. The problem is quite challenging, since individual patch

---

[*] Electronic supplementary material -Supplementary material is available in the online version of this chapter at http://dx.doi.org/10.1007/978-3-319-10593-2_10. Videos can also be accessed at http://www.springerimages.com/videos/978-3-319-10592-5

[1] The KSS code is available online at https://github.com/laszlojeni/KSS

D. Fleet et al. (Eds.): ECCV 2014, Part IV, LNCS 8692, pp. 135–150, 2014.

series or temporal series of 3D meshes are to be compared. A further sophistication appears by the changes of pace of any expression. Consider winking for example. It may be longer or shorter, and within a broad range of duration it can have identical (social) meaning. In turn, we have to generalize the recognition procedure over temporally warped signals.

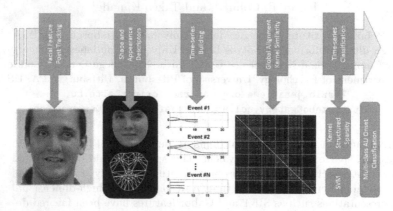

Fig. 1. Overview of the system

Efficient methods using independent component analysis [21], Haar filters [40], and hidden Markov models [4,5,37] have been applied to problems related to the estimation of facial expressions. For temporal clustering of human motion data hierarchical cluster analysis showed promising results [13]. Dynamic time warping is one of the most efficient methods that offer the comparison of temporally distorted samples [30]. Recently developed robust versions, such as the dynamic time warping (DTW) kernel and the global alignment (GA) kernel [10,11] have a great promise here.

In a recent work [22], the authors studied both DTW and GA kernels together with support vector machines (SVM) for holistic facial expressions. Performance was excellent with slight advantage for the GA kernel.

Our interest is in general social conversations, and thus we are interested in the recognition of facial actions (cf. Facial Action Units (AU) [29,28]). The dynamics in this space can reveal emotion, pain, and cognitive states in individuals and the quality of interaction between them. AUs form a large space. There are 30 or so AUs and they can combine in non-additive ways. The recognition problem is demanding. We have studied and compared two methods: (1) the multi-class Support Vector Machine procedure, where for n-classes $n(n-1)/2$ classifiers are developed and evaluation is followed by a voting procedure. This method scales quadratically with the number of classes and slows down considerably as n grows. The other method we studied (2) is structured sparse representation, where the different classes compete with each other and this competition enhances the contrast between the groups. The contrast enhancement is then followed by the winner selection step. We note that this method is also attractive since it easily generalizes to the multi-label situation.

Sparse coding [36,6] and it's structured sparse extensions [41,2] are actively researched topics in machine learning. In the original formulation, we approximate the observations with a linear combination of atoms selected from a fixed dictionary [35], whereas in the case of structured sparsity, the hidden code (i.e., the representation) can be organized into disjoint groups or even into hierarchical structures, such as trees. Furthermore, sparse recovery may involve large ensembles of kernel machines [19]. It was shown recently [2,15,27] that structured sparsity allows significant performance gains beyond the simplistic sparse and compressible models that dominate the literature. For a more detailed survey see [1]. We will use a particular and convenient form. We will optimize structured sparse recovery in a feature space defined by the time-series kernel.

Our contributions are as follows:

Time-series based analysis. Previous work on the use of sparse representation for facial expression recognition [42,25] was limited to individual frames without respect to temporal organization. Our goal is analysis of time series.

Implicit reconstruction in the time-series space. By applying time-series kernels, we can implicitly take into account spatio-temporal similarities. According to our extensive numerical experiments, this method is advantageous in the studied applications.

Structured sparse coding. We show that structured sparse coding is competitive with multi-class SVM method for holistic expressions, facial action units, and also hand gestures. For holistic expressions performance was comparable. For AUs the structured sparse method was 10% more accurate than multi-class SVM. For hand gestures KSS was better with a slight margin.

The paper is organized as follows (see Fig. 1 for a high-level summary of the proposed estimation): Time series of landmark points are used to represent the evolution of facial expressions; this is the topic of Section 2.1. To measure the similarity of the time-series representations we apply global alignment kernels (Section 2.2). Support vector machines and the proposed structured-sparse (KSS) coding technique based on time-series kernels are detailed in Section 2.3 and Section 2.4, respectively. The efficiency of our novel solution method is illustrated by numerical experiments in numerous spatio-temporal gesture and facial expression classification problems in Section 3. Conclusions are drawn in Section 4.

Notations. Vectors (**a**) and matrices (**A**) are denoted by bold letters. An $\mathbf{u} \in \mathbb{R}^d$ vector's Euclidean norm is $\|\mathbf{u}\|_2 = \sqrt{\sum_{i=1}^d u_i^2}$ and ℓ_q norm is $\|\mathbf{u}\|_q = \left(\sum_{i=1}^d |u_i|^q\right)^{\frac{1}{q}}$ ($q \geq 1$). Vector $\mathbf{u}_G$ is the restriction of $\mathbf{u}$ to $G \subseteq \{1, \ldots, d\}$. $\mathbf{B} = [\mathbf{A}_1; \ldots; \mathbf{A}_K] \in \mathbb{R}^{(d_1 + \ldots + d_K) \times N}$ denotes the concatenation of matrices $\mathbf{A}_k \in \mathbb{R}^{d_k \times N}$. The transpose of vector $\mathbf{u} \in \mathbb{R}^d$ is $\mathbf{u}^T$.

2   Methods

In this section we detail the components of our proposed approach.

2.1   Facial Feature Point Localization

We use representations based on facial feature points, landmarks to describe the evolution of facial events.

To localize a dense set of facial landmarks, Active Appearance Models (AAM) [26], Constrained Local Models (CLM) [31] and Supervised Descent Methods (SDM) [39] are often used. These methods register a dense parameterized shape model to an image such that its landmarks correspond to consistent locations on the face.

Of the two, person specific AAMs have higher precision than CLMs or SDMs, but they must be trained for each person before use. On the other hand, CLM and SDM methods can be used for person-independent face alignment because of the localized region templates.

In this work we used a combined 3D SDM method, where the shape model is defined by a 3D mesh and, in particular, by the 3D vertex locations of the mesh, called landmark points. Consider the shape of a 3D SDM as the coordinates of 3D vertices that make up the mesh:

$$\mathbf{x} = [x_1; y_1; z_1; \ldots; x_M; y_M; z_M], \tag{1}$$

or, $\mathbf{x} = [\mathbf{x}_1; \ldots; \mathbf{x}_M]$, where $\mathbf{x}_i = [x_i; y_i; z_i]$. We have T samples: $\{\mathbf{x}(t)\}_{t=1}^T$. We assume that – apart from scale, rotation, and translation – all samples $\{\mathbf{x}(t)\}_{t=1}^T$ can be approximated by means of the linear principal component analysis (PCA).

The 3D point distribution model (PDM) describes non-rigid shape variations linearly and composes it with a global rigid transformation, placing the shape in the image frame:

$$\mathbf{x}_i = \mathbf{x}_i(\mathbf{p}) = s\mathbf{R}(\bar{\mathbf{x}}_i + \boldsymbol{\Phi}_i\mathbf{q}) + \mathbf{t} \quad (i = 1, \ldots, M), \tag{2}$$

where $\mathbf{x}_i(\mathbf{p})$ denotes the 3D location of the ith landmark and $\mathbf{p} = \{s, \alpha, \beta, \gamma, \mathbf{q}, \mathbf{t}\}$ denotes the parameters of the model, which consist of a global scaling s, angles of rotation in three dimensions ($\mathbf{R} = \mathbf{R}_1(\alpha)\mathbf{R}_2(\beta)\mathbf{R}_3(\gamma)$), a translation $\mathbf{t}$ and non-rigid transformation $\mathbf{q}$. Here $\bar{\mathbf{x}}_i$ denotes the mean location of the ith landmark (i.e. $\bar{\mathbf{x}}_i = [\bar{x}_i; \bar{y}_i; \bar{z}_i]$ and $\bar{\mathbf{x}} = [\bar{\mathbf{x}}_1; \ldots; \bar{\mathbf{x}}_M]$).

We assume that the prior of the parameters follow a normal distribution with mean $\mathbf{0}$ and variance $\boldsymbol{\Lambda}$ at a parameter vector $\mathbf{q}$: $p(\mathbf{p}) \propto N(\mathbf{q}; \mathbf{0}, \boldsymbol{\Lambda})$ and we used PCA to determine the d pieces of $3M$ dimensional basis vectors ($\boldsymbol{\Phi} = [\boldsymbol{\Phi}_1; \ldots; \boldsymbol{\Phi}_M] \in \mathbb{R}^{3M \times d}$). Vector $\mathbf{q}$ represents the 3D distortion of the face in the $3M \times d$ dimensional subspace and it can be used for emotion classification, for example.

We used ZFace[2], which is a generic 3D face tracker that requires no individual training to track facial landmarks of persons is has never seen before. It locates 3D coordinates of a dense set of facial landmarks. We note that the 3D PDM of ZFace is consists of 56 non-rigid parameters ($\mathbf{q} \in \mathbb{R}^{56}$).

---

[2] ZFace is available from http://zface.org.

2.2 Global Alignment Kernel

To quantify the similarity of time-series (that form the input of the classifiers) we make use of kernels.

Kernel based classifiers, like any other classification scheme, should be robust against invariances and distortions. Dynamic time warping, traditionally solved by dynamic programming, has been introduced to overcome temporal distortions and has been successfully combined with kernel methods.

Let $\mathcal{X}^{\mathbb{N}}$ be the set of discrete-time time series taking values in an arbitrary space $\mathcal{X}$. One can try to align two time series $\mathbf{u} = (u_1, ..., u_n)$ and $\mathbf{v} = (v_1, ..., v_m)$ of lengths n and m, respectively, in various ways by distorting them. An alignment π has length p and $p \leq n + m - 1$ since the two series have $n + m$ points and they are matched at least at one point of time. We use the notation of [12]. An alignment π is a pair of increasing integral vectors (π_1, π_2) of length p such that $1 = \pi_1(1) \leq ... \leq \pi_1(p) = n$ and $1 = \pi_2(1) \leq ... \leq \pi_2(p) = m$, with unitary increments and no simultaneous repetitions. Coordinates of π are also known as warping functions.

Now, let $|\pi|$ denote the length of alignment π. The *cost* can be defined by means of a local divergence ϕ that measures the discrepancy between any two points u_i and v_j of vectors $\mathbf{u}$ and $\mathbf{v}$.

$$D_{\mathbf{u},\mathbf{v}}(\pi) = \sum_{i}^{|\pi|} \phi(u_{\pi_1(i)}, v_{\pi_2(i)}) \tag{3}$$

The Global Alignment (GA) kernel assumes that the minimum value of alignments may be sensitive to peculiarities of the time series and intends to take advantage of all alignments weighted exponentially. It is defined as the sum of exponentiated and sign changed costs of the individual alignments:

$$k_{GA}(\mathbf{u}, \mathbf{v}) = \sum_{\pi \in A(n,m)} e^{-D_{\mathbf{u},\mathbf{v}}(\pi)}, \tag{4}$$

where $A(n, m)$ denotes the set of all alignments between two time series of length n and m. Equation (4) can be rewritten by breaking up the alignment distances according to the local divergences: similarity function κ is induced by divergence ϕ:

$$k_{GA}(\mathbf{u}, \mathbf{v}) = \sum_{\pi \in A(n,m)} \prod_{i=i}^{|\pi|} e^{-\phi(u_{\pi_1(i)}, v_{\pi_2(i)})} \tag{5}$$

$$= \sum_{\pi \in A(n,m)} \prod_{i=i}^{|\pi|} \kappa\left(u_{\pi_1(i)}, v_{\pi_2(i)}\right), \tag{6}$$

where notation $\kappa = e^{-\phi}$ was introduced for the sake of simplicity. It has been argued that k_{GA} runs over the whole spectrum of the costs and gives rise to a smoother measure than the minimum of the costs, i.e., the DTW (dynamic time warping) distance [10]. It has been shown in the same paper that k_{GA} is positive definite provided that $\kappa/(1+\kappa)$ is positive definite on $\mathcal{X}$. Furthermore, the computational effort is similar to that of the DTW distance; it is $\mathcal{O}(nm)$. Cuturi argued in [12] that global alignment kernel induced Gram matrix do not tend to be diagonally dominated as long as the sequences to be compared have similar lengths.

In our numerical simulations, we used local kernel $e^{-\phi_\sigma}$ suggested by Cuturi, where

$$\phi_\sigma\left(x,y\right) = \frac{1}{2\sigma^2}\|x-y\|^2 + \log\left(2 - e^{-\frac{\|x-y\|^2}{2\sigma^2}}\right). \tag{7}$$

2.3 Time-series Classification using SVM

Support Vector Machines (SVMs) are very powerful for binary and multi-class classification as well as for regression problems [7]. They are robust against outliers. For two-class separation, SVM estimates the optimal separating hyper-plane between the two classes by maximizing the margin between the hyper-plane and closest points of the classes. The closest points of the classes are called support vectors; the optimal separating hyper-plane lies at half distance between them.

In case of time-series classification, we are given sample and label pairs $\{(\mathbf{u}^{(i)}, l^{(i)})\}_{i=1}^K$ with $\left(\mathbf{u}^{(i)}, l^{(i)}\right) \in \left(\mathbb{R}^d\right)^{\mathbb{N}} \times \{-1, 1\}$. Here, for class '1' and for class '2' $l^{(i)} = 1$ and $l^{(i)} = -1$, respectively. We also have a feature map $\varphi : \left(\mathbb{R}^d\right)^{\mathbb{N}} \to \mathcal{H}$, where $\mathcal{H}$ is a Hilbert-space. The kernel implicitly performs the dot product calculations between mapped points: $k(\mathbf{u}, \mathbf{v}) = \langle\varphi(\mathbf{u}), \varphi(\mathbf{v})\rangle_{\mathcal{H}}$. The support vector classification seeks to minimize the cost function

$$\min_{w,b,\xi} \frac{1}{2}\|w\|_{\mathcal{H}}^2 + C\sum_{i=1}^K \xi_i \tag{8}$$

subject to the constraints

$$l^{(i)}\left(\left\langle w, \varphi\left(\mathbf{u}^{(i)}\right)\right\rangle_{\mathcal{H}} + b\right) \geq 1 - \xi_i, \ \ \xi_i \geq 0, \tag{9}$$

where ξ_i-s are the so-called slack variables that generalize the original SVM concept with separating hyper-planes to soft-margin classifiers that have outliers that can not be separated.

We used multi-class classification, where decision surfaces are computed for all class pairs, i.e., for classes one has decision surfaces and then applies a voting strategy for decisions. We used the one-against-one procedure.

2.4 Multi-class Classification of Time Series Using Structured Sparsity

To tackle our multi-class AU learning problem, we exemplify structured-sparse coding defined for Euclidean spaces [23] to time series: (i) the occurrence is captured by a non-overlapping group structure ($\mathcal{G}$), (ii) the underlying similarity of time series is handled by the global alignment kernel (k_{GA}, see Section 2.2).

Formally, let us assume that we are given a $k = k_{GA}$ kernel [34] on $\left(\mathbb{R}^d\right)^{\mathrm{N}}$, the set of d-dimensional time-series. Since k is a kernel there exists a feature mapping

$$\varphi : \left(\mathbb{R}^d\right)^{\mathrm{N}} \to \mathcal{H} \tag{10}$$

to a Hilbert space $\mathcal{H}$, where k represents an inner product

$$k(\mathbf{u}, \mathbf{v}) = \langle \varphi(\mathbf{u}), \varphi(\mathbf{v}) \rangle_{\mathcal{H}}, \quad \forall (\mathbf{u}, \mathbf{v}) \in \left(\mathbb{R}^d\right)^{\mathrm{N}} \times \left(\mathbb{R}^d\right)^{\mathrm{N}}.$$

Let us also assume that we have a $D = [\varphi(\mathbf{d}_1), \ldots, \varphi(\mathbf{d}_M)]$ dictionary and a $\mathcal{G}$ partition on $\{1, \ldots, M\}$, i.e., $\forall G_i, G_j \in \mathcal{G}$: $G_i \cap G_j = \emptyset$ ($i \neq j$) and $\cup_{G \in \mathcal{G}} = \{1, \ldots, M\}$.

We aim to approximate an observation $\mathbf{x} \in \left(\mathbb{R}^d\right)^{\mathrm{N}}$ using the D dictionary taking into account the group-structure $\mathcal{G}$:

$$J(\boldsymbol{\alpha}) = \frac{1}{2} \left\| \varphi(\mathbf{x}) - \sum_{i=1}^{M} \varphi(\mathbf{d}_i)\alpha_i \right\|_{\mathcal{H}}^2 + \kappa\Omega(\boldsymbol{\alpha}) \to \min_{\boldsymbol{\alpha}}, \tag{11}$$

where

$$\Omega(\boldsymbol{\alpha}) = \sum_{G \in \mathcal{G}} \|\boldsymbol{\alpha}_G\|_q \quad (q \geq 1). \tag{12}$$

The occurrence of events is encoded by the Ω group-structure inducing regularizer: each $G \in \mathcal{G}$ corresponds to the activity of one type of event, by the application of Ω few events are favored. We used the so-called-ℓ_1/ℓ_2 norm ($q = 2$). Note that using $q = 1$ leads to ℓ_1-norm with no group sparsity effects. $\kappa > 0$ is a regularization parameter describing the trade-off between the two cost terms. In the sequel, optimization task (11) will be referred to as the kernel structured sparse coding problem of time series, or shortly KSS.

By applying the kernel trick, optimization of objective (11) is equivalent to

$$J(\boldsymbol{\alpha}) = \left(\frac{1}{2}\boldsymbol{\alpha}^T \mathbf{G}\boldsymbol{\alpha} - \mathbf{k}^T\boldsymbol{\alpha}\right) + \kappa\Omega(\boldsymbol{\alpha}), \tag{13}$$

where $\mathbf{k} = [k(\mathbf{x}, \mathbf{d}_1); \ldots; k(\mathbf{x}, \mathbf{d}_M)] \in \mathbb{R}^M$ and $\mathbf{G} = [G_{ij}] = [k(\mathbf{d}_i, \mathbf{d}_j)] \in \mathbb{R}^{M \times M}$ is the Gram-matrix.

Equation (13) is a finite dimensional problem, which can be optimized, for example, by FISTA (fast iterative shrinkage-thresholding algorithm) [3]. Our experiments were based on the modification of the SLEP package [20]. The supplementary material provides additional details for the implementation (Online Resource 1).

Note: according to our numerical experiences on time series, it is often advantageous to apply normalization to the dictionary atoms and to the observations

$$\|\varphi(\mathbf{d}_i)\|_{\mathcal{H}} = 1, \quad (\forall i), \qquad \|\varphi(\mathbf{x})\|_{\mathcal{H}} = 1. \tag{14}$$

This can be carried out implicitly in the proposed approach by using the modified kernel

$$\bar{k}(\mathbf{u},\mathbf{v}) = \frac{k(\mathbf{u},\mathbf{v})}{\sqrt{k(\mathbf{u},\mathbf{u})}\sqrt{k(\mathbf{v},\mathbf{v})}} = \left\langle \frac{\varphi(\mathbf{u})}{\|\varphi(\mathbf{u})\|_{\mathcal{H}}}, \frac{\varphi(\mathbf{v})}{\|\varphi(\mathbf{v})\|_{\mathcal{H}}} \right\rangle_{\mathcal{H}}. \tag{15}$$

Classification Using Structured Sparsity. In the multi-class case we investigated three different strategies for the classification of the input ($\mathbf{x}$) using the $\boldsymbol{\alpha}$ representation provided by the KSS method:

$$\hat{k} = \underset{k=1,\dots,K}{\arg\max} \|\boldsymbol{\alpha}_{G_k}\|_2, \tag{16}$$

$$\hat{k} = \underset{k=1,\dots,K}{\arg\min} \|\varphi(\mathbf{x}) - D_k\boldsymbol{\alpha}_{G_k}\|_{\mathcal{H}}, \tag{17}$$

$$\hat{k} = \underset{k=1,\dots,K}{\arg\max} \left\| \varphi(\mathbf{x}) - \sum_{i=1;i\neq k}^{K} D_i\boldsymbol{\alpha}_{G_i} \right\|_{\mathcal{H}}, \tag{18}$$

where $D = [D_1,\dots,D_K]$ is the dictionary partitioned according to $\mathcal{G}$ group structure ($K = |\mathcal{G}|$).

Intuitively, the first strategy [(16)] selects the group with the highest activity in the hidden representation $\boldsymbol{\alpha}$. The second one [(17)] chooses the group that minimizes the reconstruction error, the third one [(18)] selects the group, whose complement has the highest reconstruction error.

3   Experiments

3.1   Datasets

One motion gesture and two face datasets were used for evaluation. For gestures, we used the 6D Motion Gesture Database [9]. For emotion-specified expressions, we used the Cohn-Kanade Extended Facial Expression (CK+) Database [24]. For AU-labeled facial expressions, we used a subset of the more challenging Group Formation Task dataset [32]. See Table 1 for descriptive statistics of the datasets.

Table 1. Database statistics

Database	Domain	Type	# of Time-series	# of Classes	Dimension	Avg. length (std)
6DGM [9]	Gesture	Deliberate	5720	26	3-4	66.86 (29.84)
CK+ [24]	Face	Deliberate	327	7	56	17.97 (8.59)
GFT50 [32]	Face	Spontaneous	5000	12	166	7.51 (1.44)

6D Motion Gesture Database. The 6D Motion Gesture Database (6DMG) [9] contains comprehensive motion data, including the 3D position, orientation, acceleration, and angular speed, for a set of different motion gestures performed by different users. The dataset composed of three subsets: motion gestures, air-handwriting and air-fingerwriting. In our experiments we used the air-handwriting set. WorldViz PPT-X4 was used as the optical tracking system, which tracks infrared dots. As for inertial sensors, the Wii Remote Plus embedded MEMS accelerometers and gyroscope were used. Overall, the tracking device provided both explicit and implicit 6D spatio-temporal information, including the position, orientation, acceleration, and angular speed. To eliminate allographs or different stroke orders, the subjects were instructed to follow certain "stroke order" for each character. The database contains 26 motion characters (uppercase A to Z) from 22 participants. Each character is repeated 10 times for every subject.

Cohn-Kanade Extended Dataset. The Cohn-Kanade Extended Facial Expression (CK+) Database [24] was developed for automated facial image analysis. CK+ together with an earlier version [18] is one of the most widely used testbeds for this purpose. The database contains 123 different subjects with 593 frontal image sequences. Each sequence begins with a neutral expression and ends at the apex of an emotion expression. A total of 327 image sequences have validated annotation for seven universal emotions (anger, contempt, disgust, fear, happy, sad and surprise). These image sequences were used in the current study. For each image sequence, 3D landmarks and shape parameters were obtained using the ZFace tracker.

Group Formation Task Corpus (spontaneous). For Action Unit onset classification task we used the more challenging Group Formation Task (GFT) corpus [32]. The corpus was built to evaluate the socioemotional effects of alcohol. It consist of 36 minutes of casual social interaction in 240 3-person groups of previously unacquainted young adults. Groups were randomly assigned to one of three conditions: alcoholic drinks, placebo beverages, and non-alcohol control beverages. Participants were recorded using three hardware synchronized cameras while seated around a circular table. Mean head pose is mostly frontal but moderate head pose variation and self-occlusion are common as subjects turn toward or away from each other. Facial AU occur during speech and in both additive and non-additive combinations. In the latter, individual AU modify each other's appearance. A sample video clip is available in the supplement (Online Resource 2).

Highly trained and certified FACS coders at the Affect Analysis Group fully FACS coded 3 minutes of video from each of 50 subjects [14]. This subset, denoted as GFT50, consists of 235,032 frames, annotated with 34 AUs. We selected 12 AUs for this evaluation. All AU had high inter-observer reliability as quantified by coefficient kappa (see Table 2), even the ones with high degree of skew, which can attenuate measures of agreement [16].

Table 2. FACS reliability on the GFT50 dataset. The skew column shows the imbalance ratio of the negative and positive ground truth labels.

AU	FACS Name	Cohen's κ	skew	AU	FACS Name	Cohen's κ	skew
1	Inner Brow Raiser	0.936	12.0	12	Lip Corner Puller	0.911	1.8
2	Outer Brow Raiser	0.857	7.4	14	Dimpler	0 895	0.7
4	Brow Lowerer	0.912	160.3	16	Lower Lip Depressor	0.858	52.5
7	Lid Tightener	0.942	2.6	17	Chin Raiser	0.833	2.4
10	Upper Lip Raiser	0.961	1.8	20	Lip Stretcher	0.914	91.4
11	Nasolabial Deepener	0.971	5.4	22	Lip Funneler	0.798	152.2

3.2   Time-Series Dictionary Building

For the experiments on the gesture dataset, we used the time-series data provided within the dataset. This data includes the position (3D), velocity (3D), orientation (4D), acceleration (3D), and angular speed (3D) of the movements. We evaluated the effectiveness of these modalities separately.

For the experiments using the facial expression datasets we formed time-series from shape- and appearance-based features. In the case of the CK+ dataset, we tracked the video sequences with the ZFace tracker and built the time-series from the PCA coefficients of the 3D PDM (parameter $\mathbf{q}$ in (2)). Illustratively, this is the compressed representation of the 3D landmark locations without rigid head movements. Our PDM contains 56 non-rigid parameters.

In the case of GFT50 dataset (action unit classification task), we used appearance features beside the shape. Using the 3D information first we acquired a canonical view (without rigid movement) of the tracked faces and then extracted SIFT descriptors around the markers. We used 49 landmarks (excluding the jawline points), thus we had a 6272 dimensional representation. We compressed the data to 166 dimension by means of PCA. We retained 90% of the variance. We formed time-series from this compressed holistic SIFT representation.

Since all three datasets come with meta-data (i.e., motion character, emotion or AU labels) we framed the classification task as a supervised learning problem and formed the non-overlapping groups structures in the dictionary according to the labels. In all experiments we employed a leave-one-subject out cross-validation: we removed all time-series instances of a given subject from the dictionary for testing and used the rest of the atoms for the training. For parameter selection we applied the same protocol on the training set in a nested scheme using the remaining subjects. We repeated this procedure for each subjects.

3.3   Gesture Classification on 6DMG

In this set of experiment we studied the structured sparsity method on the 6DMG motion database. We measured the performances of the methods for gesture classification. We calculated Gram matrices using the GA kernel from the time-series provided with the dataset and performed leave-one-subject out cross validation. We searched for the best parameter (σ of GA kernel) between 0.4 and 20 and selected the parameter having the lowest mean classification error.

Table 3. The character error rates (CER) of motion character recognition using single modalities. The different attributes in the columns: position (P), velocity (V), acceleration (A), angular velocity (W), orientation (O). The best result for each modality is denoted with bold letters. The best result for each method is denoted with underline.

Classifier	P	W	O	A	V
Chen [8] (HMM)	3.72	7.92	**3.81**	7.97	6.12
This work (SVM)	3.68	**4.83**	7.82	6.15	**3.69**
This work (KSS)	**3.43**	4.95	13.15	**4.8**	3.88

The SVM regularization parameter (C) was searched within 2^{-10} and 2^{10} and the KSS regularization parameter (κ) was searched within 0 and 0.5 in a similar fashion. The results and comparison with Hidden Markov Model (HMM) are summarized in Table 3. All methods achieved the best result using the 3D position data from all the available modalities. The KSS method outperformed both the HMM and the SVM techniques.

3.4 Emotional Expression Classification on CK+

In this set of experiments we studied the structured sparsity method on the CK+ dataset. We measured the performances of the methods for emotion recognition.

First, we tracked facial expressions with the ZFace tracker and annotated all image sequences starting from the neutral expression to the peak of the emotion. The tracker estimates the rigid and non-rigid transformations. We removed the rigid ones from the faces and represented the sequences as multi-dimensional time-series built from the 56 non-rigid shape parameters (parameter q in Eq.(2)).

We calculated Gram matrices using the GA kernels and performed leave-one-subject out cross validation to maximally utilize the available set of training data. We searched for the best parameter (σ of GA kernel) between 2^{-5} and 2^{10} on a logarithmic scale with equidistant steps and selected the parameter having the lowest mean classification error. The SVM regularization parameter (C) was searched within 2^{-5} and 2^5 and the KSS regularization parameter (κ) was searched within 2^{-5} and 2^1 in a similar fashion.

The result of the classification using the different voting strategies is shown in Table 4.a. Performance scores show that the time-series kernel SVM and the KSS method perform equally well on this task, achieving F_1 scores of 0.935 and 0.932, respectively.

For detailed comparisons with other sparse and non-sparse methods, see Table 5. We report both classification accuracy (Acc) and Area Under ROC Curve (AUC) values. The time-series kernel SVM outperforms all the non-sparse methods, including frame based and fixed length dynamic techniques. The KSS method outperforms frame based sparse methods that utilize shape or Gabor features. We note that in our experiments both the time-series kernel SVM and the KSS method rely on simple shape features. An interesting comparison can be made with Jeni et al. [17], where 3D CLM based shape features were used, but

Table 4. Classification results on (a) CK+ and (b) GFT50 datasets

(a)   (b)

Metric	SVM	KSS-1	KSS-2	KSS-3	Metric	SVM	KSS-1	KSS-2	KSS-3
Macro F_1	**0.909**	0.881	0.889	0.902	Macro F_1	0.658	**0.743**	0.653	0.664
Micro F_1	**0.935**	0.916	0.922	0.932	Micro F_1	0.679	**0.761**	0.679	0.688
Avg. TPR	**0.900**	0.868	0.877	0.896	Avg. TPR	0.660	**0.763**	0.661	0.669

Table 5. Comparisons with different sparse and non-sparse methods on CK+. We include (1) Frame level methods, (2) Fixed length spatio-temporal methods and (3) Varying length time-series methods.

	Non-sparse										Sparse		
	Frame level							Fixed length		TS	Frame level		TS
	3D Shape [17]	Gabor [33]	LBP [33]	MSDF [33]	Simple BoW [33]	SS-SIFT+BoW [33]	MSDF+BoW [33]	Gabor [38]	ICA [21]	Dynamic Haar [40]	3D Shape + GA (this work)	Gabor [25]	Shape [42]	3D Shape + GA + KSS (this work)
Acc.	86.8	91.81	82.38	94.34	92.67	93.28	95.85	-	-	-	**97.9**	93.8	92.4	**97.6**
AUC	-	-	-	-	-	-	-	.978	.978	.966	**.991**	-	-	-

the experiments were limited to individual frames without respect to temporal organization. By using the precisely aligned temporal information, the time-series kernel SVM wins by a considerable (11.1%) margin. Another important comparison concerns the study of Zafeiriou et al. [42], where sparsity was used on shape features, however only on frame level. Both our time-series kernel SVM and our KSS achieve more than 5% higher accuracy, indicating that temporal information is somewhat more important than the sparse representation in this case.

3.5 Action Unit Onset Classification on GFT50

Encouraged by the results of the previous experiment, we decided to test the methods for AU onset classification in order to estimate performance in the early phase of facial events.

We tracked facial expressions and extracted time series between 5 and 10 frames from AU onsets and trained kernel SMVs for one-vs-one AU classification and KSS with the three different voting strategies. Figure 2 shows the classification performance.

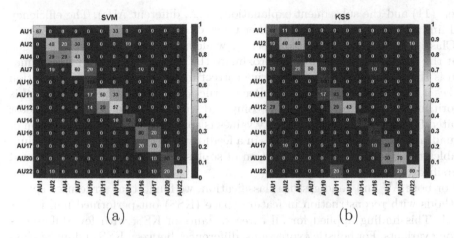

(a)   (b)

Fig. 2. Confusion matrices for early AU onset classification on the GFT50 corpus using (a) time-series kernel SVM and (b) Kernel Structured Sparsity methods

According the figures, from the three different voting strategies for the structured sparsity method the first [(16)] performed the best: its performance is superior to the multi-class time-series kernel SVM for the AU estimation task by a large (10%) margin. See Table 4.b for the comparison.

4   Conclusions

Facial expression estimation is a challenging problem for computer vision. Progress has been enabled by two factors. Large, annotated databases developed over the years were the means of developing precise texture and shape based descriptors and models. In the meantime, novel, efficient, and fast kernel-based similarity measures have been developed that can compare spatio-temporal patterns subject to time warping. We have shown that the efficiency of kernel methods can be further enhanced by sparse structured algorithms, at least for the gesture and facial expression datasets that we studied. These novel, structured methods approximate spatio-temporal patterns by a few groups of such patterns. The method achieves density within groups due to the squared norm and sparsity between them using the group-structure inducing regularizer.

Our present method has two specific features.

Contrast enhancement. Structured sparsification is used for contrast enhancement. The best group then is selected using a voting strategy.

Implicit reconstruction in feature space. By taking into account spatio-temporal similarities using time-series kernels, the reconstruction can be carried out implicitly; the representation of the input is mixed from the representations of dictionary elements belonging to a few groups.

We tested this method for detection of hand gestures, holistic emotions, and action units. For each, the method successfully represented concurrent processes (see, (11) and the subsequent explanation) (e.g., different AUs). The efficiency and limitations of this method in other types of data is a research question.

Classical sparse models try to select a few elements of the representation such that the corresponding samples approximate the input. The error of the estimation is then computed and it can drive correcting steps. Error based correction makes it a feedback approximation. Reconstruction in feature space changes this algorithmic procedure. The input is compared with the samples, and the vector created from the individual similarity values is sparsified via the minimization of a quadratic expression, which results in a feedforward procedure. This procedure enables the straightforward application of sophisticated kernels and structured sparsification simultaneously.

For both AU and hand gesture classification, we found that structured sparse methods with reconstruction in feature space (KSS) out-performed multi-class SVM. This finding applied for all three variants of KSS, with few differences among variants. For holistic expressions, differences between KSS and multi-class SVM were negligible. The lack of effective differences for holistic expressions may be due in part to ceiling effects. Detection of holistic expressions by both KSS and multi-class SVM approached 100%. An additional factor may be that the number of classes for holistic expressions was relatively small. Because SVM scales quadratically as the number of classes increases, the relatively small number of holistic expression classes may have been insufficient to attenuate performance relative to KSS. This latter possibility is a research question. In summary, by combining temporal alignment and structured sparse reconstruction, KSS was comparable to multi-class SVM for holistic expressions and achieved marked advantage in event classification for both AU and hand gesture.

Acknowledgments. Research reported in this publication was supported in part by the National Institute of Mental Health of the National Institutes of Health under Award Number MH096951; the National Development Agency, Hungary (grant agreement Research and Technology Innovation Fund. EITKIC 12.); and the Gatsby Charitable Foundation.

References

1. Bach, F., Jenatton, R., Mairal, J., Obozinski, G.: Optimization with sparsity-inducing penalties. Foundations and Trends in Machine Learning 4, 1–106 (2012)
2. Baraniuk, R.G., Cevher, V., Duarte, M.F., Hegde, C.: Model-based compressive sensing. IEEE Transactions on Information Theory 56, 1982–2001 (2010)
3. Beck, A., Teboulle, M.: A fast iterative shrinkage-thresholding algorithm for linear inverse problems. SIAM Journal on Imaging Sciences 2, 183–202 (2009)
4. Bousmalis, K., Morency, L.P., Pantic, M.: Modeling hidden dynamics of multimodal cues for spontaneous agreement and disagreement recognition. In: Automatic Face and Gesture Recognition, pp. 746–752 (2011)
5. Bousmalis, K., Zafeiriou, S., Morency, L.P., Pantic, M.: Infinite hidden conditional random fields for human behavior analysis. IEEE Transactions on Neural Networks and Learning Systems 24(1), 170–177 (2013)

6. Chandrasekaran, V., Recht, B., Parrilo, P.A., Willsky, A.S.: The convex geometry of linear inverse problems. Foundations of Computational Mathematics 12(6), 805–849 (2012)
7. Chang, C.C., Lin, C.J.: LIBSVM: A library for support vector machines. ACM Transactions on Intelligent Systems and Technology 2, 27:1–27:27 (2011), http://www.csie.ntu.edu.tw/~cjlin/libsvm
8. Chen, M.: Universal Motion-Based Control and Motion Recognition. Ph.D. thesis, Georgia Institute of Technology (2013)
9. Chen, M., AlRegib, G., Juang, B.H.: 6dmg: A new 6d motion gesture database. In: 3rd Multimedia Systems Conference, MMSys 2012, pp. 83–88. ACM, New York (2012)
10. Cuturi, M., Vert, J.P., Birkenes, Ø., Matsui, T.: A kernel for time series based on global alignments. In: International Conference on Acoustics, Speech and Signal Processing, vol. 2, pp. 413–416 (2007)
11. Cuturi, M.: Fast global alignment kernels. In: International Conference on Machine Learning (ICML), pp. 929–936 (2011)
12. Cuturi, M.: Fast global alignment kernels. In: International Conference on Machine Learning, pp. 929–936 (2011)
13. Zhou, F., de la Torre, F., Hodgins, J.K.: Hierarchical aligned cluster analysis for temporal clustering of human motion. IEEE Transactions on Pattern Analysis and Machine Intelligence 35(3), 582–596 (2013)
14. Girard, J., Cohn, J.: Ground truth FACS action unit coding on the group formation task. Tech. rep., University of Pittsburgh (2013)
15. Huang, J., Zhang, T., Metaxas, D.: Learning with structured sparsity. Journal of Machine Learning Research 12, 3371–3412 (2011)
16. Jeni, L., Cohn, J., de la Torre, F.: Facing imbalanced data–recommendations for the use of performance metrics. In: 2013 Humaine Association Conference on Affective Computing and Intelligent Interaction (ACII), pp. 245–251 (September 2013)
17. Jeni, L.A., Lőrincz, A., Nagy, T., Palotai, Z., Sebők, J., Szabó, Z., Takács, D.: 3d shape estimation in video sequences provides high precision evaluation of facial expressions. Image and Vision Computing 30(10), 785–795 (2012)
18. Kanade, T., Cohn, J.F., Tian, Y.: Comprehensive database for facial expression analysis. In: Automatic Face and Gesture Recognition, pp. 46–53 (2000)
19. Koltchinskii, V., Yuan, M.: Sparse recovery in large ensembles of kernel machines on-line learning and bandits. In: COLT, pp. 229–238 (2008)
20. Liu, J., Ji, S., Ye, J.: SLEP: Sparse learning with efficient projections (2010), http://www.public.asu.edu/~jye02/Software/SLEP/
21. Long, F., Wu, T., Movellan, J.R., Bartlett, M.S., Littlewort, G.: Learning spatiotemporal features by using independent component analysis with application to facial expression recognition. Neurocomputing 93, 126–132 (2012)
22. Lőrincz, A., Jeni, L.A., Szabó, Z., Cohn, J.F., Kanade, T.: Emotional expression classification using time-series kernels. In: Computer Vision and Pattern Recognition Workshops (CVPRW), Portland, OR (2013)
23. Lu, Y.M., Do, M.N.: A theory for sampling signals from union of subspaces. IEEE Transactions on Signal Processing 56(6), 2334–2345 (2008)
24. Lucey, P., Cohn, J.F., Kanade, T., Saragih, J., Ambadar, Z., Matthews, I.: The extended Cohn-Kanade dataset (CK+): A complete dataset for action unit and emotion-specified expression. In: Computer Vision and Pattern Recognition Workshops (CVPRW), pp. 94–101 (2010)

25. Mahoor, M., Zhou, M., Veon, K.L., Mavadati, S., Cohn, J.: Facial action unit recognition with sparse representation. In: Automatic Face Gesture Recognition and Workshops, pp. 336–342 (March 2011)
26. Matthews, I., Baker, S.: Active appearance models revisited. International Journal of Computer Vision 60(2), 135–164 (2004)
27. Obozinski, G., Wainwright, J., Jordan, M., Support, M.I.: union recovery in high-dimensional multivariate regression. Annals of Statistics 39(1), 1–17 (2011)
28. Ekman, P., Friesen, W., Hager, J.: Facial action coding system: Research nexus. Network Research Information, Salt Lake City (2002)
29. Ekman, P., Friesen, W.F.: Facial action coding system: A technique for the measurement of facial movement. Consulting Psychologists Press, Palo Alto (1978)
30. Sakoe, H., Chiba, S.: Dynamic programming algorithm optimization for spoken word recognition. IEEE Transactions on Acoustics, Speech and Signal Processing 26(1), 43–49 (1978)
31. Saragih, J.M., Lucey, S., Cohn, J.F.: Deformable model fitting by regularized landmark mean-shift. International Journal of Computer Vision 91(2), 200–215 (2011)
32. Sayette, M., Creswell, K., Dimoff, J., Fairbairn, C., Cohn, J., Heckman, B., Kirchner, T., Levine, J., Moreland, R.: Alcohol and group formation: a multimodal investigation of the effects of alcohol on emotion and social bonding. Psychological Science 23(8), 869–878 (2012)
33. Sikka, K., Wu, T., Susskind, J., Bartlett, M.: Exploring bag of words architectures in the facial expression domain. In: Fusiello, A., Murino, V., Cucchiara, R. (eds.) ECCV 2012 Ws/Demos, Part II. LNCS, vol. 7584, pp. 250–259. Springer, Heidelberg (2012)
34. Steinwart, I., Christmann, A.: Support Vector Machines. Springer (2008)
35. Tibshirani, R.: Regression shrinkage and selection via the lasso. Journal of the Royal Statistical Society. Series B (Methodological), 267–288 (1996)
36. Tropp, J.A., Wright, S.J.: Computational methods for sparse solution of linear inverse problems. In: Proceedings of the IEEE Special Issue on Applications of Sparse Representation and Compressive Sensing, pp. 948–958 (2010)
37. Valstar, M.F., Pantic, M.: Combined support vector machines and hidden markov models for modeling facial action temporal dynamics. In: Lew, M., Sebe, N., Huang, T.S., Bakker, E.M. (eds.) HCI 2007. LNCS, vol. 4796, pp. 118–127. Springer, Heidelberg (2007)
38. Wu, T., Bartlett, M., Movellan, J.R.: Facial expression recognition using Gabor motion energy filters. In: Computer Vision and Pattern Recognition Workshops (CVPRW), pp. 42–47 (2010)
39. Xiong, X., de la Torre, F.: Supervised descent method and its applications to face alignment. In: Computer Vision and Pattern Recognition (CVPR), pp. 532–539 (June 2013)
40. Yang, P., Liu, Q., Metaxas, D.N.: Boosting encoded dynamic features for facial expression recognition. Pattern Recognition Letters 30(2), 132–139 (2009)
41. Yuan, M., Lin, Y.: Model selection and estimation in regression with grouped variables. Journal of the Royal Statistical Society, Series B 68(1), 49–67 (2006)
42. Zafeiriou, S., Petrou, M.: Sparse representations for facial expressions recognition via l1 optimization. In: Computer Vision and Pattern Recognition Workshops (CVPRW), pp. 32–39 (June 2010)

Feature Disentangling Machine - A Novel Approach of Feature Selection and Disentangling in Facial Expression Analysis

Ping Liu[1], Joey Tianyi Zhou[2], Ivor Wai-Hung Tsang[3], Zibo Meng[1], Shizhong Han[1], and Yan Tong[1]

[1] Department of Computer Science, University of South Carolina, USA
[2] Center for Computational Intelligence, Nanyang Technology University, Singapore
[3] Center for Quantum Computation and Intelligent Systems, University of Technology, Australia

Abstract. Studies in psychology show that not all facial regions are of importance in recognizing facial expressions and different facial regions make different contributions in various facial expressions. Motivated by this, a novel framework, named Feature Disentangling Machine (FDM), is proposed to effectively select active features characterizing facial expressions. More importantly, the FDM aims to disentangle these selected features into non-overlapped groups, in particular, *common features* that are shared across different expressions and *expression-specific features* that are discriminative only for a target expression. Specifically, the FDM integrates sparse support vector machine and multi-task learning in a unified framework, where a novel loss function and a set of constraints are formulated to precisely control the sparsity and naturally disentangle active features. Extensive experiments on two well-known facial expression databases have demonstrated that the FDM outperforms the state-of-the-art methods for facial expression analysis. More importantly, the FDM achieves an impressive performance in a cross-database validation, which demonstrates the generalization capability of the selected features.

1 Introduction

Facial activity is one of the most important cues to perceive emotion and intention of a human. Accurate and reliable analysis of facial expressions is imperative to fulfill the demands of emerging applications, such as online/remote education, interactive games, intelligent transportation systems, and many other HCI related applications.

Previous work has shown that not all facial regions but only a few make contributions for expression analysis [3]. More specifically, the most important facial features are extracted from the regions like mouth and eyes [3], since the muscular movements in these regions invoke the expression. These discoveries indicate that features employed in facial expression analysis are sparse and thus, it is important to select the features that are the most effective to characterize facial expressions. To capture the sparsity pattern in features, sparse-coding

D. Fleet et al. (Eds.): ECCV 2014, Part IV, LNCS 8692, pp. 151–166, 2014.

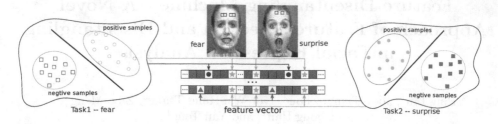

Fig. 1. An FDM performs feature selection and disentangling, simultaneously, using two expressions as an example. Green boxes in the two face images represent the common features shared across the two expressions (fear and surprise) with the corresponding bits (marked by green stars) activated in the feature vectors; blue or red boxes denote expression-specific features for the target expression (fear or surprise) with the corresponding bits (marked by blue circles or red triangles) activated. The bits marked by dark gray in the feature vector correspond to inactivated features for the target expression. Best viewed in color.

based feature learning approaches [33,8,31,14,16,2,39,32] have been employed to extract underlying "edge-like" features from facial images.

Furthermore, the evocation of different expressions may involve the muscular movements from the same facial regions, which could be treated as common features across different expressions. The existence of common features implies the relationships between different tasks, i.e., recognizing different expressions. These relationships cannot be captured in a single-task learning (STL) framework, where each facial expression is recognized individually. In contrast, multi-task learning (MTL) [29] is more suitable to exploit the potential information shared between related tasks to enhance the recognition performance for all target expressions.

Most recently, Zhong et al [40] proposed to divide the sparse features into two groups, i.e., *common features* and *expression-specific features*, through a two-stage multi-task sparse learning (MTSL) framework and achieved promising results in facial expression analysis. Specifically, *common features* that are active for all expressions are extracted by an MTSL model considering all expressions; while *expression-specific features*, learned by a separate MTSL model, are active in recognizing a specific facial expression and are important for face verification as well. Since *common features* and *expression-specific* features are learned sequentially and independently, these two groups can be overlapped.

Intuitively, it is desired to disentangle expression-specific features from the common features. Inspired by the recent work of Sparse Support Vector Machine (SSVM) [24], which employed a novel feature selection vector to precisely control the sparsity of the selected features, we propose a unified MTL framework, named *Feature Disentangling Machine* (FDM), to simultaneously select and disentangle common features and expression-specific features. As illustrated in Fig 1, a set of common features represented by green boxes in the two face images are effective to recognize both *fear* and *surprise* expressions;

while expression-specific features (represented by blue boxes for *fear* and red boxes for *surprise*) are only employed when recognizing the target expression.

Compared with the previous work [40], a novel loss function is proposed in the FDM together with a set of novel constraints to precisely control sparsity and naturally disentangle active features into common and expression-specific groups. Hence, features in any two groups are mutually exclusive. To the best of our knowledge, this is the first work to achieve this. By utilizing an MTL setting, FDM is capable of making fully use of underlying commonality between different facial expressions, which intends to enhance the generalization capability of the selected features. Furthermore, FDM is a general framework and can be applied to various multi-task problems.

Extensive experiments on two well-known facial expression databases have shown that the FDM outperforms the state-of-the-art methods in facial expression analysis. More importantly, in a cross-database experimental validation, the features selected for the Extended Cohn-Kanade (CK+) database [10,17] are also effective in recognizing expressions for the JAFFE database [18].

2 Related Work

As detailed in the surveys [19,35], extensive efforts have been devoted to facial expression analysis. Generally, facial expression recognition can be performed in three major steps: feature extraction/learning, feature selection, and classifier construction.

First, features are extracted from static images or videos to capture facial changes in appearance or geometry, which are related to a target expression. These features can be human-crafted including Gabor wavelet coefficients [37,36,25,1], Haar features [27,30], Histograms of Oriented Gradients (HOG) [9,4], histograms of Local Binary Patterns (LBP) [38,26,22], or learned in a data-driven manner including sparse-coding based approaches [33,8,31,14,16,2,39,32,15] and deep learning framework [21].

As shown in the psychological studies [3], information extracted around nose, eyes, and mouth is more critical for expression analysis. Moreover, the activation of facial regions varies among different expressions. Consequently, features selected from different facial regions should make different contributions in expression analysis. To achieve this goal, boosting-based feature selection approaches, which aim to automatically adjust the weights of features, have been employed [1,27]. Zafeiriou and Pitas [34] proposed discriminant expression-specific graphs to select expression-specific facial landmarks. However, these approaches have been performed in an STL setting, where each target expression has been treated independently despite the fact that the same set of facial muscles can be contracted when activating different facial expressions [10]. More recently, Zhong et al [40] proposed a two-stage MTSL framework to sequentially locate common and specific facial patches, which are discriminative to all expressions and a specific expression, respectively.

Compared with the previous work in feature selection, the proposed FDM considers the interactions between expression-specific and common features among different expressions in an MTL framework. More specifically, our work differs from the two-stage MTSL-based method [40] in two aspects. First, feature selection and disentangling are performed jointly in a unified framework, via minimizing a novel loss function. Second, the proposed constraints ensure that there is no overlapping for any two feature groups.

Given the selected features and a training dataset, a pre-specified classifier is employed to construct a facial expression recognizer for a target expression.

3   Methodology

In this section, we first give a brief review on SSVM [24], based on which the proposed FDM is derived. Then, the proposed FDM framework will be presented together with an efficient algorithm for solving the FDM.

3.1   A Brief Review on Sparse Support Vector Machine

Given a set of N labeled images $\{\mathbf{x}_i, y_i\}_{i=1}^{N}$, where $\mathbf{x}_i \in R^m$ is a feature vector[1] extracted from the ith sample and $y_i \in \{\pm 1\}$ represents the expression label, a linear decision hyperplane with the corresponding weight vector $\mathbf{w} = [w_1, ..., w_m]^T \in R^m$ can be estimated in a linear SVM through minimizing an objective function as follows:

$$\min_{\mathbf{w}} \Omega\left(\|\mathbf{w}\|_p\right) + \gamma \sum_{i=1}^{N} loss(-y_i \mathbf{w}^T \mathbf{x}_i) \tag{1}$$

where γ is a positive parameter to balance the complexity of the model and the fitness of the decision hyperplane. $loss(\cdot)$ is a loss function, where various choices of loss, such as quadratic loss and 0-1 loss, can be employed. Among them, hinge loss has been proven to be effective in classification problems, and is adopted in this work. $\Omega(\mathbf{w})$ is a penalty term to control the characteristics of $\mathbf{w}$. For example, l_1 norm [15] and mixed l_{21} norm [40] have been employed to model the sparsity patterns in features.

Recently, Tan et al [24] proposed SSVM, which employed a *feature selection* vector $\mathbf{d} = [d_1, \cdots, d_m]^T \in \mathcal{D}$, where $\mathcal{D} = \left\{\mathbf{d} \mid \sum_{j=1}^{m} d_j \leq \tau, d_j \in \{0, 1\}\right\}$, to select a subset of features for classification. Through specifying the value of parameter τ, the sparsity pattern in the data can be well controlled so that

$$\mathbf{w}^T \mathbf{x} = (\tilde{\mathbf{w}} \circ \mathbf{d})^T \mathbf{x} = \tilde{\mathbf{w}}^T (\mathbf{d} \circ \mathbf{x}) \tag{2}$$

where $d_j = 1$ when the jth feature is selected and otherwise $d_j = 0$; "$\circ$" denotes the element-wise multiplication.

---

[1] In this work, histograms of LBP features have been employed to represent images, while other features such as HOG and Gabor wavelet features can be employed as well. Implementation details of LBP features can be found in Section 4.

Hence, the objective function (Eq. 1) of SSVM [24] is formulated as:

$$\min_{\mathbf{d} \in \mathcal{D}} \min_{\tilde{\mathbf{w}}, \epsilon, \rho} \frac{1}{2} \|\tilde{\mathbf{w}}\|_2^2 + \frac{\gamma}{2} \sum_{i=1}^{N} \epsilon_i^2 - \rho \tag{3}$$

$$s.t. \quad y_i \tilde{\mathbf{w}}^T (\mathbf{x}_i \circ \mathbf{d}) \geq \rho - \epsilon_i, i = 1, \cdots, N.$$

where ϵ and ρ are parameters used to generate a soft margin for non-separable classification problems. Then, the optimal $\tilde{\mathbf{w}}$ can be used to construct the classifier with a subset of selected features specified by $\mathbf{d}$.

The SSVM proposed in [24] has been proven to be efficient and effective in various classification problems. However, it is in an STL setting and has not considered the interconnections between related classification problems, while facial expression recognition has been shown benefiting from MTL by exploiting information shared between different expressions [40]. By taking advantage of the underlying shared commonality, we propose an FDM to disentangle expression-specific and common features by extending the SSVM to an MTL framework. By introducing a novel joint objective function and novel constraints, the FDM aims to capture and utilize the interconnections among multiple expressions via the common features.

3.2   Formulation for the FDM

To simplify the discussion, we only discuss an MTL expression recognition problem considering two target expressions, denoted as E_1 and E_2, at the same time. Then, each image sample can be represented by a triplet $\left\{ \mathbf{x}_i, y_i^{E_1}, y_i^{E_2} \right\}, i = 1, \cdots, N$, with two expression labels ($y_i^{E_1}$ and $y_i^{E_2}$). Specifically, if only one of the target expressions, e.g., E_1, is activated in the image, $y_i^{E_1} = 1$ and $y_i^{E_2} = -1$, and vice versa; while if neither E_1 nor E_2 is activated, both the expression labels are set to -1.

In order to select *expression-specific features*, two *expression-specific feature selection* vectors denoted as $\mathbf{d}^{E_1}$ and $\mathbf{d}^{E_2}$ are introduced for tasks E_1 and E_2, respectively. In addition, a *common feature selection* vector denoted as $\mathbf{d}^{E_c}$ is used to select common features that are effective and shared in recognizing all expressions.

Therefore, the objective function in Eq. 3 can be extended to recognizing both expressions simultaneously in an MTL framework as follows:

$$\min_{\{\mathbf{d}^{E_1}, \mathbf{d}^{E_2}, \mathbf{d}^{E_c} \in \mathcal{D}\}} \min_{\{\mathbf{w}^{E_1}, \mathbf{w}^{E_2}, \epsilon^{E_1}, \epsilon^{E_2}, \rho_1, \rho_2\}} \frac{1}{2} \left(\|\mathbf{w}^{E_1}\|_2^2 + \|\mathbf{w}^{E_2}\|_2^2 \right) + \frac{\gamma}{2} \sum_{i=1}^{N} \left[(\epsilon_i^{E_1})^2 + (\epsilon_i^{E_2})^2 \right] - (\rho_1 + \rho_2)$$

$$s.t. \quad y_i^{E_1} (\mathbf{w}^{E_1})^T \left[\mathbf{x}_i \circ \left(\mathbf{d}^{E_1} + \mathbf{d}^{E_c} \right) \right] \geq \rho_1 - \epsilon_i^{E_1}, i = 1, \cdots, N,$$

$$y_i^{E_2} (\mathbf{w}^{E_2})^T \left[\mathbf{x}_i \circ \left(\mathbf{d}^{E_2} + \mathbf{d}^{E_c} \right) \right] \geq \rho_2 - \epsilon_i^{E_2}, i = 1, \cdots, N. \tag{4}$$

where the sparsity of features is controlled in the three feature selection vectors (i.e., $\mathbf{d}^{E_1}$, $\mathbf{d}^{E_2}$, and $\mathbf{d}^{E_c}$) by three parameters τ_1, τ_2, and τ_c, respectively as follows

$$\sum_{j=1}^{m} d_j^{E_1} \leq \tau_1 \qquad \sum_{j=1}^{m} d_j^{E_2} \leq \tau_2 \qquad \sum_{j=1}^{m} d_j^{E_c} \leq \tau_c \qquad d_j^{E_1}, d_j^{E_2}, d_j^{E_c} \in \{0,1\} \quad (5)$$

Furthermore, to ensure that there is no intersection between any two sets of features, i.e., a feature can be selected by at most one subset, we propose a novel constraint formulated as:

$$d_j^{E_1} + d_j^{E_2} + d_j^{E_c} \leq 1 \qquad j = 1, \cdots, m. \tag{6}$$

Therefore, by minimizing the proposed joint objective function (Eq. 4) with novel constraints (Eq. 5 and 6), the FDM framework is capable of simultaneously finding the optimal hyperplanes (represented by $\mathbf{w}^{E_1}$ and $\mathbf{w}^{E_2}$), expression-specific features, and common features, for classifying the two expressions. In the discussion below, we will present an efficient algorithm to solve the FDM.

3.3   Algorithm for Solving Feature Disentangling Machine

To solve the FDM, the Lagrange multiplier method with KKT condition is employed to transform the original inner problem (Eq. 4) into its dual formulation, and then the solution to the original problem can be found by solving the corresponding dual problem as:

$$\min_{\{\mathbf{d}^{E_1}, \mathbf{d}^{E_2}, \mathbf{d}^{E_c}\}} \max_{\boldsymbol{\alpha}, \boldsymbol{\beta}} L_{\{\mathbf{d}^{E_1}, \mathbf{d}^{E_2}, \mathbf{d}^{E_c}\}}(\boldsymbol{\alpha}, \boldsymbol{\beta}) =$$

$$\min_{\{\mathbf{d}^{E_1}, \mathbf{d}^{E_2}, \mathbf{d}^{E_c}\}} \max_{\boldsymbol{\alpha}, \boldsymbol{\beta}} -\frac{1}{2} \left\| \sum_{i} \alpha_i y_i^{E_1} \left[\left(\mathbf{d}^{E_1} + \mathbf{d}^{E_c} \right) \circ \mathbf{x}_i \right] \right\|^2 - \frac{1}{2\gamma} \boldsymbol{\alpha}^T \boldsymbol{\alpha}$$

$$-\frac{1}{2} \left\| \sum_{i} \beta_i y_i^{E_2} \left[\left(\mathbf{d}^{E_2} + \mathbf{d}^{E_c} \right) \circ \mathbf{x}_i \right] \right\|^2 - \frac{1}{2\gamma} \boldsymbol{\beta}^T \boldsymbol{\beta}$$

$$s.t. \quad \sum_{i=1}^{N} \alpha_i = 1, \quad \sum_{i=1}^{N} \beta_i = 1, \quad \alpha_i > 0, \quad \beta_i > 0, \qquad for \ i = 1, \cdots, N,$$

$$\{\mathbf{d}^{E_1}, \mathbf{d}^{E_2}, \mathbf{d}^{E_c}\} \in \mathcal{D},$$

$$where \quad \mathcal{D} = \{\{\mathbf{d}^{E_1}, \mathbf{d}^{E_2}, \mathbf{d}^{E_c}\} | \sum_{j=1}^{m} d_j^{E_1} \leq \tau_1, \sum_{j=1}^{m} d_j^{E_2} \leq \tau_2, \sum_{j=1}^{m} d_j^{E_c} \leq \tau_c,$$

$$d_j^{E_1} + d_j^{E_2} + d_j^{E_c} \leq 1, \quad d_j^{E_1}, d_j^{E_2}, d_j^{E_c} \in \{0,1\}, \qquad for \ j = 1, \cdots, m\}$$

$$(7)$$

$\boldsymbol{\alpha}$ and $\boldsymbol{\beta}$ are dual variable vectors for the inequality constraints in the inner minimization problem (Eq. 4).

The saddle point problem (7) can be lower bounded by:

$$\max_{\alpha,\beta} \min_{\{d^{E_1},d^{E_2},d^{E_c}\}} L_{\{d^{E_1},d^{E_2},d^{E_c}\}}(\alpha,\beta) =$$

$$\max_{\alpha,\beta} \min_{\{d^{E_1},d^{E_2},d^{E_c}\}} -\frac{1}{2}\left\|\sum_i \alpha_i y_i^{E_1}\left[\left(d^{E_1}+d^{E_c}\right)\circ x_i\right]\right\|^2 - \frac{1}{2\gamma}\alpha^T\alpha$$

$$-\frac{1}{2}\left\|\sum_i \beta_i y_i^{E_2}\left[\left(d^{E_2}+d^{E_c}\right)\circ x_i\right]\right\|^2 - \frac{1}{2\gamma}\beta^T\beta \tag{8}$$

$$s.t. \sum_{i=1}^n \alpha_i = 1,\ \sum_{i=1}^n \beta_i = 1,\ \alpha_i > 0,\ \beta_i > 0,\ for\ i = 1,...,N,\ \{d^{E_1},d^{E_2},d^{E_c}\} \in \mathcal{D}$$

By bringing an additional variable θ, the above optimization problem becomes:

$$\max_{\theta,\alpha,\beta} -\theta : \theta \geq -L_{\{d_t^{E_1},d_t^{E_2},d_t^{E_c}\}}(\alpha,\beta),\qquad \forall\{d_t^{E_1},d_t^{E_2},d_t^{E_c}\} \in \mathcal{D} \tag{9}$$

which is a convex Quadratically Constrained Quadratic Programming (QCQP) problem.

Define $\mu_t \geq 0$ as the dual variable for each constraint in Eq. 9 [24], the Lagrangian of Eq. 9 can be rewritten as:

$$\min_{\mu \in \mathcal{M}} \max_{\alpha,\beta} \frac{-1}{2}(\alpha \circ y^{E_1})^T(\sum_t \mu_t X_t^{E_1} X_t^{E_1 T} + \frac{1}{\gamma}\mathcal{I})(\alpha \circ y^{E_1})$$

$$\frac{-1}{2}(\beta \circ y^{E_2})^T(\sum_t \mu_t X_t^{E_2} X_t^{E_2 T} + \frac{1}{\gamma}\mathcal{I})(\beta \circ y^{E_2})$$

$$where X_t^{E_1} = \left[x_1 \circ (d_t^{E_1}+d_t^{E_c}), \cdots, x_N \circ (d_t^{E_1}+d_t^{E_c})\right]^T \tag{10}$$

$$X_t^{E_2} = \left[x_1 \circ (d_t^{E_2}+d_t^{E_c}), ..., x_N \circ (d_t^{E_2}+d_t^{E_c})\right]^T$$

$$\mathcal{M} = \{\mu|\sum \mu_t = 1, \mu_t \geq 0\}$$

where $\mathcal{I}$ represents an identity matrix.

Eq. 10 is a Multiple Kernel Learning (MKL) problem, in which the kernel matrix $\sum_t \mu_t X_t^{E_1} X_t^{E_1 T}$ and $\sum_t \mu_t X_t^{E_2} X_t^{E_2 T}$ are both convex combinations of $|\mathcal{D}|$ base kernel matrices $X_t^{E_1} X_t^{E_1 T}$ and $X_t^{E_2} X_t^{E_2 T}$. However, not all constraints in Eq. 9 are active at optimality. Therefore, the problem can be solved efficiently and effectively by cutting plane algorithm [11]. The overall algorithm of solving FDM is described here and summarized in Algorithm 1.

Denote the subset of constraints by $\mathcal{C} \in \mathcal{D}$. First, the dual variables α_i and β_i are set to $\frac{1}{N}$ for $i = 1, \cdots, N$ for initialization. The most violated feature selection vectors, denoted as $\hat{\mathcal{D}} = \{d^{E_1}, d^{E_2}, d^{E_c}\} \in \mathcal{D}$, are obtained. Then, two steps, i.e., estimating the new α and β with MKL and finding the most violated feature selection vectors ($\hat{\mathcal{D}}$), run alternatively until converge. By introducing constraints for the *expression-specific* feature selection vectors (d^{E_1} and d^{E_2}) and the *common* feature selection vector $\mathbf{d}^{Ec}$, it is ensured that the features in any two subsets are mutually exclusive. This is known as "Feature Disentangling".

MKL with a Subset of Kernel Matrices. Inspired by previous work on SSVM [24], we apply SimpleMKL [20] to solve the MKL problem defined on the subset of kernel matrices selected in $\mathcal{C}$.

In this step, since the feature selection vectors ($\mathbf{d}^{E_1}$, $\mathbf{d}^{E_2}$ and $\mathbf{d}^{Ec}$) are fixed, we can solve the MKL problem corresponding to the following primal optimization problem:

$$
\min_{\mu \in \mathcal{M}, \mathbf{w}^{E_1}, \mathbf{w}^{E_2}, \rho_1, \rho_2, \epsilon^{E_1}, \epsilon^{E_2}} \frac{1}{2} \sum_{t=1}^{K} \frac{1}{\mu_t} \|\mathbf{w}^{E_1}\|^2 + \frac{\gamma}{2} \sum_{i=1}^{N} \left(\epsilon_i^{E_1}\right)^2 - \rho_1
$$

$$
+ \frac{1}{2} \sum_{t=1}^{K} \frac{1}{\mu_t} \|\mathbf{w}^{E_2}\|^2 + \frac{\gamma}{2} \sum_{i=1}^{N} \left(\epsilon_i^{E_2}\right)^2 - \rho_2
$$

$$
s.t. \sum_{t=1}^{K} (\mathbf{w}^{E_1})^T \left[y_i^{E_1} \mathbf{x}_i \circ (\mathbf{d}^{E_1} + \mathbf{d}^{Ec}) \right] \geq \rho_1 - \epsilon_i^{E_1} \qquad \forall i = 1, \cdots, N
$$

$$
\sum_{t=1}^{K} (\mathbf{w}^{E_2})^T \left[y_i^{E_2} \mathbf{x}_i \circ (\mathbf{d}^{E_2} + \mathbf{d}^{Ec}) \right] \geq \rho_2 - \epsilon_i^{E_2} \qquad \forall i = 1, \cdots, N
$$

(11)

Since $\mathbf{d}^{E_1}$, $\mathbf{d}^{E_2}$ and $\mathbf{d}^{Ec}$ are fixed here, Eq. 11 actually becomes a combination of two SSVMs ($SSVM^{E_1}$ and $SSVM^{E_2}$). The problem can be solved by optimizing the parameters of $SSVM^{E_1}$ and $SSVM^{E_2}$ in an iterative way. For solving each sub problem $SSVM^{E_1}$ or $SSVM^{E_2}$, we employ SimpleMKL [20], following [24].

Finding the Most Violated Feature Selection Vectors by a Knapsack Problem Solver. To find $\hat{\mathcal{D}} = \{\mathbf{d}^{E_1}, \mathbf{d}^{E_2}, \mathbf{d}^{Ec}\} \in \mathcal{D}$ in Eq. 9, we propose to solve the equivalent optimization problem:

$$
\max_{\{\mathbf{d}^{E_1}, \mathbf{d}^{E_2}, \mathbf{d}^{Ec}\} \in \mathcal{D}} \frac{1}{2} \sum_{j=1}^{m} (c_j^{E_1})^2 (d_j^{E_1} + d_j^{Ec}) + \frac{1}{2} \sum_{j=1}^{m} (c_j^{E_2})^2 (d_j^{E_2} + d_j^{Ec})
$$

$$
where \quad c_j^{E_1} = \sum_{i=1}^{N} \alpha_i y_i x_{ij} \qquad c_j^{E_2} = \sum_{i=1}^{N} \beta_i y_i x_{ij}
$$

(12)

$$
s.t. \sum_{j=1}^{m} d_j^{E_1} \leq \tau_1; \sum_{j=1}^{m} d_j^{E_2} \leq \tau_2; \sum_{j=1}^{m} d_j^{Ec} \leq \tau_c;
$$

$$
d_j^{E_1} + d_j^{E_2} + d_j^{Ec} \leq 1; \ d_j^{E_1}, d_j^{E_2}, d_j^{Ec} \in \{0, 1\}; \ for \ j = 1, \cdots, m
$$

Based on Eq. 12, the problem becomes a binary and linear programming problem, more specifically, the Knapsack Problem [28]. Various methods such as dynamic programming and greedy algorithm have been proposed to solve

Initialize α_i, β_i as $\frac{1}{N}$ for $i = 1, \cdots, N$; Find the most violated feature selection
vectors $\hat{\mathcal{D}} = \{\mathbf{d}^{E_1}, \mathbf{d}^{E_2}, \mathbf{d}^{E_c}\}$ and let $\mathcal{C} = \{\hat{\mathcal{D}}\}$;
repeat
    Initialize $\mu = [1]^T$;
    repeat
    | Find the optimal μ, α and β by simpleMKL
    until *convergence*;
    Find the most violated feature selection vectors $\hat{\mathcal{D}} = \{\mathbf{d}^{E_1}, \mathbf{d}^{E_2}, \mathbf{d}^{E_c}\}$
    make $\mathcal{C} = \mathcal{C} \cup \{\hat{\mathcal{D}}\}$
until *convergence*;

Algorithm 1. Algorithm of Feature Disentangling Machine

this problem efficiently and effectively. In this work, we adopt the optimization toolbox [7] provided by MATLAB to solve the problem.

Once the optimal solution of feature selection vectors are estimated, we employ expression-specific features specified by $\mathbf{d}^{E_1}$ or $\mathbf{d}^{E_2}$, together with common features specified by $\mathbf{d}^{E_c}$ to train a classifier to recognize the target expression. In this work, the LIBLinear software [6] is adopted for constructing classifiers.

3.4 Computational Complexity

As shown in Algorithm 1, in each iteration, two major steps run alternatively: solving two sub problems of MKL and searching for the most violated feature selection vectors $\hat{\mathcal{D}}$. For the first step, linear base kernels are employed; and the LIBLinear [6], which scales linearly in the number of samples N and the feature dimensions m, is adopted in solving the two sub problems. Hence, the time complexity of the first step is $O(mN)$. For the second step, we employed the MATLAB function *bintprog* in our experiments, which uses a linear programming-based branch-and-bound algorithm with polynomial complexity [7]. Other methods like dynamic programming could be used to achieve a linear complexity of $O(m\tau)$, where τ is the maximum capacity of the Knapsack problem. For a multiclass problem with K classes, the overall computational complexity can be $O(K^2 m(N + \tau))$ using an one-versus-all strategy.

4 Experimental Results

In order to evaluate the proposed FDM framework, extensive experiments have been performed on two well-known facial expression databases: Extended Cohn-Kanade (CK+) database [10,17] and JAFFE database [18].

Preprocessing Images and Feature Extraction. For preprocessing purpose, the face regions across different facial images were aligned to remove the scale and positional variance [2] and then cropped to 96×64. Each cropped face image

---

[2] In this work, the face region was roughly aligned based on eye positions detected by an eye detector.

was further divided into 7×7 non-overlapped patches. In this work, a uniform $LBP_{8,1}$ pattern was employed to compute LBP features at each pixel location. Then, a histogram with 59 bins were calculated for each image patch. Hence, each image was represented by a feature vector with $2891(7 \times 7 \times 59)$ features. This preprocessing strategy was adopted for both databases we employed.

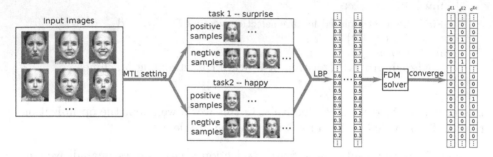

Fig. 2. An illustration of the FDM training procedure

Multi-task Learning Configuration and Experimental Setup. As shown in Fig. 2, an FDM is trained to select features for a pair of expressions simultaneously. For the FDM, the parameters τ_1 and τ_2 are set to 500 and the parameter τ_c is set to 250 empirically in all experiments. For recognizing P expressions, there are a total of $\binom{P}{2}$ FDMs needed. [3] As a result, $P-1$ sets of features can be selected and extracted for each expression, from each of which a binary classifier can be trained. In this work, the L_2-loss L_2-regularized SVM implemented in the LIBLinear [6] was adopted for constructing the binary classifiers. Given a testing image, the expression label was estimated using an average rule such that the final recognition score is an average of the $P-1$ classification scores.

4.1 Experiments on the CK+ Database

The CK+ database contains 327 expression-labeled image sequences, each of which has one of 7 expressions, i.e., anger, contempt, disgust, fear, happiness, sadness, and surprise activated. For each image sequence, only the last frame (the peak frame) is provided with an expression label. To collect more image samples from the database, we selected the last three frames from each image sequence. In addition, we also collected the first frame from each of the 327 labeled sequences for "neutral" expression. Through this way, an experimental data set named *CK-DB* with a total of 1308 images is built. Then, we employed an 8-fold cross-validation strategy. The CK-DB was divided into 8 subsets, where the subjects in any two of subsets were mutually exclusive. For each run, 7 subsets were employed for training and the remaining one for testing. We performed such 8 runs by enumerating the subset used for testing; and the recognition performance was computed as the average of the 8 runs.

---

[3] $E_1 - E_2$ and $E_2 - E_1$ are treated as the same combination.

Performance Evaluation on the CK-DB. We first compared the proposed *FDM* framework with five baseline methods. The first method, denoted as *LOG*, employed an L_2 regularized logistic classifier. The second method, denoted as L_2L_2, employed an L_2-loss SVM with L_2 regulation. Both *LOG* and L_2L_2 have no feature selection ability. The third method, denoted as L_2L_1, employed an L_2-loss SVM with L_1 regulation. The fourth method employed the *SSVM* [24]. The fifth method, denoted as FDM_{wocf}, only employed the expression-specific features selected by FDM for recognition. All the baseline methods, except the *LOG*, employed the hinge loss. The regulation term is $\|\mathbf{w}\|_{l_1}$ for L_1 regularization and $\|\mathbf{w}\|_{l_2}$ for L_2 regularization.

Quantitative experimental results were reported in terms of *average classification rate, hit rate, false positive rate, F1 score,* and *Area Under Curve (AUC) score.* As shown in Fig. 3, the proposed *FDM* outperformed all baseline methods drastically in terms of the average classification rate (**0.977**), the average hit rate (**0.978**), the average false positive rate (**0.023**), the average F1 score (**0.908**) and the average AUC score (**0.989**) of the 6 basic expressions, i.e., anger, disgust, fear, happiness, sadness, and surprise [4].

From Fig. 3, we can find that the FDM yielded a significant improvement in F1 score compared to the

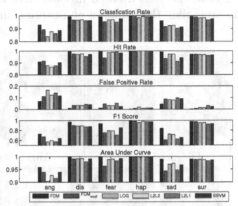

Fig. 3. From top to bottom, performance comparison on the CK-DB in terms of average classification rate, hit rate, false positive rate, F1 score and AUC score for 6 basic expressions. Best viewed in color

methods without feature selection, i.e., *LOG* (0.818) and L_2L_2 (0.822), which demonstrated the effectiveness of feature selection and disentangling. Not surprisingly, the FDM outperformed the methods with feature selection in an STL setting, i.e., L_2L_1 (0.779) and *SSVM* (0.821) thanks to the multi-task learning; it also outperformed the one without common features, i.e., FDM_{wocf} (0.814), which demonstrates the importance of the common features in expression recognition.

Furthermore, we compared the proposed FDM method with the state-of-the-art methods evaluated on CK+ or the original Cohn-Kanade database [10] [5] including methods without feature selection denoted as PGKNMF [32], selecting features by AdaBoost in an STL setting (AdaGabor [1] and LBPSVM [23]), and selecting and disentangling features sequentially based on MSTL denoted as CSPL [40]. The experimental results reported in their papers were used directly

---

[4] We did not recognize the "contempt" and "neutral" for a fair comparison with the state-of-the-art methods evaluated on the original Cohn-Kanade database [10].

[5] Cohn-Kanade database [10] is an early version of CK+ and contains a subset of CK+ data (i.e., 320 image sequences with expression labels [23]).

Table 1. Performance comparison on the CK+ database in terms of average classification rate for 6 expressions

CSPL [40]	AdaGabor [1]	LBPSVM [23]	PGKNMF [32]	**FDM**
0.899	0.933	0.951	0.835	**0.977**

for comparison. As shown in Table 1, our proposed FDM framework outperformed all the state-of-the-art methods in comparison in terms of the average classification rate (**0.977**). It is worth to mention that the FDM performed better than the MSTL-based method (CSPL) because of the jointly selecting and disentangling the common and expression-specific features.

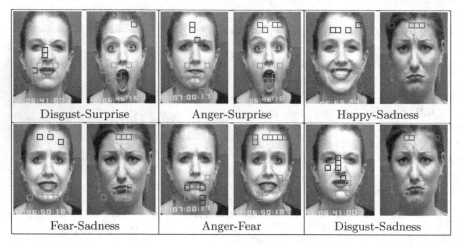

Fig. 4. An illustration of the selected image patches for recognizing the six basic expressions in CK+ database. Green boxes represent common features selected for the pair of expressions; blue or red boxes represent expression-specific features for the target expressions in the pair, respectively. For example, for the pair of *Anger-Surprise*, the features in the green boxes are selected to recognize both anger and surprise; the features in the blue boxes are only sensitive to anger, while the features in the red boxes are only sensitive to surprise. Best viewed in color.

Analysis on Patch Selection Results in the CK+ Database. To analyze what information each selected patch provides for expression recognition, a data analysis on the patch selection results was performed. As shown in Fig. 4, patches selected through FDM were marked by boxes. Only a few patches are selected for each target expression, which demonstrates the sparsity in active features. Specifically, patches enclosed in green boxes were selected as *common features* for both expressions in the FDM, while the patches enclosed in red or blue boxes were selected as expression-specific features for the corresponding expression, respectively. These selected patches contain the most discriminative information to characterize the corresponding expression.

From Fig. 4, we can find that most of the selected common patches are located around lip, which coincides with the psychological studies [3]. Furthermore, the expression-specific patches for the target expression are closely related to the facial Action Units (AUs) [5] that describe the corresponding expression. For example, the expression-specific patches selected for *anger* are either located around the lip (in the middle of the second row in Fig. 4), which are related to AU23 (Lip tighten), or around the eyebrows (in the middle of the first row in Fig. 4), which are related to AU4 (Brow Lowerer). AU23 and AU4 are the primary AUs to describe the anger expression [17]. Similar results can be found in other expressions.

4.2   Experiments on the JAFFE Database

The proposed FDM framework has been also evaluated on the JAFFE database, which consists of 213 images from 10 Japanese female subjects. For each subject, there are 3 or 4 examples of each of the six basic expressions and "neutral" expression. The experimental results on the JAFFE database are used to demonstrate the cross-database generalization ability of the FDM.

Cross-Database Validation. To evaluate the generalization ability, we performed a cross-database validation, where the features were selected and/or the classifiers were trained on the CK+ database; while the performance was tested on the JAFFE database. Particularly, we employed two different experimental settings, namely FDM^{CJ} and FDM^{CC}. In FDM^{CJ}, the features were selected by an FDM trained from CK-DB, while the classifiers were trained on JAFFE database using a leave-one-subject-out training/testing strategy. In FDM^{CC}, we employed the selected features and the trained classifiers from CK-DB to perform test directly on the JAFFE database [6].

The generalization across database is usually low in previous work. Shan et al [23] trained selected LBP features using SVMs on Cohn-Kanade database and tested the trained system on the JAFFE database. An average classification rate about 41% for 7 expressions (6 basis expressions and neutral) was obtained in their work [23]. From Table 2, we can find that both FDM^{CJ} and FDM^{CC} performed much better than [23]. Furthermore, even the training was performed on the CK-DB exclusively in FDM^{CC}, the proposed method could achieve satisfactory recognition performance on the JAFFE database. This further demonstrated that the features selected and disentangled by the FDM captured the most discriminative information for expression analysis, which can be generalized across different data sets.

Performance Evaluation on the JAFFE Database. In addition, we also evaluated the FDM trained and tested on the JAFFE database with a leave-one-subject-out training/testing strategy. To make a fair comparison, we only compared with the-state-of-the-art methods employing the leave-one-subject-out

---

[6] In order to recognize the neutral expression, feature selection and classifier training were performed on the CK-DB for FDM^{CC} and FDM^{CJ}.

Table 2. Cross-database validation, trained on the CK+ database and tested on the JAFFE database, in terms of average classification rate for 7 expressions (6 basis expressions and neutral). In [23], LBP features were employed and fed into SVM with three different kernels, i.e., linear, polynomial, and RBF, respectively. In FDM^{CJ}, the features were selected from CK+, but the classifiers were trained from the JAFFE; while FDM^{CC} employed the selected features and the trained classifiers using CK+.

Ada+SVM(Linear) [23]	Ada+SVM(Poly) [23]	Ada+SVM(RBF) [23]	FDM^{CJ}	FDM^{CC}
0.404	0.404	0.413	**0.901**	**0.882**

Table 3. Performance comparison on the JAFFE database in terms of average classification rate for 7 expressions (6 basis expressions and neutral).

SLLE [13]	SFRCS [12]	Ada+SVM(RBF) [23]	FDM^{JJ}
0.868	0.860	0.810	**0.897**

strategy and recognizing 7 expressions (six basis expressions plus "neutral"). As shown in Table 3, the FDM^{JJ} outperformed the other methods in comparison.

Note that the performance of the FDM^{CC} shown in Table 2 is similar to that of the FDM^{JJ} trained on the JAFFE Database; and the FDM^{CJ} achieved the best performance among all the methods reported in both Table 2 and 3. This implies that the FDM can be adopted in a transfer learning framework. It would be especially useful when the image dataset that was used to train the original classifiers cannot be accessed. Better recognition performance can be achieved by employing the features selected by the original classifiers together with a few labeled images in the new application.

5   Conclusion and Future Work

In this work, we propose a novel FDM framework to perform feature selection and disentangling simultaneously and jointly through a multi-task learning framework. Specifically, two types of feature selection vectors are proposed for common features and expression-specific features, respectively. Furthermore, a novel loss function and a set of constraints are formulated to precisely control the sparsity and ensure non-intersection between different feature groups. In this way, the most discriminative features for recognizing the target expression can be selected and categorized into non-overlapped groups. As demonstrated in our experiments, the proposed FDM outperformed all methods in comparison including the state-of-the-art techniques evaluated on two public facial expression databases. More importantly, the FDM yields impressive performance in the cross-database validation. In the future, we will evaluate the FDM on spontaneous facial displays. Furthermore, the FDM will be adopted to recognize facial action units (AUs), where common features learned by the FDM are expected to capture correlations among AUs.

Acknowledgments. This work was supported by National Science Foundation under CAREER Award IIS-1149787.

References

1. Bartlett, M.S., Littlewort, G., Frank, M.G., Lainscsek, C., Fasel, I., Movellan, J.R.: Recognizing facial expression: Machine learning and application to spontaneous behavior. In: CVPR, vol. 2, pp. 568–573 (2005)
2. Bociu, I., Pitas, I.: A new sparse image representation algorithm applied to facial expression recognition. In: MLSP, pp. 539–548. IEEE (2004)
3. Cohn, J.F., Zlochower, A.: A computerized analysis of facial expression: Feasibility of automated discrimination. American Psychological Society (1995)
4. Dahmane, M., Meunier, J.: Emotion recognition using dynamic grid-based HoG features. In: FG (March 2011)
5. Ekman, P., Friesen, W.V., Hager, J.C.: Facial Action Coding System: the Manual. Research Nexus, Div., Network Information Research Corp., Salt Lake City (2002)
6. Fan, R.E., Chang, K.W., Hsieh, C.J., Wang, X.R., Lin, C.J.: Liblinear: A library for large linear classification. J. Machine Learning Research 9, 1871–1874 (2008)
7. Grace, A., Works, M.: Optimization Toolbox: For Use with MATLAB: User's Guide. Math Works (2013)
8. Mahoor, M.H., Mu, Z., Veon, K.L., Mohammad, M.S., Cohn, J.F.: Facial action unit recognition with sparse representation. In: FG, pp. 336–342. IEEE (2011)
9. Hu, Y., Zeng, Z., Yin, L., Wei, X., Zhou, X., Huang, T.S.: Multi-view facial expression recognition. In: FG, pp. 1–6 (2008)
10. Kanade, T., Cohn, J.F., Tian, Y.: Comprehensive database for facial expression analysis. In: FG, pp. 46–53 (2000)
11. Kelley Jr., J.E.: The cutting-plane method for solving convex programs. Journal of the Society for Industrial & Applied Mathematics 8(4), 703–712 (1960)
12. Kyperountas, M., Tefas, A., Pitas, I.: Salient feature and reliable classifier selection for facial expression classification. Pattern Recognition 43(3), 972–986 (2010)
13. Liang, D., Yang, J., Zheng, Z., Chang, Y.: A facial expression recognition system based on supervised locally linear embedding. Pattern Recognition Letters 26(15), 2374–2389 (2005)
14. Lin, Y., Song, M., Quynh, D., He, Y., Chen, C.: Sparse coding for flexible, robust 3d facial-expression synthesis. Computer Graphics and Applications 32(2), 76–88 (2012)
15. Liu, P., Han, S., Tong, Y.: Improving facial expression analysis using histograms of log-transformed nonnegative sparse representation with a spatial pyramid structure. In: FG, pp. 1–7. IEEE (2013)
16. Liu, W., Song, C., Wang, Y.: Facial expression recognition based on discriminative dictionary learning. In: ICPR, pp. 1839–1842. IEEE (2012)
17. Lucey, P., Cohn, J.F., Kanade, T., Saragih, J., Ambadar, Z., Matthews, I.: The extended cohn-kanade dataset (ck+): A complete expression dataset for action unit and emotion-specified expression. In: CVPR Workshops, pp. 94–101 (2010)
18. Lyons, M.J., Budynek, J., Akamatsu, S.: Automatic classification of single facial images. IEEE T-PAMI 21(12), 1357–1362 (1999)
19. Pantic, M., Pentland, A., Nijholt, A., Huang, T.S.: Human computing and machine understanding of human behavior: A survey. In: Huang, T.S., Nijholt, A., Pantic, M., Pentland, A. (eds.) AI for Human Computing. LNCS (LNAI), vol. 4451, pp. 47–71. Springer, Heidelberg (2007)
20. Rakotomamonjy, A., Bach, F.R., Canu, S., Grandvalet, Y.: SimpleMKL. J. Machine Learning Research 9(11) (2008)

21. Ranzato, M., Susskind, J., Mnih, V., Hinton, G.: On deep generative models with applications to recognition. In: CVPR, pp. 2857–2864. IEEE (2011)
22. Sénéchal, T., Rapp, V., Salam, H., Seguier, R., Bailly, K., Prevost, L., et al.: Combining LGBP histograms with AAM coefficients in the multi-kernel SVM framework to detect facial action units, pp. 860–865 (2011)
23. Shan, C., Gong, S., McOwan, P.: Facial expression recognition based on Local Binary Patterns: A comprehensive study. J. IVC 27(6), 803–816 (2009)
24. Tan, M., Wang, L., Tsang, I.W.: Learning sparse svm for feature selection on very high dimensional datasets. In: ICML, pp. 1047–1054 (2010)
25. Tian, Y.I., Kanade, T., Cohn, J.F.: Evaluation of gabor-wavelet-based facial action unit recognition in image sequences of increasing complexity, pp. 229–234. IEEE (2002)
26. Valstar, M.F., Mehu, M., Jiang, B., Pantic, M., Scherer, K.: Meta-analysis of the first facial expression recognition challenge. IEEE T-SMC-B 42(4), 966–979 (2012)
27. Whitehill, J., Bartlett, M.S., Littlewort, G., Fasel, I., Movellan, J.R.: Towards practical smile detection. IEEE T-PAMI 31(11), 2106–2111 (2009)
28. Wolsey, L.A.: Integer programming. IIE Transactions 32(273-285), 2–58 (2000)
29. Xue, Y., Liao, X., Carin, L., Krishnapuram, B.: Multi-task learning for classification with dirichlet process priors. J. Machine Learning Research 8, 35–63 (2007)
30. Yang, P., Liu, Q., Metaxas, D.N.: Boosting coded dynamic features for facial action units and facial expression recognition. In: CVPR, pp. 1–6 (June 2007)
31. Ying, Z.-L., Wang, Z.-W., Huang, M.-W.: Facial expression recognition based on fusion of sparse representation. In: Huang, D.-S., Zhang, X., Reyes García, C.A., Zhang, L. (eds.) ICIC 2010. LNCS (LNAI), vol. 6216, pp. 457–464. Springer, Heidelberg (2010)
32. Zafeiriou, S., Petrou, M.: Nonlinear non-negative component analysis algorithms. IEEE T-IP 19(4), 1050–1066 (2010)
33. Zafeiriou, S., Petrou, M.: Sparse representations for facial expressions recognition via L1 optimization. In: CVPR Workshops, pp. 32–39 (2010)
34. Zafeiriou, S., Pitas, I.: Discriminant graph structures for facial expression recognition. IEEE T-Multimedia 10(8), 1528–1540 (2008)
35. Zeng, Z., Pantic, M., Roisman, G.I., Huang, T.S.: A survey of affect recognition methods: Audio, visual, and spontaneous expressions. IEEE T-PAMI 31(1), 39–58 (2009)
36. Zhang, Y., Ji, Q.: Active and dynamic information fusion for facial expression understanding from image sequences. IEEE T-PAMI 27(5), 699–714 (2005)
37. Zhang, Z., Lyons, M., Schuster, M., Akamatsu, S.: Comparison between geometry-based and Gabor-wavelets-based facial expression recognition using multi-layer perceptron. In: FG, pp. 454–459 (1998)
38. Zhao, G., Pietiäinen, M.: Dynamic texture recognition using local binary patterns with an application to facial expressions. IEEE T-PAMI 29(6), 915–928 (2007)
39. Zhi, R., Flierl, M., Ruan, Q., Kleijn, W.: Graph-preserving sparse nonnegative matrix factorization with application to facial expression recognition. IEEE T-SMC-B (99), 1–15 (2010)
40. Zhong, L., Liu, Q., Yang, P., Liu, B., Huang, J., Metaxas, D.: Learning active facial patches for expression analysis. In: CVPR (2012)

Joint Unsupervised Face Alignment and Behaviour Analysis*

Lazaros Zafeiriou, Epameinondas Antonakos,
Stefanos Zafeiriou, and Maja Pantic

Computing Department, Imperial College London, UK
{l.zafeiriou12,e.antonakos,s.zafeiriou,m.pantic}@imperial.ac.uk

Abstract. The predominant strategy for facial expressions analysis and temporal analysis of facial events is the following: a generic facial landmarks tracker, usually trained on thousands of carefully annotated examples, is applied to track the landmark points, and then analysis is performed using mostly the shape and more rarely the facial texture. This paper challenges the above framework by showing that it is feasible to perform joint landmarks localization (i.e. spatial alignment) and temporal analysis of behavioural sequence with the use of a simple face detector and a simple shape model. To do so, we propose a new component analysis technique, which we call Autoregressive Component Analysis (ARCA), and we show how the parameters of a motion model can be jointly retrieved. The method does not require the use of any sophisticated landmark tracking methodology and simply employs pixel intensities for the texture representation.

Keywords: Face alignment, time series alignment, slow feature analysis.

1 Introduction

The analysis of facial Action Units (FAUs) and expressions are important tasks in Computer Vision and Human-Computer Interaction, which have accumulated great research effort [1]. The standard approach is the application of a robust facial tracker for the facial landmark points localization and then the application of an analysis technique. The tracker can be either generic or person-specific, depending on the task and the available annotations [2,3]. On the one hand, methodologies that show exceptional performance in generic facial tracking have been recently proposed [4,5,6], capitalizing on the abundance of databases with thousands of annotated facial images in both controlled [7] and uncontrolled conditions [8,9]. On the other hand, the person-specific tracker framework requires manual annotation of a number of frames from a person's video sequence. The manual annotation of images, which is required by such methods, is a very time consuming, expensive and labour intensive procedure. Furthermore, the expressions and FAUs analysis is performed using mainly the geometric displacement

---

* Electronic supplementary material -Supplementary material is available in the online version of this chapter at http://dx.doi.org/10.1007/978-3-319-10593-2_12. Videos can also be accessed at http://www.springerimages.com/videos/978-3-319-10592-5

D. Fleet et al. (Eds.): ECCV 2014, Part IV, LNCS 8692, pp. 167–183, 2014.

of facial shape points [10,11,12] and secondarily the facial texture in the form
of hand-crafted features, i.e. Local Binary Patterns (LBPs) and SIFT features
([13],[14]). Finally, when it comes to temporal alignment of facial events, the
tracked facial landmarks are aligned after being tracked [3,15,16], usually by the
application of a person specific tracker.

In this paper we take a radically different direction. We propose a methodology
that can be used to perform joint automatic facial landmarks localization and discovery of features that can be used for analysis of temporal events (e.g. analysis
of FAU dynamics). To do so, we start by formulating a special undirected Gaussian Hidden Markov Random Field. The GHMRF is a generative model which
jointly describes (i.e. generates) the data and also captures temporal dependencies by incorporating an autoregressive chain [17] in the latent space. We show how
a novel deterministic component analysis, which we coin Autoregressive Component Analysis (ARCA), can be formulated. We further show how a motion model
can be incorporated in ARCA. Our methodology has been motivated by the success of joint alignment and low-rank matrix recovery in person specific scenarios [18,19,20] as well as previous works on parametrized component analysis [21,22].
But our method is radically different to [18], since (1) it extracts latent features
rather than image reconstructions, (2) it incorporates a non-rigid motion model
guided by a shape model rather than rigid motion used in [18][1] and (3) it incorporates time dependencies. Furthermore, our method is radically different to [24]
and [20] which are based on trained models of appearance and require annotations
of hundreds of images to allow good generalization.

By extending such methodologies in order to take into account the correlations
between sequences that depict the same facial event (i.e. FAU), we show that
the extracted features can be used to perform temporal alignment. Moreover,
we show that the proposed method achieves successful results even though it
does not utilize any robust feature-based representation of the appearance (e.g.
HOG, SIFT) as usually done in the literature, but it is instead applied on the
pixel intensities. Summarizing, the contributions of the paper are:

- We propose a novel component analysis which can perform joint reconstruction and extraction of a latent space with first order Markov dependencies.
  Hence, the proposed component analysis can be used for joint construction
  of a deformable model and extraction of smooth features for event analysis
- We show how, by incorporating a shape model, we can perform joint alignment, i.e. facial landmarks localization, and feature extraction useful for analysis of facial events. Due to the incorporation of the motion model the
  extracted dynamic latent features are robust to geometric transformations.
- We show that the latent features can be used for temporal alignment of facial
  events.

We would like to note here that the extracted features are more suitable for
unsupervised segmentation of behaviour analysis of behaviour dynamics, as well
as temporal alignment rather than recognition of expression and/or action units.

---

[1] Recently it has been empirically shown that [20,23], due to the presence of an non-
regularised low-rank term, the method in [18] fails in case of non-rigid motion.

The only prerequisites of the proposed method are the presence of (1) a simple bounding box face detector and (2) a shape model, by means of a Point Distribution Model (PDM), of the facial landmarks that we want to detect. The face detector can be as simple as the Viola-Jones object detector [25] which can return only the true positive detection of a face's bounding box. Such detectors are widely and successfully used. For example, the newest versions of Matlab have incorporated a training procedure of Viola-Jones. Additionally, such detectors are also widely employed in commercial products (e.g. even the cheapest digital camera has a robust face detector). Besides, the annotations that are needed to train such a detector can be acquired very quickly, since only a bounding box containing the image's face is required. Other detectors that can be used are efficient subwindow search [26] and deformable part-based models [27,28,24]. The statistical shape model of facial landmark points can be built easily using a small number of facial shapes. Around 50 shapes of images from the internet are sufficient in order to build a descriptive shape model that can generate multiple facial expressions and their annotation takes less than 4 hours. Finally, there are unsupervised techniques to learn the shape model directly from images [29,30].

2 Method

2.1 Definitions and Prerequisites

We assume that we have a set of facial shapes and a crude face detector, such as Viola-Jones [25]. We denote a facial shape as a $2L_S \times 1$ vector $\mathbf{s} = [x_1, y_1, \ldots, x_{L_S}, y_{L_S}]^T$, where (x_i, y_i), $i = 1, \ldots, L_S$ are the coordinates of the L_S landmark points. The PDM shape model consists of an orthonormal basis $\mathbf{U}_S \in \mathbb{R}^{2L_S \times N_S}$ of N_S eigenvectors and the mean shape $\bar{\mathbf{s}}$, which are derived from the facial shapes in our disposal. Note that the first four eigenvectors correspond to the global similarity transform that controls the face's rotation, scaling and translation. A new shape instance is generated as a linear combination of the eigenvectors weighted by the parameters $\mathbf{p} = [p_1, \ldots, p_{N_S}]^T$, thus $\mathbf{s_p} = \bar{\mathbf{s}} + \mathbf{U}_S \mathbf{p}$. Moreover, let us denote a motion model as the warp function $\mathcal{W}(\mathbf{x}, \mathbf{p})$, which maps each point within the mean (reference) shape ($\mathbf{x} \in \bar{\mathbf{s}}$) to its corresponding location in a shape instance. We employ the Piecewise Affine Warp which performs the mapping based on the barycentric coordinates of the corresponding triangles between the source and target shapes that are extracted using Delaunay triangulation. In the rest of the paper, we will denote the warp function as $\mathcal{W}(\mathbf{p})$ for simplicity.

2.2 Autoregressive Component Analysis with Spatial Alignment

In this section we propose a deterministic component analysis based on an Autoregressive (AR) statistical model. In particular, we start by formulating a probabilistic generative model which (1) captures time-variant latent features and (2) explains data generation. Hence, it can be used for joint extraction of

latent features which capture time dependencies and, in the same time, as a
linear statistical model suitable for deformable model construction.

Assume that we have a time-variant, multi-dimensional input signal, e.g. a
video sequence of N frames, denoted in vectorized form as $\mathbf{x}_i \in \mathbb{R}^F$, $i = 1, \ldots, N$,
which shows a person that performs a facial expression or FAU. The frames'
appearance is based on pixel intensities. We denote as $\mathbf{X} \in \mathbb{R}^{F \times N}$ the matrix
that has these vectorized frames as its columns, thus $\mathbf{X} = [\mathbf{x}_1, \ldots, \mathbf{x}_N]$.

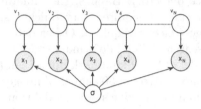

Fig. 1. Graphical model of an Autoregressive process

We assume a generative model in the form of $\mathbf{x}_i = \mathbf{U}\mathbf{v}_i + \mathbf{e}_i$, where $\mathbf{U} \in \mathbb{R}^{F \times K}$
is a subspace of K basis ($K < min(F, N)$). We also assume that $\mathbf{e}_i$ follows a zero
mean Gaussian distribution with $\sigma^2 \mathbf{I}$ covariance matrix, thus $\mathbf{e}_i \sim \mathcal{N}(\mathbf{e}_i | \mathbf{0}, \sigma^2 \mathbf{I})$.
Furthermore, in order to capture the time-variant correlations of the signals, we
assume an AR model for the latent space $\mathbf{v}_i$ as $\mathbf{v}_i | \mathbf{v}_{i-1}, \ldots, \mathbf{v}_1 \sim \mathcal{N}(\mathbf{v}_i | \phi \mathbf{v}_{i-1}, \mathbf{I})$
with $\mathbf{v}_1 \sim \mathcal{N}(\mathbf{v}_1 | \mathbf{0}, (1 - \phi^2)^{-1})$. The graphical model of the AR model is shown
in Fig. 1. That is, assume the matrix $\mathbf{V}$ of the latent features with columns $\mathbf{v}_i$,
i.e. $\mathbf{V} = [\mathbf{v}_1, \ldots, \mathbf{v}_N] \in \mathbb{R}^{K \times N}$, and its K rows denoted by $\tilde{\mathbf{v}}_j$ with size $N \times 1$.
Each row is an AR model, which is a special case of a Gaussian Markov Random
Field (GMRF) [17]

$$p(\tilde{\mathbf{v}}_j | \mathbf{L}) = \frac{|\mathbf{L}|}{\sqrt{(2\pi)^K}} e^{-\frac{1}{2}(\tilde{\mathbf{v}}_j)^T \mathbf{L} \tilde{\mathbf{v}}_j} \tag{1}$$

with the tridiagonal precision matrix $\mathbf{L} \in \mathbb{R}^{N \times N}$ given by

$$\mathbf{L} = \begin{pmatrix} 1 & -\phi & & & \\ -\phi & 1 + \phi^2 & -\phi & & \\ & \ddots & \ddots & \ddots & \\ & & -\phi & 1 + \phi^2 & -\phi \\ & & & -\phi & 1 \end{pmatrix} \tag{2}$$

The probability for all the rows of matrix $\mathbf{V}$ can be written as

$$p(\mathbf{V} | \mathbf{L}) = \prod_{j=1}^{K} p(\tilde{\mathbf{v}}_j | \mathbf{L}) = \frac{|\mathbf{L}|^N}{\sqrt{(2\pi)^{KN}}} e^{-\frac{1}{2}\sum_{j=1}^{N}(\tilde{\mathbf{v}}_j)^T \mathbf{L} \tilde{\mathbf{v}}_j} = \frac{|\mathbf{L}|^N}{\sqrt{(2\pi)^{KN}}} e^{-\frac{1}{2}\operatorname{tr}[\mathbf{V}\mathbf{L}\mathbf{V}^T]} \tag{3}$$

where tr[.] denotes the matrix trace operator. Hence, according to Fig. 1, the factorization of the joint likelihood of $\mathbf{X}, \mathbf{V}$ given σ^2, $\mathbf{L}$ and $\mathbf{U}$ has the form

$$
\begin{aligned}
p(\mathbf{X}, \mathbf{V}|\mathbf{L}, \mathbf{U}, \sigma^2) &= p(\mathbf{X}|\mathbf{V}, \mathbf{U}, \sigma^2)p(\mathbf{V}|\mathbf{L}) \\
&= \prod_{i=1}^{N} p(\tilde{\mathbf{x}}_i|\mathbf{v}_i, \mathbf{L}, \sigma^2)p(\mathbf{V}|\mathbf{L}) \\
&= \frac{1}{\sqrt{(2\pi\sigma^2)^{NF}}} e^{-\frac{1}{2\sigma^2}\sum_{i=1}^{N}(\mathbf{x}_i-\mathbf{U}\mathbf{v}_i)^T(\mathbf{x}_i-\mathbf{U}\mathbf{v}_i)} \frac{|\mathbf{L}|^N}{\sqrt{(2\pi)^{KN}}} e^{-\frac{1}{2}\operatorname{tr}[\mathbf{V}\mathbf{L}\mathbf{V}^T]} \\
&= \frac{|\mathbf{L}|^N}{\sqrt{(\sigma^2)^{NF}(2\pi)^{N(K+F)}}} e^{-\frac{1}{2}(\frac{1}{\sigma^2}\|\mathbf{X}-\mathbf{U}\mathbf{V}\|_F^2 + \operatorname{tr}[\mathbf{V}\mathbf{L}\mathbf{V}^T])}
\end{aligned}
\tag{4}
$$

where $\|.\|_F$ denotes the matrix Frobenius norm. Taking the logarithm of the above joint probability, we get a cost function with regards to $\mathbf{U}, \mathbf{V}$

$$
\begin{aligned}
g(\mathbf{U}, \mathbf{V}) &= \ln p(\mathbf{X}, \mathbf{V}|\mathbf{L}, \mathbf{U}, \sigma^2) \\
&\propto -\|\mathbf{X} - \mathbf{U}\mathbf{V}\|_F^2 - \lambda\operatorname{tr}[\mathbf{V}\mathbf{L}\mathbf{V}^T] + \text{const}
\end{aligned}
\tag{5}
$$

For simplicity, we set $\phi = 0.9$ and the variance $\sigma^2 = \frac{1}{\lambda} = 0.1$, where $\lambda \geq 0$ is a regularization parameter that controls the smoothness of the method that is used to compute the matrix $\mathbf{L}$. The first term $\|\mathbf{X} - \mathbf{U}\mathbf{V}\|_F^2$ of Eq. 5 measures how well the data can be reconstructed from the loading matrix $\mathbf{U}$ and the latent space weights $\mathbf{V}$, while the second term $\operatorname{tr}[\mathbf{V}\mathbf{L}\mathbf{V}^T]$ is a smoothing constraint over the latent space to model the undirected temporal dependencies. If we impose further orthogonality constraints on $\mathbf{U}$, we get

$$
\min_{\mathbf{U}, \mathbf{V}} \quad f(\mathbf{U}, \mathbf{V}) = \|\mathbf{X} - \mathbf{U}\mathbf{V}\|_F^2 + \lambda\operatorname{tr}[\mathbf{V}\mathbf{L}\mathbf{V}^T] \quad \text{s.t.} \quad \mathbf{U}^T\mathbf{U} = \mathbf{I}
\tag{6}
$$

where $\mathbf{I}$ denotes the identity matrix. In order to get meaningful results that explain the actual variations of images and not the variations due to misalignment, as done in all component analysis techniques [31], solving Eq. 6 requires to provide perfectly aligned images achived through manual annotations.

In this paper, we propose to take a radically different approach and jointly find the components $\mathbf{U}$, the time-variant latent space $\mathbf{V}$ and a set of parameters that align the images into a common frame, defined by the mean shape $\bar{\mathbf{s}}$. In order to do so, we introduce warp parameters on the data matrix $\mathbf{X}$. The warping of each video frame in the mean (reference) shape, given a shape estimate of the frame's displayed face ($\{\mathbf{s}_i\}$, $i = 1, \ldots, N$), returns N appearance vectors $\{\mathbf{x}_i(\mathcal{W}(\mathbf{p}_i))\}$, $\forall i = 1, \ldots, N$ of size $F \times 1$, where F is the number of pixels that lie inside the mean shape. We denote as

$$
\mathbf{X}(\mathcal{W}(\mathbf{P})) = [\mathbf{x}_1(\mathcal{W}(\mathbf{p}_1)), \ldots, \mathbf{x}_N(\mathcal{W}(\mathbf{p}_N))]
\tag{7}
$$

the $F \times N$ time-varying input data matrix that consists of the warped frames' vectors, where

$$
\mathbf{P} = [\mathbf{p}_1, \ldots, \mathbf{p}_N]
$$

is the matrix of the shape parameters of each frame. The cost function of Eq. 6 now becomes

$$
\min_{\mathbf{U}, \mathbf{V}, \mathbf{P}} \quad f(\mathbf{U}, \mathbf{V}, \mathbf{P}) = \|\mathbf{X}(\mathcal{W}(\mathbf{P})) - \mathbf{U}\mathbf{V}\|_F^2 + \lambda\operatorname{tr}[\mathbf{V}\mathbf{L}\mathbf{V}^T]
$$

$$
\text{s.t.} \quad \mathbf{U}^T\mathbf{U} = \mathbf{I}
\tag{8}
$$

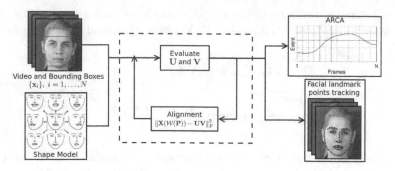

Fig. 2. Method overview. Given a video sequence with the corresponding bounding boxes and a shape model, the method performs joint facial landmarks localization and spatio-temporal facial behaviour analysis.

We solve the minimization of Eq. 8 in an alternating manner, as shown in Fig. 2. In brief, the method iteratively solves for matrices $\mathbf{U}$ and $\mathbf{V}$ based on the current estimate of the warped vectors $\mathbf{X}(\mathcal{W}(\mathbf{P}))$ and then re-estimates the shape parameters $\mathbf{P}$ of the sequence's frames. The initial shapes are estimated by applying a similarity transform on the mean shape $\bar{\mathbf{s}}$ to confront fit within the boundaries of each frame's bounding box. This means that the initial shape parameters are equal to zero ($\mathbf{p}_i = \mathbf{0}$, $\forall i = 1, \ldots, N$). Consequently, the optimizaton is solved in the following two steps:

Fix P and Minimize with Respect to $\{\mathbf{U}, \mathbf{V}\}$. In this step we have a current estimate of the shape parameters matrix $\mathbf{P}$ and thus the data matrix $\mathbf{X}(\mathcal{W}(\mathbf{P}))$. In order to find the updates $\mathbf{U}$ and $\mathbf{V}$ we follow an alternative optimization framework where we fix $\mathbf{V}$ and find $\mathbf{U}$ and then fixing $\mathbf{U}$ and finding $\mathbf{V}$

Updating $\mathbf{U}$. Given $\mathbf{V}$ the optimization problem with regards to $\mathbf{U}$ is given by

$$\mathbf{U}_o = \operatorname*{argmin}_{\mathbf{U}} f(\mathbf{U}) = \|\mathbf{X}(\mathcal{W}(\mathbf{P})) - \mathbf{U}\mathbf{V}\|_F^2 \quad \text{s.t} \quad \mathbf{U}^T\mathbf{U} = \mathbf{I}. \tag{9}$$

The solution of the above optimization problem is given by the skinny singular value decomposition (SSVD) of $\mathbf{X}(\mathcal{W}(\mathbf{P}))\mathbf{V}^T$ [32]. That is, if the SVD of $\mathbf{X}(\mathcal{W}(\mathbf{P}))\mathbf{V}^T = \mathbf{R}\mathbf{S}\mathbf{M}^T$, then

$$\mathbf{U} = \mathbf{R}\mathbf{M}^T. \tag{10}$$

Updating $\mathbf{V}$. Given $\mathbf{U}$ the optimization problem with regards to $\mathbf{V}$ is given by

$$\mathbf{V}_o = \operatorname*{argmin}_{\mathbf{V}} f(\mathbf{V}) = \|\mathbf{X}(\mathcal{W}(\mathbf{P})) - \mathbf{U}\mathbf{V}\|_F^2 + \lambda \operatorname{tr}[\mathbf{V}\mathbf{L}\mathbf{V}^T] \tag{11}$$

which gives the update

$$\mathbf{V} = \mathbf{U}^T\mathbf{X}(\mathcal{W}(\mathbf{P}))(\mathbf{I} - \lambda\mathbf{L})^{-1} \tag{12}$$

Fix $\{\mathbf{U}, \mathbf{V}\}$ and Minimize with Respect to P. In this step we have a current estimation of the basis $\mathbf{U}$ and the latent features $\mathbf{V}$ and aim to estimate the motion parameters $\mathbf{P} = [\mathbf{p}_1, \ldots, \mathbf{p}_N]$ for each frame, so that the Frobenius norm between the warped frames and the templates $\mathbf{UV}$ is minimized. This is achieved by using the efficient Inverse Compositional (IC) Image Alignment algorithm [33]. The cost function of this step can be written as

$$\min_{\mathbf{P}} \|\mathbf{X}(\mathcal{W}(\mathbf{P})) - \mathbf{UV}\|_F^2 = \min_{\{\mathbf{p}_i\}, \, i=1,\ldots,N} \sum_{i=1}^{N} \|\mathbf{x}_i(\mathcal{W}(\mathbf{p}_i)) - \mathbf{Uv}_i\|_2^2 \qquad (13)$$

where $\mathbf{v}_i$, $\forall i = 1, \ldots, N$ denotes the ith column of the matrix $\mathbf{V}$. We solve the problem of Eq. 13 by minimizing for each frame separately, as

$$\min_{\mathbf{p}_i} \|\mathbf{x}_i(\mathcal{W}(\mathbf{p}_i)) - \mathbf{y}_i\|_2^2, \, i = 1, \ldots, N \qquad (14)$$

where $\mathbf{y}_i = \mathbf{Uv}_i$ denotes the template corresponding to each frame. Within the IC optimization technique, an incremental warp is introduced on the part of the template of Eq. 14, thus the aim is to minimize

$$\min_{\Delta \mathbf{p}_i} \|\mathbf{x}_i(\mathcal{W}(\mathbf{p}_i)) - \mathbf{y}_i(\mathcal{W}(\Delta \mathbf{p}_i))\|_2^2 \qquad (15)$$

with respect to $\Delta \mathbf{p}_i$. Then, at each iteration, a compositional update rule is applied on the shape parameters, as

$$\mathcal{W}(\mathbf{p}_i) \leftarrow \mathcal{W}(\mathbf{p}_i) \circ \mathcal{W}(\Delta \mathbf{p}_i)^{-1}$$

The solution of Eq. 15 is derived by taking the first-order Taylor expansion of the template term around $\Delta \mathbf{p}_i = \mathbf{0}$ and using the identity property of the warp function $(\mathcal{W}(\mathbf{x}, \mathbf{0}) = \mathbf{x})$, as $\mathbf{y}_i(\mathcal{W}(\Delta \mathbf{p}_i)) \approx \mathbf{y}_i + \mathbf{J}_{\mathbf{y}_i}|_{\mathbf{p}=0}\Delta \mathbf{p}_i$, where $\mathbf{J}_{\mathbf{y}_i}|_{\mathbf{p}=0} = \nabla \mathbf{y}_i \left.\frac{\partial \mathcal{W}}{\partial \mathbf{p}}\right|_{\mathbf{p}=0}$ is the template Jacobian that consists of the template gradient and the warp Jacobian evaluated at $\mathbf{p} = \mathbf{0}$. Substituting this linearization to Eq. 15, the solution is given by

$$\Delta \mathbf{p}_i = \mathbf{H}^{-1} \mathbf{J}_{\mathbf{y}_i}^T|_{\mathbf{p}=0} [\mathbf{x}_i(\mathcal{W}(\mathbf{p}_i)) - \mathbf{y}_i]$$

where $\mathbf{H} = \mathbf{J}_{\mathbf{y}_i}^T|_{\mathbf{p}=0}\mathbf{J}_{\mathbf{y}_i}|_{\mathbf{p}=0}$ is the Gauss-Newton approximation of the Hessian matrix. Note that since the gradient is always computed at the template (reference frame), the warp Jacobian and the Hessian matrix inverse remain constant, which results in a small computational cost.

3   Comparison with State-of-the-Art Component Analysis Techniques

Even though component analysis is a very well-studied research field including very popular methodologies such as Principal Component Analysis (PCA)

[34], Linear Discriminant Analysis (LDA)[35] and Graph Embedding techniques [36,37], there is very limited work on deterministic component analysis techniques for discovering latent spaces that capture time dependencies[2]. One such component analysis is the so-called Slow Feature Analysis (SFA) [39], which aims to identify the most slowly varying features from rapidly temporal varying signals. More formally, given an F-dimensional time-varying input sequence, SFA seeks to determine appropriate projection bases stored in the columns of matrix $\mathbf{U} = [\mathbf{u}_1, \ldots, \mathbf{u}_K]$, that in the low dimensional space minimize the variance of the approximated first order time derivative of the latent variables $\mathbf{V} = [\mathbf{v}_1, \ldots, \mathbf{v}_N] = \mathbf{U}^T\mathbf{X}$, subject to zero mean, unit covariance and decorrelation constraints

$$\min_{\mathbf{U}} \text{tr}[\mathbf{U}^T\dot{\mathbf{X}}\dot{\mathbf{X}}^T\mathbf{U}] \quad \text{s.t.} \quad \mathbf{V1} = \mathbf{0}, \ \mathbf{U}^T\mathbf{X}\mathbf{X}^T\mathbf{U} = \mathbf{I} \tag{16}$$

where $\mathbf{1}$ is a $N \times 1$ vector with all its elements equal to $\frac{1}{N}$. The matrix $\dot{\mathbf{X}} \in \mathbb{R}^{F\times(N-1)}$ approximates the first order time derivative of $\mathbf{X}$, evaluated by taking the temporal differences between successive sample observations, as

$$\dot{\mathbf{X}} = [\mathbf{x}_2 - \mathbf{x}_1, \mathbf{x}_3 - \mathbf{x}_2, \ldots, \mathbf{x}_N - \mathbf{x}_{N-1}] = \mathbf{X}\mathbf{Q} \tag{17}$$

where $\mathbf{Q}$ is an $N \times (N-1)$ matrix with elements $q_{i,i} = -1$, $q_{i+1,i} = 1$ and 0 elsewhere. The optimal $\mathbf{U}$ from Eq. 16 is given as the eigenvectors of $[\mathbf{X}\mathbf{X}^T]^{-1}[\dot{\mathbf{X}}\dot{\mathbf{X}}^T]$ that correspond to the smallest eigenvalues. We should note that since SFA introduces an ordering to the derived latent variables sorted by the temporal slowness, the smallest eigenvectors correspond to the slowest varying features. In the following, we show that an orthogonal variant of SFA can be derived as a special case of ARCA. In particular, assuming a uniform prior for $p(\mathbf{v}_1)$ (i.e. $\phi = 1$), then the precision matrix $\mathbf{L}$ can be decomposed as $\mathbf{L} = \mathbf{Q}\mathbf{Q}^T$ and by substituting $\mathbf{V} = \mathbf{U}^T\mathbf{X}$ in Eq. 6, the optimization problem can be reformulated as

$$\begin{aligned}
\min_{\mathbf{U}} f(\mathbf{U}) &= ||\mathbf{X} - \mathbf{U}\mathbf{U}^T\mathbf{X}||_F^2 + \lambda\text{tr}[\mathbf{U}^T\mathbf{X}\mathbf{L}\mathbf{X}^T\mathbf{U}] \\
&= \text{tr}[\mathbf{X}^T\mathbf{X}] - \text{tr}[\mathbf{U}^T\mathbf{X}\mathbf{X}^T\mathbf{U}] + \lambda\text{tr}[\mathbf{U}^T\mathbf{X}\mathbf{Q}\mathbf{Q}^T\mathbf{X}^T\mathbf{U}] \\
&= -\text{tr}[\mathbf{U}^T\mathbf{X}\mathbf{X}^T\mathbf{U}] + \lambda\text{tr}[\mathbf{U}^T\dot{\mathbf{X}}\dot{\mathbf{X}}^T\mathbf{U}] + \text{const} \\
&= \text{tr}[\mathbf{U}^T(\lambda\dot{\mathbf{X}}\dot{\mathbf{X}}^T - \mathbf{X}\mathbf{X}^T)\mathbf{U}] + \text{const} \quad \text{s.t.} \quad \mathbf{U}^T\mathbf{U} = \mathbf{I}.
\end{aligned} \tag{18}$$

where $\mathbf{U}$ stores the K non-zero eigenvectors that correspond to the K smallest eigenvalues of $\lambda\dot{\mathbf{X}}\dot{\mathbf{X}}^T - \mathbf{X}\mathbf{X}^T$. Hence, the optimization problem of Eq. 18 gives a similar result, but imposes an extra orthogonality on $\mathbf{U}$.

4   Experiments

The experiments aim to demonstrate that the proposed unsupervised procedure is able to locate landmarks so as to perform image alignment and in the same

---

[2] There is very rich literature about Gaussian Linear Dynamical Models, i.e. Kalman filters [38], but this is a totally different way of modelling time series, which in principle cannot be easily combined with spatial warping techniques as the ARCA.

time extract latent features that can reveal the dynamics of facial behaviour, directly from image intensities. The gold standard in unsupervised behaviour analysis is (a) to track facial landmark points and (b) use their motion to perform analysis. For example in [2,10] person specific trackers were used, which require manual annotation, and in [15,3] a generic tracker was employed followed by a manual correction step. The goals of the experiments are two fold: (1) to show that the method can correctly track landmarks from a crude face detector and (2) to show that the extracted features can represent the dynamics of the behaviour. To do so, we use two databases: MMI[40,41] that has posed FAUs and UvA-Nemo Smile (UNS) [42] that displays more complex spontaneous behaviour. MMI consists of more than 400 videos annotated in terms of FAUs and the temporal phases in which a subject performs one or more FAUs. We use 61 of those videos, which are the ones that we manually annotated with 68 landmarks in order to compare. UvA-Nemo Smile database is a large-scale database having more than 1000 smile videos (597 spontaneous and 643 posed) from 400 subjects. Similarly to the MMI database, we conduct experiments on 25 videos with spontaneous smiles, which we manually annotated in terms of the smile's temporal phases and the 68 facial landmark points.

In ARCA we employ a shape model trained on 50 shapes of Multi-Pie database [7], annotated with the same $L_S = 68$ landmark configuration. The model consists of $N_S = 15$ eigenvectors and the mean (reference) shape has a resolution of 169×171, thus the dimensionality of our data matrix is $F = 28899$. Moreover, the faces' bounding boxes of all the videos are detected using the Viola-Jones object detection algorithm [25]. Finally, the proposed method is applied using 5 global iterations. In Section 4.1 we show results on the spatio-temporal behaviour analysis of the videos and in Section 4.3 we present the facial landmarks localization performance. Throughout the experiments, we set the regularization parameter that controls the smoothness of the proposed method equal to $\lambda = 10$ and we limit the number of extracted basis to $K = 30$.

4.1 Spatio-temporal Behaviour Analysis Results in MMI Database

In this section we provide experimental results for the task of unsupervised facial behaviour analysis. Specifically, we investigate how accurately the proposed method can capture the transitions between the temporal phases during the activation of various FAUs and compare against SFA. The temporal phases of a performed FAU are: (1) *Neutral* when the face is relaxed, (2) *Onset* when the action initiates, (3) *Apex* when the muscles reach the peak intensity and (4) *Offset* when the muscles begin to relax. The performance of the methods is evaluated by comparing the slowest varying features extracted by both methods with the ground truth annotations. To identify which of the extracted feature corresponds to the most slowly varying one we computed the first order time derivative for each obtained latent variable and keep the one with minimum: $\mathbf{v}_i^T \mathbf{L} \mathbf{v}_i$. For comparison we apply SFA on the ground truth shape [3]. More precisely, we measure

---

[3] The result of SFA on texture did not capture the dynamics.

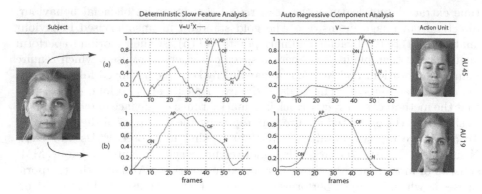

Fig. 3. Application of SFA and ARCA on a video from MMI database displaying a subject performing: (a) Blink (AU 45) and (b) Tongue Show (AU 19). The red marks indicate the ground truth moments at which the FAU's temporal phases change (ON - neutral to onset, AP - onset to apex, OF - apex to offset, N - offset to neutral).

the similarity between the ground truth and the extracted features by monitoring the alignment cost using the dynamic time warping (DTW) algorithm. Therefore, a low measured cost means that the FAUs transitions are captured more accurately by the extracted feature.

Figure 3 shows the performance of the proposed method against SFA in terms of capturing the FAU temporal phases from a subject that performs two AUs in the same video sequence. More specifically, Figs. 3(a) and 3(b) show the results obtained when the subject performs AU45 (i.e. blink) and AU19 (i.e tongue show) respectively. In each plot the red marks correspond to the ground truth points at which the FAU's temporal phase changes. The graphs of both sequences indicate that the proposed method outperforms the SFA algorithm since it detects the dynamics of the FAU more accurately and captures the temporal phases more smoothly.

Figure 4 shows the error between the extracted features and the ground truth annotations for the MMI database's videos with the application of both the ARCA and SFA. More precisely, Fig. 4(a) shows the error from 53 videos in which the subject performs mouth-related FAUs, while Fig. 4(b) shows the error from 35 videos in which the subject performs eyes-related FAUs. Table 1 summarizes these results for each temporal phase separately. The presented results indicate that the proposed method significantly outperforms SFA on the unsupervised detection of the temporal phases of FAUs, almost in all temporal phases and for all relevant regions of the face.

Next we test the ability of the ARCA method to provide low dimensional texture features that can be used for temporal alignment of behaviour. To do so, we combine the extracted features from ARCA with DTW. We compare this method with Canonical Time Warping (CTW) [2], which jointly discovers low dimensional features that can be used for temporal alignment of sequences. For CTW, we used the textures aligned using the ground truth shapes. In the

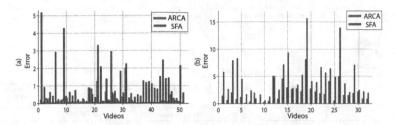

Fig. 4. Total error between the extracted features and ground truth annotations on the MMI database. The plots compare the performance of the proposed method and SFA with: (a) Mouth-related AUs (b) Eyes-related AUs.

Table 1. Error between the extracted features and ground truth annotations for each temporal phase on the MMI database. The results compare the performance of the fully automatic ARCA method against SFA on ground truth shape.

Method	Neutral			Onset			Apex			Offset		
	Mouth	Eyes	Brows	Mouth	Eyes	Brows	Mouth	Eyes	Brows	Mouth	Eyes	Brows
ARCA	**0.341**	**2.299**	**0.388**	**0.215**	**0.104**	**0.053**	**0.516**	**0.252**	**0.266**	**0.2534**	1.298	**0.2638**
SFA	1.054	3.943	2.154	0.675	0.329	0.277	2.541	2.889	0.705	0.506	**1.076**	1.084

example shown in Fig. 5 two different subjects perform AU10 (Upper Lip Raiser) in different moments. As can be observed in Fig. 5(b), ARCA+DTW was able to align accurately all the temporal phases, while the low dimensional features provided by CTW were not able to align the sequences, as indicated by its respective alignment path 5(c) solid line. For further alignment examples, please see the supplementary material. Fig. 5(d) shows several frames illustrating the alignment.

4.2 Behaviour Analysis of Spontaneous Smiles in UVS Database

As it is widely shown spontaneous behaviour differs greatly to posed behaviour both in duration and dynamics [1]. In particular, in spontaneous behavior it is very often that we do not have a single smooth transition but we have many valleys and plateaus. In order to evaluate whether the proposed methodology can capture this complex transitions we used the spontaneous smiles of UNS database.

Figure 6 shows an example in which the subject performs an FAU with many transitions. This means that the performed FAU has more than one onset and apex phases. During the first apex phase (frames 24 to 94) the subject is smiling with a normal intensity. However, the smile intensifies during frames 94 to 102 and reaches its second peak at frame 103. As can be seen in the graph, the proposed method manages to capture all the transitions of the temporal phases more accurately and smoothly compared to SFA. Moreover, Table 2 summarizes the results on all UNS database videos. Specifically, it reports the mean error

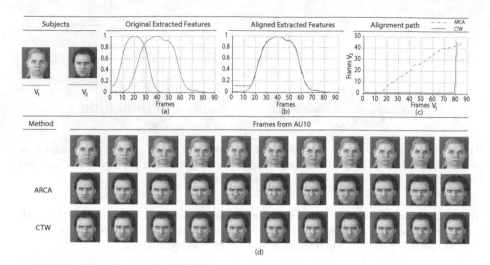

Fig. 5. Aligning the AU10 performed by two different subjects. (a)Original features (b)Aligned features (c) Alignment path. (d) Frames detected form the ARCA method (second row) and CTW method (third row).

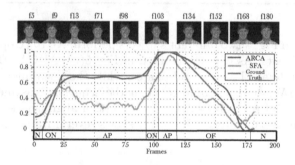

Fig. 6. Comparison of ARCA (blue) and SFA (green) with the annotated ground truth (red) on a spontaneous video sequence from UNS database. The subject performs an FAU with multi-temporal phases (ON-Onset, AP-apex, OF-offset, N-neutral).

of each temporal phase along with the overall error of the whole performed FAU. Similar to the MMI experiments, the results show that ARCA significantly outperforms SFA on the unsupervised detection of the multi temporal phases of AUs in all temporal phases.

4.3   Landmark Points Localization Results

In this section we present experimental results for the task of automatic facial landmarks localization. We evaluate the error between an estimated shape and the ground truth with the point-to-point RMSE measure normalized with respect to the face's size. Specifically, denoting as $\mathbf{s}^f$ and $\mathbf{s}^g$ the fitted and ground

Table 2. Error between the extracted features and ground truth annotations for each temporal phase on the UNS database. The results compare the performance of the fully automatic ARCA method against SFA on ground truth shape.

Method	Neutral	Onset	Apex	Offset	Overall
ARCA	**0.147**	**0.087**	**0.791**	**0.050**	**0.1524**
SFA	2.068	0.610	8.250	0.497	2.081

truth shapes respectively, the normalized RMSE between them is $RMSE = \sum_{i=1}^{L_S} \frac{\sqrt{(x_i^f - x_i^g)^2 + (y_i^f - y_i^g)^2}}{L_S d}$ where $d = (\max_x \mathbf{s}^g - \min_x \mathbf{s}^g + \max_y \mathbf{s}^g - \min_y \mathbf{s}^g)/2$ is face's size.

Figures 7a and 7b provide a proof that the cost function converges. Specifically, Fig. 7a shows the evolution of the mean cost function error of Eq. 13 over all MMI database's videos with respect to the iterations. As can be seen, the error monotonically decreases. Additionally, Fig. 7b visualizes the evolution of the mean normalized RMSE between the fitted shapes and the ground truth annotations over all MMI database's videos with respect to the iterations. Note that the plot shows the RMSE evaluated based on two masks: one with all the 68 landmarks and one with 51 which are a subset of the 68 ones by removing the boundary (jaw) points. Figure 8 shows the evolution of the subspace for an indicative MMI video. The initial and final subspace are visualized in the top and bottom rows of the figure respectively. As can be seen, the initial bases display misaligned and blurred faces. However, in the resulting subspace, the facial areas are distinctive and clear. We think that this improvement is significant given the automatic nature of the proposed method and the fact that we use pixel intensities for the appearance representation and not any other sophisticated descriptor. Moreover, note that the convergence demonstrated by Figs. 7a,7b and 8 is achieved in only 5 global iterations of the method.

Finally, we conduct an experiment to compare the fitting accuracy of ARCA with three other landmark localization methods trained on manual annotations.

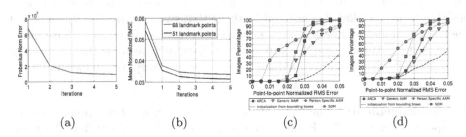

(a)   (b)   (c)   (d)

Fig. 7. Face alignment results. 7a: Plot of the mean cost function error of Eq. 13 over all MMI videos per iteration. 7b: Plot of the mean normalized RMSE over all MMI videos per iteration. 7c, 7d: Comparison of the fitting accuracy of ARCA with methods trained on manual annotations for MMI and UNS respectively.

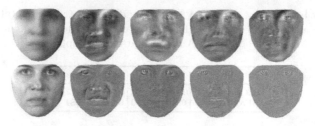

Fig. 8. Indicative example of the subspace evolution on an MMI video. *Top row:* Initial subspace. *Bottom row:* Final subspace after five iterations.

The first one is a person specific Active Appearance Model (AAM) trained using a small number of images for each subject. The second is a generic AAM trained on hundreds of "in-the-wild" images (captured in totally unconstrained conditions) from LFPW database [43]. The third methodology is Supervised Descent Method (SDM) [5], which uses the powerful SIFT features. For this technique, we utilize the implementation provided by the authors which has pre-trained models built on thousands of images. We use the same initialization for all methods except SDM, for which we use the built-in initialization technique included in the online implementation. Figures 7c and 7d show the results on MMI and UNS databases respectively. ARCA performs better than the generic AAM. Moreover, it has worse performance than SDM and it is more robust but less accurate than the person-specific AAM. Note that the initialization of SDM is much better than the one of the rest of the methods, which partially explains the performance difference. We think that these results are remarkable given the automatic character of the proposed method and the fact that it is based on pixel intensities and not on any other powerful feature-based representation.

5   Conclusions

Contrary to what is practised in facial behaviour analysis, we show that it is possible to extract low-dimensional features that can capture the dynamics of the behaviour and jointly perform landmark localization. To do so we have introduced ARCA, Autoregressive component analysis, and we show that it possible to combine it with a motion model governt by a simple sparse shape model.

Acknowledgements. The work of Lazaros Zafeiriou has been funded by the European Community 7th Framework Programme [FP7/2007-2013] under grant agreement no. 288235 (FROG). The work of Epameinondas Antonakos and Stefanos Zafeiriou was funded in part by the EPSRC project EP/J017787/1 (4DFAB). The work by Maja Pantic was funded in part by the European Community 7th Framework Programme [FP7/2007-2013] under grant agreement no. 611153 (TERESA).

References

1. Zeng, Z., Pantic, M., Roisman, G.I., Huang, T.S.: A survey of affect recognition methods: Audio, visual, and spontaneous expressions. IEEE Transactions on Pattern Analysis and Machine Intelligence (TPAMI) 31(1), 39–58 (2009)
2. Zhou, F., De la Torre, F.: Canonical time warping for alignment of human behavior. In: Conference on Neural Information Processing Systems (NIPS), pp. 2286–2294 (2009)
3. Nicolaou, M.A., Pavlovic, V., Pantic, M.: Dynamic probabilistic cca for analysis of affective behaviour. In: Fitzgibbon, A., Lazebnik, S., Perona, P., Sato, Y., Schmid, C. (eds.) ECCV 2012, Part VII. LNCS, vol. 7578, pp. 98–111. Springer, Heidelberg (2012)
4. Tzimiropoulos, G., Alabort-i-Medina, J., Zafeiriou, S., Pantic, M.: Generic active appearance models revisited. In: Lee, K.M., Matsushita, Y., Rehg, J.M., Hu, Z. (eds.) ACCV 2012, Part III. LNCS, vol. 7726, pp. 650–663. Springer, Heidelberg (2013)
5. Xiong, X., De la Torre, F.: Supervised descent method and its applications to face alignment. In: IEEE Proceedings of Int'l Conf. on Computer Vision and Pattern Recognition (CVPR) (2013)
6. Asthana, A., Zafeiriou, S., Cheng, S., Pantic, M.: Robust discriminative response map fitting with constrained local models. In: IEEE Proceedings of Int'l Conf. on Computer Vision and Pattern Recognition (CVPR) (2013)
7. Gross, R., Matthews, I., Cohn, J., Kanade, T., Baker, S.: Multi-pie. Image and Vision Computing (JIVC) 28(5), 807–813 (2010)
8. Sagonas, C., Tzimiropoulos, G., Zafeiriou, S., Pantic, M.: A semi-automatic methodology for facial landmark annotation. In: IEEE Proceedings of Int'l Conf. on Computer Vision and Pattern Recognition Workshop (CVPR-W 2013), 5th Workshop on Analysis and Modeling of Faces and Gestures (AMFG 2013), Portland Oregon, USA (June 2013)
9. Sagonas, C., Tzimiropoulos, G., Zafeiriou, S., Pantic, M.: 300 faces in-the-wild challenge: The first facial landmark localization challenge. In: IEEE Proceedings of Int'l Conf. on Computer Vision Workshop (ICCV-W 2013), 300 Faces in-the-Wild Challenge (300-W), Sydney, Australia (December 2013)
10. Zhou, F., De la Torre, F., Cohn, J.F.: Unsupervised discovery of facial events. In: IEEE Proceedings of Int'l Conf. on Computer Vision and Pattern Recognition (CVPR), pp. 2574–2581. IEEE (2010)
11. Zhou, F., De la Torre, F., Hodgins, J.K.: Hierarchical aligned cluster analysis for temporal clustering of human motion. IEEE Transactions on Pattern Analysis and Machine Intelligence (TPAMI) 35(3), 582–596 (2013)
12. Antonakos, E., Pitsikalis, V., Rodomagoulakis, I., Maragos, P.: Unsupervised classification of extreme facial events using active appearance models tracking for sign language videos. In: IEEE Proceedings of Int'l Conf. on Image Processing (ICIP), Orlando, FL, USA (October 2012)
13. Zhang, W., Shan, S., Chen, X., Gao, W.: Local gabor binary patterns based on mutual information for face recognition. International Journal of Image and Graphics 7(04), 777–793 (2007)
14. Ha, S.W., Moon, Y.H.: Multiple object tracking using sift features and location matching. International Journal of Smart Home 5(4) (2011)
15. Zafeiriou, L., Nicolaou, M.A., Zafeiriou, S., Nikitidis, S., Pantic, M.: Learning slow features for behaviour analysis. In: IEEE Proceedings of Int'l Conf. on Computer Vision (ICCV) (November 2013)

16. Zhou, F., De la Torre, F.: Generalized time warping for multi-modal alignment of human motion. In: 2012 IEEE Conference on Computer Vision and Pattern Recognition (CVPR) (2012)
17. Rue, H., Held, L.: Gaussian Markov random fields: theory and applications. CRC Press (2004)
18. Peng, Y., Ganesh, A., Wright, J., Xu, W., Ma, Y.: Rasl: Robust alignment by sparse and low-rank decomposition for linearly correlated images. IEEE Transactions on Pattern Analysis and Machine Intelligence (TPAMI) 34(11), 2233–2246 (2012)
19. Zhao, C., Cham, W.K., Wang, X.: Joint face alignment with a generic deformable face model. In: 2011 IEEE Conference on Computer Vision and Pattern Recognition (CVPR), pp. 561–568. IEEE (2011)
20. Sagonas, C., Panagakis, Y., Zafeiriou, S., Pantic, M.: Raps: Robust and efficient automatic construction of person-specific deformable models. In: Proceedings of IEEE Int'l Conf. on Computer Vision and Pattern Recognition (CVPR 2014) (June 2014)
21. De la Torre, F., Black, M.J.: Robust parameterized component analysis: theory and applications to 2d facial appearance models. Computer Vision and Image Understanding 91(1), 53–71 (2003)
22. De la Torre, F., Nguyen, M.H.: Parameterized kernel principal component analysis: Theory and applications to supervised and unsupervised image alignment. In: IEEE Conference on Computer Vision and Pattern Recognition, CVPR 2008, pp. 1–8. IEEE (2008)
23. Cheng, X., Fookes, C., Sridharan, S., Saragih, J., Lucey, S.: Deformable face ensemble alignment with robust grouped-l1 anchors. In: 10th IEEE International Conference and Workshops on Automatic Face and Gesture Recognition (FG 2013), pp. 1–7 (2013)
24. Cheng, X., Sridharan, S., Saragih, J., Lucey, S.: Rank minimization across appearance and shape for aam ensemble fitting. In: 2013 IEEE International Conference on Computer Vision (ICCV), pp. 577–584. IEEE (2013)
25. Viola, P., Jones, M.: Rapid object detection using a boosted cascade of simple features. In: IEEE Proceedings of Int'l Conf. on Computer Vision and Pattern Recognition (CVPR) (2001)
26. Lampert, C.H., Blaschko, M.B., Hofmann, T.: Efficient subwindow search: A branch and bound framework for object localization. IEEE Transactions on Pattern Analysis and Machine Intelligence (TPAMI) 31(12), 2129–2142 (2009)
27. Zhu, X., Ramanan, D.: Face detection, pose estimation, and landmark localization in the wild. In: IEEE Proceedings of Int'l Conf. on Computer Vision and Pattern Recognition (CVPR), pp. 2879–2886 (2012)
28. Orozco, J., Martinez, B., Pantic, M.: Empirical analysis of cascade deformable models for multi-view face detection. In: IEEE Proceedings of Int'l Conf. on Image Processing (ICIP) (2013)
29. Jiang, T., Jurie, F., Schmid, C.: Learning shape prior models for object matching. In: IEEE Proceedings of Int'l Conf. on Computer Vision and Pattern Recognition (CVPR) (2009)
30. Kokkinos, I., Yuille, A.: Unsupervised learning of object deformation models. In: IEEE Proceedings of Int'l Conf. on Computer Vision (ICCV) (2007)
31. Yang, J., Frangi, A.F., Yang, J.Y., Zhang, D., Jin, Z.: Kpca plus lda: a complete kernel fisher discriminant framework for feature extraction and recognition. IEEE Transactions on Pattern Analysis and Machine Intelligence (TPAMI) 27(2), 230–244 (2005)

32. Zou, H., Hastie, T., Tibshirani, R.: Sparse principal component analysis. Journal of Computational and Graphical Statistics 15(2), 265–286 (2006)
33. Baker, S., Matthews, I.: Lucas-kanade 20 years on: A unifying framework. International Journal of Computer Vision (IJCV) 56(3), 221–255 (2004)
34. Jolliffe, I.: Principal component analysis. Wiley Online Library (2005)
35. Welling, M.: Fisher linear discriminant analysis. Department of Computer Science. University of Toronto 3 (2005)
36. Roweis, S.T., Saul, L.K.: Nonlinear dimensionality reduction by locally linear embedding. Science 290(5500), 2323–2326 (2000)
37. He, X., Niyogi, P.: Locality preserving projections. In: NIPS, vol. 16, pp. 234–241 (2003)
38. Roweis, S., Ghahramani, Z.: A unifying review of linear gaussian models. Neural Computation 11(2), 305–345 (1999)
39. Wiskott, L., Sejnowski, T.J.: Slow feature analysis: Unsupervised learning of invariances. Neural Computation 14(4), 715–770 (2002)
40. Valstar, M.F., Pantic, M.: Induced disgust, happiness and surprise: an addition to the mmi facial expression database. In: Proceedings of Int'l Conf. on Language Resources and Evaluation (LREC), Workshop on EMOTION, Malta (May 2010)
41. Valstar, M.F., Pantic, M.: Mmi facial expression database, http://www.mmifacedb.com/
42. Dibeklioglu, H., Salah, A.A., Gevers, T.: Uva-nemo smile database, http://www.uva-nemo.org/
43. Belhumeur, P.N., Jacobs, D.W., Kriegman, D.J., Kumar, N.: Localizing parts of faces using a consensus of exemplars. In: IEEE Proceedings of Int'l Conf. on Computer Vision and Pattern Recognition (CVPR) (2011)

Learning a Deep Convolutional Network
for Image Super-Resolution

Chao Dong[1], Chen Change Loy[1], Kaiming He[2], and Xiaoou Tang[1]

[1] Department of Information Engineering,
The Chinese University of Hong Kong, China
[2] Microsoft Research Asia, Beijing, China

Abstract. We propose a deep learning method for single image super-resolution (SR). Our method directly learns an end-to-end mapping between the low/high-resolution images. The mapping is represented as a deep convolutional neural network (CNN) [15] that takes the low-resolution image as the input and outputs the high-resolution one. We further show that traditional sparse-coding-based SR methods can also be viewed as a deep convolutional network. But unlike traditional methods that handle each component separately, our method jointly optimizes all layers. Our deep CNN has a lightweight structure, yet demonstrates state-of-the-art restoration quality, and achieves fast speed for practical on-line usage.

Keywords: Super-resolution, deep convolutional neural networks.

1   Introduction

Single image super-resolution (SR) [11] is a classical problem in computer vision. Recent state-of-the-art methods for single image super-resolution are mostly example-based. These methods either exploit internal similarities of the same image [7,10,23], or learn mapping functions from external low- and high-resolution exemplar pairs [2,4,9,13,20,24,25,26,28]. The external example-based methods are often provided with abundant samples, but are challenged by the difficulties of effectively and compactly modeling the data.

The sparse-coding-based method [25,26] is one of the representative methods for external example-based image super-resolution. This method involves several steps in its pipeline. First, overlapping patches are densely extracted from the image and pre-processed (*e.g.*, subtracting mean). These patches are then encoded by a low-resolution dictionary. The sparse coefficients are passed into a high-resolution dictionary for reconstructing high-resolution patches. The overlapping reconstructed patches are aggregated (or averaged) to produce the output. Previous SR methods pay particular attention to learning and optimizing the dictionaries [25,26] or alternative ways of modeling them [4,2]. However, the rest of the steps in the pipeline have been rarely optimized or considered in an unified optimization framework.

In this paper, we show the aforementioned pipeline is equivalent to a deep convolutional neural network [15] (more details in Section 3.2). Motivated by

D. Fleet et al. (Eds.): ECCV 2014, Part IV, LNCS 8692, pp. 184–199, 2014.

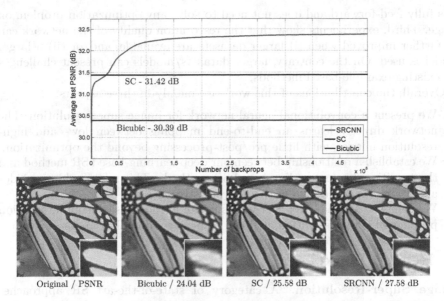

Fig. 1. The proposed Super-Resolution Convolutional Neural Network (SRCNN) surpasses the bicubic baseline with just a few training iterations, and outperforms the sparse-coding-based method (SC) [26] with moderate training. The performance may be further improved with more training iterations. More details are provided in Section 4.1 (the Set5 dataset with an upscaling factor 3). The proposed method provides visually appealing reconstruction from the low-resolution image.

this fact, we directly consider a convolutional neural network which is an end-to-end mapping between low- and high-resolution images. Our method differs fundamentally from existing external example-based approaches, in that ours does not explicitly learn the dictionaries [20,25,26] or manifolds [2,4] for modeling the patch space. These are implicitly achieved via hidden layers. Furthermore, the patch extraction and aggregation are also formulated as convolutional layers, so are involved in the optimization. In our method, the entire SR pipeline is fully obtained through learning, with little pre/post-processing.

We name the proposed model Super-Resolution Convolutional Neural Network (SRCNN)[1]. The proposed SRCNN has several appealing properties. First, its structure is intentionally designed with simplicity in mind, and yet provides superior accuracy[2] comparing with state-of-the-art example-based methods. Figure 1 shows a comparison on an example. Second, with moderate numbers of filters and layers, our method achieves fast speed for practical on-line usage even on a CPU. Our method is faster than a series of example-based methods, because

---

[1] The implementation is available at
http://mmlab.ie.cuhk.edu.hk/projects/SRCNN.html.

[2] Numerical evaluations in terms of Peak Signal-to-Noise Ratio (PSNR) when the ground truth images are available.

it is fully feed-forward and does not need to solve any optimization problem on usage. Third, experiments show that the restoration quality of the network can be further improved when (i) larger datasets are available, and/or (ii) a larger model is used. On the contrary, larger datasets/models can present challenges for existing example-based methods.

Overall, the contributions of this work are mainly in three aspects:

1. We present a convolutional neural network for image super-resolution. The network directly learns an end-to-end mapping between low- and high-resolution images, with little pre/post-processing beyond the optimization.
2. We establish a relationship between our deep-learning-based SR method and the traditional sparse-coding-based SR methods. This relationship provides a guidance for the design of the network structure.
3. We demonstrate that deep learning is useful in the classical computer vision problem of super-resolution, and can achieve good quality and speed.

2   Related Work

Image Super-Resolution. A category of state-of-the-art SR approaches [9,4,25,26,24,2,28,20] learn a mapping between low/high-resolution patches. These studies vary on how to learn a compact dictionary or manifold space to relate low/high-resolution patches, and on how representation schemes can be conducted in such spaces. In the pioneer work of Freeman *et al.* [8], the dictionaries are directly presented as low/high-resolution patch pairs, and the nearest neighbour (NN) of the input patch is found in the low-resolution space, with its corresponding high-resolution patch used for reconstruction. Chang *et al.* [4] introduce a manifold embedding technique as an alternative to the NN strategy. In Yang *et al.*'s work [25,26], the above NN correspondence advances to a more sophisticated sparse coding formulation. This sparse-coding-based method and its several improvements [24,20] are among the state-of-the-art SR methods nowadays. In these methods, the patches are the focus of the optimization; the patch extraction and aggregation steps are considered as pre/post-processing and handled separately.

Convolutional Neural Networks. Convolutional neural networks (CNN) date back decades [15] and have recently shown an explosive popularity partially due to its success in image classification [14]. Several factors are of central importance in this progress: (i) the efficient training implementation on modern powerful GPUs [14], (ii) the proposal of the Rectified Linear Unit (ReLU) [18] which makes convergence much faster while still presents good quality [14], and (iii) the easy access to an abundance of data (like ImageNet [5]) for training larger models. Our method also benefits from these progresses.

Deep Learning for Image Restoration. There have been a few studies of using deep learning techniques for image restoration. The multi-layer perceptron (MLP), whose all layers are fully-connected (in contrast to convolutional), is applied for natural image denoising [3] and post-deblurring denoising [19]. More closely related to our work, the convolutional neural network is applied for natural image denoising [12] and removing noisy patterns (dirt/rain) [6]. These restoration problems are more or less denoising-driven. On the contrary, the image super-resolution problem has not witnessed the usage of deep learning techniques to the best of our knowledge.

3 Convolutional Neural Networks for Super-Resolution

3.1 Formulation

Consider a single low-resolution image. We first upscale it to the desired size using bicubic interpolation, which is the only pre-processing we perform[3]. Denote the interpolated image as $\mathbf{Y}$. Our goal is to recover from $\mathbf{Y}$ an image $F(\mathbf{Y})$ which is as similar as possible to the ground truth high-resolution image $\mathbf{X}$. For the ease of presentation, we still call $\mathbf{Y}$ a "low-resolution" image, although it has the same size as $\mathbf{X}$. We wish to learn a mapping F, which conceptually consists of three operations:

1. **Patch extraction and representation:** this operation extracts (overlapping) patches from the low-resolution image $\mathbf{Y}$ and represents each patch as a high-dimensional vector. These vectors comprise a set of feature maps, of which the number equals to the dimensionality of the vectors.
2. **Non-linear mapping:** this operation nonlinearly maps each high-dimensional vector onto another high-dimensional vector. Each mapped vector is conceptually the representation of a high-resolution patch. These vectors comprise another set of feature maps.
3. **Reconstruction:** this operation aggregates the above high-resolution patch-wise representations to generate the final high-resolution image. This image is expected to be similar to the ground truth $\mathbf{X}$.

We will show that all these operations form a convolutional neural network. An overview of the network is depicted in Figure 2. Next we detail our definition of each operation.

Patch Extraction and Representation. A popular strategy in image restoration (*e.g.*, [1]) is to densely extract patches and then represent them by a set of pre-trained bases such as PCA, DCT, Haar, etc. This is equivalent to convolving the image by a set of filters, each of which is a basis. In our formulation, we involve the optimization of these bases into the optimization of the network. Formally, our first layer is expressed as an operation F_1:

$$F_1(\mathbf{Y}) = \max(0, W_1 * \mathbf{Y} + B_1), \tag{1}$$

---

[3] Actually, bicubic interpolation is also a convolutional operation, so can be formulated as a convolutional layer. However, the output size of this layer is larger than the input size, so there is a fractional stride. To take advantage of the popular well-optimized implementations such as *convnet* [14], we exclude this "layer" from learning.

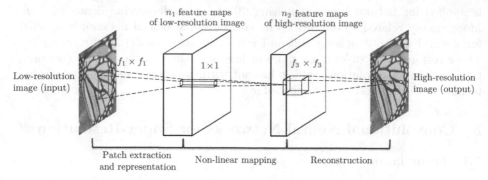

Fig. 2. Given a low-resolution image **Y**, the first convolutional layer of the SRCNN extracts a set of feature maps. The second layer maps these feature maps nonlinearly to high-resolution patch representations. The last layer combines the predictions within a spatial neighbourhood to produce the final high-resolution image $F(\mathbf{Y})$.

where W_1 and B_1 represent the filters and biases respectively. Here W_1 is of a size $c \times f_1 \times f_1 \times n_1$, where c is the number of channels in the input image, f_1 is the spatial size of a filter, and n_1 is the number of filters. Intuitively, W_1 applies n_1 convolutions on the image, and each convolution has a kernel size $c \times f_1 \times f_1$. The output is composed of n_1 feature maps. B_1 is an n_1-dimensional vector, whose each element is associated with a filter. We apply the Rectified Linear Unit (ReLU, $\max(0, x)$) [18] on the filter responses[4].

Non-linear Mapping. The first layer extracts an n_1-dimensional feature for each patch. In the second operation, we map each of these n_1-dimensional vectors into an n_2-dimensional one. This is equivalent to applying n_2 filters which have a trivial spatial support 1×1. The operation of the second layer is:

$$F_2(\mathbf{Y}) = \max\left(0, W_2 * F_1(\mathbf{Y}) + B_2\right). \qquad (2)$$

Here W_2 is of a size $n_1 \times 1 \times 1 \times n_2$, and B_2 is n_2-dimensional. Each of the output n_2-dimensional vectors is conceptually a representation of a high-resolution patch that will be used for reconstruction.

It is possible to add more convolutional layers (whose spatial supports are 1×1) to increase the non-linearity. But this can significantly increase the complexity of the model, and thus demands more training data and time. In this paper, we choose to use a single convolutional layer in this operation, because it has already provided compelling quality.

---

[4] The ReLU can be equivalently considered as a part of the second operation (Non-linear mapping), and the first operation (Patch extraction and representation) becomes purely linear convolution.

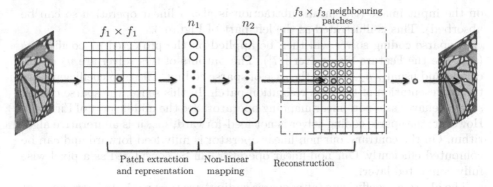

Fig. 3. An illustration of sparse-coding-based methods in the view of a convolutional neural network

Reconstruction. In the traditional methods, the predicted overlapping high-resolution patches are often averaged to produce the final full image. The averaging can be considered as a pre-defined filter on a set of feature maps (where each position is the "flattened" vector form of a high-resolution patch). Motivated by this, we define a convolutional layer to produce the final high-resolution image:

$$F(\mathbf{Y}) = W_3 * F_2(\mathbf{Y}) + B_3. \tag{3}$$

Here W_3 is of a size $n_2 \times f_3 \times f_3 \times c$, and B_3 is a c-dimensional vector.

If the representations of the high-resolution patches are in the image domain (*i.e.*, we can simply reshape each representation to form the patch), we expect that the filters act like an averaging filter; if the representations of the high-resolution patches are in some other domains (*e.g.*, coefficients in terms of some bases), we expect that W_3 behaves like first projecting the coefficients onto the image domain and then averaging. In either way, W_3 is a set of linear filters.

Interestingly, although the above three operations are motivated by different intuitions, they all lead to the same form as a convolutional layer. We put all three operations together and form a convolutional neural network (Figure 2). In this model, all the filtering weights and biases are to be optimized.

Despite the succinctness of the overall structure, our SRCNN model is carefully developed by drawing extensive experience resulted from significant progresses in super-resolution [25,26]. We detail the relationship in the next section.

3.2 Relationship to Sparse-Coding-Based Methods

We show that the sparse-coding-based SR methods [25,26] can be viewed as a convolutional neural network. Figure 3 shows an illustration.

In the sparse-coding-based methods, let us consider that an $f_1 \times f_1$ low-resolution patch is extracted from the input image. This patch is subtracted by its mean, and then is projected onto a (low-resolution) dictionary. If the dictionary size is n_1, this is equivalent to applying n_1 linear filters ($f_1 \times f_1$)

on the input image (the mean subtraction is also a linear operation so can be absorbed). This is illustrated as the left part of Figure 3.

A sparse coding solver will then be applied on the projected n_1 coefficients (*e.g.*, see the Feature-Sign solver [17]). The outputs of this solver are n_2 coefficients, and usually $n_2 = n_1$ in the case of sparse coding. These n_2 coefficients are the representation of the high-resolution patch. In this sense, the sparse coding solver behaves as a non-linear mapping operator. See the middle part of Figure 3. However, the sparse coding solver is not feed-forward, *i.e.*, it is an iterative algorithm. On the contrary, our non-linear operator is fully feed-forward and can be computed efficiently. Our non-linear operator can be considered as a pixel-wise fully-connected layer.

The above n_2 coefficients (after sparse coding) are then projected onto another (high-resolution) dictionary to produce a high-resolution patch. The overlapping high-resolution patches are then averaged. As discussed above, this is equivalent to linear convolutions on the n_2 feature maps. If the high-resolution patches used for reconstruction are of size $f_3 \times f_3$, then the linear filters have an equivalent spatial support of size $f_3 \times f_3$. See the right part of Figure 3.

The above discussion shows that the sparse-coding-based SR method can be viewed as a kind of convolutional neural network (with a different non-linear mapping). But not all operations have been considered in the optimization in the sparse-coding-based SR methods. On the contrary, in our convolutional neural network, the low-resolution dictionary, high-resolution dictionary, non-linear mapping, together with mean subtraction and averaging, are all involved in the filters to be optimized. So our method optimizes an end-to-end mapping that consists of all operations.

The above analogy can also help us to design hyper-parameters. For example, we can set the filter size of the last layer to be smaller than that of the first layer, and thus we rely more on the central part of the high-resolution patch (to the extreme, if $f_3 = 1$, we are using the center pixel with no averaging). We can also set $n_2 < n_1$ because it is expected to be sparser. A typical setting is $f_1 = 9$, $f_3 = 5$, $n_1 = 64$, and $n_2 = 32$ (we evaluate more settings in the experiment section).

3.3   Loss Function

Learning the end-to-end mapping function F requires the estimation of parameters $\Theta = \{W_1, W_2, W_3, B_1, B_2, B_3\}$. This is achieved through minimizing the loss between the reconstructed images $F(\mathbf{Y}; \Theta)$ and the corresponding ground truth high-resolution images $\mathbf{X}$. Given a set of high-resolution images $\{\mathbf{X}_i\}$ and their corresponding low-resolution images $\{\mathbf{Y}_i\}$, we use Mean Squared Error (MSE) as the loss function:

$$L(\Theta) = \frac{1}{n} \sum_{i=1}^{n} ||F(\mathbf{Y}_i; \Theta) - \mathbf{X}_i||^2, \tag{4}$$

where n is the number of training samples. The loss is minimized using stochastic gradient descent with the standard backpropagation [16].

Using MSE as the loss function favors a high PSNR. The PSNR is a widely-used metric for quantitatively evaluating image restoration quality, and is at least partially related to the perceptual quality. It is worth noticing that the convolutional neural networks do not preclude the usage of other kinds of loss functions, if only the loss functions are derivable. If a better perceptually motivated metric is given during training, it is flexible for the network to adapt to that metric. We will study this issue in the future. On the contrary, such a flexibility is in general difficult to achieve for traditional "hand-crafted" methods.

4   Experiments

Datasets. For a fair comparison with traditional example-based methods, we use the same training set, test sets, and protocols as in [20]. Specifically, the training set consists of 91 images. The **Set5** [2] (5 images) is used to evaluate the performance of upscaling factors 2, 3, and 4, and **Set14** [28] (14 images) is used to evaluate the upscaling factor 3. In addition to the 91-image training set, we also investigate a larger training set in Section 5.2.

Comparisons. We compare our **SRCNN** with the state-of-the-art SR methods: the **SC** (sparse coding) method of Yang *et al.* [26], the **K-SVD**-based method [28], **NE+LLE** (neighbour embedding + locally linear embedding) [4], **NE+NNLS** (neighbour embedding + non-negative least squares) [2], and the **ANR** (Anchored Neighbourhood Regression) method [20]. The implementations are all from the publicly available codes provided by the authors. For our implementation, the training is implemented using the *cuda-convnet* package [14].

Implementation Details. As per Section 3.2, we set $f_1 = 9$, $f_3 = 5$, $n_1 = 64$ and $n_2 = 32$ in our main evaluations. We will evaluate alternative settings in the Section 5. For each upscaling factor $\in \{2, 3, 4\}$, we train a specific network for that factor[5].

In the training phase, the ground truth images $\{\mathbf{X}_i\}$ are prepared as 32×32-pixel[6] sub-images randomly cropped from the training images. By "sub-images" we mean these samples are treated as small "images" rather than "patches", in the sense that "patches" are overlapping and require some averaging as post-processing but "sub-images" need not. To synthesize the low-resolution samples $\{\mathbf{Y}_i\}$, we blur a sub-image by a proper Gaussian kernel, sub-sample it by the upscaling factor, and upscale it by the same factor via bicubic interpolation. The 91 training images provide roughly 24,800 sub-images. The sub-images are extracted from original images with a stride of 14. We attempted smaller strides but did not observe significant performance improvement. From our observation, the training set is sufficient to train the proposed deep network. The training (8×10^8 backpropagations) takes roughly three days, on a GTX 770 GPU.

---

[5] In the area of denoising [3], for each noise level a specific network is trained.

[6] The input size is 33×33 for an upscaling factor 3, so can be divided by 3.

Following [20], we only consider the luminance channel (in YCrCb color space) in our experiments, so $c = 1$ in the first/last layer. The two chrominance channels are bicubic upsampled only for the purpose of displaying, but not for training/testing. Note that our method can be extended to directly training on color images by setting $c = 3$. We use $c = 1$ in this paper mainly for fair comparison with previous methods, as most of them only concern the luminance channels.

To avoid border effects during training, all the convolutional layers have no padding, and the network produces a smaller output (20×20). The MSE loss function is evaluated only by the difference between the central 20×20 crop of $\mathbf{X}_i$ and the network output. In processing test images, the convolutional neural network can be applied on images of arbitrary sizes. All the convolutional layers are given sufficient zero-padding during testing, so that the output image is of the same size as the input. To address the border effects, in each convolutional layer, the output (before ReLU) at each pixel is normalized by the number of valid input pixels, which can be computed beforehand.

The filter weights of each layer are initialized by drawing randomly from a Gaussian distribution with zero mean and standard deviation 0.001 (and 0 for biases). The learning rate is 10^{-4} for the first two layers, and 10^{-5} for the last layer. We empirically find that a smaller learning rate in the last layer is important for the network to converge (similar to the denoising case [12]).

4.1 Quantitative Evaluation

As shown in Tables 1 and 2, the proposed SRCNN yields the highest average PSNR in all experiments. Note that our SRCNN results are based on the checkpoint of 8×10^8 backpropagations. Specifically, as shown in the Table 1 (Set5), the average gains achieved by SRCNN are 0.51 dB, 0.47 dB, and 0.40 dB, higher than the next best approach, ANR [20], on all the three upscaling factors. We note that Set5 may not be a conclusive test set due to the limited number of test samples, but the results are indicative that the proposed model can handle different upscaling factors well. On the larger Set14 dataset, our SRCNN consistently outperforms other methods by a large margin (≥ 0.3 dB on average). A similar trend is observed when we used SSIM [22,21] as the performance metric, the results of which could be found in the supplementary file. It is worth pointing out that SRCNN surpasses the bicubic baseline at the very beginning of the learning stage (see Figure 1), and with moderate training, SRCNN outperforms existing state-of-the-art methods (see Figure 6). Yet, the performance is far from converge. We conjecture that better results can be obtained given longer training time (see Figure 6). In Section 5.2, we will show that our method also benefits from more training data.

Figures 7, 8 and 9 show the super-resolution results of different approaches by an upscaling factor 3. As can be observed, the SRCNN produces much sharper edges than other approaches without any obvious artifacts across the image. In spite of the best average PSNR values, the proposed SRCNN does not achieve the highest PSNR on images "baby" and "head" from Set5. Nevertheless, our results are still visually appealing (see Figure 10).

Table 1. The results of PSNR (dB) and test time (sec) on the Set5 dataset

Set5 [2] images	Scale	Bicubic		SC [26]		K-SVD [28]		NE+NNLS [2]		NE+LLE [4]		ANR [20]		SRCNN	
		PSNR	Time	PSNR	Time	PSNR	Time	PSNR	Time	PSNR	Time	PSNR	Time	PSNR	Time
baby	2	37.07	-	-	-	38.25	7.0	38.00	68.6	38.33	13.6	**38.44**	2.1	38.30	0.38
bird	2	36.81	-	-	-	39.93	2.2	39.41	22.5	40.00	4.2	40.04	0.62	**40.64**	0.14
butterfly	2	27.43	-	-	-	30.65	1.8	30.03	16.6	30.38	3.3	30.48	0.50	**32.20**	0.10
head	2	34.86	-	-	-	35.59	2.1	35.48	19.2	35.63	3.8	**35.66**	0.57	35.64	0.13
woman	2	32.14	-	-	-	34.49	2.1	34.24	19.3	34.52	3.8	34.35	0.57	**34.94**	0.13
average	2	33.66	-	-	-	35.78	3.03	35.43	29.23	35.77	5.74	35.83	0.87	**36.34**	0.18
baby	3	33.91	-	34.29	76.0	35.08	3.3	34.77	28.3	35.06	6.0	**35.13**	1.3	35.01	0.38
bird	3	32.58	-	34.11	30.4	34.57	1.0	34.26	8.9	34.56	1.9	34.60	0.39	**34.91**	0.14
butterfly	3	24.04	-	25.58	26.8	25.94	0.81	25.61	7.0	25.75	1.4	25.90	0.31	**27.58**	0.10
head	3	32.88	-	33.17	21.3	33.56	1.0	33.45	8.2	33.60	1.7	**33.63**	0.35	33.55	0.13
woman	3	28.56	-	29.94	25.1	30.37	1.0	29.89	8.7	30.22	1.9	30.33	0.37	**30.92**	0.13
average	3	30.39	-	31.42	35.92	31.90	1.42	31.60	12.21	31.84	2.58	31.92	0.54	**32.39**	0.18
baby	4	31.78	-	-	-	33.06	2.4	32.81	16.2	32.99	3.6	**33.03**	0.85	32.98	0.38
bird	4	30.18	-	-	-	31.71	0.68	31.51	4.7	31.72	1.1	31.82	0.27	**31.98**	0.14
butterfly	4	22.10	-	-	-	23.57	0.50	23.30	3.8	23.38	0.90	23.52	0.24	**25.07**	0.10
head	4	31.59	-	-	-	32.21	0.68	32.10	4.5	32.24	1.1	**32.27**	0.27	32.19	0.13
woman	4	26.46	-	-	-	27.89	0.66	27.61	4.3	27.72	1.1	27.80	0.28	**28.21**	0.13
average	4	28.42	-	-	-	29.69	0.98	29.47	6.71	29.61	1.56	29.69	0.38	**30.09**	0.18

Table 2. The results of PSNR (dB) and test time (sec) on the Set14 dataset

Set14 [28] images	scale	Bicubic		SC [26]		K-SVD [28]		NE+NNLS [2]		NE+LLE [4]		ANR [20]		SRCNN	
		PSNR	Time	PSNR	Time	PSNR	Time	PSNR	Time	PSNR	Time	PSNR	Time	PSNR	Time
baboon	3	23.21	-	23.47	126.3	23.52	3.6	23.49	29.0	23.55	5.6	23.56	1.1	**23.60**	0.40
barbara	3	26.25	-	26.39	127.9	**26.76**	5.5	26.67	47.6	26.74	9.8	26.69	1.7	26.66	0.70
bridge	3	24.40	-	24.82	152.7	25.02	3.3	24.86	30.4	24.98	5.9	25.01	1.1	**25.07**	0.44
coastguard	3	26.55	-	27.02	35.6	27.15	1.3	27.00	11.6	27.07	2.6	27.08	0.45	**27.20**	0.17
comic	3	23.12	-	23.90	54.5	23.96	1.2	23.83	11.0	23.98	2.0	24.04	0.42	**24.39**	0.15
face	3	32.82	-	33.11	20.4	33.53	1.1	33.45	8.3	33.56	1.7	**33.62**	0.34	33.58	0.13
flowers	3	27.23	-	28.25	76.4	28.43	2.3	28.21	20.2	28.38	4.0	28.49	0.81	**28.97**	0.30
foreman	3	31.18	-	32.04	25.9	33.19	1.3	32.87	10.8	33.21	2.2	33.23	0.44	**33.35**	0.17
lenna	3	31.68	-	32.64	68.4	33.00	3.3	32.82	29.3	33.01	6.0	33.08	1.1	**33.39**	0.44
man	3	27.01	-	27.76	111.2	27.90	3.4	27.72	29.5	27.87	6.1	27.92	1.1	**28.18**	0.44
monarch	3	29.43	-	30.71	112.1	31.10	4.9	30.76	43.3	30.95	8.8	31.09	1.6	**32.39**	0.66
pepper	3	32.39	-	33.32	66.3	34.07	3.3	33.56	28.9	33.80	6.6	33.82	1.1	**34.35**	0.44
ppt3	3	23.71	-	24.98	96.1	25.23	4.0	24.81	36.0	24.94	7.8	25.03	1.4	**26.02**	0.58
zebra	3	26.63	-	27.95	114.4	28.49	2.9	28.12	26.3	28.31	5.5	28.43	1.0	**28.87**	0.38
average	3	27.54	-	28.31	84.88	28.67	2.95	28.44	25.87	28.60	5.35	28.65	0.97	**29.00**	0.39

4.2 Running Time

Figure 4 shows the running time comparisons of several state-of-the-art methods, along with their restoration performance. All baseline methods are obtained from the corresponding authors' MATLAB implementation, whereas ours are in C++. We profile the running time of all the algorithms using the same machine (Intel CPU 3.10 GHz and 16 GB memory)[7]. Our method takes 0.39 sec per image on average in Set14 (Table 2), whereas other methods are several times or even orders of magnitude slower. Note the speed gap is not mainly caused by the different MATLAB/C++ implementations; rather, the other methods need to solve complex optimization problems on usage (e.g., sparse coding or embedding), whereas our method is completely feed-forward. We also note that the processing time of our approach is highly linear to the test image resolution, since all images go through the same number of convolutions.

---

[7] The running time may be slightly different from that reported in [20] due to different machines.

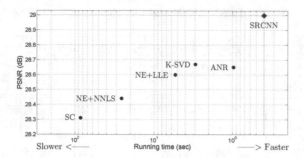

Fig. 4. The proposed SRCNN achieves the state-of-the-art super-resolution quality, whilst maintains high and competitive speed in comparison to existing external example-based methods. The chart is based on Set14 results summarized in Table 2.

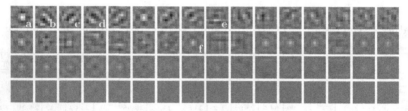

Fig. 5. The figure shows first-layer filters trained on 91 images with an upscaling factor 2. The filters are organized based on their respective variances.

5   Further Analyses

5.1   Learned Filters for Super-Resolution

Figure 5 shows examples of learned first-layer filters trained on 91 images (24,800 sub-images) by an upscaling factor 2. Please refer to our published implementation for the patterns of upscaling factors 3 and 4. Interestingly, each learned filter has its specific functionality. For instance, the filters a and f are like Laplacian/Gaussian filters, the filters b, c, and d are like edge detectors at different directions, and the filter e is like a texture extractor. We observe some "dead" filters, whose weights are all nearly zeros, similar to those observed in [27]. Nevertheless, patterns may emerge in some of these dead filters given long enough training time. We will investigate this phenomenon in future work.

5.2   Learning Super-Resolution from ImageNet

As shown in the literature, deep learning generally benefits from big data training. In the above experiments, we use a standard training set that consists of 91 images to ensure fair comparison with existing methods. In this section, we show that our deep model could achieve better performance given a large training set. We use a total of 395,909 images from the ILSVRC 2013 ImageNet detection training partition for SRCNN learning. These images are decomposed into over

5 million sub-images using a stride of 33. We use the same network settings as the above experiments, *i.e.* $f_1 = 9$, $f_3 = 5$, $n_1 = 64$ and $n_2 = 32$. The training time on ImageNet is about the same as on 91 images since the number of back-propagations is the same. The experiments are tested on Set5 with an upscaling factor 3. The test convergence curve trained on ImageNet and results of other methods are shown in Figure 6. As can be observed, with the same number of backpropagations (*i.e.*, 8×10^8), the SRCNN+ImageNet achieves **32.52 dB**, higher than 32.39 dB yielded by the original SRCNN trained on 91 images (or 24,800 sub-images). The results positively indicate that SRCNN performance may be further boosted using a larger and more diverse image training set.

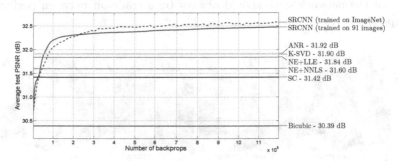

Fig. 6. The test convergence curve trained on ImageNet and results of other methods on the Set5 dataset

5.3   Filter Number

In comparison to other CNN structures [14], we use a relatively small network scale to achieve the state-of-the-art performance in super-resolution. In general, the performance would still improve if we enlarge the network scale, *e.g.* adding more layers and filters, at the cost of running time. Here, we evaluate the performance of using different numbers of filters. Specifically, based on our network default setting of $n_1 = 64$ and $n_2 = 32$, we conduct two additional experiments: (i) one is with a larger network with $n_1 = 128$ and $n_2 = 64$, and (ii) the other is with a smaller network with $n_1 = 32$ and $n_2 = 16$. Similar to Section 5.2, we also train the two models on ImageNet and test on Set5 with an upscaling factor 3. The results are shown in Table 3. It is clear that superior performance could be achieved using more filters. However, if a fast restoration speed is desired, a small network scale is preferred, which could still achieve better performance than the state-of-the-art.

Table 3. The results of using different filter numbers in SRCNN. Training is performed on ImageNet whilst the evaluation is conducted on the Set5 dataset.

Set5 [2]	$n_1 = 128, n_2 = 64$		$n_1 = 64, n_2 = 32$		$n_1 = 32, n_2 = 16$	
images	PSNR	Time	PSNR	Time	PSNR	Time
	32.60	0.60	32.52	0.18	32.26	0.05

5.4   Filter Size

In this section, we examine the network sensitivity to different filter sizes. In previous experiments, we set filter size of the first layer as $f_1 = 9$ and that of the last layer as $f_3 = 5$. Here, we enlarge the filter size to $f_1 = 11$ and $f_3 = 7$. All the other settings remain the same with Section 5.2. The results with an upscaling factor 3 on Set5 are 32.57 dB, which is slightly higher than the 32.52 dB reported in Section 5.2. This suggests that a reasonably larger filter size could grasp richer structural information, which in turn lead to better results. However, the deployment speed will also decrease with a larger filter size. Therefore, the choice of the network scale should always be a trade-off between performance and speed.

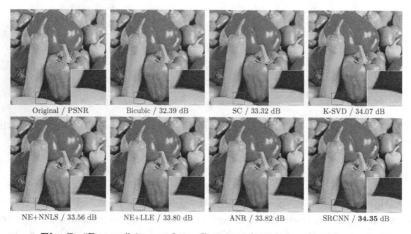

Fig. 7. "Pepper" image from Set14 with an upscaling factor 3

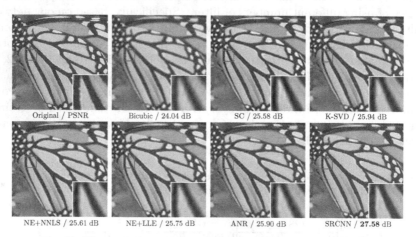

Fig. 8. "Butterfly" image from Set5 with an upscaling factor 3

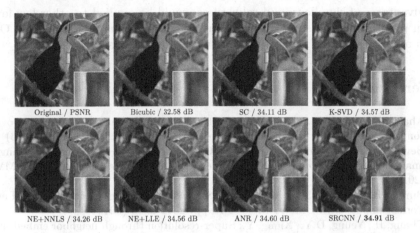

Fig. 9. "Bird" image from Set5 with an upscaling factor 3

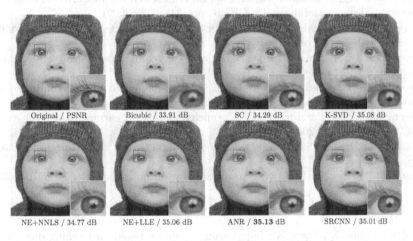

Fig. 10. "Baby" image from Set5 with an upscaling factor 3

6   Conclusion

We have presented a novel deep learning approach for single image super-resolution (SR). We show that conventional sparse-coding-based image super-resolution methods can be reformulated into a deep convolutional neural network. The proposed approach, SRCNN, learns an end-to-end mapping between low- and high-resolution images, with little extra pre/post-processing beyond the optimization. With a lightweight structure, the SRCNN has achieved superior performance than the state-of-the-art methods. We conjecture that additional performance can be further gained by exploring more hidden layers/filters in the network, and different training strategies. Besides, the proposed structure, with its advantages of simplicity and robustness, could be applied to other low-level vision problems, such as image deblurring or simultaneous SR+denoising. One could also investigate a network to cope with different upscaling factors.

References

1. Aharon, M., Elad, M., Bruckstein, A.: K-SVD: An algorithm for designing over-complete dictionaries for sparse representation. TSP 54(11), 4311–4322 (2006)
2. Bevilacqua, M., Roumy, A., Guillemot, C., Morel, M.L.A.: Low-complexity single-image super-resolution based on nonnegative neighbor embedding. In: BMVC (2012)
3. Burger, H.C., Schuler, C.J., Harmeling, S.: Image denoising: Can plain neural networks compete with BM3D? In: CVPR, pp. 2392–2399 (2012)
4. Chang, H., Yeung, D.Y., Xiong, Y.: Super-resolution through neighbor embedding. In: CVPR (2004)
5. Deng, J., Dong, W., Socher, R., Li, L.J., Li, K., Fei-Fei, L.: ImageNet: A large-scale hierarchical image database. In: CVPR, pp. 248–255 (2009)
6. Eigen, D., Krishnan, D., Fergus, R.: Restoring an image taken through a window covered with dirt or rain. In: ICCV, pp. 633–640 (2013)
7. Freedman, G., Fattal, R.: Image and video upscaling from local self-examples. TOG 30(2), 12 (2011)
8. Freeman, W.T., Jones, T.R., Pasztor, E.C.: Example-based super-resolution. Computer Graphics and Applications 22(2), 56–65 (2002)
9. Freeman, W.T., Pasztor, E.C., Carmichael, O.T.: Learning low-level vision. IJCV 40(1), 25–47 (2000)
10. Glasner, D., Bagon, S., Irani, M.: Super-resolution from a single image. In: ICCV, pp. 349–356 (2009)
11. Irani, M., Peleg, S.: Improving resolution by image registration. CVGIP 53(3), 231–239 (1991)
12. Jain, V., Seung, S.: Natural image denoising with convolutional networks. In: NIPS, pp. 769–776 (2008)
13. Jia, K., Wang, X., Tang, X.: Image transformation based on learning dictionaries across image spaces. TPAMI 35(2), 367–380 (2013)
14. Krizhevsky, A., Sutskever, I., Hinton, G.: ImageNet classification with deep convolutional neural networks. In: NIPS, pp. 1097–1105 (2012)
15. LeCun, Y., Boser, B., Denker, J.S., Henderson, D., Howard, R.E., Hubbard, W., Jackel, L.D.: Backpropagation applied to handwritten zip code recognition. Neural Computation, 541–551 (1989)
16. LeCun, Y., Bottou, L., Bengio, Y., Haffner, P.: Gradient-based learning applied to document recognition. Proceedings of the IEEE 86(11), 2278–2324 (1998)
17. Lee, H., Battle, A., Raina, R., Ng, A.Y.: Efficient sparse coding algorithms. In: NIPS, pp. 801–808 (2006)
18. Nair, V., Hinton, G.E.: Rectified linear units improve restricted Boltzmann machines. In: ICML, pp. 807–814 (2010)
19. Schuler, C.J., Burger, H.C., Harmeling, S., Scholkopf, B.: A machine learning approach for non-blind image deconvolution. In: CVPR, pp. 1067–1074 (2013)
20. Timofte, R., De Smet, V., Van Gool, L.: Anchored neighborhood regression for fast example-based super-resolution. In: ICCV, pp. 1920–1927 (2013)

21. Wang, Z., Bovik, A.C., Sheikh, H.R., Simoncelli, E.P.: Image quality assessment: from error visibility to structural similarity. TIP 13(4), 600–612 (2004)
22. Yang, C.Y., Yang, M.H.: Fast direct super-resolution by simple functions. In: ICCV, pp. 561–568 (2013)
23. Yang, J., Lin, Z., Cohen, S.: Fast image super-resolution based on in-place example regression. In: CVPR, pp. 1059–1066 (2013)
24. Yang, J., Wang, Z., Lin, Z., Cohen, S., Huang, T.: Coupled dictionary training for image super-resolution. TIP 21(8), 3467–3478 (2012)
25. Yang, J., Wright, J., Huang, T., Ma, Y.: Image super-resolution as sparse representation of raw image patches. In: CVPR, pp. 1–8 (2008)
26. Yang, J., Wright, J., Huang, T.S., Ma, Y.: Image super-resolution via sparse representation. TIP 19(11), 2861–2873 (2010)
27. Zeiler, M.D., Fergus, R.: Visualizing and understanding convolutional neural networks. Tech. rep. (2013)
28. Zeyde, R., Elad, M., Protter, M.: On single image scale-up using sparse-representations. In: Boissonnat, J.-D., Chenin, P., Cohen, A., Gout, C., Lyche, T., Mazure, M.-L., Schumaker, L. (eds.) Curves and Surfaces 2011. LNCS, vol. 6920, pp. 711–730. Springer, Heidelberg (2012)

Discriminative Indexing
for Probabilistic Image Patch Priors

Yan Wang[1,*], Sunghyun Cho[2,**], Jue Wang[2], and Shih-Fu Chang[1]

[1] Dept. of Electrical Engineering, Columbia University, USA
{yanwang,sfchang}@ee.columbia.edu
[2] Adobe Research, USA
sodomau@postech.ac.kr, juewang@adobe.com

Abstract. Newly emerged probabilistic image patch priors, such as Expected Patch Log-Likelihood (EPLL), have shown excellent performance on image restoration tasks, especially deconvolution, due to its rich expressiveness. However, its applicability is limited by the heavy computation involved in the associated optimization process. Inspired by the recent advances on using regression trees to index priors defined on a Conditional Random Field, we propose a novel discriminative indexing approach on patch-based priors to expedite the optimization process. Specifically, we propose an efficient tree indexing structure for EPLL, and overcome its training tractability challenges in high-dimensional spaces by utilizing special structures of the prior. Experimental results show that our approach accelerates state-of-the-art EPLL-based deconvolution methods by up to 40 times, with very little quality compromise.

1 Introduction

Image priors have been widely used in many ill-posed image restoration problems, such as deconvolution and denoising, to help resolve the ambiguity. One classic family of image priors is defined on image gradients, which assume that the magnitude of image gradients follows certain distributions such as exponential distributions [1], hyper Laplacian distributions [2], or a mixture of Gaussians [3]. These priors are computationally efficient using simple gradient filters and the Half-Quadratic Splitting optimization framework [2]. However, due to the extremely small spatial support of gradient filters, gradient priors cannot faithfully capture image structures.

To address this issue, image priors with larger spatial support have been proposed. One popular direction is to formulate the image restoration problem within a Conditional Random Field (CRF) framework, and associate nonadjacent pixels by connecting them in the field. Field of Experts (FoE) [4] as a typical example, constructs a CRF on all the pixels and define priors on the cliques of the CRF, with pixels within each local patch fully connected. While

---

* This work was done when Yan Wang worked as an intern at Adobe Research.
** Sunghyun Cho is now with Samsung Electronics.

D. Fleet et al. (Eds.): ECCV 2014, Part IV, LNCS 8692, pp. 200–214, 2014.
© Springer International Publishing Switzerland 2014

providing much larger spatial support than the gradient priors, the complicated field structure also suffers from the optimization tractability problem. To this end, approximate inference is often adopted, still resulting in slow speed.

While other challenges such as pixel saturation [5] and outliers [6] also exist in the image restoration field, the critical problem of optimization framework still remains open, and an emerging trend is to define probabilistic priors on image patches (i.e *probabilistic patch-based prior*), without explicit connections among pixels despite the natural pixel sharing between adjacent patches. An exemplar is Expected Patch Log-Likelihood (EPLL) [7], which shows state-of-the-art performance on image deblurring and competitive results on denoising and inpainting. These methods use Half-Quadratic Splitting for optimization which is more efficient than the inference of the CRFs. Unfortunately, they still require an excessive amount of computation which severely limits their practical usage. For example, the non-blind deconvolution method of Zoran and Weiss takes tens of minutes for an one megapixel image [7] on a decent PC. It becomes even worse for blind deconvolution, where the non-blind deconvolution component needs to be applied repeatedly and typically requires hours to finish [8].

Prior Indexing. The speed issue of the non-gradient priors is a well-known problem and various approaches have been proposed to address it. For the random-field-based priors, Jancsary *et al.* [9] restrict the potential functions of the CRF to be Gaussian functions for faster inference. To compensate for the performance drop from limiting forms of potential functions, regression trees are trained to discriminatively determine the mean and covariance of the potential functions, resulting in a Regression Tree Field formulation [10] that provides state-of-the-art performance for denoising and inpainting. This method can be interpreted as using random forests to pre-index a flexible prior defined on cliques in the random field. A similar idea of using pre-trained tree structures to efficiently construct a Regression Tree Field is also used in deblurring recently [11].

For the newly emerged probabilistic patch-based prior direction, however, little exploration has been done in expediting the associated optimization process, albeit such expedition can potentially benefit a series of practical applications and possibly reveal more insights about the patch-based priors. Inspired by the pre-indexing view of the Regression Tree Fields, we propose to pre-index the probabilistic patch-based priors to speed up their optimization. And we adopt EPLL as an example to demonstrate the novel prior indexing approach.

Challenges. However, indexing the patch-based priors is fairly challenging and the existing approaches are not readily extended to its unique settings. First, the image patches lie in a relatively high dimensional space. This makes straightforward lookup tables, as used in the hyper Laplacian prior [2], not able to work properly because of the huge memory consumption. Content-based hashing is known to be compact and fast, especially for high-dimensional data, but its accuracy is insufficient for image restoration tasks. Second, from the motivation of acceleration, we have a tight budget in the tree depth and the natural image patches have special structures different from the common distributions. Therefore as we will

show shortly, existing tree indexing structures as used in [9][11] also suffer from
the computational cost problem in our settings.

To address the challenges, we propose an efficient and compact tree indexing
structure, whose training algorithm is specifically tailored for the patch distributions of natural images for efficient computation. Specifically, we observe that
the EPLL prior can be well approximated with one single Gaussian in each optimization step, although such Gaussians may be different in each step. Therefore
we propose to train a tree structure to efficiently determine the mean and covariance of the Gaussian, with a training algorithm similar to decision tree but
using a more efficient candidate generation scheme.We take image deblurring as
the primary application because of the state-of-the-art performance EPLL shows
on it. Complexity analysis and experimental results show our indexing approach
leads to significant acceleration, while preserving the power of patch-based priors. Qualitative experiments also demonstrate the potential of proposed indexing
approach in deblurring real-life photos and image denoising.

Our main technical contributions include:

1. A novel framework of indexing patch-based natural image priors using decision trees (Section 3).
2. An efficient way of constructing the indexing tree by exploring the special
   structure of the parametric patch prior components (Section 4).

2   Observations and Our General Framework

2.1   Background and Notations

Before introducing our approach in more detail, we first provide a formal description of the problem. Image degradation is typically modeled as

$$\mathbf{y} = A\mathbf{x} + \mathbf{n}, \tag{1}$$

where $\mathbf{y}$, $\mathbf{x}$ are $\mathbf{n}$ are vectors representing an observed blurry image, its latent
image to be recovered, and noise. For denoising, $A = I$, an identity matrix. For
deconvolution, A is a convolution matrix.

The restored image $\hat{\mathbf{x}}$ can be estimated using Maximum A Posteriori (MAP)
estimation, with a Gaussian likelihood function and Gaussian noise:

$$\hat{\mathbf{x}} = \underset{\mathbf{x}}{\arg\min} \left\{ \frac{\lambda}{2} \|\mathbf{y} - A\mathbf{x}\|^2 - \log p(\mathbf{x}) \right\}, \tag{2}$$

where λ is a parameter to control the restoration strength.

GMM based Patch Prior proposed by Zoran and Weiss [7] is defined as:

$$p(\mathbf{x}) \propto \prod_i p(\mathbf{x}_i) = \prod_i \sum_{k=1}^{K} \pi_k \mathcal{N}(\mathbf{x}_i | \mu_k, \Sigma_k), \tag{3}$$

where i is a pixel index, and $\mathbf{x}_i$ is a patch centered at the i-th pixel. A Gaussian
Mixture Model (GMM) $\{\mu_k, \Sigma_k, \pi_k\}_{k=1}^{K}$ is learned from a large collection of

natural image patches, with k as the index of the Gaussian components, μ_k, Σ_k and π_k as the mean, covariance and weights of the Gaussians respectively.

Directly optimizing Equation (2) is difficult due to the coupling of the two terms. For efficient optimization, auxiliary variables $\{\mathbf{z}_i\}$ can be introduced as done in [7], reformulating Equation (2) with a popular half-quadratic scheme as:

$$\hat{\mathbf{x}} = \underset{\mathbf{x}}{\operatorname{argmin}} \left\{ \frac{\lambda}{2} \|\mathbf{y} - A\mathbf{x}\|^2 + \frac{\beta}{2} \sum_i \|\mathbf{z}_i - \mathbf{x}_i\|^2 - \sum_i \log p(\mathbf{z}_i) \right\}, \tag{4}$$

The optimization starts from a small value of β, and develops by fixing $\mathbf{x}$ to solve for $\mathbf{z}$ (the z-step), and fixing $\mathbf{z}$ to solve for $\mathbf{x}$ (the x-step) alternatingly, with increasing β values. When β becomes large enough, the optimal $\hat{x}$ and $\hat{z}$ will be nearly the same with negligible difference.

Bottleneck. While the x-step can be computed quickly as the first and second terms in Equation (4) are quadratic, the z-step is a much slower optimization process. With fixed $\mathbf{x}$, the z-step tries to solve the following problems for all i:

$$\hat{\mathbf{z}}_i = \underset{\mathbf{z}_i}{\operatorname{argmin}} \left\{ \frac{\beta}{2} \|\mathbf{z}_i - \mathbf{x}_i\|^2 - \log \sum_{k=1}^{K} \pi_k \mathcal{N}(\mathbf{z}_i|\mu_k, \Sigma_k) \right\}, \tag{5}$$

which is a complex and expensive non-linear optimization problem involving a lot of matrix multiplications. To alleviate the optimization difficulty, Zoran and Weiss [7] only use the Gaussian component with the largest conditional likelihood $p(k|P_i\mathbf{x})$ instead of all the components to do the optimization. More specifically, with the chosen Gaussian $\hat{k}_i$, they solve the following simplified problem:

$$\hat{\mathbf{z}}_i = \underset{\mathbf{z}_i}{\operatorname{argmin}} \left\{ \frac{\beta}{2} \|\mathbf{z}_i - \mathbf{x}_i\|^2 - \log \mathcal{N}(\mathbf{z}_i|\mu_{\hat{k}_i}, \Sigma_{\hat{k}_i}) \right\}. \tag{6}$$

However, this approximation still needs a huge amount of computation. Specifically, to find $\hat{k}_i$ for the i-th patch, we need to compute

$$\arg\max_k p(k|\mathbf{x}_i) \propto p(\mathbf{x}_i|k)p(k)$$

$$= \int_{\mathbf{z}_i} p(\mathbf{x}_i|\mathbf{z}_i)p(\mathbf{z}_i|k)p(k)$$

$$= \int_{\mathbf{z}_i} \mathcal{N}(\mathbf{x}_i|\mathbf{z}_i, \beta^{-1}I)\mathcal{N}(\mathbf{z}_i|\mu_k, \Sigma_k)\pi_k$$

$$= \pi_k \mathcal{N}(\mathbf{x}_i|\mu_k, \beta^{-1}I + \Sigma_k) \tag{7}$$

for *all the K Gaussian components*, resulting in $2K$ expensive matrix multiplication operations *for every patch*.

That is, the bottleneck of EPLL lies in using the naive linear scan to solve the optimization problem in Equation (7).

2.2 Observations and Our Approach

Given that Equation (7) is a discrete optimization problem for which efficient gradient-based methods cannot be applied, we propose to use a discriminative tree structure to output an approximate $\hat{k}_i$ directly based on a series of simple operations. This can also be interpreted from an information retrieval perspective, i.e. instead of an exhaustive scan on all the candidates, we use a series of quick tests to determine the rough area in the feature space that the patch lies in, and directly adopt the corresponding $\hat{k}_i$ as the approximate solution. Another interpretation from a machine learning perspective is, it is equivalent to treating Equation (7) as a classification problem and using a discriminative classifier to directly predict the most likely class.

One immediate concern one may have is that this is only an approximated solution, which may affect the quality of the restored image. However, our experiments show that with properly constructed indexing trees, we can achieve a high approximation accuracy in real applications. Furthermore, as we will show shortly, for the patches that are harder to be classified properly, on which error is more likely to be introduced, the value of final $\hat{k}_i$ actually has less effects on the quality of the restored patch $\hat{z}_i$. Therefore, such indexing on the patch-based priors can provide significant acceleration with very little quality compromise.

Now the question is: is it possible to build an efficient index for dominant Gaussian identification? Fortunately the patch-based prior has its special structures which allow us to further improve its efficiency. If we take a closer look at the GMM learned from natural image patches, most Gaussian components have very elongated shapes, i.e. Σ_k has only a few large eigenvectors, and they do not overlap each other much except for small parts [12]. This leads us to believe that it may be possible to use a hierarchy of simple classifiers, e.g. linear classifiers, to break the high-dimensional space to different subspaces that belong to different Gaussians. One subsequent concern is that since all the mixture components share the same center which is the origin as observed in [7], such overlap may confuse the linear classifiers. We found this is not a big deal because what the optimizer in Equation (6) does is to push the patch a bit to the center along the path determined by the dominant Gaussian, and it makes little difference when the patch is already close to the shared center even if a wrong Gaussian is identified and used for it.

Our Approach. We thus propose to build a decision tree based on linear classifiers to index the dominant Gaussian components in EPLL. However, traditional decision tree algorithms cannot be directly applied here because its random generation scheme of classifier candidates is extremely inefficient in a high-dimensional space. To make the training process more stable and efficient, we utilize the structure of the GMM and overcome the challenges of candidate classifier generation with a Gibbs sampling approach. A filter-based fast inference of Markov Random Field [13] is also employed to improve indexing accuracy.

3 Index-Assisted Patch Prior Optimization

In this section we assume the decision tree has already been built, and describe how to quickly find the most dominant component $\hat{k}_i$, which gives the largest $p(k|\mathbf{x}_i)$ for a given noisy patch $\mathbf{x}_i$. Specifically, from a given noisy patch $\mathbf{x}_i$, the search process goes from the root of the tree to one of the leaves. Each non-leaf node in the tree has a linear classifier $\mathbf{sgn}(\mathbf{w}^T\mathbf{x}+b)$, determining where $\mathbf{x}_i$ goes in the next level as follows:

$$\text{Next}(\mathbf{x}_i|\mathbf{w},b) = \begin{cases} \text{Left child} & \mathbf{w}^T\mathbf{x}_i + b \geq 0, \\ \text{Right child} & \mathbf{w}^T\mathbf{x}_i + b < 0. \end{cases} \tag{8}$$

While traversing the tree from its root to a leaf node, the space of patches is recursively bisected by the linear classifiers, ending with a polyhedron $L_i = \{\mathbf{x}|W_i\mathbf{x} + B_i \leq 0\}$, with W_i and B_i determined by the traversal path of $\mathbf{x}_i$. We store the expected probability of each Gaussian component dominating a random point within this polyhedron $\phi_{ik} = \mathbb{E}_{\mathbf{x}\in L_i}[\text{Prob}(\hat{\mathcal{N}}(\mathbf{x}) = \mathcal{N}_k)]$ in the leaf node, and then use it to approximate the probability of $\mathbf{x}_i$ having $\mathcal{N}_k$ as the dominant Gaussian.

Note that this tree testing process is very efficient. First, each linear classifier only requires a dot product operation. Second, only a few levels of tree nodes (e.g. 12 levels) are enough for reasonable accuracy in practice. This makes it even faster than the hashing-based approaches which typically require more than 20 bits for reasonable accuracy.

Refinement Using MRFs. To find the dominant Gaussian $\hat{k}_i$ for a given patch $\mathbf{x}_i$, instead of the winner-take-all selection of k with the largest ϕ_{ik}, which will introduce possibly large errors, we use a discrete Markov Random Field (MRF) to infer the final $\hat{k}_i$s, with the enforcement on the spatial consistency in terms of the dominant Gaussians. Specifically, the potential function of the MRF is defined as:

$$\Psi(\{\hat{k}_i\}) = \lambda_1 \sum_i \Psi_1(\hat{k}_i) + \lambda_2 \sum_{\text{Neighbors } i,j} \Psi_2(\hat{k}_i, \hat{k}_j) \tag{9}$$

where $\Psi_1(\hat{k}_i) = -\phi_{i\hat{k}_i}$, and $\Psi_2(\hat{k}_i, \hat{k}_j)$ is defined as:

$$\Psi_2(\hat{k}_i, \hat{k}_j) = \begin{cases} 0 & \text{if } \hat{k}_i = \hat{k}_j \\ |I_i - I_j|^2 & \text{otherwise} \end{cases}. \tag{10}$$

I_i and I_j are the average intensities of the patches $\mathbf{x}_i$ and $\mathbf{x}_j$, respectively. Equation (9) is minimized to find the refined dominant Gaussians $\{\hat{k}_i\}$ for all the patches, where we adopt an approximation approach, cost-volume filtering [13]. Similarly to Loopy Belief Propagation, the cost-volume filters update the marginal distribution stored in each node. However, instead of message collection and passing, such updates are performed with the guided filter [14], which is accelerated by integral images and extremely fast. More specifically, K "images" with intensities as ϕ_{ik} are first collected, and the guided filter is applied on every "image", with the smoothed input from the x-step as the guidance.

Wiener Filtering. Once the dominant mixture component $\hat{k}_i$ for each patch $\mathbf{x}_i$ is found, it is fed to the optimizer for Equation (6), which has a close form solution as the Wiener filter:

$$\hat{\mathbf{z}}_i = (\Sigma_{\hat{k}_i} + \sigma^2 I)^{-1}(\Sigma_{\hat{k}_i}\mathbf{x}_i + \sigma^2 I \mu_{\hat{k}_i}). \tag{11}$$

Time Complexity. Given an index tree with depth D for a K-component GMM defined on $n \times n$ patches, since on each level we only need to apply one dot product, the tree traversal for each patch requires $O(n^2 D)$ operations. The cost-volume filtering needs $O(K)$ time for each patch. Therefore the overall time complexity is $O(mn^2 D + mK)$ for an image with m patches, with a very small coefficient for $O(K)$, which is from the guided filter. In contrast, the original EPLL needs $O(mn^4 K)$ time.

4   Prior Index Construction

Given an observed patch $\mathbf{x}$, we expect the trained index tree to output the k which approximately maximizes $p(k|\mathbf{x})$ (Equation (7)). As $p(k|\mathbf{x})$ also depends on β, which is the pre-defined parameter for the alternating optimization, we build different index trees with respect to different values of β , with the algorithm introduced in this section.

Although the testing phase of our index tree is similar to a decision tree, the training algorithm of decision trees cannot be directly applied here. In the decision tree training algorithm, given a set of training examples, many *classifier candidates* are *randomly* generated, each of which will divide the training examples into two partitions. And then the best classifier with the largest *information gain* computed from the partitions will be selected and stored in the node. This can be viewed as a naive optimizer randomly searching for the classifier with the largest information gain. When incorporated with linear classifiers, this works fine on low-dimension data. However, with the increase of the dimensionality, the feasible space to search is expanding much faster than the small space where the good solutions lie. This leads to the failure of the naive random search optimizer when the dimensionality of $\mathbf{x}$ is not trivially small, *i.e.* a huge number of trials are required before it reaches the optimal or even near-optimal solutions.

To demonstrate such inefficiency of the random search scheme, we collect two million 8×8 training patches with ground truth labels of the dominant Gaussian. The traditional decision tree training algorithm is applied on the dataset, with 1000 candidates randomly generated for every node. It takes 48 hours to obtain a 12-level tree on a Core i7 3.0GHz desktop computer with a MATLAB implementation, and we plot the average entropy of each level as the green curve in Figure 1. From the figure, we can see that even after 12 levels, the average entropy is still close to 0.6, indicating the distributions in the leaf nodes are still not far away from uniform and contains not much information. Given we have a high expectation on the testing speed thus a tight budget on the tree depth, decision tree training algorithm actually does not fit our problem settings.

To mitigate this challenge, we exploit the special structure of the GMM learned from natural image patches, and formulate the candidate classifier generation as an optimization problem coupled with random sampling. The recursive greedy training framework of the decision tree is still used in our approach due to its simplicity and robustness. In the following paragraphs, we will discuss each step of our training process in more detail.

Training Data Generation. To train an index tree for a given β, we collect a set of noisy patches $\{\mathbf{x}\}$ from the output of the x-steps of EPLL [7] as the X for training because that is the input our index will face in real applications. The ground truth labels Y are then determined with Equation (7). While there is no theoretical clue about how many training examples are "enough", we will revisit this step in Section 5 for the practical concern of the size of the training dataset.

Candidate Classifier Generation. Given a set of noisy patches X and the ground truth labels Y, the problem we are facing is to find a linear classifier $\mathbf{sgn}(\hat{\mathbf{w}}^T\mathbf{x} + \hat{b})$ so that the information gain is maximized:

$$\hat{\mathbf{w}}, \hat{b} = \underset{\mathbf{w},b}{\operatorname{argmax}} E(Y) - \frac{|Y_+|}{|Y|} E(Y_+) - \frac{|Y_-|}{|Y|} E(Y_-), \tag{12}$$

in which $E(\cdot)$ is the entropy function, and Y_+ and Y_- are the positive and negative partitions divided by the classifier:

$$Y_+ = \{y_i | \mathbf{w}^T\mathbf{x}_i + b \geq 0, \ \forall i\}, \quad \text{and}$$
$$Y_- = \{y_i | \mathbf{w}^T\mathbf{x}_i + b < 0, \ \forall i\}. \tag{13}$$

It has been shown that naive random search does not work for high dimensional $\mathbf{x}$. Given this problem is non-differentiable with the discrete training examples, we do not use classical continuous optimization methods such as gradient descent or BFGS. Instead, we adopt a Gibbs sampling approach, while some heuristics are introduced to restrict the space from which the candidates are generated.

There are two important observations of the learned GMM. First, for most components, only a few strongest eigenvectors of the covariance matrix take the most energy of the Gaussian. This indicates it is possible to dramatically reduce the computation complexity by only doing sampling based on these a few strong *principal directions*, which are the eigenvectors of the Gaussians' covariance matrices. Second, all of the Gaussian components share the same center which is the origin, as observed in [7]. This can be explained with the inherent symmetry of the natural image patches.

These two properties inspire us a simple heuristic to generate a classifier candidate for two principal directions from two Gaussians. Take Figure 2 for an example, if two 2-D Gaussians are given with the two principal directions $\mathbf{e}_1$ and $\mathbf{e}_2$ marked as red, a reasonable guess of the decision (hyper)plane would be

$$\mathbf{w} = \lambda_1 \mathbf{e}_1 - \lambda_2 \mathbf{e}_2, \tag{14}$$

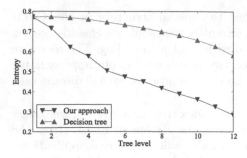

Fig. 1. Comparison of how the entropy decreases in different levels of the index tree, with different training schemes. The traditional decision tree training algorithm is plotted in green, with the proposed approach in blue.

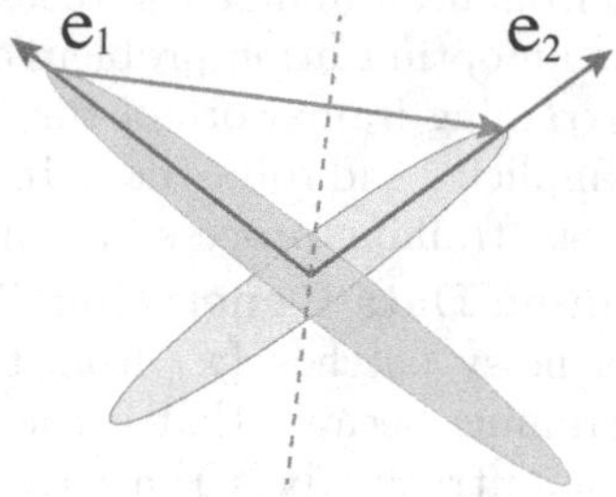

Fig. 2. A toy example of the proposed heuristic to generate a candidate classifier from two given principal directions e_1, e_2. The dashed green line shows the generated classifier when $b = 0$, with the green arrow as its normal vector.

in which λ_1, λ_2 are the corresponding eigenvalues of e_1, e_2, as the green arrow shows. Note $-e_1$ and $-e_2$ are also the principal directions. Therefore this scheme will actually generate four $\mathbf{w}$-s.[1]

With this candidate generation scheme, the problem turns to how to sample the principal directions such that we can partition the training data "effectively". With the expectation of minimizing the tree depth with a target accuracy, we add a balance factor to the objective function in Equation (12). More specifically, we expect the positive and negative examples predicted by the classifier $\mathbf{sgn}(\hat{\mathbf{w}}^T \mathbf{x} + \hat{b})$ is roughly the same in number. Given this is hard to optimize, we further relax it to expect the average projection values to be as small as possible. Then the objective function becomes,

$$E(Y) - \frac{|Y_+|}{|Y|}E(Y_+) - \frac{|Y_-|}{|Y|}E(Y_-) - \gamma \left| \sum_{\mathbf{x}} \left(\mathbf{w}^T \mathbf{x} + b \right) \right|, \qquad (15)$$

s.t. $\|\mathbf{w}\|^2 = 1$ generated from Equation (14).

Here $\gamma = 0.5$ is a parameter controlling the strength of the balance factor.

Note both the terms in Equation (15), the information gain and the balance factor, would only change when some example $\mathbf{x}_i$ changes its predicted label. That is, it will change faster if the $\mathbf{w}$ swipes along some high-density area with more training examples, while slower in the low-density areas. Therefore it is reasonable to sample more $\mathbf{w}$-s from the regions with low GMM probabilistic densities, which are the analogy to stationary points in the continuous case. More specifically, we put more priority in sampling the decision boundaries between

---

[1] One classifier may not be able to distinguish the two Gaussians shown in Figure 2. But a simple two-level decision trump from the four candidate classifiers would have enough discrimination power.

Algorithm 1. Index construction for patch priors.

Input: the patch prior $\{\pi_k, \mu_k, \Sigma_k\}_{k=1}^K$, training examples X, the ground truth labels Y, and the max tree depth D

Output: a decision tree T based on linear classifiers

1 **if** $D = 0$ **then**
2 | **return** a leaf node with label distribution of Y.
3 **end**
4 **foreach** $1 \leq I \leq I_{max}$ **do**
5 | Sample two Gaussians k_1, k_2 without replacement with probability $p(k) = \pi_k$.
6 | Given each Gaussian k from k_1, k_2 , sample one eigenvector from the eigenvectors of the covariance matrix $\{e_{ki}\}$ with probability $p(i|k) = \lambda_{ki}$, where λ_{ki} are the corresponding eigenvalues.
7 | Use Equation (14) to generate w-s given the two eigenvectors e_1, e_2.
8 | Sample b from $\mathcal{N}(0, 1)$.
9 **end**
10 Collect all the candidate w and b, store the one maximizing Equation (15) in the tree node T.
11 Train the left and right child of T with $(D - 1)$ tree depth and Y_+, Y_- as training data, which are defined in Equation (13).
12 **return** T.

---

two principal directions with large eigenvalues. That is, given the weights of the Gaussians $\{\pi_k\}$, we first sample two Gaussians with probability $p(k) = \pi_k$, and then sample one principal direction from the eigenvectors of the covariance matrix of each Gaussian $\{e_{ki}\}$ with corresponding eigenvalues as the probability $p(i|k) = \lambda_{ki}$. After that, Equation (14) is applied on the principal directions to obtain the final w-s, which forms a Gibbs sampling process. Since all the Gaussians share the same center as the origin, we use $\mathcal{N}(0, 1)$ to sample the b-s.

A complete algorithm is illustrated in Algorithm 1. We apply the proposed approach to the same data in the experiment shown in Figure 1, and obtain much better training efficiency, with average entropy below 0.3 in the 12th level, which is plotted as the blue curve in Figure 1. This proves the effectiveness of our training scheme, and in the next section, we will do more justification on our approach, followed by the evaluations on actual applications.

5 Experiments

We conduct a series of experiments to quantitatively verify (1) how well the discriminative prior indexing performs for dominant Gaussian identification; and (2) how well the proposed approach performs on real applications in terms of quality and speed. In this section we first quantitatively evaluate the proposed method in non-blind image deblurring, and then justify its components, especially on the performance of domainant Gaussian identification. Other applications including deblurring real-life photos and denoising are also demonstrated.

5.1   Evaluation on Non-blind Image Deblurring

Dataset and Evaluation Protocol. We use the standard benchmark [15], which contains 48 blurry photos and 12 motion kernels collected from real life for the evaluation. Different deblurring approaches are applied on the input images, and average PSNRs among all the kernels on each image are reported as quantitative measurements. We compare our deblurring approach with tree-based indexing with several state-of-the-art algorithms, including Discriminative non-blind deblurring [11] (referred as Schmidt), ℓ_0 based deblurring [16] (referred as Xu), and Cho's fast deblurring [17] (referred as Cho).

Implementation Details. We collect two million patches from 100 training images from the Berkeley Segmentation Dataset [18], convolve them with one blur kernel different from all the testing kernels, and add Gaussian noise to obtain the training data. Then an index tree with 12 levels is trained for each β in Half-Quadratic Splitting is trained using Algorithm 1 for our deblurring approach. As observed in [12], increasing the component number of the GMM hardly improves EPLL's performance after it reaches 10. Subsequently we adopt a 10-component GMM as the prior for both our approach and the EPLL baseline.

We implement our algorithm in MATLAB, with the core components such as the index tree testing written in C++. We further integrate Fast Fourier Transform to accelerate the x-step [1], resulting in a comprehensive fast non-blind deblurring algorithm, whose running time is adopted as the time of our approach. All the running time is measured on a desktop computer with a Core i7 3.0GHz CPU.

Results and Discussions. The average PSNRs of all approaches are shown in Table 1. Ours_C shows our PSNRs based on the kernels estimated from Cho's approach [17], and Ours_X is based on Xu's kernel [16]. We can see our non-blind deblurring component improves the performance of both Cho's and Xu's approaches in most cases. Although our PSNR is slightly worse than Schmidt's approach [11], the running time per each RGB image is 2 minites in average, which is about 20 times faster than [11][2] and 40 times faster than EPLL. Also note that this is achieved when the blur kernel for index construction is dramatically different from the blur kernels used in the test images. It suggests that our index construction is not sensitive to the blur kernel used for training.

5.2   Evaluation on Prior Indexing and Parameter Tuning

We also evaluate the performance of our prior indexing in terms of component identification accuracy. With the same training data and training algorithm in Section 5.1, we vary the depth of the decision trees to explore how it affects the indexing performance. The classification accuracy of the dominant Gaussian is calculated with ground truth from brute-force search, and is averaged on all the stages and all the test images as the evaluation protocol.

---

[2] The authors of [11] didn't report the running time on [15], but on smaller images. We project their running time to [15] based on the (linear) time complexity on resolution.

Table 1. Average PSNRs of each testing image on non-blind deblurring. $Ours_C$ and $Ours_X$ indicate our non-blind deblurring approach based on kernels estimated from Cho and Xu.

Img	1	2	3	4
Cho [17]	30.61	26.03	31.32	27.98
Xu [16]	31.64	26.64	31.45	28.42
Schmidt [11]	32.05	26.99	32.13	28.90
$Ours_C$	30.75	26.12	32.28	28.00
$Ours_X$	31.69	26.68	32.31	28.65

Table 2. Quantitative evaluation results on image denoising. The PSNR in dB is shown for each baseline and noise level (σ) setting. The average running time (in seconds) is shown in the rightmost column.

σ	0.1	0.25	0.5	1.0	Time
BM3D[19]	30.33	26.92	23.91	17.85	4.4
$BM3D_S$ [20]	30.46	26.62	23.22	19.73	782
$K\text{-}SVD_G$ [21]	29.39	25.57	22.68	19.31	60.1
$K\text{-}SVD_I$ [21]	29.76	25.68	22.70	19.38	177.7
EPLL [7]	29.57	26.13	23.44	20.62	61.7
Our approach	29.47	26.08	23.49	20.62	4.5

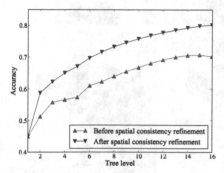

(a) Component identification accuracy along with different tree depth.

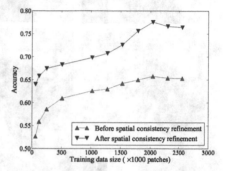

(b) Component identification accuracy along with training data size.

Fig. 3. Quantitative evaluation on the dominant Gaussian identification

The results with different tree depth settings are plotted in Figure 3(a), where we also show the classification accuracy before and after the spatial consistency refinement step. Firstly, it shows that the identification accuracy reaches 80% with 16 levels of tree nodes. Given we have 10 components in the GMM, this proves that the tree index does a reasonable job in approximating the brute-force search with merely a few dot product operations. Considering the trade-off between quality and efficiency, we use 12 level trees in all the other experiments. In addition, it also suggests that the cost-volume based MRF inference improves the identification accuracy by 10% consistently over the raw identification results. This verifies our observation on the spatial coherence of the distributions of dominant Gaussians.

Training Data Collection. With the same training and testing image sets, we also explore how many training patches are required for achieving reasonable quality of dominant Gaussian identification. Figure 3(b) plots the identification accuracy against different training data sizes. It suggests that with a 12-level tree, the accuracy saturates after the training dataset reaches two million patches.

Input photo and kernel   EPLL [5]   Our approach

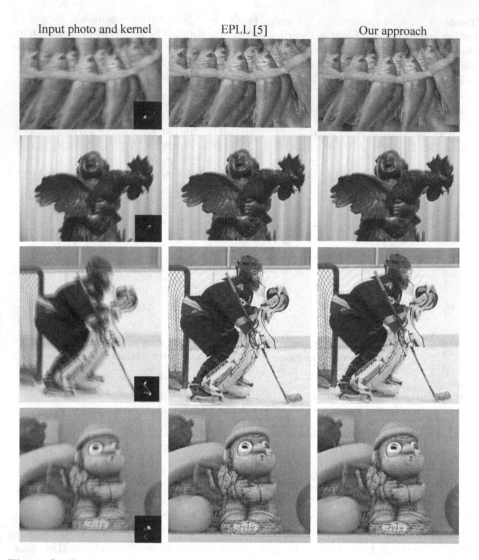

Fig. 4. Qualitative evaluation on deblurring high-resolution photos from real life. The input with the motion kernel estimated with [17], the deblurring results of EPLL and the proposed approach are shown from left to right.

We thus use this setting for all the experiments, including the non-blind image deblurring, deblurring high-reslution photos and image deblurring.

5.3   Deblurring High-Resolution Photos from Real Life

To demonstrate the capability to handle real-life data of our deblurring approach, we collect some blurred photos taken from real life, run [17]'s approach to estimate a blur kernel, and then apply the proposed algorithm on the R, G, B channels seperately. While all the collected photos have resolution larger than 800×800, EPLL [7] needs more than half an hour to deblur each image, and therefore is not practical for deblurring applications in real life. On the other hand, our algorithm generally outputs the result within 3 minutes. Figure 4 shows a comparison between the results from our approach and EPLL. From the figure, we can see that the proposed approach is able to achieve deblurring results with nearly unnoticable difference from the original patch-based approaches.

5.4   Evaluation on Image Denoising

To demonstrate the potential of the proposed approach in other low-level vision applications, we also report the performance on denoising. We use the standard benchmark in denoising, eight 512×512 gray-scale standard test images *Babara, Boat, Cameraman, Hill, House, Lena, Man* and *Peppers* for this evaluation. Gaussian noise with standard variance as 0.1, 0.25, 0.5 and 1 is added to the original images respectively as the noisy inputs. Average PSNR as well as the running time for all the images are measured for different noise levels. We compare our approach with the state-of-the-art denoising algorithms BM3D[19], BM3D-SAPCA[20] (referred as $BM3D_S$), K-SVD[21] with global dictionary (referred as K-SVD$_G$) and learned dictionary from the noisy image (referred as K-SVD$_I$), and EPLL[7], with the authors' implementations and recommended parameters. The quantitative results are reported in Table 2. The results show that the performance of EPLL is slightly worse than BM3D and BM3D-SAPCA, which is reasonable given that the latter two are specially designed for denoising. Our approach achieves very similar performance to EPLL, with < 0.1dB PSNR drop on average, but is much faster than EPLL and other denoising methods except BM3D. We further confirmed that there are no noticeable differences between our and EPLL's results.

6   Conclusion

We have presented an indexing method to improve the efficiency of applying patch-based image priors to image restoration tasks. We show that directly applying the traditional decision tree training algorithm is not optimal in our case due to the high dimensionality of the patch data. We therefore propose a training algorithm with a novel classifier candidate generation scheme utilizing the structure of the patch prior. Experimental results show that our approach achieves up to 40 times acceleration, and at the same time comparable high quality results with the original EPLL approach. The performance is also competitive with other state-of-the-art deconvolution algorithms.

There are also several interesting directions for future exploration, such as how to analytically construct the index solely from the prior model and how to apply the index to other vision problems.

References

1. Yang, J., Zhang, Y., Yin, W.: An efficient TVL1 algorithm for deblurring multichannel images corrupted by impulsive noise. Journal on Scientific Computing 31(4) (2009)
2. Krishnan, D., Fergus, R.: Fast image deconvolution using hyper-laplacian priors. In: NIPS (2009)
3. Fergus, R., Singh, B., Hertzmann, A., Roweis, S., Freeman, W.T.: Removing camera shake from a single photograph. In: ToG (SIGGRAPH) (2006)
4. Roth, S., Blacky, M.: Fields of experts. IJCV 82(2), 205–229 (2009)
5. Whyte, O., Sivic, J., Zisserman, A.: Deblurring shaken and partially saturated images. In: Proceedings of the IEEE Workshop on Color and Photometry in Computer Vision, with ICCV 2011 (2011)
6. Cho, S., Wang, J., Lee, S.: Handling outliers in non-blind image deconvolution. In: ICCV (November 2011)
7. Zoran, D., Weiss, Y.: From learning models of natural image patches to whole image restoration. In: ICCV (2011)
8. Sun, L., Cho, S., Wang, J., Hays, J.: Edge-based blur kernel estimation using patch priors. In: ICCP (2013)
9. Jancsary, J., Nowozin, S., Rother, C.: Loss-specific training of non-parametric image restoration models: A new state of the art. In: Fitzgibbon, A., Lazebnik, S., Perona, P., Sato, Y., Schmid, C. (eds.) ECCV 2012, Part VII. LNCS, vol. 7578, pp. 112–125. Springer, Heidelberg (2012)
10. Jancsary, J., Nowozin, S., Sharp, T., Rother, C.: Regression Tree Fields - an Efficient, Non-Parametric Approach to Image Labeling Problems. In: CVPR (2012)
11. Schmidt, U., Rother, C., Nowozin, S., Jancsary, J., Roth, S.: Discriminative non-blind deblurring. In: CVPR (2013)
12. Zoran, D., Weiss, Y.: Natural images, gaussian mixtures and dead leaves. In: NIPS (2012)
13. Rhemann, C., Hosni, A., Bleyer, M., Rother, C., Gelautz, M.: Fast cost-volume filtering for visual correspondence and beyond. In: CVPR (2011)
14. He, K., Sun, J., Tang, X.: Guided image filtering. In: Daniilidis, K., Maragos, P., Paragios, N. (eds.) ECCV 2010, Part I. LNCS, vol. 6311, pp. 1–14. Springer, Heidelberg (2010)
15. Köhler, R., Hirsch, M., Mohler, B., Schölkopf, B., Harmeling, S.: Recording and playback of camera shake: benchmarking blind deconvolution with a real-world database. In: Fitzgibbon, A., Lazebnik, S., Perona, P., Sato, Y., Schmid, C. (eds.) ECCV 2012, Part VII. LNCS, vol. 7578, pp. 27–40. Springer, Heidelberg (2012)
16. Xu, L., Zheng, S., Jia, J.: Unnatural l0 sparse representation for natural image deblurring. In: CVPR (June 2013)
17. Cho, S., Lee, S.: Fast motion deblurring. ToG (SIGGRAPH ASIA) 28(5) (2009)
18. Martin, D., Fowlkes, C., Tal, D., Malik, J.: A database of human segmented natural images and its application to evaluating segmentation algorithms and measuring ecological statistics. In: ICCV (2001)
19. Dabov, K., Foi, A., Katkovnik, V., Egiazarian, K.: Image denoising by sparse 3D transform-domain collaborative filtering. TIP (8) (August 2007)
20. Dabov, K., Foi, A., Katkovnik, V., Egiazarian, K.: BM3D image denoising with shape-adaptive principal component analysis. In: SPARS (2009)
21. Elad, M., Aharon, M.: Image denoising via sparse and redundant representations over learned dictionaries. TIP 15(12), 3736–3745 (2006)

Modeling Video Dynamics
with Deep Dynencoder

Xing Yan, Hong Chang, Shiguang Shan, and Xilin Chen

Key Lab of Intelligent Information Processing of Chinese Academy of Sciences (CAS),
Institute of Computing Technology, CAS, Beijing, 100190, China
{xing.yan,hong.chang,shiguang.shan,xilin.chen}@vipl.ict.ac.cn

Abstract. Videos always exhibit various pattern motions, which can
be modeled according to dynamics between adjacent frames. Previous
methods based on linear dynamic system can model dynamic textures
but have limited capacity of representing sophisticated nonlinear dynamics. Inspired by the nonlinear expression power of deep autoencoders, we
propose a novel model named dynencoder which has an autoencoder at
the bottom and a variant of it at the top (named as dynpredictor). It
generates hidden states from raw pixel inputs via the autoencoder and
then encodes the dynamic of state transition over time via the dynpredictor. Deep dynencoder can be constructed by proper stacking strategy
and trained by layer-wise pre-training and joint fine-tuning. Experiments
verify that our model can describe sophisticated video dynamics and synthesize endless video texture sequences with high visual quality. We also
design classification and clustering methods based on our model and
demonstrate the efficacy of them on traffic scene classification and motion segmentation. ...

Keywords: Video Dynamics, Deep Model, Autoencoder, Time Series,
Dynamic Textures.

1 Introduction

Video dynamics, representing as various object motions, widely exist in real-
world video data, e.g., regular rigid motion like moving escalator and windmill,
chaotic motion like smoke and water waves, sophisticated motion caused by camera panning or zooming, etc. Modeling video dynamics is challenging but very
important for subsequent vision tasks, such as dynamic texture (DT) synthesis,
video classification, motion segmentation and so on.

One popular way to address this challenge is via linear dynamic system (LDS),
a probabilistic generative model defined over space and time, which estimates
hidden states using Principal Component Analysis (PCA) and describes their
trajectory as time evolves. LDS can model videos with smooth motions and
has been applied to computer vision tasks such as DT synthesis [9], video segmentation [10][7] and video classification [18][5][17]. However, LDS has obvious
disadvantages due to its simplistic linearity so that many variants have been

D. Fleet et al. (Eds.): ECCV 2014, Part IV, LNCS 8692, pp. 215–230, 2014.

proposed. To overcome visible decay and discontinuities of sequences synthesized by LDS, closed-loop LDS (CLDS) [28] is proposed. However, the model is still linear and may fail to model some discontinuous rigid motions. Kernel-DT model is proposed in [6], where the nonlinear observation function is learned using kernel-PCA while the hidden states change linearly. kernel-DT can capture more motions such as camera panning, but may have the same weaknesses as LDS due to the linear state transition. By treating nonlinear DT as temporally multiple linear DTs, piecewise linear dynamic systems (PLDS) [27] automatically divides the video sequence and models each segment with an LDS. It can tackle videos with camera switching. But piecewise linearity is too different from nonlinearity. In short, above LDS-based approaches try to model video dynamics, but do have weaknesses more or less.

Other ways to model video dynamics for texture synthesis is via nonparametric methods. Masiero and Chiuso [15] propose to estimate the state distribution and generate samples from the implicit model. Liu et al. [13] assume the spectral parameters of image sequences lie on a low-dimensional manifold and use a mixture of linear subspaces to model it. In [2], the observation data are embedded into a higher dimensional phase space, where the predictions computed through kernel regression. Unlike LDS-based models, these nonparametric methods have no application reported such as video classification.

Once each video has been modeled by a dynamic system, we can not only synthesize dynamic textures, but also perform video classification by defining distance or kernel between pair of models. Some researchers [18][6] use the Martin distance [14] between two LDSs (or the kernel version) and achieve good performance in DT recognition. They also use probabilistic kernel based on the Kullback-Leibler divergence [5] for traffic scene classification. With proper distance definition, video clustering and segmentation can be done as well [10].

Deep learning methods have recently been proposed with notable successes in some areas including computer vision, beating the state-of-the-art [3]. Deep models, such as Deep Belief Network and stacked autoencoders, have much more expressive power than traditional shallow models and can be efficiently trained with layer-wise pre-training and fine-tuning [3][11]. Stacked autoencoders have been successfully used as a robust feature extractor [24]. Besides, they can also be used to model complex relationships between variables due to the composition of several levels of nonlinearity [24]. For example, Xie et al. [26] model relationship between noisy and clean images using stacked denoising autoencoders. Their method achieves state-of-the-art performance in image denoising and inpainting tasks. However, deep autoencoders are rarely used to model time series data, although there have been some works on using variants of Restricted Boltzmann Machine (RBM) for specific time series data, i.e., human motion [23][22]. Some other deep models address video data with convolutional learning of spatio-temporal features [21][12].

In this paper, we propose a novel hierarchical model named deep dynencoder to model video dynamics, i.e., the relationship between all pairs of adjacent frames in an image sequence. We stack an ordinary autoencoder and a variant

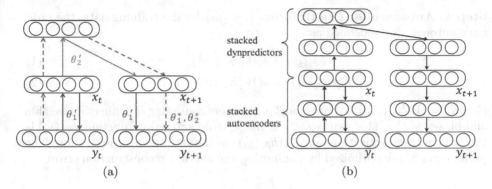

Fig. 1. Model architecture: (a) the basic dynencoder (the parameters θ_1' and θ_2' are obtained from layer-wise pre-training, while the red dashed arrows represent the fine-tuning process of the model parameters); (b) deep dynencoder

of it to form a basic dynencoder, which can be further deepened through proper stacking strategy. After layer-wise pre-training and fine-tuning, the model can capture various video dynamics including regular rigid motions, chaotic motions and camera motions such as panning or zooming. Given a DT sequence for training and an initial frame, our model can synthesize an endless DT sequence with impressive high visual quality. Similar with [6][18][10], we define a distance measure between two videos based on our model and apply it to traffic scene classification and motion segmentation. The performances of classification and segmentation are close to or higher than the state-of-the-art.

To summarize, our contributions are threefold. First, we propose deep dynencoder for modeling video dynamics and effective algorithm for training. Second, our method performs outstandingly in DT synthesis, showing its ability of describing sophisticated video dynamics. Third, we associate our model with a distance measure definition and demonstrate its usefulness on vision tasks including classification and segmentation.

2   Model Description

In this section, we first give the formulation and training method of the basic dynencoder for video modeling. Then we introduce how to construct the deep dynencoder with a stacking strategy. Notice that a video sequence is denoted by $Y = \{y_t\}_{t=1}^{T}$, where $y_t \in \mathbb{R}^m$ contains raw pixel values of the frame at time t.

2.1   Dynencoder

Dynencoder is a three-layer network constructed by stacking a variant of autoencoder on top of an ordinary one, as shown in Figure 1(a). For a video sequence, the autoencoder at the bottom generates hidden states (or compresses the input) from raw frames, while its variant (we name it *dynpredictor*) at the top encodes the dynamic of the hidden states and predicts new states.

Step 1. Autoencoder Pre-training. Let $\{y_t\}$ be the training data, the ordinary autoencoder is defined as:

$$h_{\theta_1}(y_t) = s(W_1^1 y_t + b_1^1),\tag{1}$$

$$f_{\theta_1}(h_{\theta_1}(y_t)) = s(W_2^1 h_{\theta_1}(y_t) + b_2^1).\tag{2}$$

Here $\theta_1 = \{W_1^1, b_1^1, W_2^1, b_2^1\}$ are model parameters consisting of connection weights and biases. $s(x) = (1 + \exp(-x))^{-1}$ is the sigmoid activation function. $h_{\theta_1}(y_t)$ is the hidden layer activation and $f_{\theta_1}(h_{\theta_1}(y_t))$ is the output layer activation. The parameters θ_1 are optimized by minimizing the average reconstruction error:

$$\theta_1' = \arg\min_{\theta_1} \frac{1}{T} \sum_{t=1}^{T} \|f_{\theta_1}(h_{\theta_1}(y_t)) - y_t\|_2^2.\tag{3}$$

It reveals that the hidden layer activation $h_{\theta_1}(y_t)$ can be seen as a compressed representation of y_t, as well as the hidden state of y_t.

Step 2. Dynpredictor Pre-training. After training the autoencoder, we can take hidden layer activations $\{h_{\theta_1}(y_t)\}$ as the input of a dynpredictor and train it. This means that the dynpredictor is put on the top of the autoencoder, as shown in Figure 1(a). Let $x_t = h_{\theta_1}(y_t)$, the layer activations of dynpredictor are computed similarly:

$$h_{\theta_2}(x_t) = s(W_1^2 x_t + b_1^2),\tag{4}$$

$$f_{\theta_2}(h_{\theta_2}(x_t)) = s(W_2^2 h_{\theta_2}(x_t) + b_2^2).\tag{5}$$

Here $\theta_2 = \{W_1^2, b_1^2, W_2^2, b_2^2\}$ are model parameters consisting of connection weights and biases. $h_{\theta_2}(x_t)$ and $f_{\theta_2}(h_{\theta_2}(x_t))$ are the hidden and output layer activations respectively. Note that the dynpredictor is different from autoencoder in that we optimize the parameters θ_2 by minimizing the following error:

$$\theta_2' = \arg\min_{\theta_2} \frac{1}{T-1} \sum_{t=1}^{T-1} \|f_{\theta_2}(h_{\theta_2}(x_t)) - x_{t+1}\|_2^2.\tag{6}$$

That is, dynpredictor is not used for reconstructing the input, but predicting the input at next time step.

After that, the output layer activations $\{f_{\theta_2}(h_{\theta_2}(x_t))\}$ are mapped back to the output layer of the autoencoder below. Therefore, when given y_t, the calculation process of dynencoder is:

$$F(y_t) = f_{\theta_1}(f_{\theta_2}(h_{\theta_2}(h_{\theta_1}(y_t)))).\tag{7}$$

Step 3. Joint Fine-tunning. The above two steps can be considered as the layer-wise pre-training strategy in deep learning. After pre-training with $\{y_t\}$, it is obvious that the dynencoder with parameters $\{\theta_1', \theta_2'\}$ tends to output video frame of the next time step when given the current one, i.e., $F(y_t) \approx y_{t+1}$. Similar to deep learning, fine-tuning can be performed to make the prediction more accurate. With initialized parameters $\{\theta'_1, \theta'_2\}$ and target sequence $\{y_{t+1}\}$, we fine-tune the parameters as:

$$\{\theta_1^\star, \theta_2^\star\} = \arg \min_{\{\theta_1, \theta_2\}} \frac{1}{T-1} \sum_{t=1}^{T-1} \|F(y_t) - y_{t+1}\|_2^2. \tag{8}$$

After joint fine-tuning, the dynencoder represents the mapping $y_t \to y_{t+1}$ more precisely. Actually, it can model the underlying relationship between temporally adjacent two inputs and encode the video dynamic into parameters. More specifically, the dynencoder maps the observation data to hidden states (and vice versa) via autoencoder and describes the dynamic of hidden states via dynpredictor. The mapping line is: $y_t \to x_t \to x_{t+1} \to y_{t+1}$. So given an initial frame, a trained dynencoder can generate an endless video of the same dynamic.

2.2   Deep Dynencoder

Like deep autoencoders, we can also stack many building blocks to get deep dynencoder. In the architecture of dynencoder, there are two kinds of building blocks: autoencoder and dynpredictor. So, the model can be deepened by adding more autoencoders at the bottom and more dynpredictors on the top, as shown in Figure 1(b). If we have stacked M autoencoders with parameters $\{\theta_i\}_{i=1}^{M}$ and N dynpredictors with parameters $\{\theta_i\}_{i=M+1}^{M+N}$ from bottom to top, the resulting deep dynencoder maps input y_t to output $F(y_t)$ by:

$$F(y_t) = f_{\theta_1} \circ \cdots \circ f_{\theta_{M+N}} \circ h_{\theta_{M+N}} \circ \cdots \circ h_{\theta_1}(y_t), \tag{9}$$

where $\circ$ represents function composition. In other words, the layers are activated bottom-top-bottom.

Given $\{y_t\}$, the $M+N$ building blocks are pre-trained one by one from bottom to top in the same way as stacked autoencoders. For example, $\{h_{\theta_1}(y_t)\}$ are used to train the second autoencoder, and so on. The hidden layer activations of the top autoencoder $\{h_{\theta_M} \circ \cdots \circ h_{\theta_1}(y_t)\}$, i.e., the hidden states $\{x_t\}$, are used to train the first dynpredictor . Then $\{h_{\theta_{M+1}}(x_t)\}$ are used to train the second dynpredictor, and so on. Finally, we get the pre-training parameters $\{\theta'_1, \dots, \theta'_{M+N}\}$ and use them as initializations in the following fine-tuning step:

$$\{\theta_i^\star\} = \arg \min_{\{\theta_i\}} \frac{1}{T-1} \sum_{t=1}^{T-1} \|F(y_t) - y_{t+1}\|_2^2. \tag{10}$$

The deep dynencoder can model more complex dynamics $y_t \to y_{t+1}$.

It is worth noting that the training strategy need to be modified slightly when stacking two dynpredictors. At the pre-training step, unlike autoencoder aiming at reconstructing input, dynpredictor tries to predict the hidden states of next time $\{x_{t+1}\}$. If we train the second dynpredictor using the same method as the first one and stack them, the network will tend to output x_{t+2} when inputting x_t. After pre-training, the deep dynencoder tends to output y_{t+2} when inputting y_t, which is not what we want. A simple solution is stacking only one dynpredictor on top of several autoencoders. A better solution of stacking multiple dynpredictors is interpolating between two adjacent inputs to form a new data set $\{x_t, x_{t+\frac{1}{2}}\}_{t=1}^T$. Then, two stacked dynpredictors tends to represent the mapping $x_t \to x_{t+1}$, and $x_{t+\frac{1}{2}} \to x_{t+\frac{3}{2}}$ simultaneously. Since interpolating between $\{x_t\}$ directly may lack some sense, we can adopt video frame interpolation first to get $\{y_{t+\frac{1}{2}}\}$ and treat $\{y_t, y_{t+\frac{1}{2}}\}$ as training data of bottom autoencoders to get $\{x_t, x_{t+\frac{1}{2}}\}$. After pre-training, $\{y_{t+\frac{1}{2}}\}$ and $\{x_{t+\frac{1}{2}}\}$ are abandoned to eliminate their influence, i.e., we still perform the optimization according to Equation (10). This strategy can be adopted when stacking more dynpredictors. In fact, the basic dynencoder including one autoencoder and one dynpredictor can model complex videos well. We will verify this in the experiment section.

2.3   Discussion

Dynencoder preserves some similarities with LDS. The formulation of LDS contains a couple of equations representing the observation and state transition processes, which are just the objectives of autoencoder and dynpredictor respectively, in our model. But they are significantly different as dynencoder is completely nonlinear while LDS is linear. Even some variants of LDS remain linear to some extent, e.g., in kernel-DT, hidden states change linearly. With the help of nonlinear representation capability, dynencoder can model video dynamics better than LDS-based models do.

It is clear that computational complexity of training our model is the same as training stacked autoencoders, which mainly depends on the optimization algorithm adopted in each optimization problem described above. Two popular algorithms can be adopted: L-BFGS or nonlinear conjugate gradient method. The latter is faster in each iteration and the L-BFGS needs less iterations. It is well known that the computational complexity of training a deep model is high when the input dimension is high (all pixel intensities of an image). Training with multicore computing or GPU acceleration will save a lot of time.

One may doubt why the regularization term that tends to decrease the magnitude of the weights is absent in our formulations. Actually, regularization term is to prevent overfitting and improve predictive performance. In some cases (e.g., DT synthesis), the model may be required to reconstruct the original sequence with small error. The regularization term may cause opposite effect so that it is absent in this paper. Furthermore, we can set the dimensions of hidden layers of dynencoder to be small to prevent overfitting.

Our method has potential to model any time series data beyond computer vision field, e.g., large amounts of financial data or medical time series. It may need some modifications to match different data types and tasks, e.g., it might be necessary to add regularization term in some cases. We do not give much discussion here because our focus in this paper is modeling video dynamics.

3   Vision Applications of Deep Dynencoder

We give approaches to DT synthesis, video classification and video segmentation using our proposed deep dynencoder. For classification and segmentation, a distance definition between two videos is given and the effectiveness of it is verified in the experiment section.

3.1   DT Synthesis

DT synthesis is a classical problem in computer vision and computer graphics. Our model can naturally be used to synthesize DT of any length. Given a training sequence $\{y_t\}_{t=1}^{T}$, we learn deep dynencoder with the training strategy described above and get the output mapping F of the model according to Equation (9). Given an initial frame y_1', an endless sequence $\{y_t'\}$ can be obtained iteratively:

$$y_{t+1}' = F(y_t').   \tag{11}$$

The synthesis process is real-time as many previous methods are.

3.2   Video Classification

In order to do video classification, we need to define a distance measure, which many classification algorithms, such as kNN and SVM, rely on. In LDS-based classification methods [18][6], Martin distance is adopted which is originally a metric for autoregressive moving average process (ARMA) [14]. Unfortunately, it seems that no distance has been defined between two neural networks.

Wolf et al. [25] introduce an one-shot similarity (OSS) kernel which compares two vectors representing images. They train two classifiers for each vector and apply them on the opposite vector. Two classification confidence scores are obtained and averaged to get the similarity. Inspired by OSS switching classifiers, we develop a distance definition between two videos $Y_a = \{y_t^a\}_{t=1}^{T_a}$ and $Y_b = \{y_t^b\}_{t=1}^{T_b}$ by switching models. Treating Y_a and Y_b as training data respectively, we learn two deep dynencoders M_a and M_b with output mapping F_a and F_b. Then we switch the models and measure how M_a fit Y_b well and M_b fit Y_a well. The average fitting errors are adopted as:

$$d_a^2 = \frac{1}{T_a - 1} \sum_{t=1}^{T_a - 1} \| F_b(y_t^a) - y_{t+1}^a \|_2^2,   \tag{12}$$

$$d_b^2 = \frac{1}{T_b - 1} \sum_{t=1}^{T_b - 1} \| F_a(y_t^b) - y_{t+1}^b \|_2^2.   \tag{13}$$

The distance measure between Y_a and Y_b is then defined as:

$$d(Y_a, Y_b) = \frac{d_a + d_b}{2}.   \tag{14}$$

Because video dynamics are represented by our models, this distance can reflect difference of two videos in dynamic nature. After calculating all distances between videos in a video database, any classification algorithms that rely on distance measure, e.g., kernel-SVM, can be adopted for classifying videos. Although the distance defined above is not a distance metric and the kernel using it cannot be proved positive definite, this does not affect its usefulness for classifying videos. Experiment in video classification in the next section will show the efficacy of our model together with the distance.

3.3   Video Segmentation

Distance definition also makes video clustering feasible and video segmentation can be done through the clustering of spatiotemporal patches, as [10] and [7] do. Because our model represents video dynamics or motions well, our method can segment a video into regions of homogeneous motion, i.e., can do motion segmentation. Specifically, a collection of overlapped video tubes of dimensions $p \times p \times q$ are extracted from each location in the video. Then we cluster them using algorithm like K-medoids with distance defined above. If the segmentation boundaries need not change over time, q is equal to the length of the video sequence. The segmentation result is then obtained using a voting scheme: each pixel in a tube receives a vote for its clustering result. The pixel is then assigned to the cluster with the most votes.

4   Experiments

We evaluate our method on the tasks of DT synthesis, traffic scene classification and motion segmentation, and compare its performance against popular methods in each task. In all the experiments, the raw grey scale pixel values of each video are used to train a deep dynencoder. Each frame is reshaped to a vector. Dimensions of hidden layers of dynencoder are set to be small factors times the dimension of the input, e.g., 0.1, 0.05 etc. Too high dimensions may cause overfitting while too low ones may decrease the representation ability of the model. It is easy to choose suitable dimensions. All the optimizations in our training are solved with non-linear conjugate gradient algorithm.

In the tasks related to classification, we train deep dynencoders for all videos in the video database $\mathcal{Y}$ and calculate distances between them. Then the distances are used to train a kernel-SVM classifier with an RBF-kernel. The bandwidth parameter σ^2 is estimated as:

$$\sigma^2 = \frac{1}{2}\text{median}\{d^2(Y_a, Y_b)\}_{Y_a, Y_b \in \mathcal{Y}}, \tag{15}$$

where Y_a and Y_b are two videos in the database $\mathcal{Y}$. Then we get the kernel $k(Y_a, Y_b) = \exp(-\frac{1}{2\sigma^2}d^2(Y_a, Y_b))$. We train kernel-SVM using LIBSVM [8].

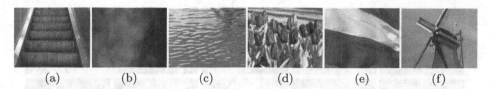

Fig. 2. Six examples in the DynTex database: (a) Escalator, (b) Steam, (c) River, (d) Flowers, (e) Flag (f) Windmill

Table 1. Comparison between mean squared errors given by five synthesis methods

Sequence\Method	LDS	Kernel-DT	Stable LDS	CLDS	Basic Dynencoder
Escalator	5.83	5.47	7.54	**4.87**	13.95
Steam	431.91	118.33	91.59	95.41	**89.88**
River	90.37	92.45	81.60	126.86	**35.65**

4.1 DT Synthesis

In this experiment, we evaluate the performance of our method in DT synthesis. We use DT sequences from the DynTex database [16] as training data respectively. Figure 2 shows some examples such as Escalator, Steam and River. Original sequences all have 250 frames of size 720×576 and we down sample them to 120×96 grey scale images. For each of these sequences, we train a dynencoder using 100 or 120 frames and synthesize a new DT sequence which is 10 times as long as the original one. Both qualitative images and quantitative measurements between synthesized and original videos are provided for comparisons.

We first compare basic dynencoder to some well-known LDS-based methods: LDS, kernel-DT, and CLDS, on some sequences in DynTex database. We implement these comparative methods and select parameters of each to produce best results. Qualitative results over two challenging sequences Steam and River are shown in Figure 3. One can see that LDS and kernel-DT produce unsatisfactory DT sequences which tend to explode or converge over time, while CLDS and dynencoder produce DT sequences with high quality. The reason why the sequence produced by LDS or kernel-DT explodes or converges is because of the eigenvalue property of the transition matrix, which is analyzed in [28] where CLDS is proposed. The sequence tends to explode when the transition matrix has eigenvalues greater than 1 and tends to converge if all the eigenvalues are less than 1. Stable LDS [4] tries to solve this by adding constraints on the eigenvalues. We apply it to the DT sequences using the released code and add the results into comparison (no images shown due to space limit). Quantitative results of all methods through mean squared errors between original frames and new synthesized frames are provided in Table 1. It reveals that our method gives close results comparing to other methods over simple sequences (such as Escalator) and achieves better performance over challenging sequences (Steam and River).

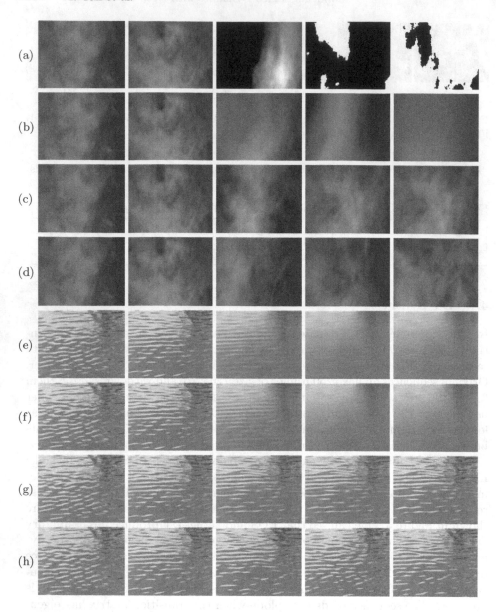

Fig. 3. Comparison between four synthesis methods. 120 frames are used for training and 1200 frames are synthesized. From left to right, the columns are the 1-st, 80-th, 200-th, 600-th, 1200-th frames of synthesized sequences. The results in each row are given by: (a) LDS, (b) Kernel-DT, (c) CLDS, (d) Dynencoder, (e) LDS, (f) Kernel-DT, (g) CLDS, (h) Dynencoder.

It is worth noting that sometimes the quantitative result given by CLDS may be unfair for itself (e.g., the result on sequence River in Table 1) because CLDS is unlike other three methods that it is not based on predicting new frames but on

Table 2. Comparison between CLDS and multilayered dynencoders through mean squared errors

Sequence\Method	CLDS	Dynencoder 1+1	Dynencoder 2+1	Dynencoder 2+2
Flowers	60.51	17.68	15.68	**11.88**
Flag	129.73	144.13	128.20	**118.82**
Windmill	21.97	73.04	47.66	**21.16**

Table 3. Comparison in traffic scene classification task. We achieve the best performance than others.

Method	Accuracy
LDS [19]	87.50% ± 0.87
CS-LDS [19]	89.06% ± 2.16
KL-SVM [5]	95%
NLSSA [1]	94.49% ± 2.02
Dynencoder 1+1	94.09% ± 1.71
Dynencoder 2+1	94.87% ± 1.75
Dynencoder 2+2	**96.06% ± 1.39**

stitching video clips getting from the original video. It is not proper to calculate predicting error for it sometimes.

CLDS achieves good performance over many sequences in our experience. It is a technique combining two steps: concatenating video clips that have similar boundaries and smoothing between the boundaries. The reason why CLDS works well may be that in most cases it can find clips that have similar boundaries. If not, the smooth process may fail and discontinuities may occur. To show this, we handcrafted a new sequence with camera motion in it. The sequence is obtained by applying a sliding window of changeable size over the sequence Flowers, which changes itself through zooming and panning in turn and will not return to the starting location exactly. Over this sequence, we compare the CLDS method not only to basic dynencoder, but also deep dynencoders with more layers to see the influence of the number of layers. The synthesis results are shown in Figure 4, in which Dynencoder $M + N$ represents the deep dynencoder consisting of M autoencoders and N dynpredictors. We can infer from the figure that CLDS fails to find clips that have similar boundaries and the smooth process does not work well. So discontinuities occur near the boundaries while our method generates more continuous sequences. Only there are some obvious discontinuities in sequence synthesized by dynencoder 1+1. Besides, we implement multilayered dynencoders over other two sequences and quantitatively compare their mean squared errors, as shown in Table 2. As we expected, dynencoder with more layers yields better performance.

4.2   Traffic Scene Classification

In this experiment, we use the UCSD traffic video database [5] to classify videos based on the density of traffic and evaluate the dynencoder and the distance

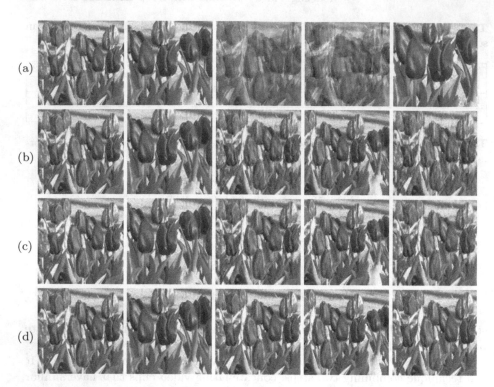

Fig. 4. Comparison between CLDS and multilayered dynencoders. 100 frames are used for training and 1000 frames are synthesized. From left to right, the columns are the 1-st, 60-th, 102-th, 380-th, 690-th, 918-th frames of synthesized sequences. The results in each row are given by: (a) CLDS, (b) Dynencoder 1+1, (c) Dynencoder 2+1, (d) Dynencoder 2+2.

definition. The database consists of 254 videos of highway traffic which are partitioned into 3 classes corresponding to the amount of traffic congestion (Figure 5 shows some examples). There are 44 sequences of heavy traffic, 45 of medium traffic, and 165 of light traffic. Each video contains between 42 to 52 frames of size 320×240 and is converted, resized and clipped to 48×48 grey scale images. All the data after preprocessing are provided in the database, and four trials of train/test splits (75% for training and 25% for testing) are suggested. We set the parameter C of SVM to be 2 without selection and report the average classification accuracy and standard deviation over the four trials.

We compare the performance of our method with three LDS-based methods: LDS [19], compressive sensing LDS (CS-LDS) [19], and probabilistic kernels (KL-SVM) [5]. We also compare it to another method named Non-Linear Stationary Subspace Analysis (NLSSA) [1]. All the results are listed in Table 3, in which Dynencoder $M + N$ represents the deep dynencoder consisting of M autoencoders and N dynpredictors. It can be seen that deeper model gets better results and Dynencoder $2 + 2$ outperforms all other methods and achieves the

Fig. 5. Examples of traffic videos in the UCSD database. From left to right, the amounts of traffic congestion are: heavy, heavy, medium, medium, light, light.

highest accuracy 96.06%. It confirms the fact that deep dynencoder represents video dynamics well and the distance definition is efficacious.

4.3 Motion Segmentation

We do segmentation experiment on real-world video sequences depicting vehicle traffic on a bridge or highway using our method described in Section 3. Each sequence has 51 grey scale frames of size 160×113 and the size of spatiotemporal patches is set to be $5 \times 5 \times 51$. Patches with pixel-level temporal variances of less than 10 are marked as static background. We use K-medoids algorithm for clustering with $K = 3$ or 4. Finally, the segmentation maps are postprocessed with a 5×5 majority smoothing filter.

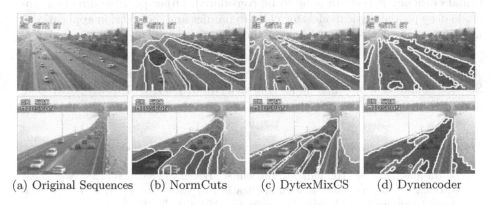

(a) Original Sequences   (b) NormCuts   (c) DytexMixCS   (d) Dynencoder

Fig. 6. Original video sequences and segmentation results given by three methods

Segmentation results of the basic dynencoder are compared with those produced by an LDS-based method DytexMixCS [7] and a traditional optical-flow-based method NormCuts [20]. It is difficult to give quantitative evaluation on the results, so we qualitatively show the segmented video frames[1] in Figure 6. As we can see, our method segments the videos into regions of traffic which are moving away from the camera and moving towards the camera. Although there are some small incorrect segmented regions, our results are better than those

---

[1] The original videos and the results of comparison methods are from the companion web site of [7].

produced by other methods in some ways. DytexMixCS and NormCuts segment the region with traffic moving away from (or moving towards) the camera into more than one main region because of perspective effects while our method does not. It means that our method can handle strong perspective effects.

5   Conclusion and Discussion

We have proposed a hierarchical model named deep dynencoder to model video dynamics, that relies on the combination of autoencoder and dynpredictor. We describe the architecture of basic dynencoder and show how to construct deep dynencoder by proper stacking strategy. Effective training algorithm is also given, which includes layer-wise pre-training and joint fine-tuning. Our model can be applied to DT synthesis and the outstanding synthesis performance verify its ability of capturing various video dynamics. With a defined distance measure between videos, our model can also be applied to video classification and clustering. Experimental results on traffic scene classification and motion segmentation confirm the effectiveness of our model and the distance definition as well.

In our experimental comparisons, we only report results on small-scale data. In our future research, we will set up more complex deep models with large-scale training data, from which more attractive results are expected. The computational efficiency is then an issue to be considered. Other possible directions include deep probabilistic models for video dynamics and more vision applications, like some general video segmentation and classification tasks.

Acknowledgement. This work is partially supported by the National Natural Science Foundation of China under contract No. 61390510, 61025010, 61379083, and 61272319.

References

1. Baktashmotlagh, M., Harandi, M., Bigdeli, A., Lovell, B., Salzmann, M.: Non-linear stationary subspace analysis with application to video classification. In: International Conference on Machine Learning, pp. 450–458 (2013)
2. Basharat, A., Shah, M.: Time series prediction by chaotic modeling of nonlinear dynamical systems. In: IEEE International Conference on Computer Vision, pp. 1941–1948 (2009)
3. Bengio, Y.: Learning deep architectures for AI. Foundations and Trends in Machine Learning 2(1), 1–127 (2009)
4. Boots, B., Gordon, G.J., Siddiqi, S.M.: A constraint generation approach to learning stable linear dynamical systems. In: Advances in Neural Information Processing Systems 20, pp. 1329–1336 (2008)
5. Chan, A., Vasconcelos, N.: Probabilistic kernels for the classification of autoregressive visual processes. In: IEEE Conference on Computer Vision and Pattern Recognition, vol. 1, pp. 846–851 (2005)
6. Chan, A., Vasconcelos, N.: Classifying video with kernel dynamic textures. In: IEEE Conference on Computer Vision and Pattern Recognition, pp. 1–6 (2007)

7. Chan, A., Vasconcelos, N.: Modeling, clustering, and segmenting video with mixtures of dynamic textures. IEEE Transactions on Pattern Analysis and Machine Intelligence 30(5), 909–926 (2008)
8. Chang, C.C., Lin, C.J.: Libsvm: a library for support vector machines. ACM Transactions on Intelligent Systems and Technology 2(3), 27 (2011)
9. Doretto, G., Chiuso, A., Wu, Y., Soatto, S.: Dynamic textures. International Journal of Computer Vision 51(2), 91–109 (2003)
10. Doretto, G., Cremers, D., Favaro, P., Soatto, S.: Dynamic texture segmentation. In: IEEE International Conference on Computer Vision (October 2003)
11. Erhan, D., Bengio, Y., Courville, A., Manzagol, P.A., Vincent, P., Bengio, S.: Why does unsupervised pre-training help deep learning? Journal of Machine Learning Research 11, 625–660 (2010)
12. Le, Q.V., Zou, W.Y., Yeung, S.Y., Ng, A.Y.: Learning hierarchical invariant spatiotemporal features for action recognition with independent subspace analysis. In: IEEE Conference on Computer Vision and Pattern Recognition (2011)
13. Liu, C.B., Lin, R.S., Ahuja, N., Yang, M.H.: Dynamic textures synthesis as nonlinear manifold learning and traversing. In: BMVC, pp. 859–868 (2006)
14. Martin, R.: A metric for ARMA processes. IEEE Transactions on Signal Processing 48(4), 1164–1170 (2000)
15. Masiero, A., Chiuso, A.: Nonlinear temporal textures synthesis: a monte carlo approach. In: Leonardis, A., Bischof, H., Pinz, A. (eds.) ECCV 2006, Part II. LNCS, vol. 3952, pp. 283–294. Springer, Heidelberg (2006)
16. Péteri, R., Fazekas, S., Huiskes, M.: Dyntex: A comprehensive database of dynamic textures. Pattern Recognition Letters 31(12), 1627–1632 (2010)
17. Ravichandran, A., Chaudhry, R., Vidal, R.: Categorizing dynamic textures using a bag of dynamical systems. IEEE Transactions on Pattern Analysis and Machine Intelligence 35(2), 342–353 (2013)
18. Saisan, P., Doretto, G., Wu, Y.N., Soatto, S.: Dynamic texture recognition. In: IEEE Conference on Computer Vision and Pattern Recognition, vol. 2 (2001)
19. Sankaranarayanan, A.C., Turaga, P.K., Baraniuk, R.G., Chellappa, R.: Compressive acquisition of dynamic scenes. In: Daniilidis, K., Maragos, P., Paragios, N. (eds.) ECCV 2010, Part I. LNCS, vol. 6311, pp. 129–142. Springer, Heidelberg (2010)
20. Shi, J., Malik, J.: Normalized cuts and image segmentation. IEEE Transactions on Pattern Analysis and Machine Intelligence 22(8), 888–905 (2000)
21. Taylor, G.W., Fergus, R., LeCun, Y., Bregler, C.: Convolutional learning of spatiotemporal features. In: Daniilidis, K., Maragos, P., Paragios, N. (eds.) ECCV 2010, Part VI. LNCS, vol. 6316, pp. 140–153. Springer, Heidelberg (2010)
22. Taylor, G.W., Hinton, G.E.: Factored conditional restricted boltzmann machines for modeling motion style. In: Annual International Conference on Machine Learning, pp. 1025–1032. ACM (2009)
23. Taylor, G.W., Hinton, G.E., Roweis, S.T.: Modeling human motion using binary latent variables. In: Advances in Neural Information Processing Systems 19, p. 1345 (2007)
24. Vincent, P., Larochelle, H., Lajoie, I., Bengio, Y., Manzagol, P.A.: Stacked denoising autoencoders: Learning useful representations in a deep network with a local denoising criterion. Journal of Machine Learning Research 11, 3371–3408 (2010)
25. Wolf, L., Hassner, T., Taigman, Y.: The one-shot similarity kernel. In: IEEE International Conference on Computer Vision, pp. 897–902 (2009)
26. Xie, J., Xu, L., Chen, E.: Image denoising and inpainting with deep neural networks. In: Advances in Neural Information Processing Systems, pp. 350–358 (2012)

27. Yan, X., Chang, H., Chen, X.: Temporally multiple dynamic textures synthesis using piecewise linear dynamic systems. In: IEEE International Conference on Image Processing (2013)
28. Yuan, L., Wen, F., Liu, C., Shum, H.-Y.: Synthesizing dynamic texture with closed-loop linear dynamic system. In: Pajdla, T., Matas, J(G.) (eds.) ECCV 2004. LNCS, vol. 3022, pp. 603–616. Springer, Heidelberg (2004)

Good Image Priors for Non-blind Deconvolution:
Generic *vs*. Specific

Libin Sun[1], Sunghyun Cho[2,*], Jue Wang[2], and James Hays[1]

[1] Brown University, Providence, RI 02912, USA
[2] Adobe Research, Seattle, WA 98103, USA
{lbsun,hays}@cs.brown.edu, sodomau@postech.ac.kr, juewang@adobe.com

Abstract. Most image restoration techniques build "universal" image priors, trained on a variety of scenes, which can guide the restoration of any image. But what if we have more specific training examples, *e.g.* sharp images of similar scenes? Surprisingly, state-of-the-art image priors don't seem to benefit from from context-specific training examples. Re-training generic image priors using ideal sharp example images provides minimal improvement in non-blind deconvolution. To help understand this phenomenon we explore non-blind deblurring performance over a broad spectrum of training image scenarios. We discover two strategies that become beneficial as example images become more context-appropriate: (1) *locally* adapted priors trained from region level correspondence significantly outperform globally trained priors, and (2) a novel multi-scale *patch-pyramid* formulation is more successful at transferring mid and high frequency details from example scenes. Combining these two key strategies we can qualitatively and quantitatively outperform leading generic non-blind deconvolution methods when context-appropriate example images are available. We also compare to recent work which, like ours, tries to make use of context-specific examples.

Keywords: deblur, non-blind deconvolution, gaussian mixtures, image pyramid, image priors, camera shake.

1 Introduction

Deblurring is a long-standing challenge in the field of computer vision and computational photography because of its ill-posed nature. In non-blind deconvolution, even though the point spread function (PSF) is known, restoring coherent high frequency image details can still be very difficult. In this paper, we address the problem of non-blind deconvolution with the help of similar (but not identical) example images, and explore deblurring performance across a spectrum of example image scenarios. For each type of training data, we evaluate various strategies for learning image priors from these examples. In contrast to popular methods that apply a single universal image prior to all pixels in the image [12,15,10,22,16], we adapt the prior to local image content and introduce

---

* Sunghyun Cho is now with Samsung Electronics.

D. Fleet et al. (Eds.): ECCV 2014, Part IV, LNCS 8692, pp. 231–246, 2014.
© Springer International Publishing Switzerland 2014

a multi-scale patch modeling strategy to fully take advantage of the example images and show improved recovery of image details. Unlike the recent instance-level deblurring method of [7], we do not require accurate dense correspondence between image pairs and hence generalize better to a wide variety of example image scenarios.

In a typical deblurring framework, a blurry image y is often modeled as a convolution between a PSF k and a sharp image x, with additive noise n:

$$y = k * x + n. \tag{1}$$

In non-blind deconvolution, both y and k are given, and n is often assumed to be i.i.d Gaussian with known variance. A typical choice of image prior is to encode the heavy-tailed characteristics on image gradients [12,15,10], and regularize the deconvolution process via some form of sparsity constraints on image gradients:

$$x = \mathrm{argmin}_x \, ||y - k * x||^2 + \lambda(||D_x x||^\alpha + ||D_y x||^\alpha) \tag{2}$$

where λ is proportional to the noise variance. For Gaussian priors ($\alpha = 2$), there exist fast closed-form solutions via Fourier transform [12,1]. However, Gaussian priors are not appropriate for capturing the heavy-tailedness of natural images, hence produce oversmoothed image gradients. Sparsity priors based on Laplace distribution ($\alpha = 1$) [12] and hyper-Laplacian distributions ($0.5 \leq \alpha \leq 0.8$) [10] have been shown to work well. Other forms of parameterization have also been introduced, such as the generalized Gaussian distribution [2] and mixture of Laplacians [14]. Constraints on image gradients alone are usually insufficient and methods that are able to reason about larger neighborhoods lead to state-of-the-art performance [17,25,23,18,19]. In particular, Zoran and Weiss [25] model image patches via a simple Gaussian mixture model (GMM). This prior turns out to be extremely powerful for removing blur and noise. More recently, discriminative methods trained on corrupted/sharp patch pairs [18,19] have shown impressive performance without specifically modeling the image prior. However, a common problem for these generic methods is that restoring coherent high frequency details remains a challenging task. Deblurred results often contain artifacts such as broken lines and painterly structure details (see Fig. 1).

One likely cause is that given only very local image evidence based on a few adjacent pixels [12,10,2] or image patches [17,21,25,13,23], there is insufficient contextual information to drive the solution away from the conservative smooth state. In addition, most existing methods apply a single image prior to the whole image, which will inevitably introduce a bias towards smooth solutions, since natural images are dominated by smooth gradients.

To combat the tendency to oversmooth details, several recent works consider a content-aware formulation of image priors to accommodate the spatially-varying statistical properties in natural images [2,3,26]. While such content-aware approaches are promising, it is difficult to choose the right prior in the presence of blur and noise. For example, [2,3] estimate content-aware parametric priors based on the downsampled input image. The power of such internal statistics can be rather limited when faced with limited resolution or large blur. However, constructing expressive, content-aware image priors becomes feasible if we have access to sharp example images that are similar to the input.

In the digital age, photographers are likely to take many photos of the same physical scene over time, and this is the type of context we exploit to restore an image and enable content-aware adaptation of image priors. As an experiment, we randomly picked 100 query photos on `Flickr` and found instance level scene matches right next to the query in their respective photostream 42% of the time. This is probably a conservative estimate because photographers are exercising editorial restraint and tend to only publish good and unique photos. For photos where the shutter count was visible, 29% of the time the photographer had taken additional (non-uploaded) photos between instance level matching scenes. It is frustrating for photographers that restoring a blurry photo, even when they can often provide *sharp* photos of the same scene, remains a problem seldom considered by the research community, with the exception of [7], which requires a dense correspondence between the input and the example. However, in the presence of blur and noise, such dense correspondence is unreliable and cannot handle occlusions (see Fig. 1).

Given the recent advances in blur kernel estimation [5,15,1,22,20,9] and the fact that non-blind deconvolution can be regarded as separate step in the deblurring process, we consider the stand-alone problem of by-example *non-blind* deconvolution: given a blurry input image, a known PSF, and one or more *sharp* images with shared content, how can we reliably remove blur and restore coherent image details?

2   Overview

In order to explore non-blind deconvolution performance over a broad range of example image scenarios, we need to define a general deconvolution framework. We extend the EPLL/GMM framework from Zoran and Weiss [25] by augmenting the single-scale patch priors to a multi-scale formulation (Sec. 3). Once the form of image prior and deconvolution method is defined, we consider two training strategies: global training using data from example images, or local training using specific subsets of example data based on a region level correpondence (Sec. 4). Based on this setup, we can investigate various baseline methods that incorporate (1) different parameters in the prior configuration, and (2) different training strategies. We evaluate the performance of these baselines for each example image scenario (Sec. 5) and discover a set of key strategies that show significant benefit from having better example images. Finally, we compare experimental results (Sec. 6) using both synthetically blurred and real photos, against leading methods in generic non-deconvolution as well as by-example deblurring.

3   Patch-Pyramid Prior

Our work builds on Zoran and Weiss [25] in which a single-scale patch prior is trained from DC-removed patches. Natural images exhibit diverse yet structured content in different frequency bands that are tightly coupled. A single-scale

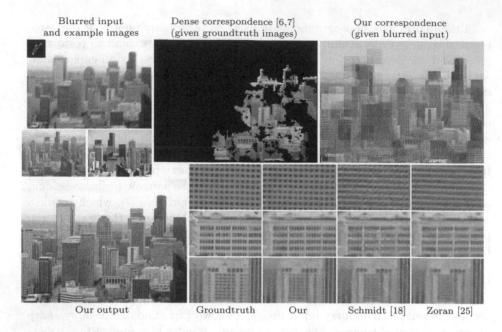

Fig. 1. The synthetically blurred input and sharp example images show different views of downtown Seattle. Even when given the groundtruth input image, the core correspondence algorithm in [6,7] returns partial (22%) correspondence from example 1 and zero matches from example 2. Our algorithm is able to establish meaningful region level correspondences, and locally adapt the prior to produce significantly more details than state-of-the-art non-blind deconvolution methods.

patch model lacks the ability to learn such statistical dependencies. We propose to jointly model multi-scale concentric patches extracted from an image pyramid, which we call *patch-pyramids*. This naturally extends the spatial scale of the patches without a geometric increase in dimensionality as would happen at a single scale. Furthermore, by capturing how mid and high frequency details covary, image details can be restored more coherently to remove common artifacts such as smudged-out structures, zigzag edges, and painterly appearance.

Consider an image x_1 and its Gaussian pyramid layers $\{x_1, \ldots, x_m\}$. Given a fixed patch width w, we denote a *patch-pyramid* by $[x_1^m]^i$, meaning a collection of m patches centered at the same relative coordinates i in each layer of the Gaussian pyramid. For conciseness, we use $[x]^i$ to denote patch-pyramid at relative location i with some fixed size. We use bold fonts to indicate matrices. $[\mathbf{x}]^i \in \mathcal{R}^{mw^2}$ is formed by concatenating patches in each layer of the pyramid.

We treat patch-pyramids with DC removed per layer as random variables and model the joint occurence of these m layers via a Gaussian Mixture Model (GMM). For simplicity, a $w \times w \times m$ GMM prior means that the model is trained using patch size w with m layers.

Let $\mathbf{x}$ and $\mathbf{y}$ be the latent and observed image. We follow the EPLL framework of [25] to minimize:

$$f_p(\mathbf{x}|\mathbf{y}) = \frac{\lambda}{2}||\mathbf{A}\mathbf{x} - \mathbf{y}||^2 - \sum_i \log p([\mathbf{x}]^i) \qquad (3)$$

where $\mathbf{A}$ represents the blur operator, $\lambda = \frac{mw^2}{\sigma^2}$, σ^2 is the noise variance in the image formation process, and $p([\mathbf{x}]^i) \sim \sum_k \pi_k N([\mathbf{x}]^i; \boldsymbol{\mu}_k, \boldsymbol{\Sigma}_k)$ is the density function of the GMM prior for patch-pyramids. $\{\pi_k, \boldsymbol{\mu}_k, \boldsymbol{\Sigma}_k\}$ are the mixture weight, mean, and covariance of the kth Gaussian component, respectively. The single-scale patch model in [25] is a special case when $m = 1$ and $\boldsymbol{\mu} = \mathbf{0}$.

3.1   Optimization

To optimize Eqn. (3) directly is challenging. A common strategy is to intro-duce auxiliary variables to assist the optimization process via half quadratic split [10,25]. To achieve this, we introduce auxiliary patch-pyramids $[\mathbf{z}]^i$ to each location i and minimize the following global objective:

$$c_{p,\beta}(\mathbf{x}, \{[\mathbf{z}]^i\}|\mathbf{y}) =$$
$$\frac{\lambda}{2}||\mathbf{A}\mathbf{x} - \mathbf{y}||^2 + \sum_i \frac{\beta}{2}(([\mathbf{x}]^i - [\mathbf{z}]^i)^T \boldsymbol{\Sigma}_{noise}^{-1}([\mathbf{x}]^i - [\mathbf{z}]^i)) - \log p([\mathbf{z}]^i) \quad (4)$$

The diagonal matrix $\boldsymbol{\Sigma}_{noise}$ reflects the varying relative noise level in each layer, with diagonal entries $\sigma_j^2, j \in \{1, 2, ..., m\}$, each repeating w^2 times. How-ever, the noise across layers is correlated due to the effect of filtering and downsampling in the Gaussian pyramid. We empirically found the relationship $\sigma_{j+1}^2 = \sigma_j^2/2$ to work well in our experiments. We set $\sigma_1^2 = 1$.

The optimization iterates between updating the auxiliary variables $[\mathbf{z}]^i$ (Sec. 3.2) and solving the latent image $\mathbf{x}$ (Sec. 3.3). Over iterations, β increases to tighten the coupling of $[\mathbf{z}]^i$ and $[\mathbf{x}]^i$ via the second term, which enables con-vergence. We empirically found the schedule $\beta = 60 \cdot [1, 2, 4, ...]$ to work well, typically converging within 8 iterations as shown in Fig. 4.

3.2   Z-Step

Given the current estimate for $\mathbf{x}$, finding $[\mathbf{z}]^i$ amounts to solving for the MAP estimate, but computing the exact MAP solution is intractable. We follow the approximation procedure from [25] to obtain a Wiener filtering solution:

$$[\mathbf{z}]^i = (\boldsymbol{\Sigma}_{k_{max}} + \beta \boldsymbol{\Sigma}_{noise})^{-1} (\boldsymbol{\Sigma}_{k_{max}}[\mathbf{x}]^i + \beta \boldsymbol{\Sigma}_{noise} \boldsymbol{\mu}_{k_{max}}) \qquad (5)$$

where k_{max} is the index of the Gaussian component with the highest responsi-bility.

3.3   X-Step

Keeping $[\mathbf{z}]^i$ fixed, we solve for $\mathbf{x}$ by the following update:

$$\hat{\mathbf{x}} = \left(\lambda \mathbf{A}^T \mathbf{A} + \sum_i \sum_j \beta_j (\mathbf{P}_{ij} \mathbf{H}_j)^T (\mathbf{P}_{ij} \mathbf{H}_j)\right)^{-1} \left(\lambda \mathbf{A}^T \mathbf{y} + \sum_i \sum_j \beta_j (\mathbf{P}_{ij} \mathbf{H}_j)^T [\mathbf{z}]_j^i\right)$$

(6)

where j indexes over layers in the pyramid, $\mathbf{H}_j$ is the Toeplitz matrix representation of the Gaussian filtering and downsampling operators associated with layer j, $\beta_j = \beta/\sigma_j^2$, $[\mathbf{z}]_j^i$ is the jth layer patch in $[\mathbf{z}]^i$, and $\mathbf{P}_{ij}$ is the matrix operator extracting the patch at location i in layer j.

4   Locally Adapted Priors

Clearly, the prior in Eqn. (3) plays a central role in the deblurring processs. But how much can the prior benefit from example images? One way is to learn the GMM parameters globally using training data collected from the example images. Unfortunately, globally trained priors do not seem to benefit from having *better* example images, as we will show in Sec. 5. This may be because image statistics vary significantly across image locations and using a single global image prior for all image content inevitably compromises image details for smoothness. Instead, we show that priors can be adapted to local image content to provide significantly better recovery of image details.

To construct locally adapted priors, we operate on a half-overlapping grid of image crops and seek local correspondence as shown in Fig. 2. First, a fast L_2-based deconvolution is performed to provide a rough estimate of the latent image, which is then divided into half-overlapping 64×64 crops. For each crop, a HOG descriptor [4] is computed and compared against a database of crops extracted from the sharp example images. We apply scale (factor of $1, 0.9, 0.8$) and rotation ($-3, 0, 3$ degrees) adjustments to each example image to better fit query image content. To reduce noise, we downsample the image by 0.5 in each dimension and apply Gaussian blur before computing the HOG features. A visualization of the nearest neighbor (NN) crops overlay is shown in Fig. 2, where salient image content is matched to reasonable example crops in the presence of noise. Additional visualizations across various example image scenarios can be found in Fig. 4.

Given the above crop-level correspondences, we train independent local GMM priors using patch data collected from 20 nearest neighbors for each query. For each query crop q_i, we adaptively choose the number of Gaussian components $K_i \in [K_{min}, K_{max}]$ according to gradient complexity in the training data. Specifically, we first run canny edge detection on the sharp example images, and the total count of edge pixels N_i in the 20-NN crops for each q_i is recorded. We linearly scale K_i's by $K_i = K_{min} + (K_{max} - K_{min})(N_i - N_{min})/(N_{max} - N_{min})$, where N_{min} and N_{max} are the smallest and largest count among all queries. We

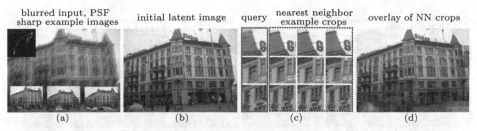

blurred input, PSF
sharp example images   initial latent image   query   nearest neighbor
example crops   overlay of NN crops

(a)   (b)   (c)   (d)

Fig. 2. (a) Input blurred image with known PSF and sharp example images, (b) initial latent image, (c) best matching example image crops for several query crops from the input, (d) visualization of the nearest neighbor crops overlaid on the input image. The initial latent image is very noisy, the nearest neighbor crops are misaligned and incoherent. Neither alone is a satisfactory image restoration, but we will use the information from both sources to restore blurry photos.

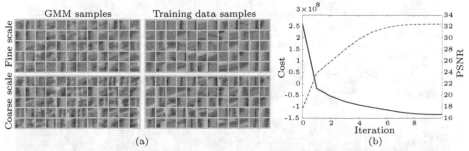

(a)   (b)

Fig. 3. (a) Using patch-pyramids from nearest neighbor crops for the bottom query crop in Fig. 2(c), we train a $7{\times}7{\times}2$ local GMM and compare its random samples (left) against patches drawn directly from training data (right). The prior captures intricate coupling in different frequency bands. (b) The global objective function in Eqn. (3) converges over iterations with a fixed schedule for β, while the PSNR of the latent image increases. Locally trained $7{\times}7{\times}2$ priors are used to restore the input image in Fig. 2.

set $K_{min} = 5, K_{max} = 50$ and learn the GMM via the Expectation-Maximization (EM) algorithm.

Due to the overlapping structure, each pixel is governed by at most four different local GMM priors. To be consistent with the overall objective in Eqn. (3), we choose the solution that gives the highest posterior log likelihood during the MAP approximation of $[\mathbf{z}]^i$ (see Sec. 3.2).

5   How Do Example Images Help?

In order to answer this question, we consider how performance is affected by (1) various example image scenarios and (2) different parameters in our prior. Since the state-of-the-art by-example deblurring method of [7] requires instance-level examples, it is hard to evaluate its performance across a wide spectrum of examples. In this section only, we use the groundtruth image content for

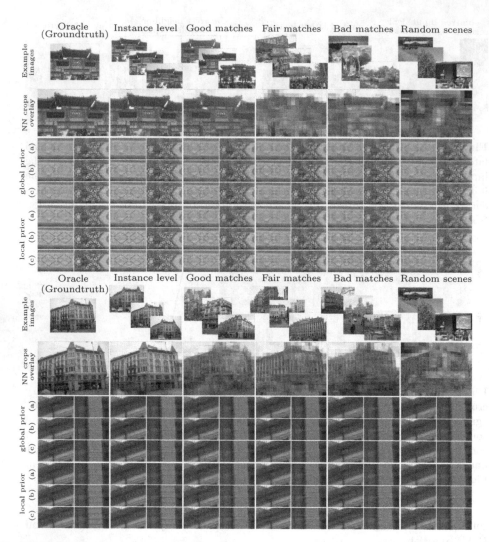

Fig. 4. Comparing various baselines across example scenarios and prior configurations. From top to bottom: various scenarios of example images, from the best possible (groundtruth) to similar scenes, to irrelevant images (random scenes); averaged overlay of 20 nearest neighbor crops; output using globally trained priors and locally adapted priors. Results obtained using $7 \times 7 \times 1$, $5 \times 5 \times 2$ and $5 \times 5 \times 3$ GMM priors are shown in row (a), (b) and (c) respectively. Better image details can be recovered by (1) using better example images and (2) local training of patch-pyramid priors.

retrieving similar scenes as well as finding crop-level correspondences so that we can more accurately experimentally manipulate the quality of training data.

We consider a number of scenarios of example images: oracle, instance-level, scene matches, and random scenes. The test images are synthetically formed based on the landmark dataset of [24] (see Sec. 6.1 for details). The oracle

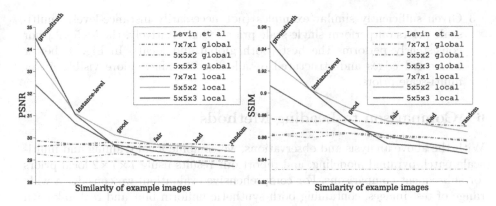

Fig. 5. Quantitative evaluation of different image priors across example images at various levels of similarity. The six groups of example images are the same visualized in Figure 4. Both PSNR and SSIM scores are reported. Each point is obtained by averaging scores from 20 test images.

scenario assumes that the groundtruth image is available for training the GMM priors. The instance-level examples come directly from the dataset of [24]. Scene matches are computed using the method and database described in [8]. The "good" scene matches (rank 1 to 3) are very similar scenes at similar scale under similar illumination, but typically not instance-level matches. The "fair" scene matches (rank 10-12) are usually less similar but still reasonable. The "bad" scene matches (rank 1998-2000) might only be of the same broad scene category. Finally, we select three random scenes from the database of [8] to act as the worst case scenario. See Figure 4 for examples of each set of training images.

For each example scenario, we consider six alternative prior configurations: (1) the prior can be either globally or locally trained, and (2) the patch-pyramid dimensions can be $7 \times 7 \times 1, 5 \times 5 \times 2, 5 \times 5 \times 3$. For the globally trained priors, we randomly sample 2×10^6 patch-pyramids from the example images (with scale and rotation adjustments) and learn a 50-component GMM via mini-batch EM.

So how do example images help? Our experiments show that the answer is rather subtle: it depends on the priors. In Fig. 4, we show how the deblurring results change as the training examples become less similar to the blurry input. Using a test set of 20 images (see Sec. 6.1), we present quantitative evaluation of these baselines in Fig. 5.

We summarize several key observations below:

1 Better example images do help, but it also depends on the priors being used. Locally adapted priors appear to be very sensitive to example images, whereas global priors are not.

2 Given instance-level example images, local priors significantly outperform global priors. This is because local priors can provide fine-grained content-aware constraints whereas global priors apply a universal treatment to all image content, often introducing a bias towards smoothness.

3 Given sufficiently similar examples (not necessarily instance-level), multi-scale priors outperform single-scale priors. Quantitatively, the $5 \times 5 \times 2$ prior consistently performs the best (both global and local). In Fig. 4, better connected edges and structured details become much more visible under multi-scale priors.

6   Comparison to Leading Methods

With the above analysis and observations, we combine local training and multi-scale patch-pyramid modeling, and report our results using $7 \times 7 \times 2$ local priors for subsequent comparisons. For comprehensive evaluation, we consider a wide range of test images, containing both synthetic uniform blur and real unknown camera shake. We present quantitative and qualitative comparisons against leading methods in both generic and by-example deblurring methods.

6.1   Synthetically Blurred Images

For quantitative evaluation, we generate 20 synthetically blurred test images using four kernels (number 2, 4, 6, 8) from Levin *et al.* [11] and five color images with examples taken from [24]. 1% i.i.d Gaussian noise is added to the luminance channel. Evaluation is based on only the gray scale output images with the outer ring of 30 pixels removed. Color information is only used to assist the correspondence step in [7] and our pipeline (see Sec. 4). In Table 1, we show quantitative comparisons based on PSNR and SSIM scores. For comparisons against non-blind deconvolution methods [12,10,25,18], we assume the groundtruth PSF is known. In this case, our performance is better than the compared methods 100% of the time. A visual comparison of deblurred results can be found in Fig. 6.

When comparing to the recent by-example blind deblurring method of [7], we assume the groundtruth PSF is unknown, and run our system with the estimated blur kernels provided by the authors of [7] to ensure fair comparison. We report PSNR and SSIM performance in Table 1. In this case, we outperform the method of HaCohen *et al.* [7] 85% of the time. A qualitative comparison is shown in Fig. 8. Please note that a single example image is manually selected by the authors of [7] (out of all the examples we supplied) to generate their results since their system does not support multiple example images.

Our method clearly outperforms existing methods in terms of PSNR and SSIM scores, and is capable of restoring coherent mid to high level frequencies such as straight lines and structured details. The recent methods of [25,18] are very competitive without using context-specific example images, but can be quite limited in terms of recovering high frequency details, as shown in Fig. 1 and Fig. 6.

6.2   Real Photos with Unknown Blur

In Fig. 7, we show comparison on a test image from [7], where the input image exhibits unknown and spatially varying blur. Our latent image is produced with

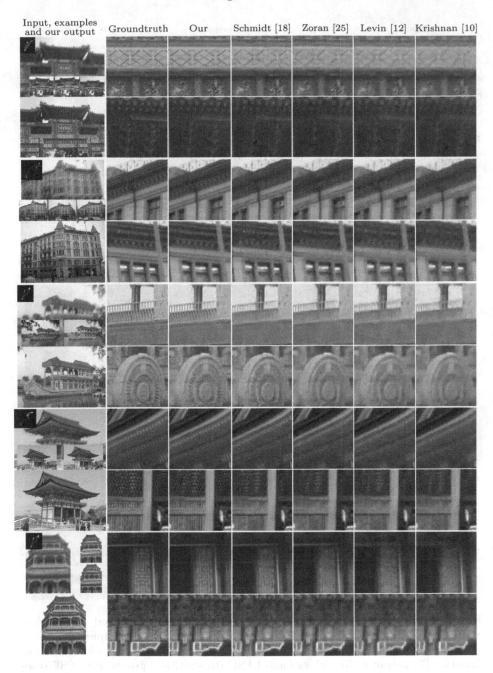

Fig. 6. Comparison on uniformly blurred synthetic test images. Groundtruth PSF's are assumed known and used by all competing methods.

Fig. 7. Test image from HaCohen *et al.* [7] with spatially varying PSF estimates. Our approach is highly competitive without requiring dense correspondence.

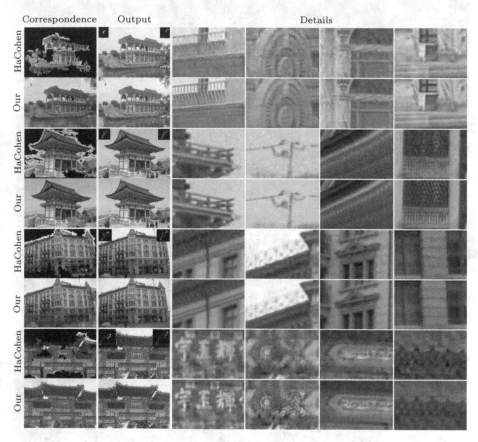

Fig. 8. Comparisons against the state-of-the-art by-example method of HaCohen *et al.* [7] on our uniformly blurred synthetic test images. Four examples are shown. Within each example, the first row shows (from left to right): dense correspondence found by [7], output of [7] with estimated PSF (top-left) and groundtruth PSF (top-right), close-up of [7]. The second row shows (from left to right): our nearest neighbor example crop overlay, our output, our close-up. The PSF estimates are supplied by the authors of [7]. All results are generated using the same input blurry images and PSF estimates, hence directly comparable. The last example shows a failure case due to inaccurate PSF estimate.

Table 1. Quantitative evaluation against existing methods. Methods [12,10,25,18] utilize universally learned image information for deconvolution, while [7] and our method focus on by-example deblurring. For fair comparison, our results in the last column are produced with the estimated PSF from [7]. Both methods make use of example images.

method	given groundtruth PSF					given estimated PSF	
	Levin[12]	Krishnan[10]	Zoran[25]	Schmidt[18]	Our	HaCohen[7]	Our
PSNR	28.94	28.43	29.85	29.90	**31.79**	27.00	**27.60**
SSIM	0.852	0.831	0.869	0.879	**0.915**	0.817	**0.843**

the PSF estimates from [7], and shows competitive restoration of details. In Fig. 9, we present additional results with unknown blur. All images are taken with the same camera. For most of the test cases, we were unable to obtain successful dense corrrespondences using the online code provided by the NRDC algorithm [6], which is at the heart of [7].

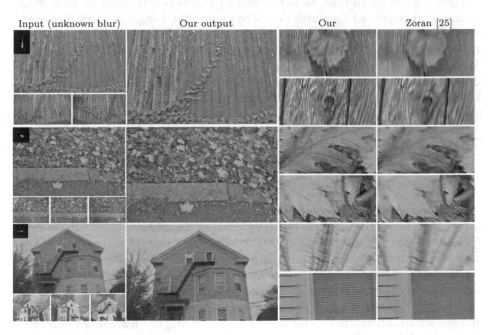

Input (unknown blur)   Our output   Our   Zoran [25]

Fig. 9. Except for the third row, the core correspondence algorithm at the heart of [7] yields zero successful matches. For the third test image, it cannot explain more than 70% of the image. All input images are real photos with unknown blur. We estimate the blur kernel using [1].

Input and examples   Our output   Groundtruth   Our   Zoran [25]

Fig. 10. An example where our method produces convincing textures but also inappropriate high frequency content in background smooth regions (bottom crop)

6.3 Limitations

While our system achieves competitive restoration of details, it requires heavy computation especially in the training stage. Using our unoptimized MATLAB implementation, training a 50-component $5 \times 5 \times 2$ GMM global prior takes roughly 5 hours on an Intel Xeon E5-2650 CPU, whereas training its local prior counterpart requires 12 minutes over a compute grid using 120 cores. However, we find that simply changing the stopping criteria for EM lets us speed up training by a factor of 100 at the expense of a 0.03 drop in PSNR on average. We speculate that further speedup can be obtained by reducing the number of parameters to learn via PCA and by optimizing our code. Finally, incorrect synthesis of details can occur near texture transitions, as shown in Fig. 10.

7   Conclusion

In this work, we have provided a novel analysis for by-example non-blind deconvolution by comparing performance against quality of example images for various scenarios using patch-based priors. In particular, we show that locally adapted priors with multi-scale patch-pyramid modeling leads to significant performance gains. We propose a method relying on mid-level correspondence of image crops that does not require dense correspondence at the pixel level. By modeling local image content using multi-scale patch-pyramids, our approach can efficiently take advantage of the sharp example images to restore coherent mid to high frequency image details. We conduct extensive evelution based on images with both synthetic and real blur, comparing against leading methods in non-blind deconvolution as well as the state-of-the-art by-example deblurring method. By-example deblurring is a promising direction to alleviate the fundamental difficulty of existing algorithms to restore coherent high frequency details, and our method is one step closer to achieving high quality deblur results. For future work, we would like to investigate how our approach can be extended to utilize non-instance level (but still similar) example images and explore ways to improve blind deconvolution via examples.

References

1. Cho, S., Lee, S.: Fast motion deblurring. ACM Transactions on Graphics (2009)
2. Cho, T.S., Joshi, N., Zitnick, C.L., Kang, S.B., Szeliski, R., Freeman, W.T.: A content-aware image prior. In: CVPR (2010)
3. Cho, T.S., Zitnick, C.L., Joshi, N., Kang, S.B., Szeliski, R., Freeman, W.T.: Image restoration by matching gradient distributions. IEEE Transactions on Pattern Analysis and Machine Intelligence (2012)
4. Dalal, N., Triggs, B.: Histograms of oriented gradients for human detection. In: CVPR (2005)
5. Fergus, R., Singh, B., Hertzmann, A., Roweis, S.T., Freeman, W.T.: Removing camera shake from a single photograph. ACM Transactions on Graphics (2006)
6. HaCohen, Y., Shechtman, E., Goldman, D., Lischinski, D.: Non-rigid dense correspondence with applications for image enhancement. ACM Transactions on Graphics (2011)
7. HaCohen, Y., Shechtman, E., Lischinski, D.: Deblurring by example using dense correspondence. In: ICCV (2013)
8. Hays, J., Efros, A.A.: Im2gps: estimating geographic information from a single image. In: CVPR (2008)
9. Köhler, R., Hirsch, M., Mohler, B., Schölkopf, B., Harmeling, S.: Recording and playback of camera shake: benchmarking blind deconvolution with a real-world database. In: Fitzgibbon, A., Lazebnik, S., Perona, P., Sato, Y., Schmid, C. (eds.) ECCV 2012, Part VII. LNCS, vol. 7578, pp. 27–40. Springer, Heidelberg (2012)
10. Krishnan, D., Fergus, R.: Fast image deconvolution using hyper-laplacian priors. In: NIPS (2009)
11. Levi, E.: Using Natural Image Priors: Maximizing Or Sampling? Hebrew University of Jerusalem (2009), http://leibniz.cs.huji.ac.il/tr/1207.pdf
12. Levin, A., Fergus, R., Durand, F., Freeman, W.T.: Image and depth from a conventional camera with a coded aperture. ACM Transactions on Graphics (2007)
13. Levin, A., Nadler, B., Durand, F., Freeman, W.T.: Patch complexity, finite pixel correlations and optimal denoising. In: Fitzgibbon, A., Lazebnik, S., Perona, P., Sato, Y., Schmid, C. (eds.) ECCV 2012, Part V. LNCS, vol. 7576, pp. 73–86. Springer, Heidelberg (2012)
14. Levin, A., Weiss, Y.: User assisted separation of reflections from a single image using a sparsity prior. TPAMI (2007)
15. Levin, A., Weiss, Y., Durand, F., Freeman, W.T.: Understanding and evaluating blind deconvolution algorithms. In: CVPR (2009)
16. Levin, A., Weiss, Y., Durand, F., Freeman, W.T.: Efficient marginal likelihood optimization in blind deconvolution. In: CVPR (2011)
17. Roth, S., Black, M.J.: Fields of experts: A framework for learning image priors. In: CVPR (2005)
18. Schmidt, U., Rother, C., Nowozin, S., Jancsary, J., Roth, S.: Discriminative non-blind deblurring. In: CVPR (2013)
19. Schuler, C., Burger, H., Harmeling, S., Schölkopf, B.: A machine learning approach for non-blind image deconvolution. In: CVPR (2013)
20. Sun, L., Cho, S., Wang, J., Hays, J.: Edge-based blur kernel estimation using patch priors. In: ICCP (2013)
21. Weiss, Y., Freeman, W.T.: What makes a good model of natural images? In: CVPR (2007)

22. Xu, L., Jia, J.: Two-phase kernel estimation for robust motion deblurring. In: Daniilidis, K., Maragos, P., Paragios, N. (eds.) ECCV 2010, Part I. LNCS, vol. 6311, pp. 157–170. Springer, Heidelberg (2010)
23. Yu, G., Sapiro, G., Mallat, S.: Solving inverse problems with piecewise linear estimators: From gaussian mixture models to structured sparsity. Transactions on Image Processing (2012)
24. Yue, H., Sun, X., Yang, J., Wu, F.: Landmark image super-resolution by retrieving web images. IEEE Transactions on Image Processing (2013)
25. Zoran, D., Weiss, Y.: From learning models of natural image patches to whole image restoration. In: ICCV (2011)
26. Zuo, W., Zhang, L., Song, C., Zhang, D.: Texture enhanced image denoising via gradient histogram preservation. In: CVPR (2013)

Image Deconvolution Ringing Artifact Detection and Removal via PSF Frequency Analysis

Ali Mosleh[1], J.M. Pierre Langlois[1], and Paul Green[2]

[1] École Polytechnique de Montréal, Canada
[2] Algolux, Canada
{ali.mosleh,pierre.langlois}@polymtl.ca, paul.green@algolux.com

Abstract. We present a new method to detect and remove ringing artifacts produced by the deconvolution process in image deblurring techniques. The method takes into account non-invertible frequency components of the blur kernel used in the deconvolution. Efficient Gabor wavelets are produced for each non-invertible frequency and applied on the deblurred image to generate a set of filter responses that reveal existing ringing artifacts. The set of Gabor filters is then employed in a regularization scheme to remove the corresponding artifacts from the deblurred image. The regularization scheme minimizes the responses of the reconstructed image to these Gabor filters through an alternating algorithm in order to suppress the artifacts. As a result of these steps we are able to significantly enhance the quality of the deblurred images produced by deconvolution algorithms. Our numerical evaluations using a ringing artifact metric indicate the effectiveness of the proposed deringing method.

Keywords: deconvolution, image deblurring, point spread function, ringing artifacts, zero-magnitude frequency.

1 Introduction

Despite considerable advancements in camera lens stabilizers and shake reduction hardware, blurry images are still often generated due to the camera motion during the exposure time. Hence, effective restoration is required to deblur captured images. Assuming that the imaging system is shift invariant, it can be modeled as

$$b = l \oplus k + \omega, \tag{1}$$

where $b \in \mathbb{R}^{MN}$ is the blurred captured image, $l \in \mathbb{R}^{MN}$ is the latent sharp image, $k \in \mathbb{R}^{MN \times MN}$ is the point spread function (PSF) that describes the degree of blurring of the point object captured by the camera, $\omega \in \mathbb{R}^{MN}$ is the additive noise, and $\oplus$ denotes the 2D convolution operator. Hence, the objective of the deblurring process is to recover l from b. Image deconvolution is often used for that purpose. One may neglect the noise and consider a naive solution for this inverse problem as

$$l = \mathcal{F}^{-} \left(\frac{\mathcal{F}(b)}{\mathcal{F}(k)} \right), \tag{2}$$

D. Fleet et al. (Eds.): ECCV 2014, Part IV, LNCS 8692, pp. 247–262, 2014.

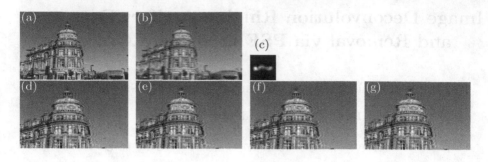

Fig. 1. Deblurred images with ringing artifacts. (a) Ground-truth image. (b) Degraded image. (c) Blur kernel (PSF). (d)-(g) Deblurring results using RL, [6], [12], and [21]. The images are rescaled for a better illustration. (The figures in this paper are best viewed on screen, rather than in print).

where $\mathcal{F}(.)$ denotes the 2D Fourier transform operator. Even if the PSF k is known precisely, this approach results in amplified singularities in the presence of a very small amount of noise. This occurs due to the characteristics of blur kernels and the unknown Fourier transform of the random noise function [1]. Hence, numerous deconvolution algorithms have been developed to estimate the latent sharp image. They include Wiener [2] and Richardson-Lucy (RL) [3, 4] techniques, least squares minimization [5], Bayesian inference [6–8], advanced variational based [9–13], and stochastic framework [14] methods.

A challenging problem in latent image restoration is the presence of wave-like artifacts called ringing that appear near strong edges. Ringing examples are illustrated in Fig. 1. These light and dark ripples are mainly due to the Gibbs phenomenon [15] as the Fourier sums overshoot at discontinuities (i.e., image edges), and this overshoot does not die out while the frequency increases. This phenomenon can be amplified if the noise ω is not modeled accurately and if the PSF k is noisy or inaccurately estimated [6]. The latter case is even more serious in blind deconvolution approaches [16–19] that involve PSF estimation from the blurred image.

Several researchers have considered the ringing issue and tried to reduce the artifacts in deconvolution schemes. Yuan et al. [20] addressed ringing artifacts by adapting edge-preserving bilateral filters to the conventional RL algorithm in a residual multiscale deconvolution approach. Shan et al. [6] proposed a spatially random noise model to separate errors in noise and PSF estimation. They also proposed to impose a smoothness constraint on the latent image to suppress ringing artifacts in the deconvolution process. Cho et al. [21] recognized saturated pixels, pixels degraded by non-Gaussian noise, and a non-linear camera response function violate the linear blur model of Eq. (1) and cause severe ringing artifacts. The camera temporal shutter modulation proposed by Raskar et al. [22] generates a very flat frequency spectrum. This eliminates zeros from the PSF to overcome the occurrence of zeros in the denominator in the deconvolution process and consequently to reduce artifacts. The idea of taking into account the zero frequencies of the PSF was also employed in the design of the coded aperture of Levin et al. [23] in removal of the out of focus blur. Increasing the weight of the regularizer term in the variational-based deconvolution techniques can also suppress the ringing artifacts. However, this over-smooths the recovered image and removes its edges [10–12]. Employing appropriate priors in such regularization schemes may reduce the potential artifacts as done partially by using cross-channel priors introduced by Heide et al. [24]. A means of ringing artifact detection can be quite effective to add ringing a priori knowledge to the deconvolution algorithm.

Ringing artifact detection algorithms were initially developed to evaluate the quality of compressed images impaired by ringing artifacts [25, 26]. These algorithms are not practical in detection of ringing artifacts produced in the deconvolution process, since the nature of ringing artifacts is different in image compression and image deconvolution. This yields a need for deconvolution-specific algorithms to detect ringing artifacts. The deblurred image is passed through a bank of Gabor-like wavelets by Zuo et al. [27], then the vertical and horizontal oscillation peaks are counted in the image filter responses as a metric for ringing artifacts. Since the employed filters are neither adapted to the content of the image nor to the PSF, high frequency patterns and textures in the image are falsely classified as artifacts in the filter response. A ringing detection procedure was proposed by Liu et al. [28]. It consists of generating a pyramid of different scales of the recovered image and finding the gradient difference between each level of the pyramid. Such ringing artifact detectors are appropriate only for quality assessment of the deblurred image and are not directly involved in an approach to produce artifact-free deblurred images.

In this paper, we first propose a deconvolution ringing artifact detection scheme based on the inspection of the saddle points and identifying the zeros in the PSF frequency response. Specific 2D Gabor wavelets with appropriate directionality and wavelength properties are then generated for the PSF components responsible for ringing artifacts. The produced 2D wavelets are used to localize the artifacts in the deblurred image. Next, the ringing artifacts are removed from the image by employing the produced wavelets in a variational-like regularization algorithm. We in fact suppress the artifacts by minimizing the image response to the generated Gabor filters. We introduce a priori knowledge of the ringing artifact locations in the restored image, by taking into account frequency details of the PSF and employing Gabor filters. The deblurring process independence of the proposed method is so that it can be applied on the result of any deconvolution approach. We show that besides its simplicity, this scheme significantly enhances the deconvolution results in terms of ringing artifact reduction which is still a challenge in image restoration.

The rest of the paper is organized as follows. In Section 2, the PSF frequency analysis and ringing artifact detection scheme is presented. In Section 3, a regularization algorithm is introduced to remove the artifacts by employing the artifact detection filters in a variational-based minimization. We then present experimental results in Section 4, followed by our conclusions in Section 5.

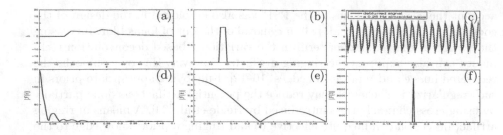

Fig. 2. 1D signal restoration using Eq. (2). (a-c) Blurred signal, PSF, and deblurred signal in the time domain. (d-f) Blurred signal, PSF, and deblurred signal in the frequency domain.

2   Ringing Artifact Detection

The principle of deblurring consists of decoupling the blur function from the observed image as in Eq. (2). However, mainly since the noise is neglected, this model generates severe artifacts. Although this model has been modified to include reasonable noise models in the modern deconvolution techniques, the inevitable presence of zero values in the denominator of Eq. (2) is a problematic source of ringing artifacts. This issue is shown in Fig. 2 for a 1D signal restoration. A 1D signal is convolved with the PSF shown in Fig. 2(b) to generate the blurred signal Fig. 2(a). This signal is then deblurred using Eq. (2) and the result is shown in Fig. 2(c). By inspecting the Fourier transform of the PSF (Fig. 2(e)) we find that at the frequency of 0.25 Hz the PSF has zero magnitude. In other words, PSF components that belong to the 0.25 Hz band have very low power. These components generate large amplitude oscillations at the same frequency in the deblurred signal (Fig. 2(f)). Therefore, in the time domain of the deblurred signal, components that belong to the 0.25 Hz frequency band dominate the signal. This effect appears as a sinusoidal pattern with a high amplitude in the deblurred signal and is considered a ringing artifact. From the large amplitude of the reconstructed signal Fig. 2(c) (-20 to 20) compared to that of the blurred signal Fig. 2(a) (0 to 5) we can infer how corrupted the deblurring result is. Such zero power frequency components in a 2D PSF can be largely responsible for disturbing ringing artifacts in 2D signals i.e., images. The fact that ringing artifacts follow a sinusoidal pattern inspired the deconvolution artifact detection techniques of Zuo et. al [27] and Liu et al. [28]. This is even more promising that from our PSF frequency analysis we can predict the frequency of this sinusoidal wave. This is shown for the 1D case in Fig. 2(c) by a superimposed sinusoidal signal indicated by a red diagram whose frequency of 0.25 Hz is chosen by inspection of the PSF frequency spectrum Fig. 2(e).

2.1   Using Gabor Filters

The Gabor filter is a traditional choice for obtaining localized frequency information. A 2D Gabor filter offers an efficient localization of spatial and frequency information. Frequency and orientation representations of 2D Gabor filters have been shown to be appropriate for texture discrimination [29]. Since the impulse response of a Gabor filter is a sinusoidal wave plane, it can be an effective tool to detect the image ringing artifacts that follow sinusoidal patterns. The 2D Gabor filter is defined as

$$g(x,y) = \frac{1}{2\pi\sigma_x\sigma_y} e^{-\frac{1}{2}\left(\frac{x^2}{\sigma_x^2} + \frac{y^2}{\sigma_y^2}\right)} e^{-j2\pi((u_0 x + v_0 y) + \phi)}. \tag{3}$$

The Gabor function can be viewed as a sinusoidal plane of particular frequency and orientation, modulated by a Gaussian envelope. In Eq. (3) (x,y) denotes the spatial location, σ_x and σ_y are respectively the horizontal and vertical standard deviations of the Gaussian envelope, u_0 and v_0 are respectively the x-axis and y-axis frequencies of the sinusoidal plane, and ϕ is the phase offset.

The spatial frequency of the ringing artifacts in a deblurred image can be determined by inspecting the Fourier transform of the PSF. The coordinate of a zero value in the Fourier transform of the PSF represents the spatial frequency of the ringing components in the deblurred image. Substituting u_0 and v_0 in Eq. (3) by the spatial frequency of a zero magnitude frequency component of the PSF results in an appropriate filter to localize the image artifacts produced by that frequency component. The parameters σ_x and σ_y of the Gaussian kernel in the filter can be selected based on the deblurred image contents. They should not be either too high to taper the image edges and misclassify them as ringing artifacts, or too low to miss the low intensity ringing artifacts. We need to ensure that the image ringing pattern with a delay or an advance (different phase offsets) will be detected by the filter. Hence, first one filter is produced with $\phi = 0$ and another one is generated with $\phi = \pi/2$, then the generated filters with different phase offsets are superimposed to make a single filter.

As an example of the process consider Fig. 3, where a blurred synthetic image and its PSF are shown in Fig. 3(b). This image is deblurred using the RL method as illustrated in Fig. 3(c). As seen in this figure, compared with the ground-truth image Fig. 3(a), the deblurring result contains ringing artifacts especially in the brighter region of the image. In order to have a better insight, the diagram of the first 140 pixel intensities at row 200 of the deblurred image is shown by the blue plot in Fig. 3(g). From the frequency spectrum of the PSF Fig. 3(e), the low-magnitude component with spatial frequencies $u_0 = -0.045$ and $v_0 = 0.001$ is picked as the source of ringing artifacts. (The procedure to select such frequencies is discussed in Section 2.2.) The Gabor filter exhibited in Fig. 3(d) is generated using Eq. (3) by utilizing these horizontal and vertical frequencies. The filter is then convolved with the deblurred image to localize the sinusoidal artifacts. The thresholded filter response of the deblurred image Fig. 3(h) reveals the regions that contain artifacts in the deblurred image. The Gabor filter response at row 200 of the image is illustrated in Fig. 3(g) (red dashed plot), along with the deblurred pixel intensities (blue plot). In this case, the Gabor filter generated with the frequencies obtained from the PSF, effectively fits and localizes the wave-like artifacts produced in the deconvolution process.

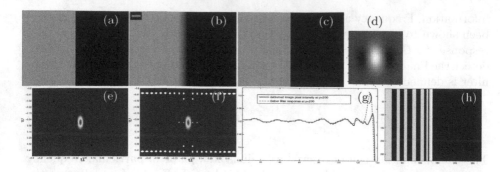

Fig. 3. Ringing detection by employing Gabor filter and the PSF frequency details. (a) Ground-truth image (originally 256 × 256). (b) Synthetically blurred image and its PSF. (c) Deblurred image that contains ringing artifacts. (d) Generated Gabor filter for artifact detection (enlarged for a better illustration). (e) The blur PSF in Frequency domain. (f) Saddle points and zero points in the frequency spectrum of the PSF. (g) Pixel intensity values and Gabor filter response values on row 200 of the image. (h) Thresholded image Gabor filter response to locate the ringing regions

2.2   Artifact Detection Algorithm

The ringing artifact detection algorithm first analyses the PSF to locate the zero-magnitude components in the Fourier domain. Then, for each component a Gabor filter is generated. There may exist many zero-magnitude frequency components in the PSF but not all of them are useful in the artifact detection process. The zero values located far from the center of the frequency spectrum may cause ringing but the frequency of their produced ringing is too high to be perceivable. Therefore, we avoid them in the process to reduce the number of Gabor filters employed in the scheme. Such kind of frequency components are marked with the white dots in the Fourier transform of the PSF shown in Fig. 3(f). Also, a sharp transient in the frequency domain of the PSF denotes an apparent oscillatory decay in the PSF which is the cause of the dominant ringing in the restored image. Hence, we reduce the number of required Gabor filters to the number of zero-magnitude frequency components of the PSF that lie on the saddle points of the PSF Fourier transform. This is done by creating a map of local minimum points in the Fourier domain using a morphological operator:

$$
m(\acute{p}, \acute{q}) = \begin{cases} 1 & \text{if } \left(\hat{K}(\acute{p}, \acute{q}) < \hat{K}(p, q), \forall p \in [p - \ell, p + \ell] \wedge \ \forall q \in [q - \ell, q + \ell] \right) \\ & \wedge \left((p, q) \neq (\acute{p}, \acute{q}) \wedge \hat{K}(\acute{p}, \acute{q}) < \delta \right) \\ 0 & \text{otherwise} , \end{cases}
$$

(4)

where $\hat{K} = |\mathcal{F}(k)|$ denotes the magnitude matrix of the Fourier transform of the PSF indexed by q and p, and ℓ determines the number of neighbouring values in $\hat{K}$. δ is a small value near zero used as a threshold to determine the low values, and m is the map of local minima of $\hat{K}$. The white crosses in Fig. 3(f) are the appropriate points found by Eq. (4) in the PSF frequency spectrum.

Algorithm 1. Ringing articfact detection.

Require: Deblurred image l, deconvolution PSF k, Gabor filter parameters σ_x and σ_y

1: Generate r an $M \times N$ matrix of zeros
2: Generate m using Eq. (4)
3: $j = 0$
4: **for** $(p, q) = (1, 1)$ to $(p, q) = (M, N)$ **do**
5:    **if** $m(p, q) = 1$ **then**
6:       $j = j + 1$
7:       $u_0 \leftarrow$ map p to frequency
8:       $v_0 \leftarrow$ map q to frequency
9:       Generate g^j using Eq. (3)
10:      Find filter response $y^j = l \oplus g^j$
11:      $\acute{y}^j \leftarrow$ Binerize y^j
12:      $r = r \vee \acute{y}^j$
13:    **end if**
14:   $N_{freq} = j$
15: **end for**
16: **return** $r, \{g^1, g^2, ..., g^{N_{freq}}\}$

In the next step, a set of Gabor filters is generated using the spatial frequencies determined by m. Each filter is then applied on the deblurred image l to produce different responses that represent ringing patterns with different frequencies and orientations. The filtering results are then binarized and superimposed to make a mask of all regions that contain ringing in the image. Algorithm 1 outlines all the steps of the ringing artifact detection method, where $\vee$ denotes the element-wise binary or operator to superimpose results. The principal objective of this algorithm is localizing the artifact regions. However, as will be discussed in the next section, in order to remove the artifacts we need the set of Gabor filters generated by Algorithm 1. Hence, in addition to the map of ringing regions r, the set of Gabor filters is returned by this algorithm for a later artifact removal procedure.

The ringing detection algorithm may falsely classify the image edges as part of the ringing pattern especially if the ringing occurs near strong edges. To avoid this issue, the process should be performed only on the smooth regions and not the edges. This cannot be done by simply running an edge detector to preserve the edges before the artifact detection step since the ringing artifacts would be detected by the edge detection schemes. Instead, we propose to analyse the local contrast of the image and run the algorithm on low contrast regions where there is no edge pixel. Typically, contrast is estimated by Weber's formula: $C_l = (l_o - l_b)/l_b$ where l_o and l_b are the luminance of the object and its surrounding background, respectively. More complex contrast analysis can be performed by employing discrete cosine transform and wavelets [30, 31]. We use the local mean $mean(l)$ and standard deviation $std(l)$ of the image intensity to estimate the contrast of a region with its background [32] $C_l = std(l)/mean(l)$. This value is computed for all existing blocks (e.g., 4×4 pixels) in the input image, then the regions with large C_l are removed from the binary mask generated at line 11 in Algorithm 1. Hence, edges are not detected as part of the ringing artifacts.

3   Ringing Artifact Removal

Let g^j be a Gabor filter generated from the jth zero-magnitude frequency component of the PSF. Hence, for a PSF employed in the deblurring process with N_{freq} zero-magnitude frequency components, we generate a set of Gabor filters $g^1, g^2, ..., g^{N_{freq}}$ to detect the ringing artifacts in the deblurred image l. The ringing artifacts detected by analysing the PSF frequency components and Gabor filters can be suppressed through a regularization scheme. Our artifact suppression technique, similar to the total variation [9] and Tikhonov regularization [33] methods widely used in inverse imaging problems, consists of a likelihood term and a regularizer as follows:

$$\underset{f}{\text{minimize}}\, \frac{\mu}{2}||f - l||^2 + \sum_{j=1}^{N_{freq}} ||g^j f||_1, \tag{5}$$

where the left term is the likelihood function weighted by the regularization parameter μ and the right term is the regularizer. In (5), l is the observed (already deblurred with ringing artifacts) image and f is the reconstructed image. In fact, some a priori knowledge about the unknown image (i.e., ringing artifacts and their locations) is added to the likelihood function by employing the regularizer. Note that $||.||_1$ is the L_1 norm, $||.||$ is the L_2 norm and $||.||^2$ is its square, and for brevity $g^j f \equiv f \oplus g^j$ where $\oplus$ denotes the 2D convolution operator.

Despite its simple formulation, problem (5) is computationally challenging to solve. This is mainly due to the non-differentiability and non-linearity of the regularizer [34]. According to [35] and [36], such regularization problems can be addressed using the half-quadratic penalty method. Therefore, we follow the variable splitting scheme employed in [10–12, 37] to solve (5). We introduce auxiliary variables $u = \{u^1, ..., u^{N_{freq}}\}$ to transfer $g^j f$ out of the non-differentiable term $||.||_1$ in (5) to model the optimization as

$$\underset{f,u}{\text{minimize}}\, \frac{\mu}{2}||f - l||^2 + \frac{\beta}{2} \sum_{j=1}^{N_{freq}} ||g^j f - u^j||^2 + \sum_{j=1}^{N_{freq}} ||u^j||_1, \tag{6}$$

with a penalty parameter β. The value of this penalty parameter has an important role in convergence of (6) [10]. When $\beta \to \infty$, the solution of the approximation problem (6) converges to that of (5). Using the information r obtained about the locations of the ringing regions, β is adapted so that the regulirizer term has the least effect on the pixels that do not belong to the ringing regions. Consider β as an $N \times M$ matrix whose elements indexed by (x, y) defined as

$$\beta(x, y) = \begin{cases} \beta_0 & \text{if } r(x, y) = 0 \\ \tilde{\beta} & \text{otherwise}, \end{cases} \tag{7}$$

where $\tilde{\beta} \to \infty$ and β_0 is a small constant in the deringing process. Hence, the weight of artifact-free pixels remains small in (6) and the ringing minimization is carried out only on the pixels identified by r in Algorithm 1. Note that in (6) the multiplication is performed element-wise on β.

The optimization problem (6) can be performed by alternating between two steps in an iterative scheme. In one step we solve for f, given values of u:

$$\underset{f}{\text{minimize}} \frac{\mu}{2}||f - l||^2 + \frac{\beta}{2} \sum_{j=1}^{N_{freq}} ||g^j f - u^j||^2, \tag{8}$$

and in another step we solve for u, given values of f:

$$\underset{u}{\text{minimize}} \frac{\beta}{2} \sum_{j=1}^{N_{freq}} ||g^j f - u^j||^2 + \sum_{j=1}^{N_{freq}} ||u^j||_1. \tag{9}$$

which is in fact solving N_{freq} sub-problems of:

$$\underset{u^j}{\text{minimize}} \frac{\beta}{2}||g^j f - u^j||^2 + ||u^j||_1 \tag{10}$$

3.1 f Sub-problem

Given u which is obtained from the previous iteration, we need to solve (8) to approximate a new f. A fixed value for u yields a quadratic form for (8). Hence, the solution for this problem can be the solution for the normal equation as

$$\left(\sum_{j=1}^{N_{freq}} g^{j^T} g^j + \frac{\mu}{\beta} h \right) f = \left(\sum_{j=1}^{N_{freq}} g^{j^T} u^j \right) + \frac{\mu}{\beta} l, \tag{11}$$

where h is an $N \times M$ matrix of ones. Using the Fourier transform, (11) can be rewritten as

$$f = \mathcal{F}^{-1} \left(\frac{\sum_{j=1}^{N_{freq}} \mathcal{F}(g^j)^* \mathcal{F}(u^j) + \frac{\mu}{\beta}\mathcal{F}(l)}{\sum_{j=1}^{N_{freq}} \mathcal{F}(g^j)^* \mathcal{F}(g^j) + \frac{\mu}{\beta}\mathcal{F}(h)} \right), \tag{12}$$

where the multiplications are element-wise and $*$ denotes the complex conjugate.

3.2 u Sub-problem

Finding an optimal u is subject to minimizing (10) independently for each Gabor filter, in total N_{freq} times. This minimization can be done using the conventional approaches such as Newton-Raphson. It was shown in [10, 37] that such type of problems can be reduced to a shrinkage scheme so we can avoid the computational challenges of the conventional optimization methods. Hence, each component of u^j indexed by i can be approximated as follows:

$$u_i^j = \max\left(|(g^j f)_i| - \frac{1}{\beta_i}, 0 \right) \text{sgn}(g^j f)_i, \tag{13}$$

where $\max(.)$ returns the maximum and $\text{sgn}(.)$ is the sign function.

Algorithm 2. Ringing artifact suppression.

Require: Deblurred image l, Gabor filters $g^1, ..., g^{N_{freq}}$, r, β_0, β_{max}, μ
1: $f = l$, $\tilde{\beta} = \beta_0$
2: **while** $\tilde{\beta} < \beta_{max}$ **do**
3:    Find β using Eq. (7)
4:    **for** $j = 1$ to N_{freq} **do**
5:       Given f, find u^j using Eq. (13)
6:    **end for**
7:    Given u, find f using Eq. (12)
8:    $\tilde{\beta} = \tilde{\beta} \times 2$
9: **end while**
10: **return** f

Fig. 4. Sample blurry images and their blur kernels used in our tests and the Gabor filters generated for artifact removal. (a) Image 1: The original image is synthetically blurred using the motion blur PSF available in [28]. (b) Image 2: The blurry image and its estimated PSF are provided by Shan et al. [6]. (c) Image 3: The blurry image and the PSF are captured using a dual-camera set-up. The kernels in (a), (b) and (c) are 4 times larger than the original sizes, for a better view. (d-f) Gabor filters used in artifact detection and removal for the image shown in (a), (b), and (c) respectively.

3.3   Summary of the Artifact Removal Algorithm

The optimization process is outlined in Algorithm 2. We minimize (6) by alternating between the f and u sub-problems. As mentioned before, for the optimization problem to converge we need to satisfy $\beta \to \infty$ for the corresponding ringing pixels. Therefore, we initiate $\tilde{\beta}$ with β_0 and increment it during the iterations. The iterations stop once $\tilde{\beta} = \beta_{max}$. It is worth noting that the fixed parameters in Eq. (8), such as $\mathcal{F}(g^1), \mathcal{F}(g^2), ..., \mathcal{F}(g^{N_{freq}})$ and their conjugates, $\mathcal{F}(l)$, and $\mathcal{F}(h)$ can be precomputed to save some computational time.

4   Experimental Results

We evaluated the performance of the proposed artifact detection and removal scheme on images. To this end, a set of blurry images were used. Three different types of blurry image and PSF pairs belong to this set. The first type of blurry images were created synthetically with known PSFs, as presented in [28]. An example of such images and PSFs is shown in Fig. 4(a). Another type of images were captured by camera that contain motion (handshake) blur. Using a blind

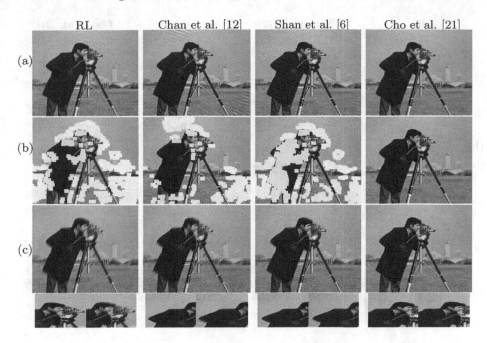

Fig. 5. Deblurring Image 1 synthetically blurred using a known PSF. (a) Deblurring results using different algorithms. (b) Detected ringing regions. (c) Deringing results.

deconvolution approach, a PSF was estimated for each image. An example of such images and their PSFs is shown in Fig. 4(b) provided by Shan et al. [6]. Finally, we built a dual-camera framework similar to that of Ben-Ezra and Nayar [38] to estimate the PSF from the camera motion in the exposure time. Fig. 4(c) shows an image and its corresponding PSF captured using this framework. The blurry images were deblurred by employing different algorithms: (i) RL [3, 4], (ii) Chan et al.'s method [12] that uses total variation norm prior and L_2 variant prior, (iii) the algorithm of Shan et al. [6] using a smoothness prior, and (iv) that of Cho et al. [21] by handling ringing prone pixels. The deblurring results are demonstrated in Fig. 5(a), Fig. 6(a) and Fig. 7(a). The input parameters for the deblurring algorithms [6, 12, 21] such as regularization weights and smoothness factors are chosen so that they do not generate over-smoothened and cartoon-like results. As seen in these figures, all of the employed deconvolution schemes generate ringing artifacts, except Cho et al.'s algorithm for Image 1. This image is synthetically blurred and its PSF is precise. Hence, it is deblurred well using Cho et al.'s method where ringing prone outliers are well-handled. Algorithm 1 was performed on the deblurred images to locate the artifacts generated in the deconvolution stage. Then, the filters produced by Algorithm 1 were used in Algorithm 2 to suppress the ringing artifacts.

In the ringing detection step, the Gaussian parameters were set as $\sigma_x = 8$ and $\sigma_y = 8$ in Algorithm 1. Also, $\delta = 0.0001$ and $\ell = 5$ so that 11×11 points

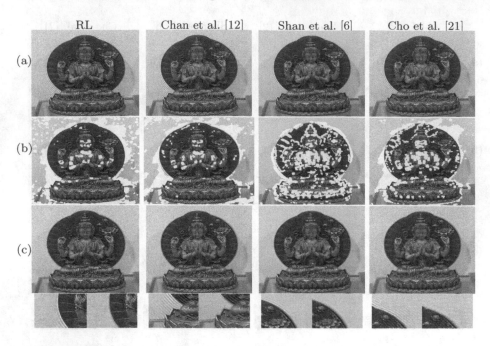

Fig. 6. Deblurring Image 2 using a PSF estimated through blind deconvolution. (The horizontal pattern in the background is part of the original scene and should not be mistaken by ringing patterns.)(a) Deblurring results using different algorithms. (b) Detected ringing regions. (c) Deringing results.

are considered in Eq. (4). Due to the symmetry of the Fourier transform of the PSF, half of the detected minima points can be discarded. This reduces the number of Gabor filters required in the detection process. Ringing artifact detection results are presented in Fig. 5(b), Fig. 6(b), Fig. 7(b). The generated sets of Gabor filters obtained for these examples are shown in Fig. 4(d)-(f). The detected ringing mask for each example is superimposed on the deblurred image with a yellow color. Almost all ringing regions in the deblurred images were detected by the algorithm. The deblurring process is more challenging for the blurry images in Fig. 6 and 7 than for the image presented in Fig. 5. The PSF used in the deblurring process of the image in Fig. 6 was estimated through blind deconvolution. Hence, it may not accurately represent the blur function of the imaging system and can be a different source of ringing artifacts. The same issue may arise from the PSF of Fig. 7 produced using the hybrid-imaging framework. Such PSFs contain sharp discontinuities due to the quantization and interpolation mechanisms employed in the PSF estimation procedure. Moreover, they likely do not represent all of the points of the image [39]. Thus, these PSFs violate the spatial invariance assumption of Eq. (1). Among our test images, the PSF of Image 3 is the extreme case of producing ringing artifacts. Despite such challenges, the ringing artifact detection algorithm detected almost all of the

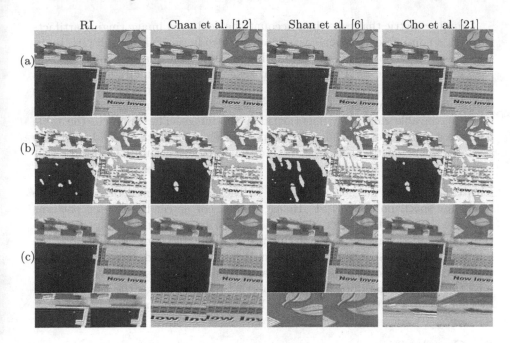

Fig. 7. Deblurring Image 3 using a camera motion-based PSF captured with a hybrid imaging system. (a) Deblurring results using different algorithms. (b) Detected ringing regions. (c) Deringing results

Table 1. Ringing artifact measurement for different algorithms and deringing results

	Deblurring Algorithms:	RL	Chan et al. [12]	Shan et al. [6]	Cho et al. [21]
Image 1	Deblurring	0.00037	0.00210	0.00089	0.00010
	Deblurring and Deringing	0.00016	0.00022	0.00031	0.00010
Image 2	Deblurring	0.02440	0.00470	0.00112	0.00406
	Deblurring and Deringing	0.00290	0.00282	0.00091	0.00270
Image 3	Deblurring	0.00580	0.00481	0.00673	0.00510
	Deblurring and Deringing	0.00201	0.00163	0.00210	0.00170

ringing regions in the deblurring results of these examples. This is largely due to the fact that artifacts caused by zero-magnitude frequency components of a PSF dominate the ringing patterns present in a deblurred image. Algorithm 2 employs the detected ringing regions and the generated Gabor filters by Algorithm 1 in order to provide a priori knowledge to the regularization scheme to enhance the deblurred images. Algorithm 2 was performed on the deblurring results of the deconvolution schemes. In our simulations, $\beta_0 = 1$ and $\beta_{max} = 64$. Hence, the algorithm runs for 6 iterations. Another important parameter is the weight μ of the likelihood term in the deringing problem (5). A typical value for μ is 1000, so that the process does not remove or over-smooth the essential details of the image. Fig. 5(c), Fig. 6(c) and Fig. 7(c) illustrate the apparent enhancement carried out by the deringing process.

A quality metric that takes into account the deblurred image ringing artifacts through a non-reference scheme was recently introduced by Lui et al. [28]. In order to provide an objective evaluation, this non-reference quality assessment was used in our experiments. Table 1 summarizes the obtained quality measurements for the deblurred images using different approaches and their post-deconvolution deringing results. A high value obtained for a deblurred image indicates that more perceivable ringing artifacts exist in the image. The values in the table indicate a high performance for the proposed ringing artifact removal algorithm and also the artifact detection algorithm that provides accurate Gabor filters.

Limitations. The method is adapted to the artifacts caused by zeros in the frequency spectrum of the PSF. Hence, it may not detect the ringing patterns generated due to other facts such as non-linearity of a camera response function, non-Gaussian noise, and violating the spatially invariant assumption of the imaging system. Also, the algorithm is customized by considering the local contrast factor to detect the most perceivable ringing artifacts. Therefore, it may miss the ringings that appear in high contrast regions such as the one produced by Chan et al.'s method near the right hand of the statue in Fig 6(b).

5   Conclusions

We proposed a new approach to suppress the ringing artifacts produced by image deblurring methods. The artifact removal algorithm is a variational-like regularization scheme that benefits from a novel a priori knowledge in reconstructing an artifact-free image from the deblurred image. The prior is the locations and intensities of the ringing artifacts determined efficiently by a set of Gabor filters. We proposed to generate Gabor filters for each deblurred image with regards to its PSF frequency components. Hence, each produced Gabor filter has specific orientation and frequency details obtained by inspecting the zero-magnitude frequency components of the PSF. Each filter is able to localize a ringing pattern in the deblurred image. We used such filters in the ringing removal process and introduced an independent algorithm to detect ringing artifacts for other purposes such as quality assessment. Our experimental results indicate high performance for both the artifact detection and artifact removal methods.

Although the proposed ringing artifact removal scheme was designed as a post-processing tool to enhance the results of any type of the image deblurring algorithms, the linearity property of Gabor filters makes the introduced prior fairly straight forward to be employed directly in variational-based deconvolution algorithms. The proposed a priori knowledge can be employed along with the total variation norm prior [10], Hyper-Laplacian prior [11], and/or the cross-channel prior [24] in a deconvolution algorithm in order to produce ringing-free deblurred images.

Acknowledgment. This work was supported in part by Mitacs.

References

1. Hansen, P.C., Nagy, J.G., O'Leary, D.P.: Deblurring Images: Matrices, Spectra, and Filtering. Society for Industrial and Applied Mathematics (2006)
2. Gonzlez, R.C., Woods, R.E.: Digital Image Processing. Prentice Hall, NJ (2002)
3. Richardson, W.H.: Bayesian-based iterative method of image restoration. J. Opt. Soc. Am. 62(1), 55–59 (1972)
4. Lucy, L.B.: An iterative technique for the rectification of observed distributions. Astronomical Journal 79(6), 745–754 (1974)
5. Mesarovic, V.Z., Galatsanos, N.P., Katsaggelos, A.K.: Regularized constrained total least squares image restoration. IEEE Transactions on Image Processing 4(8), 1096–1108 (1995)
6. Shan, Q., Jia, J., Agarwala, A.: High-quality motion deblurring from a single image. ACM Transactions on Graphics (SIGGRAPGH) 27(3), 73:1–73:10 (2008)
7. Babacan, S.D., Molina, R., Do, M.N., Katsaggelos, A.K.: Bayesian blind deconvolution with general sparse image priors. In: Fitzgibbon, A., Lazebnik, S., Perona, P., Sato, Y., Schmid, C. (eds.) ECCV 2012, Part VI. LNCS, vol. 7577, pp. 341–355. Springer, Heidelberg (2012)
8. Levin, A., Weiss, Y., Durand, F., Freeman, W.T.: Efficient marginal likelihood optimization in blind deconvolution. In: IEEE Conference on Computer Vision and Pattern Recognition (CVPR), pp. 2657–2664 (2011)
9. Rudin, L., Osher, S., Fatemi, E.: Nonlinear total variation based noise removal algorithms. Physica D: Nonlinear Phenomena 60(1), 259–268 (1992)
10. Wang, Y., Yang, J., Yin, W., Zhang, Y.: A new alternating minimization algorithm for total variation image reconstruction. SIAM Journal on Imaging Sciences 1(3), 248–272 (2008)
11. Krishnan, D., Fergus, R.: Fast image deconvolution using hyper-laplacian priors. In: Advances in Neural Information Processing Systems, pp. 1033–1041 (2009)
12. Chan, S.H., Khoshabeh, R., Gibson, K.B., Gill, P.E., Nguyen, T.Q.: An augmented Lagrangian method for total variation video restoration. IEEE Transactions on Image Processing 20(11), 3097–3111 (2011)
13. Chan, T., Golub, G., Mulet, P.: A nonlinear primal-dual method for total variation-based image restoration. SIAM Journal on Scientific Computing 20(6), 1964–1977 (1999)
14. Gregson, J., Heide, F., Hullin, M.B., Rouf, M., Heidrich, W.: Stochastic Deconvolution. In: IEEE Conference on Computer Vision and Pattern Recognition (CVPR), pp. 1043–1050 (June 2013)
15. Yuan, L., Sun, J., Quan, L., Shum, H.Y.: Image deblurring with blurred/noisy image pairs 26(3), 1–10 (2007)
16. Fergus, R., Singh, B., Hertzmann, A., Roweis, S.T., Freeman, W.T.: Removing camera shake from a single photograph 25(3), 787–794 (2006)
17. Levin, A., Weiss, Y., Durand, F., Freeman, W.T.: Understanding and evaluating blind deconvolution algorithms. In: IEEE Conference on Computer Vision and Pattern Recognition (CVPR), pp. 1964–1971 (2009)
18. Levin, A.: Blind motion deblurring using image statistics. In: Advances in Neural Information Processing Systems, pp. 841–848 (2006)
19. Xu, L., Jia, J.: Two-phase kernel estimation for robust motion deblurring. In: Daniilidis, K., Maragos, P., Paragios, N. (eds.) ECCV 2010, Part I. LNCS, vol. 6311, pp. 157–170. Springer, Heidelberg (2010)
20. Yuan, L., Sun, J., Quan, L., Shum, H.Y.: Progressive inter-scale and intra-scale non-blind image deconvolution 27(3), 74:1–74:10 (2008)

21. Cho, S., Wang, J., Lee, S.: Handling outliers in non-blind image deconvolution. In: IEEE International Conference on Computer Vision (ICCV), pp. 495–502 (2011)
22. Raskar, R., Agrawal, A., Tumblin, J.: Coded exposure photography: motion deblurring using fluttered shutter. ACM Transactions on Graphics (SIGGRAPH) 25, 795–804 (2006)
23. Levin, A., Fergus, R., Durand, F., Freeman, W.T.: Image and depth from a conventional camera with a coded aperture. ACM Transactions on Graphics (SIGGRAPH) 26(3), 70 (2007)
24. Heide, F., Rouf, M., Hullin, M.B., Labitzke, B., Heidrich, W., Kolb, A.: High-quality computational imaging through simple lenses. ACM Transactions on Graphics (SIGGRAPH) (2013)
25. Liu, H., Klomp, N., Heynderickx, I.: A perceptually relevant approach to ringing region detection. IEEE Transactions on Image Peocessing 19(6), 1414–1426 (2010)
26. Liu, H., Klomp, N., Heynderickx, I.: A no-reference metric for perceived ringing artifacts in images. IEEE Transactions on Circuits and Systems for Video Technology 20(4), 529–539 (2010)
27. Zuo, B.X., Ming, D.L., Tian, J.W.: Perceptual ringing metric to evaluate the quality of images restored using blind deconvolution algorithms. Optical Engineering 48(3), 037004–037004 (2009)
28. Liu, Y., Wang, J., Cho, S., Finkelstein, A., Rusinkiewicz, S.: A no-reference metric for evaluating the quality of motion deblurring. ACM Transactions on Graphics (SIGGRAPH Asia) (2013)
29. Jain, A.K., Farrokhnia, F.: Unsupervised texture segmentation using gabor filters. In: IEEE International Conference on Systems, Man and Cybernetics, pp. 14–19 (1990)
30. Peli, E.: Contrast sensitivity function and image discrimination. Journal of Optical Society of America 18(2), 283–293 (2001)
31. Tang, J., Kim, J., Peli, E.: Image enhancement in the JPEG domain for people with vision impairment. IEEE Transactions on Biomedical Engineering 51(11), 2013–2023 (2004)
32. Reinhard, E., Shirley, P., Ashikhmin, M., Troscianko, T.: Second order image statistics in computer graphics. In: Symposium on Applied Perception in Graphics and Visualization, pp. 99–106 (2004)
33. Tikhonov, A., Arsenin, V.: Solutions of Ill-posed Problems. Winston and Sons, Washington (1977)
34. Goldstein, T., Osher, S.: The split Bsregman method for L1-regularized problems. SIAM Journal on Imaging Sciences 2(2), 323–343 (2009)
35. Geman, D., Reynolds, G.: Constrained restoration and the recovery of discontinuities. IEEE Transactions on Pattern Analysis and Machine Intelligence 14(3), 367–383 (1992)
36. Geman, D., Yang, C.: Nonlinear image recovery with half-quadratic regularization. IEEE Transactions on Image Processing 4(7), 932–946 (1995)
37. Yang, J., Zhang, Y., Yin, W.: An efficient TVL1 algorithm for deblurring multichannel images corrupted by impulsive noise. SIAM Journal on Scientific Computing 31(4), 2842–2865 (2009)
38. Ben-Ezra, M., Nayar, S.: Motion-based motion deblurring. IEEE Transactions on Pattern Analysis and Machine Intelligence 26(6), 689–698 (2004)
39. Tai, Y.W., Du, H., Brown, M.S., Lin, S.: Image/video deblurring using a hybrid camera. In: IEEE Conference on Computer Vision and Pattern Recognition (CVPR), pp. 1–8 (2008)

View-Consistent 3D Scene Flow Estimation over Multiple Frames

Christoph Vogel[1], Stefan Roth[2], and Konrad Schindler[1]

[1] Photogrammetry and Remote Sensing, ETH Zurich, Switzerland
[2] Department of Computer Science, TU Darmstadt, Germany

Abstract. We propose a method to recover dense 3D scene flow from stereo video. The method estimates the depth and 3D motion field of a dynamic scene from *multiple consecutive frames* in a sliding temporal window, such that the estimate is *consistent across both viewpoints of all frames* within the window. The observed scene is modeled as a collection of planar patches that are consistent across views, each undergoing a rigid motion that is approximately constant over time. Finding the patches and their motions is cast as minimization of an energy function over the continuous plane and motion parameters and the discrete pixel-to-plane assignment. We show that such a view-consistent multi-frame scheme greatly improves scene flow computation in the presence of occlusions, and increases its robustness against adverse imaging conditions, such as specularities. Our method currently achieves leading performance on the KITTI benchmark, for both flow and stereo.

1 Introduction

The 3D scene flow is a dense description of surface geometry and 3D motion in a dynamic scene. Scene flow estimation analyzes images from two (or more) cameras taken at two (or more) time steps, and delivers depth and 3D motion densely for every pixel. Hence, it can be seen as a generalization of optical flow to 3D, or alternatively as stereo for dynamic scenes. Like these two classical problems, scene flow estimation is ill-posed due to the 3D equivalent of the aperture problem, and requires some form of regularization. Dense 3D shape and motion are useful for a variety of tasks, including motion capture [26], 3D video generation for 3D-TV [12] and driver assistance (*e.g.*, the Daimler *6D-vision* project [16,19,33]).

To this date most scene flow methods in the literature, *e.g.* [1,30,33], base their reconstruction on two consecutive stereo pairs, and declare one of the four images as a *reference view*, for which the shape and motion vectors are computed. The starting point for this work are two rather straightforward observations: *(i)* the two frames typically originate from a longer stereo video sequence, hence it seems wasteful not to exploit longer time intervals; and *(ii)* there is no conceptual reason for a privileged reference view, since imaging problems (occlusions, lack of contrast, *etc.*) affect all images equally. In the present paper we address these two points. Specifically, we propose to *simultaneously estimate depth and 3D*

D. Fleet et al. (Eds.): ECCV 2014, Part IV, LNCS 8692, pp. 263–278, 2014.

Fig. 1. Consistency over multiple frames makes scene flow estimation robust against severe disturbances like the windscreen wiper. *(left)* Input frames. *(middle)* The left view at time $t = 0$. *(right)* Our scene flow estimate for that viewpoint (shown, from left to right, as disparity and reprojected 2D flow field).

motion over longer time intervals, in such a way that the results are consistent across all views within that interval (see Fig. 1).

It seems evident that, at reasonable frame rates, physically plausible scenes exhibit temporal consistency over more than just two frames. We conjecture that long-term constraints may actually be more helpful for scene flow than for 2D optical flow, where the majority of today's top-performing methods only uses two frames. A scene flow reconstruction resides in 3D space rather than in its 2D projection, hence constraints caused by physical object properties like inertia remain valid in the long term, and can be exploited more directly.

The key motivation for, moreover, estimating the scene flow in all views and demanding consistency (rather than estimating it only in a single reference view) is to overcome viewpoint-dependent adversities like specularities and occlusions, where the image data is not consistent (see Fig. 1). Under difficult imaging conditions (large motions, specular reflections, occlusions, shadows) considering all views equally in our experience greatly improves robustness against outliers, and additionally allows for more reliable and accurate occlusion reasoning.

We propose to integrate both consistency across time and across views into a *single energy function*, such that one can jointly solve for a reconstruction by taking into account all evidence (rather than reconstructing independently for different frames or reference views and merging the results in post-processing). Having said that, we restrict the estimation to short temporal windows of up to 4 frames to limit the computational cost of our integrated solution. Moreover, going to longer and longer time intervals yields diminishing returns, and in many scenarios (*e.g.*, autonomous driving) immediate feedback is required, such that a time-lag of more than one or two frames is not acceptable.

Our approach leverages the scene flow representation of [28], *i.e.* the scene is modeled as a collection of planar and rigidly moving patches. This parameterization is more constrained than others in the literature, *e.g.* [1,25,33], but has been shown to be valid for road scenarios and other typical scenes of interest. It is well suited for our view-consistent multi-frame approach, since it drastically reduces the number of unknowns per frame, and inherently provides an (over-)segmentation into patches with simple geometry and motion, which can be expected to remain stable over time. In order to go beyond two time steps we additionally assume that the 3D motion (translation and rotation) of each segment is nearly constant within the examined time interval. Empirically this assumption is valid for the segment sizes and time intervals considered.

This paper makes the following contributions: *(i)* We propose a novel 3D scene flow model that does not rely on an arbitrary reference view, but rather reconstructs 3D shape and motion w.r.t. every image in a time interval, while enforcing consistency of the reconstruction across views; *(ii)* we extend dense scene flow estimation to more than two time steps, with a temporally consistent piecewise-planar segmentation of the scene and a prior that favors constant 3D velocity over time; and *(iii)* we formulate a consistent energy that includes both these aspects, along with a corresponding inference scheme, and can – at least conceptually – handle any number of viewpoints and any number of time steps.

We evaluate our method on the challenging KITTI dataset of real street scenes, using the stereo and flow benchmarks. Compared to two-frame scene flow computation with a fixed reference view [28], the proposed view-consistent estimation over four frames reduces the average endpoint error from 2.5 to 1.4 pixels, and improves the KITTI error metric by 45% for flow, respectively 36% for stereo. In the evaluation on full images, including occlusion areas, our method currently achieves the best results on the benchmark, for both optical flow and stereo. We further show on some particularly hard examples that our model is remarkably robust against missing evidence, outliers, and occlusions.

2   Related Work

Scene flow estimation is usually traced back to Vedula *et al.* [26]. With the goal of multi-camera motion capture, optical flow is first estimated independently for each camera and then triangulated to obtain a 3D motion field. Later work, mostly based on only two views, is dominated by variational approaches. Among these, some again decouple the estimation by first estimating stereo correspondence and then finding flow fields consistent with the disparities, *e.g.* [19,33]. In contrast, [11] still uses a 2D parametrization, but exploits correlations between depth and motion by estimating them jointly. [25] additionally allows for changes in the relative pose of the stereo rig, and alternates between updating the scene flow and the relative pose. To alleviate the bias of regularization in 2D, [1] directly parameterizes the scene flow with depth and 3D motion vectors, and shows that smoothing in 3D improves the reconstructed motion fields. [30] replaces the total variation regularization of the motion field with a prior that penalizes deviations from local rigidity. Taking the idea of rigidity further, [28] proposes to model the scene as a collection of planar regions, each moving rigidly over time. The representation has also been used for tracking with multiple cameras [7]. Here, we adopt the parameterization of [28], which proved to work well on realistic data. As we will show, this allows one to include consistency checks between different views, thus moving away from a single reference view, and to incorporate temporal contraints on a region's motion.

Temporal smoothness assumptions for multi-frame 2D optical flow date back to at least [17], but were limited to small displacements. [2] instead extrapolates motion fields from previous time steps and encourages similarity between the predicted and the estimated flow. This allows for larger displacements, but inference is restricted to the current frame, *i.e.* the past motion field influences the current one, but not vice versa. Later [34] jointly reasons over three consecutive frames, assuming a constant 2D motion field. In contrast, assuming constant 3D scene flow over time here allows us to address more general scenes. [31] relaxes the constant velocity assumption to soft constraints that encourage first and second order smoothness of the motion field. [8] instead uses a soft constraint that requires the 2D motions to lie in a low-rank trajectory space. [21,22] avoid simple temporal smoothing, and instead jointly estimate the flow and a segmentation into a small number of layers, enforcing constant pixel-to-layer membership. The rationale is that even if the motion changes rapidly, the scene structure should persist over time. In a similar manner, [20] segments a video into several motion layers with long-term temporal consistency. While they estimate a 2D parametric motion for each layer, their primary goal is high-level motion segmentation. Here we make a similar assumption, but for 3D shape and motion: we also group pixels to (planar, rigidly moving) segments and enforce consistency of the segmentation over time. In contrast to motion layers, our model with hundreds of small segments can represent a wider range of scenes.

An important observation here is that exploiting temporal consistency over longer time intervals is easier with an explicit 3D model of shape and motion, because smoothness assumptions are more likely to hold in the 3D scene than in its projections. This fact is exploited in [19], where a Kalman filter at each pixel propagates the geometry and motion estimated by [33] across frames. The prediction is used to detect and remove outliers, but changes neither the present nor the past flow estimate. [12] constructs longer motion trajectories from frame-to-frame stereo and flow. Trajectories that pass several heuristic plausibility checks are included in the final optimization as soft constraints, similar to including feature matches in two-frame optical flow [5]. [18] parameterizes the scene flow in 3D, and also proceeds sequentially, first estimating frame-to-frame scene flow and then smoothing it over time with tensor voting. [6,13] represent the scene with an explicit deformable 3D mesh, which is fitted to video data. All three approaches target motion capture in controlled settings with many cameras.

Also related to our work are methods that employ (over-)segmentation to make discontinuities explicit, starting with [32] for flow and [23] for stereo matching. While such early work was constrained by the initial segmentation, more recent methods infer or refine the segmentation together with the scene depth [3,4,35], the 1D epipolar flow [36], or the 2D optical flow [24]. The representation of [28], which we use here, adapts this idea to scene flow.

Moving away from an arbitrary reference frame, and treating all views equally, has been prominently used in stereo vision in the form of a left-right consistency check. In its simplest form the consistency between the forward and backward disparities is checked in post-processing, *e.g.* [10], but it can also be included directly in the objective [4]. We extend the latter strategy to ensure consistency of the scene flow across all images in a temporal window.

3   Method

Our formulation follows [28] to represent the 3D scene geometry and motion as a collection of piecewise planar regions that move rigidly over time. More specifically, we define the problem of 3D scene flow estimation as determining two assignments, a mapping $\mathcal{S}$ that assigns pixels to spatially localized segments (super-pixels), and a mapping $\mathcal{P}$ that assigns a planar 3D geometry and rigid motion to each segment. These mappings implicitly define the 3D geometry and motion at every pixel. Note that the spatial segmentation $\mathcal{S}$ is free of semantic meaning. Pixels belonging to a moving plane do not necessarily form a connected component. Moreover, an over-segmentation is actually crucial to account for non-planar or articulated objects, as well as to accurately preserve motion and depth discontinuities. There are two key distinctions to the formulation of [28]: First, we not only estimate the scene flow for a reference view, but for all views (in space and time). The main benefit is that we can check consistency of the representation across views, which makes the estimate more robust and allows for improved occlusion handling. This also means that the notion of the segmentation is extended to all views, with the challenge of obtaining a consistent segmentation of the scene over time. Second, we aim to estimate scene flow from more than 2 frames, hence extend the notion of rigid motion through time by assuming constant translational and rotational velocity of the moving planes.

Notation. We formulate our model for the classical two camera stereo-rig configuration, although no actual limitation on the number of cameras exists. We distinguish *left* and *right* camera through a subscript l,r. Superscripts $t \in T = \{-1, 0, 1, \ldots\}$ indicate the time step of image acquisition. Despite computing scene flow in all cameras and not having a reference view for representation, we still designate the *left* camera at time step 0 as a canonical view that defines a common coordinate system. This canonical view simplifies the notation and later serves as evaluation basis. W.l.o.g. we assume the camera matrix $\mathbf{K}$ to be identical for both cameras, with projection matrices $(\mathbf{K}|\mathbf{0})$ for the left and $(\mathbf{M}|\mathbf{m})$ for the right camera. For now we assume that the camera rig does not move itself; in Sec. 3.4 we show how to cope with camera ego-motion.

A 3D moving plane $\pi \equiv \pi(\mathbf{R}, \mathbf{t}, \overline{\mathbf{n}})$ is defined by 9 parameters: the rotation matrix $\mathbf{R}$, a translation vector $\mathbf{t}$, and a scaled normal $\overline{\mathbf{n}}$. Note that we assume the motion parameters to describe the rigid motion in one forward time step. Recall that the moving plane is defined in the coordinate system of the canonical view. Assuming that all planes are visible in the canonical view, they cannot pass the origin. We thus define $\overline{\mathbf{n}} \equiv \overline{\mathbf{n}}_l^0$ via the plane equation $\mathbf{x}^\mathsf{T}\overline{\mathbf{n}} = 1$, which holds for all 3D points $\mathbf{x}$ on the plane. Over the course of this section we will need to transform the moving plane also into views (coordinate systems) other than the canonical one. The respective scaled normal can be found by observing that the normal equation must still hold after a rigid transformation. *E.g.*, consider the left camera at time step 1: for all points $\mathbf{x}$ on the transformed normal we have

$$\mathbf{x}^\mathsf{T}\overline{\mathbf{n}}_l^1 = 1 \Leftrightarrow (\mathbf{R}^{-1}\mathbf{x} - \mathbf{R}^{-1}\mathbf{t})^\mathsf{T}\overline{\mathbf{n}}_l^0 = 1 \Leftrightarrow \mathbf{x}^\mathsf{T}\mathbf{R}\overline{\mathbf{n}}_l^0 - \mathbf{t}^\mathsf{T}\mathbf{R}\overline{\mathbf{n}}_l^0 = 1 \Leftrightarrow \overline{\mathbf{n}}_l^1 = \frac{\mathbf{R}\overline{\mathbf{n}}_l^0}{1 + \mathbf{t}^\mathsf{T}\mathbf{R}\overline{\mathbf{n}}_l^0}. \quad (1)$$

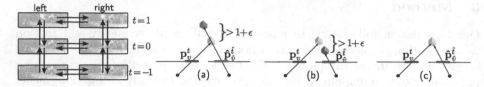

Fig. 2. *(left)* Data terms in the three-frame case: Consistency is enforced for spatial and direct temporal neighbors (black arrows). *(right)* Illustration of the per pixel data term: (a) impossible case, (b) occlusion (c) normal case (see text for more details.)

Our scene parameterization, furthermore, allows for a simple transformation of pixel locations to their corresponding position in other views using the homography induced by its assigned moving plane. The homographies from the canonical view I_l^0 to the other views given the moving plane π are written as:

$$\prescript{0}{l}{\mathbf{H}}_r^0(\pi) = (\mathbf{M} - \mathbf{m}\bar{\mathbf{n}}^\mathsf{T})\mathbf{K}^{-1} \tag{2a}$$

$$\prescript{0}{l}{\mathbf{H}}_l^1(\pi) = \mathbf{K}(\mathbf{R} - \mathbf{t}\bar{\mathbf{n}}^\mathsf{T})\mathbf{K}^{-1} \tag{2b}$$

$$\prescript{0}{l}{\mathbf{H}}_r^1(\pi) = (\mathbf{MR} - (\mathbf{Mt} + \mathbf{m})\bar{\mathbf{n}}^\mathsf{T})\mathbf{K}^{-1}. \tag{2c}$$

Homographies between arbitrary view pairs can be obtained by concatenating the transformations above, first transforming back to the canonical view and then into the desired frame, *e.g.* $\prescript{1}{l}{\mathbf{H}}_r^1(\pi) = \prescript{0}{l}{\mathbf{H}}_r^1(\pi) \cdot \prescript{0}{l}{\mathbf{H}}_l^1(\pi)^{-1}$.

Energy. We formally define the problem of 3D scene flow estimation as the minimization of an energy $E(\mathcal{P}, \mathcal{S})$ over two (sets of) mappings: First, the mappings $\mathcal{S} = \{\mathcal{S}_v^t\}$ with $\mathcal{S}_v^t : I_v^t \to S_v^t$ assign each pixel of camera v at time t to a segment from the set S_v^t, hence define a super-pixel segmentation of each view. This is in contrast to [28], which only infers a segmentation of the reference view. Second, the mappings $\mathcal{P} = \{\mathcal{P}_v^t\}$ with $\mathcal{P}_v^t : S_v^t \to \Pi$ select a rigidly moving plane for each segment from a candidate set Π of possible moving 3D planes. We define the energy function as

$$E(\mathcal{P}, \mathcal{S}) = E_D(\mathcal{P}, \mathcal{S}) + \lambda E_R(\mathcal{P}, \mathcal{S}) + \mu E_S(\mathcal{S}). \tag{3}$$

The most crucial term is the data term E_D, which unlike [28] not only considers photo-consistency w.r.t. a reference frame, but rather enforces photo-consistency across all neighboring views. Moreover, it considers whether corresponding pixels have a consistent geometric configuration and handles occlusions. The regularization term E_R evaluates the smoothness of motion and geometry at segment boundaries in all images. The final term E_S assesses the quality of the spatial segmentation per view. In the following we first describe our model for only two time steps, and later explain how to extend it to multiple frames in time.

3.1   View-Consistent Data Term

Since we compute 3D scene flow for all views involved, we define a data term for each image. In particular, we check the consistency of the scene flow in each view with its direct neighbors in time, and with the other view(s) at the same time step (Fig. 2, left). With consistency we, on the one hand, mean classical photo-consistency of the images at the corresponding pixel locations; the correspondence is determined from the assigned moving plane $\pi \equiv \pi(\mathbf{R}, \mathbf{t}, \bar{\mathbf{n}})$. On the other hand, because each pixel (in each view) is associated with a moving plane, we can additionally ensure that corresponding pixel locations are geometrically consistent, and detect occlusions. To that end we have to compare depth values induced by the respective moving planes (Fig. 2, right). Note that this form of cross checking is rather different from the occlusion reasoning in [28], and only possible here because we no longer have a reference frame, but instead estimate the scene flow for all views.

Suppose we want to check consistency between a pixel location $\mathbf{p} \equiv \mathbf{p}_v^t$ in view v at time t and its corresponding pixel location $\hat{\mathbf{p}}_{\hat{v}}^{\hat{t}}$ in view $\hat{v}$ at time $\hat{t}$. Denoting the moving 3D plane of a pixel $\mathbf{p}$ as $\pi_{\mathbf{p}} = \mathcal{P}_v^t(\mathcal{S}_v^t(\mathbf{p}))$, the corresponding pixel location in the other view is determined as $\hat{\mathbf{p}}_{\hat{v}}^{\hat{t}} = {}_v^t\mathbf{H}_{\hat{v}}^{\hat{t}}(\pi_{\mathbf{p}})\mathbf{p}$. To check geometric consistency, we furthermore determine the depth d of a pixel $\mathbf{p}$ w.r.t. the camera center of an image I_v^t through the inverse scalar product

$$d(\mathbf{p}, \bar{\mathbf{n}}_v^t(\pi)) := \langle \mathbf{K}^{-1}\mathbf{p}, \bar{\mathbf{n}}_v^t(\pi) \rangle^{-1}. \tag{4}$$

This allows us to define our data term for consistency of pixel $\mathbf{p}$ in view v at time-step t and its moving plane $\pi_{\mathbf{p}}$ with the adjacent view $\hat{v}$ at time-step $\hat{t}$ as

$$\varrho(\mathbf{p}, \hat{\mathbf{p}}_{\hat{v}}^{\hat{t}}) := \begin{cases} \theta_{\text{occ}} & \text{if} \quad d(\hat{\mathbf{p}}_{\hat{v}}^{\hat{t}}, \bar{\mathbf{n}}_{\hat{v}}^{\hat{t}}(\pi_{\mathbf{p}}))/d(\hat{\mathbf{p}}_{\hat{v}}^{\hat{t}}, \bar{\mathbf{n}}_{\hat{v}}^{\hat{t}}(\pi_{\hat{\mathbf{p}}_{\hat{v}}^{\hat{t}}})) > 1 + \epsilon \\ \theta_{\text{imp}} & \text{if} \quad d(\hat{\mathbf{p}}_{\hat{v}}^{\hat{t}}, \bar{\mathbf{n}}_{\hat{v}}^{\hat{t}}(\pi_{\hat{\mathbf{p}}_{\hat{v}}^{\hat{t}}}))/d(\hat{\mathbf{p}}_{\hat{v}}^{\hat{t}}, \bar{\mathbf{n}}_{\hat{v}}^{\hat{t}}(\pi_{\mathbf{p}})) > 1 + \epsilon \\ \theta_{\text{oob}} & \text{otherwise if} \quad \hat{\mathbf{p}}_{\hat{v}}^{\hat{t}} \notin I_{\hat{v}}^{\hat{t}} \\ \rho(\mathbf{p}, \hat{\mathbf{p}}_{\hat{v}}^{\hat{t}}) + \theta_{\text{mvp}} & \text{otherwise if} \quad \pi_{\mathbf{p}} \neq \pi_{\hat{\mathbf{p}}_{\hat{v}}^{\hat{t}}} \\ \rho(\mathbf{p}, \hat{\mathbf{p}}_{\hat{v}}^{\hat{t}}) & \text{otherwise.} \end{cases} \tag{5}$$

The first two cases consider the relative distance in depth to differentiate between occlusions and implausible geometric configurations, similar to comparing disparity values in the stereo case [4]. In particular, a pixel $\mathbf{p}$ in the first view is being occluded in the second view, if the depth of the moving plane $\pi_{\mathbf{p}}$ is greater than that of the corresponding plane $\pi_{\hat{\mathbf{p}}_{\hat{v}}^{\hat{t}}}$ (both depths determined in the second view). Since we cannot check photo-consistency in case of an occlusion, we assert a fixed penalty θ_{occ}. On the other hand, if the depth of the moving plane $\pi_{\mathbf{p}}$ is smaller than that of the corresponding plane $\pi_{\hat{\mathbf{p}}_{\hat{v}}^{\hat{t}}}$, then an implausible geometric configuration occurs. The 3D point corresponding to the plane stored in pixel $\hat{\mathbf{p}}_{\hat{v}}^{\hat{t}}$ would be occluded and hence cannot have been observed in the pixel $\hat{\mathbf{p}}_{\hat{v}}^{\hat{t}}$. We penalize this using the fixed penalty θ_{imp}. The ϵ parameter adds some "softness" to the relative depth comparisons, in order to alleviate aliasing problems induced by the pixel grid resolution and because practical considerations limit us to a finite proposal set of moving planes. Using the third case, we penalize a pixel moving out of the viewing frustum using the fixed penalty θ_{oob}.

The fifth case is the default case when pixels are in geometric correspondence. Specifically, we use the robust census transform ρ_C [37] over a 7×7 neighborhood to measure the photo-consistency, truncated at half the maximum possible data cost $\rho(\cdot, \cdot) = \min\{\rho_C(\cdot, \cdot), 0.5\max(\rho_C)\}$ at a pixel. We impose an additional penalty θ_{mvp} in the fourth case, if pixels are in geometric correspondence, but their moving planes are not the same. This encourages corresponding segments from two views to pick the same moving 3D plane, leading to a view-consistent segmentation.

In practice, we penalize pixels moving out of bounds and classical occlusions identically and set $\theta_{oob} = \theta_{occ} = 0.5\max(\rho_C)$. In our experience this ensures a small number of non-submodular edges in the corresponding graph (see Sec. 3.5) and therefore leads to good results. Due to aliasing, we cannot penalize physically implausible configurations with an infinite penalty; we instead set $\theta_{imp} := 2\theta_{oob}$, as such a limited penalty prevents deadlocks in the optimization. Note that we rarely encounter implausible configurations in the final estimate. The penalty for not assigning the same plane to pixels in geometric correspondence is empirically set to $\theta_{mvp} := 5/16\,\theta_{oob}$, thus allows for deviations from our prior assumption.

Since we compute scene flow for all views involved, we need to sum the per-pixel contribution from Eq. (5) over all pixels of all frames and their considered neighboring views (Fig. 2):

$$E_D(\mathcal{P}, \mathcal{S}) := \sum_{t \in T} \sum_{v \in \{l,r\}} \sum_{\mathbf{p} \in I_v^t} \left(\sum_{\hat{v} \neq v} \varrho(\mathbf{p}, \hat{\mathbf{p}}_{\hat{v}}^t) + \sum_{\substack{\hat{t} \in T \\ |\hat{t}-t|=1}} \varrho(\mathbf{p}, \hat{\mathbf{p}}_v^{\hat{t}}) \right). \qquad (6)$$

It is important to note that each view pair is considered twice by the data term, since both of the views have their own scene flow representation.

3.2 Shape and Motion Regularization

The spatial regularization term promotes piecewise smooth geometry and 3D motion in all views considered. For each of the views, we closely follow [28]. In particular, discontinuities can only occur at segment boundaries, as all pixels within a segment are on the same moving plane. If adjacent pixels are assigned to different moving planes, a penalty is defined by integrating a squared distance function, evaluated at points along the shared edge. Because of the piecewise planarity, the integral can be evaluated in closed form and simplifies to measuring distances only at the endpoints of the shared edge, see [28]. To achieve a certain robustness against object and motion discontinuities, the integrated distance is further embedded into a robust cost function. More formally, assuming that the two adjacent pixels $\mathbf{p}$ and $\mathbf{q}$ lie on different moving planes $\pi_\mathbf{p} = \mathcal{P}(\mathcal{S}(\mathbf{p}))$ and $\pi_\mathbf{q} = \mathcal{P}(\mathcal{S}(\mathbf{q}))$, then we can define the induced penalty as:

$$e_R(\mathbf{p}, \mathbf{q}) := w_{\mathbf{p}, \mathbf{q}}\big(\psi\left(||\mathbf{d}_1||^2 + ||\mathbf{d}_2||^2 + \langle\mathbf{d}_1, \mathbf{d}_2\rangle + \gamma^2||\mathbf{d}_n||^2\right) + \qquad (7)$$
$$\psi\left(||\mathbf{d}_1^m||^2 + ||\mathbf{d}_2^m||^2 + \langle\mathbf{d}_1^m, \mathbf{d}_2^m\rangle + \gamma^2||\mathbf{d}_n^m||^2\right)\big). \qquad (8)$$

Here the vectors $\mathbf{d}_1$ and $\mathbf{d}_2$ describe the distance in geometry, and $\mathbf{d}_1^m$ and $\mathbf{d}_2^m$ the distance in motion at the two endpoints of the shared edge. The vectors $\mathbf{d}_n$

and $\mathbf{d}_n^m$ define the distance of the normals before and after the moving plane induced motion is applied. While it appears natural to measure these distances in 3D space, current scene flow benchmarks are biased toward 2D accuracy, hence a 2D regularization delivers better results. Therefore, we use disparity for geometry regularization, and 2D flow and disparity difference across time to regularize the motion. Robustness is achieved using a truncated penalty function $\psi(y) := \min(\sqrt{y}, \eta)$; we set $\eta := 20$ and $\gamma := 1$ for both geometry and motion.

The weight $w_{\mathbf{p},\mathbf{q}}$ allows to take into account the image structure and the length of the edge between the pixels. Since we found the weighting scheme from [28] based on bilateral filtering to be noisy, we instead follow [34] and employ the anisotropic diffusion tensor $D^{\frac{1}{2}} = \exp(-\alpha|\nabla I|)gg^{\mathsf{T}} + g^{\perp}(g^{\perp})^{\mathsf{T}}$ with $\alpha = 5$, thereby assuming $I \in [0,1]$. The direction of the image gradient $g = \nabla I/|\nabla I|$ is determined in the middle between $\mathbf{p}$ and $\mathbf{q}$ via bicubic interpolation. We then define the weight as

$$w_{\mathbf{p},\mathbf{q}} := |D^{\frac{1}{2}}\overrightarrow{\mathbf{p}\mathbf{q}}|. \tag{9}$$

Because we compute the scene flow simultaneously in all images, we also apply regularization on all views and define the full spatial regularizer as

$$E_R(\mathcal{P}, \mathcal{S}) := \sum_{t \in T} \sum_{v \in \{l,r\}} \sum_{(\mathbf{p},\mathbf{q}) \in \mathcal{N}(I_v^t)} w_{\mathbf{p},\mathbf{q}} e_R(\mathbf{p}, \mathbf{q}). \tag{10}$$

Here, $\mathcal{N}$ are all neighboring pixels of the respective image (8-neighborhood).

3.3 Spatial Segmentation Regularization

The segmentation regularizer promotes the spatial coherence of the underlying over-segmentation. We again define the energy for all views considered:

$$E_S(\mathcal{S}) = \left(\sum_{\substack{t \in T, \\ v \in \{l,r\}}} \sum_{\substack{(\mathbf{p},\mathbf{q}) \in \mathcal{N}(I_v^t), \\ \mathcal{S}(\mathbf{p}) \neq \mathcal{S}(\mathbf{q})}} w_{\mathbf{p},\mathbf{q}} \right) + \sum_{\mathbf{p} \in I_l^0} \begin{cases} 0, & \exists \mathbf{e} \in \mathcal{E}(s_i):\|\mathbf{e}-\mathbf{p}\|_{\infty} < N_S \\ \infty, & \text{else.} \end{cases} \tag{11}$$

The first term takes the form of a pairwise Potts model, which encourages segment boundaries to coincide with the image edges. We use the weights from the diffusion tensor (Eq. 9) to take into account the edge contrast. The second term restricts the size of a segment within the canonical view (maximum extent of $2N_S - 1$ with $N_S = 20$) and binds them to their respective seed point $\mathbf{e} \in \mathcal{E}(s_i)$. The seed points are spaced on a regular grid. The key motivation behind this is that it reduces the time needed for optimizing the mapping $\mathcal{S}$, because only a limited set of segments needs to be considered at any pixel. Note that the second term only needs to be applied to the canonical view, since the data term from Eq. (5) encourages the segmentations in the other views to be consistent.

This segmentation regularizer is based on ideas of [27], where a similar energy is used to compute an over-segmentation of one image, and is also employed in [28], but only w.r.t. the reference image.

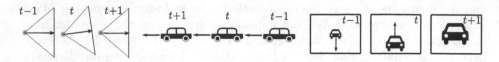

Fig. 3. Variation in camera pitch limits the validity of the constant velocity model. *(left)* A scene observed by a moving camera with varying pitch. *(right)* Camera images with induced 2D flow (black arrow). We compensate camera pitch by removing the ego-motion of the camera.

3.4 Multiple Frame Extension

Extending our formulation to more than two frames seems straightforward on a first glance: The spatial and segmentation regularizers can be trivially extended to any number of frames, but the data term is more subtle. As discussed, we generally assume motion of constant translational and rotational velocity in case we have more than just two time steps. Note that in many applications this assumption is valid, especially because we restrict ourselves to only a short time interval. Consequently, one could extend the data term by defining appropriate homographies between the views. Assuming constant velocity in rotation and translation, this can be achieved by concatenation of terms from Eq. (2). Care must be taken to use the correct normal, which must be transformed into the appropriate view coordinate system. This can be similarly achieved by repeated application of Eq. (1), again assuming constant velocity.

In certain applications, *e.g.* the automotive application in our experiments, the constant velocity assumption is challenged by a common and high-frequent pitching motion of the stereo rig, which can arise from undulations in the road surface or from not perfectly securing the rig. Because the motion between two time steps is always estimated relative to the respective camera coordinate system, even small changes in relative camera position already lead to significant changes in the relative geometry and motion (Fig. 3). Therefore we extend our formulation to incorporate ego-motion estimates for the different time steps.

In particular, we first estimate the relative ego-motion $\mathbf{E}^t = [\mathbf{Q}^t|\mathbf{s}^t]$ between all consecutive time steps t and $t+1$. When computing the homographies between subsequent time steps, we first apply the motion induced by the moving plane representation (disregarding any ego-motion) and then the relative ego-motion: Since the rotation $\mathbf{R}$ and the translation $\mathbf{t}$ of a moving plane come from a proposal (see below), which is computed for the canonical view unaware of any ego-motion, we need to disregard the relative ego-motion of the canonical view $\mathbf{E}^0$ first by applying $(\mathbf{E}^0)^{-1} = [(\mathbf{Q}^0)^{-1}| - (\mathbf{Q}^0)^{-1}\mathbf{s}^0]$. For example, in case of computing a homography between frame t and $t+1$ in the left view, we have

$$
{}_l^t\mathbf{H}_l^{t+1}(\pi) = \mathbf{K}\Big(\mathbf{Q}^t(\mathbf{Q}^0)^{-1}\mathbf{R} - \big(\mathbf{Q}^t(\mathbf{Q}^0)^{-1}(\mathbf{t} - \mathbf{s}^0) + \mathbf{s}^t\big)(\overline{\mathbf{n}}_l^t)^\mathsf{T}\Big)\mathbf{K}^{-1}. \tag{12}
$$

Other homographies can be corrected for ego-motion accordingly.

3.5   Optimization and Proposal Generation

Our piecewise rigid model energy (Eq. 3) amounts to a CRF with continuous, 9-dimensional variables for motion and geometry, and discrete variables for the pixel-to-plane assignment. Like [28] we perform inference in two steps with fusion moves [14]. First, starting from a fixed segmentation $\mathcal{S}$ we select a moving plane for each segment from a finite set of proposals; then we update the segmentation $\mathcal{S}$, given the geometry and motion $\mathcal{P}$ of the segments. To bootstrap this two-step procedure one needs an initial segmentation $\mathcal{S}$. [28] proposes to start from an intensity-based super-pixel segmentation. We found that the initial segmentation is not critical, and instead start from a regular checkerboard grid (16 pixel edge length) as trivial "segmentation". The center points of the grid cells also serve as seed points $\mathbf{e} \in \mathcal{E}$ (see Eq. 11). Optimization w.r.t. $\mathcal{S}$ will eventually refine the segmentation and adjust it to depth and motion boundaries, consistently in all views. Aside from being more efficient, the grid structure also reduces aliasing from an uneven size of the segments across views.

When first solving for $\mathcal{P}$, we can treat the segments as large pixels and ignore the segmentation term E_S, as it is independent of $\mathcal{P}$. To cope with aliasing induced by the initial (not view-consistent) grid segmentation we relax the consistency constraint and set $\epsilon := 0.1$ and $\theta_{\mathrm{mvp}} := 3/16 \, \theta_{\mathrm{oob}}$. This softer setting ensures that proposals are not prematurely discarded because of the inaccurate initial segmentation. Edge weights (Eq. 9) are summed along the segment edges.

For our fusion move framework we need a set of moving plane proposals. These are generated by running 2D stereo [10] and optical flow [29], and refining the output with a two-frame version of our method, leading to a significant reduction of the initial proposal set. The refinement, done only in the canonical view for the same grid segmentation, resembles the segment-to-plane assignment step of [28]. For the multi-frame case we generate proposals for all consecutive frame pairs ($t = -1$ and $t = 0$ for 3 time steps, and also $t = 1$ for 4 time steps). To avoid unnecessarily inflating the proposal set, proposals from other time steps are only kept if they differ significantly from already extracted ones nearby. Proposals are considered valid only in a 192×144 pixel (12×9 cells) neighborhood centered at the seed point in the canonical frame, to speed up optimization. During a fusion move we project the neighborhood into all other views and only instantiate the graph for segments within the projected box.

Once the segment-to-plane mapping $\mathcal{P}$ has been found, we infer the pixel-to-segment assignment $\mathcal{S}$ in a similar manner. *I.e.*, we discard all unused moving plane proposals and optimize again, this time labeling individual pixels rather than grid cells. The region constraint from Eq. (11) ensures the locality of the fusion move. Because our consistency decisions are made on a per pixel basis we can penalize inconsistencies more strictly now and set $\epsilon := 0.015$.

Our local expansion strategy allows to optimize multiple non-overlapping image regions in parallel. With our current implementation we observe runtimes of 23s (2 time steps) and 46s (3 time steps) to solve for $\mathcal{P}$, respectively 18s and 32s to solve for $\mathcal{S}$. Timings were measured for 0.5 Mpixel images on a dual *Intel Core i7*, working with ~ 1850 segments and proposals from 3 time steps.

Fig. 4. Example from the KITTI training set (#191). *(left)* Consistent super-pixel segmentation *(right)* Active data term ϱ (Eq. 5). Colors denote normal photo-consistency (*green*), out of bounds (*red*), occluded (*light blue*), and implausible (*dark blue*).

4   Evaluation

For our evaluation we fix the remaining parameters to of our algorithm to $\lambda = 1/50$ and $\mu = \lambda/5$, and scale the census transform to deliver values between 0 and 1.6, thus $\max \rho(\cdot, \cdot) = 0.8$ in Eq. (5). We begin by illustrating the internal representation of our model in Fig. 4. On the left we depict the (consistent) over-segmentation overlaid on two consecutive frames and beside it the assigned states of the data term ϱ from Eq. (5), for the same images.

4.1   Qualitative Evaluation

We first show a hard example from the KITTI benchmark (Fig. 5). Most optical and scene flow methods fail on these images because of severe lens flares in both cameras. However, the presence and the location of the artifacts are not consistent through all views (although they are rather consistent in consecutive frames). Our method is able to exploit the absence of a consistent depth and motion pattern for the flare, and reconstructs the scene flow reasonably well, with only 3.7% of the disparities and 8.1% of the flow vectors (including occluded areas) outside the standard 3-pixel error threshold of KITTI. We note that the improvement is achieved only through view- and multi-frame consistency – imaging artifacts that exhibit a consistent motion pattern across all images still can lead to erroneous reconstructions (which is however rather unlikely because the two views stem from physically different cameras).

In Fig. 6 we present further results on difficult outdoor scenes from [15]. On the left the input images are shown, on the right are the disparities and the flow (reprojected to 2D) estimated with our method from 3 consecutive stereo pairs. Only qualitative results are given, as no ground truth is available. The examples show that even under adverse imaging conditions our model correctly recovers not only the dominant background, but also the motion of smaller, independent objects. The scenes feature challenges such as reflections on the wet road, strong occlusions at a crossroads, and saturated headlights. The most difficult examples even include flares from headlights on the wet windscreen, and heavy snowfall. Also from this dataset is the example shown in Fig. 1, in which the windscreen wiper occludes a large part of the viewing field. This particular scene is extremely hard to reconstruct with only a single reference view.

Fig. 5. A hard example (KITTI training set, #74). *(left)* Input frames. *(right)* Reconstructed scene flow, reprojected to disparity and 2D flow field (from left to right).

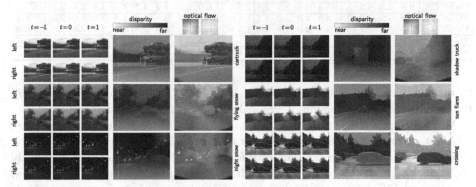

Fig. 6. Results for challenging examples from [15]. *(left)* Input frames. *(right)* Reconstructed scene flow, reprojected to disparity and 2D flow field. *Best viewed on screen.*

4.2 KITTI Benchmark

We quantitatively evaluate the performance of our algorithm on the KITTI dataset [9]. The images were acquired with a calibrated stereo rig at a resolution of 1240×376 pixels. The cameras are mounted on top of a car together with a laser scanner, which delivers semi-dense ground truth. KITTI has become a standard testbed for modern stereo and optical flow algorithms. It is challenging mainly for two reasons, *(i)* very large displacements in both stereo (> 150 pixels) and flow (> 250 pixels); and *(ii)* having real outdoor scenes under realistic lighting, with shadows, saturation, specular reflections, lens flare, *etc*.

The benchmark consists of a "training" set of 194 images with public ground truth and a test set of 195 images, for which the ground truth is withheld. The data is provided in stereo video snippets of 20 frames, so that our multi-frame method can be applied. We analyze different variants of our method on the training set, and run it on the test set to compare to the state of the art.

Table 1 summarizes the results of the evaluation on the training images. As error measures we use the average end point error (AEP) and the KITTI metric, *i.e.* the percentage of pixels that deviate by more than $2/3/4/5$ pixels from the ground truth. Both metrics are calculated both for the complete images ($\checkmark$), and only for the non-occluded pixels ($\times$). The following variants are evaluated: view-consistent estimation for two frames (*VC-2F*), three frames (*VC-3F*) and four frames (*VC-4F*). To separate the impact of propagating proposals over multiple frames from the impact of multi-frame optimization, we also test a variant in which proposals are extracted from 3 frames, but model optimization is done only for two frames (*VC-2F+*). As a baseline we also run our method for only

Table 1. *KITTI* metric (% of flow vectors / disparities above 2/3/4/5 pixels of endpoint error) and average endpoint error [px], for the complete *KITTI* training set

Occ pix.	Flow KITTI metric √ 2px 3px 4px 5px	Flow KITTI metric × 2px 3px 4px 5px	AEP √ ×	Stereo KITTI metric √ 2px 3px 4px 5px	Stereo KITTI metric × 2px 3px 4px 5px	AEP √ ×
PRSF [28]	9.9 7.3 6.0 5.2	5.8 4.1 3.3 2.8	2.5 1.2	8.0 5.6 4.4 3.7	7.0 4.8 3.8 3.1	1.2 1.0
VC-2F	8.0 5.5 4.2 3.4	4.4 2.9 2.2 1.7	1.4 0.8	6.8 4.7 3.6 3.0	5.8 3.9 3.0 2.5	1.0 0.8
VC-2F+	7.4 4.9 3.7 3.0	4.2 2.6 1.9 1.5	1.3 0.7	6.4 4.3 3.3 2.8	5.5 3.7 2.8 2.3	0.9 0.8
VC-3F	6.6 4.1 3.0 2.3	4.1 2.6 1.9 1.5	1.1 0.7	5.5 3.7 2.8 2.3	5.0 3.3 2.5 2.1	0.8 0.7
VC-4F	6.5 4.0 3.0 2.4	4.0 2.5 1.9 1.5	1.1 0.7	5.3 3.6 2.7 2.2	4.9 3.3 2.5 2.0	0.8 0.7

two frames and using a single reference view (*PRSF*). The baseline is essentially the same as the basic version of [28], called "PRSPix-2D" in that paper.

Moving from a single reference view to view-consistent estimation (*PRSF vs. VC-2F*) already yields significant improvements. In the standard KITTI metric (3px error threshold) the gains are 25% for flow, and 16% for stereo (respectively 29% and 19% in visible areas). In line with these results also the AEP is reduced by 44% and 17% (respectively, 33% and 20%), showing that view-consistency is especially helpful in the presence of occlusions.

Including proposals from the previous frame (*VC-2F+*) already improves the results further. A much larger improvement however is brought about by moving to three frames (*VC-3F*). Note in particular the strong gains in occluded areas, which significantly reduce the errors on the full images despite the small number of affected pixels. When adding a fourth frame (*VC-4F*) we observe diminishing returns, with only marginal improvements over the three-frame case. Compared to the baseline, our best result reduces the KITTI error on the full images by 45% for flow and by 36% for stereo. The corresponding AEPs drop by 56%, respectively 33%. We submitted the three-view version *VC-3F* to the official KITTI benchmark. In the evaluation on full images including occluded areas ("Out-All") the proposed scene flow method current achieves the best results for both flow and stereo, among > 40 submissions. Note that in contrast to the nearest competitor, our method can handle scenes with independently moving objects (see Fig. 6), which are rare in this benchmark, but not in general scenes.

5   Conclusion

In this paper we have addressed the question of how to exploit consistency over time and between viewpoints for dense 3D scene flow estimation. For piecewise planar and rigid scenes, we have shown a way to leverage information from multiple consecutive frames of a stereo video, and thereby significantly improve both shape and 3D motion estimation. The proposed model has proven remarkably robust against outliers, occlusions and missing evidence, and makes it possible to estimate depth and motion of road scenes even under adverse imaging conditions, where most methods fail. In future work we plan to handle deviations from the constant velocity assumption in a more flexible manner.

References

1. Basha, T., Moses, Y., Kiryati, N.: Multi-view scene flow estimation: A view centered variational approach. In: CVPR (2010)
2. Black, M.J., Anandan, P.: Robust dynamic motion estimation over time. In: CVPR (1991)
3. Bleyer, M., Rother, C., Kohli, P.: Surface stereo with soft segmentation. In: CVPR (2010)
4. Bleyer, M., Rother, C., Kohli, P., Scharstein, D., Sinha, S.N.: Object stereo – Joint stereo matching and object segmentation. In: CVPR (2011)
5. Brox, T., Malik, J.: Large displacement optical flow: Descriptor matching in variational motion estimation. TPAMI 33(3), 500–513 (2011)
6. Courchay, J., Pons, J.-P., Monasse, P., Keriven, R.: Dense and accurate spatiotemporal multi-view stereovision. In: Zha, H., Taniguchi, R.-i., Maybank, S. (eds.) ACCV 2009, Part II. LNCS, vol. 5995, pp. 11–22. Springer, Heidelberg (2010)
7. Devernay, F., Mateus, D., Guilbert, M.: Multi-camera scene flow by tracking 3-D points and surfels. In: CVPR (2006)
8. Garg, R., Roussos, A., Agapito, L.: A variational approach to video registration with subspace constraints. IJCV, 1–29 (2013)
9. Geiger, A., Lenz, P., Urtasun, R.: Are we ready for autonomous driving? In: CVPR (2012)
10. Hirschmüller, H.: Stereo processing by semiglobal matching and mutual information. TPAMI 30(2), 328–341 (2008)
11. Huguet, F., Devernay, F.: A variational method for scene flow estimation from stereo sequences. In: ICCV (2007)
12. Hung, C.H., Xu, L., Jia, J.: Consistent binocular depth and scene flow with chained temporal profiles. IJCV 102(1-3), 271–292 (2013)
13. Klaudiny, M., Hilton, A.: Cooperative patch-based 3D surface tracking. In: Proc. of the 8th International Conference on Visual Media Production (2011)
14. Lempitsky, V., Rother, C., Roth, S., Blake, A.: Fusion moves for Markov random field optimization. TPAMI 32(8), 1392–1405 (2010)
15. Meister, S., Jähne, B., Kondermann, D.: Outdoor stereo camera system for the generation of real-world benchmark data sets. Optical Engineering 51(02) (2012)
16. Müller, T., Rannacher, J., Rabe, C., Franke, U.: Feature- and depth-supported modified total variation optical flow for 3D motion field estimation in real scenes. In: CVPR (2011)
17. Murray, D.W., Buxton, B.F.: Scene segmentation from visual motion using global optimization. TPAMI 9(2), 220–228 (1987)
18. Park, J., Oh, T.H., Jung, J., Tai, Y.-W., Kweon, I.S.: A tensor voting approach for multi-view 3D scene flow estimation and refinement. In: Fitzgibbon, A., Lazebnik, S., Perona, P., Sato, Y., Schmid, C. (eds.) ECCV 2012, Part IV. LNCS, vol. 7575, pp. 288–302. Springer, Heidelberg (2012)
19. Rabe, C., Müller, T., Wedel, A., Franke, U.: Dense, robust, and accurate motion field estimation from stereo image sequences in real-time. In: Daniilidis, K., Maragos, P., Paragios, N. (eds.) ECCV 2010, Part IV. LNCS, vol. 6314, pp. 582–595. Springer, Heidelberg (2010)
20. Schoenemann, T., Cremers, D.: High resolution motion layer decomposition using dual-space graph cuts. In: CVPR (2008)
21. Sun, D., Sudderth, E.B., Black, M.J.: Layered image motion with explicit occlusions, temporal consistency, and depth ordering. In: NIPS (2010)

22. Sun, D., Wulff, J., Sudderth, E., Pfister, H., Black, M.: A fully-connected layered model of foreground and background flow. In: CVPR (2013)
23. Tao, H., Sawhney, H.S.: Global matching criterion and color segmentation based stereo. In: WACV (2000)
24. Unger, M., Werlberger, M., Pock, T., Bischof, H.: Joint motion estimation and segmentation of complex scenes with label costs and occlusion modeling. In: CVPR (2012)
25. Valgaerts, L., Bruhn, A., Zimmer, H., Weickert, J., Stoll, C., Theobalt, C.: Joint estimation of motion, structure and geometry from stereo sequences. In: Daniilidis, K., Maragos, P., Paragios, N. (eds.) ECCV 2010, Part IV. LNCS, vol. 6314, pp. 568–581. Springer, Heidelberg (2010)
26. Vedula, S., Baker, S., Collins, R., Kanade, T., Rander, P.: Three-dimensional scene flow. In: CVPR (1999)
27. Veksler, O., Boykov, Y., Mehrani, P.: Superpixels and supervoxels in an energy optimization framework. In: Daniilidis, K., Maragos, P., Paragios, N. (eds.) ECCV 2010, Part V. LNCS, vol. 6315, pp. 211–224. Springer, Heidelberg (2010)
28. Vogel, C., Schindler, K., Roth, S.: Piecewise rigid scene flow. In: ICCV (2013)
29. Vogel, C., Roth, S., Schindler, K.: An evaluation of data costs for optical flow. In: Weickert, J., Hein, M., Schiele, B. (eds.) GCPR 2013. LNCS, vol. 8142, pp. 343–353. Springer, Heidelberg (2013)
30. Vogel, C., Schindler, K., Roth, S.: 3D scene flow estimation with a rigid motion prior. In: ICCV (2011)
31. Volz, S., Bruhn, A., Valgaerts, L., Zimmer, H.: Modeling temporal coherence for optical flow. In: ICCV (2011)
32. Wang, J.Y.A., Edward, A.H.: Representing moving images with layers. IEEE Transactions on Image Processing 3, 625–638 (1994)
33. Wedel, A., Rabe, C., Vaudrey, T., Brox, T., Franke, U., Cremers, D.: Efficient dense scene flow from sparse or dense stereo data. In: Forsyth, D., Torr, P., Zisserman, A. (eds.) ECCV 2008, Part I. LNCS, vol. 5302, pp. 739–751. Springer, Heidelberg (2008)
34. Werlberger, M., Trobin, W., Pock, T., Wedel, A., Cremers, D., Bischof, H.: Anisotropic Huber-L1 optical flow. In: BMVC (2009)
35. Yamaguchi, K., Hazan, T., McAllester, D., Urtasun, R.: Continuous Markov random fields for robust stereo estimation. In: Fitzgibbon, A., Lazebnik, S., Perona, P., Sato, Y., Schmid, C. (eds.) ECCV 2012, Part V. LNCS, vol. 7576, pp. 45–58. Springer, Heidelberg (2012)
36. Yamaguchi, K., McAllester, D., Urtasun, R.: Robust monocular epipolar flow estimation. In: CVPR (2013)
37. Zabih, R., Woodfill, J.: Non-parametric local transforms for computing visual correspondence. In: Eklundh, J.-O. (ed.) ECCV 1994. LNCS, vol. 801, pp. 151–158. Springer, Heidelberg (1994)

Hand Waving Away Scale

Christopher Ham[1], Simon Lucey[2], and Surya Singh[1]

[1] Robotics Design Lab, The University of Queensland, Australia
[2] Robotics Institute, Carnegie Melon University, USA
{c.ham,spns}@uq.edu.au, slucey@cs.cmu.edu

Abstract. This paper presents a novel solution to the metric reconstruction of objects using any smart device equipped with a camera and an inertial measurement unit (IMU). We propose a batch, vision centric approach which only uses the IMU to estimate the metric scale of a scene reconstructed by any algorithm with Structure from Motion like (SfM) output. IMUs have a rich history of being combined with monocular vision for robotic navigation and odometry applications. These IMUs require sophisticated and quite expensive hardware rigs to perform well. IMUs in smart devices, however, are chosen for enhancing interactivity - a task which is more forgiving to noise in the measurements. We anticipate, however, that the ubiquity of these "noisy" IMUs makes them increasingly useful in modern computer vision algorithms. Indeed, we show in this work how an IMU from a smart device can help a face tracker to measure pupil distance, and an SfM algorithm to measure the metric size of objects. We also identify motions that produce better results, and develop a heuristic for estimating, in real-time, when enough data has been collected for an accurate scale estimation.

Keywords: Smart devices, IMU, metric, 3D reconstruction.

1 Introduction

Obtaining a metric reconstruction of the 3D world is a problem that has largely been ignored by the computer vision community when using monocular or multiple uncalibrated cameras. This ignorance is well founded, Structure from Motion (SfM) [1] dictates that a 3D object/scene can be reconstructed up to an ambiguity in scale. The vision world, however, is changing. Smart devices (phones, tablets, etc.) are low cost, ubiquitous and packaged with more than just a monocular camera for sensing the world. Even digital cameras are being bundled with a plethora of sensors such as GPS (global positioning system), light intensity, and IMUs (intertial measurement units).

The idea of combining measurements of an IMU and a monocular camera to make metric sense of the world has been well explored by the robotics community [2,3,4,5,6,7]. Traditionally, however, the community has focused on odometry and navigation which requires accurate and as a consequence expensive IMUs while using vision largely in a periphery manner. IMUs on modern smart devices, in contrast, are used primarily to obtain coarse measurement of the forces being applied to the device for the purposes of enhancing user interaction. As a consequence costs can be reduced by selecting noisy, less accurate sensors. In isolation they are largely unsuitable for making metric sense of the world.

D. Fleet et al. (Eds.): ECCV 2014, Part IV, LNCS 8692, pp. 279–293, 2014.

Fig. 1. Scale ambiguitiues can introduce detection ambiguities. These two toys are similar in shape but vary greatly in size. How could a toy detector know the difference if they are not in the same shot or share a common reference?

In this paper we explore an offline vision centric strategy for obtaining metric reconstructions of the outside world using noisy IMUs commonly found in smart devices. Specifically, we put forward a strategy for estimating everything about the world using vision except scale. We rely only on the IMU for the scale estimate. The strength of our strategy lies in the realisation that when the entire subject remains in the frame, scale does not change over time. Assuming that IMU noise is largely uncorrelated and there is sufficient motion during the collection of the video, we hypothesise that such an approach should converge eventually towards an accurate scale estimate even in the presence of significant amounts of IMU noise.

Applications in Vision: By enabling existing vision algorithms (operating on IMU enabled digital cameras such as smart devices) to make metric measurements of the world, they can be improved and new applications discovered. Figure 1 demonstrates how the lack of metric scale not only introduces ambiguities in SfM style applications, but in other common tasks in vision such as object detection. For example, a standard object detection algorithm could be employed to detect a toy dinosaur in a visual scene. However, what if the task is not only to detect the type of toy, but to disambiguate between two similar toys that differ only in scale? Unless the shot contains both toys (see right-most image in Figure 1) or some other reference object, there would be no simple way visually to separate them. Similarly, a pedestrian detection algorithm could know that a doll is not a person. In biometric applications an extremely useful biometric trait for separating people is the scale of the head (e.g. pupil distance), which goes largely unused by current facial recognition algorithms. Alternatively, a 3D scan of an object using a smart device could be 3D printed to precise dimensions using our approach combined with SfM algorithms.

Contributions: In this paper we make the following contributions.

- We propose an elegant batch-style objective for recovering scale with a noisy IMU and monocular vision. A strength of our approach is that it can be seamlessly integrated with any existing vision algorithm that is able to obtain accurate SfM style camera motion matrices, and the 3D structure of the object of interest up to an ambiguity in scale and reference frame. (Section 3.2)
- A novel strategy for aligning video and IMU input on a smart device using gravity. Most[1] smart devices do not synchronise the IMU and video. If the IMU and video inputs are not sufficiently aligned, we demonstrate that the scale estimate accuracy in practice is severely degraded. A strength of our alignment strategy, which takes advantage of gravity rather than removing it, is that it is independent of device and operating system. (Section 3.4)
- Finally, we propose an approach for ascertaining in real-time when enough device motion has occurred to ensure an accurate measure of scale can be obtained through our method. (Section 3.5)

We demonstrate the utility of our approach for obtaining metric scale across a number of visual tasks such as obtaining a metric reconstruction of a chessboard, estimating pupil distance, and obtaining a metric 3D reconstruction of a toy dinosaur. This is the first work of its kind, to our knowledge, to get such accurate (in all our experiments we achieved scale estimates within $1 - 2\%$ of ground-truth) metric reconstructions using a canonical smart device's monocular camera and IMU.

2 Related Work

2.1 Non-IMU Methods

There are ways to obtain a metric understanding of the world using monocular vision on a smart device that do not require an IMU. They all pivot on the idea of obtaining a metric measurement of something already observed by the vision algorithm and propogating the corresponding scale. There are a number of apps [8,9] which achieve this using vision. However, they all require some kind of external reference in order to estimate the metric scale factor of the vision, such as credit cards or knowing height of the camera from the ground (assuming the ground is flat).

2.2 IMU Methods

Online Methods: Our paper in many ways overlaps with existing robotics literature for combining monocular camera and IMU inputs. It differs in that many of these algorithms are focussed on navigation and odometry, and so the algorithms must execute in real-time.

Works by Jones et al. [6], Nützi et al. [2], Weiss et al. [3], and Li et al. [7] all show how the camera motion of any visual SLAM (simultaneous localisation and mapping) algorithm can be fused with accelerometer and gyroscope measurements using a

---

[1] We tested our proposed approach on both iOS and Android smart devices, neither of which provided global timestamps for the video input.

Kalman Filter. The IMU measurements (at 100Hz or more) are integrated to estimate motion and errors are corrected each time the SLAM is updated (20Hz).

Weiss et al. [3] take the idea a step further by automatically detecting failures in the SLAM output and use only the IMU until the SLAM algorithm recovers. The objectives of Weiss' work are similar to ours in that their implementation is modular to any SLAM algorithm that provides position and orientation, and they assess the quality of the scale estimate in their results.

Li et al. [7] account for rolling-shutter distortion that occurs in low quality cameras. Unlike the above mentioned methods they do apply their approach to a smart device. However, they still focus mainly on navigation, and the odometry. SLAM feature tracking, and sensor fusion are all tightly integrated and nonmodular.

Offline Methods: Offline methods are advantageous, as they do not require close integration with the vision algorithm when computing scale. They can often times give more accurate estimates of scale, as they attempt to solve the problem using all the data at the same time (i.e. in batch) unlike online methods. Offline methods have a further advantage in that they allow a "plug and play" strategy for incorporating various object-centric vision algorithms (e.g. face trackers, chessboard trackers, etc.) with little to no modification.

Jung and Taylor [4] present an offline method to fuse IMU and camera data in batch using spline approximations, with only a handful of camera frames being used to estimate the camera trajectory. Like previous online works the focus of this work was on recovering odometry. We believe one of the core motivations for the use of splines was to reduce computational requirements. Splines allow the data to be broken up into "epochs", reducing the dimensionality of the final problem, however this also reduces the resolution. This causes problems if the camera is moving too quickly.

Skoglund et al. [5] propose another offline method that enhances an SfM problem by including IMU data in the objective. The camera and IMU are high quality and secured to a custom rig. The IMU motion is first integrated so that its trajectory can be compared with that of the camera's. Unlike with smart devices, the high quality of sensors allows this to be done without introducing too many compounding errors. An estimation of scale is obtained but is not the central focus of the work.

Tanskanen et al. [10] demostrate a pipeline for real-time metric 3D reconstruction, however they never discuss the accuracy of the metric scale estimation. Finite segments of large motions are detected heuristically and estimates for the displacement measured by the IMU and by the camera are compared. An estimation of the scene scale is obtained by executing a batch least squares which minimises the difference between these two displacement estimates. This is accurate enough to help increase the robustness of the 3D reconstruction but the accuracy of the dimensions of the final model is unclear.

3   Recovery of Scale

Using SfM (Structure from Motion) algorithms, or algorithms tailored for specific objects (such as chessboards, faces, cars) we can determine the 3D camera pose and scene accurately up to scale. This section describes a batch, vision centric approach which, other than the camera, only uses a smart device's IMU to estimate the metric scale. All that is required from the vision algorithm is the position of the center of the camera, and its orientation in the scene.

3.1 In One Dimension

The scale factor from vision units to real units is time invariant and so with the correct assumptions about noise, an estimation of its value should converge to the correct answer with more and more data. Let us consider the trivial one dimensional case

$$\arg\min_{s} \ \eta\{s\nabla^2\mathbf{p}_V - \mathbf{Da}_I\} \tag{1}$$
$$\text{s.t. } s > 0,$$

where $\mathbf{p}_V$ is the position vector containing samples across time of the camera in vision units, $\mathbf{a}_I$ is the metric acceleration measured by the IMU, ∇^2 is the discrete temporal double deriviative operator, and $\mathbf{D}$ is a convolutional matrix that antialiases and downsamples the IMU data. Scale by definition must be greater than zero, we include this here to remain general to the method used to solve the problem. $\eta\{\}$ is some penalty function; the choice of $\eta\{\}$ depends on the noise of the sensor data. This could commonly be the ℓ2-norm^2, however we remain agnostic to entertain other noise assumptions. Downsampling is necessary since IMUs and cameras on smart devices typically record data at 100 Hz and 30 Hz, respectively. Blurring before downsampling reduces the effects of aliasing.

The approach here allows us to be modular with the way camera motion is obtained and allows us to compare accelerations rather than positions. This idea differs from work such as [11] and [10] which incorporates the scale estimation into an SfM algorithm by comparing the position of the camera with the position integrated from IMU data (prone to drift and compounding errors).

Equation 1 makes the following assumptions: (i) measurement noise is unbiased and Gaussian (in the case that $\eta\{\}$ is ℓ2-norm^2), (ii) the IMU only measures acceleration from motion, not gravity, (iii) the IMU and camera samples are temporally aligned and have equal spacing. In reality, this is not the case. First, IMUs (typically found in smart devices) have a measurement bias that is variant to temperature [12]. Second, acceleration due to gravity is omnipresent. However, most smart device APIs provide a "linear acceleration" which has gravity removed. Third, smart device APIs provide a global timestamp for IMU data but timestamps on video frames are relative to the begining of the video, and so we cannot trivially obtain their alignment. These timestamps do reveal, however, that the spacing between samples in all cases is uniform with little variance. Subsection 3.3 describes the method used to temporally align the data.

These facts allow us to modify our assumptions: (i) when used over a period of 1-2 minutes IMU noise is Gaussian and has a constant bias, (ii) the "linear acceleration" provided by device APIs is sufficiently accurate, (iii) the IMU and camera measurements have been temporally aligned and have equal spacing.

For simplicity we let the acceleration of the vision algorithm, $\mathbf{a}_V = \nabla^2\mathbf{p}_V$. Given the modified assumptions we introduce a bias factor into the objective

$$\arg\min_{s,b} \eta\{s\mathbf{a}_V - \mathbf{D}(\mathbf{a}_I - \mathbf{1}b)\} \ . \tag{2}$$

Note we also omit the $s > 0$ constraint from Equation 1 as it unnecessarily complicates the objective. If a solution to s is found that violates this constraint the solution can be immediately discounted.

3.2 In Three Dimensions

In the following subsection we consider the case where the smart device is moving and rotating in 3D space. Most SfM algorithms will return the position and orientation of the camera in scene coordinates, and IMU measurements are in local, body-centric coordinates. To compare them we need to orient the acceleration measured by the camera with that of the IMU. We define the acceleration matrix such that each row is the (x, y, z) acceleration for each video frame

$$\mathbf{A}_V = \begin{pmatrix} a_1^x & a_1^y & a_1^z \\ \vdots & \vdots & \vdots \\ a_F^x & a_F^y & a_F^z \end{pmatrix} = \begin{pmatrix} \Phi_1^{\mathsf{T}} \\ \vdots \\ \Phi_F^{\mathsf{T}} \end{pmatrix}. \tag{3}$$

Then we rotate the vectors in each row to obtain the body-centric acceleration measured by the vision algorithm

$$\hat{\mathbf{A}}_V = \begin{pmatrix} \Phi_1^{\mathsf{T}} \mathbf{R}_1^V \\ \vdots \\ \Phi_F^{\mathsf{T}} \mathbf{R}_F^V \end{pmatrix} \tag{4}$$

where F is the number of video frames, $\mathbf{R}_n^V$ is the orientation of the camera in scene coordinates at the nth video frame.

Similarly to $\mathbf{A}_V$, we form an $N \times 3$ matrix of IMU accelerations, $\mathbf{A}_I$, where N is the number of IMU measurements.

We also need to ensure that IMU measurements are spatially aligned with the camera coordinate frame. Since the camera and IMU are on the same circuit board, this is an orthogonal transformation, $\mathbf{R}_I$, that is determined by the API used by the smart device [13,14]. We use the rotation to find the IMU acceleration in local camera coordinates.

This leads to the following objective, noting that antialiasing and downsampling have no effect on constant bias

$$\underset{s,\mathbf{b}}{\arg\min}\, \eta \{s \cdot \hat{\mathbf{A}}_V + \mathbf{1} \otimes \mathbf{b}^{\mathsf{T}} - \mathbf{D}\mathbf{A}_I\mathbf{R}_I\}. \tag{5}$$

3.3 Temporal Alignment

Temporal alignment is important for accurate results - Figure 7 shows that scale estimation is not possible without it. Equations 2 and 5 assume that the camera and IMU measurements are temporally aligned. This subsection describes a method to determine the delay between the signals and thus align them for processing.

The optimum alignment between two signals can be found by first calculating their cross-correlation. The cross-correlation is then normalised by dividing each of its elements by the number of elements from the original signals that were used to calculate it. The index of the maximum normalised cross-correlation value is chosen as the delay between the signals.

Before aligning the two signals, an initial estimate of the biases and scale can be obtained using Equation 5. These values can be used to adjust the acceleration signals in order to improve the results of the cross-correlation. The optimisation and alignment are alternated until the alignment converges.

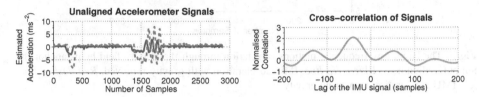

Fig. 2. Showing the result of the normalised cross-correlation of the camera and IMU signals. *Blue-solid line*: camera acceleration scaled by initial solution. *Red-dashed line*: IMU acceleration. The delay that gives the best alignment here is approximately 40 samples.

3.4 Gravity as a Friend

The above method for finding the delay between two signals can struggle with smaller motions when data is particularly noisy. Reintroducing gravity has two advantages: (i) it behaves as an anchor to significantly improve the robustness of the alignment, (ii) allows us to remove the black box gravity estimation built in to smart devices with IMUs.

Instead of comparing the estimated camera acceleration and linear IMU acceleration, we add the gravity vector, g, back into the camera acceleration and compare it with the raw IMU acceleration (which already contains gravity). Grabity is oriented, much like the vision acceleration, with the IMU acceleration before superimposing

$$\hat{\mathbf{G}} = \begin{pmatrix} \mathbf{g}^\mathsf{T}\mathbf{R}_1^V \\ \vdots \\ \mathbf{g}^\mathsf{T}\mathbf{R}_F^V \end{pmatrix}. \tag{6}$$

Since the accelerations are in the camera reference frame the reintroduction of gravity essentially captures the pitch and roll of the smart device. The red dashed line in Figure 3 shows that the gravity component is of relatively large magnitude and low frequency. This can improve the robustness of the alignment dramatically.

If the alignment of the vision scene with gravity is already known, it can simply be added to the camera acceleration vectors before estimating the scale. However, to keep our method general we extend the above objectives to include the gravity term

$$\arg\min_{s,\mathbf{b},\mathbf{g}} \eta\{s\hat{\mathbf{A}}_V + \mathbf{1} \otimes \mathbf{b}^T + \hat{\mathbf{G}} - \mathbf{D}\mathbf{A}_I\mathbf{R}_I\} \tag{7}$$

where g is linear in $\hat{\mathbf{G}}$.

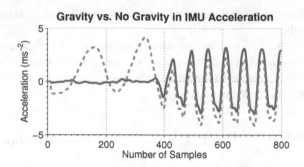

Fig. 3. The large, low frequency motions of rotation through the gravity field helps anchor the temporal alignment. *Blue solid line*: IMU acceleration with gravity removed. *Red dashed line*: raw IMU acceleration measuring gravity.

Note that Equation 7 does not attempt to constrain gravity to its known constant value. This is addressed by alternating between solving for $\{s, \mathbf{b}\}$ and $\mathbf{g}$ separately where $\mathbf{g}$ is normalised to its known magnitude when solving for $\{s, \mathbf{b}\}$. This is iterated until the scale estimation converges.

3.5 Classifying Useful Data

When recording video and IMU samples offline it is important to know when one has sufficient samples. We classify which parts of the signal are useful by ensuring it contains enough excitation. This is achieved by centering a window at sample, n, and computing the spectrum through short time Fourier analysis. A sample is classified as useful if the amplitude of certain frequencies is above a chosen threshold.

The selection of the frequency range and threshold is investigated in the experiments in Section 4.1. Note that the minimum size of the window is limited by the lowest frequency one wishes to classify as useful.

4 Experiments

In the following experiments, sensor data is collected from iOS and Android devices using custom built applications. The applications record video while logging IMU data at 100Hz to a file. These files are then processed in batch as described in the experiments. For all the experiments, the cameras' intrinsic calibration matrices have been determined beforehand, and the camera is pitched and rolled at the beginning of each sequence to help temporal alignment of sensor data (Section 3.4).

The choice of $\eta\{\}$ depends on the assumptions of the noise in the data. In many cases we obtained good empirical performance with the $\ell 2$-norm^2 penalty (Equation 8. However, we also explored alternate penalty functions such as the grouped-$\ell 1$-norm that are less sensitive to outliers. We obtain camera motion in three different ways: (i) track a chessboard of unknown size, (ii) use pose estimation of a face-tracking algorithm [15], (iii) use the output of an SfM algorithm.

4.1   Chessboard Experiments

On an iPad, we assess the accuracy of the of scale estimation described in Section 3.2 and the types of trajectories that produce the best results. Using a chessboard allows us to be agnostic from objects and obtaining the pose estimation from chessboard corners is well researched. We used OpenCV's *findChessboardCorners* and *solvePnP* functions.

The trajectories in these experiments were chosen in order to test the number of axes that need to be excited, the trajectories that work best, the frequencies that help the most, and the required amplitude of the motions. They can be placed into the four following categories (shown in Figure 4):

(a) Orbit Around: The camera remains the same distance to the centroid of the object while orbiting around,

(b) In and Out: The camera moves linearly toward and away from the object,

(c) Side Ways: The camera moves linearly and parallel to the object's plane,

(d) Motion 8: The camera follows a figure of 8 shaped trajectory - in or out of plane.

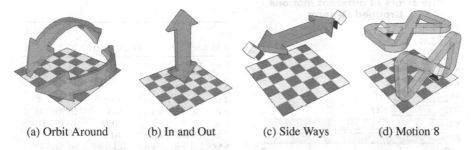

(a) Orbit Around   (b) In and Out   (c) Side Ways   (d) Motion 8

Fig. 4. The above diagrams show the different categories of trajectories. The accuracies of different combinations of these trajectories are assessed. In each case, the camera is is always looking at the subject.

Different sequences of the four trajectories were tested. The use of different penalty functions, and thus different noise assumptions, is also explored. Figure 5 shows the accuracy of the scale estimation when we choose the $\ell2$-norm^2 (Equation 8). Figure 6 shows the results when we choose the grouped-$\ell1$-norm (Equation 9). There is an obvious overall improvement when using the grouped-$\ell1$-norm, suggesting that a Gaussian noise assumption is not strictly observed.

$$\eta_{\ell2}\{\mathbf{X}\} = \sum_{i=1}^{F} \|\mathbf{x}_i\|_2^2 \qquad (8)$$

$$\eta_{\ell2\ell1}\{\mathbf{X}\} = \sum_{i=1}^{F} \|\mathbf{x}_i\|_2 \qquad (9)$$

$$\text{where } \mathbf{X} = [\mathbf{x}_1, \ldots, \mathbf{x}_F]^\mathsf{T} \qquad (10)$$

Both Figures 5 and 6 show that, in general, it is best to excite all axes of the smart device. The most accurate scale estimation was achieved by combination of *In and Out (b)* and *Sideways (c)* motion (along both the x and y axes) and is shown in Figure 8.

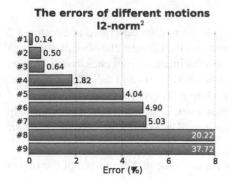

		Excitation (s)		
# Motions	Frequency (Hz)	X	Y	Z
1 b + c(X and Y axis)	~1	20	30	45
2 b + c(X and Y axis)	~1.2	35	25	70
3 b + c(X and Y axis)	~0.8	10	7	5
4 b + c(X and Y axis)	~0.7	10	10	10
5 b	~0.75	0	0	160
6 b + c(X and Y axis)	~0.8	5	3	4
7 b + c(X and Y axis)	~1.5	7	6	4
8 a(X and Y axis) + b	0.4-0.8	30	30	47
9 b + d(in plane)	~0.8	50	50	10

Fig. 5. The percentange error in scale estimations for different motions on an iPad. Linear trajectories produce more accurate estimations. Labelled according to Figure 4.

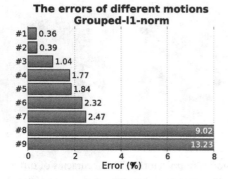

		Excitation (s)		
# Motions	Frequency (Hz)	X	Y	Z
1 b + c(X and Y axis)	~0.8	10	7	5
2 b + c(X and Y axis)	~0.7	10	10	10
3 b + c(X and Y axis)	~0.8	5	3	4
4 b + c(X and Y axis)	~1.5	7	6	4
5 b + c(X and Y axis)	~1	20	30	45
6 b	~0.75	0	0	160
7 b + c(X and Y axis)	~1.2	35	25	70
8 a(X and Y axis) + b	0.4-0.8	30	30	47
9 b + d(in plane)	~0.8	50	50	10

Fig. 6. The same sequences in Figure 5 are used to estimate scale using the group L1 norm. Overall improvement suggests a non-Gaussian noise distribution. Labelled according to Figure 4.

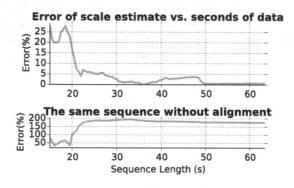

Fig. 7. The scale estimation converges (with the addition of data) to the ground truth over time for $b + c$ motions in all axes. For completeness we also show the error when the camera and IMU signals are not temporally aligned.

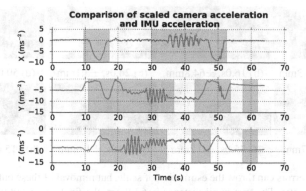

Fig. 8. The sequence $b + c(X,Y)$ excites multiple axes which increases the accuracy of scale estimations. *Blue solid line*: scaled camera acceleration. *Red dashed line*: IMU acceleration. For completeness we highlight, in shaded areas, the segments that are classified as useful motions.

Figure 7 shows the estimate of scale as a function of the length of the sequence used. It shows that scale estimate improves with the addition of new data to have an error of less than 2% with just 55 seconds of motion. This method does not focus on odometry, thus removing the risk of divergence that can occur when integrating accelerometer data.

From these observations, we build a real-time heuristic for knowing when enough data has been collected. Upon inspection of the results shown in Figure 5 we can construct the following criteria for sufficiently accurate results: (i) all axes should be excited with (ii) more than 10 seconds of motions of amplitude larger than $2ms^{-2}$.

| (a) 7.0s, ±63.0mm | (b) 10.0s, ±51.4mm | (c) 12.0s, ±43.3mm | (d) 14.0s, ±8.6mm |

| (e) 30.0s, ±5.4mm | (f) 40.0s, ±4.0mm | (g) 50.0s, ±0.6mm | (h) 68.0s, ±0.2mm |

Fig. 9. Circles show the variance in the pupil distance estimation over time. True pupil distance is 62.3mm; final estimated pupil distance is 62.1mm (0.38% error).

4.2   Measuring Pupil Distance

In this experiment, we test our method's ability to accurately measure the distance between one's pupils with an iPad. Using a facial landmark tracking SDK [15], we can

(a) 10.0s, ±75.3mm   (b) 16.0s, ±64.8mm   (c) 24.0s, ±3.1mm   (d) 50.0s, ±1.8mm

(e) 60.0s, ±0.7mm   (f) 75.0s, ±0.2mm   (g) 85.0s, ±1.6mm   (h) 115.0s, ±0.7mm

Fig. 10. Tracking errors can throw the estimation of scale, but removal of these outliers [16] helps the estimation recover. The true pupil distance is 62.8mm; the final estimated pupil distance is 63.5mm (1.1% error).

obtain the camera pose relative to the face and locations of facial landmarks (with local variations to match the indiviual). We assume that, for the duration of the sequence, the face keeps the same expression and that the head remains still. To reflect this, the facial landmark tracking SDK was modified to solve for only one expression in the sequence rather than one at each video frame.

Due to the motion blur that the cameras in smart devices are prone to, the pose estimation from the face tracking algorithm can drift and occasionally fail. These errors violate the Gaussian noise assumptions. Improved results were obtained using a grouped-ℓ1-norm, but we found in practice even better performance could be obtained through the use of an outlier detection strategy [16] (see Appendix A) in conjunction with the canonical ℓ2-norm^2 penalty. It is this strategy we use for the remainder of the experiments in this paper.

Figure 9 shows the deviation of the estimated pupil distance from the true value at selected frames from a video taken on an iPad. With only 68 seconds of data, our algorithm can measure pupil distance with sufficient accuracy. Figure 10 shows a similar sequence for a different person. It can be observed that the face tracking, and thus pose estimation, drifts occasionally. In spite of this, the scale estimation is still able to converge over time.

4.3   3D Scanning

In the final experiment, SfM is used to obtain a 3D scan of an object using an Android smart phone. The estimated camera motion from this is used to evaluate the metric scale of the vision coordinates. This is then used to make metric measurements of the virtual object which are compared with those of the original.

The results of these 3D scans can be seen in Figure 11 where a basic model was obtained using VideoTrace [17]. The dimensions estimated by our algorithm are within 1% of the real values. This is sufficiently accurate to help a toy classifier disambiguate the two dinosaur toys shown in (Figure 1).

(a) Measuring the real Rex: 184mm   (b) Measuring the virtual Rex: 0.5653 units =
                                                        182.2mm (estimated scale = 322.23)

Fig. 11. The real length of Rex (a) is compared with the length of the 3D reconstruction scaled
by our algorithm (b). Sequence recorded on an Android smart phone.

5   Conclusion

This paper has presented a batch technique for obtaining the metric scale of the SfM
like output from a vision algorithm using only the IMU on a smart device with less
than 2% error. We have made three main contributions that make this possible. First,
we realised that by comparing the acceleration of the camera in vision units with the
acceleration of the IMU (which we know to be metric), we can find the optimum scale
factor to minimise their difference. Second, we have described a method to align sensor
measurements which do not have a common timestamp origin (typical on smart device
platforms) that uses acceleration from gravity to help anchor the alignment. Finally, we
have formed a heuristic to estimate when enough useful data has been collected to make
an accurate measurement of metric scale.

Acknowledgements. This research was supported by the Commonwealth Scientific
and Industrial Research Organisation.

References

1. Hartley, R.I., Zisserman, A.: Multiple View Geometry in Computer Vision, 2nd edn. Cambridge University Press (2004) ISBN: 0521540518
2. Nützi, G., Weiss, S., Scaramuzza, D., Siegwart, R.: Fusion of IMU and vision for absolute
   scale estimation in monocular slam. Journal of Intelligent & Robotic Systems 61(1-4), 287–
   299 (2011)
3. Weiss, S., Achtelik, M.W., Lynen, S., Achtelik, M.C., Kneip, L., Chli, M., Siegwart, R.:
   Monocular vision for long-term micro aerial vehicle state estimation: A compendium. Journal of Field Robotics 30(5), 803–831 (2013)
4. Jung, S.H., Taylor, C.J.: Camera trajectory estimation using inertial sensor measurements
   and structure from motion results. In: IEEE International Conference on Computer Vision
   and Pattern Recognition (CVPR), vol. 2, pp. II–732. IEEE (2001)

5. Skoglund, M., Sjanic, Z., Gustafsson, F.: Initialisation and estimation methods for batch optimisation of inertial/visual slam. Technical report, Department of Electrical Engineering Linköpings Universitet (2013)

6. Jones, E., Vedaldi, A., Soatto, S.: Inertial structure from motion with autocalibration. In: Workshop on Dynamical Vision (2007)

7. Li, M., Kim, B.H., Mourikis, A.I.: Real-time motion tracking on a cellphone using inertial sensing and a rolling-shutter camera. In: IEEE International Conference on Robotics and Automation (ICRA), pp. 4712–4719 (2013)

8. Smart Tools co.: Smart Measure Pro. Google Play Store (2013), http://goo.gl/JDRu5

9. Kamens, B.: RulerPhone - Photo Measuring. Apple App Store (2010–2013), http://goo.gl/CRaIOk

10. Tanskanen, P., Kolev, K., Meier, L., Camposeco, F., Saurer, O., Pollefeys, M.: Live metric 3d reconstruction on mobile phones (2013)

11. Konolige, K., Agrawal, M., Solà, J.: Large-scale visual odometry for rough terrain. In: Kaneko, M., Nakamura, Y. (eds.) Robotics Research. STAR, vol. 66, pp. 201–212. Springer, Heidelberg (2010)

12. Aggarwal, P., Syed, Z., Niu, X., El-Sheimy, N.: A standard testing and calibration procedure for low cost mems inertial sensors and units. Journal of Navigation 61(02), 323–336 (2008)

13. Android Documentation: SensorEvent - Android Developers (2013), http://goo.gl/fBFBU

14. iOS Documentation: UIAcceleration Class Reference (2010), http://goo.gl/iwJjKN

15. Cox, M.J., Nuevo, J.S., Lucey, S.: Deformable model fitting by regularized landmark mean-shift. International Journal of Computer Vision (IJCV) 91(2), 200–215 (2011)

16. Rosner, B.: Percentage points for a generalized ESD many-outlier procedure. Technometrics 25(2), 165–172 (1983)

17. van den Hengel, A., Dick, A., Thormählen, T., Ward, B., Torr, P.H.: Videotrace: rapid interactive scene modelling from video. ACM Transactions on Graphics (TOG) 26, 86 (2007)

A   Outlier Detection

In practice, the output of different tracking algorithms can produce noise which violates the Gaussian noise assumption, Figure 12 shows how tracking errors cause spikes in the acceleration measured by tracking a face. After obtaining an initial estimate of scale, Generalised ESD (extreme Studentised deviate) [16] is used to detect samples whose errors do not follow a Gaussian assumption. These samples are excluded and a new scale estimation is obtained. This method requires only two iterations. Generalised ESD takes two parameters: the sensitivity of outlier detection, α, and an upper bound of the number of outliers to detect, k. In our experiments, the performance of this method was not sensitive to the tuning of these parameters.

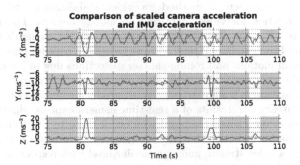

Fig. 12. A comparision of the acceleration measured by the IMU and that estimated by the visual tracking. Outliers violating a Gaussian error assumption have been detected and removed by Generalised ESD. *Blue solid line*: scaled camera acceleration. *Red dashed line*: IMU acceleration.

A Non-Linear Filter for Gyroscope-Based Video Stabilization

Steven Bell[1], Alejandro Troccoli[2], and Kari Pulli[2]

[1] Stanford University, Stanford, CA, USA
sebell@stanford.edu
[2] NVIDIA Research, Santa Clara, CA, USA
{atroccoli,karip}@nvidia.com

Abstract. We present a method for video stabilization and rolling-shutter correction for videos captured on mobile devices. The method uses the data from an on-board gyroscope to track the camera's angular velocity, and can run in real time within the camera capture pipeline. We remove small motions and rolling-shutter distortions due to hand shake, creating the impression of a video shot on a tripod. For larger motions, we filter the camera's angular velocity to produce a smooth output. To meet the latency constraints of a real-time camera capture pipeline, our filter operates on a small temporal window of three to five frames. Our algorithm performs better than the previous work that uses a gyroscope to stabilize a video stream, and at a similar level with respect to current feature-based methods.

Keywords: video stabilization, rolling-shutter, gyroscopes.

1 Introduction

Cell phones and other mobile devices have rapidly become the most popular means of recording casual video. Unfortunately, because cell phones are hand-held and light-weight devices operated by amateurs in the spur of the moment, most videos are plagued by camera shake. Such shake is at best mildly distracting, and at worst completely unbearable to watch. Additionally, most mobile cameras use a rolling shutter sensor, where each horizontal scanline of pixels is sequentially exposed and read out. When the camera moves during the exposure, each image row captures a slightly different viewpoint, resulting in a distorted image. Vertical motions cause the image to be squeezed or stretched vertically, and horizontal motions shear the image so that vertical lines tilt to left or right.

At the same time, cell phones have gained the processing resources and features that make real-time, on-device video processing possible. The majority of mid-to-high range mobile devices contain a multi-core CPU complex, a graphics processing unit (GPU) and an inertial measurement unit (IMU) with a 3-axis gyroscope. In this paper we address the challenge of performing video stabilization on such devices, using the gyroscope for motion tracking. Unlike most proposed stabilization methods, which operate as a post-processing step on a captured

D. Fleet et al. (Eds.): ECCV 2014, Part IV, LNCS 8692, pp. 294–308, 2014.

video, our method can run in real-time as part of the camera capture pipeline. In addition, our motion filter does a better job at removing camera shake than previous methods that stabilize the video stream using gyroscope data [1].

Correcting a video frame before it is sent to the hardware video encoder is beneficial in several ways. First, our algorithm has access to uncompressed data, which is an improvement over off-line methods that need to decode and re-encode and degrade the video quality when doing so. Moreover, because encoding methods such as H.264 rely on finding patches of image data which match between frames, removing frame-to-frame shake and increasing the temporal consistency of a video may improve the encoding quality and reduce the final storage size. Finally, it is important to consider that many (perhaps most) videos shot with cell phones are watched on the same device instead of being uploaded to a sharing site. Likewise, video chatting, because of its real-time peer-to-peer nature, requires that any stabilization be done on the device without inducing any lag.

Motion tracking is greatly simplified when using a phone's on-board 3-axis gyroscope. The camera orientation can be computed from the gyroscope measurements using a handful of multiplications and additions, while image-based methods must analyze thousands or even millions of pixels. As a result, motion estimation using the gyroscope can dramatically reduce CPU utilization, memory bandwidth, and battery usage compared to image-based methods. A typical MEMS gyroscope consumes about 4 milliwatts [2], while the power consumed by the CPU and memory traffic can easily be tens or hundreds of milliwatts.

Additionally, image-based methods can fail when features are sparse or when large objects move in the foreground. A gyroscope, by contrast, always reports the device motion regardless of how much and in which way the objects in the scene move. Furthermore, the gyroscope measurements allow us to estimate intra-frame camera orientations which we can use to accurately correct rolling shutter on a per-frame basis.

Compared to state-of-the-art stabilizers [3], our method provides a similar level of stabilization quality at a fraction of the processing cost, with no degradation due to foreground object motion.

2 Background and Prior Work

Video stabilization removes jitter from videos based on the assumption that high-frequency motions are unintended and are the consequence of hand tremor. It is essentially a three-stage process, consisting of a motion estimation stage, a filtering stage that smooths the measured motion, and a re-synthesis stage that generates a new video sequence as observed by a virtual camera moving under the filtered motion.

Two-dimensional stabilization involves tracking image keypoints to find the camera motion between frames, usually modeled as an affine or projective image warp [3–7]. The video is re-synthesized by defining a virtual crop window that is transformed according to the smoothed camera path. Matsushita *et al.* [7] smooth the camera motion by applying a Gaussian kernel to a local window of 2D transforms. Gleicher *et al.* [4] take a different approach by segmenting the camera path into shorter paths that follow a particular motion model, as defined by cinematic conventions. Grundmann *et al.* [5] integrate this kind of motion segmentation with saliency, blur, and crop window constraints in a unified optimization framework.

Image-based tracking methods suffer when depth variations induce pixel motions that, due to parallax, are not easily modeled by homographies. Furthermore, a rolling-shutter imaging sensor can introduce non-rigid frame-to-frame correspondences that cannot simply be modeled by a global frame-to-frame motion model. To address rolling-shutter, Baker *et al.* [8] estimate and remove the high-frequency jitter of the camera using temporal super-resolution of low-frequency optical flow. Following up on their earlier work, Grundmann *et al.* [3] developed a model based on a mixture of homographies that track the intra-frame motions and produces stabilized videos with corrected rolling-shutter distortions. Liu *et al.* [6] employ a mesh-based, spatially-variant motion representation coupled with an adaptive space-time path optimization that can handle parallax and correct for rolling-shutter effects.

Three-dimensional video stabilization techniques track the camera motion in the world 3D space using structure-from-motion methods [9, 10]. These 3D methods can deal with parallax distortions caused by depth variations in the scene, and synthesize the output using image warps that take into account the scene structure. Still, the motion estimation is brittle if there are not enough features or sufficient parallax; and these methods are, in general, computationally expensive.

Gyroscopes are an attractive alternative to feature-based motion estimation, since they sidestep many failure cases. Karpenko *et al.* [1] and Hanning *et al.* [11] describe video stabilization techniques for mobile devices which use the built-in gyroscope to track the camera orientation. Both of these methods apply a linear low-pass filter to the gyroscope output. Karpenko *et al.* [1] use a Gaussian kernel, while Hanning *et al.* [11] apply a variable-length Hann window to adaptively smooth the camera path. In contrast, we introduce a nonlinear filtering method which completely flattens small motions regardless of frequency, and performs low-pass smoothing when the virtual camera must move to keep the crop window inside the input frame. When the camera is nearly still, our virtual camera is fixed, removing all jitter. When moving, our method acts like a variable IIR filter, mixing the input velocity with the virtual camera velocity in a way that smooths the output, while guaranteeing that it tracks the input so that the crop window never leaves the input frame. This nonlinearity is necessary because a very low cutoff frequency is required to smooth out low-frequency motions such as those induced by walking. A large low-pass FIR or IIR filter introduces lag. Moreover, any linear filter with a low enough cutoff frequency to flatten low-frequency bouncing will also do a poor job tracking the input when the camera is intentionally moved.

None of the previous cited work has a suitable real-time implementation that eliminates camera shake. Karpenko *et al.* [1] implemented a truncated causal

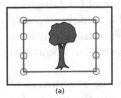 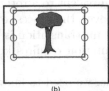 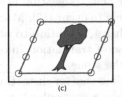 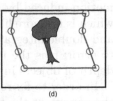

Fig. 1. Example crop polygons (shown in red) for a variety of scenarios: (a) no motion, (b) vertical motion causes shrinking, (c) horizontal motion causes shearing, and (d) a combination of motions causes a complex rolling-shutter distortion

low-pass filter for their real-time implementation of viewfinder stabilization on an iPhone. However, as mentioned in their paper, the truncated low-pass filter attenuates camera shake, but does not completely remove it. They suggest that for video recording it might be possible to hold back video frames for a longer period of time to achieve a smoother result, and leave this implementation for future work. But there is a limit on the number of frames that can be buffered, and as we show in Section 4, a Gaussian low-pass filter that buffers five frames still does not eliminate shake, while our method does.

Our primary contribution in this work is a novel smoothing algorithm that uses the gyroscope to track the camera motion and is suitable for real-time implementation. By using a nonlinear filter, we are able to produce static segments connected by smooth motions, while tracking the input and using little to no frame buffering.

3   Algorithm Description

Conceptually, video stabilization can be achieved by creating a crop rectangle that moves with the scene content from frame to frame as the camera shakes around. The position of the crop rectangle within the input frame may vary wildly, but the content within the crop rectangle remains stable, producing a smooth output. Our method is based on this idea, but instead of moving a crop rectangle, we move a crop polygon, and the region within the polygon is projectively warped to create the output video. This more flexible model allows us to model the distortions introduced by the sensor's rolling shutter, as illustrated by Figure 1.

3.1   Camera Tracking Using the Gyroscope

We model the camera motion as a rotation in a global coordinate frame. The gyroscope provides a series of discrete angular velocity measurements with time-stamps, which we integrate to produce a function of time that describes the camera orientation. In theory we could be more precise by also measuring translation with the device's accelerometer, but in practice this is difficult and of limited value. If the camera is 3 meters away from a flat scene, then the image motion induced by a 1 cm translation is equivalent to a rotation of 0.19 degrees, which is far more likely to occur [12]. Moreover, the process of estimating gravity and double-integrating acceleration to obtain translation is extremely sensitive to error; plus the use of translation information requires knowledge about the depth of objects in the scene.

In order to fix rolling shutter distortions, we need to know the orientation of the camera at the time a particular row was exposed. Given the timestamp for the first row of a frame t_0, the timestamp for row r is

$$t_r = t_0 + \frac{r}{f_l} f_t, \tag{1}$$

where f_t is the total frame time (i.e., the time elapsed between the start of two consecutive frames) and f_l is the frame length in image rows. The frame length is the sum of the image height (in pixels), plus the number of blanking rows, where no data is read out. Both of these values depend on the image sensor and capture mode, but we assume that they are known and constant for the duration of the video. If these values are not provided by the sensor driver, they can also be obtained by calibration [13, 14].

We can find the device orientation corresponding to a point x in an image by calculating its corresponding row timestamp and interpolating the camera orientation from known samples. Due to hardware and software latencies, there is a small offset between the frame timestamps and the gyroscope timestamps. We assume this offset t_d is known and constant for the duration of the capture. In practice, we calibrate this offset as detailed in section 3.5.

We use a projective camera model with focal length f and center of projection (c_x, c_y); these three parameters define the entries of the camera intrinsic matrix K. The parameters are calibrated off-line using the OpenCV library [15]. With the K matrix known, the relationship between corresponding points $\mathbf{x}_1$ and $\mathbf{x}_2$ on two different frames captured by a rolling-shutter sensor subject to rotational motion is

$$\mathbf{x}_2 = K R_c(t_2) R_c^{-1}(t_1) K^{-1} \mathbf{x}_1, \tag{2}$$

where the rotation matrix R_c represents the camera orientation in the camera's coordinate system as a function of time, and t_1 and t_2 are the row timestamps for points $\mathbf{x}_1$ and $\mathbf{x}_2$.

We can re-write Equation 2 with respect to the gyroscope coordinate system and time origin as

$$\mathbf{x}_2 = K T R_g(t_2 + t_d) R_g^{-1}(t_1 + t_d) T^{-1} K^{-1} \mathbf{x}_1, \tag{3}$$

where R_g is the orientation derived from the gyroscope, T is the transformation between the camera and the gyroscope coordinate systems, and t_d is the afore-mentioned time offset between the gyroscope and camera data streams. Since most mobile devices have the gyroscope and camera rigidly mounted with axes parallel to each other, T is simply a permutation matrix. In our implementation, the transformation T is known since the Android operating system defines a coordinate system for sensor data [16].

3.2   Motion Model and Smoothing Algorithm

We parametrize the camera path with the camera's orientation and angular velocity at each frame. We represent the physical and virtual camera orientations at frame k with the quaternions $\mathbf{p}(k)$ and $\mathbf{v}(k)$. The physical and virtual angular velocities are computed as the discrete angular changes from frame k to frame $k+1$, and are represented as $\mathbf{p}_\Delta(k)$ and $\mathbf{v}_\Delta(k)$. Since the framerate is constant, time is implicit in this representation of the velocity. For each new frame k, our smoothing algorithm computes $\mathbf{v}(k)$ and $\mathbf{v}_\Delta(k)$ using the virtual parameters from the last frame, and the physical camera parameters from the last frame, the current frame, and optionally a small buffer of future frames (5 or less).

Our smoothing algorithm creates a new camera path that keeps the virtual camera static when the measured motion is small enough to suggest that the actual intention is to keep the camera static, and that otherwise follows the intention of the measured motion with smooth changes in angular velocity. As a first step, we hypothesize a new orientation for the virtual camera by setting

$$\hat{\mathbf{v}}(k) = \mathbf{v}(k-1) \cdot \mathbf{v}_\Delta(k-1), \qquad (4)$$

where $\cdot$ denotes the quaternion product. Simply, this equation is computing a new camera orientation by rotating the camera from its last known orientation while keeping its angular velocity. Given this hypothetical camera orientation $\hat{\mathbf{v}}(k)$, we use Equation 2 to compute the coordinates of the corners of the resulting crop polygon. In virtual camera space, the crop polygon is a fixed rectangle centered at the image center, but in physical camera space, it may be be skewed or warped, and moves around within the frame, as shown in Figure 1. The crop polygon is smaller than the input size, which leaves a small amount of "padding" between the polygon borders and the input frame edges, as shown in Figure 2. We divide this padding into two concentric zones, which we will refer to as the "inner region" and "outer region". When the hypothetical crop polygon lies within the inner region of the image we assert that the hypothesis $\hat{\mathbf{v}}(k)$ is good and make it the current camera orientation. In practice, we find it advantageous to let the motion decay to zero in this case, which biases the virtual camera towards remaining still when possible. Thus, if the crop polygon remains completely within the inner region, we reduce the angular change by a decay factor d and set the new virtual camera configuration to:

$$\mathbf{v}_\Delta(k) = \mathrm{slerp}(\mathbf{q}_I, \mathbf{v}_\Delta(k-1), d), \qquad (5)$$

and

$$\mathbf{v}(k) = \mathbf{v}(k-1) \cdot \mathbf{v}_\Delta(k-1). \qquad (6)$$

Here $\mathbf{q}_I$ represents the identity quaternion, and the slerp function is the spherical linear interpolation [17] between the two quaternions. In our implementation, we set the mixing weight to $d \approx 0.95$, so that the angular change is only slightly reduced each frame.

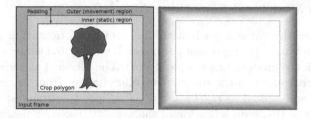

Fig. 2. Left: Crop polygon and the division of the padding space. Right: Velocity mixing weight. Dark blue represents a strong weight (taking the input velocity); white represents a small weight (keeping the current velocity).

If any part of the hypothetical crop polygon lies outside the inner region, we update the virtual camera's angular velocity to bring it closer to the physical camera's rate of change:

$$\mathbf{v}_\Delta(k) = \text{slerp}(\mathbf{p}'_\Delta(k), \mathbf{v}(k-1), \alpha). \tag{7}$$

Here $\mathbf{p}'_\Delta$ is the orientation change that preserves the relative position of the crop polygon from one frame to the next, calculated as

$$\mathbf{p}'_\Delta(k) = \mathbf{p}(k) \cdot \mathbf{p}^*(k-1) \cdot \mathbf{v}(k-1), \tag{8}$$

where $\mathbf{p}^*$ denotes the quaternion conjugate that inverts the rotation. This equation calculates the physical camera motion from the previous to the current frame in the virtual camera reference coordinate system. The term α is a mixing weight that is chosen based on how much padding remains between the crop polygon and the edge of the frame, as illustrated in the right hand side of Figure 2. Intuitively, if the crop polygon is only slightly outside the inner region, α should be close to 1, assigning a higher weight to the current velocity. Conversely, if the hypothetical crop polygon is near the edge (or even outside), α should be 0, so that the input velocity is matched, and the crop polygon remains in the same position relative to the input frame. We calculate α with

$$\alpha = 1 - w^\beta, \tag{9}$$

where $w \in (0, 1]$ is the maximum protrusion of the crop polygon beyond the inner region, and β is an exponent that determines the sharpness of the response. In the extreme case where any corner of the crop polygon would fall outside the input frame, w takes a value of 1, forcing α to 0 and causing the virtual camera to keep up with the physical camera.

This algorithm works well, but it occasionally has to make quick changes in velocity when the crop rectangle suddenly hits the edge. If frames can be buffered within the camera pipeline for a short time before being processed, then a larger time window of gyroscope data can be examined, and sharp changes can be preemptively avoided. In the remainder of this section, we extend our algorithm to use data from a look-ahead buffer to calculate a smoother path.

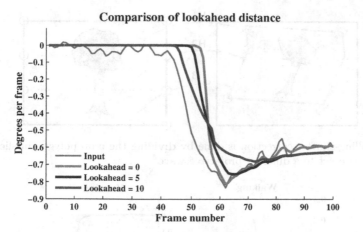

Fig. 3. Comparison of paths for varying lookahead distances. Larger lookahead values require more data to be buffered, but produce smoother output paths.

We can span a larger window of frames by projecting the virtual camera orientation forward in time and comparing it to the actual orientation at the "future" time. Let a be the number of frames to look ahead, and hypothesize

$$\mathbf{v}(k + a) - \mathbf{v}(k - 1) \cdot \mathbf{v}_\Delta(k)^{a+1}. \tag{10}$$

We can then compute $\mathbf{v}_\Delta(k+a)$ and $\mathbf{v}(k+a)$ as we described for the no-lookahead case. If the projection of the crop polygon a frames into the future is outside the inner region, we can update $\mathbf{v}_\Delta(k)$ to

$$\mathbf{v}_\Delta(k) = \mathrm{slerp}(\mathbf{v}_\Delta(k + a), \mathbf{v}_\Delta(k), \gamma), \tag{11}$$

where γ is a mixing factor that defines how much of the lookahead angular change we should mix with the current one. Using values of γ close to 1 provides a preemptive nudge in the right direction, without being a hard constraint. Note that we do not update the virtual camera position that we computed without lookahead, we only update the virtual camera velocity that we will be using for the next frame.

Figure 3 shows a comparison of paths for a range of lookahead distances (measured in frames). Larger lookahead values produce smoother paths, since they effectively "predict" large motions and gently cause the output to start moving. But it is important to note that our algorithm can work without lookahead and still produce good results.

3.3   Output Synthesis and Rolling-Shutter Correction

Once we have computed the new orientation of the virtual camera, we can synthesize the output by projectively warping the crop polygon from the video input to the virtual camera. Our crop polygon is essentially a sliced rectangle with multiple

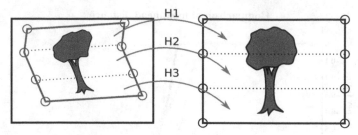

Fig. 4. Rolling-shutter correction is done by dividing the crop polygon in slices, each of which is subject to a different projective warp

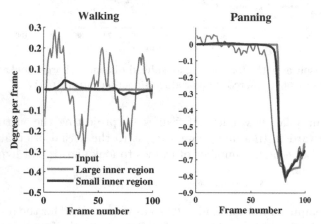

Fig. 5. Single-axis comparison of the effects of the inner region size on the smoothing result. A larger inner region can filter small motions more aggressively (left), but often produces sharper motions when the camera moves abruptly (right).

knee-points on the vertical edges, as shown in Figure 4. The knee-points allow us to use a different transform for every slice of the polygon and fix rolling-shutter distortions. For every slice we compute a homography matrix according to Equation 2. We fix the rotation matrix $R_c(t_2)$ to the orientation of the virtual output camera, and compute $R_c(t_k)$, the orientation of the input camera at each knee-point, from the gyroscope data. We set the coordinates of the crop polygon as texture coordinates of an OpenGL shader program that projectively maps the crop polygon from the input frame to the virtual camera. Note that in order to effectively correct for rolling-shutter effects, the gyroscope sampling rate should be higher than the frame read-out time. In our implementation we sample the gyroscope at 200 Hz and use a total of 10 slices, or 9 knee-points per vertical edge.

3.4   Parameter Selection

The most important parameters are the size of the output crop polygon and the amount of padding allocated to the inner and outer regions. The crop size is a trade-off between smoothing and image quality: larger crop polygons preserve more of the input image, but leave less padding for smoothing out motions. The padding allocation is a trade-off between completely removing motion and the smoothness of the remaining motion. As illustrated in Figure 5, a large inner region (green) is able to flatten out larger motions such as walking, but must move more abruptly when the crop window approaches the edge of the frame.

3.5   Gyroscope and Camera Calibration

We solve for the time offset t_d using a calibration procedure that we developed for this purpose. We place a calibration pattern, which consists of an asymmetric grid of circles, in front of the camera. Then we record a video and the gyroscope readings while rotating the camera vigorously. The circles are easily tracked across frames, even in the presence of motion blur and rolling shutter effects. We use the centroid of each circle as a feature point, and solve for t_d iteratively by minimizing the sum of re-projection errors according to Equation 3. By repeating the calibration on multiple data sets we determined that the offset t_d is nearly constant. We also considered the possibility of doing an on-line calibration, by tracking key-points as each frame is captured [18], but the off-line method proved sufficient for our purposes.

The integration of any static offset in the gyroscope measurements will result in an estimated orientation that slowly drifts away from the ground truth. However, our stabilization algorithm is not affected by such drift because it smooths the relative change of orientation. We measure orientation changes in a window of one to five frames, and in such a short time span, the integration drift is negligible.

4   Results

We experimented with a prototype Android tablet, in which we installed a modified version of the Android OS that reads and saves the gyroscope measurements while recording video. Using this tablet we recorded a series of videos representing typical use cases of casual video captured by a cell phone. For comparison here, we discuss three scenes: a video recorded while walking, a video focusing on a fountain, and panning video tracking a walking person. For the stabilization algorithm, we set the width and height of the crop rectangle to be 80% of the original video size, allocate the remaining 20% in width and height equally to the inner and outer regions, and set the lookahead to 5 frames. The results show that our method eliminates the high-frequency jitter while keeping the camera as still as possible. To compare against previous work we also implemented video stabilization using a Gaussian low-pass filter of the derived gyroscope orientations as done by Karpenko et al. [1], using a local window of eleven frames, giving a forward lookahead of 5 frames as in our method and the same 80% crop ratio. All original videos and results are included in the supplementary material that accompanies this paper.

Figure 6 shows a quantitative comparison of the camera's angular velocity rate of change for the original video, a stabilized video produced with the Gaussian

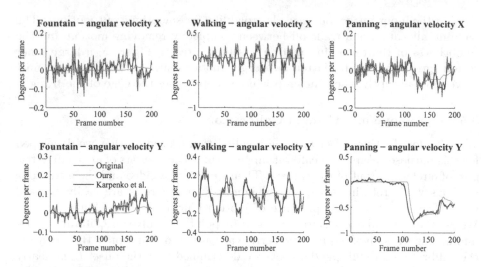

Fig. 6. Angular velocities of the camera in the X and Y axis. We show three different scenes: a handheld camera pointed at a fountain as steadily as possible (left), a camera held by a person walking (middle) and a camera panning while tracking a moving object (right). Our method (green) can eliminate most of the small camera motions. On the other hand, the Gaussian filter with a small window of support proposed in [1] can remove high-frequency motions, but fails to completely remove camera shake.

filtering of [1], and a stabilized video produced with our method. Our method dramatically reduces the jitter in angular velocity, and even removes it when possible, thus producing smoother results. The fountain video shows that we can effectively simulate a static camera. Our method keeps the virtual camera fixed for the first hundred and fifty frames and, when moving, follows the actual camera smoothly. In the walking video, our method removes most of the angular acceleration, producing an output video which is pleasing to view. The smoothed camera path is nearly free of rotational motions, but still contains small vertical periodic motions due to translations of the camera while walking. This is a limitation of our method, which cannot track translational camera motion; we discuss how to address this in the future work section. Finally, the panning video highlights that our method can produce a smooth virtual panning camera; the graph of angular velocity in the Y axis shows that our result follows the velocity of the original camera. The green line follows the original velocity (red line) during frames in the range [100, 150] at the same rate, though slightly shifted in time. This is by design, since our method tries to keep the static camera for as long as possible and then follows the original camera velocity. "Catching up" with the motion to center the crop window would require introducing additional accelerations.

To further benchmark our method against the state-of-the-art in video stabilization, we uploaded the videos to YouTube and ran the stabilization tool, which is based on the work of Grundmann *et al.* [3]. Qualitatively, our method

Fig. 7. Four different frames of the Fountain video blended together. The frames were sampled at a 10 frame interval from: (a) the original video, (b) the video stabilized using a truncated Gaussian filtering, (c) the video stabilized by YouTube, (d) the video stabilized using our method. The blended results on (a) and (b) look blurry, due to the motion of the camera. In contrast, the results from (c) and (d) look sharp, since both methods were able to eliminate the camera motion.

stabilization results are similar to those produced by the YouTube stabilization. In Figure 7 we show the results of blending together four frames taken at 10-frame intervals. The blended image from the original video is blurry, due to the motion of the camera. On the other hand, the blended images generated by sampling the stabilized videos produced from our and Grundmann's method show sharp results, showing both methods were able to remove the camera motion. Grundmann's method can dynamically adjust the size of the crop window, which we can observe is larger than ours in some cases, therefore retaining a larger area of the frame and reducing the zoom effect in the stabilized video. Our method keeps the size of the crop polygon fixed, but there is no impediment to making it a dynamic part of the virtual camera configuration, as we discuss in the next section. Additional comparisons are included with the supplementary material video.

To fix rolling-shutter effects we determined from the sensor driver that the effective frame length of our 1080p video recordings was 2214 lines. This corresponds to a read-out period of 16 ms and a blanking period of 17 ms. This is fast enough that it is difficult to perceive rolling-shutter wobble effects within a single frame. However, the effects quickly become visible in a video, even with moderate shake. Figure 8 visually shows the effect of rolling shutter correction

Fig. 8. Static visualization of rolling-shutter correction. The left image shows the average of four frames sampled at 10-frame intervals, without rolling shutter correction. Stabilization is applied using the top of the frame as a reference, but rolling shutter wobble causes the bottoms of the frames to be badly aligned. The right image shows the same four frames with rolling shutter correction applied. The wobble is greatly reduced, and the entire frame is much sharper.

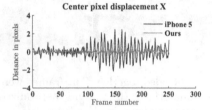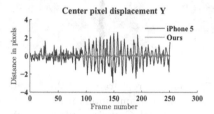

Fig. 9. Frame-to-frame displacement of the image center for a video sequence captured with our real-time implementation and an iPhone 5. Our algorithm is able to reduce motion for low-amplitude high-frequency shakes, as shown in the plot above.

by comparing a series of frames in a video with rolling shutter wobble. The supplementary video contains additional video which demonstrates the efficacy of our method.

While the comparisons above were done offline in order to run the same video through multiple filters, we have also implemented our algorithm within the Android video capture stack, where it runs in real time. The filter itself, running as a single thread on the CPU, operates in 160 microseconds. The image warp, implemented as an OpenGL shader on the tablet's GPU, runs in 15 ms.

Using this real-time implementation and fixing the crop ratio to 90% of the original frame size, we ran our prototype tablet side-by-side with an iPhone 5, both fixed rigidly to a supporting frame. A qualitative comparison of the video sequence shows both look similar, with some instances in which our algorithm produces better results, such as regions of high-frequency low-amplitude shakes, as shown in Figure 9.

Our source videos, results and supplementary material video are available at https://research.nvidia.com/publication/non-linear-filter-gyroscope-based-video-stabilization.

5   Conclusions and Future Work

We have presented a novel solution for video stabilization with rolling-shutter correction using the gyroscope in a mobile device. Our method is fast and can run in real-time within the camera processing pipeline. The stabilization can work on each incoming frame as it is received, but can also benefit from an optional buffer window that holds up to five frames. By using the gyroscope to track the camera motion we are able to do better in some scenes than most feature-based methods, which fail when there is lack of texture, excessive blur, or large foreground moving objects. We also improve on previous techniques that use the gyroscope for camera motion by using a novel filtering approach that results in smoother motions. To achieve this we assume the intention of the person recording the video is to keep the camera as static as possible or make a smooth linear motion. These assumptions hold for a wide range of videos.

Our method may under-perform the state-of-the-art in feature tracking methods on videos where the camera is subject to large translations. Translational motion cannot be tracked by the gyroscope. While it might be possible to use the accelerometer that accompanies the gyroscope in most mobile devices, estimation of translation from the accelerometer readings is less robust due to the double integration of the accelerometer data. In addition, large translations will cause occlusions and dis-occlusions in the image due to the parallax. In this case, projectively warping the crop polygon can cause distortions near the occlusion boundaries. Unfortunately, more sophisticated methods that can handle parallax [6] cannot run in real-time.

Our method can run on scenes with no trackable features or large motion of foreground objects, which feature-based might struggle with. In addition, our method works at a fraction of the computational time and cost because we don't need to compute features at all.

We intend to improve the system in the future in several ways. Firstly, our current algorithm keeps a fixed-size crop window; better stabilization might be achieved if we can vary the crop size smoothly across frames. In addition, we would like to explore the possibility of adding the ability to handle small translations by visual tracking of a sparse set of features. This tracking will be simplified by that fact that the camera rotation is already accounted for from the gyroscope data, and could be further conditioned to be done only when a significant change in acceleration is detected by the accelerometer. Finally, we would like to explore the possibility of storing the gyroscope readings as a separate track of the output video file, to enable further off-line stabilization using the gyroscope data if desired.

Acknowledgments. We thank Orazio Gallo for his helpful suggestions and feedback on earlier revisions of this paper.

References

1. Karpenko, A., Jacobs, D., Baek, J., Levoy, M.: Digital video stabilization and rolling shutter correction using gyroscopes. Technical Report CTSR 2011-03, Department of Computer Science, Stanford University (2011)
2. Invensense Corporation: MPU-6050 Product Specification, http://invensense.com/mems/gyro/documents/PS-MPU-9250A-01.pdf
3. Grundmann, M., Kwatra, V., Castro, D., Essa, I.: Calibration-free rolling shutter removal. In: IEEE ICCP (2012)
4. Gleicher, M.L., Liu, F.: Re-cinematography: improving the camera dynamics of casual video. ACM Multimedia (2007)
5. Grundmann, M., Kwatra, V., Essa, I.: Auto-directed video stabilization with robust l1 optimal camera paths. In: IEEE CVPR (2011)
6. Liu, S., Yuan, L., Tan, P., Sun, J.: Bundled camera paths for video stabilization. ACM TOG 32(4) (2013)
7. Matsushita, Y., Ofek, E., Ge, W., Tang, X., Shum, H.Y.: Full-frame video stabilization with motion inpainting. IEEE PAMI 28(7) (2006)
8. Baker, S., Bennett, E., Kang, S.B., Szeliski, R.: Removing rolling shutter wobble. In: IEEE CVPR (2010)
9. Liu, F., Gleicher, M., Jin, H., Agarwala, A.: Content-preserving warps for 3D video stabilization. ACM TOG 28(3) (2009)
10. Liu, F., Gleicher, M., Wang, J., Jin, H., Agarwala, A.: Subspace video stabilization. ACM TOG 30(1) (2011)
11. Hanning, G., Forslow, N., Forssén, P., Ringaby, E., Tornqvist, D., Callmer, J.: Stabilizing cell phone video using inertial measurement sensors. In: IEEE ICCV Workshops (2011)
12. Joshi, N., Kang, S.B., Zitnick, C.L., Szeliski, R.: Image deblurring using inertial measurement sensors. ACM TOG 29(4) (2010)
13. Forssen, P., Ringaby, E.: Rectifying rolling shutter video from hand-held devices. In: IEEE CVPR (2010)
14. Oth, L., Furgale, P., Kneip, L., Siegwart, R.: Rolling shutter camera calibration. In: IEEE CVPR (2013)
15. Various: OpenCV library, http://code.opencv.org
16. Google: Android operating system developers' API guide, http://developer.android.com/guide/topics/sensors/sensors_overview.html
17. Shoemake, K.: Animating rotation with quaternion curves. ACM TOG 19(3) (1985)
18. Li, M., Mourikis, A.: 3-D motion estimation and online temporal calibration for camera-IMU systems. In: IEEE ICRA (2013)

Multi-modal and Multi-spectral Registration for Natural Images

Xiaoyong Shen[1], Li Xu[2], Qi Zhang[1], and Jiaya Jia[1]

[1] The Chinese University of Hong Kong, China
[2] Image & Visual Computing Lab, Lenovo R&T,
Project Website, Hong Kong, China
http://www.cse.cuhk.edu.hk/leojia/projects/multimodal

Abstract. Images now come in different forms – color, near-infrared, depth, etc. – due to the development of special and powerful cameras in computer vision and computational photography. Their cross-modal correspondence establishment is however left behind. We address this challenging dense matching problem considering structure variation possibly existing in these image sets and introduce new model and solution. Our main contribution includes designing the descriptor named robust selective normalized cross correlation (RSNCC) to establish dense pixel correspondence in input images and proposing its mathematical parameterization to make optimization tractable. A computationally robust framework including global and local matching phases is also established. We build a multi-modal dataset including natural images with labeled sparse correspondence. Our method will benefit image and vision applications that require accurate image alignment.

Keywords: multi-modal, multi-spectral, dense matching, variational model.

1 Introduction

Data captured in various domains, such as RGB and near-infrared (NIR) image pairs [35], flash and no-flash images [22,1], color and dark flash images [18], depth and color images, noisy and blurred images [38], and images captured under changing light [24], are used commonly now in computer vision and computational photography research. They are multi-modal or multi-spectral data generally involving natural images. Although there are rigid and nonrigid methods developed for multi-modal medical image registration [23,21,17,2]. In computer vision, quite a few prior methods still assume already aligned input images, making them readily usable in applications to generate new effects.

For example, the inputs in [18,22,1,38,26,8] are produced from the same or calibrated cameras. The dynamic scene images used in [24] are aligned before HDR construction. In [35], a multi-spectral image restoration method was developed based on correctly relating pixels. It is clear when alignment is not a satisfied condition in prior, registering input images considering camera motion,

D. Fleet et al. (Eds.): ECCV 2014, Part IV, LNCS 8692, pp. 309–324, 2014.

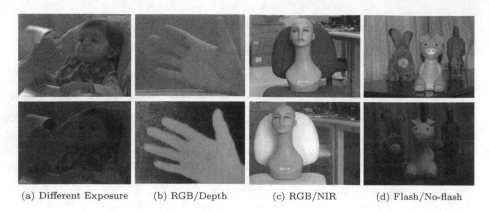

(a) Different Exposure   (b) RGB/Depth   (c) RGB/NIR   (d) Flash/No-flash

Fig. 1. Multi-modal images that need alignment. (a) Images from [24] captured under different exposure settings in dynamic scene. (b) RGB and depth image pair. (c) RGB and NIR images. (d) Flash and no-flash images captured at different time.

object deformation, and depth variation will be inevitable. It is challenging when large intensity, color, and gradient variation presents.

For images taken continuously from nearby cameras, or containing similar structure, state-of-the-art matching methods such as nonrigid image registration [7,36,16,29], optical flow estimation [13,5,6,41,5,3], and stereo matching [11,27] can help align them. But multi-modal images, like those in Fig. 1, cannot be easily dealt with. Color, gradient, and even structure similarity, which are commonly considered to establish constraints, are not applicable anymore, as detailed later in this paper. Moreover, the image pairs shown in Fig. 1 are with nonrigid displacement due to depth variation and dynamic moving objects, which makes matching very difficult.

In medical imaging, multi-modal registration methods are based on global or local statistic information like mutual information to search for region correspondence. They are mostly limited to gray level medical images and do not suit rich-detail natural image matching. For general multi-spectral image matching, Irani et al. [15] proposed a framework for multi-sensor image global alignment. Cross correlation on the directional Laplacian energy map was used to measure patch similarity. Variational frameworks ([12] and [37]) can estimate small displacements in multi-modal images. These methods do not work similarly well on heavy outlier images or those with large nonrigid displacement. General matching tools, such as SIFT flow [19], also do not handle multi-spectral images and lack sub-pixel accuracy in computation.

We aim to match general multi-modal and multi-spectral images with significant displacement and obvious structure inconsistency. We analyze and compare possible measures, and propose a new matching cost, named robust selective normalized cross correlation (RSNCC), to handle gradient and color variation, and possible structure divergence caused by noise, inconsistent shadow and reflection from object surface. In solution establishment, we provide new parameterization to separate the original descriptor into a few mathematically meaningful terms that explain optimality. Our method contains global and local phases to remove large displacements and estimates residual pixel-wise correspondence respectively. To verify our system, we build a dataset containing different kinds of image pairs with labeled point correspondence.

2 Related Work

Surveys of image matching were provided in [42,28,33]. We review in this paper related image registration methods and variational optical flow estimation.

The correspondence of images captured by different modalities is complex. The difference between multi-spectral images was analyzed in [15,35]. We coarsely categorize previous work into feature-based and patch-based methods. The feature-based methods extract multi-spectral invariant sparse feature points and then establish their correspondence for optimal transform. Hrkac et al. [14] aligned visible and infrared images by extracting corner points and getting the global correspondence via minimizing Hausdorff distance. Firmenichy et al. [9] proposed a multi-spectral interest points detection algorithm for global registration. Han et al. [10] used hybrid visual features like lines and corners to align visible and infrared images captured in controlled environment. These methods do not aim at very accurate dense matching due to feature sparseness.

Several methods employed local patch similarity to find correspondence. The effective measures include mutual information and cross correlation. Mutual information is robust for multi-modal medical image alignment, as surveyed in [23]. Hermosillo et al. [12] proposed a variational framework to match multi-modal images based on this measure. Zhang et al. [40] and Palos et al. [21] further enhanced the variational framework to solve the multi-modal registration problem. Yi et al. [37] adaptively considered global and local mutual information. As for cross correlation methods, Irani et al. [15] proposed the Laplacian energy map and computed cross correlation on it to measure multi-sensor image similarity. Cross correlation of gradient magnitude was used by Kolar et al. [17] to register autofluorescent and infrared retinal images. Recently, Andronache et al. [2] combined mutual information and cross correlation to match the multi-modal images. These measures are effective, but sometimes still suffer from outlier and large displacement influence during dense matching.

Our framework is related to modern optical flow estimation [13]. In modern methods, the data term usually enforces brightness or gradient constancy [5,6,41]. Robust functions, such as L_1 norm and Charbonnier function, were used by [5,3,31,39] in regularization. For large displacement handling, Xu et al. [34] improved the coarse-to-fine strategy by supplementing feature- and patch-based matching. We note optical flow methods cannot solve our problem since it relies on the brightness and gradient constancy constraints, which no longer hold for multi-spectral image matching. Based on the variational framework, Liu et al. [19] achieved general scene image matching using SIFT features.

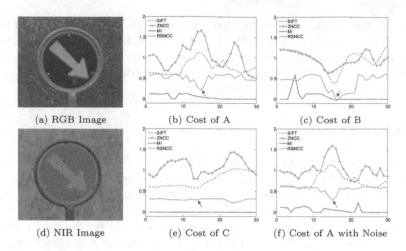

Fig. 2. Matching cost comparison. (a) and (d) are the RGB and NIR images presented in [4]. Points A, B and C are inconsistent on structure/gradient. A is with gradient reverse; B has gradient magnitude variation; and C is with gradient loss. (b), (c) and (e) are the matching costs under different descriptors along A, B and C's scanlines. (f) is the matching cost of A with added noise on (a) and (d). The arrows point to the ground-truth matching points.

3   Problem Understanding

Images from different sensors are ubiquitous, as shown in Fig. 1. Their matching is thus a fundamental problem. We in what follows take the RGB and NIR image pairs as examples as they contain many different structures and intensity levels. We analyze the difficulties in dense image matching.

Let I_1 and I_2 be the two multi-spectral or multi-modal images, $p = (x, y)^T$ be pixel coordinates of the two images, and $w_p = (u_p, v_p)^T$ be the displacement of pixel p, which indicates p in I_1 mapping to $p + w_p$ in I_2. $I_{1,p}$ and $I_{2,p}$ are the intensities (or color vectors) of I_1 and I_2 for pixel p respectively.

For dense image matching, the cost for pixel p between two input images can be generally expressed as

$$E^{\mathcal{D}}(p, w_p) = \text{dist}\big(\mathcal{D}_1(p), \mathcal{D}_2(p + w_p)\big), \tag{1}$$

where $\mathcal{D}_1(p)$ and $\mathcal{D}_2(p + w_p)$ are matching descriptors for pixels p and $p + w_p$ in I_1 and I_2 respectively. $\text{dist}(\cdot)$ is a function to measure the descriptor distance.

Color and Gradient. As shown in Fig. 2(a) and (d), an RGB/NIR image pair captured by visual and NIR cameras contains structure inconsistency. Obviously, general color and gradient constancy between corresponding pixels that was used in many alignment methods under the Euler or robust Euler distance cannot be employed. Irani et al. [15] and Kolar et al. [17] computed similarity on gradient magnitude. Although it relaxes the color constancy condition, it is still not enough in many cases. Matching accuracy could reduce when only using the gradient correspondence.

SIFT Features. Another common type of matching costs are based on SIFT descriptors [20] that work well for images captured under similar exposures. We note SIFT may not be appropriate for multi-spectral matching with the following two reasons. First, SIFT is not invariant to gradient reversal existing in input images, as shown at point A in Fig. 2(a) and (d). Although Firmenichy et al. [9] proposed gradient direction invariant SIFT, the performance is reduced compared with traditional SIFT. In (c), the minimum of SIFT descriptor difference does not correspond to the ground truth matching point. Second, SIFT descriptor is not that powerful to differentiate between true and false correspondences especially in featureless regions given its output scores.

Mutual Information. Mutual information (MI) is used popularly in medical image registration. However, for natural image with rich details, MI has its limitation. As shown in Fig. 2, the cost of MI in the 15×15 patch fails to find the correct correspondence. MI may also be sensitive to noise as shown in Fig. 2(f). The drawback of MI to measure small local patch similarity was explained by Andronache et al. [2]. For the variational frameworks [12,37] using local patch mutual information, only small displacements are computed.

4   Our Matching Cost

In order to handle structure inconsistency and notable gradient variation in multi-spectral and multi-modal images, we propose a matching cost given by

$$E^{\mathrm{RSNCC}}(p, w_p) = \rho\big(1 - |\Phi_I(p, w_p)|\big) + \tau\rho\big(1 - |\Phi_{\nabla I}(p, w_p)|\big). \qquad (2)$$

This function is a robust selective normalized cross correlation (RSNCC) addressing a few of the concerns presented above. $\rho(x)$ is a robust function and weight τ is used to combine two terms defined respectively on color and gradient domains. We present details as follows.

4.1 Φ Definition

$\Phi_I(p, w_p)$ is the normalized cross correlation between the patch centered at p in I_1 and patch $p + w_p$ in I_2 in the intensity or color space. $\Phi_{\nabla I}(p, w_p)$ is the one defined similarly in the gradient space. This definition is also extendible to other definitions. By generalizing I and ∇I as feature $F \in \{I, \nabla I\}$, $\Phi_F(p, w_p)$ in feature space F is given by

$$\Phi_F(p, w_p) = \frac{(F_{1,p} - \overline{F}_{1,p}) \cdot (F_{2,p+w_p} - \overline{F}_{2,p+w_p})}{\|F_{1,p} - \overline{F}_{1,p}\| \|F_{2,p+w_p} - \overline{F}_{2,p+w_p}\|}, \qquad (3)$$

where $F_{1,p}$ and $F_{2,p}$ are pixels' feature vectors in patch p in I_1 and patch $p+w_p$ in I_2 respectively. $\overline{F}_{1,p}$ and $\overline{F}_{2,p+w_p}$ are the means of $F_{1,p}$ and $F_{2,p+w_p}$ respectively.

The normalized cross correlation defined in Eq. (3) can represent structure similarity of the two patches under feature F even if the two patches are transformed in color and geometry locally.

Difference from Other Definitions. Our cost definition in Eq. (2) has a robust function $\rho(x)$. It handles transform more complex than a linear one defined only using Pearson's distance $1 - \Phi_I(p, w_p)$.

In addition, our data cost models the absolute value of $\Phi_F(p, w_p)$ that minimizes the matching cost on either positive or negative correlation in Eq. (2), which is the major difference compared to other matching methods only working on similar-appearance natural images. This definition is effective to handle gradient reversal ubiquitous for NIR-RGB and positive-negative images, which produce negative correlation. This is why we call it a selective model.

An example is shown in Fig. 2(b) where point A is with different gradient directions in the input images. Even in this challenging local correspondence problem that was seldom studied in previous work in natural image matching, optimizing our function can lead to reasonable results.

Color and Gradient. The combination of $\Phi_I(p, w_p)$ and $\Phi_{\nabla I}(p, w_p)$ is helpful to improve the stability in matching especially when intensity or color of the two patches differs a lot. For instance, point B in Fig. 2(a) and (d) is with different edge magnitudes in the corresponding patches. Our method can find the correspondence while zero-mean normalized cross-correlation (ZNCC), SIFT and MI fail, as shown in (c). In addition, the combination makes matching more robust to noise, which is shown in Fig. 2(f) with more explanations in our experiment section.

However, the matching cost we defined is complex with respect to w_p. We linearize it by a two-order approximation. To achieve this, a robust function is carefully chosen and per-pixel Taylor expansion is employed.

4.2 Robust Function

$\rho(x)$ in Eq. (2) is a robust function to help reject outliers. The outliers include structure divergence caused by shadow, highlight, dynamic objects, to name a few. We show one example in Fig. 3.

$\rho(x)$ should also be robust to errors generated in $1 - |\Phi_F(p, w_p)|$, which is not continuous. This makes general robust functions, such as Charbonnier, not differentiable. To address this issue, we propose $\rho(x)$ as

$$\rho(x) = -\frac{1}{\beta} \log(e^{-\beta|x|} + e^{-\beta(2-|x|)}), \tag{4}$$

where β is a parameter. To understand this function, we plot $\rho(x)$ and $\rho'(x)$ by varying β in Fig. 4. A large x does not cause an excessive penalty in $\rho(x)$. Note when $\beta \to \infty$, $\rho(x)$ becomes a nice approximation of the robust L_1 norm. Besides, it makes RSNCC continuous and solvable by continuous optimization.

This robust function is effective in image matching. For the inconsistent shadow structure in Fig. 3, our model handles it better than direct matching.

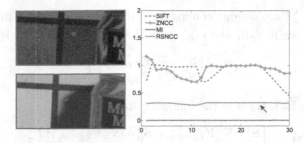

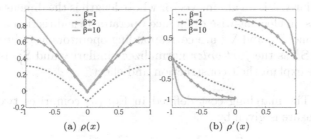

Fig. 3. Outlier example. The left two patches contain shadow only in one input. It should be regarded as an outlier in matching. The plots of matching costs in a scanline show that our method can safely ignore this outlier.

Fig. 4. Robust function with different β.

4.3   Matching Cost and Derivation

After setting $\rho(x)$ as Eq. (4), the matching cost (2) is written as

$$E^{\text{RSNCC}}(p, w_p) = -\frac{1}{\beta} \log \left(e^{-\beta(1-\Phi_I(p,w_p))} + e^{-\beta(1+\Phi_I(p,w_p))} \right)$$
$$- \frac{\tau}{\beta} \log \left(e^{-\beta(1-\Phi_{\nabla I}(p,w_p))} + e^{-\beta(1+\Phi_{\nabla I}(p,w_p))} \right). \qquad (5)$$

In addition, the term $\Phi_F(p, w_p)$, which is the patch normalized cross correlation between I_1 and I_2 according to the feature space $F \in \{I, \nabla I\}$, is highly nonconvex. We decompose it by linearization in Taylor expansion, which yields

$$\Phi_F(p, w_p + \delta w_p) \approx \Phi_F(p, w_p) + (\mathbf{A}_p^F)^T \delta \mathbf{w}_p + \frac{1}{2} \delta \mathbf{w}_p^T \mathbf{B}_p^F \delta \mathbf{w}_p, \qquad (6)$$

where $\delta \mathbf{w}_p$ is the vector form of all δw_p of patch p. $\mathbf{A}_p^F$ is the first-order approximation coefficient matrix and $\mathbf{B}_p^F$ is the second-order matrix that only includes diagonal elements. In this expansion and Eq. (5), local displacement field updated in iterations for patch p is expressed as

$$\min \left((\omega_p^I \mathbf{A}_p^I + \omega_p^{\nabla I} \mathbf{A}_p^{\nabla I})^T \delta \mathbf{w}_p + \frac{1}{2} \delta \mathbf{w}_p^T (\omega_p^I \mathbf{B}_p^I + \omega_p^{\nabla I} \mathbf{B}_p^{\nabla I}) \delta \mathbf{w}_p \right), \qquad (7)$$

where ω_p^I and $\omega_p^{\nabla I}$ are weights coming from the derivative robust function. That is, $\omega_p^I = \rho'(1 - |\Phi_I(p, w_p)|)$ and $\omega_p^{\nabla I} = \tau\rho'(1 - |\Phi_{\nabla I}(p, w_p)|)$. $\mathbf{A}_p^F$ is given by

$$\mathbf{A}_p^F = \begin{bmatrix} \mathbf{S}_p^1 \circ \nabla_x \mathbf{F}_{2,p+w_p} \\ \mathbf{S}_p^1 \circ \nabla_y \mathbf{F}_{2,p+w_p} \end{bmatrix} \mathbf{1}, \tag{8}$$

and $\mathbf{B}_p^F = \mathrm{diag}(\widehat{\mathbf{B}}_p)$. $\widehat{\mathbf{B}}_p$ is in the following form:

$$\widehat{\mathbf{B}}_p = \begin{bmatrix} \mathbf{S}_p^1 \circ \nabla_x^2 \mathbf{F}_{2,p+w_p} + \mathbf{S}_p^2 \circ (\nabla_x \mathbf{F}_{2,p+w_p})^2 \\ \mathbf{S}_p^1 \circ \nabla_y^2 \mathbf{F}_{2,p+w_p} + \mathbf{S}_p^2 \circ (\nabla_y \mathbf{F}_{2,p+w_p})^2 \end{bmatrix} \mathbf{1}, \tag{9}$$

where $\circ$ represents element-wise multiplication, $\mathbf{F}_{1,p}$ is the updated $F_{1,p}$ denoted in Eq. (3), with each row being a feature vector for the pixel in patch p. $\mathbf{F}_{2,p+w_p}$ is defined similarly. $\mathbf{1}$ is an all-one vector whose length is the dimension of feature space F. ∇_x is an element-wise difference operator in x-direction and ∇_x^2 is the second order one. ∇_y and ∇_y^2 are corresponding operators in y-direction.

We denote $\mathbf{S}_p^1$ as the *first-order* normalized similarity and $\mathbf{S}_p^2$ as the *second-order* one. We explain their construction and effect.

$\mathbf{S}_p^1$ **and** $\mathbf{S}_p^2$. The matching cost defined in Eq. (3) comprises two parts. The *similarity* measure is given by

$$\mathcal{S}_p = (F_{1,p} - \overline{F}_{1,p}) \cdot (F_{2,p+w_p} - \overline{F}_{2,p+w_p}), \tag{10}$$

and the *confidence* term contains

$$\mathcal{C}_{1,p} = \|F_{1,p} - \overline{F}_{1,p}\|, \quad \mathcal{C}_{2,p} = \|F_{2,p+w_p} - \overline{F}_{2,p+w_p}\|. \tag{11}$$

Now coming to the definition of normalized similarity in two orders, $\mathbf{S}_p^1$ describes the confidence of matching for each pixel under the normalized cross correlation descriptor. It is normalized by the *similarity* and *confidence* as

$$\mathbf{S}_p^1 = \frac{1}{\mathcal{C}_{1,p}\mathcal{C}_{2,p}}\left(\mathbf{F}_{1,p} - \overline{F}_{1,p} - \frac{\mathcal{S}_p}{\mathcal{C}_{2,p}^2}(\mathbf{F}_{2,p+w_p} - \overline{F}_{2,p+w_p})\right). \tag{12}$$

To get $\mathbf{S}_p^2$, we first denote *normalized cross similarity* as

$$\mathbf{C}_p = \frac{1}{\mathcal{C}_{1,p}\mathcal{C}_{2,p}}\frac{(\mathbf{F}_{1,p} - \overline{F}_{1,p}) \circ (\mathbf{F}_{2,p+w_p} - \overline{F}_{2,p+w_p})}{\mathcal{C}_{2,p}^2}, \tag{13}$$

which describes correlation of the two patches. Given the two-order normalized descriptor of $\mathbf{F}_{2,p+w_p}$ as

$$\mathbf{D}_{p,2} = \frac{1}{\mathcal{C}_{1,p}\mathcal{C}_{2,p}}\frac{\mathcal{S}_p(\mathbf{F}_{2,p+w_p} - \overline{F}_{2,p+w_p})^2}{\mathcal{C}_{2,p}^4}, \tag{14}$$

$\mathbf{S}_p^2$ becomes the linear combination of $\mathbf{C}_p$ and $\mathbf{D}_{p,2}$ as

$$\mathbf{S}_p^2 = 3\mathbf{D}_{p,2} - 2\mathbf{C}_p - \frac{1}{\mathcal{C}_{1,p}\mathcal{C}_{2,p}}\frac{\mathcal{S}_p(\overline{N} - 1)^2}{\mathcal{C}_{2,p}^2 \overline{N}^2}, \tag{15}$$

where $\overline{N}$ is the number of pixels in the patch. The last (third) term is a bias imposed by the different similarity of the two patches.

Note that our two-order approximation is different from the form in [32], where the latter handles similar-exposure natural images for motion estimation and assumes that the displacement field is constant locally. Our approximation is pixel-wise with new expressions, thus modeling complex correspondence in multi-spectral and multi-modal images.

5   Matching Framework

To produce matching on challenging images, our solver contains phases for global transform and local dense matching respectively. Global matching estimates large position transform caused by camera position variation or scene motion. Then the local phase estimates residual errors and compensates them considering pixel-wise correspondence.

5.1   Global Matching

The global phase estimates a homography matrix H for image-wise translation, rotation and scaling. The corresponding function is written as

$$E(H) = \sum_p E^{\mathrm{RSNCC}}(p, w_p), \tag{16}$$

where $w_p = (u_p, v_p)$ is under the homography constraint for every pixel. It is further expressed as

$$[u_p, v_p, 1]^T = [x_p, y_p, 1]^T (H - I)^T, \tag{17}$$

where I is the identity matrix. We apply gradient decent to get optimal H. The first and second order derivatives of $E(H)$ are obtained following the chain rule. For quick and robust computation, we employ the coarse-to-fine scheme and estimate H increment in each layer.

The RSNCC matching cost used here can robustly find similar structures and reject outliers. As shown in Fig. 5, our method estimates background transform despite large structure inconsistency in shadow and noise. Due to depth variation, a few pixels in Fig. 5(d) still contain errors. They are further refined in what follows.

5.2   Local Dense Matching

After global transform, we perform pixel-wise residual displacement estimation incorporating regularization terms. The function is written as

$$E(\mathbf{w}) = \sum_p E^{\mathrm{RSNCC}}(p, w_p) + \lambda_1 \sum_p \psi(\|\nabla w_p\|^2) + \lambda_2 \sum_{q \in N(p)} \|w_p - w_q\|, \tag{18}$$

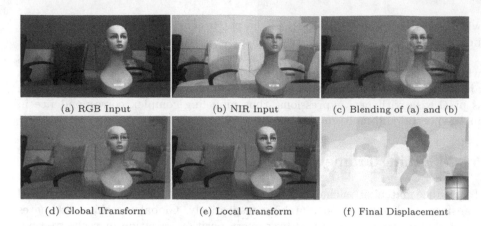

(a) RGB Input   (b) NIR Input   (c) Blending of (a) and (b)

(d) Global Transform   (e) Local Transform   (f) Final Displacement

Fig. 5. Two-phase matching. (a) and (b) RGB/NIR pair. (c) Blending result. (d) Blending result of (a) and the globally transformed (b). (e) Blending result of (a) and locally transformed (b). (f) Final displacement estimate from (b) to (a) coded in color. Structures are aligned.

where $\mathbf{w} = (\mathbf{u}^T, \mathbf{v}^T)^T$ is the vector form of w_p. $\mathbf{u}$ and $\mathbf{v}$ are vectors of u_p and v_p respectively. For simplicity's sake, we denote the three terms as $E_D(\mathbf{w})$, $E_S(\mathbf{w})$, and $E_{NL}(\mathbf{w})$. λ_1 and λ_2 are two parameters.

The robust regularization term $E_S(\mathbf{w})$ is common for enforcing spatial smoothing. $\psi(x)$ is the robust penalty function in the Charbonnier form $\psi(x^2) = \sqrt{x^2 + \epsilon^2}$ with ϵ setting to $1E - 4$ in all our experiments. This function is a differentiable variant of L_1 norm, availing optimization. $E_{NL}(\mathbf{w})$ is a nonlocal median filter. It can efficiently remove noise, as described in [25].

Optimization. Local dense matching is performed in a coarse-to-fine manner for high accuracy to optimize $E(\mathbf{w})$. In each level, $E(\mathbf{w})$ is updated and propagated to the next level for variable initialization. To handle the non-convex $E(\mathbf{w})$ in each level, we decompose it into two sub-functions both finding optimal solutions by the scheme of variable-splitting [30]. The two functions are

$$E(\mathbf{w}, \widehat{\mathbf{w}}) = E_D(\mathbf{w}) + \lambda_1 E_S(\mathbf{w}) + \frac{1}{\theta}\|\mathbf{w} - \widehat{\mathbf{w}}\|^2, \tag{19}$$

$$E(\widehat{\mathbf{w}}, \mathbf{w}) = \frac{1}{\theta}\|\widehat{\mathbf{w}} - \mathbf{w}\|^2 + \lambda_2 E_{NL}(\widehat{\mathbf{w}}), \tag{20}$$

where $\widehat{\mathbf{w}}$ is an auxiliary variable. When $\theta \to 0$, the decomposition approaches the original $E(\mathbf{w})$.

Our method minimizes Eqs. (19) and (20) respectively. The minimum of Eq. (20) can be obtained by the method of [25]. We solve Eq. (19) based on the variational configuration using iterative reweighted least squares. In each step, we update the result by a small $\delta\mathbf{w}$ after optimizing $E(\mathbf{w} + \delta\mathbf{w}, \widehat{\mathbf{w}})$. It is done by setting $\frac{\partial E(\mathbf{w}+\delta\mathbf{w}, \widehat{\mathbf{w}})}{\partial \delta\mathbf{w}} = 0$. Details are provided in the our project website (link in the title page). Our local matching improves pixel-wise alignment, as illustrated in Fig. 5(e) and (f).

6 Experiments and Evaluation

We implement our algorithm in MATLAB. The processing time of a 1200×800 image is less than three minutes on a 3.2GHz Core i7 PC. In our experiments, we set $\beta = 1.0$ in the robust function and patch size 9×9 to compute RSNCC. The weight τ is set to 1.0 in all our experiments. In local dense matching, λ_1 ranges from 0.1 to 0.5 and λ_2 is set to 0.01. In both the global and local matching phases, we employ five scales with down-sampling rate 0.8 during the coarse-to-fine optimization. More details are provided in our project website.

6.1 Evaluation

We build a dataset including four typical kinds of image pairs – RGB/NIR, RGB/Depth, different exposure, and flash/no-flash. The RGB/NIR images are captured by RGB and NIR cameras while the RGB/Depth images are captured by Microsoft Kinect. The different exposure image pairs and the flash/no-flash pairs are captured by the same camera with exposure and camera pose variation. These images contain depth variation or dynamic moving objects, needing rigid and nonrigid transformation estimation. To get the ground truth displacement, we select 100 corner points and label their correspondence. The images are shown in our website (link in the title page). In total, these images provide $2K$ ground truth correspondences and we employ them to evaluate our method.

Evaluation of our method and other state-of-the-arts is reported in Table 1. We compare the general scene matching SIFT Flow [19] and the modified SIFT Flow using the gradient direction invariant SIFT [9]. We implement the variational mutual information method [12]. SIFT Flow does not handle gradient reversal. The gradient invariant SIFT produces a level of errors for matching as well. Variational mutual information does not handle large displacement and correspondingly yields relatively large errors. Our method does not have these problems. As our matching cost is flexible to incorporate other features, we evaluate employing features proposed in [15] and of color, gradient, and the

Table 1. Evaluation of methods on our dataset. The quantities in each column are the mean errors on one labeled image pair. * denotes the SIFT implementation in [9].

	RGB/NIR	RGB/Depth	Flash/No-flash	Different Exposure	All
SIFT Flow [19]	10.11	18.32	8.76	10.03	11.47
SIFT Flow*	8.03	16.17	8.90	11.67	10.56
Method by [12]	12.03	15.19	16.57	13.24	13.81
Ours with [15]	2.34	4.57	6.87	3.68	3.96
Ours with color	2.55	4.83	6.64	3.43	4.00
Ours with gradient	2.28	4.46	6.03	3.02	3.61
Ours	**1.89**	**4.17**	**4.56**	**2.25**	**2.95**

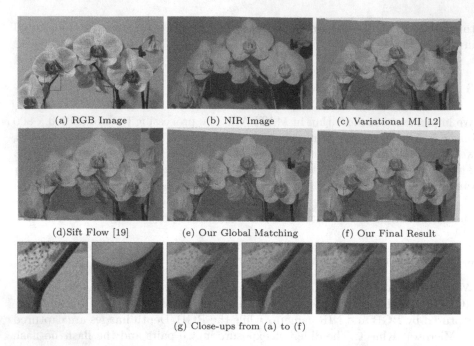

(a) RGB Image   (b) NIR Image   (c) Variational MI [12]

(d)Sift Flow [19]   (e) Our Global Matching   (f) Our Final Result

(g) Close-ups from (a) to (f)

Fig. 6. Matching of RGB and NIR images with structure variation and nonrigid transform by different methods. (c)-(f) Blending result by warping (b) to (a). (g) Close-ups.

combination of color and gradient. The result in Table 1 proves that our current feature is the best among the four for this matching task.

Examples in Figs. 6 and 7 compare our method to others. The inputs in Fig. 6 are the RGB and NIR images with significant gradient, noise and shadow variation. Fig. 7 is an example to match a series of different exposure images. Both examples are with nonrigid transform and large displacements. Our results are with good quality thanks to the new matching cost and robust two-phase matching framework.

6.2   Applications

Our framework benefits computer vision and computational photography applications that need to align multi-spectral and multi-modal images. We apply it to HDR construction and multi-modal image restoration.

HDR Image Construction. Our method can match different exposure images for restoration of high dynamic range images. As shown in Fig. 7, Our results are with high quality. We employ the method proposed in [24] to merge low dynamic range images into a HDR one, where the tone mapping result is shown in (i). Our method yields rich details compared to that of [24].

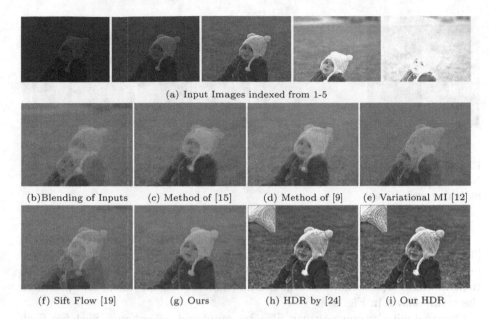

(a) Input Images indexed from 1-5

(b)Blending of Inputs (c) Method of [15] (d) Method of [9] (e) Variational MI [12]

(f) Sift Flow [19] (g) Ours (h) HDR by [24] (i) Our HDR

Fig. 7. Different exposure images matching and HDR construction example. (a) Inputs from [24]. (b) Blending result of the inputs. (c)-(g) Blending results by warping all images to image 3 by different methods. (h) HDR Tone mapping result of [24]. (i) Our tone mapping result using the matched (g). More results and complete images are contained in our website.

Multi-Modal Image Restoration. We show an example of depth and RGB image matching in Fig. 8. Depth images captured by Kinect or other equipments are not accurately aligned with the corresponding RGB images as shown in Fig. 8(c). The depth image is also with noise and missing values. Simple smoothing by filter might damage original structures. Our method matches the smoothed depth image to the RGB one. It not only aligns structure but also helps restore it damaged by filtering as shown in Fig. 8(d) and (e).

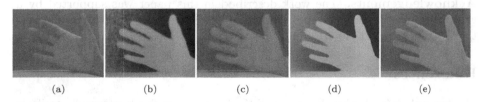

(a) (b) (c) (d) (e)

Fig. 8. RGB and depth matching and restoration. (a)-(b) are the RGB and depth raw data captured by Microsoft Kinect. (c) shows the blending result. (d) is the result using the framework of [35] but applying our matching method. (e) shows the blending of our depth and RGB images, which are aligned well.

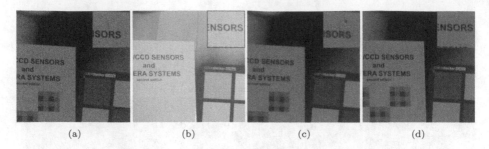

(a)	(b)	(c)	(d)

Fig. 9. Multi-spectral image restoration. (a) and (b) are input noisy RGB image and NIR image with displacements. (c) and (d) are the restoration results without and with matching respectively.

NIR image is also a good guidance to restore noisy RGB image as described in [35]. Since RGB and NIR images are often captured by different cameras, they need to be aligned before restoration. The alignment is very challenging due to their nonrigid transformation. Our method handles this problem, and produces the result shown in Fig. 9.

Our matching framework can also be employed to enhance flash/no-flash images that require alignment. Several examples are contained in the project website.

7   Conclusion and Limitation

We have presented an effective dense matching framework for multi-spectral and multi-modal images. Unlike other methods working on natural or medical images under various constraints, we address more challenging issues, including structure inconsistency and existence of strong outliers caused by shadow and highlight. We proposed a robust matching scheme, optimized in two phases.

Our method inevitably has several limitations. First, if the two images contain quite different structures, the estimated displacement field could be wrong completely. Second, our method may cause large errors on regions that do not contain necessarily informative edges or textures for credible structure matching.

Acknowledgements. The work described in this paper was supported by a grant from the Research Grants Council of the Hong Kong Special Administrative Region (Project No. 412911).

References

1. Agrawal, A.K., Raskar, R., Nayar, S.K., Li, Y.: Removing photography artifacts using gradient projection and flash-exposure sampling. ToG 24(3), 828–835 (2005)
2. Andronache, A., von Siebenthal, M., Székely, G., Cattin, P.C.: Non-rigid registration of multi-modal images using both mutual information and cross-correlation. Medical Image Analysis 12(1), 3–15 (2008)

3. Black, M.J., Anandan, P.: The robust estimation of multiple motions: Parametric and piecewise-smooth flow fields. CVIU 63(1), 75–104 (1996)
4. Brown, M., Susstrunk, S.: Multi-spectral sift for scene category recognition. In: CVPR, pp. 177–184 (2011)
5. Brox, T., Bruhn, A., Papenberg, N., Weickert, J.: High accuracy optical flow estimation based on a theory for warping. In: Pajdla, T., Matas, J.(G.) (eds.) ECCV 2004. LNCS, vol. 3024, pp. 25–36. Springer, Heidelberg (2004)
6. Bruhn, A., Weickert, J.: Towards ultimate motion estimation: Combining highest accuracy with real-time performance. In: ICCV, pp. 749–755 (2005)
7. Chui, H., Rangarajan, A.: A new point matching algorithm for non-rigid registration. Computer Vision and Image Understanding 89(2), 114–141 (2003)
8. Fattal, R., Lischinski, D., Werman, M.: Gradient domain high dynamic range compression. ToG 21(3), 249–256 (2002)
9. Firmenichy, D., Brown, M., Süsstrunk, S.: Multispectral interest points for rgb-nir image registration. In: ICIP, pp. 181–184 (2011)
10. Han, J., Pauwels, E.J., de Zeeuw, P.M.: Visible and infrared image registration in man-made environments employing hybrid visual features. Pattern Recognition Letters 34(1), 42–51 (2013)
11. Heo, Y.S., Lee, K.M., Lee, S.U.: Robust stereo matching using adaptive normalized cross-correlation. PAMI 33(4), 807–822 (2011)
12. Hermosillo, G., Chefd'Hotel, C., Faugeras, O.D.: Variational methods for multi-modal image matching. IJCV 50(3), 329–343 (2002)
13. Horn, B.K.P., Schunck, B.G.: Determining optical flow. Artif. Intell. 17(1-3), 185–203 (1981)
14. Hrkać, T., Kalafatić, Z., Krapac, J.: Infrared-visual image registration based on corners and hausdorff distance. In: Ersbøll, B.K., Pedersen, K.S. (eds.) SCIA 2007. LNCS, vol. 4522, pp. 383–392. Springer, Heidelberg (2007)
15. Irani, M., Anandan, P.: Robust multi-sensor image alignment. In: ICCV, pp. 959–966 (1998)
16. Jian, B., Vemuri, B.C.: Robust point set registration using gaussian mixture models. PAMI 33(8), 1633–1645 (2011)
17. Kolár, R., Kubecka, L., Jan, J.: Registration and fusion of the autofluorescent and infrared retinal images. International Journal of Biomedical Imaging (2008)
18. Krishnan, D., Fergus, R.: Dark flash photography. ToG 28(3) (2009)
19. Liu, C., Yuen, J., Torralba, A., Sivic, J., Freeman, W.T.: Sift flow: Dense correspondence across different scenes. In: Forsyth, D., Torr, P., Zisserman, A. (eds.) ECCV 2008, Part III. LNCS, vol. 5304, pp. 28–42. Springer, Heidelberg (2008)
20. Lowe, D.G.: Distinctive image features from scale-invariant keypoints. IJCV 60(2), 91–110 (2004)
21. Palos, G., Betrouni, N., Coulanges, M., Vermandel, M., Devlaminck, V., Rousseau, J.: Multimodal matching by maximisation of mutual information and optical flow technique. In: IEEE International Conference on Engineering in Medicine and Biology Society, pp. 1679–1682 (2004)
22. Petschnigg, G., Szeliski, R., Agrawala, M., Cohen, M.F., Hoppe, H., Toyama, K.: Digital photography with flash and no-flash image pairs. ToG 23(3), 664–672 (2004)
23. Pluim, J.P.W., Maintz, J.B.A., Viergever, M.A.: Mutual information based registration of medical images: A survey. IEEE Transaction on Medical Imaging 22(8), 986–1004 (2003)
24. Sen, P., Kalantari, N.K., Yaesoubi, M., Darabi, S., Goldman, D.B., Shechtman, E.: Robust patch-based hdr reconstruction of dynamic scenes. ToG 31(6), 203 (2012)

25. Sun, D., Roth, S., Black, M.J.: Secrets of optical flow estimation and their principles. In: CVPR, pp. 2432–2439 (2010)
26. Sun, J., Kang, S.B., Xu, Z., Tang, X., Shum, H.Y.: Flash cut: Foreground extraction with flash and no-flash image pairs. In: CVPR (2007)
27. Sun, J., Zheng, N., Shum, H.Y.: Stereo matching using belief propagation. PAMI 25(7), 787–800 (2003)
28. Szeliski, R.: Image alignment and stitching: A tutorial. Foundations and Trends in Computer Graphics Vision 2(1), 1–104 (2006)
29. Tsin, Y., Kanade, T.: A correlation-based approach to robust point set registration. In: Pajdla, T., Matas, J.(G.) (eds.) ECCV 2004. LNCS, vol. 3023, pp. 558–569. Springer, Heidelberg (2004)
30. Wang, Y., Yang, J., Yin, W., Zhang, Y.: A new alternating minimization algorithm for total variation image reconstruction. SIAM Journal on Imaging Sciences 1(3), 248–272 (2008)
31. Wedel, A., Rabe, C., Vaudrey, T., Brox, T., Franke, U., Cremers, D.: Efficient dense scene flow from sparse or dense stereo data. In: Forsyth, D., Torr, P., Zisserman, A. (eds.) ECCV 2008, Part I. LNCS, vol. 5302, pp. 739–751. Springer, Heidelberg (2008)
32. Werlberger, M., Pock, T., Bischof, H.: Motion estimation with non-local total variation regularization. In: CVPR, pp. 2464–2471 (2010)
33. Xiong, Z., Zhang, Y.: A critical review of image registration methods. International Journal of Image and Data Fusion 1(2), 137–158 (2010)
34. Xu, L., Jia, J., Matsushita, Y.: Motion detail preserving optical flow estimation. PAMI 34(9), 1744–1757 (2012)
35. Yan, Q., Shen, X., Xu, L., Zhuo, S., Zhang, X., Shen, L., Jia, J.: Cross-field joint image restoration via scale map. In: ICCV (2013)
36. Yang, J., Blum, R.S., Williams, J.P., Sun, Y., Xu, C.: Non-rigid image registration using geometric features and local salient region features. In: CVPR, pp. 825–832 (2006)
37. Yi, Z., Soatto, S.: Nonrigid registration combining global and local statistics. In: CVPR (2009)
38. Yuan, L., Sun, J., Quan, L., Shum, H.Y.: Image deblurring with blurred/noisy image pairs. ToG 26(3) (2007)
39. Zach, C., Pock, T., Bischof, H.: A duality based approach for realtime TV-L1 optical flow. Pattern Recognition, 214–223 (2007)
40. Zhang, Z., Jiang, Y., Tsui, H.: Consistent multi-modal non-rigid registration based on a variational approach. Pattern Recognition Letters 27(7), 715–725 (2006)
41. Zimmer, H., Bruhn, A., Weickert, J., Valgaerts, L., Salgado, A., Rosenhahn, B., Seidel, H.-P.: Complementary optic flow. In: Cremers, D., Boykov, Y., Blake, A., Schmidt, F.R. (eds.) EMMCVPR 2009. LNCS, vol. 5681, pp. 207–220. Springer, Heidelberg (2009)
42. Zitová, B., Flusser, J.: Image registration methods: a survey. Image and Vision Computing 21(11), 977–1000 (2003)

Using Isometry to Classify
Correct/Incorrect 3D-2D Correspondences

Toby Collins and Adrien Bartoli

ALCoV-ISIT, UMR 6284 CNRS/Université d'Auvergne, Clermont-Ferrand, France

Abstract. Template-based methods have been successfully used for surface detection and 3D reconstruction from a 2D input image, especially when the surface is known to deform isometrically. However, almost all such methods require that keypoint correspondences be first matched between the template and the input image. Matching thus exists as a current limitation because existing methods are either slow or tend to perform poorly for discontinuous or unsmooth surfaces or deformations. This is partly because the 3D isometric deformation constraint cannot be easily used in the 2D image directly. We propose to resolve that difficulty by detecting incorrect correspondences using the isometry constraint directly in 3D. We do this by embedding a set of putative correspondences in 3D space, by estimating their depth and local 3D orientation in the input image, from local image warps computed quickly and accurately by means of Inverse Composition. We then relax isometry to inextensibility to get a first correct/incorrect classification using simple pairwise constraints. This classification is then efficiently refined using higher-order constraints, which we formulate as the consistency between the correspondences' local 3D geometry. Our algorithm is fast and has only one free parameter governing the precision/recall trade-off. We show experimentally that it significantly outperforms state-of-the-art.

1 Introduction

An open problem in computer vision is to automatically determine correspondences between two images of a deformable 3D surface. Solving this problem is required in several applications, including estimating the nonrigid shape of the surface (known as template-based 3D reconstruction in the literature [2–5]), as a cue for nonrigid object detection [6, 7], and nonrigid Structure-from-Motion [8, 9]. There are several approaches to this problem, and these can be broadly broken into two main axes. In the first axis are the *Graph-Based Assignment* (GBA) methods [10–12]. These solve the problem by constructing graphs that encode the geometric relationship between correspondences. Solving GBA amounts to an NP-hard binary programming problem, and much of the ongoing research focuses on finding efficient and tight relaxations to this problem. In the second axis are the *Hard Matching with Outlier Detection* (HMOD) methods [5, 6, 1, 4, 13, 14]. HMOD methods work by first matching points using local texture information computed from a keypoint descriptor algorithm. Each point

D. Fleet et al. (Eds.): ECCV 2014, Part IV, LNCS 8692, pp. 325–340, 2014.

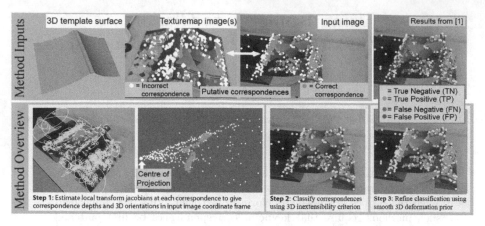

Fig. 1. Summary of the problem tackled and our 3-step solution (example is from our *OpenBook* dataset). As inputs we have 715 2D putative correspondences computed between a 3D template's texturemap and an input image. Of these 429 are correct correspondences (*i.e.* positives) and 286 are incorrect correspondences (*i.e.* negatives). In the bottom-right we show the final output of our method, which correctly classifies 713 correspondences, with 0 false negatives and 2 false positives. In the top-right is the output from [1], which gives 97 false negatives and 85 false positives. Best viewed in colour.

in one image is assigned to the point in the second image with the closest descriptor. Thus, a *hard* correspondence decision is made using only local texture information. A second stage is then performed to determine which correspondences are correct and incorrect by measuring their geometric compatibility via a deformable model. This second stage is sometimes referred to as *outlier detection* in the literature. So far HMOD methods have been preferred over GBA methods for use in template-based 3D reconstruction and nonrigid object detection. The main reason is that they are typically much faster than GBA methods. With efficient implementations the fastest HMOD methods perform in realtime [6] and can handle thousands of feature points, whereas accurate GBA methods are far slower, and may take several minutes to process a few hundred points [10]. Furthermore, unlike HMOD methods, most GBA methods are designed to work when the same features are detected in both images, however this is typically not the case in real conditions with scene clutter or occlusion.

There are three main limitations to state-of-the-art HMOD methods. Firstly, they tend not to be able to handle cases when the number of incorrect correspondences is large (*e.g.* 50% and beyond). This can often occur when dealing with surfaces with poorly discriminative texture, or when the imaging conditions are quite different such as strong lighting change or noise. Secondly, state-of-the-art HMOD methods are either fast, and use a simplified convex model of deformation [13, 6], or use a more realistic physical deformation model, but are either slow to execute and do not scale well to large, complex surfaces with complex topology [5], or cannot handle discontinuous motion such as surface tearing [4]

We present a new HMOD method that does not suffer these limitations and show experimentally that it considerably improves on state-of-the-art (Fig. 1). Our approach is based on using local physical 3D deformation constraints to detect incorrect correspondences. Specifically we use quasi-isometry, which means the amount of stretching induced by the deformation is small. This is a property exhibited by many materials, and which has been exploited before to solve the HMOD problem [5, 4, 15]. However those methods require a costly iterative optimisation process that alternates between registering the surface and detecting incorrect correspondences. We show that the problem can be solved more efficiently using the fact that the deformation of an isometric surface can be locally approximated by smoothly-varying rigid transforms. Our method involves estimating these transforms from the putative correspondences and because it models deformation only locally, and so scales well to large meshes with complex topology, can handle discontinuous surfaces and/or deformation, and is very parallelisable.

2   Previous Work

All prior HMOD methods work by fitting a deformable model using the putative correspondences and detecting incorrect correspondences as those which disagree with the fitted model. The methods differ along two main axes. Along the first axis is the *spatial extent* of the deformable model. *Global methods* work using global deformable models [6, 1, 4, 5] which model the entire deformation of the surface. *Local methods* work by breaking the surface into multiple regions and fitting a local deformable model to each region independently. Along the second axis are *HMOD-3D* and *HMOD-2D* methods which use 3D and 2D deformable models respectively. Previous HMOD-3D methods deform the surface in 3D space using the putative correspondences. Their main advantage is that they can use constraints that have physical meaning which are unaffected by changing the camera viewpoint or camera parameters. All prior HMOD-3D methods are global methods which constrain the surface deformation using isometry [4, 5, 15]. Some of these have proposed detecting incorrect correspondences and fitting the deformable model as a joint optimisation problem [15], however this was very slow and reported to take 15 minutes with examples of only 40 correspondences. Faster HMOD-3D methods work by alternating between registering a mesh of the deforming surface and detecting incorrect correspondences [4, 5]. During optimisation higher confidence is gradually placed on the model's prediction, which leads to more incorrect correspondences being detected. These alternation methods have been shown to work well on very smooth, low complexity surfaces. However the alternation is costly because at each iteration the full 3D shape of the surface is estimated. However these are prohibitively slow to process large, complex 3D surfaces in realtime, and cannot handle discontinuous deformation.

HMOD-2D methods do not model the 3D deformation of the surface. Instead they model the 2D-2D deformation between a single image of the surface (typically called a *template image*), and the input image. Because they do not involve 3D properties they cannot exploit surface isometry, and must use general assumptions on the 2D-2D flowfield. All prior HMOD-2D methods assume this flowfield is smooth (either globally or piecewise). A global HMOD-2D method was presented in [6] which first proposed the alternation strategy used by [4, 5]. This method is fast but breaks down when the flowfield is discontinuous, which occurs if the surface self-occludes or has sharp edges. Another global method was recently presented [1]. This assumes the 4D correspondence manifold is approximately planar and works by fitting this 4D hyperplane using RANSAC. This works well in some cases, such as simple, smooth bending of paper, but fails for more complex deformations. A local method was presented by [13] which uses affine and low-complexity Thin-Plate Spline (TPS) local models. The method is fast and is highly parallelisable. Because smoothness is assumed only locally, it can handle discontinuous 2D-2D flowfields, however the method does not cope well with correct correspondence ratios below 60%. There are no previous *local HMOD-3D methods*, and our proposed method fills this gap.

3   Problem Setup and Approach Overview

3.1   Problem Setup

Our problem setup is illustrated in Fig. 2. We define a 3D template similarly to the template-based 3D reconstruction literature. The template consists of a 3D mesh model defined in world coordinates which is textured using a set of registered *texturemap images*: $\mathcal{T} = \{\mathcal{T}_1, \mathcal{T}_2, .., \mathcal{T}_T\}$. Each $\mathcal{T}_t$ is an RGB photograph of the 3D mesh model with a known pose. We assume the 3D template has been constructed using a 3D acquisition device such as a structured-light scanner with fully-calibrated RGB cameras. We assume the template's silhouette in each $\mathcal{T}_t$ is known, and a set of 2D image features located within the silhouette is provided. We use affine-covariant SIFT features [16] in our experiments but this could be computed with any method. We then perform ray-intersection with the template to compute the 3D positions of the features in world coordinates.

For the input image, 2D features are then computed and putatively matched to the template's features by finding the one with the closest descriptor. An optional step is performed to remove low-confidence correspondences using Lowe's ratio test [17]. We denote the list of 3D-2D putative correspondences between the 3D template and 2D input image with $\mathcal{K} = \{(t_j, \mathbf{q}_j, \mathbf{Q}_j), \mathbf{p}_j\}$. For the jth correspondence, we have a *3D template feature*, denoted by $(t_j, \mathbf{q}_j, \mathbf{Q}_j)$ and a *2D input image feature* $\mathbf{p}_j$. $t_j \in \{1..T\}$ holds the index of the texturemap image from which the 3D template feature was detected, $\mathbf{q}_j \in \mathbb{R}^2$ holds its 2D position in the texturemap image and $\mathbf{Q}_j \in \mathbb{R}^3$ holds its 3D position in world coordinates. $\mathbf{p}_j \in \mathbb{R}^2$ holds the 2D position of the corresponding input image feature. We assume the input image's camera is intrinsically calibrated, and define $\mathbf{p}_j$ in normalised pixel coordinates. The unknown 3D position of $\mathbf{p}_j$ in camera coordinates is denoted by $\mathbf{P}_j \in \mathbb{R}^3$ where $\mathbf{p}_j = \pi(\mathbf{P}_j) + \varepsilon$, where ε denotes

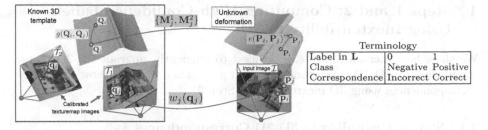

Fig. 2. Problem setup illustrated with two putative correspondences. Terms in green and red indicate known and unknown quantities respectively.

measurement noise and $\pi([x, y, z]^\top) \overset{\text{def}}{=} \frac{1}{z}[x, y]^\top$ is the normalised perspective projection function.

Our goal is to classify which members of $\mathcal{K}$ are correct and which are incorrect correspondences. We define the positive class to be correct correspondences and the negative class to be incorrect correspondences. The problem is posed as finding the binary label vector $\mathbf{L} \in \{0, 1\}^n$, $n \overset{\text{def}}{=} |\mathcal{K}|$ where $\mathbf{L}(j) = 1$ means the jth correspondence is classified positive and $\mathbf{L}(j) = 0$ means it is classified negative (Fig. 2).

3.2   Approach Overview

Our method involves determining $\mathbf{L}$ efficiently using *local* 3D deformation models. We use the fact that for isometric surfaces 3D deformation can be locally approximated by smoothly-varying rigid transforms. The method is broken down into three core steps (Fig. 1). In the first step we take each putative correspondence in $\mathcal{K}$ and *upgrade* it to a 3D-3D correspondence. This is done by estimating the local transform induced by the correspondence, and then inferring the depth of the correspondence in the camera coordinate frame, using a very fast solution inspired by [18]. The transforms are initialised using Affine Covariant Normalisation (ACN) [19], then efficiently refined with Inverse-Compositional iterations [20, 21]. In the second stage we use the 3D-3D correspondences to construct a graph that encodes pairwise inextensibility (in 3D space). Inextensibility is a relaxation of isometry, which says that the Euclidean distance between any two points on an isometric surface should not exceed their geodesic distance (which is known *a priori* from the template). We use this constraint to find an initial labelling $\mathbf{L}_0$ with an approach inspired by [14]. In the third step we refine $\mathbf{L}_0$ with a fast iterative approach by introducing local models with higher-order constraints. Specifically, we enforce that the deformation can be modelled by local, smoothly varying rigid transforms, and estimate these transforms robustly whilst refining $\mathbf{L}$. In practice only a few refinement iterations are needed.

4   Steps 1 and 2: Computing High-Confidence Labels Using Inextensibility in 3D

We show how inextensibility can be used to efficiently upgrade 3D-2D correspondences to 3D-3D correspondences (Step 1). Then we show how to classify correspondences using 3D inextensibility (Step 2).

4.1   Step 1: Upgrading to 3D-3D Correspondences

Principle. We upgrade each correspondence using the constraints that isometry imposes on the local 2D transformation between the template's texturemap image and the input image. This approach is inspired by [18, 22] where it was shown that depth information can be recovered analytically from this transform. Those methods assume that the deformable template and input images are already registered, which was achieved by conformally flattening the template and computing a *global* warp between the flat template and the input image. In our problem we do not know this warp (because knowing it would mean knowing $\mathbf{L}$). Furthermore we want to be able to compute depths for templates with arbitrary topology (including non-flattenable templates). Our solution is to fit a localised warp, but for each correspondence *individually*.

For the jth correspondence $((t_j, \mathbf{Q}_j, \mathbf{q}_j), \mathbf{p}_j) \in \mathcal{K}$, we compute a local warp w_j : $\mathbb{R}^2 \to \mathbb{R}^2$ that transforms the 2D point $\mathbf{q}_j$ in $\mathcal{T}_{t_j}$ to the 2D point $\mathbf{p}_j$ in the input image $\mathcal{I}$ (Fig. 2). Once estimated, by measuring the Jacobian $J_{w_j}(\mathbf{q}_j) \in \mathbb{R}^{2 \times 2}$ of the warp, we can compute the depth $z_j \in \mathbb{R}^+$ of $\mathbf{p}_j$ with respect to the input image's camera [18, 22]. Thus we are able to *upgrade* the 3D-2D correspondence to a 3D-3D correspondence, which we denote by the pair $(\mathbf{Q}_j, \mathbf{P}_j)$ with $\mathbf{P}_j \overset{\text{def}}{=} z_j [\mathbf{p}_j^\top, 1]^\top$. In addition to $\mathbf{P}_j$, the analytic solution also provides us with two estimates of the rotation matrix that rotates $\mathbf{Q}_j$ to $\mathbf{P}_j$ [23]. This means we have for each correspondence two estimates of the local rigid transform from $\mathbf{Q}_j$ to $\mathbf{P}_j$. We denote these by $\mathcal{M}_j = \{\mathbf{M}_j^1, \mathbf{M}_j^2\}$, $\mathbf{M}_j^s \in SE_3$. We now address the question of how to fit the local warps in order to compute $J_{w_j}(\mathbf{q}_j)$, and hence compute z_j and $\mathcal{M}_j$.

Computing the warp Jacobians. Our approach to compute $J_{w_j}(\mathbf{q}_j)$ is to fit the warp using pixel intensity information surrounding $\mathbf{q}_j$ and $\mathbf{p}_j$. This is summarised in two steps:

1. **Coarse approximation**. We first compute a coarse estimate of $J_{w_j}(\mathbf{q}_j)$ using ACN. By using a feature matching algorithm that performs ACN as part of descriptor extraction then this step is done for us and so is at no additional cost. In our experiments we use VLFeat's `vl_covdet`.
2. **Direct refinement with a local warp**. We then construct a low-complexity 2D-2D parametric warp centred at each $\mathbf{q}_j$. The warp is initialised using the affine transform from Step 1 and refined efficiently by IC iterations [20, 21].

For Step 2 it is important to use low complexity warps. This is necessary to prevent overfitting, improve convergence and to reduce computation time. We have found good results can be achieved using a TPS warp with only four control points. We define a circular support region centred at $\mathbf{q}_j$ of radius r_j. There is a trade-off in choosing r_j. Too small, and the region may contain insufficient image structure with which to estimate $J_w(\mathbf{q}_j)$. Too large and the motion in the region may be too complex to describe with a simple model. A strategy for selecting r_j is to use the characteristic scale of the feature at $\mathbf{q}_j$. The characteristic scale gives the size of the image region surrounding $\mathbf{q}_j$ with which its descriptor was computed. Because feature descriptors do not normally provide invariance beyond very simple transforms (at most affine transforms), a correct putative correspondence implies the image transform at this scale must be simple. Furthermore if the correspondence is correct then the characteristic scale is large enough to encompass sufficient discriminative image structure, which usually implies there is enough structure with which to estimate $J_{w_j}(\mathbf{q}_j)$. We optimise the TPS parameters using IC iterations, which are extremely fast, using a centre-weighted Normalised Sum-of-Square Difference (NSSD) data cost. We provide implementation details for this optimisation in the supplementary material. After optimisation, we compute $J_{w_j}(\mathbf{q}_j)$ by differentiating the local warp at $\mathbf{q}_j$, from which we compute $\mathbf{P}_j$ and the local rigid transforms $\mathcal{M}_j$.

4.2 Step 2: Classifying Correspondences Using Pairwise Inextensibility

We now use the upgraded 3D-3D correspondences to efficiently gain an initial correspondence labelling $\mathbf{L}_0 \in \{0,1\}^n$ using pairwise *3D* inextensibility constraints (Fig. 2). The approach is inspired by [14], however it it different because in [14] *2D* inextensibility is enforced. The latter can be violated between two correct correspondences when e.g. viewing the surface at different depths, different orientations, using different image resolutions or using different focal lengths. By contrast for isometric surfaces, *3D* inextensibility is never violated, and is totally independent of the imaging conditions. We use $g(\mathbf{Q}_i, \mathbf{Q}_j)$ to denote the geodesic distance between points $\mathbf{Q}_i$ and $\mathbf{Q}_j$, and $e(\mathbf{P}_i, \mathbf{P}_j) \overset{\text{def}}{=} \|\mathbf{P}_i - \mathbf{P}_j\|_2$ to denote the Euclidean distance between $\mathbf{P}_i$ and $\mathbf{P}_j$. $g(\mathbf{Q}_i, \mathbf{Q}_j)$ can be pre-computed efficiently offline when the 3D template was built, and the online cost of evaluating it is negligible. If i and j are correct correspondences, then in the absence of noise $g(\mathbf{Q}_i, \mathbf{Q}_j) \geq e(\mathbf{P}_i, \mathbf{P}_j)$. This is a relaxation of the isometric constraint $g(\mathbf{Q}_i, \mathbf{Q}_j) = g(\mathbf{P}_i, \mathbf{P}_j)$, which we cannot apply because we do not have measurements of $g(\mathbf{P}_i, \mathbf{P}_j)$. The relaxation is however still powerful because if j is an incorrect correspondence then $\mathbf{P}_j$ tends to be distributed very randomly within the camera's frustum. This is illustrated in Fig. 1 (Step 1). The randomisation of the incorrect correspondences means that when either i, j, or both i and j are incorrect, often $e(\mathbf{P}_i, \mathbf{P}_j)$ will exceed $g(\mathbf{Q}_i, \mathbf{Q}_j)$, and this tells us correspondences i and j are not geometrically compatible. We define a pairwise binary compatibility matrix as follows:

$$\mathbf{U}(i,j) = \begin{cases} 1 & \text{if } g(\mathbf{Q}_i, \mathbf{Q}_j) \geq e(\mathbf{P}_i, \mathbf{P}_j) - \tau_e \\ 0 & \text{otherwise} \end{cases} \tag{1}$$

This compatibility score is more discriminative when $\mathbf{Q}_i$ and $\mathbf{Q}_j$ are close because when $g(\mathbf{Q}_i, \mathbf{Q}_j)$ is smaller the bound on $e(\mathbf{P}_i, \mathbf{P}_j)$ is tighter. τ_e is a tolerance term used to handle uncertainty caused by the fact that the local warps will have some noise, and hence induce noise in $\mathbf{P}_i$ and $\mathbf{P}_j$. To select τ_e recall that the template has been normalised to fit within the unit cube, and so τ_e does not need to be adapted depending on the template's size. We have found $\tau_e = 5\%$ to work well across all our experiments.

$\mathbf{U}$ can be interpreted as a graph with n nodes, where each node is a correspondence and an edge appears between a pair of nodes if they respect the inextensibility constraint. The set of correct correspondences should therefore form a strongly-connected component in the graph, and so we can estimate $\mathbf{L}$ by establishing which nodes belong to this component. We do this in a similar manner to [14], but because $\mathbf{U}$ is binary the selection process can be simplified because we do not need the eigendecomposition of $\mathbf{U}$. Let $\mathbf{m}_i \in \{0,1\}^n$ denote the ith row of $\mathbf{U}$. First two empty sets are constructed; a set $\mathcal{P} = \emptyset$ holding all positives, and a set $\mathcal{N} = \emptyset$ holding all negatives. We then find $i^* = \arg\max_i \sum_j \mathbf{m}_i(j)$ (*i.e.* the best-connected correspondence) and insert i^* into $\mathcal{P}$. We then find the correspondence which has not yet been classified that has the highest number of connections: $i^* = \arg\max_{i \notin \mathcal{P} \cup \mathcal{N}} \sum_j \mathbf{m}_i(j)$. We test whether i^* is geometrically compatible with $\mathcal{P}$ by computing the compatibility score:

$$c(i^*, \mathcal{P}) = \frac{1}{|\mathcal{P}|} \sum_{j \in \mathcal{P}} \mathbf{U}(i^*, j) \tag{2}$$

This gives the proportion of members of $\mathcal{P}$ that are geometrically compatible with i^*. We insert i^* into $\mathcal{P}$ if $c(i^*, \mathcal{P}) > \tau_c$, otherwise it is inserted into $\mathcal{N}$. We use $\tau_c = 90\%$, which provides robustness during selection if $\mathcal{P}$ contains some incorrect correspondences. This selection process continues until all correspondences have been assigned to $\mathcal{P}$ or $\mathcal{N}$. We then initialise $\mathbf{L}$ with $\mathbf{L}_0(k) = \mathbb{1}(j \in \mathcal{P})$, where $\mathbb{1}(\cdot)$ denotes the indicator function.

5   Step 3: Fast Label Refinement with Higher-Order Constraints

$\mathbf{L}_0$ serves as an initial classification, but it may contain errors. An example of these errors is shown in Fig. 1 (Step 2). By using a high value of $\tau_c = 90\%$ the number of false positives is usually low. False negatives mainly occur when the local warp of a correspondence fails to converge to the right solution, which can lead to a poor estimate of $\mathbf{P}_j$. The main reasons for this are when (*i*) there is a photoconstancy violation in the local warp's region (such as a specularity) or when (*ii*) the warp's region crosses a discontinuity.

Our classification refinement method is based on the fact that if there is a neighbouring correspondence i which is correct, from $\mathcal{M}_i$ we have two estimates for the local transform that maps the template at point $\mathbf{Q}_i$ to the input image. We can therefore use these to validate whether j is a correct or incorrect correspondence. Assuming rigidity holds locally at i and j, if either $\pi\left(\mathbf{M}_i^1[\mathbf{Q}_j^\top, 1]^\top\right)$ or $\pi\left(\mathbf{M}_i^2[\mathbf{Q}_j^\top, 1]^\top\right)$ is close to $\mathbf{p}_j$, then j is likely to be a correct correspondence. Otherwise j is likely to be an incorrect correspondence. One challenge with doing this is that we do not know if i is a correct correspondence. Our solution is to use i if it has been classified positive in $\mathbf{L}_0$, but in a way that is robust to false positives.

For each j we construct a list of positives $\mathcal{S}_j = \{i \in 1..n, \mathbf{L}_0(i) = 1, i \neq j\}$. All members of $\mathcal{S}_j$ then vote for the predicted position of $\mathbf{p}_j$. First, for each i we find the rigid transform in $\mathcal{M}_i$ that agrees with $\mathbf{p}_j$ the most. We define this by $\mathbf{M}_i^*(j)$:

$$\mathbf{M}_i^*(j) = \arg\min_{\mathbf{M} \in \mathcal{M}_i} \left\| \pi \left(\mathbf{M}[\mathbf{Q}_j^\top, 1]^\top \right) - \mathbf{p}_j \right\|_2^2 \tag{3}$$

We then compute a robust prediction $\hat{\mathbf{p}}_j$ for $\mathbf{p}_j$. We do this using a weighted median of the individual predictions in $\mathcal{S}_j$ in a neighbourhood of size σ_j:

$$\hat{\mathbf{p}}_j = \underset{i \in \mathcal{S}_j}{\mathrm{wmed}} \left\{ \pi \left(\mathbf{M}_i^*(j)[\mathbf{Q}_j^\top, 1]^\top \right), v_i^j(\sigma_j) \right\}$$
$$v_i^j \overset{\mathrm{def}}{=} \begin{cases} \exp(-g(\mathbf{Q}_j, \mathbf{Q}_i)^2/\sigma_j^2) & \text{if } \|\mathbf{Q}_j - \mathbf{Q}_i\|_2 < 3\sigma_j \\ 0 & \text{otherwise} \end{cases} \tag{4}$$

v_i^j is a weight function which gives more influence to i if it is close to j. We use a truncated Gaussian for this, which means only a subset of nearby correspondences are used to compute $\hat{\mathbf{p}}_j$ (and thus improve efficiency). The weighted median provides robustness if $\mathcal{S}_j$ has false positives. It also provides robustness if local rigidity holds for some, but not all members of $\mathcal{S}_j$. We then reclassify j according to $\mathbf{L}(j) \leftarrow \mathbb{1}(\|\hat{\mathbf{p}}_j - \mathbf{p}_j\|_2 < \tau_p)$.

The free parameter τ_p governs the degree to which $\hat{\mathbf{p}}_j$ must agree with $\mathbf{p}_j$ for us to classify j as a positive. Thus τ_p provides a recall/precision tradeoff, with a lower τ_p meaning fewer false positives but potentially more false negatives. τ_p is a free parameter which can be set according to the application. We have found a good default value to be $\tau_p = 2\%$.

The weight function's bandwidth is given by σ_j. This should be adapted to reflect the extent of rigidity of the deformation about $\mathbf{Q}_j$. We automatically adapt σ_j using $\mathbf{L}_0$ and a fast minimisation of the prediction error. Specifically, we compute:

$$\sigma_j = \arg\min_\sigma \|\hat{\mathbf{p}}_j(\sigma) - \mathbf{p}_j\|_2^2 \tag{5}$$

where $\hat{\mathbf{p}}_j(\sigma)$ denotes the dependency of $\hat{\mathbf{p}}_j$ on σ. We solve Eq. (5) by quantising σ_j in 10 levels in the range 1% to 30%, and using the one that minimises Eq. (5).

We have found that $\mathbf{L}$ can usually be improved further by performing a few reclassification iterations. The algorithm pseudocode is simple and presented in Table 1, Step 3. There are a few cases which must be handled. The first is if j began negative but was reclassified positive. If this occurs it is likely that its warp was not estimated correctly in Step 2, leading to a poor estimate of its 3D position and orientation. We recompute this 3D information using neighbouring positives and a Pose from n Points (PnP) computation. Specifically we take a neighbour i if it is a member of $\mathcal{S}_j$ and $\|\pi \left(\mathbf{M}_i^*(j)[\mathbf{Q}_j^\top, 1]^\top \right) - \mathbf{p}_j\|_2 < \tau_p$ (i.e. its transform can predict well the position of j in the image). If there are more than two such neighbours, we recompute $\mathcal{M}_j$ by performing PnP using the correspondences from j and these neighbours. To perform PnP we use RPnP

Table 1. Classifying correct/incorrect 3D-2D correspondences using isometry: algorithm summary

---

Inputs (§3.1)
- Putative 3D-2D correspondences $\mathcal{K} = \{(t_j, \mathbf{Q}_j, \mathbf{q}_j), \mathbf{p}_j\}$
- Recall/precision threshold τ_p (default to 2% of the image diagonal)

Step 1: Upgrade $\mathcal{K}$ to 3D-3D correspondences (§4.1)
  1. For $j = 1 \rightarrow |\mathcal{K}|$ use IC iterations to compute local warp w_j that transforms $\mathbf{q}_j$ to $\mathbf{p}_j$
  2. Use $J_{w_j}(\mathbf{q}_j)$ to estimate $\mathbf{P}_j$ and local rigid transforms $\mathcal{M}_j$ mapping $\mathbf{Q}_j$ to $\mathbf{P}_j$
Step 2: Initialise $\mathbf{L}_0$ using 3D-3D pairwise inextensibility constraints (§4.2)
  1. Construct compatibility matrix $\mathbf{U} \in \{0, 1\}^{|\mathcal{K}| \times |\mathcal{K}|}$
  2. Compute $\mathbf{L}_0$ from $\mathbf{U}$ with greedy selection process
Step 3: Refine $\mathbf{L}_0$ using higher-order constraints (§5)
  1. $\mathbf{L} \leftarrow \mathbf{L}_0$
  2. While $\mathbf{L}$ changes or 10 iterations have not passed **do**
  3.   For $j = 1 \rightarrow |\mathcal{K}|$
  4.   Compute $\mathcal{S}_j$, σ_j, $\{w_i^j\}$ and $\hat{\mathbf{p}}_j$ (Eq. (4,5))
  5. $\mathbf{L}'(j) \leftarrow \begin{cases} 0 & |\mathcal{S}_j| = 0 \\ \mathbb{1}(\|\hat{\mathbf{p}}_j - \mathbf{p}_j\|_2 < \tau_p) & \text{otherwise} \end{cases}$
  6. $\mathbf{L} \leftarrow \mathbf{L}'$

Output class vector $\mathbf{L} \in \{0, 1\}^{|\mathcal{K}|}$

---

[24], and put into $\mathcal{M}_j$ all rigid poses returned by RPnP. We use RPnP because it is fast and can handle cases when the problem is ambiguous (which is often the case when doing local PnP [25]). A second case that must be handled is when $\mathcal{S}_j$ is empty. This occurs when all correspondences excluding j are negative. In practice this only usually happens when the template is not visible in the input image. Thus if $\mathcal{S}_j$ is empty we conclude the template is not visible and set $\mathbf{L}(j) \leftarrow 0$.

6   Experimental Results

We present a range of experiments to compare the performance of our method against state-of-the-art. We compare against [13, 6, 1, 5], which we refer to by Piz-IJCV12, Pil-IJCV08, Tran-ECCV12, and Salz-CVPR09 respectively. We use the authors' original code for Piz-IJCV12, Tran-ECCV12 and Salz-CVPR09, and the implementation of Pil-IJCV08 from [1].

Obtaining ground truth. There are several existing datasets for deformable isometric surfaces (e.g. [26, 27]). However these do not include ground-truth correspondences and are generally quite simple and involve developable surfaces such as sheets of paper or cloth. We have created three new real ground-truth datasets involving more complex surfaces and deformations. Computing dense ground truth correspondences for deforming surfaces is notoriously difficult and tedious [28]. Our approach was based on the idea that although the 3D-2D non-rigid registration problem is hard, when the surface is isometric, registering two deformed surfaces in 3D is far simpler and can be done automatically or semi-automatically [29, 30]. We captured a test surface in several deformed states and performed dense multiview Structure-from-Motion to obtain a texturemapped 3D template for each deformed state, and the camera parameters for each image. We then semi-automatically co-registered the 3D templates with a method based on [29] to provide us with dense correspondence between the 3D templates, and hence dense registration between different images of the surface in different deformed states.

The OpenBook dataset. The OpenBook dataset comprises four deformed states $(S_1 \rightarrow S_4)$ of a book cover (Fig. 3 (top row)), with 14 images taken for each deformed state. Images were captured with a standard 1020p point-and-shoot camera and we used Agisoft's Photoscan to perform dense multiview reconstruction. We use C_i to denote the set of images capturing the ith deformed state. A selection of images from C_3 are shown in Fig. 3 (second row). We then used each state in turn as the 3D template, and used all images for all other deformed states as input images. Thus in this dataset there is a total of $4 \times 3 \times 14 = 168$ different template/input image pairs. To allow a comparison between our method and the HMOD-2D methods we used only features detected in one of the template's texturemap images. This is because the HMOD-2D methods cannot trivially handle features coming from different texturemap images.

We use affine-covariant features using *VLFeat*'s implementation with default parameters. Putative correspondences were found using a Lowe ratio threshold of 1.1 [31]. Typically this resulted in between 200-800 putative correspondences per input image. Correspondences which were within 10 pixels of their ground truth positions were marked as true correspondences, and the rest as false. The proportion of incorrect correspondences in each image had a mean of 62%. For all methods we generated ROC curves by varying each method's detection threshold (we use the same procedure as [1] to do this). For our method the detection threshold is governed by τ_p (§5), with a default of 2.0% of the input image's diagonal). In Fig. 3 (third row) we show the ROC curves, with one ROC curve generated for each deformed state. We can see that our method performs significantly better than all others. At a false negative rate of 4.5% our method successfully classified all incorrect correspondences. The worst performing method is Salz-CVPR09. The reason is because it often eliminates many correct correspondences early in the annealing stage and cannot recover in later iterations. In the fourth row of Fig. 3 we show how the previous methods typically fail. Piz-IJCV12 fails if there is a small number of correct correspondences within each correspondence's neighbourhood. When this occurs a good local 2D model cannot be found, and this leads to false negatives. Tran-ECCV12 fails in general when the image transform is not simple and globally smooth. Pil-IJCV08 also fails when the image transform is not globally smooth. Salz-CVPR09 fails systematically when the incorrect correspondence ratio is beyond approximately 40%. Note that our method can correctly handle correspondences on the book's spine, which proved difficult for the other methods.

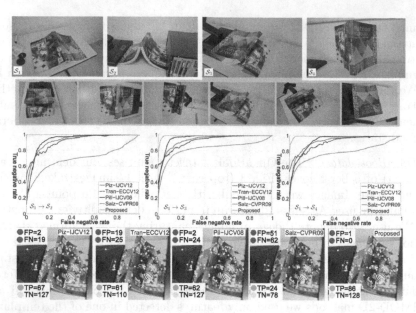

Fig. 3. Results on the OpenBook dataset. There are 86 true and 129 false putative correspondences in the example in the third row. FP and FN denote the number of false positives and false negatives for each method. Best viewed in colour.

The ALCoV Baseball Cap dataset [22]. This dataset consists of two image sets of a baseball cap in two deformed states S_1 and S_2. C_1 and C_2 are of sizes 29 and 16 respectively. We show sample images from C_1 and C_2 in the first row of Fig. 4. The dataset is challenging due to the texture on the cap being repetitive and there being considerable change in illumination. Between 488 and 1,404 affine covariant SIFT features were detected in these images. We used C_1 to build the 3D template, which consists of 12,205 vertices, and used each image in C_2 as an input image. We compared all methods using their default values for detection precision. The results are summarised in the three graphs in Fig. 4 (bottom) showing false negative, true negative and average errors across all 16 input images. We can see that our method performs vastly better than all others in terms of false negative rate, with a mean value of just 1.19%. The true negative rate for our method was joint highest with Pil-IJCV08, however Pil-IJCV08 gives many more false negatives because its deformation model cannot suitably handle the 2D flowfield induced by the cap's deformation, which causes many false negatives. The second and third rows of Fig. 4 show the results on a typical input image from C_2. We present timing information of the methods in Fig. 4 (bottom-right). Note that the implementations are sub-optimal non-parallelised Matlab implementations, and considerable speedups could be made with optimised code. We fully expect our method to be realtime on a standard PC with a good C++/GPGPU implementation.

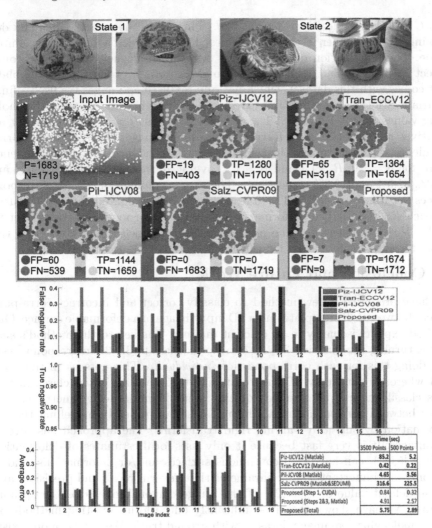

Fig. 4. Results on the ALCoV Baseball Cap dataset. P and N denote the number of positives and negatives. FP and FN denote the number of false positives and false negatives for each method. Timing information is shown in bottom-right. Best viewed in colour.

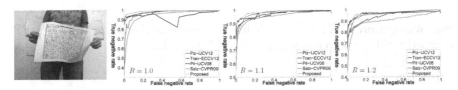

Fig. 5. Results on the CVLAB Bending Paper dataset. Best viewed in colour.

The CVLAB Bending Paper dataset [26]. This dataset is a short video of a deforming sheet of paper lasting 193 frames. Fig. 5 (top left) shows one example frame. The deformation of the paper is very low-frequency, and so we would expect Pil-IJCV08 and Tran-ECCV12 to work well. We used the 3D template that comes with this dataset, which has one texturemap image. We used affine-covariant SIFT features and ran three tests by varying Lowe's ratio threshold using values of $R = 1.0$, $R = 1.1$ and $R = 1.2$. When $R = 1.0$ it means that all putatives are kept (*i.e.* each feature in the input images has a putative correspondence with a feature in the template image). The incorrect correspondence ratios for $R = 1.0$, $R = 1.1$ and $R = 1.2$ (averaged over the whole sequence) are 77.1%, 32.5% and 12.3% respectively. The average number of correct correspondences per frame are 481, 421, 390 respectively. We computed three ROC curve for each R (Fig. 5). The performance difference of our method with respect to Pil-IJCV08 is smaller than the previous datasets, which is expected given the dataset's simple deformation for which Pil-IJCV08 is designed for.

7   Conclusion and Future Work

We have presented a new method to classify correct and incorrect correspondences between a 3D template and a 2D input image of a deformable surface. Our method exploits isometry in an efficient manner. The key to the method's success is turning the putative 3D-2D correspondences to 3D-3D correspondences, and doing this for each correspondence *individually*. This gets us in the position where we can apply 3D inextensibility to obtain an initial classification. This classification is then refined quickly using higher-order geometric consistency between correspondences, which is based on robustly modelling the 3D deformation by smoothly varying rigid transforms. The approach has several advantages. It is very fast because it only uses local estimates of deformation (unlike [5, 4]), can handle discontinuous surfaces and/or deformations, and it has only one important tuning parameter that governs recall and precision, and whose default value of $\tau_p = 2\%$ of the image diagonal gives close to optimal results. We have shown that it significantly outperforms existing methods on more challenging real image datasets with ground truth. We will turn our existing Matlab implementation (which takes a few seconds to run), into a realtime C++/GPGPU implementation and we believe that our algorithm will broaden the use of template-based 3D reconstruction methods. We will be testing new applications of those in our future research.

Acknowledgments. This research has received funding from the EU's FP7 through the ERC research grant 307483 FLEXABLE.

References

1. Tran, Q.-H., Chin, T.-J., Carneiro, G., Brown, M.S., Suter, D.: In defence of ransac for outlier rejection in deformable registration. In: Fitzgibbon, A., Lazebnik, S., Perona, P., Sato, Y., Schmid, C. (eds.) ECCV 2012, Part IV. LNCS, vol. 7575, pp. 274–287. Springer, Heidelberg (2012)

2. Bartoli, A., Gérard, Y., Chadebecq, F., Collins, T.: On template-based recon-struction from a single view: Analytical solutions and proofs of well-posedness for developable, isometric and conformal surfaces. In: CVPR (2012)
3. Salzmann, M., Fua, P.: Linear local models for monocular reconstruction of de-formable surfaces. PAMI 33, 931–944 (2011)
4. Östlund, J., Varol, A., Ngo, D.T., Fua, P.: Laplacian meshes for monocular 3D shape recovery. In: Fitzgibbon, A., Lazebnik, S., Perona, P., Sato, Y., Schmid, C. (eds.) ECCV 2012, Part III. LNCS, vol. 7574, pp. 412–425. Springer, Heidelberg (2012)
5. Salzmann, M., Fua, P.: Reconstructing sharply folding surfaces: A convex formu-lation. In: CVPR (2009)
6. Pilet, J., Lepetit, V., Fua, P.: Fast non-rigid surface detection, registration and realistic augmentation. IJCV (2008)
7. Alcantarilla, P.F., Bartoli, A.: Deformable 3D reconstruction with an object database. In: BMVC (2012)
8. Torresani, L., Hertzmann, A., Bregler, C.: Nonrigid structure-from-motion: Esti-mating shape and motion with hierarchical priors. PAMI 30 (2008)
9. Taylor, J., Jepson, A.D., Kutulakos, K.N.: Non-rigid structure from locally-rigid motion. In: CVPR (2010)
10. Zhou, F., De la Torre, F.: Deformable graph matching. In: CVPR (2013)
11. Duchenne, O., Bach, F.R., Kweon, I.S., Ponce, J.: A tensor-based algorithm for high-order graph matching. In: CVPR (2009)
12. Torresani, L., Kolmogorov, V., Rother, C.: Feature correspondence via graph matching: Models and global optimization. In: Forsyth, D., Torr, P., Zisserman, A. (eds.) ECCV 2008, Part II. LNCS, vol. 5303, pp. 596–609. Springer, Heidelberg (2008)
13. Pizarro, D., Bartoli, A.: Feature-based deformable surface detection with self-occlusion reasoning. IJCV (2012)
14. Leordeanu, M., Hebert, M.: A spectral technique for correspondence problems using pairwise constraints. In: ICCV (2005)
15. Shaji, A., Varol, A., Torresani, L., Fua, P.: Simultaneous point matching and 3D deformable surface reconstruction. In: CVPR (2010)
16. Mikolajczyk, K., Schmid, C.: Scale and affine invariant interest point detectors. IJCV 60, 63–86 (2004)
17. Lowe, D.G.: Distinctive image features from scale-invariant keypoints. IJCV (2004)
18. Bartoli, A., Gerard, Y., Chadebecq, F., Collins, T.: On template-based recon-struction from a single view: Analytical solutions and proofs of well-posedness for developable, isometric and conformal surfaces. In: CVPR (2012)
19. Mikolajczyk, K., Tuytelaars, T., Schmid, C., Zisserman, A., Matas, J., Schaffal-itzky, F., Kadir, T., Van Gool, L.: A comparison of affine region detectors. IJCV (2005)
20. Matthews, I., Baker, S.: Active appearance models revisited. IJCV (2004)
21. Brunet, F., Gay-Bellile, V., Bartoli, A., Navab, N., Malgouyres, R.: Feature-driven direct non-rigid image registration. IJCV (2011)
22. Bartoli, A., Collins, T.: Template-based isometric deformable 3D reconstruction with sampling-based focal length self-calibration. In: CVPR (2013)
23. Collins, T., Bartoli, A.: Infinitesimal plane-based pose estimation. IJCV (July 2014)
24. Li, S., Xu, C., Xie, M.: A robust O(n) solution to the perspective N point problem. PAMI (2012)

25. Schweighofer, G., Pinz, A.: Robust pose estimation from a planar target. Pattern Analysis and Machine Intelligence (PAMI) 28, 2024–2030 (2006)
26. Varol, A., Salzmann, M., Fua, P., Urtasun, R.: A constrained latent variable model. In: CVPR (2012)
27. Salzmann, M., Hartley, R., Fua, P.: Convex optimization for deformable surface 3-d tracking. In: ICCV (2007)
28. Baker, S., Scharstein, D., Lewis, J., Roth, S., Black, M., Szeliski, R.: A database and evaluation methodology for optical flow. IJCV (2011)
29. Huang, Q.X., Adams, B., Wicke, M., Guibas, L.J.: Non-rigid registration under isometric deformations. Comput. Graph. Forum (2008)
30. Tam, G.K.L.: quan Cheng, Z., kun Lai, Y., Langbein, F.C., Liu, Y., Marshall, D., Martin, R.R., fang Sun, X., Rosin, P.L.: Registration of 3D point clouds and meshes: A survey from rigid to non-rigid. Visualization and Computer Graphics (2013)
31. Lowe, D.G.: Distinctive image features from scale-invariant keypoints. IJCV (2004)

Bilateral Functions for Global Motion Modeling

Wen-Yan Daniel Lin[1], Ming-Ming Cheng[2], Jiangbo Lu[1], Hongsheng Yang[3],
Minh N. Do[4], and Philip Torr[2]

[1] Advanced Digital Sciences Center, Singapore
[2] Oxford University, UK
[3] University of North Carolina at Chapel Hill, USA
[4] University of Illinois at Urbana-Champaign, USA

Abstract. This paper proposes modeling motion in a bilateral domain that augments spatial information with the motion itself. We use the bilateral domain to reformulate a piecewise smooth constraint as continuous global modeling constraint. The resultant model can be robustly computed from highly noisy scattered feature points using a global minimization. We demonstrate how the model can reliably obtain large numbers of good quality correspondences over wide baselines, while keeping outliers to a minimum.

1 Introduction

Finding point-to-point correspondence between images is a fundamental vision problem. Applications include recognition, structure from motion, self-localization, warping, etc. For wide baselines, researchers typically focus on matching scattered, feature points which are distinctive and easy to match. Despite substantial success in feature descriptor design [1,2,3], basing correspondence solely on local information remains an unstable, outlier prone process.

Researchers usually handle outliers at the application level through task-specific motion models[1], that are often integrated into a RANSAC [4,5] outlier removal framework. Some of the most successful techniques, are based around identifying specific motion types/aspects that are amenable to global parameterization. Examples include epipolar geometry [6] for different views of a static scene, homography [7,8] for planar or pure rotational motion and non-rigid thin-plate splines [9] for smooth deformations. We believe the high reliance on task-specific global models highlights two issues:

A) Strength of global modeling: Global models have many features important to the correspondence problem. These are:

- Robustness: By defining a global rigidity/ smoothness, model computation can potentially tolerate high noise levels and even handle correlated noise [10].
- Scattered Samples: Models can be computed on a sub-set of available data and the results extrapolated. This approach permits computational efficiency and a natural interface with sparse feature matchers.

---

*This work was supported by the research grant for the Human Sixth Sense Programme at the Advanced Digital Sciences Center from Singapore's Agency for Science, Technology and Research (A*STAR).

[1] **Motion model:** a finite global parameter set that defines an aspect of a continuous motion field.

D. Fleet et al. (Eds.): ECCV 2014, Part IV, LNCS 8692, pp. 341–356, 2014.
© Springer International Publishing Switzerland 2014

- Generalization: Models can verify existing data and hypothesize new data points.

B) Lack of a general motion model: Creating a general motion model for image correspondence is difficult. Not only are correspondence points scattered and noisy, the primary underlying constraint is piecewise smoothness, with the potential for large motion discontinuities. Thus, modeling requires detection and change of parametrization at motion boundaries; a process that risks preserving outlier clusters and destroys the model's global properties. Yet, exclusively focusing on easily modeled motion aspects discards a great deal of information. This increases the brittleness of more general models like the epipolar constraint, while restricting the flexibility of robust models like homography. Our paper fills the gap by reformulating the piecewise-smoothness as a robust, global constraint. This allows model fitting, outlier removal and matching set expansion to begin before reaching the application level.

Our key concept is a general definition of motion coherence. Traditionally, coherence [11] is equated to spatial (x, y) smoothness, i.e. a motion model is coherent if the motion or its proxy[2] varies smoothly over the spatial domain. In contrast, we suggest a motion model be considered coherent if the motion/proxy varies smoothly in some low dimensional domain.

Fig. 1. Inset: a one-dimensional discontinuous set of motion hypothesis Main figure: the same data (black dots) over the bilateral domain with a likelihood motion proxy. Note: the bilateral domain expresses discontinuous data as a smooth field.

In particular, an extended domain that includes the motion itself, x, y, u, v, allows modeling of (spatially) piecewise smooth motions with a smoothly varying motion proxy. A detailed explanation is given in Sec. 3. We term such functions, which achieve smoothness by incorporating the desired output as part of the function domain, *bilateral functions*. Fig. 1 illustrates a bilateral function with a likelihood motion proxy. The bilateral domain makes it possible to fit a global function to (spatially) piecewise smooth motion data via the traditional as-smooth-as-possible data modeling. This can be solved by minimizing a global cost. The global smoothness makes bilateral motion model computation highly robust and it can be computed directly from noisy correspondence without RANSAC's [4] hypothesis and test framework. Once computed, models can robustly validate new matching hypothesis. This provides large numbers of correspondence points over wide baselines, while keeping outliers to a minimum (zero in many cases). Fig. 2 illustrates our performance.

To summarize our paper's contributions:

- We propose a bilateral model as a principled means of imposing a piecewise motion constraint via a global cost minimization. Our model is sufficiently robust to handle high noise levels without RANSAC's hypothesis and test framework.

---

[2] **Motion proxy:** a value which indicates but does not define the motion (an example is likelihood or a single affine parameter)

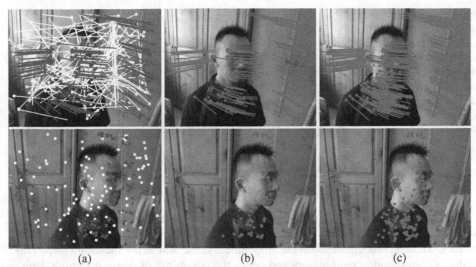

(a)   (b)   (c)

Fig. 2. An example of our global method for finding correspondences. Circles represent feature locations and lines their motion. a) Noisy feature correspondence (inliers highlighted in dark blue). b) Our global model eliminates outliers. The model is directly computed from the noisy matches in (a). c) The global model allows us to robustly expand the set of matches.

– We utilize the bilateral model to remove outliers from feature correspondences and expand the existing matching set. The resultant algorithm procures large numbers of correspondences while keeping outliers to a minimum. over wide baselines.

2   Related Works

Formulation: The piecewise smooth motion constraint has a long history in computer vision. Examples range from piecewise smooth flow estimation [12,13] to plane-fitting stereo [14]. However, to our knowledge, piecewise smoothness has always been enforced with some form of motion boundary discovery. Rather than the usual piecewise smooth approaches, our formulation builds on the global coherence [11,15,16,10] framework which fits a smooth, continuous field over scattered points. By applying the field on the bilateral domain, the global coherence accommodates discontinuities, while retaining its original robustness.

RANSAC: For rigid parametric models, RANSAC [4,17,18] provides a general means of removing outliers from feature correspondence. Of particular relevance are recent piecewise planar RANSAC techniques [18], which handle general motion. Unfortunately, they relinquish the global model, forcing tight thresholding (that removes many inliers). The lack of a global model also makes generalization for matching set expansion difficult. Interestingly, our bilateral coherence constraint is sufficiently robust to directly fit highly noisy data, without RANSAC's hypothesis and test framework. This enables our flexible non-rigid model. If additional parametric constraints are appropriate, RANSAC can be applied as a post-processor to further improve correspondence.

Fig. 3. An image pair with huge motion. The warp projects the second image onto the first. While this is not a difficult feature correspondence scene, the large occlusions makes it difficult for optical flow.

Optical flow [21,22,20], graph matching [23], surface modeling [24]: An alternative to modeling feature correspondences is optical flow or graph matching techniques. These approaches embed the smoothness constraint at the matching step. This reduces correspondence ambiguity and opens the possibility of dense matching. However, wide baselines introduce extensive occlusion which can turn the linkage of every pixel/feature through a neighbor-wise smoothness into a liability as seen in Fig. 3. For such scenes, our integration of bilateral modeling with point correspondence provides a natural means of handling high occlusion. This is discussed in more detail in the supplementary material.

Others: Outlier detection can also be achieved by local mesh techniques developed by Pizarro and Bartoli [25]. However, the lack of a global model reduces its effectiveness at higher noise level.

As our name suggests, bilateral functions are inspired by bilateral filters [26] that use the same domain change technique for edge preserving image de-noising. Bilateral filters have also been applied to optical flow computation [27]. However, they do not deal with the scattered point sets. Further, their window based approach makes identifying outlier clusters difficult. By extending the bilateral concept as a function domain, we overcome both these restrictions.

Interestingly, bilateral functions are related to patch-match [28] and quasi-dense correspondence algorithms [29,30]. These techniques grow seed correspondences by iteratively searching their neighborhood. This growing mechanics is similar manner to minimization of a bilateral likelihood function as elaborated in Sec. 3.2. However, patch-match does not compute an explicit model and it is unclear how its formulation can extend to outlier removal or multi-image matching.

3   Formulation

We begin with an intuitive explanation of our approach. Our underlying function is based on the motion coherence used in [11,15,16,10]. These techniques formulate a non-rigid motion fitting problem in terms of finding the smoothest $f_k(\mathbf{p})$ function that is consistent with given data. In these cases, $\mathbf{p}$ represents pixel coordinates, while the range of $f_k(\mathbf{p})$ represents motion or its proxy.

The smoothness (or infinite differentiability) implies a continuity constraint

$$\lim_{\Delta \mathbf{p} \mapsto 0} f_k(\mathbf{p} + \Delta \mathbf{p}) - f_k(\mathbf{p}) = 0, \quad \mathbf{p} = \begin{bmatrix} x \, y \end{bmatrix}^T \in \mathbb{R}^2, \tag{1}$$

which forces the function value in the neighborhood of $\mathbf{p}$ to be similar. This causes the function to incur large errors at discontinuous motion boundaries.

Our formulation changes the domain of $f_k(\mathbf{p})$ to a bilateral one spanning both the spatial and motion dimensions i.e. $\mathbf{p} = \begin{bmatrix} x \, y \, u \, v \end{bmatrix}^T$. This might mean that points with different velocities are no longer near each other. Thus, we can assign very different function values to points with adjacent spatial coordinates, while retaining the constraint that $f_k(\mathbf{p})$ must be smooth. If the motion difference $(\Delta u, \Delta v)$ between two points in the domain $\mathbf{p}$ tends to infinity, the point separation also tends to infinity, reducing their influence on each other. This occurs irrespective of their spatial coordinates and ensures the smoothness penalty in the bilateral domain does not tend to infinity as the magnitude of the motion's spatial discontinuity increases.

The (spatial) piecewise smoothness of the true underlying motion, creates large clusters of inlier points that are similar in both spatial and motion values, while sharing similar motion proxies. These points can be fitted at minimal cost to the smoothing function. In contrast, outliers appear as isolated point clusters requiring their own unique motion proxies. These incur a high smoothness cost if fit. The overall problem can now cast as finding the globally smoothest function consistent with the data. As we do not modify the as-smooth-as possible requirement, the global curve fitting [10] retains all is original robustness. Fig. 1 provides a visualization of the bilateral domain.

Preliminaries: We discuss two different bilateral functions in Sec. 3.1, Sec. 3.2. Sec. 3.3 gives an intuitive explanation of their properties while implementation is discussed in Sec. 3.4. Formally, we denote spatial locations as $\mathbf{x} = \begin{bmatrix} x \, y \end{bmatrix}^T$ and motion as $\mathbf{m} = \begin{bmatrix} u \, v \end{bmatrix}^T$. The set of N correspondences across two images is $\{\mathbf{x}_j, \mathbf{m}_j, \mathbf{a}_j\}$. $\mathbf{x}_j$ denotes pixel locations, $\mathbf{m}_j$ their corresponding motion hypothesis, and $\mathbf{a}_j$ is a 4×1 vector representing the relative affine orientation derived from local feature's orientation.

3.1 Bilaterally Varying Affine

A bilaterally varying affine is a set of affine parameters which vary smoothly in a bilateral domain. $\mathbf{p} = \begin{bmatrix} x \, y \, u \, v \end{bmatrix}^T$ is a point in $D = 4$ dimension bilateral domain and q is a scalar. For simplicity, we focus on the X motion direction first. The given correspondences are observed data:

$$observed\ data = \{\mathbf{p}_j = [\mathbf{x}_j; \mathbf{m}_j], \hat{q}_{xj} = x_j + u_j\} \tag{2}$$

where j is the correspondence index, and $\{\hat{q}_{xj}\}$ are noisy observations of model $q_x(\mathbf{p})$ evaluated at locations $\{\mathbf{p}_j\}$. We define $q_x(\mathbf{p})$ as a linear sum of smooth functions

$$q_x(\mathbf{p}) = f_1(\mathbf{p})x + f_2(\mathbf{p})y + f_3(\mathbf{p}), \tag{3}$$

where each $f_k(.)$ represents an affine parameter.

Our goal is to fit the smoothest possible, continuous, $f_k(.)$ functions to observed, $\{\hat{q}_{xj}\}$ data. Individual $f_k(.)$ functions are composed of two terms, $f_k(\mathbf{p}) = H_k + \phi_k(\mathbf{p})$.

H_k is an optional scalar offset and $\phi_k(\mathbf{p})$ is a smooth function with attached motion coherence [11,15,10] penalty:

$$\Psi_k = \int_{\mathbb{R}^D} \frac{|\bar{\phi}_k(\omega)|^2}{\bar{g}(\omega)} \, d\omega. \tag{4}$$

$\bar{\phi}_k(.)$ denotes the Fourier transform of a function $\phi_k(.)$, while $\bar{g}(\omega)$ is the Fourier transform of a Gaussian with spatial distribution γ. Hence, (4) achieves smoothness by penalizing high frequency terms.

We seek the $f_k(\mathbf{p})$ functions which minimize the cost

$$E = \sum_{j=1}^{N} C(\hat{q}_{xj} - q_x(\mathbf{p}_j)) + \lambda \sum_{k=1}^{3} \Psi_k \tag{5}$$

where $C(.)$ represents the Huber cost

$$C(z) = huber(z) = \begin{cases} z^2 & \text{if } |z| \le \epsilon \\ 2\epsilon|z| - \epsilon^2 & \text{if } |z| > \epsilon \end{cases} \tag{6}$$

that penalizes deviation of the estimated function predictions from given $\hat{q}_{xj}$ observations. λ represents the weight given to the smoothness constraint Ψ_k.

From [10], we know that both the continuous functions $f_k(\mathbf{p})$ and the coherence terms Ψ_k can be re-expressed in terms of a finite number of variables given by the N-dimensional vectors $\mathbf{w}_k$ and scalars H_k:

$$f_k(\mathbf{p}) = H_k + \sum_{j=1}^{N} \mathbf{w}_k(j)g(\mathbf{p} - \mathbf{p}_j, \gamma), \quad \Psi_k = \mathbf{w}_k^T G \mathbf{w}_k, \quad k \in \{1, 2, 3\} \tag{7}$$

where $g(\mathbf{z}, \gamma) = e^{-|\mathbf{z}|^2/\gamma^2}$ and $G(i, j) = g(\mathbf{p}_i - \mathbf{p}_j, \gamma)$. This allows us to minimize the energy in (5) with gradient descent as it is convex in terms of the variables $H_k, \mathbf{w}_k$. The Huber based energy in (5) allows the robust, non-parametric fitting of smooth curves by leveraging the smoothness constraint to ignore individual outliers and outlier clusters [10]. Note that the resultant bilateral affine model (3), is not a one-to-one mapping function. Rather it validates a match location $\mathbf{p}$ by checking the cost $(q_x - (x + u))^2$.

Similarly, for the Y direction, repeating the same steps as X but replacing $k \in \{1, 2, 3\}$ with $k \in \{4, 5, 6\}$ respectively and replacing $\hat{q}_{xj}$ with $\hat{q}_{yj} = y_j + v_j$, one obtains the bilateral affine model

$$q_y(\mathbf{p}) = f_4(\mathbf{p})x + f_5(\mathbf{p})y + f_6(\mathbf{p}). \tag{8}$$

Note that the formulation used here is not restricted to bilateral affines, with different choices of $f_k(.)$ domain and range leading to different functions as we demonstrate in the following subsection.

3.2   Likelihood Proxy

Another potential motion proxy is likelihood. For this proxy, we choose an 8 dimensional bilateral domain over spatial position, motion and relative feature affine parameters. A point in the domain given by $\mathbf{p} = [\mathbf{x}; \mathbf{m}; \mathbf{a}]$. The function range is set from

[0 1]. Each match j hypothesizes a 1 value at location $\mathbf{p}_j$. Thus the *observed data* in (2) takes the form:

$$observed\ data = \{\mathbf{p}_j = [\mathbf{x}_j; \mathbf{m}_j; \mathbf{a}_j], \hat{q}_j = 1\}.$$

We can fit a likelihood surface, $f(\mathbf{p})$, to the *observed data* in a manner similar to the bilaterally varying affine of Sec. 3.1. In this case, we have only one smooth function, $q = f(\mathbf{p})$. $f(\mathbf{p})$ is subject to the smoothness constraint

$$\Psi = \int_{\mathbb{R}^8} \frac{|\overline{f}(\omega)|^2}{\overline{g}(\omega)}\, d\omega. \tag{9}$$

Similar to (5), we seek the final $f(\mathbf{p})$ that minimizes the cost

$$E = \sum_{j=1}^{N} huber(1 - f(\mathbf{p}_j)) + \lambda\Psi. \tag{10}$$

Without the H_k offset terms in Sec. 3.1, the Fourier smoothness in (9) causes the $f(\mathbf{p})$ function to return to zero unless given correspondence data biases it to 1. The robust fitting provided by both the Huber function and the smoothness requirement ensures that the cost in (10) does not fit the given data blindly but rejects correspondence clusters without sufficient support.

As in (7), from [10] we know that $f(\mathbf{p})$ and Ψ can be re-parametrized in terms of a N-dimensional $\mathbf{w}$ vector.

$$f(\mathbf{p}) = \sum_{j=1}^{N} \mathbf{w}(j)g(\mathbf{p} - \mathbf{p}_j, \gamma), \quad \Psi = \mathbf{w}^T G \mathbf{w} \tag{11}$$

This allows gradient descent minimization of cost in (10), which is convex in $\mathbf{w}$.

$f(\mathbf{p})$ in (11) forms a motion proxy which indicates whether matches at a specific $\mathbf{p}$ location should be considered an inlier. An example with a simplified $\mathbf{p} = [x\ u]^T$ is shown in Fig. 1. Interestingly, algorithms that iteratively grow seed matches [28,29,30] exploit a similar coherence. By biasing the matching search radius towards the surroundings of pre-existing matches, they implicitly update a bilateral field with likelihood potentials similar to Fig. 1. This may explain why, despite having no explicit smoothing function, such techniques provide matching results with a strong sense of overall coherence (albeit with some outliers).

3.3 One-to-Many Mapping

Observe that the bilateral motion models indicate likely motion directions, rather than specify a one-to-one mapping between images. While inconvenient, the one-to-many mapping reflects the reality of multiple motion layers. For a foreground image point, its alternative motion hypothesis reflects the estimated motion of the occluded background. For a background image point, the alternative motion hypothesis suggests its position if it were actually part of the foreground. Due to this ambiguity, bilateral motion models must be integrated with some image measure (such as gray-level value or SIFT descriptors) to provide a final match location. In practice, for independently obtained matching hypothesis, the motion model can reliably distinguish between inliers and outliers, through a thresholding based on deviation from the model. The discrimination is surprisingly good. Even when the given point correspondences contain many outliers, the computed motion model can preserve a large fraction of the inliers, while eliminating all outliers. An example can be seen in the inlier recall of Fig. 2c) with more rigorous analysis performed in Sec. 4.1. Apart from validating matches, the model can also be used to search for desired features as discussed in Sec. 5.2.

3.4 Implementation

This section gives a broad overview of the computation of bilateral models from feature correspondence. We primarily use A-SIFT [1] for matching. The SIFT threshold is set at $t = 0.82$. This incurs many more outliers than the typical $t = 0.66$. However, for wide baselines, it provides nearly an order of magnitude more inlier matches as seen in Fig. 8. The inliers at the relaxed threshold are also more evenly distributed, allowing for better motion modeling. The spatial coordinates of features are Hartley normalized [31] to allow parameters to be invariant to image size. We compute the likelihood field given by $f(\mathbf{p})$ in (11) by finding the $\mathbf{w}$ that minimizes the energy function E in (10). We accept as inliers all matches with likelihood greater than 0.5 (i.e. $f(\mathbf{p}_j) > 0.5$). This thresholding is deliberately weak and there are still outliers remaining. The inlier set obtained from the likelihood function is used to obtain a bilaterally varying affine in (3), (8) by finding the H_k, $\mathbf{w}_k$ values that minimize the energy in (5). A match $\mathbf{p} = [\, x\ y\ u\ v\,]^T$ is accepted if $(q_x(\mathbf{p}) - (x + u))^2 + (q_y(\mathbf{p}) - (y + v))^2 < 0.01$. The likelihood cost has lower long range ambiguity (removes extreme outliers) but does not validate matches finely (will accept matches with some localization error). Its simpler formulation also makes it more stable. The bilateral affine penalizes localization error but will occasionally accept gross outliers if they coincide with the affine. While the stages can theoretically be integrated into a single cost, they are computed separately for speed. If there too many points, we perform random sub-sampling to keep computation time constant.

Once the bilateral model is computed, we can use it to validate matching hypothesis. In this paper, our matching hypothesis are SIFT matches with no nearest neighbor thresholding but other methods of generating hypothesis can be considered. Fig. 4 gives a system overview.

Fig. 4. System overview: to obtain large numbers of high quality matches, we compute bilateral motion fields according to noisy hypothesis set, and use the model to validate hypothesized matching without nearest neighbor thresholding.

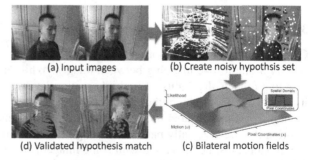

(a) Input images

(b) Create noisy hypothsis set

(d) Validated hypothesis match

(c) Bilateral motion fields

4 Experiments and Discussion

This section focuses on empirical evaluation. Images are evaluated at 480×640 resolution. For data with known camera pose, an inlier is a match whose deviation from epipolar geometry is less than 5 pixels. An outlier is one that deviates more than 40 pixels (due to large scale changes, this is not especially generous). The strict threshold for inliers and outliers, ensures that algorithms are neither penalized nor rewarded based on classification of ambiguous matches. We urge readers to view the supplementary material which contains many images and visualizations of the empirical results.

4.1 Inlier-Outlier Discrimination for Measuring Motion Model Quality

The bilateral motion model does not define a one-to-one correspondence between images, making direct quantitative evaluation difficult. However, the overall correctness of the model and robutsness of its computation can be indirectly measured via its ability to discriminate between inlier and outlier correspondences. While many modern outlier removal techniques work robustly at standard 0.66 A-SIFT thresholds, our evaluation uses a more challenging 0.82 threshold[3]. For wide baselines, this also has the practical advantage of providing many more inliers as illustrated in Fig. 8. *Occ* [25] (an excellent outlier detector for general motion) forms the baseline. One measure of inlier-outlier

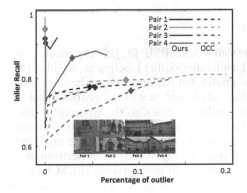

Fig. 5. Recall and % outliers between image pairs, with varying algorithm parameters (diamonds indicate default parameters). Occ [25] is the baseline. The recall value where the curves first intersect outliers = 0 represents the maximum number of inliers that can be retained if no outliers are tolerated. Apart from highly repetitive scenes (blue and red curves), our curves are vertical lines on the outliers = 0 axis. Our default parameters provide over 90% recall with no outliers for many scenes.

discrimination is the percentage of of inliers sacrificed to eliminate outliers. We perform this analysis on wide baseline image pairs chosen from Strecha's dataset [32] . Results are shown in Fig. 5. Pair 1, 2 are the first and last images of [33]'s "cannonical" sampling of Strecha's Dataset. Pair 3, 4 are chosen as difficult cases for our algorithms as they involve both wide baselines and strong image self similarity. Observe that local fitting of *Occ* trades a large percentage of inliers to remove the final few outliers. In contrast, for the "canonical" Pair 1, 2, our lines are vertical on the outlier = 0 axis, indicating little need to trade inlier recall for outlier removal. For repetitive scenes like Pairs 3, 4, there is indeed a trade-off but performance is still substantially better.

---

[3] Ideally, we would evaluate directly on matches without thresholding. However, the noise level is too high for all tested algorithms.

We also use the entire viewpoint change section of Hienly's dataset [33] for evaluation. This includes many images with extreme illumination and viewpoint changes. For
each set, we use the first image as a base and match the rest to it. We compared our
results against epipolar RANSAC [34] and MLESAC [35], implemented by [36]. We
also evaluated piecewise homographic RANSAC (RCM homo) [18] and Occ [25], run
at their default parameters. Results are shown below

	Ours	epipolar RANSAC [34,35]	RCM homo [18]	Occ [25]
Images with outliers	**5/35**	18/35, 24/35	6/35	25/35
Precision (1-% outliers)	0.987	0.947, 0.963	0.966	0.983
Inlier recall	0.928	0.873, 0.886	0.561	0.733
F-Measure	**0.957**	0.908, 0.923	0.709	0.839

Our bilateral motion models provide good recall and precision compared to other outlier
rejection methods. Our recall is even comparable with epipolar RANSAC which is a
valid motion model for test images. Apart from precision and recall, the flexibility of
bilateral models allow us to tune parameters to a level where recall remains high despite
having zeros outliers for many image pairs. As discussed in Fig. 5, for other methods,
removing the last few outliers often involves discarding a large percentage of inliers. It
is important to bear in mind that these methods are not mutually exclusive. As we do
not enforce the epipolar constraint, RANSAC can still be run as a post-processor on our
correspondences.

4.2 Independent Motion

We evaluate independent motion on images from AdelideRMF [37]. Every image pair
contains large independent motions. Ground truth inlier-outlier labeling is provided for
noisy pre-computed correspondences. As the small set of background matches are automatically labeled outliers, the dataset systematically lowers precision statistics of some
scenes. Thus, the number of images with no outliers is not directly meaningful. Images used are the same as those in [18] and results for other RANSAC algorithms on
the same data can be found in [18]. As feature orientation is not given, we modified
our algorithm to use only spatial location information. Fig. 6 shows our performance
improvement over multi-fundamental (RCM fund), multi-homographic (RCM homo)
RANSAC [18] and Occ.

Fig. 6. Ex-
ample of our
performance
on independent
motion data [37].
Statistics for
inlier recall and
precision are
given below.

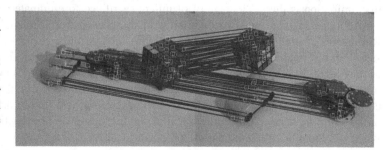

	Ours Precision	Ours Recall	RCM fund Precision	RCM fund Recall	RCM homo Precision	RCM homo Recall	Occ Precision	Occ Recall
dinobooks	0.8062	0.8927	0.7519	0.9902	1.0000	0.1659	0.8672	0.5415
toycubecar	1.0000	0.9063	0.8880	0.8672	1.0000	0.7734	0.9878	0.6328
cubebreadtoychips	0.9712	0.9874	0.9271	0.9582	1.0000	0.3264	0.9943	0.7238
carchipscube	1.0000	0.8762	0.9196	0.9810	1.0000	0.8000	1.0000	0.7429
breadtoycar	0.9892	0.8364	0.8560	0.9727	1.0000	0.5364	1.0000	0.6909
breadcubechips	1.0000	0.8591	0.9013	0.9195	1.0000	0.6443	1.0000	0.6779
breadcartoychips	1.0000	0.9935	0.8284	0.7161	1.0000	0.6516	1.0000	0.5548
biscuitbookbox	1.0000	0.9444	0.8710	1.0000	1.0000	0.6790	0.9926	0.8272
average	0.9708	0.9120	0.8679	0.9256	1.0000	0.5721	0.9802	0.6740
F-Measure	**0.94**		0.90		0.73		0.80	

Limitations Our algorithm assumes piecewise smooth motion and treats small sets of independently moving matches as outliers. This makes it unsuited for tasks like correspondence on pedestrian scenes, as the algorithm will only focus on the background. In extreme scenarios (large viewpoint change and lighting changes), scenes with strong self similarity can cause ambiguities unresolvable by global coherence. For moderate motions, matches are sufficiently well distributed for global coherence to handle self similar images. Visual examples are given in the supplementary material.

5 Applications

As a general motion model, bilateral functions can extend to many correspondence related problems. This section discusses examples such as expanding a correspondence set, drift free multi-image correspondence and template image search.

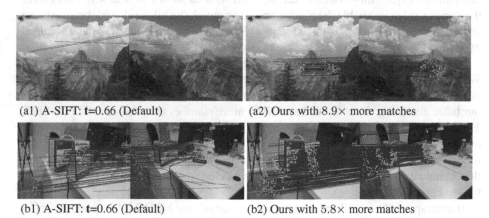

(a1) A-SIFT: t=0.66 (Default)   (a2) Ours with 8.9× more matches

(b1) A-SIFT: t=0.66 (Default)   (b2) Ours with 5.8× more matches

Fig. 7. Top: two views of half-dome, taken a few miles apart, causing parallax in the foreground. Bottom: an office scene with re-arranged stationary. Observe that our algorithm provides many more matches and fewer outliers than standard A-SIFT.

Fig. 8. Inlier numbers (log scale) versus increasing displacement for the *herzjesu* sequence [32]. Vertical bars represents the $-log_{10}$(fraction of inliers). Thresholding varies from 1 (no thresholding) to 0.66 (typical SIFT threshold). A-SIFT controls outlier numbers, at the cost of rejecting many inliers. Our bilateral models retain most inliers, while having no outliers (short vertical bars).

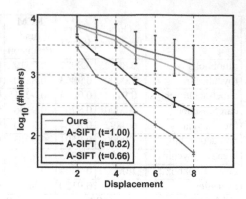

5.1 Additional Correspondence

Applications like Structure from Motion rely on matching algorithms to deliver many correspondences while controlling outlier numbers. Typically, outliers are controlled by a ratio test of nearest neighbor matches. A match is accepted, only if its descriptor matching score (zero is best) is below a certain fraction of the second best match. A typical ratio threshold is $t = 1/1.5 = 0.66$ [38]. This threshold ensures that as baselines increase, the number of outliers remain restricted to a small handful but at the price of removing an enormous percentage of the inliers (often over 90%) from wide baseline image pairs. A typical SIFT threshold is shown by the red, $t = 0.66$ curve in Fig. 8, while the maximum number of inliers is shown by the blue $t = 1$ curve.

Our bilateral models can procure many additional correspondence as seen in Fig. 7). These results rely on two properties of bilateral functions. Firstly, as shown in Sec. 4.1, the functions can be run on SIFT thresholds that are much weaker than usual. This produces substantially more, better distributed potential inlier matches. The accompanying explosion of outliers can be controlled as shown in Sec. 4.1. This makes the correspondences usable. Secondly, once computed, the bilateral model can validate new matching hypothesis, using the steps in Sec. 3.4. These hypothesis can be obtained by setting $t = 1$. This produces the green curve of Fig. 8.

We applied this algorithm to the 35 image pairs of the Heinly dataset of Sec. 4.1. We incurred no new outlier images compared to our basic outlier rejection technique in Sec. 4.1 (number remained at 5). However, we average of 225% more matches than our basic algorithm. Overall, we have 470% more matches than standard 0.66 A-SIFT. This occurs despite the high noise level at $t = 1$, with image pairs having an average of only 25% inliers. Note that the averages mask extreme cases. In one example, our model successfully filtered an inlier ratio of below 5%. It had 4100% more matches than standard A-SIFT with no outliers. More modest improvements are recorded when the baseline is narrow.

If correspondence numbers are important, quasi-dense NRDC [30] techniques offer a viable alternative. While NRDC provides many more matches, its average correspondence error of 5.94 pixels is significantly higher than our 3.16, and it had 17/35 images with outliers, compared to our 5/35. However, the bilateral model's primary advantage lies in a graceful handling of difficult scenes. Fig. 9 shows NRDC's error distribution has a heavy tail. This is due to large sections of erroneous correspondence on difficult scenes. Ideally, NRDC should be fused with our bilateral functions, however, this is a research direction we have not yet explored.

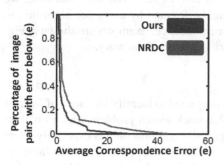

Fig. 9. Tail distribution of average correspondence error for test image pairs. In difficult cases, NRDC gives extremely high average errors (in one case reaching 43 pixels). In contrast, bilateral models have stabler error, with average error exceeding 15 pixels only once.

5.2 Drift-Free Multi-Image Correspondence

Multi-image correspondence is a perennial computer vision problem. Many algorithms like factorization [39], tri-focal tensor [40] and camera calibration [41] require correspondence across multiple wide-baseline images. However, feature matchers seldom reliably match the same feature across multiple frames, while feature trackers are prone

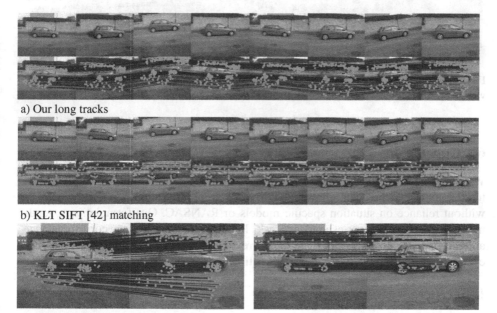

a) Our long tracks

b) KLT SIFT [42] matching

c) Zoom in on our first and last view   d) Zoom in on KLT's first and last view

Fig. 10. Matching across the car sequence. Observe that KLT-SIFT tracking drifts. A clear example can be seen at the car's front wheel.

to drift. Bilateral motion models can solve this problem as they can find a specified feature's matching location in another image. This is achieved by proposing potential matching locations which are verified using local information. By matching all images to a base frame, the formulation avoids drift. In fact, to save computational time, we automatically choose the widest baseline (quickly detected by using our algorithm to match low resolution images) pair to begin correspondence. Examples are shown in Fig. 10. Implementation details and more results are in the supplementary.

5.3   Needle in the Haystack

When multiple agents operate collaboratively, they need to identify locations of interest to each other. This becomes a needle-in-the-haystack search problem which involves locating a template within a much larger image. Bilateral matching is especially adept at this problem as it produces many matches and few outliers. This creates a large response gap between image pairs from similar and different locations, an ideal situation when comparing sub-images. In practice, we decompose the large image into multiple sub-images. These are ranked based on similarity to the template using gist [43]. Bilateral matching is applied on the top 10 candidates to perform the final selection and matching. Results are shown in Fig. 11. Details and alternative solutions are discussed in the supplementary.

(a) Input Images   (b) Matching

Fig. 11. Examples of our algorithm localizing a template in a large image. Note that the template was taken at street level while the target image is from an overlooking roof.

6   Conclusion

We proposed a principled solution for modeling of general motion from noisy, scattered features matches. This allows reliable recovery of large numbers of inlier matches without reliance on situation specific models or RANSAC. Our formulation extends naturally to associated correspondence tasks like drift free multi-image correspondence and template localization. Applying the current formulation for dense correspondence estimation [44] is an interesting future direction.

References

1. Morel, J., Yu, G.: Asift: A new framework for fully affine invariant image comparison. SIAM Journal on Imaging Sciences 2(2), 438–469 (2009)
2. Lowe, D.G.: Distinctive image features from scale-invariant keypoints. IJCV 60(2), 91–110 (2004)

3. Bay, H., Tuytelaars, T., Van Gool, L.: SURF: Speeded up robust features. In: Leonardis, A., Bischof, H., Pinz, A. (eds.) ECCV 2006, Part I. LNCS, vol. 3951, pp. 404–417. Springer, Heidelberg (2006)
4. Fischler, M.A., Bolles, R.C.: Random sample consensus: A paradigm for model fitting with applications to image analysis and automated cartography. Comm. of the ACM 24, 381–395 (1981)
5. Raguram, R., Frahm, J.-M., Pollefeys, M.: A comparative analysis of ransac techniques leading to adaptive real-time random sample consensus. In: Forsyth, D., Torr, P., Zisserman, A. (eds.) ECCV 2008, Part II. LNCS, vol. 5303, pp. 500–513. Springer, Heidelberg (2008)
6. Longuet-Higgins, H.C.: A computer algorithm for reconstructing a scene from two projections. Nature, 133–135 (1981)
7. Brown, M., Lowe, D.: Automatic panoramic image stitching using invariant features. IJCV 1(74), 59–73 (2007)
8. Serradell, E., Özuysal, M., Lepetit, V., Fua, P., Moreno-Noguer, F.: Combining geometric and appearance priors for robust homography estimation. In: Daniilidis, K., Maragos, P., Paragios, N. (eds.) ECCV 2010, Part III. LNCS, vol. 6313, pp. 58–72. Springer, Heidelberg (2010)
9. Sprengel, R., Rohr, K., Stiehl, H.S.: Thin-plate spline approximation for image registration. In: Proc. of Engineering in Medicine and Biology Society (1996)
10. Lin, W.Y., Cheng, M.M., Zheng, S., Lu, J., Crook, N.: Robust non-parametric data fitting for correspondence modeling. In: IEEE ICCV (2013)
11. Yuille, A.L., Grywacz, N.M.: The motion coherence theory. In: IEEE ICCV (1988)
12. Black, M.J., Anandan, P.: The robust estimation of multiple motions: Parametric and piecewise-smooth flow fields. Computer Vision and Image Understanding (1996)
13. Ye, M., Haralick, R.M., Shapiro, L.G.: Estimating piecewise-smooth optical flow with global matching and graduated optimization. PAMI (2003)
14. Sinha, S.N., Steedly, D., Szeliski, R.: Piecewise planar stereo for image-based rendering. In: ICCV (2009)
15. Myronenko, A., Song, X., Carreira-Perpinan, M.: Non-rigid point set registration: Coherent point drift. In: NIPS (2007)
16. Lin, W.Y., Liu, S., Matsushita, Y., Ng, T.T., Cheong, L.F.: Smoothly varying affine stitching. In: IEEE CVPR (2011)
17. Raguram, R., Frahm, J.M.: Recon: Scale-adaptive robust estimation via residual consensus. In: ICCV (2011)
18. Pham, T.T., Chin, T.J., Yu, J., Suter, D.: The random cluster model for robust geometric fitting. In: CVPR (2012)
19. Weinzaepfel, P., Revaud, J., Harchaoui, Z., Schmid, C.: Deepflow: Large displacement optical flow with deep matching. In: ICCV (2013)
20. Brox, T., Malik, J.: Large displacement optical flow: Descriptor matching in variational motion estimation. IEEE TPAMI (2010)
21. Horn, B., Schunck, B.: Determining optical flow. Artificial Intelligence (1981)
22. Lucas, B., Kanade, T.: An iterative image registration technique with an application to stereo vision. In: Proceedings of Imaging Understanding Workshop (1981)
23. Torresani, L., Kolmogorov, V., Rother, C.: Feature correspondence via graph matching: Models and global optimization. In: Forsyth, D., Torr, P., Zisserman, A. (eds.) ECCV 2008, Part II. LNCS, vol. 5303, pp. 596–609. Springer, Heidelberg (2008)
24. Garg, R., Roussos, A., Agapito, L.: Dense variational reconstruction of non-rigid surfaces from monocular video. In: CVPR (2013)
25. Pizarro, D., Bartoli, A.: Feature-based deformable surface detection with self-occlusion. IJCV (2012)

26. Tomasi, C., Manduch, R.: Bilateral filtering for gray and color images. In: IEEE ICCV (1998)
27. Xiao, J., Cheng, H., Sawhney, H.S., Rao, C., Isnardi, M.: Bilateral filtering-based optical flow estimation with occlusion detection. In: Leonardis, A., Bischof, H., Pinz, A. (eds.) ECCV 2006, Part I. LNCS, vol. 3951, pp. 211–224. Springer, Heidelberg (2006)
28. Barnes, C., Shechtman, E., Goldman, D.B., Finkelstein, A.: The generalized PatchMatch correspondence algorithm. In: Daniilidis, K., Maragos, P., Paragios, N. (eds.) ECCV 2010, Part III. LNCS, vol. 6313, pp. 29–43. Springer, Heidelberg (2010)
29. Lhuiller, M., Quan, L.: A quasi-dense approach to surface reconstruction from uncalibrated images. PAMI (2005)
30. HaCohen, Y., Shechtman, E., Goldman, D.B., Lischinski, D.: Non-rigid dense correspondence with applications for image enhancement. ACM TOG (2011)
31. Hartley, R.I.: In defense of the eight-point algorithm. IEEE TPAMI 19(6), 580–593 (1997)
32. Strecha, C., von Hansen, W., Gool, L.V., Fua, P., Thoennessen, U.: On benchmarking camera calibration and multi-view stereo for high resolution imagery. In: CVPR (2008)
33. Heinly, J., Dunn, E., Frahm, J.-M.: Comparative evaluation of binary features. In: Fitzgibbon, A., Lazebnik, S., Perona, P., Sato, Y., Schmid, C. (eds.) ECCV 2012, Part II. LNCS, vol. 7573, pp. 759–773. Springer, Heidelberg (2012)
34. Kovesi, P.D.: MATLAB and Octave functions for computer vision and image processing, http://www.csse.uwa.edu.au/~pk/research/matlabfns/
35. Torr, P.H.S., Zisserman, A.: Mlesac: A new robust estimator with application to estimating image geometry. Computer Vision and Image Understanding (2010)
36. Konouchine, A., Gaganov, V., Veznevets, V.: A new maximum likelihood robust estimator. Computer Vision and Image Understanding (2005)
37. Wong, H.S., Chin, T.J., Yu, J., Suter, D.: Dynamic and hierarchical multi-structure geometric model fitting. In: ICCV (2011)
38. Vedaldi, A., Fulkerson, B.: VLFeat: An open and portable library of computer vision algorithms (2008)
39. Tomasi, C., Kanade, T.: Shape and motion from image streams under orthography: a factorization method. IJCV (1992)
40. Torr, P., Zisserman, A.: Robust parameterization and computation of the trifocal tensor. Image and Vision Computing 15, 591–605 (1997)
41. Agrawal, M.: Practical camera auto calibration using semidefinite programming. In: WMVC (2007)
42. Sharma, A.: (2004), http://www.cs.cmu.edu/abhishek/softwares.html
43. Oliva, A., Torralba, A.: Modeling the shape of the scene: A holistic representation of the spatial envelope. IJCV (2001)
44. Yang, H., Lin, W.Y., Lu, J.: Daisy filter flow: A generalized discrete approach to dense correspondences. In: CVPR (2014)

VCDB: A Large-Scale Database
for Partial Copy Detection in Videos

Yu-Gang Jiang, Yudong Jiang, and Jiajun Wang

School of Computer Science, Shanghai Key Laboratory of Intelligent
Information Processing, Fudan University, Shanghai, China
ygj@fudan.edu.cn

Abstract. The task of partial copy detection in videos aims at finding
if one or more segments of a query video have (transformed) copies in a
large dataset. Since collecting and annotating large datasets of real partial copies are extremely time-consuming, previous video copy detection
research used either small-scale datasets or large datasets with simulated
partial copies by imposing several pre-defined transformations (e.g., photometric or geometric changes). While the simulated datasets were useful
for research, it is unknown how well the techniques developed on such
data work on real copies, which are often too complex to be simulated. In
this paper, we introduce a large-scale video copy database (VCDB) with
over 100,000 Web videos, containing more than 9,000 copied segment
pairs found through careful manual annotation. We further benchmark
a baseline system on VCDB, which has demonstrated state-of-the-art
results in recent copy detection research. Our evaluation suggests that
existing techniques—which have shown near-perfect results on the simulated benchmarks—are far from satisfactory in detecting complex real
copies. We believe that the release of VCDB will largely advance the
research around this challenging problem.

Keywords: Video copy detection, benchmark dataset, frame matching,
temporal alignment.

1   Introduction

With the popularity of video capture devices and network sharing activities,
a huge amount of videos are being transmitted online. This brings increased
concerns about copyright issues due to the very low cost of copying a video (or
a small fraction in it) and massively distributing it on the Internet. Therefore,
video copy detection, which aims at automatically identifying copies in a large
dataset, has received significant research attention.

The task of video copy detection is very challenging because of the complex
content variations that widely exist among the copied segments, such as scale
and lighting changes. Research on copy detection has benefited significantly from
the invention of local invariant features like the SIFT [1]. Indexing structures
such as the inverted file have also been popularly adopted to enable efficient detection [2]. While great progress has been made, many recent works focused only

D. Fleet et al. (Eds.): ECCV 2014, Part IV, LNCS 8692, pp. 357–371, 2014.
© Springer International Publishing Switzerland 2014

Fig. 1. Three pairs of frames extracted from copied video segments in VCDB. All the copies were found directly from the Internet through careful manual annotation. The complex forms of transformations in VCDB pose new challenges to video copy detection research, as the existing datasets were mostly generated "artificially" by imposing a very few number of pre-defined transformations.

on entire video-level copy detection [3, 4], where a query video and a reference video normally share very long copied segments. Annotations in these datasets were provided only at video-level, i.e., whether or not two videos are copies of each other, preventing research on finer-grained partial copy detection where the copied segments are short and may be even just one single frame. Precise partial copy detection is desired particularly in large datasets so that copyright protection becomes easier.

Because the manual annotation of real partial copies is very difficult and extremely time consuming, recent research on partial copy detection has mostly been done on small scale datasets with *simulated* copies [2], produced by imposing pre-defined transformations like modifications in scale and contrast. While the simulated datasets have been very useful, it is unknown how well the state-of-the-art approaches work on real copies, many of which are too complex to be simulated by just applying a few pre-defined transformations.

This paper introduces a large-scale video copy detection database (VCDB)[1] that aims to address the aforementioned shortcomings of the existing datasets. We construct a dataset of over 100,000 videos downloaded from the Internet, covering a wide range of topics like movies and sports. Through careful manual annotation, approximately 9,200 partial copies were found between around 6,000 pairs of videos. Figure 1 shows a few example frames in the found video segment copies, where the transformations between each pair are very complex. To set up a good baseline and understand the limitations of the existing solutions, we benchmark a popular method that has demonstrated state-of-the-art copy detection results in the literature. We also compare a few popular techniques in this area and provide insightful discussions.

The main contribution of this work is the construction of a large dataset with realistic partial video copies, which requires significant efforts in both design and annotation. Through benchmarking state-of-the-art techniques on the new

---

[1] Available at: http://www.yugangjiang.info/research/VCDB/

comprehensive dataset, we observe that the systems that have produced near-perfect results on the simulated datasets like TRECVID [5, 6] are still far from satisfactory. This opens up new opportunities to continue further research around this problem to make copy detection algorithms practically more effective.

The rest of the paper is organized as follows. We review related works in Section 2. Section 3 describes the construction and annotation of VCDB. Section 4 briefly introduces the baseline system and Section 5 discusses the evaluation results. Finally, Section 6 concludes this paper.

2 Related Work

We first discuss related datasets for video copy detection, and then review a few representative approaches.

Video Copy Detection Datasets: Although the problem of video copy detection has been investigated for decades, very few benchmark datasets have been constructed. Many researchers constructed their own datasets and did not release them for cross-site comparison. For instance, Indyk et al. [7] downloaded 2,000 clips of news, music videos and movie trailers. The duration of these clips is between 2 and 5 minutes. Copies were generated by the authors using pre-defined transformations including inserting TV logos and using various cam-cordings, frame rates, etc. Joly et al. [8] collected 1,040 hours of TV video data stored in MPEG1 format, containing contents in various categories like commercials, news, sports and TV shows. Copies were also created by imposing some transformations.

Perhaps the first well-known public benchmark is the Muscle-VCD, created by Law-To et al. [9], which contains around 100 hours of videos collected from the Internet, TV archives and movies. Videos are in different resolutions and formats. There are two kinds of queries representing two practical situations: (1) ST1: entire video copy (normally between 5 minutes and 1 hour), where the videos may be slightly recoded and/or noised. (2) ST2: partial video copy, where two videos only share one or more short segments. This scenario was also simulated by using video-editing softwares to impose a few transformations. The "transformed" segments were later used as queries to search their original versions in the dataset. The duration of a segment normally ranges from 1 second to 1 minute.

The importance of video copy detection was also recognized by the U.S. National Institute of Standards and Technology, whose annual TRECVID evaluation [10] included a separate task on copy detection in 2008. Each year a benchmark dataset was generated and released only to the registered participants of the task. The TRECVID datasets were constructed in a very similar way to the Muscle-VCD. The 2008 edition, used in several recent works like [6, 2], contains 200 hours of TV programs and around 2,000 query clips. Each query was generated using a software to randomly extract a segment from the dataset and impose a few pre-defined transformations. The copy detection task

Table 1. Comparison of video copy detection datasets, sorted by construction year. VCDB is the only one containing real partial copies.

	Reference	Year	Partial Copy	Type of Copies
Indyk et al.	[7]	1999	N	Real
Joly et al.	[8]	2003	Y	Simulated
Muscle-VCD	[9]	2007	Y	Simulated
CC_Web	[3]	2007	N	Real
TRECVID 2008	[10]	2008	Y	Simulated
UQ_Video	[4]	2011	N	Real
VCDB	—	2014	Y	Real

of TRECVID was terminated in 2011 because near-perfect results were reported. However, as will be shown later in this paper, the existing approaches cannot detect many real partial copies.

Different from the datasets mentioned earlier, which are all simulated based on pre-defined transformations, a few datasets have real video copies directly obtained from the Internet. The CC_Web dataset constructed by Wu et al. [3] has been popularly used, which consists of 12,790 videos collected from the video search results of Google, YouTube and Yahoo!. Another recent dataset, called UQ_Video [4], was constructed by extending the CC_Web with more background distraction videos. Both datasets were created for near-duplicate video detection, which by definition is different from the copy detection problem. For instance, two videos containing the same scenes but originally captured from two different cameras could be near-duplicates but not copies. Many copies in the two datasets are easy to be detected as the transformations among them are very limited. In addition, the labels in the datasets are only available on video-level, indicating whether or not two videos are copies of each other without the timestamps of the copied segments. Therefore they are not suitable for evaluating the techniques of partial copy detection. We summarize these datasets and compare them with VCDB in Table 1.

Video Copy Detection Approaches: Several noteworthy copy detection systems have been proposed in the past decade. We briefly describe a few representative ones. Works on entire video-level copy detection relied on the use of global features like color histogram and local features like the LBP [11, 3, 4]. Reasonably good results were obtained as the samples used in the experiments were mostly simple with limited content variations.

To accurately locate partial copies, particularly those under severe content transformations, more advanced techniques are needed. In [5], local features are extracted and quantized using the bag-of-visual-words (BoV) representations, which are then indexed by an inverted file structure for efficient retrieval. In [2], local descriptors were also used, but were quantized into an aggregated representation similar to the Fisher Vectors [12, 13]. The aggregated features were then encoded using an indexing structure for efficient frame retrieval or matching.

Finally, a modified Hough voting scheme was used to fuse the frame matching results and produce segment level copy predictions. Similarly, another system introduced by Tan et al. [14] used standard bag-of-words representations of the local descriptors, which were indexed in an inverted file structure. The matched local descriptors across two frames were further filtered by a geometric consistency verification method, which is able to reject outlier wrong matches that are geometrically not consistent to a majority of matches. After that, a temporal network model was constructed and the partial video copies can be found by solving a network flow optimization problem.

As can be summarized from the above works, most copy detection systems start from the extraction of local features, which are then used for frame-level matching. Finally, the frame matching results are sent into a temporal alignment method to identify the copied segments. The main differences of these systems lie in the choices of the efficient descriptor matching method (e.g., using the product quantization [15] or its extended version [16]), the geometric verification scheme (e.g., using the Weak Geometric Consistency [5] or its variant [17]), or the final copy segment identification algorithm. The first two steps, i.e., the local descriptor matching and geometric verification, are technically very similar to the approaches for image-based object retrieval, which has been extensively studied in the vision community [18, 5, 19–22].

3   Creating VCDB

3.1   Database Collection

All the videos in VCDB were downloaded from video-sharing websites YouTube and MetaCafe. In order to collect representative partial copies, we started from 28 carefully selected queries, covering a wide range of topics such as commercials, movies, music videos, public speeches, sports, etc. We downloaded the top returned search results of the queries from the two websites, and manually picked on average around 20 videos per query. These videos are all relevant to the query and many of them share partial copies. In total we have 528 videos (approximately 27 hours) in the core dataset, forming around 6,000 candidate pairs ($\binom{20}{2} \times 28$) requiring manual annotation.

To make the task of copy detection in VCDB close to the realistic application scenario, we further downloaded 100,000 videos from YouTube as background distraction videos. We skimmed over these distraction videos to reduce the chance of having copies of videos in the core dataset. The final VCDB consists of both the core dataset and the distraction videos.

3.2   Annotation

Annotating 6,000 pairs of videos on frame level is an extremely difficult task, particularly when many copies in the core dataset are short segments. Figure 2 gives an example of multiple partial copies between two videos. Manually identifying the boundaries of the segments is very time-consuming. Different from

Fig. 2. An example of a video pair containing multiple partial copies. Similar cases are frequently seen in VCDB.

simple image or video annotation tasks that can be performed on crowdsourcing websites like the Amazon MTurk, the task of annotating partial copies is sophisticated as it requires more inputs with precise operations. This makes it very difficult to design a good interface on the MTurk for the novice workers. We therefore employed seven part-time annotators, who were well trained before performing the task.

An annotation tool was developed with careful design to finish the task efficiently. Each time two videos were shown to an annotator, who can view them separately or in parallel with different start times to compare them. The annotator can then input the timestamps of all the found copied segments. To speed up the effort, the transitivity property of the video copies was utilized in the annotation tool. Specifically, if two segments are copies of the same segment in another video, they are very likely to be copies of each other. Notice that the transitivity property does not always hold, since the bridging segment may contain two different scenes (a.k.a. picture-in-picture) that are copies of the two segments respectively (see an example of picture-in-picture in the middle of Figure 1). Therefore, the tool will automatically recommend these *candidate* segment pairs from transitivity propagation to the annotator for confirmation. This function can largely reduce the annotation time, because the annotator rarely needs to manually specify the boundary frames of these segments. The entire annotation process finished in about one month (around 700 man-hours).

3.3   Statistics

As a benchmark dataset, it is important that the copies in VCDB are representative and diverse. In total, 9,236 pairs of partial copies were found. Figure 3 gives one example copy from videos downloaded by each of the 28 queries. As can be clearly seen, there are a wide range of content transformations among the partial copies in VCDB, which cannot be fully covered by the very few predefined transformations used in generating the existing datasets with simulated copies.

We manually went through all the 9,236 pairs to count the number of copies according to a few major transformations popularly used in generating the simulated datasets. We found that around 36% of them contain "insertion of

Fig. 3. Example frame copies from the videos downloaded by the 28 queries, respectively. Ordered from left to right and top to bottom, the corresponding queries are topics about commercials (3), movies (11), music video (1), public speeches (3), sports (6), surveillance event (1), and others (3).

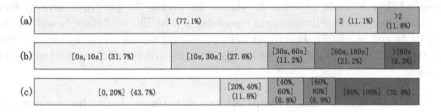

Fig. 4. Statistics of VCDB: (a) the number of partial copies per video pair, among those having at least one copy; (b) the duration of the partial copies; and (c) the percentage of the duration of the copy segments in the corresponding parent videos. See texts for more explanations.

patterns", 18% are from "camcording", 27% have scale changes, and 2% contain "picture in picture" patterns. These percentages are quite different from that in the simulated datasets. Many "insertion of patterns" copies exist in the practical scenario because of the logos of different TV channels, and the "picture in picture" patterns frequently seen in the simulated copies do not seem to be popular in real cases.

Figure 4 further shows some statistics of VCDB. We see that, among the video pairs that have at least one partial copy, nearly 80% of them contain just

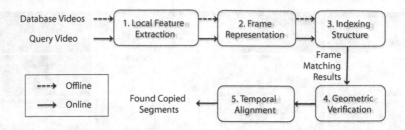

Fig. 5. The general framework of a video copy detection system.

one copied segment and as high as 20% contain two or more partial copies. In addition, 32% of the found copied segments are less than 10 seconds and another 28% are between 10 and 30 seconds, which are very short. More importantly, according to Figure 4(c), we see that 44% of the copies are shorter than 1/5 of their parent videos and only 31% of them occupy over 80% of the parent videos. This confirms the fact that most copies in VCDB are partial video segments.

4   The Baseline System

To evaluate the capability of current copy detection techniques, and also to understand the difficulty of VCDB, we benchmark a system that has produced strong performances on various datasets. This also sets up a good baseline for future systems to compare against. Most state-of-the-art video copy detection systems follow a basic pipeline as shown in Figure 5. The first several core components of the baseline system (modules 1–4 of Figure 5) are based on the work of Herve et al. [5]. For temporal alignment, we adopt and compare two options [14, 2]. In the following we briefly describe the techniques used in all the modules.

Feature Extraction and Frame Representation: First, frames are uniformly sampled from the videos and local SIFT descriptors are computed on each of the frames. The popular BoV representation is then used to quantize the SIFT features from each frame. The codebook used in generating the BoV representations is constructed by hierarchical k-means, which segments the SIFT feature space into many Voronoi cells.

Indexing and Hamming Embedding: The inverted file structure is adopted to index the frames for efficient online frame matching. Hamming embedding is used [5] to alleviate the effect of quantization errors in the traditional BoV representation. Specifically, the key idea of Hamming embedding is to partition each Voronoi cell into a few subspaces. Each subspace is represented by a very short binary code, so that the feature similarity within the cell can be measured by the Hamming distance that can be efficiently computed. With Hamming embedding, two SIFT feature matches only when they fall in the same Voronoi cell and their Hamming distance within the cell is smaller than a threshold. This is better than directly using more Voronoi cells (i.e., more clusters) because using more cells will incur significant quantization error [23].

Geometric Verification: The SIFT matches found by the inverted file and Hamming embedding are not always correct. One important reason is that the BoV representation and the indexing structure do not capture any geometric information such as the orientations of the local image patches. The matching accuracy can be improved by geometric verification as a post-processing step to exclude "wrong" matches that are not consistent with a majority of matches geometrically. For this, a weak geometric consistency (WGC) method [5] is adopted. WGC is based on the angle and scale parameters of the SIFT descriptors, which are used to adjust the matching scores of video frames. The underlying assumption is that the matching score of a frame pair should be enhanced if the matched SIFT features are transformed by consistent angles and scales. Similarly the score should be reduced if the matched features are transformed inconsistently. As both the angle and the scale parameters are embedded in the SIFT descriptors, WGC can be very efficiently computed. For more details of the Hamming embedding and the WGC, readers are referred to [5].

Alignment by Temporal Network: Two frames are considered to be a copy pair if they have a sufficient number of matched SIFT features over a threshold. The next step is to align the matched frames and identify the copied video segments, by considering both the visual similarity and the temporal information. Note that this alignment process also has the capability of further filtering the wrong frame matches by checking temporal (in)consistency. We adopt two methods to achieve this goal. The first one was proposed by Tan et al. [14], who formulated the problem by network flow optimization. Given a query video Q and a database video R, a temporal network is constructed by querying the top-k similar frames from R using Q. After that directed edges are established across the frames in the top-k lists by chronologically linking the frames according to their timestamps. The value (edge weight) of the link (edge) is the similarity value between the corresponding frames. Finally, optimization is performed to identify the longest path (segment) by considering three constraints: the maximum difference between the timestamps of two successively aligned frames, the minimum length of a copied segment, and the minimum similarity value between the matched frames.

Alignment by Temporal Hough Voting: The second temporal alignment method adopted in this work is called temporal Hough transform proposed in [2]. Denote $s(t_q, t_d) > 0$ as the matching score between a query frame at time t_q and a reference database frame at time t_d. A histogram $h(\delta)$ is computed to accumulate the frame matching scores for the matched pair within a window of δ frames: $h(\delta) = \sum_{t_q \in Y} s(t_q, t_q + \delta)$, where Y is the set of timestamps of the query and $s(t_q, t_q + \delta) = 0$ if the timestamp $t_q + \delta$ does not exist in the database video. Peaks are then searched in the histogram, and the matched segments are identified around the peaks. In addition, because consecutive frames in videos can be visually very similar, we often see bursts of matches which bias the scores returned by the Hough histogram. To alleviate this issue, a re-weighting scheme is adopted to normalize the matching scores. The normalized scores are used as input to compute the histogram $h(\delta)$. This alignment method was used in a system [2] that produced competitive results on the TRECVID dataset of simulated partial copies.

Discussions: Here we briefly discuss the rationale of selecting the baseline techniques. One important guideline is that the selected techniques should be representative and have shown consistently good results on multiple datasets. We underline that, although the methods of [5] and [2] were proposed a few years ago, to our knowledge they still represent a state-of-the-art solution, and systems developed on top of them have demonstrated outstanding performance in competitions such as the TRECVID [10]. Very few new copy detection methods have been developed recently. This is probably because the near-perfect results on the traditional simulated databases have delivered a wrong signal that the video copy detection problem might already be successfully solved. Perhaps the most related approach proposed recently is by Revaud et al. [16], who used a different frame representation called VLAD [13] and an extended version of the product quantization [15] for event retrieval in large video databases. We also implemented this pipeline on VCDB but observed slightly worse results than the adopted baseline. This is probably because the approach was designed for similar video event retrieval, which emphasizes more on similar semantics, not necessarily the same visual patterns, and therefore did not enforce strong geometric consistency of the matched local feature points.

5   Experiments

In this section we discuss experimental results. While our main purpose is to analyze the results of the aforementioned techniques on VCDB, we also conduct experiments on a small and popular benchmark, the Muscle-VCD dataset [9], in order to ensure that all the methods are correctly implemented and to examine the power of the baseline system.

5.1   Muscle-VCD

For this dataset, we focus on the ST2 of partial copies as described in Section 2. In total there are 21 query segments, and performance is evaluated by QF=1 − $|missed\ frames|/|groundtruth\ frames|$ and QS=$(|correct| - |false\ alarm|)/$ $|returned\ segments|$, following [9]. Throughout all the experiments in this work, we use uniform frame sampling to extract two frames every second. Note that using more frames may lead to slightly better results, but evaluating this factor is beyond the focus of this paper.

Using the baseline system with the first temporal alignment method, i.e., the temporal network, we achieve 0.81 for QS and 0.70 for QF. To our knowledge

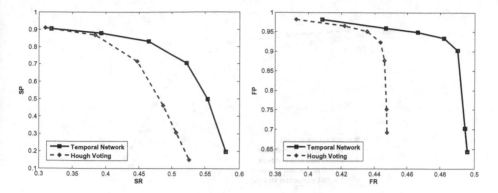

Fig. 6. Precision-recall curves of the baseline system on the core dataset of VCDB, using the two temporal alignment methods respectively. **Left:** segment-level results. **Right:** frame-level results. Overall, the performance is much worse than that reported on the existing datasets with simulated copies, indicating that partial copy detection in realistic videos remains a challenging problem that deserves future research.

the best results achieved on this dataset are 0.86 and 0.76 respectively for the two criteria, reported in [14] where a similar method to the baseline system was used. The small performance gap is mainly due to the use of different geometric verification methods. An improved version of the WGC was used in [14], while our baseline uses the standard WGC.

5.2   VCDB

This subsection presents results on VCDB. We first report performance on the core dataset, and then discuss the results of large scale experiments by incrementally adding the background distraction videos. Each segment of the 9,236 pairs is used as a query. Performance is measured by the standard precision and recall, which are widely adopted and can nicely reflect the power of a copy detection system. A detected pair of copied segments is considered correct if both segments have intersection frames with a ground-truth pair. We do not set a minimum percentage of the overlapped time window because hitting a ground-truth pair with one single frame will be adequate in practical applications such as copyright protection. More formally, the segment-level precision (SP) and recall (SR) are defined as: SP=$|correctly\ retrieved\ segments|/|all\ retrieved\ segments|$ and SR=$|correctly\ retrieved\ segments|/|groundtruth\ copy\ segments|$. In addition, we also measure frame-level precision and recall on the core dataset as auxiliary criteria to understand how accurate the baseline system is, which are defined as: FP=$|correctly\ retrieved\ frames|/|all\ retrieved\ frames|$ and FR=$|correctly\ retrieved\ frames|/|groundtruth\ copy\ frames|$.

Results on the core dataset are shown in Figure 6. To plot the precision-recall curves, we adjust the thresholds of the frame matching scores and the minimum numbers of matched frames needed for temporal alignment to achieve different

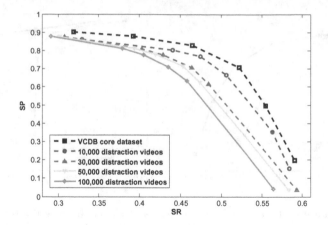

Fig. 7. Precision-recall curves of large-scale copy detection on VCDB, using the temporal network method with different numbers of background distraction videos

levels of detection precisions and recall rates. We compare the two temporal alignment methods on this core dataset. The only technical difference behind the two curves is the use of different alignment methods. As can be observed from the figure, the temporal network method produces better results in most cases, which shows the effectiveness of explicitly enforcing the several constraints in an optimization framework. This method is slightly slower than the Hough voting based method but is practically acceptable as the number of matched frames is limited after thresholding. In addition, we see that the frame-level recall tends to be saturated at 0.5 for the temporal network method and at 0.45 for the Hough voting. This indicates that around half of the copied frames are difficult to be identified by the baseline system.

Overall, the results on this core dataset are far from satisfactory. The baseline system with the temporal network alignment method achieves very impressive results on the Muscle-VCD dataset, but can only attain a segment-level recall of around 0.48 at a similar precision of 0.80. The frame-level recall is similar at the same level of precision. This clearly verifies our argument that partial copy detection under realistic scenario is much more challenging.

Next we move on to the large scale copy detection experiments by gradually adding the background distraction videos. We use four distraction set sizes with 10,000, 30,000, 50,000, and 100,000 (the entire VCDB) videos respectively. Results are visualized in Figure 7. As expected, the performance drops with an increasing number of the added distraction videos. However, the degradation is quite insignificant considering the large number of distraction videos included in the experiments, particularly when recall is smaller than 0.4. This indicates that the baseline system is not very sensitive to background noises, which is quite appealing as robustness is very important in large scale real applications. In addition, similar to the trends shown from the small-scale experiment on the VCDB core dataset, one can observe from Figure 7 that the existing

Fig. 8. Four frame pairs that are difficult to be detected, which contain very severe and complex content variations

techniques face difficulties in locating nearly 50% of the partial copies. These copies are valuable resources as they pose new challenges for future research. Figure 8 shows examples of a few failure cases.

6   Conclusions

We have introduced a new dataset called VCDB for partial copy detection in videos, which is—to our knowledge—the only large scale dataset containing realistic partial video copies. Most previous video copy detection research used simulated datasets, on which near-perfect results have been frequently reported. Because of this, copy detection is sometimes considered as a solved problem. This has largely limited the needed progress of copy detection research. With over 9,000 carefully annotated partial copies and over 100,000 videos, VCDB goes far beyond the existing benchmarks and poses new challenges to the research around this problem.

We evaluated a baseline system on VCDB, which is built upon techniques that have produced state-of-the-art performances on related tasks. The performance of the system is far from satisfactory, indicating that VCDB is arguably a good benchmark for future investigations. We also compared two temporal alignment methods on VCDB and observed that the temporal network method with optimization using explicit constraints tends to be a better solution. The best recall rate on VCDB is just close to 0.60 when the precision significantly drops to 0.20. This suggests that future research on copy detection should pay particular attention on the frame matching stage to overcome the difficulties caused by the severe content variations.

Acknowledgments. This work was supported in part by a National 863 Program (#2014AA015101), a Key Technologies Research and Development Program (#2013BAH09F01), a grant from the National Natural Science Foundation of China (#61201387), four grants from the Science and Technology Commission of Shanghai Municipality (#13PJ1400400, #13511504503, #12511501602 and #14511106900), and a grant from Ministry of Education (#20120071120026), China.

References

1. Lowe, D.: Distinctive image features from scale-invariant keypoints. IJCV 60(2), 91–110 (2004)
2. Douze, M., Jégou, H., Schmid, C., Pérez, P.: Compact video description for copy detection with precise temporal alignment. In: Daniilidis, K., Maragos, P., Paragios, N. (eds.) ECCV 2010, Part I. LNCS, vol. 6311, pp. 522–535. Springer, Heidelberg (2010)
3. Wu, X., Hauptmann, A.G., Ngo, C.W.: Practical elimination of near-duplicates from web video search. In: ACM MM (2007)
4. Song, J., Yang, Y., Huang, Z., Shen, H.T., Hong, R.: Multiple feature hashing for real-time large scale near-duplicate video retrieval. In: ACM MM (2011)
5. Jegou, H., Douze, M., Schmid, C.: Hamming embedding and weak geometric consistency for large scale image search. In: Forsyth, D., Torr, P., Zisserman, A. (eds.) ECCV 2008, Part I. LNCS, vol. 5302, pp. 304–317. Springer, Heidelberg (2008)
6. Douze, M., Jegou, H., Schmid, C.: An image-based approach to video copy detection with spatio-temporal post-ltering. IEEE TMM 12(4), 257–266 (2010)
7. Indyk, P., Iyengar, G., Shivakumar, N.: Finding pirated video sequences on the internet. Technical Report, Stanford University (1999)
8. Joly, A., Frelicot, C., Buisson, O.: Robust content-based video copy identification in a large reference database. In: Bakker, E.M., Lew, M., Huang, T.S., Sebe, N., Zhou, X.S. (eds.) CIVR 2003. LNCS, vol. 2728, pp. 414–424. Springer, Heidelberg (2003)
9. Law-To, J., Joly, A., Boujemaa, N.: Muscle-VCD-2007: a live benchmark for video copy detection (2007), http://www-rocq.inria.fr/imedia/civr-bench/
10. U.S. National Institute of Standards and Technology: TREC video retrieval evaluation, http://trecvid.nist.gov/
11. Law-To, J., Chen, L., Joly, A., Laptev, I., Buisson, O., Gouet-Brunet, V., Boujemaa, N., Stentiford, F.: Video copy detection: a comparative study. In: CIVR (2007)
12. Perronnin, F., Dance, C.R.: Fisher kernels on visual vocabularies for image categorization. In: CVPR (2007)
13. Jegou, H., Douze, M., Schmid, C., Perez, P.: Aggregating local descriptors into a compact image representation. In: CVPR (2007)
14. Tan, H.K., Ngo, C.W., Hong, R., Chua, T.S.: Scalable detection of partial near-duplicate videos by visual-temporal consistency. In: ACM MM (2009)
15. Jegou, H., Douze, M., Schmid, C.: Product quantization for nearest neighbor search. IEEE TPAMI 33(1), 117–128 (2011)
16. Revaud, J., Douze, M., Schmid, C., Jegou, H.: Event retrieval in large video collections with circulant temporal encoding. In: CVPR (2013)
17. Zhao, W.L., Ngo, C.W.: Flip-invariant sift for copy and object detection. IEEE TIP 22(3), 980–991 (2013)
18. Philbin, J., Chum, O., Isard, M., Sivic, J., Zisserman, A.: Object retrieval with large vocabularies and fast spatial matching. In: CVPR (2007)

19. Perronnin, F., Liu, Y., Sanchez, J., Poirier, H.: Large-scale image retrieval with compressed fisher vectors. In: CVPR (2010)
20. Arandjelovi, R., Zisserman, A.: Three things everyone should know to improve object retrieval. In: CVPR (2012)
21. Avrithis, Y., Tolias, G.: Hough pyramid matching: Speeded-up geometry re-ranking for large scale image retrieval. IJCV (2013)
22. Zhang, S., Yang, M., Wang, X., Lin, Y., Tian, Q.: Semantic-aware co-indexing for image retrieval. In: ICCV (2013)
23. Philbin, J., Chum, O., Isard, M., Sivic, J., Zisserman, A.: Lost in quantization: Improving particular object retrieval in large scale image databases. In: CVPR (2008)

Single-Image Super-Resolution: A Benchmark

Chih-Yuan Yang[1], Chao Ma[1,2], and Ming-Hsuan Yang[1]

[1] University of California at Merced, USA
[2] Shanghai Jiao Tong University, China
{cyang35,cma26,mhyang}@ucmerced.edu

Abstract. Single-image super-resolution is of great importance for vision applications, and numerous algorithms have been proposed in recent years. Despite the demonstrated success, these results are often generated based on different assumptions using different datasets and metrics. In this paper, we present a systematic benchmark evaluation for state-of-the-art single-image super-resolution algorithms. In addition to quantitative evaluations based on conventional full-reference metrics, human subject studies are carried out to evaluate image quality based on visual perception. The benchmark evaluations demonstrate the performance and limitations of state-of-the-art algorithms which sheds light on future research in single-image super-resolution.

Keywords: Single-image super-resolution, performance evaluation, metrics, Gaussian blur kernel width.

1 Introduction

The goal of single-image super-resolution (SISR) algorithms is to generate high-resolution (HR) images from a low-resolution (LR) image input. Numerous SISR algorithms have been recently proposed with different assumptions and evaluation criteria. Broadly speaking, SISR algorithms can be categorized based on their tasks. While domain-specific SISR algorithms focus on specific classes of images such as faces [35,42], scenes [33], and graphics artwork [18], generic SISR algorithms [10,38,8,3,27,30,11,46,9,34,32,12,5,39,44,43] are developed for all kinds of images where the priors are typically based on primitive image properties such as edges and segments. In order to evaluate the performance of a SISR algorithm, human subject studies or ground truth images are used [33,43]. In this work, we focus on performance evaluation of state-of-the-art SISR algorithms under different settings based on a set of ground truth images.

Generic SISR algorithms in the literature are usually evaluated with different images and metrics with certain assumptions (e.g., scaling factor and Gaussian kernel width). In addition, the LR images may be generated from different processes (e.g., different downsampling processes). It is thus of great interest to systematically and thoroughly evaluate state-of-the-art SISR algorithms within one framework. For fair comparisons, the ground truth and LR test images should be the same for all evaluated methods. Scaling factors and blur kernel width

D. Fleet et al. (Eds.): ECCV 2014, Part IV, LNCS 8692, pp. 372–386, 2014.

should be considered in performance evaluation. In addition, a wide range of images and metrics should be used for thorough examinations.

In this work, numerous state-of-the-art SISR methods are evaluated systematically and thoroughly. Two large sets of images are used in the experiments. The Berkeley segmentation dataset [20] is widely used for low-level vision problems, and the LIVE1 dataset [28] is commonly used for image quality assessment. We use a wide range of scaling factors and blur kernel width to examine the performance of SISR methods under different assumptions. The HR images generated by SISR methods are evaluated by full-reference metrics and human visual perception. We present the evaluation results and show the limitations of state-of-the-art methods. The findings from these large-scale experiments not only confirm what is commonly believed but also suggest new research directions for SISR. In addition, a code library of state-of-the-art SISR algorithms is available[1] to the public for ease of reproducing experimental results and evaluating novel algorithms on a common platform.

2   Related Work

Generic SISR algorithms aim to generate high-quality HR images from a single LR input image by exploiting certain image priors. According to the image priors, generic SISR algorithms can be categorized into several types of approaches.

Prediction Models. SISR algorithms in this category generate HR images from LR inputs through a predefined mathematical formula without training data. Interpolation-based methods (bilinear, bicubic, and Lanczos) generate HR pixel intensities by weighted averaging neighboring LR pixel values. Since interpolated intensities are locally similar to neighboring pixels, these algorithms generate good smooth regions but insufficient large gradients along edges and at high-frequency regions. The IP method [16] exploits a predefined downsampling model from a HR image to a LR image. Given an initial HR image, this method iteratively generates a LR image through the predefined downsampling model and compensates the difference map in LR back to the HR image. Since a generated HR image is designed to best match the LR input image under the linear downsampling model, the contrast along edges is better enhanced than the results generated by bicubic interpolation.

Edge Based Methods. Edges are important primitive image structures that play a prime role in visual perception. Several SISR algorithms have been proposed to learn priors from edge features for reconstructing HR images. Various edge features have been proposed such as the depth and width of an edge [8] or the parameter of a gradient profile [30]. Since the priors are primarily learned from edges, the reconstructed HR images have high-quality edges with proper sharpness and limited artifacts. However, edge priors are less effective for modeling other high-frequency structures such as textures.

---

[1] https://eng.ucmerced.edu/people/cyang35

Image Statistical Methods. Various image properties can be exploited as priors to predict HR images from LR images. The heavy-tailed gradient distribution [15] is exploited in [27] for SISR. The sparsity property of large gradients in generic images is exploited in [17] to reduce the computational load and in [41] to regularize the LR input images. Total variation has also been used as a regularization term for generating HR images [1,48].

Patch Based Methods. Given a set of paired LR and HR training images, patches can be cropped from the training images to learn mapping functions. The exemplar patches can be generated from external datasets [10,2], the input image itself [11,9], or combined sources [44]. Various learning methods of the mapping functions have been proposed such as weighted average [31,2], kernel regression [17], support vector regression [23], Gaussian process regression [13], sparse dictionary representation [46,7,5,24,45,39,47,19,14]. In addition to equally averaging overlapped patches, several methods for blending overlapped pixels have been proposed including weighted averaging [11,44], Markov Random Fields [10], and Conditional Random Fields [38].

3   Benchmark Settings

We use two sets of images as the ground truth to thoroughly evaluate the SISR algorithms from diverse sources. From the ground truth HR images, we generate LR test images using various settings of scaling factor and blur kernel width. We generate the SR images by the originally released code [27,17,46,5,43,36] or our implementation [16,30,11,9] if the code is not available. The generated SR image are used to evaluate the performance of SISR algorithms and quality assessment metrics. In order to evaluate the performance of metrics, we conduct human subject studies to generate perceptual scores of the SR images.

Test Image Sets. We use two image sets as the HR ground truth data for evaluation. The first set contains 200 images from the Berkeley segmentation dataset [20], which is widely used for SISR evaluations [11,9,32,12]. All images are of 321×481 pixels covering diverse contents acquired in a professional photographic style. The second set contains 29 undistorted high-quality images from the LIVE1 dataset [28], which is widely used for image quality assessment [26]. The resolution of these images ranges from 480×720 to 512×768 pixels.

Test Image Formation. There are several ways to generate LR test images from the ground truth images [27,30,36] such that the generated LR test images may be numerically different. For clarity, we present an image formulation to address this problem. Given a ground truth HR image I_h, a scaling factor s, and a Gaussian blur kernel width σ, we generate a test LR image I_l by

$$I_l(x_l, y_l) = \sum_{x,y} w(x - x_u, y - y_u)I_h(x, y) + \varepsilon, \tag{1}$$

where $x_l \in \{1, \ldots, m\}$ and $y_l \in \{1, \ldots, n\}$ are indices of I_l; $x \in \{1, \ldots, s \times m\}$ and $y \in \{1, \ldots, s \times n\}$ are indices of I_h; and ε denotes noise. The noise term

Table 1. List of evaluated methods. Language column, M: MAT-LAB, MC: Mixture of MATLAB and C/C++, E: Executable binary code. Learning column, N: No learning approach involved, E: External exemplar images are required, S: Self-similar exemplars are used. The execution time is measured on a machine with a 2.7 GHz Quad Core CPU with an image of 128 × 128 pixels (shown on the right).

The test image

Method	Language	Learning	Factors and Execution Time (sec.)					
			2x	3x	4x	5x	6x	8x
Bicubic Interpolation	MC	N	0.002	0.002	0.003	0.004	0.004	0.005
IP [16]	M	N	0.140	0.172	0.091	0.059	0.046	0.077
SLJT [27]	E	E	5.913	11.90	21.29	29.19	39.78	73.49
SSXS [30]	M	E	37.39	92.92	156.2	N.A.	N.A.	N.A.
GBI [11]	MC	S	364	807	3851	9028	21668	53762
KK [17]	MC	E	7.715	17.14	49.06	N.A.	N.A.	N.A.
YWHM [46]	M	E	321	598	1229	1956	2477	4795
FF [9]	M	S	1779	1513	2557	N.A.	N.A.	N.A.
DZSW [5]	M	E	266	568	887	1271	1721	2764
YY [43]	M	E	15.38	15.55	15.84	18.18	19.35	20.48
TSG [36]	M	E	0.948	1.126	1.405	1.873	2.093	3.189

ε is introduced from discretization while storing I_l into an uncompressed 8-bit image. We compute the HR coordinates (x_u, y_u) from the and LR ones (x_l, y_l) by

$$x_u = s(x_l - 0.5) + 0.5,$$
$$y_u = s(y_l - 0.5) + 0.5. \tag{2}$$

The weight w is determined by σ as

$$w(\Delta x, \Delta y) = \frac{1}{Z} e^{-(\Delta x^2 + \Delta y^2)/2\sigma^2}, \tag{3}$$

where Z is a normalization term. The formation is compatible with most SR methods [16,11,17,30,46,43,36] where the reconstructed images are well aligned with the ground truth images.

Evaluated SISR Methods. For fair comparisons, we evaluate the methods using the original binaries or source code [27,46,17,5,43,36]. In addition, we implement four state-of-the-art algorithms when the source or binary code is not available [16,30,11,9]. Table 1 lists the evaluated algorithms and their execution time under different scaling factors. We note these methods are implemented in different programming languages. For algorithms where the blur kernel width is an adjustable parameter [16,27,11,46,5,43], we set the same values as used in the LR image formation. We only evaluate the SSXS, KK, and FF methods [30,17,9] under scaling factors 2, 3, and 4 because the released code or priors only support these scaling factors. When the training code and dataset are available [46,5,43,36], we re-train the priors for all 54 settings. For algorithms that require other parameter settings [27,30,46,5,9,43,36], the default values in the released code or manuscripts are used.

Human Subject Studies. We conduct human subject studies to evaluate the effectiveness of existing metrics for performance evaluation of SR algorithms. We select 10 images from the BSD200 dataset [20] as the ground truth data. The selected images cover a wide range of high-frequency levels in order to generate a representative subset of the entire BSD200 dataset. (See the supplementary material for their high-frequency levels). From each ground truth image, 9 LR images are generated using Eq. 1 under different settings (the scaling factors of 2, 3, and 4, and the Gaussian kernel width of 0.4, 1.2, and 2.0). From each LR image, we use 6 state-of-the-art methods to generate the SR images, and in total we generate 540 SR images. We collect 16,200 perceptual scores from 30 participants evaluating the 540 SR images without knowing the ground truth images or the method names. The SR images are displayed in a random order to avoid bias to favor certain methods. Subjects are asked to give scores between 0 to 10 to assess the image quality based on their visual perception.

4 Benchmark Evaluation Results

Fig. 1 shows the quantitative evaluation results using two full-reference metrics PSNR and SSIM, which are widely used in the SISR literature [2,30,17,46,43,36]. While each row represents one scaling factor, the x and y axes show the Gaussian kernel width (σ) and the mean values of all the images in a dataset. We do not show the evaluation results of three test methods (SLJT, DZSW, and FF) because the generated SR images do not align with the ground truth images and thus their scores are ineffectively low (the complete comparisons are shown in the supplementary material). The misalignment in the SLJT and DZSW methods is caused by a LR image formation different from Eq. 1 used in our experiments where we sample the central pixels but they sample the pixels at the top-left corner of non-overlapping patches. The FF method uses non-dyadic filter banks to upsample images layer-by-layer in small scaling factors, which does not lead to fully aligned SR images with the ground truth.

Blur Kernel Width and Scaling Factor. Although it is widely accepted that the blur kernel significantly affects the performance of SISR algorithms [21,6], the proper values of blur kernel width have not been thoroughly investigated. Our benchmark evaluations shown in Fig. 1 indicate that the influence of the Gaussian kernel width is consistent across the two test datasets (BSD200 and LIVE1) and the two metrics (PSNR ans SSIM) for various settings of scaling factor and kernel width. Although the settings of peak performance are algorithm-dependent, a clear trend can be observed that a larger kernel width is required to generate good performance for a larger scaling factor. According to the experimental results, we suggest to use kernel width with ranges of (0.4-0.6), (0.8-1.0), and (1.2-1.4) for scaling factors 2, 3, and 4, respectively, which are different from some given kernel width in the literature [30,43].

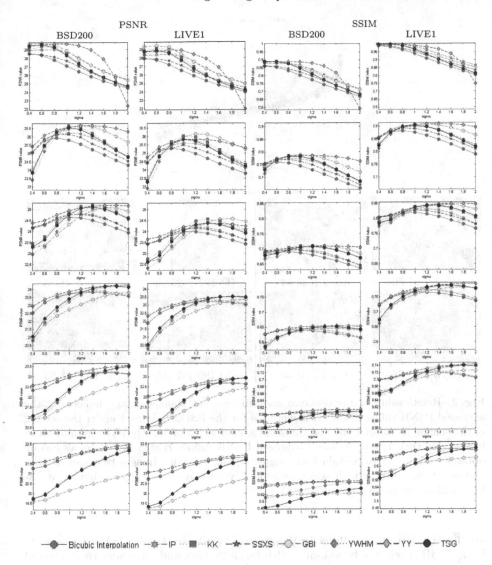

Fig. 1. Performance evaluation. Eight SISR methods are evaluated using two image sets (BSD200 and LIVE1) and two metrics (PSNR and SSIM) under six scaling factors and nine values of Gaussian kernel width. From top to bottom, each row shows results with a scaling factor of 2, 3, 4, 5, 6, and 8. The plots show mean values for all SR images of a dataset. The BSD200 dataset contains 200 images of 321×481 pixels, and the LIVE1 dataset contains 29 images ranging from 768×512 to 480×720 pixels.

We explain these results by considering the LR image formation Eq. 1 where σ determines the richness of information preserved in the LR images from the ground truth images. If the value is too large, numerous ground truth pixels will be assigned with similar weights in Eq. 1 and the generated LR image will be blurry, which means that little visual information is preserved for reconstructing

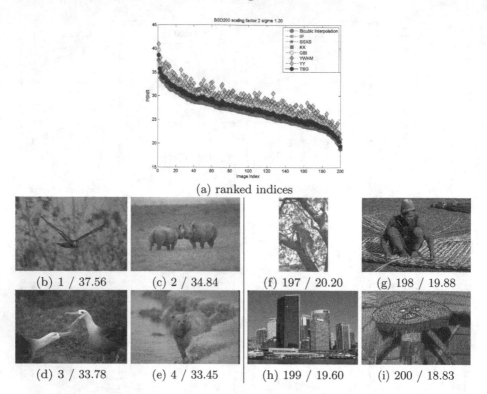

(a) ranked indices

| (b) 1 / 37.56 | (c) 2 / 34.84 | (f) 197 / 20.20 | (g) 198 / 19.88 |

| (d) 3 / 33.78 | (e) 4 / 33.45 | (h) 199 / 19.60 | (i) 200 / 18.83 |

Fig. 2. Relationship of performance and images. (a) Ranked image indices by the averaged PSNR values of the eight methods for the BSD200 dataset under the setting of the scaling factor of 2 and the Gaussian kernel width of 1.2. (b-i) The ground truth images and their ranked indices / averaged PSNR values. Higher PSNR values can be obtained when images contain fewer high-frequency details. Images best viewed on a high-resolution display with adequate zoom level where each image is shown with at least 320 × 480 pixels (full-resolution).

an effective HR image similar to the ground truth. If the value is too small, only limited HR pixels will be assigned with large weights and all others are neglected by small weights, which result in reduced information in the LR images. When the σ value is properly set for a given scaling factor, most information is preserved in the LR images, which are likely to reconstruct HR images similar to the ground truth images.

Performance Limitations and Potential Solutions. Our human subject studies show that a scaling factor of 4 is the limit of state-of-the-art SISR methods evaluated in this paper. The perceptual scores of upsampled SR images with a scaling factor of 4 are all close to the lower bound designed in the subject studies, which means that the image quality is too low to be evaluated. We investigate the reasons of this limitation by exploring the numerical evaluation results which can be viewed as objective quality indices. Fig. 2 shows the ranked results under one setting (the scaling factor of 2 and the Gaussian kernel with of 1.2) of the BSD200 dataset based on the averaged PSNR value of eight SISR methods. An observation is that the performance is primarily determined by the images rather than the SR methods, and we find similar results using the other dataset and metric (SSIM). The image ranks only change slightly even under different settings of scaling factors and Gaussian kernel width. After checking individual images in the dataset, we find that the richness of large magnitude high-frequency details is the key factor. Fig. 2(b)-(e) and Fig. 2(f)-(i) show two sets of images with the highest and lowest PSNR indices where images with more highly contrast pixels lead to smaller PSNR values, and vice versa.

We explain the performance limitation of the evaluated SR algorithms. Except the bicubic interpolation and IP [16] methods, all SR algorithms rely on statistical priors to predict HR features from LR ones. The priors of cross-scale self-similarity used in the GBI method [11] is also a specialized statistical prior as shown in [9,49]. In order to process a wide range of images and to train the priors with limited computational resources, the features of the tested algorithm are all extracted from small patches. According to the statistics of natural images [15], the patches containing large magnitude of gradients are rare in natural images. Since a LR patch can be generated from various HR patches through the downsampling process of Eq. 1, any learned statistical priors must be able to generate predicted HR features close to the majority of the training HR features for high-quality SR images. As a result, rare patches are less likely to be effectively reconstructed and this leads to low PSNR and SSIM indices.

These findings are useful for developing effective SR algorithms. First, it is useful to divide training data into non-overlapping subsets where HR features of large magnitude of gradients will not be averaged by other features significantly. Such an approach has been adopted in [43,36] and our experimental results show that the algorithm performs well against other algorithms in most settings. Second, it is reasonable to enlarge the feature dimension in order to increase the distinguishability of LR patches. This approach is used in [32] where patches are extended to segments in order to reconstruct effective high-frequency details. However, the ensuing high computational load and large amount of training data will be challenging for this approach to scale up due to the curse of dimensionality. Third, it is ideal to classify training data and to analyze image contents to facilitate specific priors for each class. This idea has been used in [12,42] for specific domains such as textures and faces. However, it remains an open question how to generate a sufficient number of classes and parse images for generic SR.

Evaluation Metrics. The PSNR and SSIM index are the most widely used metrics in SR problems, but they do not reflect image quality well [44]. As explained in Section 3, we conduct human subject studies to validate the effectiveness of metrics for SR images. Fig. 3 shows the relationship between perceptual scores on the X axes and metric indices on the Y axes. Effective metrics should generate quality indices where the ranks are similar to the ones of perceptual scores. We evaluate the performance of a metric by the Spearman's rank correlation

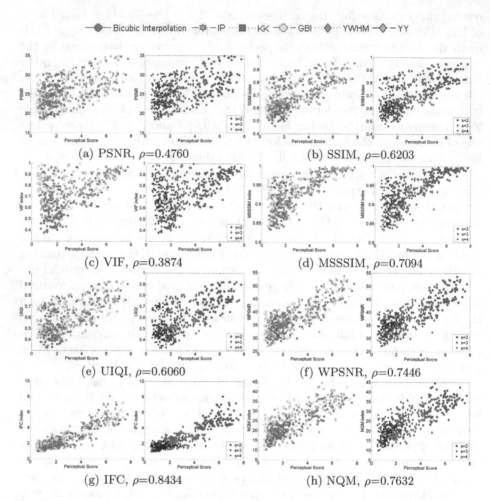

Fig. 3. Relationship between perceptual scores and metric indices for eight image quality metrics. Since the metric ranges are different, we compute the performance by the Spearman's rank correlation coefficient (denoted by ρ), which is not affected by the ranges. The left and right plots distinguish from different SR methods and scaling factors (denoted by s) by colors, which are best viewed on a color display. Experimental results show that SR images should be evaluated by the IFC metric due to the better effectiveness instead of the widely used metrics PSNR and SSIM.

coefficient [22], which is not affected by different ranges of quality indices generated by different metrics.

Our experimental results indicate that for SR images four metrics are more effective such as the multi-scale structure similarity index (MSSSIM) [40], information fidelity criterion (IFC) [29], weighted peak signal-to-noise ratio (WPSNR), and noise quality measure (NQM) [4]. Overall, the IFC index has highest correlation with perceptual scores for SR evaluation. We examine the effectiveness of the IFC metric for SR images by the extracted features and specialized application for natural images. First, the IFC metric is designed to evaluate the loss of image information so that it extracts wavelet features with focus on high-frequency details rather than low-frequency components. This metric matches human perception well as visual perception is more sensitive to high-frequency details of SR images rather than low-frequency components. Second, the IFC metric is developed based on natural scene statistics using the Gaussian scale mixtures [37] and the BSD200 dataset contains numerous such images.

We note that the extracted features by the VIF method put more weight on edges which are of great importance for visual perception. As a result, SR images with sharp edges have large VIF values even though they are not visually pleasant. Fig. 3(c) shows that many points in the upper left region have low perceptual scores but high VIF indices, especially for images generated by the GBI method. We compare a set of the generated images in Fig. 4 where the one generated by the GBI method contains apparently over-sharpened edges than other methods, which indicates the VIF metric is not effective for SR performance evaluation. It is worth noticing that the weights computed in the WPSNR metric significantly improve the performance over the widely used PSNR metric (where the weights can be viewed as the same). The weights of WPSNR in our experiments are computed by a function [25] that models contrast sensitivity of perception in terms of spatial frequency. As a result, patches in a SR image carrying signals n mid frequency ranges will be assigned with larger weights, and the smooth regions and complicated textures will have smaller weights. Thus the WPSNR metric performs well with the assigned weights.

Evaluations of SISR Methods. As shown in Table 1, the bicubic interpolation and IP [16] methods perform well with low computational load. The IP method almost always outperforms the bicubic interpolation method in terms of visual quality by iteratively restoring high-frequency details based on a difference map between the LR test image and a downsampled image of the estimated HR result. The restored high-frequency map enhances contrast of edges and textures, and makes a SR image more similar to the ground truth image than the one generated by bicubic interpolation. However, the IP method is limited by the accuracy of the restored high-frequency map. Since it is simply interpolated from a LR difference map, the HR results are better when the compensated difference is limited with small scaling factor as shown in Fig. 1. The low computational load of the back-projection method makes it widely used as a post-processing step to refine contrast in state-of-the-art SISR methods [11,46].

The GBI method [11] generates sharp contours as it uses a small scaling factor (1.25) to upsample intermediate images in a pyramid. The exploited self-exemplar priors are effective for contour patches because the image structures remain similar after being downsampled with a small scaling factor. Furthermore, it utilizes the back-projection compensation to enhance the contrast in every upsampling iteration. Due to the generated sharp contours, the GBI method works well for some settings such as scaling factor of 3 with σ greater than 0.6, and the scaling factor of 4 with σ greater than 1.4. However, the performance of the GBI

(a) Ground truth
Perceptual score/VIF index

(b) GBI [11]
1.88/0.8891

(c) YWHM [46]
1.63/0.7226

(d) YY [43]
2.00/0.7208

(e) KK [17]
2.5/0.6880

(f) IP [16]
2.00/0.6554

Fig. 4. A set of super-resolution images and their perceptual scores and VIF indices. (b)-(f) Five SR images generated under the same setting (the scaling factor of 4, and the Gaussian kernel width of 1.2). Since the VIF metric uses edge features to evaluate image quality, images with sharp edges likely generate large VIF indices. The GBI method generates over-sharpened edges in (b) compared to the ground truth image in (a) and distorted image structures like the flowers at the bottom, which lead to a low perceptual score but a large VIF index. Images best viewed on a high-resolution display with adequate zoom level where each image is shown with at least 320 × 480 pixels (full-resolution).

method is limited because of three factors. First, this method exploits self-similar exemplar patches only from the input LR image through a pyramid. When the scaling factor is large, it may be difficult for a patch to find similar ones in the exemplar set through the pyramid (i.e., lack of sufficient exemplar patches).

Second, the repeated usage of the back-projection results in over-contrasted contours. As shown in Fig. 4(b), the contours along the face and arms of the wood figure are over-contrasted, and the image structures of the flowers at the bottom are distorted. Thus the performance of the GBI method decreases significantly when the scaling factor is greater than 4 (more details can be found in the supplementary material). Third, the method requires high computational load as a result of searching for similar patches in a pyramid. As shown in Table 1, it is the most computationally expensive method among all.

The YWHM, YY, and TSG methods [46,43,36] all upsample high-frequency components (pixel gradients or patch difference) from LR to HR through learned mapping functions, and the main difference is about learning approaches. While the YWHM and TSG methods learn a pair of sparse dictionaries, the YY method trains numerous simple linear functions. The difference between the YWHM and TSG methods is usage of the dictionaries. Indeed the YWHM method uses the dictionaries to generate sparse coefficients while the TSG method uses the dictionaries as sets of anchor points in LR/HR feature spaces, which is more similar to the YY method in this manner. Since the computational load of generating sparse coefficients is skipped, the TSG method gains significant advantages on execution time over the YWHM method as shown in Table 1 while their performance is similar as shown in Fig. 1.

We discuss the difference of the YY and TSG methods since both partition the LR feature space into numerous subspaces in order to map LR features to HR space by individual linear functions. The most significant difference lies in anchor points used to partition the LR feature space where they are evenly scattered in the YY method due to the L2-norm distance but restricted in a unit sphere in the TSG method because they are all bases of a sparse dictionary. The difference of anchor points lead to the differences of computational load and performance. The unit-length anchor points used in the TSG method have advantages on computation in which the cost of finding anchor points is lower as highest correlation can be easily computed by inner product. However, this step in the YY method is computed by L2-norm distances which is computationally more expensive. On the contrary, the evenly scattered anchor points used in the YY method lead to better performance for most settings as shown in Fig. 1 because the regression functions can be learned more directly and effectively. As features extracted from training images are directly grouped by the evenly scattered anchor points, the source patches are visually similar which in turn facilitates learning better regression functions.

We find that the YY method performs poorly when the scaling factor is 2 and the σ value is 2.0, which can be attributed to sensitivity of the learned functions. When the scaling factor is small but σ is large, most generated LR patches are smoothed, and thus the feature values of difference patches are close to zero. However, the HR source patches are highly varied and the feature values are large. As a result, this linear regression model is likely to have a large condition number and leads to numerically instability. As shown in Fig. 5, the artifacts are the noise caused from many high-frequency details.

(a) σ=1.6   (b) σ=1.8   (c) σ=2.0

Fig. 5. A set of super-resolution images to show the sensitivity of learned regression functions in the YY method [43]. (a)-(c) The ground truth image and scaling factor of 2 are the same while the only difference is the parameter of Gaussian kernel width (σ) used in the low-resolution image formation Eq. 1. The artifacts caused by sensitivity of linear regression can be found along contours. Images best viewed on a high-resolution display with adequate zoom level where each image is shown with at least 320 × 480 pixels (full-resolution).

5   Conclusion

In this paper, several state-of-the-art SISR methods are thoroughly studied. Hundreds of images are evaluated using various scaling factors and Gaussian kernel width values. Comprehensive experimental results show how state-of-the-art SISR methods perform with respect to scaling factor, Gaussian kernel and image contents. The benchmark evaluations demonstrate the performance and limitations of state-of-the-art algorithms quantitatively and qualitatively. The developed code library of state-of-the-art SISR algorithms provides a common platform for ease of reproducing experimental results and evaluating novel algorithms for future research.

Acknowledgment. This work is supported in part by the NSF CAREER Grant #1149783 and NSF IIS Grant #1152576. C. Ma is sponsored by CSC fellowship.

References

1. Aly, H.A., Dubois, E.: Image up-sampling using total-variation regularization with a new observation model. TIP 14(10), 1647–1659 (2005)
2. Chang, H., Yeung, D.Y., Xiong, Y.: Super-resolution through neighbor embedding. In: CVPR (2004)

3. Dai, S., Han, M., Xu, W., Wu, Y., Gong, Y.: Soft edge smoothness prior for alpha channel super resolution. In: CVPR (2007)
4. Damera-Venkata, N., Kite, T.D., Geisler, W.S., Evans, B.L., Bovik, A.C.: Image quality assessment based on a degradation model. TIP 9(4), 636–650 (2000)
5. Dong, W., Zhang, L., Shi, G., Wu, X.: Image deblurring and super-resolution by adaptive sparse domain selection and adaptive regularization. TIP 20(7), 1838–1857 (2011)
6. Efrat, N., Glasner, D., Apartsin, A., Nadler, B., Levin, A.: Accurate blur models vs. image priors in single image super-resolution. In: ICCV (2013)
7. Elad, M., Zeyde, R., Protter, M.: Single image super-resolution using sparse representation. In: SIAM Imaging Science (2010)
8. Fattal, R.: Image upsampling via imposed edge statistics. In: SIGGRAPH (2007)
9. Freedman, G., Fattal, R.: Image and video upscaling from local self-examples. TOG 30(2), 1–11 (2011)
10. Freeman, W.T., Jones, T.R., Pasztor, E.C.: Example-based super-resolution. IEEE Computer Graphics and Applications, pp. 56–65 (March/April 2002)
11. Glasner, D., Bagon, S., Irani, M.: Super-resolution from a single image. In: ICCV (2009)
12. HaCohen, Y., Fattal, R., Lischinski, D.: Image upsampling via texture hallucination. In: ICCP (2010)
13. He, H., Siu, W.C.: Single image super-resolution using Gaussian process regression. In: CVPR (2011)
14. He, L., Qi, H., Zaretzki, R.: Beta process joint dictionary learning for coupled feature spaces with application to single image super-resolution. In: CVPR (2013)
15. Huang, J., Mumford, D.: Statistics of natural images and models. In: CVPR (1999)
16. Irani, M., Peleg, S.: Improving resolution by image registration. CGVIP 53(3), 231–239 (1991)
17. Kim, K.I., Kwon, Y.: Single-image super-resolution using sparse regression and natural image prior. PAMI 32(6), 1127–1133 (2010)
18. Kopf, J., Lischinski, D.: Depixelizing pixel art. In: SIGGRAPH (2011)
19. Lu, X., Yuan, H., Yan, P., Yuan, Y., Li, X.: Geometry constrained sparse coding for single image super-resolution. In: CVPR (2012)
20. Martin, D., Fowlkes, C., Tal, D., Malik, J.: A database of human segmented natural images and its application to evaluating segmentation algorithms and measuring ecological statistics. In: ICCV (2001)
21. Michaeli, T., Irani, M.: Nonparametric blind super-resolution. In: ICCV (2013)
22. Moore, D., McCabe, G.P., Craig, B.: Introduction to the Practice of Statistics, 7th edn. W.H. Freeman (2005)
23. Ni, K., Nguyen, T.: Image superresolution using support vector regression. TIP 16(6), 1596–1610 (2007)
24. Purkait, P., Chanda, B.: Image upscaling using multiple dictionaries of natural image patches. In: Lee, K.M., Matsushita, Y., Rehg, J.M., Hu, Z. (eds.) ACCV 2012, Part III. LNCS, vol. 7726, pp. 284–295. Springer, Heidelberg (2013)
25. Robson, J.G.: Spatial and temporal contrast-sensitivity functions of the visual system. Journal of the Optical Society of America (1966)
26. Saad, M.A., Bovik, A.C., Charrier, C.: Blind image quality assessment: A natural scene statistics approach in the DCT domain. TIP 21(8), 3339–3352 (2012)
27. Shan, Q., Li, Z., Jia, J., Tang, C.K.: Fast image/video upsampling. In: SIGGRAPH Asia (2008)
28. Sheikh, H.R., Sabir, M.F., Bovik, A.C.: A statistical evaluation of recent full reference image quality assessment algorithms. TIP 15(11), 3340–3451 (2006)

29. Sheikh, H.R., Bovik, A.C., de Veciana, G.: An information fidelity criterion for image quality assessment using natural scene statistics. TIP 14(12), 2117–2128 (2005)
30. Sun, J., Sun, J., Xu, Z., Shum, H.Y.: Image super-resolution using gradient profile prior. In: CVPR (2008)
31. Sun, J., Zheng, N.N., Tao, H., Shum, H.Y.: Image hallucination with primal sketch priors. In: CVPR (2003)
32. Sun, J., Zhu, J., Tappen, M.F.: Context-constrained hallucination for image super-resolution. In: CVPR (2010)
33. Sun, L., Hays, J.: Super-resolution from internet-scale scene matching. In: ICCP (2012)
34. Tai, Y.W., Liu, S., Brown, M.S., Lin, S.: Super resolution using edge prior and single image detail synthesis. In: CVPR (2010)
35. Tappen, M.F., Liu, C.: A Bayesian approach to alignment-based image hallucination. In: Fitzgibbon, A., Lazebnik, S., Perona, P., Sato, Y., Schmid, C. (eds.) ECCV 2012, Part VII. LNCS, vol. 7578, pp. 236–249. Springer, Heidelberg (2012)
36. Timofte, R., Smet, V.D., Gool, L.V.: Anchored neighborhood regression for fast example-based super-resolution. In: ICCV (2012)
37. Wainwright, M.J., Simoncelli, E.P., Willsky, A.S.: Random cascades on wavelet trees and their use in analyzing and modeling natural images. Applied and Computational Harmonic Analysis 11, 89–123 (2001)
38. Wang, Q., Tang, X., Shum, H.: Patch based blind image super resolution. In: ICCV (2005)
39. Wang, S., Zhang, L., Liang, Y., Pan, Q.: Semi-coupled dictionary learning with applications to image super-resolution and photo-sketch synthesis. In: CVPR (2012)
40. Wang, Z., Simoncelli, E., Bovik, A.C.: Multi-scale structural similarity for image quality assessment. In: IEEE Conference Record of the Thirty-Seventh Asilomar Conference on Signals, Systems, and Computers (2003)
41. Xiong, X., Sun, X., Wu, F.: Robust web image/video super-resolution. TIP 19(8), 2017–2028 (2010)
42. Yang, C.Y., Liu, S., Yang, M.H.: Structured face hallucination. In: CVPR (2013)
43. Yang, C.Y., Yang, M.H.: Fast direct super-resolution by simple functions. In: ICCV (2013)
44. Yang, J., Lin, Z., Cohen, S.: Fast image super-resolution based on in-place example regression. In: CVPR (2013)
45. Yang, J., Wang, Z., Lin, Z., Shu, X., Huang, T.: Bilevel sparse coding for coupled feature spaces. In: CVPR (2012)
46. Yang, J., Wright, J., Huang, T., Ma, Y.: Image super-resolution via sparse representation. TIP (2010)
47. Yang, S., Wang, M., Chen, Y., Sun, Y.: Single-image super-resolution reconstruction via learned geometric dictionaries and clustered sparse coding. TIP 21(9), 4016–4028 (2012)
48. Zhang, H., Yang, J., Zhang, Y., Huang, T.S.: Non-local kernel regression for image and video restoration. In: Daniilidis, K., Maragos, P., Paragios, N. (eds.) ECCV 2010, Part III. LNCS, vol. 6313, pp. 566–579. Springer, Heidelberg (2010)
49. Zontak, M., Irani, M.: Internal statistics of a single natural image. In: CVPR (2011)

Well Begun Is Half Done:
Generating High-Quality Seeds
for Automatic Image Dataset Construction from Web

Yan Xia[1], Xudong Cao[2], Fang Wen[2], and Jian Sun[2]

[1] University of Science and Technology of China
[2] Microsoft Research Asia, Beijing, China

Abstract. We present a fully automatic approach to construct a large-scale, high-precision dataset from noisy web images. Within the entire pipeline, we focus on generating high quality seed images for subsequent dataset growing. High quality seeds are essential as we revealed, but they have received relatively less attention in previous works with respect to how to automatically generate them. In this work, we propose a density score based on rank-order distance to identify positive seed images. The basic idea is images relevant to a concept typically are tightly clustered, while the outliers are widely scattered. Through adaptive thresholding, we guarantee the selected seeds as numerous and accurate as possible. Starting with the high quality seeds, we grow a high quality dataset by dividing seeds and conducting iterative negative and positive mining. Our system can automatically collect thousands of images for one concept/class, with a precision rate of 95% or more. Comparisons with recent state-of-the-arts also demonstrate our method's superior performance.

1 Introduction

High quality datasets (e.g. LabelMe [15] and ImageNet [7]) play vital roles in the tasks of computer vision and push relevant researches forward [12]. However extensive human effort is required in order to label tens of millions of images, and existing datasets can not cover all tasks or user specific classes such as "wearing glasses". In this context, automatic dataset construction has emerged: given noisy images crawled from search engines, the images which belong to the query concept/class such as "waterfall", are labeled as positive samples (the rest are negative outliers/distractors) in un- or semi-supervised way.

The pipeline of existing methods [10,16,14,13,5,3] for automatic dataset construction can be summarized into two steps: generating a group of labeled images i.e. seed images or seeds; and growing the dataset from the starting seeds by iterative "self training". But previous works mainly focus on the second step, paying relative less attention to the first step – the seeds are either labeled by human [10,14,13,5] (high cost) or labeled according to top-ranked images [14,13] or noisy surrounding text [1,16] (low quality).

In this work, we study the impacts of the first step, i.e., generating seeds, on automatic dataset construction. We find that high quality seeds are critical to achieving

D. Fleet et al. (Eds.): ECCV 2014, Part IV, LNCS 8692, pp. 387–400, 2014.

high recall and precision for the constructed dataset (see Section 2). With this mind, we propose a novel and fully automatic approach to generate high quality seeds. The basic observation/assumption underline of our approach is that the positive samples are densely clustered while the negative outliers are widely scattered. In this context, we can identify the images with high density as positive seeds.

To realize this basic idea, we need to handle the heterogeneous problem: the L2 distance is incomparable across different concepts. For example, the average distance between "human" images is usually larger than the average distance between "waterfall" images. We handle this problem by transforming the L2 distance to rank-order distance [19], which is more robust to the heterogeneous problem. Based on the rank-order distance, we define the density of an image as the number of neighbors within a certain distance, and choose images with high densities above a certain threshold as the seeds. For various concepts, we adaptively set the thresholds, because the proportions of the positive samples are concept-dependent. The threshold is automatically determined by balancing the following considerations: the average density of selected seeds should be high, while the selected seeds should be similar to each other but dissimilar from the outliers.

We grow the dataset from the seeds using iterative negative mining [6,9] and positive mining [14]. We develop seed dividing as a preprocessing step in the creation of the dataset to alleviate the multi-modal problem in negative and positive mining. We exploit k-means to divide the seeds into multiple groups and train separated classifiers on each of them. Substantial improvements are observed in the multi-modal case.

We apply the features obtained by deep learning [12,8,18] in the task of automatic dataset construction. As deep learning features are very capable of capturing the semantic meaning of images, we expect substantial improvement and revisit the task of automatic dataset construction.

2   Seeds Quality Matters

Intuitively, the larger the amount and the higher the precision of seeds, the better the quality of the constructed dataset. We measure the seeds' quality using seeds ratio and seeds precision. *Seeds ratio* measures the amount of seeds relative to the total number of the crawled images. *Seeds precision* measures the percentage of the true positive relative to the total number of selected seeds.

To quantitatively study the dataset quality as a function of seeds quality, we artificially build a dataset of "crawled" images: the positive samples are from one class of ImageNet and the negative outliers are randomly crawled web images. In this way, we quantitatively vary the seeds ratio and seeds precision, and study their influences on the quality of the constructed dataset.

We find high seeds precision is critical to dataset quality (Fig. 1(a)). For example, the recall and precision are 91% and 95% given a high seeds precision of 100%, but the recall and precision drop dramatically to 74% and 91% when the seeds precision decreases to 80%. We also find that a certain seeds ratio (e.g. 20%) is necessary for good recall (Fig. 1(b)).

In this context, we need adequate and accurate seeds to benefit the final constructed dataset. We propose our approach with this factor under consideration.

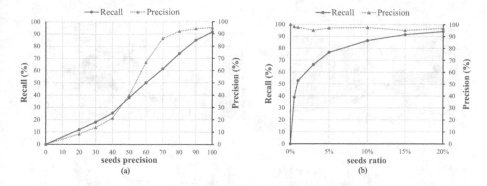

Fig. 1. The impact of seeds quality on the constructed dataset. (a) seeds precision vs. dataset quality. (b) seeds ratio vs. dataset quality. In (a), seeds ratio is fixed to 15%. In (b), seeds precision is fixed to 100%. One concept is taken as a representative example in this figure. Similar patterns are also observed in other concepts.

3 Our Approach

To automatically construct a dataset, we firstly crawl large-scale noisy images from web, and generate clean seed images from the crawled images. Then we grow the dataset starting from the seeds. We will detail these three steps in this section.

3.1 Image Crawling

Herein we describe how we construct the initial set containing tens of thousands images. Since Google and Bing can only return 1000 results at most for one query, which is far from what we need, we enlarge the number of crawled images in two ways: (i) We exploit searching filters provided by search engines. For example, we vary the image layout (square, wide or tall) and size (small, medium or large), and combine these filters to crawl more images. The top 300 results are downloaded in each combination. Then about 2000–4000 images are crawled for one text query. (ii) We utilize automatic query expansion [2]. For example, given a target concept such as "waterfall", we expand 10–20 relevant queries such as "cascading waterfall", "waterfall in Europe" and so on. Then we use the expanded queries to crawl more images.

After downloading, we remove small images (width or height < 160 px) and duplicates. The remaining images form the initial set for subsequent seeds generating and dataset growing.

3.2 Seeds Generating

We exploit the topological structure of crawled images to generate seeds un-supervisedly. According to the topological structure, most positive images are densely clustered while the outliers are widely scattered. In other words, images in denser areas are more likely to be seeds. Therefore we can rank the crawled images by a certain density

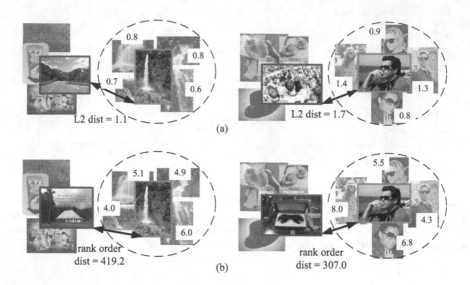

Fig. 2. (a) The L2 distances between the positive image and its nearest outlier are 1.1 and 1.7 for concept "waterfall" and "wearing glasses" respectively. Distance values are shown near images. Note that for concept "wearing glasses", there exists some positive neighbors with L2 distances larger than 1.1. (b) The rank-order distances between images in a dense area are much smaller.

measurement and select the top-ranked samples as the seeds. To translate this basic idea into a good algorithm, we need to deal with two issues.

Firstly, it is not effective to directly measure density in the Euclid space, because of the heterogenous problem: the L2 distance is incomparable across different concepts. As shown in Fig. 2(a), for the concept "waterfall", the L2 distance between a positive image and its nearest outlier is 1.1; while this value is 1.7 for concept "wearing glasses". These distance values are measured by deep learning features we extract. This implies that, for a same distance, a sample could be within the concept "wearing glasses", but beyond the concept "waterfall". This makes it hard to define a good density measurement in Euclid space.

Secondly, it is clear that samples with a very high density are positive, and samples with a very small density are negative. But it is not easy to draw a line in the middle to decide how many top images are selected: selecting too many images leads to low seeds precision, while selecting too few leads to low seeds ratio. In addition, the proportion of positive images differs for different concepts, which requires adaptive threshold.

Rank-Order Distance. We use rank-order distance [19] to address the heterogenous problem. We denote the initial set as $X = \{x_i : 1 \leq i \leq N\}$. Rank-order distance is defined as:

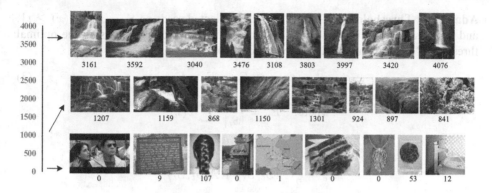

Fig. 3. Images and their density scores (shown below images)

$$d(x_i, x_j) = \frac{D(i,j) + D(j,i)}{\min(O_i(j), O_j(i))}, \tag{1}$$

$$D(i,j) = \sum_{k=0}^{O_i(j)} O_j(f_i(k)), \quad 1 \le i, j \le N,$$

where O_i is denoted as an order list ranked by the L2 distance from x_i to other images. $O_i(j)$ is the order of x_j in O_i. $f_i(k)$ returns the kth image in O_i. (see [19] for details)

Rank-order distance is used here because it is defined on the structure of neighborhood. If two images have similar neighbors, then the distance between the two images is small, otherwise the distance is large. Because of the topological structures of different concepts are similar, rank-order distance is comparable across different concepts. Moreover, rank-order distance is more robust to outliers. The distances between images in a dense area are around 100 times smaller than those between outliers, but this difference is insignificant when measured in Euclid space, as illustrated in Fig. 2(b).

Density Score. With the rank-order distance, we define the measurement of density as the number of neighbors within a certain distance ($d = 15$ in our implementation). Formally, the neighborhood graph on X is defined as:

$$h(x_i, x_j) = \begin{cases} 1, & d(x_i, x_j) < d \\ 0, & d(x_i, x_j) > d \end{cases} \tag{2}$$

and the density score of x is $v(x) = \sum_{i=1...N} h(x_i, x)$.

To understand how well the density score works, we visualize the crawled images under the concept "waterfall" in Fig. 3, along with their density scores. We find that for a high density (around 4,000), all images belong to "waterfall"; for a medium density (around 1,000), most images belong to "waterfall", and the rest belong to relevant concepts such as "fast-flow river" or "small waterfall"; for a small density (about 0), most images are irrelevant. It is interesting to mention that the image with a 107 density score (in the third row, third from left) says that "a long ponytail" looks similar to "waterfall".

Adaptively Thresholding. Denote the set of selected seeds as $S_t = \{x : v(x) \geq t\}$, and outliers $\overline{S}_t = X - S_t$. For various concepts, we propose choosing the optimal threshold t^* by maximizing the following objective function:

$$t^* = \underset{t}{\operatorname{argmax}} E_u + E_i - E_e \tag{3}$$

$$\text{where:} \quad E_u = \frac{1}{|S_t|} \sum_{x \in S_t} v(x),$$

$$E_i = A(S_t, S_t),$$

$$E_e = \frac{1}{2}(A(S_t, \overline{S}_t) + A(\overline{S}_t, S_t)).$$

Here $A(S_t, R_t)$ is the similarity between two sets, which is defined hierarchically: first we define the similarity between two samples x and y as the amount of their common neighbors, i.e., $h(x, :)h(y, :)^T$; then we define the similarity between a sample and a set as the maximum similarity between this sample and the samples in the set, i.e., $g(x, R_t) = \max_{y \in R_t, y \neq x} h(x, :)h(y, :)^T$; finally we define the similarity between two sets as the average similarity between the samples of one set to the other set, i.e., $A(S_t, R_t) = \frac{1}{|S_t|} \sum_{x \in S_t} g(x, R_t)$.

So in Equation(3), the three terms E_u, E_i, E_e mean the following:

(1) E_u: the unary term. It equals to the average density of all selected seeds.
(2) E_i: the intra-seeds similarity term. It is the self similarities of the set of seeds.
(3) E_e: the extra-seeds similarity term. It is the cross similarity between the set of seeds and the set of outliers.

As there is only one unknown variable in the optimization, we use binary search to efficiently find the optimal threshold t^* and select S_{t^*} as seeds.

3.3 Dataset Growing

Given the generated seeds, we can grow the dataset in an iterative self-training way: (i) train a classifier using the seeds as the positive and an irrelevant reference set as the negative; (ii) apply the classifier to all crawled images; (iii) add images with high scores and remove those with low scores; (iv) iterate. Here an irrelevant reference set is introduced to anchor the iterative training and screen out outliers.

With this in mind, in order to reduce training cost, we first do **negative mining**: we train a linear svm classifier on the positive seeds and the negative reference set; apply the classifier to the negative set only; the hard negative samples are selected to form a new negative set; iterate. By doing this, we obtain hard negative samples, which are more effective in identifying the boundary of positive samples. We next do **positive mining**. This procedure is similar to the aforementioned self-training process, expect that the negative samples are not the whole reference set, but the hard negative samples.

In our implementation, we use NUS-WIDE [4] as the reference set. This dataset contains about 250K images crawled from Flicker, and we find 100K of these are enough for good performance. Usually 2%~6% (i.e. 2K~6K) images are selected as hard negative samples in negative mining.

Fig. 4. Five groups of seeds after seeds dividing

Seeds Dividing. Generally, images under one concept may be multi-modal due to different scenes, viewpoints, illumination and so on. This fact will degrade the negative and positive mining because linear svm does not handle multi-modal problem so well. Therefore we propose dividing the seeds into multiple groups as a pre-processing step to alleviate the multi-modal problem. Given the divided groups, we train classifiers on each group separately.

We use k-means to divide the seeds into m groups ($m = 5$ in our experiments as a tradeoff between cost and performance). Take "waterfall" as an example again. In Fig. 4, seeds of "waterfall" are divided into five groups. Between different groups, there are apparent appearance gaps/differences, but within the same group the appearance variations are relatively smaller. Intuitively, we can tell the proposed seed dividing simplifies the classification task. With simpler tasks, linear svm can fit better and generalize better, resulting in better performance.

4   Experiments

In this section, we compare the proposed method with recently state-of-the-arts and demonstrate our performance in both quantitative and qualitative ways. We also experimentally investigate different components of our method to reveal more understandings.

Deep Learning Features. Recently, deep learning features trained on ImageNet [7] have been successfully applied in many vision tasks such as image classification [12,8,18] and object detection [17]. We first apply deep learning [12,8,18] features to the task of automatic dataset construction. Similar to [12], we train a seven-layer convolutional neural network on ImageNet 2010 and use it to extract features from images – 2048-dimensional features are extracted from the first fully-connected layer.

Evaluation Datasets. We use two datasets to quantitatively compare and analyze our method. The first one is Web-23 [14], containing 23 concepts with positive images and outliers. We also construct a synthetic dataset: we choose 16 concepts and gather corresponding images from ImageNet as the positive samples (see Table 1), and use randomly crawled web images as the negative outliers. Note these subsets are excluded from the training of the deep neural network. Each concept in the synthetic dataset is formed by mixing positive and negative samples ar a ratio of 1:1.

Table 1. The 16 concepts in the synthetic dataset and the number of positive images within

concept	bird	tower	building window	bus	car	car mirror	wheel	fireplace
#images	7196	9439	7799	11037	7046	3288	1981	1359
concept	bread	dish	hamburger	pizza	porridge	corn	garden	tree
#images	6850	10216	2473	2337	8879	1157	2388	2081

4.1 Comparison Experiments

Seeds Comparison. We conduct experiments to compare different seeds generating methods and their impacts on the constructed dataset. We compare our method with the recent state-of-the-art [3] on the synthetic dataset. [3] uses exemplar-LDA [11] classifiers to vote the seeds, on which multiple classifiers are trained to find more positive samples. We call this method ELDA for simplicity.

In our method, a density score based on rank-order distance is used for identifying seeds. A more straight forward approach is to define the density score based on L2 distance. We use this naive approach as a baseline. We also compare with ELDA which is a highly competitive method. For various seeds ratios (5%, 10% and 20%), we compare the seeds precision of different methods. Average results of 16 concepts are reported in Table 2, from which we can tell: (i) our method is significantly better than the baseline approach, because rank-order distance is more robust than L2 distance; (ii) compared to ELDA, the precision of our method is still 6%~9% higher, see visualized comparison in Fig. 5. We also apply our dataset growing method to both our and ELDA's seeds to isolate the quality of seeds for study. As shown in Table 2, our recall is 5%~7% higher than ELDA while the precision of both methods are comparable.

If adaptive thresholding is applied, we will have 98% seeds precision and 18% seeds recall. This result presents good balance between seeds ratio and seeds precision. Such a good balance translates into high dataset quality: 74.2% recall and 98.3% precision, better than any pre-defined threshold (i.e. selecting top 5%, 10%, and 20%).

To further investigate the impact of seeds on constructed datasets, we splice seeds generating and dataset growing in different methods. As shown in Table. 3, by replacing the seeds of ELDA with ours, recall/precision increase from 70.3%/91.9% to 72.4%/97.7%. If we replace the seeds in our method with ELDA's, recall/precision drop from 74.2%/98.3% to 72.1%/93.8%. These results imply that: (i) better seeds lead to better system performance; (ii)our seeds generalize well to ELDA's dataset growing process.

Table 2. Seeds comparison. The datasets are constructed by corresponding seeds and our dataset growing method.

Seeds Ratio	Seeds Precision			Recall/Precision of constructed dataset	
	L2	ELDA [3]	Ours	ELDA [3]	Ours
5%	75.7	90.9	99.7	52.0/95.4	59.0/98.5
10%	72.6	89.6	98.9	61.8/94.0	68.8/96.6
20%	70.2	88.0	94.2	73.3/93.8	78.2/92.2

ELDA   ours

Fig. 5. Seeds comparison visualization. We first generate image rank lists for our and ELDA method. Then we randomly sample images at the 20% quantile position of the rank lists.

System Comparison. We conduct system comparison with OPTIMOL([14]) and ELDA([3]). Results on Web-23 are shown in Fig. 6. The values of OPTIMOL are from [14,13], and the seeds' amount K in ELDA is set to be the same with ours. From Fig. 6, it can be seen that our method collects more images than the other methods, with a higher level of precision.

We also compare with ELDA on the synthetic dataset. In this experiment, we manually set the K so that the corresponding seeds ratio are 5%, 10% and 20% respectively. The comparison results are shown in Table 4 , from which we can see that: (i) our method consistently outperforms ELDA, no matter measured by recall or precision; (ii) larger seeds ratios generally lead to higher recall and lower precision.

4.2 Components Evaluation

Here we study the contributions of different components to our entire system. Basically our system contains three components: seeds generating, negative and positive mining and seeds dividing. We break down those components and design three experiments to analyze their contributions to the entire system.

- *Seeds*: only seeds generating, with dataset growing.
- *Seeds+NegPosMining*: negative and positive mining without seeds dividing.
- *Seeds+Divide+NegPosMining*: our full system, including all components.

Table 3. Seeds' impact on constructed datasets. The amount of ELDA's seeds is set to be the same with ours.

Seeds Generating	Dataset Growing	Recall	Precision
Ours	Ours	74.2	98.3
Ours	ELDA's	72.4	97.7
ELDA's	Ours	72.1	93.8
ELDA's	ELDA's	70.3	91.9

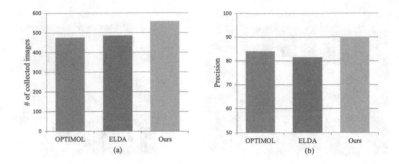

Fig. 6. System comparison on Web-23 dataset.

From the results in Fig. 7, we can see that: *First,* the recall of *Seeds* is around 20%~40%. This is fairly good. Considering the typical amount of crawled images is more than 10K per concept, such recall can offer us over 2K images with very high precision (95% or more). *Second,* the negative and positive mining effectively improve the recall, which is around 50%~80% after mining. *Third,* the system is further improved by seeds dividing, which helps the final recall achieve 70%~90%. This means that we generally can collect more than 7K images for one concept.

We also observe that: for some concepts, like "bird" and "tower", recalls of our system are much higher than that obtained without seed dividing. This is because images under these concepts have diverse visual appearances. This indicates that seeds dividing is essential to our dataset construction system.

Table 4. System comparison on the synthetic dataset

concept	Ours recall/precision	ELDA's recall/precision		
		5% seeds	10% seeds	20% seeds
bird	70.0/98.3	21.2/90.8	32.1/86.3	53.7/82.3
tower	69.9/95.5	22.0/89.1	33.5/85.2	56.6/83.8
building window	89.7/96.3	20.9/85.6	38.3/82.0	51.2/78.7
bus	76.4/98.6	20.9/92.5	39.1/90.2	59.4/87.3
car	82.2/98.0	16.3/93.9	29.3/91.3	56.2/89.7
car mirror	52.6/99.1	18.9/83.6	28.6/81.6	46.9/80.9
wheel	56.1/99.8	9.6/97.4	29.3/93.2	43.7/89.5
fireplace	75.1/99.4	20.2/97.2	36.8/94.9	48.1/92.6
bread	73.8/97.9	17.3/90.3	29.3/88.3	55.0/85.9
dish	70.6/98.1	20.4/92.1	36.0/90.6	59.4/88.6
hamburger	75.7/98.6	10.6/95.3	31.9/94.0	45.2/93.1
pizza	85.5/99.4	21.5/94.7	39.3/94.2	64.7/91.0
porridge	88.1/99.3	17.0/90.6	39.2/88.9	50.7/87.5
corn	65.3/99.2	8.7/98.1	20.3/93.6	37.8/90.5
garden	83.8/98.4	10.1/89.0	29.1/86.2	41.8/81.2
tree	72.9/96.7	11.1/93.2	25.2/90.9	41.1/88.8

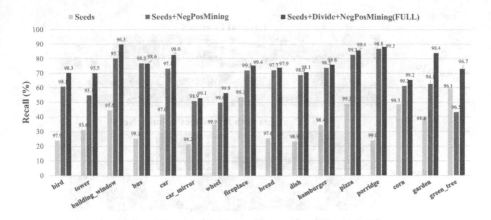

Fig. 7. Components Evaluation. The height of a bar stands for recall and the numbers above the bar is precision. (best viewed in color).

4.3   Dataset Constructed by Our System

Our system has now constructed a dataset which contains 80 concepts, averaging 7K images per concept. It takes nearly a month, and most of the time is spent on downloading images from Internet. The processing time for seeds generating and dataset growing

Table 5. Some concepts in our constructed dataset and corresponding statistics

	concept	#images crawled	#images collected	precision of collected images	#images in ImageNet
general concepts	bus	35232	16585	94.5	>15590
	train	24485	10087	96.8	>10041
	tree	39457	19885	96.0	>14433
concepts with few images in ImageNet	cabin	16224	6649	96.3	2546
	crowd	23943	9150	99.3	1296
	ferris wheel	10120	5283	98.8	1795
	fried egg	8087	5104	97.5	1295
	meeting room	11119	6681	98.0	1354
	sculpture	37213	15732	98.0	2677
	sun	24855	6816	99.3	1341
	tattoo	33364	21201	97.0	1685
	tree root	16554	8547	97.5	1769
concepts not exist in ImageNet	fly in sky	17813	5141	96.5	0
	team photo	9919	4829	98.5	0
	wearing glasses	15723	5082	92.4	0
	waterfall	18766	9368	98.5	0
	view from plane	3350	1274	98.3	0

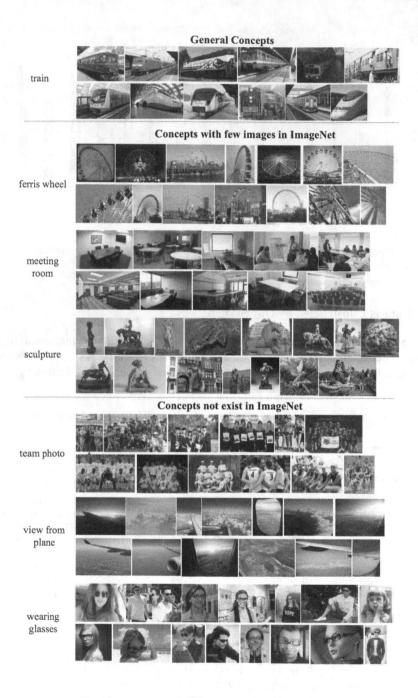

Fig. 8. Exemplar images from our constructed dataset

is just around 3 hours per concept. Exemplary images from this dataset are shown in Fig. 8. We also present the statistics of some representative concepts in Table 5, including image amounts and corresponding precisions. We estimate the precision from a manually labeled subset (500 images per concept) of the entire dataset. The average precision is 95%.

Our constructed dataset demonstrates two desired properties which could be a good supplementary to existing large-scale datasets such as ImageNet: (i) apart from a handful of generic concepts such as "bus" and "train", most concepts in ImageNet only contain 1,000~2,000 images, while our method can enlarge that amount by 5 times on average; (ii) Although a large range of concepts has been covered by ImageNet, the uncovered range is even larger. For example, there is no concept such as "wearing glasses" or "view from sky" in ImageNet, but our system can automatically collect many precise images for these concepts.

5 Conclusion and Future Work

In this work, we present a fully automatic system to construct large-scale, high-precision dataset from noisy web images. The system can collect thousands of images for one concept with very high precision – 95% or more. The superior performance is mainly due to the proposed seeds generating, negative and positive mining, as well as seeds dividing. Currently we only use visual features, and it is worth studying how to appropriately exploit text and web-ranking to further improve the system performance.

References

1. Berg, T.L., Forsyth, D.A.: Animals on the web. In: Computer Vision and Pattern Recognition, vol. 2, pp. 1463–1470 (2006)
2. Carpineto, C., De Mori, R., Romano, G., Bigi, B.: An information-theoretic approach to automatic query expansion. ACM Transactions on Information Systems (TOIS) 19(1), 1–27 (2001)
3. Chen, X., Shrivastava, A., Gupta, A.: Neil: Extracting visual knowledge from web data. In: International Conference on Computer Vision, vol. 3 (2013)
4. Chua, T.S., Tang, J., Hong, R., Li, H., Luo, Z., Zheng, Y.T.: Nus-wide: A real-world web image database from national university of singapore. In: Proc. of ACM Conf. on Image and Video Retrieval (2009)
5. Collins, B., Deng, J., Li, K., Fei-Fei, L.: Towards scalable dataset construction: An active learning approach. In: Forsyth, D., Torr, P., Zisserman, A. (eds.) ECCV 2008, Part I. LNCS, vol. 5302, pp. 86–98. Springer, Heidelberg (2008)
6. Dalal, N., Triggs, B.: Histograms of oriented gradients for human detection. In: Computer Vision and Pattern Recognition, vol. 1, pp. 886–893 (2005)
7. Deng, J., Dong, W., Socher, R., Li, L.J., Li, K., Fei-Fei, L.: Imagenet: A large-scale hierarchical image database. In: Computer Vision and Pattern Recognition, pp. 248–255 (2009)
8. Donahue, J., Jia, Y., Vinyals, O., Hoffman, J., Zhang, N., Tzeng, E., Darrell, T.: Decaf: A deep convolutional activation feature for generic visual recognition. arXiv:1310.1531 (2013)
9. Felzenszwalb, P.F., Girshick, R.B., McAllester, D., Ramanan, D.: Object detection with discriminatively trained part-based models. Pattern Analysis and Machine Intelligence 32(9), 1627–1645 (2010)

10. Feng, H., Chua, T.S.: A bootstrapping approach to annotating large image collection. In: Proceedings of the 5th ACM SIGMM International Workshop on Multimedia Information Retrieval, pp. 55–62 (2003)
11. Hariharan, B., Malik, J., Ramanan, D.: Discriminative decorrelation for clustering and classification. In: Fitzgibbon, A., Lazebnik, S., Perona, P., Sato, Y., Schmid, C. (eds.) ECCV 2012, Part IV. LNCS, vol. 7575, pp. 459–472. Springer, Heidelberg (2012)
12. Krizhevsky, A., Sutskever, I., Hinton, G.: Imagenet classification with deep convolutional neural networks. In: NIPS, pp. 1106–1114 (2012)
13. Li, L.J., Fei-Fei, L.: Optimol: automatic online picture collection via incremental model learning. International Journal of Computer Vision 88(2), 147–168 (2010)
14. Li, L.J., Wang, G., Fei-fei, L.: Optimol: automatic online picture collection via incremental model learning. In: Computer Vision and Pattern Recognition (2007)
15. Russell, B.C., Torralba, A., Murphy, K.P., Freeman, W.T.: Labelme: a database and web-based tool for image annotation. International Journal of Computer Vision 77(1-3), 157–173 (2008)
16. Schroff, F., Criminisi, A., Zisserman, A.: Harvesting image databases from the web. In: International Conference on Computer Vision, pp. 1–8 (2007)
17. Szegedy, C., Toshev, A., Erhan, D.: Deep neural networks for object detection. In: Advances in Neural Information Processing Systems, pp. 2553–2561 (2013)
18. Zeiler, M.D., Fergus, R.: Visualizing and understanding convolutional neural networks. arXiv:1311.2901 (2013)
19. Zhu, C., Wen, F., Sun, J.: A rank-order distance based clustering algorithm for face tagging. In: Computer Vision and Pattern Recognition, pp. 481–488 (2011)

Zero-Shot Learning via Visual Abstraction

Stanislaw Antol[1], C. Lawrence Zitnick[2], and Devi Parikh[1]

[1] Virginia Tech, Blacksburg, VA, USA
[2] Microsoft Research, Redmond, WA, USA

Abstract. One of the main challenges in learning fine-grained visual categories is gathering training images. Recent work in Zero-Shot Learning (ZSL) circumvents this challenge by describing categories via attributes or text. However, not all visual concepts, *e.g.*, two people dancing, are easily amenable to such descriptions. In this paper, we propose a new modality for ZSL using *visual abstraction* to learn difficult-to-describe concepts. Specifically, we explore concepts related to people and their interactions with others. Our proposed modality allows one to provide training data by manipulating abstract visualizations, *e.g.*, one can illustrate interactions between two clipart people by manipulating each person's pose, expression, gaze, and gender. The feasibility of our approach is shown on a human pose dataset and a new dataset containing complex interactions between two people, where we outperform several baselines. To better match across the two domains, we learn an explicit mapping between the abstract and real worlds.

Keywords: zero-shot learning, visual abstraction, synthetic data, pose.

1 Introduction

Fine-grained object classification has gained significant attention in recent years. One of its main challenges is gathering training images. For example, though it may be easy to find images of birds, it might be very difficult to find images of specific species of birds, *e.g.*, "least auklet." Zero-Shot Learning (ZSL) [7,16,18, 30] addresses this scenario by providing an alternative approach that does not require any example training images. Instead, a user may provide other forms of side information, such as semantic visual attributes [16] (*e.g.*, "has black forehead," "has rounded wings") or textual descriptions of categories [7].

While semantic attributes or text-based descriptions provide an intuitive method for describing a variety of visual concepts, generating semantic descriptions is tedious or unreasonable for many visual concepts. For instance, how would a user semantically describe "a person sitting" to a recognition system that did not understand the concept of "sitting"? The problem is further exacerbated if the category is related to the interaction of multiple objects. For instance, consider the specific dancing poses between two people shown in the upper-right of Figure 1. Describing these scenes to a computer would require a lengthy textual description and still might not capture the full nuance.

D. Fleet et al. (Eds.): ECCV 2014, Part IV, LNCS 8692, pp. 401–416, 2014.

Fig. 1. Our approach: First, we have people create abstract illustrations (left) using our interface for various categories. Then we train models of these categories on illustration data. Finally, we test our models on real images (right).

To address this issue, we propose a new modality for ZSL that utilizes visual abstraction. The underlying intuition, shared by work in sketch-based image retrieval [6,24], is that it can be easier to communicate a visual concept through an abstract visual representation rather than a textual description. Thus, instead of a textual description like an attribute list, our proposed modality allows a supervisor to create abstract illustrations (left side of Figure 1).

In this paper, we use visual abstraction to train models for recognizing visual classes related to the pose of individuals or the interaction between two people. These concepts are of high interest in computer vision and are difficult to describe with traditional ZSL approaches. We introduce a novel image dataset, INTERACT, of 60 fine-grained interactions between pairs of people depicting various combinations of verbs and propositions (*e.g.*, "running after," "running to," "arguing with"). We test our approach on this dataset and a subset of the PARSE [21] dataset. We introduce a simple and intuitive interface that allows a supervisor to train these visual models. This interface lets users illustrate visual categories by varying the poses, expressions, gazes, and genders of people built from a collection of clipart. We present results for category-level ZSL (where each concept has a semantic name but is still hard to semantically *describe*, such as "dancing with") and instance-level ZSL (where each concept is very specific, such as a specific "dancing with" pose, and may not even have a semantic name). Surprisingly, our models, trained only on abstract illustrations (*i.e.*, visual abstractions), are effective at the category-level classification task on *real* images, even if only a single illustration depicting the concept is provided. As more example illustrations are provided, performance is further improved (Figure 4).

We create models that can generalize from abstract visualizations to real images by using a novel set of features. We analyze the role of different feature types (*e.g.*, contact between people, expressions) and show that some are more informative than others. When creating these example illustrations, users may visualize the semantically important aspects of the poses and interactions in more detail, but may have a fuzzier or even skewed notion of the other aspects.

Moreover, our easy-to-use interface results in biases in the illustrations (*e.g.*, the interface does not allow for out-of-plane rotation). To account for these human tendencies, as well as interface biases, we learn an explicit mapping from the features extracted from illustrations to the features extracted from real images. This allows us to improve performance on instance-level ZSL. Our visual abstraction interface, code, and datasets are publicly available.

2   Related Work

We discuss existing work on zero-shot learning, learning with synthetic data, learning semantic relations, pose estimation, and action recognition.

Zero-Shot Learning (ZSL): The problem of learning models of visual concepts without example images of the concepts is called Zero-Shot Learning. Attributes (mid-level, visual, and semantic features) [9,10,15,16] provide a natural interface for ZSL [16], where an unseen class is described by a list of attributes. Equipped with a set of pre-trained attribute classifiers, a test image can be probabilistically matched to each of these attribute signatures and be classified as the category with the highest probability. Instead of using a list of attributes, recent work [7] has leveraged more general textual descriptions of categories to build visual models of these categories. Our work takes a fundamentally different approach to ZSL. We propose a strictly visual modality to allow a supervisor to train a model for visual concepts that may not be easily *describable* in semantic terms, *e.g.*, poses of people, interactions between people.

Learning With Synthetic Data: Our work introduces the use of abstract visualizations as a modality to train visual models in a ZSL setting. Previously, papers have explored the use of synthetic data to aid in the training of vision algorithms. In many object recognition tasks, it is common to perturb the training data using affine warps to augment the training data [14]. Computer-generated scenes may also be used to evaluate recognition systems [13]. Shotton *et al.* [23] used synthetically generated depth data depicting humans to learn a human pose detector from this depth data. Unlike these approaches, we are trying to learn high-level, complex concepts where it is not feasible to automatically generate synthetic data, so we must rely on humans to create our synthetic data. Most similar to our work, the problem of semantic scene understanding using abstract scenes was studied in [31]. They use a dataset of simple sentences corresponding to abstract scenes to learn a mapping from sentences to abstract scenes. Recently, sequences of abstract scenes were used to predict which objects will move in the near future [11]. Unlike these works, we use abstraction to learn visual models that can be applied to *real* images. Sketch-based image retrieval [6, 24] allows users to search for an image by sketching the concept. Sketching complex interactions between people would be time consuming, and likely inaccurate for most lay users. More importantly, our modality has the potential to augment the abstract scenes with a large variety of visual cues (*e.g.*, gender, ethnicity, clothing, background) that would be cumbersome for users to convey via sketches.

Learning Semantic Relations: Previous papers have studied relations between people [26] and other objects [22, 29]. Most similar to the learning semantic relations part of our work, Yang *et al.* [26] used contact points to detect six different interactions between people. Sadeghi *et al.* [22] and Yao *et al.* [29] both model the relationship of people and objects when their combination creates a canonical pose or "visual phrase." Unlike all of this previous work, we are able to train our models for a larger number of concepts without relying on any training images. Several papers have studied the relations of people in groups using videos [4, 17], such as "queuing in line" or whether people are looking at each other [19]. While our approach only considers relations between people in the 2D image space, recently Chakraborty *et al.* [3] explored determining human relations using 3D information from a single image.

Pose Estimation and Action Recognition: Automatically estimating human pose [2, 27] and recognizing human actions [1, 28] in images has received a lot of attention in the vision community. These efforts are orthogonal to the focus of our work. We propose a new modality that enables us to train a vision system to recognize fine-grained interactions between people without any example images depicting those interactions. This can be augmented with any pose estimation technique at test time.

3   Datasets

To evaluate our approach, we need real images to *test* our visual models. For evaluation, we use two datasets: INTERACT, a new dataset that we introduce here, and the standard PARSE dataset [21].

3.1   INTERACT

Many fine-grained visual categories exist between *pairs of people*. While some datasets exist for a small number of these categories [26], we collected a new dataset with a significantly larger number of visual classes, INTERACT.

Interactions: Our dataset focuses on two people interacting via different verb phrases. They include transitive verbs (*e.g.*, "A is pushing B"), joint activities (*e.g.*, "A is dancing *with* B"), movement verbs with directional prepositions (*e.g.*, "A is walking *to* B"), and posture verbs with locational prepositions (*e.g.*, "A is sitting *next to* B"). We combine different verbs with different prepositions to get 60 verb phrases, including ones that share a verb but contain different prepositions, such as "running *to*" and "running *away from*." The full list of interactions can be found in the supplementary material (on the project website).

Real Image Collection: We crowdsourced our image collection on Amazon Mechanical Turk (AMT). We asked 3 workers to collect 20 images that meet the following criteria: they are all different photographs, they depict the sentence "Person A is *verb phrase* Person B," and all contain exactly 2 people. Note that we did not require them to have each person's entire body in the image (*e.g.*, some body parts can be cropped out), which makes this dataset challenging (*e.g.*, right side of Figure 1). This resulted in 3,600 initial images.

Real Image Annotations: We also used AMT to collect various image annotations that are needed for our features via different custom interfaces. The pose annotation interface prompted the worker with one of our images and its corresponding sentence. We highlighted whether the worker should be annotating Person A or Person B in the sentence. The worker annotates the person's 14 body parts (right side of Figure 3). The worker provides their best guess if the part is occluded and responds "not present" if it is not within the image border. We had 5 workers annotate each person in each image and averaged them for the final ground truth pose annotations. In addition, workers annotated ground truth eye gaze (*i.e.*, looking to the image left or right), facial expression (*i.e.*, one of six prototypic emotional expressions [5] plus a neutral expression), and gender of each person via separate interfaces. We selected the mode of their responses for our final annotation. In addition to collecting the annotation of interest, two interfaces asked one additional question each. One asked if the prompted image contained exactly two main people or not and the other asked if the annotated pose overlaid on the prompted image was of good quality or not. We used the last two annotation queries to remove poor quality work. Additionally, a GIST-based [20] image matching scheme was used to remove duplicates. Removing these images gave us our final annotated dataset with 3,172 images (52.9 images per category on average). Some examples can be found in the bottom part of Figure 1 and the rightmost two columns of Figure 5. More details about our interfaces and our procedure can be found in the supplementary material.

3.2 PARSE

We also use a subset of the standard PARSE [21] dataset, which originally contains 305 images of *individuals* in various poses. We created a list of categories that frequently appear in the PARSE dataset (*e.g.*, "is dunking," "is diving for an object"). From the images that belong to these categories, we removed those that were used to train the pose detector [26]. Some categories (*e.g.*, "is standing") had disproportionately large number of images, so we removed images at random from these categories. This leaves us with 108 images in our dataset (7.7 images per category on average). We also collected the same annotations as in Section 3.1, except for pose (since ground truth pose annotations are already available with the dataset). See the supplementary material for more details.

4 Our Approach

In this section, we present our new modality for ZSL. We begin by introducing our user interface for collecting visual illustrations for training. We then describe the novel features that are extracted from our abstract illustrations and real images. Finally, we describe the approach used to train our models. The results of various experiments follow in Section 5.

Fig. 2. User interface (with random initialization) used to collect abstract illustrations on AMT. Workers were able to manipulate pose, expression, gaze direction, and gender.

4.1   Visual Abstraction Interface

For our domain of interest, we conjectured that our concepts depend primarily on four main factors: pose, eye gaze, facial expression, and gender. Some other factors that we do not model, but may also be important are clothing, the presence of other objects, and scene context. A screenshot of our user interface is shown in Figure 2. Initially, two people (one blond-haired and one brown-haired) are shown with random poses, gaze directions (*i.e.*, "flip"), expressions, and genders. We allow our subjects to continuously manipulate the poses (*i.e.*, joint angles and positions) of both people by dragging on the various body parts. They may horizontally flip the people to change their perceived eye gaze direction. The facial expressions are chosen from the same selection as is used for the annotation of real images (Section 3.1). Finally, the subjects may select one of the two predominant genders for each clipart person.

To collect our training data for category-level ZSL, we prompt the user with a sentence to illustrate using the interface (*e.g.*, "Person A is dancing with Person B.", "A person is dunking."). To promote diversity, we encouraged them to imagine any objects or background, as long as the poses are consistent with the imagined scene (*e.g.*, a worker can imagine a chair and illustrate someone sitting on it). The interface includes buttons to annotate which clipart person corresponds to which person in the sentence. Some illustrations are shown on the left side of Figure 1 and in the left three columns of Figure 5. For the PARSE concepts, the interface is the same except that only one person is present.

For instance-level ZSL, we modify our previous interface. Instead of sentences, we first (briefly, for 2 seconds) show the user a real image and then they recreate it (from memory) as best they can. The stated goal is to recreate the real image so another person would be able to select the shown image from a collection of real images. This mimics the scenario when a person is searching for a specific image: they might be clear on the semantically important aspects while having a fuzzier or skewed notion of other aspects. Another bias of the illustrations occurs when it is impossible to recreate the real image exactly due to the limitations of the interface, such as not being able to change the height of the clipart people, the interface not allowing for out-of-plane rotation, *etc.*

4.2   Relation and Appearance Features

Using the annotations described in Section 3.1 (*i.e.*, pose, gaze, expression, and gender) for persons denoted by i and j, we compute a set of relation and appearance features. Some of our relation features are distance-based and some are angle-based. All distance-based features use Gaussians placed at different positions to capture relative distance. The Gaussians' σ parameters are proportional to the *scale* of each person. A person's scale is defined as the distance between their head and the center of their shoulders and hips. Unless otherwise noted, all angles/orientations are w.r.t. the image frame's x-axis. They are represented by 12 dimensional unit histograms with each bin corresponding to $\pi/6$ radians. Soft assignments are made to the histograms using linear weighting. The first two sets of features, Basic and Gaze, account for both people. The remaining five feature sets are described for a single person and must be evaluated twice (swapping i and j) and concatenated. The feature sets are described below.

Basic: This feature set encodes basic relation properties between two people, such as relative orientation and distance. We calculate each person's body angle (in the image frame). This is calculated from the image coordinates for the head and mid-point between shoulders. We place Gaussians at the center of the people and then use the distance between them to evaluate the Gaussian functions. We also calculate the angle (in the image frame) between the centers of the two people. This gives us a total of $2 * (12 + 1) + 12 = 38$ features. They can be thought of as simplifying the people into two boxes (possibly having different scale parameters) with certain orientations and looking at the relative positions and angle between their centers.

Gaze: The gaze feature set is encoded using 5 binary features, corresponding to i looking at j, j looking at i, both people are looking at each other, both people are looking away from each other, and both people are looking in the same direction. To determine if i is looking at j, we check if j's neck is in the *appropriate region* of the image. The image is divided into two parts by extending the line between i's head and neck and the appropriate region is defined to be the area where i is looking (which depends on i's gaze direction). Once we have both i looking at j and *vice versa* features, we compute the remaining three gaze features via the appropriate logic operations (*e.g.*, if i is looking at j and j is looking at i, then the looking-at-each-other feature is true).

Global: This feature set encodes the general position of the joints in reference to a body. Three Gaussians are placed in a 3×1 grid on the image based on the body's size and orientation (the blue circles in Figure 3). The positions of one person's 8 joints (two for each limb) are evaluated using all Gaussians from both Gaussian sets (*i.e.*, person i's joints relative to person i's global Gaussians and person j's global Gaussians), giving us a total of $8 * 3 * 2 = 48$ features.

Contact: This feature set encodes the specific location of the joints in reference to other body parts. For each person, we place Gaussians at 13 positions: 3

Fig. 3. (Left) Illustration of the part locations labeled for each person (red dots). We illustrate the standard deviations of the Gaussians used to compute normalized features (Section 4.2) for a joint's general location (blue circles) and whether there is contact with another part (green circles). (Right) The corresponding labeled part locations on a real image (from INTERACT) acquired from one of our annotation tasks.

for each limb and 1 for the head (the green circles in Figure 3). The positions of 8 joints (two for each limb) are then evaluated on the Gaussians placed on *themselves* (*e.g.*, is i's left hand near i's head) and the *other person* (*e.g.*, is i's right elbow near j's left shoulder) for a total of $8 * 13 * 2 = 208$ features.

Orientation: This final pose-based feature set encodes the relative (*i.e.*, *not* w.r.t. the image frame) joint angles. They are computed by finding the relative angle between parent and child joint positions (*e.g.*, left elbow and left shoulder). We compute 8 joint angles (two for each limb) for a total of $8 * 12 = 96$ features.

Expression: We convert expression into a set of 7 binary variables.

Gender: We convert gender into a set of 2 binary variables.

Thus, concatenating all of these features gives us a total of $38 + 5 + 2 * (48 + 208 + 96 + 7 + 2) = 765$ features, which are all between 0 and 1.

For the PARSE dataset, where each image only contains a single person, each of the previous feature sets are modified accordingly (if at all). The Basic feature set becomes only the body angle. The Gaze feature set is replaced with 2 binary variables that indicate if the person is looking to their left or right, respectively. The Global feature set is halved. The Contact feature set is also halved. This gives us a total of $12 + 2 + 24 + 104 + 96 + 7 + 2 = 247$ features.

By design, our illustration interfaces provide (without any additional annotation) the same data that was collected for the real images. Thus, we can use the same features for both abstract illustrations and real images.

4.3   Zero-Shot Learning Models

In category-level ZSL, we are trying to create a model that can classify an image as belonging to one of the given semantic classes (*e.g.*, "dancing with"). We use multiple one-vs-all linear Support Vector Machines (SVMs), trained on the abstract illustration features. At test time, these classifiers are used to determine the category of the real images. In instance-level ZSL, we are trying to decide if an image represents a specific concept, *i.e.*, given a test real image, we wish to determine which specific abstract visualization (instance) corresponds to the real image. For this, we use Nearest Neighbor matching. Since our features are from two different domains, learning a mapping between them could improve the matching performance. This is described next.

4.4   Mapping From Abstract to Real for the Instance-level Model

We learn a mapping between the domain of abstract images and the domain of real images. To learn such a mapping, we need examples that correspond to the same thing in both domains. We use some of our instance-level illustrations (Section 4.1) as these abstract-real pairs. The mapping can learn to correct for both user and interface biases discussed in Section 4.1.

Simpler techniques, such as Canonical Correspondence Analysis [12], did not learn a good mapping between the abstract and real worlds. We found that General Regression Neural Networks (GRNN) [25] did better. We also found that converting from our abstract features into "real" features performed better than converting real features into "abstract" features. Thus, the GRNN's input is all of the abstract features and its output is all of the real features.

5   Experimental Results

In this section, we describe our experiments which show that our new modality for ZSL is able to create models that can learn category-level (Section 5.1) and instance-level (Section 5.2) visual concepts. We perform an ablation study on different feature sets, showing their performance contribution (Section 5.3). Finally, we utilize a state-of-the-art pose detector on both INTERACT and PARSE datasets to investigate our approach in a more automatic setting (Section 5.4).

5.1   Category-Level Zero-Shot Learning

We begin by experimenting with the ability of our novel modality to learn our category-level concepts, *i.e.*, classifying images into one of the semantic descriptions, such as "A is kicking B." To acquire the required training illustrations, we ran our visual abstraction interface with sentence prompts (described in Section 4.1) on AMT. We had 50 workers create an abstract illustration for each of the 60 semantic concepts from INTERACT (Section 3.1) and the 14 semantic concepts from PARSE (Section 3.2). After removing poor quality work, we are left with 3,000 and 696 illustrations, respectively.

The setup for all category-level ZSL experiments (unless otherwise noted) is described here. Using the abstract illustrations, we train multiple one-vs-all linear SVMs (liblinear [8]) with the cost parameter, C, set to 0.01, which worked reasonably well across all experiments. For INTERACT, there is ambiguity (at test time) as to which person is Person A and which person is Person B. To account for this, we evaluate each of the classifiers using both orderings, select the

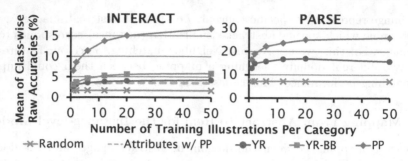

Fig. 4. We evaluate category-level ZSL performance on both datasets as described in Section 5.1. As we increase the number of ZSL training illustrations, our classification performance improves, but it begins to saturate. With both using perfect poses, our model (PP) does much better than the attribute DAP model (Attributes w/ PP). We also show results (described in Section 5.4) with output from a pose detector (YR) and, for INTERACT, a pose detector assisted by ground truth bounding boxes (YR-BB).

most confident score on orderings, and then predict the label of the classifier with the highest confidence. Our category-level classification metric is the mean of the class-wise raw accuracies. We observe performance as the number of training illustrations per category is increased. For each number of training illustrations, we average over 50 random selections of training illustrations (per category).

Results for our model with perfect poses, PP, are shown in Figure 4. It can be seen that even one illustration is able to perform several times better than random on both of our datasets. Adding additional training illustrations improves performance, although it begins to saturate around 20 training examples. For INTERACT, we reach ~17% using all illustrations. We compare this to a stronger baseline: attribute-based ZSL. We define a vocabulary of 79 attributes, such as "A's hand is touching B's knee," gender, and gaze. For attribute ZSL, we use the DAP model from Lampert *et al.* [16]. Our approach significantly outperforms this approach (~3.5%), demonstrating the benefit of our new modality for ZSL. More details about the baseline are in the supplementary material.

Some qualitative results are shown in Figure 5. Confusion matrices for the model are shown in the supplementary material. We also did a human agreement study on AMT for INTERACT. On average, the correct verb phrase for an image was selected only ~51% of the time (averaged over 10 workers per image), which demonstrates how ambiguous this classification task can be. A similar human agreement study was done for the illustrations to identify the most canonical (*i.e.*, top) illustrations per category. Using the top illustrations instead of random ones to train our model provided modest improvements when using fewer training illustrations. If we treat any of the human labels that were collected during the INTERACT human agreement experiment as a valid label, we find that the PP model's performance increases to ~37% (at 50 illustrations per category).

5.2   Instance-Level Zero-Shot Learning

We also test the ability of our new modality to learn instance-level concepts. To acquire the necessary training illustrations, we ran our visual abstraction interface with image prompts (as described in Section 4.1) on AMT. We showed a real image (one of 3,172 from INTERACT and one of 305 from PARSE) for two seconds to the workers, who recreated it using the interface. Through a pilot study, just as in [6], we found two seconds to be sufficient for people to capture the more salient aspects of the image. It is unlikely that a user would have every detail of the instance in mind when trying to train a model for a specific concept and we wanted to mimic this in our setup. We had 3 workers recreate each of the images, and after manually removing work from problematic workers, we are left with 8,916 and 914 illustrations for INTERACT and PARSE, respectively.

We perform classification via nearest-neighbor matching. If the real image's features match the features of any of the (up to) 3 illustration instances that workers created for it, we have found a correct label. We vary K, the number of nearest neighbors that are considered, and evaluate the percentage of real images that have a correct label within those K neighbors. We normalized K by the total number of illustrations. We need a training dataset to learn a mapping between the abstract and real worlds, i.e., training the GRNN from Section 4.4. For IN-TERACT, we split the categories into 39 seen categories for training and 21 unseen categories for testing to minimize learning biases specific to specific categories (i.e., verb phrases). The results are averaged over 10 random seen/unseen category splits. For PARSE, the training data corresponds to the 197 images

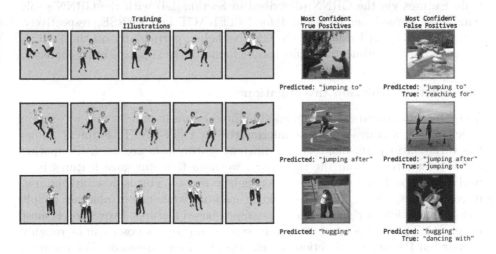

Fig. 5. The left columns show 5 random illustrations (of 50) used for classifier training. Columns 6 and 7 contain the most confident true positive and false positive for a given category, respectively. Mistakes include choosing a semantically reasonable verb (top), choosing the incorrect preposition (middle), and incorrect prediction due to the pose similarity between two classes (bottom). More examples are in the supplement.

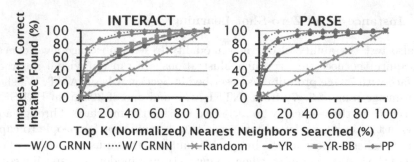

Fig. 6. We evaluate instance-level classification, showing the percent of images (y-axis) with the correct label being found within the top K (dataset size normalized) guesses (x-axis). We outperform random and see some benefit of learning a mapping (see Section 4.4) between the domains, particularly for the PARSE dataset.

that were not assigned a semantic category nor were used in the pose detector training (as discussed in Section 3.2). The training required for this mapping can be thought of as analogous to training the attribute predictors in the DAP model [16] for ZSL. One needs to train the attribute classifiers before one can use attribute descriptions with DAP. Similarly, we learn the mapping between the real and abstract world offline on a held out set of categories.

The results are shown in Figure 6. We see that our models are doing orders of magnitude better than chance just looking at the closest nearest neighbor and the gap increases as we search through neighbors that are further away. We also evaluate our approach by performing matching after transforming the train features via the GRNN (described in Section 4.4) with the GRNN's sole parameter, spread, set to 5 and 1 for INTERACT and PARSE, respectively. Using the mapping learned by the GRNNs helps, particularly on the PARSE dataset. More experimental results can be found in the supplementary material.

5.3   Feature Ablation Investigation

To better understand our system and the interactions in our dataset, we explore which of our features are most informative on INTERACT. Figure 7 shows the variation in performance when different feature sets are used. Comparing the first and third from the right bars, we note that our gaze features have negligible impact (actually performing slightly worse). This is possibly because, in real images, people might be looking head-on, whereas our abstract people can only look left or right. Of the appearance-based features, expression is most beneficial. This makes sense intuitively, since two people's poses can be roughly similar but the perceived action can change based on expression. For instance, when two people are wrestling *vs.* when they are hugging (*e.g.*, Figure 1). In both cases, arms can be around the other person's body, but expressions will change from angry to happy. Of the pose-based features, the Global feature is the most informative on its own. It indirectly captures contact and joint angles, so it is reasonable that it performs better than Contact or Orientation alone.

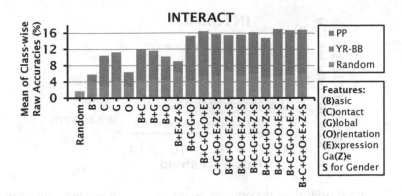

Fig. 7. We plot classification performance for INTERACT using different subsets of features. Some features, like Global, are more informative than others. Of the appearance-based features, Expression turns out to be most informative, presumably when body pose features are similar (*e.g.*, "wrestling" *vs.* "hugging").

5.4   Automatic Pose Evaluation

In this section, we do an evaluation of our category-level ZSL task using the current state-of-the-art pose detector developed by Yang and Ramanan [27]. We utilized the pre-trained PARSE model and detected the pose on both the INTERACT and the PARSE datasets. For the expression, gaze, and gender features, we continue to use human annotations. These results (YR) are shown in Figures 4, 6, and 7. As expected, due to the pose detector being developed for PARSE, automatic detection on the PARSE dataset yields reasonable performance (compared to perfect pose). The results on INTERACT do not perform nearly as well, although it still outperforms the baselines. To boost the performance of the pose detector on INTERACT, we also experimented with providing ground truth bounding boxes (YR-BB), which results in better performance.

INTERACT is significantly more challenging than PARSE for automatic pose detection. Thus, it is not surprising that incorrectly detected poses confuse our models. Properties that make INTERACT particularly challenging include: images from arbitrary perspectives, more difficult (for the detector) poses (*e.g.*, "crawling," "lying"), overlapping people (*e.g.*, "hugging," "standing in front of"), and incomplete poses (*i.e.*, not all body parts are present). We investigated this latter point by selecting images from INTERACT based on the number of parts present in the image. There are 14 parts per person and we ensure that both people have at least a certain number of parts. Requiring all parts to be within the image reduces INTERACT to 1,689 images (from 3,172). 91.5% of our images contain at least 7 parts per person. More of these details can be found in the supplementary material. We re-evaluate our category-level ZSL performance (at 50 training illustrations per category) as we vary the part threshold and show our results in Figure 8. Although there is some noise, both the perfect pose and automatic pose detection methods show an increase in accuracy as we require

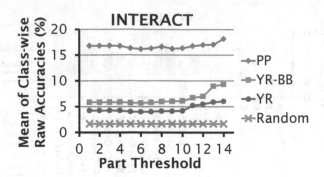

Fig. 8. We plot classification performance as we vary the minimum number of parts both people have (see Section 5.4). While the perfect pose approach only has minor improvements, both detection approaches improve more when all people are fully visible, showing that current detectors do not work well when parts are missing.

more parts to be within the image border. This result suggests that there is a lot to gain by furthering research into more robust pose detectors. We would like to reiterate that we have part annotations even in the case of occlusion, which probably accounts for some of the automatic detector's performance difference with perfect poses. We hope the introduction of INTERACT will help the community advance pose detectors in more practical settings.

6   Conclusions

We propose a new modality for Zero-Shot Learning (ZSL) of concepts that are too difficult to describe in terms of attributes or text in general (*e.g.*, "holding hands with"). A user illustrates the concept through visual abstraction. We demonstrate its utility for classifying poses of people and interactions between two people. We introduce a new dataset containing 60 fine-grained verb phrases describing interactions between pairs of people. We present results for category-level ZSL (where the concept has a semantic name, *e.g.*, "crouching with") and instance-level ZSL (where the concept is specific and may not have a semantic name). We report results on our new dataset, as well as a standard single-person pose dataset. We also learn a mapping from abstract-world features to real-world features. Our approach outperforms several baselines. We also analyze the information captured by various subsets of features, such as contact and expression. Our interface, code, and datasets are made publicly available.

Acknowledgements. We thank Yi Yang and Deva Ramanan for making their implementation publicly available. We thank Micah Hodosh and Julia Hockenmaier for their initial discussions. We also would like to thank the hundreds of Turkers, without whom this work would not have been possible.

References

1. Ali, S., Shah, M.: Human action recognition in videos using kinematic features and multiple instance learning. PAMI (2010)
2. Bourdev, L., Malik, J.: Poselets: Body part detectors trained using 3d human pose annotations. In: ICCV (2009)
3. Chakraborty, I., Cheng, H., Javed, O.: 3d visual proxemics: Recognizing human interactions in 3d from a single image. In: CVPR (2013)
4. Choi, W., Shahid, K., Savarese, S.: Learning context for collective activity recognition. In: CVPR (2011)
5. Darwin, C.: The Expression of the Emotions in Man and Animals. Oxford University Press (1998)
6. Eitz, M., Hildebrand, K., Boubekeur, T., Alexa, M.: Sketch-based image retrieval: Benchmark and bag-of-features descriptors. IEEE Transactions on Visualization and Computer Graphics (2011)
7. Elhoseiny, M., Saleh, B., Elgammal, A.: Write a classifier: Zero-shot learning using purely textual descriptions. In: ICCV (2013)
8. Fan, R.E., Chang, K.W., Hsieh, C.J., Wang, X.R., Lin, C.J.: LIBLINEAR: A library for large linear classification. JMLR (2008)
9. Farhadi, A., Endres, I., Hoiem, D., Forsyth, D.: Describing objects by their attributes. In: ICCV (2009)
10. Ferrari, V., Zisserman, A.: Learning visual attributes. In: NIPS (2007)
11. Fouhey, D.F., Zitnick, C.L.: Predicting object dynamics in scenes. In: CVPR (2014)
12. Hotelling, H.: Relations between two sets of variates. Biometrika (1936)
13. Kaneva, B., Torralba, A., Freeman, W.T.: Evaluation of image features using a photorealistic virtual world. In: ICCV (2011)
14. Krizhevsky, A., Sutskever, I., Hinton, G.: Imagenet classification with deep convolutional neural networks. In: NIPS (2012)
15. Kumar, N., Berg, A.C., Belhumeur, P.N., Nayar, S.K.: Attribute and simile classifiers for face verification. In: ICCV (2009)
16. Lampert, C.H., Nickisch, H., Harmeling, S.: Learning to detect unseen object classes by between-class attribute transfer. In: CVPR (2009)
17. Lan, T., Wang, Y., Yang, W., Mori, G.: Beyond actions: Discriminative models for contextual group activities. In: NIPS (2010)
18. Larochelle, H., Erhan, D., Bengio, Y.: Zero-data learning of new tasks. In: AAAI (2008)
19. Marin-Jimenez, M., Zisserman, A., Eichner, M., Ferrari, V.: Detecting people looking at each other in videos. IJCV (2013)
20. Oliva, A., Torralba, A.: Modeling the shape of the scene: A holistic representation of the spatial envelope. IJCV (2001)
21. Ramanan, D.: Learning to parse images of articulated bodies. In: NIPS (2007)
22. Sadeghi, M.A., Farhadi, A.: Recognition using visual phrases. In: CVPR (2011)
23. Shotton, J., Fitzgibbon, A., Cook, M., Sharp, T., Finocchio, M., Moore, R., Kipman, A., Blake, A.: Real-time human pose recognition in parts from single depth images. In: CVPR (2011)
24. Smeulders, A.W.M., Worring, M., Santini, S., Gupta, A., Jain, R.: Content-based image retrieval at the end of the early years. PAMI (2000)
25. Specht, D.F.: The general regression neural network-rediscovered. Neural Networks (1993)

26. Yang, Y., Baker, S., Kannan, A., Ramanan, D.: Recognizing proxemics in personal photos. In: CVPR (2012)
27. Yang, Y., Ramanan, D.: Articulated pose estimation with flexible mixtures-of-parts. In: CVPR (2011)
28. Yao, B., Fei-Fei, L.: Action recognition with exemplar based 2.5d graph matching. In: ECCV (2012)
29. Yao, B., Fei-Fei, L.: Modeling mutual context of object and human pose in human-object interaction activities. In: CVPR (2010)
30. Yu, X., Aloimonos, Y.: Attribute-based transfer learning for object categorization with zero/one training example. In: ECCV (2010)
31. Zitnick, C.L., Parikh, D., Vanderwende, L.: Learning the visual interpretation of sentences. In: ICCV (2013)

Discovering Groups of People in Images

Wongun Choi[1], Yu-Wei Chao[2], Caroline Pantofaru[3], and Silvio Savarese[4]

[1] NEC Laboratories, USA
[2] University of Michigan, Ann Arbor, USA
[3] Google, Inc, USA
[4] Stanford University, USA

Abstract. Understanding group activities from images is an important yet challenging task. This is because there is an exponentially large number of semantic and geometrical relationships among individuals that one must model in order to effectively recognize and localize the group activities. Rather than focusing on directly recognizing group activities as most of the previous works do, we advocate the importance of introducing an intermediate representation for modeling groups of humans which we call *structure groups*. Such groups define the way people spatially interact with each other. People might be facing each other to talk, while others sit on a bench side by side, and some might stand alone. In this paper we contribute a method for identifying and localizing these structured groups in a single image despite their varying viewpoints, number of participants, and occlusions. We propose to learn an ensemble of discriminative interaction patterns to encode the relationships between people in 3D and introduce a novel efficient iterative augmentation algorithm for solving this complex inference problem. A nice byproduct of the inference scheme is an approximate 3D layout estimate of the structured groups in the scene. Finally, we contribute an extremely challenging new dataset that contains images each showing multiple people performing multiple activities. Extensive evaluation confirms our theoretical findings.

Keywords: Group discovery, Social interaction, Activity recognition.

1 Introduction

In day-to-day environments we observe various types of complex group activities such as people conversing, waiting in a line, listening to a lecture, and eating together. Consider the images in Figure 1 - each shows multiple people involved in multiple different activities. To understand these scenes, we need to understand all of the activities, and to localize the activities we need to divide the people into groups with consistent spatial configurations consisting of individuals' poses, their relative poses, and their geometric patterns. For example, a group of people in conversation are often all sitting or standing while facing each other; a group of people standing in line may all face the same direction and stand one-behind-the-next; a group listening to a lecture might sit or stand while all face the same direction side-by-side. We call these consistent spatial configurations of people *structured groups*.

Structured groups are building blocks which can be composed to recognize and localize higher-level semantic group activities when combined with contextual information.

D. Fleet et al. (Eds.): ECCV 2014, Part IV, LNCS 8692, pp. 417–433, 2014.
© Springer International Publishing Switzerland 2014

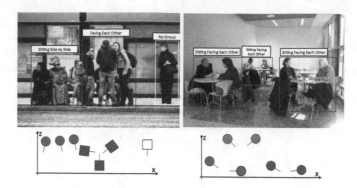

Fig. 1. Natural images often contain people forming multiple groups. Such groups can be categorized by the way people spatially interact with each other. People might be facing each other to talk, while others sit on a bench side by side, and some might stand alone. An image may contain multiple instances of the same group category. *Group discovery* is the problem of finding such *structured groups* despite their varying viewpoints, number of participants, and occlusions. In this paper we propose a framework for group discovery from a single image. Our approach is also capable of localizing the structure groups in 2D and half as shown in the lower part of the figure. Each person is depicted with a different color and symbol which corresponds to the structured group it belongs to (see figure 2 for a list of structure groups). Different colors corresponds to different group instances.

For example, a line of people queuing plus two people at the front conversing plus a store context equals a group of people paying for something. Or a group of people sitting side-by-side plus a teacher at the front teaching plus a classroom context equals a lecture. Moreover, by identifying the members of a structured group, we can segment the people in a scene into different localized interactions. This will enable methods for identifying multiple activities in a given image.

In this paper, we focus on the problem of discovering structured groups of people and contribute a method for identifying and localizing these groups in a single image. We call this problem *group discovery*. Our approach seeks to 1) divide people into different classes of structured groups wherein participating individuals share the same patterns of interactions; 2) localize these groups in the 3D space; and 3) provide semantic descriptions to each structured group.

There are multiple challenges related to this problem domain. Detecting people in crowded scenes is extremely difficult due to occlusions and size variation. Also, once a person is found, it is still difficult to identify his/her pose and location. Moreover, given noisy detections but an unknown number of groups, the number of group assignments grows exponentially large. Finally, structured groups change their geometry and appearance because of viewpoint changes and other topological transformations.

To address these challenges, we contribute a method to segment people into semantically meaningful groups. We propose to use discriminative interaction patterns to encode the relationships between people in 3D. Capturing the relative poses and positions in 3D makes the approach viewpoint invariant. Importantly, the interaction patterns do not need to be supervised during training. As a key contribution, we propose an efficient *iterative augmentation* algorithm for solving the challenging inference problem. A nice byproduct of the inference scheme is an approximate 3D layout estimate of the

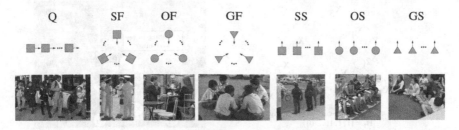

Fig. 2. The structured groups. Squares represent standing people, the circles are people sitting on chairs, and the triangles are people sitting on the ground. Arrows indicate individuals' orientations. See Sec. 2 for details.

structured groups in the scene. Finally, we contribute an extremely challenging new dataset that contains images each showing multiple people performing multiple activities.

1.1 Related Work

In the last decade, significant effort has been put toward understanding human activities at different levels of granularity. Several approaches have been proposed for classifying the activity of a single person, including [21,9,24,23]. Unfortunately, the activity of a single person in isolation is a poor indicator of the activity of a group of people.

Additional work has looked at the interactions between pairs of people [28,36,26,35], and the collective activities of larger groups [6,5,19,29,16]. However most of these approaches perform image (or video) classification, assuming that there is only one activity. They do not localize the activities and hence have difficulty identifying multiple activities in the same scene. Recently, Desai and Ramanan [8] proposed a relational phraselet to model the relationship between two people (or generally two objects) and identify the poses, but the model is limited to a pair of people. Eichner and Ferrari [10] focus on human pose estimation in a group context, but they assume only a single group in the image. Pellegrini et al. [27] consider the problem of tracking people in crowded scenes. Using short tracks extracted from video data they jointly cluster people into groups and derive their longer trajectories. Leal-Taixe et al. [22] extend this idea further to incorporate more generalized interactions between people.

Recently, a number of methods were proposed to detect single person activities in video sequences [4,13,12]. Although they can localize multiple activities in the temporal direction, only one activity can be identified in one time slice. Odashima *et al.* [25] and Amer *et al.* [1] proposed methods to localize multiple collective activities, but they either leverage naive holistic models or evaluated only on datasets which contain limited view point and intraclass variability.

There is a long list of works addressing the problem of image segmentation [30,32,18]. These works take either individual pixels or superpixels as the basic unit, and segment the images into coherent regions. Unlike traditional bottom-up 2D pixel-based segmentation problems, the basic units in our work are human detections.

In this paper, we focus on discovering structured groups of people in images. These groups form the building blocks for detecting and classifying higher-level activities.

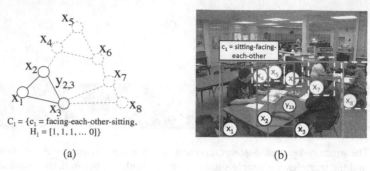

(a)   (b)

Fig. 3. An illustration of our model. Image I is represented by a set of individual detections $\mathbb{X}$. A group C_i (green bounding box) is represented by class c_i (sitting facing each other) and participating individuals (shown as solid black nodes in (a) and solid red bounding boxes in (b)) who are set to 1 in H_i. Individuals who are not group members are shown as dashed black nodes in (a) and white bounding boxes in (b). The group configuration potential is measured by the individual properties x_i and interaction $y_{i,j}$ between all participating individuals. (We model a fully connected graph, but omit edges in the figure for clarity.)

As a contribution, we introduce the concept of *discriminative interaction* patterns that capture the characteristics of pairwise configurations. Unlike [26,35,5], which have a predefined set of pairwise interaction classes, we automatically discover an expressive dictionary of discriminative interactions. In Sec. 2, we describe our model representation that ties together structured groups, individuals and image observations. Sec. 3 explains our feature representation as well as the discriminative interactions. Secs. 4 and 5 describe how we solve the inference problem and learn the model parameters.

2   Model

The purpose of our model is to group together individual hypotheses into structured groups as they are observed in images (Fig. 3). We aim to localize and segment people into 7 different types of structured groups. The categories are defined based on geometric relationships between participants. The first type is *"queuing"* (Q), a linear configuration of people, most of whom are facing the principal direction of the distribution. The second type is *"standing facing-each-other"* (SF), which is defined by a set of people in close proximity facing into a central point. Similarly, we define *"sitting facing-each-other"* (OF) and *"sitting on the ground facing-each-other"* (GF). Additionally, we define *"standing side-by-side"* (SS) that is characterized by a linear distribution of people with view point perpendicular to their distribution. Similarly, we introduce *"sitting side-by-side"* (OS) and *"sitting on the ground side-by-side"* (GS). Theses primitive types of structured groups provide useful information to understand social interaction among people. Examples of the structured groups are given in Fig. 2.

Let us define the set of individuals in an image I as $\mathbb{X} = \{x_1, x_2, ..., x_n\}$. Each x_i encodes the properties of an individual. In this work we assume that a detector is available that can estimate each individual's detection confidence, their pose, and their location in the image. The feature representation will be explained in detail in Section 3.

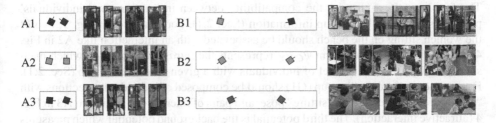

(a) intra-group interactions (attraction)　　　(b) inter-group interactions (repulsion)

Fig. 4. A set of interactions examples learned from training data. The (a) and (b) show interactions learned from intra-group and inter-group pairs, respectively. Each row shows the 3D configuration of interactions from top view and the associated pairs in the training data. The pair examples show that our learned interactions are view-point invariant.

Notice that the detector can be noisy and produce false alarm or missed detections, as well as poor localization and erroneous pose classification results.

Given a set of bounding boxes corresponding to person detections, we wish to identify the structured groups $\mathbb{C} = \{C_1, C_2, ..., C_m\}$ in the image. Examples of structured groups are shown in Fig.2. Each group description, C_k, consists of a binary membership vector $H_k = \{h_1^k, h_2^k, ..., h_n^k\}$ indicating which individuals are in the group, and a class label c_k taking one of $\mathcal{C}$ group labels. We also define a background group B that consists of the binary membership vector H_B indicating individuals that do not belong to any group. We assume that one individual can belong to at most one group, that is $\forall i, \sum_k h_i^k + h_i^B = 1$.

As an intermediate step between the individual detections and the group interactions, we model the interactions between pairs of people. During training, the detections, locations and poses of the people are given, however the interactions between pairs of people are not given and must be learned. Some examples of these learned interactions are presented in Fig. 4. Let $\mathbb{Y} = \{y_{1,2}, ..., y_{n-1,n}\}$ be the interaction variables that encode the relationships between pairs. Each y can have $\mathcal{Y}$ discrete interaction labels that are learned from training data, as described in Sec. 3.4. These interaction labels encode different types of interactions that tend to occur within the same group instances (attraction interaction) or that tend to occur across different group instances (repulsion interactions) (See Fig. 4).

We now want to use this model to discover structured groups. Discovery is formulated in an energy minimization framework as follows:

$$\hat{\mathbb{C}} = \operatorname*{argmin}_{\mathbb{C}} E(\mathbb{C}, \mathbb{X}, I) \tag{1}$$

where $\hat{\mathbb{C}}$ denotes the optimal set of structured groups and $E(\cdot)$ is an energy function. In order to capture both the characteristic pattern of each group as well as the compatibility between different groups, we define the energy function using a compositional model as follows (hereafter, we drop I for clarity):

$$E(\mathbb{C}, \mathbb{X}) = \min_{\mathbb{Y}}(\Psi_{XY}(\mathbb{X}, \mathbb{Y}) + \sum_i \Psi_{CXY}(C_i, \mathbb{X}, \mathbb{Y}) + \Psi_{BX}(B, \mathbb{X}) + \Psi_{RY}(\mathbb{C}, \mathbb{Y})) \tag{2}$$

The first term Ψ_{XY} encodes the compatibility between interactions and individuals' properties, which is bottom-up information (Sec. 2.1). For example, in Fig. 1, two of the women sitting on the bench should be associated with an interaction like A2 in Fig. 4, but not A1. The second term Ψ_{CXY} represents the *intragroup potential* which measures the compatibility of a set of individuals with a given structured group (Sec. 2.1). For instance, a "queuing" group (G1) should be composed of individual detections with "standing" poses rather than "sitting" pose, and pairs of interactions similar to A3 in Fig. 4 (attractive interaction). The third potential is the background potential which measures the probability of a solitary person, while the last potential is the intergroup potential that measures the probability of two people begin in different groups (repulsive interaction). In the following subsections, we describe each potential function. We then discuss the details of the feature representation in Sec. 3.

2.1 Potentials

Bottom-up Interaction Potential The first potential encodes the compatibility between the properties of pairs of individuals (x_i, x_j) and the interaction variable $y_{i,j}$:

$$\Psi_{XY}(\mathbb{X}, \mathbb{Y}) = \sum_{i<j} w_{xy}^{\top} \psi_{xy}(x_i, x_j, y_{i,j}) \tag{3}$$

where the feature vector $\psi_{xy}(\cdot)$ encodes the observed interaction patterns between two people, and model parameters w_{xy} measure the compatibility between interaction patterns and a specific type of interaction (Sec. 3.4 and Fig. 5).

Intragroup Potential The second term encodes the intragroup potential. This reflects the characteristic patterns of each structured group as a function of individuals' appearances (Sec. 3.3) and their interaction variables. $\Psi(C_k, \mathbb{Y}, \mathbb{X})$ is designed to maximize the compatibility of individual's appearances and the relational patterns between individuals with a given type of structured group.

$$\Psi_{CXY}(C_k, \mathbb{Y}, \mathbb{X}) = \sum_{i} h_i^k w_{xc}^{\top} \psi_{xc}(x_i, c_k) + \sum_{i<j} h_i^k h_j^k w_{yc}^{\top} \psi_{yc}(y_{i,j}, c_k) \tag{4}$$

where w_{xc} and w_{yc} are model parameters, $\psi_{xc}(\cdot)$ encodes a person's appearance information (Sec. 3.3), and $\psi_{yc}(\cdot)$ is a feature vector encoding the co-occurrence of an interaction label and group label. The co-occurrence feature is a vectorized two dimensional matrix where only the specified elements have a value of 1, and others are 0.

Background Potential This potential captures individuals that do not belong to any group (background).

$$\Psi_{BX}(B, \mathbb{X}) = \sum_{i} h_i^B w_{xb}^{\top} \psi_{xb}(x_i) \tag{5}$$

where w_{xb} is the parameter and $\psi_{xb}(\cdot)$ encodes a person's appearance (Sec. 3.3).

Intergroup Potential This potential captures interactions of individuals belonging to different groups (repulsive interaction). $\Psi_{RY}(\mathbb{C}, \mathbb{Y})$ is formulated similarly to the intragroup potential.

$$\Psi_{RY}(\mathbb{C}, \mathbb{Y}) = \sum_{i<j}(1 - \sum_{k} h_i^k h_j^k) w_{yr}^\top \psi_{yr}(y_{i,j}) \tag{6}$$

where w_{yr} are the model parameters and $\psi_{yr}(\cdot)$ is a feature vector encoding the occurrence of a repulsive interaction label. Notice that unlike the intragroup potential, we accumulate all *ungrouped* pairs in Eq.6 that do not contribute to any intragroup potential in Eq.4. In turn, all the interaction labels either contribute to one group's intragroup potential (if attractive) or intergroup potential (if repulsive).

2.2 Model Characteristics

Our model has a number of favorable characteristics for discovering structured groups in images. First, it permits an arbitrary number of groups $\mathbb{C} = \{C_1, ...C_m\}$ in each image and provides a principled measurement of the groups' compatibility using both individuals' and interaction information. Secondly, it explicitly models whether an individual is a member of a group, so we can identify how people are clustered. Notice that we can even segment individuals participating in different instances of the same group type, which is very challenging when using distance-based clustering. This is enabled by the attractive and repulsive interaction model through the intragroup and intergroup potentials. Thirdly, our model also identifies which person detections are valid, which in turn improves the robustness of the group discovery despite noisy bottom-up detection results. Finally, the interaction variables $y_{i,j}$ enable us to share interaction patterns across different structured group categories, which would not be possible if the features were directly connected to the class $\mathbb{C}$ without regard to $\mathbb{Y}$.

3 Feature Representation

In the previous section we described the potential functions that make up our model. Each of these potential functions relies on one or more feature representations. Here, we describe the details of those representations. For each image, we detect people and represent each detection with a pose confidence and the corresponding location of the person in 3D. Using this information, we encode the pairwise relationships using interaction features (Sec. 3.4) and the individuals' contextual information using the unary group feature (Sec. 3.3).

3.1 Individual Pose Feature

Given an image, we first detect individual people using the Poselet detector [2]. We represent each detection hypothesis bounding box using a combination of the Poselet activation vector, MDP activation vector [33] and HOG descriptor [7]. Instead of using such a high dimensional vector directly to encode individual properties, we train SVM classifiers [3] equipped with histogram intersection kernel for individual pose classes and assign the confidence vector (probabilistic estimation) to individual feature p_i (e.g. we train person v.s. no person, standing v.s. sitting on an object v.s. sitting on the ground, and 8 viewpoints $\times$ 3 poses classifiers). These individual pose vectors are used to represent the unary and interaction features.

3.2 3D Estimation

In order to robustly encode the relationship between people in images, we propose to estimate each person in 3D using a technique similar to [14]. Each person z_i is parametrized by their 3D location, height, and pose. The camera Θ is represented by its focal length, pitch angle, and height (we assume zero yaw and roll angles). With the assumption that every person is located on the same ground plane, the camera parameter Θ and the presented human $Z = \{z_1, \ldots, z_n\}$ are estimated by optimizing the function:

$$E(\Theta, Z, I) = \omega_{\Theta I}\Psi(\Theta, I) + \omega_{\Theta Z}\Psi(\Theta, Z) + \omega_{ZI}\Psi(Z, I) + \omega_{\Theta}\Psi(\Theta). \quad (7)$$

The first term captures the compatibility between the camera parameter Θ and the image feature. The second term captures how well the humans in configuration H fit into the scene given the camera parameter Θ. The third term captures how likely the human configuration H is given the observed image. The last term accounts for the prior on Θ. Given the function E, we solve Θ and Z in a two-step fashion. We first solve Θ using the RANSAC algorithm, which iterates between 1) sampling three people and their pose from the detection set and 2) computing the sample score E by optimizing Θ given the sampled people. Once we generate enough samples, the optimized camera parameter Θ is obtained from the sample with the highest score E. Finally, we compute Z (locations, heights, and poses of all human) by maximizing E given Θ.

3.3 Individual Unary Feature

Inspired by [6,20], we represent an individual's "appearance" information with a contextual descriptor that captures the relative distribution of other people in the scene. Similarly to [6], we discretize the space around the individual into multiple radial and angular bins and pool the pose confidence vectors of other detections. In order to make the descriptor robust under noisy detections, two nearest bin centers are obtained for each dimension (angular and radial) and the pose confidence vectors are assigned with linear interpolation weights. We use 8 angular bin centers and 3 radial bin centers.

Given the contextual descriptor for each individual, we represent the unary feature $\phi_x(x_i)$ using the confidence value of SVM classifier trained on the group categories. In order to deal with outliers (NA) and false positive (FP) detections, we add two more categories to the category set. With $\phi_x(x_i)$, $\psi_{xc}(x_i, c_k)$ (Eq. 4) are obtained by shifting $|\mathcal{C}| * c_k$ dimensions to make it compatible with the parameters in w_{xc}, where $\mathcal{C}$ is the set of structured group categories including NA and FP.

3.4 Pair Interaction Feature

The interaction pattern between two individuals is encoded by a spatial descriptor with view invariant relative pose encoding. Given the 3D locations of two individual detections z_i, z_j and two pose features p_i, p_j, we represent the pairwise relationship using

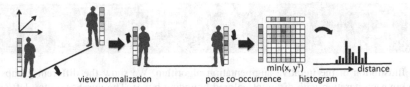

view normalization   pose co-occurrence   histogram

Fig. 5. We obtain the interaction feature via 1) view normalization, 2) pose co-occurrence encoding, 3) semantic compression and 4) spatial histogram. Given the 3D coordinates of two detections, the location of individuals are transformed to a canonical view and the corresponding pose features are shifted accordingly. Subsequently, the co-occurrence pattern is encoded by taking minimum of the transformed pose confidence values. The elements that deliver the same semantic concepts are accumulated to reduce the feature dimension and provide semantic invariance. Finally, the compressed representation is assigned to the spatial bin corresponding to the distance between the two individuals.

view normalization, pose co-occurrence encoding, semantic compression and a spatial histogram (see Fig. 5 for illustration).

The view normalization is performed by rotating the two people in 3D space by θ with respect to their midpoint, making their connecting line perpendicular to the camera view point. In this step, the pose features are also shifted accordingly (e.g. if $\theta = 45'$, shift 1 dimension with a cycle). Then, the co-occurrence feature is obtained by building a 2-dimensional matrix in which each element (r, c) corresponds to $min(p_i(r), p_j(c))$. Although the feature is view invariant, there are still elements in the matrix that deliver the same semantic concepts (e.g. left-left and right-right). To reduce such unnecessary variance and obtain a compact representation, we perform another transformation by multiplying a semantic compression matrix Sc to the vector form of the co-occurrence feature. The matrix Sc is learned offline by enumerating all possible configurations of view points and grouping the pairs that are equivalent when rotated by 180 degrees. Finally, we obtain the pair interaction descriptor by building a spatial histogram based on the 3D distance between the two (bin centers at 0.2, 0.6, 2.0 and 6.5 m). Here, we use linear interpolation similarly to contextual feature in Sec. 3.3. Given the interaction descriptor for each pair, we represent the interaction feature $\phi_{xx}(x_i, x_j)$ using the confidence value from an SVM classifier trained on a dictionary of interaction labels $\mathcal{Y}$.

Each interaction label is defined as a characteristic 3D spatial relationship between a pair of people. The key property is that each interaction label must be view-invariant, so that we can propagate a view invariant signal to the group model using $\psi_{yc}(y_{i,j}, c_k)$. To achieve view invariance, we obtain a set of interaction labels by agglomeratively clustering all possible pairs of individuals using a similarity metric S defined below. Given 3D location as well as poses of a pair z_i, z_j, we first align each of them by rotating along the center, so the $\theta = 0$. The similarity metric S between (z_i, z_j) and (z_k, z_l) is defined as follows:

$$S((z_i, z_j), (z_k, z_l)) = \lambda(d_{ij} - d_{kl})^2 + \gamma[\Delta(\theta_i, \theta_k)^2 + \Delta(\theta_j, \theta_l)^2] \qquad (8)$$

where d_{ij} is the distance between z_i and z_j and θ_i is the individual pose angles of z_i after the alignment. $\Delta(\theta_i, \theta_k)$ computes the difference between θ_i and θ_k. The weights

Iteration 1   Iteration 2   Iteration 3   Iteration 4

Fig. 6. Illustration of the iterative augmentation algorithm. We show the different groups discovered in each iteration with different colored bounding boxes. The number on top-left corner shows overall energy value given the configuration and numbers on bottom-left corner of each group shows the energy contribution of each group. Notice that the algorithm tends to group larger people in one iteration since a larger incorrect group minimizes overall objective value better than a smaller but correct group. Our algorithm is capable of fixing such mistakes made in earlier iterations and arrives at an optimal solution in a few iterations.

λ and γ are empirically set to 2.5 and 1. Any clusters containing more than T instances are kept as possible interaction labels. In practice, we set $T = 10$. In order to learn both intragroup and intergroup interaction labels, we perform the dictionary learning separately for the pairs observed in the same groups and the pairs observed across different groups. Some examples of learned interaction labels are shown in Fig. 4.

Given the SVM interaction classifier confidences vector ϕ_{xx} , the $\psi_{xy}(x_i, x_j, y_{i,j})$ (Eq.3) are obtained by taking the confidence value of the interaction label $y_{i,j}$.

4   Inference

Given the potentials and features defined thus far, we can model the interactions between people in an image. To find the optimal set of groups $\hat{\mathbb{C}}$ that minimize equation 1, we need to perform inference on this model. The inference problem, however, is very challenging since there are an unknown number of groups $\mathbb{C}$ with different group types in a scene. To cope with the challenges, we propose the *iterative-augmentation* algorithm.

Let us define the group augmentation operator $\oplus$ as $\mathbb{C}_k \oplus C_{new} = \mathbb{C}_k^- \cup C_{new}$ where $\forall i, k, h_i^{k-} = 0$ if $h_i^{new} = 1$, $h_i^{k-} = h_i^k$ otherwise (h_i^k represents the membership of individuals to a group, Sec. 2). Clearly, the operator is not commutative and gives priority for the new group to *include* individuals as participants while keeping the assignment constraint $\sum_h h_i^k + h_i^B = 1$.

The iterative augmentation algorithm starts the inference with an empty set of groups $\hat{\mathbb{C}}_0 = \emptyset$. Then, in each iteration we find a single group that minimize the function:

$$\nabla\Psi(C_k; \hat{\mathbb{C}}_{k-1}, \mathbb{X}, \mathbb{Y}) = \Psi(\hat{\mathbb{C}}_{k-1} \oplus C_k, \mathbb{X}, \mathbb{Y}) - \Psi(\hat{\mathbb{C}}_{k-1}, \mathbb{X}, \mathbb{Y}) \tag{9}$$

The new group $\hat{\mathbb{C}}_k$ is obtained by $\hat{\mathbb{C}}_{k-1} \oplus C_k$. The key property of this algorithm is that it can fix mistakes made in early iterations (see Fig. 6) and can find the optimal solution if it finds optimal C_k for Eq. 9. We optimize Eq. 9 by applying a variational method on each group type $\hat{c}$. Fixing the group type $\hat{c}$, the optimization space can be represented by the membership vector $\hat{H}_k$. With a slight abuse of notation, we can reformulate the optimization problem with a fully connected conditional random field (CRF) as:

$$\nabla\Psi(\hat{H}_k) = \sum_i \psi_u(\hat{h}_i^k) + \sum_{i<j} \psi_p(\hat{h}_i^k, \hat{h}_j^k) \tag{10}$$

Since this CRF is fully connected and contains high order cliques, it is not possible to obtain globally optimal solution in an efficient way. Instead, the energy function is approximated with a mean field distribution $Q(\hat{H}_k) = \prod_i Q(\hat{h}_i^k)$ that minimizes the KL divergence between Q and $P(\hat{H}_k) = \frac{1}{Z}exp(-\nabla\Psi(\hat{H}_k))$ using mean-field message passing (MFMP) [17]. Given the approximate distribution Q, the optimal solution is found by taking the maximizing state of each variable in the marginal distribution. Please see the supplemental material for details of the reformulation and the derivation of the mean-field message passing algorithm. In practice, we run both the MFMP algorithm and the greedy algorithm and take the solution gives better objective value. [1] Although the interaction labels $\mathbb{Y}$ could be optimized jointly in this algorithm by incorporating a high order potential, in practice we obtain $\mathbb{Y}$ separately using the bottom-up signal for computational reasons. Computing the joint model efficiently is future work.

5 Model Learning

To train our model, we need to learn the parameters w that maximize its discriminative power. We learn these from training data that contains supervised annotations of 1) bounding boxes around individual people, 2) pose labels for individual people, and 3) the group annotations. Group annotations are done by labeling each person to his associated group instances, or to not belonging to any groups. For instance, in Fig. 1 (right), the man in the gray jacket and the women in front of him belong to a "sitting-facing-each-other" group while the others are belong to different instances of the same group type.

Given the interaction dictionary $\mathcal{Y}$ (Sec. 3.4) and a set of training images $\{\mathbb{X}_i, \mathbb{C}_i\}_i$, the model parameters are learned using the structured support vector machine framework [15]. In order to obtain the group association $\mathbb{C}_i$ and interaction labels $\mathbb{Y}_i$, we find the optimal association between detections $\mathbb{X}_i$ and ground truth human annotations by computing the intersection-over-union (IOU) between the two. If the IOU is larger than 0.5, we transfer the ground truth group association and interaction labels to the corresponding detections and pairs of detections. If not, we assign a false positive group and a false positive interaction label to any pair that is connected to the detection. Then, using the complete set of information $\{\mathbb{X}_i, \mathbb{Y}_i, \mathbb{C}_i\}_i$, we obtain the corresponding model parameters w using the following structural SVM formulation:

$$\min_{w,\xi} \frac{1}{2}\|w\|^2 + C\sum_i \xi^i, \ s.t. \ \Psi_{\mathcal{Y},w}(\mathbb{C},\mathbb{X}_i,\mathbb{Y}_i) - \Psi_{\mathcal{Y},w}(\mathbb{C}_i,\mathbb{X}_i,\mathbb{Y}_i) \le \xi^i - \delta(\mathbb{C},\mathbb{C}_i), \ \forall i, \mathbb{C}$$

(11)

where C is a hyper parameter in an SVM and ξ^i are slack variables. $\delta(\mathbb{C},\mathbb{C}_i)$ represents the loss function of a discovered group $\mathbb{C}$. More details of the learning procedure can be found in the supplemental materials.

---

[1] We observe that two algorithms are complementary to each other in the experiments. Among all the experiments, MFMP achieves a better solution (with smaller objective values) for 41% of the times, while greedy win for 33% of the times.

Table 1. Classification accuracy of input features. Poselet detections are used in this experiment. We show both average per class accuracy and overall accuracy as the data is unbalanced.

# classes	Pose			Interaction	Group Context
	2	4	25	59	9
Train	83.1 / 83.6	78.0 / 77.7	42.5 / 47.6	34.1 / 48.1	52.6 / 66.7
Test	79.6 / 80.5	71.0 / 66.9	41.7 / 33.6	28.8 / 35.2	43.0 / 52.7

6 Experimental Evaluation

Dataset: We test our algorithm on a newly proposed challenging dataset, *Structured Group Dataset* (SGD)[2]. The dataset is contains 588 images with 5,415 human annotations and 1,719 groups (excluding outliers). We mirror all the images to get 1,176 images with 10,830 humans and 3,438 groups. The groups are categorized into 7 different types of structured groups. Examples of the structured groups are shown in the Fig. 2. We contribute supervised annotations of individual person properties - bounding boxes, individual poses (standing, sitting on an object, sitting on the floor), and 8 different view points (front, front-left, ..., back-right). We also provide annotations of all groups. Please see the supplemental material for examples and statistics.

Experimental Setup: In order to provide an extensive evaluation of the method, we run 5 fold training and testing over the entire dataset. In each split, we learn the pose classifier, the interaction dictionary and classifier, and contextual group classifier in sequential order. To prevent overfitting we train each low level classifier using 10 fold cross validation over the training set and assign the classifier output in each fold separately. The cross-validated confidence values are used as features for model learning. The entire training data are used to provide features for the testing data. Please see the Tab. 1 for the classification accuracies for the first set of training and testing splits.

Evaluation Metric: Evaluating structured groups is complex. To evaluate whether a group is correct we first need to determine if the individuals were detected correctly and if they were, whether they belong in the same group. Assigning individual detections to ground truth detections must be done carefully to provide a fair evaluation. For example, there could be many detection boxes overlapping with a ground truth annotation. Evaluating the grouping is also complex as accidentally dividing or merging clusters can vastly affect the outcome [34].

In the following experiments, we report two metrics. First, we report the precision, recall, and corresponding F1-measure ($2PR/(P + R)$) value of our solution. Group detections are evaluated using the intersection over union ratio of the group participants. This is computed by dividing the number of individuals that are both included in a ground truth group and a discovered group (intersection) by the number of individuals that are either participating in the ground truth group or the discovered group (union).

---

[2] The dataset and our code are available at http://cvgl.stanford.edu/projects/groupdiscovery/.

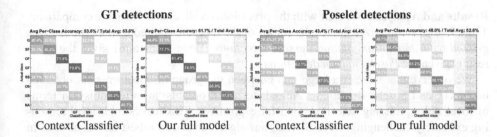

Fig. 7. Confusion tables for group category classification with GT and poselet detections. We compare the accuracy of the output of context feature alone (Sec. 3.3 and the final output of our model. In both GT and poselet detection experiments, we observe significant improvements.

If the ratio is larger than 0.5, we declare the discovered group a true positive. Following the PASCAL evaluation convention [11], only one group is associated with a ground truth group. This measure can evaluate the segmentation accuracy of individuals into groups as well as the categorization accuracy of each discovered group. When evaluating the group discovery with poselet detections, we ignore the ground truth annotations that do not match with any detection hypothesis to separate the error caused by detector itself. Second, we show the individual person labeling accuracy in a confusion table to evaluate the assignment of individuals to semantic groups.

Baseline Method: As a baseline for our evaluation, we propose to group objects based on proximity. A similarity matrix is constructed based on the estimated 3D distance between people and Normalized Cuts [31] is used to cluster the people into k groups. NCuts requires k to be given (denoting NCut+K), so we provide the correct ground truth number of groups in each image (including groups for outliers and false positive detections). This is a very important piece of information that our system does not have, so this baseline is very strong. The group category label is assigned by taking the votes of individual contextual classifier outputs (Sec. 3.3) and no interaction labels are considered here.

Component Evaluations: To better understand the contributions of the components of our system, we also compare against multiple reduced versions of our model as follows.

- (w/out interactions) We exclude the intragroup and intergroup interactions by replacing the pairwise edges in our graph with conventional distance-based edges. Interaction labels are replaced by 4 distance labels corresponding to the distance bins used in the pair interaction feature (Sec. 3.4).
- (w/out 3D) We use only 2D information instead of the estimated 3D information when computing the interaction feature. The distance between people is normalized by their average width.

We also provide all results on both detected persons as given by the Poselet detector [2] (Poselet) and on the ground truth person detections (GT) to separate the system performance from the performance of the person detection algorithm used.

Results and Analysis: We start with the precision, recall, and F1 measure comparison. Table 2 (top) summarizes the results for all of the baseline and reduced methods given *ground truth human annotation person detections*. Table 2 (bottom) gives the same results given the *Poselet human detections*.

We observe that there is a large gap between the group discovery results obtained using GT and poselet detections. Actual detection outputs are often noisy in terms of localization, missing detections and false positives. This makes high-level reasoning extremely challenging. Nevertheless, our algorithm shows robust results as seen in qualitative examples shown in Fig. 8 and the quantitative metrics shown in the Tab. 2.

We also notice that conventional clustering (NCuts) does not perform well even though the ground truth number of clusters are given and the same unary features are provided for the categorization. This confirms that the data set is extremely difficult and a more complex approach is required.

Let us consider the partial models. The partial model without pairwise interactions does not perform as well as the full model. This implies that reasoning about the interaction between pairs of people is critical for finding groups.

The 2D-based model achieves much lower accuracy than the 3D-based model. This is not surprising given that the 2D model is not view or distance invariant.

Our experiments also show that the algorithm can effectively estimate the number of groups present in the scene. We found that the mean absolute error of the predicted number of groups per image is 0.59 when GT detections are used, and 0.71 when poselet detections are used. The mean true number of groups is 4.25 for entire test set.

Fig. 8. Qualitative examples of the results obtained using our full model with poselet detections. We show the image configuration of groups on the left and corresponding 3D configuration on the right. Different colors represent different groups, the type of each structured group is overlayed on the bottom-left of one participant. In 3D visualization, squares represent standing people, circles represent people sitting on an object, and triangles represent people sitting on the ground. The view point of each individual is shown with a line. The gray triangle is the camera position. The poses are obtained by using the individual pose classification output for visualization purposes. The figures show that our algorithm is capable of correctly associating individuals into multiple different groups while estimating the type of each group. Notice that our algorithm can successfully segment different instances of the same group type that appear in proximity. A distance-based clustering method would not be able to differentiate them. The last figure shows a typical failure case due to only reasoning about people while ignoring objects (such as the tables). Detections that are not assigned to outlier (NA), false positive (FP) or background are not shown to avoid clutter.

Table 2. Precision, recall, and F1 measure given ground truth detections (top) and Poselet detections (bottom). Each column shows the precision and recall for each structured group category. Our model shows clear improvement over the baseline NCut+K and partial models. In some cases NCut+K does better than our model, but note that we provided the ground truth number of groups to NCut algorithm that is not available in practice. The best numbers in each column are bold.

Method	P/R	Q	SF	OF	GF	SS	OS	GS	Avg
		Group Discovery with **Ground Truth** Detections							
NCuts+K	Prec	12.29	47.80	50.13	43.55	25.94	47.25	**43.03**	38.57
	Recall	**35.50**	40.91	**76.73**	**76.00**	25.23	39.21	**30.87**	**46.35**
	F1	18.26	44.09	60.64	55.37	25.58	42.86	**35.95**	42.10
w/o interactions	Prec	6.76	39.48	44.88	56.34	21.68	40.08	21.89	33.01
	Recall	1.91	55.06	56.52	60.00	14.22	38.96	19.13	35.11
	F1	2.98	45.99	50.03	58.11	17.17	39.51	20.42	34.03
w/o 3D	Prec	32.29	44.96	46.98	52.23	36.51	38.18	26.63	39.68
	Recall	11.83	57.92	52.66	58.50	15.83	36.29	19.57	36.09
	F1	17.32	50.62	49.66	55.19	22.08	37.21	22.56	37.80
full model	Prec	**41.86**	**55.78**	**62.48**	**60.19**	**39.08**	**53.85**	37.65	**50.13**
	Recall	27.48	**64.55**	65.56	65.00	21.33	**40.86**	26.52	44.47
	F1	**33.18**	**59.85**	**63.98**	**62.50**	**27.60**	**46.46**	31.12	**47.13**
		Group Discovery with **Poselet** Detections							
NCuts+K	Prec	6.47	11.81	16.58	19.38	13.52	18.00	8.39	13.45
	Recall	**29.03**	34.96	34.19	53.39	**24.37**	44.95	12.00	33.27
	F1	10.58	17.66	22.33	28.44	17.39	25.71	9.88	19.16
w/o interactions	Prec	9.32	18.25	20.49	29.80	16.37	20.72	11.11	18.01
	Recall	8.87	30.49	36.25	50.00	14.21	39.63	10.00	27.06
	F1	9.09	22.83	26.18	37.34	15.21	27.21	10.53	21.63
w/o 3D	Prec	16.95	21.13	26.97	34.90	25.14	20.77	9.84	22.24
	Recall	16.13	28.86	43.19	**56.78**	22.34	**37.50**	6.00	30.11
	F1	16.53	24.40	33.21	**43.23**	23.66	26.73	7.45	25.58
full model	Prec	**25.74**	**26.40**	**30.61**	**36.21**	**30.57**	**23.01**	**13.19**	**26.53**
	Recall	28.23	**42.28**	**50.13**	53.39	**24.37**	33.78	12.00	**34.88**
	F1	**26.93**	**32.50**	**38.01**	43.15	**27.12**	**27.37**	**12.57**	**30.14**

Finally we study the accuracy of classifying the group category for each individual, with results in the confusion tables in Fig. 7. For each individual, the category label is derived from the label of its group. The result suggest that reasoning with the full model improves individual classification over the baseline unary classifier that only looks at local context. We show results for both ground truth and detected persons.

7   Conclusion

In this paper, we tackled a new challenging problem, *group discovery* in images. As a key contribution, we introduced the concept of discriminative interaction patterns and proposed a view invariant interaction feature to robustly encode the patterns. The interaction patterns enabled us to segment different instances of groups properly.

Our *iterative augmentation* algorithm effectively found the number of structured groups in images and identified their participants. We demonstrated the effectiveness of our algorithm using both quantitative and qualitative experimental results on a new and difficult dataset. This approach is now ready to be used as a step toward higher-level activity understanding.

Acknowledgement. The work is partially supported by an ONR award N0001411 10389.

References

1. Amer, M.R., Xie, D., Zhao, M., Todorovic, S., Zhu, S.C.: Cost-sensitive top-down/bottom-up inference for multiscale activity recognition. In: ECCV (2012)
2. Bourdev, L., Malik, J.: Poselets: Body part detectors trained using 3d human pose annotations. In: International Conference on Computer Vision (ICCV) (2009), http://www.eecs.berkeley.edu/~lbourdev/poselets
3. Chang, C.C., Lin, C.J.: LIBSVM: a library for support vector machines (2001), software available at http://www.csie.ntu.edu.tw/~cjlin/libsvm
4. Chen, C.Y., Grauman, K.: Efficient activity detection with max-subgraph search. In: CVPR (2012)
5. Choi, W., Savarese, S.: A unified framework for multi-target tracking and collective activity recognition. In: ECCV (2012)
6. Choi, W., Shahid, K., Savarese, S.: What are they doing? : Collective activity classification using spatio-temporal relationship among people. In: VSWS (2009)
7. Dalal, N., Triggs, B.: Histograms of oriented gradients for human detection. In: CVPR (2005)
8. Desai, C., Ramanan, D.: Detecting actions, poses, and objects with relational phraselets. In: ECCV (2012)
9. Dollar, P., Rabaud, V., Cottrell, G., Belongie, S.: Behavior recognition via sparse spatio-temporal features. In: VS-PETS (2005)
10. Eichner, M., Ferrari, V.: We are family: Joint pose estimation of multiple persons. In: ECCV (2010)
11. Everingham, M., Van Gool, L., Williams, C.K.I., Winn, J., Zisserman, A.: The PASCAL Visual Object Classes Challenge 2012 (VOC2012) Results. http://www.pascal-network.org/challenges/VOC/voc2012/workshop/index.html
12. Hoai, M., De la Torre, F.: Max-margin early event detectors. In: CVPR (2012)
13. Hoai, M., Lan, Z.Z., De la Torre, F.: Joint segmentation and classification of human actions in video. In: CVPR (2011)
14. Hoiem, D., Efros, A.A., Hebert, M.: Putting objects in perspective. IJCV (2008)
15. Joachims, T., Finley, T., Yu, C.N.: Cutting-plane training of structural svms. Machine Learning (2009)
16. Khamis, S., Morariu, V.I., Davis, L.S.: Combining per-frame and per-track cues for multi-person action recognition. In: European Conference on Computer Vision (2012)
17. Koller, D., Friedman, N.: Probabilistic graphical models: principles and techniques. MIT press (2009)
18. Ladicky, L., Russell, C., Kohli, P., Torr, P.H.S.: Graph cut based inference with co-occurrence statistics. In: ECCV (2010)
19. Lan, T., Wang, Y., Yang, W., Mori, G.: Beyond actions: Discriminative models for contextual group activities. In: NIPS (2010)

20. Lan, T., Wang, Y., Mori, G., Robinovitch, S.: Retrieving actions in group contexts. In: International Workshop on Sign Gesture Activity (2010)

21. Laptev, I., Lindeberg, T.: Space-time interest points. In: ICCV (2003)

22. Leal-Taixe, L., Fenzi, M., Kuznetsova, A., Rosenhahn, B., Savarese, S.: Learning an image-based motion context for multiple people tracking. IEEE Conference on Computer Vision and Pattern Recognition (CVPR) (2014)

23. Liu, J., Luo, J., Shah, M.: Recongizing realistic actions from videos "in the wild". In: CVPR (2009)

24. Niebles, J.C., Wang, H., Fei-Fei, L.: Unsupervised learning of human action categories using spatial-temporal words. IJCV (2008)

25. Odashima, S., Shimosaka, M., Kaneko, T., Fukui, R., Sato, T.: Collective activity localization with contextual spatial pyramid. In: ECCV Workshops and Demonstrations (2012)

26. Patron-Perez, A., Marszałek, M., Zisserman, A., Reid, I.D.: High five: Recognising human interactions in TV shows. In: BMVC (2010)

27. Pellegrini, S., Ess, A., Gool, L.V.: Improving data association by joint modeling of pedestrian trajectories and groupings. In: European Conference on Computer Vision (ECCV) (2010)

28. Ryoo, M.S., Aggarwal, J.K.: Spatio-temporal relationship match: Video structure comparison for recognition of complex human activities. In: ICCV (2009)

29. Ryoo, M.S., Aggarwal, J.K.: Stochastic representation and recognition of high-level group activities. IJCV (2010)

30. Shi, J., Malik, J.: Normalized cuts and image segmentation. PAMI (2000)

31. Shi, J., Malik, J.: Normalized cuts and image segmentation. PAMI 22(8), 888–905 (2000)

32. Shotton, J., Winn, J., Rother, C., Criminisi, A.: Textonboost for image understanding: Multi-class object recognition and segmentation by jointly modeling texture, layout, and context. IJCV (2009)

33. Singh, S., Gupta, A., Efros, A.A.: Unsupervised discovery of mid-level discriminative patches. In: European Conference on Computer Vision (2012), http://arxiv.org/abs/1205.3137

34. Unnikrishnan, R., Pantofaru, C., Hebert, M.: Toward objective evaluation of image segmentation algorithms. PAMI 29(6), 929–944 (2007)

35. Yang, Y., Baker, S., Kannan, A., Ramanan, D.: Recognizing proxemics in personal photos. In: CVPR (2012)

36. Yao, A., Gall, J., Van Gool, L.: A hough transform-based voting framework for action recognition. In: CVPR (june 2010)

Untangling Object-View Manifold
for Multiview Recognition and Pose Estimation

Amr Bakry and Ahmed Elgammal

Department of Computer Science, Rutgers University
Piscataway, NJ, USA

Abstract. The problem of multi-view/view-invariant recognition remains one of the most fundamental challenges to the progress of the computer vision. In this paper we consider the problem of modeling the combined object-viewpoint manifold. The shape and appearance of an object in a given image is a function of its category, style within category, viewpoint, and several other factors. The visual manifold (in any chosen feature representation space) given all these variability collectively is very hard and even impossible to model. We propose an efficient computational framework that can untangle such a complex manifold, and achieve a model that separates a view-invariant category representation, from category-invariant pose representation. We outperform the state of the art in the three widely used multiview dataset, for both category recognition, and pose estimation.

1 Introduction

Visual object recognition is a challenging problem. This is mainly due to the large variations in appearance of objects within a given category, as well as variation of the appearance of an object due to viewpoint, illumination, occlusion, articulation, clutter, *etc.*. Impressive work have been done in the last decade on developing computer vision systems for generic object recognition. Research has spanned a wide spectrum of recognition-related issues, however, the problem of multi-view/view-invariant recognition remains one of the most fundamental challenges to the progress of the computer vision.

The problems of object classification from multi-view setting (view-invariant recognition) and pose recovery are coined together. Inspired by Marr's 3D object-centric doctrine [14], traditional 3D pose estimation algorithms often solved the recognition, detection, and pose estimation problems simultaneously (*e.g.* [7,11,13,24]), through 3D object representations, or through invariants. However, such models were limited in their ability to capture large within-class variability and were mainly focused on recognizing instances of objects. In the last two decades the field has shifted to study 2D representations based on local features and parts, with encoding the geometry loosely (*e.g.* pictorial structure like methods [6,5]) or without encoding the geometry at all (*e.g.* bag of words methods [29,25].) Encoding the geometry and the constraints imposed by objects' 3D structure are essential. Most research on generic object recognition

D. Fleet et al. (Eds.): ECCV 2014, Part IV, LNCS 8692, pp. 434–449, 2014.

bundle all viewpoints of a category into one representation; or learn view-specific classifiers from limited viewpoints, *e.g.* frontal cars, side view cars, rear cars, *etc.*.

In the context of multiview recognition and pose estimation, there is a growing recent interest in developing representations that captures 3D geometric constraints in a flexible way to handle the categorization problem. The work of Savarese and Fei-Fei [21,22] was pioneering in that direction. In [21,22] a part-based model was proposed where canonical parts are learned across different views, and a graph representation is used to model the object canonical parts. Successful recent approaches have proposed learning category-specific detection models that is able to estimate object pose (*e.g.* [15,18,23,19]). This has an adverse side-effect of not being scalable to a large number of categories while dealing with high within-class variations. Typically papers on this area focus primarily on evaluating the detection, and secondarily on evaluating pose estimation performance, and do not evaluate the categorization performance. In contrast to category-specific representations, in this paper we focus on developing a common representation for recognition and pose estimation, which can scale up to deal with a large number of classes.

In this paper we consider the problem of modeling the combined object-viewpoint manifold. The shape and appearance of an object in a given image is a function of its category, style within category, viewpoint, and several other factors. Given all these variability collectively, the visual manifold (in any chosen feature representation space) is very hard and even impossible to model. The main goal of this paper is to find a computational framework that can untangle such a complex manifold. In particular, we aim at untangling the object-viewpoint manifold, to achieve a model that separates a view-invariant category representation, from category-invariant pose representation.

This paper is builds over the model introduced in [30], which mainly proposed to model the category as a "style" variable over the view manifold of objects. This unconventional way is motivated by three observations: 1) low-dimensionality of the manifold of different views for a given object; 2) the prior knowledge of the view-manifold topology; 3) view manifolds of different objects (under the same view setting) share the same topology (ignoring degeneracy) but differ in their geometry, i.e, view manifolds of different objects are deformed version of each other. In contrast, considering the inter-class and the intra-class variability, even from a give view point, the resulting visual manifold is expected to be quite challenging to model, and can be of infinite dimensions. In [30] a computational framework was introduced that capitalizes on these observations, and models the deformation of different objects' view manifolds. The deformation space is then parameterized to reach a latent view-invariant category space, which is used in recognition. The overall model in [30] is a generative model, where hypotheses about the category and pose were used, within a sampling-based inference approach to minimize the reconstruction error, given a test image.

There is a mounting evidence of a feedforward computation in the brian [3] for the immediate categorization task. This motivated us to seek a forward model, that capitalizes on the same manifold structure observations used in [30], however avoids the challenging inference problem. The sampling-based inference, in [30], constitutes a major limitation to the computational framework. Even though the pose space is very low in dimensionality (one or two depending on the view setting), the view-invariant category latent space is high in dimensionality, which makes sampling not effective with no guarantee of convergence to the correct answer. In contrast, the current work presents several realizations, which leads to feed-forward computational models that do not require sampling-based inference.

The organization of the paper is as follows. Sec 2 describes the framework. Sec 3 describes how sampling-free inference can be achieved. Sec 4 illustrates experimental validation of the approach.

2   Framework

This section explains the intuition behind the the proposed framework and introduces the mathematical framework.

2.1   Framework Overview

Consider collections of images containing instances of different object classes and different views of each instance. The shape and appearance of an object in a given image is a function of its category, style within category, viewpoint, besides other factors that might be nuisances for recognition. Our discussion do not assume any specific feature representation of the input, we just assume that the images are vectors in some input space. The visual manifold given all these variability collectively is impossible to model. Let us first simplify the problem. Let us assume that the object is detected in the training images (so there is no 2D translation or in-plane rotation manifold). Let us also assume we are dealing with rigid objects (to be relaxed), and ignore the illumination variations (assume using an illumination invariant feature representation). Basically, we are left with variations due to category, within category, and viewpoint, *i.e.* , we are dealing with a combined *view-object manifold*.

The underlying principle in our framework is that multiple views of an object lie on an intrinsically low-dimensional manifold (*view manifold*) in the input space. The view manifolds of different objects are distributed in that descriptor space. To recover the category and pose of a test image we need to know which manifold this image belongs to, and what is the intrinsic coordinate of that image within that manifold. This basic view of object recognition and pose estimation is not new, and was used in the seminal work of Murse and Nayar [16]. In that work, PCA was used to achieve linear dimensionality reduction of the visual data, and the manifolds of different objects were represented as parameterized curves in the embedding space. However, dimensionality reduction techniques, whether linear or nonlinear, will just project the data to a lower dimension, and will not be able to achieve the desired untangled representation.

The main challenge is how to achieve an untangled representation of the visual manifold. The key is to utilize the low-dimensionality and known topology of the view manifold of individual objects. To explain the point, let us consider the

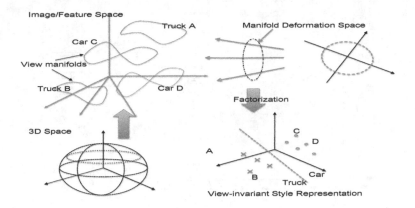

Fig. 1. Framework for untangling the view-object manifold.

simple case where the different views are obtained from a viewing circle, *e.g.* a camera looking at an object on a turntable. The view manifold of each object in this case is a one-dimensional closed manifold embedded in the input space. However, that simple closed curve deforms on the input space as a function of the object geometry and appearance. The visual manifold can be degenerate, for example, imaging a texture-less sphere from different views result in the same image, *i.e.* , the view manifold in this case is degenerate to a single-point.

Ignoring degeneracy, the view manifolds of all objects share the same topology but differ in geometry, and are all homeomorphic to each other. Therefore, capturing and parameterizing the deformation of a given object's view manifold tells us fundamental information about the object category and within category. *The deformation space* of these view manifolds captures a view-invariant signature of objects, analyzing such space provides a novel way to tackle the categorization and within-class parameterization. Therefore, a fundamental aspect in our framework, is that we use the view-manifold deformation as an invariant for categorization and modeling the within-class variations. If the views are obtained from a full or part of the view-sphere around the object, the resulting visual manifold should be a deformed sphere as well. In general, the dimensionality of the view manifold of an object is bounded by the dimensionality of viewing manifold (degrees of freedom imposed by the camera-object relative pose).

2.2 Manifold Parameterization

Here, we summarize the mathematical framework proposed in [30], which is the basic for our model, and highlight the challenges. The input are different views of each object instance, where the number views do not have to be same, and the views do not have to be aligned across objects.

Let us denote the view manifold of object instance s in the input space by $\mathcal{D}^s \subset \mathbb{R}^D$ where D is the dimensionality of the input space. Assuming that all manifolds $\mathcal{D}^s$ are not degenerate (we will discuss this issue shortly), then they

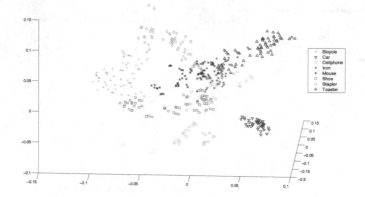

Fig. 2. Plotting of a three-dimensional unsupervised projection of the view-invariant style parameterization of 473 instances from 3DObjects dataset [21] (obtained from a training set of 3784 images from 8 views). Points of different categories show in different colors and point style. The plot clearly shows the separation between different objects, even in a three-dimensional projection.

are all topologically equivalent, and homeomorphic to each other[1]. Moreover, suppose we can achieve a common view manifold representation across all objects, denoted by $\mathcal{M} \subset \mathbb{R}^e$, in a Euclidean embedding space of dimensionality e. All manifolds $\mathcal{D}^s$ are also homeomorphic to $\mathcal{M}$. In fact all these manifold are homeomorphic to a unit circle in 2D for the case of a viewing circle, and a unit-sphere ($\mathbf{S^2}$) for the case of full view sphere.

We can achieve a parameterization of each manifold deformation by learning object-dependent regularized mapping functions $\gamma_s(\cdot) : \mathbb{R}^e \to \mathbb{R}^D$ that map from $\mathcal{M}$ to each $\mathcal{D}^s$. Given a Reproducing Kernel Helbert Space (RKHS) of functions and its corresponding kernel $K(\cdot, \cdot)$, from the representer theorem [8,20] it follows that such functions admit a representation in the form

$$\gamma_s(\mathbf{v}) = \boldsymbol{C}^s \cdot \psi(\mathbf{v}) , \tag{1}$$

where $\boldsymbol{C}^s$ is a $D \times N_\psi$ mapping coefficient matrix, and $\psi(\cdot) : \mathbb{R}^e \to \mathbb{R}^{N_\psi}$ is a nonlinear kernel map, i.e. $\psi(\mathbf{v}) = [K(\mathbf{v}, \mathbf{v}_1), \cdots, K(\mathbf{v}, \mathbf{v}_{N_\psi})]^T$, defined using a set basis of points $\{\mathbf{v}_i \in \mathbb{R}^e\}_{i=1 \cdots N_\psi}$ on $\mathcal{M}$ (The basis points can be arbitrary and does not need to correspond to actual data points [20]).

In the mapping in Eq. 1, the geometric deformation of manifold $\mathcal{D}^s$, from the common manifold $\mathcal{M}$, is encoded in the coefficient matrix $\boldsymbol{C}^s$. Therefore, the space of matrices $\mathbb{C} = \{\boldsymbol{C}^s\}$ encodes the variability between manifolds of different objects, and can be used to parameterize such manifolds. Notice that

---

[1] A function $f : X \to Y$ between two topological spaces is called a homeomorphism if it is a bijection, continuous, and its inverse is continuous. In our case the existence of the inverse is assumed but not required for computation, *i.e.*, we do not need the inverse for recovering pose. We mainly care about the mapping in a generative manner from $\mathcal{M}$ to $\mathcal{D}^s$.

the dimensionality of these matrices $(D \times N_\psi)$ does not depend on the number of views available each object. We can parameterize the variability across different manifolds in a subspace in the space of coefficient matrices.

Of course the visual manifold can be degenerate or it can be self intersecting, because of the projection from 3D to 2D and lack of visual features, *e.g.* images of a textureless sphere. In such cases the homeomorphic assumption does not hold. The key to tackle this challenge is in learning the mapping in a generative manner from $\mathcal{M}$ to $\mathcal{D}^s$, not in the other direction. By enforcing the known non-degenerate topology on $\mathcal{M}$, the mapping from $\mathcal{M}$ to $\mathcal{D}^s$ still exists, still is a function, and still captures the manifold deformation. In such cases the recovery of object pose might be ambiguous and ill-posed. In fact, such degenerate cases can be detected by rank-analysis of the mapping matrix C^s.

The space of manifold deformation functions, encoded by the coefficient matrices C^s is a high-dimensional rich space. Note that all the views of a given object is represented by a single point in that space, parameterizing the geometry of the view manifold of that object, and hence encoding information about its 3D geometry. By projecting the coefficient matrices to a low-dimensional latent space, we can reach a view-invariant representation. Such a representation can be achieved in an unsupervised way or in a supervised way using class labels; in a linear or nonlinear way. In the simplest case, using linear projection, we can achieve a generative model of the data in the form

$$z = \gamma(\mathbf{v}, \mathbf{s}) = \mathcal{A} \times_2 \mathbf{s} \times_3 \psi(\mathbf{v}), \tag{2}$$

where $\mathcal{A}$ is a third order tensor of dimensionality $D \times d \times N_\psi$, $\times_i$ is the mode-i tensor product as defined in [12]. The variable $\mathbf{v}$ is a representation of the viewpoint that evolves around the common manifold $\mathcal{M}$, which is explicitly modeled. In this model, the variable $\mathbf{s} \in \mathbb{R}^d$ is a parameterization of manifold $\mathcal{D}^s$ that encodes the variation in category/instance of an object in a view-invariant way. We denote that space by "style" space. Therefore, that space can be used to train category classifiers in a view-invariant way. In this model, both the viewpoint and object/style latent representations, $\mathbf{v}$ and $\mathbf{s}$, are continuous.

Given features from a single test image, denoted by $\mathbf{z}$, recovering the pose and category reduces to an inference problem, where the goal is to find $\mathbf{s}^*$ and viewpoint $\mathbf{v}^*$ that minimize a reconstruction error, i.e.,

$$\arg\min_{\mathbf{s}, \mathbf{v}} \|\mathbf{z} - \mathcal{A} \times_2 \mathbf{s} \times_3 \psi(\mathbf{v})\| \tag{3}$$

Once $\mathbf{s}^*$ is recovered, a category classifier trained on the style space can be used for categorization. There are different ways to do inference here, for example typical MCMC sampling, or gradient-based optimization can be used.

While the view variable is constrained to a 1D or 2D manifold for the cases of a viewing circle or a viewing sphere, respectively, inference in the style space is very challenging if its dimensionality is high. There is a fundamental tradeoff here: Lowering the dimensionality can lead to efficient inference, on the expense of losing the discriminative power of the space; in contrast, keeping the dimensions of the style space high will make the inference unlikely to converge. This is a fundamental limitation of the model, which we try to resolve by avoiding sampling all together, and investigating feed-forward solutions.

3   From Inference to Feed Forward

We propose a feedforward realization of the model that does not involve inference of the latent variables, yet still capitalizes on the advantages of the model. There are three motivations behind investigating such a feedforward realization of the model. First, biologically motivated, inspired by the extensive evidence of a cascade of feedforward computation in the brain for solving the immediate categorization problem [2], we would like to capitalize on the view-invariant property of the style space to achieve a realization of the model that can be implemented in a feedforward manner. Second, computationally, solving the inference problem in Eq 3 requires a sampling or a gradient-based search, which might not be desired for real-time applications. Third, from accuracy point of view, there is a tradeoff in choosing the dimensionality of the style space, (recall the style space is a achieved using linear or nonlinear projection of the high-dimensional manifold deformation space). Inference in high-dimensional spaces is notoriously not efficient nor effective. Reducing the dimensionality would lead to efficient inference, on the expense of losing discriminative power in categorization.

View-Invariant Category Manifolds: Let the set of view manifold parameterization matrices be $\{\mathbf{C}^i\}$, where $i = 1, \cdots, M$, is the index of the instances in the training data. Let us assume the case where the factorization in Eq 2 is achieved in an unsupervised way, by finding the subspace spanning these matrices. In that case, the factorization is achieve by SVD of the matrix

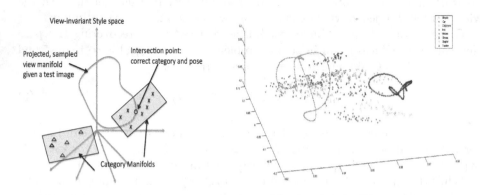

Fig. 3. Left: Illustration of recovering pose and category by manifold intersection in a view-invariant space. Right: Example of Style-projected Inconsistent View Manifold for two images

$[\mathbf{c}_1 \cdots \mathbf{c}_M] = \mathbf{U}\boldsymbol{\Sigma}\mathbf{V}^\top$, where $\mathbf{c}_i$ is a vectorization of $\mathbf{C}^i$. The columns of $\mathbf{V}^\top$, corresponding to the styles of all training instances. Let us denote these style vectors by $\{\mathbf{s}_i \in \mathbb{R}^d\}_1^M$. Instances of the same category lie on a linear manifold (subspace) in the style space; we call that the *view-invariant category manifold*, and denote it by $\mathcal{C}^k$, where k denotes the category index. Such manifolds capture the within-category variability and also facilitate modeling other variabilities, hence relaxing the rigidity assumption. Figure 2 shows an example of the view-invariant space, with different category clearly separated. For the case where no dimensionality reduction take place, *i.e.* $d = M$, the style vectors for the instances of each category would provide orthonormal basis for that category's subspace.

Style-projected Inconsistent View Manifold: The key to achieve a feedforward realization is, again, in utilizing the low-dimensionality and known topology of the view manifold. Given a test image $\mathbf{z}$ we need to solve the inference problem in Eq 3 for the view ($\mathbf{v}$) and style ($\mathbf{s}$) variables. If we know the viewpoint, the problem reduces to solving a least-squares problems for the style variable, which can be achieved by solving the linear system $(\mathcal{A} \times_3 \psi(\mathbf{v}))\mathbf{s} = \mathbf{z}$. Suppose we have a sequence of images of the same object from different viewpoints, $\{\mathbf{z}_i\}_1^n$, and we know the corresponding latent view representation $\{\mathbf{v}_i\}_1^n$, the solutions for the linear system above for every pair $(\mathbf{z}_i, \mathbf{v}_i)$ should all coincide in a single point $\mathbf{s}^*$, since the style-space is view-invariant. However, we only have a single test image, and we do not know the corresponding latent view representation. Instead, if we sample the latent view manifold $\{\hat{\mathbf{v}}_i\}_1^n$ and solve the linear systems $(\mathcal{A} \times_3 \psi(\hat{\mathbf{v}}_i))\hat{\mathbf{s}}_i = \mathbf{z}$, we get a sequence of solutions $\{\hat{\mathbf{s}}_i\}$, which constitutes a projection of the view manifold into the style space, using inconsistent pairs $\{(\mathbf{z}, \hat{\mathbf{v}}_i)\}$. Such projection will also constitute a manifold, we call that *style-projected inconsistent view manifold*, denote it by $\hat{\mathcal{M}}_\mathbf{z}$, formally define it as

$$\hat{\mathcal{M}}_\mathbf{z} = \{\hat{\mathbf{s}}_i = \mathbf{V}_i^\dagger \mathbf{z}\}_1^n$$

where $\mathbf{V}_i = \mathcal{A} \times_3 \psi(\hat{\mathbf{v}}_i)$ is a $d \times D$ matrix, and † denotes the Moore-Penrose pseudoinverse. Note that each image will have its own inconsistent view manifold, hence the use of the subscript. Figure 3 shows examples of these manifolds for sample images.

Ideally the correct style $\mathbf{s}^*$ will be a point on that projected view manifold, corresponding to the solution for the pair $(\mathbf{z}, \mathbf{v}^*)$, where $\mathbf{v}^*$ is the closest sampled view to the correct viewpoint. Ideally also the correct style will be the intersection point between $\hat{\mathcal{M}}_\mathbf{z}$ and the correct category's manifold $\mathcal{C}^k$. Notice that finding the intersection point directly corresponds to finding the correct viewpoint as well. Figure 3 illustrates this process. Realistically, these manifolds might not intersect, especially since we are using sparse sampling of views. Moreover, the category manifolds are hard to model, given the sparse data available at training anyway. Therefore, we need to investigate different ways to achieve an approximate solution. The brute-force method would be a nearest neighbor search between $\{\hat{\mathbf{s}}_i\}_1^n$ and the set of style vectors of the all training instances.

Instead we can parameterize $\hat{\mathcal{M}}$ and/or $\mathcal{C}$ and use interpolation to find closest points between them.

Based on the concept explained above, in what follows we propose four different solutions to solve for pose, instance, and category, given image $\mathbf{z}$.

Manifold Intersection: Parametrizing the projected view manifold is easy since its topology and dimensionality is known. The category manifolds are linear in the style space. A simple way to find an approximate solution is to find the point on $\hat{\mathcal{M}}_\mathbf{z}$ closest to each category subspace, This can be achieved by

$$\underset{i,k}{\operatorname{argmin}} \|\mathbf{V}_i^\dagger \mathbf{z} - \mathbf{A}_k \mathbf{A}_k^\top \mathbf{V}_i^\dagger \mathbf{z}\| \tag{4}$$

where $\mathbf{A}_k$ is the matrix of orthonormal basis for category k. Unlike the optimization in Eq 3, where the search was over continuous spaces for style and view, here the problem reduces to discrete search over categories and sample views. The trade-off in choosing the style dimensionality is no-longer an issue here. The main trade-off here comes from sampling the viewpoint/pose space, however, in most pose estimation applications, only coarse estimation of the viewpoint is needed anyway. However, dense sampling might be necessary to obtain good approximation of the intersection with category manifold, which directly impact the categorization accuracy. This leads to the following three alternative solutions.

View-specific Projections: Given a test image $\mathbf{z}$, the correct style $\mathbf{s}^*$ will be a point on the projected view manifold for that image $\hat{\mathcal{M}}_\mathbf{z}$, which is most consistent with the correct view $\mathbf{v}^*$, *i.e.* minimizes the reconstruction error. The problem then reduces to minimizing

$$\|\mathbf{z} - \mathcal{A} \times_2 (\mathbf{V}_i^\dagger \mathbf{z}) \times_3 \psi(\hat{\mathbf{v}}_i)\|$$

Since $\mathbf{V}_i = \mathcal{A} \times_3 \psi(\hat{\mathbf{v}_i})$, the above equation reduces to

$$i^* = \underset{i}{\operatorname{argmin}} \|\mathbf{z} - \mathbf{V}_i \mathbf{V}_i^\dagger \mathbf{z}\| \equiv \underset{i}{\operatorname{argmax}} \|\mathbf{V}_i \mathbf{V}_i^\dagger \mathbf{z}\| \tag{5}$$

Basically, this marginalizes the instance/category and provides a way to find the best viewpoint, among the sampled latent viewpoints, that is most consistent with test image. Once the best view, i^*, is found, the style can be directly obtained as $\mathbf{s}^* = \mathbf{V}_{i^*}^\dagger \mathbf{z}$. The geometric interpretation of this solution relies on noticing that the each of the matrices $\mathbf{V}_i \mathbf{V}_i^\dagger$ is an orthogonal projection operator into a view-dependent object-invariant subspace spanned by the columns of $\mathbf{V}_i$. Eq 5 is equivalent to finding the view-dependent subspace (spanned by the columns of $\mathbf{V}_i$) where $\mathbf{z}$ is closest to. In that sense, the images in the training data are used to learn these view-dependent object-invariant operators.

One important aspect that we should highlight is that the number of view-specific projector in this model is not restricted by the number of views in the training data. Since manifold parameterization is used to learn the view manifold for each instance, we can sample the view manifold at any arbitrary points $\{\hat{\mathbf{v}}_i\}_1^n$, and hence we can reach any desired number of view-specific projectors.

Instance-specific Projections: Using the same rational above, we can also obtain instance-specific view-invariant projectors by marginalizing out the view. Given a test image $\mathbf{z}$, and hypothesizing its corresponding style $\mathbf{s}$, an encoding of the view can be obtained by solving the linear system $(\mathcal{A} \times_2 \mathbf{s})\psi = \mathbf{z}$. Recall that $\psi(\mathbf{v})$ is a vector of nonlinear RBF kernels on $\mathbf{v}$, hence we can not obtain $\mathbf{v}$ directly, instead an encoding in an empirical kernel space. Given the set of style vectors $\{\mathbf{s}_i\}_1^M$ obtained from the instances in training data, let us define $D \times N_\psi$ instance-specific matrices $\{\mathbf{B}_i = \mathcal{A} \times_2 \mathbf{s}_i\}_1^M$. The solution for the view representation can be written as $\psi(\mathbf{v}) = \mathbf{B}_i^\dagger \mathbf{z}$. Substituting in the reconstruction error equation, we can reach

$$i^* = \operatorname*{argmin}_i \|\mathbf{z} - \mathbf{B}_i \mathbf{B}_i^\dagger \mathbf{z}\| \equiv \operatorname*{argmax}_i \|\mathbf{B}_i \mathbf{B}_i^\dagger \mathbf{z}\| \tag{6}$$

This marginalizes the viewpoint and provides a set of instance-specific view-invariant orthogonal projectors $\{\mathbf{B}_i \mathbf{B}_i^\dagger\}_1^M$. Eq 6 is equivalent to finding the instance-specific view-invariant subspace (spanned by the columns of $\mathbf{B}_i$) where $\mathbf{z}$ is closest to. Once the closest instance subspace is obtained, the pose can be recovered by finding the closest view in the empirical kernel map space

$$\operatorname*{argmin}_j \|\mathbf{B}_{i*}^\dagger \mathbf{z} - \psi(\mathbf{v}_j)\| \tag{7}$$

Notice that, if the full dimensions of the style space is retained, *i.e.* d=M, the matrices $\mathbf{B}_i$'s reduce to the original coefficient matrices $\mathbf{C}^i$'s. In terms of scalability, the instance-specific solution will not scale well since one projection has to be computed for every instance in the training data, a problem that we will discuss next, to reach category-specific projections

Category-specific Projections: The scalability issues highlighted above motivates finding category-specific view-invariant projections, rather than instance-specific ones. The goal is to find a good category representation from the set of matrices $\mathcal{B}_k = \{\mathbf{B}_i | i \in \text{class } k\}$. Equivalently, each of these instance-specific matrices can be represented by an orthonormal basis matrix $\mathbf{U}_i \in \mathbb{R}^D \times N_\psi$. In other words, each instance corresponds to a point on a Grassmann manifold $G(D, N_\psi)$ (the subspace spanned by its column). This put into our disposal all the tools available for Grassmann manifold analysis [4] to obtain a good category-specific representations. For example k-means clustering on Grassmann manifold [28] can be used to achieve a representative category-specific subspace.

Given the set of instance-specific matrices $\mathcal{B}_k$ for the k-th category, we can reach a representation of that category's subspace by merging the subspaces of all its instances. Let $\mathbb{B}_k$ be a $D \times (N_\psi M_k)$ matrix constructed by stacking all the matrices in $\mathcal{B}_k$, where M_k is the number of instances of class k. The column span of this matrix is the union of all the column spans of the instance-specific matrices for this class. Therefore, a category-specific view-invariant projector can be achieved by $\mathbb{B}_k \mathbb{B}_k^\dagger = \mathbf{U}_k \mathbf{U}_k^\top$, where $\mathbb{B}_k = \mathbf{U}_k \mathbf{\Sigma}_k \mathbf{V}_k$ is the truncated SVD of $\mathbb{B}_k$. Category and pose can be recovered in the same way as in Eq 6 and 7, by replacing the instance-specific matrices with the category-specific ones.

Discussion: At this point, it is important to contrast the solutions based on the view-specific, instance-specific, and category-specific projections. In terms of scalability, the instance-specific solution will not scale well since one projection has to be computed for every instance in the training data. In contrast the view-specific solution provides a more scalable solution, since the number of views can always be restricted. The view-specific projection also allows the use of discriminative classifiers, *e.g.* SVM in the style space, since it provides a solution for the s^*, in contrast, the instance-specific and the category-specific just find the closest instance or category subspace. Another advantage of the view-specific solution, is that it allows expanding the model to add new objects, even with a single image from a single view point. This can be achieved by computing the corresponding style representation, as mentioned above. A reader might question, why this solution would yield a feedforward computational model. Notice that all projectors are learned offline during training. Finding the best point, whether using nearest neighbor search, or svm classifiers, is also a feedforward computation. Although we do not address detection in this paper, it can be achieved through a sliding window approach. However, the challenge is to learn a model for clutter. This can be achieved by projecting clutter training patches using the view-specific projectors, and learning a clutter/object classifier in the style space.

4   Experiments

We validated our framework using three multiview datasets: 3DObjects [21], U-Washigton-RGBD datasets [9], and Multi-View Car Dataset [17]. Since we target categorization, instance recognition and pose estimation, in all reported experiments we use ground-truth localizations of objects.

Results on 3DObjects

3DObjects dataset contains objects from 10 different categories: car, stapler, iron, shoe, monitor, computer mouse, head, bicycle, toaster and cellphone. Each object is imaged from 24 poses on a viewing sphere (8 azimuth angles $\times$ 3 zenith angles), and from 3 scales. We used the entire (all classes) 3DObjects dataset to evaluate the performance of the proposed framework on both object categorization and viewpoint estimation. Similar to [21,22] we test our model on an 8-category classification task (excluding heads and monitors). However, unlike [21,22], we do not exclude the farthest scale (which is more challenging). Figure 2 shows the learned view-invariant "style" vectors of each object instance, which clearly shows separation between different classes, even in a three-dimensional projection. Because of the limited number of zenith angles (3), we treat each zenith angle as a different viewing circle; *i.e.* all viewing manifolds are considered homeomorphic to a unit circle. To compare to published results, we used a train/test split similar to [21]; we randomly selected 7 object instances out of 10 in each category to build the proposed model, and the rest 3 instances for testing. We used HOG [1] features (20x20x31) as the input space representation. For parameterizing the view manifold, we used 8 RBF centers, (*i.e.* $N_\psi = 8$).

Table 1. 3DObjects: Category recognition and pose estimation results (%) for several configurations

	Categorization Accuracy				Pose Estimation		
	View-specific	Instance-specific	Category-specific	Manifold intersection	View specific	Instance-specific	Manifold intersection
# v SVM 5NN 7NN S-Dists							
8	81.86 83.07 79.73	89.65	90.01	76.46	81.86	70.08	63.83
16	82.46 83.74 79.67	89.65	90.01	76.21	80.67	70.08	60.32
20 90.53 82.1 83.34 79.55		89.65	90.01	69.30	80.34	70.08	46.19

Table 1 shows the categorization and pose estimation accuracies using the different setting explained in Sec 3. Different rows show the results with different number of sampled views along the view manifold latent space, which is the number of view-specific projectors. For the case of view-specific projectors, after recovering the pose and the style, we evaluated four different classifiers on the style space: one-vs-all linear SVM, 5NN, 7NN, and the distance to the different category subspaces (similar to Eq 4 after choosing the best view, *i.e.* minimizing over categories only), denoted as S-Dists. For the view-specific case, the SVM classifier yields the best results. Interestingly, the three types of projectors gave very similar results ($\approx 90\%$). Notice, by construction, that changing the number of sampled views has no effect on the recognition accuracy of the instance-specific or the category-specific projectors. For the pose estimation, we estimate the azimuth angle. Given that the ground truth only has 8 azimuth viewpoints, for the cases where we sample more than 8 views, we approximate the result to the nearest 8 bin case. Not surprisingly, the view-specific projector gave the best results for pose estimation. Overall, the view-specific projector give the best results for both category recognition and pose estimation. Table 4-I shows comparison to some of the published results on this dataset[2].

In a machine with *2.3 GHz Intel Core i7 CPU and 16 GB 1600 MHz DDR3 memory*, each frame of this dataset takes about 4.6 microseconds to be processed (using MATLAB code), excluding the HOG feature extraction, for the instance-specific case.

Results on RGBD

We evaluated the different setting with the RGB-D dataset [9], which is the largest available multi-view dataset, consisting of 300 instances of 51 tabletop object categories. Each object is rotated on a turn-table and captured using an Xbox Kinect, providing synchronized RGB and depth images. For each object three pitch angles are used: 30,45,60 degrees. Training is done on using 30 and 60 degrees sequences and testing is done on the 45 degree sequences. We use HOG descriptors [1] in both RGB and depth. Unlike the 3DObject dataset, which include completely different objects, the RGB-D is challenging because it has large number of objects, with high appearance similarity among them. Also

---

[2] We mainly compared to approaches that perform categorization and pose estimation. We do not compare to approaches that perform category-pacific detection and pose estimation, since such a comparison will not be fair.

Table 2. RGB-D: Instance, Category, and Pose recognition results (%) using several configurations

| | View-Specific | | | | | | Instance-Specific-I | | | Instance-Specific-II | | |
| | SVM (classes) | | S-Dists (Instances) | | | | | | | (Height-mean) | | |
Features	Category	Pose	Instance	Category	Pose	Instance	Category	Pose	Instance	Category	Pose
Setting I											
RGB			60.36	76.95	72.51	66.48	85.66	72.24	80.10	94.84	76.63
RGB+D	88.31	73.23	63.80	82.36	73.23	66.19	89.62	71.93	78.63	95.77	75.44
Setting II											
RGB	83.23	72.69	66.24	82.49	74.13	68.24	86.71	73.13			
Depth	51.87	59.02	17.88	39.80	59.02	34.42	71.55	61.30	38.86	76.04	61.65
RGB+D			62.09	82.04	73.36				79.73	96.01	76.01

many objects are almost textureless with symmetric geometry, which makes the pose estimation ill-posed in such cases (*e.g.* an apple or an orange)

Table 2 shows the results over different configuration. We use two different setting for manifold parameterization: Setting I uses 11 RBF centers, while Setting II used 20 RBF centers. In both settings we samples 32 viewpoints on the view latent space to generate the view-specific projectors. The description of the different classifiers/metrics is similar to the case of 3D Objects. For the instance-specific projectors we compared two settings: in the first we used the two different heights for each instance to construct a different projector, while in the second setting, we combined the two heights to obtain one instance-specific projector (taking the average of the two style vectors for each instance). We report the instance, category, and pose estimation accuracies. The best results is achieved using the instance-specific projectors.

Table 3 summarizes the results, and compares to the state-of-the-art results [10,30]. Comparison to [30] is particularly important since our approach is based on the same formulation. The percentage evaluation metric used is the same as [10]. Following from [10], Average Pose (C) are computed only on test images whose categories were correctly classified. We report the results of our instance-specific projector-II from Table 2. We compared the results using different features (RGB and/or Depth). For all feature settings, our instance-specific projector outperforms both [10,30] for instance, category, and pose estimation.

Although our framework is based on [30], and it might be considered as an approximation of it, however we outperforms [30] in all settings. The reason, as we hypothesized in Sec 3, is that our approach avoids the sampling-based inference, which has a fundamental dimensionality-accuracy tradeoff, which we do not have. Moreover, our approach is much more efficient. Using Matlab code, on Dell PRECISION 490 with *Intel(R) Xeon (5160@ 3.00GHz 3.00 GHz) CPU - 8 GB memory and 64-bits Windows-7 os* machine (this configuration is far from powerful), we find that the average running time using Instance-Specific approach in this dataset is about 9.2 milliseconds. While the running time of the View-specific approach (with K-NN classifier) is about 0.279 microseconds on the same machine, which shows the power and speed of our framework. This is compared to less than two seconds per frame reported in [30], *i.e.* , our approach much faster and more accurate.

Table 3. Instance and Category recognition, and pose estimation accuracy (%) on the RGBD dataset. Compared to the state of the art [30] and [10].

Method	Instance	Category	Avg. Pose	Avg. Pose (C)
Ours (RGB)	80.10	94.84	76.63	79.78
[30] (RGB)	74.36	92.00	61.59	80.01
Ours (Depth)	38.86	76.04	61.65	70.79
[30] (Depth)	36.18	74.49	26.06	66.36
ours (RGB+Depth)	79.73	96.01	76.01	78.42
[30] (RGB+Depth)	74.79	93.10	61.57	80.01
[10] (RGB+Depth)	78.40	94.30	53.50	56.80

Table 4. Categorization and Pose estimation - comparison with state-of-the-art

Table 4-I Categorization - 3DObjects					Table 4-II Pose Estimation - Multiview Cars			
	View-Spec Instance-Spec Zhang et al Savarese et al				Method	Split	16 views	8 views
	Projectors	Projectors	[30]	[21]	Ozuysal et al.[17]	50% split	41.69	71.20
Average	90.53%	89.56%	80.07%	75.65%	Teney and Piater [26]	50% split	78.10	79.70
Bicycle	99.54%	99.54%	99.79%	81.00%	Torki and Elgammal [27]	50% split	70.31	80.75
Car	99.31%	100.00%	99.03%	69.31%	Zhang et al. [30]	50% split	87.77	88.48
Cellphone	98.15%	96.29%	66.74%	76.00%	proposed- 16 views	50% split	**93.94**	**94.13**
Iron	86.11%	90.74%	75.78%	77.00%	proposed- 20 views	50% split	**94.64**	**94.73**
Mouse	52.58%	44.60%	48.60%	86.14%	proposed- 32 views	50% split	**94.84**	**94.84**
Shoe	94.07%	92.59%	81.70%	62.00%	Torki and Elgammal [27]	leave one out	63.73	76.84
Stapler	98.10%	96.21%	82.66%	77.00%	Zhang et al. [30]	leave one out	90.34	90.69
Toaster	98.15%	99.54%	86.24%	74.26%	proposed -32 views	leave one out	**95.38**	**95.38**

Results on EPFL-CARS

The Multi-View Car Dataset [17], is a challenging dataset, which captures 20 rotating cars in an auto show. It provides finely discretized viewpoint groundtruth, that can be calculated using the time of capturing assuming a constant velocity. Table 4-II shows the view estimation results in comparison to the state of the art. All results are generated using view-specific projectors. We build the parameterizations using 15 Gaussian-RBF centers, and the input space is HOG features. We compared the results using 50% splits and leave-one-out splits, which are the typical splits reported in other papers, we report the average over different splits. More detailed experiments available at the supplementary material.

5   Conclusion

We presented a framework for untangling the object-viewpoint visual manifold. We described different approaches based on the framework which learn view-specific object-invariant, instance-specific view-invariant, or category-specific view-invariant projectors from the input space, and described how to solve for the pose and category in each case. Experiment on three multi-view dataset showed the potentials of our proposed approach, we outperform the reported state-of-the-art approaches for recognition and pose estimation on these datasets. Moreover, the approach is shown to be very efficient. The view-specific projectors are the most promising and most scalable approach. We did not target detection in this paper, however, detection can be achieved by running the approach in a sliding window manner, which is a subject of our future research.

References

1. Dalal, N., Triggs, B.: Histograms of oriented gradients for human detection. In: CVPR (2005)
2. DiCarlo, J.J., Cox, D.D.: Untangling invariant object recognition. Trends in Cognitive Sciences 11(8), 333–341 (2007)
3. DiCarlo, J.J., Zoccolan, D., Rust, N.C.: How does the brain solve visual object recognition? Neuron 73(3), 415–434 (2012)
4. Edelman, A., Arias, T.A., Smith, S.T.: The geometry of algorithms with orthogonality constraints. SIAM J. Matrix Anal. Appl. 20(2), 303–353 (1998)
5. Felzenszwalb, P.F., Girshick, R.B., McAllester, D., Ramanan, D.: Object detection with discriminatively trained part-based models. IEEE Transactions on Pattern Analysis and Machine Intelligence, PAMI (2010)
6. Felzenszwalb, P.F., Huttenlocher, D.P.: Pictorial structures for object recognition. IJCV 61(1), 55–79 (2005)
7. Grimson, W., Lozano-Perez, T.: Recognition and localization of overlapping parts from sparse data in two and three dimensions. In: Proceedings of the1985 IEEE International Conference on Robotics and Automation, vol. 2, pp. 61–66. IEEE (1985)
8. Kimeldorf, G.S., Wahba, G.: A correspondence between bayesian estimation on stochastic processes and smoothing by splines. The Annals of Mathematical Statistics 41, 495–502 (1970)
9. Lai, K., Bo, L., Ren, X., Fox, D.: A large-scale hierarchical multi-view rgb-d object dataset. In: 2011 IEEE International Conference on Robotics and Automation (ICRA), pp. 1817–1824. IEEE (2011)
10. Lai, K., Bo, L., Ren, X., Fox, D.: A scalable tree-based approach for joint object and pose recognition. In: Twenty-Fifth Conference on Artificial Intelligence, AAAI (2011)
11. Lamdan, Y., Wolfson, H.: Geometric hashing: A general and efficient model-based recognition scheme (1988)
12. Lathauwer, L.D., de Moor, B., Vandewalle, J.: A multilinear singular value decomposiiton. SIAM Journal on Matrix Analysis and Applications 21(4), 1253–1278 (2000)
13. Lowe, D.G.: Three-dimensional object recognition from single two-dimensional images. Artificial Intelligence 31(3), 355–395 (1987)
14. Marr, D.: Vision: A computational investigation into the human representation and processing of visual information. W.H. Freeman (1982)
15. Mei, L., Liu, J., Hero, A., Savarese, S.: Robust object pose estimation via statistical manifold modeling. In: 2011 IEEE International Conference on Computer Vision (ICCV), pp. 967–974. IEEE (2011)
16. Murase, H., Nayar., S.: Visual learning and recognition of 3d objects from appearance. International Journal of Computer Vision 14, 5–24 (1995)
17. Ozuysal, M., Lepetit, V., Fua, P.: Pose estimation for category specific multiview object localization. In: CVPR (2009)
18. Payet, N., Todorovic, S.: From contours to 3d object detection and pose estimation. In: ICCV (2011)
19. Pepik, B., Stark, M., Gehler, P., Schiele, B.: Teaching 3d geometry to deformable part models. In: 2012 IEEE Conference on Computer Vision and Pattern Recognition (CVPR), pp. 3362–3369. IEEE (2012)

20. Poggio, T., Girosi, F.: Network for approximation and learning. Proceedings of the IEEE 78(9), 1481–1497 (1990)
21. Savarese, S., Fei-Fei, L.: 3d generic object categorization, localization and pose estimation. In: ICCV (2007)
22. Savarese, S., Fei-Fei, L.: View synthesis for recognizing unseen poses of object classes. In: Forsyth, D., Torr, P., Zisserman, A. (eds.) ECCV 2008, Part III. LNCS, vol. 5304, pp. 602–615. Springer, Heidelberg (2008)
23. Schels, J., Liebelt, J., Lienhart, R.: Learning an object class representation on a continuous viewsphere. In: 2012 IEEE Conference on Computer Vision and Pattern Recognition (CVPR), pp. 3170–3177. IEEE (2012)
24. Shimshoni, I., Ponce, J.: Finite-resolution aspect graphs of polyhedral objects. IEEE Transactions on Pattern Analysis and Machine Intelligence 19(4), 315–327 (1997)
25. Sivic, J., Russell, B.C., Efros, A.A., Zisserman, A., Freeman, W.T.: Discovering objects and their location in images. In: ICCV (2005)
26. Teney, D., Piater, J.: Continuous pose estimation in 2d images at instance and category levels. In: 2013 International Conference on Computer and Robot Vision, pp. 121–127 (2013)
27. Torki, M., Elgammal, A.: Regression from local features for viewpoint and pose estimation. In: Proceedings of International Conference on Computer Vision, ICCV (2011)
28. Turaga, P., Veeraraghavan, A., Srivastava, A., Chellappa, R.: Statistical computations on grassmann and stiefel manifolds for image and video-based recognition. IEEE Transactions on Pattern Analysis and Machine Intelligence 33(11), 2273–2286 (2011)
29. Willamowski, J., Arregui, D., Csurka, G., Dance, C.R., Fan, L.: Categorizing nine visual classes using local appearance descriptors. In: IWLAVS (2004)
30. Zhang, H., El-Gaaly, T., Elgammal, A., Jiang, Z.: Joint object and pose recognition using homeomorphic manifold analysis. In: AAAI (2013)

Parameterizing Object Detectors in the Continuous Pose Space

Kun He[1], Leonid Sigal[2], and Stan Sclaroff[1]

[1] Computer Science Department, Boston University, USA
[2] Disney Research Pittsburgh, USA
{hekun,sclaroff}@cs.bu.edu, lsigal@disneyresearch.com

Abstract. Object detection and pose estimation are interdependent problems in computer vision. Many past works decouple these problems, either by discretizing the continuous pose and training pose-specific object detectors, or by building pose estimators on top of detector outputs. In this paper, we propose a structured kernel machine approach to treat object detection and pose estimation jointly in a mutually benificial way. In our formulation, a unified, continuously parameterized, discriminative appearance model is learned over the entire pose space. We propose a cascaded discrete-continuous algorithm for efficient inference, and give effective online constraint generation strategies for learning our model using structural SVMs. On three standard benchmarks, our method performs better than, or on par with, state-of-the-art methods in the combined task of object detection and pose estimation.

Keywords: object detection, continuous pose estimation.

1 Introduction

We focus on the combined problems of object detection and pose estimation. Given an image x containing some object, we seek to localize the object in x, while estimating its pose at the same time. We can encode the prediction output as $y = (B, \theta)$, where B is a structured output indicating the object's location, and θ is a real-valued vector indicating the object's pose. Fig. 1 shows three examples; in these examples, B is a rectangular bounding box for the detected object, while θ gives 1D or 2D angles specifying the object's orientation.

Object detection and pose estimation are interdependent problems, and it is challenging to simultaneously infer both the object's location and pose in uncontrolled images. Many past works have broken this problem into two stages

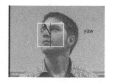

Fig. 1. Three examples of joint object detection and pose estimation

D. Fleet et al. (Eds.): ECCV 2014, Part IV, LNCS 8692, pp. 450–465, 2014.
© Springer International Publishing Switzerland 2014

to simplify the situation. Some approaches, *e.g.* [1–3], discretize the pose space and then learn pose-specific detectors. While having considerable success, the complexity of such approaches scales with the granularity of the discretization of the pose space, and generalization to continuous pose estimation is difficult. On the other hand, regression methods, *e.g.* [4–6], produce continuous pose estimates given detection results as input. However, the outputs from actual object detectors in practice are often not optimized for successive stages, resulting in suboptimal pose estimation performance.

In contrast, we argue that object detection and pose estimation should be solved jointly in a mutually beneficial way. We also argue that object pose should not be treated as a discrete variable: the continuous pose space usually has a smooth underlying structure that can be lost in discretization. We thus solve the combined problem within a unified structured prediction framework, simultaneously estimating the object's location and pose.

We take a kernel machine approach, where localization and pose are jointly modeled using a product of two kernels: a structural kernel for localization, and a pose kernel for continuous parameterization. In order to solve the associated nonconvex inference problem, we devise a cascaded inference algorithm that efficiently generates diverse proposals to explore the search space. For learning our model using the structural SVM, we propose a mini-batch online learning algorithm with simple but effective constraint generation strategies, which significantly decreases training time. To summarize, our contributions are:

1. We formulate object detection and continuous pose estimation jointly as a structured prediction problem. Our method learns a *single, continuously parameterized*, object appearance model over the entire pose space.
2. We design a cascaded discrete-continuous inference algorithm to effectively optimize a nonconvex objective involving a complicated search space.
3. We give an online mini-batch constraint generation strategy that can significantly speed up the training of structural SVMs.

In experiments with three standard benchmarks in the combined task of object detection and pose estimation, our method performs better than, or on par with, state-of-the-art methods that are typically more complicated.

2   Related Work

Multi-view object detection is an extensively studied problem. Representative works include [1, 7, 8]. These works predominantly treat the object pose or viewpoint estimation problem as a multiclass classification problem, by discretizing the viewsphere and learning view-specific object detectors.

More recently, in light of the success of the Deformable Part Model (DPM) [9] in generic object detection, view-based DPM mixture models have been introduced [2, 3, 10] to train a collection of view-specific DPMs, or even provide limited 3D reasoning [8, 11–13]. The learning of different view-specific DPMs in such works is loosely coupled by either implicit latent variable assignments [2, 3] or explicit part sharing [10–12]. However, all these models inherently deal with discretized views, and strongly coupling part appearance across views is difficult (*e.g.* via expensive part selection mechanisms). While both [11] and [12] claim to learn object models on a continuous viewsphere (in [12] leveraging high-quality 3D CAD models), both works in practice resort to fine discretizations of the pose space. In contrast, our approach continuously models the pose space by means of continuous parameterization of object detectors, and tightly couples the learning across the entire space.

For the standalone problem of object pose estimation, various regression methods [4–6], also including methods relying on statistical manifold modeling [14, 15], have been proposed. While these methods are able to perform continuous pose estimation, they assume that the object localization is given. In practice, clean object foreground masks are hard to come by, and outputs from actual object detectors are rarely optimized for the subsequent regression stage. This mismatch ultimately degrades the pose estimation performance of regression methods. In contrast, we avoid this mismatch by learning a unified model that performs detection and pose estimation jointly.

A closely related work to ours is Yuan *et al.* [16], who learn "parameter sensitive detectors" for binary classification. Pose parameterization in [16] is achieved by multiplying a pose kernel $K_\theta(\theta, \theta')$ with the original kernel, and inference is performed by discretizing the pose and testing pose-specific classifiers. While we also use a multiplicative decomposition of the joint kernel, we formulate the problem in the structured-output domain, and produce continuous solutions for pose during inference.

Ionescu *et al.* [17] propose a structural SVM approach for joint object localization and continuous state estimation, also using a multiplicative joint kernel. Inference is performed in an alternating fashion where localization is initialized using a generic object detector. However, single initialization is suboptimal for our nonconvex objective; instead, our cascaded inference efficiently generates diverse initializations to better explore the search space. Also, we propose novel online constraint generation strategies for structural SVMs. The resulting online algorithm significantly outperforms the cutting plane method used in [17].

3   Mathematical Formulation

Suppose we are given a training set of n pairs $\{(x_i, y_i)\}_{i=1}^n$ where each example $x_i \in \mathcal{X}$ is a training image, and each label y_i belongs to a structured output space $\mathcal{Y}$. We focus on predicting bounding boxes and viewing angles, and take the structured output space $\mathcal{Y}$ to be $\Re^4 \times [0, 2\pi)^d$, where $d \leq 3$ is the number of angles (a complete parameterization of the viewsphere needs 3 angles).

Our goal is to learn a scoring function $f : \mathcal{X} \times \mathcal{Y} \to \Re$ such that the label y assigned to x maximizes $f(x, y)$. We parameterize f as $f(x, y) = \langle \mathbf{w}, \Psi(x, y) \rangle$, where $\mathbf{w}$ is a parameter vector, and $\Psi(x, y)$ is a *joint feature map*. The inner product $\langle \cdot, \cdot \rangle$ is defined in a reproducing kernel Hilbert space (RKHS), instantiated by a *joint kernel function* K: $K(x, y, x', y') = \langle \Psi(x, y), \Psi(x', y') \rangle$.

We intend to learn the scoring function f via regularized loss minimization. Assuming that the conditions of the Representer Theorem [18] are met, f has the following implicit representation, where $\mathcal{V}$ is the index set of "support vectors" $\{(x_j, y_j)\}$, and α_j are scalars:

$$f(x, y) = \langle \mathbf{w}, \Psi(x, y) \rangle = \sum_{j \in \mathcal{V}} \alpha_j K(x, y, x_j, y_j). \tag{1}$$

It is key to design the joint kernel K for our task. Given two input-output pairs $(x, (B, \theta))$ and $(x', (B', \theta'))$, we define K to be the product of two valid Mercer kernels K_s and K_p:

$$K(x, y, x', y') = K_s(\phi(x, B), \phi(x', B')) \cdot K_p(\theta, \theta'). \tag{2}$$

Here, $\phi(x, B)$ represents the feature vector extracted from the image region inside bounding box B in image x. The structural kernel K_s measures the similarity between two such feature vectors. The pose kernel K_p measures the similarity between poses θ and θ'. The joint kernel achieves a high value only for input-output pairs with similar inputs and similar outputs.

In this work, we are interested in the case where K_s is linear, i.e. $K_s(\phi, \phi') = \phi^T \phi'$, for efficiency considerations. On the other hand, in order for K_p to smoothly capture the complex effects of varying pose, we choose to use a non-linear RBF kernel: $K_p(\theta, \theta') = \exp\left(-\gamma d(\theta, \theta')^2\right)$ where $d(\theta, \theta')$ is a distance measure, e.g. Euclidean distance or geodesic distance. Then, given image x and model $\mathbf{w}$, the inference problem in our model becomes:

$$\max_{y \in \mathcal{Y}} \langle \mathbf{w}, \Psi(x, y) \rangle = \max_{(B, \theta) \in \mathcal{Y}} \sum_{j \in \mathcal{V}} \alpha_j \phi(x, B)^T \phi(x_i, B_j) \exp\left(-\gamma d(\theta, \theta_j)^2\right). \tag{3}$$

This is a complicated nonconvex optimization problem. In the next section, we will describe a cascaded solution to optimizing Eq.(3).

4   Cascaded Inference

Solving Eq.(3) is difficult: there are a large number of bounding boxes B in an image, and the objective is nonconvex in θ whenever there is a negative α_j. However, if either B or θ is fixed, the problem becomes significantly simplified and better studied: given B, θ can be estimated by regression; given θ, B can be obtained by a θ-specific detector. Both can be seen as extreme cases of a general cascaded scheme: first prune the search space, and then refine the answer.

Inspired by the reasoning above, we also propose to use a two-step cascade consisting of a pruning step and a refining step. However, we shall take the middle ground and keep multiple candidates for both B and θ after the first step, in order to avoid problems associated with the two extreme approaches, as discussed in Section 2.

Specifically, the pruning step returns a reduced search space $\tilde{\mathcal{Y}} = \{(B_k, \Theta_k)\}_{k=1}^K$, where each pair consists of a candidate bounding box B_k and an associated range Θ_k of plausible poses, e.g. $\Theta_k = \{\theta \mid d(\theta, \theta_k) < \delta\}$ for some θ_k and δ. The refining step performs further optimization and returns a final solution pair (B^*, θ^*).

4.1 Refining Step

Barring a somewhat unconventional ordering, we shall first study the problem of refinement, in order to highlight desired properties for the pruning step. Assume for now that $\tilde{\mathcal{Y}}$ is given, and for $\forall k \in \{1, \ldots, K\}, \forall j \in \mathcal{V}$, denote $\eta_k^j = \alpha_j \phi(x_j, B_k)^T \phi(x, B_j)$. Then, the problem of refinement can be cast as:

$$\max_k \max_{\theta \in \Theta_k} \sum_{j \in \mathcal{V}} \eta_k^j \exp\left(-\gamma \, d(\theta, \theta_j)^2\right). \tag{4}$$

We employ a gradient ascent approach for optimizing Eq.(4) with respect to θ, as the use of a smoothly differentiable pose kernel permits the use of gradient algorithms, e.g. L-BFGS. For each B_k, we optimize over $\theta \in \Theta_k$ to find its matching pose θ_k, and finally maximize over k to pick the best-scoring pair (B^*, θ^*).

However, as Eq.(4) still is nonconvex in general, Θ_k's should be restricted in size so that there are few local optima. Also, the candidate bounding boxes $\{B_k\}$ should contain diverse elements so as to explore the search space. Lastly, K necessarily needs to be small since continuous optimization is a relatively costly operation. To summarize, the pruning step should:

- efficiently generate diverse B_k's to explore the solution space,
- produce small Θ_k's to reduce the number of local optima, and
- produce a small K to reduce the number of continuous refinements.

4.2 Pruning Step

Now we are ready to propose our pruning strategy: uniformly divide the θ space into M intervals $\{\Theta_1, \ldots, \Theta_M\}$, specify a "seed pose" $\{\theta_1, \ldots, \theta_M\}$ within each interval (e.g. the geometric centers), and sample pose-specific detectors from the model to generate proposals for B.

Since our method learns a continuously parameterized object appearance model Eq.(1) over the entire pose space, we can efficiently sample pose-specific detectors from the unified model. For any fixed θ, our model reduces to a single linear classifier $\mathbf{w}_\theta$ (this observation is also made by [16]):

$$\mathbf{w}_\theta = \sum_{j \in \mathcal{V}} \alpha_j \exp\left(-\gamma \, d(\theta, \theta_j)^2\right) \phi(x_j, B_j), \quad m = 1, \ldots, M. \tag{5}$$

Our strategy satisfies all the desired properties: we can control the size of the intervals to limit the number of local optima within them; we can leverage existing techniques to efficiently evaluate the classifiers and generate bounding box proposals; and it is easy to control the number of generated proposals.

Given detectors $\{\mathbf{w}_1, \ldots, \mathbf{w}_M\}$, we reuse existing techniques, for example sliding windows, to generate diverse bounding box proposals. Then, the refining step performs gradient-based continuous optimization using the seed poses as starting points. If the intervals are relatively small, single stage refinement is sufficient (we observe this to be the case in practice); coarse sampling can be handled by cascades where the solution is refined in a hierarchical fashion: first refining Θ to a smaller interval, constructing a better tuned detector specific to Θ, refining localization using this new detector, etc.

We emphasize that the pose-specific detectors are sampled from the original unified model by fixing θ; thus, their scores are directly comparable, since the scores are essentially given by the unified model. This contrasts with many 1-vs-all methods, where the classifier scores for different classes may be uncalibrated.

4.3   Generating Diverse Proposals: Branch-and-Bound

With the M pose-specific detectors sampled from our model, bouding box proposals can be generated typically in time that is linear in M. We further speed this up via a branch-and-bound algorithm that is capable of generating diverse proposals in sublinear time. Our algorithm generalizes the Efficient Subwindow Search (ESS) [19] by Lampert $et\ al.$ and operates on an augmented state space, encoding both object location and pose.

The input to our algorithm are the pose-specific detectors $\{\mathbf{w}_1, \mathbf{w}_2, \ldots, \mathbf{w}_M\}$ sampled from our unified model. Sets of candidate solutions, or $states$, are sorted in a priority queue Q according to a merit function indicating their promisingness. The algorithm iterates by splitting the most promising state in Q and inserting the resulting states back into Q, until it gets a singleton state. The amortized time complexity for branch-and-bound is on the order of $O(\log_2 M)$.

State Representation: A state is parameterized as $s = (w, h, x_0, x_1, y_0, y_1, \theta)$, where w and h encode the bounding box size, x_0 and x_1 bound the x coordinate of its upper-left corner, and y_0 and y_1 bound the y coordinate. θ is one of $\{\theta_1, \ldots, \theta_M\}$. For each combination of the first six parameters, there are M unique states containing different values of θ.

Bounding Classifier Scores: If state s contains pose θ_m, then the corresponding classifier $\mathbf{w}_m$ is used to generate bounds for the set of bounding boxes contained in s. Once $\mathbf{w}_m$ is chosen, the scenario reduces to that of bounding the score of a single linear classifier over a set of rectangular regions. In this case, Lampert $et\ al.$ [19] showed that tight bounds can be constructed for Bag-of-Words (BOW) features. We refer interested readers to [19] for the full derivation of the bounding techniques.

Diverse Solutions: Instead of terminating the algorithm after obtaining the first singleton state, we store the state in an output buffer and continue the algorithm, until K singleton states have been returned (obtaining top-K solutions) or until the score is below a threshold (obtaining all "good" solutions). Non-maximum suppression is used to enforce diversity.

5   Learning

For learning our unified model for joint object detection and continuous pose estimation within a kernel machine framework, we use the structural SVM [20] to learn a large-margin model $\mathbf{w}$. The structural SVM is formulated as:

$$\min_{\mathbf{w},\xi} \frac{1}{2}\|\mathbf{w}\|^2 + \frac{C}{n}\sum_{i=1}^{n}\xi_i \qquad (6)$$

$$s.t. \quad \langle \mathbf{w}, \Psi(x_i, y_i)\rangle - \langle \mathbf{w}, \Psi(x_i, \bar{y}_i)\rangle \geq \Delta(y_i, \bar{y}_i) - \xi_i, \quad \forall i, \forall \bar{y}_i \in \mathcal{Y}, \qquad (7)$$

where the loss term $\Delta(y_i, \bar{y}_i)$ encodes the penalty of predicting $\bar{y}_i$ instead of y_i. To jointly handle object localization and pose, we use a combined loss:

$$\Delta(y_i, y) = \Delta((B_i, \theta_i), (B, \theta)) = \beta\Delta_{loc}(B_i, B) + (1 - \beta)\Delta_{pose}(\theta_i, \theta). \qquad (8)$$

The localization loss is based on bounding box overlap [21]: $\Delta_{loc}(B, B') = 1 - \frac{Area(B \cap B')}{Area(B \cup B')}$, and pose loss is proportional to angular difference: $\Delta_{pose} \propto \angle(\theta, \theta')$.

The structural SVM usually is solved by constraint generation algorithms such as the cutting plane algorithm [20] or its one-slack reformulation [22]. To find a violated constraint for training pair (x_i, y_i), the following loss-augmented inference problem is solved:

$$\bar{y}_i = \arg\max_{y\in\mathcal{Y}} \ \Delta(y_i, y) + \langle \mathbf{w}, \Psi(x_i, y)\rangle \qquad (9)$$

$$\approx \arg\max_{B,\theta_m} \beta\Delta_{loc}(B_i, B) + (1 - \beta)\Delta_{pose}(\theta_i, \theta_m) + \mathbf{w}_m^T\phi(x, B). \qquad (10)$$

Eq.(9) has the same structure as the test-time inference problem Eq.(3) and can also be solved by the two-step cascade. The pruning step Eq.(10) samples seed poses $\{\theta_m|m = 1, \ldots, M\}$ and performs branch-and-bound, and then continuous refinement can be applied. However, we found that fine-sampling poses (e.g. 16 equally spaced poses for the 1D case) without doing refinement actually works well in practice.

We briefly describe how to bound the loss term here. Firstly, given state s and the set $\mathcal{B}(s)$ of bounding boxes it contains, Δ_{loc} can be bounded as

$$\Delta_{loc}(B_i, B) = 1 - \frac{Area(B_i \cap B)}{Area(B_i \cup B)} \leq 1 - \frac{\min_{B\in\mathcal{B}(s)} Area(B_i \cap B)}{\max_{B\in\mathcal{B}(s)} Area(B_i \cup B)}, \qquad (11)$$

which can be computed by considering the intersection and union regions of the set $\mathcal{B}(s)$. Secondly, $(1-\beta)\Delta_{pose}(\theta_i, \theta_m)$ is in fact a constant in any state, since θ_m is fixed. We add this constant to the upper and lower bounds for the localization loss to get bounds for the overall loss term.

We also generate multiple diverse solutions for the loss-augmented inference, as this speeds up empirical convergence for structural SVM learning, as shown in [23]. With branch-and-bound, this can be done in the same fashion as generating multiple solutions for test-time inference; the diversity of solutions can be enforced by performing non-maximum suppression on the loss values.

5.1   Online Mini-Batch Algorithm

In learning a continuously parameterized model over the pose space, all training examples are tightly coupled into a single learning problem. Efficient structural SVM learning algorithms are needed to keep the complexity of learning manageable. However, cutting plane methods [20, 22], which typically perform constraint generation over the training set multiple times, are usually slow to converge in practice. Instead of traversing the training set multiple times and revisiting examples for which constraints are likely to be satisfied already, we focus on learning from subsets of "important" examples and generating multiple diverse constraints per iteration.

We cast the learning problem into an online version by considering mini-batches of training examples. In iteration t, a subset S_t is sampled from the training set, and new constraints are generated only for examples in S_t. Model updates can be done using SMO-style dual updates [24, 25]. We then seek appropriate sampling strategies for finding "important" subsets that contribute to improving the current model. In practice, we consider two strategies: 1) sample according to the slack variables ξ_i, and 2) randomly permute the training set and take sequential mini-batches.

The rationale behind the first strategy is that a large ξ_i indicates severe constraint violation and an important example for improving the model. The second strategy deems the next subset of unseen examples as important. Despite their simplicity, in our experiments, both strategies enable the online algorithm to provide a speedup of an order of magnitude over cutting plane methods, while achieving comparable or better prediction performance.

6   Experiments

We evaluated our method on three publicly available datasets: EPFL Cars [7], Pointing'04 [26], and 3D Objects [1].

We intend to keep our object appearance models simple so as to cleanly demonstrate the effects of continuous pose parameterization. Therefore, all of our appearance models are *single rectangular templates*, using the linear kernel as K_s, without any notion of mixture components or parts. For pose parameterization, we use Gaussian RBF kernels as K_p. The RBF bandwidth γ and SVM's trade-off parameter C are determined via cross validation. During learning, we weight the localization and pose losses equally ($\beta = 0.5$).

To assess detection performance, we follow the Pascal VOC protocol [21] to compute the Average Precision (AP) for predicted bounding boxes. For continuous pose estimation, we report the Mean Angular Error (MAE). For completeness, we also quantize our continuous pose estimates into M bins and report the Mean Precision of Pose Estimation (MPPE), defined as the average along the diagonal of the M-way confusion matrix in [3].

In all experiments, in addition to comparing with leading methods, we compare to a baseline that learns 1-vs-all SVM classifiers for discretized poses with the same feature. Each SVM is initially trained using ground truth bounding

Table 1. Performance comparison on the EPFL Cars dataset [7]. Multi-view methods using 16 viewpoint bins [3, 12, 27] are listed. Regression methods [4–6] use ground truth bounding boxes (GT) as input. AP and MPPE: higher is better. MAE: lower is better. Top two results for each category in bold.

Method	Baseline	BnB	Refined	[3]	[12][b]	[27]	[6]	[5]	[4]	[15]
AP (%)	88.0	**100**	**100**	97	**97.5**	89.5	GT	GT	GT	GT
MAE°	36.7	**17.0**	**15.8**	27.2[a]	–	–	24.2	31.2	33.1	24.0
Median AE°	12.2	8.0	**6.2**	–	**6.9**	24.8	–	–	–	–
MPPE (%)	46.8	63.8	64.0	**66.1**	**69.0**	–	–	66.1[c]	70.3[c]	87.8[c]

[a] Obtained from direct correspondence with [3]'s authors.
[b] We cite [12]'s "3D^{2}PM-C Lin" variant with 16 viewpoint bins.
[c] [4, 5, 15] report percentages of $AE < 22.5°$, or 8-bin MPPEs.

(a)   (b)

Fig. 2. EPFL Cars results: (a) typical success cases; (b) example errors. Ground truth: yellow. Detection/pose estimation: green (correct), red (incorrect).

boxes associated with the target pose as positive examples, and ground truth bounding boxes with other poses as negatives. Then hard negative mining is applied on the training set to iteratively add negative examples and retrain the SVM until convergence.

6.1   EPFL Cars Dataset

The EPFL Cars dataset [7] contains 20 different cars with views captured roughly 2°-3° apart on rotating platforms. This dataset has been studied in many previous works, *e.g.* [3, 12, 27], and is suitable for studying continuous pose estimation due to its relatively fine-grained and accurate pose annotations. A major challenge in this dataset is handling the near-180° confusions (*e.g.* front-back, left-right) or flipping errors, as noted in [7].

Setup. We first extract dense SIFT features from training images and cluster them into a codebook of 500 visual words using K-means, and construct our image feature as a 3-level spatial pyramid of visual words, with dimensionality 10500. The LLC encoding scheme of [28] is used, and L_2 normalization is applied to the feature vectors [29].

Following the standard test protocol in [7], we train on the first 10 car instances and test on the remaining 10. At test time, the initial solutions for each image are obtained using branch-and-bound with M=16 equally spaced seed poses. We then perform continuous pose refinement and pick the top-scoring solution, since each image contains exactly one car in EPFL Cars.

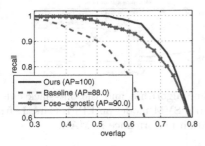 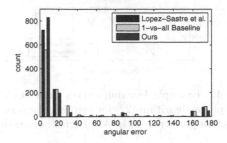

Fig. 3. Results on EPFL Cars. Left: closeup of overlap-recall curves for our method, the baseline, and a pose-agnostic detector learned with bounding box annotations. Right: histograms of angular errors for our method, the baseline, and Lopez-Sastre *et al.* [3].

Results. Example results are shown in Fig. 2. We report our results both with respect to initial solutions (`BnB`) and continuously refined solutions (`Refined`) in Table 1, and compare them to competing methods.

Our method achieves **100%** AP and **15.8°** MAE, and outperforms all previous methods that report AP and MAE by a large margin, including regression methods [4–6] that use ground truth bounding boxes as input. We also achieve **6.2°** *Median* Angular Error, which is significantly better than [27]'s 24.8° and comparable to [12]'s 6.9° (16 viewpoint bins) and 4.7° (36 viewpoint bins). Note that [12] builds a much richer model by learning 3D part-based models directly from high-quality CAD models; in contrast, our model is a single part-free 2D object template, parameterized by pose, and learned on the original training set. When we quantize our continuous pose estimates into 16 bins, we obtain a 64.0% MPPE, which is comparable to the 69.0% and 66.1% reported by [12] and [3]. To our knowledge, our method gives the current state-of-the-art results in detection and continuous pose estimation on EPFL Cars.

To analyze detection results, in Fig. 3 we plot the overlap-recall curve [29]. The lowest overlap with ground truth for our detections is 53%, giving 100% AP when using the 50% overlap threshold. The 1-vs-all baseline produces a significantly worse overlap-recall curve, with the lowest overlap being just 14%. We also compare to a pose-agnostic detector trained using only bounding box annotations; its learning can be achieved in our formulation by only considering the localization loss, or setting $\beta = 1$ in Eq.(8). This improves the lowest overlap with ground truth to 23%, but still produces a noticeably worse overlap-recall curve compared to ours. We thus conclude that incorporating pose information into the detector helps improve detection performance.

Next, in Fig. 3 we plot the histograms of angular errors for our method, the 1-vs-all baseline, and Lopez-Sastre *et al.* [3], who learn a mixture of view-specific DPMs. We report [3]'s result since it gives the previous best performance with the original training set. The numbers of flipping errors (angular errors of more than 150°) for the three methods are: 52 (Ours), 129 (baseline), and 123 ([3]). We reduce the number of flipping errors in both methods by more than half. This confirms the benefit of learning a unified model over the pose space.

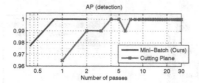
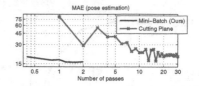

Fig. 4. Example learning curves from our online algorithm and the one-slack cutting plane algorithm [22] for learning the structural SVM model on EPFL Cars. Left: detection performance in AP. Right: pose estimation performance in MAE.

Online Mini-Batch Learning. We also compared our mini-batch online algorithm against the one-slack cutting plane algorithm [22] in learning our structural SVM model on EPFL Cars. We use the sequential mini-batch sampling strategy due to its simplicity. The time complexity is measured in *passes over training set*, or the average number of loss-augmented inference operations per training example. Learning curves for both methods are shown in Fig. 4.

Our online algorithm converges after two passes over training set, while the cutting plane algorithm typically requires 20–30 passes to converge, and to a worse solution (identical AP, higher MAE). We attribute the fast convergence of the online algorithm to the more frequent model updates and the ability to focus on "important" examples. The cutting plane algorithm emphasizes consistently improving the model with respect to the whole training set, but this may result in 1) increased computational efforts, and 2) the loss of emphasis on important examples, since their effects can be "averaged out". Our observations are consistent with those in the online learning community, *e.g.* [25].

6.2   Pointing'04 Dataset

Next, we turn to the problem of head pose estimation in the Pointing'04 dataset [26]. This dataset contains 2790 face images of 15 human subjects, captured from a total of 93 distinct poses parameterized by two angles (*pitch, yaw*). The images all have clean backgrounds and are not challenging for the detection task; therefore, we only evaluate pose estimation performance by making use of ground truth bounding boxes, as also done in [5, 6]. The approximately annotated poses are at least 15° apart in Pointing'04

Setup. We use the same features as Hara *et al.* [6] by cropping out the face regions from the images and extracting HOG descriptors from three scales, resulting in a 2124 dimensional feature vector. We follow the standard protocol in [26] and report five-fold cross validation MAEs for *pitch* and *yaw*. However, with five folds the randomness in splitting data was found to be statistically significant. We thus tried 10 random five-fold splits, and report the mean and standard deviation for five-fold MAEs from the 10 trials. The best five-fold MAEs (having the lowest average) are also reported.

Results. Table 2 summarizes the results. Our method consistently outperforms the baseline by an average of 2.07° and 1.78° in *pitch* and *yaw* respectively, which again speaks to the benefit of learning a unified parameterized model.

Table 2. Head pose estimation performances on the Pointing'04 dataset. Results for our method (**BnB** and **Refined**) are reported from 10 random trials of five-fold cross validation, in the format of **mean±std/best**. Top two results for each category in bold.

MAE°	Baseline	BnB	Refined	KRF[6]	[5]	kPLS[30]	[26]
pitch	6.37±.17	4.30±.16/**4.01**	5.25±.15/4.95	**2.51**	6.73	6.61	15.9
yaw	7.14±.16	5.36±.15/**5.20**	5.91±.14/5.71	**5.29**	5.94	6.56	10.1
average	6.76±.16	4.83±.13/**4.61**	5.58±.13/5.33	**3.90**	6.34	6.59	13.0

 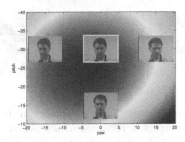

Fig. 5. Left: four training examples annotated with $(30°, 30°)$ in the Pointing'04 dataset. Approximate annotations affect the quality of our continuous model. Left: a test example (yellow box) annotated with $(-30°, 0°)$ and its three neighbors overlayed on top of the score map produced by our model. Although the scoring function does not peak exactly at $(-30°, 0°)$, it remains the top-scoring discrete pose.

A seemingly surprising fact is that the continuous refinement step yields higher MAEs. We note that this has to do with annotation quality. As illustrated in Fig. 5, pose annotations in Pointing'04 are at least 15° apart, and also carry noticeable label noise. Compared to the case of EPFL Cars (2°-3° apart and less noisy), this more significantly affects the quality of continuous parameterization. As a result, the scoring function in general does not peak exactly at discretized poses, which can result in nonzero angular errors even for poses already correctly estimated by discrete initialization. However, continuous refinement is highly consistent with discrete initialization, altering nearest-neighbor assignments to discrete poses only 0.36% of the time. Despite the coarse parameterization, we still significantly improve upon the discretized 1-vs-all baseline.

We also compare to previous methods [5, 6, 26, 30] in Table 2. Our method significantly outperforms Fenzi *et al.* [5], Haj *et al.* [30] and Gourier *et al.* [26] despite the use of more complex models in all three methods (1-NN classifier, kernel Partial Least Squares, and facial structure detection, respectively). Our best average MAE of 4.61° is slightly higher than [6]'s 3.90°, but note that our result is achieved by linear classifiers, while [6] employs a highly nonlinear kernel regression forest that also performs feature selection. We would also like to point out that [6], as well as [5, 30], is a regression method that requires clean input, whereas our method is fully capable of doing joint object detection and pose estimation, as we demonstrate in the other two experiments.

Table 3. 3D Objects: performance comparison for classes `bicycle` and `car`. Results for our method (**BnB**) are from 10 random trials, in the format of `mean±std/best`. Top two results for each category in bold.

Method		Baseline	BnB	[12]	[3]	[11]	[27]	[2]
bicycle	AP (%)	78.2±5.2	95.1±1.4/**96.8**	**97.6**	91	87.0	–	–
	MPPE (%)	98.7±2.1	94.0±3.3/**97.6**	**98.9**	90	87.7	–	96.2
car	AP (%)	85.4±8.8	98.2±3.9/97.8	**99.9**	96	94.9	**99.2**	–
	MPPE (%)	97.7±3.2	87.9±3.4/**93.0**	**97.9**	89	82.6	84.9	92.0

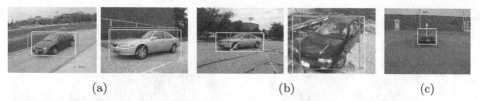

(a)   (b)   (c)

Fig. 6. Example results on car images in the 3D Objects dataset [1]: (a) typical success cases; (b) correct detections, wrong poses; (c) complete failure. Note the variation in actual poses in images having the same pose annotation (first four images).

6.3   3D Objects Dataset

We also evaluate our method in object detection and discrete pose classification on the 3D Objects dataset [1]. The dataset contains 8 object classes each having 10 instances, roughly annotated with 8 discrete viewpoints spaced at 45° apart. With such sparse views, object appearances tend to form discrete clusters rather than vary smoothly, making discrete classification methods more suitable. In fact, previous methods relying on mixtures of view-specific DPMs [3, 12] have obtained very competitive results on the 3D Objects dataset.

We shall only evaluate our branch-and-bound algorithm with discrete poses on the 3D Objects dataset, since its granularity of pose samples and accuracy of annotation are both insufficient for learning our continuously parameterized detector. Nevertheless, we are still interested in evaluating whether or not coarse parameterization and feature sharing can improve detector performance.

Setup. We use the same feature representation that we used with EPFL Cars: 3-level spatial pyramid of 500 SIFT visual words, with LLC encoding and L_2 normalization. We focus on the `bicycle` and `car` classes, as they are the most representative and they have been extensively studied in the literature.

As noted in [11], despite the large number of studies on 3D Objects, different test configurations have been reported, making a fully comprehensive comparison difficult. As in experiments with Pointing'04, we tried 10 different splits of the dataset, each time using images from 7 object instances for training, and the rest for testing. For viewpoint classification, we compute MPPE on the set of correct detections. We report from the 10 trials both the average and best performance (having the highest average of AP and MPPE).

Results. Table 3 reports results obtained by our method (BnB). We achieve significant improvements in AP over the baseline for both bicycle and car, on average by 16.9% and 12.8%, respectively. This again shows the benefit of pose parameterization for object detectors. However, the baseline does have higher MPPEs than BnB. Since the MPPE is computed on correct detections, this means that the 1-vs-all SVMs learned by the baseline are highly specific to their correponding views. However, collectively they produce many more misdetections for which pose estimates are hardly useful. The 1-vs-all SVMs are independently learned, and give essentially uncalibrated scores; this can lead to mutual confusions and degradation of collected detection performance.

We show example detection and pose estimation results for the car class in Fig. 6. Many of our pose classification errors are next-bin errors (by 45°) due to approximate annotations (see Fig. 6(b) for an example).

As can be seen in Table 3, our best results (96.8% AP and 97.6% MPPE for bicycle, 97.8% AP and 93.0% MPPE for car) are collectively better than those from all competing methods only except [12], while our average performance is also competitive. Again, we note that [12] learns rich 3D part-based models directly from high-quality CAD models, while our method learns a single parameterized 2D object template from roughly annotated images. Remarkably, our method consistently outperforms another more complicated system by Schels et al. [11], who also learn from CAD models and construct a dense part-based object representation over the viewsphere by fine-sampling viewpoints.

7   Conclusion

We propose a structured formulation to jointly perform object detection and pose estimation, by learning a single, continuously parameterized, discriminative object appearance model over the entire pose space. To solve the associated nonconvex inference problem, we design a cascaded algorithm with an efficient pruning step to generate diverse proposals, and a refining step that performs continuous optimization. For efficient model learning, we give simple but effective costraint generation strategies for a mini-batch online structural SVM learning algorithm, which converges significantly faster than batch algorithms. On three standard benchmarks in the combined task of object detection and pose estimation, our method performs better than, or on par with, state-of-the-art systems that are usually of higher complexity.

We focus on 1D and 2D viewing angles in this paper as this provides a very common parameterization of object appearance, appropriate for nearly any object and imaging scenario. Nevertheless, our formulation is general and can work with other continuous or even discrete factors that parameterize object appearance, such as articulated pose, directional lighting, phenotypes, and object subcategories. We are interested in exploring these factors in future work.

Acknowledgments. This work was supported in part by U.S. NSF grants 0910908 and 1029430.

References

1. Savarese, S., Fei-Fei, L.: 3D generic object categorization, localization and pose estimation. In: ICCV (2007)
2. Gu, C., Ren, X.: Discriminative mixture-of-templates for viewpoint classification. In: Daniilidis, K., Maragos, P., Paragios, N. (eds.) ECCV 2010, Part V. LNCS, vol. 6315, pp. 408–421. Springer, Heidelberg (2010)
3. Lopez-Sastre, R.J., Tuytelaars, T., Savarese, S.: Deformable part models revisited: A performance evaluation for object category pose estimation. In: ICCV 2011 Workshops (2011)
4. Torki, M., Elgammal, A.: Regression from local features for viewpoint and pose estimation. In: ICCV (2011)
5. Fenzi, M., Leal-Taixé, L., Rosenhahn, B., Ostermann, J.: Class generative models based on feature regression for pose estimation of object categories. In: CVPR (2013)
6. Hara, K., Chellappa, R.: Growing Regression Forests by Classification: Applications to Object Pose Estimation. In: Fleet, D., Pajdla, T., Schiele, B., Tuytelaars, T. (eds.) ECCV 2014, Part II. LNCS, vol. 8690, pp. 552–567. Springer, Heidelberg (2014)
7. Ozuysal, M., Lepetit, V.: P.Fua: Pose estimation for category specific multiview object localization. In: CVPR (2009)
8. Stark, M., Goesele, M., Schiele, B.: Back to the future: Learning shape models from 3D CAD data. In: BMVC (2010)
9. Felzenszwalb, P.F., Girshick, R.B., McAllester, D., Ramanan, D.: Object detection with discriminatively trained part-based models. IEEE TPAMI 32(9) (2010)
10. Zhu, X., Ramanan, D.: Face detection, pose estimation, and landmark localization in the wild. In: CVPR (2012)
11. Schels, J., Liebelt, J., Lienhart, R.: Learning an object class representation on a continuous viewsphere. In: CVPR (2012)
12. Pepik, B., Gehler, P., Stark, M., Schiele, B.: 3D^{2}PM - 3D deformable part models. In: Fitzgibbon, A., Lazebnik, S., Perona, P., Sato, Y., Schmid, C. (eds.) ECCV 2012, Part VI. LNCS, vol. 7577, pp. 356–370. Springer, Heidelberg (2012)
13. Xiang, Y., Savarese, S.: Estimating the aspect layout of object categories. In: CVPR (2012)
14. Mei, L., Liu, J., Hero, A., Savarese, S.: Robust object pose estimation via statistical manifold modeling. In: ICCV (2011)
15. Zhang, H., El-Gaaly, T., Elgammal, A., Jiang, Z.: Joint object and pose recognition using homeomorphic manifold analysis. In: AAAI (2013)
16. Yuan, Q., Thangali, A., Ablavsky, V., Sclaroff, S.: Multiplicative kernels: Object detection, segmentation and pose estimation. In: CVPR (2008)
17. Ionescu, C., Bo, L., Sminchisescu, C.: Structural SVM for visual localization and continuous state estimation. In: ICCV (2009)
18. Hofmann, T., Schölkopf, B., Smola, A.J.: Kernel methods in machine learning. The Annals of Statistics, 1171–1220 (2008)
19. Lampert, C.H., Blaschko, M.B., Hofmann, T.: Efficient subwindow search: A branch and bound framework for object localization. IEEE TPAMI 31(12) (2009)
20. Tsochantaridis, I., Joachims, T., Hofmann, T., Altun, Y.: Large margin methods for structured and interdependent output variables. JMLR 6(9) (2005)
21. Everingham, M., Van Gool, L., Williams, C.K.I., Winn, J., Zisserman, A.: The PASCAL visual object classes (VOC) challenge. IJCV 88(2) (2010)

22. Joachims, T., Finley, T., Yu, C.N.J.: Cutting-plane training of structural SVMs. Machine Learning 77(1) (2009)

23. Guzman-Rivera, A., Kohli, P., Batra, D.: Faster training of structural SVMs with diverse M-best cutting-planes. In: AISTATS (2013)

24. Platt, J.C.: Fast training of support vector machines using sequential minimal optimization. In: Advances in Kernel Methods, pp. 185–208. MIT Press, Cambridge (1999)

25. Bordes, A., Usunier, N., Bottou, L.: Sequence labelling SVMs trained in one pass. In: Daelemans, W., Goethals, B., Morik, K. (eds.) ECML PKDD 2008, Part I. LNCS (LNAI), vol. 5211, pp. 146–161. Springer, Heidelberg (2008)

26. Gourier, N., Hall, D., Crowley, J.L.: Estimating face orientation from robust detection of salient facial structures. In: ICPR 2004 Workshops (2004)

27. Glasner, D., Galun, M., Alpert, S., Basri, R., Shakhnarovich, G.: Viewpoint-aware object detection and pose estimation. In: ICCV (2011)

28. Wang, J., Yang, J., Yu, K., Lv, F., Huang, T., Gong, Y.: Locality-constrained linear coding for image classification. In: CVPR (2010)

29. Vedaldi, A., Gulshan, V., Varma, M., Zisserman, A.: Multiple kernels for object detection. In: ICCV (2009)

30. Haj, M.A., Gonzalez, J., Davis, L.S.: On partial least squares in head pose estimation: How to simultaneously deal with misalignment. In: CVPR (2012)

Jointly Optimizing 3D Model Fitting and Fine-Grained Classification

Yen-Liang Lin[1], Vlad I. Morariu[2], Winston Hsu[1], and Larry S. Davis[2]

[1] National Taiwan University, Taipei, Taiwan
[2] University of Maryland, College Park, MD, USA
yenliang@cmlab.csie.ntu.edu.tw, whsu@ntu.edu.tw,
{morariu,lsd}@umiacs.umd.edu

Abstract. 3D object modeling and fine-grained classification are often treated as separate tasks. We propose to optimize 3D model fitting and fine-grained classification jointly. Detailed 3D object representations encode more information (e.g., precise part locations and viewpoint) than traditional 2D-based approaches, and can therefore improve fine-grained classification performance. Meanwhile, the predicted class label can also improve 3D model fitting accuracy, e.g., by providing more detailed class-specific shape models. We evaluate our method on a new fine-grained 3D car dataset (FG3DCar), demonstrating our method outperforms several state-of-the-art approaches. Furthermore, we also conduct a series of analyses to explore the dependence between fine-grained classification performance and 3D models.

1 Introduction

Fine-grained recognition methods have been proposed to address different types of super-ordinate categories (e.g., birds [10,5,6,8], dogs [18] or cars [23,14]), and many of these methods focus on finding distinctive 2D parts for distinguishing different classes [6,27,5,2] or seeking better pose-invariant feature representations [29]. Recently, researchers [8,14] have used 3D models for fine-grained classification. While these methods have shown some success in tackling viewpoint variations within the objects, their non-deformable 3D model representations limit the ability of these approaches to adjust to different shapes of objects.

At the same time, 3D object modeling has also received renewed attention recently [20,12,21,16,30]. Many methods have been proposed to fit a 3D model to a 2D image [16,30,24]. However, their objective functions are usually highly nonlinear and a suboptimal initialization leads to convergence to poor minima. One common approach is to try multiple starting points [30]; however, this increases the time to reach convergence and it is also unclear how many starting points are sufficient for good results.

In this paper, we investigate these two challenging problems together and show that they can provide benefit to each other if they are solved jointly. We propose a novel approach that optimizes 3D model fitting and fine-grained classification in a joint manner. 3D model representations can convey more information than

D. Fleet et al. (Eds.): ECCV 2014, Part IV, LNCS 8692, pp. 466–480, 2014.
© Springer International Publishing Switzerland 2014

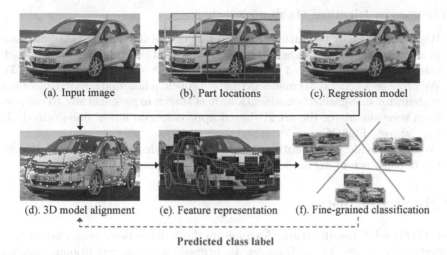

(a). Input image   (b). Part locations   (c). Regression model

(d). 3D model alignment   (e). Feature representation   (f). Fine-grained classification

Predicted class label

Fig. 1. System overview of the proposed method. Given an input image (a), our method first extracts rough part locations based on deformable part models (DPM) (b) and then uses regression models to estimate image landmark locations (c). Next, we fit the 3D model landmarks (yellow circles) of our 3D deformable model to the predicted 2D landmark locations (magenta circles) (d), extract part-based features relative to the 3D geometry (e) and feed these features into SVM classifiers for fine-grained classification (f). After classification, the predicted class labels are then further exploited to iteratively refine the model fitting results.

traditional 2D-based approaches, e.g., viewpoint and precise part locations, and can therefore benefit fine-grained classification. Also, the semantic label of each part is typically defined in modern CAD file formats, which reduces the naming effort by users [6]. Additionally, the predicted class label provides a better class-specific shape prior, which improves model fitting by alleviating the local minima problem for non-linear objective functions. Instead of using a rough 3D ellipsoid [8] or a massive bank of classifiers [14], we adopt a more general and flexible 3D modeling approach, which is based on a highly detailed and deformable 3D model constructed by Principal Components Analysis (PCA) on a set of 3D CAD models.

The system overview is depicted in Fig. 1. Given an input image (a), we first apply a deformable part model (DPM) [9] to obtain rough part locations (b) and feed them as features to a pre-trained regression model for estimating landmark locations (c). The 3D object geometry is recovered by fitting a deformable 3D model to those estimated 2D landmark locations (d). Then, we represent each image by the concatenation of feature descriptors (e.g., HOG [4] or Fisher vector [22]) for each landmark (e). SVM-based classifiers are utilized for fine-grained classification (f). Predicted classes are then exploited to derive better shape parameters to refine the 3D model fitting results in an iterative manner.

The main contributions of this work include:

- We simultaneously optimize 3D model fitting and fine-grained classification in a joint manner. As shown in our experimental results, they benefit each other and lead to improved performance on both tasks (see Tables. 1 and 3).
- We propose a general 3D model fitting approach, a landmark-based Jacobian system, for fine-grained classification; it is shown experimentally to outperform several state-of-the-art 2D-based approaches on a new fine-grained 3D car dataset (FG3DCar).
- We also provide an in-depth analysis of various design decisions to explore the dependence of 3D models and fine-grained classification.

2   Related Work

Fine-Grained Classification: Various methods have been proposed to find distinctive 2D parts. In [6] Duan et al. propose a latent conditional random field model that automatically discovers discriminative attributes. Yao et al. [27] select important regions by a random forest with discriminative decision trees. Deng et al. [5] introduce a human-in-the-loop approach to select discriminative bubbles. Gavves et al. [10] localize distinctive details by roughly aligning objects. Some researchers also seek better feature representations for pose invariance [29].

However, there is currently little research employing 3D models for fine-grained classification. Farrell et al. [8] fit an ellipsoid to 2D images of birds and use it to construct a pose-normalized feature representation. However, a rough ellipsoid might not be suitable for other categories (e.g., car). The most related work to ours is [14], which lifts 2D-based features into 3D space to better associate features across different viewpoints. However, they use a massive bank of classifiers (i.e., example-based) to match 3D models to 2D images, which is time consuming and not applicable to different object shapes.

3D Modeling: At the same time, there has been renewed attention in representing objects in 3D rather 2D [9,19,15]. 3D model representations can convey more information than traditional 2D-based approaches, such as viewpoint, precise part locations, model shape and semantic meaning of parts, and can benefit high-level object reasoning. There are some recent works tailoring 2D part-based methods (e.g., DPM [9]) toward 3D geometric reasoning [21,20], however these approaches only provide coarse bounding boxes in either 2D or 3D space. To go beyond a bounding box representation, Hejrati et al. [12] recover a coarse 3D model from 2D part locations with non-rigid SfM. Some recent works go even further by fitting a more detailed 3D model to 2D images [30,16,24]. However, the objective functions for these methods are usually highly nonlinear and often get trapped in local minima. One possible solution to this problem is by sampling [30], that is, having multiple starting points and selecting the best solution. However, this lengthens the time to convergence and it is still not clear how many starting points are needed for good results.

Inspired by some co-optimization approaches for other tasks [28,15,1], we combine 3D model fitting and fine-grained classification jointly and show that they benefit each other. We propose a more general 3D modeling approach for fine-grained classification based on the Active Shape Model (ASM) formulation, which is more flexible and effective than using a large set of classifiers [14] or a rough ellipsoid [8]. Furthermore, we exploit classification results (i.e., class labels) to derive better shape priors for improving 3D model fitting accuracy. Both processes collaborate iteratively.

Algorithm 1. Overall algorithm

Input: Given an input image I
Output: Class label c^*, shape s^* and pose x^*.
1: Find part locations and component $(z, m) = DPM(I)$
2: Estimate image landmark locations $\hat{l} = regression(z, m)$ Eq. (2)
3: Initialize shape: $\mathbf{s}^{(0)} \leftarrow \mathbf{u}$ (mean shape) and pose: $\mathbf{x}^{(0)} \leftarrow \mathbf{x}_{init}$ parameters
4: **for** $t = 1$ to T **do**
5:     $(\mathbf{s}^{(t)}, \mathbf{x}^{(t)}) \leftarrow FitModeltoImage(\mathbf{s}^{(t-1)}, \mathbf{x}^{(t-1)})$ Eq. (5) & Eq. (6)
6:     $f(I) \leftarrow ExtractFeatureVector(\mathbf{s}^{(t)}, \mathbf{x}^{(t)})$ Eq. (11)
7:     $c \leftarrow Classification(f(I))$
8:     Refine shape parameters $\mathbf{s}^{(t)} \leftarrow \Phi(c)$
9: **end for**

---

3   3D Deformable Car Model

To cope with large shape variations, we build our 3D representation based on the Active Shape Model (ASM) formulation [3]. Each instance (3D model) is represented by a collection of 3D points. These points have the same semantic meaning (i.e., are located on the same car parts) across different 3D models. Then we perform PCA to derive mean $\mathbf{u}$ and n eigen-vectors $\Omega = [\mathbf{w}_1, \mathbf{w}_2, ..., \mathbf{w}_n]$.

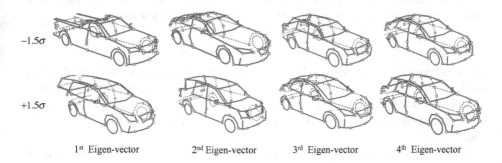

Fig. 2. The top four eigen-vectors derived from Active Shape Model (ASM) are visualized with the shape parameters $\pm 1.5\sigma$ (eigen-value), where landmarks are drawn as yellow circles and (hidden) model segments estimated from 3D geometry are drawn as (blue dotted) red lines.

Any 3D model can be represented as a linear combination of n eigen-vectors with shape parameters $\mathbf{s} = [s_1, ..., s_n]^T$:

$$P'(\mathbf{s}) = \mathbf{u} + \sum_{i=1}^{n} s_i \mathbf{w}_i \tag{1}$$

In our experiments, we use 11 3D CAD models of cars for training our 3D deformable model, including 3 sedans, 2 wagons, 1 pickup truck, 1 crossover, 2 hatchbacks, and 2 SUVs. There are total 256 salient points and 342 triangular faces; from them we manually select 64 landmarks covering important appearance and shape features for car images (see Fig. 2).

4   Regression Model for Landmark Estimation

To fit our 3D model to images, we locate the corresponding landmarks in the 2D image using a set of regression models based on part locations from DPM.

Our approach differs from the previous approaches that find the correspondences between image edges and model segments based on some low-level features (e.g., edge intensity) [16,24], which often fail due to cluttered background or complex edges on the surface of cars. Also, we avoid training a part detector for each landmark individually [17,30], which ignores the geometric relations between parts and may generate a noisy detection map with several local maxima. Instead, we exploit part locations generated from a state-of-the-art part-based method (e.g., [9]) to estimate the image landmark positions, which implicitly encodes both appearance of and geometric relationships between landmarks.

More formally, the input is a set of training images with detected part locations: $z = \{\beta_1, \beta_2, ...\beta_o\}$, where β_i denotes the pixel coordinates for the bounding box of each part (see Fig. 1 (b)), component number m from DPM, and manually annotated landmark positions $l = \{l_1, l_2, \cdots, l_N\}$, where l_i specifies a 2D position (x, y) for i-th landmark (see Sec. 6.1 for more details of obtaining ground truth landmark locations). We then train a regression model for each landmark under each component using the part locations as input features:

$$l_i \approx f(z) \tag{2}$$

We use linear Support Vector Regressor as our regression model to train each landmark position x, y separately. At test time, we use the pre-trained regression models to estimate image landmarks $\hat{l} = \{\hat{l}_1, \hat{l}_2, \cdots, \hat{l}_N\}$ given the part locations and component number from DPM. Example estimated landmarks are shown in Fig. 1 (c).

Given the mean car shape and initial pose, the goal of model fitting is to adjust the pose and shape parameters to minimize the distances between model and image landmarks. For initial pose, we roughly estimate the translation, rotation and scale from the DPM model [9]. For shape, the mean shape is adopted in the first iteration and can be further refined by exploiting the predicted class label. There do exist approaches for solving shape and pose parameters [16,30,24],

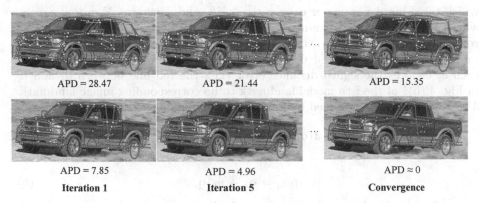

Fig. 3. Illustration of the local minimum problem when using an improper initial shape; ground truth pose and corresponding landmarks are used in this example. The model fitting accuracy is measured by average pixel distance (APD) (Eq. 12). **Top:** initialization by mean shape. **Bottom:** initialization by type shape (i.e., mean of all pickup truck shapes). Yellow circles are the landmarks on the model edges and green circles are the corresponding image landmarks from ground truth. This example illustrates that model fitting accuracy is strongly affected by the initial shape parameters due to the non-linearity of the target objective function. This motivates us to leverage the class label to obtain a better shape prior to improve model fitting accuracy.

however, their objective functions are usually non-linear and their fitting performance is sensitive to initialization. Additionally, the underlying shape distribution of cars is not a single normal distribution represented by a PCA model. There are several disjoint modes for different car classes and thus a generated car shape (controlled by shape parameters) might not be physically possible (e.g., the bottom example of 1st eigen-vector in Fig. 2).

Fig. 3 gives an example of 3D model fitting results when adopting different initial shape parameters; here ground-truth pose and landmark correspondences are used. Some car samples, e.g., pickup truck, are quite different from the mean shape, and optimizing shape starting from the mean shape is a very challenging even using ground-truth pose and landmark correspondences. To alleviate these problems, we use the predicted class label to refine our shape parameters, where the mapping function $\Phi(\cdot) : \mathbb{R}^1 \to \mathbb{R}^n$ that maps the class label to the shape parameters is learned in advance from our training samples (Sec. 6.1). To instantiate this idea, we modify the edge-based Jacobian system from [16] to landmark-based (Fig. 4), since edge-based approaches are susceptible to noise and clutter. Our method is general and could be also applied to other 3D model fitting approaches (e.g., [30]). For model fitting, the task can be formulated as minimizing an error function $F : \mathbb{R}^{n'} \to \mathbb{R}^N$ [16]:

$$\mathbf{q}^* = \arg\min_{\mathbf{q} \in Q} F(\mathbf{q}), \tag{3}$$

$$F(\mathbf{q}) = \mathbf{e} = (e_1, e_2, ...e_N), \tag{4}$$

which takes input parameter $\mathbf{q} = [s, x]^T \in \mathbb{R}^{n'}$ and generates N output errors, where s denotes shape parameters (n dimensions), x are pose parameters (3 rotation and 3 translation), Q is the parameter space. The total number of input parameters is $n' = n + 6$. The error vector $\mathbf{e}$ contains all error terms and each e_i denotes the signed distance error (i.e., the red line between u_i and v_i in Fig. 4 (b)) of the i-th model landmark to its corresponding image landmark. The solution can be obtained by iteratively solving a Jacobian system:

$$\mathbf{J}(\mathbf{q}_k)\Delta\mathbf{q} = -F(\mathbf{q}_k) = \mathbf{e}, \tag{5}$$

$$\mathbf{q}_{k+1} = \mathbf{q}_k + \eta\Delta\mathbf{q}, \tag{6}$$

where $\mathbf{J}$ is the Jacobian matrix, and η is the learning rate (η is set to 0.1 in our experiments). To compute each Jacobian row $\mathbf{J}_i$ more easily, the error function can be split into to 3 composite functions and the Jacobian matrices can be computed by the chain rule:

$$e_i = F_i(\mathbf{q}) = F_i^1(F_i^2(F_i^3(\mathbf{q}))), \tag{7}$$

$$\mathbf{J}_i = \mathbf{J}_i^1\mathbf{J}_i^2\mathbf{J}_i^3, \tag{8}$$

where F_i^3 generates the corresponding 3D point, X_i, of landmark i from the input parameters $\mathbf{q}$; F_i^2 projects X_i into 2D image space u_i; and, F_i^1 measures the distance error between the projected landmark u_i and its corresponding image landmark v_i. We modify the distance error function and its Jacobian matrix to:

$$F_i^1(u_i) = n_i^T R(\theta)(v_i - u_i), \tag{9}$$

$$\mathbf{J}_i^1 = -n_i^T R(\theta), \tag{10}$$

where R is the rotation matrix and θ is the angle between $v_i - u_i$ and n_i^T (see Fig. 4). This modification enables the model to search for the most similar image landmark derived by our regression models (Sec. 4) without being constrained to the normal direction used in the original formulation. In other words, our model possesses the ability to match landmark-to-landmark instead of edge-to-edge; see [16] for more details.

5   Feature Representation for Classification

The appearance of cars in an image can change dramatically with respect to viewing angle and self-occlusion becomes an important issue for fine-grained categorization. We leverage the proprieties from 3D models to better deal with these problems.

To eliminate the need to model the direction that the car is facing in the image, we use the estimated pose from 3D model fitting to flip (mirror image) the car

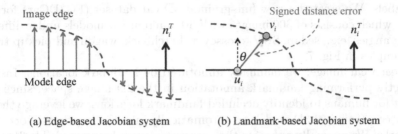

(a) Edge-based Jacobian system   (b) Landmark-based Jacobian system

Fig. 4. Comparison of edge-based [16] (a) and our landmark-based Jacobian system (b), where image and model edge are depicted in dotted blue and black line, u_i and v_i are the i-th model landmark and corresponding image landmark and n_i^T is the normal direction of the model edge. Our landmark-based Jacobian system finds the corresponding image landmarks by using regression models (encoding both appearance and geometric features) rather than low-level edge features (searching along the normal direction) as in the traditional edge-based approach. Therefore, our landmark-based Jacobian system is more efficient (only landmarks are needed for computing the Jacobian matrix) and robust to clutter and noise.

(for example, so that all cars point to the left of the image). Not surprisingly, flipping improves performance noticeably (Table. 2).

After flipping, we extract a feature descriptor φ_i from a window ($W \times W$, $W = 55$ in our experiments) centered around each landmark and concatenate them into a high-dimensional vector as our final feature representation:

$$f(I) = [v_1(\mathbf{q})\varphi_1, v_2(\mathbf{q})\varphi_2, ..., v_N(\mathbf{q})\varphi_N], \qquad (11)$$

where $v_i(\mathbf{q})$ is a binary indicator function for visibility, which can be computed by normal direction of model faces. In other words, the final feature vector is modified by zero-filling the features corresponding to occluded landmarks as predicted by 3D geometry. Since those landmarks are self-occluded, their locations would be less stable compared to the visible ones and their features are less predictive of object class. The trimmed feature representation further boosts classification performance.

We explore two different feature descriptors: HOG [4] and Fisher vector [22], both of which are commonly used in classification. After feature extraction, we use a multi-class Linear SVM [7] to determine the class label.

6   Experiments

We present experiments to validate the effectiveness of our approach for fine-grained classification and 3D model fitting.

6.1   Fine-Grained 3D Car Dataset

Existing fine-grained car datasets (e.g., [13,23]) are not suitable for our purposes, since they are not annotated with both landmark locations and fine-grained class labels. We created a new fine-grained 3D car dataset (FG3DCar) for this study[1], which consists of 300 images with 30 different car models under different viewing angles, e.g., sedan, SUV, crossover, hatchback, wagon and pickup truck. See examples in Fig. 7.

For each car image, we manually annotated 64 landmark locations. Instead of directly performing landmark annotation in the 2D image space, since it is difficult for humans to identify occluded landmark locations, we leverage the geometric constraints of 3D models to automatically infer the locations of occluded landmarks. We manually annotate the correspondences between visible 3D landmarks of our deformable 3D model and their 2D projections on the image, and iteratively adjust the shape and pose parameters to minimize the distance errors between the correspondences based on our modified Jacobian system. Our deformable 3D model is constructed from a set of 3D CAD models with manually aligned 3D points as discussed in Sec. 3. Our annotations provide not only the location and visibility state of each landmark but also the final shape parameters for each car instance.

We evenly split the images into a train/test set for evaluating classification performance. The mapping function $\Phi(\cdot) : \mathbb{R}^1 \to \mathbb{R}^n$ as mentioned in Sec. 4 is learnt by averaging the shape parameters within the same class from our training dataset. Foreground images are used, following standard criteria in fine-grained classification [23,14], and resized to height = 300 pixels. Note that the reported numbers in the following experiments (e.g., fitting accuracy) are based on this image scale.

6.2   Baselines

We compare our approaches with several state-of-the-art 2D-based methods: LLC [26], PHOW [25] and Fisher vector (FV) [22]. We only report the main parameter settings of the baseline methods here; for more details please refer to the original papers. For LLC, we train a codebook with 2048 entries and use 3-layer spatial pyramid (i.e., 1×1, 2×2 and 4×4). For FV, we reduce the dimensionality of SIFT feature to 64 by applying Principal Component Analysis (PCA) and use Gaussian Mixture Model (GMM) with different numbers of components (e.g., $K = 32, 64, 256$). Power- and L2 normalization schemes are also applied [22]. To roughly encode the spatial relationship of FV, we also combine FV with a [2x2] spatial pyramid. For both methods, we use linear SVM classifiers with the cost parameter $C = 10$. For PHOW, we train the same-sized codebook and 3-layer spatial pyramid as LLC and use a homogeneous kernel map for the χ^2 kernel. For our approach, we only use $K = 32$ components of FV on each landmark due to the high dimensionality of our final part-based feature representation.

To validate the effectiveness of these baseline methods, we apply them on a public fine-grained car dataset [23] (denoted as BMVC dataset). Experimental

---

[1] We will publicly release our dataset, landmark annotations, and source code at www.cmlab.csie.ntu.edu.tw/~yenliang/FG3DCar/

Table 1. Classification comparison. We report the results of our method and several state-of-the-art methods: LLC [26], PHOW [25] and Fisher vector (FV) [22] on BMVC [23] and a new fine-grained 3D car dataset (FG3DCar). The baseline methods show very competitive results on BMVC dataset compared to best reported methods [23,14] (not publicly available), demonstrating their effectiveness for fair comparison. We compare our method with these baselines on FG3DCar dataset (The reasons why we did not evaluate our method on BMVC dataset are explained in Sec. 6.2). Our 3D part-based representation shows superior performance compared to the baseline methods (shown in bold font), validating the feasibility of using 3D models to improve fine-grained classification performance. To further analyze where future work should focus, we also investigate classification performance under idealized cases (last two rows); the results show that better alignment (GT alignment) would lead to further improvements. See Sec. 6.3 for more detailed explanations.

Method	BMVC [23]	FG3DCar
LLC [26]	84.5%	51.3%
PHOW+χ^2 [25]	89.0%	54.7%
FV [22](K=32, 64, 256)	88.3%, 90.7%, 93.9%	62.0%, 64.7%, 70.0%
FV [22] [2x2](K=32, 64, 256)	90.9%, 91.7%, 92.6%	60.0%, 64.0%, 69.3%
structDPM [23]	93.5%	-
BB-3D-G [14]	94.5%	-
Regression + FV	-	82.7%
3D-part (mean prior)+(HOG/FV) (ours)	-	55.3% / **88.7%**
3D-part (class prior)+(HOG/FV) (ours)	-	57.3% / **90.0%**
3D-part+GT model prior+(HOG/FV)	-	70.0% / 90.0%
3D-part+GT alignment+(HOG/FV)	-	90.7% / 95.3%

results (left column in Table. 1) show that they achieve very competitive results compared to best reported methods [23,14][2]. Also, the classification performance on BMVC dataset is saturated, which is why we chose not to incur the cost of manual annotating 3D pose and did not evaluate our method on this dataset (since our regression models are currently trained based on manually annotated landmark locations). Instead, we will compare our methods with these baselines on our new and more challenging fine-grained 3D car dataset.

6.3   Fine-Grained Classification Results

We compare our 3D part-based representation to several 2D-based state-of-the-art approaches on our FG3DCar dataset. Empirically, we find that the convergence of our approach is achieved after 2 iterations (i.e., T in Alg. 1) for most cases when using Fisher vectors. Therefore, we only report the results for the first and second iteration, which are also denoted as "mean prior" and "class prior" respectively. In addition, we also provide an in-depth analysis of different

---

[2] The source codes of methods [23,14] are not publicly available.

choices of feature descriptors and 3D features, and also study the idealized cases for the task of fine-grained classification.

3D Versus 2D Representation. Table. 1 summarizes the overall classification accuracy for different methods. The overall performance of baseline methods on our dataset is lower than the BMVC dataset, implying that our dataset is more challenging as it contains more classes (i.e., 30 classes for ours versus 14 classes for BMVC). From the results, our 3D part-based representation (3D-part+mean/class prior+FV) significantly outperforms baseline methods, confirming the feasibility of using 3D models to improve fine-grained classification accuracy - they provide more precise part locations and tolerance to viewpoint changes. Moreover, the classification performance is further improved by using class prior (see mean prior vs. class prior in Table. 1), as it more closely matches to the instance shape, which supports the proposed iterative approach for further improvements.

In Table. 2, we investigate the impact of using 3D features (e.g., flipping and visibility). Flipping improves over un-flipped by 10% and visibility modeling further improves the results by 3%. It is worth noting that even when we do not use flipping and visibility, our method still outperforms baseline methods, gaining from the precise landmark locations derived from 3D models[3].

Fisher Vector Versus HOG. In Table. 1, we observe that the Fisher vector significantly outperforms HOG. We hypothesize that this is because Fisher vector adopts a bag-of-visual-words (BOW)-like feature representation, which ignores spatial relationships and thus can tolerate a higher amount of local displacement. We also find that the classification accuracy of HOG significantly improved (55.3% to 70.0%) when using ground truth model prior (3D-part+GT model prior+HOG) (i.e., perfect shape parameters), indicating that HOG needs more accurate alignment to obtain good classification accuracy compared to the classification-oriented Fisher vector. To better understand the effectiveness of HOG and Fisher vector, we further investigate the classification accuracy of these two features under different degrees of misalignment. To do this, we generate test data by adding Gaussian noise to the ground truth (e.g., translation), where the degree of misalignment is quantified by mean average pixel distance (mean APD):

$$\frac{1}{K}\sum_{i=1}^{K} APD_i, \ APD = \frac{1}{N}\sum_{j=1}^{N} dist(m_j, g_j) \qquad (12)$$

Here, m_j and g_j correspond to j-th landmark on the fitted model and ground truth. K is the number of testing images and N is the number of landmarks. Fig. 5 plots the classification accuracy versus mean average pixel distance using

---

[3] Geometric constraints (e.g., shape, visibility) from 3D models further improved the results from regression model. Based on our 3D model representation, we believe more sophisticated image rectification techniques (e.g., [11]) can be utilized for further improvements, but leave these for future work.

different features. The result further confirms that Fisher vector is less sensitive to misalignment than HOG.

Idealized Case. To understand where future work should focus, we also evaluate our model with idealized perfect shape parameters (GT model prior) and landmark alignment (GT alignment) from ground truth data. We find that the model prior does not improve performance, due to the imperfect image landmark locations estimated by DPM and our regression model. Using ground truth alignment, the performance is increased to 95%, suggesting the possible future benefit from improving landmark estimation accuracy. We will discuss this issue in Sec. 6.4.

Table 2. Different settings of 3D features are analyzed for the method: 3D-part+class prior+FV. The results show that using flipping and visibility state further improve the classification accuracy. Even if we do not use flipping and visibility, our method still outperforms baseline methods (77.3% vs. 70%), gaining from the precise landmark locations derived from 3D models.

Flipping	Visibility	Classification accuracy
No	No	77.3%
Yes	No	87.3%
Yes	Yes	90.0%

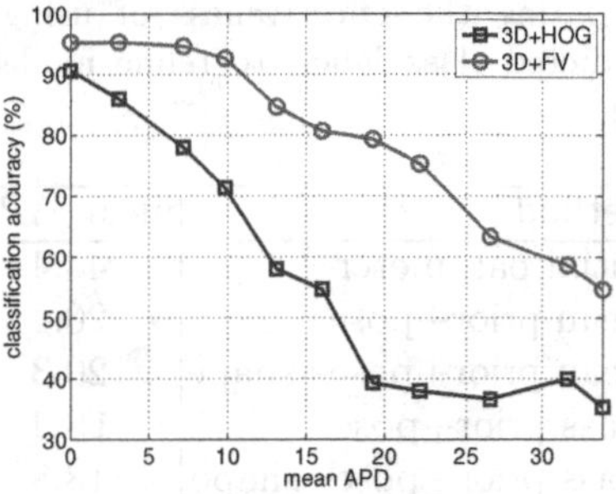

Fig. 5. Comparison of Fisher vector and HOG under different levels of misalignment. Fisher vector can tolerate more displacement error than HOG.

6.4   3D Model Fitting Results

Having discussed the power of our 3D part-based representation for fine-grained classification, we now describe experiments to evaluate the model fitting accuracy. There are two main sources of error for model fitting: initial parameters and estimated landmarks. We analyze their effects in the following paragraphs.

Class Versus Mean Shape Prior. Table. 3 shows the model fitting results, where "pose" indicates optimizing pose parameters only (keeping shape parameters fixed), while "pose+shape" optimizes both shape and pose parameters. Our results show that the class shape prior outperforms the mean shape prior, as it more closely matches the instance shape than the mean shape prior for highly non-linear objective functions as mentioned in Sec. 4. In Fig. 6, we further investigate this by evaluating the mean APD for each category. We see the largest improvement for those categories (e.g., pickup truck) that deviate the most from the mean shape, validating the utility of using the class label to improve the 3D model fitting. We also evaluate the edge-based Jacobian [16]; it obtains lower model fitting accuracy (e.g., mean APD = 43.6 and 45.0 for mean prior+pose and mean prior+pose+shape) than our landmark-based Jacobian, since it is susceptible to noise and clutter. Fig. 7 shows some fitting results of our system.

Pose Versus Pose + Shape. We find that optimizing pose alone yields better results than optimizing both pose and shape for the class prior case. A possible reason is that imperfect landmark positions estimated from DPM and our regression models introduce errors into the shape model parameters. Therefore, optimizing pose alone allows the shape model slightly compensate prediction errors from regression models and lead to better fitting results. Meanwhile, if

Table 3. Model fitting accuracy with different shape priors. Class prior achieves better fitting accuracy than mean prior, validating the effectiveness of using the predicted class labels to refine model fitting.

Method	mean APD
Initial parameter	44.4
Mean prior+pose	20.4
Mean prior+pose+shape	20.3
Class prior+pose	**18.1**
Class prior+pose+shape	18.8

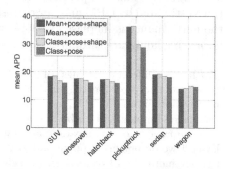

Fig. 6. Mean APD for each category. Class prior provides more benefit to the model fitting accuracy for those categories (e.g., pickup truck) that deviates far from the mean shape.

Fig. 7. Comparison of model fitting results. Top row shows the output of mean prior+pose+shape, and the bottom shows our final fitting results: class prior+pose. Our approach can produce better fitting results (e.g., the backside of pickup truck, SUV, hatchback and the grille part of Alfa romeo) compared to the mean prior, because it can more closely match to the target shape (benefiting from the predicted class label) and avoids falling into local minima for our non-linear objective function.

Fig. 8. Some failure cases of our system mainly caused by wrongly estimated part locations from DPM and errors introduced by regression models

the class label can be estimated correctly, the role of shape optimization might not be as important. We conjecture that the fitting performance can be further improved if we have more training images for each category so that we can train better regression models.

7   Conclusions and Future Work

In this work, we have presented an iterative approach for simultaneously optimizing 3D model fitting and fine-grained classification. By leveraging 3D models, we improved fine-grained classification performance over several state-of-the-art 2D-based methods, confirming the ability of our model to deliver more informative features than previous work. At the same time, we also showed that the predicted class label can further improve the 3D model fitting results. In future work, we seek further improvements on landmark estimation accuracy by using class label information and incorporate image rectification techniques (e.g., [11]) to better associate images across different viewpoints.

References

1. Andriluka, M., Roth, S., Schiele, B.: People-tracking-by-detection and people-detection-by-tracking. In: CVPR (2008)
2. Berg, T., Belhumeur, P.N.: Poof: Part-based one-vs-one features for fine-grained categorization, face verification, and attribute estimation. In: CVPR (2013)
3. Cootes, J.G.T.F., Taylor, C.J., Cooper, D.H.: Active shape models—their training and application. In: CVIU (1995)
4. Dalal, N., Triggs, B.: Histograms of oriented gradients for human detection. In: CVPR (2005)
5. Deng, J., Krause, J., Fei-Fei, L.: Fine-grained crowdsourcing for fine-grained recognition. In: CVPR (2013)
6. Duan, K., Parikh, D., Crandall, D., Grauman, K.: Discovering localized attributes for fine-grained recognition. In: CVPR (2012)
7. Fan, R.E., Chang, K.W., Hsieh, C.J., Wang, X.R., Lin, C.J.: LIBLINEAR: A library for large linear classification. Journal of Machine Learning Research 9, 1871–1874 (2008)

8. Farrell, R., Oza, O., Zhang, N., Morariu, V.I., Darrell, T., Davis, L.S.: Birdlets: Subordinate categorization using volumetric primitives and pose-normalized appearance. In: ICCV (2011)
9. Felzenszwalb, P., Girshick, R., McAllester, D., Ramanan., D.: Object detection with discriminatively trained part based models. TPAMI (2010)
10. Gavves, E., Fernando, B., Snoek, C.G.M., Smeulders, A.W.M., Tuytelaars, T.: Fine-grained categorization by alignments. In: ICCV (2013)
11. Guo, Y., Rao, C., Samarasekera, S., Kim, J., Kumar, R., Sawhney, H.: Matching vehicles under large pose transformations using approximate 3d models and piecewise mrf model. In: CVPR (2009)
12. Hejrati, M., Ramanan, D.: Analyzing 3d objects in cluttered images. In: NIPS (2012)
13. Krause, J., Deng, J., Stark, M., Fei-Fei, L.: Collecting a large-scale dataset of fine-grained cars. In: CVPR-FGCV2 (2013)
14. Krause, J., Stark, M., Deng, J., Fei-Fei, L.: 3d object representations for fine-grained categorization. In: International IEEE Workshop on 3D Representation and Recognition (2013)
15. Leibe, B., Leonardis, A., Schiele, B.: Robust object detection with interleaved categorization and segmentation. IJCV (2007)
16. Leotta, M.J., Mundy, J.L.: Vehicle surveillance with a generic, adaptive, 3d vehicle model. TPAMI (2011)
17. Li, Y., Gu, L., Kanade, T.: Robustly aligning a shape model and its application to car alignment of unknown pose. TPAMI (2011)
18. Liu, J., Kanazawa, A., Jacobs, D., Belhumeur, P.: Dog breed classification using part localization. In: Fitzgibbon, A., Lazebnik, S., Perona, P., Sato, Y., Schmid, C. (eds.) ECCV 2012, Part I. LNCS, vol. 7572, pp. 172–185. Springer, Heidelberg (2012)
19. Özuysal, M., Lepetit, V., Fua, P.: Pose estimation for category specific multiview object localization. In: CVPR (2009)
20. Pepik, B., Gehler, P., Stark, M., Schiele, B.: 3d2pm - 3d deformable part models. In: Fitzgibbon, A., Lazebnik, S., Perona, P., Sato, Y., Schmid, C. (eds.) ECCV 2012, Part VI. LNCS, vol. 7577, pp. 356–370. Springer, Heidelberg (2012)
21. Pepik, B., Stark, M., Gehler, P., Schiele, B.: Teaching 3d geometry to deformable part models. In: CVPR (2012)
22. Perronnin, F., Sánchez, J., Mensink, T.: Improving the fisher kernel for large-scale image classification. In: Daniilidis, K., Maragos, P., Paragios, N. (eds.) ECCV 2010, Part IV. LNCS, vol. 6314, pp. 143–156. Springer, Heidelberg (2010)
23. Stark, M., Krause, J., Pepik, B., Meger, D., Little, J.J., Schiele, B., Koller, D.: Fine-grained categorization for 3d scene understanding. In: BMVC (2012)
24. Tsin, Y., Genc, Y., Ramesh, V.: Explicit 3d modeling for vehicle monitoring in non-overlapping cameras. In: AVSS (2009)
25. Vedaldi, A., Fulkerson, B.: VLFeat: An open and portable library of computer vision algorithms (2008), http://www.vlfeat.org/
26. Wang, J., Yang, J., Yu, K., Lv, F., Huang, T., Gong, Y.: Locality-constrained linear coding for image classification. In: CVPR (2010)
27. Yao, B., Khosla, A., Fei-Fei, L.: Combining randomization and discrimination for fine-grained image categorization. In: CVPR (2011)
28. Chai, Y., Lempitsky, V., Zisserman, A.: Symbiotic segmentation and part localization for fine-grained categorization. In: ICCV (2013)
29. Zhang, N., Farrell, R., Darrell, T.: Pose pooling kernels for sub-category recognition. In: CVPR (2012)
30. Zia, M.Z., Stark, M., Schiele, B., Schindler, K.: Detailed 3d representations for object recognition and modeling. PAMI (2013)

Pipelining Localized Semantic Features
for Fine-Grained Action Recognition

Yang Zhou[1], Bingbing Ni[2], Shuicheng Yan[3], Pierre Moulin[4], and Qi Tian[1]

[1] University of Texas at San Antonio, USA
[2] Advanced Digital Sciences Center, Singapore
[3] National University of Singapore, Singapore
[4] University of Illinois at Urbana-Champaign, USA
myh511@my.utsa.edu, bingbing.ni@adsc.com.sg, eleyans@nus.edu.sg,
moulin@ifp.uiuc.edu, qi.tian@utsa.edu

Abstract. In fine-grained action (object manipulation) recognition, it is important to encode object semantic (contextual) information, i.e., which object is being manipulated and how it is being operated. However, previous methods for action recognition often represent the semantic information in a global and coarse way and therefore cannot cope with fine-grained actions. In this work, we propose a representation and classification pipeline which seamlessly incorporates localized semantic information into every processing step for fine-grained action recognition. In the feature extraction stage, we explore the geometric information between local motion features and the surrounding objects. In the feature encoding stage, we develop a semantic-grouped locality-constrained linear coding (SG-LLC) method that captures the joint distributions between motion and object-in-use information. Finally, we propose a semantic-aware multiple kernel learning framework (SA-MKL) by utilizing the empirical joint distribution between action and object type for more discriminative action classification. Extensive experiments are performed on the large-scale and difficult fine-grained MPII cooking action dataset. The results show that by effectively accumulating localized semantic information into the action representation and classification pipeline, we significantly improve the fine-grained action classification performance over the existing methods.

1 Introduction

Recently, fine-grained action analysis has raised a lot of research interests due to its potential applications in smart home, medical surveillance, daily living assist and child/elderly care, where action videos are captured indoor with fixed camera. Although background motion (i.e. one of main challenges for general action recognition) is more controlled compared to general action recognition, it is widely acknowledged that fine-grained action recognition (some examples are listed in Figure 8) is very challenging due to large intra-class variability, small inter-class variability, large variety of action categories, complex motions and complicated interactions. Fine-grained actions, especially the manipulation

D. Fleet et al. (Eds.): ECCV 2014, Part IV, LNCS 8692, pp. 481–496, 2014.

sequences involve a large amount of interactions between hands and objects, therefore how to model the interactions between human hands and objects (i.e., context) plays an important role in action representation and recognition. Contextual information has been explored in earlier action recognition works. Feifei et al. [28] modeled objects and human poses jointly by leveraging the mutual context model in human action images. Lan et al. [12,11] introduced the action context descriptor to encode action of individual person and people nearby. Choi et al. [6] proposed to learn crowd action context to recognize collective activities. Marszalek et al. [16] exploited the high correlation between human actions and natural dynamic scenes. Object contextual information has been commonly used for recognizing actions which involves human and object interactions [17,26,24,10]. Feifei et al. [27] jointly modeled the attributes (i.e., actions) and parts (i.e., objects or poselets related to actions) by learning a set of sparse bases that are shown to carry much semantic meaning. However, these methods often represent the human and object contextual information in a global and coarse way, e.g., co-occurrence, which is not sufficient for representing fine-grained actions. This is because in fine-grained actions, local manipulation motion details (e.g., subtle movements of hand in operating an object) are much more important than global co-occurrence information.

The recently proposed local dense motion trajectories [22] has achieved the state-of-the-art performance in action recognition. Local motion trajectory is capable of describing subtle movement, which is suitable for representing fine-grained motion feature. Inspired by this observation, we propose **localized semantic features** (LS) based on local dense motion trajectories. Namely, we extract object occurrence information (i.e., object detection scores) surrounding each local motion trajectory and we augment the semantic features to the motion features. Therefore, we can know which object is being manipulated (object semantic feature) and how it is being manipulated (motion feature) in a localized manner (i.e., per motion trajectory). These complementary information are very important in representing fine-grained actions. Various previous methods have combined semantic features with low-level features for recognition, but they only used global context. For example, Cao et al. [3] only considered grouped feature pooling using global scene type. Chao et al. [5] considered only global label information instead of local semantic.

Further more, we propose a representation and classification pipeline which seamlessly incorporates the localized semantic features into every processing step for fine-grained action recognition. More details are given as follows. In the feature extraction stage, we explore the geometric information between local motion features and the surrounding objects. In the feature encoding stage, we develop a semantic-grouped locality-constrained linear coding (SG-LLC) method that captures the joint distribution between motion and object semantic features. Finally, we propose a semantic-aware multiple kernel learning (SA-MKL) framework by utilizing the empirical joint distributions between action and object type for more discriminative action classification. The proposed pipeline is experimented thoroughly on the fine-grained MPII cooking action dataset [20], which is the

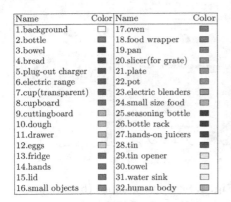

Name	Color	Name	Color
1.background	☐	17.oven	■
2.bottle	■	18.food wrapper	■
3.bowl	■	19.pan	■
4.bread	■	20.slicer(for grate)	■
5.plug-out charger	■	21.plate	■
6.electric range	■	22.pot	■
7.cup(transparent)	■	23.electric blenders	■
8.cupboard	■	24.small size food	■
9.cuttingboard	■	25.seasoning bottle	■
10.dough	■	26.bottle rack	■
11.drawer	■	27.hands-on juicers	■
12.eggs	■	28.tin	■
13.fridge	■	29.tin opener	☐
14.hands	■	30.towel	☐
15.lid	■	31.water sink	☐
16.small objects	■	32.human body	■

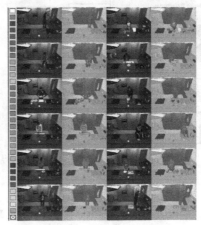

Fig. 1. Color code for 32 types object-of-interest

Fig. 2. Sample object detection maps

large-scale and very challenging dataset for fine-grained action recognition. The results show that the localized semantic action representation and classification pipeline can step-by-step improve the action classification performance, which significantly outperforms the existing methods on the MPII cooking dataset in terms of multi-class precision, recall and per-class average precision.

To summarize, our contributions are three-fold: 1) we propose an end-to-end solution on utilizing **localized semantic** features (i.e., object contextual information of **local** dense trajectories in the spatial-temporal volume) in fine-grained action analysis, which includes novel **localized semantic** feature encoding, pooling and classification; 2) we propose a novel MKL modeling and optimization framework for **semantic-aware** classifier learning, which utilizes the prior knowledge of kernel weights; 3) the proposed fine-grained action recognition pipeline achieves about 10% improvement over the existing methods on the challenging fine-grained action dataset.

2 Methodology

2.1 Localized Semantic Feature Extraction

As introduced in the previous section, our basic idea is to augment local motion features with *localized semantic features* (LS), to enrich the descriptions for representing manipulation movement that involves subtle human and object interactions. To this end, we first extract local dense motion trajectories [22] from input videos. To describe motion, different types of motion feature descriptors are computed in a spatial-temporal volume (i.e., spatial size of 2×2 with temporal length of 15) around the 3D neighborhood of the tracked points along the trajectory. Following [22], we use four types of motion feature descriptors in-

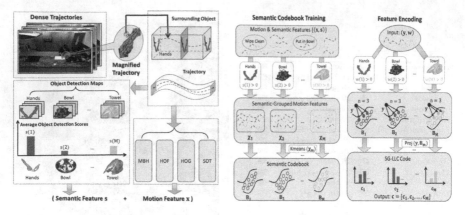

Fig. 3. Localized semantic feature extraction

Fig. 4. Semantic-grouped (best viewed with color) feature encoding

cluding histogram of oriented gradients (HOG), histogram of optic flows (HOF), motion boundary histogram (MBH) and shape of trajectory (SOT).

During human-object interaction, local motion features describe *how a certain object is being manipulated*. For fine-grained actions, different action types share similar motion patterns, for example, local motions are almost the same among actions "put on plate", "put on pot", "put on dough". Therefore, we should augment each local motion feature with *localized semantic feature* to encode *which object is being manipulated*, i.e., whether the action is related to "plate", "pot" or "dough"? In other words, the localized semantic feature descriptor encodes the local object-in-use contextual information for each local motion trajectory. To compute localized semantic features, for each input video frame, we first build object detection maps for various types of objects. Assume we have M objects of interest, then each position on the detection map is represented by a M-dimensional object detection score vector. For a trajectory, we average the object detection score vectors in the spatial-temporal volume along its tracked points and form a M-dimensional localized semantic feature vector.

Object detection maps are computed as follows. We first apply superpixel segmentation using SLIC [1] on each input frame. The 1624×1224 pixels video frame is over-segmented into around 2000 superpixels, with the regularization parameter being set as 10. We then represent each superpixel with a concatenated feature vector consisting of histogram of oriented gradient (HOG) [7] and HSV color histogram. Multiple linear support vector machine classifiers are applied to calculate the object detection scores. We build our training object patch (superpixel) dataset by randomly sampling 12000 video frames from the training videos. In average, we have annotated around 2000 training patches for each object type. In addition, we use the conditional random field model to spatially regularize the object detection map for better detection accuracy. For the MPII cooking dataset, 32 types of object-of-interest are defined in data-driven approach, which are summarized in Figure 1, some object detection maps are shown in Figure 2. The feature extraction process is illustrated in Figure 3.

Discussion: One might argue that pre-detection of objects gives *unfair* advantages to our method over conventional holistic action recognition method [22]. We clarify that: 1) we do not target general action recognition problem on action datasets such as YouTube [15], Hollywood2 [16], UCF sport [25], etc., where object detection is infeasible. Instead, fine-grained action recognition is more suitable for applications such as indoor assisted living, occupational therapy (with fixed camera), where object detection is quite feasible. Indeed, to detect object-of-interest is compulsory task in these applications; 2) for fine-grained actions with frequent and delicate hand-object interactions, to detect object and associate it locally with motion features is a natural, reasonable and promising approach. Holistic approaches such as bag of dense trajectories [22] or STIPs [13] cannot well deal with fine-grained action recognition, even though their implementations are easier without the need for object detection.

2.2   Semantic-Grouped Feature Encoding

The next important building block for image and video classification is local feature encoding. State-of-the-art local feature encoding schemes include vector quantization (or bag-of-words) [8], locality-constrained linear coding (LLC) [23], fisher kernel [18], etc. Usually, a codebook is trained using the training features, any input feature vector can be encoded using the codebook either by searching its nearest codebook item (visual word) or by computing the linear combination of codebook items that well approximates it (i.e., LLC).

In this work, each local motion feature is augmented with a localized semantic feature vector, which indicates which object(s) the motion feature is associated with. This contextual information motivates us to propose an enhanced feature encoding scheme. The basic idea is as follows. As the localized semantic features tell us to which object(s)-of-interest the motion feature is related, when we encode a local motion feature descriptor, we should encourage that the codebook items it selects are also related to the same object(s)-of-interest. We believe that the advantages of this localized semantic feature grouped feature encoding are two-fold: firstly, it implicitly embeds the information of *which object(s) is being manipulated* into the encoded feature representation; secondly, because the codebook motion features that are related to the same object(s)-of-interest are considered for approximating the input motion feature, the similarity between the input motion feature and the selected codebook items is higher, thus more accurate encoding (i.e., lower reconstruction error) can be achieved. The proposed semantic-grouped feature encoding is illustrated in Figure 4 and more details are introduced as follows.

We denote by $(\mathbf{x}, \mathbf{s})$ the pair of motion descriptor $\mathbf{x}$ and the corresponding localized semantic feature vector $\mathbf{s}$. Namely, $\mathbf{x}$ represents the concatenation of HOG, HOF, MBH and SOT feature descriptors and $\mathbf{s}$ is a M-dimensional object detection score vector. Let $\mathcal{X}$ be a set of features extracted from the training video clips, i.e., $\mathcal{X} = \{(\mathbf{x}^1, \mathbf{s}^1), \cdots, (\mathbf{x}^N, \mathbf{s}^N)\}$. The total number of training features is N. According to the localized semantic features $\{\mathbf{s}^i\}$, we further group the whole training feature set $\mathcal{X}$ into M subsets $\mathcal{X} = \bigcup \mathcal{X}_m, m = 1, \cdots, M$. Each $\mathcal{X}_m$ only contains the set of features that are related to object-of-interest type m, i.e., $\mathbf{s}(m) > 0$, we denote by $\mathbf{s}(m)$ the m-th element of vector $\mathbf{s}$. Note that one feature can be related to multiple objects-of-interest (i.e., the trajectory is surrounded by multiple objects), therefore different $\mathcal{X}_m$ may be overlapped. For each $\mathcal{X}_m$, we use the K-means clustering algorithm to train a codebook of motion features B_m. Note that each B_m is a $D \times N_m$ matrix, i.e., D is the motion feature dimension and N_m is the number of basis for codebook B_m. We denote by B_0 the codebook trained using the whole training set $\mathcal{X}$. Therefore our codebook can be denoted as $B = [B_0, B_1, \cdots, B_M]$. Each sub-codebook $B_m, m = 1, \cdots, M$ is related to m-th type of object-of-interest.

Given an input feature descriptor $(\mathbf{y}, \mathbf{w})$, i.e., local motion feature $\mathbf{y}$ and localized semantic feature $\mathbf{w}$ vector pair, the encoding objective is to minimize the following cost function with respect to encoding coefficients $\mathbf{c} = [\mathbf{c}_0; \mathbf{c}_1; \cdots; \mathbf{c}_M]$:

$$\min_{\mathbf{c}} \|\mathbf{y} - [B_0, B_1, \cdots, B_M][\mathbf{c}_0; \mathbf{c}_1; \cdots; \mathbf{c}_M]\|_2^2 \qquad (1)$$

$$s.t. \quad \sum_{m=0}^{M} |\mathbf{c}_m| \le \varepsilon, \quad \varepsilon > 0, \qquad (2)$$

$$\sum_{m=1}^{M} (1 - \mathrm{w}_m) |\mathbf{c}_m| \le \tau, \quad \tau > 0, \qquad (3)$$

here $\mathbf{c}_m$ is the encoding coefficient on sub-codebook B_m. The first constraint Eqn. (2) encourages that: 1) only a few sub-codebooks are selected for reconstructing the input local motion feature vector $\mathbf{y}$ and 2) the codebook items are sparsely selected. The second constraint Eqn. (3) encourages that the sub-codebooks which are not related to the motion feature $\mathbf{y}$ (i.e., the sub-codebook

---

Algorithm 1. Semantic-grouped locality-constrained linear coding

input: feature descriptor pair $(\mathbf{y}, \mathbf{w})$, number of nearest neighbors n, regularization term β of sparse coding solver, sub-codebooks $B_1, \cdots, B_M$.

Initialize $\tilde{B} = [\ ]$, $\beta = 500$, $n = 5$, compute $\mathbf{c}_0$ with LLC encoding on B_0.
for $m = 1, \cdots, M$ **do**
   if $\mathbf{w}(m) > 0$
      Choose n nearest neighbors of $\mathbf{y}$ from B_m as $\tilde{B}_m$.
      Push $\tilde{B}_m$ into $\tilde{B}$, i.e., $\tilde{B} = [\tilde{B}, \tilde{B}_m]$.
   else
      $\mathbf{c}_m = 0$.
end
Solve $\mathbf{c}$ following sparse coding solver in [23]:
   (1) $\tilde{\mathbf{c}} = \mathbf{C} + \beta \mathrm{diag}(\mathbf{C}) \backslash \mathbf{1}$, where $\mathbf{C} = (\tilde{B} - \mathbf{1}\mathbf{y}^{\mathrm{T}})(\tilde{B} - \mathbf{1}\mathbf{y}^{\mathrm{T}})^{\mathrm{T}}$.
   (2) $\mathbf{c} = \tilde{\mathbf{c}} / \mathbf{1}^{\mathrm{T}} \tilde{\mathbf{c}}$,
Assign $\mathbf{c}$ to the corresponding positions of $\mathbf{c}_m$, i.e., $\mathbf{w}(m) > 0$.

output: SG-LLC code $\mathbf{c} = [\mathbf{c}_0; \mathbf{c}_1; \cdots; \mathbf{c}_M]$.

m that $\mathbf{w}(m)$ is near zero) are not selected for reconstructing $\mathbf{y}$. Applying these two constraints ensures that only a few codebook items which are related to the object-in-use of the motion feature $\mathbf{y}$ are selected for approximating the input motion feature vector $\mathbf{y}$.

Finding the exact solution to Eqn. (1) is possible by various sparse coding solvers including generic QP solvers (e.g., CVX), ℓ^1-regularized Least Squares solver [14], etc. However, for a large-scale dataset as MPII cooking, exact solution for encoding millions of local motion features is extremely expensive. In practice, we develop an approximate optimization algorithm which is shown in Algorithm 1. The basic idea is to first choose n nearest codebook items from the sub-codebooks which are selected by non-zero semantic scores of the input motion feature, and then perform reconstruction using the codebook items. We note that this approximated optimization for feature encoding is similar to the locality-constrained linear coding algorithm (LLC). Therefore, our feature encoding algorithm is named as *Semantic-Grouped Locality-constrained Linear Coding (SG-LLC)*.

2.3   Semantic-Aware Motion Feature Pooling and Classification

After local motion feature encoding, the next building blocks for action classification are to perform local motion feature pooling and classifier learning. Feature pooling is to aggregate local features to form a video level representation (i.e., to form a representation vector). In this subsection, we show how localized semantic features can help enhance the pooling and classifier training stage, i.e., to achieve more discriminative video level representation and classification. The procedure is shown in Figure 5.

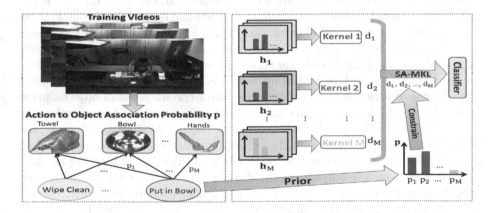

Fig. 5. Semantic-Aware multiple kernel learning (SA-MKL) utilizing action to object association probability (Eqn. (4)) as prior information

Semantic-Partitioned Feature Pooling: A traditional motion feature pooling scheme is global pooling, i.e., a frequency vector of all encoded local motion features within the video volume is calculated, named as the bag-of-words frequency vector representation $\mathbf{h}$. With localized semantic feature vector for each local motion feature, we can perform *finer* pooling. More specific, global pooling ignores the object-in-use contextual information and the local motion features associated with different irrelevant objects are pooled together, therefore, the resulting histogram representation is noisy (i.e., confused by motion features occurring on different objects) and less discriminative. On the contrary, if we utilize the localized semantic information, we can pool the local motion features *object-wise*. Namely, local motion features that are associated with the same object are pooled together and we can have multiple pooled histogram representations where each corresponds to the distribution of motions related to one type of object. It is obvious this new histogram representation possesses richer and finer descriptive information than globally pooled histogram.

The proposed pooling process is as follows. Suppose for video volume V, we have a set of extracted local motion features $\mathcal{X} = \{(\mathbf{x}^1, \mathbf{s}^1), \cdots, (\mathbf{x}^N, \mathbf{s}^N)\}$. Each local feature $\mathbf{x}$ is encoded as $\mathbf{c}$. According to localized semantic features we can group (partition) the local motion feature set $\mathcal{X}$ into M subsets $\mathcal{X} = \bigcup \mathcal{X}_m, m = 1, \cdots, M$, where each $\mathcal{X}_m$ only contains motion features which are associated with m-th object-of-interest, i.e., $\mathbf{s}(m) > 0$. We then calculate the pooled vector (histogram) within each $\mathcal{X}_m$ and result in M histogram vectors as $\{\mathbf{h}_1, \cdots, \mathbf{h}_M\}$. We also denote $\mathbf{h}_0$ as the pooled histogram vector using all local motion features in the video volume, i.e., $\mathcal{X}$.

Semantic-Aware Multiple Kernel Learning: Now we have $M + 1$ feature channels for each video clip (i.e., each feature channel corresponds to one object-associated histogram $\mathbf{h}_m, m = 0, 1, \cdots, M$), a straightforward feature fusion and classification scheme is to calculate $M + 1$ kernel matrices $\{\mathbf{K}_0, \mathbf{K}_1, \cdots, \mathbf{K}_M\}$ and combine them for classifier training. There are two major kernel combination ways include: 1) average kernel combination [21]; and 2) kernel weights learning, i.e., multiple kernel learning [2]. Traditional multiple kernel learning methods do not rely on any prior knowledge about the kernel weights $\{d_1, \cdots, d_M\}$, i.e., the value of d_m means how important kernel $\mathbf{K}_m$ is. However, for our problem, as each type of action is strongly correlated with certain types of objects, prior knowledge on the kernel weights are available. For example, to recognize the action "put in bowl", the kernels related to object "hands" and "bowl" are important. To take advantage of the prior knowledge brought by the localized semantic feature, we therefore propose a novel multiple kernel learning method which can leverage the empirical joint distributions between action and object type. Namely, the empirical action-object association probability estimated from the training data guides the learning of kernel weights $\{d_1, \cdots, d_M\}$.

To begin with, we define the empirical action-object association probability for action a (we ignore the superscript for action a in the rest of paper) and object m as:

$$p_m^a = \frac{\sum\limits_{i=1}^{N_{tr}} (y_i = 1 \wedge \mathbf{h}_m^i > \mathbf{0})}{\sum\limits_{i=1}^{N_{tr}} (y_i = 1)}, \quad m = 1, \cdots, M, \tag{4}$$

here N_{tr} denotes the number of training video clips, and $y_i \in \{+1, -1\}$ denotes binary classification label for video level representation $\mathbf{h}^i$. The numerator represents the number of training video clips which have action label a and there is object-use on the m-th object. The denominator denotes the number of positive training video clips for action a.

We consider one-versus-all classification in this work. 64 action types are defined in dataset, and a total of 64 binary classifiers $f(\mathbf{h})$ are learned. For each binary classifier (i.e., to classify action a), we define the following decision function:

$$f^a(\mathbf{h}) = f_0^a(\mathbf{h}) + \Delta f^a(\mathbf{h}), \tag{5}$$

here $f_0^a(\mathbf{h}) = \mathbf{w}_0^T \phi_0(\mathbf{h}_0) + b$ is the base classifier trained from the globally pooled histogram vector $\mathbf{h}_0$. $\Delta f^a(\mathbf{h})$ is a linear combination of object-specific classifiers learned from their corresponding object-specific histogram vector $\mathbf{h}_m, m = 1, \cdots, M$, which is defined as in Eqn. (6):

$$\Delta f^a(\mathbf{h}) = \sum_{m=1}^{M} d_m \mathbf{w}_m^T \phi_m(\mathbf{h}_m) + b \tag{6}$$

$$s.t. \quad \mathbf{d} \geq \mathbf{0}, \quad ||\mathbf{d}||_\infty \leq 1,$$

where $\mathbf{d} = [d_1, \cdots, d_M]^T$ are the weights for combining different classifiers. The combined classifier can be learned by optimizing the following objective function:

$$\min_{d_m} \min_{\mathbf{v}_{m,b,\xi_i}} \frac{1}{2} \sum_{m=1}^{M} \frac{||\mathbf{v}_m||}{d_m} + \frac{\lambda}{2} \sum_{m=1}^{M} |d_m - p_m| + C \sum_{i=1}^{N_{tr}} \xi_i \tag{7}$$

$$s.t. \quad y_i \left(\mathbf{w}_0^T \phi_0(\mathbf{h}_0^i) + \sum_{m=1}^{M} \mathbf{v}_m^T \phi_m(\mathbf{h}_m^i) + b \right) \geq 1 - \xi_i,$$

$$\xi_i \geq 0, i = 1, \cdots, N_{tr}, \quad \mathbf{d} \geq \mathbf{0}, \quad ||\mathbf{d}||_\infty \leq 1,$$

where we set $C = 100$ as the multiple kernel learning regularization parameter. $\mathbf{K}_m(\mathbf{h}_m^i, \mathbf{h}_m^j) = \phi_m(\mathbf{h}_m^i)^T \phi_m(\mathbf{h}_m^j)$. p_m is the action-object association probability for object m, which is defined in Eqn. (4). $\lambda, d_1, \cdots, d_M$ are the parameters we need to learn. Note that the second objective, i.e., $|d_m - p_m|$ enforces that the kernel weights to approximate the values of action-object association probability p_m. λ adjusts the weight between kernel $\mathbf{K}_0$ and semantic kernels $\mathbf{K}_1, \cdots, \mathbf{K}_M$. Large λ will encourage that the learned object-specific kernel weight follows the empirical action-object association probability.

To solve the objective Eqn. (7), we alternatively optimize w.r.t. the variables $d_m, \mathbf{v}_m, b, \xi_i$ using the following two steps.

Firstly, we optimize $\mathbf{v}_m$, b, ξ_i with fixed d_m. By introducing the non-negative Lagrangian multipliers $\boldsymbol{\alpha} = [\alpha_1, \cdots, \alpha_{N_{tr}}]^{\mathrm{T}}$, the dual can be derived as follows:

$$\max_{\boldsymbol{\alpha}} \boldsymbol{\alpha}^{\mathrm{T}}\mathbf{1} - \frac{1}{2}(\boldsymbol{\alpha} \odot \mathbf{y})^{\mathrm{T}}(\sum_{m=1}^{M} d_m \mathbf{K}_m + \mathbf{K}_0)(\boldsymbol{\alpha} \odot \mathbf{y}) \tag{8}$$

$$s.t. \quad \boldsymbol{\alpha}^{\mathrm{T}}\mathbf{y} = 0, \quad 0 \leq \boldsymbol{\alpha} \leq C,$$

where $\boldsymbol{\alpha} \odot \mathbf{y}$ denotes the element-wise product between two vectors $\boldsymbol{\alpha}$ and $\mathbf{y}$. Because Eqn. (8) is a standard dual problem, we can solve it with the SVM solvers such as libsvm [4]. With the dual primal coefficients $\boldsymbol{\alpha}$ derived from the SVM solvers, we compute the primal variables $\mathbf{v}_m$ as:

$$\mathbf{v}_m = d_m \sum_{i=1}^{N_{tr}} \alpha_i y_i \phi_m(\mathbf{h}_m^i), m = 1, \cdots, M. \tag{9}$$

Secondly, we optimize d_m with fixed $\mathbf{v}_m, b, \xi_i$, the problem in Eqn. (7) reduces to:

$$\min_{d_m} \frac{1}{2}\sum_{m=1}^{M} \frac{\|\mathbf{v}_m\|}{d_m} + \frac{\lambda}{2}\sum_{m=1}^{M} |d_m - p_m| \tag{10}$$

$$s.t. \quad \mathbf{d} \geq 0, \quad \|\mathbf{d}\|_\infty \leq 1.$$

By taking the derivative over d_m, the closed-form solution is given in Eqn. (11):

$$d_m = \max\{\sqrt{\frac{\|\mathbf{v}_m\|}{\lambda}}, p_m\}. \tag{11}$$

The optimization procedure is given in Algorithm 2. Finally, the classifier for a novel input $\mathbf{h} = \{\mathbf{h}_0, \mathbf{h}_1, \cdots, \mathbf{h}_M\}$ is expressed as Eqn. (12):

$$f^a(\mathbf{h}) = \sum_{i=1}^{N_{tr}} \alpha_i y_i \left[\sum_{m=1}^{M} d_m \mathbf{K}_m(\mathbf{h}, \mathbf{h}^i) + \mathbf{K}_0(\mathbf{h}, \mathbf{h}^i)\right] + b. \tag{12}$$

Algorithm 2. Optimization for Semantic-Aware Multiple Kernel Learning

---

input: $\mathbf{d}^0$, λ, ϵ, $\{\mathbf{K}_0, \mathbf{K}_1, \cdots, \mathbf{K}_M\}$, $\{p_1, \cdots, p_M\}$

Initialize $d_m^0 = 1/M$ ($m = 1, \cdots, M$), $\lambda = 0.2$, $\epsilon = 10^{-4}$.

repeat

    Compute $\boldsymbol{\alpha}^t$ by solving Eqn. (8) using SVM solver with $\mathbf{d}^t$.

    Compute $\mathbf{v}_m$ by Eqn. (9) and solve $\mathbf{d}^{t+1}$ by Eqn. (11).

    t=t+1.

until $\|\mathbf{d}^{t+1} - \mathbf{d}^t\| < \epsilon$

output: $\boldsymbol{\alpha}$, $\mathbf{d}$, λ

---

3   Experiment

3.1   Dataset and Configurations

We perform extensive experiments on the MPII cooking [20] dataset, which is a recent fine-grained cooking action dataset published on CVPR 2012. Considering the scale and complexity, it is very challenging for fine-grained action recognition.

Totally, 5609 video segments are annotated for 65 action categories such as "open drawer", "cut slices", "cut into dices", "wash hands" or "background" ("background" is dropped in evaluation as indicated in [20]). Following the same experimental setting as in [20], 5 out of 12 subject are used to train the model, the remaining 7 subjects are used to perform leave-one-person-out cross-validation. We evaluate classification performance in terms of multi-class precision (Pr), recall (Rc) and per-class average precision (AP).

For codebook training, the base codebook $\mathbf{B}_0$ is clustered into 4000 centers, all the other object-specific codebooks have 500 cluster centers. For the original holistic bag-of-words on dense motion trajectories method [22], the size of codebook is also set as 4000 for all types of descriptors for fair comparison. All the experiments are conducted on a powerful 16-core computing server. Each step is paralleled if applicable, and our pipeline (with object detection) involves 9 hours of running time in total.

In the following, we first evaluate the effectiveness of every component of our proposed localized semantic feature based fine-grained action recognition pipeline, which includes both semantic-grouped feature encoding and semantic-aware multiple kernel learning. Then we quantitatively compare the classification performance of our method with state-of-the-art results on the MPII cooking dataset with in-depth discussions on the algorithmic behavior of our approach.

3.2   Results and Discussions

Effectiveness of Semantic-Grouped Feature Encoding: We show the effectiveness of proposed SG-LLC in Table 1. We compare various state-of-the-art encoding methods including: vector quantization encoding (VQ), locality-constrained linear coding (LLC) and our proposed semantic-grouped locality-

Table 1. Comparison among different encoding methods in terms of multi-class precision (%)

	VQ	LLC	SG-LLC
HOG	39.6	42.2	46.2
HOF	41.3	42.8	45.7
MBHx	42.4	44.9	49.3
MBHy	45.6	47.1	51.8
SOT	39.2	42.3	47.6
Combined	49.4	52.5	57.3

Table 2. Comparison among different multiple kernel learning methods in terms of multi-class precision (%)

	AK-SVM	MKL	SA-MKL
HOG+SG-LLC	46.2	47.1	48.7
HOF+SG-LLC	45.7	46.9	48.3
MBHx+SG-LLC	49.3	50.5	52.4
MBHy+SG-LLC	51.8	53.1	54.7
SOT+SG-LLC	47.6	47.9	49.3
Combined+SG-LLC	57.3	58.2	60.1

constrained encoding (SG-LLC). To be comprehensive, these encoding techniques are tested on individual feature descriptor and their combination (Combined). From the comparison results shown in Table 1, we observe that the SG-LLC coding consistently and significantly enhances the discriminative power for all types of motion feature descriptors as well as their combination. More specific, SG-LLC is much more discriminative than LLC (i.e., which does not consider localized semantic information), and the improvement from LLC to SG-LLC is over 5% for most feature descriptors. This demonstrates that the encoding method to embed localized semantic information into motion feature encoding is beneficial. We also study our algorithmic performance by varying the number of nearest neighbors parameter n for our algorithm SG-LLC, i.e., $n = 2, 5, 20, 40$. As illustrated in Figure 6, $n = 5$ gives the best performance, and larger n will induce more noise and decrease classification performance.

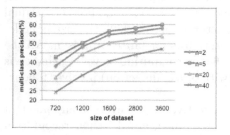 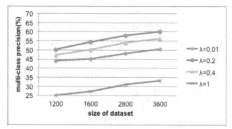

Fig. 6. Classification test on 7 cross-validation rounds under different n

Fig. 7. Classification test on 7 cross-validation rounds under different λ

Effectiveness of Semantic-Aware Motion Feature Pooling and Classification: We show in Table 2 that after semantic-grouped feature encoding (SG-LLC), our proposed semantic-aware motion feature pooling and multiple kernel learning (SA-MKL) can further boost the classification performance. To this end, Table 2 compares our proposed SA-MKL with conventionally used average kernel (AK-SVM) in action recognition [22] as well as conventional multiple kernel learning method (MKL). For MKL, we use the state-of-the-art implementation of SimpleMKL [19]. We test on different types of motion features (which are encoded by the proposed SG-LLC method) and the results show that 1) MKL outperforms average kernel due to its kernel selection capability and 2) our proposed SA-MKL further outperforms traditional MKL as our SA-MKL method utilizes prior information for the kernel weights through semantic information extraction for kernel learning, i.e., action class-object type contextual information. We also study the effect of the parameter λ used for adjusting the weight between kernel $\mathbf{K}_0$ and kernels $\mathbf{K}_1, \cdots, \mathbf{K}_M$. Figure 7 illustrates the classification performance by varying λ. As can be seen from Figure 7, small λ improves classification performance, which is benefited from prior semantic information, and $\lambda = 0.2$ achieves the best result. Performance starts to drop from $\lambda = 0.4$ because of the magnified semantic noise.

Table 3. Stage-by-stage classification performance(%) of our proposed pipeline

	Pr	Rc	AP
Holistic Dense Trajectories [22]	49.4	44.8	59.2
Holistic + Pose [20]	50.4	45.1	57.9
Dense Trajectory + LS	53.9	48.9	64.4
SG-LLC + AK-SVM	57.3	52.4	68.4
SG-LLC + SA-MKL	**60.1**	**54.3**	**70.5**

Comparison with the State-of-the-Art: We compare our approach with the state-of-the-art performance achieved by the holistic dense motion trajectory approach [22] (naive combination of motion features with pose features is used in [20], which achieves minor improvement). To study the algorithmic behavior of our pipeline (i.e., to show the stage-by-stage improvement of the pipeline), we also compare our method with: 1) naive combination of the dense motion trajectory bag-of-words features and the localized semantic bag-of-words features (Dense trajectory + LS, Average Kernel is used) and 2) our proposed SG-LLC encodings but without semantic-aware pooling and multiple kernel learning (SG-LLC + Average Kernel). Comparison results are shown in Table 3. In our experiment, we set λ and n to be 0.2 and 5 empirically. The results show that naive combination of local motion features and localized semantic features improves the holistic dense trajectory method. However, by exploring novel ways to embed the localized semantic features into feature coding, pooling and classification steps, we can obtain a total of more than 10% performance increase accumulated by every stage of our proposed pipeline, which is much better than merely using the semantic feature and combining it naively with the original motion feature descriptors (about 6% more increase than naive combination of dense trajectory and LS). Also each proposed step (i.e., SG-LLC and SA-MKL) consistently benefits the final fine-grained action classification performance.

To prove the effectiveness of our approach on fine-grained actions, we specifically pick up classification results of five fine-grained action groups (i.e., "cut", "put in/on", "take & put in", "take out", "open/close") and compare our approach with holistic dense trajectories in Figure 8, we observe that our method significantly outperforms the holistic approach on the fine-grained action recognition. We find that recognition on actions of "put in/on" have been significantly improved, which are benefited from excellent object detection performance on objects such as bowel, bread/dough or cutting-board (i.e., manipulated objects in the "put in/on" video clips). However, actions of "put on plate" are not improved as expected because the plate is always occluded and difficult for detection. We also observe that "cut" actions are not improved significantly compared to "put in/on", the reasons can be two-fold: 1) the intra-class variability is especially large and 2) the object detection is extremely difficult for the manipulated objects (e.g., knife, fruits, vegetables) because they are in very small size. Nevertheless, "cut" actions are still improved by incorporating the localized semantic information into further steps of our pipeline.

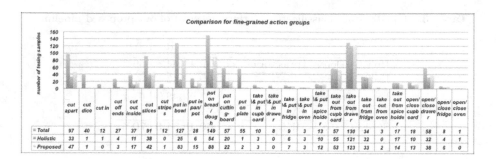

Fig. 8. Holistic [22] and our proposed approach are compared among five major fine-grained action groups (i.e.,"cut","put in/on","take & put in","take out","open/close") in terms of per-class classification accuracy (true positive out of total)

There are still two major issues for our approach. First of all, object detection performance is far from good enough. For example, the object-of-interest list is coarse and incomplete, some defined object categories are difficult to detect (e.g., small size objects such as knife or vegetables, we group them as one object type in our work). Secondly, motions including human body or background motions (i.e., with mainly useless patterns) still count for a large part of dense trajectories, thus actions such as "cut" or "put" are easily confused by the intensive noise.

In the future work, we will make the localized semantic feature more discriminative and less noisy, e.g., by using better object detection method. Note that according to the large deformation and small size nature of the manipulated objects, superpixel based object detection is more suitable than DPM [9] in our scenario. But we believe the performance can be further improved if better tuned object detection method is applied. We can also leverage object co-occurrence information in the localized semantic feature extraction.

4   Conclusion

In summary, we propose a fine-grained action recognition pipeline which seamlessly incorporates localized semantic information into every processing step. The pipeline includes localized semantic feature extraction, semantic-grouped feature encoding, semantic-aware motion feature pooling and classification. We evaluate our approach on the MPII cooking fine-grained action dataset and achieve significant improvement over the existing methods, which is quite promising to be applied in applications such as daily living assist or medical assistance.

Acknowledgment. The study is supported by a research grant for the Human Sixth Sense Programme at the Advanced Digital Sciences Center from Singapores Agency for Science, Technology and Research(A*STAR), and supports from ARO grant W911NF-12-1-0057, Faculty Research Awards by NEC Laboratories of America, National Science Foundation of China (NSFC) 61128007, 2012 UTSA START-R Research Award.

References

1. Achanta, R., Shaji, A., Smith, K., Lucchi, A., Fua, P., Süsstrunk, S.: Slic super-pixels. EPFL 149300 (2010)
2. Bach, F.R., Lanckriet, G.R., Jordan, M.I.: Multiple kernel learning, conic duality, and the smo algorithm. In: ICML, pp. 6–13 (2004)
3. Cao, L., Mu, Y., Natsev, A., Chang, S.-F., Hua, G., Smith, J.R.: Scene aligned pooling for complex video recognition. In: Fitzgibbon, A., Lazebnik, S., Perona, P., Sato, Y., Schmid, C. (eds.) ECCV 2012, Part II. LNCS, vol. 7573, pp. 688–701. Springer, Heidelberg (2012)
4. Chang, C.-C., Lin, C.-J.: Libsvm: a library for support vector machines. TIST 2(3), 1–27 (2011)
5. Chao, Y.-W., Yeh, Y.-R., Chen, Y.-W., Lee, Y.-J., Wang, Y.-C.F.: Locality-constrained group sparse representation for robust face recognition. In: ICIP, pp. 761–764 (2011)
6. Choi, W., Shahid, K., Savarese, S.: Learning context for collective activity recognition. In: CVPR, pp. 3273–3280 (2011)
7. Dalal, N., Triggs, B.: Histograms of oriented gradients for human detection. In: CVPR, pp. 886–893 (2005)
8. Fei-Fei, L., Perona, P.: A bayesian hierarchical model for learning natural scene categories. In: CVPR, pp. 524–531 (2005)
9. Felzenszwalb, P.F., Girshick, R.B., McAllester, D., Ramanan, D.: Object detection with discriminatively trained part-based models. T-PAMI 32(9), 1627–1645 (2010)
10. Koppula, H.S., Gupta, R., Saxena, A.: Learning human activities and object affordances from rgb-d videos. CoRR (2012)
11. Lan, T.: Beyond actions: Discriminative models for contextual group activities. Ph.D. thesis, Applied Science: School of Computing Science (2010)
12. Lan, T., Wang, Y., Mori, G., Robinovitch, S.N.: Retrieving actions in group contexts. In: Kutulakos, K.N. (ed.) ECCV 2010 Workshops, Part I. LNCS, vol. 6553, pp. 181–194. Springer, Heidelberg (2012)
13. Laptev, I., Marszalek, M., Schmid, C., Rozenfeld, B.: Learning realistic human actions from movies. In: CVPR, pp. 1–8 (2008)
14. Lee, H., Battle, A., Raina, R., Ng, A.: Efficient sparse coding algorithms. In: NIPS, pp. 801–808 (2006)
15. Liu, J., Luo, J., Shah, M.: Recognizing realistic actions from videos "in the wild". In: CVPR, pp. 1996–2003 (2009)
16. Marszalek, M., Laptev, I., Schmid, C.: Actions in context. In: CVPR, pp. 2929–2936 (2009)
17. Moore, D., Essa, I., Hayes, M.: Exploiting human actions and object context for recognition tasks. In: ICCV, Greece (1999)
18. Perronnin, F., Sánchez, J., Mensink, T.: Improving the fisher kernel for large-scale image classification. In: Daniilidis, K., Maragos, P., Paragios, N. (eds.) ECCV 2010, Part IV. LNCS, vol. 6314, pp. 143–156. Springer, Heidelberg (2010)
19. Rakotomamonjy, A., Bach, F.R., Canu, S., Grandvalet, Y.: Simplemkl. JMLR 9(11), 2491–2521 (2008)
20. Rohrbach, M., Amin, S., Andriluka, M., Schiele, B.: A database for fine grained activity detection of cooking activities. In: CVPR, pp. 1194–1201 (2012)
21. Ullah, M.M., Parizi, S.N., Laptev, I.: Improving bag-of-features action recognition with non-local cues. In: BMVC, vol. 10, pp. 1–11 (2010)

22. Wang, H., Klaser, A., Schmid, C., Liu, C.L.: Action recognition by dense trajectories. In: CVPR, pp. 3169–3176 (2011)
23. Wang, J., Yang, J., Yu, K., Lv, F., Huang, T., Gong, Y.: Locality-constrained linear coding for image classification. In: CVPR, pp. 3360–3367 (2010)
24. Wang, Y., Mori, G.: Hidden part models for human action recognition: Probabilistic versus max margin. T-PAMI 33(7), 1310–1323 (2011)
25. Willems, G., Tuytelaars, T., Van Gool, L.: An efficient dense and scale-invariant spatio-temporal interest point detector. In: Forsyth, D., Torr, P., Zisserman, A. (eds.) ECCV 2008, Part II. LNCS, vol. 5303, pp. 650–663. Springer, Heidelberg (2008)
26. Wu, J., Osuntogun, A., Choudhury, T., Philipose, M., Rehg, J.: A scalable approach to activity recognition based on object use. In: ICCV, pp. 1–8 (2007)
27. Yao, B., Jiang, X., Khosla, A., Lin, A.L., Guibas, L., Fei-Fei, L.: Human action recognition by learning bases of action attributes and parts. In: ICCV (2011)
28. Yao, B., Khosla, A., Fei-Fei, L.: Classifying actions and measuring action similarity by modeling the mutual context of objects and human poses. In: ICML (2011)

Robust Scene Text Detection with Convolution Neural Network Induced MSER Trees

Weilin Huang[1,2], Yu Qiao[1], and Xiaoou Tang[2,1]

[1] Shenzhen Key Lab of Comp. Vis and Pat. Rec.,
Shenzhen Institutes of Advanced Technology, Chinese Academy of Sciences, China
[2] Department of Information Engineering,
The Chinese University of Hong Kong, China

Abstract. Maximally Stable Extremal Regions (MSERs) have achieved great success in scene text detection. However, this low-level pixel operation inherently limits its capability for handling complex text information efficiently (e. g. connections between text or background components), leading to the difficulty in distinguishing texts from background components. In this paper, we propose a novel framework to tackle this problem by leveraging the high capability of convolutional neural network (CNN). In contrast to recent methods using a set of low-level heuristic features, the CNN network is capable of learning high-level features to robustly identify text components from text-like outliers (e.g. bikes, windows, or leaves). Our approach takes advantages of both MSERs and sliding-window based methods. The MSERs operator dramatically reduces the number of windows scanned and enhances detection of the low-quality texts. While the sliding-window with CNN is applied to correctly separate the connections of multiple characters in components. The proposed system achieved strong robustness against a number of extreme text variations and serious real-world problems. It was evaluated on the ICDAR 2011 benchmark dataset, and achieved over 78% in F-measure, which is significantly higher than previous methods.

Keywords: Maximally Stable Extremal Regions (MSERs), convolutional neural network (CNN), text-like outliers, sliding-window.

1 Introduction

With the rapid evolvement and popularization of high-performance mobile and wearable devices in recent years, scene text detection and localization have gained increasing attention due to its wide variety of potential applications. Although recent progresses in computer vision and machine learning have substantially improved its performance, scene text detection is still an open problem. The challenge comes from extreme diversity of text patterns and highly complicated background information. For example, texts appeared in a natural image can be in a very small size or in a low contrast against the background color, and even regular texts can be distorted significantly by strong lightings, occlusion, or blurring. Furthermore, a large amount of noise and text-like outliers, such as

D. Fleet et al. (Eds.): ECCV 2014, Part IV, LNCS 8692, pp. 497–511, 2014.

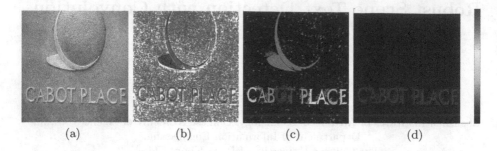

(a)   (b)   (c)   (d)

Fig. 1. The text detection pipeline of our method. The input image is shown in (a). We first apply the MSERs operator on the input image to generate a number of text component candidates (b). We then apply the CNN classifier to generate a component confidence map (c). The components with positive confident scores are applied for constructing text-lines, which are scored by the mean values the components included. The final detection results are generated by a simple thresholding on (d).

windows, leaves, and bricks, can be included in the image background, and often cause many false alarms in detection.

There are mainly two groups of methods for scene text detection in the literature, sliding-window based and connected component based methods. The sliding-window based methods detect text information by sliding a sub-window in multiple scales through all locations of an image [11,3,9,28,29,18,1]. Text and non-text information is then distinguished by a trained classifier, which often uses manually designed low-level features extracted from the window, such as SIFT and Histogram of Oriented Gradients (HoG) [6]. The main challenge lies in the design of local features to handle the large variance of texts, and computational demand for scanning a large amount of windows, which may increase to N^2 for an image with N pixels. Hand crafted features like SIFT and HoG are effective to describe image content information, but these features are not optimized for text detection.

The connected component based methods achieved the state-of-the-art performance in scene text detection. They first separate text and non-text pixels by running a fast low-level filter and then group the text pixels with similar properties (e. g. intensity, stroke width, or color) to construct component candidates [23,24,22,34,7,31,10,32,2]. Stroke width transform (SWT) [7,31,10] and Maximally Stable Extremal Regions (MSERs) [16,23,24,22,34] are two representative low-level filters applied for scene text detection with great success. The main advantages of these methods are the computational efficiency by detecting text components in an one pass computation in complexity of $O(N)$, and providing effective pixel segmentations, which greatly facilitate the subsequent recognition task.

It has been shown that MSERs based methods have high capability for detecting most text components in an images [24]. However, they also generate a large number of non-text components at the same time, leading to high ambiguity between text and non-text in MSERs components. Robustly separating them has been a key issue for improving the performance of MSERs based methods. Efforts have been devoted to handling this problem, but most of current methods for MSERs pruning focus on developing low-level features, such as heuristic characteristics or geometric properties, to filter out non-text components [23,24,22,34]. These low-level features are not robust or discriminative enough to distinguish true texts from text-like outliers, which often have similar heuristic or geometric properties with true texts. Besides, the MESRs methods are based on pixel level operations, and hence are highly sensitive to noise or single pixel corruption. This may lead to incorrect component connections, such as a single component includes multiple characters, which significantly affect the performance of text-line construction in the subsequent step.

In order to tackle these inherent problems, this paper aims to develop a robust text detection system by embedding the high-capability deep learning method into the MSERs model, and taking the advantages of both MESRs and sliding-window methods. The main contributions of the paper are:

1. We apply deep convolutional neural network to learn high-level features from the MSREs components. This high-capability classifier correctly distinguishes texts from a large amount of non-text components, and shows high discriminant ability and strong robustness against complicated background components (see Fig. 1 and 2), and therefore greatly improves capability of the MSERs based methods.
2. We incorporate the CNN classifier with sliding-window model and non-maximal suppression (NMS) to handle the multiple characters connection problem of the MSREs, and also recover missing characters, as shown in Fig. 3. Our method provides better character candidates than previous MSERs methods. This improvement is a crucial technique for bottom-up scheme to construct text-lines.
3. Our system have the advantages of both MSERs and sliding window methods. Comparing to traditional sliding-window methods, our method not only reduces the number of search window, but also enhances the detection of low contrast texts by using MSREs, as shown in Fig. 2 (a) and (b).
4. Our method achieves state-of-the-art results on the most cited ICDAR 2011 benchmark with over 78% in F-measure, which improves current results with a large margin.

The rest of paper is organized as follow. Section 2 describes all details of the proposed system. Experimental verifications are produced on Section 3, followed by the conclusions in Section 4.

2 Our System

The proposed text detection system includes three main steps, as shown in Fig. 1. Text components are first generated by applying the MSERs detector on the input image. Then, each MSERs component is assigned a confident value by using a trained CNN classifier. Finally, the text components with high confident scores are employed for constructing the final text-lines. Besides, we also propose a novel approach to enhance character separation by applying siding window with the CNN classifier for error-connected MSERs components. Details of the system are presented bellow.

2.1   MSERs Component Generation

MSERs define an extremal region as a connected component of an image whose pixels have intensity contrast against its boundary pixels [16,25]. The intensity contrast is measured by increasing intensity values, and controls the region areas. A low contrast value would generate a large number of low-level regions, which are separated by small intensity difference between pixels. When the contrast value increases, a low-level region can be accumulated with current level pixels or merged with other lower level regions to construct a higher level region. Therefore, an extremal region tree can be constructed when it reaches the largest contrast (e.g. 255 in a gray-scale image). An extremal region is defined as a maximally stable extremal region (MSER) if its variation is lower than both its parent and child [16,25]. Therefore, a MSER can be considered as a special extremal region whose size remains unchanged over a range of thresholds.

The MSERs has been one of the most widely-used region detectors. For text region detection, it can be assumed that pixel intensity or color within a single text letter is uniform, while the intensity contrast between text and background regions typically exists. Each individual character can be detected as a extremal region or a MSER. Two promising properties make the MSER detector effective in text detection. First, the MSERs detector is computationally fast and can be computed in linear time of the number of pixels in a image [25]. Second, it is a powerful detector with high capability for detecting low quality texts, such as low contrast, low resolution and blurring. With this capability, MSER is able to detect most scene texts in a natural images, leading to high recall on the detection. However, the capability of the MSER is penalized by the increasing number of false detections. It would substantially increase the difficulty to identity true texts from a large number of non-text false alarms, which is one of the main challenge for current MSERs based methods. Previous work often balance the two factors by using a MSERs threshold, which can be changed from 1 to 255 for a gray-scale image.

For text detection system, our goal is to detect as many text components as possible in this step. Because it is difficult or impossible to recover the missed characters in the subsequent processes. The MSERs threshold is set to its lowest value 1 which makes it possible to capture most challenging cases, as shown in the top row of Fig. 2. As shown, although they are a number of error detections, the true text characters in highly difficult cases are also correctly detected. This makes it possible to construct a robust system to correctly detect those challenge texts and result in a high recall. But at the same time, it needs a powerful classifier to identify those low-quality texts from a large number of non-text components. A high capability classifier based on deep convolutional neural network is present bellow.

2.2 Deep Convolutional Neural Network

Deep learning has been applied to a number of challenging tasks in computer vision with breakthrough improvements achieved in last several years. It has been shown that deep network is capable of leaning meaningful high-level features and semantic representations for visual recognition through a hierarchal architecture with multiple-layers feature convolutions. The deep structure of the CNN allows it to refine feature representation and abstract sematic meaning gradually. The traditional CNN network has achieved great success on digit and hand-written character recognition [12,13]. Scene text detection in natural image is a high-level visual task, which is difficult to be solved completely by a set of low-level operations or manually designed features. In contrast to previous works, which often use a set of heuristic features to distinguish text and non-text components [23,24,22,34,31,10], we take the advantages of deep learning and adapt

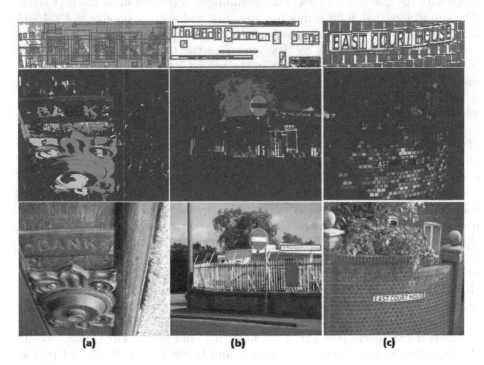

Fig. 2. The performance of the MSERs detector and the CNN classifier for low contrast (a) and low quality texts (b), and text-like outliers (c). The top row are the MESRs detections on text areas. The middle row are the confident maps generated by the CNN classifier. The pixels are displayed by their higher confident scores if they belong to multiple components. The bottom row are the detection results.

a deep convolutional neural network to robustly classify the generated MESRs components.

The structure of the CNN text classifier is similar to that applied in [29,4]. The network includes two convolutional layers, each of which has a convolution and an average pooling steps. The number of filters for the two layers are 64 and 96, respectively. The input patch is with fixed size of 32 × 32. Similar to [29,4,5,19], the first layer is trained in an unsupervised way by using a variant of K-means described in [4] to learn a set of filters $D \in \mathbb{R}^{k \times n_1}$ from a set of 8 × 8 patches randomly extracted from training patches, k is the dimension of the convolution kernel, and is 64 for the kernel size with 8 × 8, $n_1 = 64$ is the number of the filters in the first layer in our system. The responses (r) of the first layer is computed as [29],

$$r = \max\{0, |D^T \mathbf{x}| - \theta\} \tag{1}$$

where $\mathbf{x} \in \mathbb{R}^{64}$ is an input vector for an 8 × 8 convolutional kernel, and $\theta = 0.5$. The resulted first layer response maps are with size of 25 × 25 × 64. Then average pooling with window size of 5 × 5 is applied to the response maps to get reduced maps with the size of 5 × 5 × 64. The second layer is stacked upon the first layer. The sub-window patch for computing response and average pooling is 4 × 4 and 2 × 2, respectively. The final output of the two layers is a 96 dimension feature vector, which is input to a SVM to generate the final confident score of the MSERs component. The parameters in the second layer are fully connected and are trained by back-propagating the SVM classification error.

Given a MESR component, we applied the trained CNN classifier to decide whether it is a text component by assigning a confident score to it. In our experiments, we discarded the MSERs components which include very small numbers of pixels (e.g. less than 0.01% of the total pixel number in an image), and keep all other components as input to the CNN classifier. For each retained MSER component, we computed the aspect ratio of its boundary box. If the width of the box is larger than its height, we directly resized the image component into the size of 32 × 32; otherwise, we extracted a square patch with the same center of the boundary box and with the side length equal to the height of box, and then resized it into 32 × 32. This alignment scheme makes the input patches consistent with the synthetic training samples used in our experiments, which were originally generated by Wang et. al. [28,29]. Two examples for both cases are shown in Fig. 3. The final confident maps for three challenge images are shown in the middle row of the Fig. 2. As shown, our CNN classifier generally assigns higher scores to text components, even for those MSERs with very low quality of the text characters (see Fig. 2 (a) and (b)), and at the same time, classify the text-like outliers (such as the masks and bricks in Fig. 2 (b) and (c)) as low confident scores, demonstrating strong robustness and highly discriminative capability for filtering the non-text components.

The performance of the SWT methods highly depend on the edge detector, which is often not feasible in many challenge cases. Compared to the SWT based methods, MSER operator is capable of detecting more true text components,

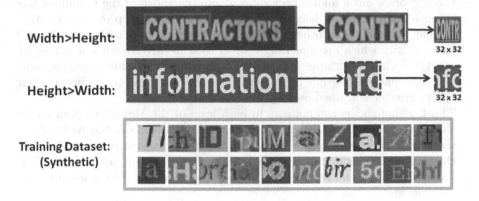

Fig. 3. MESRs component alignment with size of 32×32 and synthetic training samples

often leading to a higher recall. But at the same time, the MESRs methods also generate a larger number of non-text components. It means that the high performance of the MSERs methods heavily depend on a powerful component classifier. Thus we designed the CNN network by leveraging its high learning capability to improve the performance of the MSERs methods. Besides, in our system, the MESRs method and the CNN classifier are strongly compensated to each other. Comparing to general siding-window methods, the MSER operator provides two promising properties. It not only reduces the number of searching windows dramatically by two orders of magnitude, but also provides a significant enhancement on low quality texts, which are difficult to be detected correctly by a general sliding-window method. In our experiment, the average number of the MSERs components in an image input to the CNN classifier is 516 in the ICDAR 2011 database.

2.3 Component Splitting with MSERs Tree

As pointed out in the literature, most connected component based methods suffer from inherent limitations of low-level filters, which easily cause error connections between multiple characters or with background components in some difficult cases, such as low quality or seriously affected texts [24,2,10]. In order to tackle this problem, we proposed a high-level approach by incorporating CNN scores and MSERs tree structure with a sliding window model.

We define an error-connected component as a MSER component including multiple text characters. As mentioned, implementation of the sliding-window model is computationally expensive. We show that only a small number of the MSERs components are considered as the error-connected components by selecting them using the output CNN scores and the structure of MSERs tree. It can be observed that an error-connected component generally has three remarkable characteristics.

- First, it often has a high aspect ratio where the width of the boundary box is much longer than its height (e.g. the example in the top row of Fig. 3).
- Second, differing from other non-text components, such as long horizontal lines or bars which are generally scored with negative confident values by our CNN classifier, the error-connected component actually includes some text information (multiple characters), but it is not very strong, because our CNN classifier is trained on single-character components.
- Third, although the components in high-level of the MSERs trees often include multiple text characters, such as the components in the roots of the tree. Most of these components can be further separated correctly by their children components, which often have higher confident scores than their parents. Thus, we do not consider these components as the error-connected components.

Therefore, the error-connected components are defined as the components having high aspect ratios (e.g. $width/height > 2$ in our experiments) and positive CNN scores, (1) but cannot be further separated in their MSERs trees; or (2) all components in their children sets do not have a higher CNN score than them. The first situation includes the texts having multiple characters truly connected, which cannot be separated by most low-level filters. The components in the second situation often include error separations (resulted in the low or negative confident scores for all their children components), which are caused by some challenging cases.

To present the proposed splitting scheme, we selected an error-connected MSER component sample, as shown in Fig 4. The component has high aspect ratio and positive CNN scores, which is higher than the scores of its children. We applied a sliding window with our CNN classifier to scan through the component, which returns an one dimension continuous confident scores. Finally, non-maximal suppression (NMS) method [20] was applied to the continuous scores to estimate the locations for each single characters. The details of the component splitting method are described in Algorithm 1.

As shown in Fig. 4, the proposed high-level component splitting method effectively handles the component connection problem of the MSERs methods, and often generates better component candidates with high confident values for subsequent text-line construction and recognition. Note that, by integrating MSERs tree structure and CNN confident map for carefully choosing the error-connected components, only a small number of components are selected for splitting. While each component is scanned just once by a sliding window with a single scale (32×32) and the size of component is often small. Therefore, the increase of the computational cost for the proposed splitting method is relatively trivial. With powerful CNN classifier and efficient splitting scheme, a large number of non-text components have been identified correctly and only a small number of text components (with positive confident scores in our experiments) are retained to construct the final text-lines.

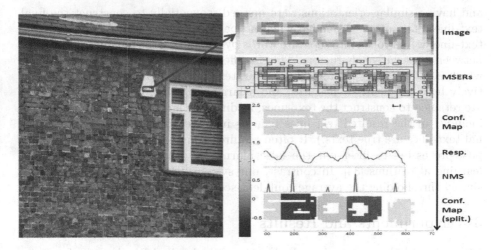

Fig. 4. Error-connected component slitting by sliding window model with the CNN classifier

---

Algorithm 1. Error-connected Component Splitting

Require: Selected error-connected components, MSERs Tree Structure and CNN confident map.

Ensure: Revised MSERs Tree and CNN confident map.

1: Given N error-connected components
2: **for** $k = 1 \rightarrow N$ **do**
3:   Get the confident score of the current component, W_k
4:   Normalize the size of component into $32 \times X$
5:   Use sliding window (32×32) with CNN to compute confident scores S_k
6:   Apply NMS [20] for estimating the peak values (P_k) in S_k as,
7:

$$P_k(x) = \begin{cases} S_k(x) & \text{if } S_k(x) \geqslant S_k(x + \Delta x), \Delta x < \Theta \\ 0 & otherwise \end{cases} \quad (2)$$

8:   Generate new components at location x, where $P_k(x) > 0$, $\{P_k^1, P_k^2, \ldots, P_k^m\}$
9:   **if** $\max(P_k^1, P_k^2, \ldots, P_k^s) > W_k$ **then**
10:     Replace children set of current component with new generated ones
11:     Update confident map with new scores and locations, as shown in Fig 4
12:   **end if**
13: **end for**
14: **return** Revised MSERs tree and new CNN confident map

The text-line construction is now simple and straightforward. Similar to previous work in [7,10], we first grouped two neighboring components into a pair if they have similar geometric and heuristic properties, such as similar intensities, colors, heights, and aspect ratios. Then, the pairs including a same component and having similar orientations were merged sequentially to construct the final text-lines. The process is ended when no pairs can be merged further. Finally, text-lines were broken into separate words by computing the horizontal distances between consecutive characters. This is different from Yin *et al.*'s method [34], which is difficult to sperate text and non-text MSERs components discriminatively by using heuristic features, and a large number of non-text components are retained to construct the text-lines, leading to a large number of false alarms included in the resulted text-lines (e.g. as indicated in [34], only 9% of the final text-lines are true texts.). It often requires a further computationally costly post-processing to filter out the false alarms by using sophisticated machine learning algorithms [34]. In contrast, our system discards the false alarms by simply thresholding the average confident scores of the text-lines.

3   Experiments and Results

We evaluated the proposed method on two widely cited benchmarks for scene text detection, the ICDAR 2005 [15,14] and the ICDAR 2011 [26] Robust Reading Competition databases.

3.1   Datasets and Evaluation Method

The ICDAR 2005 dataset includes 509 color images having sizes varied from 307×93 to 1280×960. 258 images are included in the training set, while 251 images are used for test. There are 229 training images and 255 testing ones for the ICDAR 2011 dataset. The detection performance were evaluated in the word level in both datasets, which include totally 1114 and 1189 words in their test sets, respectively.

For evaluation, we followed the ICDAR 2011 competition evaluation protocol, which was proposed by Wolf et al. [30]. This evaluation method presents object level precision and recall based on constraints on detection quality. It evaluates both quantity and quality of rectangle matches through all images in the database, and considers not only one-to-one matching, but also one-to-many and many-to-one matchings. The quality of detection or matching is controlled by two parameters which penalizes more on parts matching than larger detection. Specifically, the evaluation is computed by *Precision*, *Recall*, and *F-measure* which are defined bellow,

$$Precision = \frac{\sum_i^N \sum_j^{|D^i|} M_D(D_j^i, G^i)}{\sum_i^N |D^i|} \tag{3}$$

$$Recall = \frac{\sum_i^N \sum_j^{|G^i|} M_G(G_j^i, D^i)}{\sum_i^N |G^i|} \tag{4}$$

$$F_{measure} = 2 \times \frac{Precision \times Recall}{Precision + Recall} \tag{5}$$

where N is the total number of images in a dataset. $|D^i|$ and $|G^i|$ are the number of detection and ground true rectangles in the i-th image. $M_D(D^i_j, G^i)$ and $M_G(G^i_j, D^i)$ are the matching scores for detection rectangle D_j and ground true rectangle G_j. Their values are set to 1 for one-to-one matching, 0.8 for one-to-many matching and 0 for no matching. Two rectangles are considered as matched when their overlapping ratio is higher than a defined threshold, which controls the quality of the matching.

3.2 Experiments and Results

The CNN classifier was trained by using 15000 toy samples generated by Wang et al. [29]. There are 5000 positive and 10000 negative samples in the training dataset, and all samples are resized into 32×32. Some examples are shown in Fig. 3. The training data on the two datasets were not applied for training in our experiments, which shows strong generalization power of the proposed system. In our experiments, the MSERs operator was run twice on each image, corresponding to both black-to-white and white-to-black texts. Each MSER component was classified by the trained CNN classifier and only the component with positive confident score was used for text-line construction. A text-line with an average component score lower than 1.2 was considered as a fail detection. The final detected boundary boxes for each image are the non-overlap combination of the boxes from both sides. The full evaluation results on the two databases are presented in Table 1 and 2, along with the detection results on several challenging images displayed in Fig. 5.

The proposed method achieved excellent performance on both databases and the improvements are significant in terms of $Precision$, $Recall$, and $F_{measure}$. In the most recent ICDAR 2011 dataset, our method improved the most closed performance with $2 \sim 3\%$ in all three terms and reached the $F_{measure}$ score over 78%. Note that the evaluation scheme of the SFT-TCD method [10] did not follow the standard protocol of the ICDAR 2011. It was evaluated based on each single image and the mean values of all images in the dataset were reported. The improvements by our method mainly gain from two facts. On the one hand, the powerful MSERs detector is able to detect most true texts, which resulted in a high $Recall$. One the other hand, high capability of the CNN classifier with high-level splitting scheme robustly identify true text components from non-text ones, leading to a large improvement on $Precision$.

Fig. 5 shows the successful detection results on a number of challenging cases, which indicate that our system is highly robust to large variations in texts including small font size, low contrast, and blurring. The images also show that our system is robust against strong lighting and highly noise background effects. Fig. 6 shows two failure cases in our experiments. For the left one, our method missed a number of true text-lines. It is mainly caused by the strong masks covering the texts, which significantly break the low-level structure of texts. The text components in the right image do not include strong text information and are easily confused with its background.

Fig. 5. Successful text detection results with extreme variances and significant affects

Fig. 6. Failure cases

Table 1. Experimental results on the ICDAR 2005 dataset

Method	Year	$Precision$	$Recall$	$F - measure$
Our method	–	**0.84**	**0.67**	**0.75**
SFT-TCD [10]	2013	0.81	0.74	0.72
Yao et al. [31]	2012	0.69	0.66	0.67
Chen et al. [2]	2012	0.73	0.60	0.66
Epshtein et al. [7]	2010	0.73	0.60	0.66
Yi and Tian [33]	2013	0.71	0.62	0.63
Neumann and Matas [23]	2011	0.65	0.64	0.63
Zhang and Kasturi [35]	2010	0.73	0.62	–
Yi and Tian [32]	2011	0.71	0.62	0.62
Becker et al. [14]	2005	0.62	0.67	0.62
Minetto et al. [17]	2010	0.63	0.61	0.61
Chen and Yuille [3]	2004	0.60	0.60	0.58

Table 2. Experimental results on the ICDAR 2011 dataset

Method	Year	$Precision$	$Recall$	$F - measure$
Our method	–	**0.88**	**0.71**	**0.78**
Yin et al. [34]	2014	0.86	0.68	0.76
Neumann and Matas [21]	2013	0.85	0.68	0.75
SFT-TCD [10]	2013	0.82	0.75	0.73
Neumann and Matas [22]	2013	0.79	0.66	0.72
Shi et al. [27]	2013	0.83	0.63	0.72
Neumann and Matas [24]	2012	0.73	0.65	0.69
González et al. [8]	2012	0.73	0.56	0.63
Yi and Tian [32]	2011	0.67	0.58	0.62
Neumann and Matas [23]	2011	0.69	0.53	0.60

4   Conclusions

We have presented a robust system for scene text detection and localization in natural images. Our main contribution lies in effectively leveraging the high capacity of the deep learning model to tackle two main problems of current MSERs methods for text detection, and enable our system with strong robustness and highly discriminative capability to distinguish texts from a large amount of non-text components. A sliding window model was intergraded with the CNN classifier to further improve text character detection on challenging images. Our method has achieved the state-of-the-art performance on two benchmark datasets, convincingly verifying the efficiency of the proposed method.

Acknowledgments. This work is supported by National Natural Science Foundation of China (913201 01), Shenzhen Basic Research Program (JCYJ20120903092050890, JCYJ2012061 7114614438, JCYJ20130402113127496), 100 Talents Programme of Chinese Acad emy of Sciences, and Guangdong Innovative Research Team Program (No. 201001 D0104648280). Yu Qiao is the corresponding author.

References

1. Bissacco, A., Cummins, M., Netzer, Y., Neven, H.: Photoocr: reading text in uncontralled conditions (2013), ICCV
2. Chen, H., Tsai, S., Schronth, G., Chen, D., Grzeszczuk, R., Girod, B.: Robust text detection in natural images with edge-enhanced maximally stable extremal regions. In: ICIP (2012)
3. Chen, X., Yuille, A.: Detecting and reading text in natural scenes. In: CVPR (2004)
4. Coates, A., Carpenter, B., Case, C., Satheesh, S., Suresh, B., Wang, T., Wu, D.J., Ng, A.Y.: Text detection and character recognition in scene images with unsupervised feature learning. In: ICDAR (2011)
5. Coates, A., Lee, H., Ng, A.Y.: An analysis of single-layer networks in unsupervised feature learning. In: AISTATS (2011)
6. Dalal, N., Triggs, B.: Histograms of oriented gradients for human detection. In: CVPR (2005)
7. Epshtein, B., Ofek, E., Wexler, Y.: Detecting text in natural scenes with stroke width transform. In: CVPR (2010)
8. González, A., Bergasa, L., Yebes, J., Bronte, S.: Text location in complex images. In: ICPR (2012)
9. Hanif, S., Prevost, L.: Text detection and localization in complex scene images using constrained adaboost algorithm. In: ICDAR (2009)
10. Huang, W., Lin, Z., Yang, J., Wang, J.: Text localization in natural images using stroke feature transform and text covariance descriptors. In: ICCV (2013)
11. Kim, K., Jung, K., Kim, J.: Texture-based approach for text detection in images using support vector machines and continuously adaptive mean shift algorithm. IEEE Trans. Pattern Analysis and Machine Intelligence 25, 1631–1639 (2003)
12. LeCun, Y., Boser, B., Denker, J., Henderson, D., Howard, R., Hubbard, W.: Handwritten digit recognition with a back-propagation network. In: NIPS (1989)
13. LeCun, Y., Bottou, L., Bengio, Y., Haffner, P.: Gradient-based learning applied to document recognition. Proceedings of the IEEE 86, 2278–2324 (1998)
14. Lucas, S.: Icdar 2005 text locating competition results. In: ICDAR (2005)
15. Lucas, S., Panaretos, A., Sosa, L., Tang, A., Wong, S., Young, R.: Icdar 2003 robust reading competitions. In: ICDAR (2003)
16. Matas, J., Chum, O., Urban, M., Pajdla, T.: Robust wide baseline stereo from maximally stable extremal region. In: BMVC (2002)
17. Minetto, R., Thome, N., Cord, M., Fabrizio, J., Marcotegui, B.: Snoopertext: A multiresolution system for text detection in complex visual scenes. In: ICIP (2010)
18. Mishra, A., Alahari, K., Jawahar, C.V.: Top-down and bottom-up cues for scene text recognition. In: CVPR (2012)
19. Netzer, Y., Wang, T., Coates, A., Bissacco, A., Wu, B., Ng, A.Y.: Reading digits in natural images with unsupervised feature learning
20. Neubeck, A., Gool, L.: Efficient non-maximum suppression. In: ICPR (2006)

21. Neumann, L., Matas, J.: On combining multiple segmentations in scene text recognition. In: ICDAR (2013)
22. Neumann, L., Matas, J.: Scene text localization and recognition with oriented stroke detection. In: ICCV (2013)
23. Neumann, L., Matas, K.: Text localization in real-world images using eficiently pruned exhaustive search. In: ICDAR (2011)
24. Neumann, L., Matas, K.: Real-time scene text localization and recognition. In: CVPR (2012)
25. Nistér, D., Stewénius, H.: Linear time maximally stable extremal regions. In: Forsyth, D., Torr, P., Zisserman, A. (eds.) ECCV 2008, Part II. LNCS, vol. 5303, pp. 183–196. Springer, Heidelberg (2008)
26. Shahab, A., Shafait, F., Dengel, A.: Icdar 2011 robust reading competition challenge 2: Reading text in scene images. In: ICDAR (2011)
27. Shi, C., Wang, C., Xiao, B., Zhang, Y., Gao, S.: Scene text detection using graph model built upon maximally stable extremal regions. Pattern Recognition 34, 107–116 (2013)
28. Wang, K., Babenko, B., Belongie, S.: End-to-end scene text recognition. In: ICCV (2011)
29. Wang, T., Wu, D.J., Coates, A., Ng, A.Y.: End-to-end text recognition with convolutional neural network. In: ICPR (2012)
30. Wolf, C., Jolion, J.-M.: Object count/area graphs for the evaluation of object detection and segmentation algorithms. International Journal on Document Analysis and Recognition 8, 280–296 (2006)
31. Yao, C., Bai, X., Liu, W., Ma, Y., Tu, Z.: Detecting texts of arbitrary orientations in natural images. In: CVPR (2012)
32. Yi, C., Tian, Y.: Text string detection from natural scenes by structure-based partition and grouping. IEEE Trans. Image Processing 20, 2594–2605 (2011)
33. Yi, C., Tian, Y.: Text extraction from scene images by character appearance and structure modeling. Computer Vision and Image Understanding 117, 182–194 (2013)
34. Yin, X.C., Yin, X., Huang, K., Hao, H.W.: Robust text detection in natural scene images. IEEE Trans. Pattern Analysis and Machine Intelligence (to appear)
35. Zhang, J., Kasturi, R.: Character energy and link energybased text extraction in scene images. In: ACCV (2010)

Deep Features for Text Spotting

Max Jaderberg, Andrea Vedaldi, and Andrew Zisserman

Visual Geometry Group, Department of Engineering Science,
University of Oxford, UK

Abstract. The goal of this work is text spotting in natural images. This is divided into two sequential tasks: detecting words regions in the image, and recognizing the words within these regions. We make the following contributions: first, we develop a Convolutional Neural Network (CNN) classifier that can be used for both tasks. The CNN has a novel architecture that enables efficient feature sharing (by using a number of layers in common) for text detection, character case-sensitive and insensitive classification, and bigram classification. It exceeds the state-of-the-art performance for all of these. Second, we make a number of technical changes over the traditional CNN architectures, including no downsampling for a per-pixel sliding window, and multi-mode learning with a mixture of linear models (maxout). Third, we have a method of automated data mining of Flickr, that generates word and character level annotations. Finally, these components are used together to form an end-to-end, state-of-the-art text spotting system. We evaluate the text-spotting system on two standard benchmarks, the ICDAR Robust Reading data set and the Street View Text data set, and demonstrate improvements over the state-of-the-art on multiple measures.

1 Introduction

While text recognition from scanned documents is well studied and there are many available systems, the automatic detection and recognition of text within images – text spotting (Fig.1) – is far less developed. However, text contained within images can be of great semantic value, and so is an important step towards both information retrieval and autonomous systems. For example, text spotting of numbers in street view data allows the automatic localization of houses numbers in maps [20], reading street and shop signs gives robotic vehicles scene context [39], and indexing large volumes of video data with text obtained by text spotting enables fast and accurate retrieval of video data from a text search [26].

Text spotting in natural images is usually divided into two tasks [12]: text detection, and word recognition. Text detection involves generating candidate bounding boxes that are likely to contain lines of text, while word recognition takes each candidate bounding box, and attempts to recognize the text depicted within it, or potentially reject the bounding box as a false positive detection.

In this paper we show that a very high quality character classifier can improve over the state-of-the-art for both the word detection and recognition tasks of this pipeline. To achieve this we use a Convolutional Neural Network (CNN) [27]

D. Fleet et al. (Eds.): ECCV 2014, Part IV, LNCS 8692, pp. 512–528, 2014.

(a)   (b)

Fig. 1. (a) An end-to-end text spotting result from the presented system on the SVT dataset. (b) Randomly sampled cropped word data automatically mined from Flickr with a weak baseline system, generating extra training data.

and generate a per-pixel text/no-text saliency map, a case-sensitive and case-insensitive character saliency map, and a bigram saliency map. The text saliency map drives the proposal of word bounding boxes, while the character and bigram saliency maps assist in recognizing the word within each bounding box through a combination of soft costs. Our work is inspired by the excellent performance of CNNs for character classification [6, 8, 47]. Our contributions are threefold:

First, we introduce a method to share features [44] which allows us to extend our character classifiers to other tasks such as character detection and bigram classification at a very small extra cost: we first generate a single rich feature set, by training a strongly supervised character classifier, and then use the intermediate hidden layers as features for the text detection, character case-sensitive and insensitive classification, and bigram classification. This procedure makes best use of the available training data: plentiful for character/non-character but less so for the other tasks. It is reminiscent of the Caffe idea [14], but here it is not necessary to have external sources of training data.

A second key novelty in the context of text detection is to leverage the convolutional structure of the CNN to process the entire image in one go instead of running CNN classifiers on each cropped character proposal [27] . This allows us to generate efficiently, in a single pass, all the features required to detect word bounding boxes, and that we use for recognizing words from a fixed lexicon using the Viterbi algorithm. We also make a technical contribution in showing that our CNN architecture using maxout [21] as the non-linear activation function has superior performance to the more standard rectified linear unit.

Our third contribution is a method for automatically mining and annotating data (Fig.1). Since CNNs can have many millions of trainable parameters, we require a large corpus of training data to minimize overfitting, and mining is useful to cheaply extend available data. Our mining method crawls images from the Internet to automatically generate word level and character level bounding box annotations, and a separate method is used to automatically generate character level bounding box annotations when only word level bounding box annotations are supplied.

In the following we first describe the data mining procedure (Sect. 2) and then the CNN architecture and training (Sect. 3). Our end-to-end (image in, text out) text spotting pipeline is described in Sect. 4. Finally, Sect. 5 evaluates the method on a number of standard benchmarks. We show that the performance exceeds the state of the art across multiple measures.

Related Work. Decomposing the text-spotting problem into text detection and text recognition was first proposed by [12]. Authors have subsequently focused solely on text detection [7, 11, 16, 50, 51], or text recognition [31, 36, 41], or on combining both in end-to-end systems [40, 39, 49, 32–34, 45, 35, 6, 8, 48].

Text detection methods are either based on connected components (CCs) [11, 16, 50, 49, 32–35] or sliding windows [40, 7, 39, 45]. *Connected component methods* segment pixels into characters, then group these into words. For example, Epshtein *et al.* take characters as CCs of the stroke width transform [16], while Neumann and Matas [34, 33] use Extremal Regions [29], or more recently oriented strokes [35], as CCs representing characters. *Sliding window methods* approach text spotting as a standard task of object detection. For example, Wang *et al.* [45] use a random ferns [38] sliding window classifier to find characters in an image, grouping them using a pictorial structures model [18] for a fixed lexicon. Wang & Wu *et al.* [47] build on the fixed lexicon problem by using CNNs [27] with unsupervised pre-training as in [13]. Alsharif *et al.* [6] and Bissacco *et al.* [8], also use CNNs for character classification – both methods over-segment a word bounding box and find an approximate solution to the optimal word recognition result, in [8] using beam search and in [6] using a Hidden Markov Model.

The works by Mishra *et al.* [31] and Novikova *et al.* [36] focus purely on text recognition – assuming a perfect text detector has produced cropped images of words. In [36], Novikova combines both visual and lexicon consistency into a single probabilistic model.

2 Data Mining for Word and Character Annotations

In this section we describe a method for automatically mining suitable photo sharing websites to acquire word and character level annotated data. This annotation is used to provide additional training data for the CNN in Sect. 5.

Word Mining. Photo sharing websites such as Flickr [3] contain a large range of scenes, including those containing text. In particular, the "Typography and Lettering" group on Flickr [4] contains mainly photos or graphics containing text. As the text depicted in the scenes are the focus of the images, the user given titles of the images often include the text in the scene. Capitalizing on this weakly supervised information, we develop a system to find title text within the image, automatically generating word and character level bounding box annotations.

Using a weak baseline text-spotting system based on the Stroke Width Transform (SWT) [16] and described in Sect. 5, we generate candidate word detections for each image from Flickr. If a detected word is the same as any of the image's title text words, and there are the same number of characters from the SWT detection phase as word characters, we say that this is an accurate word detection, and use this detection as positive text training data. We set the parameters so that the recall of this process is very low (out of 130000 images, only 15000 words were found), but the precision is greater than 99%. This means the precision is high enough for the mined Flickr data to be used as positive training data, but the recall is too low for it to be used for background no-text training data. We will refer to this dataset as *FlickrType*, which contains 6792 images, 14920 words, and 71579 characters. Fig. 1 shows some positive cropped words randomly sampled from the automatically generated FlickrType dataset.

Although this procedure will cause a bias towards scene text that can be found with a simple end-to-end pipeline, it still generates more training examples that can be used to prevent the overfitting of our models.

Automatic Character Annotation. In addition to mining data from Flickr, we also use the word recognition system described in Sect. 4.2 to automatically generate *character* bounding box annotations for datasets which only have *word* level bounding box annotations. For each cropped word, we perform the optimal fitting of the groundtruth text to the character map using the method described in Sect. 4.2. This places inter-character breakpoints with implied character centers, which can be used as rough character bounding boxes. We do this for the SVT and Oxford Cornmarket datasets (that are described in section 5), allowing us to train and test on an extra 22,000 cropped characters from those datasets.

3   Feature Learning Using a Convolutional Neural Network

The workhorse of a text-spotting system is the character classifier. The output of this classifier is used to recognize words and, in our system, to detect image regions that contain text. Text-spotting systems appear to be particularly sensitive to the performance of character classification; for example, in [8] increasing the accuracy of the character classifier by 7% led to a 25% increase in word recognition. In this section we therefore concentrate on maximizing the performance of this component.

To classify an image patch x in one of the possible characters (or background), we extract a set of features $\Phi(x) = (\phi_1(x), \phi_2(x), ..., \phi_K(x))$ and then learn a binary classifier f_c for each character c of the alphabet C. Classifiers are learned to yield a posterior probability distribution $p(c|x) = f_c(\Phi(x))$ over characters and the latter is maximized to recognize the character $\bar{c}$ contained in patch x: $\bar{c} = \mathrm{argmax}_{c \in C}\, p(c|x)$. Traditionally, features Φ are manually engineered and optimized through a laborious trial-and-error cycle involving adjusting the features and re-learning the classifiers. In this work, we propose instead to *learn* the representation using a CNN [27], jointly optimizing the performance of the features as well as of the classifiers. As noted in the recent literature, a well designed learnable representation of this type can in fact yield substantial performance gains [25].

CNNs are obtained by stacking multiple layers of features. A *convolutional layer* consist of K linear filters followed by a non-linear response function. The input to a convolutional layer is a *feature map* $z_i(u, v)$ where $(u, v) \in \Omega_i$ are spatial coordinates and $z_i(u, v) \in \mathbb{R}^C$ contains C scalar features or *channels* $z_i^c(u, v)$. The output is a new feature map z_{i+1} such that $z_{i+1}^k = h_i(W_{ik} * z_i + b_{ik})$, where W_{ik} and b_{ik} denote the k-th filter kernel and bias respectively, and h_i is a non-linear activation function such as the *Rectified Linear Unit* (ReLU) $h_i(z) = \max\{0, z\}$. Convolutional layers can be intertwined with *normalization*, *subsampling*, and *max-pooling layers* which build translation invariance in local neighborhoods. The process starts with $z_1 = x$ and ends by connecting the last feature map to a logistic regressor for classification. All the parameters of the model are jointly optimized to minimize the classification loss over a training set using Stochastic Gradient Descent (SGD), back-propagation, and other improvements discussed in Sect. 3.1.

Instead of using ReLUs as activation function h_i, in our experiments it was found empirically that *maxout* [21] yields superior performance. Maxout, in particular when used in the final classification layer, can be thought of as taking the maximum response over a mixture of n linear models, allowing the CNN to easily model multiple modes of the data. The maxout of two feature channels z_i^1 and z_i^2 is simply their pointwise maximum: $h_i(z_i(u, v)) = \max\{z_i^1(u, v), z_i^2(u, v)\}$. More generally, the k'-th maxout operator $h^{k'}$ is obtained by selecting a subset $G_{k'i} \subset \{1, 2, \dots, K\}$ of feature channels and computing the maximum over them: $h_i^{k'}(z_i(u, v)) = \max_{k \in G_{k'i}} z_i^k(u, v)$. While different grouping strategies are possible, here groups are formed by taking g consecutive channels of the input map: $G_{1i} = \{1, 2, \dots, g\}$, $G_{2i} = \{g + 1, g + 2, \dots, 2g\}$ and so on. Hence, given K feature channels as input, maxout constructs $K' = K/g$ new channels.

3.1   Training and Implementation Details

This section discusses the details of learning the character classifiers. Training is divided into two stages. In the first stage, a case-insensitive CNN character classifier is learned. In the second stage, the resulting feature maps are applied to other classification problems as needed. The output is four state-of-the-art CNN classifiers: a character/background classifier, a case-insensitive character classifier, a case-sensitive character classifier, and a bigram classifier.

Stage 1: Bootstrapping the Case-Insensitive Classifier. The case-insensitive classifier uses a four-layer CNN outputting a probability $p(c|x)$ over an alphabet C including all 26 letters, 10 digits, and a noise/background (no-text) class, giving a total of 37 classes (Fig. 2) The input $z_1 = x$ of the CNN are grayscale cropped character images of 24×24 pixels, zero-centered and normalized by subtracting the patch mean and dividing by the standard deviation.

Due to the small input size, no spatial pooling or downsampling is performed. Starting from the first layer, the input image is convolved with 96 filters of size

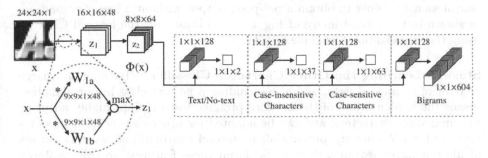

Fig. 2. Convolutional Neural Networks. The method uses four CNNs. These share the first two layers, computing "generic" character features and terminate in layers specialized into text/no-text classification, case-insensitive and case-sensitive character classification, and bigram classification. Each connection between feature maps consists of convolutions with maxout groups.

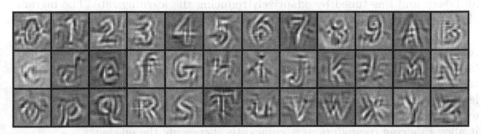

Fig. 3. Visualizations of each character class learnt from the 37-way case-insensitive character classifier CNN. Each image is synthetically generated by maximizing the posterior probability of a particular class. This is implemented by back-propagating the error from a cost layer that aims to maximize the score of that class [43, 17].

9×9, resulting in a map of size 16×16 (to avoid boundary effects) and 96 channels. The 96 channels are then pooled with maxout in group of size $g = 2$, resulting in 48 channels. The sequence continues by convolving with 128, 512, 148 filters of side 9, 8, 1 and maxout groups of size $g = 2, 4, 4$, resulting in feature maps with 64, 128, 37 channels and size $8 \times 8, 1 \times 1, 1 \times 1$ respectively. The last 37 channels are fed into a soft-max to convert them into character probabilities. In practice we use 48 channels in the final classification layer rather than 37 as the software we use, based on `cuda-convnet` [25], is optimized for multiples of 16 convolutional filters – we do however use the additional 12 classes as extra no-text classes, abstracting this to 37 output classes.

We train using stochastic gradient descent and back-propagation, and also use dropout [22] in all layers except the first convolutional layer to help prevent overfitting. Dropout simply involves randomly zeroing a proportion of the parameters; the proportion we keep for each layer is 1, 0.5, 0.5, 0.5. The training data is augmented by random rotations and noise injection. By omitting any downsampling in our network and ensuring the output for each class is one pixel in size, it is immediate to apply the learnt filters on a full image in a convolutional manner to obtain a per-pixel output without a loss of resolution, as shown in the second image of Fig 4. Fig. 3 illustrates the learned CNN by using the visualization technique of [43].

Stage 2: Learning the Other Character Classifiers. Training on a large amount of annotated data, and also including a no-text class in our alphabet, means the hidden layers of the network produce feature maps highly adept at discriminating characters, and can be adapted for other classification tasks related to text. We use the outputs of the second convolutional layer as our set of discriminative features, $\Phi(x) = z_2$. From these features, we train a 2-way text/no-text classifier[1], a 63-way case-sensitive character classifier, and a bigram classifier, each one using a two-layer CNN acting on $\Phi(x)$ (Fig. 2). The last two layers of each of these three CNNs result in feature maps with 128-2, 128-63, and 128-604 channels respectively, all resulting from maxout grouping of size $g = 4$. These are all trained with $\Phi(x)$ as input, with dropout of 0.5 on all layers, and fine-tuned by adaptively reducing the learning rate. The bigram classifier recognises instances of two adjacent characters, *e.g.* Fig 6.

These CNNs could have been learned independently. However, sharing the first two layers has two key advantages. First, the low-level features learned from case-insensitive character classification allows *sharing training data* among tasks, reducing overfitting and improving performance in classification tasks with less informative labels (text/no-text classification), or tasks with fewer training examples (case-sensitive character classification, bigram classification). Second, it allows *sharing computations*, significantly increasing the efficiency.

4   End-to-End Pipeline

This section describes the various stages of the proposed end-to-end text spotting system, making use of the features learnt in Sect. 3. The pipeline starts with a detection phase (Sect. 4.1) that takes a raw image and generates candidate bounding boxes of words, making use of the text/no-text classifer. The words contained within these bounding boxes are then recognized against a fixed lexicon of words (Sect. 4.2), driven by the character classifiers, bigram classifier, and other geometric cues.

4.1   Text Detection

The aim of the detection phase is to start from a large, raw pixel input image and generate a set of rectangular bounding boxes, each of which should contain the image of a word. This detection process (Fig. 4) is tuned for high recall, and generates a set of candidate word bounding boxes.

---

[1] Training a dedicated classifier was found to yield superior performance to using the background class in the 37-way case-sensitive character classifier.

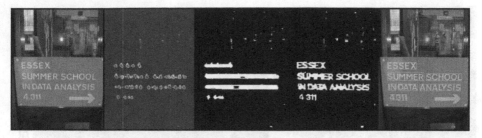

Fig. 4. The detector phase for a single scale. From left to right: input image, CNN generated text saliency map using that text/no-text classifier, after the run length smoothing phase, after the word splitting phase, the implied bounding boxes. Subsequently, the bounding boxes will be combined at multiple scales and undergo filtering and non-maximal suppression.

The process starts by computing a **text saliency map** by evaluating the character/background CNN classifier in a sliding window fashion across the image, which has been appropriately zero-padded so that the resulting text saliency map is the same resolution as the original image. As the CNN is trained to detect text at a single canonical height, this process is repeated for 16 different scales to target text heights between 16 and 260 pixels by resizing the input image.

Given these saliency maps, word bounding boxes are generated independently at each scale in two steps. The first step is to **identify lines of text**. To this end, the probability map is first thresholded to find local regions of high probability. Then these regions are connected in text lines by using the *run length smoothing algorithm* (RLSA): for each row of pixels the mean μ and standard deviation σ of the spacings between probability peaks are computed and neighboring regions are connected if the space between them is less than $3\mu - 0.5\sigma$. Finding connected components of the linked regions results in candidate text lines.

The next step is to **split text lines into words**. For this, the image is cropped to just that of a text line and Otsu thresholding [37] is applied to roughly segment foreground characters from background. Adjacent connected components (which are hopefully segmented characters) are then connected if their horizontal spacings are less than the mean horizontal spacing for the text line, again using RLSA. The resulting connected components give candidate bounding boxes for individual words, which are then added to the global set of bounding boxes at all scales. Finally, these bounding boxes are filtered based on geometric constraints (box height, aspect ratio, *etc.*) and undergo non-maximal suppression sorting them by decreasing average per-pixel text saliency score.

4.2   Word Recognition

The aim of the word recognition stage is to take the candidate cropped word images $I \in \mathbb{R}^{W \times H}$ of width W and height H and estimate the text contained in them. In order to recognize a word from a fixed lexicon, each word hypothesis is scored

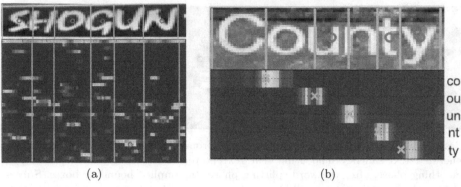

(a) (b)

Fig. 5. (a) The optimal placing of breakpoints for the word "SHOGUN" in the image, with the 1D character response map for 37 character classes below. Each row of the response map is the horizontal CNN response for a particular character, with classes in row order from top to bottom: no-text, 0-9, a-z (*i.e.* first row is the no-text class response, last row is the "z" class response). (b) The optimal breakpoint placing for "County" with the bigram responses of only the ground-truth text bigrams shown below. Green lines show the placed breakpoints b^w with red circles showing the implied character center.

using a generative model that combines multiple visual cues. The computational complexity is therefore linear in the lexicon size.

The input to the word recognition are the 2D character probability maps (case sensitive and insensitive) and bigram probability maps generated using the CNN classifiers. Restricted to the cropped word region, this results in a $W \times H$ map for each character hypothesis. These $W \times H$ maps are reduced to $W \times 1$ responses by averaging along the columns (averaging uses a Gaussian weight centered on the middle row). Grouping the 1D responses per classifier type, this result in matrices $P \in \mathbb{R}^{37 \times W}$, $Q \in \mathbb{R}^{63 \times W}$, $R \in \mathbb{R}^{604 \times W}$ for the case-insensitive, case-sensitive, and bigram classifier classifiers respectively (Fig. 5).

Given matrices P, Q, R, the next step is to score each word hypothesis $w = (c_1, c_2, \ldots, c_{L_w})$. Let $b^w = (b_1^w, b_2^w, \ldots, b_{L_w+1}^w)$ denote the breakpoints between characters (where b_1^w marks the beginning of the first character and the $b_{L_w}^w$ the end of the last one). The word-breakpoints hypothesis (w, b^w) receives score

$$s(w, b^w, P, Q, R) = \frac{1}{|b^w|} \left(\sum_{i=1}^{|b^w|} m_i(b_i^w, R) + \sum_{i=2}^{|b^w|} \phi(b_i^w, b_{i-1}^w, P, Q, R) \right). \quad (1)$$

For each word hypothesis w the optimal location of breakpoints are determined using dynamic programming and the word with best score $s(w, I) = \max_{b^w} s(w, b^w, P, Q, R)$ is recognized.

The unary scores $m_i(b_i^w, R)$ combine the following cues: distance from expected breakpoint placement, distance to out of image bounds, no-text class score, the bigram score, and, for the first and last breakpoint, the distance from the edge of the image. The pairwise score $\phi(b_i^w, b_{i-1}^w, P, Q, R)$ combines:

Table 1. A description of the various datasets used to evaluate on. # *im.* denotes the total number of images in the dataset, and # *words* the total number of word occurrences.

Label	Description	Lex. size	# im.	# words
IC03	ICDAR 2003 [1] test dataset.	–	251	860
IC03-50	ICDAR 2003 [1] test dataset with fixed lexicon.	50	251	860
IC03-Full	ICDAR 2003 [1] test dataset with fixed lexicon.	860	251	860
SVT	SVT [46] test dataset.	–	250	647
SVT-50	SVT [46] test dataset with fixed lexicon.	50	250	647

the character score at the midpoint between breakpoints, the no-text score at the character center, the deviation from the average width of the character, and a dynamic contribution from the left and right bigram responses relative to the character score – this allows bigram responses to take control when it is difficult to classify the character in focus, but easy to classify characters on either side. Also it is ensured that there is no violation of the sequence of characters in the word and that the character centers are all in the region of the word image. Each score is weighted and linearly combined, with the parameters found by grid search on a validation set.

Given the recognized word, the bounding box is adjusted to match the estimated breakpoints and added to a list of candidate recognized word regions. The final step is to perform non-maximal suppression on this set of bounding boxes in order to eliminate duplicate detections.

5   Experiments

This section evaluates our method on a number of standard text-spotting benchmarks. Data and technical details are discussed next, with results in Sect. 5.1.

Datasets. We train and evaluate on a number of datasets. The **four ICDAR datasets** – ICDAR 2003 [1], 2005 [28], 2011 [42], and 2013 [24] – containing a varied array of photos of the world that contain scene text. ICDAR 2003, 2005, and 2013 have word and character bounding box annotations, whereas the ICDAR 2011 dataset contains only word bounding box annotations. The **Street View Text dataset** (SVT) [46] contains images downloaded from Google Street View of road-side scenes, and only has case-insensitive word bounding box annotations. The labelled text can be very challenging with a wide variety of fonts, orientations, and lighting conditions. **KAIST** provide a scene text dataset [5] consisting of 3000 images of indoor and outdoor scenes containing text, with both a mixture of photos from a high-resolution digital camera and a low-resolution mobile phone camera. Word and character bounding boxes are provided as well as segmentation maps of characters, and the words are a mixture of English and Korean. The **Oxford Cornmarket Scene Text** dataset [39] provides high resolution images of a busy street scene, with case-insensitive, word level bounding

Fig. 6. Some training samples used for bigram classification as seen by the CNN. From left to right, the top row labels are "de", "sf", "aw", "lp", "oa", and "ad".

box annotations. Not all text is labelled, but there are some difficult samples. The **Chars74k** [10] and the **StanfordSynth** [47]. Both datasets contain small single-character images of all 62 characters (0-9, a-z, A-Z). Chars74k comprises a set of characters from natural images, and a set of synthetically generated characters. The StanfordSynth characters are all synthetically generated, but are very representative of natural scene characters, whereas the Chars74k synthetic characters are not.

Classifier Training Data. The case-insensitive character classifier is learned on 163k cropped 24 × 24 pixel characters from ICDAR 2003, 2005, 2011, 2011, 2013 training sets, KAIST, the natural images from Chars74k (we do not use the synthetically generated images), StanfordSynth, and FlickrType. After this training, the characters in the SVT training set and Oxford Cornmarket dataset are automatically annotated, and training continues including those samples, giving a total of 186k characters. No-text data is generated from all four ICDAR training datasets (all other datasets do not annotate all text occurrences). The case-sensitive character classifier is trained on the same data, excluding FlickrType and automatically annotated characters, giving 107k training samples. Wherever possible, the characters were cropped and resized to maintain their original aspect ratio.

The bigram classifier performs 604-way classification – the number of unique bigrams present in the ICDAR 2003 and SVT lexicons. We train on 24 × 24 pixel samples, generated by centering a window with width 1.5 times that of the height at the breakpoint between two characters, cropping the image, and resizing to 24 × 24 pixels, thus squashing the aspect ratio. We use the character annotations from the ICDAR 2003, 2005, 2011, 2011, 2013 training sets, KAIST dataset, FlickrType and the automatically annotated datasets giving a total of 92k samples. However, due to the relative distribution of bigrams in natural text, some bigram classes have no training data, while others have thousands of samples – on average there are 152 image samples per bigram class.

Weak Baseline System. The Flickr mining process described in Sect. 2 uses a weak baseline end-to-end text spotting system based on the Stroke Width Transform (SWT) [16]. First, the SWT word detection algorithm is run as described in [16]. The SWT labels each pixel with a value of the width of the stroke it is estimated to belong to. Regions of similar stroke width are combined into connected components and are character candidates. Using simple heuristics [16], these character candidates are grouped together to form words, generating word bounding boxes, character bounding boxes, as well as rough character

Table 2. The accuracy of classifiers for 36-way character classification, 62-way case-sensitive character classification, 2-way text detection, and 604-way bigram classification on ground-truth cropped patches. For the SVT dataset the character-level annotation is automatically generated by our system. *Value read from graph.

Method	Character Classifier (%)		Case-sensitive Character Classifier(%)	Text/No-text Classifier (%)		Bigram Classifier (%)
	IC03	SVT	IC03	IC03	SVT	IC03
Wang & Wu [47]	-	-	83.9	97.8*	-	-
Alsharif [6]	89.8	-	86.0	-	-	-
Proposed	**91.0**	**80.3**	**86.8**	**98.2**	**97.1**	**72.5**

segmentations. This process is run with multiple sets of parameters, as the SWT is very sensitive to changes in them, producing a large number of word detection candidates. A random forest classifier based on [7] is then used to produce a text saliency map for each candidate bounding box, rejecting false positive SWT word detections. For each remaining word detection candidate, the rough SWT character segmentations are used to generate a color model to fully segment characters using Graph Cut [9], after which the word detections are filtered based on profile features described in [15]. Finally, the segmented word detection is fed in to an off-the-shelf OCR package, Tesseract [2], for case-insensitive character recognition. When tested on the standard benchmarks, this baseline system achieves an unconstrained end-to-end word recognition f-measure of 0.50 on ICDAR 2003 ([33] get 0.41, higher is better) and 0.42 on ICDAR 2011 ([35] get 0.45).

5.1 Results

This section compares the performance of our system against the standard benchmarks and state-of-the-art. It also reports the performance of the individual components of the system. The evaluation datasets are given in Table 1.

CNN Classifiers. Table 2 shows the results of the trained classifiers on IC-DAR 2003 cropped characters (IC03) and SVT automatically annotated cropped characters, as well as ICDAR 2003 cropped bigrams. To make results comparable with published ones, the background class is ignored in this case. The 37-way case-insensitive character classifier and case-sensitive classifier both achieve state-of-the-art performance, as does the text/no-text classifier used for detection. Our bigram classifier gives a recognition accuracy of 72.5%, a good result for a problem with 604 classes.

Although the CNNs are large (2.6 million parameters for the case-insensitive classifier), the method does not require any unsupervised pre-training as is done in [47], and incorporating the unsupervised approach described in [47, 13] gives no improvement. Empirically, maxout and dropout were found to be essential

Fig. 7. Five randomly chosen cropped groundtruth cropped words out of only 33 that were recognized incorrectly in the IC03-50 cropped word benchmark

Table 3. Left: Ground-truth cropped word recognition accuracy (%) on different datasets. **Right**: End-to-end word recognition F-measure results (%). These methods report PASCAL VOC style 50% overlap match measure for the detection.

Method	Cropped Words			Method	End-to-End		
	IC03-50	IC03-Full	SVT-50		IC03-50	IC03-Full	SVT-50
Wang [45]	76.0	62.0	57.0	Wang [45]	68	51	38
Mishra [31]	81.8	67.8	73.2	Weak Baseline	-	55	41
Novikova [36]	82.8	-	72.9	Wang & Wu [47]	72	67	46
Wang & Wu [47]	90.0	84.0	70.0	Alsharif [6]	77	70	48
Alsharif [6]	93.1	88.6	74.3	Proposed	**80**	**75**	**56**
Goel [19]	-	-	77.3				
PhotoOCR [8]	-	-	**90.4**				
Proposed	**96.2**	**91.5**	86.1				

to achieve this performance. For example, replacing maxout with ReLU non-linearities (this equates to reducing the number of filters to give the same layer output dimensionality) causes slight overfitting hence worse accuracy (-3.3% accuracy for case-insensitive character classification). We also found experimentally that pooling and downsampling have no effect on classifier accuracy.

Sharing feature maps between tasks improves results compared to learning independent models: $+3\%$ accuracy for text/no-text, $+1\%$ accuracy for the case-sensitive character classifier, and $+2.5\%$ accuracy for the bigram classifier. Including the FlickrType mined data also gives an extra 0.8% accuracy for the case-insensitive character classifier, illustrating the importance of more training data. On the contrary, learning on more synthetic data from Chars74k dataset (black and white renderings of different fonts) and Wang *et al.* [45] harmed recognition accuracy by causing the CNN to overfit to the synthetic data.

Fixed Lexicon Cropped Word Recognition. The cropped word recognition accuracy of the recognition sub-system (Tab. 3) is evaluated following the protocol of [45] (in particular, words smaller than two characters are ignored). For each word, a set of hypothesis is formed adding to the ground-truth text a small number of distractors. These distractors are: in IC03-full the full lexicon, in IC03-50 the 50 words from [45], and in SVT, 50 selected words.

Our word recognition system gives state of the art accuracy on the ICDAR 2003 benchmarks, improving on state of the art by 3.1% for the 50 word lexicon and 2.4% for the full lexicon. The total recognition accuracy of 96.2% for the 50 word lexicon makes only 33 mistakes out of 860 test images, and many of the

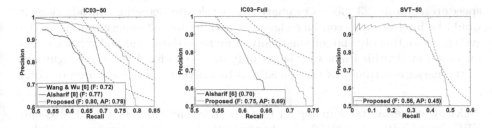

Fig. 8. The precision/recall curves on the IC03-50 dataset (left), IC03-Full (middle), and SVT-50 dataset (right) with lines of constant F-measure. The results from [47, 6] were extracted from the papers.

misclassified examples can be very difficult to classify even for a human (Fig. 7). On the SVT dataset, we achieve an accuracy of 86.1%, which while 4.3% off state-of-the-art, improves on the next best result [19] by 8.8%. This is a competitive result considering our method is trained on two orders of magnitude less data, and so must use a smaller model than the state-of-the-art PhotoOCR [8] method.

End-to-End Word Recognition. The results of our end-to-end system are evaluated on the ICDAR 2003 test set with different sized lexicons and the SVT dataset (Tab. 3, Fig. 8). A recognition result is considered to be correct if the bounding box has at least 50% overlap with the ground truth and the text is correct. The detector described in Sect. 4.1 is tuned for high recall and generates word bounding boxes with localization P/R (precision/recall) of 0.19/0.80 (IC03) and 0.04/0.72 (SVT). After word recognition, detection results are re-ranked by word recognition score, P/R curves generated, and the P/R/F-measure at the maximum F-measure working point is reported [47, 45, 6]. Our end-to-end pipeline outperforms previous works, with P/R/F-measure of 0.90/0.73/0.80 for IC03-50, 0.89/0.66/0.75 for IC03-Full, and 0.73/0.45/0.56 for SVT-50. Interestingly, due to the fact that our pre-recognition bounding boxes are generated by a detector trained from the same data as the character recognizer, we find that the difference between the localization and recognition scores to be inline with the cropped word recognition results: at maximum recall, 95% of correctly *localized* words are subsequently correctly *recognized* in IC03-50. When removing the bigram response maps from the word recognition process, F-measure drops significantly from 0.8 to 0.76 for IC03-50 and from 0.56 to 0.50 for SVT-50.

6   Conclusions

In this paper we have presented a text spotting system using a single set of rich, learnt features, that achieve state-of-the-art performance on a number of benchmarks. These results illustrate the power of jointly learning features to build multiple strong classifiers as well as mining additional training data in publicly available resources such as Flickr. One additional potential advantage, to be explored in future work, is that by implementing sliding window detection as a byproduct of the convolutional network, our method allows the use of CNN speedup methods [23, 30] to dramatically accelerate detection. In addition, it would be interesting to continue classifier learning by self-supervision using the system to continually and automatically mine more data, and find other sources for this. Finally, this framework is not only limited to fixed lexicon recognition, as the major contributions are agnostic as to whether a lexicon is used or not.

Acknowledgements. Funding for this research is provided by the EPSRC and ERC grant VisRec no. 228180, and thanks to Prof. Ingmar Posner for his insights in discussions.

References

1. http://algoval.essex.ac.uk/icdar/datasets.html
2. https://code.google.com/p/tesseract-ocr/
3. http://www.flickr.com/
4. http://www.flickr.com/groups/type/
5. http://www.iapr-tc11.org/mediawiki/index.php/kaist_scene_text_database
6. Alsharif, O., Pineau, J.: End-to-End Text Recognition with Hybrid HMM Maxout Models. In: ICLR (2014)
7. Anthimopoulos, M., Gatos, B., Pratikakis, I.: Detection of artificial and scene text in images and video frames. Pattern Analysis and Applications, 1–16 (2011)
8. Bissacco, A., Cummins, M., Netzer, Y., Neven, H.: PhotoOCR: Reading text in uncontrolled conditions. In: ICCV (2013)
9. Boykov, Y., Jolly, M.P.: Interactive graph cuts for optimal boundary and region segmentation of objects in N-D images. In: Proc. ICCV, vol. 2, pp. 105–112 (2001)
10. de Campos, T., Babu, B.R., Varma, M.: Character recognition in natural images, pp. 591–604 (2009)
11. Chen, H., Tsai, S., Schroth, G., Chen, D., Grzeszczuk, R., Girod, B.: Robust text detection in natural images with edge-enhanced maximally stable extremal regions. In: Proc. International Conference on Image Processing (ICIP), pp. 2609–2612 (2011)
12. Chen, X., Yuille, A.L.: Detecting and reading text in natural scenes. In: Proceedings of the 2004 IEEE Computer Society Conference on Computer Vision and Pattern Recognition, CVPR 2004, vol. 2, p. II–366. IEEE (2004)
13. Coates, A., Carpenter, B., Case, C., Satheesh, S., Suresh, B., Wang, T., Wu, D.J., Ng, A.Y.: Text detection and character recognition in scene images with unsupervised feature learning. In: 2011 International Conference on Document Analysis and Recognition (ICDAR), pp. 440–445. IEEE (2011)
14. Donahue, J., Jia, Y., Vinyals, O., Hoffman, J., Zhang, N., Tzeng, E., Darrell, T.: Decaf: A deep convolutional activation feature for generic visual recognition. arXiv preprint arXiv:1310.1531 (2013)
15. Dutta, S., Sankaran, N., Sankar, K., Jawahar, C.: Robust recognition of degraded documents using character n-grams. In: International Workshop on Document Analysis Systems (DAS), pp. 130–134. IEEE (2012)
16. Epshtein, B., Ofek, E., Wexler, Y.: Detecting text in natural scenes with stroke width transform. In: Proc. CVPR, pp. 2963–2970. IEEE (2010)
17. Erhan, D., Bengio, Y., Courville, A., Vincent, P.: Visualizing higher-layer features of a deep network. Tech. rep. University of Montreal (2009)

18. Felzenszwalb, P., Huttenlocher, D.: Pictorial structures for object recognition. IJCV 61(1) (2005)
19. Goel, V., Mishra, A., Alahari, K., Jawahar, C.: Whole is greater than sum of parts: Recognizing scene text words. In: 2013 12th International Conference on Document Analysis and Recognition (ICDAR), pp. 398–402. IEEE (2013)
20. Goodfellow, I.J., Bulatov, Y., Ibarz, J., Arnoud, S., Shet, V.: Multi-digit number recognition from street view imagery using deep convolutional neural networks. In: ICLR (2014)
21. Goodfellow, I.J., Warde-Farley, D., Mirza, M., Courville, A., Bengio, Y.: Maxout networks. arXiv preprint arXiv:1302.4389 (2013)
22. Hinton, G.E., Srivastava, N., Krizhevsky, A., Sutskever, I., Salakhutdinov, R.R.: Improving neural networks by preventing co-adaptation of feature detectors. arXiv preprint arXiv:1207.0580 (2012)
23. Jaderberg, M., Vedaldi, A., Zisserman, A.: Speeding up convolutional neural networks with low rank expansions. arXiv preprint arXiv:1405.3866 (2014)
24. Karatzas, D., Shafait, F., Uchida, S., Iwamura, M., Mestre, S.R., Mas, J., Mota, D.F., Almazan, J.A., de las Heras, L.P., et al.: Icdar 2013 robust reading competition. In: 2013 12th International Conference on Document Analysis and Recognition (ICDAR), pp. 1484–1493. IEEE (2013)
25. Krizhevsky, A., Sutskever, I., Hinton, G.E.: Imagenet classification with deep convolutional neural networks. In: NIPS, vol. 1, p. 4 (2012)
26. Lalonde, M., Gagnon, L.: Key-text spotting in documentary videos using adaboost. In: Electronic Imaging 2006, p. 60641N. International Society for Optics and Photonics (2006)
27. LeCun, Y., Bottou, L., Bengio, Y., Haffner, P.: Gradient-based learning applied to document recognition. Proceedings of the IEEE 86(11), 2278–2324 (1998)
28. Lucas, S.M.: Icdar 2005 text locating competition results. In: Proceedings of the Eighth International Conference on Document Analysis and Recognition 2005, pp. 80–84. IEEE (2005)
29. Matas, J., Chum, O., Urban, M., Pajdla, T.: Robust wide baseline stereo from maximally stable extremal regions. In: Proc. BMVC, pp. 384–393 (2002)
30. Mathieu, M., Henaff, M., LeCun, Y.: Fast training of convolutional networks through FFTs. CoRR abs/1312.5851 (2013)
31. Mishra, A., Alahari, K., Jawahar, C., et al.: Scene text recognition using higher order language priors. In: 23rd British Machine Vision Conference on BMVC 2012 (2012)
32. Neumann, L., Matas, J.: A method for text localization and recognition in real-world images. In: Kimmel, R., Klette, R., Sugimoto, A. (eds.) ACCV 2010, Part III. LNCS, vol. 6494, pp. 770–783. Springer, Heidelberg (2011)
33. Neumann, L., Matas, J.: Text localization in real-world images using efficiently pruned exhaustive search. In: Proc. ICDAR, pp. 687–691. IEEE (2011)
34. Neumann, L., Matas, J.: Real-time scene text localization and recognition. In: Proc. CVPR, vol. 3, pp. 1187–1190. IEEE (2012)
35. Neumann, L., Matas, J.: Scene text localization and recognition with oriented stroke detection. In: 2013 IEEE International Conference on Computer Vision (ICCV 2013), pp. 97–104. IEEE, California (2013)
36. Novikova, T., Barinova, O., Kohli, P., Lempitsky, V.: Large-lexicon attribute-consistent text recognition in natural images. In: Fitzgibbon, A., Lazebnik, S., Perona, P., Sato, Y., Schmid, C. (eds.) ECCV 2012, Part VI. LNCS, vol. 7577, pp. 752–765. Springer, Heidelberg (2012)

37. Otsu, N.: A threshold selection method from gray-level histograms. IEEE Transactions on Systems, Man, and Cybernetics 9(1), 62–66 (1979)
38. Ozuysal, M., Fua, P., Lepetit, V.: Fast keypoint recognition in ten lines of code. In: Proc. CVPR (2007)
39. Posner, I., Corke, P., Newman, P.: Using text-spotting to query the world. In: Proc. of the IEEE/RSJ Int. Conf. on Intelligent Robots and Systems, IROS (2010)
40. Quack, T.: Large scale mining and retrieval of visual data in a multimodal context. Ph.D. thesis, ETH Zurich (2009)
41. Rath, T., Manmatha, R.: Word spotting for historical documents. IJDAR 9(2-4), 139–152 (2007)
42. Shahab, A., Shafait, F., Dengel, A.: Icdar 2011 robust reading competition challenge 2: Reading text in scene images. In: Proc. ICDAR, pp. 1491–1496. IEEE (2011)
43. Simonyan, K., Vedaldi, A., Zisserman, A.: Deep inside convolutional networks: Visualising image classification models and saliency maps. In: Workshop at International Conference on Learning Representations (2014)
44. Torralba, A., Murphy, K.P., Freeman, W.T.: Sharing features: efficient boosting procedures for multiclass object detection. In: Proc. CVPR, pp. 762–769 (2004)
45. Wang, K., Babenko, B., Belongie, S.: End-to-end scene text recognition. In: Proc. ICCV, pp. 1457–1464. IEEE (2011)
46. Wang, K., Belongie, S.: Word spotting in the wild. In: Daniilidis, K., Maragos, P., Paragios, N. (eds.) ECCV 2010, Part I. LNCS, vol. 6311, pp. 591–604. Springer, Heidelberg (2010)
47. Wang, T., Wu, D.J., Coates, A., Ng, A.Y.: End-to-end text recognition with convolutional neural networks. In: 2012 21st International Conference on Pattern Recognition (ICPR), pp. 3304–3308. IEEE (2012)
48. Weinman, J.J., Butler, Z., Knoll, D., Feild, J.: Toward integrated scene text reading. IEEE Trans. Pattern Anal. Mach. Intell. 36(2), 375–387 (2014)
49. Yang, H., Quehl, B., Sack, H.: A framework for improved video text detection and recognition. Int. Journal of Multimedia Tools and Applications, MTAP (2012)
50. Yi, C., Tian, Y.: Text string detection from natural scenes by structure-based partition and grouping. IEEE Transactions on Image Processing 20(9), 2594–2605 (2011)
51. Yin, X.C., Yin, X., Huang, K.: Robust text detection in natural scene images. CoRR abs/1301.2628 (2013)

Improving Image-Sentence Embeddings Using Large Weakly Annotated Photo Collections

Yunchao Gong[1], Liwei Wang[2], Micah Hodosh[2], Julia Hockenmaier[2],
and Svetlana Lazebnik[2]

[1] University of North Carolina at Chapel Hill, USA
yunchao@cs.unc.edu
[2] University of Illinois at Urbana-Champaign, USA
{lwang97,mhodosh2,juliahmr,slazebni}@illinois.edu

Abstract. This paper studies the problem of associating images with descriptive sentences by embedding them in a common latent space. We are interested in learning such embeddings from hundreds of thousands or millions of examples. Unfortunately, it is prohibitively expensive to fully annotate this many training images with ground-truth sentences. Instead, we ask whether we can learn better image-sentence embeddings by augmenting small fully annotated training sets with millions of images that have weak and noisy annotations (titles, tags, or descriptions). After investigating several state-of-the-art scalable embedding methods, we introduce a new algorithm called Stacked Auxiliary Embedding that can successfully transfer knowledge from millions of weakly annotated images to improve the accuracy of retrieval-based image description.

1 Introduction

Describing images with natural language sentences is an ambitious goal at the intersection of computer vision and natural language processing. Previous approaches to this problem can be roughly categorized into two groups: novel sentence generation and retrieval-based description. Approaches in the former group, e.g., [1–6], use natural language models or templates for generating sentences, and learn predictors to "fill in" or compose parts of these models. However, image descriptions automatically composed in this way can often be unnatural. More importantly, as argued by Hodosh et al. [7], it is difficult to objectively compare the quality of novel sentences produced by different generation methods for an image – not least because the sentences can vary in specificity, or exhibit different types of quirks or artifacts. Retrieval-based systems, e.g., [7–9], describe images by retrieving pre-existing sentences from a dataset. One representative method, that of Ordonez et al. [8], uses millions of images from Flickr and their corresponding descriptions as a source of image captions. For each query image, it finds similar images in the Flickr database and transfers the descriptions of these retrieved images to the query. However, since this method relies on image-to-image matching to transfer sentences, it cannot return any sentences

D. Fleet et al. (Eds.): ECCV 2014, Part IV, LNCS 8692, pp. 529–545, 2014.

that have no images associated with them. Hybrid retrieval- and generation-based methods are also possible: in follow-up to [8], Kuznetsova et al. [10] adopt a template-based approach of composing parts of retrieved sentences to create more query-specific and relevant descriptions.

To automatically evaluate the quality of image captioning systems, many previous works have relied on the BLEU score [11], which is based on the n-gram precision of the caption returned by a system against a human-produced reference caption (or set of captions). However, BLEU was originally developed for machine translation, and it has widely recognized shortcomings for the much more open-ended image description task [7, 2, 8]: BLEU penalizes captions that are relevant to the image but do not happen to overlap with the reference set; it does not measure vision output quality directly; and it has poor correlation with human judgment. As an automatic alternative to BLEU, Hodosh et al. [7] propose a retrieval-based protocol: given a query image, use the model being evaluated to retrieve sentences from a pool that also contains some reference sentences associated with that image, and see how highly the model ranks them. This protocol can be used with any systems that can score image-sentence pairs. It can still underestimate performance by not reflecting when the system returns a valid caption that was not originally associated with the image, but Hodosh et al. [7] show that recall of the original caption has better correlation with human judgment than BLEU.

In this paper, we adopt the retrieval-based protocol of [7], as well as their idea of image-to-sentence retrieval in a joint image-sentence embedding space. To establish a baseline, they use Kernel Canonical Correlation Analysis (KCCA) [12] with multiple visual and linguistic kernels to map images and sentences into a space where similarity between them can be computed directly. They train this embedding on 6,000 images associated with five ground-truth captions each. However, to enable substantial further progress in techniques for mapping between images and sentences, we believe that a much larger amount of training data is required. This leads to two fundamental challenges:

1. Nonlinear image-sentence embedding methods, such as KCCA, tend not to scale to large training sets.
2. Obtaining high-quality sentence descriptions for millions of images is a prohibitively expensive task.

To address the first challenge, we conduct a comparative evaluation of scalable image-sentence embedding methods and show that linear Canonical Correlation Analysis (CCA) with proper normalization [13] outperforms several state-of-the-art alternatives in terms of both accuracy and efficiency, and is therefore a promising framework on top of which to build a large-scale image-to-sentence retrieval approach. To address the second challenge, we ask: *Can the addition of a large amount of Internet images with noisy textual annotations to a smaller set of images with clean sentence annotations help us induce a better latent space?* Figure 1 shows an illustration of this scenario. It is a multi-view transfer learning setting that, to our knowledge, has not been studied before. It has

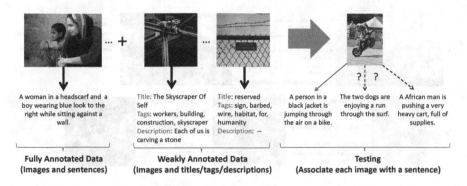

Fig. 1. The problem setting of our paper. We want to use large amounts of Flickr images annotated with noisy tags, titles, and descriptions to help with learning of an image-sentence embedding on a small dataset of images and clean ground truth sentences. At test time, we embed images and sentences in the learned latent space and perform image-to-sentence retrieval.

connections to multi-view learning [13, 7], transfer learning [14–16], and methods that use Internet data to help recognition [17–21]. Starting with the normalized CCA formulation, we propose a novel transfer learning approach we call Stacked Auxiliary Embedding (SAE) and show its effectiveness in transferring knowledge from two large-scale Flickr datasets of a million images each.

The rest of our presentation is organized as follows. Section 2 will introduce our datasets, evaluation protocols, and feature representations for images and text. In Section 3, we begin by conducting a comparative evaluation of several scalable image-sentence embedding models in the fully supervised scenario – i.e., trained on tens of thousands of images annotated with ground-truth sentences. Next, in Section 4, we take the winning embedding, CCA with normalization [13] and consider how to improve it by adding millions of images weakly annotated with noisy tags, titles, and descriptions. We introduce our Stacked Auxiliary Embedding model and demonstrate that it outperforms a number of alternative baselines in terms of image-sentence retrieval accuracy.

2   Datasets, Protocols, and Features

2.1   Datasets

We begin by describing our datasets for learning image-sentence embeddings. Our fully annotated data comes from the dataset of Young et al. [22], which is an expanded version of the one from [7]. This dataset, referred to as **Flickr30K**, contains 31,783 images collected from different Flickr groups and focusing on events involving people and animals. Each image is associated with five sentences independently written by native English speakers from Mechanical Turk. Sample data from Flickr30K is shown in Figure 2(a).

For the weakly annotated data for the transfer task, we experiment with two datasets of about a million images each that do not overlap with Flickr30K or

Fig. 2. (a) Sample images and sentences from the Flickr30K dataset [22]. (b) Sample images from the Flickr1M dataset. These images come with titles, tags, and descriptions, some of which may be missing.

each other. For the first one, referred to as **Flickr1M**, we used queries based on the most frequent 350 keywords in Flickr30K to download more than two million additional images from Flickr. After removing duplicates and images lacking tags, we were left with one million images. We use these images and their tags, titles and descriptions as weak supervision. Sample data from Flickr1M is shown in Figure 2(b). As our second weakly annotated dataset, we use the **SBU1M** dataset of [8], which also comes from Flickr, but has very different statistics from Flickr30K because it was collected totally independently. We took the Flickr IDs of the SBU1M images and downloaded all their titles, tags and descriptions. We are interested in experimenting on both datasets because we would like to investigate to what an extent the success of transfer embedding methods depends on the similarity between the fully and the weakly supervised domains.

2.2   Evaluation Protocol

As stated in the Introduction, we follow the retrieval-based protocol of [7, 22]. For the Flickr30K dataset, we use the 3,000 test images from the split of [22] and for each test image, we keep only the first sentence out of five. Each method being evaluated is used to separately map the 3,000 images and 3,000 sentences to the learned latent space, and then each of these images is used as a query to retrieve the sentences based on some similarity measure in the latent space. If the ground-truth sentence is within the top k retrieved sentences, we mark this query as successful, otherwise, it is a failure. We report Recall@10, which is the percentage of query images that have successfully found their ground truth sentence within $k = 10$ nearest neighbors (numbers for other k exhibit exactly the same trends). To learn the latent spaces, we use fixed training subsets ranging in size from 5,000 to 25,000, together with all five sentences per each image. That is, if we report results for a given training set size, we are in fact using five times as many image/sentence pairs. We also use a disjoint set of 3,000 validation images (also from the split of [22]) to tune parameters.

Table 1. Recall@10 for CNN activations versus a combination of standard visual features. The standard features consist of a 960-dimensional GIST [23], a 512-dimensional RGB histogram, and three local descriptors densely sampled on a regular grid: CSIFT [24], RGBSIFT [24], and HOG [25]. Each local descriptor type is quantized using a codebook of size 500 and VLAD-pooled [26] to obtain 6,400-dimensional image descriptors. GIST and RGB histograms are PCA-reduced to 500 dimensions and VLAD to 1,000 dimensions, and concatenated to get 4,000-dimensional combined descriptors. The sentence features are 3,000-dimensional BoW vectors and the embedding model is normalized CCA (Section 3).

method / training set size	5,000	15,000	25,000
Standard combined features (4,000 dim.)	11.07	18.40	22.13
CNN activations (4,096 dim.)	**19.77**	**27.03**	**31.13**

2.3 Visual and Textual Features

We represent the visual content of images using activations from a deep convolutional neural network (CNN) [27]. CNNs have recently produced state-of-the-art results on a wide range of recognition tasks. Specifically, we use the 4,096-dimensional activations from the sixth hidden layer of the Decaf system [28] pre-trained on ImageNet [29]. Table 1 confirms that CNN activations give significantly higher accuracy on our problem than a combination of standard visual descriptors like GIST and bags of visual words.

For the textual features, we use a standard bag-of-words (BoW) representation. In the following, we will refer as a "document" to each separate piece of text associated with an image: a sentence, a title, a set of tags, or a description. We first pre-process all the documents with WordNet's lemmatizer [30] and remove stop words. After that, we construct a dictionary by taking a few thousand most common words, and represent documents as tf-idf-weighted BoW vectors. Table 2 compares different dictionary sizes for sentence features. We have found that using 3,000 words is sufficient for good performance. For sentences, we have also experimented with a bigram feature, but did not observe any improvement.

For our weakly labeled datasets, Flickr1M and SBU1M, each image is associated with up to three document types: tags, titles, and descriptions (Figure 2(b)). Among other things, we are interested in investigating which of these types (or their combination) gives the best cues for transfer learning. Table 3 compares the BoW features constructed from each document type separately, as well as a single BoW feature computed from a concatenation of all of them. Surprisingly, titles achieve the highest performance despite having the shortest average length. Thus, while tags are more commonly used, titles might actually be the most informative source of annotations from Flickr. On the other hand, descriptions of the Flickr images are by far the longest, but their predictive power is the worst. In the end, combining all three document types achieves the best performance, so in the following experiments, we will use the combined text feature for Flickr1M and SBU1M.

Table 2. Recall@10 for sentence features with different dictionary sizes and different training set sizes. The embedding technique is normalized CCA (Section 3).

dictionary / training set size	5,000	15,000	25,000
1,000	19.03	23.30	26.53
3,000	19.77	27.03	31.13
5,000	20.20	27.40	31.07

Table 3. Recall@10 for different text cues on the weakly annotated datasets, together with the average number of words for each type of cue. We train normalized CCA (Section 3) on Flickr1M or SBU1M and directly apply it to the Flickr30K test set (the Flickr30K training set is not used). All text is represented using 3,000-dimensional tf-idf-weighted BoW vectors.

	Average length	Flickr1M→ Flickr30K	SBU1M → Flickr30K
Title	2.93	17.83	14.57
Tag	5.09	15.97	12.90
Description	23.41	16.67	14.57
Combined	31.03	**18.33**	**15.50**

3 Fully Supervised Image-Sentence Embedding

To provide a foundation for developing transfer embeddings, we first conduct a comparative evaluation of scalable methods for joint embedding of images and sentences in the fully supervised scenario, i.e., training on images paired with clean ground-truth sentences and no auxiliary data of any kind. The methods we compare include textbook baselines of ridge regression and canonical correlation analysis (CCA), as well as several state-of-the-art methods: CCA with normalization [13], Wsabie with stochastic gradient descent [31], and Wsabie with an adaptive learning rate [32, 33].

Assuming images and sentences are represented by vectors of dimension d and D, respectively, our training data consists of a set of images $X \in \mathbb{R}^{n \times D}$ and associated sentences $Y \in \mathbb{R}^{n \times d}$, for n image/sentence pairs. Each image x corresponds to a row in X, and each sentence y corresponds to a row in Y. The goal of all the embedding methods is to find matrices $W \in \mathbb{R}^{D \times c}$ and $U \in \mathbb{R}^{d \times c}$ to map images and sentences respectively as XW and YU to a common c-dimensional latent space in which image-to-sentence retrieval can be done by directly computing a distance or similarity function between pairs of projected image and sentence features.

Ridge Regression: Socher et al. [34] suggest mapping images to a sentence space for zero-shot learning by minimizing the sum of squared distances between the two views. This formulation is close to ridge regression, which we take as our first baseline. The projection matrix U for sentences is given by the top c PCA directions of Y. Then the mapping W from the image features X to the PCA-projected sentence features $\hat{Y} = YU$ is found by minimizing $\|\hat{Y} - XW\|_F^2 + \lambda\|W\|_F^2$. The optimal W is found in closed form as $(X^TX + \lambda I)^{-1}X^T\hat{Y}$. The regularization parameter λ is found on the validation set. Given a query image feature x, image-to-sentence retrieval is performed by projecting this feature as xW and finding the closest k sentences $\hat{y} = yU$ according to their Euclidean distance $\|xW - yU\|_2$.

Canonical Correlation Analysis (CCA) [35] aims to find projections W and U for the two views X and Y such that the normalized correlation between the projected data is maximized:

$$\max_{W,U} \text{ trace}(W^T X^T Y U) \quad \text{s.t.} \quad W^T X^T X W = I, \; U^T Y^T Y U = I. \quad (1)$$

The CCA objective function can be solved as a generalized eigenvalue problem, and entries of the top c leading eigenvectors are concatenated to form W and U. As with ridge regression, the distance function for image-to-sentence retrieval in the projected space is Euclidean.

Normalized Canonical Correlation Analysis: Recently, Gong et al. [13] reported significantly improved results for cross-modal retrieval by scaling the columns of the CCA projection matrices by a power of the corresponding eigenvalues, and using cosine similarity instead of Euclidean distance. Specifically, given the projection matrices W and U obtained by solving the CCA objective (eq. 1) with columns corresponding to c eigenvectors, and their eigenvalues $\lambda_1, \ldots, \lambda_c$, the similarity between image x and sentence y is measured as:

$$\frac{\left(xW \text{ diag}(\lambda_1^t, \ldots, \lambda_c^t)\right)\left(yU \text{ diag}(\lambda_1^t, \ldots, \lambda_c^t)\right)^T}{\|xW \text{ diag}(\lambda_1^t, \ldots, \lambda_c^t)\|_2 \|yU \text{ diag}(\lambda_1^t, \ldots, \lambda_c^t)\|_2}, \quad (2)$$

where t is the power to which the eigenvalues are taken (we use $t = 4$, the same value as in [13]). The cosine similarity is a natural choice for test data as it is exactly the quantity that the CCA objective function is maximizing for the training data. In this work, we would like to see whether this similarity also improves image-to-sentence retrieval, a task that was not considered in [13].

Wsabie with SGD: Weston et al. [31] have proposed the Wsabie approach for mapping images and tags to the same space using stochastic gradient descent. Several other works, e.g., [36], have also reported good results for this model. We adapt Wsabie to our problem as follows. Given the training set of n image/sentence pairs, we iterate through them in random order. For each pair of image feature x_i and positive sentence y_i, we keep sampling negative sentences (i.e., sentences not originally associated with this image) until we find a negative sentence y_j that violates the margin constraint:

$$x_i W U^T y_j^T > x_i W U^T y_i^T - 1$$

(here, we use correlation as the similarity function between images and sentences in the latent space). Assuming we have sampled s sentences until we find a violation, we estimate the rank of the positive sentence given the current model by $r_i = \lfloor \frac{n-1}{s} \rfloor$. Then we weight the amount of margin violation by the ranking

Table 4. Recall@10 for different image-sentence embedding methods

method / training set size	5,000	15,000	25,000
Ridge regression	10.63	11.40	12.77
CCA	8.76	12.37	15.43
CCA+Normalization	**19.77**	**27.03**	**31.13**
Wsabie with SGD	15.43	17.86	18.10
Wsabie with AdaGrad	18.20	24.33	26.60

loss $L(r) = \sum_l^r 1/l$ as in [31]. For a small rank (corresponding to a good model), the value of the loss is small, and for a large one, it is large. This leads to the following stochastic objective function:

$$\sum_{i=1}^n L(r_i) \max(0, 1 - x_i W U^T y_i^T + x_i W U^T y_j^T) \tag{3}$$

$$\text{s.t. } \|w_k\|_2^2 \le \alpha, \ \|u_k\|_2^2 \le \alpha, \ k = 1, \dots, c, \tag{4}$$

where w_k and u_k denote the columns of W and U. To minimize the objective function, whenever we find a violation, we take a gradient step to adjust the weights (entries of U and W) and project them to enforce the constraints (eq. 4). We initialize the weights using a random Gaussian with zero mean and unit variance, tune the learning rate by searching a grid of values [0.01, 0.05, 0.1, 0.2, 0.5, 1] on the validation set, and run the algorithm for 300 epochs. The parameter α is also tuned on the validation set using a grid of [50, 100, 150, 200]. At retrieval time, we use normalized correlation or cosine similarity between projected images and sentences: $(xWU^Ty^T)/(\|xW\|_2\|yU\|_2)$ (we have found it to work better than unnormalized correlation or Euclidean distance).

Wsabie with AdaGrad: We also minimize the loss of eq. (3) with AdaGrad [32, 33], a per-dimensional learning rate adjustment method that has been shown to improve performance of SGD. We tune the global learning rate over a grid of [0.2, 0.4, 0.6, 0.8, 1] on the validation set. Once again, we initialize the weights using a random Gaussian and train for 300 epochs. As with the regular Wsabie, we use cosine similarity for image-to-sentence retrieval.

Comparative Evaluation. Table 4 compares the performance of the above image-sentence embedding methods. For all methods, we set the dimension of the latent space to $c = 96$, which we have found to work the best in all cases. We can see that neither ridge regression nor vanilla CCA are competitive with the rest of the approaches. However, when combined with the normalized similarity function (eq. 2), CCA yields dramatically better performance, which is consistent with the findings of [13] on other cross-modal search tasks. As for Wsabie, the SGD version is better than CCA but much worse than normalized CCA, while Wsabie with AdaGrad is only 2-5% below normalized CCA. The advantage of normalized CCA over Wsabie with AdaGrad is probably due to two reasons. First, our experiments seem to indicate that cosine similarity (i.e., normalized correlation) works the best for image-to-sentence retrieval in the latent space, and the CCA objective function, unlike the Wsabie one, directly optimizes this measure. Furthermore, CCA finds the globally optimal solution in closed form.

By contrast, our current Wsabie objective (eq. 3) is already non-convex and SGD might not be able to obtain its global optimum (and reformulating the objective in terms of normalized correlation would only make matters worse).

In terms of computational requirements, normalized CCA is faster and easier to tune than Wsabie. CCA only requires solving a generalized eigenvalue problem involving the cross-covariance matrix. The complexity of this step scales roughly quadratically in the combined input feature dimension and is insensitive to training set size. In practice, it is very fast: on our four-core Xeon 3.33GHz machine with 64GB RAM, it takes 5 minutes for 5,000 training examples or 15 minutes for one million. On the other hand, training for Wsabie involves multiple passes over the data and validation for parameter tuning. For 5,000 examples, just one epoch of Wsabie already takes around 15 minutes on the same machine, and the time scales linearly with the training set size. Thus, we will use the normalized CCA approach as the basis for our transfer embedding model.

4   Transfer Embedding

In this section, we get to the main focus of our work: adding a large amount of weakly annotated images to a smaller amount of fully annotated ones to learn a better image-sentence embedding. In this setting, the weakly annotated data comes from the Flickr1M or SBU1M datasets (described in Section 2.1), and the fully annotated data comes from Flickr30K. Training is done on one of Flickr1M or SBU1M, plus the training subset of Flickr30K. Testing is done on the same test subset of Flickr30K as all the preceding experiments.

Fig. 3. A Flickr30K query image (left) with its nearest neighbors (according to CNN visual features) from Flickr30K (top) and Flickr1M (bottom). Associated sentences (resp. Flickr text) are shown beneath the retrieved images. Words relevant to the content of the query are manually highlighted in blue for visualization purposes.

4.1   Stacked Auxiliary Embedding

Our basic assumption is that images and annotations in Flickr1M share some similarity with the images and sentences in Flickr30K. To illustrate this, Figure 3 shows a sample image from Flickr30K together with its nearest neighbors in Flickr1M and Flickr30K. We can see that the Flickr1M neighbors have much more relevant content to the query than the Flickr30K ones. This suggests that Flickr1M can provide additional useful information for learning the embedding (although, as will be shown in Section 4.3, a naive attempt to transfer text from nearest neighbors via the method of [21] does not succeed).

We follow related work where embedded features learned from auxiliary sources are concatenated with the original features to form a stacked representation [37, 38]. As the first step, we use CCA to learn a joint c_1-dimensional embedding from our weakly annotated dataset, say Flickr1M. Let $A \in \mathbb{R}^{d \times c_1}$ and $B \in \mathbb{R}^{D \times c_1}$ denote the resulting projection matrices for visual and textual features, respectively, with each column already scaled by the t-th power of its eigenvalue. We then apply these projections to X and Y, the visual and textual feature vectors from the Flickr30K training set. Next, we nonlinearly transform the embedded features XA and YB using a mapping $\phi(\cdot)$ and concatenate the result with the original features to form the stacked representation:

$$\hat{X} = [X, \phi(XA)], \qquad \hat{Y} = [Y, \phi(YB)]. \tag{5}$$

The goal of $\phi(\cdot)$ is to raise the dimensionality of its input and help avoid degradation of the stacked model. We use the random Fourier feature (RFF) mapping [39]: $\phi(\boldsymbol{x}) = \sqrt{2}\cos(\boldsymbol{x}R + \boldsymbol{b})$, where R is drawn from Normal$(0, \sigma^2)$ (σ is set to the average distance to the 50th nearest neighbor) and $\boldsymbol{b}$ is drawn from Unif$[0, 1]$. For the CCA embedding, we set the output dimensionality to $c_1 = 128$, and then use RFF to raise the dimensionality to 3,000 (note that we have found the results to be insensitive to the exact choice of these values). We have also tested other nonlinear functions such as sigmoid or tanh, but found they do not work well for our case.

Given the augmented Flickr30K features $\hat{X}$ and $\hat{Y}$ as defined by eq. (5), we again learn a CCA model on top of them to obtain the projections $\hat{W}$ and $\hat{U}$ for images and sentences. The dimensionality of the final output space is 96 as in Section 3 (this value is much more sensitive than the $c_1 = 128$ of the first round of CCA and needs to be tuned on the validation set). At test time, we apply the entire sequence of learned transformations to the test images and sentences and use the cosine similarity of eq. (2) to perform image-to-sentence retrieval.

We dub our method **Stacked Auxiliary Embedding (SAE)**. It is inspired by stacked denoising autoencoders [40, 41] and the recent work on using stacked corrupted features for domain adaptation [38]. Like these approaches, we also use an embedding learned from noisy data to augment the feature representation. Unlike them, we are trying to use a large amount of noisily annotated images as auxiliary sources, instead of randomly added corruptions. Also, to our knowledge, we are the first to apply such techniques to a multi-view setting.

4.2   Baseline Models

We compare our proposed SAE model to a number of baselines.

Fully Supervised Only: We only use the clean annotated images and sentences from Flickr30K to learn the normalized CCA model. This corresponds to the setting of Section 3.

Weakly Supervised Only: We only use the images and noisy textual information (titles, tags, descriptions) from Flickr1M or SBU1M to learn the normalized CCA model, and no clean data from Flickr30K.

Joint Training: We treat the fully and weakly annotated training samples as being the same, merge them together into a single dataset, and train a normalized CCA embedding. That is, if X and Y denote the image and sentence features of the Flickr30K training set, and F and T denote the image and noisy text features of Flickr1M or SBU1M, we concatenate them vertically as $[X; \beta F]$ and $[Y; \beta T]$. The weight β controls the contribution of the weakly annotated data.

Text Feature: This method was proposed by Wang et al. [21] for using large noisily annotated image collections to improve image classification. To obtain the text feature for each image in the Flickr30K dataset, we find its k nearest neighbors in the weakly annotated dataset based on visual similarity of CNN features. Then we construct a single text feature for each Flickr30K image by averaging the BoW vectors (formed from combined titles, tags, and descriptions) of the retrieved images. We denote the new text feature as as $\hat{T}$. Next, we concatenate the original visual features and text features as $\hat{X} = [X, \hat{T}]$, and perform CCA on $\hat{X}$ and the clean sentences Y to obtain the image-sentence embedding. We have experimented with different values of k and did not find much variation in performance, so we report results for $k = 50$ in the following.

Stacked Training: We first learn a c_1-dimensional CCA embedding of images and text from Flickr1M or SBU1M, and embed the images and sentences from Flickr30K in that latent space. Then we learn another CCA embedding on top of these features. This corresponds to setting $\hat{X} = XA$ and $\hat{Y} = YB$ in eq. (5).

SAE (Linear): We apply our SAE framework, only without the nonlinear mapping. That is, we set $\hat{X} = [X, XA]$ and $\hat{Y} = [Y, YB]$ in eq. (5). Together with stacked training, this baseline examines whether every component of SAE is indeed necessary in order to obtain good performance.

4.3   Empirical Results

Table 5 compares SAE to all the baselines. We separately report results for using Flickr1M and SBU1M as the weakly annotated domains. The most important observation is that none of the methods except SAE can consistently exceed the fully supervised baseline – i.e., they are unable to benefit from the million weakly annotated images. For joint training, we have varied the weight β of the weakly annotated dataset (two of the values tried are shown in the table), but could only obtain an improvement for the smallest amount of fully annotated data (5,000 examples). For stacked training, we could not obtain any improvement

Table 5. Recall@10 for methods that train both on the weakly annotated images and Flickr30K. See Section 4 for description of methods and parameters.

method / training set size	Flickr1M			SBU1M		
	5,000	15,000	25,000	5,000	15,000	25,000
Fully Supervised Only	19.77	27.03	31.13	19.77	27.03	31.13
Weakly Supervised Only	18.33	18.33	18.33	15.10	15.10	15.10
Joint Training ($\beta = 0.01$)	20.80	25.90	28.47	20.87	25.87	28.47
Joint Training ($\beta = 1$)	20.63	23.50	25.37	20.07	24.10	25.63
Text Feature ($k = 50$)	19.67	27.00	30.97	19.63	27.03	30.93
Stacked Training ($c_1 =256$)	19.30	22.93	24.30	19.13	21.97	22.73
Stacked Training ($c_1 =1024$)	15.10	22.83	26.17	15.17	22.63	25.87
SAE (linear)	23.53	28.57	30.73	22.67	28.43	30.97
SAE (nonlinear)	**23.60**	**29.80**	**32.83**	**23.17**	**29.50**	**32.40**

Table 6. Recall@10 for training the SAE model on different numbers of weakly annotated images. The number of Flickr30K training images is 5,000.

Internet dataset size	Flickr1M	SBU1M
0 (fully annotated only)	19.77	19.77
1,000	20.93	20.20
10,000	20.23	20.53
100,000	21.90	22.60
1,000,000	**23.60**	**23.17**

by varying the dimensionality c_1 of the intermediate embedding learned from the weakly annotated dataset, or by nonlinearly transforming the output of the intermediate embedding. Text features also fail to make a difference over the fully supervised baseline.

By contrast, both the linear and the nonlinear versions of our proposed SAE method achieve a substantial improvement over the fully supervised model, with the nonlinear consistently being the best. Figure 4 shows the top-ranked sentences for a few sample images for the fully supervised baseline vs. SAE. Note that even the incorrect sentences retrieved by SAE tend to contain many keywords closely related to the content of the image. Interestingly, we get very similar results with SAE by using either Flickr1M or SBU1M. This is unexpected, as we have specifically downloaded Flickr1M to match the statistics of Flickr30K – indeed, by looking at the results of the weakly supervised baseline (second line of Table 5), we can see that directly training on Flickr1M does produce a better embedding for Flickr30K than training on SBU1M (18.33% vs. 15.10%). However, after applying SAE, the advantage of Flickr1M disappears, which suggests that a sufficiently complex statistical model is somehow able to extract roughly the same information from any sufficiently large-scale weakly annotated dataset.

Next, Tables 5 and 6 allow us to examine how the performance of SAE changes when we vary the amounts of fully and weakly supervised training data. By comparing the first and last lines of Table 5, it is easy to ascertain that as we increase the number of Flickr30K training examples, the benefit afforded by the Flickr1M or SBU1M examples diminishes. Nevertheless, even when we use the largest number of fully supervised training examples available (25,000), SAE still gives us around 1.3-1.5% improvement. It is important to note that Flickr30K is already the largest dataset of images and sentences available to date; increasing the amount of available fully annotated data by orders of magnitude is likely to be prohibitively expensive, whereas weakly annotated data can be downloaded in unlimited quantities essentially for free. To our knowledge, SAE is the first attempt at combining the two sources of annotation to improve image description. Our main contribution is to confirm that weakly labeled data can improve image-sentence embeddings *in principle* – and, as our extensive baseline comparisons show, getting any kind of improvement is not trivial. Future research should result in methods that can give bigger improvements.

Finally, it is interesting to compare the absolute accuracy of our image-to-sentence retrieval to other results reported in the literature. In fact, Hodosh et al. [7] have intended their dataset and protocol to constitute a standard benchmark that can be used to automatically compare different methods as "black

(a) Fully Supervised Only   **(b) SAE**

Fig. 4. Image-to-sentence retrieval examples for our fully supervised model vs. SAE. Sentences in red are the ground truth. In the other sentences, words relevant to the query image are manually highlighted in blue for visualization purposes.

boxes" to gauge the absolute state of the art. For their own KCCA approach, they report a Recall@10 of 30.3% on a 6K/1K training/test split of their original Flickr8K dataset. For the visual features, they use spatial pyramid kernels on color, texture, and SIFT features. While this representation is not exactly equivalent to our "standard" visual features (Table 1, top line), we expect it to have a similar expressive power. For the text features, they use a sophisticated trigram kernel with distributional and alignment-based similarities – a representation we could not easily accommodate in our linear CCA framework. For comparison, our fully supervised normalized CCA model trained and tested on the same 6K/1K split with the "standard" visual features has a Recall@10 of 30.1% – a remarkably similar number despite our system being totally unrelated to that of [7]. For the SAE approach with additional Flickr1M training data we get 38.2% – a significant improvement. With the CNN visual features, the numbers for our CCA and SAE models go up to 43.8% and 48.8%, respectively. In the future, we would like to experiment with encoding more complex linguistic features in our linear CCA framework to see what additional benefit we can obtain from improving that part of the representation (Hodosh et al. [7] have observed a big advantage for their trigram feature over a simple BoW).

5 Discussion

Our paper is the first to show that Internet images annotated with noisy titles, tags, and descriptions can provide useful information for improving joint embeddings of images and sentences for the application of retrieval-based image description, despite the fact that these sources of textual information have very different distributions and are collected in completely different ways. We have introduced a novel method named Stacked Auxiliary Embedding that convincingly outperforms a number of alternatives, and is, in fact, the only method we have considered that is able to obtain a non-trivial improvement over the baseline that uses fully supervised image-sentence data only.

Apart from this main contribution, we have obtained several other interesting findings along the way. In particular, we have shown that CNN features work much better than traditional visual features for our task, with very affordable dimensionality. This adds to the growing list of recent results in the vision community showing the effectiveness of pre-trained CNN activations as a generic representation for recognition. We have also found that Flickr image titles seem to be more discriminative than the more commonly used tags, despite being much shorter. Next, we have confirmed the somewhat surprising findings of [13] that a simple modification of the similarity function used for retrieval with CCA dramatically improves its accuracy, to the point of outperforming sophisticated state-of-the-art ranking models such as Wsabie. While we were able to improve Wsabie in turn with the addition of AdaGrad, normalized CCA still emerged as the more accurate and scalable method.

In the future, we would like to gain more insight into what makes SAE effective. While our baseline comparisons have empirically confirmed the necessity of every implementation choice (i.e., stacking, nonlinearly transforming the intermediate embedded features, and concatenating them with the original features), the resulting technique is frustratingly opaque.

Acknowledgments. Lazebnik's research was partially supported by NSF grants 1228082 and 1302438, the DARPA Computer Science Study Group, Xerox UAC, Microsoft Research, and the Sloan Foundation. Hockenmaier's research was partially supported by NSF grants 1053856 and 1205627. Gong was supported by the 2013 Google Ph.D. Fellowship in Machine Perception.

References

1. Farhadi, A., Hejrati, M., Sadeghi, M.A., Young, P., Rashtchian, C., Hockenmaier, J., Forsyth, D.: Every picture tells a story: Generating sentences from images. In: Daniilidis, K., Maragos, P., Paragios, N. (eds.) ECCV 2010, Part IV. LNCS, vol. 6314, pp. 15–29. Springer, Heidelberg (2010)
2. Kulkarni, G., Premraj, V., Dhar, S., Li, S., Choi, Y., Berg, A.C., Berg, T.L.: Baby talk: Understanding and generating image descriptions. In: CVPR (2011)
3. Li, S., Kulkarni, G., Berg, T.L., Berg, A.C., Choi, Y.: Composing simple image descriptions using web-scale n-grams. In: CoNLL (2011)
4. Mitchell, M., Han, X., Dodge, J., Mensch, A., Goyal, A., Berg, A., Yamaguchi, K., Berg, T., Stratos, K., Daumé, I.H.: Midge: Generating image descriptions from computer vision detections. In: EACL (2012)
5. Fidler, S., Sharma, A., Urtasun, R.: A sentence is worth a thousand pixels. In: CVPR (2013)
6. Yao, B.Z., Yang, X., Lin, L., Lee, M.W., Zhu, S.C.: I2T: Image parsing to text description. Proceedings of the IEEE 98 (2010)
7. Hodosh, M., Young, P., Hockenmaier, J.: Framing image description as a ranking task: Data, models and evaluation metrics. Journal of Artificial Intelligence Research (2013)
8. Ordonez, V., Kulkarni, G., Berg, T.L.: Im2Text: Describing images using 1 million captioned photographs. In: NIPS (2011)
9. Socher, R., Le, Q.V., Manning, C.D., Ng, A.Y.: Grounded compositional semantics for finding and describing images with sentences. In: ACL (2013)
10. Kuznetsova, P., Ordonez, V., Berg, A.C., Berg, T.L., Choi, Y.: Collective generation of natural image descriptions. In: ACL (2012)
11. Papineni, K., Roukos, S., Ward, T., Zhu, W.J.: Bleu: a method for automatic evaluation of machine translation. In: ACL, pp. 311–318 (2002)
12. Hardoon, D., Szedmak, S., Shawe-Taylor, J.: Canonical correlation analysis; an overview with application to learning methods. Neural Computation 16 (2004)
13. Gong, Y., Ke, Q., Isard, M., Lazebnik, S.: A multi-view embedding space for modeling internet images, tags, and their semantics. IJCV (2013)

14. Gong, B., Grauman, K., Sha, F.: Connecting the dots with landmarks: Discriminatively learning domain-invariant features for unsupervised domain adaptation. In: ICML, pp. 222–230 (2013)
15. Saenko, K., Kulis, B., Fritz, M., Darrell, T.: Adapting visual category models to new domains. In: Daniilidis, K., Maragos, P., Paragios, N. (eds.) ECCV 2010, Part IV. LNCS, vol. 6314, pp. 213–226. Springer, Heidelberg (2010)
16. Shrivastava, A., Malisiewicz, T., Gupta, A., Efros, A.A.: Data-driven visual similarity for cross-domain image matching. ACM SIGGRAPH ASIA 30(6) (2011)
17. Hays, J., Efros, A.A.: Scene completion using millions of photographs. ACM Transactions on Graphics (SIGGRAPH) 26(3) (2007)
18. Guillaumin, M., Ferrari, V.: Large-scale knowledge transfer for object localization in imageNet. In: CVPR, 3202–3209 (2012)
19. Guillaumin, M., Verbeek, J., Schmid, C.: Multimodal semi-supervised learning for image classification. In: CVPR, 902–909 (2010)
20. Quattoni, A., Collins, M., Darrell, T.: Learning visual representations using images with captions. In: CVPR (2007)
21. Wang, G., Hoiem, D., Forsyth, D.: Building text features for object image classification. In: CVPR (2009)
22. Young, P., Lai, A., Hodosh, M., Hockenmaier, J.: From image descriptions to visual denotations: New similarity metrics for semantic inference over event descriptions. In: TACL (2014)
23. Oliva, A., Torralba, A.: Modeling the shape of the scene: a holistic representation of the spatial envelope. IJCV (2001)
24. van de Sande, K.E.A., Gevers, T., Snoek, C.G.M.: Evaluating color descriptors for object and scene recognition. PAMI 32(9), 1582–1596 (2010)
25. Dalal, N., Triggs, B.: Histograms of oriented gradients for human detection. In: CVPR (2005)
26. Jégou, H., Douze, M., Schmid, C., Perez, P.: Aggregating local descriptors into a compact image representation. In: CVPR (2010)
27. Krizhevsky, A., Sutskever, I., Hinton, G.E.: ImageNet classification with deep convolutional neural networks. In: NIPS (2012)
28. Donahue, J., Jia, Y., Vinyals, O., Hoffman, J., Zhang, N., Tzeng, E., Darrell, T.: DeCAF: A deep convolutional activation feature for generic visual recognition. CoRR abs/1310.1531 (2013)
29. Deng, J., Dong, W., Socher, R., Li, L.J., Li, K., Fei-Fei, L.: ImageNet: A large-scale hierarchical image database. In: CVPR (2009)
30. Loper, E., Bird, S.: Nltk: The natural language toolkit. In: Proceedings of the ACL 2002 Workshop on Effective Tools and Methodologies for Teaching Natural Language Processing and Computational Linguistics, vol. 1 (2002)
31. Weston, J., Bengio, S., Usunier, N.: Wsabie: Scaling up to large vocabulary image annotation. In: IJCAI (2011)
32. Duchi, J., Hazan, E., Singer, Y.: Adaptive subgradient methods for online learning and stochastic optimization. JMLR (2011)
33. Zeiler, M.D.: ADADELTA: An adaptive learning rate method. arXiv preprint arXiv:1212.5701 (2012)
34. Socher, R., Ganjoo, M., Sridhar, H., Bastani, O., Manning, C.D., Ng, A.Y.: Zero-shot learning through cross-modal transfer. In: NIPS (2013)
35. Hotelling, H.: Relations between two sets of variables. Biometrika 28, 312–377 (1936)
36. Gordo, A., Rodrıguez-Serrano, J.A., Perronnin, F., Valveny, E.: Leveraging category-level labels for instance-level image retrieval. In: CVPR (2012)

37. Gopalan, R., Li, R., Chellappa, R.: Domain adaptation for object recognition: An unsupervised approach. In: ICCV (2011)

38. Xu, Z., Chen, M., Weinberger, K.Q., Sha, F.: From sBoW to dCoT: Marginalized encoders for text representation. In: CIKM (2011)

39. Rahimi, A., Recht, B.: Random features for large-scale kernel machines. In: NIPS (2007)

40. Vincent, P., Larochelle, H., Bengio, Y., Manzagol, P.A.: Extracting and composing robust features with denoising autoencoders. In: ICML, pp. 1096–1103 (2008)

41. Bengio, Y.: Learning deep architectures for AI. Foundations and Trends in Machine Learning 2(1), 1–127 (2009)

Strengthening the Effectiveness of Pedestrian Detection with Spatially Pooled Features

Sakrapee Paisitkriangkrai, Chunhua Shen*, and Anton van den Hengel

The University of Adelaide, Australia
chunhua.shen@adelaide.edu.au

Abstract. We propose a simple yet effective approach to the problem of pedestrian detection which outperforms the current state-of-the-art. Our new features are built on the basis of low-level visual features and spatial pooling. Incorporating spatial pooling improves the translational invariance and thus the robustness of the detection process. We then directly optimise the partial area under the ROC curve (pAUC) measure, which concentrates detection performance in the range of most practical importance. The combination of these factors leads to a pedestrian detector which outperforms all competitors on all of the standard benchmark datasets. We advance state-of-the-art results by lowering the average miss rate from 13% to 11% on the INRIA benchmark, 41% to 37% on the ETH benchmark, 51% to 42% on the TUD-Brussels benchmark and 36% to 29% on the Caltech-USA benchmark.

1 Introduction

Pedestrian detection is a challenging but an important problem due to its practical use in many computer vision applications such as video surveillance, robotics and human computer interaction. The problem is made difficult by the inevitable variation in target appearance, lighting and pose, and by occlusion. In a recent literature survey on pedestrian detection [1] the authors evaluated several pedestrian detectors and concluded that combining multiple features can significantly boost the performance of pedestrian detection.

Hand-crafted low-level visual features have been applied to several computer vision applications and shown promising results [2, 3, 4, 5, 6, 7]. Inspired by the recent success of spatial pooling on object recognition and pedestrian detection problems [8, 9, 10, 11], we propose to perform the spatial pooling operation to create the new feature type. Our new detector yields competitive results to the state-of-the-art on major benchmark data sets. A further improvement is achieved when we combine the new feature type and channel features from [12]. We confirm the observation made in [1]: carefully combining multiple features often improves detection performance. The new multiple channel detector outperforms the state-of-the-art by a large margin. Despite its simplicity, our

---

* Corresponding author.

D. Fleet et al. (Eds.): ECCV 2014, Part IV, LNCS 8692, pp. 546–561, 2014.
© Springer International Publishing Switzerland 2014

new approach outperforms all reported pedestrian detectors, including several complex detectors such as LatSVM [13] (a part-based approach which models unknown parts as latent variables), ConvNet [9] (deep hierarchical models) and DBN-Mut [14] (discriminative deep model with mutual visibility relationship).

Dollár et al. propose to compare different detectors using the miss rate performance at 1 false positive per image (FPPI) as a reference point [15]. This performance metric was later revised to the log-average miss rate in the range 0.01 to 1 FPPI as this better summarizes practical detection performance [1]. This performance metric is also similar to the average precision reported in text retrieval and PASCAL VOC challenge. As the performance is assessed over the partial range of false positives, the performance of the classifier outside this range is ignored as it is not of practical interest. Many proposed pedestrian detectors optimize the miss rate over the complete range of false positive rates, however, and can thus produce suboptimal results both in practice, and in terms of the log-average miss rate. In this paper, we address this problem by optimizing the log-average miss rate performance measure directly, and in a more principled manner. This is significant because it ensures that the detector achieves its best performance within the range of practical significance, rather than over the whole range of false positive rates, much of which would be of no practical value. The approach proposed ensures that the performance is optimized not under the full ROC curve but only within the range of practical interest, thus concentrating performance where it counts, and achieving significantly better results in practice.

Main Contributions. (1) We propose a novel approach to extract low-level visual features based on spatial pooling for the problem of pedestrian detection. Spatial pooling has been successfully applied in sparse coding for generic image classification problems. The new feature is simple yet outperforms the original covariance descriptor of [5] and LBP descriptor of [7]. (2) We discuss several factors that affect the performance of boosted decision tree classifiers for pedestrian detection. Our new design leads to a further improvement in log-average miss rate. (3) Empirical results show that the new approach, which combines our proposed features with existing features [12, 7] and optimizes the log-average miss rate measure, outperforms all previously reported pedestrian detection results and achieves state-of-the-art performance on INRIA, ETH, TUD-Brussels and Caltech-USA pedestrian detection benchmarks.

Related Work. Numerous pedestrian detectors have been proposed over the past decade along with newly created pedestrian detection benchmarks such as INRIA, ETH, TUD-Brussels, Caltech and Daimler Pedestrian data sets. We refer the reader to [1] for an excellent review on pedestrian detection frameworks and benchmark data sets. In this section, we briefly discuss several recent state-of-the-art pedestrian detectors that are not covered in [1].

Sermanet et al. train a pedestrian detector using a convolutional network model [9]. Instead of using hand designed features, they propose to use unsupervised sparse auto encoders to automatically learn features in a hierarchy. Experimental results show that their detector achieves competitive results on major benchmark data sets. Benenson et al. investigate different low-level aspects of pedestrian detection [16]. The authors show that by properly tuning low-level features, such as feature selection, pre-processing the raw image and classifier training, it is possible to reach state-of-the-art results on major benchmarks. From their paper, one key observation that significantly improves the detection performance is to apply image normalization to the test image before extracting features.

Lim *et al.* propose novel mid-level features, known as sketch tokens [17]. The feature is obtained from hand drawn sketches in natural images and captures local edge structure such as straight lines, corners, curves, parallel lines, *etc.* They combine their proposed features with channel features of [18] and train a boosted detector. By capturing both simple and complex edge structures, their detector achieves the state-of-the-art result on the INRIA test set. Park *et al.* propose new motion features for detecting pedestrians in a video sequence [8]. By factoring out camera motion and combining their proposed motion features with channel features [18], the new detector achieves a five-fold reduction in false positives over previous best results on the Caltech pedestrian benchmark.

2 Our Approach

Despite several important work on object detection, the most practical and successful pedestrian detector is still the sliding-window based method of Viola and Jones [6]. Their method consists of two main components: feature extraction and the AdaBoost classifier. For pedestrian detection, the most commonly used features are HOG [2] and HOG+LBP [7]. Dollár *et al.* propose Aggregated Channel Features (ACF) which combine gradient histogram (a variant of HOG), gradients and LUV [12]. ACF uses the same channel features as ChnFtrs [18], which is shown to outperform HOG [16, 18].

To train the classifier, the procedure known as bootstrapping is often applied, which harvests hard negative examples and re-trains the classifier. Bootstrapping can be repeated several times. It is shown in [19] that at least two bootstrapping iterations are required for the classifier to achieve good performance. In this paper, we build our detection framework based on [12]. We first propose the new feature type based on a modified low-level descriptor and spatial pooling. We then discuss how the miss rate performance measure can be further improved using structural SVM. Finally, we discuss our improvements to [12] in order to achieve state-of-the-art detection results on most benchmark data sets.

2.1 Spatially Pooled Features

Spatial pooling has been proven to be invariant to various image transformations and demonstrate better robustness to noise [20, 21, 22]. Several empirical results have indicated that a pooling operation can greatly improve the recognition performance. Pooling combines several visual descriptors obtained at nearby locations into some statistics that better summarize the features over some region of interest (pooling region). The new feature representation preserves visual information over a local neighbourhood while discarding irrelevant details and noises. Combining max-pooling with unsupervised feature learning methods have led to state-of-the-art image recognition performance on object recognition. Although these feature learning methods have shown promising results over hand-crafted features, computing these features from learned dictionaries is still a time-consuming process for many real-time applications. In this section, we further improve the performance of low-level features by adopting the pooling operator commonly applied in unsupervised feature learning and supervised convolutional neural networks. This simple operation can enhance the feature robustness to noise and image transformation. In the following section, we investigate two visual descriptors which have shown to complement HOG in pedestrian detection, namely covariance descriptors and LBP. It is important to point out here that our approach is not limited to these two features, but can be applied to any low-level visual features.

Covariance Matrix. A covariance matrix is positive semi-definite. It provides a measure of the relationship between two or more sets of variates. The diagonal entries of covariance matrices represent the variance of each feature and the non-diagonal entries represent the correlation between features. The variance measures the deviation of low-level features from the mean and provides information related to the distribution of low-level features. The correlation provides the relationship between multiple low-level features within the region. In this paper, we follow the feature representation as proposed in [5]. However, we introduce an additional edge orientation which considers the sign of intensity derivatives. Low-level features used in this paper are:

$$[x, \ y, \ |I_x|, \ |I_y|, \ |I_{xx}|, \ |I_{yy}|, \ M, \ O_1, \ O_2]$$

where x and y represent the pixel location, and I_x and I_{xx} are first and second intensity derivatives along the x-axis. The last three terms are the gradient magnitude ($M = \sqrt{I_x^2 + I_y^2}$), edge orientation as in [5] ($O_1 = \arctan(|I_x|/|I_y|)$) and an additional edge orientation O_2 in which,

$$O_2 = \begin{cases} \mathtt{atan2}(I_y, I_x) & \text{if } \mathtt{atan2}(I_y, I_x) > 0, \\ \mathtt{atan2}(I_y, I_x) + \pi & \text{otherwise.} \end{cases}$$

The orientation O_2 is mapped over the interval $[0, \pi]$. Although some O_1 features might be redundant after introducing O_2, these features would not deteriorate the performance as they are unlikely to be selected by the boosting learner. Our preliminary experiments show that using O_1 alone yields slightly worse performance than combining O_1 and O_2. With the defined mapping, the input image is mapped to a 9-dimensional feature image. The covariance descriptor of a region is a 9×9 matrix, and due to symmetry, only the upper triangular part is stored, which has only 45 different values.

LBP. Local Binary Pattern (LBP) is a texture descriptor that represents the binary code of each image patch into a feature histogram [23]. The standard version of LBP is formed by thresholding the 3×3-neighbourhood of each pixel with the centre pixel's value. All binary results are combined to form an 8-bit binary value (2^8 different labels). The histogram of these 256 different labels can be used as texture descriptor. The LBP descriptor has shown to achieve good performance in many texture classification [23]. In this work, we transform the input image from the RGB color space to LUV space and apply LBP to the luminance (L) channel. We adopt an extension of LBP, known as the uniform LBP, which can better filter out noises [7]. The uniform LBP is defined as the binary pattern that contains at most two bitwise transitions from 0 to 1 or vice versa.

Spatially Pooled Covariance. In this section, we improve the spatial invariance and robustness of the original covariance descriptor by applying the operator known as spatial pooling. There exist two common pooling strategies in the literature: average pooling and max-pooling. We use max-pooling as it has been shown to outperform average pooling in image classification [22, 20]. We divide the image window into *dense patches* (refer to Fig. 1). For each patch, covariance features are calculated over pixels within the patch. For better invariance to translation and deformation, we perform spatial pooling over a fixed-size spatial region (*pooling region*) and use the obtained results to represent covariance features in the pooling region. The pooling operator thus summarizes multiple covariance matrices within each pooling region into a single matrix which represents covariance information. We refer to the feature extracted from each pooling region as spatially pooled covariance (sp-Cov) feature. Note that extracting covariance features in each patch can be computed efficiently using the integral image trick [24]. Our sp-Cov differs from covariance features in [5] in the following aspects:

1. We apply spatial pooling to a set of covariance descriptors in the pooling region. To achieve this, we ignore the geometry of covariance matrix and stack the upper triangular part of the covariance matrix into a vector such that pooling is carried out on the vector space. For simplicity, we carry out pooling over a square image region of fixed resolution. Considering pooling over a set of arbitrary rectangular regions as in [25] is likely to further improve the performance of our features.

2. Instead of normalizing the covariance descriptor of each patch based on the whole detection window [5], we calculate the correlation coefficient within each patch. The correlation coefficient returns the value in the range $[-1, 1]$. As each patch is now independent, the feature extraction can be done in parallel on the GPU.

Implementation. We extract sp-Cov using multi-scale patches with the following sizes: 8×8, 16×16 and 32×32 pixels. Each scale will generate a different set of visual descriptors. Multi-scale patches have also been used in [26]. In this paper, the use of multi-scale patches is important as it expands the richness of our feature representations and enables us to capture human body parts at different scales. In our experiments, we set the patch spacing stride (step-size) to be 1 pixel. The pooling region is set to be 4×4 pixels and the pooling spacing stride is set to 4 pixels in our experiments.

Spatially Pooled LBP. Similar to sp-Cov, we divide the image window into small patches and extract LBP over pixels within the patch. The histogram,

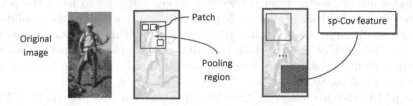

Fig. 1. Architecture of our pooled features. In this example, sp-Cov are extracted from each fixed sized pooling region.

which represents the frequency of each pattern occurring, is computed over the patch. For better invariance to translation, we perform spatial pooling over a pooling region and use the obtained results to represent the LBP histogram in the pooling region. We refer to the new feature as spatially pooled LBP (sp-LBP) feature.

Implementation. We apply the LBP operator on the 3×3-neighbourhood at each pixel. The LBP histogram is extracted from a patch size of 4×4 pixels. We extract the 58-dimension LBP histogram using a C-MEX implementation of [27]. For sp-LBP, the patch spacing stride, the pooling region and the pooling spacing stride are set to 1 pixel, 8×8 pixels and 4 pixels, respectively. We also experiment with combining the LPB histogram extracted from multi-scale patches but only observe a slight improvement in detection performance at a much higher feature extraction time. Instead of extracting LBP histograms from multi-scale patches, we combine sp-LBP and LBP as channel features.

Discussion. Although we make use of spatial pooling, our approach differs significantly from the unsupervised feature learning pipeline, which has been successfully applied to image classification problem [26, 11]. Instead of pooling encoded features over a pre-trained dictionary, we compute sp-Cov and sp-LBP by performing pooling directly on covariance and LBP features extracted from local patches. In other words, our proposed approach removes the dictionary learning and feature encoding from the conventional unsupervised feature learning [26, 11]. The advantage of our approach over conventional feature learning is that our features have much less dimensions than the size of visual words often used in generic image classification [11]. Using too few visual words can significantly degrade the recognition performance as reported in [21] and using too many visual words would lead to very high-dimensional features and thus make the classifier training become computationally infeasible.

2.2 Optimizing the Partial Area under ROC Curve

As the performance of the detector is usually measured using the log-average miss rate, we optimize the pAUC (the partial AUC) between any two given false positive rates $[\alpha, \beta]$, similar to the work of [28]. Unlike [28], in which weak learners are selected based on the pAUC criterion, we use AdaBoost to select weak learners as it is more efficient. In order to achieve the best performance, we build a feature vector from the weak learners' output and learn the pAUC classifier in the final stage. For each predicted positive patch, the confidence score is re-calibrated based on this pAUC classifier. This post-learning step is similar to the work of [29], in which the authors learn the asymmetric classifier from the output of AdaBoost's weak learners to handle the node learning goal in the cascade framework.

The pAUC risk for a scoring function $f(\cdot)$ between two pre-specified FPR $[\alpha, \beta]$ can be defined [30] as :

$$\hat{R}_\zeta(f) = \sum_{i=1}^{m}\sum_{j=j_\alpha+1}^{j_\beta} \mathbf{1}(f(\boldsymbol{x}_i^+) < f(\boldsymbol{x}_{(j)_{f|\zeta}}^-)). \tag{1}$$

Here $\boldsymbol{x}_i^+$ denotes the i-th positive training instance and $\boldsymbol{x}_{(j)_{f|\zeta}}^-$ denotes the j-th negative training instance sorted by f in the set $\zeta \in \mathcal{Z}_\beta$. Both $\boldsymbol{x}_i^+$ and $\boldsymbol{x}_{(j)_{f|\zeta}}^-$ represent the output vector of weak classifiers learned from AdaBoost. Clearly (1) is minimal when all positive samples, $\{\boldsymbol{x}_i^+\}_{i=1}^m$, are ranked above $\{\boldsymbol{x}_{(j)_{f|\zeta}}^-\}_{j=j_\alpha+1}^{j_\beta}$, which represent negative samples in our prescribed false positive range $[\alpha, \beta]$ (in this case, the log-average miss rate would be zero). The structural SVM framework can be adopted to optimize the pAUC risk by considering a classification problem of all $m \times j_\beta$ pairs of positive and negative samples. In our experiments, the pAUC classifier is trained once at the final bootstrapping iteration and most of the computation time is spent in extracting features and bootstrapping hard negative samples. See the supplementary material for more details on the structural SVM problem.

2.3   Design Space

In this section, we further investigate the experimental design of the ACF detector [12]. For experiments on shrinkage and spatial pooling, we use the proposed sp-Cov as channel features. For experiments on the depth of decision trees, we use channel features of [12]. All experiments are carried out using AdaBoost with the shrinkage parameter of 0.1 as a strong classifier and level-3 decision trees as weak classifiers (if not specified otherwise). We use three bootstrapping stages and the final model consists of 2048 weak classifiers with soft cascade. We heuristically set the soft cascade's reject threshold to be -10 at every node. We trained all detectors using the INRIA training set and evaluated the detector on INRIA, ETH and TUD-Brussels benchmark data sets.

Shrinkage. Hastie *et al.* show that the accuracy of boosting can be further improved by applying a weighting coefficient known as shrinkage [31]. The explanation given in [32] is that a shrinkage version of boosting simply converges to the ℓ_1 regularized solution. It can also be viewed as another form of regularization for boosting. At each iteration, the weak learner's coefficient is updated by

$$F_t(\boldsymbol{x}) = F_{t-1}(\boldsymbol{x}) + \nu \cdot \omega_t h_t(\boldsymbol{x}) \tag{2}$$

Here $h_t(\boldsymbol{x})$ is AdaBoost's weak learner at the t-th iteration and ω_t is the weak learner's coefficient at the t-th iteration. $\nu \in (0, 1]$ can be viewed as a learning

Table 1. Log-average miss rate when varying shrinkage parameters. Shrinkage can further improve the final detection performance. † The model consists of 4096 weak classifiers while other models consist of 2048 weak classifiers.

Shrinkage	INRIA	ETH	TUD-Br.	Avg.
None	14.4%	40.8%	48.7%	34.6%
$\nu = 0.5$	12.5%	43.7%	50.3%	35.5%
$\nu = 0.2$	11.6%	41.4%	50.4%	34.4%
$\nu = 0.1$	12.8%	42.0%	47.8%	**34.2%**
$\nu = 0.05$	14.0%	43.1%	51.4%	36.2%
$\nu = 0.05^\dagger$	12.8%	42.6%	48.6%	34.7%

Table 2. Log-average miss rate of our features with and without applying spatial pooling

	Covariance			LBP		
	INRIA	ETH	TUD-Brussels	INRIA	ETH	TUD-Brussels
without pooling	14.2%	42.7%	48.6%	25.8%	47.8%	**55.5%**
with pooling	**12.8%**	**42.0%**	**47.8%**	**23.7%**	**46.2%**	55.8%

rate parameter. The smaller the value of ν, the higher is the overall accuracy as long as the number of iterations is large enough. The authors of [32] report that shrinkage often produces better generalization performance compared to linear search algorithms.

We compare four different shrinkage parameters from {0.05, 0.1, 0.2, 0.5} with the conventional AdaBoost. When applying shrinkage, we lower the soft cascade's reject threshold by a factor of ν as weak learners' coefficients have been diminished by a factor of ν. The log-average miss rate of different detectors is shown in Table 1. We observe that applying a small amount of shrinkage ($\nu \leq 0.2$) often improves the detection performance. From Table 1, setting the shrinkage value to be too small ($\nu = 0.05$) without increasing the number of weak classifiers can hurt the performance as the number of boosting iterations is not large enough for the boosting to converge. For the rest of our experiments, we set the shrinkage parameter to be 0.1 as it gives a better trade-off between the performance and the number of weak classifiers.

Spatial Pooling. In this section, we compare the performance of the proposed feature with and without spatial pooling. For sp-Cov and sp-LBP without pooling, we extract both low-level visual features with the patch spacing stride of 4 pixels and no pooling is performed. Using these low-level features and LUV colour features, we trained four detectors using the INRIA training set. Log-average miss rates of both features are shown in Table 2. We observe that it is beneficial to apply spatial pooling as it increases the robustness of the features against small deformations and translations. We observe a reduction in miss rate by more than one percent on the INRIA test set. Since we did not combine sp-LBP with HOG as in [7], sp-LBP performs slightly worse than sp-Cov.

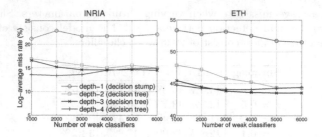

Fig. 2. Log-average miss rates of different tree depths on INRIA (left) and ETH (right) benchmark data sets

Depth of Decision Trees. The authors of [18] and [16] report that the depth-2 decision tree produces the best performance in their experiments. However, we observe that the depth-3 decision tree offers better generalization performance. To conduct our experiments, we trained 4 different pedestrian detectors with decision trees of depth 1 (decision stump) to 4 (containing 15 stumps). Our experiments are based on the ACF detector of [12] which combines gradient histogram (O), gradient (M) and LUV features. The ACF detector linearly quantizes feature values into 256 bins to speed up the conventional decision tree training [33]. We trained the pedestrian detector using the INRIA training set and evaluated the detector on both INRIA and ETH benchmark data sets. Fig. 2 plots the log-average miss rate on the vertical axis and the number of weak classifiers on the horizontal axis. We observe that the pedestrian detection performance improves as we increase the depth of decision trees. Similar to [16], we observe that using decision stumps as weak learners can lead to significant underfitting, *i.e.*, the weak learner can not separate pedestrian patches from non-pedestrian patches. On the other hands, setting the tree depth to be larger than two can lead to a performance improvement, especially on the ETH data set. For the rest of our experiments, we set the depth of decision trees to be three as it achieves good generalization performance and is faster to train than the depth-4 decision tree.

3   Experiments

We train two detectors: one using the INRIA training set and one using the Caltech-USA training set. For INRIA, each pedestrian training sample is scaled to a resolution of 64×128 pixels. Negative patches are collected from INRIA background images. We follow the work of [12] to train the boosted pedestrian detector. Each detector is trained using three bootstrapping stages and consists of 2048 weak classifiers. The detector trained on the INRIA training set is evaluated on all benchmark data sets except the Caltech-USA test set[1]. On both

---

[1] Park et al. [8] report a performance improvement on the Caltech-USA when they retrain the detector using the Caltech-USA training set. We follow the setup discussed in [8].

ETH and TUD-Brussels data sets, we apply the automatic colour equalization algorithms (ACE) [34] before we extract channel features [16]. We upscale both ETH and TUD-Brussels test images to 1280×960 pixels. For Caltech-USA, the resolution of the pedestrian model is set to 32×64 pixels. We exclude occluded pedestrians from the Caltech training set [8]. Negative patches are collected from the Caltech-USA training set with pedestrians cropped out. To obtain final detection results, greedy non-maxima suppression is applied with the default parameter as in Addendum of [18]. We use the log-average miss rate to summarize the detection performance. For the rest of our experiments, we evaluate our pedestrian detectors on the reasonable subset (pedestrians are at least 50 pixels in height and at least 65% visible).

3.1   Improved Covariance Descriptor

In this experiment, we evaluate the performance of the proposed sp-Cov. sp-Cov consists of 9 low-level image statistics. We exclude the mean and variance of two image statistics (pixel locations at x and y co-ordinates) since they do not capture discriminative information. We also exclude the correlation coefficient between pixel locations at x and y co-ordinates. Hence there is a total of 136 channels (7 low-level image statistics $+ 3 \cdot 7$ variances $+ 3 \cdot 35$ correlation coefficients $+ 3$ LUV color channels)[2]. It is important to note here that our features and weak classifiers are different from those in [5]. There the authors calculate the covariance distance in the Riemannian manifold. As eigen-decomposition is performed, the approach of [5] is computationally expensive. We speed up the weak learner training by proposing our modified covariance features and train the weak learner using the decision tree. The new weak learner is not only simpler than [5] but also highly effective.

We compare our detector with the original covariance descriptor [5] in Fig. 3. We plot HOG [2] and HOG+LBP [7] as the baseline. Similar to the result reported in [16], where the authors show that HOG+BOOSTING reduces the average miss-rate over HOG+SVM by more than 30%, we observe that applying our sp-Cov features as the channel features significantly improves the detection performance over the original covariance detector (a reduction of more than 5% miss rate at 10^{-4} false positives per window). More experiments on sp-Cov with different subset of low-level features, multi-scale patches and spatial pooling parameters can be found in the supplementary.

Next we compare the proposed sp-Cov with ACF features (M+O+LUV) [12]. Since ACF uses fewer channels than sp-Cov, for a fair comparison, we increase ACF's discriminative power by combining ACF features with LBP[3] (M+O+LUV+LBP). The results are reported in Table 3. We observe that sp-Cov yields competitive results to M+O+LUV+LBP. From the table, sp-Cov performs better on the INRIA test set, worse on the ETH test set and on par with M+O+LUV+LBP on

---

[2] Note here that we extract covariance features at 3 different scales.

[3] In our implementation, we use an extension of LBP, known as the uniform LBP, which can better filter out noises [7]. Each LBP bin corresponds to each channel.

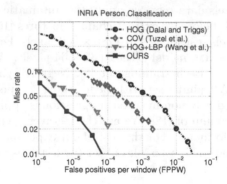

Fig. 3. ROC curves of our sp-Cov features and the conventional covariance detector [5] on the INRIA test image

Table 3. Log-average miss rates of various feature combinations

	# channels	INRIA	ETH	TUD-Br.
M+O+LUV+LBP	68	14.5%	39.9%	47.0%
sp-Cov+LUV	136	12.8%	42.0%	47.8%
sp-Cov+M+O+LUV	143	**11.2%**	39.4%	46.7%
sp-Cov+sp-LBP+M+O+LUV	259	**11.2%**	**38.0%**	**42.5%**

the TUD-Brussels test set. We observe that the best performance is achieved by combining sp-Cov and sp-LBP with M+O+LUV.

3.2 Improving Average Miss Rate with pAUC^{struct}

In this experiment, we evaluate the effect of re-calibrating the final confidence score with pAUC^{struct}. Instead of using the weighted responses from AdaBoost, we re-rank the confidence score of predicted pedestrian patches using a scoring function of pAUC^{struct}. The performance is calculated by varying the threshold value in the false positive range of $[0.01, 1]$ FPPI. Since the partial area under the ROC curve is determine on a logarithmic scale [1], it is non-trivial to determine the best pAUC^{struct} parameters α and β which maximize the detection rate between 0.01 and 1 false positive per image. In our experiment, we heuristically set α to be 0 and perform a cross-validation to find the best pAUC^{struct} regularization parameter C (see Supplementary) and the false positive rate β. In this section, we first train the baseline pedestrian detector as discussed in Section 2.3. The baseline detector achieves the log-average miss rate of 21.3%. Next we perform the post-learning step by re-ranking the confidence score of positive and negative samples based on the pAUC criterion. Using cross-validation on the INRIA training set, the post-learning step improves the log-average miss rate by 0.6%. Fig. 4 plots the log average miss rate with respect to the pAUC^{struct} regularization parameter C and the false positive rate β. From the figure, the following parameters ($C = 2^4$ and $\beta = 0.7$) perform best with a miss rate of 20.7%.

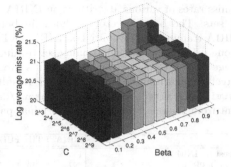

Fig. 4. Cross-validation results (log-average miss rate) as the pAUC^{struct} regularization parameter C and the false positive rate β change. Without pAUC^{struct}, the detector achieves the miss rate of 21.3%. The detector with post-tuning ($C = 2^4$ and $\beta = 0.7$) performs best with a miss rate of 20.7% (an improvement of 0.6%).

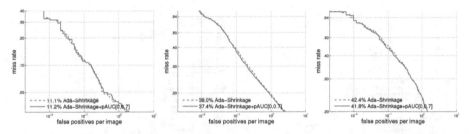

Fig. 5. Detection performance of our detectors with pAUC^{struct} post-tuning on INRIA (*left*), ETH (*middle*) and TUD-Brussels (*right*) benchmark data sets

In the next experiment, we evaluate the detector with the post-learning step on INRIA, ETH and TUD-Brussels benchmark data sets. ROC curves along with their log-average miss rates between $[0.01, 1]$ FPPI are shown in Fig. 5. Based on our results, applying pAUC^{struct} improves the log-average miss rate of the original detector on both ETH and TUD-Brussels benchmark data sets by 0.6%. However we do not observe an improvement on the INRIA test set. Our conjecture is that the INRIA test set consists of high-resolution human in a standing position which might be easier to detect than those appeared in ETH and TUD-Brussels data sets. No improvement in detection performance is observed on the INRIA test set as compared to the detection results on ETH and TUD-Brussels data sets.

3.3 Comparison with State-of-the-Art Results

In the next experiment, we compare our combined features with state-of-the-art detectors. Recently Lim et al. [17] propose sketch tokens (ST) feature which achieves the state-of-the-art result on the INRIA test set (a miss rate of 13.3%). Our new detector outperforms ST by achieving a miss rate of 11.2%. Our best performance is achieved when we apply pAUC^{struct} to the combined features (a

Table 4. Log-average miss rates of various algorithms on INRIA, ETH, TUD-Brussels and Caltech-USA test sets. The best detector is shown in boldface. We train two detectors: one using INRIA training set (evaluated on INRIA, ETH and TUD-Brussels test sets) and another one using Caltech-USA training set (evaluated on Caltech-USA test set). The log-average miss rate of our detection results are calculated using the Caltech pedestrian detection benchmark version 3.2.0. † Results reported here are taken from http://www.vision.caltech.edu/Image_Datasets/CaltechPedestrians/ and are slightly different from the one reported in the original paper.

Approach	INRIA	ETH	TUD-Brussels	Caltech-USA
Sketch tokens [17] (Prev. best on INRIA†)	13.3%	N/A	N/A	N/A
DBN-Mut [14] (Prev. best on ETH†)	N/A	41.1%	N/A	48.2%
MultiFtr+Motion+2Ped [35] (Prev. best on TUD-Brussels)	N/A	N/A	50.5%	N/A
SDtSVM [8] (Prev. best on Caltech-USA)	N/A	N/A	N/A	36.0%
Roerei [16] (2-nd best on INRIA† & ETH†)	13.5%	43.5%	64.0%	48.4%
Ours (sp-Cov+sp-LBP+M+O+LUV)	11.1%	38.0%	42.4%	29.4%
Ours (sp-Cov+sp-LBP+M+O+LUV + pAUC^{struct})	11.2%	**37.4%**	**41.8%**	**29.2%**

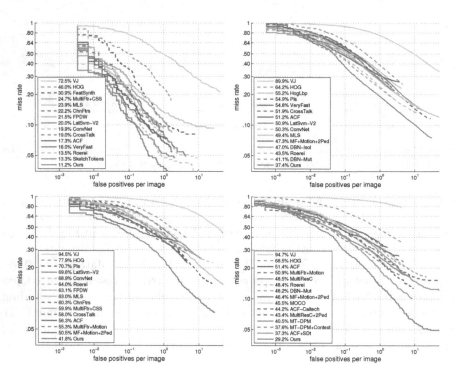

Fig. 6. ROC curves of our proposed approach on INRIA, ETH, TUD-Brussels and Caltech-USA pedestrian detection benchmarks

miss rate of 11.1%). As shown in Table 4, the combined features + pAUC^{struct} outperform all previous best results on four major pedestrian detection benchmarks. Fig. 6 compares our best results (the last row in Table 4) with other state-of-the-art methods. Fig. 7 shows the spatial distribution of regions selected

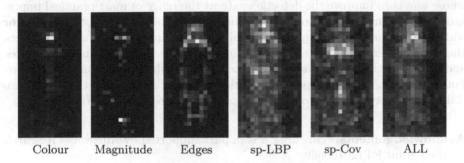

| Colour | Magnitude | Edges | sp-LBP | sp-Cov | ALL |

Fig. 7. Spatial distribution of selected regions based on their feature types. White pixels indicate that a large number of features are selected in that area. Often selected regions correspond to human contour and human body.

by different feature types. White pixels indicate that a large number of features are selected in that region. From the figure, most selected regions typically contain human contours (especially the head and shoulders). Colour features are selected around the human face (skin colour) while edge features are mainly selected around human contours (head, shoulders and feet). sp-LBP features are selected near human head and human hips while sp-Cov features are selected around human chest and regions between two human legs.

It is important to point out that our significant improvement comes at the cost of increased computational complexity. We briefly list these additional computational costs compared to [12] here. (i) Additional CPU time to extract two additional features: sp-Cov and sp-LBP. (ii) The time taken to re-compute the confidence score of positive patches. To be more specific, we additionally calculate the dot product of the weak learners' output and pAUC^{struct} variables (new coefficients for weak learners), $i.e.$, $\boldsymbol{w}^\top \boldsymbol{h}$ where $\boldsymbol{w}$ is pAUC^{struct} variables, $\boldsymbol{h} = [h_1(\cdot), \cdots, h_t(\cdot)]$ and $h_k(\cdot)$ is the k-th weak learner. (iii) Additional CPU time to perform the global normalization (ACE). In our experiment, applying the colour normalization on a 640×480 pixels image takes approximately 0.3 seconds. This fast result is already based on an approximation of ACE [36], which estimates a slope function with an odd polynomial approximation and uses the DCT transform to speed up the convolutions. Using a single core Intel Xeon CPU 2.70GHz processor, our detector currently operates at approximately 0.126 frames per second (without global normalization) and 0.119 frames per second (with global normalization) on the Caltech data sets (detecting pedestrians larger than 50 pixels).

4   Conclusion

In this paper we propose a simple yet effective feature extraction method based on spatially pooled low-level visual features. To achieve optimal log-average miss rate performance measure, we learn another set of weak learners' coefficients whose aim is to improve the detection rate at the range of most practical importance. The combination of our approaches contributes to a pedestrian detector which outperforms all competitors on all of the standard benchmark datasets. Based on our experiments, we observe that the choice of discriminative features and implementation details are crucial to achieve the best detection performance. Future work includes incorporating motion information through the use of spatial and temporal pooling to further improve the detection performance.

Acknowledgements. This work was in part supported by Australian Research Council grant FT120100969.

References

[1] Dollár, P., Wojek, C., Schiele, B., Perona, P.: Pedestrian detection: An evaluation of the state of the art. IEEE Trans. Pattern Anal. Mach. Intell. 34, 743–761 (2012)

[2] Dalal, N., Triggs, B.: Histograms of oriented gradients for human detection. In: Proc. IEEE Conf. Comp. Vis. Patt. Recogn., vol. 1 (2005)

[3] Shen, C., Wang, P., Paisitkriangkrai, S., van den Hengel, A.: Training effective node classifiers for cascade classification. Int. J. Comp. Vis. 103 (2013)

[4] Paisitkriangkrai, S., Shen, C., Zhang, J.: Fast pedestrian detection using a cascade of boosted covariance features. IEEE Trans. Circuits Syst. Video Technol. 18, 1140–1151 (2008)

[5] Tuzel, O., Porikli, F., Meer, P.: Pedestrian detection via classification on Riemannian manifolds. IEEE Trans. Pattern Anal. Mach. Intell. 30, 1713–1727 (2008)

[6] Viola, P., Jones, M.J.: Robust real-time face detection. Int. J. Comp. Vis. 57, 137–154 (2004)

[7] Wang, X., Han, T.X., Yan, S.: An HOG-LBP human detector with partial occlusion handling. In: Proc. IEEE Int. Conf. Comp. (2009)

[8] Park, D., Zitnick, C.L., Ramanan, D., Dollár, P.: Exploring weak stabilization for motion feature extraction. In: Proc. IEEE Conf. Comp. Vis. Patt. Recogn. (2013)

[9] Sermanet, P., Kavukcuoglu, K., Chintala, S., LeCun, Y.: Pedestrian detection with unsupervised multi-stage feature learning. In: Proc. IEEE Conf. Comp. Vis. Patt. Recogn. (2013)

[10] Wang, X., Yang, M., Zhu, S., Lin, Y.: Regionlets for generic object detection. In: Proc. IEEE Int. Conf. Comp. Vis. (2013)

[11] Yang, J., Yu, K., Gong, Y., Huang, T.: Linear spatial pyramid matching using sparse coding for image classification. In: Proc. IEEE Conf. Comp. Vis. Patt. Recogn. (2009)

[12] Dollár, P., Appel, R., Belongie, S., Perona, P.: Fast feature pyramids for object detection. IEEE Trans. Pattern Anal. Mach. Intell. 1 (2014)

[13] Felzenszwalb, P., Girshick, R., McAllester, D., Ramanan, D.: Object detection with discriminatively trained part based models. IEEE Trans. Pattern Anal. Mach. Intell. 32, 1627–1645 (2010)

[14] Ouyang, W., Zeng, X., Wang, X.: Modeling mutual visibility relationship with a deep model in pedestrian detection. In: Proc. IEEE Conf. Comp. Vis. Patt. Recogn. (2013)

[15] Dollár, P., Wojek, C., Schiele, B., Perona, P.: Pedestrian detection: A benchmark. In: Proc. IEEE Conf. Comp. Vis. Patt. Recogn. (2009)

[16] Benenson, R., Mathias, M., Tuytelaars, T., Gool, L.V.: Seeking the strongest rigid detector. In: Proc. IEEE Conf. Comp. Vis. Patt. Recogn. (2013)

[17] Lim, J.J., Zitnick, C.L., Dollár, P.: Sketch Tokens: A learned mid-level representation for contour and object detection. In: Proc. IEEE Conf. Comp. Vis. Patt. Recogn. (2013)

[18] Dollár, P., Tu, Z., Perona, P., Belongie, S.: Integral channel features. In: Proc. of British Mach. Vis. Conf. (2009)

[19] Walk, S., Majer, N., Schindler, K., Schiele, B.: New features and insights for pedestrian detection. In: Proc. IEEE Conf. Comp. Vis. Patt. Recogn., San Francisco, US (2010)

[20] Boureau, Y., Roux, N.L., Bach, F., Ponce, J., LeCun, Y.: Ask the locals: multi-way local pooling for image recognition. In: Proc. IEEE Int. Conf. Comp. Vis. (2011)

[21] Chatfield, K., Lempitsky, V., Vedaldi, A., Zisserman, A.: The devil is in the details: an evaluation of recent feature encoding methods. In: Proc. of British Mach. Vis. Conf. (2011)

[22] Coates, A., Ng, A.: The importance of encoding versus training with sparse coding and vector quantization. In: Proc. Int. Conf. Mach. Learn. (2011)

[23] Ojala, T., Pietikainen, M., Maenpaa, T.: Multiresolution gray-scale and rotation invariant texture classification with local binary patterns. IEEE Trans. Pattern Anal. Mach. Intell. 24, 971–987 (2002)

[24] Tuzel, O., Porikli, F., Meer, P.: Region covariance: A fast descriptor for detection and classification. In: Leonardis, A., Bischof, H., Pinz, A. (eds.) ECCV 2006. Part II. LNCS, vol. 3952, pp. 589–600. Springer, Heidelberg (2006)

[25] Jia, Y., Huang, C., Darrell, T.: Beyond spatial pyramids: Receptive field learning for pooled image features. In: Proc. IEEE Conf. Comp. Vis. Patt. Recogn. (2012)

[26] Bo, L., Ren, X., Fox, D.: Multipath sparse coding using hierarchical matching pursuit. In: Proc. IEEE Conf. Comp. Vis. Patt. Recogn. (2013)

[27] Vedaldi, A., Fulkerson, B.: VLFeat: An open and portable library of computer vision algorithms. In: Int. Conf. on Multimedia (2010)

[28] Paisitkriangkrai, S., Shen, C., van den Hengel, A.: Efficient pedestrian detection by directly optimizing the partial area under the roc curve. In: Proc. IEEE Int. Conf. Comp. Vis. (2013)

[29] Wu, J., Brubaker, S.C., Mullin, M.D., Rehg, J.M.: Fast asymmetric learning for cascade face detection. IEEE Trans. Pattern Anal. Mach. Intell. 30, 369–382 (2008)

[30] Narasimhan, H., Agarwal, S.: SVM_{pAUC}^{tight}: A new support vector method for optimizing partial auc based on a tight convex upper bound. In: ACM Int. Conf. on Knowl. Disc. and Data Mining (2013)

[31] Hastie, T., Tibshirani, R., Friedman, J.: The Elements of Statistical Learning: Prediction, Inference and Data Mining. Springer (2009)

[32] Friedman, J., Hastie, T., Tibshirani, R.: Additive logistic regression: A statistical view of boosting. Ann. Stat. 28, 337–407 (2000)

[33] Appel, R., Fuchs, T., Dollár, P., Perona, P.: Quickly boosting decision a trees-pruning underachieving features early. In: Proc. Int. Conf. Mach. Learn. (2013)

[34] Rizzi, A., Gatta, C., Marini, D.: A new algorithm for unsupervised global and local color correction. Patt. Recogn. 24, 1663–1677 (2003)

[35] Ouyang, W., Wang, X.: Single-pedestrian detection aided by multi-pedestrian detection. In: Proc. IEEE Conf. Comp. Vis. Patt. Recogn. (2013)

[36] Getreuer, P.: Automatic color enhancement (ACE) and its fast implementation. Image Proc. On Line 2012 (2012)

Selecting Influential Examples: Active Learning with Expected Model Output Changes

Alexander Freytag*, Erik Rodner*, and Joachim Denzler

Computer Vision Group, Friedrich Schiller University Jena, Germany
{firstname.lastname}@uni-jena.de
http://www.inf-cv.uni-jena.de

Abstract. In this paper, we introduce a new general strategy for active learning. The key idea of our approach is to measure the expected change of model outputs, a concept that generalizes previous methods based on expected model change and incorporates the underlying data distribution. For each example of an unlabeled set, the expected change of model predictions is calculated and marginalized over the unknown label. This results in a score for each unlabeled example that can be used for active learning with a broad range of models and learning algorithms. In particular, we show how to derive very efficient active learning methods for Gaussian process regression, which implement this general strategy, and link them to previous methods. We analyze our algorithms and compare them to a broad range of previous active learning strategies in experiments showing that they outperform state-of-the-art on well-established benchmark datasets in the area of visual object recognition.

Keywords: active learning, Gaussian processes, visual recognition, exploration-exploitation trade-off.

1 Introduction

Over the last decade, the amount of accessible data has been growing dramatically and our community discovered the benefits of "big data" for learning robust recognition models [2,11]. However, in several important applications, *e.g.*, defect detection [15] or fine-grained categorization of rare categories [7], collecting labeled samples turns out to be a hard and expensive task, where labeling uninformative samples should be avoided as much as possible. Therefore, actively selecting an informative set of samples to label is important, especially if the labeling budget is strictly limited. Furthermore, it is necessary for *life-long learning* of visual objects, where we are interested in incrementally enriching object models with minimal user interaction.

In active learning, we are interested in reducing expensive manual labeling efforts. This goal is achieved by identifying a subset of unlabeled samples from a huge pool, such that the resulting accuracy (classification or regression accuracy depending on the application) of a model learned using the additional subset is maximized. The challenges are that the labels of the selected examples are only available after the selection

---

* A. Freytag and E. Rodner were supported by a FIT scholarship from the DAAD.

D. Fleet et al. (Eds.): ECCV 2014, Part IV, LNCS 8692, pp. 562–577, 2014.

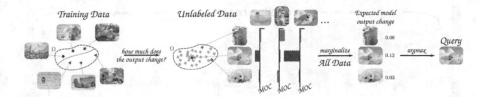

Fig. 1. Illustration of the active learning strategy introduced in this paper: an initial model is trained from labeled samples (blue and green). Unlabeled samples (gray) are evaluated with respect to the change of model outputs after adding them to the train set. For three exemplary samples (red, orange, and pink), the resulting model output change (MOC) for three different images is visualized. The sample leading to the strongest output change marginalized over all data Ω is finally queried.

and that the accuracy for unseen data can not be correctly measured beforehand and a proxy for it needs to be optimized. Although approximations exist based on estimated labels [16] or estimated confidence [1], they have to perform time-consuming extensive model evaluations and updates. Furthermore, estimating class labels is especially prone to errors in the presence of only few labeled data – which is the working range of nearly all active learning scenarios.

To circumvent these drawbacks, a variety of different strategies has been proposed, which are based on *what one assumes to be important* for higher accuracies, *e.g.*, a rapid exploration of the whole feature space [10], the identification of 'hard samples' among unlabeled points with respect to the current model [17], or combinations of existing techniques [1,4]. Although being intuitive in their different ways, none of these strategies can actually guarantee an impact of active learning on future model decisions.

In this paper, we therefore introduce a new general active learning strategy facing the problem by predicting the influence of an unlabeled example on future model decisions. If the unlabeled example is likely to change future decisions of the model when being labeled, it is regarded as an informative sample. An illustration of our strategy is visualized in Fig. 1. In the toy example, the final query is likely to change model outputs for a whole set of samples and is therefore preferred over samples which would lead to almost no changes. In summary, the contributions of this paper are two-fold: (1) we present a novel active learning strategy applicable to different applications and models, and (2) we derive an efficient algorithm based on Gaussian process regression from our general strategy.

The active learning strategy most similar to ours is to calculate the expected model change [6,20], which is mostly realized by measuring the Euclidean distance between the current model parameters and the expected model parameters after labeling. As we show in this paper, this strategy completely ignores the underlying data distribution, which is not the case for our approach, where we consider the change of model *outputs* instead of model parameters. Our technique is rather general and can be used for several different learning methods; however, we show that in the case of Gaussian process regression (or kernel ridge regression), the expected model output change can be efficiently calculated without learning from scratch. Furthermore, several active learning methods derived from the new approach are empirically compared with each other

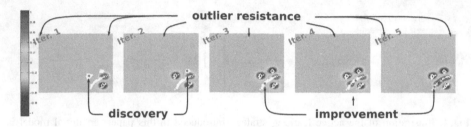

Fig. 2. Visualizing our active learning technique (EMOC). Figure is best viewed in color and by zooming in. Current classification scores are color coded, and thickness of unlabeled samples corresponds to their active learning scores, with large scores being preferred. You are invited to compare also against results of different strategies given in the supplementary material.

and we demonstrate in our experimental evaluation on well-known visual recognition datasets the advantage of expected model output change as a tool for active learning.

Why Yet Another Active Learning Technique?   While facing active learning and diving through the enormous amount of great work done in this field, we sought for gaining clarity about which technique to use in which scenario. We investigated several playgrounds, among it a 2D toy example simple on first sight (see Fig. 2 and supplementary material). To our surprise, the majority of existing approaches struggled heavily due to either a focus too strong on outliers, or poor discovery abilities (see Table 1 in the suppl. mat. for an overview of our findings). The only positive exception, however, performed surprisingly poor in experiments on real-world data. As a consequence, we found the necessity to develop a technique inheriting advantages of previous active learning approaches, *i.e.*, being capable of discovering new clusters of data while being resistant to outliers, and on the same time focusing on regions where unconfident classification boundaries badly need improvements. In the remainder of the paper, we derive our technique from a theoretical position, prove it on real-world data, and, without further anticipating, show here already on the 2D problem that our technique offers the desired properties (see Fig. 2).

After reviewing related work in Sect. 2, we derive the main principle of our approach in Sect. 3. How to obtain efficient query strategies by utilizing Gaussian process models is shown in Sect. 4 and fast approximations are derived. Sect. 5 shows that the typical trick of density weighting in active learning can be motivated as a very rough approximation of our approach. We finally analyze the derived strategies on well-established benchmark datasets for visual object recognition in Sect. 6.

2   Related Work

As mentioned earlier, active learning techniques aim for selecting samples that lead to the highest improvement in accuracies, or similarly reduce the error as fast as possible. Since accuracies can not be reliably estimated in the absence of test data, multitudes of proxies and heuristics have been developed, which can be grouped into several general strategies. We review a prominent subset of them and list a few representative works.

Rapid Exploration. In order to quickly obtain label information for the whole feature space, exploration strategies prefer samples maximally far away from all current training samples, like KFF by [1] or the Gaussian process predictive variance [10]. However, since recognition problems are often characterized by low-dimensional manifolds of the original input space, these techniques often struggle with querying outliers rarely related to the class distribution.

Maximum Uncertainty. Similar to exploration, techniques relying on classifier uncertainty aim for selecting samples the current model is most uncertain about. In contrast to the previous strategy, this is done in a supervised manner taking the current model boundaries into account. Exemplary techniques are given in [21] and [10] for Support Vector Machines (SVM) or Gaussian process classifiers (GP), respectively.

Maximization of Expected Model Change. To balance exploration and exploitation and additionally ensure that queried samples affect the current model, techniques in this area favor samples that result in the largest model change after retraining. Since the process of model retraining is costly, techniques had been restricted to parametric models where the model change can be traced back to the change of the gradient of the objective function [20]. In our earlier work [6], we extended this strategy to nonlinear GP regression models by exploiting efficient closed-form updates. However, a theoretical connection to the goal of error reduction is missing and assuming that a large model change results in an acceptable change of predictions is not valid in general.

Reduction of Estimated Classification Error. To overcome the previous shortcomings, this strategy directly aims at reducing the unknown classification error of the current model under a specified loss function. The technique most famous here was introduced by [16], where the true conditional distribution is approximated with the prediction of the current model, which leads to an expected entropy minimization scheme. Although being closest to the goal of active learning, techniques of this strategy suffer from two drawbacks: (i) they often have to face the computational costs of model retraining for every unlabeled sample and additionally have to evaluate the error on all available data, and (ii) the estimation of unknown labels needed for error evaluations is crucial and prone to errors especially in the presence of only few training data.

Work Most Similar to our Approach. The active learning approach we introduce in this paper is located *in between* the general strategies of *Maximization of expected model change* and *Reduction of estimated classification error*. While the first one does not take the actual change of model decisions into account at all, the latter requires perfectly reliable estimates of class labels used for empirical risk estimation. Both drawbacks are less present in our strategy. Additionally, we show that the density re-weighting technique introduced by [19] can be derived as an approximation of our proposed method. Furthermore, [22] present a technique to actively pick unlabeled nodes in a CRF to improve semantic segmentation quality based on the amount of CRF nodes flipping their state, which is generalized in our approach as well. For the choice of a GP regression model, we show how to transfer the work in [6] to our approach, which thereby additionally exploits the density information available in unlabeled data.

3   Expected Model Output Change (EMOC)

In pool-based active learning, a set $\mathfrak{L} \in \Omega^n$ of n labeled examples with labels $\boldsymbol{y} \in \mathcal{Y}^n$ and a set $\mathfrak{U} \subset \Omega$ of unlabeled examples is given from a problem domain Ω and an algorithm should select an example $\boldsymbol{x}' \in \mathfrak{U}$ to be labeled by an annotator, $i.e.$, assigned an output value $y' \in \mathcal{Y}$. The selection aims at improving the accuracy of a model $f : \Omega \rightarrow \mathcal{Y}$ ($e.g.$, a classifier for $\mathcal{Y} = \{-1, 1\}$ or a regressor for $\mathcal{Y} = \mathbb{R}$) learned by the given training data. In this paper, we deal with selecting one example at a time also known as myopic active learning.

As reviewed in the last section, several quite different active learning strategies exist. However, what we ultimately look for are high accuracy models with less annotated data, $i.e.$, we should select unlabeled examples $\boldsymbol{x}'$ that lead to the maximum increase in accuracy when being labeled and used to improve the current predictor. Unfortunately, we can never precisely predict the change in accuracy after adding a sample to the labeled pool in advance[1]. Therefore, we would like to raise the question: *Given a pool of unlabeled samples – some of them changing your model* outputs *when being labeled and added, others do not change anything – which one would you query?*

In absence of further knowledge, we argue that examples that lead to high expected model output changes should be queried. Therefore, we consider *how strongly a new sample $\boldsymbol{x}'$ influences the model decisions marginalized over all possible inputs $\boldsymbol{x} \in \Omega$ and over its yet unknown output $y' \in \mathcal{Y}$:*

$$\Delta f(\boldsymbol{x}') = \mathbb{E}_{y' \in \mathcal{Y}} \, \mathbb{E}_{\boldsymbol{x} \in \Omega} \left(\mathcal{L} \left(f_{(\mathfrak{L},\boldsymbol{y})}(\boldsymbol{x}), f_{([\mathfrak{L},\boldsymbol{x}'],[\boldsymbol{y},y'])}(\boldsymbol{x}) \right) \right) , \qquad (1)$$

where $f_{(\cdot,\cdot)}$ is a model trained from labeled data and $\mathcal{L}$ is a loss function measuring the difference between model outputs. In the following, we skip the dependency of $\mathfrak{L}, \boldsymbol{y}, \boldsymbol{x}'$ and y' on f in the notation and instead write $f(\boldsymbol{x})$ and $f'(\boldsymbol{x})$ for models before and after including $(\boldsymbol{x}', y')$ as additional training sample:

$$\Delta f(\boldsymbol{x}') = \int_{\mathcal{Y}} \left(\int_{\Omega} \mathcal{L}(f(\boldsymbol{x}), f'(\boldsymbol{x})) \, p(\boldsymbol{x}) \, \mathrm{d}\boldsymbol{x} \right) p(y'|\boldsymbol{x}') \mathrm{d}y'.$$

The active learning algorithm we propose evaluates $\Delta f(\boldsymbol{x}')$ for all unlabeled examples $\boldsymbol{x}' \in \mathfrak{U}$ and selects the example with the maximum value. In the following, we motivate the usefulness of this strategy for active learning and derive a specific algorithm from it by defining probability estimators, loss functions, and model classes.

EMOC Is an Upper Bound for Loss Reduction.   Using EMOC for active learning can be motivated as an upper bound for the expected loss reduction. The additional assumption we need is that the loss function $\mathcal{L}$ obeys the following triangle inequality for $a, b, c \in \mathcal{Y}$:

$$\mathcal{L}(a, b) \leq \mathcal{L}(a, c) + \mathcal{L}(c, b) . \qquad (2)$$

---

[1] Note that we can not even precisely measure the accuracy of our system before the update and instead have to rely on approximations based on validation and test sets.

Furthermore, we assume that the model $g(x)$ learned from all possible data of the problem domain Ω exists[2] and that

$$\epsilon_f = \mathbb{E}_{x \in \Omega} \left(\mathcal{L} \left(f(x), g(x) \right) \right) , \tag{3}$$

is giving us an error measure for f. The expected decrease in loss for f' can now be defined as $\Delta\epsilon = \mathbb{E}_{y' \in \mathcal{Y}}(\epsilon_f - \epsilon_{f'})$ and the following shows that the expected model output change defined in Eq. (1) is an upper bound [22]:

$$\Delta\epsilon = \mathbb{E}_{y' \in \mathcal{Y}} \, \mathbb{E}_{x \in \Omega} \left(\mathcal{L}(f(x), g(x)) - \mathcal{L}(f'(x), g(x)) \right)$$
$$\leq \mathbb{E}_{y' \in \mathcal{Y}} \, \mathbb{E}_{x \in \Omega} \left(\mathcal{L}(f(x), f'(x)) \right) = \Delta f(x').$$

It is impossible to directly maximize the loss reduction term on the left-hand side for active learning, because g is unknown. Therefore, our active learning methods search for the unlabeled example x' with highest upper bound in loss reduction given by EMOC. It should be noted that this of course does not guarantee a proper decrease in the loss, but it at least does not limit it in advance by selecting examples that do not change model outputs at all.

Possible Choices for $\mathcal{L}(\cdot, \cdot)$ and $p(x)$. The choice of $\mathcal{L}$ naturally complies with the problem settings faced. The absolute difference $|f(x) - f'(x)|$ in model response is well suited for regression tasks with continuous output values. For classification tasks, where $\mathcal{Y}$ is a discrete set, the common choice for measuring model output changes would be the classification loss, where $\mathcal{L}(a, b)$ is 1 for $a \neq b$ and zero everywhere else. However, we will see that for classification decisions based on thresholding underlying continuous model outputs, simpler losses can be used that avoid estimating a threshold (Sect. S1 in the supplementary material). Marginalization over y' is done by computing estimates based on the current model output and we discuss the details in the next section. In the future, we are planning to investigate also losses suitable for multi-class classification tasks.

What remains is how to model the probability distribution over the input space in practice, *i.e.*, how to specify $p(x)$. Since we only have access to the set $\mathcal{S} = \mathcal{L} \cup \mathcal{U}$ of labeled examples $\mathcal{L}$ and unlabeled examples $\mathcal{U}$, we approximate $p(x)$ with the empirical density distribution:

$$p(x) \approx \frac{1}{|\mathcal{S}|} \sum_{x_j \in \mathcal{S}} \delta(x - x_j) , \tag{4}$$

where $\delta(x)$ is the Dirac function. Note that this implies a representative data distribution in $\mathcal{S}$, which however is one of the main assumptions for active learning. In summary, EMOC scores (see Eq. (1)) for models with continuous outputs can be calculated based on empirical estimates for given data by:

$$\Delta f(x') = \mathbb{E}_{y' \in \mathcal{Y}} \left(\frac{1}{|\mathcal{S}|} \sum_{x_j \in \mathcal{S}} |f(x_j) - f'(x_j)| \right) , \tag{5}$$

independent of the learning algorithm for f.

---

[2] For classification, we need this requirement for g because the label space is not $\mathbb{R}$. However, for regression, we could even assume that g is the ground-truth function.

4   Efficient EMOC with GP Regression

Our active learning strategy introduced in the previous section applies to a broad span of possible models and a naive approach to calculate the scores is to train a new predictor f' for each unlabeled example $x' \in \mathfrak{U}$ by adding the example to the training set, retrain the predictor, and evaluate it on the whole set of examples given. In the following, we show that this is not necessary when using Gaussian process regression models. Furthermore, we also show how the marginalization over y' can be directly done.

Gaussian process regression is a kernel approach with the following decision function:

$$f(x) = \sum_{i=1}^{n} \alpha_i \, \kappa(x_i, x) = \alpha^T k(x) \tag{6}$$

where κ is a given kernel function. The weight vector α of the model is the result of kernel ridge regression and given by $\left(\mathbf{K} + \sigma_n^2 \cdot \mathbf{I}\right)^{-1} y$, where $\mathbf{K}$ is the kernel matrix of the training set $\mathfrak{L}$, y is the vector of outputs of $\mathfrak{L}$, and σ_n^2 their assumed noise variance [13]. For the model in Eq. (6), the influence of a new sample on all possible predictions can therefore be computed as follows:

$$\Delta f(x') = \mathbb{E}_{y' \in \mathcal{Y}} \left(\frac{1}{|\mathcal{S}|} \sum_{x_j \in \mathcal{S}} |k(x_j)^T \alpha - \bar{k}(x_j)^T \bar{\alpha}| \right)$$

$$= \mathbb{E}_{y' \in \mathcal{Y}} \left(\frac{1}{|\mathcal{S}|} \sum_{x_j \in \mathcal{S}} |\bar{k}(x_j)^T \left(\begin{bmatrix} \alpha \\ 0 \end{bmatrix} - \bar{\alpha} \right) | \right)$$

where $\bar{k}(x) = [k(x) \quad \kappa(x', x)]$ and $\bar{\alpha} = \bar{\mathbf{K}}^{-1} \begin{bmatrix} y \\ y' \end{bmatrix}$ is the updated weight vector computed using the regularized kernel matrix $\bar{\mathbf{K}}$ of $\mathfrak{L} \cup \{x'\}$.

Efficient Model Updates.   Instead of computing expected model output changes from scratch by retraining the model with each unlabeled example, GP regression allows us to compute the new model and therefore also the change $\Delta\alpha$ of model coefficients efficiently and in closed form for a given output y':

$$\Delta\alpha \doteq \begin{bmatrix} \alpha \\ 0 \end{bmatrix} - \bar{\alpha} = \frac{y' - k^T \alpha}{\sigma_{f_*}^2 + \sigma_n^2} \left[\begin{matrix} \left(\mathbf{K} + \sigma_n^2 \cdot \mathbf{I}\right)^{-1} k \\ -1 \end{matrix} \right], \tag{7}$$

where $\sigma_{f_*}^2$ is the predictive variance of x' and k is the vector of pairwise kernel values of the training set and x'. A proof is given in [6] and is based on block-wise matrix inversion. Please note that similar derivations for linear models are also possible and known for several decades [12].

EMOC for Classification with Label Regression.   With GP regression as an illustrative example, we focused on models with a continuous output. For classification, we assume the final output to be obtained by maximizing a given $p(y \mid f(x))$. In fact, a prominent set of popular models used for binary classification, such as SVMs [18], GP-regression [13], or LDA [9], first compute continuous scores for test samples which are then transformed to discrete responses, *e.g.*, by comparing against an application-specific threshold. For the case of GP classification, using GP regression scores as proposed by [10] leads to treating outputs as continuous values with Gaussian random noise and allows for skipping approximate inference necessary for direct GP classification [13]. Since we focus on binary classification settings in the rest of this paper, we argue to compute model output changes directly on the continuous scores, which reflects the non-ordinal nature of these models, avoids tricky threshold determinations, and will also be important to develop a fast version of our active learning algorithms. Furthermore, we will see in the experiments that label regression leads to an even better classification performance than proper classification models with approximate inference (supplementary material, Sect. S1).

Although our computed model output changes are based on continuous scores, the labels y' are still binary, *i.e.*, $y' \in \{-1, 1\}$, and we need a method to compute the expectation with respect to y' in Eq. (1). We know that the output of GP regression is not only a deterministic estimate but rather a predictive Gaussian distribution with mean $f(x')$ and variance $\sigma_{f_*}^2$. Therefore, we compute $p(y' = 1|x')$ by calculating the probability that a sample from this distribution is positive, which directly corresponds to the manner in which classification decisions are done in [10][3]. This probability can be calculated in closed form:

$$p(y' = 1|x') = \frac{1}{2} - \frac{1}{2} \cdot \text{erf}\left(-f(x')/\sqrt{2\sigma_{f_*}^2}\right) \tag{8}$$

using the error function $\text{erf}(z)$ and is related to the cumulative Gaussian noise model presented by [13]. In summary, the inner part of $\Delta f(x')$ is evaluated using Eq. (7) for $y' = 1$ as well as $y' = -1$, and both values are used to compute a weighted average using the probability in Eq. (8).

Fast Approximated EMOC.   Even with the efficient model updates presented, we have to compute $\bar{k}(x_j)^T \Delta \alpha$ for every unlabeled example x_j, which can be a huge computational burden for large sets of unlabeled examples. Fortunately, the computation time necessary to evaluate EMOC can be significantly reduced by the following approximation:

$$\Delta f(x') = \mathbb{E}_{y' \in \mathcal{Y}}\left(\frac{1}{|\mathcal{S}|} \sum_{x_j \in \mathcal{S}} |\bar{k}(x_j)^T \Delta \alpha|\right) \tag{9}$$

$$\leq \mathbb{E}_{y' \in \mathcal{Y}}\left(\frac{1}{\mathcal{S}} \sum_{x_j \in \mathcal{S}} \bar{k}(x_j)^T \text{abs}(\Delta \alpha)\right) \tag{10}$$

---

[3] A more sophisticated estimation might also marginalize over possible thresholds, and future work should focus on integrating this aspect efficiently.

where abs($\cdot$) denotes element-wise absolute value. Since the model change $\Delta\alpha$ itself is independent of x_j, we can write this in short form as

$$\Delta f_{\text{fast}}(x') = \mathbb{E}_{y'}\left(\sum_{i=1}^{n+1}\left(|\Delta\alpha_i|\frac{1}{S}\sum_{x_j \in S}\kappa\left(x, x_j\right)\right)\right). \tag{11}$$

The computational benefit of the approximation introduced above is two-fold: (i) the asymptotic runtime reduces (see Table 2), and (ii) instead of demanding the kernel matrix consisting of kernel values between every two samples of S, computing the approximated version only needs the resulting row sums. Additionally, note that the approximation has an interesting interpretation: the right-hand side can be seen as a Parzen density estimation

$$\text{PDE}(x; S) \propto \frac{1}{|S|}\sum_{x_j \in S}\kappa(x, x_j) \tag{12}$$

of each of the corresponding training samples estimated with both labeled and unlabeled data ($S = \{\mathcal{L} \cup \mathfrak{U}\}$). Therefore, the changes of model coefficients are weighted with respect to the data likelihood, $i.e.$, an outlier with a high change in α should not have a huge impact on EMOC and therefore also not on the selection process during active learning. Note that kernel density estimation takes place in a possibly high-dimensional input space, however, we have not seen any issues with respect to the curse of dimensionality in our experiments.

5 Density Weighting as a Special Case of EMOC

In the following section, we do not propose any novel method, but show that a further approximation of the EMOC principle leads to density-weighted queries [19]. This connection emphasizes the importance of density weighting for active learning in general, which will be further studied in our experiments. Density weighting has been known for quite a while for active learning, but to the best of our knowledge, we are the first ones presenting it as an approximation of a very general active learning strategy.

Let us now denote the vector containing density values of all labeled samples with $p_{\mathcal{L}} : p_{\mathcal{L}}^{(i)} = \text{PDE}(x_i; S)$ and let further be $p_{x'} = \text{PDE}(x'; S)$ the data density value of the new sample. We can then even further approximate $\Delta f_{\text{fast}}(x')$:

$$\Delta f_{\text{fast}}(x') = \mathbb{E}_{y'}\left(\left|\Delta\alpha^{\mathrm{T}} \cdot \begin{bmatrix} p_{\mathcal{L}} \\ p_{x'} \end{bmatrix}\right|\right) \tag{13}$$

$$\leq \mathbb{E}_{y'}\left(\|\Delta\alpha\|_1 \cdot \left\|\begin{bmatrix} p_{\mathcal{L}} \\ p_{x'} \end{bmatrix}\right\|_1\right) \tag{14}$$

$$\propto \mathbb{E}_{y'}\left(\|\Delta\alpha\|_1 \cdot |p_{x'}|\right), \tag{15}$$

where we used the fact that only terms depending on x' are important for the selection process during active learning.

Consequently, we notice that this very rough and simplified approximation of our proposed active learning strategy is equivalent to taking queries based on expected model change, *e.g.*, using [6], and to multiply the scores with a Parzen density estimate of the corresponding unlabeled sample. This indeed seems intuitive, since we now can ensure that the samples being queried not only affect the model, but are also likely to occur in dense regions of the space with respect to our current subspace of interest. Note that in contrast to [6], we marginalize over y' instead of using only the most likely y' as proposed by the authors.

Extension to Arbitrary Query Strategies.   Based on the previous ideas, we will use the following straight-forward replacements of arbitrary query strategies[4] $\mathcal{Q}(x)$ in order to integrate the data density:

$$\mathcal{Q}^*(x) = p_x \cdot \mathcal{Q}(x) \; . \tag{16}$$

The suggested replacement is a heuristic, which is easy to apply and motivated by our approach. We thereby ensure that samples of high density areas[5] are preferred over outliers from non-important, sparse regions. We show in our experiments that this modification improves the performance of previous active learning methods and therefore also offers a fairer comparison to our new active learning methods based on expected model output change.

Note that the idea for density-based re-weighting of query scores was already introduced in [19] for the task of sequence labeling. However, the authors proposed it as a heuristic without a clear theoretical motivation and simply note that they would *recommend it in practice*. In contrast to that, we place this technique in a proper theoretical background by deriving it as a special approximation of the more general active learning approach introduced in this paper. Furthermore, the Parzen estimates in Eq. (12) use all the given samples $\mathcal{S} = \{\mathcal{L} \cup \mathfrak{U}\}$ in contrast to $\mathcal{S} = \mathfrak{U}$ as proposed in [19]. This is reasonable, since (1) density estimates do not have to be adapted during the query process, which naturally changes $\mathfrak{U}$ and (2) we estimate densities for the actual problem setting, *i.e.*, we rely on all information and data we have and not only on an arbitrary subset.

6   Experimental Results

For an experimental evaluation, we have been interested in the following aspects (i) how do active learning techniques derived from our strategy compare to previous state-of-the-art strategies (see Sect. 6.1), (ii) how strongly does the density-based re-weighting affect learning accuracies of state-of-the-art techniques (see Sect. 6.2), (iii) how powerful is the EMOC approach under ideal settings, where we assume a perfect label estimation for model updates (see Sect. 6.3), and is label regression enough for classification (supplementary material, Sect. S1)? To answer these questions, we follow the experimental setup of [6] and use the corresponding evaluation protocol[6]. We conduct

---

[4] If $\mathcal{Q}$ is designed to query samples with minimum score, multiply by $1 - p(x)$ instead.

[5] Density is considered with respect to the current problem and its induced data distribution.

[6] Evaluation protocol was taken from
https://github.com/cvjena/activeLearning-GP

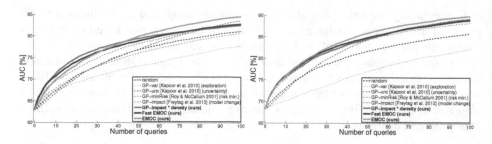

Fig. 3. Active Learning on binary tasks derived from **ImageNet** (*left*) and **Caltech 256** (*right*). We compare against active learning strategies 'rapid exploration', 'maximum uncertainty', 'maximization of expected model change', and 'reduction of estimated classification error'. See text for further details. The figure is best viewed in color.

experiments on two well-established benchmark datasets for image categorization: ImageNet [3] and Caltech-256 [8]. Source code of our techniques and experiments will be made publicly available at our homepage http://www.inf-cv.uni-jena.de/ active_learning.

6.1 Comparison to State-of-the-Art

Experimental Setup.   As done in [6], we derive 100 random binary tasks from the ImageNet challenge consisting of a single positive and 9 negative classes. Every task is repeated with 10 random initializations, which finally results in 1,000 experiments to allow for reliable conclusions. Images are represented using the publicly available bag-of-words-features of ILSVRC 2010[7] and we evaluate our EMOC approach when using GP regression models as introduced in Sect. 4. In particular, we rely on the exact model output change as introduced in Eq. (4) (*EMOC*), its approximation given in Eq. (13) (*Fast EMOC*), as well as the density-weighted model change (*GP-impact · density*, see Eq. (15)), which is an extension of [6] derived from the EMOC principle. We compare against passive learning (*random*), which is the naive baseline for all active learning settings. Apart from that, we chose representative state-of-the-art methods for the reviewed strategies: *GP-var* (using examples with a high predictive GP variance) and *GP-unc* (seek for small ratios of predictive GP mean and variance) have been introduced by [10] and are representative for the rapid exploration and maximum uncertainty strategy, respectively. Additionally, we compare against the technique introduced in [6] (*GP-impact*) for the expected model change strategy, and the approach of [16] transferred to GP (*GP-minRisk*) for reduction of estimated classification error principle. See Sect. S4 in the supplementary material for further details of the experimental setup.

Evaluation.   Active learning curves on tasks derived from ImageNet are shown in the left plot of Fig. 3. Dashed curves correspond to strategies existing in the literature, whereas our techniques are plotted in solid lines. First of all, we observe that the rapid exploration strategy leads to worse classification accuracies then passive learning,

---

[7] http://www.image-net.org/challenges/LSVRC/2010

Table 1. Experimental results for ImageNet and Caltech 256: Average AUC value (in %) after 50 queries for **100** random binary **tasks** averaged over 10 random initializations. (*) Our approach significantly outperforms all other approaches verified by a paired t-Test and $p < 10^{-3}$.

Strategy	ImageNet	Caltech 256
Random	76.83	81.70
Predictive variance [10] (GP-var)	73.11	77.06
Classification uncertainty [10] (GP-unc)	76.97	84.31
Reduction of classification error [16] (GP-minRisk)	76.08	84.59
Model change [6] (GP-impact)	78.32	84.56
EMOC strategy (Ours)*	**80.03**	**85.88**

which indicates the preference of outliers being queried. In contrast, nearly all remaining methods improve random sampling. Interestingly, empirical risk minimization leads to results slightly inferior to passive learning, emphasizing the negative influence of wrongly estimated labels. In contrast, queries based on expected model output change result in a significant improvement, confirming the intuition that samples resulting in different model *responses* are worth being labeled. As argued in Sect. 4, this partly originates from the fact that previous methods focus on less important aspects of unlabeled examples, *e.g.*, looking for unexplainable samples (as done by GP-uncertainty) might result in *interesting* samples, but without a clear relation to improvement of accuracy.

To further verify our findings, we performed experiments with an identical setup on the Caltech-256 dataset and visualized results in the right plot of Fig. 3. The results clearly indicate the before-mentioned relation between different active learning approaches. Uncertainty-based strategies obviously have problems querying useful samples if the size of training data is relatively small. Apart from that, the results are consistent with the observations from the ImageNet experiment. In addition, Table 1 contains average AUC values obtained after 50 queries. Our approach outperforms all other strategies significantly (paired t-Test, $p < 10^{-3}$). It has to be emphasized again that we obtained this result from experiments with 100 different recognition tasks and 10 different initializations. Furthermore, we compare against representative approaches of five active learning strategies.

With respect to the approximations of the EMOC principle, we further observe that for few labeled data in the ImageNet experiment, the approximation performs better then the exact EMOC scores, whereas for a larger number the relation switches. This suggests that the introduced approximations are less affected by randomly initialized training sets, whereas exact EMOC scores are especially valuable when the current model can be trained more robustly.

Evaluation in a One-vs-All Scenario. We also evaluated our approach in binary tasks created in a one-vs-all manner as done by [10] (see supplementary material for further details). As can be seen in Fig. 4, we observe a similar performance benefit of our methods as in the previous experiments. Visualizations of queried images for the airplane task as well as some hand-picked, interesting queries for remaining scenarios are given in the supplementary material (see Sect. S5, Fig. 1).

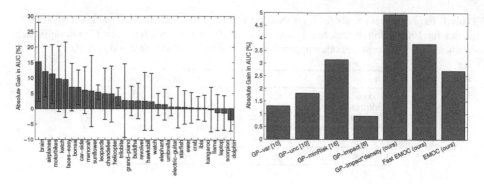

Fig. 4. Active learning improvement over passive baseline after 20 queries for 30 one-vs-all binary tasks derived from Caltech-256. *Left:* Results on all 30 individual classes with our Fast EMOC technique. *Right:* Averaged results for all compared techniques.

Table 2. Computation times needed performing active selection with our method and approximations (Sect. 4) and n labeled examples as well as u unlabeled examples

Method	GP-impact [6]	[6] · density	Fast EMOC	EMOC
Time ($n = 10, u = 990$)	$7.81 \cdot 10^{-4}$ s	$7.64 \cdot 10^{-4}$ s	$8.08 \cdot 10^{-4}$ s	$2.38 \cdot 10^{-2}$ s
Asymptotic time	$\mathcal{O}(n^2 u)$	$\mathcal{O}(n^2 u)$	$\mathcal{O}(n^2 u)$	$\mathcal{O}(n^2 u + n u^2)$

Runtime Evaluation.   An empirical comparison of computation times[8] for the derived methods when querying the first sample in the previous experiments is given in Table 2. As expected, exact EMOC computation is significantly slower than its approximated versions, which are as fast as existing strategies. Furthermore, the asymptotic time reveals that in case of a large number u of unlabeled examples, Fast EMOC should be the method of choice, because the selection time only depends linearly on the number of unlabeled samples. The approach of [16] has the same asymptotic time as exact EMOC, but we observed a speed-up of 1.6 over [16] in practice.

6.2   Importance of Density-Based Re-weighting

As mentioned earlier, density-based re-weighting of query scores is not limited to our introduced strategies, but can be extended to arbitrary active learning techniques. In the left plot of Fig. 5, we show the resulting gains when applying the re-weighting scheme to GP active learning strategies introduced in the literature. First of all, we observe that learning results are improved in almost all cases. Apart from this, it is also intuitive why some of the methods can only benefit from the heuristic in late stages of learning (like *GP-var*), whereas others can draw a partial advantage in early stages (*e.g., GP-impact*). For example, as stated in [6], relying on the highest estimated model change leads to an implicit balancing between exploration and exploitation. Consequently, in early stages of learning, where the exploration aspect is usually more important, the density-based

---

[8] Computation times have been measured using a Matlab implementation on a 3.4 GHz CPU without parallelization and excluding precomputed kernel values.

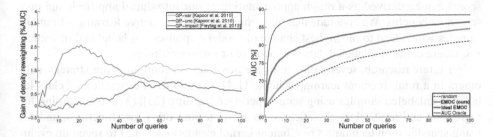

Fig. 5. *Left*: Gain of density-based re-weighting of active learning scores for several active learning strategies. *Right*: Performance of our EMOC method in a real active learning setting with unknown label y' (EMOC), when label y' is known during selection with EMOC (Ideal EMOC), and when the ground-truth label is used to greedily maximize AUC (AUC oracle).

re-weighting leads to exploration more focused on dense clusters than on outliers. In later stages, where exploration is less necessary, a focus too strong on dense regions is also less important and might even decrease performance.

6.3 Ideal EMOC

In a last experiment, we analyze the performance of our approach for a perfect estimation of model updates, *i.e.*, an artificial setup with known labels y'. Although we could directly use them for performance optimization on $\mathfrak{U}$, we are instead interested in the upper bound for EMOC. Therefore, we follow the previous experimental setup, and replace the expectation over possible labels in Eq. (1) by ground-truth labels for the unlabeled pool. As can be seen in the right plot of Fig. 5, working with correct label estimations again significantly improves learning rates. This observation is interesting by considering the experimental results in Sect. 6.1, where the EMOC strategy already outperformed existing techniques. Consequently, it would be highly beneficial to better infer unknown labels, especially if only few labeled samples are available and the initial model might be learned poorly. The right plot of Fig. 5 also contains the results of a perfect AUC oracle, where examples are chosen that maximize the AUC performance on $\mathfrak{U}$. The plot of this method is the upper bound for all myopic active learning methods.

7 Conclusions

We presented a new general active learning strategy based on calculating the expected change of model outputs when an unlabeled example would be labeled and incorporated. The main motivation is that examples with a high overall impact on the model *outputs* are most informative during learning. Our approach is flexible and allowed us to derive several new active learning methods. In particular, we showed how to compute expected model output changes efficiently for Gaussian process regression models. An extensive experimental evaluation revealed that our strategies outperform several existing active learning techniques on established benchmark datasets for image categorization. We further showed that density-based re-weighting of arbitrary active learning scores can be derived as a rough approximation of our introduced approach and presented its benefits. We conclude that our general strategy for active learning – to query samples which lead to the highest change of model responses – is beneficial in scenarios, where collecting labeled data is expensive or time-consuming.

For future research, several directions are possible: (1) combining our strategy with others in a reinforcement learning scheme [1,4], (2) improved estimation of class labels for unlabeled samples using semi-supervised learning [23], (3) active learning for regression and multi-class classification tasks by testing other loss functions, and (4) using sparsification techniques or efficient kernel evaluations [14,5] to speed up evaluation in the presence of large-scale data, such as the whole ImageNet dataset

References

1. Baram, Y., El-Yaniv, R., Luz, K.: Online choice of active learning algorithms. Journal of Machine Learning Research (JMLR) 5, 255–291 (2004)
2. Deng, J., Berg, A.C., Li, K., Fei-Fei, L.: What does classifying more than 10,000 image categories tell us? In: Daniilidis, K., Maragos, P., Paragios, N. (eds.) ECCV 2010, Part V. LNCS, vol. 6315, pp. 71–84. Springer, Heidelberg (2010)
3. Deng, J., Dong, W., Socher, R., Li, L.J., Li, K., Fei-Fei, L.: Imagenet: A large-scale hierarchical image database. In: Conference on Computer Vision and Pattern Recognition, CVPR (2009)
4. Ebert, S., Fritz, M., Schiele, B.: Ralf: A reinforced active learning formulation for object class recognition. In: Conference on Computer Vision and Pattern Recognition (CVPR), pp. 3626–3633 (2012)
5. Freytag, A., Rodner, E., Bodesheim, P., Denzler, J.: Rapid uncertainty computation with gaussian processes and histogram intersection kernels. In: Lee, K.M., Matsushita, Y., Rehg, J.M., Hu, Z. (eds.) ACCV 2012, Part II. LNCS, vol. 7725, pp. 511–524. Springer, Heidelberg (2013)
6. Freytag, A., Rodner, E., Bodesheim, P., Denzler, J.: Labeling examples that matter: Relevance-based active learning with gaussian processes. In: Weickert, J., Hein, M., Schiele, B. (eds.) GCPR 2013. LNCS, vol. 8142, pp. 282–291. Springer, Heidelberg (2013)
7. Göring, C., Rodner, E., Freytag, A., Denzler, J.: Nonparametric part transfer for fine-grained recognition. In: Conference on Computer Vision and Pattern Recognition, CVPR (accepted for publication, 2014)
8. Griffin, G., Holub, A., Perona, P.: Caltech-256 object category dataset. Tech. Rep. 7694. California Institute of Technology (2007)
9. Hariharan, B., Malik, J., Ramanan, D.: Discriminative decorrelation for clustering and classification. In: Fitzgibbon, A., Lazebnik, S., Perona, P., Sato, Y., Schmid, C. (eds.) ECCV 2012, Part IV. LNCS, vol. 7575, pp. 459–472. Springer, Heidelberg (2012)
10. Kapoor, A., Grauman, K., Urtasun, R., Darrell, T.: Gaussian processes for object categorization. International Journal of Computer Vision (IJCV) 88, 169–188 (2010)
11. Krizhevsky, A., Sutskever, I., Hinton, G.E.: Imagenet classification with deep convolutional neural networks. In: Advances in Neural Information Processing Systems, NIPS (2012)
12. Plackett, R.L.: Some theorems in least squares. Biometrika 37(1/2), 149–157 (1950)
13. Rasmussen, C.E., Williams, C.K.I.: Adaptive Computation and Machine Learning. Adaptive Computation and Machine Learning. The MIT Press, Cambridge (2006)
14. Rodner, E., Freytag, A., Bodesheim, P., Denzler, J.: Large-scale gaussian process classification with flexible adaptive histogram kernels. In: Fitzgibbon, A., Lazebnik, S., Perona, P., Sato, Y., Schmid, C. (eds.) ECCV 2012, Part IV. LNCS, vol. 7575, pp. 85–98. Springer, Heidelberg (2012)

15. Rodner, E., Wacker, E.S., Kemmler, M., Denzler, J.: One-class classification for anomaly detection in wire ropes with gaussian processes in a few lines of code. In: Conference on Machine Vision Applications (MVA), pp. 219–222 (2011)
16. Roy, N., McCallum, A.: Toward optimal active learning through sampling estimation of error reduction. In: International Conference on Machine Learning (ICML), pp. 441–448 (2001)
17. Schohn, G., Cohn, D.: Less is more: Active learning with support vector machines. In: International Conference on Machine Learning (ICML), pp. 839–846 (2000)
18. Schölkopf, B., Smola, A.J.: Learning with kernels: Support Vector Machines, Regularization, Optimization, and beyond. Adaptive Computation and Machine Learning. The MIT Press, Cambridge (2002)
19. Settles, B., Craven, M.: An analysis of active learning strategies for sequence labeling tasks. In: Conference on Empirical Methods in Natural Language Processing (EMNLP), pp. 1070–1079. Association for Computational Linguistics (2008)
20. Settles, B., Craven, M., Ray, S.: Multiple-instance active learning. In: Advances in Neural Information Processing Systems (NIPS), pp. 1289–1296. MIT Press (2008)
21. Tong, S., Koller, D.: Support vector machine active learning with applications to text classification. Journal of Machine Learning Research (JMLR) 2, 45–66 (2002)
22. Vezhnevets, A., Buhmann, J.M., Ferrari, V.: Active learning for semantic segmentation with expected change. In: Conference on Computer Vision and Pattern Recognition (CVPR), pp. 3162–3169 (2012)
23. Zhu, X., Lafferty, J., Ghahramani, Z.: Combining active learning and semi-supervised learning using gaussian fields and harmonic functions. In: Workshop on the Continuum from Labeled to Unlabeled Data in Machine Learning and Data Mining (ICML-WS), pp. 58–65 (2003)

Efficient Sparsity Estimation via Marginal-Lasso Coding

Tzu-Yi Hung[1], Jiwen Lu[2], Yap-Peng Tan[1], and Shenghua Gao[3]

[1] School of Electrical and Electronic Engineering,
Nanyang Technological University, Singapore
[2] Advanced Digital Sciences Center, Singapore
[3] ShanghaiTech University, Shanghai, China

Abstract. This paper presents a generic optimization framework for efficient feature quantization using sparse coding which can be applied to many computer vision tasks. While there are many works working on sparse coding and dictionary learning, none of them has exploited the advantages of the marginal regression and the lasso simultaneously to provide more efficient and effective solutions. In our work, we provide such an approach with a theoretical support. Therefore, the computational complexity of the proposed method can be two orders faster than that of the lasso with sacrificing the inevitable quantization error. On the other hand, the proposed method is more robust than the conventional marginal regression based methods. We also provide an adaptive regularization parameter selection scheme and a dictionary learning method incorporated with the proposed sparsity estimation algorithm. Experimental results and detailed model analysis are presented to demonstrate the efficacy of our proposed methods.

Keywords: Sparsity estimation, marginal regression, sparse coding, lasso, dictionary learning, adaptive regularization parameter.

1 Introduction

Sparse coding has been successfully applied to many machine learning and computer vision tasks, including image classification [30,31,8], face recognition [28,5], activity-based person identification [22,15], etc. Sparse coding refers to a feature quantization mechanism which obtains a codebook to encode each input signal as a sparse histogram feature based on the linear combination of a few visual words. Due to its soft assignment principal, it can make the quantization error much smaller [9,22]. Moreover, sparse coding is more robust to the noise and easily incorporating into the bag-of-feature (BoF) framework.

The least absolution shrinkage and selection operator which is also known as lasso [27] in short is a popular sparse coding model in statistics signal processing which has wildly used in sparsity estimation. It simultaneously minimizes the quantization error, and impose an L_1 penalty with a regularization parameter λ which controls the sparsity of the coefficients. While there exists many efficient algorithms [20,7,29], however, finding the lasso solutions remain a computational task with the complexity $O(p^3 + dp^2)$ where d refers to the input feature dimension, and p refers to the amount of visual

D. Fleet et al. (Eds.): ECCV 2014, Part IV, LNCS 8692, pp. 578–592, 2014.

words in the dictionary. Thus, it hardly supports large scale data analysis efficiently and effectively [6,23,11,1].

Recently, marginal regression, has been revisited and shown its efficient performance for visual word selection and sparsity estimation [6,11,1]. For each feature, it calculates the correlation with each visual word and imposes a tuning parameter to achieve the sparsity. While marginal regression is simple and fast with the complexity $O(dp)$, it usually considers and utilizes a fixed tuning parameter which is not always the good cut-off point for each feature and could result in a large quantization error since some coefficients may be shrunk too much, but some may be included too much noise. Hence, how to determine a suitable cut-off point becomes an typical problem in featuring coding. To address this, the sure independent screening (SIS) [6] method imposes an L_1-norm penalty and an energy constraint E to each marginal regression coefficient vector. It sorts coefficients in terms of their absolute values and selects the top k coefficients whose L_1 norm is bounded by E so that each sparse code can be represented by similar sparsity level. However, this method may also cause a large quantization error, because marginal regression works well when visual words have low correlation in the dictionary [1,23]; however, in general, they are highly correlated, and thus may fail to clarify the relationship between visual words and the input feature.

While there are many works working on sparse coding and dictionary learning, none of them has exploited the advantages of the marginal regression and the lasso simultaneously to provide more efficient and effective solutions. To this end, we provide in this paper such an approach with a theoretical support. We propose an efficient sparsity estimation approach using Marginal-Lasso Coding (MLC) which quantizes each feature into a small set of visual words using marginal regression combined with the lasso framework. Our model represents each sparse code with similar sparsity level bounded by a global sparsity energy and simultaneously shrinks individual coefficients to alleviate the bias of sparse codes caused by the highly correlated visual words. Moreover, our approach automatically determines the shrinking regularization parameter for each feature and further designs a self-ratio energy constraint of sparsity level which is different from the traditional constraint with a case-dependent chosen value.

Contribution: 1) We propose an efficient Marginal-Lasso Coding (MLC) framework for feature quantization with sparsity estimation, regularization parameter selection and dictionary learning. 2) We exploit the advantages of the marginal regression and the lasso simultaneously to provide more efficient and effective solutions. 3) We determine the regularization parameter automatically and adaptively for each individual feature and provide a self-ratio energy bound. 4) We provide a theoretical support for the proposed model. 5) We successfully apply the proposed method to various recognition tasks.

2   Related Work

Our approach is related to the general sparse coding model which has been widely used for sparse representation [28,27,30,22], and there exist many algorithms to estimate sparse codes, such as least angle regression [4], gradient descent [7,29], and feature-sign search [20]. The feature-sign search method [20,8,31] is a popular and efficient solution for sparsity estimation. It continuously selects and updates potential candidates in an active set to maintain these nonzero coefficients and their corresponding signs until reaching the constraint. However, with a large dictionary size, the active set would become large and the feature-sign searching process may be hard to terminate [1,23]. While these methods aim to obtain a small quantization error, they have a large computational cost [6,11]. Therefore, different from traditional sparsity estimation techniques which estimate sparse codes by continuously selecting variables to the active set based on the searching criteria, we incorporate marginal regression coefficients into the sparse coding model which is more efficient for sparsity estimation.

Recently, Fan and Lv [6] proposed a sure independent screening (SIS) method using marginal regression to obtain sparse codes efficiently and can easily deal with large-scale problems. Genovese *et al.* [11] provided a statistical comparison of the lasso and marginal regression. Due to the promising performance in terms of accuracy and speed, Krishnakumar *et al.* [1] applied marginal regression to learn sparse representation for visual tasks. While these solutions use hard-thresholding-type methods, we propose in this work a soft-thresholding-type method with a theoretical support to use marginal regression combined with the lasso model for sparsity estimation.

3 Efficient Sparsity Estimation via Marginal-Lasso Coding

3.1 Sparsity Estimation via Marginal Regression

Consider a regression model $x = Us + z$ with an input feature $x \in \mathbb{R}^d$, a coefficient vector $s \in \mathbb{R}^p$, a column-wisely normalized dictionary $U = [u_1, \ldots, u_p] \in \mathbb{R}^{d \times p}$ ($p \gg d$) and a noise vector $z \in \mathbb{R}^d$. The feature quantization task is to quantize an input feature x into a feature histogram s with a few non-zero elements so that the linear combination of U and s can gain a minimized quantization error. The mathematical expression can be shown as follows:

$$\min_s \frac{1}{2}\|x - Us\|_2^2 \tag{1}$$

To estimate the sparse code s, we first compute the component-wise marginal regression coefficients $\hat{a}$:

$$\hat{a} \equiv U^T x \tag{2}$$

where $\hat{a}^{(k)} = u_k^T x$ is the kth element of $\hat{a}$ and u_k is the kth column of the dictionary U. Then, we threshold the coefficients in terms of their absolute values using a tuning parameter $t > 0$ [3,11] so that the coefficients whose absolute values are larger than t are kept and the rest are set to zero. The mathematical expression can be written as follows:

$$\hat{s}^{(k)} = \begin{cases} \hat{a}^{(k)} & \text{if } |\hat{a}^{(k)}| > t \\ 0 & \text{otherwise} \end{cases} \tag{3}$$

According to Eq. 3, however, utilizing a fixed tuning parameter may cause a large quantization error since it is not always the good cut-off point for each feature. Instead of cut-off point selection, we can select the top k large coefficients in terms of their absolute values whose L_1-norm is bounded by a constraint E [6,1]. The equation can be reformulated as follows:

$$\hat{s}^{(k)} = \begin{cases} \hat{a}^{(k)} & \text{if } k \in B \\ 0 & \text{otherwise} \end{cases} \tag{4}$$

where

$$B = \{J_1, \dots, J_r : r \le p : \sum_{k=1}^{r} |\hat{a}^{(J_k)}| \le E\} \tag{5}$$

We sort the coefficients in terms of their absolute values in descending order which denotes by indexes $J_1, \dots, J_p$ where $|\hat{s}^{(J_1)}| > |\hat{s}^{(J_2)}| > \cdots > |\hat{s}^{(J_p)}|$. The two thresholding approaches above are hard-thresholding-type methods.

3.2 Marginal-Lasso Coding

While marginal regression has shown its effectiveness, there still exists three limitations: (i) Marginal regression works well when the columns of dictionary have low correlation [1,23]. However, in general, the columns of over-complete dictionaries are usually highly correlated, and thus, in a linear regression model, their coefficients can become poorly determined and exhibit high variance. (ii) In addition, the fixed regularization parameter may cause a large quantization error. Some coefficients may be shuck too much and some may be included too much noise. (iii) Moreover, the existing marginal regression solutions are hard-thresholding-type methods, and there are no theoretical supports.

To address this, we consider the following conditions: (1) The regularization parameter should be chosen adaptively and automatically for each feature to minimize individual estimate of expected quantization error. (2) The L_1-norm in the lasso framework should be considered locally for visual word selection and coefficient shrinkage to alleviate the bias of sparse codes caused by the highly correlated visual words. (3) The L_1-norm in the constraint should be bounded locally and globally for sparse representation. To this end, we introduce a Marginal-Lasso Coding (MLC) method to better characterize input features and provide a theoretically soft-thresholding-type solution. Similar to the existing works, we first compute the marginal regression coefficients of each feature via Eq. 2. Then, we consider the following optimization problem:

$$\min_{s, \lambda} \frac{1}{2} \|U^T x - s\|_2^2 + \lambda \|s\|_1 \tag{6}$$

$$\text{subject to } \|s\|_1 \le E$$

The first term is the quantization error, and the second term is a local L_1 penalty with an adaptive regularization parameter λ which controls the cut-off point selection and the shrinkage of coefficients. The global sparsity constraint E bounds each sparse code to the similar sparsity level. In this model, we aim to estimate a sparse code and a parameter λ so that the quantization error can be minimized and the coefficients can be shrunk simultaneously for sparse representation. When considering multiple features, the optimization problems can be refined as follows:

$$\min_{\substack{s_1,\ldots,s_N \\ \lambda_1,\ldots,\lambda_N}} \frac{1}{2}\|U^T X - S\|_F^2 + \sum_{i=1}^{N} \lambda_i \|s_i\|_1$$

$$\text{subject to } \|s_i\|_1 \leq E \quad \forall i \tag{7}$$

where $X = [x_1, \ldots, x_N] \in \mathbb{R}^{d \times N}$ be a set of features, and $S = [s_1, \ldots, s_N] \in \mathbb{R}^{p \times N}$ be a set of corresponding sparse codes. Since the sparsity energy E is case-dependent variable, we provide here another self-ratio energy e such that each feature can obtain its sparse code by proportionally shrinking their marginal coefficients to the desired level. The constraint can be reformulated as follows:

$$\min_{\substack{s_1,\ldots,s_N \\ \lambda_1,\ldots,\lambda_N}} \frac{1}{2}\|U^T X - S\|_F^2 + \sum_{i=1}^{N} \lambda_i \|s_i\|_1$$

$$\text{subject to } \frac{\|f_\lambda(U^T x)\|_1}{\|U^T x\|_1} \leq e \quad \forall i \tag{8}$$

where $f_\lambda(A)$ refers to the solution of Eq. 3 with $\hat{a} = A$ and $t = \lambda$. While Eq. 7 considers the similar L_1-norm between sparse codes, Eq. 8 considers the similar self-ratio between each other.

3.3 Sparsity Estimation

When λ is fixed, we can solve the optimization problem of Eq. 6 by rewriting the objective as follows:

$$\min_s \frac{1}{2}\|\hat{a} - s\|_2^2 + \lambda\|s\|_1 \tag{9}$$

Minimizing the Eq. 9 is equivalent to minimize individual element errors with their corresponding absolute values. Thus, we can rewrite the objective as follows:

$$\min_s \frac{1}{2}\sum_{k=1}^{p}(\hat{a}^{(k)} - s^{(k)})^2 + \lambda|s^{(k)}| \tag{10}$$

Since the marginal regression coefficients are computed independently for each element, hence, we can decompose the problem into p separate optimization tasks. For each task k, the optimization problem can be defined as follows:

$$\min_{s^{(k)}} (\hat{a}^{(k)} - s^{(k)})^2 + \lambda|s^{(k)}| \tag{11}$$

Then, by solving the above optimization problem, we can obtain a soft-thresholding-type optimal solution of each element $s^{*(k)}$:

$$s^{*(k)} = \begin{cases} \hat{a}^{(k)} - \lambda & \text{if } \hat{a}^{(k)} > \lambda \\ \hat{a}^{(k)} + \lambda & \text{if } \hat{a}^{(k)} < -\lambda \\ 0 & \text{otherwise} \end{cases}$$

$$= \text{sign}(\hat{a}^{(k)})(|\hat{a}^{(k)}| - \lambda)_+ \tag{12}$$

where $sign(j)$ refers to the sign of j, and $(l)_+$ means to keep the value when l is positive and set it to zero when l is negative. The L_1-norm can be defined as the sum of absolute elements $\|s^*\|_1 = \sum_{k=1}^{p} |sign(\hat{a}^{(k)})(|\hat{a}^{(k)}| - \lambda)_+|$. In Eq. 12, the regularization parameter λ controls the element selection and the shrinkage of the coefficients. If λ equals to zero, then $\|s^*\|_1 = \|\hat{a}\|_1$. Instead, if $\lambda > 0$, then some coefficients will be directly set to zero and others will be shrunk towards zero automatically so that $\|s^*\|_1 < \|\hat{a}\|_1$. By maximizing $\|s^*\|_1$ bounded by the global sparsity constraint E, the individual λ^* can be calculated as follows:

$$\lambda^* = \arg\max_{\lambda} \|s^*\|_1 = \arg\max_{\lambda} \sum_{k=1}^{p} |sign(\hat{a}^{(k)})(|\hat{a}^{(k)}| - \lambda)_+| \tag{13}$$

$$\text{subject to } \|s^*\|_1 \leq E$$

By doing so, we can estimate each element of the sparse code $s^{*(k)} = sign(\hat{a}^{(k)})(|\hat{a}^{(k)}| - \lambda^*)_+$ which is a soft-thresholding-type solution. When considering a set of features, the optimization problem of Eq. 7 or 8 can be solved via Algorithm 1.

4   Marginal-Lasso Coding for Dictionary Learning

The dictionary U is a set of normalized visual words denoting by each column u_k. To learn the dictionary, we iteratively optimize U and S by obtaining S with a fixed U and updating U based on a given S. The sparsity estimation S via the marginal-lasso model has been introduced in the previous subsection. In this subsection, we introduce the dictionary learning method. Since marginal regression works well when the columns in the dictionary have low correlation [6,11,1,23], we formulate the optimization problem of the dictionary learning as follows:

$$\min_{U} \sum_{i=1}^{N} \|x_i - Us_i\|_2^2 + \gamma\|U^TU - I\|_F^2 \tag{18}$$

$$\text{subject to } u_k^T u_k \leq 1 \quad \forall k$$

We simultaneously minimize the quantization errors denoting by the first term and the correlations between columns in the second term with a regularization parameter γ. This optimization problem can be solved via the first-order gradient descent method [23,1]:

$$U_{q+1} = \Pi_U \{U_q - \beta\nabla F(U_q)\} \tag{19}$$

where

$$F(U) = \sum_{i=1}^{N} \|x_i - Us_i\|_2^2 + \gamma\|U^TU - I\|_F^2 \tag{20}$$

and

$$\nabla F(U_q) = 2(U_q SS^T - XS^T) + 4\gamma(U_q U_q^T U_q - U_q) \tag{21}$$

$\nabla F(U_q)$ is the gradient of $F(U)$ with respect to U at each iteration q, parameter β is the step size, and Π_U is the projection function which maps each column u_k to the

---

Algorithm 1. Efficient Sparsity Estimation via Marginal-Lasso Coding

Require: Data $X = [x_1, \ldots, x_N] \in \mathbb{R}^{d \times N}$, a learned dictionary $U = [u_1, \ldots, u_p] \in \mathbb{R}^{d \times p}$, and a specific value of the sparsity constraint E or a self-ratio constraint e

Ensure: Sparse coefficients $S = [s_1, \ldots, s_N] \in \mathbb{R}^{p \times N}$

1: For x_i $\forall i$, compute the marginal regression coefficients

$$\hat{a}_i^{(k)} = \frac{u_k^T x_i}{\|u_k\|_2^2} \quad \forall k \tag{14}$$

2: Calculate the regularization parameter λ_i for each x_i $\forall i$ based on the sparsity constraint E of Eq. 6 and 13

$$\lambda_i^* = \arg\max_{\lambda_i} \|s_i^*\|_1 = \arg\max_{\lambda_i} \sum_{k=1}^p |\text{sign}(\hat{a}_i^{(k)})(|\hat{a}_i^{(k)}| - \lambda_i)_+| \tag{15}$$

$$\text{subject to } \|s_i\|_1 \leq E$$

Or calculate the regularization parameter λ_i for each x_i $\forall i$ based on the self-ratio constraint e in Eq. 8

$$\lambda_i^* = \arg\max_{\lambda_i} \|s_i^*\|_1 = \arg\max_{\lambda_i} \sum_{k=1}^p |\text{sign}(\hat{a}_i^{(k)})(|\hat{a}_i^{(k)}| - \lambda_i)_+| \tag{16}$$

$$\text{subject to } \frac{\|f_{\lambda_i}(U^T x_i)\|_1}{\|U^T x_i\|_1} \leq e$$

3: Obtain sparse codes

$$s_i^{*(k)} = \begin{cases} \hat{a}_i^{(k)} - \lambda_i^* & \text{if } \hat{a}_i^{(k)} > \lambda_i^* \\ \hat{a}_i^{(k)} + \lambda_i^* & \text{if } \hat{a}_i^{(k)} < -\lambda_i^* \\ 0 & \text{otherwise} \end{cases} \tag{17}$$

L_2-norm unit ball. More specifically, the dictionary is learned iteratively by finding the local minimum along the gradient direction based on the small step size and normalizing each column vector with length smaller or equal to one until convergence. The sparsity estimation and the dictionary learning process is shown in Algorithm 2.

5   Experimental Results

In this section, we describe the experimental settings and analyze the proposed method on the image classification, action recognition and activity-based human identification tasks. We denote the proposed marginal-lasso coding approach by MLC with Matlab implementation. We compare the proposed method with 5 algorithms: (1) The lasso model with feature-sign search (LASSO-FS): the code has been implemented by its authors in Matlab [20]. (2) The lasso model with least angle regression (LASSO-LAR): we used the code from SPAMS software implemented by C++ [23]. (3) The marginal regression model with the hard-thresholding method (MR-Hard): we implemented it in

---

Algorithm 2. Sparsity Estimation and Dictionary Learning

Require: Data $X = [x_1, \ldots, x_N] \in \mathbb{R}^{d \times N}$, an initial normalized dictionary $U = [u_1, \ldots, u_p] \in \mathbb{R}^{d \times p}$, and an energy bound with value E or self-ratio e
Ensure: Learned dictionary $U \in \mathbb{R}^{d \times p}$, sparse coefficients $S = [s_1, \ldots, s_N] \in \mathbb{R}^{p \times N}$
1: **repeat**
2:     Obtain sparse code via Algorithm 1 using the latest dictionary.

$$\min_{\substack{s_1, \ldots, s_N \\ \lambda_1, \ldots, \lambda_N}} \frac{1}{2} \|U^T X - S\|_F^2 + \sum_{i=1}^N \lambda_i \|s_i\|_1 \tag{22}$$

$$\text{subject to } \|s_i\|_1 \leq E \quad \forall i$$

3:     Update the dictionary based on the sparse codes obtained from the previous step.

$$\min_U \sum_{i=1}^N \|x_i - U s_i\|_2^2 + \gamma \|U^T U - I\|_F^2 \tag{23}$$

$$\text{subject to } u_k^T u_k \leq 1 \quad \forall k$$

4: **until** convergence

Matlab according to Eq. 3. (4) The marginal regression model with the soft-thresholding method (MR-Soft): we implemented it in Matlab according to Eq. 3 with soft thresholding. (5) The marginal regression model with the sure independence screening method (MR-SIS): we implemented it in Matlab according to Eq. 4.

5.1 Image Classification

We evaluate the performance of the proposed method for the image classification task on USPS and Scene 15 datasets. USPS is a handwritten digits dataset [14,31] which consists of 7291 training images and 2007 test images of size 16×16 with digits 0 to 9. We represent each sample by a 256-dimensional vector. The dictionary sizes are selected from $32, 64, 128, 256, 512, 1024$ under different training sizes. For the penalty constraint, we adopt self-ratio in Eq. (8), and the parameters are set empirically via cross-validation. To evaluate the performance, we train a linear SVM classifier and compare to original regression (OR) and sparse coding (SC) methods. Table 1 shows the results under different sizes of training samples from 100 to 7291. As shown, the proposed MLC method outperforms the other two methods in most of the cases and obtains the best accuracy result 95.3 under 5000 training sample size.

Scene 15 [24,21,19] contains 4485 images with 15 categories. Each category consists of ranging from 200 to 400 images with average size of 300×250 pixels. This dataset is very diverse from indoor such as living room, kitchen, office, store, etc., to outdoor including street, inside city, building, mountain, forest, etc. Following the same setting as the previous works [19,30], we randomly select 100 images per category as training samples and the rest as test samples and incorporate the proposed method with spatial pyramid matching which denotes by MLcSPM. Table 2 shows the results. As shown, our MLcSPM method outperforms other methods, especially for the

Table 1. Recognition accuracy (%) of different methods on the USPS dataset

Method \ Size of training set	100	500	1000	2000	5000	7291
OR	81.7	88.4	90.1	91.4	92.3	93.8
SC	79.6	88.0	90.4	91.8	92.9	94.5
MLC	74.5	91.1	92.9	94.2	95.3	94.0

Table 2. Recognition accuracy (%) of different methods on the Scene 15 dataset

Method \ Size of training set	100
KSPM [19]	81.40
KC [10]	76.67
ScSPM [30]	80.28
HardSPM	75.72
SoftSPM	79.48
SISSPM	81.37
MLcSPM	82.54

popular lasso-based ScSPM scheme. Further, the proposed MLcSPM outperforms other marginal regression based methods.

5.2   Action Recognition

We analyze the characteristic of the proposed method using the KTH action recognition dataset. The KTH dataset [26] contains 25 persons. Each person performed 6 different activities, including boxing, handclapping, handwaving, jogging, running, and walking, respectively. There are 4 scenarios under each activity, including outdoors, outdoors with scale variation, outdoors with different clothes and indoors, respectively, resulting 599 video sequences in total. We follow the original experimental setup which divides clips into 2391 subclips with 863 clips for the test set (9 subjects) and 1528 clips for the training set (16 subjects). We use three space-time local feature descriptors in the experiments, HOG, HOF and HOGHOF [18] obtained by a 3D-Harris detector [17], and quantize each local feature into a sparse code via Algorithm 1. After that, we represent each video clip using the maximum pooling method and use a non-linear support vector machine [2] with a X^2 kernel [18]. We select the parameters using cross validation. To speedup the dictionary learning process, we firstly learn an initial dictionary using online dictionary learning method [23] with 100 runs as the warm start.

Comparison between Hard-Thresholding and Soft-Thresholding: We encode each HOF local feature using a hard-thresholding technique, MR-Hard, and a soft-thresholding technique, MR-Soft, respectively, with dictionary size 4000 in the training set as the tunning parameter t varies. Fig. 1 (a) shows the average L_1-norm energy of sparse codes under different t. As shown, using the soft-thresholding scheme is a more effective way for variable selection and coefficient shrinkage. Further, the soft-thresholding

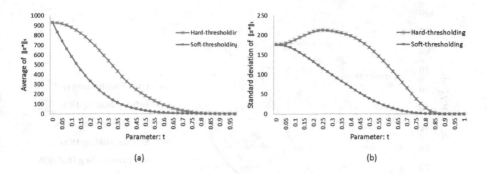

Fig. 1. Comparison of the soft and hard-thresholding schemes. (a) The average L_1-norm energy of sparse codes under different t. As shown, using the soft-thresholding scheme is a more effective way for variable selection and coefficient shrinkage. (b) The average standard deviation of the L_1-norm energy between sparse codes as t changes. Sparse codes obtained via the soft-thresholding scheme are much stable than those obtained via the hard-thresholding scheme under different t.

scheme achieves smaller standard deviation between sparse codes as t varies as shown in Fig. 1 (b). In the recognition point of view, Fig. 2 shows the recognition accuracy of MR-Soft and MR-Hard with the HOG, HOF, and HOGHOF features respectively under different t. The accuracy of the MR-soft method is much better than that of the MR-Hard method. Therefore, we can conclude that soft-thresholding technique such as MR-Soft is much stable and robust than hard-thresholding technique such as MR-Hard.

Energy Discussion: The sparsity constraint E in Eq. 6 needs to be specified a value, and the value may vary with different datasets. Instead, the self-ratio constraint e in Eq. 8 aims to keep the certain ratio of the marginal regression coefficients in terms of L_1-norm energy. For example, the self-ratio $e = 5\%$ means that, for each feature, only 5% of its marginal regression coefficients in terms of the L_1 norm can be kept and the rest will be set to zero. Thus, we can obtain sparse codes more easily by assigning a desired ratio. Fig. 3 shows the recognition accuracy between different values of the self-ratio constraint e. The results show that we obtain around 90% recognition accuracy by setting the self-ratio e from 5% to 35%, and obtain poor recognition accuracy (below 10%) by setting e from 75% to 100%. Therefore, we can conclude that sparse representation helps signal interpretation.

Speed Comparison: In this subsection, we examine the feature quantization speed using different sparsity estimation methods under three different feature descriptors, HOG, HOF and HOGHOF, respectively. The dictionary sizes are set from 1000 to 4000. It is worth mentioning that all the methods except for LASSO-LAR were implemented in Matlab, and thus it would be unfair to compare them with the LASSO-LAR method together since C++ program of LASSO-LAR has a built-in speed advantage. Nevertheless, as shown in Table 3, the marginal regression related methods still take significantly less time than those of the lasso solutions. In addition, MR-SIS and MLC have

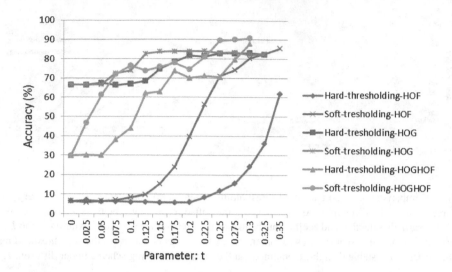

Fig. 2. Accuracy of soft and hard-thresholding with the HOG, HOF and HOGHOF features as t varies. The accuracy of MR-soft is much better than that of MR-Hard in terms of recognition accuracy under three different features.

comparable quantization speed but perform slower than MR-Hard and MR-soft since the former two consider the L_1-norm energy constraint, and the latter two do not.

Feature Quantization Error: Except for the speed comparison, Table 3 also shows the quantization errors. As shown, LASSO-FS and LASSO-LAR achieve the lowest quantization error. For the marginal regression related methods, the energy-based methods (MR-SIS and MLC) achieve lower quantization error than those without L_1-norm energy (MR-Hard and MR-Soft) constraint. In addition, the soft-thresholding-like methods achieve lower quantization error than the hard-thresholding-like methods pairwisely, i.e. MR-Soft against MR-Hard, and MLC against MR-SIS.

Recognition Accuracy: Table 4 shows the recognition accuracy under three different features with the dictionary size 4000. In this experiment, we select the sparsity constraint E via cross validation, and compare the proposed MLC model to other marginal related methods: MR-Hard, MR-Soft and MR-SIS. As shown, the proposed MLC approach obtains the best results, and the MR-Hard method obtains the worst and performs poorly under the HOF feature. In addition, the energy-based methods (MLC and MR-SIS) performs better than those without the energy constraint (MR-Hard and MR-Soft), and the soft-thresholding-type methods have better performance against the hard-thresholding-type methods pairwisely (MLC against MR-SIS and MR-Soft against MR-Hard).

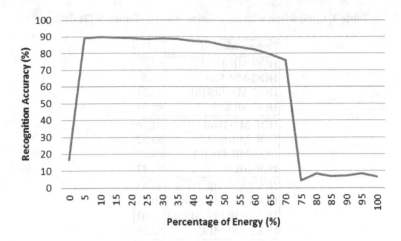

Fig. 3. Recognition accuracy under different self-ratios

Table 3. Comparison with the existing methods for the KTH dataset. The results are shown in terms of speed and quantization error. Notice that here we random sampled 1,258 features from the training set. The actual numbers of the local features in the KTH dataset are 261,946 for the training set and 136,219 for the test set.

Method \ Dictionary size	time (sec)				Reconstruction error			
	1000	2000	3000	4000	1000	2000	3000	4000
HOG-LASSO-FS [20]	8.08	9.71	18.83	19.77	0.04	0.03	0.03	0.03
HOG-LASSO-LAR [4]	1.69	3.61	5.81	7.67	0.04	0.03	0.03	0.03
HOG-MR-Hard	0.03	0.05	0.08	0.11	781.94	3438.42	8079.61	14863.70
HOG-MR-Soft	0.03	0.06	0.09	0.12	68.40	319.07	764.57	1423.95
HOG-MR-SIS [6]	0.54	1.01	1.48	2.03	2.92	2.90	12.13	4.68
HOG-MLC	0.47	0.92	1.44	1.93	2.20	2.43	2.47	2.57
HOF-LASSO-FS [20]	5.47	6.95	13.89	14.96	0.03	0.03	0.03	0.02
HOF-LASSO-LAR [4]	1.15	2.64	4.61	6.07	0.03	0.03	0.03	0.02
HOF-MR-Hard	0.03	0.06	0.09	0.12	7317.76	32218.46	77688.51	142454.52
HOF-MR-Soft	0.03	0.07	0.10	0.14	1258.00	5818.47	14413.56	26806.27
HOF-MR-SIS [6]	0.65	1.19	1.80	2.34	17.02	29.80	39.24	65.60
HOF-MLC	0.64	1.21	1.86	2.48	3.35	3.27	3.12	3.09
HOGHOF-LASSO-FS [20]	7.73	9.34	17.83	18.46	0.07	0.06	0.05	0.05
HOGHOF-LASSO-LAR [4]	1.60	3.52	5.79	7.78	0.07	0.06	0.05	0.05
HOGHOF-MR-Hard	0.03	0.06	0.09	0.12	595.99	2366.80	5247.93	9215.52
HOGHOF-MR-Soft	0.03	0.06	0.10	0.14	47.14	192.52	431.67	765.61
HOGHOF-MR-SIS [6]	0.52	0.97	1.45	1.93	2.90	2.95	3.03	2.91
HOGHOF-MLC	0.44	0.88	1.34	1.79	2.18	2.33	2.43	2.47

Table 4. Comparison with the existing methods for the KTH dataset

Feature-Method	KTH
HOG-MR-Hard	82.27
HOG-MR-Soft	82.39
HOG-MR-SIS [6]	84.01
HOG-MLC	85.98
HOF-MR-Hard	61.76
HOF-MR-Soft	85.52
HOF-MR-SIS [6]	89.11
HOF-MLC	92.47
HOGHOF-MR-Hard	87.83
HOGHOF-MR-Soft	90.73
HOGHOF-MR-SIS [6]	90.03
HOGHOF-MLC	92.35

Summary: While the lasso-like models (LASSO-FS and LASSO-LAR) achieve the lowest quantization error, they take more time to obtain sparse codes. Instead, the marginal regression models without energy constraint (MR-Hard and MR-Soft) can reach the fastest speed to generate sparse codes; however, they also gain the highest quantization errors. While MR-SIS can compete with our model in terms of the quantization error, we reach better recognition accuracy than that of MR-SIS as shown in Table 4 because the proposed approach is a soft-thresholding method which is more stable and robust. There are two main differences between the MR-SIS model and the proposed MLC model: 1) While the idea of MR-SIS is frequently used of the hard-thresholding technique in the applications, it has no theoretical support. We integrates marginal regression and the lasso model with a theoretical support which is a soft-thresholding scheme. 2) We estimate the regularization parameter for each individual input feature and gain the lower quantization error than that of the MR-SIS model.

5.3 Activity-Based Human Identification

The activity-based human identification task aims to recognize the identity of a person based on his/her activities. We performed the experiment on two publicly available databases, weizmann [13] and MOBISERV-AIIA [16], respectively. In the dataset, each clip contains a person performing one activity. For each image frame, we extract human body silhouette which is similar to the way in [25,12,16,22,15]. An initial dictionary is learned via the online learning method proposed in [23] to speed up the learning process. The weizmann dataset contains 215 clips with 9 persons performing 9 different activities. The bend activity is excluded due to lack of samples. We randomly select one clip per action per class as training data, and use the remaining as test data. The MOBISERV-AIIA dataset contains 12 persons performing eating and drinking activities with 2 clothing scenarios in four different days. We adopt 2 kinds of the activities, drinking with a cup and eating with a fork, with 776 clips in total. We randomly choose one-day sequences as test samples and use the rest as the training samples.

The parameters are determined via cross validation. Table 5 shows the recognition accuracy based on the 10% self-ratio sparsity constraint. In this application, the soft-thresholding-type methods (MLC and MR-Soft) work better than the hard-thresholding-type methods (MR-Hard and MR-SIS). In addition, MLC outperforms MR-Soft.

Table 5. Comparison with the existing methods for the weizmann and the MOBISERV-AIIA datasets

backslashboxMethodDataset	weizmann	MOBISERV-AIIA
MR-Hard	69.40	62.69
MR-Soft	79.85	70.47
MR-SIS [6]	77.61	67.88
MLC	85.82	73.06

6   Conclusion

In this paper, we have proposed a novel feature quantization approach for sparsity estimation by exploiting the advantages of the marginal regression and the lasso simultaneously to provide more efficient and effective solutions. The proposed approach has been evaluated on three visual applications: image classification, action recognition and activity-based human identification. Experimental results have shown that our method can achieve excellent performance in terms of speed, quantization error and recognition accuracy. All these sufficiently demonstrate the efficacy of our proposed methods.

Acknowledgment. This work is supported by the research grant for the Human Cyber Security Systems (HCSS) Program at the Advanced Digital Sciences Center from the Agency for Science, Technology and Research of Singapore.

References

1. Balasubramanian, K., Yu, K., Lebanon, G.: smooth sparse coding via marginal regression for learning sparse representations. In: ICML (2013)
2. Chang, C.C., Lin, C.J.: Libsvm: A library for support vector machines. ACM Trans. Intell. Syst. Technol. 2(3), 27:1–27:27 (2011)
3. Donoho, D.L.: For most large underdetermined systems of linear equations the minimal l1-norm solution is also the sparsest solution. Comm. Pure Appl. Math. 59, 797–829 (2004)
4. Efron, B., Hastie, T., Johnstone, I., Tibshirani, R.: Least angle regression. Annals of Statistics (2004)
5. Elhamifar, E., Vidal, R.: Robust classification using structured sparse representation. In: CVPR (2011)
6. Fan, J., Lv, J.: Sure independence screening for ultrahigh dimensional feature space. Journal of the Royal Statistical Society: Series B (Statistical Methodology) 70(5), 849–911 (2008)
7. Friedman, J., Hastie, T., Hofling, H., Tibshirani, R.: Pathwise coordinate optimization (2007)
8. Gao, S., Tsang, I., Chia, L.: Laplacian sparse coding, hypergraph laplacian sparse coding, and applications. IEEE Transactions on Pattern Analysis and Machine Intelligence(2012)

9. Gao, S., Tsang, I.W.H., Chia, L.T., Zhao, P.: Local features are not lonely - laplacian sparse coding for image classification. In: 2013 IEEE Conference on Computer Vision and Pattern Recognition (2010)

10. van Gemert, J.C., Geusebroek, J.-M., Veenman, C.J., Smeulders, A.W.M.: Kernel codebooks for scene categorization. In: Forsyth, D., Torr, P., Zisserman, A. (eds.) ECCV 2008, Part III. LNCS, vol. 5304, pp. 696–709. Springer, Heidelberg (2008)

11. Genovese, C.R., Jin, J., Wasserman, L., Yao, Z.: A comparison of the lasso and marginal regression. J. Mach. Learn. Res. 13(1), 2107–2143 (2012)

12. Gkalelis, N., Tefas, A., Pitas, I.: Human identification from human movements. In: ICIP, pp. 2585–2588 (2009)

13. Gorelick, L., Blank, M., Shechtman, E., Irani, M., Basri, R.: Action as space-time shapes. PAMI 29(12), 224–2253 (2007)

14. Hull, J.: A database for handwritten text recognition research. PAMI 16(5), 550–554 (1994)

15. Hung, T.-Y., Lu, J., Tan, Y.-P.: Graph-based sparse coding and embedding for activity-based human identification. In: ICME (2013)

16. Iosifidis, A., Tefas, A., Pitas, I.: Activity based person identification using fuzzy representation and discriminant learning. TIFS 7(2), 530–542 (2012)

17. Laptev, I.: On space-time interest points. International Journal of Computer Vision 64(2-3), 107–123 (2005)

18. Laptev, I., Marszalek, M., Schmid, C., Rozenfeld, B.: Learning realistic human actions from movies. In: CVPR (2008)

19. Lazebnik, S., Schmid, C., Ponce, J.: Beyond bags of features: Spatial pyramid matching for recognizing natural scene categories. In: CVPR, pp. 2169–2178 (2006)

20. Lee, H., Battle, A., Raina, R., Ng, A.Y.: Efficient sparse coding algorithms. In: Schölkopf, B., Platt, J., Hoffman, T. (eds.) Advances in Neural Information Processing Systems, vol. 19, pp. 801–808. MIT Press, Cambridge (2007)

21. Li, F.F., Perona, P.: A bayesian hierarchical model for learning natural scene categories. In: CVPR, pp. 524–531 (2005)

22. Lu, J., Hu, J., Zhou, X., Shang, Y.: Activity-based human identification using sparse coding and discriminative metric learning. In: ACM Multimedia (2012)

23. Mairal, J., Bach, F., Ponce, J., Sapiro, G.: Online learning for matrix factorization and sparse coding. J. Mach. Learn. Res. 11, 19–60 (2010)

24. Oliva, A., Torralba, A.: Modeling the shape of the scene: A holistic representation of the spatial envelope. IJCV 42(3), 145–175 (2001)

25. Sarkar, S., Phillips, P.J., Liu, Z., Vega, I.R., Grother, P., Bowyer, K.W.: The humanID gait challenge problem: data sets, performance, and analysis. PAMI 27(2), 162–177 (2005)

26. Schuldt, C., Laptev, I., Caputo, B.: Recognizing human actions: A local svm approach. In: ICPR, pp. 32–36 (2004)

27. Tibshirani, R.: Regression shrinkage and selection via the lasso. Journal of the Royal Statistical Society. Series B (Methodological) 58(1), 267–288 (1996)

28. Wright, J., Yang, A., Ganesh, A., Sastry, S., Ma, Y.: Robust face recognition via sparse representation. IEEE Transactions on Pattern Analysis and Machine Intelligence 31(2), 210–227 (2009)

29. Wu, T., Lange, K.: Coordinate descent algorithms for lasso penalized regression. Annals of Applied Statistics (2008)

30. Yang, J., Yu, K., Gong, Y., Huang, T.: Linear spatial pyramid matching using sparse coding for image classification. In: IEEE Conference on Computer Vision and Pattern Recognition, CVPR 2009, pp. 1794–1801 (June 2009)

31. Zheng, M., Bu, J., Chen, C., Wang, C., Zhang, L., Qiu, G., Cai, D.: Graph regularized sparse coding for image representation. IEEE Transactions on Image Processing 20(5), 1327–1336 (2011)

Continuous Conditional Neural Fields for Structured Regression

Tadas Baltrušaitis[1], Peter Robinson[1], and Louis-Philippe Morency[2]

[1] Computer Laboratory, University of Cambridge, UK
{tadas.baltrusaitis,peter.robinson}@cl.cam.ac.uk
[2] Institute for Creative Technologies, University of Southern California, CA
morency@ict.usc.edu

Abstract. An increasing number of computer vision and pattern recognition problems require structured regression techniques. Problems like human pose estimation, unsegmented action recognition, emotion prediction and facial landmark detection have temporal or spatial output dependencies that regular regression techniques do not capture. In this paper we present continuous conditional neural fields (CCNF) – a novel structured regression model that can learn non-linear input-output dependencies, and model temporal and spatial output relationships of varying length sequences. We propose two instances of our CCNF framework: Chain-CCNF for time series modelling, and Grid-CCNF for spatial relationship modelling. We evaluate our model on five public datasets spanning three different regression problems: facial landmark detection in the wild, emotion prediction in music and facial action unit recognition. Our CCNF model demonstrates state-of-the-art performance on all of the datasets used.

Keywords: Structured regression, Landmark detection, Face tracking.

1 Introduction

As an extension to the conventional regression problem, structured regression algorithms are designed to take advantage of the relationships between output variables. A number of computer vision problems such as human pose estimation and unsegmented action recognition exhibit temporal output structure. Structured regression is also desirable when modelling 2D spatial relationships for landmark detection problems. Another important aspect of many prediction problems is the need for modelling variable length sequences or variable size 2D grids. This is both because we might have varying length video sequences as training data; and because we would like our approaches to generalise to sequences of arbitrary length.

In this paper we present the *continuous conditional neural field* (CCNF) model that can perform structured regression. The key features of CCNF are: (1) a structured regression model; (2) captures non-linearities between input and output; (3) can easily define temporal and spatial relationships (long and short

D. Fleet et al. (Eds.): ECCV 2014, Part IV, LNCS 8692, pp. 593–608, 2014.

distance); (4) ability to model arbitrary and different length sequences; (5) simple and efficient single pass inference.

We propose two instances of our CCNF framework: Chain-CCNF for time series modelling, and Grid-CCNF for spatial relationship modelling. We evaluate CCNF on five public datasets spanning three very different and challenging regression problems: facial landmark detection in the wild, emotion prediction in music and facial action unit recognition.[1] This work is a generalisation of our work on Grid-CCNF [1].

First we present a brief overview of structured prediction and regression techniques (Section 1.1). This is followed by the description of our CCNF model (Section 2). The two instances of the model are evaluated in Sections 3 and 4.

1.1   Prior Work

The most often used techniques for regression problems in computer vision and pattern recognition communities are linear and logistic regression, support vector regression (SVR), neural networks, and relevance vector machines (RVM) [2]. These approaches are designed to model input-output dependencies disregarding the output-output structure. SVR models have been used for modelling alignment probabilities of facial landmarks [3,4], inferring continuous emotions from music [5] and human behaviour [6], and the recognition of facial action units in videos [7]. RVM is another popular approach and has been used for emotion prediction from facial expressions [8] and speech [9].

The greatest amount of work on structured prediction concentrates on discrete outputs (classification). Popular approaches include conditional random fields (CRF) [10], Hidden Markov Models [2] structural SVM [11] and Markov Random Field models [12]. Another example of a structured classification method that is suitable for temporal modelling is the Conditional Neural Fields Model [13], which augments CRF with the ability to model non-linear relationships. It is possible to convert regression problems to classification ones through quantisation. However, this can lead to loss of information and of relationships between neighbouring classes, moreover, the number of classes to be used is often unclear.

There has been some recent work exploring structured regression as well. One such example is the Output-Associative Relevance Vector Machine (OA-RVM), that has been used for emotion prediction from facial expressions [8]. Other examples include SVR models for structured output [14] and the twinned Gaussian process model that exploits the output dependencies of multi-variate output [15]. Both of these approaches have been used for human pose estimation. However, few of the above mentioned approaches are suitable for modelling arbitrary length sequences, such as varying length time-series, directly.

Another structured regression approach is the continuous conditional random fields (CCRF) [16] model, that extends the CRF model to the continuous case. CCRF model relies on initial prediction from an unstructured regression model

---

[1] Code available at https://github.com/TadasBaltrusaitis/CCNF

such as SVR [17], making the training procedure more complex. Our approach does not suffer from this problem as all of its parameters are optimised jointly.

2   Continuous Conditional Neural Fields

In this section we introduce and define our CCNF model for structured regression. The model definition is presented in Section 2.1, followed by description of learning and inference in Section 2.2. Section 2.3 presents two specific instantiations of our model.

2.1   Model Definition

In our discussion we adopt the following notation: $\boldsymbol{x} = \{\mathbf{x}_1, \mathbf{x}_2, \ldots, \mathbf{x}_n\}$ is a set of observed input variables ($\mathbf{x}_i \in \mathcal{R}^m$), $\mathbf{y} = \{y_1, y_2, \ldots, y_n\}$ is a set of output variables ($y_i \in \mathcal{R}$) that we wish to predict, n is the size of the set (length of sequence or the number of pixels we are interested in), and m is the dimensionality of input vector.

CCNF is an undirected graphical model that can learn the conditional probability of a continuous valued vector $\mathbf{y}$ depending on continuous $\boldsymbol{x}$. A graphical illustration of our two model instances – Chain-CCNF and Grid-CCNF, can be seen in Figure 1. We define our CCNF model as:

$$P(\mathbf{y}|\boldsymbol{x}) = \frac{\exp(\varPsi)}{\int_{-\infty}^{\infty} \exp(\varPsi)d\mathbf{y}} \tag{1}$$

Our potential function is defined as:

$$\varPsi = \sum_i \sum_{k=1}^{K1} \alpha_k f_k(y_i, \boldsymbol{x}, \boldsymbol{\theta}_k) + \sum_{i,j} \sum_{k=1}^{K2} \beta_k g_k(y_i, y_j) + \\ \sum_{i,j} \sum_{k=1}^{K3} \gamma_k l_k(y_i, y_j) \tag{2}$$

We define three types of feature functions in our model – vertex features (f_k) and two types of edge features (g_k, l_k), see Figure 1 for an illustration.

Vertex features f_k represent the mapping from the input $\mathbf{x}_i$ to output y_i through a single layer neural network and $\boldsymbol{\theta}_k$ is the weight vector for a particular neuron k. The corresponding α_k for vertex feature f_k represents the reliability of the kth neuron.

$$f_k(y_i, \boldsymbol{x}, \boldsymbol{\theta}_k) = -(y_i - h(\boldsymbol{\theta}_k, \mathbf{x}_i))^2, \tag{3}$$

$$h(\boldsymbol{\theta}, \mathbf{x}) = \frac{1}{1 + e^{-\boldsymbol{\theta}^T \mathbf{x}}}; \tag{4}$$

Edge features g_k represent the similarities between observations y_i and y_j, allowing the model to enforce smoothness. This is controlled by the neighbourhood measure $S^{(g_k)}$, which allows us to control where the smoothness is to be enforced (which nodes should be connected). If $S_{i,j}^{(g_k)} > 0$ there exists a similarity connection between y_i and y_j; if $S_{i,j}^{(g_k)} = 0$ they are not connected. It is

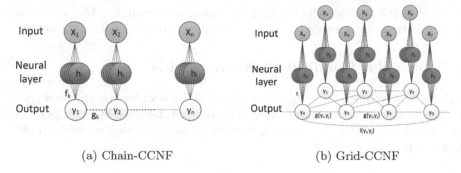

(a) Chain-CCNF   (b) Grid-CCNF

Fig. 1. Two instances of our CCNF model: Chain-CCNF and Grid-CCNF. Solid lines represent vertex features (f_k), dashed lines represent edge features (g_k or l_k). The input vector $\mathbf{x}_i$ is connected to the relevant output y_i through the vertex features that combine the neural layer (Θ) and the vertex weights $\boldsymbol{\alpha}$. The outputs are further connected with edge features g_k (similarity) or l_k (sparsity). Only direct links from $\mathbf{x}_i$ to y_i are presented here, but extensions are straightforward.

important to note that CCNF supports connections between any of the nodes, allowing us to create long range dependencies and still retain tractable training and inference.

$$g_k(y_i, y_j) = -\frac{1}{2}S_{i,j}^{(g_k)}(y_i - y_j)^2;$$ (5)

Edge features l_k represent the sparsity (or inhibition) constraint between observations y_i and y_j. For example the model is penalised if both y_i and y_j are high, but is not penalised if both of them are zero (note that we are constrained to certain types of edge and vertex features in order to keep model learning and inference tractable). This is controlled by the neighbourhood measure $S^{(l_k)}$ that allows us to define regions where sparsity/inhibition should be enforced. This feature is particularly useful if we want to model output as a unimodal probability density (which is the case for landmark detection).

$$l_k(y_i, y_j) = -\frac{1}{2}S_{i,j}^{(l_k)}(y_i + y_j)^2.$$ (6)

The feature functions are parametrised by parameters that need to be learned: $\boldsymbol{\alpha} = \{\alpha_1, \alpha_2, \ldots \alpha_{K1}\}$, $\boldsymbol{\Theta} = \{\boldsymbol{\theta}_1, \boldsymbol{\theta}_2, \ldots \boldsymbol{\theta}_{K1}\}$, $\boldsymbol{\beta} = \{\beta_1, \beta_2, \ldots \beta_{K2}\}$, and $\boldsymbol{\gamma} = \{\gamma_1, \gamma_2, \ldots \gamma_{K3}\}$. The number of edge feature functions (K2, and K3) is dependent on the CCNF instance (see Section 2.3) and the number of vertex feature functions K1 depends on the nature of the regression problem and can be determined during model validation.

2.2 Learning

In this section we describe how to estimate the parameters $\{\boldsymbol{\alpha}, \boldsymbol{\beta}, \boldsymbol{\gamma}, \boldsymbol{\Theta}\}$. It is important to note that all of the parameters are optimised jointly. We learn the temporal/spatial structure alongside the mapping from features to the prediction, which is not the case in a model like CCRF.

We are given training data $\{\mathbf{x}^{(q)}, \mathbf{y}^{(q)}\}_{q=1}^{M}$ of M sets, where each $\mathbf{x}^{(q)} = \{\mathbf{x}_1^{(q)}, \mathbf{x}_2^{(q)}, \ldots, \mathbf{x}_n^{(q)}\}$ is a set of inputs and each $\mathbf{y}^{(q)} = \{y_1^{(q)}, y_2^{(q)}, \ldots, y_n^{(q)}\}$ is a set of real valued outputs, n can be different for each set.

In learning we want to optimise the $\boldsymbol{\alpha}$, $\boldsymbol{\beta}$, $\boldsymbol{\gamma}$ and $\boldsymbol{\Theta}$ parameters that maximise the conditional log-likelihood of CCNF on the training sequences:

$$L(\boldsymbol{\alpha}, \boldsymbol{\beta}, \boldsymbol{\gamma}, \boldsymbol{\Theta}) = \sum_{q=1}^{M} \log P(\mathbf{y}^{(q)}|\mathbf{x}^{(q)}) \tag{7}$$

$$(\boldsymbol{\alpha}^*, \boldsymbol{\beta}^*, \boldsymbol{\gamma}^*, \boldsymbol{\Theta}^*) = \arg\max_{\boldsymbol{\alpha}, \boldsymbol{\beta}, \boldsymbol{\gamma}, \boldsymbol{\Theta}} (L(\boldsymbol{\alpha}, \boldsymbol{\beta}, \boldsymbol{\gamma}, \boldsymbol{\Theta})) \tag{8}$$

Because of the careful vertex and edge feature selection, Equation 1 can be transformed into a multivariate Gaussian form (a more detailed derivation can be found in the Appendix in the supplementary material):

$$P(\mathbf{y}|\mathbf{x}) = \frac{1}{(2\pi)^{\frac{n}{2}}|\Sigma|^{\frac{1}{2}}} \exp(-\frac{1}{2}(\mathbf{y} - \boldsymbol{\mu})^T \Sigma^{-1}(\mathbf{y} - \boldsymbol{\mu})). \tag{9}$$

This is achieved by collecting the quadratic $\mathbf{y}$ terms in the exponent into the covariance matrix:

$$\Sigma^{-1} = 2(A + B + C) \tag{10}$$

$$A_{i,j} = \begin{cases} \sum_{k=1}^{K1} \alpha_k, & i = j \\ 0, & i \neq j \end{cases} \tag{11}$$

$$B_{i,j} = \begin{cases} (\sum_{k=1}^{K2} \beta_k \sum_{r=1}^{n} S_{i,r}^{(g_k)}) - (\sum_{k=1}^{K2} \beta_k S_{i,j}^{(g_k)}), & i = j \\ -\sum_{k=1}^{K2} \beta_k S_{i,j}^{(g_k)}, & i \neq j \end{cases} \tag{12}$$

$$C_{i,j} = \begin{cases} (\sum_{k=1}^{K2} \gamma_k \sum_{r=1}^{n} S_{i,r}^{(l_k)}) + (\sum_{k=1}^{K2} \gamma_k S_{i,j}^{(l_k)}), & i = j \\ \sum_{k=1}^{K2} \gamma_k S_{i,j}^{(l_k)}, & i \neq j \end{cases} \tag{13}$$

The diagonal matrix A represents the contribution of $\boldsymbol{\alpha}$ terms (vertex features) to the covariance matrix, and the symmetric B and C represent the contribution of the $\boldsymbol{\beta}$, and $\boldsymbol{\gamma}$ terms (edge features).

It is useful and convenient for inference to define a vector d, that describes the linear terms in the distribution, and μ which is the mean value of the Gaussian form of the CCNF distribution:

$$d = 2\alpha^T (1 + \exp(-\Theta X))^{-1}, \tag{14}$$

$$\mu = \Sigma d. \tag{15}$$

Above X is a matrix where the ith column is x_i, Θ is the concatenated neural network weights, and exp is an element-wise exponential function.

Intuitively d is the contribution from the the vertex features. These are the terms that contribute directly from input features x towards y. Σ on the other hand, controls the influence of the edge features on the output. Finally, μ is the expected value of the distribution.

In order to guarantee that our partition function is integrable, we constrain $\alpha_k > 0$ and $\beta_k > 0, \gamma_k > 0$ [16]. The log-likelihood can be maximised using a gradient based method such as constrained limited memory Broyden-Fletcher-Goldfarb-Shanno (L-BFGS) algorithm [18]. In order to make the optimisation more accurate and faster we the partial derivatives of the $\log P(y|x)$ can be used:

$$\frac{\partial \log(P(y|x))}{\alpha_k} = -y^T y + 2y^T H_{k,*}^T - 2H_{*,k}\mu + \mu^T \mu + \text{tr}(\Sigma) \tag{16}$$

$$\frac{\partial \log(P(y|x))}{\beta_k} = -y^T \frac{\partial B}{\partial \beta_k} y + \mu^T \frac{\partial B}{\partial \beta_k} \mu + \text{tr}(\Sigma \frac{\partial B}{\partial \beta_k}), \tag{17}$$

$$\frac{\partial \log(P(y|x))}{\gamma_k} = -y^T \frac{\partial C}{\partial \gamma_k} y + \mu^T \frac{\partial C}{\partial \gamma_k} \mu + \text{tr}(\Sigma \frac{\partial C}{\partial \gamma_k}), \tag{18}$$

$$\frac{\partial \log(P(y|x))}{\theta_{i,j}} = y^T \frac{\partial b}{\partial \theta_{i,j}} - \mu^T \frac{\partial b}{\partial \theta_{i,j}} \tag{19}$$

$$b_i = 2 \sum_{k=1}^{K1} \alpha_k h(\theta_k, x_i), \tag{20}$$

Above, $H = (1 + \exp(-\Theta X))^{-1}$, where the exponential is applied element-wise. $H_{k,*}$ notation refers to a row vector corresponding to the kth row respectively (k^{th} column for $H_{*,k}$), and tr is the matrix trace.

Regularisation. To prevent over-fitting of the model, we assume that the parameters have a Gaussian prior and constrain the diagonal inverse covariance matrix by a small number of hyper-parameters. We split the model parameters into three different groups: α, θ, and $[\beta, \gamma]$, and assume that the parameters among different groups are independent of each other. This leads to the following log-likelihood function:

$$L(\boldsymbol{\alpha}, \boldsymbol{\beta}, \boldsymbol{\gamma}, \boldsymbol{\Theta}) = \sum_{q=1}^{M} \log P(\mathbf{y}^{(q)}|\boldsymbol{x}^{(q)}) + \lambda_\alpha ||\boldsymbol{\alpha}||$$
$$+ \lambda_\beta ||\boldsymbol{\beta}|| + \lambda_\beta ||\boldsymbol{\gamma}|| + \lambda_\theta ||\boldsymbol{\Theta}|| \tag{21}$$

The variances $\lambda_\alpha, \lambda_\beta, \lambda_\theta$ are determined automatically during model validation.

Inference. Since the CCNF model can be viewed as a multivariate Gaussian, inferring $\mathbf{y}'$ values that maximise $P(\mathbf{y}|\boldsymbol{x})$ (from Equation 1) is straightforward. The prediction is the mean (expected) value of the distribution:

$$\mathbf{y}' = \arg\max_{\mathbf{y}}(P(\mathbf{y}|\boldsymbol{x})) = \boldsymbol{\mu} = \Sigma\boldsymbol{d}. \tag{22}$$

Such straightforward and efficient inference is a major advantage of our model when compared to other structured prediction approaches, such as CNF.

Note that because of the sigmoid activation function, outputs y_i are limited the 0-1 range. However, most regression problems can be mapped to this range and later mapped back to their original ranges.

2.3 CCNF Instances

We propose two instances of the CCNF model that can exploit different output relationships. The first instance is called Chain-CCNF and can be used for time series and sequence modelling (illustrated in Figure 1a). The model has neighbouring nodes in time series connected using a single similarity edge feature:

$$S_{i,j}^{(l)} = \begin{cases} 1, & |i - j| = 1 \\ 0, & \text{otherwise} \end{cases} \tag{23}$$

This allows to capture the smoothness of the time-series signal. Even though, this example only connects neighbouring nodes it is easily extended to capture distant dependencies.

The second instance is called Grid-CCNF and it models spatial relationships. This model is illustrated in Figure 1b. Grid-CCNF is particularly suited for vision problems where regression across the image is needed, for example a probability density across an image. Sections 3 and 4 compare Chain- and Grid- CCNF to other popular regression models.

3   Chain-CCNF Experiments

We performed a set of experiments that explored the use of Chain-CCNF for time series modelling on two tasks: emotion prediction in music on the MTurk dataset [19] and facial action unit recognition on the DISFA dataset [20]. The following sections present the datasets, baselines, methodology and results.

3.1   Datasets

MTurk is a music extracts dataset labelled on the arousal-valence (AV) dimensional emotion space using Mechanical Turk [19]. Paid participants were asked to label 15-second excerpts with continuous emotion ratings on the AV space. The songs in the dataset cover a wide range of genres: pop, various types of rock and hip-hop/rap. MTurk dataset consists 240 15-second clips, with ≈ 17 ratings each - we used the ratings averaged over one second windows as ground truth. In addition, the dataset contains a standard set of features extracted from those musical clips. We used four types of features provided in the dataset: mel-frequency cepstral coefficients, chromagram, spectral contrast and statistical spectrum descriptors. They were concatenated into a single vector of 100 features per observation. Features were averaged over a one second window and their Z-scores were computed on the training set (same scalings used on the test set). For CCNF training the ground truth was scaled to [0,1], and the inverse scalings were used for testing.

DISFA - Denver Intensity of Spontaneous Facial Action database [20] contains 27, 4 minute long, videos of spontaneous facial expression, annotated for action units (AU) [21]. DISFA contains over 130,000 annotated frames from 27 adult participants. For every video frame, the intensity of 12 AUs was manually annotated on a six-point ordinal scale (0 and five increasing levels of intensity). AUs are a way to quantify facial muscle action and are a way to describe facial expressions. For our experiment these were treated as continuous values from 0 to 5 and not discrete classes.

For feature extraction we used an approach similar to the one proposed by Jeni et al.[7]. First, we extracted 25×25 pixel areas around facial feature points (provided with DISFA dataset). The areas of interest are also normalised for scale and rotation using affine transforms to frontal face and 32 pixel interocular distance. Only the areas around relevant feature points are extracted for each AU. For example for AU1 (inner brow raiser) prediction, we used the areas around eyebrow and eye-corner feature points. Each area of interest was normalised on a per subject basis to extract subject specific changes in appearance.

To reduce feature dimensionality of appearance features, we performed sparse non-negative matrix factorisation on each area of interest [22]. Unseen samples were projected on the non-negative basis using non-negative least squares (the basis was recomputed for each training fold). As an additional feature to appearance, we used the non-rigid shape parameters of a Point Distribution Model inferred from the provided landmark locations (the model was trained on the Multi-PIE dataset [23]).

Given the unbalanced nature of this dataset (most of the time neutral expression is shown), we rebalanced the training subset by keeping all sub-sequences with at least one AU activated and adding some temporal padding before and after. This lead to $\approx 40k$ frames per each AU with sequences of ≈ 100 frames. Note, that this rebalancing was only performed on the training set, for testing we used the original sequences. For CCNF training the ground truth was scaled to [0,1], and the inverse scalings were used for testing.

3.2 Baseline Models

We compared our Chain-CCNF model to the following approaches:

SVR which is a widely used model for regression. SVR treats each element in a sequence independently and does not perform structured regression. We explored both linear-kernel and radial basis kernel SVR.

Neural Network another popular regression technique. We used a version of CCNF model without edge features, which reduces to a neural network as time dependencies are not modelled any more. This allows us to evaluate the effect of the temporal CCNF features.

CCRF is a structured regression approach that can model temporal relationships [17,24]. The process of CCRF training requires an extra step, it first needs to train an SVR model to use its predictions as input to the CCRF model.

3.3 Methodology

For the **MTurk** dataset, a separate model was trained for each emotional dimension: one for arousal and one for valence. A 5-fold cross-validation testing was used for all of the experiments. When splitting the dataset into folds, it was made sure that all of the feature vectors from a single song were in the same fold. The reported test results were averaged over 5 folds. All experiments were performed on the same training and testing sets.

For hyper-parameter selection, 2-fold cross-validation (splitting into equal parts) was used on the training dataset. The automatically chosen hyper-parameters were used for training on the whole training dataset.

To evaluate the results, we used three metrics suggested for emotion prediction in music evaluation [25]: average Euclidean distance (combined dimensions), average root mean squared error and average squared Pearson correlation coefficient (per dimension).

We used leave-one-subject out testing in our experiments on the **DISFA** datasets, as done in previous work [20]. For hyper-parameter validation we used hold-out validation, with 2/3rds of the data used for training and the rest for validation for training all of the approaches.

To evaluate the results on the DISFA dataset, we used the Pearson correlation coefficient and RMSE across all test sequences (concatenating predictions from each test fold and then computing the error metrics).

3.4 Results and Discussion

CCNF consistently outperforms the baselines on most of the evaluation metrics on the MTurk dataset (Table 1). Not only is accuracy improved, but the results are substantially better than those of linear-kernel SVR, radial basis function SVR. Friedman's ANOVA ($\chi^2(3) = 49.6, p < 0.001$) on mean per-sequence Euclidean errors with follow up Wilcoxon tests on the Euclidean metric revealed that CCNF performs statistically significantly better than the other baselines.

Table 1. Results comparing the CCNF approach to the CCRF and SVR with linear and RBF kernels for emotion prediction on the MTurk dataset

MODEL	AROUSAL CORR.	VALENCE CORR.	AROUSAL RMS	VALENCE RMS	EUCLIDEAN DISTANCE
SVR-Lin	0.636	0.174	0.179	0.186	0.130
SVR-RBF	0.649	0.232	0.176	0.180	0.126
Neural Network	0.647	0.201	0.176	0.185	0.127
CCRF [24]	**0.744**	0.265	0.150	0.175	0.121
CCNF	0.732	**0.289**	**0.145**	**0.166**	**0.116**

Table 2. Results comparing the CCNF approach to other baselines on the DISFA dataset. The Pearson correlation metric and RMSE were computed on concatenated predictions across all of the 27 subjects. We also present a comparison against the best performing model from Sandbach et al.[12] (Built 1) for AUs reported in their paper.

MODEL	AU1	AU2	AU4	AU5	AU6	AU9	AU12	AU15	AU17	AU20	AU25	AU26	AVG.
	CORRELATION												
SVR [7]	0.35	0.34	0.48	0.28	0.42	0.31	**0.71**	0.38	0.17	0.13	0.81	0.47	0.40
MRF [12]	**0.56**	**0.55**	0.44	0.17	0.14	0.01	-	-	-	-	-	-	-
CCRF [24]	0.44	0.37	0.43	0.40	0.38	0.26	0.65	0.35	0.31	**0.14**	0.77	0.46	0.41
CCNF	0.48	0.50	**0.52**	**0.48**	**0.45**	**0.36**	0.70	**0.41**	**0.39**	0.11	**0.89**	**0.57**	**0.49**
	RMSE												
SVR [7]	0.74	0.70	1.09	**0.27**	0.78	0.64	**0.71**	0.41	0.59	**0.39**	0.81	0.67	0.65
MRF [12]	**0.62**	**0.59**	1.10	0.34	0.90	**0.61**	-	-	-	-	-	-	-
CCRF [24]	0.65	0.62	**1.04**	**0.27**	**0.72**	**0.61**	0.75	**0.39**	**0.57**	0.45	0.87	0.66	**0.63**
CCNF	0.74	0.63	1.13	0.33	0.75	0.67	**0.71**	0.46	0.67	0.58	**0.63**	**0.63**	0.66

For action unit recogntion the results of our experiment can be seen in Table 2. The CCNF model can be seen outperforming the other proposed baselines on most AUs for the correlation metric. Interestingly, CCNF does not do better on the RMSE metric than the baselines on some of the AUs while substantially outperforming the same baselines on the correlation metric (AU5, AU15, AU17). This is because RMSE is not a reliable metric for evaluating regressors on such an unbalanced dataset dominated by neutral expressions. This leads to an uninformed regressor that always predicts 0 performing well on RMSE metric.

None of the regressors are able to learn to recognise AU20 reliably. This is possibly because of two reasons: the features used are not discriminative enough, and there not enough positive training samples in the dataset – only 99 events for the action unit, when compared to 296 and 321 events for AU25 and AU26.

These results show the importance of modelling temporal and non-linear relationships for both emotion prediction in music and action unit recognition and the ability of CCNF to do so effectively.

4   Grid-CCNF Experiments

We conducted a set of experiments to evaluate our Grid-CCNF model as a patch expert in the constrained local model (CLM) – a popular framework for facial landmark detection [3,26]. Patch experts evaluate the probability of a landmark alignment at a particular pixel location and are a crucial part of CLM. The alignment probability is often modelled using a regressor trained to output 0 when landmark is not aligned and 1 when it is aligned. The evaluation of a patch expert in an area of interest leads to a *response map*. Landmark detection is done by optimising the CLM model over these response maps.

There has been a number of different patch experts proposed: various SVR models and logistic regressors, or even simple template matching techniques. The most popular patch expert by far is the linear SVR in combination with a logistic regressor [27,3,4]. Linear SVRs are used because of their computational simplicity and potential for efficient implementation on images using convolution.

There are some desirable properties for a response map from a patch expert[3,4]: the high probabilities should be be centred around the true landmark location, it should be smooth, preferably convex, and not have ambiguous peaks. Because of these desired properties, patch expert is a great use case for our Grid-CCNF model: (1) non-linear relationships between input pixel values and the output responses lead to better accuracy, and (2) ability to enforce similarity and sparsity relationships lead to a smoother and more convex response map.

To achieve desired similarity properties we define two similarity edge features: $S^{(g_1)}$ returns 1 (otherwise return 0) only when the two nodes i and j are direct (horizontal/vertical) neighbours in a grid; $S^{(g_2)}$ returns 1 (otherwise 0) when i and j are diagonal neighbours in a grid. For sparsity we define a single sparsity edge feature using the neighbourhood region $S^{(l)}$ that returns 1 only when two nodes i and j are between 4 and 6 edges apart (where edges are counted from the grid layout of our Grid-CCNF patch expert).

To train our Grid-CCNF patch expert, we need to define the output variables y_i. Given an image, with a true landmark location at $\mathbf{z} = (u, v)^T$, landmark alignment probability at $\mathbf{z}_i$ is modelled as $y_i = \mathcal{N}(\mathbf{z_i}; \mathbf{z}, \sigma)$ ($\sigma = 1$).

4.1   Datasets

In order to evaluate the ability of Grid-CCNF to generalise on unseen datasets we evaluated our approach on four different datasets: Annotated Faces in the Wild (**AFW**)[28], **IBUG** [29], and 300 Faces in-the-Wild Challenge (**300-W**) [29] and **LFPW + Helen** [30,31] datasets. The datasets contain 135, 337, 600, and 554 images respectively. They all contain uncontrolled images of faces *in the wild*: in indoor-outdoor environments, under varying illuminations, in presence of occlusions, under different poses, and from different quality cameras. Note that LFPW and Helen were used as training datasets for CLM, CCNF, and AAM models, but same images were not used for testing.

4.2   Baseline Models

We used a number of state-of-the-art facial landmark detectors to compare to our CLM model that using Grid-CCNF patch experts:

CLM + SVR model that uses linear SVR patch experts and regularised landmark mean-shift fitting [3]. Same training data and initialisation was used for this model as for our CLM with Grid-CCNF. Note that we use a more accurate CLM model that that presented by Saragih *et al.*[3], our model includes a multi-modal (patch experts trained on raw pixel and gradient images) and multi-scale formulation leading to more accurate landmark detection.

Tree based face and landmark detector, proposed by Zhu and Ramanan [28]. It has shown good performance at locating the face and the landmark features on a number of datasets. We used a model trained on *in the wild* dataset [27].

DRMF – discriminative response map fitting implementation provided by the authors [27]. It was trained on LFPW [30] and Multi-PIE [23] datasets.

SDM – Supervised Descent Method implementation from the authors [32]. This approach is trained on the Multi-PIE and LFW [33] datasets. It relies on face detection from a Viola-Jones face detector.

AAM - Active Appearance Model using the inverse compositional image alignment algorithm [34]. This model was trained on *in the wild* data.

The above baselines were trained to detect 49, 66, or 68 feature points, making exact comparisons difficult. However, they all share 49 feature points, on which the error metrics were computed in our experiments.

4.3   Methodology

For Grid-CCNF and SVR patch expert training we used two datasets: Labelled Face Parts in the Wild (LFPW) [30] and Helen [31]. Both of them contain unconstrained images of faces in indoor and outdoor environments. In total 1029 training images were used, each of which was sampled at 6 locations (5 away from the true landmark location and 1 near it) in window sizes of 19×19 pixels - this led to 6 sequences of 81 samples per image. Each of the samples was an 11×11 pixel support region. Each training sample was normalised using their Z-score. For SVR each of the samples was treated independently. The models were trained using the LIBLINEAR package [35] with default parameters. For Grid-CCNF training the following parameters were used: 7 vertex features, $\lambda_\alpha = 10^2, \lambda_\beta = 10^3, \lambda_\Theta = 1$.

Nine sets of patch experts were trained in total: at three orientations – $-20°, 0°, 20°$ yaw; and three scales – 17, 23 and 30 pixel of interocular distance. Labels from the Helen and LFPW datasets were used to learn the point distribution model, using non-rigid structure from motion [36].

For fitting we used a multi-scale approach, with 15×15 pixel areas of interest for each scale. For model fitting we used regularised landmark mean-shift [3].

To initialise model fitting, we used the bounding boxes initialised using the tree based face detector [28]. In order to deal with pose variation the model was initialised at three orientations – $(0, 0, 0), (0, \pm 30, 0)$ degrees of roll, pitch and

Table 3. Results comparing CCNF patch expert to SVR patch expert on the LFPW and Helen datasets. Notice how CCNF can learn the relationship between input pixels and expected response map much better than SVR (all differences statistically significant according to a Wilcoxon signed-rank test, $p < .001$).

SCALE	CCNF		SVR[3]	
	RMS	CORR.	RMS	CORR.
0.25	**0.083**	**0.33**	0.094	0.20
0.35	**0.086**	**0.27**	0.092	0.16
0.5	**0.089**	**0.22**	0.090	0.12
Avg.	**0.086**	**0.27**	0.092	0.16

yaw. The converged model with the highest alignment likelihood was chosen as the correct one. Note that SDM code provided by the authors does not allow to use bounding box or rotation initialisation. hence the images were cropped to the face area to make them easier for the internal face detector (however, it still failed in more difficult cases).

4.4 Results and Discussion

Before performing any landmark detection, we studied how CCNF patch experts compare to SVR ones at learning the expected patch response maps. We evaluated the patch experts on an unseen 1/5th of the images in the training datasets (LFPW and Helen). The results of this can be seen in Table 3. The results demonstrate that Grid-CCNF can learn the relationship between pixel values and expected alignment better than SVR at all of the training scales. The differences are statistically significant (see Table 3 caption).

The second experiment, compared the proposed CLM model that uses Grid-CCNF as a patch expert against other landmark detectors. The results of this experiment can be seen in Figure 2. Our approach can be seen outperforming all of the other baselines tested. The differences are statistically significant (see Figure 2 caption). This illustrates the greater generalisability of our proposed model over other approaches. This improved performance comes both from the learning capacity and the non-linearity of the neural network and the modelled sparsity and similarity constraints of our CCNF. Linear SVR is unable to accurately discriminate facial landmarks when their appearance varies due to large changes in illumination and pose.

Training time for $68 \times 3 \times 3 = 612$ patch experts took ≈ 9 hours on a single quad core Intel i7 machine. We exploited the fact that patch experts of a profile face in one direction are just mirror images of a profile face in another direction, same fact was exploited for symmetric frontal face patch experts.

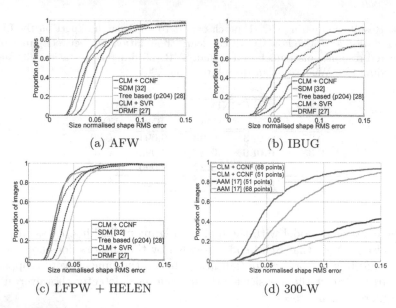

(a) AFW

(b) IBUG

(c) LFPW + HELEN

(d) 300-W

Fig. 2. Landmark detection using our **CLM + CCNF** model and other state-of-the-art methods. The benefit of our approach in generalising on unseen data is clear. Note that for 300-W dataset, error rates using just internal (51) and all of the points (68) are reported. CLM + CCNF has statistically significantly smaller RMS values compared to all of the other approaches on all of the datasets ($p < .001$), according to Friedman's ANOVA and Wilcoxon signed-rank follow up tests.

Finally, part of Grid-CCNF inference across an image area of interest can be performed using convolution, leading to fast landmark detection. Landmark detection speed depends on the area of interest, our CCNF implementation is able to reach 30 frames per second for landmark detection in videos and 5 images per second for more complex in the wild images.

5   Conclusions

We presented the Continuous Conditional Neural Field model for structured regression. Our model can exploit spatial and temporal relationships inherent in pattern recognition problems. It also learns non-linear dependencies between input and output. The flexibility of CCNF is demonstrated through evaluation on six datasets spanning three challenging regression tasks: landmark detection, emotion prediction in music and continuous intensity action unit recognition.

Our CCNF model showed statistically significant improvement over state-of-the-art approaches for all of the tasks, both in terms of prediction accuracy - evaluated using root mean squared error, and prediction structure - evaluated using the correlation coefficient. Finally, we make all of our code available for experiment recreation on the public datasets.

Acknowledgements. We acknowledge funding support from from the European Community's Seventh Framework Programme (FP7/2007- 2013) under grant agreement 289021 (ASC-Inclusion). The effort described here is partially supported by the U.S. Army. Any opinion, content or information presented does not necessarily reflect the position or the policy of the United States Government, and no official endorsement should be inferred.

References

1. Baltrusaitis, T., Morency, L.P., Robinson, P.: Constrained local neural fields for robust facial landmark detection in the wild. In: IEEE International Conference on Computer Vision Workshops (2013)
2. Bishop, C.M.: Pattern Recognition and Machine Learning. Springer-Verlag New York, Inc. (2006)
3. Saragih, J., Lucey, S., Cohn, J.: Deformable Model Fitting by Regularized Landmark Mean-Shift. IJCV (2011)
4. Wang, Y., Lucey, S., Cohn, J.: Enforcing convexity for improved alignment with constrained local models. In: CVPR (2008)
5. Han, B.J., Rho, S., Dannenberg, R.B., Hwang, E.: Smers: Music emotion recognition using support vector regression. In: ISMIR (2009)
6. Valstar, M., Schuller, B., Smith, K., Eyben, F., Jiang, B., Bilakhia, S., Schnieder, S., Cowie, R., Pantic, M.: AVEC 2013 – The Continuous Audio / Visual Emotion and Depression Recognition Challenge (2013)
7. Jeni, L.A., Girard, J.M., Cohn, J.F., De La Torre, F.: Continuous au intensity estimation using localized, sparse facial feature space. In: FG (2013)
8. Nicolaou, M.A., Gunes, H., Pantic, M.: Output-associative RVM regression for dimensional and continuous emotion prediction. IVC (2012)
9. Wang, F., Verhelst, W., Sahli, H.: Relevance vector machine based speech emotion recognition. In: D'Mello, S., Graesser, A., Schuller, B., Martin, J.-C. (eds.) ACII 2011, Part II. LNCS, vol. 6975, pp. 111–120. Springer, Heidelberg (2011)
10. Sutton, C., McCallum, A.: Introduction to Conditional Random Fields for Relational Learning. In: Introduction to Statistical Relational Learning. MIT Press (2006)
11. Tsochantaridis, I., Hofmann, T., Joachims, T., Altun, Y.: Support vector machine learning for interdependent and structured output spaces. In: ICML (2004)
12. Sandbach, G., Zafeiriou, S., Pantic, M.: Markov random field structures for facial action unit intensity estimation. In: IEEE International Conference on Computer Vision, Workshop on Decoding Subtle Cues from Social Interactions (2013)
13. Peng, J., Bo, L., Xu, J.: Conditional neural fields. In: NIPS (2009)
14. Bo, L., Sminchisescu, C.: Structured output-associative regression. In: CVPR (2009)
15. Bo, L., Sminchisescu, C.: Twin gaussian processes for structured prediction. IJCV (2010)
16. Qin, T., Liu, T.Y., Zhang, X.D., Wang, D.S., Li, H.: Global ranking using continuous conditional random fields. In: NIPS (2008)
17. Baltrušaitis, T., Banda, N., Robinson, P.: Dimensional affect recognition using continuous conditional random fields. In: FG (2013)
18. Byrd, R.H., Lu, P., Nocedal, J., Zhu, C.: A limited memory algorithm for bound constrained optimization. SIAM Journal on Scientific Computing 16(5), 1190–1208 (1994)

19. Speck, J.A., Schmidt, E.M., Morton, B.G., Kim, Y.E.: A comparative study of collaborative vs. traditional musical mood annotation. In: ISMIR (2011)
20. Mavadati, S.M., Member, S., Mahoor, M.H., Bartlett, K., Trinh, P., Cohn, J.F.: Disfa: A spontaneous facial action intensity database. IEEE T-AFFC (2013)
21. Ekman, P., Friesen, W.V.: Manual for the Facial Action Coding System. Consulting Psychologists Press, Palo Alto (1977)
22. Kim, J., Park, H.: Toward faster nonnegative matrix factorization: A new algorithm and comparisons (2008)
23. Gross, R., Matthews, I., Cohn, J., Kanade, T., Baker, S.: Multi-pie. IVC 28(5), 807–813 (2010)
24. Imbrasaitė, V., Baltrušaitis, T., Robinson, P.: Emotion tracking in music using Continuous Conditional Random Fields and relative feature representation. In: IEEE International Conference on Multimedia and Expo (2013)
25. Imbrasaitė, V., Baltrušaitis, T., Robinson, P.: What really matters? a study into peoples instinctive evaluation metrics for continuous emotion prediction in music. In: Affective Computing and Intelligent Interaction (2013)
26. Martins, P., Caseiro, R., Henriques, J.F., Batista, J.: Discriminative bayesian active shape models. In: Fitzgibbon, A., Lazebnik, S., Perona, P., Sato, Y., Schmid, C. (eds.) ECCV 2012, Part III. LNCS, vol. 7574, pp. 57–70. Springer, Heidelberg (2012)
27. Asthana, A., Zafeiriou, S., Cheng, S., Pantic, M.: Robust discriminative response map fitting with constrained local models. In: CVPR (2013)
28. Zhu, X., Ramanan, D.: Face detection, pose estimation, and landmark localization in the wild. In: IEEE CVPR (2012)
29. Sagonas, C., Tzimiropoulos, G., Zafeiriou, S., Pantic, M.: 300 faces in-the-wild challenge: The first facial landmark localization challenge. In: ICCV (2013)
30. Belhumeur, P.N., Jacobs, D.W., Kriegman, D.J., Kumar, N.: Localizing parts of faces using a consensus of exemplars. In: CVPR (2011)
31. Le, V., Brandt, J., Lin, Z., Bourdev, L., Huang, T.S.: Interactive facial feature localization. In: Fitzgibbon, A., Lazebnik, S., Perona, P., Sato, Y., Schmid, C. (eds.) ECCV 2012, Part III. LNCS, vol. 7574, pp. 679–692. Springer, Heidelberg (2012)
32. Xiong, X., De la Torre, F.: Supervised descent method and its applications to face alignment. In: CVPR (2013)
33. Huang, G.B., Ramesh, M., Berg, T., Learned-Miller, E.: Labeled Faces in the Wild: A Database for Studying Face Recognition in Unconstrained Environments (2007)
34. Matthews, I., Baker, S.: Active appearance models revisited. IJCV 60(2), 135–164 (2004)
35. Fan, R.E., Kai-Wei, C., Cho-Jui, H., Wang, X.R., Lin, C.J.: Liblinear: A library for large linear classification. The Journal of Machine Learning Research 9 (2008)
36. Torresani, L., Hertzmann, A., Bregler, C.: Nonrigid structure-from-motion: estimating shape and motion with hierarchical priors. TPAMI 30(5), 878–892 (2008)

Learning to Rank Using High-Order Information

Puneet Kumar Dokania[1], Aseem Behl[2], C.V. Jawahar[2], and M. Pawan Kumar[1]

[1] Ecole Centrale de Paris
INRIA Saclay, France
[2] IIIT Hyderabad, India

Abstract. The problem of ranking a set of visual samples according to their relevance to a query plays an important role in computer vision. The traditional approach for ranking is to train a binary classifier such as a support vector machine (SVM). Binary classifiers suffer from two main deficiencies: (i) they do not optimize a ranking-based loss function, for example, the average precision (AP) loss; and (ii) they cannot incorporate high-order information such as the *a priori* correlation between the relevance of two visual samples (for example, two persons in the same image tend to perform the same action). We propose two novel learning formulations that allow us to incorporate high-order information for ranking. The first framework, called *high-order binary* SVM (HOB-SVM), allows for a structured input. The parameters of HOB-SVM are learned by minimizing a convex upper bound on a surrogate 0-1 loss function. In order to obtain the ranking of the samples that form the structured input, HOB-SVM sorts the samples according to their *max-marginals*. The second framework, called *high-order average precision* SVM (HOAP-SVM), also allows for a structured input and uses the same ranking criterion. However, in contrast to HOB-SVM, the parameters of HOAP-SVM are learned by minimizing a difference-of-convex upper bound on the AP loss. Using a standard, publicly available dataset for the challenging problem of action classification, we show that both HOB-SVM and HOAP-SVM outperform the baselines that ignore high-order information.

1 Introduction

Many tasks in computer vision require the development of automatic methods that sort a given set of visual samples according to their relevance to a query. For example, consider the problem of action classification (or more precisely action ranking). The input is a set of samples corresponding to bounding boxes of persons, and an action such as 'jumping'. The desired output is a ranking where a sample representing a jumping person is ranked higher than a sample representing a person performing a different action. Other related problems include image classification (sorting images according to their relevance to a user query) and object detection (sorting all the windows in a set of images according to their relevance to an object category). As the desired output of the aforementioned problems is a ranking, the accuracy of an approach is typically reported using a ranking-based measure such as the average precision (AP).

D. Fleet et al. (Eds.): ECCV 2014, Part IV, LNCS 8692, pp. 609–623, 2014.

A popular way of solving a problem that requires us to rank a set of samples is to train a binary classifier. The positive class of the classifier corresponds to the relevant samples and the negative class corresponds to the non-relevant samples. Once a classifier is learned on a training set, a new set of samples is sorted according to the scores assigned to the samples by the classifier. Perhaps the most commonly used classifier is the support vector machine (SVM) [23]. However, the SVM framework has two main drawbacks. First, an SVM minimizes an upper bound on the 0-1 loss function (that is, the fraction of misclassifications) instead of a loss function that depends on the AP. Second, an SVM only uses first-order information to classify a sample, that is, the score of a sample depends only on itself and not on other samples in the dataset. In other words, an SVM does not explicitly incorporate *a priori* high-order information, which can be very useful in improving the accuracy of ranking. For example, in action classification, most of the persons present in the same image tend to perform the same action. In object detection, two objects of the same category tend to have the similar aspect ratio. In pose estimation, people in the same scene tend to have similar poses (sitting down to watch movie). In document retrieval, documents containing same or similar words are more likely to belong to the same class.

At first glance, the two drawbacks seem to be easily fixable using a generalization of the SVM framework, known as structured output support vector machines (SSVM) [20,22]. Given a structured input, the SSVM framework provides a linear prediction rule to obtain a structured output. Specifically, the score of a putative output is the inner product of the parameters of an SSVM with the joint feature vector of the input and the output. The prediction requires us to maximize the score over all possible outputs for an input. Given a training dataset, the parameters of an SSVM are learned by minimizing a regularized convex upper bound on a user-specified loss function. In the past decade, several customized algorithms have been developed to solve the optimization problem that learns the SSVM parameters [6,8,13,20,22]. While the optimization algorithms for SSVM differ significantly in their details, they share the common characteristic of iteratively performing *loss-augmented inference*. In other words, given the current estimate of the parameters, they compute the output that jointly maximizes the sum of the score and the loss function. Loss-augmented inference can be viewed as the optimal cutting-plane or the subgradient of the learning objective, which exploits its central role in the optimization.

The SSVM framework places no restriction on the form of the loss function and on the structure of the input and the output. Thus, it appears the ideal framework to (i) optimize the AP loss; and (ii) incorporate high-order information. However, in order to successfully employ an SSVM, we need an efficient algorithm for loss-augmented inference. In that regard, the first drawback can be addressed using AP-SVM [24], which is a special form of SSVM. In the AP-SVM framework, the input is a set of samples and the output is a ranking. The loss value for a putative output is one minus the AP of the corresponding ranking with respect to the ground truth ranking. The joint feature vector of the input and the output is a weighted sum of the feature vectors for all samples, where the weights are governed by the ranking. Yue *et al.* [24] showed that, for this choice of joint feature vector, loss-augmented inference can be performed optimally using an efficient greedy algorithm. Furthermore, they showed that the prediction of AP-SVM is exactly the same as the prediction of the standard SVM, that is, to sort the samples according to their individual scores. Since the joint feature vector of AP-SVM depends only on the feature vectors of the individual samples, AP-SVM does not incorporate high-order information. A straightforward way to address this deficiency would be to modify the joint feature vector such that it depends on feature vectors of pairs of samples, or more generally, on feature vectors of subsets of samples. For example, Rosenfeld *et al.* [19] recently proposed a framework to optimize the area under curve (AUC) while considering the high-order information. However, similar approach cannot be used for optimizing AP based loss function since it does not decompose over single variable. Therefore, such a modification can not be introduced trivially into the AP-SVM formulation.

We present two alternate frameworks to incorporate high-order information for ranking. The first framework, which we call high-order binary SVM (HOB-SVM), takes its inspiration from the standard SVM. The input of HOB-SVM is a set of samples. The output is a binary label for each sample, where the label 1 indicates that the sample is relevant and 0 indicates that the sample is not relevant. The joint feature vector of HOB-SVM depends not only on the feature vectors of the individual samples, but also on the feature vectors of subsets of samples. In this work, we restrict the subsets to be of size two, but our frameworks can easily be generalized to other subset sizes. The loss function of HOB-SVM is a weighted 0-1 loss, which allows us to efficiently perform loss-augmented inference using graph cuts [12]. Practically speaking, the difficulty with employing HOB-SVM is that it provides a single score for the entire labeling of a dataset, whereas we need scores corresponding to each sample in order to find the ranking. To address this difficulty, we propose to rank the samples using the difference between the *max-marginal* for assigning a sample to the relevant class and the max-marginal for assigning it to the non-relevant class. Intuitively, difference of max-marginals measure the positivity of a particular sample while capturing high-order information. Empirically, we show that the difference of max-marginals provides an accurate ranking. The main advantage of HOB-SVM is that its parameters can be estimated efficiently by solving a convex optimization problem. However, its main disadvantage is that, similar to SVM, it optimizes a surrogate loss function instead of the AP loss.

The second framework, which we call high-order AP-SVM (HOAP-SVM), takes its inspiration from AP-SVM and HOB-SVM. Similar to AP-SVM, the input of HOAP-SVM is a set of samples, its output is a ranking of the samples, and its loss function is the AP loss. However, unlike AP-SVM, the score of a ranking is equal to the weighted sum of the difference of max-marginals of the individual samples. Since the max-marginals capture high-order information, and the loss function depends on the AP, HOAP-SVM addresses both the aforementioned deficiencies of traditional classifiers such as SVM. The main disadvantage of HOAP-SVM is that estimating its parameters requires solving a difference-of-convex program

[7]. While we cannot obtain an optimal set of parameters for HOAP-SVM, we show how a local optimum of the HOAP-SVM learning problem can be computed efficiently by the concave-convex procedure [25]. Using standard, publicly available datasets, we empirically demonstrate that HOAP-SVM outperforms the baselines by effectively utilizing high-order information while optimizing the correct loss function. For the sake of clarity, the proofs of all the propositions presented in the paper are given in the accompanying technical report. To facilitate the use of HOB-SVM and HOAP-SVM, we have made our code and data available online at http://cvn.ecp.fr/projects/ranking-highorder.

2 Preliminaries

2.1 Structured Output SVM

An SSVM, parameterized by $\mathbf{w}$, provides a linear prediction rule to obtain a structured output $\mathbf{y} \in \mathcal{Y}$ from a structured input $\mathbf{x} \in \mathcal{X}$. Formally, let $\Psi(\mathbf{x}, \mathbf{y})$ denote the joint feature vector of the input $\mathbf{x}$ and the output $\mathbf{y}$. The prediction for a given input $\mathbf{x}$ is obtained by maximizing the score over all possible outputs, that is, $\mathbf{y} = \mathrm{argmax}_{\overline{\mathbf{y}} \in \mathcal{Y}} \mathbf{w}^\top \Psi(\mathbf{x}, \overline{\mathbf{y}})$.

Given a dataset that consists of n samples, that is, $\mathcal{D} = \{(\mathbf{x}_i, \mathbf{y}_i^*), i = 1, \cdots, n\}$, the parameters of an SSVM are estimated by minimizing a regularized upper bound on the empirical risk. The risk is measured using a user-specified loss function $\Delta(\cdot, \cdot)$. In more detail, the parameters are estimated by solving the following convex optimization problem:

$$\min_{\mathbf{w}} \frac{1}{2}||\mathbf{w}||^2 + \frac{C}{n}\sum_{i=1}^{n}\xi_i, \tag{1}$$

$$\mathbf{w}^\top \Psi(\mathbf{x}_i, \mathbf{y}_i^*) - \mathbf{w}^\top \Psi(\mathbf{x}_i, \overline{\mathbf{y}}) \geq \Delta(\mathbf{y}_i^*, \overline{\mathbf{y}}) - \xi_i, \forall \overline{\mathbf{y}} \in \mathcal{Y}, \forall i \in \{1, \cdots, n\}.$$

Intuitively, the above problem encourages a margin (proportional to $\Delta(\mathbf{y}_i^*, \overline{\mathbf{y}})$) between the score of the ground-truth output $\mathbf{y}_i^*$ and all other outputs $\overline{\mathbf{y}}$. The hyperparameter C controls the trade-off between the training error and the model complexity. Inspite very large number of constraints, it has been shown that the above problem can be optimized efficiently using cutting-plane algorithm [8] which requires iteratively solving the loss-augmented inference problem (to find the most-violated constraint), that is, $\hat{\mathbf{y}}_i = \mathrm{argmax}_{\overline{\mathbf{y}}} \mathbf{w}^\top \Psi(\mathbf{x}_i, \overline{\mathbf{y}}) + \Delta(\mathbf{y}_i^*, \overline{\mathbf{y}})$.

2.2 AP-SVM

The AP-SVM classifier is a special case of SSVM. The input of an AP-SVM is a set of n samples, which we denote by $\mathbf{X} = \{\mathbf{x}_i, i = 1, \cdots, n\}$. Each sample can either belong to the positive class (that is, the sample is relevant) or the negative class (that is, the sample is not relevant). The indices for the positive and negative samples are denoted by $\mathcal{P}$ and $\mathcal{N}$ respectively. In other words, if $i \in \mathcal{P}$ and $j \in \mathcal{N}$ then $\mathbf{x}_i$ belongs to positive class and $\mathbf{x}_j$ belongs to the negative class.

The desired output is a ranking matrix $\mathbf{R}$ of size $n \times n$, such that (i) $\mathbf{R}_{ij} = 1$ if $\mathbf{x}_i$ is ranked higher than $\mathbf{x}_j$; (ii) $\mathbf{R}_{ij} = -1$ if $\mathbf{x}_i$ is ranked lower than $\mathbf{x}_j$; and (iii) $\mathbf{R}_{ij} = 0$ if $\mathbf{x}_i$ and $\mathbf{x}_j$ are assigned the same rank. During training, the ground-truth ranking matrix $\mathbf{R}^*$ is defined as: (i) $\mathbf{R}^*_{ij} = 1$ and $\mathbf{R}^*_{ji} = -1$ for all $i \in \mathcal{P}$ and $j \in \mathcal{N}$; (ii) $\mathbf{R}^*_{ii'} = 0$ and $\mathbf{R}^*_{jj'} = 0$ for all $i, i' \in \mathcal{P}$ and $j, j' \in \mathcal{N}$.

Joint Feature Vector. For a sample $\mathbf{x}_i$, let $\psi(\mathbf{x}_i)$ denote its feature vector. For example, in action classification, $\psi(\mathbf{x}_i)$ can represent poselet [2] or bag-of-visual-words [3]. Similar to [24], we specify a joint feature vector as

$$\Psi(\mathbf{X}, \mathbf{R}) = \gamma \sum_{i \in \mathcal{P}} \sum_{j \in \mathcal{N}} \mathbf{R}_{ij}(\psi(\mathbf{x}_i) - \psi(\mathbf{x}_j)), \gamma = \frac{1}{|\mathcal{P}||\mathcal{N}|} \tag{2}$$

In other words, the joint feature vector is the scaled sum of the difference between the features of all pairs of samples having different classes.

Parameters and Prediction. The parameter vector of the classifier is denoted by $\mathbf{w}$. Given the parameters $\mathbf{w}$, the ranking of an input $\mathbf{X}$ is predicted by maximizing the score, that is, $\mathbf{R} = \text{argmax}_{\overline{\mathbf{R}}} \mathbf{w}^\top \Psi(\mathbf{X}, \overline{\mathbf{R}})$. Yue *et al.* [24] showed that the above optimization can be performed efficiently by sorting the samples $\mathbf{x}_k$ in descending order of the score $\mathbf{w}^\top \psi(\mathbf{x}_k)$.

Loss Function. Given a training dataset, our aim is to learn a classifier that provides a high AP measure. Let $\text{AP}(\mathbf{R}^*, \mathbf{R})$ denote the AP of the ranking matrix $\mathbf{R}$ with respect to the ground truth ranking $\mathbf{R}^*$. The $\text{AP}(\mathbf{R}^*, \mathbf{R})$ is defined as: $\text{AP}(\mathbf{R}, \mathbf{R}^*) = \frac{1}{|\mathcal{P}|} \sum_k Prec(k)\delta(Rec(k))$, where $|\mathcal{P}|$ is the number of positive samples in the ground truth $\mathbf{R}^*$, $Prec(k)$ is the precision upto top k samples given by $\mathbf{R}$, and $\delta(Rec(k))$ is the change in recall when moving from $(k-1)^{th}$ to k^{th} sample. The value of the $\text{AP}(\cdot, \cdot)$ lies between 0 and 1, where 0 corresponds to a completely incorrect ranking $-\mathbf{R}^*$ and 1 corresponds to the correct ranking $\mathbf{R}^*$. In order to maximize the AP, we will minimize a loss function defined as $\Delta(\mathbf{R}^*, \mathbf{R}) = 1 - \text{AP}(\mathbf{R}^*, \mathbf{R})$.

Parameter Estimation. Given the input $\mathbf{X}$ and the ground-truth ranking matrix $\mathbf{R}^*$, we would like to learn the parameters of the classifier such that regularized upper bound on the empirical AP loss is minimized. Specifically, the model parameters are obtained by solving the following convex optimization problem:

$$\min_{\mathbf{w}} \frac{1}{2}||\mathbf{w}||^2 + C\xi, \tag{3}$$

$$\mathbf{w}^\top \Psi(\mathbf{X}, \mathbf{R}^*) - \mathbf{w}^\top \Psi(\mathbf{X}, \mathbf{R}) \geq \Delta(\mathbf{R}^*, \mathbf{R}) - \xi, \forall \mathbf{R}$$

Problem (3) is specified over an exponential number of $\mathbf{R}$. Nonetheless, Yue *et al.* [24] showed that it can be optimized efficiently by providing an optimal greedy algorithm to solve the corresponding loss-augmented inference problem, that is, $\hat{\mathbf{R}} = \text{argmax}_{\overline{\mathbf{R}}} \mathbf{w}^\top \Psi(\mathbf{X}, \overline{\mathbf{R}}) + \Delta(\mathbf{R}^*, \overline{\mathbf{R}})$.

3   High-Order Binary SVM (HOB-SVM)

We now describe our two frameworks for ranking while incorporating high-order information. As mentioned earlier, we will restrict our description to second-order information. However, extending our frameworks to general high-order information is trivial. We start with the simpler framework, which we call *High-Order Binary* SVM (HOB-SVM). This will allow us to define the terminology necessary to develop a more principled framework (HOAP-SVM) in the next section.

The input of a HOB-SVM is a set of n samples $\mathbf{X} = \{\mathbf{x}_i, i = 1, \cdots, n\}$. Similar to the AP-SVM, a sample can either belong to the positive class or a negative class. However, the output of HOB-SVM is not a ranking, but an assignment of a class for each sample. In other words, the output is a vector $\mathbf{Y} = \{y_i, i = 1, \cdots, n\}$ where $y_i \in \{0, 1\}$. The label '0' implies that the sample has been assigned to the negative class, whereas the label '1' implies that the sample has been assigned to the positive class. During training, the ground-truth output $\mathbf{Y}^*$ assigns all relevant samples to the positive class and all non-relevant samples to the negative class. Once again, given $\mathbf{Y}^*$, we denote the indices of the positive and the negative samples as $\mathcal{P}$ and $\mathcal{N}$ respectively.

Joint Feature Vector. The joint feature vector of the input $\mathbf{X}$ and the output $\mathbf{Y}$ consists of two parts. The first part $\Psi_1(\mathbf{X}, \mathbf{Y})$ captures first-order information, and is henceforth referred to as the unary joint feature vector. The second part $\Psi_2(\mathbf{X}, \mathbf{Y})$ captures second-order information, and is henceforth referred to as the pairwise joint feature vector. In more detail, let $\psi(\mathbf{x}_i) \in \mathbb{R}^d$ denote the feature vector of the sample $\mathbf{x}_i$. The unary joint feature vector is defined as follows:

$$\Psi_1(\mathbf{X}, \mathbf{Y}) = \begin{pmatrix} \sum_{i, y_i = 1} \psi(\mathbf{x}_i) \\ \sum_{i, y_i = 0} \psi(\mathbf{x}_i) \end{pmatrix}. \tag{4}$$

The unary joint feature vector is of dimensionality $2d$. The first d dimensions correspond to the sum of the feature vectors of the samples belonging to the positive class. The last d dimensions correspond to the sum of the feature vectors of the samples belonging to the negative class. Clearly, $\Psi_1(\mathbf{X}, \mathbf{Y})$ only captures the first-order information.

As mentioned earlier, our aim is to use second-order information to improve ranking. In other words, if we know *a priori* that two samples $\mathbf{x}_i$ and $\mathbf{x}_j$ are more likely to belong to the same class (henceforth referred to as similar samples), then we would like to encourage them to either both be labeled as relevant or as non-relevant. Let $\mathcal{E}$ denote the set of all pairs of similar samples. In other words, if samples $\mathbf{x}_i$ and $\mathbf{x}_j$ are similar, then $(i, j) \in \mathcal{E}$. We define the pairwise joint feature vector as follows:

$$\Psi_2(\mathbf{X}, \mathbf{Y}) = \eta \left(\sum_{(i,j) \in \mathcal{E}, y_i \neq y_j} \Phi(\psi(\mathbf{x}_i), \psi(\mathbf{x}_j)) \right) \tag{5}$$

where $\Phi(\psi(\mathbf{x}_i), \psi(\mathbf{x}_j))$ is a vector such that each of its elements is inversely proportional to the difference between the corresponding elements of its two input vectors and η controls the trade-off between the first-order and high-order information. In our work, we define $\Phi(\mathbf{z}_i, \mathbf{z}_j) = \exp(-(\mathbf{z}_i - \mathbf{z}_j)^2)$. All the operations are performed in an element-wise manner. In other words, $\Psi_2(\mathbf{X}, \mathbf{Y})$ is a d dimensional vector that is the sum of pairwise feature vectors over all pairs of similar samples having different classes.

Parameters and Prediction. Similar to the joint feature vector, the parameters of a HOB-SVM consist of two parts: the unary parameters $\mathbf{w}_1 \in \mathbb{R}^{2d}$ and the pairwise parameters $\mathbf{w}_2 \in \mathbb{R}^d$. Given an input $\mathbf{X}$, the output $\mathbf{Y}$ is predicted by maximizing the score, that is,

$$\mathbf{Y} = \operatorname*{argmax}_{\mathbf{Y}} \mathbf{w}^\top \Psi(\mathbf{X}, \mathbf{Y}), \mathbf{w} = \begin{pmatrix} \mathbf{w}_1 \\ \mathbf{w}_2 \end{pmatrix}, \Psi(\mathbf{X}, \mathbf{Y}) = \begin{pmatrix} \Psi_1(\mathbf{X}, \mathbf{Y}) \\ \Psi_2(\mathbf{X}, \mathbf{Y}) \end{pmatrix}. \qquad (6)$$

Note that, in general, the above problem is NP-hard. However, when $\mathbf{w}_2 \le 0$, it can be optimized efficiently using graph cuts [12]. This follows from the fact that each element of the pairwise joint feature vector is non-negative (see equation (5)), and hence the score of an output $\mathbf{Y}$ is a supermodular function of $\mathbf{Y}$. In what follows, we will always estimate the parameters of a HOB-SVM under the constraint that $\mathbf{w}_2 \le 0$. Moreover, our approaches can also be used without this constraint by employing approximate inference algorithms such as [11,14,18].

Loss Function. Although we would ideally like to optimize the AP loss, as mentioned earlier, this results in a difficult loss-augmented inference problem when the joint feature vector captures high-order information. Hence, inspired by the success of SVM for ranking, we use a surrogate loss function defined as follows:

$$\Delta(\mathbf{Y}^*, \mathbf{Y}) = \frac{J \sum_{i, y_i^* = 1} \delta(y_i = 0) + \sum_{j, y_j^* = 0} \delta(y_j = 1)}{J |\mathcal{P}| + |\mathcal{N}|}, \qquad (7)$$

where $\delta(\cdot)$ is 1 if its argument is true and 0 otherwise. The terms $|\mathcal{P}|$ and $|\mathcal{N}|$ are the total number of positive and negative samples (as specified by the ground-truth assignment $\mathbf{Y}^*$) respectively. The hyperparameter J is set to $|\mathcal{N}|/|\mathcal{P}|$. In other words, $\Delta(\mathbf{Y}^*, \mathbf{Y})$ is the weighted fraction of misclassifications.

Parameter Estimation. Given the dataset $(\mathbf{X}, \mathbf{Y}^*)$, the parameters of HOB-SVM are obtained by solving the following convex optimization problem:

$$\min_{\mathbf{w}} \frac{1}{2} \|\mathbf{w}\|^2 + C\xi, \qquad (8)$$

$$\mathbf{w}^\top \Psi(\mathbf{X}, \mathbf{Y}) - \mathbf{w}^\top \Psi(\mathbf{X}, \overline{\mathbf{Y}}) \ge \Delta(\mathbf{Y}^*, \overline{\mathbf{Y}}) - \xi, \forall \overline{\mathbf{Y}}, \mathbf{w}_2 \le 0.$$

Even though the number of constraints in the above problem are exponential in the number of samples n, it can be optimized efficiently by iteratively solving the loss-augmented inference problem, that is, $\hat{\mathbf{Y}} = \operatorname{argmax}_{\overline{\mathbf{Y}}}(\mathbf{w}^\top \Psi(\mathbf{X}, \overline{\mathbf{Y}}) + \Delta(\mathbf{Y}^*, \overline{\mathbf{Y}}))$. The restriction $\mathbf{w}_2 \le 0$ allows us to solve the above problem efficiently using graph cuts [12]. The problem (8) is similar to training graphical models with approximate inference [5,6,15,21].

Using HOB-SVM for Ranking. From a theoretical point of view, the main disadvantage of HOB-SVM is that it optimizes a surrogate loss function instead of the AP loss. In the next section, we will describe a novel framework that addresses this disadvantage. From a practical point of view, the main disadvantage of HOB-SVM is that it provides a single score for the entire assignment $\mathbf{Y}$. In other words, instead of assigning an individual score for each sample, it assigns one score $\mathbf{w}^{\top}\Psi(\mathbf{X}, \mathbf{Y})$ for all the samples taken together. This prevents us from specifying a ranking of the samples. To address this issue, we propose a simple yet intuitive solution: (i) compute the difference between the max-marginal of a sample being assigned to the positive class and the max-marginal of it being assigned to the negative class; and (ii) sort the samples according to the difference in max-marginals. Max-marginal captures high-order information and the difference of max-marginals measures our confidence on a particular sample belonging to the positive class. Formally, we define the max-marginal of a sample $\mathbf{x}_i$ belonging to the positive class $m_i^+(\mathbf{w})$ and negative class $m_i^-(\mathbf{w})$ as:

$$m_i^+(\mathbf{w}) = \mathbf{w}^{\top}\Psi(\mathbf{X}, \mathbf{Y}_i^+), \mathbf{Y}_i^+ = \operatorname*{argmax}_{\mathbf{Y}, y_i=1} \mathbf{w}^{\top}\Psi(\mathbf{X}, \mathbf{Y}). \tag{9}$$

$$m_i^-(\mathbf{w}) = \mathbf{w}^{\top}\Psi(\mathbf{X}, \mathbf{Y}_i^-), \mathbf{Y}_i^- = \operatorname*{argmax}_{\mathbf{Y}, y_i=0} \mathbf{w}^{\top}\Psi(\mathbf{X}, \mathbf{Y}). \tag{10}$$

The max-marginals for all the samples can be computed efficiently using the *dynamic graph cuts* algorithm [9,10]. Given the max-marginals $m_i^+(\mathbf{w})$ and $m_i^-(\mathbf{w})$, the score of a sample $\mathbf{x}_i$ is defined as

$$s_i(\mathbf{w}) = m_i^+(\mathbf{w}) - m_i^-(\mathbf{w}). \tag{11}$$

Note that, if the two labelings $\mathbf{Y}_i^+$ and $\mathbf{Y}_i^-$ defined in equations (9)-(10) respectively differ only in the label assigned to the sample $\mathbf{x}_i$, this implies that the sample $\mathbf{x}_i$ has no influence in determining the labels of the other samples in the dataset. In this case, the difference in max-marginals does not depend on the feature vectors of any other samples except the sample $\mathbf{x}_i$. However, if the sample $\mathbf{x}_i$ does influence the labels of the other samples (that is, $\mathbf{Y}_i^+$ and $\mathbf{Y}_i^-$ differ significantly), then the difference in the max-marginals depends on several samples in the dataset. The ranking is obtained by sorting the samples in descending order of their scores $s_i(\mathbf{w})$. As will be seen in section 5, this intuitive way of scoring a sample provides an improved ranking over the baselines.

4   High-Order Average Precision SVM (HOAP-SVM)

While HOB-SVM allows us to incorporate high-order information via the pairwise joint feature vector, it suffers from the deficiency of using a surrogate loss function. Specifically, instead of optimizing the AP loss in order to estimate the parameters, it optimizes a weighted 0-1 loss. However, the way that HOB-SVM obtains a ranking points us to the direction of resolving this deficiency. We begin by presenting the high-level overview of our approach. We observe that the score of a ranking according to an AP-SVM is the weighted sum of the scores of the individual samples. The reason why AP-SVM fails to capture high-order information is that the score of the individual sample depends on no other sample in the dataset. This is in contrast to the score employed by HOB-SVM (see equation (11)). Hence, it would be desirable to extend AP-SVM such that the score of the ranking is the weighted sum of the difference of max-marginals of individual samples. This is precisely our next learning framework, which we call *High-Order* AP-SVM (HOAP-SVM). In what follows, we describe HOAP-SVM in detail.

The input of HOAP-SVM is a set of n samples $\mathbf{X} = \{\mathbf{x}_i, i = 1, \cdots, n\}$. Similar to AP-SVM, a sample can belong to the positive class or the negative class. The output of HOAP-SVM is a ranking matrix $\mathbf{R}$, defined in a similar manner to AP-SVM. During training, the ground-truth ranking matrix $\mathbf{R}^*$ assigns each positive sample to a higher rank than all negative samples. Once again, the indices of positive and negative samples is represented as $\mathcal{P}$ and $\mathcal{N}$ respectively.

Score of a Ranking. The parameters of HOAP-SVM are denoted by $\mathbf{w}$. Given an input $\mathbf{X}$ and a ranking $\mathbf{R}$, the score for the ranking specified by HOAP-SVM is defined as follows:

$$S(\mathbf{X}, \mathbf{R}; \mathbf{w}) = \gamma \sum_{i \in \mathcal{P}} \sum_{j \in \mathcal{N}} \mathbf{R}_{ij}(s_i(\mathbf{w}) - s_j(\mathbf{w})), \qquad (12)$$

where $s_i(\mathbf{w})$ is as specified in equation (11). In other words, the score of a ranking is the weighted sum of the difference of max-marginals for each sample, where the weights are specified by the ranking.

Prediction. Given an input $\mathbf{X}$, the ranking $\mathbf{R}$ is predicted by maximizing the score over all possible rankings, that is,

$$\mathbf{R} = \operatorname*{argmax}_{\mathbf{R}} S(\mathbf{X}, \mathbf{R}; \mathbf{w}). \qquad (13)$$

Proposition 1. *Problem (13) can be solved efficiently by sorting the samples in descending order of their scores $s_i(\mathbf{w})$.*

In other words, the prediction for HOAP-SVM is the same as the prediction for HOB-SVM. Recall that the score $s_i(\mathbf{w})$ can be computed efficiently using dynamic graph cuts [9,10].

Parameter Estimation. Given the input $\mathbf{X}$ and the ground-truth ranking $\mathbf{R}^*$, the parameters of HOAP-SVM are learned by optimizing the AP loss. To this end, we propose to estimate $\mathbf{w}$ by solving the following optimization problem:

$$\min_{\mathbf{w}} \frac{1}{2}||\mathbf{w}||^2 + C\xi, \qquad (14)$$
$$S(\mathbf{X}, \mathbf{R}^*; \mathbf{w}) - S(\mathbf{X}, \mathbf{R}; \mathbf{w}) \geq \Delta(\mathbf{R}^*, \mathbf{R}) - \xi, \forall \mathbf{R}, \mathbf{w}_2 \leq 0.$$

Here, $\Delta(\mathbf{R}^*, \mathbf{R})$ is the AP loss, that is, one minus the AP of the ranking $\mathbf{R}$ with respect to $\mathbf{R}^*$. The following proposition establishes the suitability of the above problem for learning an HOAP-SVM.

Proposition 2. *Problem (14) minimizes a regularized upper bound on the* AP *loss of the predicted ranking.*

Optimization. While problem (14) provides a valid upper bound on the AP loss, it is not a convex program. Hence, it cannot be optimized efficiently to obtain an optimal set of parameters for HOAP-SVM. However, in what follows, we show that problem (14) is a difference-of-convex program. By identifying the convex and the concave part of problem (14), we show how a locally optimal set of parameters can be obtained efficiently using the concave-convex procedure (CCCP) [25].

We begin by specifying the following shorthand notation that will be useful in simplifying problem (14). Given a ranking $\mathbf{R}$ we define functions $f(\mathbf{w}; \mathbf{R})$ and $g(\mathbf{w}; \mathbf{R})$ of the parameters $\mathbf{w}$ as

$$f(\mathbf{w}; \mathbf{R}) = \gamma \sum_{i \in \mathcal{P}} m_i^-(\mathbf{w}) \left(\sum_{j \in \mathcal{N}} (\mathbf{R}_{ij}^* - \mathbf{R}_{ij}) \right) + \gamma \sum_{j \in \mathcal{N}} m_j^+(\mathbf{w}) \left(\sum_{i \in \mathcal{P}} (\mathbf{R}_{ij}^* - \mathbf{R}_{ij}) \right),$$

$$g(\mathbf{w}; \mathbf{R}) = \gamma \sum_{i \in \mathcal{P}} m_i^+(\mathbf{w}) \left(\sum_{j \in \mathcal{N}} (\mathbf{R}_{ij}^* - \mathbf{R}_{ij}) \right) + \gamma \sum_{j \in \mathcal{N}} m_j^-(\mathbf{w}) \left(\sum_{i \in \mathcal{P}} (\mathbf{R}_{ij}^* - \mathbf{R}_{ij}) \right) \tag{15}$$

Proposition 3. *For any valid ranking matrix* $\mathbf{R}$*, the functions* $f(\mathbf{w}; \mathbf{R})$ *and* $g(\mathbf{w}; \mathbf{R})$ *are convex in* $\mathbf{w}$*.*

Using our shorthand notation problem (14) can be rewritten as follows:

$$\min_{\mathbf{w}} \frac{1}{2} ||\mathbf{w}||^2 + C\xi, \tag{16}$$
$$\xi \geq \Delta(\mathbf{R}^*, \mathbf{R}) + f(\mathbf{w}; \mathbf{R}) - g(\mathbf{w}; \mathbf{R}), \forall \mathbf{R}.$$

The above problem is obtained by substituting the value of the score of the ranking, defined in equation (12), into problem (14). Using proposition 3, it follows that problem (16) is a difference-of-convex program. This allows us to obtain a locally optimal set of parameters for the HOAP-SVM formulation using the CCCP approach outlined in Algorithm 1. The CCCP algorithm consists of two steps. In the first step, given the current set of parameters $\mathbf{w}_t$, we obtain a linear approximation $l(\mathbf{w}; \mathbf{R})$ of the function $g(\mathbf{w}; \mathbf{R})$ such that $l(\mathbf{w}_t; \mathbf{R}) = g(\mathbf{w}_t; \mathbf{R}), l(\mathbf{w}; \mathbf{R}) \leq g(\mathbf{w}; \mathbf{R}), \forall \mathbf{w}$. In other words, the linear function $l(\mathbf{w}; \mathbf{R})$ is a lower bound on the function $g(\mathbf{w}; \mathbf{R})$ such that the lower bound is tight at the current parameters $\mathbf{w}_t$. While at first sight the problem of obtaining the linear approximation for each ranking matrix $\mathbf{R}$ may appear to be highly expensive, the following proposition shows how this step can be performed in a computationally efficient manner.

Proposition 4. *Given the current set of parameters* $\mathbf{w}_t$*, let*

$$\bar{\mathbf{Y}}_i^+ = \underset{\mathbf{Y}, y_i = 1}{\operatorname{argmax}} \mathbf{w}_t^\top \Psi(\mathbf{X}, \mathbf{Y}), \bar{\mathbf{Y}}_j^- = \underset{\mathbf{Y}, y_j = -1}{\operatorname{argmax}} \mathbf{w}_t^\top \Psi(\mathbf{X}, \mathbf{Y}). \tag{18}$$

Algorithm 1. The CCCP algorithm for learning HOAP-SVM parameters.

---

input Samples $\mathbf{X}$, ranking $\mathbf{R}^*$, tolerance ϵ, initial parameters $\mathbf{w}_0$.

1: $t \leftarrow 0$.

2: **repeat**

3:    For all $\mathbf{R}$, find a linear lower bound $l(\mathbf{w};\mathbf{R})$ tight at $\mathbf{w}_t$ using proposition 4.

4:    Update the parameters by solving the following convex optimization problem:

$$\mathbf{w}_{t+1} = \underset{\mathbf{w}}{\operatorname{argmin}} \ \frac{1}{2}\|\mathbf{w}\|^2 + C\xi, \tag{17}$$

$$\xi \geq \Delta(\mathbf{R}^*,\mathbf{R}) + f(\mathbf{w};\mathbf{R}) - l(\mathbf{w};\mathbf{R}), \forall \mathbf{R}.$$

   The loss-augmented inference can be solved efficiently using proposition 5.

5:    $t \leftarrow t+1$.

6: **until** Objective of problem (16) does not decrease more than ϵ.

The following linear function is a lower bound on $g(\mathbf{w};\mathbf{R})$ that is tight at $\mathbf{w}_t$:

$$l(\mathbf{w};\mathbf{R}) = \gamma\sum_{i\in\mathcal{P}}\mathbf{w}^\top\Psi(\mathbf{X},\bar{\mathbf{Y}}_i^+)\left(\sum_{j\in\mathcal{N}}(\mathbf{R}_{ij}^* - \mathbf{R}_{ij})\right) + \gamma\sum_{j\in\mathcal{N}}\mathbf{w}^\top\Psi(\mathbf{X},\bar{\mathbf{Y}}_j^-)\left(\sum_{i\in\mathcal{P}}(\mathbf{R}_{ij}^* - \mathbf{R}_{ij})\right)$$

An upshot of the above proposition is that the linear lower bound of $g(\mathbf{w};\mathbf{R})$ can be computed efficiently for any $\mathbf{R}$ by pre-computing the labelings $\bar{\mathbf{Y}}_i^+$ and $\bar{\mathbf{Y}}_j^-$, which are independent of $\mathbf{R}$. The labelings $\bar{\mathbf{Y}}_i^+$ and $\bar{\mathbf{Y}}_j^-$ can be obtained efficiently using dynamic graph cuts [9,10].

In the second step of CCCP, we obtain a convex optimization problem by substituting the linear approximation $l(\mathbf{w};\mathbf{R})$ in place of the convex function $g(\mathbf{w};\mathbf{R})$. We update the parameters by solving the resulting convex optimization problem. To this end, we use the cutting-plane algorithm [8] in order to handle exponentially many constraints. Cutting-plane algorithm requires us to iteratively find the most-violated ranking $\hat{\mathbf{R}}$. The following proposition makes the cutting-plane algorithm efficient.

Proposition 5. *Given the upperbounded scores $\bar{m}_i^+(\mathbf{w}) = \mathbf{w}^\top\Psi(\mathbf{X},\bar{\mathbf{Y}}_i^+)$, $\bar{m}_j^-(\mathbf{w}) = \mathbf{w}^\top\Psi(\mathbf{X},\bar{\mathbf{Y}}_j^-)$, and the scores for the current parameters $m_i^+(\mathbf{w}) = \mathbf{w}^\top\Psi(\mathbf{X},\mathbf{Y}_i^+)$, $m_j^-(\mathbf{w}) = \mathbf{w}^\top\Psi(\mathbf{X},\mathbf{Y}_j^-)$, the following problem gives the most violated ranking.*

$$\hat{\mathbf{R}} \leftarrow \underset{\mathbf{R}}{\operatorname{argmax}}\left\{\eta\sum_{i\in\mathcal{P},j\in\mathcal{N}}\mathbf{R}_{ij}(\bar{s}_i(\mathbf{w}) - \bar{s}_j(\mathbf{w})) + \Delta(\mathbf{R},\mathbf{R}^*) - \eta\sum_{i\in\mathcal{P},j\in\mathcal{N}}\mathbf{R}_{ij}^*(\bar{s}_i(\mathbf{w}) - \bar{s}_j(\mathbf{w}))\right\}$$

where, $\bar{s}_i(\mathbf{w}) = (\bar{m}_i^+(\mathbf{w}) - m_i^-(\mathbf{w}))$ and $\bar{s}_j(\mathbf{w}) = (m_j^+(\mathbf{w}) - \bar{m}_j^-(\mathbf{w}))$. The greedy algorithm of [24] can be used to find the $\hat{\mathbf{R}}$ efficiently.

Upon convergence, the CCCP algorithm provides a locally optimal set of parameters for the HOAP-SVM framework.

Table 1. *The AP over five folds for the best setting of the hyperparameters obtained using the cross-validation. Our frameworks outperforms* SVM *and* AP-SVM *in all the 10 action classes. Note that* HOAP-SVM *is initialized with* HOB-SVM.

Actions/ Methods	Jump	Phone	Play inst	Read	Ride bike	Run	Take photo	Use comp	Walk	Ride horse	Average
SVM	56.0	35.5	42.6	33.8	81.9	78.4	33.9	37.2	61.7	85.9	54.7
AP-SVM	57.5	34.4	46.3	35.5	83.0	79.3	33.3	42.7	63.1	86.6	56.2
HOB-SVM	60.9	**36.1**	48.1	35.7	84.1	**81.5**	35.1	45.8	63.0	**87.9**	57.8
HOAP-SVM	**63.4**	34.5	**48.8**	**38.3**	**84.3**	81.0	**36.5**	**48.7**	**65.3**	87.7	**58.9**

Table 2. *The AP of all the four methods. The training is performed over the entire 'trainval' dataset of PASCAL VOC 2011 using the best hyperparameters obtained during 5-fold cross-validation. The testing is performed on the 'test' dataset and evaluated on the PASCAL VOC server. Note that* HOAP-SVM *is initialized using* HOB-SVM.

Actions/ Methods	Jump	Phone	Play inst	Read	Ride bike	Run	Take photo	Use comp	Walk	Ride horse	Average
SVM	51.1	29.7	40.5	20.6	81.1	76.7	20.0	27.7	56.7	84.2	48.82
AP-SVM	54.0	**33.8**	42.3	26.5	82.5	76.7	23.7	32.8	**57.7**	84.2	51.42
HOB-SVM	56.3	**33.8**	42.8	24.3	82.5	80.5	**27.7**	32.8	53.6	84.5	51.88
HOAP-SVM	**59.5**	**33.8**	**47.5**	**27.2**	**84.0**	**82.6**	26.1	**36.4**	55.1	**85.3**	**53.75**

5   Experiments

We now demonstrate the efficacy of our learning frameworks on the challenging problem of action classification [3,16]. The input for action classification is an action class such as 'jumping' or 'running' and a set of samples $\mathbf{X} = \{\mathbf{x}_i = (\mathbf{I}_i, \mathbf{b}_i), i = 1, \cdots, n\}$. Here, $\mathbf{I}_i$ is the image corresponding to the i-th sample, and $\mathbf{b}_i$ is a tight bounding box around a person present in the image. The desired output is a ranking of the samples according to their relevance to the action. Recall that our main hypothesis is that high-order information can help improve the ranking accuracy. To test our hypothesis, we require a set of similar samples such that samples $\mathbf{x}_i$ and $\mathbf{x}_j$ are more likely to belong to the same class (relevant or non-relevant) if $(i, j) \in \mathcal{E}$. In the action classification experiments, we define $\mathcal{E} = \{(i, j), \mathbf{I}_i = \mathbf{I}_j\}$, that is, the set of all pairs of bounding boxes that are present in the same image. Note that one could use any other similarity criterion in the proposed frameworks. Below we describe our experimental setup in detail.

Dataset. We use PASCAL VOC 2011 [4] action classification dataset, which consists of 4846 images depicting 10 action classes. The dataset is divided into two subsets: 2424 'trainval' images for which we are provided the bounding boxes of the person in the image together with their action classes; and 2422 'test' images for which we are only provided with the person bounding boxes.

Features. Given a sample $\mathbf{x}_i = (\mathbf{I}_i, \mathbf{b}_i)$, we use the concatenation of standard poselet-based feature vector [2] of the bounding box $\mathbf{b}_i$ and GIST feature vector

Fig. 1. *Top 8 samples ranked by all the four methods for 'reading' action class. First row – SVM, Second row – AP-SVM, Third row – HOB-SVM, and Fourth row – HOAP-SVM. Note that, the first false positive is ranked 2nd in case of SVM (first row) and 3rd in case of AP-SVM (second row), this shows the importance of optimizing the AP loss. On the other hand, in case of HOB-SVM (third row), the first false positive is ranked 4th and the 'similar samples' (2nd and 3rd) are assigned similar scores, this illustrates the importance of using high-order information. Furthermore, HOAP-SVM (fourth row) has the best AP among all the four methods, this shows the importance of using high-order information and optimizing the correct loss. Note that, in case of HOAP-SVM, the 4th and 5th ranked samples are false positives (underlying action is close to reading) and they both belong to the same image (our similarity criterion). This indicates that high-order information sometimes may lead to poor test AP in case of confusing classes (such as 'playinginstrument' vs 'usingcomputer') by assigning all the connected samples to the wrong label. Same effect can be seen in HOB-SVM for 7th and 8th ranked samples.*

[17] of the image $\mathbf{I}_i$ to specify the sample features $\psi(\mathbf{x}_i)$. The poselet feature consists of 2400 activation scores of action-specific poselets and 4 object activation scores. The GIST feature is a 512 dimensional feature vector that captures the overall scene depicted in the image. This results in a sample feature of size 2916. The sample features used to specify the unary and the pairwise joint feature vectors are shown in equations (4) and (5). As each pair of similar samples comes from the same image, we defined the joint pairwise feature vector using only the poselet features. The size of the joint feature vector is therefore 8748.

Methods. We compare our proposed approaches, namely HOB-SVM and HOAP-SVM, with the standard binary SVM (obtained by setting $\mathbf{w}_2 = 0$ in HOB-SVM) and AP-SVM (obtained by setting $\mathbf{w}_2 = 0$ in HOAP-SVM) that ignore high-order information. The baselines, SVM and AP-SVM requires one hyperparameter C, and HOB-SVM and HOAP-SVM requires two hyperparameters C and η. The common hyperparameter C is the trade-off between the regularization and the empirical loss, and η is the trade-off between the first order information and the high-order information. Note that the 'test' dataset was not used for cross-validation. We obtained the best setting of the hyperparameters for each method independently via a 5-fold cross-validation on the entire 'trainval' dataset. We consider the following putative values: $C \in \{10^{-1}, 10^0, \ldots, 10^4\}$ and $\eta \in \{10^{-4}, 10^0, \ldots, 10^4\}$. The J parameter in (7) is fixed to $|\mathcal{N}|/|\mathcal{P}|$.

Results. Table 1 shows the average AP over all the five folds for the best hyperparameter setting. By incorporating high-order information HOB-SVM provides an improvement in the ranking compared to the commonly used SVM classifier for all 10 action classes. Furthermore, even though HOB-SVM employs a surrogate loss function, it provides more accurate rankings compared to AP-SVM for 9 action classes. By optimizing the AP loss function, while incorpoating high-order information, HOAP-SVM outperforms SVM in 9 action classes, AP-SVM in all 10 action classes, and HOB-SVM in 7 action classes. Table 2 shows the AP values obtained for the 'test' set when the methods are trained using the best hyperparameter setting over the entire 'trainval' set. Table 2 clearly shows that HOB-SVM outperforms SVM classifier in 9 action classes and AP-SVM in 5 along with 3 ties. On the other hand, HOAP-SVM outperforms SVM classifier in all the 10 classes, AP-SVM in 8 along with 1 tie, and HOB-SVM in 8 along with 1 tie.

The paired t-test shows that: (a) HOB-SVM is statistically better than SVM for 6 action classes, (b) HOB-SVM is not statistically better than AP-SVM, (c) HOAP-SVM is statistically better than SVM for 6 action classes, and (d) HOAP-SVM is statistically better than AP-SVM for 4 action classes.

The effects of incorporating high-order information is illustrated in Fig. 1. While high-order information can introduce errors in the ranking, in general it provides boost in the overall performance.

6   Discussion

We proposed two new learning frameworks that incorporate high-order information to improve the accuracy of ranking. The first framework, HOB-SVM, uses a surrogate loss function, which allows us to compute its parameters by solving a convex optimization problem. The second framework, HOAP-SVM, minimizes the AP loss, which results in a difference-of-convex optimization problem. Both HOB-SVM and HOAP-SVM outperform baseline methods that do not make use of high-order information. By minimizing the correct loss function, HOAP-SVM outperforms HOB-SVM. An interesting direction for future work would be to allow for weakly supervised learning by extending the recently proposed *latent* AP-SVM [1] formulation to use high-order information. While such a learning formulation can be easily obtained with the introduction of latent variables, it is not clear whether the resulting optimization problem can be solved efficiently.

Acknowledgements. This work is partially funded by the European Research Council under the European Community's Seventh Framework Programme (FP7/2007-2013)/ERC Grant agreement number 259112, and the Ministere de l'education nationale, de l'enseignement superieure et de la recherche.

References

1. Behl, A., Jawahar, C.V., Kumar, M.P.: Optimizing average precision using weakly supervised data. In: CVPR (2014)
2. Bourdev, L., Malik, J.: Poselets: Body part detectors trained using 3D human pose annotations. IJCV (2009)
3. Delaitre, V., Laptev, I., Sivic, J.: Recognizing human actions in still images: a study of bag-of-features and part-based representations. In: BMVC (2010)
4. Everingham, M., Gool, L., Williams, C., Winn, J., Zisserman, A.: The pascal visual object classes (voc) challenge. IJCV (2010)
5. Finley, T., Joachims, T.: Training structural SVMs when exact inference is intractable. In: ICML (2008)
6. Franc, V., Savchynskyy, B.: Discriminative learning of max-sum classifiers. JMLR (2008)
7. Horst, R., Thoai, N.: DC programming overview. Journal of Optimization Theory and Applications (1999)
8. Joachims, T., Finley, T., Yu, C.: Cutting-plane training of structural SVMs. Machine Learning (2009)
9. Kohli, P., Torr, P.: Measuring uncertainty in graph cut solutions efficiently computing min-marginal energies using dynamic graph cuts. In: Leonardis, A., Bischof, H., Pinz, A. (eds.) ECCV 2006. Part II. LNCS, vol. 3952, pp. 30–43. Springer, Heidelberg (2006)
10. Kohli, P., Torr, P.: Dynamic graph cuts for efficient inference in Markov random fields. PAMI (2007)
11. Kolmogorov, V.: Convergent tree-reweighted message passing for energy minimization. PAMI (2006)
12. Kolmogorov, V., Zabih, R.: What energy functions can be minimized via graph cuts. PAMI (2004)
13. Komodakis, N.: Efficient training for pairwise or higher order crfs via dual decomposition. In: CVPR (2011)
14. Komodakis, N., Paragios, N., Tziritas, G.: MRF energy minimization and beyond via dual decomposition. PAMI (2011)
15. Kulesza, A., Pereira, F.: Structured learning with approximate inference. In: NIPS (2007)
16. Maji, S., Bourdev, L., Malik, J.: Action recognition from a distributed representation of pose and appearance. In: CVPR (2011)
17. Oliva, A., Torralba, A.: Modeling the shape of the scene: A holistic representation of the spatial envelope. IJCV (2001)
18. Pearl, J.: Probabilistic Reasoning in Intelligent Systems: Networks of Plausible Inference. Morgan Kaufmann (1988)
19. Rosenfeld, N., Meshi, O., Globerson, A., Tarlow, D.: Learning structured models with the AUC loss and its generalizations. In: AISTAT (2014)
20. Taskar, B., Guestrin, C., Koller, D.: Max-margin Markov networks. In: NIPS (2003)
21. Taskar, B., Lacoste-Julien, S., Jordan, M.I.: Structured prediction, dual extragradient and bregman projections. JMLR (2006)
22. Tsochantaridis, I., Hofmann, T., Joachims, T., Altun, Y.: Support vector machine learning for interdependent and structured output spaces. In: ICML (2004)
23. Vapnik, V.: Statistical learning theory. Wiley (1998)
24. Yue, Y., Finley, T., Radlinski, F., Joachims, T.: A support vector method for optimizing average precision. In: SIGIR (2007)
25. Yuille, A., Rangarajan, A.: The concave-convex procedure. Neural Computation (2003)

Support Vector Guided Dictionary Learning

Sijia Cai[1,3], Wangmeng Zuo[2], Lei Zhang[3,*], Xiangchu Feng[4], and Ping Wang[1]

[1] School of Science, Tianjin University, China
[2] School of Computer Science and Technology, Harbin Institute of Technology, China
[3] Dept. of Computing, The Hong Kong Polytechnic University, China
[4] Dept. of Applied Mathematics, Xidian University, China
cssjcai@gmail.com, cslzhang@comp.polyu.edu.hk

Abstract. Discriminative dictionary learning aims to learn a dictionary from training samples to enhance the discriminative capability of their coding vectors. Several discrimination terms have been proposed by assessing the prediction loss (e.g., logistic regression) or class separation criterion (e.g., Fisher discrimination criterion) on the coding vectors. In this paper, we provide a new insight on discriminative dictionary learning. Specifically, we formulate the discrimination term as the weighted summation of the squared distances between all pairs of coding vectors. The discrimination term in the state-of-the-art Fisher discrimination dictionary learning (FDDL) method can be explained as a special case of our model, where the weights are simply determined by the numbers of samples of each class. We then propose a parameterization method to adaptively determine the weight of each coding vector pair, which leads to a support vector guided dictionary learning (SVGDL) model. Compared with FDDL, SVGDL can adaptively assign different weights to different pairs of coding vectors. More importantly, SVGDL automatically selects only a few critical pairs to assign non-zero weights, resulting in better generalization ability for pattern recognition tasks. The experimental results on a series of benchmark databases show that SVGDL outperforms many state-of-the-art discriminative dictionary learning methods.

Keywords: Dictionary learning, support vector machine, sparse representation, Fisher discrimination.

1 Introduction

Sparsity has become an appealing concept for data representation and it has been successfully applied in a variety of fields, e.g., compressed sensing [1], image restoration [2, 3], subspace clustering [4] and image classification [5, 6], etc. In sparse representation, a signal is approximated by the linear combination of a few bases sparsely selected from an over-complete set of atoms, i.e., a dictionary. Such a sparse coding strategy can be explained from the perspective of neuroscience [7] and it brings some desirable properties for signal reconstruction [8]. In sparse representation, the dictionary can be simply predefined as some

---

* Corresponding author.

D. Fleet et al. (Eds.): ECCV 2014, Part IV, LNCS 8692, pp. 624–639, 2014.

off-the-shelf dictionaries such as wavelets [9], but it has been demonstrated that learning a dictionary from exemplar images can lead to much better signal reconstruction performance [10]. Some typical reconstructive dictionary learning methods include K-means, method of optimal direction (MOD) [11], K-SVD [10] and analysis K-SVD [12].

Sparse representation can also be used for pattern recognition. The sparse representation based classification (SRC) has achieved competitive performance on face recognition [13]. Moreover, sparse coding as a soft vector quantization technique [14] adopted in Bag-of-Words based image representation [15] has also been recognized as a thought-provoking idea in image classification [5, 6]. Similar to signal reconstruction, in pattern classification a discriminative dictionary learned from given examples can also improve much the performance.

A number of discriminative dictionary learning (DDL) methods [16–25] have been proposed. One type of DDL methods dedicate to improving the discriminative capability of signal reconstruction residual. Rather than learning a dictionary for all classes, these methods exploit structural assumption on dictionary design and impose the learned dictionary with category-specific property, e.g., learning a sub-dictionary for each class [18, 22, 23]. Ramirez et al. [22] introduced the structured incoherence term to promote the independence of the sub-dictionaries associated with different classes. Gao et al. [23] learned both the category-specific sub-dictionaries and a shared dictionary for fine-grained image categorization. However, these dictionary learning methods might not be scalable to the problems with a large number of classes.

Another type of DDL methods aim to seek the optimal dictionary to improve the discriminative capability of coding vectors. These methods learn concurrently a dictionary and a classifier by incorporating some prediction loss on the coding vectors. In this spirit, Zhang et al. [16] extended the original K-SVD algorithm by simultaneously learning a linear classifier. Jiang et al. [19, 20] introduced a label consistent regularization term to enforce the discrimination of coding vectors. The so-called LC-KSVD algorithm exhibits good classification performance. Mairal et al. [17] proposed a supervised dictionary learning scheme by exploiting logistic loss function and further presented a general task-driven dictionary learning (TDDL) framework [21]. Wang et al. [25] formulated the dictionary learning problem from a max-margin perspective and learned the dictionary by using a multi-class hinge loss function. By considering the discrimination from both reconstruction residual and coding vectors, Yang et al. [18] proposed a Fisher discrimination dictionary learning (FDDL) method, where the category-specific strategy is adopted for learning a structured dictionary and the Fisher discrimination criterion is imposed on the coding vectors to enhance class discrimination.

In most of the above DDL methods, the discrimination of the learned dictionary is enforced by either imposing structural constraints on dictionary or imposing a discrimination term on the coding vectors. Several discrimination terms have been proposed by assessing the prediction loss (e.g., logistic regression) or class separation criterion (e.g., Fisher discrimination criterion) on coding vectors

[16–20, 22]. In this paper, we provide a new scheme for DDL, where the discrimination term is formulated as the weighted summation of the squared distances between all pairs of coding vectors. This weighted squared distance principle has been widely adopted in unsupervised manifold regularization, where the coding vectors can preserve the geometric structure of original data samples to benefit clustering and classification. Recent advances in sparse coding, such as GraphSC [26], LLC [27] and LSC/HLSC [28, 29], utilized the similarity between pairs of samples to assign the weight and achieved significant improvements in Bag-of-Words based image classification. Unlike these methods, we incorporate the sample label information into the design of weight. With the proposed scheme, the design of discrimination term can be regarded as the design of a paradigm of weight assignment, which provides a new insight in developing new DDL models. Actually, the discrimination term on coding vectors in the FDDL method can be explained as a special case of our model, where the weights are deterministic and are simply determined by the numbers of samples of each class.

To make weight assignment more adaptive and flexible, we then propose a parameterization method, which consequently leads to the proposed support vector guided dictionary learning (SVGDL) model. One promising property of SVGDL is that, by incorporating the weight parameterization with the symmetry, consistency and balance constraints, the optimization problem on weight assignment is equivalent to the dual form of linear support vector machines (SVM) [30]. This property allows us to use the multi-class linear SVM [5] for efficient DDL. Another important insight from SVGDL is that, most weights will be zero and only the weights of pairs of support vectors are nonzero. Such a fact indicates that the weights are sparse and only the coding vectors near the decision boundaries play a crucial role in learning a discriminative dictionary. Compared with FDDL, SVGDL adaptively assigns weights to pairs of coding vectors in the support vector set, and is superior in terms of classification performance.

Another interesting point of SVGDL is its robustness to the regularizer of coding vectors. Almost all DDL methods impose the sparse ℓ_0-norm or ℓ_1-norm regularizers on coding vectors. However, some recent works [31, 32] argue that sparsity may not be always helpful for classification. Mehta and Gray [33] analyzed the working mechanism and generalization error bound of predictive sparse coding, but several open problems remain on the necessity of sparsity in DDL. Furthermore, the complexity of ℓ_1-norm sparse coding generally is much higher than that of ℓ_2-norm coding, and the inefficiency would be exacerbated for DDL with ℓ_1-norm regularizer when the number of atoms or training samples is high. For SVGDL, fortunately, our experimental results show that the classification performance is insensitive to the choice of ℓ_2-norm or ℓ_1-norm regularizer. This can be owed to the fact only a few support coding vectors (with non-zero weights) are automatically selected to guide the learning of dictionary, i.e., the sparsity lies in the weights but not the coding vectors. Consequently, the time complexity of SVGDL can be greatly reduced, especially in the testing stage where the coding step can be replaced by matrix-vector multiplication.

2   Problem Formulation

Assume that $x \in \mathbb{R}^m$ is a m dimensional signal with class label $y \in \{1, 2, \ldots, C\}$. The training set with n samples is denoted as $X = [X_1, X_2, \ldots, X_C] = [x_1, x_2, \ldots, x_n] \in \mathbb{R}^{m \times n}$, where X_c is the subset of n_c training samples from class c. Denote the learned dictionary by $D = [d_1, d_2, \ldots, d_K] \in \mathbb{R}^{m \times K}$ ($K > m$ and $K \ll n$), where d_is are the atoms. $Z = [z_1, z_2, \ldots, z_n]$ are the coding vectors of X over D. A general DDL model can be described as:

$$< D, Z >= \arg\min_{D,Z} \ \mathcal{R}(X, D, Z) + \lambda_1 \|Z\|_p^p + \lambda_2 \mathcal{L}(Z), \qquad (1)$$

where λ_1 and λ_2 are the trade-off parameters, $\mathcal{R}(X, D, Z)$ is the reconstruction term, p denotes the parameter of the ℓ_p-norm regularizer (e.g., ℓ_1-norm or ℓ_2-norm), and $\mathcal{L}(Z)$ denotes the discrimination term for Z.

Note that apart from the discrimination term, discrimination can also be enforced by imposing structural constraints on the learned dictionary. For example, FDDL [18] learns the structured dictionary $D = [D_1, D_2, \ldots, D_C]$, where D_c is the sub-dictionary corresponding to class c. Then $\mathcal{R}(X, D, Z)$ can be divided into the sum of the reconstruction errors under the sub-dictionaries. Although this class-customized setting for dictionary learning is effective when there are sufficient training samples for each class, it is not scalable to the problem with a great number of classes. Thus, in our formulation we only consider the discrimination term and learn a single dictionary shared between all classes.

Intuitively, the discrimination can be assessed by the similarity of pairs of coding vectors from the same class and the dissimilarity of pairs of coding vectors from different classes. Thus, it is reasonable to use the weighted sum of the squared distances of pairs of coding vectors as an indicator of discrimination capability, resulting in the discrimination term:

$$\mathcal{L}(Z, w_{ij}) = \sum_{i,j} \|z_i - z_j\|_2^2 w_{ij}. \qquad (2)$$

Next we will show that the Fisher discrimination criterion adopted in FDDL can be reformulated as a special case of the discrimination term in Eq. (2).

In FDDL, the discrimination term is defined as $\mathcal{L}(Z) = tr(S_W(Z)) - tr(S_B(Z))$, where $tr(S_W(Z))$ and $tr(S_B(Z))$ denote the within-class and between-class scatters, respectively. Based on the definitions of S_W and S_B, $\mathcal{L}(Z)$ in FDDL can be reformulated as the weighted sum of the squared distances of pairs of coding vectors. We have the following **Lemma 1**.

Lemma 1. *Denote by $\bar{z}_c$ and $\bar{z}$ the mean vectors of Z_c and Z, respectively, where Z_c is the set of coding vectors of samples from class c. Then $\mathcal{L}(Z)$ in FDDL is equivalent to the weighted sum of the squared distances of pairs of coding vectors:*

$$\mathcal{L}(Z) = \sum_{c=1}^{C} \Big(\sum_{y_i=c, y_j=c} \big(\frac{1}{n_c} - \frac{1}{2n} \big) \|z_i - z_j\|_2^2 + \sum_{y_i=c, y_j \neq c} \big(-\frac{1}{2n} \big) \|z_i - z_j\|_2^2 \Big). \qquad (3)$$

Please refer to **Appendix A** for the proof of **Lemma 1**.

From Eq. (3), we can see that if two samples are from the same class, the weight $\frac{1}{n_c} - \frac{1}{2n}$ is positive, and the Fisher discrimination term would encourage to learn a dictionary that minimizes the difference between coding vectors from the same class. Meanwhile, if two samples are from different classes, the weight $-\frac{1}{2n}$ is negative, and the Fisher discrimination term would encourage to learn a dictionary that maximizes the difference between coding vectors from different classes.

Using the discrimination term in Eq. (2), we define a general model for DDL:

$$< D, Z >= \arg\min_{D,Z} \|X - DZ\|_F^2 + \lambda_1\|Z\|_p^p + \lambda_2 \sum_{i,j} \|z_i - z_j\|_2^2 w_{ij}, \quad (4)$$

where $w_{ij} \geq 0$ when x_i and x_j are from the same class, and $w_{ij} < 0$ when x_i and x_j are from different classes. One choice of the discrimination term is the Fisher discrimination criterion. However, as we show above, the weight assignment adopted in the Fisher discrimination term is deterministic. The weight of pairwise coding vectors from different classes is fully determined by the number of samples n, and the weight of pairwise coding vectors from the same class is fully determined by n and the number of samples of this class n_c. Note that some pairs of coding vectors may play more important roles than other pairs in learning a discriminative dictionary. The deterministic weight assignment in Fisher discrimination term ignores this fact and thus may result in less effective classification. In the next section we propose a parameterization method for adaptive weight assignment.

3   Support Vector Guided Dictionary Learning

3.1   A Parameterized Perspective on Discrimination

Rather than directly assigning weight w_{ij} for each pair, we assume that all the weights w_{ij} can be parameterized as a function with variable β, and define the parameterized formulation of the discrimination term $\mathcal{L}(Z)$ as follows:

$$\mathcal{L}(Z, w_{ij}(\beta)) = \sum_{i,j} \|z_i - z_j\|_2^2 w_{ij}(\beta). \quad (5)$$

In order to choose a proper manner for the parameterization of w_{ij}, we claim that the following three properties should be satisfied:

   a) Symmetry: $w_{ij}(\beta) = w_{ji}(\beta)$;
   b) Consistency: $w_{ij}(\beta) \geq 0$ if $y_i = y_j$, and $w_{ij}(\beta) \leq 0$ if $y_i \neq y_j$;
   c) Balance: $\sum_{j=1}^n w_{ij}(\beta) = 0, \forall i$.

The above three properties give a specific explanation of the model in Eq. 4. The symmetry can be achieved naturally; the consistency means that the weight w_{ij} should be non-negative when z_i and z_j are from the same class while the weight w_{ij} should be non-positive when z_i and z_j are from different classes; since the number of pairs with different class labels is much larger than that with the same class label, the balance constraint is introduced to balance the contributions of positive and negative weights.

We then give an instance of the constructed parameterization for $w_{ij}(\beta)$. For convenience, we consider the two-class classification problem with label $y_i \in$

$\{-1, 1\}$. Then we can define $w_{ij}(\beta) = y_i y_j \beta_i \beta_j$ and $\sum_{j=1}^{n} y_j \beta_j = 0$, where the variable $\beta = [\beta_1, \beta_2, \ldots, \beta_n]$ is a nonnegative vector. It is obvious to see that $w_{ij}(\beta)$ satisfies all the three properties above. Based on this setting of $w_{ij}(\beta)$, we can then transform $\mathcal{L}(Z, w_{ij}(\beta))$ into the new form as described in the following **Lemma 2**.

Lemma 2. *Let* $w_{ij}(\beta) = y_i y_j \beta_i \beta_j$. *If* $\sum_{j=1}^{n} y_j \beta_j = 0$, *then the discrimination term* $\mathcal{L}(Z)$ *can be written as:*

$$\mathcal{L}(Z, w_{ij}(\beta)) = -2 \sum_{i,j} y_i y_j \beta_i \beta_j z_i^T z_j = \beta^T K \beta, \tag{6}$$

where K is the negative semidefinite matrix.

Please refer to **Appendix B** for the proof of **Lemma 2**.

Since K is a negative semidefinite matrix, to obtain an extremum of β, we could maximize the objective function of $\mathcal{L}(Z, w_{ij}(\beta))$:

$$\begin{aligned} <\beta> = \arg\max_{\beta} \quad & \beta^T K \beta + r(\beta) \\ \text{s.t.} \quad & \beta_i \geq 0, \forall i, \sum_{j=1}^{n} y_j \beta_j = 0, \end{aligned} \tag{7}$$

where $r(\beta)$ is some regularization term to avoid the trivial solution with $\beta = 0$. Overall, we have the following parameterized formulation of DDL:

$$<D, Z> = \arg\min_{D,Z} (\|X - DZ\|_F^2 + \lambda_1 \|Z\|_p^p + \lambda_2 \max_{\beta \in dom(\beta)} (\sum_{i,j} \|z_i - z_j\|_2^2 w_{ij}(\beta) + r(\beta))), \tag{8}$$

where the domain $dom(\beta)$ of variable β is $dom(\beta) : \beta \succeq 0, \sum_{j=1}^{n} y_j \beta_j = 0$ according to the previous definition. We can see that the general weight assignment in coding space falls into the appropriate selection of $dom(\beta)$, $w_{ij}(\beta)$ and $r(\beta)$. In particular, the model in Eq. (4) is a special case of Eq. (8) when β is given by a fixed matrix $[w_{ij}]$.

3.2 Dictionary Learning Model

By choosing $r(\beta) = 4 \sum_{i=1}^{n} \beta_i$ and adopting the $w_{ij}(\beta)$ and $dom(\beta)$ described above, the model in Eq. (8) can be rewritten as:

$$\begin{aligned} <D, Z> = \arg\min_{D,Z} (\|X - DZ\|_F^2 + \lambda_1 \|Z\|_p^p + \lambda_2 \max_{\beta} (4 \sum_{i=1}^{n} \beta_i \\ - 2 \sum_{i,j} y_i y_j \beta_i \beta_j z_i^T z_j)) \\ \text{s.t.} \quad \beta_i \geq 0, \forall i \text{ and } \sum_{j=1}^{n} y_j \beta_j = 0. \end{aligned} \tag{9}$$

Note that the subproblem for β is exactly the Lagrange dual of hard-margin binary SVM, which can be solved using some classical algorithms like sequential minimal optimization (SMO) [34]. To further reduce the adverse effect of outliers, we impose β with the additional constraint $\beta_i \leq \frac{1}{2}\theta$ for all i, where θ is a fixed constant. Thus the subproblem for β reduces to the dual formulation of soft-margin binary SVM. Then we replace the subproblem of β with its primal SVM form, leading to the support vector guided dictionary learning (SVGDL) model:

$$<D, Z, u, b> = \arg\min_{D,Z,u,b} \|X - DZ\|_F^2 + \lambda_1 \|Z\|_p^p + 2\lambda_2 \mathcal{L}(Z, y, u, b), \tag{10}$$

where u is the normal to the hyperplane of SVM, b is the corresponding bias, $y = [y_1, y_2, \ldots, y_n]$ is the label vector, and $\mathcal{L}(Z, y, u, b)$ is defined as:

$$\mathcal{L}(Z, y, u, b) = \|u\|_2^2 + \theta \sum\nolimits_{i=1}^n \ell(z_i, y_i, u, b), \tag{11}$$

where $\ell(z_i, y_i, u, b)$ is the hinge loss function.

The solution $< u, b >$ can be represented as the linear combination of a few coding vectors (support vectors), i.e., we have $\beta_i \neq 0$ only if z_i is the support vector. The sparsity of β further leads to the sparsity of weight matrix $[w_{ij}]$ based on our parameterization method. Thus, the model in Eq. (4) can be written as:

$$< D, Z >= \arg\min_{D,Z} \|X - DZ\|_F^2 + \lambda_1 \|Z\|_p^p + \lambda_2 \sum_{i,j \in SV} \|z_i - z_j\|_2^2 w_{ij}(\beta), \tag{12}$$

where SV is the set of support vectors. From the model in Eq. (10), there are two distinct characteristics of SVGDL. First, unlike FDDL which adopts a deterministic method for weight assignment, SVGDL adopts an adaptive weight assignment. Second, rather than assigning non-zero weights for all pairwise coding vectors, SVGDL only assigns non-zero weights for pairwise support coding vectors, which indicates that only the coding vectors near the classification hyperplane play a dominant role in learning the discriminative dictionary. These two characteristics are consistent with our intuitive understandings: the coding vectors near the boundary are more crucial for DDL.

Another noticeable advantage of the proposed model is that the classification performance of SVGDL is insensitive to the choice of ℓ_1-norm or ℓ_2-norm regularizers on the coding vectors. Note that most existing dictionary learning methods take the sparsity as a primary requirement for learning a discriminative dictionary. However, our experimental results indicate that sparsity has little impact on the discriminative capability of the learned dictionary by SVGDL, while it will greatly increase the computational burden in both the training and testing stages. Figure 1 shows the classification accuracy of SVGDL with the ℓ_1-norm regularizer and the ℓ_2-norm regularizer on the Caltech-101 database using different numbers of training samples per class. One can see that, SVGDL with the ℓ_2-norm regularizer always achieves higher accuracy than SVGDL with the ℓ_1-norm regularizer. We argue that, other than the sparsity of coding vectors, the sparsity of the weight matrix $[w_{ij}]$ seems to play a more crucial role in learning a discriminative dictionary. To verify this, we evaluate the model in Eq. (10) by utilizing the quadratic hinge loss (will be discussed later) and squared loss, which induce the sparse and non-sparse weight matrix $[w_{ij}]$ respectively, and compare the recognition results on several face databases (the detailed settings are presented in Section 4.3). As shown in Table 1, the results using quadratic hinge loss are much better than that using squared loss, which further emphasizes the importance of sparse weight matrix. Thus, we choose ℓ_2-norm regularizer on Z for SVGDL in the later discussion due to its computational efficiency.

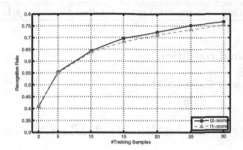

Fig. 1. Accuracy curves on Caltech-101 database using ℓ_1-norm and ℓ_2-norm for regularization in SVGDL

Table 1. The recognition rates by using quadratic hinge loss and squared loss on different face databases

	Extended Yale B	AR	Multi-PIE Test 1
Quadratic hinge loss	0.961	0.946	0.955
Squared loss	0.933	0.921	0.937

For multi-class classification, we simply adopt the one-vs-all strategy by leaning C hyperplanes $U = [u_1, u_2, \ldots, u_C]$ and the corresponding biases $b - [b_1, b_2, \ldots, b_C]$. The SVGDL is formulated as:

$$< D, Z, U, b >= \arg\min_{D,Z,U,b} \|X - DZ\|_F^2 + \lambda_1 \|Z\|_p^p + 2\lambda_2 \sum_{c=1}^{C} \mathcal{L}(Z, y^c, u_c, b_c), \quad (13)$$

where $y^c = [y_1^c, y_2^c, \ldots, y_n^c]$, $y_i^c = 1$ if $y_i = c$, and otherwise $y_i^c = -1$.

3.3 Optimization and Complexity

The SVGDL model in Eq. (13) is a not a jointly convex optimization problem for $< D, Z, U, b >$, but is convex with respect to each variable. Thus, we adopt an alternative minimization scheme for updating D, Z and $< U, b >$, respectively. The detailed procedure can be partitioned into three steps alternatingly.

When D and Z are fixed, the minimization of $< U, b >$ can be formulated as a multi-class linear SVM problem, which can be further divided into C linear one-against-all SVM subproblems. We adopt the multi-class linear SVM solver [5] proposed by Yang to learn all u_cs and b_cs one by one based on the gradient-based optimization method. The quadratic hinge loss function $\ell(z_i, y_i^c, u_c, b_c) = [\max(0, y_i^c[u_c; b_c]^T[z_i; 1] - 1)]^2$ in [5] is used in our implementation to approximate the hinge loss due to its computational simplicity and the better smooth property than hinge loss function.

When D, U and b are fixed, the coefficient matrix Z can be optimized by columns. The optimization problem related to each z_i is formulated as follows:

$$< z_i >= \arg\min_{z_i} \|x_i - Dz_i\|_2^2 + \lambda_1 \|z_i\|_2^2 + 2\lambda_2 \cdot \theta \cdot \sum_{c=1}^{C} \ell(z_i, y_i^c, u_c, b_c). \quad (14)$$

Algorithm 1. Algorithm of Support Vector Guided Dictionary Learning (SVGDL)

Input: $D_{init}, Z_{init}, U_{init}, b_{init}, X \in \mathbb{R}^{m \times n}, \lambda_1, \lambda_2, \theta$.

Output: D, U, b.

1:**do until the terminal condition**

2: **for** $c = 1$ to C **do**

3:     $u_c, b_c \leftarrow$ by one-vs-all linear SVM

4: **end for**

5: **for** $i = 1$ to n **do**

6:     $z_i \leftarrow \arg\min_{z} \; \|x_i - Dz\|_2^2 + \lambda_1\|z\|_2^2 + 2\lambda_2 \cdot \theta \cdot \sum_{c=1}^{C} \ell(z_i, y_i, u_c, b_c)$

7: **end for**

8: $D \leftarrow \arg\min_{D} \; \|X - DZ\|_F^2 \quad s.t. \; \|d_i\|^2 \leq 1, \forall i.$

9:**end do**

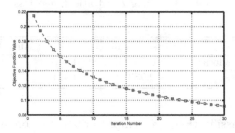

Fig. 2. The convergence of SVGDL on the AR database

In each iteration, for each c, if $y_i^c u_c^T z_i + b_c - 1 > 0$ in the previous iteration, we use $\|y_i^c u_c^T z_i + b_c - 1\|^2$ to replace the squared hinge loss, and use 0 else. We repeat this until convergence. Thus the optimization of each z_i has a closed-form solution.

When Z, U and b are fixed, the optimization problem with respect to D can be written as:

$$< D >= \arg\min_{D} \; \|X - DZ\|_F^2 \quad s.t. \; \|d_k\|^2 \leq 1, \; \forall k \in \{1, 2, \ldots, K\}, \qquad (15)$$

where the additional constraints are introduced to avoid the scaling issue of the atoms. The subproblem in Eq.(15) can be solved effectively by the Lagrange dual method [35].

We use PCA to initialize the dictionary of each class, and concatenate these sub-dictionaries as the initialized D. The initialized Z, U and b are set as zero matrices and zero vector, respectively. The stopping criterion is the relative difference between D in 2 successive iterations with a maximum iteration number. The overall optimization procedure of SVGDL is summarized in Algorithm 1.

In the training stage, the computational cost of the SVGDL algorithm comes from tree parts: $O(Cmn)$ for linear SVM, $O(K^3mn)$ for updating the coding vectors and $O(K^3mn)$ for updating the learned dictionary. Since the optimization model is non-convex, the algorithm can not converges to the global minimum. Empirically, satisfactory solutions to the desired dictionary D and the SVM classifier $< U, b >$ can be obtained with the decreasing of the objective function. Figure 2 shows an example to illustrate the convergence of SVGDL.

3.4   Classification Approach

Once the dictionary D and the classifier $< U, b >$ are learned, we perform classification as follows. For a test sample x, we first perform the coding step by projecting x with a fixed matrix P: $z = Px$, where $P = (D^T D + \lambda_1 I)^{-1} D^T$. Then we simply apply the C linear classifiers $< u_c, b_c >$, where $c \in 1, 2, \ldots, C$, on the coding vector z to predict the label of x by:

$$y = \arg \max_{c \in 1, 2, \ldots, C} u_c^T z + b_c. \tag{16}$$

In the test stage, the computational complexity of SVGDL is $O(Km)$.

4   Experiments

In this section, SVGDL is evaluated on three classification tasks, i.e., face recognition, object recognition, and sport action recognition. For face recognition, we use three face datasets: Extended Yale B [36], AR [37], and Multi-PIE [38]. For object recognition, we adopt the Caltech-101 dataset [39]. For action recognition, we use the UCF sport action dataset. SVGDL is compared with both the standard sparse representation based classification (SRC) method [13] and the state-of-the-art dictionary learning methods, including DKSVD [16], LC-KSVD [19, 20], dictionary learning with structure incoherence (DLSI) [22] and FDDL [18]. For each dataset, we report the recognition accuracy, training and test time of the competing methods. (In the following tables, "N.A." means that the training stage is not needed and "-" means that the run time is not available.)

4.1   Parameter Settings

We choose the parameter $\theta = 0.2$ and it works well in all of our experiments. Besides, there are two main parameters (λ_1, λ_2) to be tuned in the proposed SVGDL method. The parameters λ_1 and λ_2 are evaluated by 5-fold cross validation. For the face recognition tasks, we set $\lambda_1 = 0.002$ and $\lambda_2 = 0.001$ for Extended Yale B [36], $\lambda_1 = 0.002$ and $\lambda_2 = 0.001$ for AR [37], and $\lambda_1 = 0.002$ and $\lambda_2 = 0.001$ for Multi-PIE [38]. We also evaluate our method on Caltech-101 dataset [39] for object recognition task. We use the 3,000 dimensional features described in [20] for fair comparison. $\lambda_1 = 0.05$ and $\lambda_2 = 0.002$ are selected in this setup. We finally apply SVGDL on the UCF sport action dataset [40], where each sample has a dimension of 29,930 and the parameters are chosen as $\lambda_1 = 0.02$ and $\lambda_2 = 0.002$.

4.2   Visual Illustration of SVGDL

Using two individuals from the Extended Yale B database, we provide a visual illustration of the influence of SVGDL training on the coding vectors and classification hyperplane. For each individual, we select 32 images for training and use

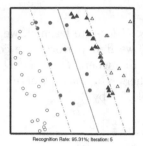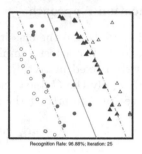

Fig. 3. The change of coding vectors and the classifying hyperplane in iterations

the remaining 32 images for test. Figure 3 plots the distributions of the coding vectors obtained using SVGDL after 5 and 25 iterations. The hyperplanes and margins are also provided to illustrate the discriminative capability of coding vectors. The solid circles and triangles are the support vectors that need to be assigned the weight to update dictionary. The green solid line and dotted line depict the separating hyperplane and margin. From Figure 3, one can see that the number of misclassified samples after 25 iterations is 2, which is less than that after 5 iterations. The margin after 25 iterations is also larger than that after 5 iterations. The recognition accuracy on the test set after 25 iterations is 96.88%, which is also higher than that after 5 iterations. All these cues indicate that SVGDL training is effective in learning a discriminative dictionary, resulting in coding vectors with better discriminative capability.

4.3   Face Recognition

We evaluate the performance of the proposed algorithm on several face recognition benchmark databases like the Extended Yale B, AR, and Multi-PIE. We compare the proposed SVGDL with two typical classification methods, including linear support vector machines (SVM) and SRC [13], five dictionary learning based methods, including DKSVD [16], LC-KSVD [19, 20], DLSI [22] and FDDL [18]. In all FR experiments, each face image has a reduced dimension of 300.

a) Extended Yale B: The Extended Yale B database consists of 2,414 frontal face images of 38 individuals. Each individual has 64 images and we randomly pick 20 images as training set and use the rest as testing set. The images were cropped to 54 × 48. The number of dictionary atoms K is fixed as 380 here. Table 2 summarizes the recognition accuracies. We can observe that SVGDL gives a significant accuracy improvement compared to other methods and it has the least testing time.

b) AR: The AR database consists of over 4,000 images of 126 individuals. For each individual, 26 face images are collected from two separated sessions. Following [18], we select 50 male individuals and 50 female individuals for the standard evaluation procedure. Focusing on the illumination and expression condition, we choose 7 images from Session 1 for training, and 7 images from Session 2 for

Table 2. The recognition rates and run time on the Extended Yale B database

Methods	SRC	SVM	DKSVD	LC-KSVD	DLSI	FDDL	**SVGDL**
Accuracy	0.900	0.888	0.753	0.906	0.890	0.919	**0.961**
Train(s)	N.A.	0.51	-	75.3	4.5e2	4.4e3	2.2e2
Test(s)	3.1e-2	3.5e-5	-	4.0e-4	4.3e-2	1.4	7.9e-6

Table 3. The recognition rates and run time on the AR database

Methods	SRC	SVM	DKSVD	LC-KSVD	DLSI	FDDL	**SVGDL**
Accuracy	0.888	0.871	0.854	0.897	0.898	0.920	**0.946**
Train(s)	N.A.	1.24	-	53.7	4.9e2	2.1e4	7.6e2
Test(s)	3.4e-2	6.1e-5	-	4.2e-4	0.16	2.5	2.0e-5

testing. The face image is of size 60×43 and the learned dictionary has 500 atoms. The results are presented in Table 3. Although the experimental setting is challenging, SVGDL still has at least 2% improvement over other methods, and it has much less time consumption compared to FDDL.

c) Multi-PIE: The CMU Multi-PIE face database consists of 337 individuals including four sessions with the variations of pose, expression and illumination. We follow the same experimental setting adopt in [18]. We chose the first 60 individuals from Session 1 for training. For each training person, we use the frontal images of 14 illuminations ({0,1,3,4, 6,7,8,11,13,14,16,17,18,19}) with neutral expression (for Test 1) or smile expression (for Test 2) for training, and use the frontal images of 10 illuminations ({0,2,4,6,8,10,12,14,16,18}) from Session 3 with neutral expression (for Test 1) or smile expression (for Test 2) for testing. The images are normalized to 100×82 and $K = 840$. The recognition results and the elapsed time of Test 1 are presented in Table 4. SVGDL performs the second best in the experiment, only lags FDDL. Note that FDDL trains sub-dictionaries for all individuals, while a single dictionary is enough to give good performance by SVGDL.

4.4 Objection Classification

We also evaluate SVGDL on the Caltech-101 dataset for object classification. This dataset contains 101 object categories and 29,780 images; each category has at least 80 images. Following [20], we randomly select 5, 10, 15, 20, 25 and 30 images per object, respectively, for training and test on the rest. We also give the run time in the case of 30 images. Figure 4 shows some samples from five classes. We find $K = 510$ is sufficient in this experiment.

Table 5 compares the classification accuracies of SVGDL with SRC, K-SVD, DKSVD, LC-KSVD and FDDL under the same experimental setting. As it can be observed, SVGDL outperforms the other methods in all cases. SVGDL, FDDL, LC-KSVD and DKSVD all give better results than SRC, which indicates that the better performance can be achieved by learning a discriminative dictionary. When 30 images involved in training, the improvements over LC-KSVD

Table 4. The recognition rates and run time on the Multi-PIE database

Methods	SRC	SVM	DKSVD	LC-KSVD	DLSI	FDDL	**SVGDL**
Test 1	0.955	0.916	0.939	93.7	0.941	**0.967**	0.955
Test 2	0.961	0.922	0.898	90.8	0.959	**0.980**	0.963
Train(s)	N.A.	1.74	-	64.8	6.3e2	5.1e4	2.2e3
Test(s)	3.0e-2	5.2e-5	-	3.7e-4	6.9e-2	3.1	2.6e-5

Fig. 4. Some sample objects from the Caltech-101 database

and FDDL by SVGDL are 2.7% and 3.6%, respectively. The shorter training and testing time also shows the superiority of SVGDL.

4.5   Action Recognition

Finally, we illustrate SVGDL on the UCF sport action dataset [40] for action recognition. There are 140 video clips in the UCF sport action dataset that are collected from various broadcast sports channels (e.g., BBC and ESPN). This dataset contains 10 sport action classes: driving, golfing, kicking, lifting, horse riding, running, skate-boarding, swinging (prommel horse and floor), swinging (high bar) and walking. We follow the common experimental settings in [20]. The number of atoms is set to $K = 50$.

The results of SVGDL are evaluated via five-fold cross validation, where one fold is used for testing and the remaining four folds for training. We compare SVGDL with Qiu *et. al.* [41], Yao *et. al.* [42], Sadanand *et. al.* [43], SRC, K-SVD, DKSVD, LC-KSVD and FDDL. The recognition accuracies, training and testing time are shown in Table 6. SVGDL outperforms the state-of-the-art methods. It is 200 times faster than FDDL, which has the second best accuracy in test.

Table 5. The recognition rates (%) and run time on the Caltech-101 dataset

training number	5	10	15	20	25	30	Train(s)	Test(s)
SRC	48.8	60.1	64.9	67.7	69.2	70.7	N.A.	1.09
K-SVD	49.8	59.8	65.2	68.7	71.0	73.2	-	-
DKSVD	49.6	59.5	65.1	68.6	71.1	73.0	-	-
LC-KSVD	54.0	63.1	67.7	70.5	72.3	73.6	1.3e4	3.7e-3
FDDL	53.6	63.6	66.8	69.8	71.7	73.1	1.1e5	12.9
SVGDL	**55.3**	**64.3**	**69.6**	**72.3**	**75.1**	**76.7**	1.5e3	1.2e-5

Table 6. The accuracies (%) and run time on the UCF sports action dataset

Methods	Qiu	Yao	Sadanand	SRC	K-SVD	DKSVD	LC-KSVD	FDDL	**SVGDL**
Accuracy	83.6	86.6	90.7	92.9	86.8	88.1	91.2	94.3	**94.4**
Train(s)	-	-	-	N.A.	-	-	2.0	8.02	15.6
Test(s)	-	-	-	1.8e-3	-	-	8.6e-4	3.4e-2	1.6e-4

5   Conclusions

This paper provided a new insight on DDL by formulating the discrimination term as the weighted summation of the squared distances between pairwise coding vectors. The proposed discrimination term not only can explain some existing discrimination term, e.g., Fisher discrimination, but also is valuable in developing novel DDL methods by designing appropriate weight assignment scheme. To overcome the limitation of Fisher discrimination, we adopt a parameterization method for adaptive weight assignment, leading to the proposed support vector guided dictionary learning (SVGDL) method. SVGDL can adaptively assign non-zero weights to only a few pairwise coding vectors which play a critical role in learning a discriminative dictionary. Furthermore, in contrast to the standard ℓ_1 sparsity based dictionary learning methods, SVGDL is more efficient by using the ℓ_2-norm regularizer on coding vectors. Experimental results on several benchmark image classification datasets showed that SVGDL outperforms many state-of-the-art DDL methods in terms of higher accuracy and faster test time.

Acknowledgements. This work is supported by the Hong Kong RGC GRF grant (PolyU 5313/13E), NSFC grant (61271093, 51275348), and the program of MoE (NCET-12-0150).

References

1. Baraniuk, R.: Compressive sensing. IEEE Signal Processing Magazine (2007)
2. Mairal, J., Elad, M., Sapiro, G.: Sparse representation for color image restoration. IEEE Transactions on Image Processing (2008)
3. Yang, J., Wright, J., Huang, T.S., Ma, Y.: Image super-resolution via sparse representation. IEEE Transactions on Image Processing (2010)
4. Elhamifar, E., Vidal, R.: Sparse subspace clustering: Algorithm, theory, and applications. IEEE Transactions on Pattern Analysis and Machine Intelligence (2013)
5. Yang, J., Yu, K., Gong, Y., Huang, T.: Linear spatial pyramid matching using sparse coding for image classification. In: CVPR (2009)
6. Shabou, A., LeBorgne, H.: Locality-constrained and spatially regularized coding for scene categorization. In: CVPR (2012)
7. Olshausen, B.A., Field, D.J.: Sparse coding with an overcomplete basis set: A strategy employed by v1? Vision research (1997)
8. Candes, E.J.: The restricted isometry property and its implications for compressed sensing. Comptes Rendus Mathematique (2008)

9. Mallat, S.: A wavelet tour of signal processing (1999)
10. Aharon, M., Elad, M., Bruckstein, A.: K-svd: An algorithm for designing overcomplete dictionaries for sparse representation. IEEE Transactions on Signal Processing (2006)
11. Engan, K., Aase, S.O., Husoy, J.: Frame based signal compression using method of optimal directions (mod). In: ISCAS (1999)
12. Rubinstein, R., Peleg, T., Elad, M.: Analysis k-svd: a dictionary-learning algorithm for the analysis sparse model. IEEE Transactions on Signal Processing (2013)
13. Wright, J., Yang, A.Y., Ganesh, A., Sastry, S.S., Ma, Y.: Robust face recognition via sparse representation. IEEE Transactions on Pattern Analysis and Machine Intelligence (2009)
14. Philbin, J., Chum, O., Isard, M., Sivic, J., Zisserman, A.: Lost in quantization: Improving particular object retrieval in large scale image databases. In: CVPR (2008)
15. Sivic, J., Zisserman, A.: Video google: A text retrieval approach to object matching in videos. In: ICCV (2003)
16. Zhang, Q., Li, B.: Discriminative k-svd for dictionary learning in face recognition. In: CVPR (2010)
17. Mairal, J., Bach, F., Ponce, J., Sapiro, G., Zisserman, A., et al.: Supervised dictionary learning. In: NIPS (2008)
18. Yang, M., Zhang, D., Feng, X.: Fisher discrimination dictionary learning for sparse representation. In: ICCV (2011)
19. Jiang, Z., Lin, Z., Davis, L.S.: Learning a discriminative dictionary for sparse coding via label consistent k-svd. In: CVPR (2011)
20. Jiang, Z., Lin, Z., Davis, L.: Label consistent k-svd: learning a discriminative dictionary for recognition. IEEE Transactions on Pattern Analysis and Machine Intelligence (2013)
21. Mairal, J., Bach, F., Ponce, J.: Task-driven dictionary learning. IEEE Transactions on Pattern Analysis and Machine Intelligence (2012)
22. Ramirez, I., Sprechmann, P., Sapiro, G.: Classification and clustering via dictionary learning with structured incoherence and shared features. In: CVPR (2010)
23. Gao, S., Tsang, I., Ma, Y.: Learning category-specific dictionary and shared dictionary for fine-grained image categorization. IEEE Transactions on Image Processing (2013)
24. Zhang, W., Surve, A., Fern, X., Dietterich, T.: Learning non-redundant codebooks for classifying complex objects. In: ICML (2009)
25. Wang, Z., Yang, J., Nasrabadi, N., Huang, T.: Look into sparse representation-based classification: A margin-based perspective. In: ICCV (2013)
26. Zheng, M., Bu, J., Chen, C., Wang, C., Zhang, L., Qiu, G., Cai, D.: Graph regularized sparse coding for image representation. IEEE Transactions on Image Processing (2011)
27. Wang, J., Yang, J., Yu, K., Lv, F., Huang, T., Gong, Y.: Locality-constrained linear coding for image classification. In: CVPR (2010)
28. Gao, S., Tsang, I.W., Chia, L.T., Zhao, P.: Local features are not lonely–laplacian sparse coding for image classification. In: CVPR (2010)
29. Gao, S., Tsang, I.H., Chia, L.T.: Laplacian sparse coding, hypergraph laplacian sparse coding, and applications. IEEE Transactions on Pattern Analysis and Machine Intelligence (2013)
30. Burges, C.J.: A tutorial on support vector machines for pattern recognition. Data Mining and Knowledge Discovery (1998)

31. Rigamonti, R., Brown, M.A., Lepetit, V.: Are sparse representations really relevant for image classification? In: CVPR (2011)
32. Zhang, D., Yang, M., Feng, X.: Sparse representation or collaborative representation: Which helps face recognition? In: ICCV (2011)
33. Mehta, N., Gray, A.G.: Sparsity-based generalization bounds for predictive sparse coding. In: ICML (2013)
34. Platt, J., et al.: Sequential minimal optimization: A fast algorithm for training support vector machines (1998)
35. Lee, H., Battle, A., Raina, R., Ng, A.Y.: Efficient sparse coding algorithms. In: NIPS (2007)
36. Lee, K.C., Ho, J., Kriegman, D.: Acquiring linear subspaces for face recognition under variable lighting. IEEE Transactions on Pattern Analysis and Machine Intelligence (2005)
37. Martınez, A., Benavente, R.: The ar face database. CVC Technical Report (1998)
38. Gross, R., Matthews, I., Cohn, J., Kanade, T., Baker, S.: Multi-pie. Image and Vision Computing (2010)
39. Fei-Fei, L., Fergus, R., Perona, P.: Learning generative visual models from few training examples: An incremental bayesian approach tested on 101 object categories. Computer Vision and Image Understanding (2007)
40. Rodriguez, M., Ahmed, J., Shah, M.: Action mach a spatio-temporal maximum average correlation height filter for action recognition. In: Indian Conference on Computer Vision, Graphics and Image Processing (2008)
41. Qiu, Q., Jiang, Z., Chellappa, R.: Sparse dictionary-based representation and recognition of action attributes. In: ICCV (2011)
42. Yao, A., Gall, J., Van Gool, L.: A hough transform-based voting framework for action recognition. In: CVPR (2010)
43. Sadanand, S., Corso, J.J.: Action bank: A high-level representation of activity in video. In: CVPR (2012)

Video Object Discovery and Co-segmentation
with Extremely Weak Supervision

Le Wang[1,*], Gang Hua[2], Rahul Sukthankar[3], Jianru Xue[1], and Nanning Zheng[1]

[1] Xi'an Jiaotong University, China
[2] Stevens Institute of Technology, USA
[3] Google Research, USA

Abstract. Video object co-segmentation refers to the problem of simultaneously segmenting a common category of objects from multiple videos. Most existing video co-segmentation methods assume that all frames from all videos contain the target objects. Unfortunately, this assumption is rarely true in practice, particularly for large video sets, and existing methods perform poorly when the assumption is violated. Hence, any practical video object co-segmentation algorithm needs to identify the relevant frames containing the target object from all videos, and then co-segment the object only from these relevant frames. We present a spatiotemporal energy minimization formulation for simultaneous video object discovery and co-segmentation across multiple videos. Our formulation incorporates a spatiotemporal auto-context model, which is combined with appearance modeling for superpixel labeling. The superpixel-level labels are propagated to the frame level through a multiple instance boosting algorithm with spatial reasoning (Spatial-MILBoosting), based on which frames containing the video object are identified. Our method only needs to be bootstrapped with the frame-level labels for a few video frames (*e.g.*, usually 1 to 3) to indicate if they contain the target objects or not. Experiments on three datasets validate the efficacy of our proposed method, which compares favorably with the state-of-the-art.

Keywords: video object discovery, video object co-segmentation, spatiotemporal auto-context model, Spatial-MILBoosting.

1 Introduction

The problem of simultaneously segmenting a common category of objects from two or more videos is known as video object co-segmentation. Compared with object segmentation from a single image, the benefit is that the appearance and/or structure information of the target objects across the videos are leveraged for segmentation. Several previous methods [9,13,27] have attempted to harness such information for video object co-segmentation.

However, these methods [9,13,27] all made the assumption that all frames from all videos contain the target object, *i.e.*, all frames are relevant. Moreover, a closer look at the video datasets employed in previous papers reveals that the object instances in

---

* Le Wang participated in this project while working at Stevens Institute of Technology as a visiting Ph.D. student supervised by Prof. Gang Hua.

D. Fleet et al. (Eds.): ECCV 2014, Part IV, LNCS 8692, pp. 640–655, 2014.

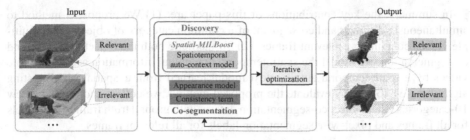

Fig. 1. The flowchart of our video object discovery and co-segmentation method

different videos are frequently the same object [9], or only exhibit small variations in color, shape, pose, size, and location [13, 27]. These limitations render such methods less applicable to real-world videos, such as those online videos gathered from a search engine in response to a specific query. The common objects in these videos are usually just of the same category, exhibiting dramatic variations in color, size, shape, pose, and viewpoint. Moreover, it is not uncommon for such videos to contain many irrelevant frames where the target objects are not present. This suggests that a practical video object co-segmentation method should also be capable of identifying the frames that contain the objects, *i.e.*, discover the objects.

We present a spatiotemporal energy minimization formulation to simultaneously discover and co-segment the target objects from multiple videos containing irrelevant frames. Fig. 1 presents the flowchart of our method. Bootstrapped from just a few (often 1-3) labeled frames indicating whether they are relevant or not, our method incurs a top-down modeling to propagate the frame-level label to the superpixels through a multiple instance boosting algorithm with spatial reasoning, namely Spatial-MILBoosting. From bottom up, the labels of the superpixels are jointly determined by a spatiotemporal auto-context model induced from the Spatial-MILBoosting algorithm and an appearance model using colors.

The learning of the spatiotemporal auto-context model, cast together with the color based appearance model as the data term, is embedded in a spatiotemporal energy minimization framework for joint object discovery and co-segmentation. Due to the embedded formulation, the learning of the spatiotemporal auto-context model (hence the object discovery), and the minimization of the energy function conducted by min-cut [6, 7] (hence the object co-segmentation), are performed iteratively until convergence. The final output of our method includes a frame-level label for each frame indicating if it contains the target object, and a superpixel-level labeling of the target object for each identified relevant frame.

As a key component of our formulation, our proposed spatiotemporal auto-context model extends the original auto-context model [31] to also capture the temporal context. Our embedded formulation also facilitates learning the model with only weak supervision with frame-level labels using the Spatial-MILBoosting algorithm. The Spatial-MILBoosting allows information to be propagated between the frame level and the superpixel level, and hence facilitates the discovery of the objects and the co-segmentation by effectively exploiting the spatiotemporal context across multiple videos.

In summary, the key contributions of this paper are: (1) We propose a method to simultaneously discover and co-segment of a common category of objects from multiple videos containing irrelevant frames. (2) To facilitate both the object discovery and co-segmentation, we model the spatiotemporal contextual information across multiple videos by a spatiotemporal auto-context model learned from a Spatial-MILBoosting algorithm. (3) To exactly evaluate the proposed method, we collect and release a new 10-categories video object co-segmentation dataset with ground truth frame-level labels for all frames and pixel-wise segmentation labels for all relevant frames.

2   Related Work

Video Object Discovery. Video object discovery has recently been extensively studied, in both unsupervised [18,42] or weakly supervised [19,24] settings. Liu and Chen [18] proposed a latent topic model for unsupervised object discovery in videos by combining pLSA with Probabilistic Data Association filter. Zhao et al. [42] proposed a topic model by incorporating a word co-occurrence prior into LDA for efficient discovery of topical video objects from a set of key frames. Liu et al. [19] engaged human in the loop to provide a few labels at the frame level to roughly indicate the main object of interest. Prest et al. [24] proposed a fully automatic method to learn a class-specific object detector from weakly annotated real-world videos. Tuytelaars et al. [32] surveyed the unsupervised object discovery methods, but with the focus on still images. In contrast, our video object discovery is achieved by propagating superpixel-level labels to frame level through a Spatial-MILBoosting algorithm.

Video Object Segmentation/Co-segmentation. Video object segmentation refers to the task of separating the objects from the background in a video, either interactively [4,28,30] or automatically [8,12,16,17,20,22,23,41]. A number of methods have focused on finding the object-like proposals for this problem [16,20,23,41]. Several methods track feature points or local regions over frames, and then cluster the resulting tracks based on pairwise [8,30] or triplet similarity measures [17,22]. Tang et al. [28] proposed an algorithm for annotating spatiotemporal segments based on video-level labels. Grundmann et al. [12] cluster a video into spatiotemporal consistent supervoxels.

Several video object co-segmentation methods [9,13,27] have been proposed recently to simultaneously segment a common category of objects from two or more videos. They made the assumption that all frames from all videos should contain the target object. Chiu and Fritz [10] proposed an algorithm to conduct multi-class video object co-segmentation, in which the number of object classes and the number of instances are unknown in each frame and video. Our method jointly discovers and co-segments the target objects from multiple videos, in which an unknown number of frames do not contain the target objects at all.

Image Co-segmentation. Our work is also related to image co-segmentation [5,11, 15,26,33,34], where the appearance or structure consistency of the foreground objects across the image collection is exploited to benefit object segmentation. The objective of image co-segmentation is to jointly segment a specific object from two or more images, and it is assumed that all images contain that object. There are also several

Table 1. Principal notations

$\mathcal{V}$	A collection of N videos	l_i^n	The label of f_i^n, $l_i^n \in \{0,1\}$, where 1 means that f_i^n is relevant, $i.e.$, f_i^n contains the target object
$\mathcal{L}$	The frame-level labels of $\mathcal{V}$		
$\mathcal{B}$	A segmentation of $\mathcal{V}$		
V^n	The nth video in $\mathcal{V}$ with N^n frames	b_i^n	A segmentation of f_i^n
L^n	The frame-level labels of V^n	s_{ij}^n	The jth superpixel in f_i^n
B^n	A segmentation of V^n	b_{ij}^n	The label of s_{ij}^n, $b_{ij}^n \in \{0,1\}$, where 1 means that s_{ij}^n belongs to the target object
f_i^n	The ith frame of V^n with N_i^n superpixels		

co-segmentation methods that conduct the co-segmentation of noisy image collections [25,38], in which several images do not contain the target objects. In our work, we focus on video object discovery and co-segmentation with noisy video collections, where many frames may not contain the target objects.

3   Problem Formulation

For ease of presentation, we first summarize the main notations in Table 1. Then we present the proposed spatiotemporal energy minimization framework for simultaneous object discovery and co-segmentation across multiple videos, along with details of the spatiotemporal context model and the Spatial-MILBoosting algorithm.

Given a set of videos $\mathcal{V}$, our objective is to obtain a frame-level label l_i^n for each frame f_i^n indicating if it is a relevant frame that contains the target objects, and a superpixel-level labeling b_i^n of the target object for each identified relevant frame f_i^n ($l_i^n = 1$). We cast this problem into a spatiotemporal energy minimization framework. Then, our energy function for simultaneous object discovery and co-segmentation from multiple videos $\mathcal{V}$ becomes

$$E(\mathcal{B}) = \sum_{s_{ij}^n \in \mathcal{V}} D_j^1(b_{ij}^n) + \sum_{s_{ij}^n \in V^n} D_j^2(b_{ij}^n)$$

$$+ \sum_{s_{ij}^n, s_{ik}^n \in \mathcal{N}_j} S_{jk}^1(b_{ij}^n, b_{ik}^n) + \sum_{s_{ij}^n, s_{uk}^n \in \bar{\mathcal{N}}_j} S_{jk}^2(b_{ij}^n, b_{uk}^n), \qquad (1)$$

$$n = 1, \ldots, N, i = 1, \ldots, N^n, j = 1, \ldots, N_i^n,$$

where $D_j^1(b_{ij}^n)$ and $D_j^2(b_{ij}^n)$ compose the data term, measuring the cost of labeling superpixel s_{ij}^n to be b_{ij}^n from a spatiotemporal auto-context model and a color based appearance model, respectively. The spatiotemporal auto-context model builds a multi-layer Boosting classifier on context features surrounding a superpixel to predict if it is associated with the target concept, where subsequent layer is working on the probability maps from the previous layer, detailed below in Sec. 3.1. Hence, $D_j^1(b_{ij}^n)$ relies on the discriminative probability maps estimated by a learned spatiotemporal auto-context model. It is learned to model the spatiotemporal contextual information across multiple videos $\mathcal{V}$, and thus is video independent. While the appearance model is estimated by capturing the color distributions of the target objects and the backgrounds for each video V^n, and thus is video dependent.

$S^1_{jk}(b^n_{ij}, b^n_{ik})$ and $S^2_{jk}(b^n_{ij}, b^n_{uk})$ compose the consistency term, constraining the segmentation labels to be both spatially and temporally consistent. $\mathcal{N}_j$ is the spatial neighborhood of s^n_{ij} in f^n_i. $\bar{\mathcal{N}}_j = \{\grave{s}^n_{ij}, \acute{s}^n_{ij}\}$ is the temporal neighborhood of s^n_{ij}, i.e., its corresponding next superpixel $\acute{s}^n_{ij}$ in f^n_{i+1} and previous superpixel $\grave{s}^n_{ij}$ in f^n_{i-1}. The superpixels are computed by using SLIC [1], due to its superiority in terms of adherence to boundaries, as well as computational and memory efficiency. However, the proposed method is not tied to any specific superpixel method, and one can choose others.

The particular spatiotemporal auto-context model embedded in the energy function is learned through a multiple instance learning algorithm with spatial reasoning (Spatial-MILBoosting), and hence it can propagate information between the frame level and the superpixel level. From top down, the label of frame is propagated to the superpixel level to facilitate the energy minimization for co-segmentation; from bottom up, the labels of superpixels are propagated to the frame level to identify which frame is relevant. Bootstrapped from just a few frame-level labels, the learning of the spatiotemporal auto-context model (hence the object discovery), and the minimization of the energy function conducted by min-cut [6, 7] (hence the object co-segmentation) are performed iteratively until it converges. At each iteration, the spatiotemporal auto-context model, the appearance model, and the consistency term are updated based on the new segmentation $\mathcal{B}$ of $\mathcal{V}$.

3.1 Spatiotemporal Auto-context Model

We extend the auto-context model originally proposed by Tu [31] and later tailored by Wang *et al.* [36, 37, 40] for video object discovery and co-segmentation. The original auto-context model builds a multi-layer Boosting classifier on image and context features surrounding a pixel to predict if it is associated with the target concept, where subsequent layer is working on the probability maps from the previous layer. In previous works, it just modeled the spatial contextual

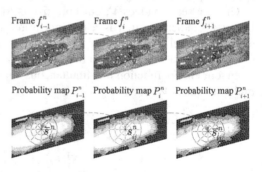

Fig. 2. The spatiotemporal auto-context feature

information, either from a single image [36, 40], or a set of labeled [31] or unlabeled [37, 38] images. Here, we extend it to capture both the spatial and temporal contextual information across multiple videos, and the extended model operates on superpixels instead of pixels.

Spatiotemporal Auto-context Feature. Let c^n_{ij} denote the context feature of superpixel s^n_{ij}, $P^n \in \mathcal{P}$ the probability map set for video V^n, P^n_i the probability map for frame f^n_i, p^n_{ij} the probability value of superpixel s^n_{ij}. The sampling structure of the spatiotemporal auto-context model on the discriminative probability maps are illustrated in Fig. 2. c^n_{ij} consists of a backward-frame part, a current-frame part and a forward-frame part as

$$\mathbf{c}^n_{ij} = \{\{\grave{p}^n_{ij}(k)\}, \{p^n_{ij}(k)\}, \{\acute{p}^n_{ij}(k)\}\}^{N_c}_{k=1}, \tag{2}$$

where $p_{ij}^n(k)$, $\check{p}_{ij}^n(k)$ and $\hat{p}_{ij}^n(k)$ are the probability values of the kth point on the sampling structure centered at s_{ij}^n in P_i^n, its corresponding previous superpixel $\check{s}_{ij}^n$ in P_{i-1}^n, and its corresponding next superpixel $\hat{s}_{ij}^n$ in P_{i+1}^n, respectively. N_c is the number of sampled points on the sampling structure for the current superpixel in each frame, and it is set to be 41 in our experiments. Here, we find the corresponding previous and next superpixels of current superpixel between neighboring frames using optical flow [39]. If the pixel number of the intersection between a superpixel in the current frame and its corresponding superpixel in neighboring frames, identified from the optical flow vector displacements of current superpixel, is larger than half of the pixel number of the current superpixel, it is selected as the temporal neighbor.

Update the Spatiotemporal Auto-context Classifier. In the first round of the iterative learning of the spatiotemporal auto-context model, the training set is built as

$$S_1 = \{\{C_{i'}^n(\alpha), l_{i'}^n(\alpha)\} | n = 1, \dots, N; i' = 1', \dots, N^{n'}; \alpha = 0, 1\}, \quad (3)$$

where i' is the index of frame $f_{i'}^n$ that was manually labeled by the user as relevant ($l_{i'}^n = 1$) or irrelevant ($l_{i'}^n = 0$). $N^{n'}$ is the number of labeled frames in video V^n, and it is set to be 1 to 3 in our experiments. $C_{i'}^n = \{c_{i'j}^n\}_{j=1}^{N_{i'}^n}$ are the context features of superpixels in $f_{i'}^n$, and $C_{i'}^n(\alpha)$ are the context features in the object ($\alpha = 1$) or background ($\alpha = 0$) of $f_{i'}^n$. We treat $C_{i'}^n(\alpha)$ as a *bag*, and $c_{i'j}^n$ as an *instance*. $l_{i'}^n(\alpha)$ is the label of bag $C_{i'}^n(\alpha)$, and it equals to 1 when both $l_{i'}^n$ and α equal to 1, and 0 otherwise. In other words, we treat the objects of the relevant frames as positive bags, the backgrounds of the relevant frames and both the objects and backgrounds of the irrelevant frames as negative bags. The initial segmentations $\mathcal{B}$ for $\mathcal{V}$ are obtained by using an objectness measure [2] and a saliency measure [14], and the probability maps $\mathcal{P}$ for $\mathcal{V}$ are initialized by averaging the scores returned by objectness and saliency.

Then, the first classifier $H(\cdot)$ is learned on S_1 using Spatial-MILBoosting, detailed immediately below. We proceed to use the learned classifier to classify all the context features of the objects and backgrounds of all frames in $\mathcal{V}$, and obtain the new probability map set $\mathcal{P}$ for $\mathcal{V}$, where the new probability of superpixel s_{ij}^n being positive is given by the learned classifier as

$$p_{ij}^n = \frac{1}{1 + \exp\left(-H(c_{ij}^n)\right)}. \quad (4)$$

The data term based on the spatiotemporal auto-context model in Eq(1) is defined as

$$D_j^1(b_{ij}^n) = -\log p_{ij}^n. \quad (5)$$

The probability of the object or background (*bag*) of frame f_i^n being positive is a "Noisy OR" defined as

$$p_i^n(\alpha) = 1 - \prod_{j=1}^{N_i^n(\alpha)} (1 - p_{ij}^n), \quad (6)$$

where $N_i^n(\alpha)$ denotes the number of superpixels (*instances*) in the object or background (*bag*) of frame f_i^n. In this way, the trained auto-context classifier can propagate superpixel-level labels indicating if the superpixels belong to the target objects to the object (or background) level label indicating if it contains the target object.

Algorithm 1. Spatial-MILBoosting - Training

Input: Training set $\{\mathbf{x}_i, l_i\}_{i=1}^N$ of N bags, where each bag $\mathbf{x}_i = \{x_{ij}\}_{j=1}^{N_i}$ containing N_i instances, the bag label $l_i \in \{0, 1\}$.

1. Initialize the instance weights $w_{ij} = 2 * (l_i - 0.5)$ and the instance classifier $H = 0$
2. Initialize estimated margins $\{\hat{y}_{ij}\}_{i,j=1}^{N,N_i}$ to 0
3. For $t = 1, \ldots, T$
   a. Set $\bar{x}_{ij} = \{\hat{y}_{ik} | x_{ik} \in \text{Nbr}(x_{ij})\}$
   b. Train weak *data* classifier h_t^d on the data $\{x_{ij}, l_i\}_{i,j=1}^{N,N_i}$ and the weights $\{w_{ij}\}_{i,j=1}^{N,N_i}$ as
      $$h_t^d(x_{ij}) = \arg\max_{\hat{h}(\cdot)} \sum_{i,j} \hat{h}(x_{ij}) w_{ij}$$
   c. Train weak *spatial* classifier h_t^s on the data $\{\bar{x}_{ij}, l_i\}_{i,j=1}^{N,N_i}$ and the weights $\{w_{ij}\}_{i,j=1}^{N,N_i}$ as $h_t^s(\bar{x}_{ij}) = \arg\max_{\hat{h}(\cdot)} \sum_{i,j} \hat{h}(\bar{x}_{ij}) w_{ij}$
   d. Set $\epsilon^d = \sum_{i,j} w_{ij} |h_t^d(x_{ij}) - l_i|$ and $\epsilon^s = \sum_{i,j} w_{ij} |h_t^s(\bar{x}_{ij}) - l_i|$
   e. Set $h_t(x_{ij}) = \begin{cases} h_t^d(x_{ij}) & \text{if} \quad \epsilon^d < \epsilon^s \\ h_t^s(\bar{x}_{ij}) & \text{otherwise} \end{cases}$
   f. Find λ_t via line search to minimize likelihood $L(H) = \prod_i (q_i)^{l_i} (1 - q_i)^{(1-l_i)}$ as $\lambda_t = \arg\max_\lambda L(H + \lambda h_t)$
   g. Update margins $\hat{y}_{ij}$ to be $\hat{y}_{ij} = H(x_{ij}) = \hat{y}_{ij} + \lambda_t h_t(x_{ij})$
   h. Compute the instance probability $q_{ij} = \frac{1}{1+\exp(-\hat{y}_{ij})}$
   i. Compute the bag probability $q_i = 1 - \prod_{j=1}^{N_i} (1 - q_{ij})$
   j. Update the instance weights $w_{ij} = \frac{\partial \log L(H)}{\partial y_{ij}} = \frac{l_i - q_i}{q_i} q_{ij}$

Output: Instance classifier $H(x_{ij}) = \sum_{t=1}^T \lambda_t h_t(x_{ij})$.

From the second round of the iterative learning process, we update the training set as

$$S_2 = \{\{\mathbf{C}_i^n(\alpha), l_i^n(\alpha)\} | n = 1, \ldots, N; i = 1, \ldots, N^n; \alpha = 0, 1\}, \tag{7}$$

and learn a new classifier on the updated context features, which are based on the discriminative probability map set $\mathcal{P}$ obtained from the previous iteration. Then, the new $\mathcal{P}$ for $\mathcal{V}$ are computed by the new spatiotemporal auto-context classifier. This process will iterate until convergence, where $\mathcal{P}$ no longer changes. Indeed, the spatiotemporal auto-context model is alternatively updated with the iterative co-segmentation of $\mathcal{V}$, i.e., the iterative minimization of the energy in Eq(1).

Spatial-MILBoosting Algorithm. Compared to the original MILBoost algorithm [35], we incorporate the spatial information between the neighboring superpixels [3] into the multiple instance boosting algorithm [19, 35] to infer whether the superpixel is positive or not, and name this algorithm Spatial-MILBoosting. To present the algorithm in a more general sense, we use $\mathbf{x}_i$, l_i and $x_{ij} \in \mathbf{x}_i$ instead of $\mathbf{C}_i^n(\alpha)$, $l_i^n(\alpha)$ and $\mathbf{c}_{ij}^n \in \mathbf{C}_i^n(\alpha)$ to denote the *bag*, its *label* and its *instance*, respectively. The training and testing details of Spatial-MILBoosting are presented in Alg. 1 and Alg. 2, respectively.

The score of the instance x_{ij} is $y_{ij} = H(x_{ij})$, where $H(x_{ij}) = \sum_{t=1}^T \lambda_t h_t(x_{ij})$ is a weighted sum of weak classifiers. The probability of the instance x_{ij} being positive is defined as a standard logistic function,

---

Algorithm 2. Spatial-MILBoosting - Testing

Input: Unlabeled testing set $\{x_{ij}\}_{i,j=1}^{N,N_i}$, and the instance classifier $H(\cdot)$.

1. Initialize estimated margins $\{\hat{y}_{ij}\}_{i,j=1}^{N,N_i}$ to 0
2. For $t = 1, \ldots, T$
   a. Set $\bar{x}_{ij} = \{\hat{y}_{ik} | x_{ik} \in \text{Nbr}(x_{ij})\}$
   b. Update margins $\hat{y}_{ij}$ to be $\hat{y}_{ij} = \hat{y}_{ij} + \lambda_t h_t(x_{ij})$

Output: Labels $\{\hat{y}_{ij}\}_{i,j=1}^{N,N_i}$.

$$q_{ij} = \frac{1}{1 + \exp(-y_{ij})}. \tag{8}$$

The probability of the bag $\mathbf{x}_i$ being positive is a "Noisy OR" as

$$q_i = 1 - \prod_{j=1}^{N_i}(1 - q_{ij}). \tag{9}$$

The goal now is to estimate λ_t and h_t, so q_{ij} approaches its true value. The likelihood assigned to a set of training bags is $L(H) = \prod_i (q_i)^{l_i} (1 - q_i)^{(1-l_i)}$, and is maximum when $q_i = l_i$, where $l_i \in \{0,1\}$ is the label of bag $\mathbf{x}_i$. To find an instance classifier that maximizes the likelihood, we compute the derivative of the log-likelihood with respect to y_{ij} as $\frac{\partial \log L(H)}{\partial y_{ij}} = w_{ij} = \frac{l_i - q_i}{q_i} q_{ij}$.

In each round t of gradient descent, one solves the optimal weak *instance* classifier $h_t(\cdot)$. Here, we train a weak *data* classifier on the data $\{x_{ij}, l_i\}_{i,j=1}^{N,N_i}$ and the weights $\{\omega_{ij}\}_{i,j=1}^{N,N_i}$ as $h_t^d(x_{ij}) = \arg\max_{\hat{h}(\cdot)} \sum_{i,j} \hat{h}(x_{ij}) w_{ij}$. Meanwhile, we train a weak *spatial* classifier on the data $\{\bar{x}_{ij}, l_i\}_{i,j=1}^{N,N_i}$ and the weights $\{\omega_{ij}\}_{i,j=1}^{N,N_i}$ as $h_t^s(\bar{x}_{ij}) = \arg\max_{\hat{h}(\cdot)} \sum_{i,j} \hat{h}(\bar{x}_{ij}) w_{ij}$, where $\bar{x}_{ij} = \{\hat{y}_{ik} | x_{ik} \in \text{Nbr}(x_{ij})\}$ are the predicted labels of the neighbors $\text{Nbr}(x_{ij})$ of the current instance x_{ij}.

The classifier which has lower training error is selected as the weak *instance* classifier $h_t(x_{ij})$,

$$h_t(x_{ij}) = \begin{cases} h_t^d(x_{ij}) & \text{if } \epsilon^d < \epsilon^s \\ h_t^s(\bar{x}_{ij}) & \text{otherwise} \end{cases}, \tag{10}$$

where $\epsilon^d = \sum_{i,j} \omega_{ij} |h_t^d(x_{ij}) - l_i|$ and $\epsilon^s = \sum_{i,j} \omega_{ij} |h_t^s(\bar{x}_{ij}) - l_i|$ are the training errors of the weak *data* classifier $h_t^d(x_{ij})$ and the weak *spatial* classifier $h_t^s(\bar{x}_{ij})$, respectively. This is the major difference of the proposed Spatial-MILBoosting algorithm and traditional MILBoost algorithm [19,35].

The parameter λ_t is determined using a line search as $\lambda_t = \arg\max_\lambda L(H + \lambda h_t)$. Then, the instance classifier $H(\cdot)$ is updated by $H(\cdot) \leftarrow H(\cdot) + \lambda_t h_t(\cdot)$.

3.2 Appearance Model

Since the appearance of the object instances (also the backgrounds) are similar within each video V^n while exhibiting large variations across $\mathcal{V}$, we independently learn the color distributions of the target objects and the backgrounds for each video V^n.

In detail, with a segmentation $\mathcal{B}$ for $\mathcal{V}$, we estimate two color Gaussian Mixture Models (GMMs) for the target objects and the backgrounds of each video V^n, denoted as $\mathbf{h}_1^n$ and $\mathbf{h}_0^n$, respectively. The corresponding data term based on the appearance model in Eq(1) is defined as

$$D_j^2(b_{ij}^n) = -\log \mathbf{h}_{b_{ij}^n}^n(s_{ij}^n), \tag{11}$$

where $D_j^2(b_{ij}^n)$ measures the contribution of labeling superpixel s_{ij}^n to be b_{ij}^n, based on the appearance model learned from video V^n.

3.3 Consistency Term

The consistency term is composed of an intra-frame consistency model and an inter-frame consistency model, and is leveraged to constrain the segmentation labels to be both spatially and temporally consistent.

Intra-frame Consistency Model. The intra-frame consistency model encourages the spatially adjacent superpixels in the same frame to have the same label. In Eq(1), the consistency term computed between spatially adjacent superpixels s_{ij}^n and s_{ik}^n in frame f_i^n of video V^n is defined as

$$S_{jk}^1(b_{ij}^n, b_{ik}^n) = \delta(b_{ij}^n, b_{ik}^n) \exp\left(-||\mathbf{I}_{ij}^n - \mathbf{I}_{ik}^n||_2^2\right), \tag{12}$$

where $\mathbf{I}$ is the color vector of the superpixel, and b_{ij}^n and b_{ik}^n are the segmentation labels of s_{ij}^n and s_{ik}^n. $\delta(\cdot)$ denotes the Dirac delta function, which is 0 when $b_{ij}^n = b_{ik}^n$, and 1 otherwise.

Inter-frame Consistency Model. The inter-frame consistency model encourages the temporally adjacent superpixels in consecutive frames to have the same label. In Eq(1), the consistency term computed between temporally adjacent superpixels s_{ij}^n and s_{uk}^n in consecutive frames of video V^n is defined as

$$S_{jk}^2(b_{ij}^n, b_{uk}^n) = \delta(b_{ij}^n, b_{uk}^n) \exp\left(-||\mathbf{c}_{ij}^n - \mathbf{c}_{uk}^n||_1\right), \tag{13}$$

where $\mathbf{c}$ is the context vector of the superpixel, and b_{ij}^n and b_{uk}^n are the segmentation labels of s_{ij}^n and s_{uk}^n. s_{uk}^n is the temporal neighbor of s_{ij}^n, i.e., its corresponding next superpixel $\hat{s}_{ij}^n$ in frame f_{i+1}^n or previous superpixel $\hat{s}_{ij}^n$ in frame f_{i-1}^n.

4 Optimization

The proposed approach is bootstrapped from a few manually annotated relevant and irrelevant frames (e.g., usually 1 to 3), and an objectness measure [2] and a saliency measure [14] to initialize the segmentation $\mathcal{B}$ and the discriminative probability map set $\mathcal{P}$ of $\mathcal{V}$. We proceed to start the first round learning of the spatiotemporal auto-context model, and propagate the superpixel labels estimated from the learned auto-context classier $H(\cdot)$ to frame-level labels $\mathcal{L}$ of $\mathcal{V}$ through the Spatial-MILBoosting algorithm. We then update the spatiotemporal auto-context model together with the appearance model and consistency term, and perform energy minimization on Eq(1) by using min-cut [6,7] to obtain an updated segmentation $\mathcal{B}$ of $\mathcal{V}$.

The learning of the spatiotemporal auto-context model (the object discovery), and the minimization of the energy function in Eq(1) (the object co-segmentation) are iteratively performed until convergence, which returns not only a frame-level label $\mathcal{L}$ of $\mathcal{V}$ and a segmentation $\mathcal{B}$ of $\mathcal{V}$, but also a spatiotemporal auto-context model.

Object Discovery. The object discovery is to identify the relevant frames containing the target objects from multiple videos $\mathcal{V}$. As we obtained a current frame-level labels $\mathcal{L}$, segmentation $\mathcal{B}$, and discriminative probability map set $\mathcal{P}$ estimated by the spatiotemporal auto-context model from the previous iteration, the probability of frame f_i^n containing the target object is updated as

$$p_i^n = 1 - (1 - p_i^n(1))(1 - p_i^n(0)), \tag{14}$$

where $p_i^n(1)$ and $p_i^n(0)$ are the probabilities of the object and background of f_i^n being positive, respectively. They are calculated by Eq(4) and Eq(6) above in Sec. 3.1. Then, the label l_i^n indicating if f_i^n is relevant can be predicted by binarizing p_i^n. l_i^n equals to 1 when f_i^n is relevant, and 0 irrelevant. In this way, the label l_i^n can be inferred from the probabilities of the object and background inside f_i^n indicating if they contain the target objects; while the probability of the object (or background) can be inferred from the probabilities of the superpixels inside it denoting if they belong to the target object.

Object Co-segmentation. The video object co-segmentation is to simultaneously find a superpixel-level labeling $\mathcal{B}$ for the relevant frames identified from $\mathcal{V}$. As we obtain a current frame-level labels $\mathcal{L}$, segmentation $\mathcal{B}$ and discriminative probability map set $\mathcal{P}$ estimated by the spatiotemporal auto-context model, we can update the video independent spatiotemporal auto-context model. Naturally, the spatiotemporal contextual information across multiple videos $\mathcal{V}$ are leveraged for the segmentation of each frame. The new segmentation B^n of each video V^n also serves to update the corresponding video dependent appearance model and consistency term. We then minimize the energy function in Eq(1) using min-cut [6,7] to obtain the new segmentation $\mathcal{B}$ of $\mathcal{V}$.

5   Experiments and Discussions

We conduct extensive experiments to evaluate our method on three datasets, including the SegTrack dataset [30], the video co-segmentation dataset [12, 27, 29], and a new 10-categories video object co-segmentation dataset collected by ourselves.

5.1   Evaluation on the SegTrack v1 and v2 Datasets

The SegTrack (v1 [30] and v2 [17]) is a video segmentation dataset consisting of 8 videos containing one object and 6 videos containing multiple adjacent/interacting objects, with full pixel-level annotations on the objects at each frame. As our method focuses on single object segmentation, we test our method on the 8 videos containing one object. By initializing all frames as relevant, we segment each video using our method.

We first compute the average per-frame pixel error rate for each video, and compare it with 8 other methods [8, 12, 17, 20, 22, 23, 41] on 3 videos from SegTrack v1 dataset [30], as summarized in Table 2. We also compare the average intersection-over-union score of

Table 2. The per-frame pixel error rates of our method and 8 other methods [8,12,17,20,22,23,41] on SegTrack v1 dataset [30]. Lower values are better.

Video	Ours	[23]	[17]-1	[17]-2	[41]	[20]	[22]	[12]	[8]
girl	**1053**	3859	1573	1564	1488	1698	5683	5777	7595
birdfall	**152**	217	188	242	155	189	468	305	468
parachute	**189**	855	339	328	220	221	1595	1202	1113

Table 3. The intersection-over-union scores of our method and 4 other video segmentation methods [12,16,17] on SegTrack v2 dataset [17]. Higher values are better.

Algorithm	girl	birdfall	parachute	frog	worm	soldier	monkey	bird of paradise
Ours	**90.5**	**70.3**	92.4	**83.1**	80.4	**85.3**	**89.8**	**94.5**
[17]-1	89.1	62.0	93.2	65.8	75.6	83.0	84.1	88.2
[17]-2	89.2	62.5	93.4	72.3	82.8	83.8	84.8	94.0
[16]	87.7	49.0	**96.3**	0	**84.4**	66.6	79.0	92.2
[12]	31.9	57.4	69.1	67.1	34.7	66.5	61.9	86.8

our method with 4 video segmentation methods [12,16,17] on the videos from SegTrack v2 dataset [17], as summarized in Table 3.

The per-frame pixel error rate is the number of pixels misclassified according to the ground truth segmentation, and is calculated as $error = N_{seg \oplus gt}$. The intersection-over-union is calculated as $N_{seg \cap gt}/N_{seg \cup gt}$, where $N_{seg \cap gt}$ and $N_{seg \cup gt}$ are the pixel numbers of the intersection and the union of the segmentation result and the ground truth segmentation, respectively. The [17]-1 and [17]-2 in Table 2 and Table 3 denote the original method [17], and the method [17] plus a refinement process using composite statistical inference, respectively. Some qualitative example results of our method are presented in Fig. 5 of the supplementary material.

As the results in Table 2 shown, our method outperforms the other 8 methods on the 3 videos. The results in Table 3 showed that our method is superior among the 4 other methods on 6 videos, but underperforms the other methods on 2 videos. The intersection-over-union score on parachute is slightly lower because of the complex background caused by difficult lighting conditions. The worm is difficult to segment since the boundaries between the worms and the background in some frames are too weak. For the birdfall, the frames are complex due to the cluttered background and the small size of the birds. In general, as the results shown, our method has the ability to segment the objects with certain variations in appearance (bird of paradise), shape (girl and frog), size (soldier), and backgrounds (parachute), but has encountered some difficulties when the objects are too small (birdfall), or the boundaries between the objects and the background are too weak (worm).

5.2 Evaluation on the Video Co-segmentation Dataset

We also test our method on videos of 3 categories, *i.e.*, 4 videos of the Cha-cha-cha category from Chroma dataset [29], 3 videos of the kite surfing category and 3 videos of the ice dancing category both from [12] and [27]. Because all frames from all videos of each category contain the target objects, we treat all frames of each category as relevant, and simultaneously segment the videos of each category using our method.

We compute the average labeling accuracy on each video of the Cha-cha-cha category, and compare them with 2 other video object co-segmentation methods [13,27], as presented in Table 4. Since the method presented in [13] produces the results in terms of dense trajectories, they use the method in [21] to turn their trajectory labels into pixel labels for comparison.

Table 4. The labeling accuracy of our method and two video object co-segmentation methods [13,27] on 4 videos of the Cha-cha-cha category. Higher values are better.

Algorithm	cha.1	cha.2	cha.3	cha.4
Ours	**97.1**	**96.9**	**97.0**	**97.5**
[13] + [21]	96	96	95	96
[27]	61	81	56	74

Table 5. Labeling accuracy on the kite surfing and ice dancing categories

Algorithm	kite.1	kite.2	kite.3	ice.1	ice.2	ice.3
Ours	93.7	94.1	95.8	97.2	96.5	98.1

The labeling accuracy is calculated as $N_{seg \odot gt}/N_{total}$, i.e., it is the ratio of the number of pixels classified correctly in accordance with the ground truth segmentation to the total number of pixels. We also present some qualitative results of our method compared with [13, 27] on the Cha-cha-cha category in Fig. 3 (a). These results showed that our method outperforms the other 2 video object co-segmentation methods [13, 27], and is not limited to the initial segmentation generated by combing the objectness and saliency measures that the method in [27] is sensitive to.

(a)

(b)

Fig. 3. Some qualitative results of our method compared with other methods [12, 13, 16, 27, 27]. (a) From left to right: original frames, results of [27], [13], [13] plus [21], and our results on the Cha-cha-cha category. (b) From left to right: original frames, results of [12], [16], [27], and our results on the kite surfing and ice dancing categories.

The average labeling accuracies computed on videos of the kite surfing and ice dancing categories by our method are presented in Table 5. We also present some qualitative results of our method compared with [12, 16, 27] on the two categories in Fig. 3 (b). They showed that our method compares favorably or is on par with [12, 16, 27].

5.3   Evaluation on the New Video Object Co-segmentation Dataset

New Video Object Co-segmentation Dataset. To exactly evaluate the efficacy of our method and to establish a benchmark for future research, we have collected 10 categories of 101 publicly available Internet videos, in which some videos include irrelevant frames. We manually assign each frame a label (1 for relevant and 0 for irrelevant),

Table 6. The new video co-segmentation dataset. "Video (R./I.)" denotes the numbers of all videos, videos only containing the relevant frames, and videos containing irrelevant frames; "Frame (R./I.)" denotes the numbers of all frames, relevant frames, and irrelevant frames in videos of each category.

Category	Video (R./I.)	Frame (R./I.)	Category	Video (R./I.)	Frame (R./I.)
airplane	11(4/7)	1763(1702/61)	balloon	10(4/6)	1459(1394/65)
bear	11(6/5)	1338(1282/56)	cat	4(3/1)	592(578/14)
eagle	13(12/1)	1703(1665/38)	ferrari	12(9/3)	1272(1244/28)
figure skating	10(7/3)	1173(1115/58)	horse	10(5/5)	1189(1134/55)
parachute	10(4/6)	1461(1421/40)	single diving	10(0/10)	1448(1372/76)

Table 7. The discovery performance of our method by varying the number of manually annotated frames (the number in the 1st row). The number in the table is the misclassified frames when 1, 2, and 3 labeled frames are provided.

Category	1	2	3	Category	1	2	3	Category	1	2	3
airplane	20	10	0	balloon	13	4	3	bear	3	3	2
cat	4	5	5	eagle	23	12	8	ferrari	11	7	6
figure skating	0	0	0	horse	5	1	1	parachute	14	10	2
single diving	18	13	5	-	-	-	-	-	-	-	-

and also manually assign pixel-wise ground truth foreground labels for each relevant frame. The statistical details of the new dataset are given in Table 6. We present some example relevant and irrelevant frames for each category of the new dataset in Fig. 6 of the supplementary material. The objects in videos of each category are of the common category, but exhibit large differences in appearance, size, shape, viewpoint, and pose.

Performance Evaluation. To better understand the contributions of the different aspects of our proposed method, we perform an ablative study. To this end, in addition to the proposed method (denoted V-1), we implemented a variant where Spatial-MILBoosting was replaced by MILBoost [35] (denoted V-2).

We first evaluate the discovery performance of our method by varying the number of manually annotated relevant and irrelevant frames. In our experiments, the number of manually annotated relevant and irrelevant frames of each video are set from 1 to 3, and they are randomly selected from each video given the ground truth frame-level labels. We present the number of misclassified frames of each category tested on the new video co-segmentation dataset in Table 7. As the results shown, our method works well when just provide each video 1 relevant or irrelevant frame, and can identify almost all the relevant frames from multiple videos when we provide 3 relevant and irrelevant frames. This validated the efficacy of the spatiotemporal auto-context model learned through the Spatial-MILBoosting algorithm.

Table 8 presents the average intersection-over-union scores of two versions of our method tested on each category of the new dataset. Some qualitative results of two versions of our method on videos of each category are presented in Fig. 4. They demonstrate the advantages of our method. In addition, it also demonstrates the advantages of

Table 8. Ablative study comparing Spatial-MILBoosting vs. MILBoost [35] on intersection-over-union on the new video co-segmentation dataset

Category	V-1	V-2	Category	V-1	V-2	Category	V-1	V-2
airplane	86.4	84.7	balloon	94.6	93.9	bear	90.5	89.3
cat	92.1	89.4	eagle	89.5	86.2	ferrari	87.7	86.3
figure skating	88.5	86.9	horse	92.0	90.7	parachute	94.0	91.7
single diving	87.7	85.2	-	-	-	-	-	-

Fig. 4. Qualitative results of two versions of our method tested on each category of the new dataset. The 1, 3, 5 and 7 columns: results of V-1; the 2, 4, 6 and 8 columns: results of V-2.

the Spatial-MILBoosting algorithm, which considers the spatial relationship of neighboring superpixels while predicting the segmentation label of superpixel.

To summarize, as shown above, our method has the capability of discovering the relevant frames from multiple videos containing irrelevant frames, and clearly co-segmenting the common objects from them.

6 Conclusion

We presented a spatiotemporal energy minimization formulation to simultaneously discover and co-segment a common category of objects from multiple videos containing irrelevant frames, which only requires extremely weak supervision (*i.e.*, 1 to 3 frame-level labels). Our formulation incorporates a spatiotemporal auto-context model to capture the spatiotemporal contextual information across multiple videos. It facilitates both the object discovery and co-segmentation through a MIL algorithm with spatial reasoning. Our method overcomes an important limitation of previous video object co-segmentation methods, which assume all frames from all videos contain the target objects. Experiments on three datasets demonstrated the superior performance of our proposed method.

Acknowledgements. This work was partly supported by China 973 Program Grant 2012CB316400, and NSFC Grant 61228303. Le Wang was supported by the Ph.D.

Short-term Academic Visiting Program of Xi'an Jiaotong University. Dr. Gang Hua was partly supported by US National Science Foundation Grant IIS 1350763, a Google Research Faculty Award, and GHs start-up funds from Stevens Institute of Technology.

References

1. Achanta, R., Shaji, A., Smith, K., Lucchi, A., Fua, P., Susstrunk, S.: SLIC superpixels compared to state-of-the-art superpixel methods. TPAMI 34(11), 2274–2282 (2012)
2. Alexe, B., Deselaers, T., Ferrari, V.: What is an object? In: CVPR, pp. 73–80 (2010)
3. Avidan, S.: SpatialBoost: Adding spatial reasoning to adaboost. In: Leonardis, A., Bischof, H., Pinz, A. (eds.) ECCV 2006. Part IV. LNCS, vol. 3954, pp. 386–396. Springer, Heidelberg (2006)
4. Bai, X., Wang, J., Simons, D., Sapiro, G.: Video SnapCut: robust video object cutout using localized classifiers. ACM Trans. on Graphics 28, 70 (2009)
5. Batra, D., Kowdle, A., Parikh, D., Luo, J., Chen, T.: iCoseg: Interactive co-segmentation with intelligent scribble guidance. In: CVPR, pp. 3169–3176 (2010)
6. Boykov, Y., Funka-Lea, G.: Graph cuts and efficient ND image segmentation. IJCV 70(2), 109–131 (2006)
7. Boykov, Y., Kolmogorov, V.: An experimental comparison of min-cut/max-flow algorithms for energy minimization in vision. TPAMI 26(9), 1124–1137 (2004)
8. Brox, T., Malik, J.: Object segmentation by long term analysis of point trajectories. In: Daniilidis, K., Maragos, P., Paragios, N. (eds.) ECCV 2010, Part V. LNCS, vol. 6315, pp. 282–295. Springer, Heidelberg (2010)
9. Chen, D.J., Chen, H.T., Chang, L.W.: Video object cosegmentation. In: ACM Multimedia, pp. 805–808 (2012)
10. Chiu, W.C., Fritz, M.: Multi-class video co-segmentation with a generative multi-video model. In: CVPR, pp. 321–328 (2013)
11. Dai, J., Wu, Y.N., Zhou, J., Zhu, S.C.: Cosegmentation and cosketch by unsupervised learning. In: ICCV (2013)
12. Grundmann, M., Kwatra, V., Han, M., Essa, I.: Efficient hierarchical graph-based video segmentation. In: CVPR, pp. 2141–2148 (2010)
13. Guo, J., Li, Z., Cheong, L.F., Zhou, S.Z.: Video co-segmentation for meaningful action extraction. In: ICCV (2013)
14. Harel, J., Koch, C., Perona, P., et al.: Graph-based visual saliency. In: NIPS, pp. 545–552 (2006)
15. Joulin, A., Bach, F., Ponce, J.: Discriminative clustering for image co-segmentation. In: CVPR, pp. 1943–1950 (2010)
16. Lee, Y.J., Kim, J., Grauman, K.: Key-segments for video object segmentation. In: ICCV, pp. 1995–2002 (2011)
17. Li, F., Kim, T., Humayun, A., Tsai, D., Rehg, J.M.: Video segmentation by tracking many figure-ground segments. In: ICCV (2013)
18. Liu, D., Chen, T.: A topic-motion model for unsupervised video object discovery. In: CVPR, pp. 1–8 (2007)
19. Liu, D., Hua, G., Chen, T.: A hierarchical visual model for video object summarization. TPAMI 32(12), 2178–2190 (2010)
20. Ma, T., Latecki, L.J.: Maximum weight cliques with mutex constraints for video object segmentation. In: CVPR, pp. 670–677 (2012)
21. Ochs, P., Brox, T.: Object segmentation in video: a hierarchical variational approach for turning point trajectories into dense regions. In: ICCV, pp. 1583–1590 (2011)

22. Ochs, P., Brox, T.: Higher order motion models and spectral clustering. In: CVPR, pp. 614–621 (2012)
23. Papazoglou, A., Ferrari, V.: Fast object segmentation in unconstrained video. In: ICCV (2013)
24. Prest, A., Leistner, C., Civera, J., Schmid, C., Ferrari, V.: Learning object class detectors from weakly annotated video. In: CVPR, pp. 3282–3289 (2012)
25. Rubinstein, M., Joulin, A., Kopf, J., Liu, C.: Unsupervised joint object discovery and segmentation in internet images. In: CVPR, pp. 1939–1946 (2013)
26. Rubinstein, M., Liu, C., Freeman, W.T.: Annotation propagation in large image databases via dense image correspondence. In: Fitzgibbon, A., Lazebnik, S., Perona, P., Sato, Y., Schmid, C. (eds.) ECCV 2012, Part III. LNCS, vol. 7574, pp. 85–99. Springer, Heidelberg (2012)
27. Rubio, J.C., Serrat, J., López, A.: Video co-segmentation. In: Lee, K.M., Matsushita, Y., Rehg, J.M., Hu, Z. (eds.) ACCV 2012, Part II. LNCS, vol. 7725, pp. 13–24. Springer, Heidelberg (2013)
28. Tang, K., Sukthankar, R., Yagnik, J., Fei-Fei, L.: Discriminative segment annotation in weakly labeled video. In: CVPR, pp. 2483–2490 (2013)
29. Tiburzi, F., Escudero, M., Bescós, J., Martínez, J.M.: A ground truth for motion-based video-object segmentation. In: ICIP, pp. 17–20 (2008)
30. Tsai, D., Flagg, M., Rehg, J.: Motion coherent tracking with multi-label MRF optimization. In: BMVC (2010)
31. Tu, Z.: Auto-context and its application to high-level vision tasks. In: CVPR, pp. 1–8 (2008)
32. Tuytelaars, T., Lampert, C.H., Blaschko, M.B., Buntine, W.: Unsupervised object discovery: A comparison. IJCV 88(2), 284–302 (2010)
33. Vicente, S., Kolmogorov, V., Rother, C.: Cosegmentation revisited: Models and optimization. In: Daniilidis, K., Maragos, P., Paragios, N. (eds.) ECCV 2010, Part II. LNCS, vol. 6312, pp. 465–479. Springer, Heidelberg (2010)
34. Vicente, S., Rother, C., Kolmogorov, V.: Object cosegmentation. In: CVPR, pp. 2217–2224 (2011)
35. Viola, P., Platt, J.C., Zhang, C.: Multiple instance boosting for object detection. In: NIPS, pp. 1417–1424 (2005)
36. Wang, L., Xue, J., Zheng, N., Hua, G.: Automatic salient object extraction with contextual cue. In: ICCV, pp. 105–112 (2011)
37. Wang, L., Xue, J., Zheng, N., Hua, G.: Concurrent segmentation of categorized objects from an image collection. In: ICPR, pp. 3309–3312 (2012)
38. Wang, L., Hua, G., Xue, J., Gao, Z., Zheng, N.: Joint segmentation and recognition of categorized objects from noisy web image collection. TIP (2014)
39. Xu, L., Jia, J., Matsushita, Y.: Motion detail preserving optical flow estimation. TPAMI 34(9), 1744–1757 (2012)
40. Xue, J., Wang, L., Zheng, N., Hua, G.: Automatic salient object extraction with contextual cue and its applications to recognition and alpha matting. PR 46(11), 2874–2889 (2013)
41. Zhang, D., Javed, O., Shah, M.: Video object segmentation through spatially accurate and temporally dense extraction of primary object regions. In: CVPR, pp. 628–635 (2013)
42. Zhao, G., Yuan, J., Hua, G.: Topical video object discovery from key frames by modeling word co-occurrence prior. In: CVPR, pp. 1602–1609 (2013)

Supervoxel-Consistent
Foreground Propagation in Video

Suyog Dutt Jain and Kristen Grauman

University of Texas at Austin, USA

Abstract. A major challenge in video segmentation is that the foreground object may move quickly in the scene at the same time its appearance and shape evolves over time. While pairwise potentials used in graph-based algorithms help smooth labels between neighboring (super)pixels in space and time, they offer only a myopic view of consistency and can be misled by inter-frame optical flow errors. We propose a higher order *supervoxel label consistency* potential for semi-supervised foreground segmentation. Given an initial frame with manual annotation for the foreground object, our approach propagates the foreground region through time, leveraging bottom-up supervoxels to guide its estimates towards long-range coherent regions. We validate our approach on three challenging datasets and achieve state-of-the-art results.

1 Introduction

In video, the *foreground object segmentation* problem consists of identifying those pixels that belong to the primary object(s) in every frame. A resulting foreground object segment is a space-time "tube" whose shape may deform as the object moves over time. The problem has an array of potential applications, including activity recognition, object recognition, video summarization, and post-production video editing.

Recent algorithms for video segmentation can be organized by the amount of manual annotation they assume. At one extreme, there are purely unsupervised methods that produce coherent space-time regions from the bottom up, without any video-specific labels [8, 12, 14, 17, 19, 21, 36, 38, 39]. At the other extreme, there are strongly supervised interactive methods, which require a human in the loop to correct the system's errors [4, 10, 20, 25, 34, 35]. Between either extreme, there are semi-supervised approaches that require a limited amount of direct supervision—an outline of the foreground in the first frame—which is then propagated automatically to the rest of the video [2, 3, 10, 27, 31, 33].

We are interested in the latter semi-supervised task: the goal is to take the foreground object segmentation drawn on an initial frame and accurately propagate it to the remainder of the frames. The propagation paradigm is a compelling middle ground. First, it removes ambiguity about what object is of interest, which, despite impressive advances [17, 19, 21, 39], remains an inherent pitfall for unsupervised methods. Accordingly, the propagation setting can accommodate a broader class of videos, e.g., those in which the object does not move much,

D. Fleet et al. (Eds.): ECCV 2014, Part IV, LNCS 8692, pp. 656–671, 2014.

or shares appearance with the background. Second, propagation from just one human-labeled frame can be substantially less burdensome than human-in-the-loop systems that require constant user interaction, making it a promising tool for gathering object tubes at a large scale. While heavier supervision is warranted in some domains (e.g., perfect rotoscoping for graphics), in many applications it is worthwhile to trade pixel-perfection for data volume (e.g., for learning object models from video, or assisting biologists with data collection).

Recent work shows that graph-based methods are a promising framework for propagating foreground regions in video [3,10,27,31,33]. The general idea is to decompose each frame into spatial nodes for a Markov Random Field (MRF), and seek the foreground-background (fg-bg) label assignment that maximizes both appearance consistency with the supplied labeled frame(s) as well as label smoothness in space and (optionally) time.

Despite encouraging results, these methods face an important technical challenge. In video, reliable foreground segmentation requires capturing *long-range* connections as an object moves and evolves in shape over time. However, current methods restrict the graph connectivity to local cliques in space and time. These local connections can be noisy: frame-to-frame optical flow is imperfect, and spatial adjacency can be a weak metric of "neighborliness" for irregularly shaped superpixels [1]. The failure to capture long-range connections is only aggravated by the fact that propagation models receive very limited supervision, i.e., the true foreground region annotated on the first frame of the video.

We propose a foreground propagation approach using *supervoxel* higher order potentials. Supervoxels—the space-time analog of spatial superpixels—provide a bottom-up volumetric segmentation that tends to preserve object boundaries [8,12,14,36,38]. To leverage their broader structure in a graph-based propagation algorithm, we augment the usual adjacency-based cliques with potentials for supervoxel-based cliques. These new cliques specify soft preferences to assign the same label (fg or bg) to superpixel nodes that occupy the same supervoxel. Whereas existing models are restricted to adjacency or flow-based links, supervoxels offer valuable longer-term temporal constraints.

We validate our approach on three challenging datasets, SegTrack [31], YouTube Objects [23], and Weizmann [13], and compare to state-of-the-art propagation methods. Our approach outperforms existing techniques overall, with particular advantage when foreground and background look similar, inter-frame motion is high, or the target changes shape between frames.

2   Related Work

Unsupervised video segmentation. Unsupervised video segmentation methods efficiently extract coherent groups of voxels. Hierarchical graph-based methods use appearance and flow to group voxels [14,38], while others group superpixels using spectral clustering [12] or novel tracking techniques [5,32]. Distinct from the region-based methods, tracking methods use point trajectories to detect cohesive moving object parts [7,18]. Any such bottom-up method tends to preserve object boundaries, but "oversegment" them into multiple parts. As such, they are not intended as object segmentations; rather, they provide a mid-level space-time grouping useful for downstream tasks.

Several recent algorithms aim to upgrade bottom-up video segmentation to *object-level* segments [17, 19, 21, 22, 39]. While the details vary, the main idea is to generate foreground object hypotheses per frame using learned models of "object-like" regions (e.g., salient, convex, distinct motion from background), and then optimize their temporal connections to generate space-time tubes. While a promising way to reduce oversegmentation, these models remain fully unsupervised, inheriting the limitations discussed above. Furthermore, none incorporates higher order volumetric potentials, as we propose.

Interactive video segmentation. At the other end of the spectrum are interactive methods that assume a human annotator is in the loop to correct the algorithm's mistakes [4, 20, 25, 35], either by monitoring the results closely, or by responding to active queries by the system [10, 33, 34]. While such intensive supervision is warranted for some applications, particularly in graphics [4, 20, 25, 35], it may be overkill for others. We focus on the foreground propagation problem, which assumes supervision in the form of a single labeled frame. Regardless, improvements due to our supervoxel idea could also benefit the interactive methods, some of which start with a similar MRF graph structure [10, 20, 25, 33] (but lack the proposed higher order potentials).

Weakly supervised video cosegmentation. An alternative way to supervise video segmentation is to provide the algorithm with a *batch* of videos, all known to contain the same object or object category of interest as foreground. Methods for this "weakly supervised" setting attempt to learn an object model from ambiguously labeled exemplars [15, 23, 28, 30]. This is very different from the propagation problem we tackle; our method gets only one video at a time and cannot benefit from cross-video appearance sharing.

Semi-supervised foreground propagation. Most relevant to our work are methods that accept a frame labeled manually with the foreground region and propagate it to the remaining clip [3, 10, 27, 31, 33]. While differing in their optimization strategies, most prior methods use the core MRF structure described above, with i) unary potentials determined by the labeled foreground's appearance/motion and ii) pairwise potentials determined by nodes' temporal or spatial adjacency. Pixel-based graphs can maintain very fine boundaries, but suffer from high computational cost and noisy temporal links due to unreliable flow [3, 33]. Superpixel-based graphs form nodes by segmenting each frame independently [10, 27, 31]. Compared to their pixel counterparts, they are much more efficient, less prone to optical flow drift, and can estimate neighbors' similarities more robustly due to their greater spatial extent. Nonetheless, their use of per-frame segments and frame-to-frame flow links limits them to short range interactions. In contrast, our key idea is to impose a supervoxel potential to encourage consistent labels across broad spatio-temporal regions.

Higher order potentials for segmentation. Our approach is inspired by higher order potentials (HOP) for multi-class static image segmentation [16]. There, multiple over-segmentations are used to define large spatial cliques in the Robust P^n model, capturing a label consistency preference for each image segment's component pixels. We extend this idea to handle video foreground propagation with supervoxel label consistency.

Two existing unsupervised methods also incorporate the Robust P^n model to improve video segmentation, but with important differences from our approach. In [8], the spatial cliques of [16] are adopted for each frame, and 3-frame temporal cliques are formed via optical flow. The empirical impact is shown for the former but not the latter, making its benefit unclear. In [32], the Robust P^n model is used to prefer consistent labels in temporally adjacent superpixels within 5-frame subsequences. Both prior methods [8, 32] rely on traditional adjacency criteria among spatial superpixel nodes to define HOP cliques, and they restrict temporal connections to a short manually fixed window (3 or 5 frames). In contrast, we propose *supervoxel* cliques and HOPs that span space-time regions of variable length. The proposed cliques often span broader areas in space-time— at times the entire video length—making them better equipped to capture an object's long term evolution in appearance and shape. Ours is the first video segmentation approach (unsupervised or semi-supervised) to incorporate label consistency over supervoxels.

3 Approach

The input to our approach is a video clip and one labeled frame in which an annotator has outlined the foreground object of interest. The output is a space-time segmentation that propagates the foreground (fg) or background (bg) label to every pixel in every frame. While the foreground object must be present in the labeled frame, it may leave and re-enter the scene at other times.

3.1 Motivation and Approach Overview

Our main objective is to define a space-time graph and energy function that respect the "big picture" of how objects move and evolve throughout the clip. Key to our idea is the use of *supervoxels*. Supervoxels are space-time regions computed with a bottom-up unsupervised video segmentation algorithm [14, 36, 38]. They typically oversegment—meaning that objects may be parcelled into many supervoxels—but the object boundaries remain visible among the supervoxel boundaries. They vary in shape and size, and will typically be larger and longer for content more uniform in its color or motion. Though a given object part's supervoxel is unlikely to remain stable through the entire length of a video, thanks to temporal continuity, it will often persist for a series of frames. For example, in Figure 1, we see a number of larger supervoxels remain steady in early frames, then some split/merge as the dog's pose changes, then a revised set again stabilizes for the latter chunk of frames. As we will see below, our approach exploits the partial stability of the supervoxels but also acknowledges their noisy imperfections.

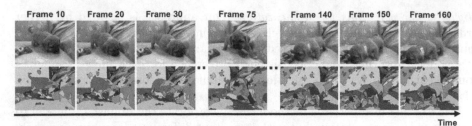

Fig. 1. Example supervoxels, using [14]. Unique colors are unique supervoxels, and repeated colors in adjacent frames refer to the same supervoxel. Best viewed in color.

While a number of supervoxel algorithms could be used, we choose the method of Grundmann et al. [14] due to its efficiency and object boundary-preserving properties [36]. The method uses appearance and motion cues to produce a hierarchy of supervoxels, and as such it can detect long-term coherence. To be concrete, whereas flat pixel-level approaches typically return regions on the order of ~5 frames, the Grundmann approach yields voxels lasting up to 400 frames for some videos. We take all supervoxels at the 15-th level of the tree, which based on preliminary visual inspection was found to be a good middle ground between very fine and coarse voxels.[1]

How should supervoxels be leveraged for propagation? To motivate our solution, first consider an analog in the *static* image segmentation domain, which is currently much more mature than video segmentation. It is now standard in static segmentation to construct MRF/CRF models using superpixel nodes rather than pixel nodes, e.g., [29]. Superpixels [11, 26] are local oversegmented spatial regions with coherent color or texture. MRF segmentations on a superpixel graph are not only faster to compute, but they also enable broader spatial connections and richer unary potentials.

A naive generalization to video would build a graph with supervoxels as nodes, connecting adjacent supervoxels in space and time. The problem is the irregular shape of supervoxels—and their widely varying temporal extents—lead to brittle graphs. As we will see in the results, the pairwise potentials in such an approach lead to frequent bleeding across object boundaries.

Instead, we propose to leverage supervoxels in two ways. First, for each supervoxel, we project it into each of its child frames to obtain spatial superpixel nodes. These nodes have sufficient spatial extent to compute rich visual features. Plus, compared to standard superpixel nodes computed independently per frame [3, 8, 10, 12, 25, 27, 31], they benefit from the broader perspective provided by the hierarchical space-time segment that generates the supervoxels. For example, optical flow similarity of voxels on the dog's textured collar may preserve it as one node, whereas per-frame segments may break it into many. Secondly, we leverage supervoxels as a higher-order potential. Augmenting the usual unary and pairwise terms, we enforce a soft label consistency constraint

---

[1] This choice could possibly be eliminated by incorporating a "flattening" stage [37].

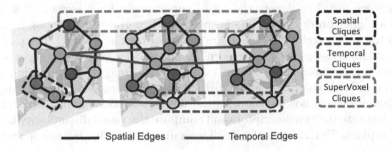

Fig. 2. Proposed spatio-temporal graph. Nodes are superpixels (projected from super-voxels) in every frame. Spatial edges exist if the superpixels have boundary overlap (black); temporal edges are computed using optical flow (red). Higher order cliques are defined by supervoxel membership (dotted green). For legibility, only a small subset of nodes and connections are depicted. Best viewed in color.

among nodes originating from the same supervoxel. Again, this provides broader context to the propagation engine.

In the following, we describe the three main stages of our approach: 1) we construct a spatio-temporal graph from the video sequence using optical flow and supervoxel segmentation (Sec. 3.2); 2) we define a Markov Random Field over this graph with suitable unary potentials, pairwise potentials, and higher order potentials (Sec 3.3); and 3) we minimize the energy of this MRF by iteratively updating the likelihood functions using label estimates (Sec 3.4).

3.2 Space-Time MRF Graph Structure

We first formally define the proposed spatio-temporal Markov Random Field (MRF) graph structure G consisting of nodes $\mathcal{X}$ and edges $\mathcal{E}$. Let $\mathcal{X} = \{X_t\}_{t=1}^T$ be the set of superpixels[2] over the entire video volume, where T refers to the number of frames in the video. X_t is a subset of $\mathcal{X}$ and contains superpixels belonging only to the t-th frame. Therefore each X_t is a collection of superpixel nodes $\{x_t^i\}_{i=1}^{K_t}$, where K_t is the number of superpixels in the t-th frame.

We associate a random variable $y_t^i \in \{+1, -1\}$ with every node to represent the label it may take, which can be either object ($+1$) or background (-1). Our goal is to obtain a labeling $\mathcal{Y} = \{Y_t\}_{t=1}^T$ over the entire video. Here, $Y_t = \{y_t^i\}_{i=1}^{K_t}$ represents the labels of superpixels belonging only to the t-th frame. Below, (t, i) indexes a superpixel node at position i and time t.

We define an edge set $\mathcal{E} = \{\mathcal{E}_s, \mathcal{E}_t\}$ for the video. $\mathcal{E}_s$ is the set of spatial edges between superpixel nodes. A spatial edge exists between a pair of superpixel nodes (x_t^i, x_t^j) in a given frame if their boundaries overlap (black lines in Figure 2). $\mathcal{E}_t$ is the set of temporal edges. A temporal edge exists between a pair of superpixels (x_t^i, x_{t+1}^j) in adjacent frames if any pixel from x_t^i tracks into x_{t+1}^j using optical flow (red lines in Figure 2). We use the algorithm of [6] to compute dense flow between consecutive frames. Let $[(t, i), (t', j)]$ index an edge between two nodes. For spatial edges, $t' = t$; for temporal edges, $t' = t + 1$.

---

[2] Throughout, we use "superpixel" to refer to a supervoxel projection into the frame.

Finally we use $\mathcal{S}$ to denote the set of supervoxels. Each element $v \in \mathcal{S}$ represents a higher order clique (one is shown with a green dashed box in Fig. 2) over all the superpixel nodes which are a part of that supervoxel. Let y_v denote the set of labels assigned to the superpixel nodes belonging to the supervoxel v.

For each superpixel node x_t^i, we compute two image features using all its pixels: 1) an RGB color histogram with 33 bins (11 bins per channel), and 2) a histogram of optical flow, which bins the flow orientations into 9 uniform bins. We concatenate the two descriptors and compute the visual dissimilarity between two superpixels $\mathcal{D}(x_t^i, x_{t'}^j)$ as the Euclidean distance in this feature space.

3.3   Energy Function with Supervoxel Label Consistency

Having defined the graph structure, we can now explain the proposed segmentation pipeline. We define an energy function over $G = (\mathcal{X}, \mathcal{E})$ that enforces long range temporal coherence through higher order potentials derived from supervoxels $\mathcal{S}$:

$$E(\mathcal{Y}) = \underbrace{\sum_{(t,i) \in \mathcal{X}} \Phi_t^i(y_t^i)}_{Unary\ potential} + \underbrace{\sum_{\substack{[(t,i),(t',j)] \in \mathcal{E} \\ t' \in \{t, t+1\}}} \Phi_{t,t'}^{i,j}(y_t^i, y_{t'}^j)}_{Pairwise\ potential} + \underbrace{\sum_{v \in \mathcal{S}} \Phi_v(y_v)}_{Higher\ order\ potential} . \quad (1)$$

The goal is to obtain the video's optimal object segmentation by minimizing Eqn. 1: $\mathcal{Y}^* = \operatorname{argmin}_{\mathcal{Y}} E(\mathcal{Y})$. The unary potential accounts for the cost of assigning each node the object or background label, as determined by appearance models and spatial priors learned from the labeled frame. The pairwise potential promotes smooth segmentations by penalizing neighboring nodes taking different labels. The higher order potential, key to our approach, ensures long term consistency in the segmentation. It can offset the errors introduced by weak or incorrect temporal connections in the adjacent frames.

Next we give the details for each of the potential functions.

Unary Potential: The unary potential in Eqn. 1 has two components, an appearance model and a spatial prior:

$$\Phi_t^i(y_t^i) = \underbrace{\lambda_{app} A_t^i(y_t^i)}_{Appearance\ prior} + \underbrace{\lambda_{loc} L_t^i(y_t^i)}_{Spatial\ prior}, \quad (2)$$

where λ_{app} and λ_{loc} are scalar weights reflecting the two components' influence.

To obtain the appearance prior $A_t^i(y_t^i)$, we use the human-labeled frame to learn Gaussian mixture models (GMM) to distinguish object vs. background. Specifically, all the pixels inside and outside the supplied object mask are used to construct the foreground G_{+1} and background G_{-1} GMM distributions, respectively, based on RGB values. To compute the likelihood that a superpixel x_t^i is object or background, we use the mean likelihood over all pixels within the superpixel:

$$A_t^i(y_t^i) = -\log \frac{1}{|x_t^i|} \sum_{p \in x_t^i} P(F_p | G_{y_t^i}), \quad (3)$$

where F_p is the RGB color value for pixel p and $|x_t^i|$ is the pixel count within the superpixel node x_t^i.

The spatial prior $L_t^i(y_t^i)$ penalizes label assignments that deviate from an approximate expected spatial location for the object:

$$L_t^i(y_t^i) = -\log P(y_t^i|(t,i)), \tag{4}$$

where (t,i) denotes the location of a superpixel node. To compute this prior, we start with the human-labeled object mask in the first frame and propagate that region to subsequent frames using both optical flow and supervoxels.[3] In particular, we define:

$$P(y_{t+1}^k|(t+1,k)) = \sum_{(i,t)\in\mathcal{B}_k} \psi\left(x_{t+1}^k, x_t^i\right) \delta\left(P(y_t^i|(t,i)) > \tau\right), \tag{5}$$

where $\mathcal{B}_k$ is the set of superpixel nodes tracked backwards from x_{t+1}^k using optical flow, and δ denotes the delta function. The δ term ensures that we transfer only from the most confident superpixels, as determined in the prior frame of propagation. In particular, we ignore the contribution of any x_t^i with confidence lower than $\tau = 0.5$.

The term $\psi(x_{t+1}^k, x_t^i)$ in Eqn. 5 estimates the likelihood of a successful label transfer from frame t to frame $t+1$ at the site x^k. If, via the flow, we find the transfer takes place between superpixels belonging to the same supervoxels, then we predict the transfer succeeds to the extent the corresponding superpixels overlap in pixel area, $\rho = \frac{|x_t^i|}{|x_{t+1}^k|}$. Otherwise, we further scale that overlap by the superpixels' feature distance:

$$\psi(x_{t+1}^k, x_t^i) = \begin{cases} \rho & \text{if } (x_{t+1}^k, x_t^i) \in v \text{ (same supervoxel)} \\ \rho\exp\left(-\beta_u \mathcal{D}(x_{t+1}^k, x_t^i)\right) & \text{otherwise,} \end{cases}$$

where β_u is a scaling constant for visual dissimilarity.

Pairwise Potential: In order to ensure that the output segmentation is smooth in both space and time, we use standard pairwise terms for both spatial and temporal edges:

$$\Phi_{t,t'}^{i,j}\left(y_t^i, y_{t'}^j\right) = \delta(y_t^i \neq y_{t'}^j)\exp\left(-\beta_p \mathcal{D}(x_t^i, x_{t'}^j)\right), \tag{6}$$

where β_p is a scaling parameter for visual dissimilarity. The penalty for adjacent nodes having different labels is contrast-sensitive, meaning we modulate it by the visual feature distance $\mathcal{D}(x_t^i, x_{t'}^j)$ between the neighboring nodes. For temporal edges, we further weigh this potential by ρ, the pixel overlap between the two nodes computed above with optical flow. Both types of edges encourage output segmentations that are consistent between nearby frames.

---

[3] If a frame other than the first is chosen for labeling, we propagate from that frame out in both directions. See Sec. 4.3 for extension handling multiple labeled frames.

Higher Order Potential: Finally, we define the supervoxel label consistency potential, which is crucial to our method. While the temporal smoothness potential helps enforce segmentation coherence in time, it suffers from certain limitations. Temporal edges are largely based on optical flow, hence they can only connect nodes in adjacent frames. This inhibits long-term coherence in the segmentation. In addition, the edges themselves can be noisy due to errors in flow.

Therefore, we propose to use higher order potentials derived from the supervoxel structure. As discussed above, the supervoxels group spatio-temporal regions which are similar in color and flow. Using the method of [14], this grouping is a result of long-term analysis of regions, and thus can overcome some of the errors introduced from optical flow tracking. For instance, in the datasets we use below, supervoxels can be up to 400 frames long and occupy up to 70% of the frame. At the same time, the supervoxels themselves are not perfect—otherwise we'd be done! Thus, we use them to define a soft preference for label consistency among superpixel nodes within the same supervoxel.

We adopt the Robust P^n model [16] to define these potentials. It consists of a higher order potential defined over supervoxel cliques:

$$\Phi_v(y_v) = \begin{cases} N(y_v)\frac{1}{Q}\gamma_{\max}(v) & \text{if } N(y_v) \leq Q \\ \gamma_{\max}(v) & \text{otherwise,} \end{cases} \tag{7}$$

where y_v denotes the labels of all the superpixel nodes within the supervoxel $v \in \mathcal{S}$, and $N(y_v)$ is the number of nodes within the supervoxel v that do not take the dominant label. That is, $N(y_v) = \min(|y_v = -1|, |y_v = +1|)$. Following [16], Q is a truncation parameter that controls how rigidly we want to enforce the consistency within the supervoxels. Intuitively, the more confident we are the supervoxels are strictly an oversegmentation, the higher Q should be.

The penalty $\gamma_{\max}(v)$ is a function of the supervoxel's size and color diversity, reflecting that those supervoxels that are inherently less uniform should incur lesser penalty for label inconsistencies. Specifically, $\gamma_{\max}(v) = |y_v| \exp(-\beta_h \sigma_v)$, where σ_v is the total RGB variance in supervoxel v.

3.4 Energy Minimization and Parameters

The energy function defined in Eqn. 1 can be efficiently minimized using the α-expansion algorithm [16]. The optimal labeling corresponding to the minimum energy yields our initial fg-bg estimate. We iteratively refine that output by re-estimating the appearance model—using only the most confident samples based on the current unary potentials—then solving the energy function again. We perform three such iterations to obtain the final output.

The only three parameters that must be set are λ_{app} and λ_{loc}, the weights in the appearance potential, and the truncation parameter Q. We determined reasonable values ($\lambda_{app} = 100$, $\lambda_{loc} = 40, Q = 0.2 \, |y_v|$) by visual inspection of a couple outputs, then fixed them for all videos and datasets. (This is minimal effort for a user of the system. It could also be done with cross-validation, when sufficient pixel-level ground truth is available for training.) The remaining

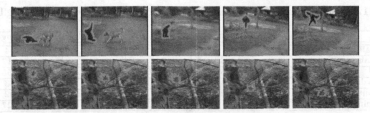

Fig. 3. Example results on SegTrack. Best viewed in color.

parameters β_u, β_p, and β_h, which scale the visual dissimilarity for the unary, pairwise, and higher order potentials, respectively, are all set automatically as the inverse of the mean of all individual distance terms.

4 Results

Datasets and metrics: We evaluate on 3 publicly available datasets: Seg-Track [31], YouTube-Objects [24], and Weizmann [13]. For SegTrack and YouTube, the true object region in the first frame is supplied to all methods. We use standard evaluation metrics: average pixel label error and intersection-over-union overlap.

Methods compared: We compare to five state-of-the-art methods: four for semi-supervised foreground label propagation [9,10,31,33], plus the state-of-the-art higher order potential method of [8]. Note that unsupervised multiple-hypothesis methods [17,19,21,39] are not comparable in this semi-supervised single-hypothesis setting. We also test the following baselines:

- **SVX-MRF:** an MRF comprised of supervoxel nodes. The unary potentials are initialized through the labeled frame, and the smoothness terms are defined using spatio-temporal adjacency between supervoxels. It highlights the importance of the design choices in the proposed graph structure.
- **SVX-Prop:** a simple propagation scheme using supervoxels. Starting from the labeled frame, the propagation of foreground labels progresses through temporally linked (using optical flow) supervoxels. It illustrates that it's non-trivial to directly extract foreground from supervoxels.
- **PF-MRF:** the existing algorithm of [33], which uses a pixel-flow (PF) MRF for propagation. This is the only video segmentation propagation algorithm with publicly available code.[4] Note that the authors also propose a method to actively select frames for labeling, which we do not employ here.
- **Ours w/o HOP:** a simplified version of our method that lacks higher order potentials (Eqn. 7), to isolate the impact of supervoxel label consistency.

4.1 SegTrack Dataset Results

SegTrack [31] was designed to evaluate object segmentation in videos. It consists of six videos, 21-71 frames each, with various challenges like color overlap in

---

[4] http://vision.cs.utexas.edu/projects/active_frame_selection/

Table 1. Average pixel errors for all existing propagation methods on SegTrack

	Ours	PF-MRF [33]	Fathi [10]	Tsai [31]	Chockalingam [9]
birdfall	**189**	405	342	252	454
cheetah	1170	1288	**711**	1142	1217
girl	2883	8575	**1206**	1304	1755
monkeydog	**333**	1225	598	563	683
parachute	**228**	1042	251	235	502
penguin	**443**	482	1367	1705	6627

Table 2. Average pixel errors (lower is better) for other baselines on SegTrack

	Ours	Ours w/o HOP	SVX-MRF	SVX-Prop
birdfall	**189**	246	299	453
cheetah	**1170**	1287	1202	1832
girl	**2883**	3286	3950	5402
monkeydog	**333**	389	737	1283
parachute	**228**	258	420	1480
penguin	**443**	497	491	541

objects, large inter-frame motion, and shape changes. Pixel-level ground truth is provided, and the standard metric is the average number of mislabeled pixels over all frames, per video. The creators also provide difficulty ratings per video with respect to appearance, shape, and motion.

Table 1 shows our results, compared to all existing propagation results in the literature. We outperform the state-of-the-art in 4 of the 6 videos. Especially notable are our substantial gains on the challenging "monkeydog" and "birdfall" sequences. Figure 3 (top row) shows examples from "monkeydog" (challenging w.r.t shape & motion [31]). Our method successfully propagates the foreground, despite considerable motion and deformation. Figure 3 (bottom row) is from "birdfall" (challenging w.r.t motion & appearance [31]). Our method propagates the foreground well in spite of significant fg/bg appearance overlap.

Our weaker performance on "cheetah" and "girl" is due to undersegmentation in the supervoxels, which hurts the quality of our supervoxel cliques and the projected superpixels. In particular, "cheetah" is low resolution and fg/bg appearance strongly overlap, making it more difficult for [14] (or any supervoxel algorithm) to oversegment. This suggests a hierarchical approach that considers fine to coarse supervoxels could be beneficial, which we leave as future work.

PF-MRF [33], which propagates based on flow links, suffers in several videos due to errors and drift in optical flow. This highlights the advantages of our broader scale nodes formed from supervoxels: our graph is not only more efficient (it requires 2-3 minutes per video, while PF-MRF requires 8-10 minutes), but it also is robust to flow errors. The prior superpixel graph methods [10, 31] use larger nodes, but only consider temporal links between adjacent frames. Thus, our gains confirm that long-range label consistency constraints are important for successful propagation.

Table 2 compares our method to the other baselines on SegTrack. SVX-Prop performs poorly, showing that tracking supervoxels alone is insufficient. SVX-MRF performs better but still is much worse than our method, which shows

Table 3. Average accuracy per class on YouTube-Objects (higher is better). Numbers in parens denote the number of videos for that class.

obj (#vid)	Ours	Ours w/o HOP	SVX-MRF	SVX-Prop	PF-MRF [33]
aeroplne (6)	**86.27**	79.86	77.36	51.43	84.9
bird (6)	**81.04**	78.43	70.29	55.23	76.3
boat (15)	**68.59**	60.12	52.26	48.70	62.44
car (7)	**69.36**	64.42	65.82	50.53	61.35
cat (16)	**58.89**	50.36	52.9	36.25	52.61
cow (20)	**68.56**	65.65	64.66	51.43	58.97
dog (27)	**61.78**	54.17	53.57	39.10	57.22
horse (14)	**53.96**	50.76	47.91	28.92	43.85
mbike (10)	60.87	58.31	45.23	42.23	**62.6**
train (5)	66.33	62.43	47.26	55.33	**72.32**

Propagation result using PF-MRF [33] | Propagation result with our method

Fig. 4. Our method resolves dragging errors common in flow-based MRFs

that it's best to enforce supervoxel constraints in a soft manner. We see that the higher order potentials (HOP) help our method in all cases (compare cols 1 and 2 in Table 2). To do a deeper analysis of the impact of HOPs, we consider the sequences rated as difficult in terms of motion and shape by [31], "monkeydog" and "birdfall". On their top 10% most difficult frames, the relative gain of HOPs is substantially higher. On "birdfall" HOPs yield a 40% gain on the most difficult frames (as opposed to 23% over all frames). On "monkeydog" the gain is 18% (compared to 13% on all frames).

4.2   YouTube-Objects Dataset Results

Next we evaluate on the YouTube-Objects [24]. We use the subset defined by [30], who provide segmentation ground truth. However, that ground truth is approximate—and even biased in our favor—since annotators marked super-voxels computed with [14], not individual pixels. Hence, we collected fine-grained pixel-level masks of the foreground object in every 10-th frame for each video using MTurk. In all, this yields 126 web videos with 10 object classes and more than 20,000 frames.[5] To our knowledge, these experiments are the first time such a large-scale evaluation is being done for the task of foreground label propagation; prior work has limited its validation to the smaller SegTrack.

Table 3 shows the results in terms of overlap accuracy. Our method outperforms all the baselines in 8 out of 10 classes, with gains up to 8 points over the best competing baseline. Note that each row corresponds to multiple videos for the named class; our method is best on average for over 100 sequences.

---

[5] Available at http://vision.cs.utexas.edu/projects/videoseg/

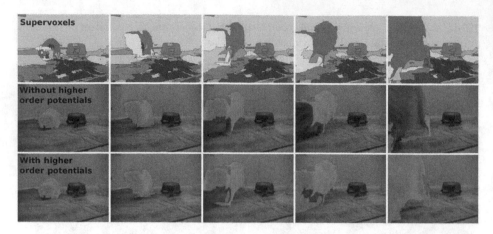

Fig. 5. Label propagation with and without HOPs (frames 31, 39, 42, 43, 51)

Fig. 6. Qualitative results highlighting our performance under fast motion, shape changes, and complex appearance. The first image in each row shows the human-labeled first frame of the video. See text for details.

On YouTube, PF-MRF [33] again suffers from optical flow errors, which introduce a "dragging effect". For example, Figure 4 shows the PF-MRF pixel flow drags as the dog moves on the sofa (left), accumulating errors. In contrast, our method propagates the fg and bg more cleanly (right). The SVX-MRF baseline is on average 10 points worse than ours, and only 25 seconds faster.

Comparing the first two columns in Table 3, we see our supervoxel HOPs have the most impact on "boat", "dog", and "cat" videos. They tend to have substantial camera and object motion. Thus, often, the temporal links based on

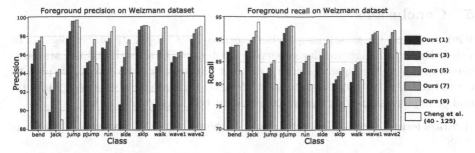

Fig. 7. Foreground precision (left) and recall (right) on Weizmann. Legend shows number of labeled frames used per result (1 to 9 for our method, 40-125 for [8]).

optical flow are unreliable. In contrast, the supervoxels, which depend on not only motion but also object appearance, are more robust. For example, Figure 5 shows a challenging case where the cat suddenly jumps forward. Without the HOP, optical flow connections alone are insufficient to track the object (middle row). However, the supervoxels are still persistent (top row), and so the HOP propagates the object properly (bottom row).

Figure 6 shows more qualitative results. Our method performs well even in the cases where there is significant object or camera motions. The cat (third row) also shows our robustness to fg-bg appearance overlap. In the failure case (last row), we intially track the cat well, but later incorrectly merge the foreground and ladder due to supervoxel undersegmentations.

4.3 Weizmann Dataset Results

Lastly, we use the Weizmann dataset [13] to compare to [8], which uses higher order spatial cliques and short temporal cliques found with flow (see Sec. 2). The dataset consists of 90 videos, from 10 activities with 9 actors each.

Figure 7 shows the results in terms of foreground precision and recall, following [8]. Whereas we output a single fg-bg estimate (2 segments), the method of [8] outputs an oversegmentation with about 25 segments per video. Thus, the authors use the ground truth on each frame to map their outputs to fg and bg labels, based on majority overlap; this is equivalent to obtaining on the order of 25 manual clicks per frame to label the output. In contrast, our propagation method uses just 1 labeled frame to generate a complete fg-bg segmentation. Therefore, we show our results for increasing numbers of labeled frames, spread uniformly through the sequence. This requires a multi-frame extension of our method—namely, we take the appearance model G_{y_t} from the labeled frame nearest to t, and re-initialize the spatial prior $L_t^i(y_t^i)$ at every labeled frame.

With just 5 labeled frames (compared to the 40-125 labeled frames used in [8]), our results are better in nearly all cases. Even with a single labeled frame, our performance is competitive. This result gives strong support for our formulation of a long-range HOP via supervoxels. Essentially, the method of [8] achieves a good oversegmentation, whereas our method achieves accurate object tubes with long range persistence.

5   Conclusions

We introduced a new semi-supervised approach to propagate object regions in video. Due to its higher order supervoxel potential, it outperforms the state-of-the-art on over 200 sequences from 3 distinct datasets. In future work, we plan to extend the idea to accommodate multiple and/or hierarchical supervoxel inputs, and to explore shape descriptors to augment the foreground models.

Acknowledgements. This research is supported by ONR award N00014-12-1-0068.

References

1. Ahuja, N., Todorovic, S.: Connected segmentation tree: a joint representation of region layout and hierarchy. In: CVPR (2008)
2. Ali, K., Hasler, D., Fleuret, F.: Flowboost: Appearance learning from sparsely annotated video. In: CVPR (2011)
3. Badrinarayanan, V., Galasso, F., Cipolla, R.: Label propagation in video sequences. In: CVPR (2010)
4. Bai, X., Wang, J., Simons, D., Sapiro, G.: Video snapcut: Robust video object cutout using localized classifiers. In: SIGGRAPH (2009)
5. Brendel, W., Todorovic, S.: Video object segmentation by tracking regions. In: ICCV (2009)
6. Brox, T., Malik, J.: Large displacement optical flow: descriptor matching in variational motion estimation. PAMI 33(3), 500–513 (2011)
7. Brox, T., Malik, J.: Object Segmentation by Long Term Analysis of Point Trajectories. In: Daniilidis, K., Maragos, P., Paragios, N. (eds.) ECCV 2010, Part V. LNCS, vol. 6315, pp. 282–295. Springer, Heidelberg (2010)
8. Cheng, H.T., Ahuja, N.: Exploiting nonlocal spatiotemporal structure for video segmentation. In: CVPR (2012)
9. Chockalingam, P., Pradeep, S.N., Birchfield, S.: Adaptive fragments-based tracking of non-rigid objects using level sets. In: ICCV (2009)
10. Fathi, A., Balcan, M., Ren, X., Rehg, J.: Combining self training and active learning for video segmentation. In: BMVC (2011)
11. Felzenszwalb, P., Huttenlocher, D.: Efficient graph-based image segmentation. IJCV 59(2) (2004)
12. Galasso, F., Cipolla, R., Schiele, B.: Video segmentation with superpixels. In: Lee, K.M., Matsushita, Y., Rehg, J.M., Hu, Z. (eds.) ACCV 2012, Part I. LNCS, vol. 7724, pp. 760–774. Springer, Heidelberg (2013)
13. Gorelick, L., Blank, M., Shechtman, E., Irani, M., Basri, R.: Actions as space-time shapes. PAMI 29(12), 2247–2253 (2007)
14. Grundmann, M., Kwatra, V., Han, M., Essa, I.: Efficient hierarchical graph based video segmentation. In: CVPR (2010)
15. Hartmann, G., et al.: Weakly supervised learning of object segmentations from web-scale video. In: Fusiello, A., Murino, V., Cucchiara, R. (eds.) ECCV 2012 Ws/Demos, Part I. LNCS, vol. 7583, pp. 198–208. Springer, Heidelberg (2012)
16. Kohli, P., Ladicky, L., Torr, P.H.S.: Robust higher order potentials for enforcing label consistency. In: CVPR (2008)
17. Lee, Y.J., Kim, J., Grauman, K.: Key-segments for video object segmentation. In: ICCV (2011)
18. Lezama, J., Alahari, K., Sivic, J., Laptev, I.: Track to the future: Spatio-temporal video segmentation with long-range motion cues. In: CVPR (2011)

19. Li, F., Kim, T., Humayun, A., Tsai, D., Rehg, J.M.: Video Segmentation by Tracking Many Figure-Ground Segments. In: ICCV (2013)
20. Li, Y., Sun, J., Shum, H.Y.: Video object cut and paste. ACM Trans. Graph. 24(3), 595–600 (2005)
21. Ma, T., Latecki, L.: Maximum weight cliques with mutex constraints for video object segmentation. In: CVPR (2012)
22. Papazoglou, A., Ferrari, V.: Fast object segmentation in unconstrained video. In: ICCV (2013)
23. Prest, A., Leistner, C., Civera, J., Schmid, C., Ferrari, V.: Learning object class detectors from weakly annotated video. In: CVPR (2012)
24. Prest, A., Leistner, C., Civera, J., Schmid, C., Ferrari, V.: Learning object class detectors from weakly annotated video. In: 2012 IEEE Conference on Computer Vision and Pattern Recognition, pp. 3282–3289. IEEE Computer Society Press, Los Alamitos (2012),
    http://ieeexplore.ieee.org/lpdocs/epic03/wrapper.htm?arnumber=6248065
25. Price, B.L., Morse, B.S., Cohen, S.: Livecut: Learning-based interactive video segmentation by evaluation of multiple propagated cues. In: ICCV (2009)
26. Ren, X., Malik, J.: Learning a classification model for segmentation. In: ICCV (2003)
27. Ren, X., Malik, J.: Tracking as repeated figure/ground segmentation. In: CVPR (2007)
28. Rubio, J.C., Serrat, J., López, A.: Video co-segmentation. In: Lee, K.M., Matsushita, Y., Rehg, J.M., Hu, Z. (eds.) ACCV 2012, Part II. LNCS, vol. 7725, pp. 13–24. Springer, Heidelberg (2013)
29. Shotton, J., Winn, J.M., Rother, C., Criminisi, A.: Textonboost: Joint appearance, shape and context modeling for multi-class object recognition and segmentation. In: Leonardis, A., Bischof, H., Pinz, A. (eds.) ECCV 2006, Part I. LNCS, vol. 3951, pp. 1–15. Springer, Heidelberg (2006)
30. Tang, K., Sukthankar, R., Yagnik, J., Fei-Fei, L.: Discriminative segment annotation in weakly labeled video. In: CVPR (2013)
31. Tsai, D., Flagg, M., Rehg, J.: Motion coherent tracking with multi-label mrf optimization. In: BMVC (2010)
32. Vazquez-Reina, A., Avidan, S., Pfister, H., Miller, E.: Multiple hypothesis video segmentation from superpixel flows. In: Daniilidis, K., Maragos, P., Paragios, N. (eds.) ECCV 2010, Part V. LNCS, vol. 6315, pp. 268–281. Springer, Heidelberg (2010)
33. Vijayanarasimhan, S., Grauman, K.: Active frame selection for label propagation in videos. In: Fitzgibbon, A., Lazebnik, S., Perona, P., Sato, Y., Schmid, C. (eds.) ECCV 2012, Part V. LNCS, vol. 7576, pp. 496–509. Springer, Heidelberg (2012)
34. Vondrick, C., Ramanan, D.: Video annotation and tracking with active learning. In: NIPS (2011)
35. Wang, J., Bhat, P., Colburn, A., Agrawala, M., Cohen, M.F.: Interactive video cutout. ACM Trans. Graph. 24(3), 585–594 (2005)
36. Xu, C., Corso, J.: Evaluation of super-voxel methods for early video processing. In: CVPR (2012)
37. Xu, C., Whitt, S., Corso, J.: Flattening supervoxel hierarchies by the uniform entropy slice. In: ICCV (2013)
38. Xu, C., Xiong, C., Corso, J.J.: Streaming Hierarchical Video Segmentation. In: Fitzgibbon, A., Lazebnik, S., Perona, P., Sato, Y., Schmid, C. (eds.) ECCV 2012, Part VI. LNCS, vol. 7577, pp. 626–639. Springer, Heidelberg (2012)
39. Zhang, D., Javed, O., Shah, M.: Video object segmentation through spatially accurate and temporally dense extraction of primary object regions. In: CVPR (2013)

Clustering with Hypergraphs:
The Case for Large Hyperedges

Pulak Purkait[1], Tat-Jun Chin[1], Hanno Ackermann[2], and David Suter[1]

[1] The University of Adelaide, Australia
[2] Leibniz Universität Hannover, Germany

Abstract. The extension of conventional clustering to *hypergraph clustering*, which involves higher order similarities instead of pairwise similarities, is increasingly gaining attention in computer vision. This is due to the fact that many grouping problems require an affinity measure that must involve a subset of data of size more than two, i.e., a *hyperedge*. Almost all previous works, however, have considered the smallest possible hyperedge size, due to a lack of study into the potential benefits of large hyperedges and effective algorithms to generate them. In this paper, we show that large hyperedges are better from both theoretical and empirical standpoints. We then propose a novel guided sampling strategy for large hyperedges, based on the concept of *random cluster models*. Our method can generate pure large hyperedges that significantly improve grouping accuracy without exponential increases in sampling costs. In the important applications of face clustering and motion segmentation, our method demonstrates substantially better accuracy and efficiency.

Keywords: Hypergraph clustering, model fitting, guided sampling.

1 Introduction

We follow the nomenclature of [1] in describing hypergraph clustering. A hypergraph $\mathcal{H} = (V, E)$ consists of a set of vertices V and hyperedges E. A hyperedge $e \in E$ is a subset of the vertices, i.e., $e \subseteq V$, and e is said to be incident with a vertex v if $v \in e$. For a weighted hypergraph $\mathcal{H}$, a weight $w(e)$ is associated with each hyperedge. The degree $\delta(e)$ of a hyperedge e is the number of vertices in e, i.e., $\delta(e) = |e|$. The degree $d(v)$ of a vertex v is the sum of all the weights of the hyperedges incident with v, i.e., $d(v) = \sum_{e \in E|v \in e} w(e)$. If all hyperedges have the same degree r, the hypergraph is said to be r-*uniform*. Clearly 2-uniform hypergraphs are normal graphs where an edge connects only two vertices.

The concept of hypergraph clustering generalises the traditional notion of clustering, whereby the affinity measure is now defined over more than a pair of vertices. In the graph partitioning view, a partitioning of $\mathcal{H}$ separates the vertices V into mutually exclusive clusters. In particular, a 2-way partitioning results in (V_1, V_2), where $V_1 \cup V_2 = V$ and $V_1 \cap V_2 = \emptyset$. The "goodness" of the partitioning is inversely proportional to the cost of the cut that separates the vertices, which in turn is a function of the weights of the hyperedges with vertices in both clusters. Methods have been proposed to find the best cut [1], given arbitrary $\mathcal{H}$. Below, we give examples of grouping problems based on hypergraph clustering.

D. Fleet et al. (Eds.): ECCV 2014, Part IV, LNCS 8692, pp. 672–687, 2014.

Multiple line fitting. Consider a set of points V in 2D which are known to lie on a set of K lines. Our goal is to cluster V into K groups based on their line membership. The traditional concept of clustering cannot be applied here, since any two points lie exactly on a line and thus have infinite affinity. To construct useful similarity measures, we must consider more than two points. Given a subset $e \subset V$ with $|e| > 2$, we can fit a line through e (e.g., via least squares) and convert the error of the fit d into an affinity measure $w(e) = \exp(-d^2/\sigma^2)$. A hyperedge e thus conveys the existence of a line with evidence $w(e)$.

Subspace clustering. Consider a set of vectors V in $\mathbb{R}^D$, e.g., face images or feature trajectories, where the vectors are known to lie on K p-dimensional subspaces. To cluster V into K groups, we must consider affinity measures defined over more than p vectors. Given a hyperedge $e \subset V$ with $|e| > p$, a subspace can be fitted (e.g., via SVD) and the fitting error converted into a weight as above.

Whilst the above examples relate to linear models, hypergraphs can also be defined using nonlinear models, e.g., projective entities like homography. The key requirement is a geometric model that describes the "shape" of the underlying clusters. The order p of the model is the minimum number of data to instantiate the model, and a valid hyperedge must thus be larger than p. Theoretically, the total number of hyperedges is $\mathcal{O}(2^{|V|})$, which is gargantuan for even small $|V|$.

In practice, therefore, approximations are necessary. An overwhelming majority (if not all) of the previous works that utilised the hypergraph formalism [2 8] limited the hyperedges to size $p+1$, i.e., the smallest possible. The resulting hypergraph is thus $(p + 1)$-uniform. Even with this limit, the number of possible hyperedges $\binom{|V|}{p+1}$ is too large for exhaustive listing. Previous works thus *sample* the set of hyperedges to construct "sparse" hypergraphs. Concurrently, limiting to the smallest size $p+1$ also maximises the chance of recovering *pure* hyperedges, i.e., those containing data that are likely from the same clusters.

Whilst computational feasibility was the overriding factor in imposing the size constraint, we nevertheless ask in this paper, *is there any benefit in using large hyperedges (size $> p + 1$) for higher-order grouping?* This is a natural question since the hypergraph formalism theoretically allows hyperedges of arbitrary size, and using the smallest allowable size seems to limit the potential. We will answer in the affirmative and provide theoretical and empirical justifications.

Secondly, *how can we sample large hyperedges without expending too much effort?* Previous guided sampling approaches for hyperedges select data one-by-one [7, 4]. Extending them to large hyperedges will inevitably expose them to the effects of exponentially decreasing probability of sampling pure hyperedges. We propose a novel guided sampling strategy to sample large hyperedges based on *random cluster models* [9, 10]. Our method generates large pure hyperedges accurately without exponential increases in computational effort.

In practical applications, our approach outperforms previous hypergraph clustering methods on face clustering and motion segmentation. Notwithstanding the usage of large hyperedges, our guided sampling strategy enables our technique to be orders of magnitude more efficient (in terms of number of hyperedges and actual time required) than previous hypergraph clustering algorithms.

1.1   Previous Work

Hypergraph clustering has a long history in VLSI [11]. There, vertices correspond to circuit elements and hyperedges correspond to wiring that may connect more than two elements. Finding the minimum cost cuts allows to divide the elements into modules with minimum interconnections. Unlike in computer vision, the hyperedges arise from the circuit design and need not be sampled.

The introduction of hypergraph clustering to computer vision and machine learning is relatively recent [3, 2]. Zhou et al. [12] generalised the popular Normalised Cut (NCut) algorithm [13] to the hypergraph setting. A more theoretical work by Agarwal et al. [1] analysed different existing hypergraph methods and showed that they can all be expressed as different clique projection techniques onto ordinary graphs. More recent works have largely followed the basic concepts, with various algorithmic extensions [4–8, 14]. Applications include face image clustering [3], motion segmentation [2, 4, 7], grouping of categorical data [12], and plane segmentation in RGBD data [8] and two-view images [6].

As mentioned earlier, for feasibility the methods [2–8] considered only $(p+1)$-uniform hypergraphs. Moreover, most of the methods either use random sampling [2, 6] or spatial proximity sampling [7] to generate hyperedges. Chen and Lerman [4] presented an incremental clustering and sampling technique which is more accurate than random or proximity sampling. However, a naive extension to large hyperedges is unworkable, since the probability to sample good hyperedges vanishes quickly with successive data selection. Pham et al. [10] proposed using random cluster models [9] to sample large clusters directly for geometric fitting, however, they did not pose their problem as hypergraph clustering. Moreover, they obtain intermediate clustering via graph cuts, which is relatively expensive. Nonetheless, we will combine the ideas from [4, 10] to design our algorithm.

By attempting to linearly reconstruct a point from a sparse set of neighbours, Sparse Subspace Clustering (SSC) [15] can be seen as generating hyperedges for clustering (a point and its selected neighbours are in the same hyperedge). However, SSC is tailored for linear models and is thus inapplicable in nonlinear/nonsubspace models such as homography and affine plane.

1.2   Dense versus Sparse Sample Reuse

It is crucial to reconcile the seemingly different tensor decomposition approach [2, 8] with hypergraph clustering [3, 1]. In [2, 8], subsets of V of size p are sampled. For each p-tuple, the model is instantiated and *evaluated* (the affinity value is calculated) with respect to all points in V. Each p-tuple thus generates a "row" in the $(p+1)$-dimensional affinity tensor, or equivalently, $|V|$ hyperedges of degree $p+1$ in a hypergraph. Govindu showed how the (sampled) affinity tensor can be flattened into a matrix and decomposed [2]. Compared to methods that directly sample hypedges of size $p+1$ without testing them with the rest of the data [3–7], evidently [2, 8] extract more information per sample. It was shown in [8] that this "dense" sampling approach outperforms "sparse" sampling, given the same sampling effort. We adopt the dense reuse idea in our paper.

2   Why Use Large Hyperedges?

2.1   Theoretical Justifications

We will motivate using NCut [13], which is arguably one of the most well known clustering techniques in computer vision. Zhou et al. [12] have generalised NCut to the hypergraph setting. Let (S, S^c) be a partitioning of the vertices V in $\mathcal{H}$, where $S \cup S^c = V$. The corresponding cut has the cut set $c(S, S^c) = \{e \in E | e \cap S \neq \emptyset, e \cap S^c \neq \emptyset\}$, i.e., the removal of the hyperedges in $c(S, S^c)$ yields the disjoint sets (S, S^c). Following [12], the volume or cost of the cut is

$$\text{vol}(S, S^c) = \sum_{e \in c(S, S^c)} w(e) \frac{|e \cap S||e \cap S^c|}{\delta(e)}. \tag{1}$$

If the hypergraph is 2-uniform, $|e \cap S| = |e \cap S^c| = 1$ and $\delta(e) = 2$ for all e, and (1) reduces to the cut cost on a normal graph. The volume of cluster S is

$$\text{vol}(S) = \sum_{v \in S} d(v). \tag{2}$$

The *normalized cut* criterion for partitioning V into (S, S^c) is

$$\text{ncut}(S, S^c) = \text{vol}(S, S^c) \left(\frac{1}{\text{vol}(S)} + \frac{1}{\text{vol}(S^c)} \right). \tag{3}$$

Similar to [13], Zhou et al. [12] showed how a relaxed version of the cost function (3), which involves continuous membership labels, can be minimised globally by an eigendecomposition of an affinity matrix; see [12] for details.

Define $\alpha(e|S, S^c) := |e \cap S||e \cap S^c|/\delta(e)$. The existence of multiplier $\alpha(e|S, S^c)$ on the weight $w(e)$ differentiates NCut on hypergraphs from normal graphs. Further, $\alpha(e|S, S^c)$ can be understood as arising from the projection of the hypergraph to a normal graph [1], where each hyperedge e is replaced by a fully connected subgraph with vertices e, and each edge in the subgraph has the weight $w(e)/\delta(e)$. The cut cost (1) is exactly the cut cost on the projected graph. We can rewrite $\alpha(e|S, S^c) = \alpha(e|\eta) := \eta(1 - \eta)\delta(e)$, where $\eta := |e \cap S|/\delta(e)$ is a *size ratio* of the partitioning of e based on the cut (S, S^c). Trivially, the range

$$\frac{1}{\delta(e)} \leq \eta \leq \frac{\delta(e) - 1}{\delta(e)} \tag{4}$$

can be established. Fig. 1(a) plots $\alpha(e|\eta)$ against η for e's of different degrees. First, it is clear that the cost of cutting a hyperedge e is the highest if e is divided into equal halves (i.e., $\eta = 0.5$). More crucially, given the same η, the multiplier $\alpha(e|\eta)$ is *always higher for larger hyperedges*, since the numerator in $\alpha(e|\eta)$ increases quadratically while the denominator increases linearly. Hence, given two hyperedges of the same weight $w(e)$ and the same η, *NCut will inherently favour preserving the larger hyperedge and cutting the smaller hyperedge.*

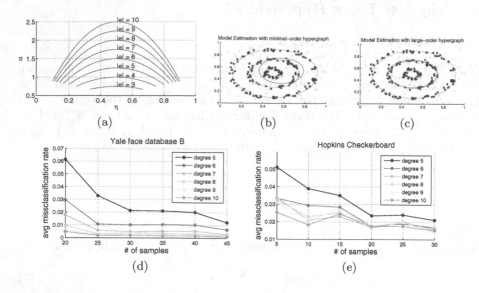

Fig. 1. (a) Plot of $\alpha(e|\eta)$ against η for e's of different degrees. (b–c) NCut segmentation (first cluster only) on a 4-uniform and 8-uniform hypergraph, respectively. (d–e) Average misclassification rate plotted against number of samples and size of hyperedges on Yale Face Database B and the 3-motion checkerboard sequences from Hopkins 155.

Effectively, the algorithm trusts larger hyperedges more than smaller hyperedges. Despite the purely algebraic motivation, the preference can be rationalised since larger hyperedges convey more evidence on the existence of a cluster than smaller hyperedges, even if the model is fitted equally well in both cases. Further, a larger data subset statistically constrains the model better and can more confidently estimate the parameters under noise. Figs. 1(b) and 1(c) show NCut segmentation results (only the first cluster is shown) for circle fitting ($p = 3$) on a 4-uniform hygergraph and a 8-uniform hypergraph. Four points cannot constrain a circle well, especially if they are spatially close, thus the result is poor. In contrast, using large hyperedges fits the circle accurately.

The algebraic derivations above were based on NCut [12]. Can we generalise the result to other hypergraph clustering algorithms? The source of the inherent bias in NCut is the hypergraph projection style that converts a hyperedge to a fully connected subgraph. Any algorithm that conducts such a projection (either implicitly or explicitly) contains this intrinsic bias. For example, it can be shown that *clique averaging* [3] and *max projection* [7] also have this property.

2.2 Empirical Justifications

The dominant factor for using the smallest allowable hyperedges previously is the lack of algorithms that can sample large hyperedges; to tackle this issue, we will propose a guided sampling algorithm in Sec. 3. In this subsection, we demonstrate the benefits of using large hyperedges via an "oracle sampler" that produces hyperedges based on ground truth cluster labels. This serves to preclude the effects of inaccuracies in an imperfect sampling technique. Any differences in the results is thus largely due to using hyperedges of different degrees.

Given data (vertices) V, we wish to cluster them into K groups, where each group lies on a model of order p. Given a fixed hyperedge degree $D > p$, we sample M subsets of size $D - 1$ from V. Half of the samples are chosen purely within true clusters (evenly among K groups), while the other half is chosen randomly to simulate sampling inaccuracies. The model is fitted on each sample via SVD and evaluated against V. Each sample thus produces $|V|$ hyperedges of degree D; recall that we adopt Govindu's [2, 8] dense sample reuse approach. We obtain an affinity matrix from all the hyperedges and conduct K-way partitioning [12]. The average misclassification rate is then obtained by comparing with the ground truth. The steps are repeated by varying D and M. Note that the model complexity is fixed at p, whereas the hyperedge degree varies with D.

We performed the above on Yale Face Database B [16] and the 26 checkerboard sequences with 3 motions from the Hopkins 155 dataset [17]. We used the frontal face images of $K = 10$ persons under 64 illumination conditions from Yale Face Database B. Under the Lambertian assumption, the images of the same face lie on a low-dimensional subspace; we chose this dimension to be $p = 4$ since this gives the best results. Each checkerboard sequence contains $K = 3$ distinct rigid motions. Under the affine camera model, the trajectories on these distinct motions can be grouped into 4-dimensional subspaces ($p = 4$). Results are presented in Figs. 1(d) and 1(e). Clearly, there is an improvement in accuracy as the degree of the hyperedges is increased.

We have shown that large hyperedges are better from both theoretical and empirical standpoints; a straightforward question that arises is how large should the hyperedges be? Our answer is "reasonably large but not too large". Very large hyperedges require more effort for fitting, and may not significantly improve the accuracy further (the trends in Figs. 1(d) and 1(e) show diminishing increases in accuracy). In all our experiments we have used hyperdeges of degrees 10–20; these numbers are significantly larger than the $p + 1$ used in previous works.

3   Guided Sampling for Large Hyperedges

Guided sampling for data subsets has primarily been used in robust model fitting [18–20]. However, following the RANSAC tradition only *minimal subsets* (of size p) have generally been considered. An exception is Pham et al. [10] who used the concept of random cluster models (RCM) [9] to sample large data subsets. However, they did not pose their work as hypergraph clustering, and their method requires graph cuts and Delaunay triangulation to produce intermediate clustering, which are relatively expensive. To construct our novel algorithm, we will draw from RCM and ISS [4]. Note that [4] considered only the smallest possible hyperedge (size $p+1$), which is only one larger than minimal subsets [18–20].

3.1 Generating Auxiliary Graph

RCM requires a spatial neighbourhood structure which is represented as a graph $G^{(0)} = (V, E^{(0)})$; whilst $G^{(0)}$ shares the same vertices V as the hypergraph $\mathcal{H}$, $G^{(0)}$ is a normal graph that encodes spatial proximity and not affinity to the geometric structures. To create $G^{(0)}$, we first perform PCA on the data $V = \{v_i\}_{i=1}^N$. This is obtained from the SVD of the mean-subtracted data matrix $\hat{V} = [\hat{v}_1 \ \hat{v}_2 \ \ldots \ \hat{v}_N]$, where $\hat{v}_i = v_i - \mu$, and $\mu = (1/N) \sum_i v_i$. Let U^l be the first-l left singular vectors of $\hat{V}$. The reduced-dimension version of V is thus $Y = (U^l)^T \hat{V}$. We create $E^{(0)}$ using k-nearest neighbours (knn) on $Y = \{y_i\}_{i=1}^N$. Two vertices v_i and v_j are connected by an edge $e = <i,j> \in E_0$ if y_i is a knn of y_j or vice versa, i.e., the edges are undirected. The weight p_e of the edge e is

$$p_e = \exp\left(-\frac{\|y_i - y_j\|^2}{2\sigma_e^2}\right), \tag{5}$$

where σ_e is a scale factor. The weight p_e for the edge e indicates how likely x_i and x_j are from the same structure, based purely on spatial proximity.

The parameters l, k and σ_e required for this step are as follows: $l = pK$ (model complexity times number of clusters), $k = 3$ for all experiments, and σ_e is obtained as the standard deviation of the nearest neighbour distances in Y.

3.2 RCM

Given $G^{(0)} = (V, E^{(0)})$, the Potts model is defined as the factor graph

$$P(f) = \frac{1}{Z} \prod_{e=<i,j> \in E^{(0)}} \exp(\beta_e \mathbf{1}(f_i = f_j)) \tag{6}$$

where Z is the partition function and $\mathbf{1}(.)$ returns 1 if its argument is true and 0 otherwise. The vector $f = \{f_i\}_{i=1}^N$ represents labels of the vertices V, where $f_i \in \{1, 2, \ldots, K\}$. If $\beta_e > 0$, $P(f)$ will assign higher probabilities to labellings f that contain large clusters. The relationship between β_e and p_e is given by

$$p_e = 1 - \exp(-\beta_e); \tag{7}$$

see [9, 10] for details. The Swendsen-Wang method [9] introduces the binary "bond" variables $d = \{d_e\}$ for each edge e to yield the extended Potts model

$$P(f,d) = \frac{1}{Z'} \prod_{e=<i,j> \in E^{(0)}} g(f_i, f_j, d_e), \tag{8}$$

where the factor g is defined as

$$g(f_i, f_j, d_e) = \begin{cases} 1 - p_e & \text{if } d_e = 0, \\ p_e & \text{if } d_e = 1 \text{ and } f_i = f_j, \\ 0 & \text{if } d_e = 1 \text{ and } f_i \neq f_j. \end{cases} \tag{9}$$

A realisation of (f, d) effectively partitions the vertices into a set of connected components. Each connected component is a subset of V such that all the bond variables between vertices in the component are turned on. Further, according to (9), vertices in a connected component must have the same labels.

Marginalising d in (8) returns the Potts model (6), while marginalising f in (8) yields the RCM $P(d)$. Let $c(d)$ be the number of connected components implied by a realisation of d. Then the RCM is

$$P(d) = \frac{1}{Z''} \prod_{e \in E^{(0)}} (p_e^{d_e}(1 - p_e)^{1-d_e}) K^{c(d)} \tag{10}$$

where K is the number of clusters. Simulating the RCM (10) is difficult. Instead, the Swendsen-Wang method simulates the extended Potts model (8) by observing that given f, the bond variables d are independent of each other and can be sampled independently. We take advantage of this characteristic to sample large clusters from V which will form large hyperedges for the hypergraph $\mathcal{H}$.

Note that each vertex v_i in $G^{(0)}$ is on average incident with k edges, i.e., $G^{(0)}$ is sparse. Hence the total number of edges (bond variables) is $\mathcal{O}(k|V|)$, i.e., linear with $|V|$. This enables highly efficient sampling for large clusters.

3.3   Simulating the RCM for Large Hyperedges

Our method alternatingly updates f and samples d. Given f, we generate a number of samples of d, which give us a set of hyperedges. Given the hyperedges, we update f by carrying out NCut [12]. Details are as follows.

At iteration t, given the current labelling $f^{(t)}$, the vertices V can be partitioned into clusters $\mathcal{C}^{(t)} = (\mathcal{C}_1^{(t)}, \ldots, \mathcal{C}_K^{(t)})$ with a label $f_i^{(t)}$ for each vertex for $v_i \in V$, where $f_i^{(t)} \in 1, 2, \ldots, K$. The clustering above can be summarised by the graph $G^{(t)} = (V, E^{(t)})$ with $E^{(t)} = \{e = <i, j> | f_i^{(t)} = f_j^{(t)}\}$. Up to this stage, the bond variables in d that straddle two vertices with different labels have been turned off (set to zero) deterministically, cf. (9). The remaining bond variables in d, i.e., those that straddle two vertices with the same labels, are then sampled by turning them on/off probabilistically. Specifically, a bond variable d_e is turned on (set to one) with probability p_e. After this step, d is fully realised.

By sampling in the above manner, a cluster $\mathcal{C}_k^{(t)}$ is partitioned into a number of subclusters $(\mathcal{C}_{k,1}^{(t)}, \mathcal{C}_{k,2}^{(t)}, \ldots, \mathcal{C}_{k,R_k}^{(t)})$. Specifically, each subcluster is a set of vertices connected by bond variables that have been turned on. We then collect all the subclusters into the set $\mathcal{CP} = \{\mathcal{P}_1, \mathcal{P}_2, \ldots, \mathcal{P}_{KR_K}\}$. The clusters in $\mathcal{CP}$ have varying sizes, as one would expect from a random cluster model. In our algorithm, however, we fix the degree of the hyperedges to be generated to D, where $D > p$. To do so, we sample a component from $\mathcal{CP}$ based on the probability

$$q(\mathcal{P}_s | \mathcal{CP}) \propto \sum_{e \in \mathcal{P}_s} p_e, \quad \forall \mathcal{P}_s \in \mathcal{CP}. \tag{11}$$

Given the chosen $\mathcal{P}_s$, we randomly sample a $(D-1)$-tuple from $\mathcal{P}_s$ and fit the geometric model of interest. The model is then evaluated against all the data in V, thus yielding $|V|$ hyperedges of degree D. One can envision a scheme where $D \in \mathbb{Z}$ is also randomly sampled. However, since we wish to more thoroughly test the effects of large hyperedges, we fix D to a constant. Of course, in the experiments, we will vary D across different instances of the sampling algorithm.

At iteration t, the above steps are repeated to produce a number of hyperedges. The newly generated hyperedges are then added to the set of hyperedges sampled thus far, and NCut [12] is executed to obtain the labelling $f^{(t+1)}$ for the next iteration. The process is terminated when either the labels f do not change significantly, or the maximum number of iterations is reached. Our method (Swendsen-Wang sampling) is summarised in Algorithm 1.

Algorithm 1. Swendsen-Wang sampling

Input: Data V, num clusters K, hyperedge degree D, iter count T and M, threshold ϵ.
Output: A set of hyperedges E of degree D for hypergraph $\mathcal{H} = (V, E)$.

1. Obtain auxiliary graph $G^{(0)} = (V, E^{(0)})$ (Sec. 3.1).
2. Initialise $f^{(1)}$ to a constant value.
3. For $t = 1, 2, \ldots, T$
   (a) From $f^{(t)}$, obtain clustering $\mathcal{C}^{(t)}$ and corresponding graph $G^{(t)} = (V, E^{(t)})$.
   (b) Repeat M times
      i. For all $e \in E^{(t)}$, turn off d_e with probability $1 - p_e$. This divides each $\mathcal{C}_k^{(t)}$ into a set of subclusters.
      ii. Collect all subclusters from $\{\mathcal{C}_k^{(t)}\}_{k=1}^K$ into $\mathcal{CP}$.
      iii. Remove from $\mathcal{CP}$ all components of size less than $D - 1$.
      iv. Select a component $\mathcal{P}_s$ from $\mathcal{CP}$ with probability $q(\mathcal{P}_s | \mathcal{CP})$ (11), then randomly select a $(D-1)$-subset s from $\mathcal{P}_s$.
      v. Fit the model onto s and evaluate it against all data in V. Add the newly generated hyperedges to the set of all hyperedges.
   (c) Apply NCut [12] on the current hypergraph $\mathcal{H}$ to obtain labels $f^{(t+1)}$.
   (d) If the difference between $f^{(t)}$ and $f^{(t+1)}$ is smaller than ϵ, terminate sampling.

---

4   Results

We conduct experiments on real datasets to verify the effectiveness and efficiency of the proposed large hyperedge sampling method. Since we use Govindu's dense sample reuse approach, a D-degree hyperedge e is composed of $e = \{s \cup v\}$, where s is a sampled $(D-1)$-tuple, and v is an arbitrary vertex in V. In all the experiments, the weight $w(e)$ of a hyperedge e is calculated as

$$w(e) = \begin{cases} \exp(-r^2(v,\phi_s)/2\sigma^2) & \text{if } v \notin s; \\ 0 & \text{otherwise,} \end{cases} \quad (12)$$

where ϕ_s is the model fitted in a least squares manner on s, and $r(v,\phi_s)$ is the residual of v with respect to ϕ_s. The parameter σ is problem dependent, and a similar parameter needs to be tuned for all hypergraph clustering methods [3, 4]. We calculate σ following [4], i.e., choose the sigma that gives the lowest subspace approximation error after segmentation by Ncut; see [4] for details.

4.1   Face Clustering

It has been established that a set of images of a the same face subjected to different illumination conditions can be modelled by a low-dimensional subspace [16]. Given a set of images of K different faces V, we wish to cluster them into K subspaces. We used the Yale Face Database B [16] in our experiment, which contains images of $K = 10$ faces under 64 different lighting conditions. As in Sec. 2.2, the dimensionality of the face subspace is chosen to be p = 2. Before clustering, we first reduce the dimensionality of V to $4K$ to construct the auxiliary graph $G^{(0)}$.

Sampling accuracy and effects of large hyperedges. We have tested with degree D in the range $\{6, 8, \ldots, 20\}$. Unlike in Sec. 2.2, here we sample without ground truth labels. Three methods were compared: random sampling (RS), iterative spectral sampling (ISS) [4], and Swendsen-Wang sampling (SWS). We extended ISS to sample large hyperedges by using the intermediate clustering information to successively select data. Here, NCut [12] was used for hypergraph clustering for all sampling methods. The average misclassification rate is plotted against the number of samples in Figs. 2(a)–(c). The sampling accuracy (% hyperedges containing data from the same cluster) is displayed in Fig. 2(d). For RS and ISS in Figs. 2(a)(b), as D is increased, the misclassification rate also increases; this reflects the inability of these methods to sample large pure hyperedges, and *not* because large hyperedges are ineffective; see Sec. 2.2. In contrast, SWS not only samples large hyperedges more accurately, the hypergraph clustering accuracy also improves as the hyperedge degree is increased; see Fig. 2(c).

In terms of computational effort, our method does not require discernibly higher run time than RS and ISS. Sec. 4.3 will examine run time more closely.

Benchmark against state-of-the-art. For our method (SWS followed by NCut), we chose degree $D = 20$ and 300 samples. We varied K from 2 to 10 and repeated our algorithm on 100 randomly chosen subpopulations of K persons. We compared against well-known methods for subspace segmentation: Generalised PCA (GPCA) [21], SCC [4], Sparse Subspace Clustering SSC [15], Spectral Local Best-fit Flat (SLBF) [22] and Agglomerative Lossy Compression (ALC) [23]; these methods have also recently been applied on Yale Face Database B. The

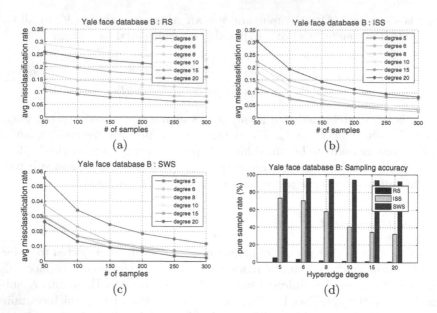

Fig. 2. (a)–(c) Misclassification rate of three methods on Yale Face Database B as hyperedge degree D is increased. (d) Sampling accuracy for different degree D.

mean percentage of misclassification along with the run time are shown in Table 1. The proposed method is on par with ALC which correctly clustered all the faces for all K. Moreover, our method is much faster than ALC.

4.2   Motion Segmentation with Sparse Trajectories

Under the affine camera model, the trajectories corresponding to the same rigid motion can be described by a subspace of dimension $p = 4$. Given a set of trajectories V containing K distinct motions, we can separate the motions by subspace clustering. Here we used the Hopkins 155 dataset. The dataset consists of 155 video sequences with 2 or 3 independent rigid motions which are sub-categorised into three types: checkerboard, traffic and articulated.

For our approach (SWS followed by NCut), we used $D = 10$ and 50 samples. To compute the auxiliary graph $G^{(0)}$ and edge weights (5), we reduce the dimension of the data in each sequence to $l = 4K$. For our method, across all sequences we observe that on average 98.34% the hyperedges generated are clean, i.e., contain trajectories from the same motion.

Table 2 presents the misclassification rates of proposed method along with the other recent methods for comparison. We also additionally compared with Local Subspace Affinity (LSA) [24] and the recent method of [25] which uses discrete cosine transform (DCT). Unlike our method, these state-of-the-art techniques are dedicated to motion segmentation. It is clear that our approach can achieve similar or better results than the other methods.

Comparing run time is nontrivial, since the methods are based on very different principles. Our approach typically takes less than 5 minutes to execute. The following subsection will examine the run time of our method more closely.

Table 1. Mean percentage of misclassification on clustering Yale face B dataset

K	2	3	4	5	6	7	8	9	10	time(s)
GPCA	0.0	49.5	0.0	26.6	9.9	25.2	28.5	30.6	19.8	$\approx 10^6$
SCC	0.0	0.0	0.0	1.1	2.7	2.1	2.2	5.7	6.6	4.93
SSC	0.0	0.0	0.0	0.0	0.0	0.0	0.0	2.4	4.6	6.12
SLBF	0.0	0.0	0.0	0.0	0.0	0.0	0.0	1.2	0.9	1.72
ALC	0.0	0.0	0.0	0.0	0.0	0.0	0.0	0.0	0.0	1878.56
Ours	0.0	0.0	0.0	0.0	0.0	0.0	0.0	0.0	0.0	1.74

Table 2. Percent misclassification error on Hopkins 155 dataset

	Two Motions			Three Motions			
Method	Chck.(78)	Trfc.(31)	Artc.(11)	Chck.(26)	Trfc.(7)	Artc.(2)	all(155)
	MN MD	MN MD	MN MD	MN MD	MN MD	MN MD	MN MD
GPCA	6.09 1.03	1.41 0.00	2.88 0.00	31.95 32.93	19.83 19.55	16.85 16.85	10.34 2.54
LSA	2.57 0.27	5.43 1.48	4.10 1.22	5.80 1.77	25.07 23.79	7.25 7.25	4.94 0.90
ALC	1.55 0.29	1.59 1.17	10.70 0.95	5.20 0.67	7.75 0.49	21.08 21.08	3.56 0.50
SCC	1.31 0.06	1.02 0.26	3.21 0.76	6.31 1.97	3.31 3.31	9.58 9.58	2.42 NA
SSC	1.12 0.00	0.02 0.00	0.62 0.00	2.97 0.27	0.58 0.00	1.42 1.42	1.24 0.00
DCT	0.71 0.00	0.05 0.00	0.96 0.00	2.44 1.29	0.05 0.00	1.60 1.60	0.87 NA
Ours	1.86 0.00	0.08 0.00	1.13 0.00	2.72 0.00	0.00 0.00	1.06 1.06	1.50 0.00
MN: mean, MD: median, NA: not available							

4.3   Motion Segmentation with Dense Trajectories

Recently there is a surge of interest in conducting video-based object segmentation by clustering the dense feature trajectories $V = \{v_i\}_{i=1}^N$ on the objects. The original proposal by Brox and Malik (BM) [26] achieves this via a conventional clustering approach, which constructs an affinity measure to compare pairs of trajectories. Using pairwise affinities restricts the motions to be 2D translations.

Ochs and Brox (OB) [7] later argued that the approach of [26] fails if the objects undertake more complex motions, which occur quite often in the videos used in [26]. Thus the affinity measure must include more than two trajectories to allow richer motion models. OB used 2D similarities (rotation, translation, and scaling) and posed motion segmentation as hypergraph clustering. Hyperedges of degree 3 are used (the hypergraph is 3-uniform). Recall that a minimum of two trajectories are needed to instantiate a 2D similarity ($p = 2$), thus $D = 3$ is the smallest possible hyperedge degree.

Even with such small hyperedges, enumerating them is not feasible since their number scales as $\mathcal{O}(|V|^3)$; recall that a short video can have thousands of dense

684   P. Purkait et al.

trajectories. OB samples the hyperedges as follows: all $|V| \times |V|$ pairs of trajectories are generated. For each pair of trajectories, 12 hyperedges are created by including in the pair a third trajectory from the 12 nearest spatial neighbours of the pair. An additional 30 hyperedges are produced by randomly including a third trajectory. As an example, the *car1* sequence (which is one of the shortest in the dataset with 19 frames) contains 4850 trajectories. OB thus generates $4850 \times 4850 \times (30 + 12) = 987,945,000$ ($\approx 10^9$) hyperedges. To compute the weight of a hyperedge, the max-error fit is obtained as follows: all three pairs of trajectories in a hyperedge are used to instantiate 2D similarities which are then evaluated with the third trajectory. The highest error is converted to an affinity value via a negative exponential. The massive number of hyperedges used contribute to significant computational expense. For example, OB requires 48 minutes to compute the affinity matrix of *car1*.

We demonstrate how our approach significantly improves the run time of hypergraph clustering for motion segmentation. Hyperedges of degree of $D = 10$ were used in our hypergraphs. Based on SWS, we generated 1000 samples of $(D - 1)$-tuples from the trajectories V of a given sequence. A 2D similarity motion was fitted on each $(D - 1)$-tuple and evaluated against the rest of the trajectories. There were thus a total of (just) $1000|V|$ hyperedges in each hypergraph. This reduces run time enormously. Moreover, as we will show later, since SWS can generate pure hyperedges accurately, these relatively few hyperedges were sufficient to produce good segmentation. Since we used large hyperedges, OB's max-error fit procedure which tests all pairs is too costly to be applied. We simply estimated the 2D similarity on each $(D - 1)$-tuple using least squares. Under these settings, we computed the affinity matrix of *car1* within 10 seconds.

Due to the significant difference in computational requirements, any comparisons must thus take run time into account. To compare against OB, we reduce a given sequence by taking just the first-10 frames of the video. We ran the implementation of BM and OB[1] on a linux 64-bit desktop. Note that the provided binaries conduct dense feature tracking from scratch; approximately 4 minutes are needed for dense tracking over 10 frames. Comparing just the *clustering step*, OB takes ≈ 1 hour and BM takes ≈ 1 minute. Using the trajectories output by OB, our method requires a relatively tiny ≈ 15 seconds for clustering.

Fig. 3 provides qualitative comparisons on *car5*, *marple8*, *marple13* and *duck* sequences (all reduced to 10 frames). Despite the much smaller computational expense, our method provides similar segmentation quality as OB. Note also that BM fails in *duck* due to the more complex motions (as reported in [7]). Quantitative comparison based on the criteria in BM and OB is also made using the evaluation code provided with the dataset. See Table 3.

The reader may suggest that our speed is due to using least squares instead of max-error fit. Note that when applied to a subset of size 3, the max-error fit is similar with least squares in time, since there are only 3 pairs to test. Thus, the major factor in the computational burden of OB is the number of hyperedges.

---

[1] Available at
http://http://lmb.informatik.uni-freiburg.de/Publications/2012/OB12/

(a) Brox and Malik [26].   (b) Ochs and Brox [7].   (c) Our method.

Fig. 3. Segmentation results in sample frames of sequences *car5*, *marple8*, *marple13* and *duck* from the Berkeley motion segmentation dataset [26]

Table 3. Results on Berkeley motion segmentation benchmark for first 10 frames

	Density	overall error	average error	over segmentation	extracted objects
BM	0.81%	7.86%	28.76%	0.35	22
OB	0.79%	7.44%	28.01%	0.38	23
Ours	0.79%	8.05%	27.84%	0.23	22

5   Conclusion

We have established theoretically the benefits of using large hyperedges in hypergraph clustering. Our theoretical analysis is then supported by comprehensive experiments. In particular, the experimental results clearly show that using large hyperedges yields better clustering accuracy - this departs from previous methods that have exclusively used the smallest possible hyperedge. We have also proposed a novel algorithm for accurately sampling large hyperedges. Notwithstanding the usage of large hyperedges, our method is very efficient to compute.

Acknowledgment. This work was supported by ARC grant DP130102524.

References

1. Agarwal, S., Branson, K., Belongie, S.: Higher order learning with graphs. In: ICML (2006)
2. Govindu, V.M.: A tensor decomposition for geometric grouping and segmentation. In: CVPR (2005)
3. Agarwal, S., Lim, J., Zelnik-Manor, L., Perona, P., Kriegman, D., Belongie, S.: Beyond pairwise clustering. In: CVPR (2005)
4. Chen, G., Lerman, G.: Spectral curvature clustering (scc). IJCV 81(3), 317–330 (2009)
5. Liu, H., Latecki, L., Yan, S.: Robust clustering as ensembles of affinity relations. In: NIPS (2010)
6. Liu, H., Yan, S.: Efficient structure detection via random consensus graph. In: CVPR (2012)
7. Ochs, P., Brox, T.: Higher order motion models and spectral clustering. In: CVPR (2012)
8. Jain, S., Govindu, V.M.: Efficient higher-order clustering on the grassmann manifold. In: ICCV (2013)
9. MacKay, D.J.C. (extra) The Swendsen-Wang method. In: Information Theory, Inference, and Learning Algorithms. Cambridge University Press (2003)
10. Pham, T.T., Chin, T.J., Yu, J., Suter, D.: The random cluster model for robust geometric fitting. In: CVPR (2012)
11. Alpert, C.J., Kahng, A.B.: Recent directions in netlist partitioning: A survey. Integration: The VLSI Journal 19(1–2), 1–81 (1995)
12. Zhou, D., Huang, J., Schölkopf, B.: Learning with hypergraphs: Clustering, classification, and embedding. In: NIPS (2006)
13. Shi, J., Malik, J.: Normalized cuts and image segmentation. IEEE TPAMI 22(8), 888–905 (2000)
14. Bulo', S.R., Pelillo, M.: A game-theoretic approach to hypergraph clustering. IEEE TPAMI 35(6), 1312–1327 (2013)
15. Elhamifar, E., Vidal, R.: Sparse subspace clustering. In: CVPR (2009)
16. Georghiades, A., Belhumeur, P., Kriegman, D.: From few to many: illumination cone models for face recognition under variable lighting and pose. IEEE TPAMI 23(6), 643–660 (2001)
17. Tron, R., Vidal, R.: A benchmark for the comparison of 3-d motion segmentation algorithms. In: CVPR (2007)
18. Tordoff, B., Murray, D.W.: Guided sampling and consensus for motion estimation. In: Heyden, A., Sparr, G., Nielsen, M., Johansen, P. (eds.) ECCV 2002, Part I. LNCS, vol. 2350, pp. 82–96. Springer, Heidelberg (2002)
19. Raguram, R., Frahm, J.-M., Pollefeys, M.: A comparative analysis of RANSAC techniques leading to adaptive real-time random sample consensus. In: Forsyth, D., Torr, P., Zisserman, A. (eds.) ECCV 2008, Part II. LNCS, vol. 5303, pp. 500–513. Springer, Heidelberg (2008)

20. Chin, T.-J., Yu, J., Suter, D.: Accelerated hypothesis generation for multi-structure robust fitting. In: Daniilidis, K., Maragos, P., Paragios, N. (eds.) ECCV 2010, Part V. LNCS, vol. 6315, pp. 533–546. Springer, Heidelberg (2010)

21. Vidal, R., Ma, Y., Sastry, S.: Generalized principal component analysis (gpca). IEEE TPAMI 27(12), 1945–1959 (2005)

22. Zhang, T., Szlam, A., Wang, Y., Lerman, G.: Hybrid linear modeling via local best-fit flats. IJCV 100(3), 217–240 (2012)

23. Ma, Y., Derksen, H., Hong, W., Wright, J.: Segmentation of multivariate mixed data via lossy data coding and compression. IEEE TPAMI 29(9), 1546–1562 (2007)

24. Yan, J., Pollefeys, M.: A general framework for motion segmentation: Independent, articulated, rigid, non-rigid, degenerate and non-degenerate. In: Leonardis, A., Bischof, H., Pinz, A. (eds.) ECCV 2006. Part IV. LNCS, vol. 3954, pp. 94–106. Springer, Heidelberg (2006)

25. Shi, F., Zhou, Z., Xiao, J., Wu, W.: Robust trajectory clustering for motion segmentation. In: ICCV (2013)

26. Brox, T., Malik, J.: Object segmentation by long term analysis of point trajectories. In: Daniilidis, K., Maragos, P., Paragios, N. (eds.) ECCV 2010, Part V. LNCS, vol. 6315, pp. 282–295. Springer, Heidelberg (2010)

Person Re-identification by Video Ranking

Taiqing Wang[1], Shaogang Gong[2], Xiatian Zhu[2], and Shengjin Wang[1]

[1] Dept. of Electronic Engineering, Tsinghua University, China
[2] School of EECS, Queen Mary University of London, UK

Abstract. Current person re-identification (re-id) methods typically rely on single-frame imagery features, and ignore space-time information from image sequences. Single-frame (single-shot) visual appearance matching is inherently limited for person re-id in public spaces due to visual ambiguity arising from non-overlapping camera views where viewpoint and lighting changes can cause significant appearance variation. In this work, we present a novel model to automatically select the most discriminative video fragments from noisy image sequences of people where more reliable space-time features can be extracted, whilst simultaneously to learn a video ranking function for person re-id. Also, we introduce a new image sequence re-id dataset (iLIDS-VID) based on the i-LIDS MCT benchmark data. Using the iLIDS-VID and PRID 2011 sequence re-id datasets, we extensively conducted comparative evaluations to demonstrate the advantages of the proposed model over contemporary gait recognition, holistic image sequence matching and state-of-the-art single-shot/multi-shot based re-id methods.

1 Introduction

In person re-identification, one matches a probe (or query) person against a set of gallery persons for generating a ranked list according to their matching similarity, typically assuming the correct match is assigned to one of the top ranks, ideally Rank-1 [50,20,11,12]. As the probe and gallery persons are often captured from a pair of non-overlapping camera views at different time, cross-view visual appearance variation can be significant. Re-identification by visual matching is inherently challenging [14]. The state-of-the-art methods perform this task mostly by matching spatial appearance features (e.g. colour and intensity gradient histograms) using a pair of single-shot person images [11,35,20,49]. However, single-shot appearance features are intrinsically limited due to the inherent visual ambiguity caused by clothing similarity among people in public spaces, and appearance changes from cross-view illumination variation, viewpoint difference, cluttered background and occlusions (Fig. 1). It is desirable to explore space-time information from image sequences of people for re-identification in public spaces.

Space-time information has been explored extensively for action recognition [34,45]. Moreover, discriminative space-time video patches have also been exploited for action recognition [37]. However, action recognition approaches are

D. Fleet et al. (Eds.): ECCV 2014, Part IV, LNCS 8692, pp. 688–703, 2014.
© Springer International Publishing Switzerland 2014

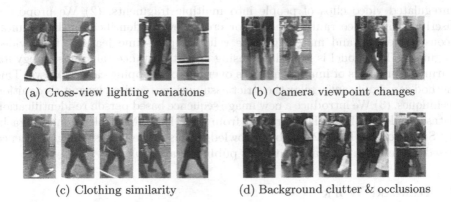

(a) Cross-view lighting variations   (b) Camera viewpoint changes

(c) Clothing similarity   (d) Background clutter & occlusions

Fig. 1. Person re-identification challenges in public space scenes [42]

not directly applicable to person re-identification because pedestrians in public spaces exhibit similar walking activities without distinctive and semantically categorisable actions unique to different people. On the other hand, gait recognition techniques have been developed for person recognition using image sequences by discriminating subtle distinctiveness in the style of walking [33,38]. Different from action recognition, gait is a behavioural biometric that measures the way people walk. An advantage of gait recognition is no assumption being made on either subject cooperation (framing) or person distinctive actions (posing). These are similar to person re-id situations. However, existing gait recognition models are subject to stringent requirements on person foreground segmentation and accurate alignment over time throughout a gait image sequence (cycle). It is also assumed that complete gait cycles were captured in target image sequences [17,31]. Most gait recognition methods do not cope well with cluttered background and/or random occlusion with unknown covariate conditions [1]. Person re-id in public spaces is inherently challenging for gait recognition (Fig. 1).

In this study, we aim to construct a discriminative video matching framework for person re-identification by selecting more reliable space-time features from videos of a person. To that end, we assume the availability of image sequences of people which may be highly noisy, i.e. with arbitrary sequence duration and starting/ending frames, unknown camera viewpoint/lighting variations during each image sequence, also with likely incomplete frames due to occlusion. We call this *unregulated* image sequences of people (Fig. 1 and Fig. 4). More specifically, we propose a novel approach to Discriminative Video fragments selection and Ranking (DVR) based on a robust space-time feature representation given unregulated image sequences of people.

The main contributions of this study are: (1) We derive a multi-fragments based space-time feature representation of image sequences of people. This representation is based on a combination of HOG3D features and optic flow energy profile over each image sequence, designed to break down automatically unregulated video clips of people into multiple fragments. (2) We propose a discriminative video ranking model for cross-view re-identification by simultaneously selecting and matching more reliable space-time features from video fragments. The model is formulated using a multi-instance ranking strategy for learning from pairs of image sequences over non-overlapping camera views. This method can significantly relax the strict assumptions required by gait recognition techniques. (3) We introduce a new image sequence based person re-identification dataset called iLIDS-VID, extracted from the i-LIDS Multiple-Camera Tracking Scenario (MCTS) [42]. To our knowledge, this is the largest image sequence based re-identification dataset that is publically available.

2   Related Work

Space-Time Features - Space-time feature representations have been extensively explored in action/activity recognition [34,43,15]. One common representation is constructed based on space-time interest points [26,10,46,5]. They facilitate a compact description of image sequences based on sparse interest points, but are somewhat sensitive to shadows and highlights in appearance [24] and may lose discriminative information [13]. Thus they may not be suitable to person re-id scenarios where lighting variations are unknown and uncontrolled. Alternatively, space-time volume/patch based representations [34] can be more robust. Mostly these are spatial-temporal extensions of image descriptors, e.g. HoGHoF [27], 3D-SIFT [39], HOG3D [25]. In this study, we adopt HOG3D [25] as space-time features for video fragment representation due to: (1) they can be computed efficiently; (2) they contain both spatial gradient and temporal dynamic information, therefore potentially more expressive [43,25]; (3) they are more robust against cluttered background and occlusions [25]. The choice of a space-time feature representation is independent of our model.

Gait Recognition - Space-time information of sequences has been extensively exploited by gait recognition [33,38,17,31]. However, these methods often make stringent assumptions on the image sequences, e.g. uncluttered background, consistent silhouette extraction and alignment, accurate gait phase estimation and complete gait cycles, most of which are unrealistic in typical person re-id scenarios. It is challenging to extract a suitable gait representation from such re-id data. In contrast, our approach relaxes significantly these assumptions by simultaneously selecting discriminative video fragments from noisy image sequences, and matching them cross-views without temporal alignment.

Temporal Sequence Matching - One approach to exploiting image sequences for re-identification is sequence matching. For instance, Dynamic Time Warping (DTW) is a popular sequence matching method widely used for action recognition [29], and more recently also for person re-id [40]. However, given two sequences with unsynchronised starting/ending frames, it is difficult to align sequences for matching, especially if the image sequences are subject to significant noise caused by unknown camera viewpoint change, background clutters and significant lighting changes. Our approach is designed to address this problem

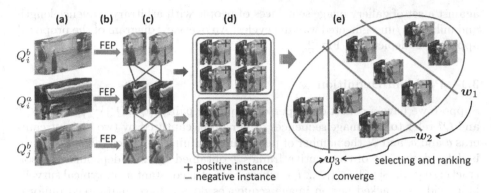

Fig. 2. Pipeline of the training phase of our DVR model. (a) Image sequences, Q_i^a denotes the image sequence of person p_i in camera a (Sec. 3.1). (b) Generating candidate fragment pools by Flow Energy Profiling (FEP) (Sec. 3.2). (c)-(d) Creating candidate fragment pairs as positive and negative instances (Sec. 3.3). (e) Simultaneously selecting and ranking the most discriminative fragment pairs (Sec. 3.3).

so to avoid any implicit assumptions on sequence alignment and camera view similarity among image frames both within and between sequences.

Multi-shot Re-identification - Multiple images of a sequence have been exploited for person re-identification. For example, interest points were accumulated across images for capturing appearance variability [16]. Manifold geometric structures from image sequences of people were utilised to construct more compact spatial descriptors of people [8]. The time index of image frames and identity consistency of a sequence were used to constrain spatial feature similarity estimation [23]. There are also attempts on training an appearance model from image sets [32] or by selecting best pairs [28]. Multiple images of a person sequence were used either to enhance local image region/patch spatial feature description [12,11,7,48], or to extract additional appearance information such as change statistics [2]. In contrast, the proposed model in this work aims to simultaneously select and match discriminative video space-time features for maximising cross-view ranking. Our experiments show the advantages of the proposed model over existing multi-shot models for person re-identification.

3   A Framework for Discriminative Video Ranking

We wish to construct a model capable of simultaneously selecting and matching discriminative video fragments from unregulated pairs of image sequences of people captured from two non-overlapping camera views (Fig. 2(a)). The model is based on (1) optic flow energy profiling over time in the image sequences, (2) HOG3D space-time feature extraction from video fragments and (3) a multi-instance learning strategy for simultaneous discriminative video fragments selection and cross-view matching by ranking. The learned model can then be deployed to perform person re-identification given unseen probe image sequences against a set of gallery image sequences of people with arbitrary sequence length and unknown/unsegmented walking cycles. An overview diagram of the proposed approach is depicted in Fig. 2.

3.1   Problem Definition

Suppose we have a collection of person sequence pairs $\{(Q_i^a, Q_i^b)\}_{i=1}^N$, where Q_i^a and Q_i^b refer to the image sequences of person p_i captured by two disjoint cameras a and b, and N the number of people in a training set. Each image sequence is defined as a set of consecutive frames I obtained by an independent person tracker, e.g. [3,18] : $Q = (I_1, ..., I_t)$, where t is not a constant as in typical surveillance videos, tracked person image sequences do not have guaranteed uniform length (arbitrary number of frames), nor number of walking cycles and starting/ending phases. For model training, we aim to learn a ranking function of image sequences $f(Q^a, Q^b)$ that satisfies the ranking constraints as:

$$f(Q_i^a, Q_i^b) > f(Q_i^a, Q_j^b), \ \forall i = \{1, ..., N\}, \ \forall j \neq i. \tag{1}$$

That is, a pair of image sequences of the same person p_i is constrained/maximised to be assigned with a top rank, i.e. the highest ranking score.

Learning a ranking function *holistically without discrimination and selection* from pairs of unsegmented and temporally unaligned person image sequences will subject the learned model to significant noise and degrade any meaningful discriminative information contained in the image sequences. This is an inherent drawback of any holistic sequence matching approach, including those with dynamic time warping applied for nonlinear mapping (see experiments in Sec. 4). Reliable human parsing/pose detection [22] or occlusion detection [47] may help, but such approaches are difficult to be scaled, especially with image sequences from crowded public scenes. The challenge is to learn a robust ranking function effective in coping with incomplete and partial image sequences by identifying and selecting most discriminative video fragments from each sequence suitable for extracting space-time features. Let us first consider generating a pool of candidates for video fragmentation.

3.2   Generating Candidates Pool for Video Fragmentation

Given the unregulated image sequences of people, it is too noisy to attempt holistically locating and extracting reliable discriminative space-time features from an entire image sequence. Instead, we consider breaking down each image sequence and generate a pool of video fragment candidates for a learning model to automatically select the most discriminative fragment(s) (Sec. 3.3).

It can be observed that motion energy intensity induced by the two legs of a walking person (or the activity of human muscles during walking) exhibits regular periodicity [44]. This motion energy intensity can be approximately estimated by optic flow. We call this Flow Energy Profile (FEP), see Fig. 3. This FEP signal is particularly suitable to address our video fragmentation problem for selecting more robust and discriminative space-time features due to: (i) Its local minimum and maximum are likely to correspond to some characteristic phases in a pedestrian's walking cycle, thus helping in estimating these characteristic walking postures (e.g. one leg is about to land); (ii) Relatively robust to changes in camera viewpoint. More precisely, given a sequence $Q = (I_1, ..., I_t)$, we first compute the optic flow field (v_x, v_y) centered at each frame I. The flow energy e of I is defined as

$$e = \sum_{(x,y) \in U} \| [\, v_x(x,y), v_y(x,y)\,] \|_2, \tag{2}$$

where U is the pixel set of the lower body, e.g. the lower half of image I. The FEP $\mathcal{E}$ of Q is then defined as $\mathcal{E} = (e_1, ..., e_t)$, which is further smoothed by a Gaussian filter to suppress noise. Finally, we generate a candidate pool (set) of video fragments $S = \{s\}$ for each image sequence Q by detecting the local minima and maxima landmarks $\{t\}$ of $\mathcal{E}$ and extracting the surrounding frames $s = (I_{t-L}, ..., I_t, ..., I_{t+L})$ of each landmark as a video fragment. We fix $L = 10$ for all our experiments, determined by cross-validation on the iLIDS-VID dataset. It is worth pointing out that many of the obtained fragments of each image sequence can have similar phases of a walking cycle since the local minimum/maximum $\{t\}$ of the FEP signal are likely to correspond to certain characteristic walking postures (Fig. 3). This increases the possibility of finding aligned video fragment pairs (i.e. centred at similar walking postures) given a pair (S^a, S^b) of video fragment sets, facilitating discriminative video fragments selection and matching during model learning (Sec. 3.3).

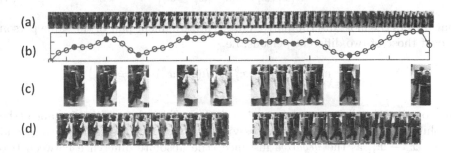

Fig. 3. (a) A person sequence of 50 frames is shown, with the motion intensity of each frame shown in (b). The red dots in (b) denote automatically detected local minima and maxima temporal landmarks in the motion intensity profile, of which the corresponding frames are shown in (c). (d) Two example video fragments (shown every 2 frames) with the landmark frames highlighted by red bounding boxes.

Video Fragment Space-Time Feature Representation - We exploit HOG3D for space-time feature representation of a video fragment, due to its advantages demonstrated for applications in action and activity recognition [25]. In order to capture spatially more localised space-time information of a person in motion, e.g. body parts such as head, torso, arms and legs, we decompose a video fragment spatially into 2×5 even cells. To encode separately the information of sub-intervals before and after the characteristic walking posture (Fig. 3 (d)) potentially situated in the middle of a video fragment, the fragment is further divided temporally into two smaller sections. Two adjacent cells have 50% overlap for increased robustness to possible spatio-temporal fragment misalignment. A space-time gradient histogram is computed in each cell and then concatenated to form the HOG3D descriptor x of the fragment s. We denote by $X = \{x\}$ the HOG3D feature set of a fragment set $S = \{s\}$.

3.3   Selecting and Ranking the Most Discriminative Fragment Pairs

Given the candidate fragment sets $\{(X_i^a, X_i^b)\}_{i=1}^N$ represented by HOG3D features, the next problem for re-identification is how to select and match the most discriminative fragment pairs from cross-view fragment *sets*. Inspired by multi-instance classification [9] where each training sample is a bag (or set) of instances, we formulate a similar strategy for *multi-instance ranking* of video fragment candidates for automatic cross-view fragment selection and matching. More specifically, we aim for person re-identification by automatically selecting the most discriminative cross-view fragment pairs such that the selected fragments optimise cross-view re-id ranking score. Formally, we denote two cross-view fragments of person p_i captured in camera a and b as $x_i^a \in X_i^a$ and $x_i^b \in X_i^b$. The objective is to learn a linear ranking function on the absolute difference of cross-view fragment pairs:

$$h(x_i^a, x_i^b) = w^\top |x_i^a - x_i^b| \tag{3}$$

that prefers the most discriminative cross-view fragment pair of the same person p_i over those of two different persons, i.e.

$$\max_{x_i^a \in X_i^a, x_i^b \in X_i^b} h(x_i^a, x_i^b) > h(x_i^a, x_j^b), \forall j \neq i. \tag{4}$$

For notation simplicity, we define $y^+ = |x_i^a - x_i^b|$ as the *positive* instance (the absolute difference between two cross-view fragments of the same person), and $y^- = |x_i^a - x_j^b|$ as the *negative* instance (the absolute difference between two cross-view fragments of two different persons). By enumerating all possible cross-view combinations between fragment sets, for every person p_i, we form a *positive* bag $B_i^+ = \{y^+\}$ with all y^+, and a *negative* bag $B_i^- = \{y^-\}$ with all y^-. After redefining the ranking function $h(x^a, x^b) = g(|x^a - x^b|) = g(y)$, Eqn. (4) can be rewritten as

$$\max_{y^+ \in B_i^+} g(y^+) > g(y^-), \forall y^- \in B_i^-. \tag{5}$$

With this constraint Eqn. (5), we aim to automatically discover and locate the most informative (most discriminative) cross-view video fragment pair within the positive bag B_i^+ for each person p_i during optimisation. To that end, we introduce a binary selection variable $\boldsymbol{v}_i$ with each entry being 0 or 1 and of unity ℓ_0 norm for each person p_i, and obtain

$$g(\boldsymbol{Y}_i \boldsymbol{v}_i) > g(\boldsymbol{y}^-), \forall \boldsymbol{y}^- \in B_i^-, \tag{6}$$

where each column of $\boldsymbol{Y}_i$ corresponds to one $\boldsymbol{y}^+ \in B_i^+$.

Optimising $\boldsymbol{w}$, $\boldsymbol{v}$ - For the optimisation of the ranking function Eqn. (3) under the constraint Eqn. (6), we relax $\boldsymbol{v}$ to be continuous with non-negative entry and unity ℓ_1 norm as in [4]. In particular, to optimise $\boldsymbol{w}$ (Eqn. (3)) subject to Eqn. (6), we formulate our problem into the standard max-margin framework,

$$\boldsymbol{w}^* = \arg\min_{\boldsymbol{w},\boldsymbol{\xi},\boldsymbol{v}} \frac{1}{2}||\boldsymbol{w}||^2 + C\boldsymbol{e}^\top \boldsymbol{\xi}$$
$$\text{s.t.} \quad \boldsymbol{v}_i^\top \boldsymbol{Y}_i^\top \boldsymbol{w} - \boldsymbol{y}_k^\top \boldsymbol{w} \geq 1 - \xi_{i,k}, \ \forall \boldsymbol{y}_k \in B_i^-, \ \xi_{i,k} \geq 0, \tag{7}$$
$$\boldsymbol{e}^\top \boldsymbol{v}_i = 1, \boldsymbol{v}_i \geq 0, \ i \in \{1,\dots,N\}, \ k \in \{1,\dots,|B_i^-|\},$$

where $\boldsymbol{e}$ refers to the vector of all ones and N the number of persons in the training set; $\boldsymbol{\xi}$ is the slack vector, with entry $\xi_{i,k}$; $\boldsymbol{v}$ denotes the selection vector for all training persons, a concatenation of personwise selector vectors $\boldsymbol{v}_i$. We solve Eqn. (7) by optimising $\boldsymbol{w}$ and $\boldsymbol{v}$ iteratively between two steps. In the *ranking* step, we fix $\boldsymbol{v}$ to optimise $\boldsymbol{w}$: this Quadratic Programming problem can be solved by the interior point algorithm. In the *selection* step, we fix $\boldsymbol{w}$ to estimate $\boldsymbol{v}$: the simplex algorithm is used to solve this Linear Programming problem. During this iterative optimisation, a pair of two well aligned cross-view fragments of the same person with less partial/missing frames and noises is more likely to be selected since they can share more similarity in the space-time feature space and thus induce a higher ranking score (Eqn. (3)). Such more discriminative video fragment pairs are favoured by model optimisation.

Initially each $\boldsymbol{v}_i$ is set to $\frac{1}{|B_i^+|}\boldsymbol{e}$. The iteration terminates when $\boldsymbol{v}$ is converged e.g. $||\boldsymbol{v}^{(q)} - \boldsymbol{v}^{(q-1)}||_2 \leq 10^{-8}$, with q the current iteration index. For efficiency consideration, only 10% instances out of each B_i^- are employed during training.

Efficient Learning - As the number of ranking constraint (Eqn. (6)) grows quadratically with the number of fragments per sequence, an efficient version of the ranking step is necessary to make model learning scalable. Motivated by [6], we relax the ranking step into a non-constrained primal problem that can be more efficiently solved by the linear conjugate gradient method as

$$\boldsymbol{w}^* = \arg\min_{\boldsymbol{w},\boldsymbol{\xi}} \frac{1}{2}||\boldsymbol{w}||^2 + C \sum_{\boldsymbol{y}_k \in \{B_i^-\}} \ell\left(0, 1 - (\boldsymbol{v}_i^\top \boldsymbol{Y}_i^\top - \boldsymbol{y}_k^\top)\boldsymbol{w}\right)^2, \tag{8}$$

where ℓ refers to the hinge loss function. Our method is thus called Primal Max-Margin Multi-Instance Ranking (PM3IR).

3.4 Re-identification by Discriminative Video Fragment Ranking

The learned ranking model can be deployed to perform person re-id by matching a probe person image sequence Q^p observed in one camera against a gallery set

$\{Q^g\}$ in another camera. Formally, the ranking score of a gallery person sequence Q^g with respect to the probe Q^p is computed as

$$f(Q^p, Q^g) = \max_{x_i \in X^p, x_j \in X^g} w^\top |x_i - x_j|, \tag{9}$$

where X^p and X^g are the HOG3D feature sets of the video fragments in sequence Q^p and Q^g, respectively. The gallery persons are then sorted in descending order of their assigned matching scores to generate a ranked list.

Combination with Existing Spatial Feature Based Models - Our approach can complement existing spatial feature based re-id approaches. In particular, we incorporate Eqn. (9) into the ranking scores γ_i obtained by other models as

$$\hat{f}(Q^p, Q^g) = \sum_i \alpha_i \gamma_i(Q^p, Q^g) + f(Q^p, Q^g). \tag{10}$$

where α_i refers to a weighting assigned to the i-th method, which is estimated by cross-validation.

4   Experiments

We conducted extensive experiments on two image sequence datasets designed for person re-identification, the PRID 2011 dataset [19] and our newly introduced dataset named iLIDS-VID [1].

iLIDS-VID Dataset - A new iLIDS-VID person sequence dataset has been created based on two non-overlapping camera views from the i-LIDS Multiple-Camera Tracking Scenario (MCTS) [42], which was captured at an airport arrival hall under a multi-camera CCTV network. It consists of 600 image sequences for 300 randomly sampled people, with one pair of image sequences from two camera views for each person. Each image sequence has variable length consisting of 23 to 192 image frames, with an average number of 73. This dataset is very challenging due to clothing similarities among people, lighting and viewpoint variations across camera views, cluttered background and occlusions (Fig. 1 and Fig. 4 (a)).

PRID 2011 Dataset - The PRID 2011 re-identification dataset [19] includes 400 image sequences for 200 people from two camera views that are adjacent to each other. Each image sequence has variable length consisting of 5 to 675 image frames [2], with an average number of 100. Compared with the iLIDS-VID dataset, it was captured in uncrowded outdoor scenes with relatively simple and clean background and rare occlusions (Fig. 4 (b)).

Evaluation Settings - From both datasets, the total pool of sequence pairs is randomly split into two subsets of equal size, one for training and one for testing. Following the evaluation protocol on the PRID 2011 dataset [19], in the

---

[1] The iLIDS-VID dataset is available at http://www.eecs.qmul.ac.uk/ xz303/ downloads_qmul_iLIDS-VID_ReID_dataset.html

[2] Sequences with more than 21 frames from 178 persons are used in our experiments.

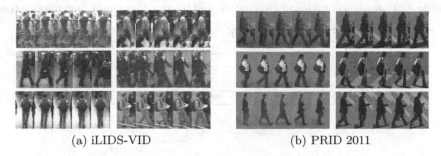

(a) iLIDS-VID   (b) PRID 2011

Fig. 4. Example pairs of image sequences of the same people appearing in different camera views from (a) the iLIDS-VID dataset, (b) the PRID 2011 dataset. Only every 3rd frame is shown and the total number of frames for each sequence is not identical.

testing phase, the sequences from the first camera are used as the probe set while the ones from the other camera as the gallery set. The results are shown in Cumulated Matching Characteristics (CMC) curves. To obtain stable statistical results, we repeat the experiments for 10 trials and report the average results.

Comparison with Gait Recognition and Temporal Sequence Matching - We compared the proposed DVR model with contemporary gait recognition and temporal sequence matching methods for person (re-)identification:
(1) Gait recognition (GEI+RSVM) [31]: A state-of-the-art gait recognition model using Gait Energy Image (GEI) [17] (computed from pre-segmented silhouettes in their datasets) as sequence representation and RankSVM [6] for recognition. A challenge for applying gait recognition to unregulated person sequences in re-id scenarios is to generate good gait silhouettes as input. To that end, we first deployed the DPAdaptiveMedianBGS algorithm in the BGSLibrary [41] to extract silhouettes from video sequences in the iLIDS-VID dataset [3]. This approach produces better foreground masking than other alternatives.
(2) Colour&LBP+DTW, HoGHoF+DTW: We applied Dynamic Time Warping [36] to compute the similarity of two sequences, using either Colour&LBP [20] or HoGHoF [27] as per-frame feature descriptor. This is similar to the approach of Simonnet et al. [40], except that they only used colour features. In comparison, Colour&LBP is a stronger representation as it encodes both colour and texture. Alternatively, HoGHoF encodes both texture and motion information.

Fig. 5 and Table 1 show comparative results between DVR, GEI+RSVM (gait), Colour&LBP+DTW and HoGHoF+DTW. It is evident that the proposed DVR outperforms significantly all others on both datasets (gait was not applied to PRID 2011 for reasons stated above).

In particular, gait recognition [31] achieves the worst re-identification accuracy on the iLIDS-VID dataset. This is largely due to very noisy GEI features avaliable from person sequences. This is evident from the examples shown in

---

[3] We can only evaluate on the iLIDS-VID dataset because the original image sequences are not included in the PRID 2011 dataset.

Table 1. Comparison with gait recognition and temporal sequence matching methods

Dataset	PRID 2011				iLIDS-VID			
Rank R	$R{=}1$	$R{=}5$	$R{=}10$	$R{=}20$	$R{=}1$	$R{=}5$	$R{=}10$	$R{=}20$
Gait Recognition [31]	-	-	-	-	2.8	13.1	21.3	34.5
Colour&LBP[20]+DTW[36]	14.6	33.0	42.6	47.8	9.3	21.7	29.5	43.0
HoGHoF[27]+DTW[36]	17.2	37.2	47.4	60.0	5.3	16.1	29.7	44.7
DVR (ours)	**28.9**	**55.3**	**65.5**	**82.8**	**23.3**	**42.4**	**55.3**	**68.4**

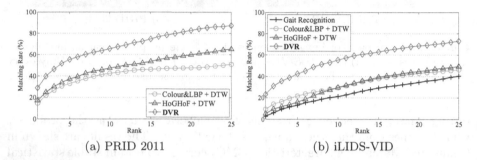

(a) PRID 2011   (b) iLIDS-VID

Fig. 5. Comparing CMC curves of the DVR model, gait recognition and temporal sequence matching based methods

Fig. 6 : The extracted gait foreground masks tend to be affected by other moving objects in the scene, whilst our DVR model trains itself by simultaneously selecting and ranking only those fragments of image sequences which suffer the least from occlusion and noise. Moreover, DTW based matching for re-id using either Colour&LBP+DTW or HoGHoF+DTW features also suffer notably from the inherent uncertain nature of re-id sequences and perform significantly poorer than the proposed DVR approach. This is largely due to: (1) Person sequences have different durations with arbitrary starting/ending frames, also potentially different walking cycles. Therefore, attempts to match holistically entire sequences inevitably suffer from mismatching with erroneous similarity measurement. (2) There is no clear (explicit) mechanism to avoid incompleteness/missing data, typical in busy scenes. (3) Direct sequence matching is less discriminative than learning an inter-camera discriminative mapping function explicitly, which is built into the DVR model by exploring multi-instance ranking.

Comparison with Single-Shot and Multi-frame/Multi-shot Spatial Feature Representations - To evaluate the effectiveness of discriminative video fragmentation and ranking using space-time features for person re-identification, we compared the proposed DVR model against a wide range of contemporary re-id models using spatial features, either in single-shot or as multiple frames (multi-shot). In order to process the iLIDS-VID dataset for the experiments, we mainly considered those methods with both their code available publically and being contemporary. They include (1) SDALF [11] (both single-shot and multi-shot versions), (2) Salience [49], (3) a combination of colour and

(a)   (b)

Fig. 6. (a) and (b) show two examples of the GEI gait features and our video fragment pairs. In both (a) and (b), the leftmost thumbnail shows GEI gait features, while the remaining thumbnails present some examples of fragment pairs, with the automatically selected pairs marked by red bounding boxes. A fragment is visualized as the weighted average of all its frames with emphasis on its central frame.

Table 2. Comparing spatial feature methods (SS: Single-Shot; MS: multi-shot)

Dataset	PRID 2011				iLIDS-VID			
Rank R	$R=1$	$R=5$	$R=10$	$R=20$	$R=1$	$R=5$	$R=10$	$R=20$
SS-Colour&LBP[20]+RSVM	22.4	41.8	51.0	64.7	9.1	22.6	33.2	45.5
SS-SDALF [11]	4.9	21.5	30.9	45.2	5.1	14.9	20.7	31.3
MS-SDALF [11]	5.2	20.7	32.0	47.9	6.3	18.8	27.1	37.3
Salience [49]	25.8	43.6	52.6	62.0	10.2	24.8	35.5	52.9
DVR (ours)	28.9	55.3	**65.5**	**82.8**	**23.3**	42.4	**55.3**	68.4
MS-Colour&LBP+RSVM	**34.3**	**56.0**	**65.5**	77.3	23.2	**44.2**	54.1	**68.8**

texture (Colour&LBP) [20] with RankSVM [6] as the distance metric. (4) Moreover, we also extended a Colour&LBP single-shot model to multi-shot by averaging the Colour&LBP features of each frame over a person sequence to focus on stable appearance cues and suppress noises, in a similar approach to [21]. We call this method MS-Colour&LBP+RSVM. Table 2 and Fig. 7 show the results. It is evident that the proposed DVR model outperforms significantly all the spatial feature based methods except our extended multi-shot MS-Colour&LBP+RSVM model, which offers slight advantage on PRID 2011 and very close performance on iLIDS-VID. This can be explained by that the DVR model with HOG3D space-time feature representation *only* utilises spatio-temporal gradient information *without* benefiting from any colour information. As colour information can often play an important role in person re-id [30], it is rather significant that using only space-time texture information (HOG3D), the proposed DVR model outperforms significantly most spatial feature based models, e.g. 10.7% and 128.4% Rank 1 improvement over Salience on PRID 2011 and iLIDS-VID, respectively. For a further analysis on the DVR model when colour information is incorporated, more details are discussed next.

Complementary to Existing Spatial Feature Representations - We further evaluated the effects from both adding additional colour information into the DVR model and combining the DVR model with existing colour and texture feature representations. The results are shown in Table 3. It is evident that significant performance gain was achieved by incorporating the DVR ranking score (Eqn. (10)). More specifically, the Rank-1 re-id performance of using multi-shot colour feature (MS-Colour) was boosted by 40.7% and 99.4% on PRID 2011

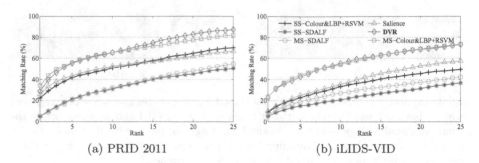

(a) PRID 2011   (b) iLIDS-VID

Fig. 7. CMC curve comparison between the proposed DVR model (without colour information) and existing spatial feature based models (SS: Single-Shot, MS: multi-shot).

Table 3. Performance from combining DVR with spatial features (MS: Multi-Shot)

Dataset	PRID 2011				iLIDS-VID			
Rank R	$R=1$	$R=5$	$R=10$	$R=20$	$R=1$	$R=5$	$R=10$	$R=20$
MS-Colour+RSVM	29.7	49.4	59.3	71.1	16.4	37.3	48.5	62.6
MS-Colour+DVR	**41.8**	**63.8**	**76.7**	**88.3**	**32.7**	**56.5**	**67.0**	**77.4**
MS-Colour&LBP+RSVM	34.3	56.0	65.5	77.3	23.2	44.2	54.1	68.8
MS-Colour&LBP+DVR	**37.6**	**63.9**	**75.3**	**89.4**	**34.5**	**56.7**	**67.5**	**77.5**
MS-SDALF [11]	5.2	20.7	32.0	47.9	6.3	18.8	27.1	37.3
MS-SDALF+DVR	**31.6**	**58.0**	**70.3**	**85.3**	**26.7**	**49.3**	**61.0**	**71.6**
Salience [49]	25.8	43.6	52.6	62.0	10.2	24.8	35.5	52.9
Salience+DVR	**41.7**	**64.5**	**77.5**	**88.8**	**30.9**	**54.4**	**65.1**	**77.1**

and iLIDS-VID respectively; Rank 1 score of MS-SDALF feature was boosted by 507.7% and 323.8% on PRID 2011 and iLIDS-VID respectively; and Rank 1 of Salience feature was boosted by 61.6% and 202.9% on PRID 2011 and iLIDS respectively.

Evaluation of Space-Time Fragment Selection - To evaluate the space-time video fragment selection mechanism in the proposed DVR model, we implemented two baseline methods without this mechanism: (1) SS-HOG3D+RSVM: Each person sequence is represented by the HOG3D descriptor of a single fragment randomly selected from the sequence; (2) MS-HOG3D+RSVM: Each person sequence is represented by the averaged HOG3D descriptors of four fragments uniformly selected from the sequence. In both these baseline methods, RankSVM [6] is used to rank the person sequence representations. The results are presented in Table 4. On the PRID 2011 dataset, the DVR model outperforms SS-HOG3D+RSVM and MS-HOG3D+RSVM in Rank 1 by 160.4% and 49.0% respectively. The performance advantage is even greater on the more challenging iLIDS-VID dataset, i.e. in Rank-1 by 206.6% and 92.6% respectively. It demonstrates clearly that in the presence of significant noise and given unregulated person image sequences, it is indispensable to automatically select discriminatively space-time features from raw image sequences in order to construct a

Table 4. The effect of space-time video fragment selection (SS: Single-Shot, MS: Multi-Shot)

Dataset	PRID 2011				iLIDS-VID			
Rank R	$R=1$	$R=5$	$R=10$	$R=20$	$R=1$	$R=5$	$R=10$	$R=20$
SS-HOG3D+RSVM	11.1	30.0	41.1	57.1	7.6	18.7	29.1	46.5
MS-HOG3D+RSVM	19.4	44.9	59.3	72.2	12.1	29.3	41.5	56.3
DVR (ours)	**28.9**	**55.3**	**65.5**	**82.8**	**23.3**	**42.4**	**55.3**	**68.4**

more robust model for person re-id. It is also noted that MS-HOG3D+RSVM outperforms SS-HOG3D+RSVM by suppressing noises benefited from temporal averaging. Although such a straightforward temporal averaging approach can have some benefits over single-shot methods, it loses important discriminative space-time information when applying uniformly temporal smoothing.

5 Conclusion

We have presented a novel DVR framework for person re-identification by video ranking using discriminative space-time feature selection. Our extensive evaluations show that this model outperforms a wide range of contemporary techniques from gait recognition, temporal sequence matching, to state-of-the-art single-shot/multi-shot/multi-frame spatial feature representation based re-id models. In contrast to existing approaches, the proposed method is capable of capturing more accurately space-time information that are discriminative to person re-identification through learning a cross-view multi-instance ranking function. This is made possible by the ability of our model to automatically discover and exploit the most reliable video fragments extracted from inherently incomplete and inaccurate person image sequences captured against cluttered background, and without any guarantee on person walking cycles and starting/ending frame alignment. Moreover, the proposed DVR model complements (improves) significantly existing spatial appearance features when combined for person re-identification. Extensive comparative evaluations were conducted to validate the advantages of the proposed model with the introduction of a new image sequence re-id dataset iLIDS-VID, which to our knowledge is currently the largest image sequence re-id dataset in the public domain.

References

1. Bashir, K., Xiang, T., Gong, S.: Gait recognition without subject cooperation. PRL 31, 2052–2060 (2010)
2. Bedagkar-Gala, A., Shah, S.K.: Part-based spatio-temporal model for multi-person re-identification. PRL 33, 1908–1915 (2012)
3. Shitrit, H.B., Berclaz, J., Fleuret, F., Fua, P.: Tracking multiple people under global appearance constraints. In: ICCV, pp. 137–144 (2011)
4. Bergeron, C., Zaretzki, J., Breneman, C., Bennett, K.P.: Multiple instance ranking. In: ICML, pp. 48–55 (2008)
5. Bregonzio, M., Gong, S., Xiang, T.: Recognising action as clouds of space-time interest points. In: CVPR, pp. 1948–1955 (2009)

6. Chapelle, O., Keerthi, S.S.: Efficient algorithms for ranking with svms. Information Retrieval 13, 201–215 (2010)
7. Cheng, D.S., Cristani, M., Stoppa, M., Bazzani, L., Murino, V.: Custom pictorial structures for re-identification. In: BMVC (2011)
8. Cong, D.N.T., Achard, C., Khoudour, L., Douadi, L.: Video sequences association for people re-identification across multiple non-overlapping cameras. In: ICIAP, pp. 179–189 (2009)
9. Dietterich, T.G., Lathrop, R.H., Lozano-Pérez, T.: Solving the multiple instance problem with axis-parallel rectangles. Artificial Intelligence, 31–71 (1997)
10. Dollár, P., Rabaud, V., Cottrell, G., Belongie, S.: Behavior recognition via sparse spatio-temporal features. In: 2nd Joint IEEE International Workshop on Visual Surveillance and Performance Evaluation of Tracking and Surveillance, pp. 65–72 (2005)
11. Farenzena, M., Bazzani, L., Perina, A., Murino, V., Cristani, M.: Person re-identification by symmetry-driven accumulation of local features. In: CVPR, pp. 2360–2367 (2010)
12. Gheissari, N., Sebastian, T.B., Hartley, R.: Person reidentification using spatiotemporal appearance. In: CVPR, pp. 1528–1535 (2006)
13. Gilbert, A., Illingworth, J., Bowden, R.: Fast realistic multi-action recognition using mined dense spatio-temporal features. In: ICCV, pp. 925–931 (2009)
14. Gong, S., Cristani, M., Loy, C.C., Hospedales, T.: The re-identification challenge. In: Person Re-Identification, pp. 1–20. Springer (2014)
15. Gong, S., Xiang, T.: Visual analysis of behaviour: From pixels to semantics. Springer (2011)
16. Hamdoun, O., Moutarde, F., Stanciulescu, B., Steux, B.: Person re-identification in multi-camera system by signature based on interest point descriptors collected on short video sequences. In: ICDSC, pp. 1–6 (2008)
17. Han, J., Bhanu, B.: Individual recognition using gait energy image. TPAMI 28, 316–322 (2006)
18. Hare, S., Saffari, A., Torr, P.H.S.: Struck: Structured output tracking with kernels. In: ICCV, pp. 263–270 (2011)
19. Hirzer, M., Beleznai, C., Roth, P.M., Bischof, H.: Person re-identification by descriptive and discriminative classification. In: Heyden, A., Kahl, F. (eds.) SCIA 2011. LNCS, vol. 6688, pp. 91–102. Springer, Heidelberg (2011)
20. Hirzer, M., Roth, P.M., Köstinger, M., Bischof, H.: Relaxed pairwise learned metric for person re-identification. In: Fitzgibbon, A., Lazebnik, S., Perona, P., Sato, Y., Schmid, C. (eds.) ECCV 2012, Part VI. LNCS, vol. 7577, pp. 780–793. Springer, Heidelberg (2012)
21. John, V., Englebienne, G., Krose, B.: Solving person re-identification in non-overlapping camera using efficient gibbs sampling. In: BMVC (2013)
22. Kanaujia, A., Sminchisescu, C., Metaxas, D.: Semi-supervised hierarchical models for 3d human pose reconstruction. In: CVPR, pp. 1–8 (2007)
23. Karaman, S., Bagdanov, A.D.: Identity inference: Generalizing person re-identification scenarios. In: Fusiello, A., Murino, V., Cucchiara, R. (eds.) ECCV 2012 Ws/Demos, Part I. LNCS, vol. 7583, pp. 443–452. Springer, Heidelberg (2012)
24. Ke, Y., Sukthankar, R., Hebert, M.: Volumetric features for video event detection. IJCV 88, 339–362 (2010)
25. Klaser, A., Marszalek, M.: A spatio-temporal descriptor based on 3d-gradients. In: BMVC (2008)
26. Laptev, I.: On space-time interest points. IJCV 64, 107–123 (2005)
27. Laptev, I., Marszalek, M., Schmid, C., Rozenfeld, B.: Learning realistic human actions from movies. In: CVPR, pp. 1–8 (2008)

28. Li, W., Wang, X.: Locally aligned feature transforms across views. In: CVPR, pp. 3594–3601 (2013)
29. Lin, Z., Jiang, Z., Davis, L.S.: Recognizing actions by shape-motion prototype trees. In: ICCV, pp. 444–451 (2009)
30. Liu, C., Gong, S., Loy, C.C.: On-the-fly feature importance mining for person re-identification. PR 47, 1602–1615 (2014)
31. Martín-Félez, R., Xiang, T.: Gait recognition by ranking. In: Fitzgibbon, A., Lazebnik, S., Perona, P., Sato, Y., Schmid, C. (eds.) ECCV 2012, Part I. LNCS, vol. 7572, pp. 328–341. Springer, Heidelberg (2012)
32. Nakajima, C., Pontil, M., Heisele, B., Poggio, T.: Full-body person recognition system. PR 36, 1997–2006 (2003)
33. Nixon, M.S., Tan, T., Chellappa, R.: Human identification based on gait, vol. 4. Springer (2010)
34. Poppe, R.: A survey on vision-based human action recognition. IVC 28, 976–990 (2010)
35. Prosser, B., Zheng, W.S., Gong, S., Xiang, T.: Person re-identification by support vector ranking. In: BMVC (2010)
36. Rabiner, L.R., Juang, B.H.: Fundamentals of speech recognition, vol. 14. PTR Prentice Hall, Englewood Cliffs (1993)
37. Sapienza, M., Cuzzolin, F., Torr, P.: Learning discriminative space-time actions from weakly labelled videos. In: BMVC (2012)
38. Sarkar, S., Phillips, P.J., Liu, Z., Vega, I.R., Grother, P., Bowyer, K.W.: The humanid gait challenge problem: Data sets, performance, and analysis. TPAMI 27, 162–177 (2005)
39. Scovanner, P., Ali, S., Shah, M.: A 3-dimensional sift descriptor and its application to action recognition. In: ACM MM, pp. 357–360 (2007)
40. Simonnet, D., Lewandowski, M., Velastin, S.A., Orwell, J., Turkbeyler, E.: Re-identification of pedestrians in crowds using dynamic time warping. In: Fusiello, A., Murino, V., Cucchiara, R. (eds.) ECCV 2012 Ws/Demos, Part I. LNCS, vol. 7583, pp. 423–432. Springer, Heidelberg (2012)
41. Sobral, A.: BGSLibrary: An opencv c++ background subtraction library. In: WVC. Rio de Janeiro, Brazil (2013)
42. UK Home Office: i-LIDS Multiple Camera Tracking Scenario Definition (2008)
43. Wang, H., Ullah, M.M., Klaser, A., Laptev, I., Schmid, C., et al.: Evaluation of local spatio-temporal features for action recognition. In: BMVC (2009)
44. Waters, R., Morris, J.: Electrical activity of muscles of the trunk during walking. Journal of Anatomy 111, 191 (1972)
45. Weinland, D., Ronfard, R., Boyer, E.: A survey of vision-based methods for action representation, segmentation and recognition. CVIU 115, 224–241 (2011)
46. Willems, G., Tuytelaars, T., Van Gool, L.: An efficient dense and scale-invariant spatio-temporal interest point detector. In: Forsyth, D., Torr, P., Zisserman, A. (eds.) ECCV 2008, Part II. LNCS, vol. 5303, pp. 650–663. Springer, Heidelberg (2008)
47. Xiao, J., Cheng, H., Sawhney, H.S., Rao, C., Isnardi, M.: Bilateral filtering-based optical flow estimation with occlusion detection. In: Leonardis, A., Bischof, H., Pinz, A. (eds.) ECCV 2006, Part I. LNCS, vol. 3951, pp. 211–224. Springer, Heidelberg (2006)
48. Xu, Y., Lin, L., Zheng, W.S., Liu, X.: Human re-identification by matching compositional template with cluster sampling. In: ICCV (2013)
49. Zhao, R., Ouyang, W., Wang, X.: Unsupervised salience learning for person re-identification. In: CVPR, pp. 3586–3593 (2013)
50. Zheng, W.S., Gong, S., Xiang, T.: Reidentification by relative distance comparison. TPAMI 35, 653–668 (2013)

Bayesian Nonparametric Intrinsic Image Decomposition[*]

Jason Chang, Randi Cabezas, and John W. Fisher III

CSAIL, MIT, USA

Abstract. We present a generative, probabilistic model that decomposes an image into reflectance and shading components. The proposed approach uses a Dirichlet process Gaussian mixture model where the mean parameters evolve jointly according to a Gaussian process. In contrast to prior methods, we eliminate the Retinex term and adopt more general smoothness assumptions for the shading image. Markov chain Monte Carlo sampling techniques are used for inference, yielding state-of-the-art results on the MIT Intrinsic Image Dataset.

Keywords: Intrinsic images, Dirichlet process, Gaussian process, MCMC.

1 Introduction

Intrinsic image analysis, first introduced in [2], is the problem of decomposing an image into various scene characteristics. Assuming a Lambertian surface model, where the perceived illumination is constant from all angles of incidence, the observed image decomposes into the product of the intrinsic shading and reflectance images. The reflectance image contains the albedo of the object surface, whereas the shading image captures the amount of reflected light from the surface. An example decomposition using the proposed approach is shown in Figure 1.

Fig. 1. An example of the intrinsic image problem. Left-to-right: original image, inferred shading and reflectance images under the proposed method.

While interesting in its own right, intrinsic image analysis is also important for other fields of computer vision. For example, the shading image can be exploited in shape-from-shading algorithms to reveal the underlying 3D structure

[*] This research was partially supported by the Office of Naval Research Multidisciplinary Research Initiative (MURI) program, award N000141110688, and the Defense Advanced Research Projects Agency, award FA8650-11-1-7154.

D. Fleet et al. (Eds.): ECCV 2014, Part IV, LNCS 8692, pp. 704–719, 2014.

of an object or to infer elements of the scene illumination, such as the number, location, and color of the light sources. Use of the reflectance image improves many segmentation algorithms, where shading effects often introduce artifacts.

We consider the problem of intrinsic reflectance and shading decomposition from a single observation. The Retinex algorithm [3,11,12], one of the first proposed solutions, detects edges in the observed image and solves for a reflectance image that has matching gradients at the detected edges. Surprisingly, many methods still require these gradient-matching terms to achieve good results. We show that these terms are not required to achieve state-of-the-art results. While aspects are related to previous methods, the presented formulation differs by: (1) using a Dirichlet process Gaussian mixture model for the reflectance image instead of setting a fixed number of components; (2) using a Gaussian process to model the shading image for added expressiveness; (3) treating the image as an observation from a *generative*, stochastic process; and (4) developing inference techniques that are robust to initialization.

2   Related Work

Many algorithms have been developed to decompose images into their intrinsic components. Some use multiple images to disambiguate the decomposition (e.g., [21]), while others use data-driven, patch-based algorithms (e.g., [6]).

The original Retinex algorithm [12], which many algorithms build upon (e.g., [3,7,8,11,14,17,20]), still performs well decades after its original inception. Results on the MIT Intrinsic Image Dataset [9] show that the original formulation in 1971 outperforms all other algorithms prior to 2009. The different flavors of Retinex all include two underlying concepts: sharp edges should occur in the reflectance image, and the shading image should be smooth. Edges in the image are first detected, typically by thresholding intensity or chromaticity gradients. Gradients of the reflectance image are then favored to match gradients in the observed image at the detected edges. This type of interaction is often referred to as the "Retinex term". A smoothness assumption in the shading image is then used to propagate the bias of the Retinex term away from the edges.

Some recent extensions to the Retinex algorithm have improved results. Many authors have observed that a small set of distinct colors can often be used to model the reflectance image (e.g., [1,8,17,18,22]). In particular, Shen et al. [17,22] group reflectance values based on a local texture patch. They develop a "match weight" for each pairwise match that is used as a heuristic to weight reflectance differences in their energy functional. Gehler et al. [8] explicitly partitions the pixels based on their reflectance colors into K clusters. However, it is unclear how to set K *a priori*, since one would expect this value to be dependent on the particular image. In contrast, we model the reflectance image with a Dirichlet process mixture model that does not predefine a model order.

Smoothness in the shading image is most commonly enforced with a Markov random field (MRF) and an L_1 or L_2 penalty on the difference of neighboring shading pixels. We note that an L_2 penalty is equivalent to using an improper

Table 1. Differences in Algorithms for Intrinsic Image Decomposition

	Gehler et al. [8]	Proposed Model
Shading Smoothness	4-connected GMRF	Gaussian process
Reflectance Prior	Uniform over fixed K clusters	Dirichlet process
Observations	Noiseless	Log-Normal noise
Probabilistic Model	Discriminative	Generative
Retinex Term	Yes	No
Inference	Iterative optimization	Marginalized MCMC

Gaussian MRF (GMRF) prior [13]. These types of model are used in [8], [17], and every method in the survey paper of [9]. In this work, we place a similar prior on the shading image. However, instead of restricting the smoothness to be a 4-connected GMRF as was done previously, we allow for a much broader class of smooth functions by placing a Gaussian process (GP) prior on the shading image. Stationary GMRFs are approximately finite realizations of GPs with stationary covariance kernels. However, as we shall see, framing the model using a GP allows us to exploit two advantages: (1) inference is simplified with GPs; and (2) changing the smoothness is a matter of altering the covariance kernel without having to explicitly adapt to a different graphical MRF structure.

The two current state-of-the-art algorithms take quite different approaches. SIRFS [1], the current best-performing algorithm on [9], differs from most methods by inferring 3D geometry and treating the shading image as a by-product of the lighting conditions and 3D surface. One might draw the conclusion from these results that modeling the 3D structure is essential to good performance; however, as we will show, that is not necessarily the case. Furthermore, training and inference in SIRFS is challenging due to the large set of parameters.

Our model can be thought of as the Bayesian nonparametric extension to the second best-performing algorithm of Gehler et al. [8]. Table 1 summarizes explicit differences between the two approaches. While [8] has shown that the Retinex term improves results, it is difficult to incorporate such a term in a *generative* model. Moreover, our experiments show that by using a more expressive shading model and improved inference, the Retinex term is unnecessary to achieve state-of-the-art results. This work also departs from [8] by placing Bayesian priors that adapt to different noise characteristics and object complexities.

3   Generative Model

As is common in intrinsic image analysis, we assume a Lambertian surface model, where an image decomposes into the product of a shading image and a reflectance image. We now present a generative model, depicted in Figure 2, that contains this explicit decomposition. For the remainder of this paper, we will work in the log domain where the log of the observed image, x, is assumed to be generated from the sum of the log shading and the log reflectance image.

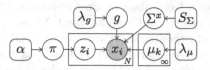

Fig. 2. The generative graphical model. See text for description. $\lambda_\mu = \{\theta, \Sigma^\mu\}$ and $\lambda_g = \{\kappa, \sigma_g^2, \nu, l\}$ denote sets of hyper-parameters.

The log reflectance image is generated from a standard Dirichlet process Gaussian mixture model (DPGMM) as follows: (1) infinite-length mixture model weights, π, are drawn from a stick-breaking process [16]; (2) the mean RGB color for each cluster, μ_k, is drawn from a multivariate Gaussian prior; and (3) the cluster assignment for each pixel, i, denoted z_i, is drawn from a categorical distribution with parameters π. The following expressions summarize this process:

$$p(\pi) = \text{GEM}(\pi \; ; \; 1, \alpha), \tag{1}$$

$$p(\mu) = \prod_k p(\mu_k) = \prod_k \mathcal{N}(\mu_k \; ; \; \theta, \Sigma^\mu), \tag{2}$$

$$p(z|\pi) = \prod_i p(z_i|\pi) = \prod_i \text{Cat}(z_i \; ; \; \pi). \tag{3}$$

The hyper-parameters, α, θ, and Σ^μ, are chosen to specify broad priors. The $3K \times 1$ vector of means is denoted by μ, where K is the number of realized clusters for 3 color channels. The log reflectance image, denoted μ_z, is then formed by setting each pixel, $[\mu_z]_i$, to the corresponding cluster mean: $[\mu_z]_i = \mu_{z_i}$. The reflectance image is then a $3N \times 1$ vector for an image with N pixels.

The log shading image, denoted g, is generated from a zero-mean Gaussian process (GP) with a stationary covariance kernel, κ. Shading images of interest (e.g., in the MIT Intrinsic Image Dataset [9]) are often generated from white-colored incident light. However, we find that allowing colored shading images generally results in better convergence. As such, we model g as a 3D Gaussian process with a covariance kernel that is a function of location and color. Furthermore, we are only interested in the values at the fixed grid locations. Since any subset of variables in a GP is jointly Gaussian, we can express the GP as

$$p(g) = \text{GP}(g \; ; \; \kappa) = \mathcal{N}(g \; ; \; 0, \Sigma^g), \tag{4}$$

where Σ^g denotes the finite-dimensional covariance matrix obtained by evaluating the kernel, κ, at the grid points. The specific covariance kernel parameters govern the smoothness properties of g and are learned from training data.

Finally, we assume that the observed pixels in the log image are drawn independently from the following Gaussian distribution:

$$p(x|\mu, z, g, \Sigma^x) = \prod_i p(x_i|\mu, z_i, g_i, \Sigma^x) = \prod_i \mathcal{N}(x_i \; ; \; \mu_{z_i} + g_i, \Sigma^x). \tag{5}$$

While one could assume a fixed observation covariance, Σ^x, we have found that it is difficult to set *a priori*, and instead treat Σ^x as a latent variable. One possibility is to use a cluster-specific covariance instead of a global covariance (e.g., via a Normal Inverse-Wishart prior). However, as described in Section 4, a global observation covariance that is also Toeplitz lends itself to efficient inference of g. As we are unaware of conjugate priors on positive definite *Toeplitz* matrices, the prior on Σ^x is uniform over a *discrete* set of covariances, S_Σ:

$$\Sigma^x = S_\Sigma(u), \quad u \sim \mathrm{Uniform}(|S_\Sigma|). \tag{6}$$

The elements of S_Σ are chosen to be 3×3 matrices with color correlations logarithmically spaced in $[2^{-10}, 2^0]$ and marginal variances logarithmically spaced in $[2^{-7}, 2^0]$. This choice does not affect results significantly as long as the range is sufficiently broad. Visualizations can be found in [4].

Relation to DPGMMs. Typical DPGMMs draw each pixel from one of the infinite Gaussians with mean μ_k, regardless of the pixel location. The proposed model departs from the DPGMM by *jointly* changing the μ_k's in space according to g. One can view each pixel, i, as being drawn from a Gaussian with spatially-varying mean, $\mu_k(i) = \mu_k + g_i$. As such, we refer to this model as the spatially-varying DPGMM (SV-DPGMM). Additional details are included in [4].

4   Posterior Inference

One motivation for generative models is that computation of marginal event probabilities are generally more robust to noise as compared to point estimates such as the maximum *a posteriori* estimate. Consequently, we reason over the full distribution of the SV-DPGMM rather than use optimization approaches. MCMC methods, such as Gibbs sampling or the Metropolis-Hastings algorithm, are commonly used in complex probabilistic models such as the SV-DPGMM.

Before developing the inference techniques, we introduce some notation. Covariance matrices are denoted by Σ, possibly superscripted by an associated random variable. Corresponding precision matrices are denoted by $\Lambda \triangleq \Sigma^{-1}$. We use i and j for pixel indices in $[1, N]$, k and ℓ for cluster indices in $[1, K]$, and m and n for color channel indices in $[1, 3]$. As the posterior inference is complex, we build the algorithm over the next three sections.

4.1   Iterative Posteriors Inference without Marginalization

Conditioned on the GP, g, the SV-DPGMM simplifies to a traditional DPGMM. We sample this via the DP Sub-Cluster method [5], which restricts each Gibbs iteration to the current non-empty clusters and proposes split and merge moves. The relevant posterior distributions can expressed as:

Algorithm 1 SV-DPGMM Iterative Inference via MCMC

1. Initialize z and g to be all 0.
2. Sample $(z, \mu, \Sigma^x | g, x)$ using the DP Sub-Clusters algorithm [5].
3. Sample $(g | \mu, \Sigma^x, z, x)$ from Equation (11) using equivalent kernel [19] techniques.
4. Repeat from Step 2 until convergence.

$$p(\pi | z) = \text{Dir}(\pi \; ; \; N_1, \ldots, N_K, \alpha), \tag{7}$$

$$p(\mu | \Sigma^x, z, g, x) = \prod_{k=1}^{K} \mathcal{N}\left(\mu_k \; ; \; \overline{\theta}(x_{\mathcal{I}_k} - g_{\mathcal{I}_k}, \Sigma^x), \overline{\Sigma}^{\mu}(x_{\mathcal{I}_k} - g_{\mathcal{I}_k}, \Sigma^x)\right), \tag{8}$$

$$p(\Sigma^x | \mu, z, g, x) \propto \sum_{u=1}^{|S_\Sigma|} p(x | \mu, z, g, \Sigma^x = S_\Sigma(u)), \tag{9}$$

$$p(z | \pi, \mu, \Sigma^x, g, x) = \prod_{i=1}^{N} \sum_{k=1}^{K} \mathbb{I}[z_i = k] \, \pi_k \, \mathcal{N}(x_i \; ; \; \mu_k + g_i, \Sigma^x), \tag{10}$$

where $\mathcal{I}_k \triangleq \{i; z_i = k\}$ is the set of pixel indices assigned to cluster k, $N_k \triangleq |\mathcal{I}_k|$ counts the number of pixels assigned to cluster k, and $\overline{\theta}$ and $\overline{\Sigma}^{\mu}$ denote posterior hyper-parameters that are functions of the data through the conjugate prior. We note that the posterior on Σ^x is just the prior weighted by the likelihood because of the uniform prior over a discrete set (see Equation (6)).

Conditioned on the cluster assignments, z, and cluster parameters, μ, the posterior on g is known to be Gaussian with the following distribution (cf. [15]):

$$p(g | \mu, z, \Sigma^x, x) = \mathcal{N}\left(g \; ; \; \Sigma^g \Lambda^{g+x}(x - \mu_z), \Sigma^g - \Sigma^g \Lambda^{g+x} \Sigma^g\right), \tag{11}$$

where $\Lambda^{g+x} \triangleq (\Sigma^{g+x})^{-1} \triangleq (\Sigma^g + \Sigma^x \otimes I_N)^{-1}$, $\otimes$ denotes the Kronecker product, and I_N denotes an $N \times N$ identity matrix. We note that $\Sigma^x \otimes I_N$ is a $3N \times 3N$ block diagonal matrix where each 3×3 block represents the observation covariance for a 3-channel, colored pixel. If the GP uses a stationary covariance kernel, sampling from Equation (11) is well approximated using equivalent kernel methods [19]. Details of the approximation are shown in [4].

Equations (7)–(11) express the conditional distributions of all latent variables. Posterior inference can then alternate between sampling these expressions, as described in Algorithm 1. This procedure is very closely related to the procedure of [8], except that we solve Equation (11) analytically while [8] utilizes conjugate gradient iterations. Algorithm 1 empirically converges to local extrema and is sensitive to initialization. The method of [8] attempts to circumvent this issue by choosing the best solution from multiple initializations.

4.2   Marginalized Posterior Inference

Both the reflectance, μ, and shading, g, contribute additively in the log domain. Consequently, errors in one can be incorrectly explained by the other. Such problems are addressed in Bayesian inference by treating one variable as a nuisance parameter and marginalizing it out. While this is often intractable, marginalization of the shading image in the SV-DPGMM results in a closed-form expression.

Since each distribution conditioned on z and Σ^x is Gaussian, the joint distribution, $p(x, \mu, g | z, \Sigma^x)$, must be jointly Gaussian, and any marginal or conditional distribution must also be Gaussian. We show in [4] that marginalizing over g results in $p(\mu | z, \Sigma_x, x) = \mathcal{N}(\mu \; ; \; \theta^*, \Sigma^*)$, where each element of the mean, θ^*, and precision, $\Lambda^* = (\Sigma^*)^{-1}$, is defined as

$$\Lambda^*_{km,\ell n} = \Lambda^\mu_{m,n} + \sum_{i \in \mathcal{I}_k} \sum_{j \in \mathcal{I}_\ell} \Lambda^{g+x}_{im,jn}, \qquad \forall k = \ell, \tag{12}$$

$$\Lambda^*_{km,\ell n} = \sum_{i \in \mathcal{I}_k} \sum_{j \in \mathcal{I}_\ell} \Lambda^{g+x}_{im,jn}, \qquad \forall k \neq \ell, \tag{13}$$

$$[\Lambda^* \theta^*]_{km} = [\Lambda^\mu \theta]_m + \sum_{i \in \mathcal{I}_k} \sum_j \sum_n x_{jn} \Lambda^{g+x}_{im,jn}. \tag{14}$$

Equations (12)–(14) define a system of $3K$ linear equations for the reflectance colors that differs from Equation (8) by *marginalizing* over the shading image. This modification avoids dependence on possibly erroneous estimates of g. The current form requires the inversion of Σ^{g+x}, a large $3N \times 3N$ matrix, which is computationally burdensome. The covariance matrix, Σ^{g+x}, is evaluated on a square grid and will be Toeplitz for stationary covariance kernels. In the limit as the domain of observations extends to infinity, the precision will also be Toeplitz. If we approximate Λ^{g+x} as Toeplitz, Equations (12)–(14) become convolutions and are efficiently computed in the Fourier domain. In practice, we find that this approximation does not work well and consider the following alternative.

We note that the system of equations in Equations (12)–(14) only contains $4.5(K^2 + K)$ variables estimated from approximately N^2 variables. We remind the reader that K is the number of reflectance clusters (typically < 10) and N is the number of pixels (typically $> 50{,}000$). As such, there are many more observations than are necessary to reliably categorize θ^* and Λ^*. We therefore approximate the posterior on μ from a random *subset* of the data, where each cluster has at least 10 pixels and there are a total of at least 1,000 pixels.

Denoting the subset of pixel indices as $\mathcal{S}$, we then define a new realization of the GP on the subset of indices as $g_\mathcal{S}$ which is distributed according to $p(g_\mathcal{S}) = \mathcal{N}(g_\mathcal{S} \; ; \; 0, \Sigma^{g_\mathcal{S}})$. Following the same formulation as above, we can then approximate the posterior on the mean colors as

$$p(\mu | z, \Sigma^x, x) \approx p(\mu | z_\mathcal{S}, \Sigma^x, x_\mathcal{S}) = \mathcal{N}(\mu \; ; \; \hat{\theta}^*, \hat{\Sigma}^*), \tag{15}$$

where the approximate mean and precision are defined as

$$\hat{\Lambda}^*_{km,\ell n} = \Lambda^\mu_{m,n} + \sum_{i \in \mathcal{I}_k \cap \mathcal{S}} \sum_{j \in \mathcal{I}_\ell \cap \mathcal{S}} \Lambda^{g_\mathcal{S}+x}_{im,jn}, \qquad \forall k = \ell, \tag{16}$$

$$\hat{\Lambda}^*_{km,\ell n} = \sum_{i \in \mathcal{I}_k \cap \mathcal{S}} \sum_{j \in \mathcal{I}_\ell \cap \mathcal{S}} \Lambda^{g_\mathcal{S}+x}_{im,jn}, \qquad \forall k \neq \ell, \tag{17}$$

$$[\hat{\Lambda}^* \hat{\theta}^*]_{km} = [\Lambda^\mu \theta]_m + \sum_{i \in \mathcal{I}_k \cap \mathcal{S}} \sum_{j \in \mathcal{S}} \sum_n x_{jn} \Lambda^{g_\mathcal{S}+x}_{im,jn}. \tag{18}$$

Due to the subsampling process, $\Lambda^{g_\mathcal{S}+x} = (\Sigma^{g_\mathcal{S}} + \Sigma^x \otimes \mathrm{I}_{|\mathcal{S}|})^{-1}$ can now be computed efficiently. We note that this approximation performs well in practice. The resulting inference procedure is summarized in Algorithm 2.

Algorithm 2 SV-DPGMM Marginalized Inference via MCMC

1. Initialize z and g to be all 0.
2. Sample $(z, \mu, \Sigma^x | g, x)$ using the DP Sub-Clusters algorithm [5].
3. Sample $(\mu | \Sigma^x, z, x)$, marginalizing out g, from Equation (15).
4. Sample $(g | \mu, \Sigma^x, z, x)$ from Equation (11) using equivalent kernel [19] techniques.
5. Repeat from Step 2 until convergence.

4.3 Marginalized Split/Merge Posterior Inference

In this section, we describe an improved procedure that changes z while marginalizing out both μ and g. As mentioned previously, we exploit the recent DP Sub-Cluster sampling algorithm [5] to sample from the posterior of z. The core idea underlying the DP Sub-Cluster algorithm is to form two "sub-clusters" for each regular-cluster, and to use the sub-clusters to propose split moves. The prior distributions for the sub-clusters are chosen such that the posteriors are of the same form as Equations (7)–(10). Conditioned on the sub-clusters, a proposed split or merge is then used in a Metropolis-Hastings MCMC [10] framework that accepts the proposal with what is known as the Hastings ratio (cf. [5] for details).

Similar to the marginalization of the shading image g, we show in [4] that a related derivation can be used to express $p(x|z, \Sigma^x)$ as

$$p(x|z, \Sigma^x) = \frac{|\Lambda^{g+x}|^{1/2} |\Lambda^\mu|^{K/2}}{(2\pi)^{3N/2} |\Lambda^*|^{1/2}} \exp\left[\tfrac{1}{2}\left(\theta^{*\top}\Lambda^*\theta^* - K\theta^\top\Lambda^\mu\theta - x^\top\Lambda^{g+x}x\right)\right] \quad (19)$$

where the dependence on z and Σ^x are implied through Equations (12)–(14) for θ^* and Λ^*. A split of cluster k into clusters $\hat{k}$ and $\hat{\ell}$ using the DP Sub-Clusters algorithm, marginalizing over μ and g, is accepted with Hastings ratio

$$H_{\text{split}} = \frac{\alpha\Gamma(N_{\hat{k}})\Gamma(N_{\hat{\ell}})}{\Gamma(N_{\hat{k}}+N_{\hat{\ell}})} \cdot \frac{p(x|\hat{z}, \Sigma^x)}{p(x|z, \Sigma^x)} \prod_{i\in\mathcal{I}_k} \frac{\overline{\pi}_{\hat{k}}\mathcal{N}(x_i\,;\overline{\mu}_{\hat{k}}, \Sigma^x) + \overline{\pi}_{\hat{\ell}}\mathcal{N}(x_i\,;\overline{\mu}_{\hat{\ell}}, \Sigma^x)}{\overline{\pi}_{\hat{z}_i}\mathcal{N}(x_i\,;\overline{\mu}_{\hat{z}_i}, \Sigma^x)}, \quad (20)$$

where $\hat{z}$ is the newly split cluster labels, and $\overline{\pi}$ and $\overline{\mu}$ are sub-cluster parameters defined in [5]. Note that $p(x|z, g, \Sigma^x)$ integrates out the mean parameter. A similar marginalization applies to merge moves, resulting in the following Hastings ratio for a proposed merge of clusters k and ℓ into cluster $\hat{k}$:

$$H_{\text{merge}} = \frac{\Gamma(N_k+N_\ell)}{\alpha\Gamma(N_k)\Gamma(N_\ell)} \cdot \frac{p(x|\hat{z}, \Sigma^x)}{p(x|z, \Sigma^x)} \prod_{i\in\mathcal{I}_{\hat{k}}} \frac{\pi_{z_i}\mathcal{N}(x_i\,;\mu_{z_i}, \Sigma^x)}{\pi_k\mathcal{N}(x_i\,;\mu_k, \Sigma^x) + \pi_\ell\mathcal{N}(x_i\,;\mu_\ell, \Sigma^x)}. \quad (21)$$

This marginalized split/merge sampling method is summarized in Algorithm 3.

5 Parameter Learning

We now present two methods for learning model parameters. The first is supervised and uses training data to find the set of parameters that works best across all training examples. The second is unsupervised and places Bayesian hyper-priors on the parameters. The only parameters to learn are those of the

---

Algorithm 3 SV-DPGMM Marginalized Split/Merge Inference via MCMC

---

1. Initialize z and g to be all 0.
2. Run DP Sub-Clusters to find likely splits conditioned on g (Σ^x is concurrently sampled within DP Sub-Clusters).
3. Sample $(z|\Sigma^x, x)$ via Metropolis-Hastings MCMC by proposing all splits or merges and accept with the Hastings ratios in Equations (20) and (21).
4. Sample $(\mu|\Sigma^x, z, x)$ marginalizing over g from Equation (15).
5. Sample $(g|\mu, \Sigma^x, z, x)$ from Equation (11) using equivalent kernel [19] techniques.
6. Repeat from Step 2 until convergence.

---

covariance kernel in the GP, g. We use the Matérn class of kernels. Additionally, as mentioned previously, allowing for small amounts of color in the shading images improves convergence. As such, we alter the Matérn kernel to the following:

$$\kappa(c, r \; ; \; \sigma_c, \sigma_g^2, \nu, l) = \sigma_c^{\mathbf{1}[c \neq 0]} \, \sigma_g^2 \, \frac{2^{1-\nu}}{\Gamma(\nu)} \left(\frac{r\sqrt{2\nu}}{l}\right)^\nu K_\nu \left(\frac{r\sqrt{2\nu}}{l}\right), \qquad (22)$$

where c is the change in the color channel, r is the change in 2D location, $K_\nu(\cdot)$ is a modified Bessel function of the second kind, and $\lambda_g \triangleq \{\sigma_c, \sigma_g^2, \nu, l\}$ is the set of hyper-parameters to learn.

Supervised Learning. In the following sections, we test on the MIT Intrinsic Image Dataset [9]. Unfortunately, because the 20 images from [9] were released in two batches, some published methods are only trained or tested on a subset of the images. For example, [8] uses 16 of the 20 images, while [1] uses all 20 images. Furthermore, each method uses different training and test sets; [8] performs leave-one-out-cross-validation (LOOCV), while [1] separates the set into 10 training images and 10 test images. For an accurate comparison, we learned separate parameters using LOOCV and the separate training/test sets used in [1]. For each image, we ran the inference algorithm under a discrete set of parameter choices. The set of parameters that minimized the arithmetic mean of RS-MSE was chosen (similar to [8]). This error metric will be described shortly.

Unsupervised Learning. An alternative, Bayesian approach for *unsupervised* learning is to place a hyper-prior on the parameters, λ_g. For simplicity, we place a uniform prior on λ_g over a discrete set of plausible values. Inference then proceeds in the same sequence as before, with the added step of sampling λ_g from the posterior distribution, $\lambda_g \sim p(\lambda_g|g) \propto p(g|\lambda_g)$. This requires computing the likelihood of a GP realization with parameters λ_g, and can be efficiently approximated with methods described in [4].

6   Post-processing for Color Constancy

One ambiguity in the shading and reflectance decomposition has not been explicitly addressed; namely, any color channel of the log-shading image can be

Original   Ground Truth   SV-DPGMM   SV-DPGMM^{post}

Fig. 3. An example of correcting color constancy as a post processing step

shifted by an arbitrary amount if the log-reflectance image is shifted by the negative of the same amount. For example, this could correspond to changing the color of the light in the shading from white to blue and adding a yellow tint to reflectance image. The SV-DPGMM approach implicitly restricts these ambiguities. Because the GP is assumed to be zero-mean with correlated color channels, the shading image largely favors white lights and grayscale shading images. This is undesirable in some situations, one of which is shown in Figure 3.

Barron and Malik [1] address this color constancy issue by placing a prior on log reflectance values and assuming spherical harmonic lighting models. We take a slightly different approach since neither is easily applicable. We learn the distribution of the log shading and log reflectance values from the ground truth training data via a kernel density estimate. It would be ideal if these distributions could be incorporated into the generative model, but the non-parametric nature of the distributions eliminate the exploited conjugacy in the inference. As such, we perform a post-processing step that finds the optimal global color-shift in the coupled shading/reflectance space. Additional details can be found in [4]. We note that this procedure can be used with any intrinsic image algorithm.

7   Experimental Results

For each image in the MIT Intrinsic Image dataset [9], we run Algorithm 3 for 50 iterations to ensure convergence, which typically occurs with 5–10 iterations. We then take the mean of 25 samples from the stationary distribution. This takes approximately 1–20 minutes, depending on the image. Since the simulated Markov chains tend to explore a local mode, we run 10 chains independently and show the resulting pixel-wise median shading and reflectance images. Each chain essentially explores a local mode of shading and reflectance, and the median of the 10 independent chains finds the mode that is in the middle. As we soon show, while this procedure slightly improves results, running a single chain still achieves state-of-the-art results. Publicly available source code can be downloaded from http://people.csail.mit.edu/jchang7/.

In the following section, we compare SV-DPGMM with Retinex and the two state-of-the-art methods from [1] and [8]. For an accurate comparison, we train the model parameters using the same training and test sets described in each of the previous methods. We compute three metrics from [1]: S-MSE, R-MSE, and RS-MSE. S-MSE and R-MSE compute the global scale-invariant shading and reflectance mean squared error, respectively. RS-MSE is the metric from [9], which computes the average of local scale-invariant MSEs. We evaluate both the arithmetic and geometric mean (denoted with a 'g') across the images. We note that [8] and [9] use the arithmetic mean while [1] uses the geometric mean.

7.1   SV-DPGMM Ablation Testing

We first compare different inference methods for SV-DPGMMs using LOOCV on the 16 images of the original dataset presented in [9]. We consider the following inference methods: iterative inference via Algorithm 1 (SV-DPGMM^{it1}); iterative inference via Algorithm 1 while sampling shading first (SV-DPGMM^{it2}); marginalized inference via Algorithm 2 (SV-DPGMM^{marg1}); marginalized inference via Algorithm 2 while sampling shading first (SV-DPGMM^{marg2}); and marginalized split/merge inference via Algorithm 3 (SV-DPGMM). Additionally, we consider a procedure which replaces all sampling steps of Algorithm 3 with optimization (SV-DPGMM^{opt}). Table 2 summarizes the different inference schemes. We see that the methods based on Algorithms 1–2 are quite sensitive since their results vary dramatically based on whether the shading or reflectance is first estimated. In contrast, Algorithm 3 computes these jointly and does not suffer from this sensitivity. Since the training is based on RS-MSE, it is reasonable that SV-DPGMM does not perform the best across all metrics.

Next, we consider the following variants of the SV-DPGMM model: unsupervised training (SV-DPGMM^{unsup}); supervised training on a single Markov chain (SV-DPGMM^{single}); supervised training and computing the median across 10 Markov chains (SV-DPGMM); and SV-DPGMM with the color constancy post-processing (SV-DPGMM^{post}). Additionally, we compare to a model using a 10-component Dirichlet *distribution* mixture model instead of the Dirichlet *process* (SV-DPGMM$^{K=10}$). The results for SV-DPGMM^{single} were obtained by averaging the *errors* for 10 Markov chains, instead of combining the 10 Markov chains with a median image. Table 3 summarizes results from the different variants. The unsupervised method generally performs worse than the supervised training. In principle, unsupervised learning has an advantage, in that it yields a set of parameters for each observed image. However, the sample space that includes the GP covariance kernel may be too complex to sufficiently explore. Combining multiple chains, using a Dirichlet *process*, and post-processing to enforce color constancy all improve results. We note that the RS-MSE does not change with post-processing since it is invariant to global shifts in any color channel.

7.2   Algorithm Comparison

Table 4 compares SV-DPGMM^{post} with the Retinex algorithm and the method of [8] with ([8]+Ret.) and without ([8]−Ret.) Retinex. S-MSE is the only metric on which the SV-DPGMM yields worse performance. Upon examination of the individual results, we have found that this abnormally high error is due to making a large error in one of the shading estimate. We remind the reader that the

Table 2. Comparing SV-DPGMM Inference Methods

	S-MSE	R-MSE	RS-MSE	gS-MSE	gR-MSE	gRS-MSE
SV-DPGMM$^{\text{it}1}$	0.0548	0.0309	0.0362	0.0202	0.0196	0.0205
SV-DPGMM$^{\text{it}2}$	0.0532	0.0238	0.0302	0.0193	0.0146	0.0181
SV-DPGMM$^{\text{marg}1}$	0.0300	0.0146	0.0248	0.0097	0.0085	0.0121
SV-DPGMM$^{\text{marg}2}$	0.0321	0.0175	0.0271	0.0106	0.0109	0.0154
SV-DPGMM	0.0321	0.0144	0.0239	0.0093	0.0078	0.0111
SV-DPGMM^{opt}	0.0352	0.0172	0.0286	0.0120	0.0104	0.0157

Table 3. Comparing SV-DPGMM Model Variations

	S-MSE	R-MSE	RS-MSE	gS-MSE	gR-MSE	gRS-MSE
SV-DPGMM^{unsup}	0.0298	0.0166	0.0260	0.0096	0.0098	0.0136
SV-DPGMM^{single}	0.0328	0.0151	0.0249	0.0100	0.0087	0.0124
SV-DPGMM$^{K=10}$	0.0321	0.0147	0.0241	0.0095	0.0083	0.0120
SV-DPGMM	0.0321	0.0144	0.0239	0.0093	0.0078	0.0111
SV-DPGMM^{post}	0.0317	0.0135	0.0239	0.0072	0.0060	0.0111

Table 4. Leave-One-Out-Cross-Validation on 16 images from [9]

	S-MSE	R-MSE	RS-MSE	gS-MSE	gR-MSE	gRS-MSE
Retinex	0.0400	0.0292	0.0297	0.0219	0.0225	0.0185
[8]−Ret.	0.0311	0.0172	0.0304	0.0107	0.0134	0.0156
[8]+Ret.	0.0287	0.0205	0.0277	0.0119	0.0150	0.0166
SV-DPGMM^{post}	0.0317	0.0135	0.0239	0.0072	0.0060	0.0111

Table 5. Separate Train/Test Validation on 20 images from [9]

	S-MSE	R-MSE	RS-MSE	gS-MSE	gR-MSE	gRS-MSE
SIRFS Reported	-	-	-	0.0064	0.0098	0.0125
SIRFS Locally Run	0.0201	0.0158	0.0247	0.0068	0.0115	0.0125
SV-DPGMM	0.0306	0.0148	0.0229	0.0113	0.0092	0.0136
SV-DPGMM^{post}	0.0303	0.0141	0.0229	0.0092	0.0074	0.0136

only differences between SV-DPGMM and [8]−Ret. are the DP prior, a more expressive GP shading smoothness, and more robust inference. Moreover, many of the simplified inference algorithms of Tables 2–3 also outperform current methods. We believe that our optimization procedure for a more expressive model is only comparable to [8] due to the particular realization converging to a local extrema. Multiple initializations can circumvent this issue, as was done in [8].

Table 5 compares results with SIRFS [1] when training on half the images and testing on the other half. We note that published results from [1] and those obtained with their public source code are slightly different. SV-DPGMM performs better in three of the six metrics without needing to model the 3D scene

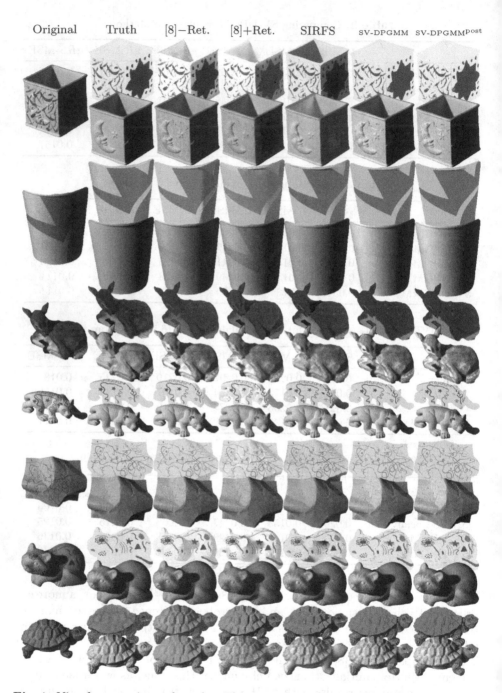

Fig. 4. Visual comparison of results. The rows show the estimated reflectance and shading images, respectively. SIRFS is trained via separate train/test sets. All other algorithms are trained using LOOCV.

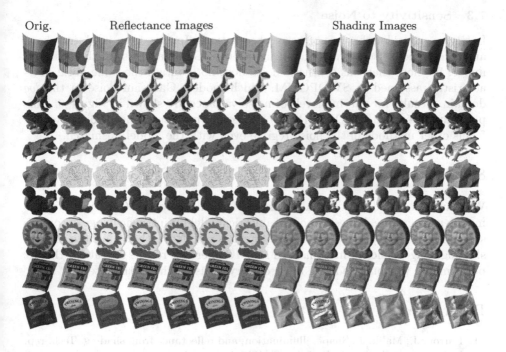

Fig. 5. Visual comparison of results. Left to right: original, reflectance images, and shading images. The reflectance and shading images from left to right: ground truth, [8]−Ret., [8]+Ret., SIRFS, SV-DPGMM, and SV-DPGMM^{post}.

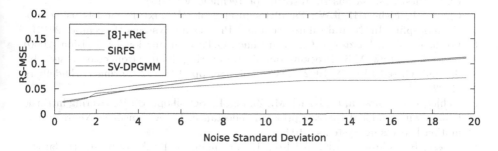

Fig. 6. Performance with additive noise

geometry. We visualize results of each algorithm from the LOOCV training in Figure 4. In general, the reflectance image is more piecewise constant in color and there is less bleeding of the reflectance into the shading. Figure 5 shows additional images. SV-DPGMM occasionally makes large errors (e.g., first row in Figure 5), which are likely due to allowing color in the shading images. The prior could be changed on a per-image basis to correct these errors.

7.3   Sensitivity to Noise

Lastly, we consider the case of noisy observations. Images from [9] do not have any camera noise, so we inject artificial additive Gaussian noise in the observed image. We note that this synthetic noise does not contain the same noise characteristics assumed in SV-DPGMM, which models Gaussian noise in the *log* domain. Results for varying levels of noise variance are shown in Figure 6. This plot illustrates that SV-DPGMM, which explicitly characterizes noise, outperforms other methods in the noisy regime even with the model mismatch.

8   Conclusion

We have presented the spatially-varying Dirichlet process Gaussian mixture model, a generative, Bayesian nonparametric model for intrinsic image decomposition. A Dirichlet process reflectance image is coupled with a Gaussian process shading image. Efficient marginalized MCMC inference results in state-of-the-art performance without modeling 3D geometry or using the Retinex term.

References

1. Barron, J., Malik, J.: Shape, illumination, and reflectance from shading. Tech. rep. Univeristy of California, Berkeley (2013)
2. Barrow, H., Tenenbaum, J.: Recovering intrinsic scene characteristics from images. Computer Vision Systems (1978)
3. Blake, A.: Boundary conditions for lightness computation in Mondrian world. Computer Vision, Graphics, and Image Processing (1985)
4. Chang, J.: Sampling in Computer Vision and Bayesian Nonparametric Mixtures. Ph.D. thesis, Massachusetts Institute of Technology (2014)
5. Chang, J., Fisher III, J.W.: Parallel sampling of DP mixture models using subclusters splits. In: Neural Information and Processing Systems (December 2013)
6. Freeman, W.T., Pasztor, E.C., Carmichael, O.T.: Learning low-level vision (2000)
7. Funt, B.V., Drew, M.S., Brockington, M.: Recovering shading from color images. In: Sandini, G. (ed.) ECCV 1992. LNCS, vol. 588, pp. 124–132. Springer, Heidelberg (1992)
8. Gehler, P.V., Carsten, R., Kiefel, M., Zhang, L., Schölkopf, B.: Recovering intrinsic images with a global sparsity prior on reflectance. In: Advances in Neural Information Processing Systems (2011)
9. Grosse, R., Johnson, M.K., Adelson, E., Freeman, W.T.: A ground-truth dataset and baseline evaluations for intrinsic image algorithms. In: International Conference on Computer Vision (2009)
10. Hastings, W.K.: Monte Carlo sampling methods using Markov chains and their applications. Biometrika 57(1), 97–109 (1970)
11. Horn, B.: Robot Vision. MIT Press, Cambridge (1986)
12. Land, E., McCann, J.: Lightness and retinex theory. Journal of the Optical Society of America (1971)
13. Malioutov, D., Johnson, J., Choi, M., Willsky, A.: Low-rank variance approximation in gmrf models: Single and multiscale approaches. IEEE Transacations on Signal Processing 56(10), 4621–4634 (2008)

14. Matsushita, Y., Nishino, I., Ikeuchi, K., Sakauchi, M.: Illumination normalization with time-dependent intrinsic images for video surveillance. IEEE Transacations on Pattern Analysis and Machine Intelligence 26(10), 1336–1347 (2004)
15. Rasmussen, C.E., Williams, C.K.I.: Gaussian Processes for Machine Learning. MIT Press, Cambridge (2006)
16. Sethuraman, J.: A constructive definition of Dirichlet priors. Statstica Sinica, 639–650 (1994)
17. Shen, L., Tan, P., Lin, S.: Intrinsic image decomposition with non-local texture cues. In: Computer Vision and Pattern Recognition (2008)
18. Shen, L., Yeo, C.: Intrinsic images decomposition using a local and global sparse representation of reflectance. In: Computer Vision and Pattern Recognition (2011)
19. Sollich, P., Williams, C.K.I.: Using the equivalent kernel to understand Gaussian process regression. In: Advances in Neural Information Processing Systems (2005)
20. Tappen, M.F., Freeman, W.T., Adelson, E.H.: Recovering intrinsic images from a single image. IEEE Transacations on Pattern Analysis and Machine Intelligence 27(9), 1459–1472 (2005)
21. Weiss, Y.: Deriving intrinsic images from image sequences. In: International Conference on Computer Vision (2001)
22. Zhao, Q., Tan, P., Dai, Q., Shen, L., Wu, E., Lin, S.: A closed-form solution to retinex with nonlocal texture constraints. IEEE Transactions on Pattern Analysis and Machine Intelligence (2012)

Face Detection without Bells and Whistles

Markus Mathias[1], Rodrigo Benenson[2], Marco Pedersoli[1], and Luc Van Gool[1,3]

[1] ESAT-PSI/VISICS, iMinds, KU Leuven, Belgium
[2] MPI Informatics, Saarbrücken, Germany
[3] D-ITET/CVL, ETH Zürich, Switzerland

Abstract. Face detection is a mature problem in computer vision. While diverse high performing face detectors have been proposed in the past, we present two surprising new top performance results. First, we show that a properly trained vanilla DPM reaches top performance, improving over commercial and research systems. Second, we show that a detector based on *rigid* templates - similar in structure to the Viola&Jones detector - can reach similar top performance on this task. Importantly, we discuss issues with existing evaluation benchmark and propose an improved procedure.

Fig. 1. Our proposed `HeadHunter` detector at the Oscars. Can you spot the one false positive, and one false negatives ? (hint: first rows).

1 Introduction

Face detection is a classic topic in computer vision. It is a relevant problem due to its many commercial application in a human-centric world, and as a building block for more sophisticated systems. Deployed in a myriad of consumer products (e.g. digital cameras, social networks, and smart phone applications), it is considered a mature technology. In this paper we focus on the canonical problem of face detection in a single frame of photographs taken "in the wild".

Because of its maturity, we consider it as an application particularly suitable to study core aspects of object detection. One can expect benchmarking

D. Fleet et al. (Eds.): ECCV 2014, Part IV, LNCS 8692, pp. 720–735, 2014.

datasets with a diverse set of methods available for comparison. However, despite the interest in the topic and the quantity of data available, due to the lack of a commonly accepted annotation guidelines and evaluation protocols, a fair comparison of face detectors on various datasets is still missing.

In this paper we intend to create a common ground to evaluate and compare different face detectors. We have selected the most relevant datasets for face detection, improved their annotations, and propose a modified evaluation protocol that reduces dataset bias.

With this new evaluation in hand, we set to understand "what makes a face detector (truly) tick?". We propose to compare the well known deformable parts model (DPM) [9] with the integral channels detector approach [7]. We also compare side by side face detectors originating from the research community and from commercial products. We show that despite significant progress, face detection has not yet reached saturation. Even more surprisingly, we present new top results while using a simpler architecture than competitors. Although we focus on face detection, most of the discussion is agnostic to the object class.

1.1 Contributions

- We point out that the evaluation of existing face datasets is biased due to different guidelines for the annotation. We provide improved annotations and a new evaluation criteria that copes better with these problems (section 2).
- We show that (despite common belief) face detection has not saturated, and there are still relevant open questions to explore (section 6).
- We show that (contrary to previously reported results), when properly used, a vanilla deformable part models (DPM) [9] reaches top performance on face detection, improving over more sophisticated DPM variants (section 4).
- We evaluate for the first time an integral channels detector [7,3] for the task of face detection (section 3). We show that top detection results on face detection can be obtained using a small set of *rigid* templates (i.e. without deformable parts).
- We explore which aspects of such rigid detector most impact quality, such as the number of components or the training data volume (section 5).
- We provide source code for both our improved evaluation toolbox and for training/evaluating our proposed face detector.

1.2 Related Work

Being a classic topic, there are probably thousands of papers specifically addressing the face detection problem. We present here a selection of what we consider landmark papers on the topic.

Nowadays the textbook version of a face detector is the Viola&Jones architecture [30]. It introduced the idea of computing an integral image over the greyscale input to enable fast evaluation of boosted weak classifiers based on Haar-like features. This detector provides high speed, but only moderate detection quality. This framework has been the source of inspiration for countless

Fig. 2. Example frames of the annotated datasets considered

variants [35]. Amongst them SURF cascades [16] is one of the top performers (recently introduced by Intel labs).

Thanks to its elegant formulation, its intuitive interpretation, and strong results the Deformable Parts Model (DPM) has established itself as the de-facto standard for generic object detection [9]. This approach combines the estimation of latent variables for alignment and clustering at training time, the use of multiple components and deformable parts to handle intra-class variance, and a healthy dose of engineering to make it all work robustly and fast enough. A tree-structured DPM trained with supervised parts positions was successfully applied to face detection and fiducial points estimation [36,33], showing improved results over vanilla DPM.

Some of the earlier work on face detection employed neural networks [22,10,20]. Although competitive at the time, it is unclear how well such a method would perform on modern benchmarks. The work of [20] introduced the intriguing idea of coupling pose estimation and face detection into a single inference problem.

Other than the discriminative approaches mentioned above competitive results have been attained by formulating the detection problem as an image retrieval problem [27,17].

Instead of proposing a new detector, [13] shows that adapting a detector to the context of the test image can significantly improve detection quality. Although very interesting, it is a form of "per image semi-supervised learning". In this paper we focus on the raw detection problem, when using only the information available in each candidate detection window.

In our experimental section we also compare to black box commercial systems such as Picasa (from Google), Face.com (acquired by Facebook), Olaworks (acquired by Intel), and Face++ (start-up based in China).

2   Datasets

For our experiments we use four datasets of faces acquired in an unconstrained setup (so called "in the wild"). AFLW [15] contains $\sim 26\,000$ annotated faces, that we use for training. For preliminary experiments (sections 5.1 to 5.4), and parameters tuning we use the Pascal Faces dataset [33] (851 Pascal VOC images with bounding boxes). For comparison with previous work we use AFW [36] (205 images with bounding boxes) and FDDB [12] (2845 images with ellipses annotations). See figure 2 for some example frames, which illustrate the "in the wild" aspect of our test data.

Unless otherwise specified detections are evaluated using the standard "intersection over union above 50 %" criterion [8], and quality is summarised using the average precision (AP).

2.1   Annotations and Evaluation Policies

The four datasets used in this paper are annotated by different research groups following different annotation strategies. As it stands, a face detector algorithm trained to output a specific bounding box policy cannot be properly evaluated directly on the different datasets.

In our preliminary experiments we found that adjusting the detector output towards the specific dataset annotations is key for competitive results. For most published methods it is unknown if adjustments to compensate different annotations have been made or not, making it difficult to perform a fair comparison. We want to improve this situation.

Differences in Annotations. Examples of dataset differences include: different policies for what constitutes a face (is a statue head a face? is a head rotated more than 90 degrees a face?), different sizes of annotation boxes (relative to the real world face, i.e. should the box span all facial landmarks, or include the whole head?), boxes centred differently (for lateral views, centred on the nose or on the cheeks?), and different minimum/maximum annotated face size.

All of these differences have a direct impact on the false positive and false negative evaluation metrics. If one method tunes for a specific dataset, then it will be unfairly penalized in another one. In this paper we take special care to design the comparisons as fairly as possible; we propose remedial measure for each of these issues. These measures require changes in the annotation and evaluation protocol for Pascal Faces and AFW (the FDDB dataset is immutable, see below).

New Annotations. The goal of new annotations is two fold: 1) Make sure that the bounding boxes are created using a uniform policy inside the dataset (this is imperative for proper evaluation). 2) To annotate all faces that might depend on the face presence policy.

For the new annotations, we adjusted the detection bounding boxes in Pascal Faces to match the guidelines defined in the supplementary material (similar to AFW one). The boxes in AFW already follow much stricter rules, and needed no major edits. Additionally, we added new annotations for overlooked faces and faces in challenging conditions such as small, occluded, or truncated faces. We labelled most of these new detections with an ignore flag. Methods should not be punished for their ability to detect challenging instances.

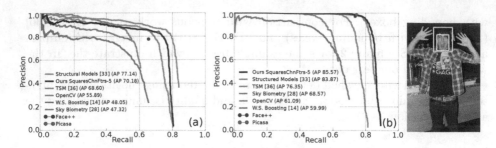

Fig. 3. Precision-recall curves of the different evaluation methods on Pascal. (a) Shows the evaluation based on the previous annotations, not compensating different guidelines. (b) Transforms the detections to reflect the test set annotation policy. (c) Green and yellow boxes show different annotation/detection policies. The green box indicates a previously missing annotations, now marked as "ignore". Detecting this face should not count as false positive.

Remedial Measures for Bounding Box Policy. Our new evaluation has a preprocessing stage that searches for a global rigid transformation of the detection output of a specific method, such as to maximize the overlap with the ground truth annotations. By searching a global scaling and translation that maximize performances we evaluate as if each method would have taken care of targeting their detections (size and position) towards the specific test set.

Note that since bounding boxes are adapted for every method in our evaluation, it becomes part of the evaluation protocol and does not advantage any specific method. The details of the estimation algorithm are provided in the supplementary material.

Remedial Measures for Different Scale Ranges. Another important aspect of the different detectors is their minimal and maximal search scale. Different search ranges result in different sets of detected bounding boxes. The search range and annotation quality/guidelines have severe impact on the overall detector quality. If one approach searches for smaller faces than specified by the dataset policy, high scoring false positives might be introduced; if a method is searching only for larger faces, it will miss out on recall. Thus using annotations and detections as-is is a no go.

For the sake of explanation let us assume a dataset has been perfectly annotated for all faces larger than 15 pixels. Different detectors will output different detection sizes, which might or might not cover the minimum size annotations. In this example, let us assume that we are interested in evaluating all faces larger than $\alpha = 30$ pixels. The naive approach would be to chop-off all annotations smaller than α, and also all detections smaller than α. However, if the detector originally triggered with a bounding box of size $\alpha - 1$ for a face of true size α, removing it will create a drop in recall (false negative). If one decides to keep detection smaller than α while dropping annotations smaller than α, then this create artificial false positives. The naive approach does not work either.

We propose to solve this problem in the following way. Given a set of annotations, the evaluation minimal size α is set to a value comfortably larger than the minimal annotation size. We introduce a second threshold β, which defines the minimal size of *detections* that we consider. We set $\beta = \sqrt{0.5 \cdot \alpha^2}$, given that our overlap over union threshold is 0.5. With β we keep all detections which would still have sufficient overlap (> 0.5 overlap over union) with a ground truth bounding box of size α, and remove all smaller ones. Finally, to avoid small false positives, we mark all annotations smaller than α with the "ignore" flag. With these two thresholds we reduce the border effects, and obtain the desired unbiased evaluation. In our evaluation we set set α to 30 pixels.

Impact of the New Protocol. To summarize our new protocol for Pascal and AFW datasets include: a) new annotations, b) a transformation of the detection bounding boxes to adapt each algorithm to each dataset, c) a new handling of detection windows on the border of the annotated scale range.

To give an impression about the importance of a proper evaluation, in figure 3 we compare the precision-recall curves of several methods on the Pascal Faces dataset. Sub-figures 3a and 3b show, respectively, results with the original annotations and the standard protocol (Pascal VOC [8]), and with our new annotations and protocol. Many detections, which are counted as errors in figure 3a are actually wrongly annotated. This produces an artificial slope on all the curves that biases the results. Importantly, notice how the change of evaluation protocol (from figure 3a to figure 3b) also produces a *different ranking* for the methods.

FDDB Dataset. This dataset has a good annotation quality, provides a publicly available evaluation toolbox, and collects results online. All of these are best practices. Unfortunately, the FDDB protocol calls for sharing the ROC curves, not the detection bounding boxes. Without these boxes it is impossible to improve the evaluation, or to have a in-depth analysis of the different detection methods. We do not (cannot) use our new evaluation protocol for the FDDB dataset.

For our own methods we convert our detection bounding boxes into ellipses based on the dataset annotation description [12]. The FDDB evaluation protocol foresees to match bounding boxes with their annotation ellipses using the Pascal VOC criterion. Changing the output format from bounding boxes to ellipses immediately increases the overlap region, showing a significant positive impact on the result curve. Here again, it is unclear which other methods make similar adjustments.

Our evaluation tools, and the new annotations for Pascal Faces and AFW, will be released together with this paper. We hope that future detection benchmarks will consider in their design the issues raised here.

3   Integral Channel Features Detector

One of the key ingredients in the classic Viola&Jones face detector [30] is the use of an integral image (summed area table) for fast features computation. This idea is generalised by the integral channels features framework described in [7]. Instead of computing an integral image over a single input greyscale channel, it is proposed to define an arbitrary set of feature channels (feature maps), such as quantised oriented image gradient, colour, linear filter responses, etc. The integral images defined over these channels allow to quickly sum over arbitrary rectangular pooling regions. The object detector is trained by boosting a forest of trees built using such rectangular pooling regions as input features.

Somewhat surprisingly, this combination of classic ingredients (oriented gradient and colour feature maps, decision trees, and Adaboost) has shown top performance on tasks such as pedestrian detection [3], traffic signs detection [19], and feature points matching [29]. It reaches higher pedestrian detection quality than more sophisticated methods using deformable parts [9], more complex features [31], non-linear kernels [18] or a deep architecture [26].

We propose to adapt the integral channels detector to the task of face detection. We purposely use a plain setup, similar to [7,3,19]. Unless otherwise specified we use simple gradient magnitude channels (six for quantised orientations, one for magnitude channel), and colour channels (LUV colour space). We use shallow boosted trees of depth two (three stumps per tree).

The main difference from previous instances of this framework is that instead of using a single template per object category, we combine a set of templates to represent the face category (so called "components") [9,25]. Each component captures a fraction of the intra-class diversity of faces. At test time all templates are evaluated, and their detections merged during non-maximum suppression.

3.1   Baseline Detector

Our baseline detector `SquaresChnFtrs-5` consists of 5 components, clustered using the yaw angle annotations. We collected a total of 15 106 samples from the AFLW database [15] to train 5 models (components) of size 80 × 80 pixels.

A frontal face detector (yaw angle ±20 degrees) and two side views (20 → 60 and 60 → 100 degrees) are trained using 6 752, 5 810, and 2 544 samples respectively. Pitch and roll are kept between ±22.5 degrees. As negative samples we use 3 652 person-free images from the Pascal VOC database [8]. The remaining two models are mirrored version of the side views. See supplementary material for details on the learned models and their training samples.

For each component the training is similar to the `SquaresChnFtrs` setup described in [3], unless otherwise specified we use the same parameters. The features are drawn from a pool containing all possible square features (28 700). We perform 4 rounds of bootstrapping to ensure that no additional false positives can be found in our negative training data. Our final component detector consists of an Adaboost classifier with 2 000 weak learners. For non-maximum suppression we join the candidate detection from all components and suppress them together using the overlap over min-area criterion as described in [7, addendum], the overlap threshold is set to 0.3.

In the experiments of section 5 we explore the design space of our detector, and in section 5.5 we describe a stronger detector than our baseline.

3.2 Detection Speed

By using aggressive (soft and crosstalk) cascades and reducing features computation across scales [2,6], it has been shown that integral channels detectors can reach fast detection rates of the order of ~ 50 Hz for 640×480 pixels images (either on GPU or multi-core CPU). The bulk of time is spent in the weak classifiers evaluation.

In our setup adding more templates to evaluate costs a linear decrease in speed. This could be mitigated by using a hard cascade where a short classifier is first evaluated (trained on all views), before deciding to evaluate all view-specific classifiers. Our implementation is not speed-aware, however even with a conservative estimate (5 components $\rightarrow$ 5 $\times$ slow-down) it seems reasonable to believe that the proposed approach can reach frame-rate detection speeds of ~ 10 Hz once tuned for speed.

4 Building the DPM Baseline

Other than considering an evolved version of the Viola&Jones detector, we would like to also consider an evolved version of the classic HOG+SVM [4]. As a reference baseline we train a DPM using the same training data as SquaresChnFtrs-5. We use publicly available DPM version 5 [9].

We define the DPM components using the same three views as Squares-ChnFtrs-5 (defined in section 3.1), due to mirroring this results in 6 components. Each component has one root template

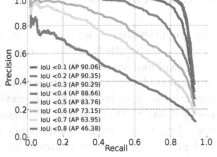

Fig. 4. For the DPM detector, the non-maximum suppression overlap (intersection over union, IoU) threshold is an important parameter. The default value of 0.5 leads to poor performance.

and 8 parts. Besides the initialization of the components we keep all other training parameters to default.

We found that a test time the non-maximum suppression (NMS) overlap threshold is a crucial parameter. Figure 4 shows our DPM evaluated over the Pascal Faces dataset using different thresholds. When using the default value 0.5 the detection performance is significantly lower than when using an an adequate one (we use 0.3). When setting the NMS threshold to the default value of 0.5, the low performance DPM results are consistent with the previously reported one [36]. In the supplementary material we have the equivalent plot for Squares-ChnFtrs-5.

As will be discussed in section 6, to our surprise, our DPM baseline turns out to match or outperform *all other methods,* including more sophisticated DPM

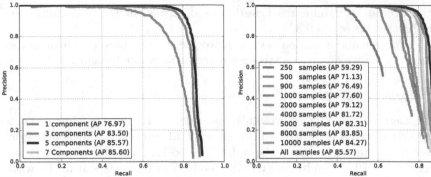

Fig. 5. Quality versus number of compon- **Fig. 6.** Quality versus number of training ents. AP: average precision. samples.

variants. We attribute the strong results to the proper use of available training data, and to noticing the importance of appropriate non-maximum suppression.

5   Experiments

We are interested in understanding which ingredients are critical for good face detection. The effect of the parameters of the integral channels detector have been explored in previous work on pedestrian detection [7,3]. A few of them are repeated for faces and reported in the supplementary material (overall we observe the same trends). In this section we present experiments (over the Pascal Faces dataset) that explore orthogonal aspects not covered by previous work, regarding view-specific components (§5.1), the amount of training data (§6), and skin aware feature channels (§5.3). Along them, when relevant, we draw parallel comparisons with the DPM approach. In all plots, the thick black line corresponds to our `SquaresChnFtrs-5` baseline detector (§3.1). In section 6 we provide a comparative evaluation with other face detectors.

5.1   How Many Multi-view Components ?

The number of components is considered to be a critical ingredient for high quality detections [5]. Figure 5 shows the impact of the number of components on the detection quality. When adding new components we only change the steps of the yaw angle (instead of introducing views which where not considered in our baseline model, such as faces with > 22.5 degree roll and pitch angles).

It can be seen that the quality of the integral channel features detector does not improve any further past 5 components. As an increase in the number of components directly maps to a decrease in detection speed, using more components seems not to be beneficial for our use case. Choosing 5 components for our baseline strikes a good balance between detection quality and detection speed. If accurate face pose detection is of interest, more components may help to get better initial pose estimates.

Our comparative experiments with DPM are done using 6 components, these are the same 5 components, plus one obtained by mirroring the frontal face (default behaviour of the DPMv5 source code [9]).

5.2 How Much Training Data ?

Collecting training data is a labour intensive task. The different methods evaluated in this paper differ in the number of training samples (900 to > 20 000) and also in the type of annotations (from simple bounding boxes to facial landmarks and face orientation). The amount and quality of the training data can highly influence the performance of a detector. Exploring the influence of the amount of annotations on all other methods is beyond the scope of this paper, we have to assume that other methods explored this option to present a competitive face detector.

To quantify how our approach scales with the amount of training data, we evaluate the impact of varying the amount of training data in terms of precision and recall. In figure 6 we plot the precision-recall curves on the Pascal Faces dataset when gradually varying the number of samples from 250 to the entire training data. Our SquaresChnFtrs-5 performs quite poorly when trained with only a few samples. By adding more training data the recall can be steadily improved without affecting precision. Our results indicate that the detection quality could further be improved by using an even larger training set.

When doing a similar experiment for our DPM we observe that with as few as 500 samples it reaches already 95 % of its final average precision (AP) value. Similar to SquaresChnFtrs-5, increasing the number of samples improves its recall.

The number of training samples also highly influences the training time. When using all available training data, SquaresChnFtrs-5 will be trained in less than 6h, while DPM needs roughly one week.

5.3 Which Colour Channels ?

One difference between our baseline detector (§3.1) and a vanilla HOG template (used in DPMs), is the use of LUV colour channels. Since faces have a discriminative colour distribution, one wonders how much colour helps for the task. In figure 8 we investigate the effect of colour for face detection. We consider the following channels (see figure 7): HOG, the gradient magnitude and quantized orientations; the L luminance channel (grey image); the U chromaticity channel, which is known to respond to skin colour; RmG is the subtraction of the red and green channels, included because $20 < R - G < 80$ is the simplest known skin colour detector [1]; Skin is a naive Bayes skin colour classifier trained on the dbskin dataset [23].

The results figure 8 shows that the colour information mainly affects the recall. Unsurprisingly the Skin channel is the most informative, we also confirm that U captures relevant information for skin detection, improving over RmG. Even the

Fig. 7. Example of colour channels considered, see section 5.3

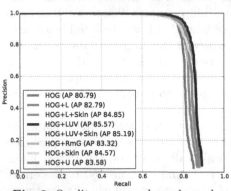

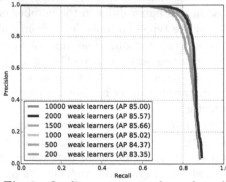

Fig. 8. Quality versus colour channels

Fig. 9. Quality versus number of weak classifiers.

weakest colour channel improves over the L greyscale channel, indicating that chromaticity is indeed relevant for the task.

Finally, when probing combinations such as HOG+L+Skin or HOG+LUV+Skin we see no improvement compared to the vanilla HOG+LUV. This indicates that, for this task, the classifier is able to extract the relevant information directly from the LUV channels, without requiring the use of custom made channels.

5.4   How Many Weak Classifiers ?

The number of weak classifiers boosted to build the strong classifier is an important parameter which is usually set to a fixed value. We observed that during training, already a small amount of weak learners is enough to successfully separate the positive and negative samples (20 stages before bootstrapping, 100 stages after the last bootstrapping stage). Since Adaboost lacks a well understood regularization mechanism [24], depending on the training data, adding more weak classifiers could lead to over-fitting.

Figure 9 shows the influence of the classifier length on the detection quality. A small amount of only 200 weak learners is already enough to get decent detection quality of 82.8% average precision. Since weak classifiers evaluation is the speed bottleneck, using a smaller number of weak learners is of special interest when targeting high detection speed.

On the other side, it can be observed that even with 10 000 Adaboost stages, the performance does still not deteriorate. This shows that when using faces for training, the system is robust to the number of weak classifiers.

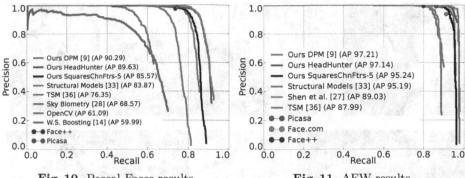

Fig. 10. Pascal Faces results   **Fig. 11.** AFW results

To match previous setups [7,3] we set the number of weak classifiers in our baseline to 2000, even though figure 9 shows that the detection quality already saturates with 1500 classifiers.

5.5 Building a Strong Face Detector

For our final face detector model we focus on quality to see how competitive a detector based on rigid templates can be. To that end we apply previous results presented in [3]. In that paper, the authors present three strategies to improve the quality of an integral channel features detector. First, we follow their suggestion by applying global normalization [21] before running the detector. Second, we train a multi-scale model by doubling each template (component) with an additional one of twice its size. Third, the templates are trained using the maximum amount of pooling features: all possible rectangles for the the baseline, and all possible squares for the largest templates (see [3]).

As can be seen by the high average precision of our baseline (e.g. figure 5), most views are well captured by our training data. On the other hand, as mentioned in section 5.2, being a rigid model, our detector has difficulties to handle unseen views (compared to a DPM, which generalizes via deformations). To improve recall we add copies of the training data with a rotation of 35 degrees. We use these to train 6 additional components that handle

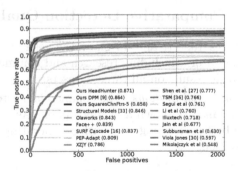

Fig. 12. FDDB results

tilted faces. Using the eleven (5 + 6) components together provides further improvement in detection quality (mainly increase in recall).

We name our final strong multi-scales model the **HeadHunter** detector. This detector consists in total of 22 templates, 11 for each scale. Each scale uses 5

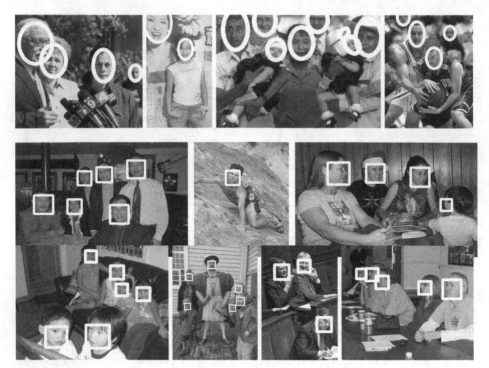

Fig. 13. Qualitative `HeadHunter` detection results from FDDB (top row), Pascal Faces (middle row), and AFW (bottom row).

templates for the frontal faces and 6 for the rotated faces. We train a total of 12 different templates, the remaining 10 templates are generated via mirroring.

6   Comparative Detection Quality

Figures 10, 11, and 12 show the results of our methods compared to many competitors (including research and commercial systems). Only a few methods provide results on all three datasets.

Commercial Systems. The commercial systems often do not provide confidence score and are shown as a single point. As can be seen these methods are among the best performing ones with an operating point clearly chosen to provide high precision.

Annotation Type. One of the highest scoring competitors to ours is the DPM based structured models method [34,33]. However, similarly to TSM (Tree Parts Model) [36], this method requires the annotation of facial landmarks, while we need only the bounding boxes. Furthermore, the method uses also context (upper body detector) to improve results, although it is not clear how important that is for the final results. We note that already a single template of our baseline (figure 5) matches the performances of TSM [36].

Common Approaches. Most approaches rely either on a Viola&Jones like frame-work (e.g. Face++,), or HOG+SVM based (e.g. TSM, Structured Models, DPM). Even if methods are based on these two frameworks the range of results can vary a lot. This underlines once again how the task of object detection is sensitive to small details and therefore in depth analysis such as this one are required.

DPM Results. Overall it is quite striking to notice that a properly trained DPM baseline obtains top performance across all datasets considered (updating pre-viously reported results, such as [36]). This is a testament to the importance of careful baselines design, the importance of low-level details (a single threshold value makes the difference between under-performing to top performing), and the value of open source release of research material.

In parallel to the preparation of this manuscript Yan et al. [32] independently reported results DPM for the AFW dataset which are consistent to our results. Their work however is not focused on detection quality, and their high performing results are left unexplained there. Our discussion of section 4 details the critical ingredients for a high quality DPM face detector.

Rigid Templates. Although our DPM reaches top performance, the experiments also show that HeadHunter, a set of rigid templates, essentially reaches the same performance. This indicates that parts are useful but not critical to reach top performance. As long as enough training data is available to cover pose diversity, a small set of rigid templates will detect faces as good as anything else.

Problem Saturation. The difference in recall at high precision between 11 and 10 indicates that when increasing dataset difficulty, existing methods fail to reach full recall. This shows there is still a measurable gap before matching human performance. The missing recall in 12 seems mainly due to out-of-focus image blur, one could consider this a separate problem. A detailed analysis of the causes of failure for each detector type still remains to be done [11].

Open Questions. Not only detection quality has not saturated, but also multiple questions remain open, for example: the DPM and HeadHunter use mainly or-thogonal strategies to improve detection quality; how can deformable parts and strong boosted templates be used together best? If blur causes missing recall in FDDB; how to best handle this case? There is not yet strong evidence that fiducial points annotation can help build better detectors; how best to exploit this data?

7   Conclusion and Future Work

In this work we have shown that even if face detection is a quite mature field, there is still room for improvements in terms of both detection performance as well as evaluation protocols. We have shown that the evaluation protocol plays an important role, analysed the current issue and provided a thorough and fair evaluation of face detectors in different datasets. We also provide a update evaluation method, which might well be suitable for other detection evaluation datasets.

It turns out that for face detection the children of two classic detection approaches, Viola&Jones and HOG+SVM, are the best performing methods. Both our DPM and integral channel features model, HeadHunter, reach top performance on the task. Rigid templates provide excellent quality for many classes, especially if sufficient training data is available. DPMs are still the method of choice if only few training samples are available and at the same time high recall is of essence. We believe that our findings are an important cue for the next generation of detectors, probably combining the capacity of representation provided the integral channel features detector with the powerful generalization induced by modelling deformations.

Acknowledgement. Many thanks to Junjie Yan for access to Pascal Faces result curves. Work supported by the EU project EUROPA2, and the Cametron project.

References

1. Al-Shehri, S.A.: A simple and novel method for skin detection and face locating and tracking. In: Masoodian, M., Jones, S., Rogers, B. (eds.) APCHI 2004. LNCS, vol. 3101, pp. 1–8. Springer, Heidelberg (2004)
2. Benenson, R., Mathias, M., Timofte, R., Van Gool, L.: Pedestrian detection at 100 frames per second. In: CVPR (2012)
3. Benenson, R., Mathias, M., Tuytelaars, T., Van Gool, L.: Seeking the strongest rigid detector. In: CVPR (2013)
4. Dalal, N., Triggs, B.: Histograms of oriented gradients for human detection. In: CVPR (2005)
5. Divvala, S.K., Efros, A.A., Hebert, M.: How important are deformable parts in the deformable parts model? In: Fusiello, A., Murino, V., Cucchiara, R. (eds.) ECCV 2012 Ws/Demos, Part III. LNCS, vol. 7585, pp. 31–40. Springer, Heidelberg (2012)
6. Dollár, P., Appel, R., Kienzle, W.: Crosstalk cascades for frame-rate pedestrian detection. In: Fitzgibbon, A., Lazebnik, S., Perona, P., Sato, Y., Schmid, C. (eds.) ECCV 2012, Part II. LNCS, vol. 7573, pp. 645–659. Springer, Heidelberg (2012)
7. Dollár, P., Tu, Z., Perona, P., Belongie, S.: Integral channel features. In: BMVC (2009)
8. Everingham, M., Van Gool, L., Williams, C.K.I., Winn, J., Zisserman, A.: The PASCAL Visual Object Classes Challenge (2008)
9. Felzenszwalb, P., Girshick, R., McAllester, D., Ramanan, D.: Object detection with discriminatively trained part-based models. PAMI (2010)
10. Garcia, C., Delakis, M.: Convolutional face finder: A neural architecture for fast and robust face detection. PAMI (2004)
11. Hoiem, D., Chodpathumwan, Y., Dai, Q.: Diagnosing error in object detectors. In: Fitzgibbon, A., Lazebnik, S., Perona, P., Sato, Y., Schmid, C. (eds.) ECCV 2012, Part III. LNCS, vol. 7574, pp. 340–353. Springer, Heidelberg (2012)
12. Jain, V., Learned-Miller, E.: Fddb: A benchmark for face detection in unconstrained settings. Tech. Rep. UM-CS-2010-009, University of Massachusetts, Amherst (2010)

13. Jain, V., Learned-Miller, E.: Online domain adaptation of a pre-trained cascade of classifiers. In: CVPR (2011)
14. Kalal, Z., Matas, J., Mikolajczyk, K.: Weighted sampling for large-scale boosting. In: Everingham, M., Needham, C.J., Fraile, R. (eds.) BMVC. British Machine Vision Association (2008)
15. Koestinger, M., Wohlhart, P., Roth, P.M., Bischof, H.: Annotated facial landmarks in the wild: A large-scale, real-world database for facial landmark localization. In: ICCV BeFIT Workshop (2011)
16. Li, J., Zhang, Y.: Learning surf cascade for fast and accurate object detection. In: CVPR (2013)
17. Ma, K., Ben-Arie, J.: Vector array based multi-view face detection with compound exemplars. In: CVPR (2012)
18. Maji, S., Berg, A., Malik, J.: Classi cation using intersection kernel support vector machines is efficient. In: CVPR (2008)
19. Mathias, M., Timofte, R., Benenson, R., Van Gool, L.: Traffic sign recognition - how far are we from the solution? In: ICJNN (2013)
20. Osadchy, M., LeCun, Y., Miller, M.: Synergistic face detection and pose estimation with energy-based models. JMLR (2007)
21. Rizzi, A., Gatta, C., Marini, D.: A new algorithm for unsupervised global and local color correction. Pattern Recognition Letters (2003)
22. Rowley, H., Baluja, S., Kanade, T.: Neural network-based face detection. PAMI (1998)
23. Ruiz-del-Solar, J., Verschae, R.: Skin detection using neighborhood information. In: FG, Seoul, Korea, May 17-19, pp. 463–468 (2004)
24. Schapire, R.E.: Explaining adaboost. In: Empirical Inference: Festschrift in Honor of Vladimir N. Vapnik (2013)
25. Schneiderman, H., Kanade, T.: Object detection using the statistics of parts. IJCV (2004)
26. Sermanet, P., Kavukcuoglu, K., Chintala, S., LeCun, Y.: Pedestrian detection with unsupervised multi-stage feature learning. In: CVPR (2013)
27. Shen, X., Lin, Z., Brandt, J., Wuk, Y.: Detecting and aligning faces by image retrieval. In: CVPR (2013)
28. SkyBiometry, http://www.skybiometry.com
29. Trzcinski, T., Christoudias, C.M., Fua, P., Lepetit, V.: Boosting binary keypoint descriptors. In: CVPR (2013)
30. Viola, P., Jones, M.: Robust real-time face detection. IJCV (2004)
31. Walk, S., Majer, N., Schindler, K., Schiele, B.: New features and insights for pedestrian detection. In: CVPR (2010)
32. Yan, J., Lei, Z., Wen, L., Li, S.Z.: The fastest deformable part model for object detection. In: CVPR (June 2014)
33. Yan, J., Zhang, X., Lei, Z., Li, S.: Face detection by structural models. Image and Vision Computing (2013)
34. Yan, J., Zhang, X., Lei, Z., Li, S.: Real-time high performance deformable model for face detection in the wild. In: ICB (2013)
35. Zhang, C., Zhang, Z.: A survey of recent advances in face detection. Tech. rep., Microsoft Research (2010)
36. Zhu, X., Ramanan, D.: Face detection, pose estimation, and landmark localization in the wild. In: CVPR (2012)

On Image Contours of Projective Shapes

Jean Ponce[1],[*] and Martial Hebert[2]

[1] Department of Computer Science,
Ecole Normale Supérieure, France
[2] Robotics Institute,
Carnegie-Mellon University, USA

Abstract. This paper revisits classical properties of the outlines of solid shapes bounded by smooth surfaces, and shows that they can be established in a purely projective setting, without appealing to Euclidean measurements such as normals or curvatures. In particular, we give new synthetic proofs of Koenderink's famous theorem on convexities and concavities of the image contour, and of the fact that the rim turns in the same direction as the viewpoint in the tangent plane at a convex point, and in the opposite direction at a hyperbolic point. This suggests that projective geometry should not be viewed merely as an analytical device for linearizing calculations (its main role in structure from motion), but as the proper framework for studying the relation between solid shape and its perspective projections. Unlike previous work in this area, the proposed approach does not require an oriented setting, nor does it rely on any choice of coordinate system or analytical considerations.

1 Introduction

Under perspective projection, the image (occluding) contour of a solid shape is the intersection of the retina with the boundary of a cone tangent to the shape's surface, with apex at the pinhole. It is the projection of the rim curve where the cone and the surface meet tangentially.

What does the occluding contour tell us about solid shape? This is the question asked, and largely answered by Jan Koenderink in his landmark 1984 paper [12]. Specifically, contradicting an earlier claim by David Marr [18] stating that inflections of image contours do not (in general) convey any information about three-dimensional shape, Koenderink proved a remarkable result: The inflections of the image contour of a solid bounded by a smooth surface are the projections of parabolic points, where the Gaussian curvature of the surface vanishes. The convex points of the contour are projections of convex points of the surface, and its concave points are the images of saddle-shaped, hyperbolic points. The concave parts of the surface themselves never show up on the contour, for they are hidden from view by the solid itself.

Koenderink's proof holds for both orthographic and perspective projection, and it is simple and elegant (see [1,5,6,8,22] for variants). It is also firmly anchored in Euclidean (differential) geometry, since it largely relies on concepts such as curve and surface normals and curvatures. This paper revisits Koenderink's question in the more general

---

[*] Willow project team. DI/ENS, ENS/CNRS/Inria UMR 8548.

D. Fleet et al. (Eds.): ECCV 2014, Part IV, LNCS 8692, pp. 736–749, 2014.

setting of projective geometry, where Euclidean measurements such as distances, angles, and curvatures are forbidden, but more primitive incidence, tangency and more generally contact properties are still available.

Lazebnik and Ponce addressed the same problem in [17], and showed that Koenderink's results are in fact valid in *oriented* projective geometry [21]. In this setting, points, lines, and planes are all oriented, which allows for deciding, for example, on which side of a plane a point lies, but requires somewhat awkward constructions such as maintaining two oriented copies of each point. We go one step further in this presentation, and prove that Koenderink's results holds in classical projective geometry, without the need for such constructions (Theorems 1 and 2). Likewise, we show that the rim turns in the same direction as the pinhole at a convex point, and in the opposite direction at a hyperbolic one (Theorem 3), a well known property in Euclidean geometry, extended to oriented projective geometry in [17].

While the paper does not introduce new theorems, it introduces new ways of manipulating concepts previously restricted to the Euclidean or oriented projective realms. Stated plainly, basic properties of the visual world that were known to be true in Euclidean or oriented projective settings are shown to be true in the much more general setting of plain projective geometry and, unlike most proofs in geometric computer vision, that require global or local coordinate systems and analytical parameterizations [1,5,6,8,12,17,22], ours are purely synthetic and do not require such an apparatus. Thus plain projective geometry is the appropriate framework for studying these properties.

We believe that the type of inquiry pursued in this paper is important because it identifies projective geometry as the natural setting for the qualitative study of the visual world: Koenderink's result (Theorems 1 and 2) tells us about the appearance of a solid shape in one image. Theorem 3 tells us about the rim moves with the viewpoint, and is therefore a first step toward understanding how the appearance of a solid changes in multiple pictures. We will come back to the latter point in Section 6.

The rest of this presentation is organized as follows: We recall basic facts about the local shape of curves and surfaces in classical (differential) projective geometry in Section 2. We prove in Section 3 that inflections of the contour are the projections of parabolic points (Theorem 1), which can be seen as a weak version of Koenderink's theorem. The strong version (Theorem 2) is proven in Section 4, and the rim motion is characterized by Theorem 3 in Section 5. We conclude by a brief discussion of future work in Section 6.

2 The Local Projective Shape of Curves and Surfaces

2.1 Basic Setting

We assume that objects of interest live in the real projective space $\mathbb{P}^m$, $m = 2$ or 3, which can be defined as the quotient of $\mathbb{R}^m \setminus \{0\}$ by the equivalence relation identifying vectors that are nonzero multiples of each other [4]. In our context, it is perhaps better viewed as a manifold, locally affine (in fact the complement of any hyperplane in $\mathbb{P}^m$ has an affine structure) but globally exempt of affine exceptions such as non-intersecting (parallel) coplanar lines or planes. Put more plainly, a projective plane (for example), looks locally just like an affine plane. On the other hand, one has to be mindful of the fact that, for example, a line does not split a projective plane into two distinct components, nor does a plane split space into two components, and it is in general meaningless to talk about the "two sides" of such a line or plane. The whole arsenal of Euclidean measurements such as length or angle is also missing, along with the notions of normal, curvature, etc. Projective transformations (or collineations) are isomorphisms between projective spaces, and they preserve relations such as incidence or contact, as well as certain numerical invariants such as cross-ratios and homogeneous coordinates.

A perspective camera is defined in $\mathbb{P}^3$ by its pinhole o and retinal plane Π. It maps any point in $\mathbb{P}^3 \setminus \{o\}$ onto the point y of the retina Π where the line joining o to x intersects that plane [20]. We are interested in this paper in qualitative relations between objects of $\mathbb{P}^3$ and their perspective projections that are invariant under projective transformations.

The objects considered in this paper are solid, opaque, rigid bodies, bounded by smooth surfaces. These bodies will be called solids for short from now on. Certain visual features such as points, lines or curves drawn on these surfaces, are observed by cameras in the form of their projections onto some retinal plane. The images of the solids themselves, their shadows, so to speak, also form solid regions on the retinas, and they are in general bounded by piecewise-smooth curves.

Our setting excludes "hanging" threads for example, but so be it, and, as argued in [13], it will simplify our arguments. In particular, this will allow us to easily generalize the familiar notions of (local) convexity and concavity to the projective setting. More importantly, the definitions below are intuitive and similar to those used in Euclidean geometry. Yet, they do not rely in any way on the Euclidean machinery of curve and surface normals and curvatures.

2.2   Flatland

Let us start in Flatland—that is, restrict the world to a (projective) plane, equipped with its natural topology. A curve of the projective plane is said to be *smooth* when it admits a unique tangent at every point. Its inflections and cusps of both kinds can be defined as usual. A *piecewise-smooth* curve is continuous and smooth everywhere except at isolated points where it may admit multiple tangents.

¿From a topological viewpoint, there are two kinds of simple (no crossing) connected curves in $\mathbb{P}^2$, one-sided curves (like straight lines), and two-sided ones, called *ovals*, that split the plane into two components, one, called the interior of the oval, homeomorphic to a disc, and the other, called its exterior, homeomorphic to a Möbius strip. We limit our attention in this section to *solid regions* ω of the plane, defined as the closure of the interior of an oval $\partial\omega$.

We shall say that a piecewise-smooth oval $\partial\omega$ is (locally) *convex* at some point x when there exists a line passing through x and (locally) contained in the (closure of the) exterior of ω, and that it is (locally) *concave* in x when there exists a line passing through that point and (locally) contained in the (closure of the) interior of ω. Convex and concave subsets of $\partial\omega$ form connected arcs of this curve, and they are separated by inflections and cusps of the second kind.

A subset ω of the affine plane is said to be convex when the segment joining any two of its points is itself a subset of ω. This definition is problematic in the projective case because there are always two "antipodal" segments joining two points. This has led previous studies of local shape in computer vision [17] to rely on notions from oriented projective geometry [21]. Limiting our attention to curves bounding solid regions avoids this difficulty.

2.3   In the Round

Let us now move to the slightly more complicated world of surfaces bounding solid bodies defined "in the round"—that is, in the projective model we will adopt from now on for the three-dimensional world surrounding us.

The tangent plane π at a point x on a smooth surface σ (whether σ is orientable or not) is the plane that contains all the tangents to the curves drawn on σ and passing through x. The point x can be classified as elliptic, hyperbolic, or parabolic according to the way σ intersects its tangent plane π there (Figure 1): At an elliptic point, the intersection of σ and π consists of x itself, and σ locally lies on one side of π there (let us emphasize that this statement is only valid *locally*—that is, in some small neighborhood of x since, like a line in a projective plane, π does not split $\mathbb{P}^3$ into two distinct components). At a hyperbolic point, on the other hand, σ and π meet along two *asymptotic curves* intersecting in x, and the surface traverses its tangent plane. Finally, at a parabolic point, σ and π intersect transversally along a curve that cusps there. Elliptic and hyperbolic subsets of smooth surfaces form connected regions, and they are separated by parabolic curves. Note that all the notions defined in this paragraph are purely projective, and depend in no way on Euclidean devices since they are entirely based on incidence and tangency relations.

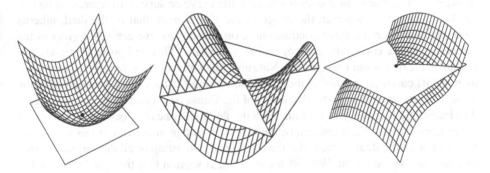

Fig. 1. The local shape of a surface. From left to right: an elliptic point, a hyperbolic point, and a parabolic point. (Reproduced with permission from the authors of [17].)

For simplicity, we define a solid as the closure of the interior of an oriented, connected and smooth surface, admitting a single tangent plane at each point. We shall say that the surface $\sigma = \partial\omega$ bounding some solid ω is (locally) *convex* at some elliptic point x when the tangent plane in x (locally) contained in the (closure of the) exterior of ω, and that it is (locally) *concave* in x when it is contained instead in the (closure of the) interior of ω.

As noted earlier, the image of ω is the intersection of the retinal plane Π with the solid cone tangent to σ with the pinhole o as its apex. The image contour formed by its boundary is an oval with piecewise-smooth boundary having at most two tangents at any point.[1] The intersection curve between the surface of the cone and σ is the rim curve γ. When x is a concave point, it cannot be visible because the line between o and x is tangent to σ, and thus locally contained in the interior of ω. We will use this fact in the proof of Theorem 2 in Section 4.

2.4   The Gauss Map

In Euclidean geometry, the Gauss map associates with every point on an oriented smooth curve γ drawn in a plane the point of the unit circle centered at the origin corresponding to the tip of its normal. Its folds correspond to inflections and cusps of the second kind. Likewise, the Gauss map associates with every point on the smooth oriented surface the point of the unit sphere centered at the origin corresponding to the tip of its normal. Interestingly, under orthographic projection, the Gaussian image of the rim is a great circle of the sphere, orthogonal to the projection direction. It is identical to the Gaussian image of the contour itself. This has been used in [10] to prove the weak version of Koenderink's theorem, namely that inflections of the contour are the projections of parabolic points, in the Euclidean case.

In projective geometry, the Gauss map associates instead with each point on a curve its tangent line (Figure 2[a,b]). Its image is the dual of the curve. This time, the cusps of the dual correspond to inflections and cusps of the second kind. Double points of the Gaussian image correspond to bitangents of the curve. The Gauss map also associates with every point on a surface its tangent plane (Figure 2[c,d]). Note that the definition of the projective Gauss map does not require the curve or surface of interest to be orientable. When it is, however, the image of the Gauss map, that is, the dual, inherits an orientation from the corresponding curve or surface, and we can talk *locally* of the orientation of the corresponding tangent line or surface. This will prove extremely important in the rest of our presentation. Note also that some of the properties of the Gauss map and its cusps established in the Euclidean setting [2] have been generalized to the projective one in [19]. In particular, cusps of the Gauss map correspond to the (tangential) intersections of the parabolic line with the flecnodal one (the locus of inflections of the asymptotic curves). Interestingly, the Gaussian image of the rim in this case is the intersection of the dual surface with the dual plane consisting of all the (primal) planes that contain the viewpoint. We will see in the next section that this can be be used to prove the weak version of Koenderink's theorem in the projective case.

Note: The proofs of the classical results used in our presentation all assume that certain genericity conditions are satisfied [7,19], that is (informally), that the surfaces considered are "sufficiently general", thus excluding quadrics, toruses, etc. We assume throughout the rest of this presentation that these genericity conditions are indeed satisfied.

---

[1] Points with multiple tangents may occur for exceptional viewpoints.

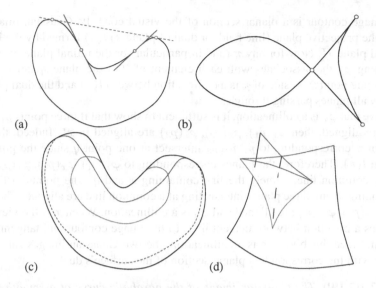

Fig. 2. Dual curves and surfaces: (a) a planar curve, with its inflections and bitangent; (b) its dual, with the cusps and double point associated with the inflections and bitangent; (c) a surface, with its parabolic line (in green) and a rim curve (in red); and (d) (part of) its dual, with the cuspidal edge associated with the parabolic line and the planar section corresponding to the rim. Best seen in color.

3 Koenderink's Theorem: Weak Version

We first characterize the type of rim points corresponding to inflections of the image contour:

Theorem 1. *Under perspective projection, the inflections of the image contour of a smooth surface are the images of parabolic points.*

The Euclidean version of this theorem was proven by Koenderink in [12]. We now show that it also holds under a pure projective setting. We do so by first clarifying the relationship between the Gaussian image of the image contour and that of the surface. We then use this result to connect Theorem 1 to a known (projective) property of the Gaussian images of curves of smooth surfaces.

Lemma 1. *Under perspective projection, the rim of a surface and its image contour have the same Gaussian image, which is a planar section of the Gaussian image of the surface itself by the dual plane associated with the viewpoint.*

Proof. By definition, the rim of a surface and the visual cone tangent to it with apex at the viewpoint share the same Gaussian image. In addition, the dual of a surface's rim is a planar section of its dual. More precisely, the Gaussian image of the rim is the intersection of the Gaussian image of the surface with the dual plane formed by all (primal) planes passing through the viewpoint.

The image contour is a planar section of the visual cone. Its Gaussian image is a curve in the projective plane (line field, or dual of plane π) $l(\pi)$ formed by the lines of the retinal plane Π. Now for any π (and in particular for the retinal plane of course), the mapping φ_x that associates with each element of $l(\pi)$ the plane spanned by that line and some point x outside of π is a collineation between $l(\pi)$ and the dual plane x^* formed by all planes passing through x.

To prove that φ_x is a collineation, it is sufficient to show that if three points p_1, p_2, p_3 in $l(\pi)$ are aligned, then $\varphi_x(p_1), \varphi_x(p_2), \varphi_x(p_3)$ are aligned in x^*. Indeed, the lines l_1, l_2, l_3 in π corresponding to p_1, p_2, p_3 intersect at one point q since the points are aligned in $l(\pi)$. Therefore, the planes corresponding to $\varphi_x(p_1), \varphi_x(p_2), \varphi_x(p_3)$ must meet at a common line, namely the line containing x and q. The points in the dual corresponding to any three planes intersecting at a common line are aligned. Therefore, $\varphi_x(p_1), \varphi_x(p_2), \varphi_x(p_3)$ are aligned and φ_x is a collineation. When x is the viewpoint, φ_x induces a bijection between tangent lines to the image contour and tangent planes to the rim. Since this bijection is a collineation, the two Gaussian images can thus be identified with the corresponding planar section of the surface's dual.   □

Lemma 2 ([7,19]). *The Gaussian image of the parabolic curve of a smooth surface consists of cuspidal edges with isolated swallowtail points.*

Theorem 1 immediately follows from Lemmas 1 and 2 by noting that a planar section of a cuspidal edge is in general a cusp (Figure 2[d]).

4   Koenderink's Theorem: Strong Version

The weak version of Koenderink's theorem does not require the observed surface σ to be oriented. Its strong version, stated below, does. In fact, we assume from now on that σ bounds an opaque solid, with a well defined interior and exterior. It enables us to characterize the concave and convex points of the image contours in addition to the inflection points already addressed in Theorem 1.

Notation. Let us define the perspective camera observing σ by its pinhole o and retina Π. Together, the surface and the camera define a conical surface κ with apex in o, tangent to σ along the rim γ. We denote by x' the perspective projection of a rim point x with tangent plane τ onto Π, and by γ' the image contour passing through x' with tangent τ'. The contour is obtained (equivalently) as the perspective projection of γ onto Π or the intersection of κ with that plane.

Theorem 2. *Under perspective projection, the convexities of the image contour of an oriented smooth surface are the images of convex points, its concavities are the projections of hyperbolic points, and its inflections are the images of parabolic points.*

The following lemma, given without proof, summarizes well known properties of a conical surface κ [11]. These will prove to be a key to the proof of Theorem 2. These properties are true whether κ is a visual cone or not.

Lemma 3. *A conical surface κ is made up entirely of parabolic points. Contrary to the generic case depicted in Figure 1[right], its intersection with its tangent plane τ at*

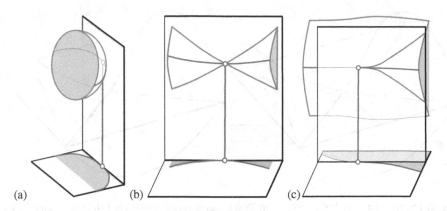

Fig. 3. Koenderink's theorem: (a) convex points project onto convex points of the image contour; (b) hyperbolic points project onto concave ones; (c) parabolic points project onto inflections.

some point x is a straight line joining its apex to x. A necessary and sufficient condition for κ to (locally) lie entirely on one side of τ at x is that there exists an open segment of a curve γ passing through x and (locally) lying entirely on that side of τ.

Proof (of Theorem 2). The conical surface κ, the rim γ, the tangent plane τ to σ in x, the contour γ' and its tangent τ' all inherit their orientation from σ (in particular, γ' is also an orientable, and in fact oriented, curve). At a convex point x (Figure 3[a]), τ is (locally) outside σ and therefore κ, and thus τ' is also outside γ', which in turn implies that the contour is convex in x'. When x is a concave point, on the other hand, τ is locally inside σ, and thus inside the opaque solid it bounds, which in turn implies that x is hidden from the pinhole o.

Consider now a hyperbolic point x (Figure 3[b]). The orientation of σ in x induces as before an orientation of the tangent plane τ, which locally splits the surface into an inner part "below" τ—that is, on the same side as the interior of the solid, and an outer part "above" this plane. Any ray passing through a point below the plane τ in a sufficiently small neighborhood of x intersects the solid's interior. Thus the rim γ must (locally) be drawn on the part of σ emerging above τ, i.e., there exists an open segment of γ containing x and entirely lying on the outer side of τ. According to Lemma 3, it follows that τ is (locally) inside κ. Likewise, τ' is locally inside κ and therefore inside γ', which in turn implies that the contour is concave in x'. The parabolic case, already covered by Theorem 1, is illustrated by Figure 3(c). □

Consider a hyperbolic point and a viewpoint moving in its tangent plane. From Theorem 2, the contour is concave everywhere it is visible—that is, within the sector that lies outside the intersection curve γ of the observed solid and its tangent plane (Figure 4). This sector is bounded by the two *asymptotic lines* tangent to the two branches of γ. As illustrated by Figure 4, the contour cusps when the viewpoint belongs to one of the asymptotic lines.

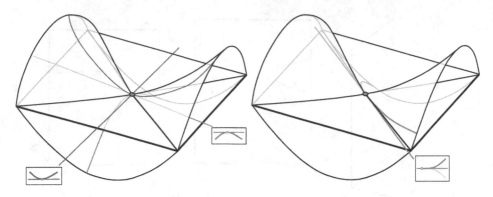

Fig. 4. The rim at a hyperbolic point. Left: Two generic visual rays (in red and green) and the corresponding rim curves. For a surface bounding a solid, one of the two rays and the corresponding rim would be (locally) in the interior of the object. Right: An asymptotic ray and the corresponding rim curve (in blue). The ray is tangent to the rim, giving birth to a cusp in the image. For a surface bounding an opaque solid, one branch of the rim and the corresponding branch of the contour at the cusp would be invisible.

5   Relative Rim and Viewpoint Motions in the Tangent Plane

Having established the relationship between the configuration of the local surface at a point on the rim and that of the local contour at its projection, we now turn our attention to the relationship between a change of viewpoint and the motion of the rim on the surface which it induces. Informally, given a pair of viewpoints in the tangent plane of a point which is on the rims corresponding to the two viewpoints, can we say something about the direction in which the rims locally turn around the point? We show in this section that the following theorem holds in the general projective case:

Theorem 3. *The rim turns in the same direction as the viewpoint in the tangent plane of a smooth oriented surface at a convex point, and in opposite ones at a hyperbolic point (Figure 5).*

In fact, this result can be shown in the Euclidean setting by showing explicitly that the Gauss map preserves orientation at elliptic points and reverses orientation at hyperbolic points [9]. The same result was shown in the *oriented* projective geometry setting by tracing oriented rays from the pinhole to the point [17]. Here, we go one step further by showing that the result holds without requiring the machinery of oriented projective geometry.

Of course, since we do not have any ready concept of signed angle or orientation at our disposal in the pure projective setting, what we mean by "turning in the same in the same direction or in the opposite direction" is not so obvious. Our first order of business is to introduce a clear definition. For that, we first need a notion of separability for pairs of lines in the same flat pencil (Figure 6).

Definition 1. *Given four distinct, coplanar and concurrent lines ξ_1, δ_1, ξ_2 and δ_2, we say that (ξ_1, ξ_2) and (δ_1, δ_2) form separable pairs when both δ_1 and δ_2 lie in the interior*

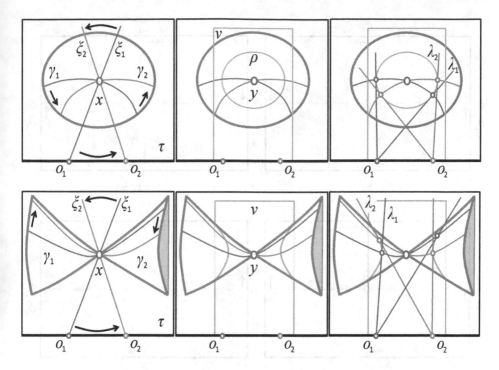

Fig. 5. Visual rays and rim curves turn in the same direction at an elliptic point (top) and in opposite directions at a hyperbolic one (bottom)

of one of the sectors delimited by ξ_1 and ξ_2 in their common plane or, equivalently, when both ξ_1 and ξ_2 lie in the interior of one of the sectors delimited by δ_1 and δ_2.

When δ_1 and δ_2 (resp. ξ_1 and ξ_2) are fixed, a sufficient condition for separability is (for example) that ξ_2 (resp. δ_2) be close enough to ξ_1 (resp. δ_1) in the natural topology of the projective line formed by a pencil of lines. Whether the elements of two separable pairs of lines turn in the same direction or not can now be defined, again in terms of separability (Figure 6).

Definition 2. *Given two separable pairs of coplanar and concurrent lines (ξ_1, ξ_2) and (δ_1, δ_2), we say that δ_1 and δ_2 turn in the same direction as ξ_1 and ξ_2 when (ξ_1, ξ_2) and (ξ_2, δ_1) are separable, and that they turn in opposite directions otherwise.*

This is indeed a projective notion, and a strictly analogous line of reasoning leads by duality to a notion of relative order for two pairs of separable points on a line.

Proof (of Theorem 3). Let us consider a point x on the surface σ with tangent plane τ, two nearby pinholes o_1 and o_2 in τ, the corresponding visual rays ξ_1 and ξ_2 through x, and the corresponding rim curves γ_1 and γ_2 with tangents δ_1 and δ_2 in the neighborhood of x (Figure 5). We assume that o_1 is fixed, and that ξ_1 and δ_1 are distinct—that is, either x is convex, or it is hyperbolic but ξ_1 is not an asymptotic direction in x. We also assume

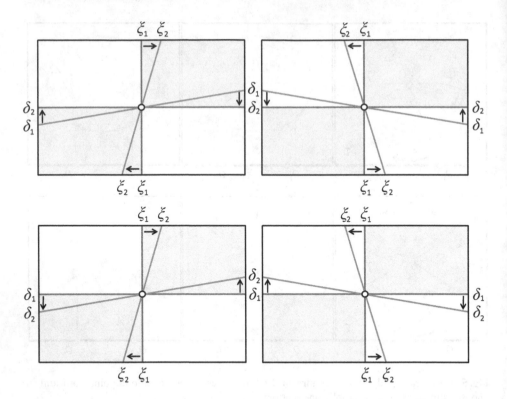

Fig. 6. Comparing the way separable pairs of lines in the same pencil turn in their plane. The lines ξ_1 and ξ_2 are separable from the lines δ_1 and δ_2 in each one of the four cases depicted. Top: The lines ξ_1 and δ_2 define two bidirectional sectors (here one is drawn in light blue, the other one is white). When ξ_2 and δ_1 lie in the same sector, (ξ_1, δ_2) and (ξ_2, δ_1) are separable, and δ_1 and δ_2 turn in the same direction as ξ_1 and ξ_2. Bottom: When (ξ_1, δ_2) and (ξ_2, δ_1) are not separable, (ξ_1, δ_1) and (ξ_2, δ_2) are separable instead, and the pairs (δ_1, δ_2) and (ξ_1, ξ_2) turn in opposite directions.

that the second pinhole o_2 is fixed, but sufficiently close to o_1 for the two pairs of lines (ξ_1, ξ_2) and (δ_1, δ_2) to be separable.

Let us now consider a plane ν in the pencil of planes passing through o_1 and o_2, close enough to τ to intersect the rim. When x is a convex point, ν is "below" (on the inner side of) τ and locally intersects σ along a non-empty, closed and (everywhere locally) convex curve ρ (Figure 5, top). The curve ρ inherits its orientation from that of σ. Given some point y in its interior, this point approaches x as ν approaches τ, and the ray η_1 passing through o_1 and y approaches ξ_1. Let us further assume from now on, without loss of generality, that ν is close enough to τ that all "inside" and "outside" relations below are meaningful (they indeed are, *locally*, in general). In particular, among the two rays passing through the first viewpoint o_1 and tangent to ρ, let us choose λ_1 to be the one with η_1 on its inner side.

Let us also denote by μ_1 the line joining y to t_1, and define similarly η_2, t_2, λ_2 and μ_2 for the second viewpoint o_2. For ν close enough to τ, the pairs (η_1, η_2) and (μ_1, μ_2)

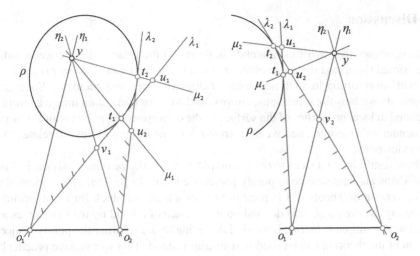

Fig. 7. Left: A convex point. Nearby rays λ_1 and λ_2 and the lines μ_1 and μ_2 joining y to the points where they graze the curve ρ. Right: A hyperbolic point. We have also highlighted the inner side of the lines λ_1 and λ_2 with hash marks.

are separable since the lines η_1 and η_2 approach the rays ξ_1 and ξ_2, and μ_1 and μ_2 approach the rim tangents δ_1 and δ_2. Finally, let u_1 (resp. u_2) denote the intersection of λ_1 and μ_2 (resp. λ_2 and μ_1), and let v_1 denote the intersection of λ_1 and η_2. We can (again) always pick ν close enough to τ that the points t_1, u_1, t_2, u_2, and v_1 are all in a small open neighborhood of y where it is meaningful to say that one of these points is on the inner or outer side of λ_1 or λ_2. In particular, t_1 (resp. t_2) is by construction on the inner side of λ_2 (resp. λ_1), thus u_1 (resp. u_2) is on the outer side of λ_2 (resp. λ_1).

Let us show that the two pairs of points (o_1, u_1) and (v_1, t_1) on λ_1 are separable. By duality, this will show in turn that the pairs (η_1, μ_2) and (η_2, μ_1) are separable. Let us define $[v_1 t_1]$ as the intersection of the line λ_1 with the sector formed by η_2 and μ_1 which does *not* contain o_1. Since t_1 and v_1 are on the inner side of λ_2 (and for ν close enough to τ), the entire segment $[v_1 t_1]$ is also on the inner side of λ_2. Since u_1 is by construction outside λ_2, it is thus also outside $[v_1 t_1]$. It follows that the two pairs of points (o_1, u_1) and (v_1, t_1) are separable, and thus the lines (η_1, μ_2) and (η_2, μ_1) are separable too. Since the lines η_1 and η_2 approach the rays ξ_1 and ξ_2, and the lines μ_1 and μ_2 approach the rim tangents δ_1 and δ_2 as ν approaches τ, if finally follows that the rim turns in the same direction as the viewpoint in x.

The same reasoning can be applied at a hyperbolic point, except that the plane ν intersecting the rim must lie "above" (on the outer side of) τ (Theorem 2), and locally intersects the surface along two curves (Figure 5, bottom). These curves inherit the orientation of σ, and we can choose some point y lying outside both these curves and approaching x as ν approaches τ. When ν is close enough to τ, we can always choose a ray λ_1 tangent to one of these curves such that y lies on the outer side of λ_1 (Figure 7[right]). A similar line of reasoning one shows that (v_1, u_2) can be separated from (o_2, t_2), and thus (ξ_1, μ_1) can be separated from (ξ_2, μ_2). Since μ_1 and μ_2 converge to δ_1 and δ_2 as ν approaches τ, the rim and the viewpoint turn in opposite directions in x.

$\square$

6 Discussion

We have shown that two fundamental questions on the relationship between a three-dimensional shape and its image contour could be answered in a purely projective setting without resorting to analytical tools or oriented projective geometry. Specifically, we have shown how the inflections, convex, and concave parts of an image contour can be related to local properties of the surface at the corresponding points with a new proof of Koenderink's theorem, and we have shown how the motion of the rim relates to that of the viewpoint.

These results are first steps toward a complete reformulation of several classical models of shape and appearance in purely projective terms. In particular, the oriented projective version of Theorem 3 is used in [17] as a building block for an algorithm for computing the *rim mesh* [15] defined on the surface of a solid by the rim curves associated with multiple cameras. It would interesting to see whether the purely projective version of the theorem can be used in a similar fashion. This would have practical implications in the context of visual hulls as well [3,16]. The geometry of the Euclidean Gauss map has also been shown to dictate (in part) the evolution of the image contour and its topology under changes in viewpoint (see [10, Ch. 20] for an overview). Using the projective Gauss map in a similar way would be very interesting. Results in this direction [19] showing that the cusps of the Gauss map correspond to the (tangential) intersections of the parabolic line with the flecnodal one, in the projective case as well as in the Euclidean one, are encouraging, and may lead to a purely projective formulation of aspect graphs [14] for example.

More generally, we have introduced new concepts and tools such as separability in order to generalize concepts such as ordering or "in betweenness" normally defined in a Euclidean or oriented projective setting to a general projective setting. We believe that they are crucial in formulating many geometric properties of solid shapes and their projections in the projective realm.

Acknowledgments. This work was supported in part by the ERC grant VideoWorld, the Institut Universitaire de France, and ONR MURI N000141010934.

References

1. Arbogast, E., Mohr, R.: 3D structure inference from image sequences. Journal of Pattern Recognition and Artificial Intelligence 5(5) (1991)
2. Banchoff, T., Gaffrey, T., McCrory, C.: Cusps of Gauss mappings. Pitman (1982)
3. Baumgart, B.G.: Geometric modeling for computer vision. Technical Report AIM-249, Stanford University, Ph.D. Thesis. Department of Computer Science (1974)
4. Berger, M.: Geometry. Springer (1987)
5. Boyer, E., Berger, M.-O.: 3D surface reconstruction using occluding contours. IJCV 22(3), 219–233 (1997)
6. Brady, J.M., Ponce, J., Yuille, A., Asada, H.: Describing surfaces. In: Hanafusa, H., Inoue, H. (eds.) Proceedings of the 2nd International Symposium on Robotics Research, pp. 5–16. MIT Press (1985)
7. Bruce, J.W.: The duals of generic hypersurfaces. Math. Scand. 48, 36–60 (1981)

8. Cipolla, R., Blake, A.: Surface shape from the deformation of the apparent contour. IJCV 9(2), 83–112 (1992)
9. do Carmo, M.P.: Differential Geometry of Curves and Surfaces. Prentice-Hall, Englewood Cliffs (1976)
10. Forsyth, D.A., Ponce, J.: Computer Vision: A Modern Approach. Prentice-Hall (2003)
11. Hilbert, D., Cohn-Vossen, S.: Geometry and the Imagination. Chelsea, New York (1952)
12. Koenderink, J.J.: What does the occluding contour tell us about solid shape? Perception 13, 321–330 (1984)
13. Koenderink, J.J.: Solid Shape. MIT Press, Cambridge (1990)
14. Koenderink, J.J., Van Doorn, A.J.: The internal representation of solid shape with respect to vision. Biological Cybernetics 32, 211–216 (1979)
15. Lazebnik, S., Boyer, E., Ponce, J.: On computing exact visual hulls of solids bounded by smooth surfaces. In: CVPR, pp. 156–161 (2001)
16. Lazebnik, S., Furukawa, Y., Ponce, J.: Projective visual hulls. IJCV 74(2), 137–165 (2007)
17. Lazebnik, S., Ponce, J.: The local projective shape of smooth surfaces and their outlines. IJCV 63(1), 65–83 (2005)
18. Marr, D.: Analysis of occluding contour. Proc. Royal Society, London B-197, 441–475 (1977)
19. McCrory, C., Shifrin, T.: Cusps of the projective Gauss map. Journal of Differential Geometry 19 (1984)
20. Ponce, J.: What is a camera? In: CVPR (2009)
21. Stolfi, J.: Oriented Projective Geometry: A Framework for Geometric Computations. Academic Press (1991)
22. Vaillant, R., Faugeras, O.D.: Using extremal boundaries for 3D object modeling. PAMI 14(2), 157–173 (1992)

Programmable Automotive Headlights

Robert Tamburo[1], Eriko Nurvitadhi[2], Abhishek Chugh[1], Mei Chen[2],
Anthony Rowe[1], Takeo Kanade[1], and Srinivasa G. Narasimhan[1]

[1] Carnegie Mellon University, Pittsburgh, PA, USA
[2] Intel Labs, Pittsburgh, PA, USA

Abstract. The primary goal of an automotive headlight is to improve safety in low light and poor weather conditions. But, despite decades of innovation on light sources, more than half of accidents occur at night even with less traffic on the road. Recent developments in adaptive lighting have addressed some limitations of standard headlights, however, they have limited flexibility - switching between high and low beams, turning off beams toward the opposing lane, or rotating the beam as the vehicle turns - and are not designed for all driving environments. This paper introduces an ultra-low latency reactive visual system that can sense, react, and adapt quickly to any environment while moving at highway speeds. Our single hardware design can be programmed to perform a variety of tasks. Anti-glare high beams, improved driver visibility during snowstorms, increased contrast of lanes, markings, and sidewalks, and early visual warning of obstacles are demonstrated.

Keywords: Adaptive headlights, reactive visual system, computational illumination.

1 Introduction

Traditional headlights consist of a small number of lamps with simple optics to direct a light beam onto the road. Starting with gas/oil lamps in the 1880s, research has been primarily geared towards developing headlights that can be electrically controlled, have a long working life, and are bright and energy efficient. The inventions of Halogen lamps, Xenon (HID) lamps [4], [5], and the more recent LED [1], [2] and Laser sources [9] have followed this research trend. These latest sources provide bright and comfortable color temperatures improving driving experiences. However, even with these new light sources the only control offered to a majority of drivers is to switch between high and low beams.

Low beams illuminate the road a short range in front of the vehicle while high beams have a longer range and wider angle. High beams are useful in a variety of situations providing better visibility farther down the road and along narrow, curvy roads. However, they cause significant glare to other drivers, bicyclists, and pedestrians. High beams also significantly reduce contrast in the presence of fog and haze, and cause bright distracting streaks during precipitation events. Even after 130 years of headlight development, more than half of vehicle crashes and fatalities occur at night despite significantly less traffic [13]. More than 300,000

D. Fleet et al. (Eds.): ECCV 2014, Part IV, LNCS 8692, pp. 750–765, 2014.

crashes and thousands of fatalities are caused by rain and snow at night annually [13]. Approximately 30% of drivers are stressed by glare causing hundreds of fatalities every year [12]. Thus, a headlight that adapts to the environment can be critical to improving safety on the road during poor visibility conditions.

Recognizing the limitations of traditional headlights, adaptive lighting systems have been developed to adjust their brightness in response to changing driving conditions. Some systems, e.g. Lincoln [6], Audi [2], Volkswagen [7], mechanically swivel the headlight based on the vehicle's turning radius allowing drivers to see around curved roads. Other systems use configurations of multiple LEDs, where individual LEDs can be automatically turned off toward the driving lane and/or the opposing lane to reduce glare, e.g., BMW [21], Audi [22], Mercedes [23], and Volvo [24]. In [9] swiveling LEDs spotlight pedestrians on sidewalks. These advanced systems have come a long way from traditional headlights, but fundamental issues remain: they are not versatile and are designed for one-off applications, they require mechanical components that reduce reliability, and their low-resolution and high latency limits them from adapting to many types of road conditions and poor visibility situations.

This paper presents a new computational illumination design for an automotive headlight that is flexible and can be programmed to perform multiple tasks at high speeds. The key idea is the introduction of a high-resolution spatial light modulator (SLM) such as the digital micro-mirror device (DMD) present in DLP projectors. A DMD divides a light beam into approximately one million beams that can be individually controlled to shape the collective beam for any situation. A sensor (camera) is co-located with the light source and a computer processes images to generate illumination patterns for the SLM. While the design may seem straightforward and follows many works on projector-camera systems in computer vision, there are many challenges in building such a system to serve as a headlight. The accuracy requirements can be high since small errors in beam positioning and flickering are easily perceived and can be more disturbing than standard headlights. High accuracy can be achieved by minimizing the time from when a camera senses the environment to when the headlight reacts (system latency). Low latency is also required to avoid the need for complex prediction algorithms to determine where an object will move next.

A prototype system was built with an ultra-low latency of 1 to 2.5 ms (variation due to factors explained in Section 4) and hence our system requires no prediction algorithm in most cases. We have conducted road demonstrations while traveling at usual traffic speeds to show the feasibility and effectiveness of the design (see website for videos [25]). Example applications include anti-glare persistent high beams, visibility improvement in snowstorms (shown with artificial snow), and illuminating roads with better contrast and lane definition. Results of providing early visual warning of obstacles can be seen at [25]. Our system is able to tackle all of these applications with a single hardware design and achieve higher light throughput than what is possible with any configuration of a small number of controllable LEDs available in current headlights.

Fig. 1. Left: Prototype of our programmable automotive headlight design (computer not pictured). The camera, spatial light modulator, and beam splitter are firmly mounted to an optical breadboard. A mirror to the side of the beam splitter deflects reflected light from the light source upward. Right: Road tests were conducted by securing the prototype to the hood of a vehicle with a suction cup-based mount. An acrylic enclosure was constructed to protect components from dust, dirt, and moisture.

2   Overview of Programmable Headlight Design

Our programmable headlight design consists of four main components: an image sensor, processing unit, spatial light modulator (SLM), and beam splitter. The *imaging sensor* observes the road environment in front of the vehicle. Additional sensors such as RADAR or LIDAR can be incorporated into the design to complement the camera. The *processing unit* analyzes image data from the sensor and controls the headlight beam via a spatial light modulator. The *spatial light modulator* (e.g., digital micro-mirror device, liquid crystal display, liquid crystal on silicon, etc.) modifies the beam from a light source by varying the intensity over space and time in two dimensions. We use a DMD because its high working frequency and small pixel size permit high-speed modulation and fine illumination control, which makes it possible for our headlight to quickly react to objects as small as snowflakes and objects as large as vehicles.

The camera and SLM are co-located along the same optical line of sight via a *beam splitter*, which virtually places the image sensor and DMD at the same location. Co-location is advantageous because it makes calculating the distance to objects unnecessary. Consequently, there is no need to perform costly computations required for depth estimation and 3D tracking. Also, a single homography will map the camera and projector image planes regardless of the scene. If the image sensor and DMD chip are placed very close to each other, the beam splitter is not required. Reactive visual systems with a similar design have been described by [11], [16], [20], but their systems are too slow for high-speed automotive applications. High latency in conjunction with road effects like wind turbulence and vibration will require complex prediction algorithms that will add latency to the system making it unusable.

3   Design and Implementation of a Prototype System

We designed and implemented a prototype with low latency and high data throughput (Figure 1), and conducted road tests to demonstrate the feasibility of our DMD-based reactive visual system design as a headlight. The camera and SLM must have a very fast frame rate, e.g., kilohertz range, to capture images of fast moving objects and to create illumination patterns that are imperceptible to drivers. Consequently, a lot of data must be transferred to and from the processing unit with minimal latency. To achieve these goals, components with high-speed interfaces were tightly integrated through hardware and software. The prototype measures 45 cm wide, 45 cm long, and 30 cm tall and is currently too large to install in a vehicle as a headlight. The current size is due to using off-the-shelf components. Specialized embedded hardware with an integrated imaging, processing, and SLM unit will be required to create a compact headlight. Road tests were conducted by securing the prototype to the hood of a vehicle with a suction-cup based vehicle mount. A custom acrylic enclosure protects the system from dust, dirt, and moisture. We demonstrate in Sections 5 and 6 that the prototype performs a variety of tasks at typical traffic speeds.

3.1   Sensing the Road Environment

A camera (Basler acA2040) with a CMOS sensor highly sensitive to light with correlated double sampling to significantly reduce noise was used to capture images. The camera is sensitive to visible and near infrared light since most objects of interest are detectable within this spectrum of light. Monochrome imagery is used to avoid the computational overhead associated with demosaicing the Bayer pattern. A global shutter with area scan is used to avoid distortion effects common with the rolling shutter. Latency is reduced via a pipelined pixel architecture that permits exposure during readout. The camera's extended CameraLink configuration has transfer rates of up to 6.8 gigabits per second. The camera is mounted to a set of linear stages for fine control during calibration.

3.2   Image Processing and System Control

A desktop computer provides an interface between the camera and SLM, performs image analysis, and controls the system. The computer was custom built using an Intel Core 3.4 GHz (i7-2600K) CPU with eight cores and hyper-threading technology. A PCI express 2.0 frame grabber (Bitflow Karbon SP) that transfers image data directly into computer memory without any buffering. The main processing tasks were parallelized to reduce latency and increase system responsiveness. The three-stage processing pipeline is shown in a timing diagram (Figure 2) with times measured from the prototype system as described in Section 4. Capture refers to the integration time of the camera. TX denotes the time to transfer image data to the host computer and the time to transfer data from the host computer to the SLM. Process refers to image analysis and system control. Illumination refers to directing light to the scene for a single cycle.

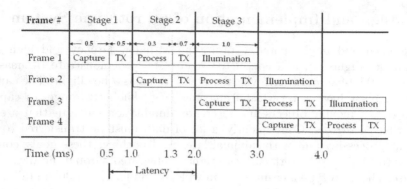

Fig. 2. Timing diagram of the three-stage pipeline with execution times in milliseconds. Capture refers to camera exposure. Process refers to analysis of images and system control. TX denotes data transfer between camera and computer or between computer and SLM. Latency is the time required to illuminate the scene after capturing an image.

Since execution time is critical, the focus of image analysis algorithms is on speed rather than accuracy. Image analyses were performed using OpenCV compiled with Intel Integrated Performance Primitives and Thread Building Blocks to maximize parallelism. Functions that perform per-pixel operations were combined using SSE2 intrinsic functions, when possible, to reduce the computation time associated with multiple iterations over the image. Pre-computable operations such as distortion correction and perspective transformation were initialized and stored in look-up tables. After analyzing images, illumination patterns are encoded and stored in an array then transmitted to the SLM.

3.3   High-Speed Illumination of the Road Environment

A DMD chip is used as a SLM for its spatial and temporal resolution. They are used in consumer DLP projectors, but are driven by video frame rates, which are well below our kilohertz target. A DLP development kit (WinTech W4100) based on the Discovery 4100 (Texas Instruments) was used as the basis of our SLM because the board contains a user programmable FPGA (Xilinx Virtex-5) to achieve fast update rates. The DMD chip is 0.7" with XGA (1024×768) resolution, which, essentially means the headlight beam can be divided into 786,432 smaller beams each of which can be turned on or off. This type of modulation gives unprecedented control over the illumination in space and time. Illumination patterns are received from the host computer by USB 2.0.

The DLP development kit does not include any optics. The optics and light source from a consumer DLP projector (InFocus IN3124) were used instead of designing custom components. We chose this projector because it uses the same DMD chipset as the development kit and uses a lamp (4800 Lumens) brighter than most vehicle high beams. The projector's native DMD chip was removed from the optics module and replaced with that of the development kit via a custom machined mount. A copper heat sink and fan were installed to improve heat dissipation. All of the native DLP electronic boards were left attached to maintain operability even though only the optics and lamp are actively used.

The FPGA was programmed to display patterns faster than 1 kHz. In our design, the FPGA receives data streamed from the host PC and produces the commands for a DMD controller to display the appropriate patterns on the DMD. Each row (1024 pixels) of the DMD is represented as a bit-vector. Transferring a 1024-bit vector for each of the 768 rows was too slow (over 1.5 ms). Instead, the rows are subsampled by a factor of four by representing 1024 pixels by a 256-bit vector. Some resolution is lost, but the visual impact is negligible. Data was further compressed to increase system speed by reading out every other row from the image sensor. The missing rows of the resulting illumination pattern are filled-in by duplicating the previous row on the FPGA. Thus, the image is down-sampled by a factor of 4 horizontally and a factor of 2 vertically.

3.4   System Calibration

Calibrating the system consists of co-locating the camera and SLM, and computing the homography between the camera and SLM image planes. To achieve co-location, a beam splitter with 50% transmission and 50% reflection (Edmund Optics) is used. The projector, rigidly affixed to the optical breadboard, illuminates an object. The camera is translated in all three cardinal directions and rotated until shadows cast by the object are no longer observed by the camera. This recursive co-location procedure takes about 10 minutes to perform.

After positioning the camera and SLM along the same optical line of sight, a perspective transform is calculated for the homography. Radial and tangential distortion by the camera lens is characterized by capturing an image of a checkerboard image and estimating the camera's intrinsic parameters and distortion coefficients. A homography is computed by first projecting a checkerboard pattern and capturing an image. The image is then undistorted and detected corner points are used to compute a perspective transform. After performing these calibration steps, the transformations are stored in look-up tables for later use and the system can be used anywhere without modification. These calibration steps were performed using functionality available in the OpenCV library.

4   Measuring System Latency

As discussed in Section 3.2, the system is pipelined in three stages: image capture and transfer, image processing and transfer, and illumination. Latency of the system is the time between capturing an image and illuminating the scene. There are several factors that contribute to latency. Image size is directly related to camera/computer and computer/SLM transfer time, and image processing time. The size and number of detected objects also has an effect on latency requiring more processing time and thus increases latency. Lastly, the computer's operating system has timing jitter and interrupts that add uncertainty to the latency.

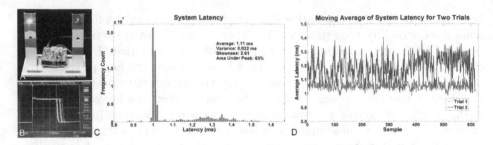

Fig. 3. A: Circuit for measuring system latency consists of an LED and a phototransistor connected to a micro-controller board (Arduino Uno). To measure the system's reaction time, the micro-controller measures the time for the system to detect the illuminated LED then illuminates/dis-illuminates the phototransistor. B: Latency is observed on an oscilloscope (typical readout shown) and measured/recorded by the micro-controller board. C: Histogram (0.01 ms per bin) shows data collected over 30 minutes. The system has some uncertainty, but typically reacts within about 1 ms. D: Moving average (1 second intervals) of latency for a trial with and without uncertainty.

To measure system latency, a circuit was built to measure the system's time to react to an illuminated LED (Figure 3A). The circuit consists of an LED, phototransistor, and micro-controller (Arduino Uno). The high-level idea is to measure the response time of the system by enabling an LED and timing how long it takes for the system to detect the LED and project light onto the phototransistor. To achieve this, the system was programmed to illuminate the phototransistor every other frame. Observing the signal from the phototransistor with an oscilloscope reveals a step response as shown in Figure 3B. The plateau of the signal corresponds to the time that the phototransistor is illuminated. Time was measured with microsecond precision and recorded with the micro-controller.

Data were collected for thirty minutes evenly divided over six separate trials to assess repeatability. During these trials, the image resolution was 800×220, exposure time was 750 μs, and frame rate was 1 kHz. Latency for all the trials is shown in Figure 3C. Across the six trials, the system most often reacts within 1 ms and 63% of the time reacts within two standard deviations from the peak. The average reaction time for all six trials was 1.11 ms with a variance of 0.032 ms. The histogram also reveals uncertainty in the system. This variability was studied by averaging every 1 second worth of data. Shown in Figure 3D are averaged data for two trials: one trial with little variability and one trial with a lot of variability. The plot shows that, in either situation, latency consistently varies by small fluctuations within a narrow band. In the worst case, the fluctuations range from 1 to 1.4 ms.

Several strategies can be utilized to account for latency variability. The uncertainty can be simply included in the illumination pattern by artificially increasing the size of detected objects. Light throughput will decrease, but accuracy will improve. Alternatively, temporal information can be used to predict the location of detected objects. Care must be taken to ensure the prediction model does not add too much time to the system's latency. At high frame rates, a linear model will suffice for most applications. The time to perform processing tasks was measured, in software, with a high resolution timer (Windows API). The average time for processing was 0.3 ms with a standard deviation of 0.04 ms (Figure 2). The time to send data to the DMD board over USB was measured for 5 minutes with an average of 0.76 ms and a standard deviation of 0.07 ms.

5   Anti-Glare High Beams

Glare from the headlights, especially high beams, of oncoming vehicles cause significant stress and distraction at best and temporary blindness at worst. Trucks and other vehicles with headlights at high positions are the worst offenders. Although, glare is not often reported as a cause of accidents, hundreds of fatal night crashes attribute glare as a contributing factor every year [15]. Glare is especially problematic for the elderly whom take eight times longer to recover from glare as compared to a 16-year old [14]. Although high beams are a nuisance to other drivers, they are beneficial on narrow, curvy, and poorly lit roads, especially in rural areas where wildlife routinely jumps onto the road.

Anti-glare headlights are currently being deployed by car companies, e.g., [21], [22], [23], [24]. The details of their systems are publicly unavailable, but it is known that these systems utilize multiple LEDs and sensors placed at different locations in the vehicle, e.g, [10], [9], [2]. Based on this information, it can be inferred that spatial resolution is limited to the number of LEDs. Camera frame rates of these headlight systems are limited to 30 - 60 Hz and thus have high latency [26], [27], [28]. In this section, it will be shown that a high-resolution SLM with low latency produces the best light throughput.

System Requirements and Comparisons. Computer simulations were performed to determine the latency required to maintain high light throughput. Camera parameters and the position of our prototype on a vehicle were used in simulations where two vehicles traveled towards each other at 225 kph on a two-lane, straight road. Detection and prediction were set to be error-free guaranteeing that only system latency contributed to light throughput. Light throughput was calculated for latencies of 2, 16, 30, 50, and 100 ms (Figure 4A). Throughput remains above 90% for all latencies tested when the vehicles are farther than 20 m apart. The reason for this is the oncoming vehicle is moving towards the camera and its position in the image has little variation. However, as the vehicles move closer towards each other, light throughput substantially decreases with higher latency. It is clear that the system needs a latency of at least 2 ms to maintain 90% light throughput when the vehicles are close to each other. The same would be true for vehicles in further lanes or on curved roads.

Computer simulations were conducted to compare the performance LED-based headlights to DMD-based headlights with the same latency. Since specific details of LED-based systems are publicly unavailable, several assumptions were made: (a) LEDs were positioned in a linear array parallel to the road and (b) all LEDs in the array that would illuminate the oncoming driver are disabled.

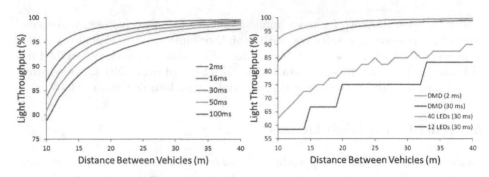

Fig. 4. Results of computer simulations of anti-glare headlights. Detection and prediction are assumed to be perfect and vehicles were traveling towards each other in adjacent lanes at a relative speed of 225 kph. Left: Light throughput as a function of distance between vehicles for different system latencies. Right: Light throughput for DMD- and LED- based anti-glare headlights for different latencies. Simulations show lower latency and higher resolution results in higher light throughput and accuracy, which will be even more relevant for curvy, multilane roads with multiple vehicles.

Simulation results are shown in Figure 4B along with those of the DMD-based system. The low spatial resolution of LED-based systems results in lower light throughput and also creates flicker (abrupt changes in light throughput) for the driver. The flicker can be reduced by turning off more LEDs, but with the trade-off of sacrificing light throughput.

Our Headlight Design as Anti-Glare High Beams. The anti-glare problem and our solution is illustrated in Figure 5A. Headlights from oncoming vehicles are detected in the captured image. Headlights are detected using the assumption that they are the brightest objects in the system's field of view. A very short exposure (100 μs) time is used and the image is thresholded. False detections can be reduced by excluding connected components that are too small to be headlights. Once the locations of the vehicles are known in the camera's reference frame, it is transformed to the headlight reference frame and the spatial light modulator blocks light in that direction. Since the resolution offered by the SLM is very high, only a small region above the detected headlight overlapping the oncoming driver's head is dis-illuminated. This type of beam blocking can be done for any number of oncoming drivers without significant loss of illumination. Compared to the system settings used to evaluate latency in Section 4, the image resolution was increased to 1000×340 to provide the largest field of view possible resulting in a system latency to 2.5 ms.

Demonstration on the Road. The system was tested on the road at night with three oncoming vehicles. Figures 5B-D show video frames captured from inside vehicles driving towards the programmable headlight. In Figure 5B, the blinding glare as the vehicles near each other is shown. Figure 5C and D show the benefit of our anti-glare headlight. Clearly, the difference in visibility is significant allowing drivers to see the road, vehicle, and surroundings. The prototype was able to function for all three drivers at the same time with little light loss.

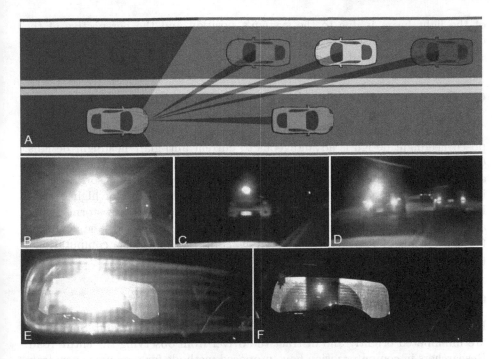

Fig. 5. A: Illustration for eliminating high beam glare. Vehicles are identified and small regions around drivers are dis-illuminated while maintaining illumination elsewhere. Drivers with programmable headlights can then potentially use high beams without worry. Middle row shows view while driving towards our prototype. B: Glare typically seen from high beams (anti-glare feature disabled). C: Reduced glare when the anti-glare feature of our headlight is enabled. D: Anti-glare headlights allow the driver to better see other vehicles on the road. E: Glare in a rear view mirror caused by a following vehicle. F: Tail lights are detected to avoid illuminating the rear-view mirror.

Fig. 6. View shown from the perspective of the vehicle equipped with our prototype. Left: Anti-glare feature is disabled acting as a typical high beam. Middle and Right: Anti-glare feature is enabled detecting multiple oncoming vehicles and reducing light only in the direction of each driver. Notice no discernable difference between images.

The average light throughput was calculated from saved images to be 93.8% with a standard deviation of 3.3%. In Figure 5F, tail lights were detected to avoid illuminating the driver's rear-view mirror and glaring them from behind. As shown in Figure 6, there is no discernible difference to the driver with the programmable headlight when the anti-glare function is enabled. The odd shape of the light beam is due to the system's position and the perspective of the capturing device. Installation in the headlight bay will create a more uniform shape and the spread of the light beam can be increased with a wide angle lens.

6   Demonstrating System Design Versatility

Thus far, computer simulations and demonstrations have shown that the proposed headlight design is advantageous to current anti-glare headlight designs. Our headlight can also be programmed to perform other tasks, whereas, other advanced lighting systems may require additional light sources, sensors, mechanical parts, etc., or are insufficient due to low spatial resolution or high latency. Here we show several tasks, such as visibility improvement in snowstorms (using artificial snow) and illuminating roads with better contrast and lane definition (visual warning of obstacles can be seen at [25]). Also shown is a computational photography application to examine high-speed events.

6.1   Improving Visibility during Snowstorms

Driving in a snowstorm at night is incredibly difficult and stressful. Snowflakes are illuminated brightly and distract the driver from observing the entire road. Researchers in computer vision have proposed methods for removing snow from videos [17], [18], [19]. Processed videos can be displayed for the driver, but current implementations are not intuitive and, at times, distracting for the driver. We can address this problem with a solution similar to that for anti-glare, i.e., reacting to detected bright objects. The main difference, however, is that the density, size, and speed of snowflakes requires high-resolution, low-latency illumination to be effective. Therefore, we exploit the high-resolution and fast illumination beam control of our prototype to distribute light between falling snowflakes to reduce backscatter directly in the driver's visual field (Figure 7). However, this application is significantly more challenging since (a) the size of snowflakes is very small compared to an easily detectable vehicle and (b) the quantity of snowflakes is several orders higher than the number of cars on the road. The goal is to send as much light as possible from the headlight to sufficiently illuminate the road for the driver while dis-illuminating snowflakes.

Computer simulations performed in [11] demonstrate that the idea is feasible. They estimate that, for a vehicle traveling at 30 kph, the system's latency needs to be 1.5 ms or less to have high light throughput and accuracy. We demonstrate improved visibility outside at night with artificial snowflakes. Snowflakes were detected by performing background subtraction and binary thresholding. To compensate for any small detection errors, dilation with a structuring element of a radius equivalent to that of a snowflake was applied. The visibility improvement can be seen by comparing Figures 7B and 7C. Even though the snowflakes fall chaotically, no prediction was required because of the system's fast speed. For comparison, the system by [11] (13 ms latency) was demonstrated for rain drops falling along a straight path and required a linear prediction model.

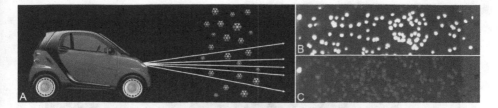

Fig. 7. A: Our headlight has unprecedented resolution over space and time so that beams of light may be sent in between the falling snow. Illustration adapted from [11]. B: Artificial snowflakes brightly illuminated by standard headlight. C: Our system avoids illuminating snowflakes making them much less visible.

Fig. 8. A: Concept of illuminating the driver's lane with high-intensity light and illuminating the adjacent lane dimly to improve the contrast of the driver's lane. B: Driver's lane more brightly illuminated than the adjacent lane. C: Demonstration while driving on an unmarked road. D: Concept of adjusting lane illumination based on the presence of other vehicles. E: Illumination for the left lane stops at the oncoming driver to avoid projecting lane patterns on the vehicle. F: Lane illumination stops in front of the vehicle in the adjacent lane and behind the vehicle in the driver's lane.

Fig. 9. A tennis ball is thrown into a bowl of ping pong balls causing them to fly through the air. A digital image was captured with a long exposure (3 seconds) to observe the trajectory of ping pong balls. Left: Image captured with scene brightly illuminated. Ball trajectories are not visible against the illuminated wall behind the scene. Right: Image captured with only the ping pong balls being illuminated. The trajectory of the balls is much more visible against the unlit background.

6.2   Improved Lane Illumination

Sometimes the road is not clearly visible and no amount of illumination from a standard headlight can assist the driver. A few examples of such situations are snow covered roads, roads without lane markings or shoulders, and poorly lit roads. Our prototype can be used to brightly illuminate only the driver's lane to provide them with a visual guide. Opposing lanes, curbs, and sidewalks can be dimly illuminated to create a strong contrast with the driver's lane and also provide sufficient illumination to see obstacles (Figure 8A). For this application, images do not need to be captured or analyzed, and objects do not need to be tracked. After computing the homography with the road plane, the headlight acts only as an illumination device. For proof-of-concept, illumination patterns were pre-determined for the stretch of road where experiments were conducted. In practice, the position and speed of the vehicle will be used to dynamically determine the illumination patterns required for the road.

In Figure 8B, the driver's lane and lane markings are fully illuminated, and the adjacent lane is dimly illuminated. The same contrast is used while driving on a dark, unmarked road in Figure 8C. The opposing lane is dimly illuminated while the driver's lane remains fully illuminated creating a demarcation line for the driver to follow. Vehicles driving on the illuminated lane will experience disorienting illumination patterns because the system is calibrated to illuminate the road plane. Therefore, the beam can be adjusted where vehicles are detected in either lane as illustrated in Figure 8D. The adjacent lane can be illuminated up to the location of an oncoming vehicle while maintaining full illumination of the driver's own lane (Figure 8E). Illumination can be controlled in the presence of vehicles in both lanes as well (Figure 8F).

6.3   Observing Events with Computational Photography

Generally speaking, our programmable headlight is a low-latency reactive visual system with many uses outside of the automotive field. It has the flexibility of illuminating or dis-illuminating any fast moving object. An interesting application is studying the trajectory of fast moving objects or fast events. Typically, to capture these types of images, an expensive camera is needed and the room needs to be brightly lit causing a decrease in contrast. Instead, with our system, only the objects of interest need to be illuminated.

For example, a handful of ping pong balls were placed in a bowl. A tennis ball was thrown into the bowl causing the ping pong balls to fly through the air. The ping pong balls were illuminated with infrared LEDs so that they would be detectable in the dark. To observe the trajectory of the ping pong balls, a long exposure (3 seconds) image was captured with a camera. The ping pong balls were detected and immediately illuminated. As shown in Figure 9, the trails are barely visible when the scene is fully illuminated, but are clearly visible when our system is used to illuminate just the ping pong balls.

7   Conclusions and Future Work

The automotive headlight should not be a passive device that can only be completely switched on or off. It should be capable of adapting to the environment to improve safety in poor visibility conditions. Moreover, the design for adaptive headlights should not be limited to a single task. It should be capable of performing many different tasks to help the driver in multiple road environments. Our headlight design provides unprecedented light beam control over space and time. We have demonstrated the flexibility of the headlight for numerous tasks: allowing drivers to use high beams without glaring any other driver on the road, allowing drivers to see better in snow, and allowing better illumination of road lanes, sidewalks and dividers. Our prototype can quickly react to the road environment within 1 to 2.5 milliseconds, and, thus does not create any flicker to be seen by the human eye. Further research and development is needed to make the prototype compact to fit within actual vehicle headlight compartments. Further engineering is required to make the system reliable in the presence of vehicular vibrations and heat. Lastly, more sophisticated algorithms and reliable software need to be developed before deploying our headlight design.

Acknowledgements. This research was funded in parts by a grant from the Intel Science and Technology Center for Embedded Computing, a grant from the U.S. Department of Transportation (Carnegie Mellon University Transportation Center (T-SET)), a gift from Ford Motor Company, a grant from the Office of Naval Research (N00014-11-1-0295), and an NSF CAREER Award (IIS-0643628). The authors also thank the NavLab group at Carnegie Mellon University, Robotics Institute for providing an experimental vehicle platform and Zisimos Economou for helping with the timing circuit.

References

1. Rice, L.: Headlight with Single LED Module. SAE Technical Paper 2010-01-0295 (2010)
2. Söllner, T.: Audi - The Leading Brand in Lighting Technology. Audi Press Release (2013)
3. Plucinsky, T.: BMW Develops Laser Light for the Car. BMW Group Press Release (2011)
4. Bölling, C.: Osram Presents Future Technologies for Car Headlights. Osram Press Release (2013)
5. Schuellerman, D.: GE Lighting Unveils High-Performance Headlamp Lighting Solutions. GE Lighting Press Release (2012)
6. Ford Motor Company: Next Generation of Ford Motor Company's Headlights Make Nighttime Driving Safer. Ford Press Release (2005)
7. Volkswagon Group: To the Point: The New Polo GTI: Extremely Strong and Exceptionally Fuel Efficient. VW Press Release (2010)
8. Boeriu, H.: 2011 BMW 5 Series. BMW Press Release (2009)
9. Wiese, M.: BMW Innovations in Vehicle Lights. "Dynamic Light Spot" for Actively Illuminating Persons, the "Glare-Free High Beam Assistant" and Full-LED Headlights Provide Even More Safety at Night. BMW Press Release (2011)
10. Mercedes Benz: Mercedes-Benz Announces New Active Multibeam LED Headlights. Press Release (2013)
11. de Charette, R., Tamburo, R., Barnum, P.C., Rowe, A., Kanade, T., Narasimhan, S.G.: Fast Reactive Control for Illumination Through Rain and Snow. In: IEEE International Conference on Computational Photography (ICCP), Seattle, Washington (2012)
12. National Highway Traffic Safety Administration: Report on Drivers' Perceptions of Headlight Glare from Oncoming and Following Vehicles (2003)
13. National Highway Traffic Safety Administration: Traffic Safety Facts 2011: A Compilation of Motor Vehicle Crash Data from the Fatality Analysis Reporting System and the General Estimates System (2011)
14. AAA Foundation for Traffic Safety: How To Avoid Headlight Glare (2013)
15. National Highway Traffic Safety Administration: Nighttime Glare and Driving Performance (2007)
16. Wang, O., Fuchs, M., Fuchs, C., Davis, J., Seidel, H.-P., Lensch, H.P.A.: A Context-Aware Light Source. In: IEEE International Conference on Computational Photography (ICCP), Cambridge, MA (2010)
17. Shen, Y., Ma, L., Liu, H., Bao, Y., Chen, Z.: Detecting and Extracting Natural Snow From Videos. Information Processing Letters 110, 1124–1130 (2010)
18. Zhen, C., Jihong, S.: A New Algorithm of Rain (Snow) Removal in Video. Journal of Multimedia 8(2) (2013)
19. Garg, K., Nayar, S.K.: Detection and Removal of Rain from Videos. In: IEEE Computer Society Conference on Computer Vision and Pattern Recognition (CVPR), vol. I, pp. 528–535 (2004)
20. Toshiyuki, A., Osamura, K., Fujisawa, M.: Controlled Illumination for the Object Recognition with Projector Camera Feedback. In: IAPR Conference on Machine Vision Applications, pp. 152–155 (2011)
21. Wiese, M.: BMW Lights the Way into the Future. BMW Press Release (2014)
22. HELLA Inc.: HELLA Develops Unique Matrix LED Headlamp System With Audi. Press Release (2014)

23. Giesen, N.: New Generation CLS with the Future's High-Resolution Precision LED Technology: Leading the way with Better Light. Daimler Group Press Release (2014)
24. Fröberg, P.: Volvo Cars Makes Driving at Night Safer and More Comfortable with Innovative, Permanent High Beam. Volvo Car Group Press Release (2013)
25. Illumination and Imaging Laboratory Project Web Page for Smart Headlights, http://cs.cmu.edu/~ILIM/SmartHeadlight
26. MobileEye Camera Matrix, http://www.mobileye.com/technology/development-evaluation-platforms/cameras
27. Advanced Driving Assistance and Active Safety Systems, http://media.opel.com/media/intl/en/opel/vehicles/opel_eye/2009.html
28. HELLA Group Website, http://www.hella.com/hella-com

ROCHADE: Robust Checkerboard Advanced Detection for Camera Calibration

Simon Placht[1,2], Peter Fürsattel[1,2], Etienne Assoumou Mengue[2],
Hannes Hofmann[1], Christian Schaller[1], Michael Balda[1],
and Elli Angelopoulou[2]

[1] Metrilus GmbH, Erlangen, Germany
[2] Pattern Recognition Lab, University of Erlangen, Nuremberg, Germany

Abstract. We present a new checkerboard detection algorithm which is able to detect checkerboards at extreme poses, or checkerboards which are highly distorted due to lens distortion even on low-resolution images. On the detected pattern we apply a surface fitting based subpixel refinement specifically tailored for checkerboard X-junctions. Finally, we investigate how the accuracy of a checkerboard detector affects the overall calibration result in multi-camera setups. The proposed method is evaluated on real images captured with different camera models to show its wide applicability. Quantitative comparisons to OpenCV's checkerboard detector show that the proposed method detects up to 80% more checkerboards and detects corner points more accurately, even under strong perspective distortion as often present in wide baseline stereo setups.

Keywords: Checkerboard Detection, Saddle-Based Subpixel Refinement, Multi Camera Calibration, Low Resolution Sensors, Lens Distortion.

1 Introduction

The goal of camera calibration is the recovery of intrinsic parameters of cameras. In the case of a multi-camera setup it also includes the estimation of their spatial relation to each other. Most calibration methods involve the detection of an object with known geometric properties in the scene.

Multiple methods which put different constraints on the calibration pattern can be used to estimate the desired parameters. Some algorithms allow or require three dimensional objects [12], circular patterns [5] or planar checkerboard patterns. Three dimensional patterns are hard to build and typically more expensive than simple planar checkerboard patterns which can be generated by a regular printer. Circle patterns are not invariant with respect to projective and nonlinear transformations like lens distortion [5,7]. Complex patterns which include self-identifying patterns [4] are also not considered in this work as they typically have higher requirements on sensor resolution and noise levels.

Rather, we focus on planar patterns in combination with Zhang's calibration method [14]. Although this calibration approach is not limited to a particular

D. Fleet et al. (Eds.): ECCV 2014, Part IV, LNCS 8692, pp. 766–779, 2014.

planar calibration pattern we consider only checkerboard patterns due to their robustness with respect to different distortions, low price and simple construction. The regular pattern and high-contrast edges of checkerboards makes them particularly suitable for automatic detection with high accuracy. However, an extreme pose of the checkerboard, low sensor resolution, image noise or lens distortion may still lead to inaccurate corner point coordinates or may even make automatic detection impossible. Wide baseline stereo camera setups are particularly prone to extreme poses and a robust pattern detector becomes a necessity.

In this work we present a novel checkerboard detector which finds checkerboards at extreme poses and on distorted images with high accuracy. Our detection method involves two steps. First, we detect the checkerboard in the image and calculate initial pixel coordinates for the inner checkerboard corners. In the second step, the initial corners are refined to subpixel accuracy with a method based on the work of Lucchese and Mitra [6]. Their approach consists of fitting a polynomial to saddlepoints in the vicinity of the initial coordinates to calculate the corner coordinates with subpixel accuracy. Typically some sort of filtering, for example Gaussian smoothing [1], is applied before fitting the polynomial. Instead of using a Gaussian we apply a cone-shaped filter kernel escpecially tailored for surface fitting around checkerboard X-junctions.

There is considerable prior work on checkerboard pattern detection. A widely used approach is OpenCV's checkerboard detection algorithm which is based on the work of Vezhnevets[1]. After thresholding the images, the algorithm tries to separate black checkerboard quads from each other by applying erosion. Next quadrangles are fitted into the black quads. By merging the corners of the quadrangles the inner checkerboard corners can be calculated. Rufli et al. [9] present an extension to this algorithm which includes different erosion kernels and a heuristic for quadrangle linking in order to make the algorithm more robust to lens distortion. However, their algorithm does not include any subpixel refinement of corner points. Wang et al. [13] present a method which fits lines into initial corner points and calculates the final corner coordinates by intersecting these lines. While this method works well with images with only small distortions, the line fitting is expected to be less accurate if the image is significantly distorted. All the aforementioned methods have in common that they require prior knowledge about the number of squares of a calibration pattern. De la Escalera et al. [3] avoid this limitiation by automatically finding checkerboard-like patterns by combining corner and line detection. In their method the Hough transform is used to find straight lines, which however may fail for images under medium or strong lens distortions. Dao et al. present [2] a method which is able to detect checkerboards even if they are not planar or partly occluded. Such a technique is particularly useful if the checkerboard pattern is not used for camera calibration but for example for geometry reconstruction but is not useful for camera calibration.

---

[1] `http://graphicon.ru/oldgr/en/research/calibration/opencv.html`

We evaluate our proposed method with real images captured with different multi-camera setups consisting of both industrial and consumer cameras. This allows us to examine the influence of lens distortion, sensor resolution and checkerboard pose on detection accuracy. Furthermore, we compare our method to OpenCV's checkerboard detector[2]. We show that OpenCV's initial detection of checkerboards is less robust with respect to the aforementioned criteria and also that our subpixel refinement method achieves higher accuracy.

This paper is organized as follows. Section 2 describes our checkerboard detection algorithm as well as the subpixel refinement method. Our experiments and results are discussed in Section 3. In the last section we draw conclusions on our evaluation and present a short outlook on future work.

2   Robust Checkerboard Advanced Detection (ROCHADE)

The localization of a checkerboard pattern in an image can be divided into two subtasks: the detection of the checkerboard pattern, including corner initialization and the refinement of the inner checkerboard corners. An inner corner is the vertex shared by four adjacent checkerboard squares (two black, two white ones) which together form a larger square.

2.1   Detection of Checkerboard Pattern

A robust checkerboard pattern detector should satisfy the following properties:

- Detection even under the presence of strong lens distortions. Due to deviations from straight lines, the shape of the checkerboard squares in the acquired image will differ from the contours of a quadrangle.
- Invariance to camera-dependent parameters (range of values, resolution).
- Robustness with respect to pose of the acquired checkerboards.
- Detection, even when the checkerboard field lengths are not constant (important for projector to camera calibration).

In order to keep the calibration procedure user-friendly, it should also work in real-time, be fully automatic and without configuration parameters that need to be adjusted to camera types and setups.

The key idea behind our checkerboard detection algorithm is an edge graph generation for the whole image. Usually the graph is disconnected, since the checkerboard is not the only acquired object. Inner checkerboard corners correspond to saddle points in the edge graph, i. e. nodes with three or more neighbors. Hence, the search space is reduced to those connected components where the number of saddle points matches the number of inner corners of the checkerboard. An outline of the processing pipeline used for checkerboard detection is given in Figure 1. A detailed description of the 7-step processing pipeline is provided below:

---

[2] In our evaluation we use OpenCV 2.4.8

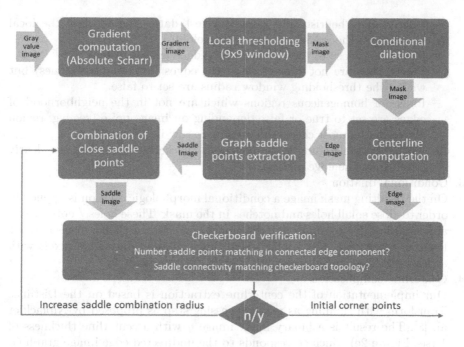

Fig. 1. The processing pipeline of the checkerboard detection algorithm

0. Downsampling

   This is an optional stage for controlling the processing time of the checker-board detection. If the input image is downsampled, the minimum field size of detectable checkerboards will increase. For the corner refinement stage described in Section 2.2 the original image size is used.

1. Gradient computation

   In order to highlight the edges/corners of the checkerboard pattern, a Scharr gradient computation with a kernel size of 3x3 is applied. We have chosen a Scharr kernel for filtering because of its better rotational symmetry compared to the more commonly used Sobel filter. Since the subsequent steps are not based on the gradient directions, we consider only the magnitude of the horizontal and vertical gradient.

2. Local thresholding

   Having computed the gradient, we generate a mask image (see Figure 2c) in which the high gradient values close to the checkerboard edges/corners are separated from the homogenous regions inside the checkerboard squares. This separation is carried out by thresholding in a $(2\tau+1) \times (2\tau+1)$ window around the current pixel. In all our experiments, we have set the thresholding window's radius to $\tau = 4$. If the gray value of the center-pixel is in the upper 60% of the windows intensity range, it is set to true in the resulting binary mask image, otherwise it is set to false. The threshold of 60% has been determined heuristically using our test data. The effect of the local thresholding on the gradient image is threefold:

- Pixels very close to the checkerboard edges are set to true.
- Pixels, that are not very close to the edges (low gradient values) but within the thresholding window radius are set to false.
- Pixels of homogeneous regions which are not in the neighborhood of edges are set to true or false depending on image noise (see e.g. region above the topmost checkerboard square row in Figure 2c).

As can be seen in Figure 2c, homogenous checkerboard regions are clearly separated from the edge regions.

3. Conditional dilation

   On the resulting mask image a conditional morphologic dilation is applied in order to close small holes and notches in the mask. These holes / notches can appear either due to sensor noise or image correction artifacts (especially for low-cost webcams). The applied conditional dilation only adds pixels with at least six "true" neighbors (out of eight) to the mask.

4. Centerline computation

   Our implementation of the centerline extraction is based on the Distance Transform with thinning as post-processing step as proposed by Niblack et al. [8]. The result is a binary mask image g with a centerline thickness of 1 (see Figure 2e) which corresponds to the undirected edge image graph G. The edge image graph G with nodes V and edges E is defined as follows:

$$G = (V, E) \tag{1}$$
$$V = \{v \mid g(v) = \text{"true"}\} \tag{2}$$
$$E = \{e = \{v_i, v_j\} \mid \text{dist}(v_i, v_j) \leq \sqrt{2}\} \ (\text{"8-connected neighborhood"}) \tag{3}$$

The set of saddle points in the edge image is defined as:

$$S = \{s \in V \mid |E_s| \geq 3\} \text{ with } E_s = \{e = \{v_i, v_j\} \in E \mid v_i = s \lor v_j = s\} \tag{4}$$

Since the checkerboard edges form a connected component in the input mask they are also connected in the resulting centerline mask. When the centerline mask is interpreted as a graph, every checkerboard edge pixel is part of a cycle.

Due to noise, the connected centerline component related to the checkerboard can contain small branches, which are not part of a cycle and which would generate additional saddle points at the connection to the grid-shaped checkerboard edge structure. In order to remove these "dead ends", we search for pixels with only one neighbor and remove all "true" pixels along the path until we reach the next saddle point. The non-cycle removal is skipped for pixels at the image border in order to enable checkerboard detection if its margin squares are projected partially beyond the image borders.

After removal of acyclic paths there may remain mini-cycles at the branch region and the edge image does not have a centerline thickness of 1 anymore. Therefore, we remove these pixels by thinning to restore the single pixel thickness criterion (which has already been achieved after initial centerline computation). This thinned centerline image can again be interpreted as a graph $G' = (V', E')$ with saddle points S'.

5. Graph saddle points extraction

The extraction of saddle points in the thinned centerline image becomes equivalent to selecting all pixels with three or more "true" neighbors in the edge image graph G' (corresponds to set S'). In the ideal case, the number of corners in the connected edge image graph now matches the number of inner corners in the checkerboard. However, the edge graph can contain multiple, nearby saddle points around a single checkerboard corner (see Figure 2f). This problem is adressed by combining closely clustered saddle points as described in step 6. The result of this step is a mask image with "true" values at the saddle locations and "false" values otherwise.

6. Combination of saddle points

Since the inner checkerboard corners may generate multiple, nearby saddle points, we cluster saddle points which are within a saddle combination distance α from each other. We keep only one saddle point for each cluster. The combination of saddle points is based on the mask image representing all saddle points (Figure 2f). It is not using the graph respresentation. The challenge of the saddle point combination is the choice of the parameter α. If it is too high, saddle points corresponding to different checkerboard corners are combined for small checkerboard field sizes. Low values on the other hand may result in having multiple saddle points for one checkerboard corner. Therefore, we start with a low value of 2, proceed with the checkerboard verification step (7) and iteratively increase the parameter α as long as we either detect a checkerboard or the empirically chosen threshold of 5 is exceeded.

7. Checkerboard verification

For the automatic detection and verification of the checkerboard pattern in the image we use both the centerline image (Figure 2e) and the mask image representing the combined saddle points (Figure 2g). We search for connected components in the centerline image and count the number of saddle points for every component. If the number of saddle points is equal to the number of checkerboard corners, we check the adjacency of the saddle points in the image graph G'. Directly adjacent saddle points in G' (corresponding to adjacent checkerboard X-junctions) are the representatives of two different saddle clusters, but with no saddle point belonging to another cluster in the shortest path between the two points. If the adjacency structure of all saddle points equals a grid structure we return the mean values of the saddle point clusters as corner intializations for the subsequent refinement step.

2.2   Refinement of Checkerboard Corners

After initializing the checkerboard corners, the corners need to be refined with sub-pixel accuracy. For checkerboard patterns typically two methods are proposed: edge approximation techniques (e.g. used by OpenCV) and surface fitting

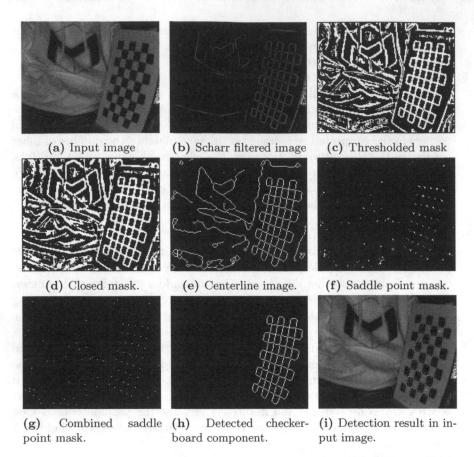

(a) Input image   (b) Scharr filtered image   (c) Thresholded mask

(d) Closed mask.   (e) Centerline image.   (f) Saddle point mask.

(g)   Combined   saddle   (h)   Detected   checker-   (i) Detection result in in-
point mask.   board component.   put image.

Fig. 2. Intermediate results of the checkerboard detection algorithm

around corner candidates [7]. Since edge approximation methods are potentially
biased because of lens distortions, we apply a modified version of the corner
point estimation strategy introduced by Lucchese and Mitra [6]. Our proposed
method consists of two steps:

1. Image filtering around the initial corner point location to obtain an intensity
   surface amenable to fitting a bivariate quadratic polynomial.
2. Fitting a bivariate polynomial of degree 2 represented by the parameters
   $a_{1,2,...,6}$ in the local neighborhood of the initial corner (x, y).

Similar to [6], we apply a lowpass filter as preprocessing step. Instead of using
a normalized Gaussian filter as a preprocessing step we apply a 2-D cone filter to
the original input image. Since a cone is sectionally linear, the convolution with
a combination of step functions (checkerboard pattern) yield sectionally defined
bivariate quadratic polynomials. The kernel c of the cone filter applied in our
tests is defined as following:

$$c_{i,j} = \max\left(0, \gamma + 1 - \sqrt{(\gamma - i)^2 + (\gamma - j)^2}\right), \tag{5}$$

where γ is the half size of the kernel and $i, j \in \{0...2\gamma\}$ are the kernel indices. The size of the cone filter should be at least chosen to be at least as large as the half window size used for surface fitting, otherwise the filtered surface will have constant regions which cannot be well approximated by a bivariate quadratic polynomial.

The polynomial fitting in the local neighborhood of the checkerboard corner is expressed by:

$$\underset{a_{1,2,...,6}}{\arg\min} \sum_{i=-\kappa}^{\kappa} \sum_{j=-\kappa}^{\kappa} \left(a_1 x_i^2 + a_2 x_i y_j + a_3 y_j^2 + a_4 x_i + a_5 y_j + a_6 - f(x_i, y_j)\right)^2 , \quad (6)$$

where $x_i = x + i$, $y_j = y + j$, f is the filtered input intensity image and κ is the half window size used for surface fitting. The saddle point of this polynomial is equal to the refined corner point.

3   Experiments

In this paper we propose a checkerboard detection technique which finds corner points of a checkerboard calibration pattern with subpixel accuracy. We evaluate this method with different sensors and different stereo camera setups with respect to detection accuracy and overall detection rate and compare it to OpenCV's checkerboard detector. All results which refer to OpenCV's checkerboard detector are computed with the detector's internal adaptive thresholding and image normalization enabled.

The evaluation section can be split into two parts. The first part covers stereo camera setups with a small baseline and cameras being verged only slightly towards each other. In these experiments we investigate the subpixel accuracy of the corner refinement stage and the influence of the number of calibration images on the accuracy of the calibration parameters. For these experiments we use only images in which checkerboards are detected both by ROCHADE and OpenCV. The subpixel accuracy is given by the error that occurs when measuring the size of known calibration patterns with a stereo camera setup. We perform these measurements with different sets of calibration parameters which are estimated with different numbers of calibration images.

In the second experiment we evaluate the robustness of the initial checkerboard detection in different setups. We compare the detection rate of the presented method with OpenCV's detection rate and additionally to the detection rate of the OCamCalib Toolbox [10] which implements an improved version of OpenCV's detector as decribed in [9].

3.1   Subpixel Accuracy

For our first experiment we use three different stereo camera setups with different sensor resolutions and lens distortions. Our first setup consists of two Mesa

SR4000 ToF cameras[3]. The Mesa SR4000 has a sensor resolution of 176 x 144 pixels, considerable lens distortion and a pixel resolution of 16 bits. In all our experiments only the 2D intensity images of the ToF sensor are used. We choose these cameras because of the low sensor resolution and the large amount of noise in the images.

The half size of the search window κ in the subpixel refinement step is set to 2 px in case of the Mesa cameras. The filtering parameter γ is set to κ (see Section 2). For better comparability the 16 bit valued images are converted to 8 bit valued images. This is required as OpenCV's checkerboard detection works only on 8 bit images. In the following experiments a simple min/max-windowing is performed, whenever necessary, on the Mesa camera images.

The second camera type we use is the Ensenso N10 stereo camera[4]. The sensor resolution of this camera is 752 x 480 pixels and its lenses introduce only a small amount of distortion. Images captured with this camera have a pixel resolution of 8 bits per pixel. For the Ensenso camera κ is set to 5 px. Again γ is set to the same value as κ.

Our third stereo setup consists of two IDS UI-1241LE[5] cameras. The distortion which is introduced by the lenses is insignficant. The images we capture have a size of 1280 x 1024 pixels with intensities represented with 8 bits per pixel. For this setup κ and γ are set to 5 px.

In all experiments we use a checkerboard with 7 x 10 squares as calibration pattern of which only the corners of the inner 5 x 8 squares are detected. Each square has an edge length of 50 mm.

The evaluation is performed with two image series per camera setup which we call the calibration images and the evaluation images. Both image series consist of image pairs which contain the checkerboard. For estimating the intrinsic and extrinsic parameters of these setups we use OpenCV's implementation of Zhang's method [14] with point correspondences derived from a subset of the calibration images. These point correspondences are either derived with OpenCV's checkerboard detector or ROCHADE.

We work with subsets of the calibration image set in order to investigate the influence of the number of used images on the overall calibration result. For each number of calibration images we estimate two sets of calibration parameters, the first estimated with point correspondences detected with ROCHADE, the second one with OpenCV's checkerboard detector. During calibration both radial and tangential lens distortion is considered.

After estimating the intrinsic and extrinsic parameters, the corners of the evaluation image series are detected with a detector $D = \{OpenCV, ROCHADE\}$. With the calibration parameters and the corner point correspondences we can then measure the length of the of the n-th checkerboard square edge $m_{j,n}$ on the j-th image by simple triangulation.

---

[3] Mesa Imaging AG, Zürich, http://www.mesa-imaging.ch

[4] Ensenso GmbH, Freiburg, http://www.ensenso.de

[5] IDS Imaging Development Systems GmbH, Obersulm,
http://www.ids-imaging.com

The mean absolute error is calculated based on the true edge length l_t for all edge measurements of all images of the evaluation image series as given by Equation 7.

$$\mu_D = \frac{1}{N_i N_e} \sum_{j}^{N_i} \sum_{n}^{N_e} |m_{j,n} - l_t| \; , \tag{7}$$

where N_i denotes the number of evaluation images and N_e the number of edges per checkerboard.

The results for the Mesa SR4000 stereo camera setup are shown in Figures 3a and 3b. One can see that the accuracy of the length measurements does not improve if more than 20 images are used during calibration. A larger number of images is not necessary because the low resolution of the images limits the accuracy for finding corners anyway. If a sufficient number of images is used during calibration the mean absolute measurement accuracy is approximately 0.71 mm with ROCHADE and 1.85 mm with OpenCV. It is worth mentioning that the accuracy of ROCHADE does not decrease noticably due to the 8 bit conversion performed before detecting the corners. One can also see that the measurement accuracy is independent of the pattern detector which is used during calibration of the stereo setup.

Figures 3c and 3d show the mean absolute measurement error for the checkerboards captured with the Ensenso N10 camera. Due to the higher resolution the corner points can be detected more accurately which leads to a significantly lower mean absolute error compared to the Mesa SR4000 camera setup. In this example the mean absolute error is approximately 0.21 mm for ROCHADE and 0.53 mm for OpenCV's detector. Again one can see that the measurement accuracy does not improve if more than approximately 30 images are used for calibration. The larger number of images required is caused by a higher resolution and less noisy images of the Ensenso camera.

The results for our third setup are given in Figures 3e and 3f. With this setup the mean absolute measurement error is almost identical for ROCHADE and OpenCV. Due to the higher resolution OpenCV's detector is able to refine checkerboard corner coordinates more accurately as gradients can be computed more reliably than in low resolution images. Furthermore, OpenCV benefits more from the camera's little lens distortion than ROCHADE as the squares and therefore gradients around intial corners are not distorted. Similar as in the previous setups the detection accuracy does not improve if more than approximately 30 images are used.

3.2   Overall Detection Rate

The overall detection rate is defined as the number of checkerboards which are detected compared to the total number of images of a series. When calibrating a new camera a certain number of point correspondences, which can be derived from detected checkerboards, is required. In this experiment, a high detection rate reflects high robustness with respect to lens distortion and extreme checkerboard poses.

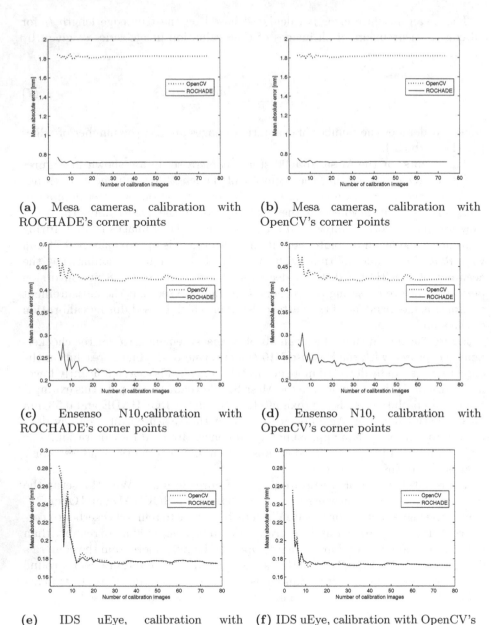

(a) Mesa cameras, calibration with ROCHADE's corner points

(b) Mesa cameras, calibration with OpenCV's corner points

(c) Ensenso N10, calibration with ROCHADE's corner points

(d) Ensenso N10, calibration with OpenCV's corner points

(e) IDS uEye, calibration with ROCHADE's corner points

(f) IDS uEye, calibration with OpenCV's corner points

Fig. 3. Mean absolute measurement errors for different camera setups with respect to the number of used calibration images

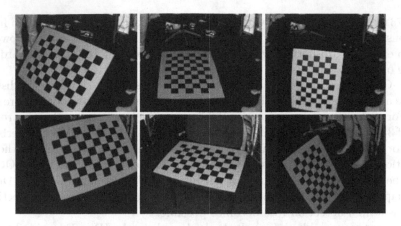

Fig. 4. Three sample image pairs of the Mesa SR4000 wide baseline image set. The top row shows the images of the first camera, the second row the corresponding images of the second camera. Images are enlarged with nearest neighbour interpolation.

Two image series are captured with a wide baseline stereo camera setup. In such a setup the detection of calibration pattern is difficult due to the extreme pose of the calibration pattern. The first setup consists of the two Mesa SR4000 cameras as described in Section 3.1 but with a baseline of approximately 103 cm. Figure 4 shows three image pairs of this series.

In our second setup we use the IDS uEye cameras we have already used in the first experiment but again with a wider baseline of approximately 224 cm.

The third image series was taken with a single GoPro Hero 3 camera. We use this camera to investigate the detection rate on high resolution images which suffer from strong lens distortion.

The results of this experiment are shown in Table 1.

Table 1. Successful checkerboard detections for ROCHADE, OpenCV and OCamCalib [10]

Camera Setup	Total images	ROCHADE	OpenCV	OCamCalib
Stereo Mesa SR4000 setup	103	91	8	50
Stereo IDS uEye setup	100	100	100	100
Single GoPro Hero 3	100	96	73	100

In the case of the Mesa SR4000 stereo camera setup 91 out of 103 checkerboard patterns are detected by ROCHADE whereas OCamCalib finds only 50 and OpenCV only 8 patterns. Note that the checkerboards are not only found but also detected highly accurately. The detected cornerpoints are suitable for estimating the intrinsic and extrinsic parameters of this stereo camera setup. When using 91 detected checkerboard patterns and performing the same evaluation as presented in Section 3.1 we achieve a mean absolute measurement error of 0.273 mm when measuring with ROCHADE. This error is smaller than in the previous experiment due to the wider baseline of the camera setup. However, due to extreme foreshortening ROCHADE fails to detect the checkerboard in a couple of images.

The GoPro Hero 3 comes with a wide angle lens which significantly distorts images and therefore makes the automatic detection of checkerboards more difficult. For evaluation purposes we use 100 images which are captured with a resolution of 3840 x 2160 pixels. Due to the higher resolution, OpenCV's checkerboard detector is able to detect a larger percentage of checkerboards than in the low resolution setup with the Mesa cameras. Similar to OpenCV's detector OCam-Calib benefits greatly from the high resolution of the evaluation images. Due to the adaptions for the detection of checkerboards captured with omnidirectional cameras a high detection rate becomes possible.

All detectors are able to find all checkerboards in the IDS uEye wide baseline stereo setup, even though the image resolution is signifcantly lower than the resolution of the previously presented GoPro camera. However, with the IDS uEye camera almost no lens distoriton is present which simplifies the detection progress.

4   Conclusion

Recent developments in real time depth imaging (Microsoft Kinect, Creative Senz3D) make the fast and accurate (multi-) camera calibration of mid and low resolution sensors more and more important. Moreover, low cost lenses used in mobile devices often show a relatively high optical distortion. Our presented checkerboard detection method outperforms OpenCV's checkerboard detector in low resolution images or highly distorted images. Especially in the low resolution case ROCHADE is more robust with respect to extreme poses of the checkerboard. Furthermore our method performs at least as good as OpenCV's detector in medium and high resolution images if no significant amounts of distortion are present. Especially in multi camera setups with wide baselines the presented algorithm still allows a highly accurate estimation of intrinsic and extrinsic camera parameters whereas a calibration with OpenCV's checkerboard detection is impossible.

We also evaluate the influence of accurate corner detection on the overall calibration of a stereo setup. In our experiments we show that the accuracy of intrinsic and extrinsic parameters does not improve with a higher accuracy of the point correspondences, provided a certain subpixel accuracy has already been achieved. Future work will include the determination of this minimum accuracy.

By presenting quantitative results we also showed that the accuracy of multi-camera calibration typically cannot be increased if more than a certain number point correspondences, or calibration images, are used. These results comply with the results published by Sun et al. in [11]. However, it might be possible to reduce this number by chosing the right checkerboard poses. Furthermore an extension of the presented algorithm is planned which does not require that the whole checkerboard is visible in the image. A Matlab implementation of the method presented in this paper can be found on our website[6].

Acknowledgements. This publication was supported by the German Federal Ministry of Education and Research as part of the Spitzencluster Medical Valley program 13GW0029A.

References

1. Chen, D., Zhang, G.: A new sub-pixel detector for x-corners in camera calibration targets. WSCG (Short Papers) 5, 97–100 (2005)
2. Dao, V.N., Sugimoto, M.: A robust recognition technique for dense checkerboard patterns. In: Pattern Recognition (ICPR), 2010 20th International Conference on. pp. 3081–3084. IEEE (2010)
3. De la Escalera, A., Armingol, J.M.: Automatic chessboard detection for intrinsic and extrinsic camera parameter calibration. Sensors 10(3), 2027–2044 (2010)
4. Fiala, M., Shu, C.: Self-identifying patterns for plane-based camera calibration. Machine Vision and Applications 19(4), 209–216 (2008)
5. Heikkila, J.: Geometric camera calibration using circular control points. IEEE Transactions on Pattern Analysis and Machine Intelligence 22(10), 1066–1077 (2000)
6. Lucchese, L., Mitra, S.K.: Using saddle points for subpixel feature detection in camera calibration targets. In: Asia-Pacific Conference on Circuits and Systems. vol. 2, pp. 191–195. IEEE (2002)
7. Mallon, J., Whelan, P.F.: Which pattern? biasing aspects of planar calibration patterns and detection methods. Pattern Recognition Letters 28(8), 921–930 (2007)
8. Niblack, C.W., Gibbons, P.B., Capson, D.W.: Generating skeletons and centerlines from the distance transform. CVGIP: Graph. Models Image Process. 54(5), 420–437 (Sep 1992)
9. Rufli, M., Scaramuzza, D., Siegwart, R.: Automatic detection of checkerboards on blurred and distorted images. In: Intelligent Robots and Systems, 2008. IROS 2008. IEEE/RSJ International Conference on. pp. 3121–3126. IEEE (2008)
10. Scaramuzza, D.: Omnidirectional Vision: from Calibration to Root Motion Estimation. Ph.D. thesis, Swiss Federal Institute of Technology Zurich (ETHZ) (February 2008)
11. Sun, W., Cooperstock, J.R.: An empirical evaluation of factors influencing camera calibration accuracy using three publicly available techniques. Machine Vision and Applications 17(1), 51–67 (2006)
12. Tsai, R.Y.: A versatile camera calibration technique for high-accuracy 3d machine vision metrology using off-the-shelf tv cameras and lenses. IEEE Journal of Robotics and Automation 3(4), 323–344 (1987)
13. Wang, Z., Wu, W., Xu, X., Xue, D.: Recognition and location of the internal corners of planar checkerboard calibration pattern image. Applied mathematics and computation 185(2), 894–906 (2007)
14. Zhang, Z.: A flexible new technique for camera calibration. IEEE Transactions on Pattern Analysis and Machine Intelligence 22(11), 1330–1334 (2000)

---

[6] http://www.metrilus.de/rochade/

Correcting for Duplicate Scene Structure in Sparse 3D Reconstruction

Jared Heinly, Enrique Dunn, and Jan-Michael Frahm

The University of North Carolina at Chapel Hill, USA

Abstract. Structure from motion (SfM) is a common technique to recover 3D geometry and camera poses from sets of images of a common scene. In many urban environments, however, there are symmetric, repetitive, or duplicate structures that pose challenges for SfM pipelines. The result of these ambiguous structures is incorrectly placed cameras and points within the reconstruction. In this paper, we present a postprocessing method that can not only detect these errors, but successfully resolve them. Our novel approach proposes the strong and informative measure of conflicting observations, and we demonstrate that it is robust to a large variety of scenes.

Keywords: Structure from motion, duplicate structure disambiguation.

1 Introduction

In the last decade, structure from motion (SfM) has been taken out of the lab and into the real world. The achieved progress is impressive and has enabled large-scale scene reconstruction from thousands of images covering different scenes around the world [2,9,11,27]. In crowd-sourced reconstructions of large-scale environments, SfM methods do not have any control over the acquisition of the images, leading to many new challenges. One major challenge that arises is the ambiguity resulting from duplicate structure, i.e. different structures with the same appearance. Fig. 1 shows an example of duplicate scene structure on Big Ben, where every side of the clock tower has the same appearance. SfM methods often erroneously register these duplicate structures as a single structure, yielding incorrect 3D camera registrations (see Fig. 1). We propose a method that can correct the misregistrations caused by the duplicate scene structure in the final SfM model (see Fig. 1 for the corrected reconstruction of Big Ben).

To correct the misregistration caused by duplicate structure, it is important to understand the nature of the ambiguity that causes the error. The most common SfM methods operate as an incremental reconstruction, i.e. they start from an initial pair or triplet and subsequently extend the reconstruction one-by-one for each remaining image. However, the decision of which image to add next to the reconstruction is not arbitrary. This choice is typically driven by an image similarity metric used to find images that are similar to the ones already registered [2,4,7,11,18,20]. It is within this process that sometimes SfM algorithms select images which do not actually overlap with the current reconstruction, but

D. Fleet et al. (Eds.): ECCV 2014, Part IV, LNCS 8692, pp. 780–795, 2014.

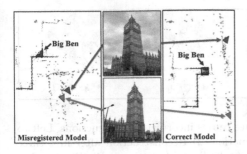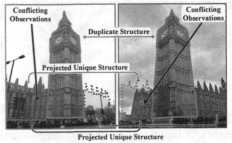

Fig. 1. Left: example camera placements in a misregistered and correct SfM model. Right: example illustration of conflicting observations between two images.

do overlap with a different instance of the duplicate structure. These images are then erroneously registered to the wrong instance of the duplicate structure. An indication for this erroneous registration is that only points on the duplicate structure register. Unfortunately, a priori knowledge of the duplicate structure is not available at registration time. Subsequent registrations extend the reconstruction further, but with the two copies of the duplicate structure combined into a single model. This erroneous reconstruction contains incorrectly placed unique structures due to the incorrect registration of the duplicate structure.

Fig. 2 shows an incremental SfM pipeline that results in erroneous geometry. The images are sequentially registered and added to the reconstruction, and upon reaching the fourth image in the set (which is taken from a different location than the first three), it registers, but only to the facades of the tower. This registration is incorrect, as the camera should have been rotated 90° around the tower. Now, when registering the remaining cameras (which should also be rotated 90°) they will correctly register to the fourth image and start to triangulate 3D structure. However, because of the fourth camera's mislocation, the new structure (and camera poses) will be incorrectly placed within the scene.

Given the difficulties of detecting erroneous registration during reconstruction, we propose a method which can correct the errors upon completion of SfM. Our method identifies incorrectly placed unique scene structures, and from this we infer the points belonging to the duplicate structure. Once our system identifies the duplicate structure, it attempts registration of cameras and points using only the distinct unique structures to obtain a correct model.

2   Related Work

Duplicate structure has been of recent interest in the research community and has motivated a variety of applications [3,8,14,22,23,25,28]. Generally, there are different types of duplicate scene structures, ranging from duplicate instances caused by 3D rotational symmetries, separate identical surfaces, or repetitive or mirrored structures often found on facades (a survey of symmetry is provided in [17]). Duplicate structures are prone to lead to misregistered scene reconstructions, though mirror symmetries do not typically contribute to these errors.

Fig. 2. Illustration of how duplicate structure causes incorrect reconstructions. Left to right: 1) Input images ordered for reconstruction, 2) Reconstruction after first three images, 3) Fourth camera registers, but only to duplicate structure on Big Ben facades, 4) Remaining images register, and an erroneous structure is created (circled in red).

Symmetric and repetitive structures can generally be detected in images through techniques that detect symmetric or repetitive patterns [5,6,13,15,16,31,32]. Methods have leveraged these patterns for urban geolocalization [3,22,25] and reconstruction of a scene from only a single image [14,23,28]. Furthermore, there has been recent work on utilizing symmetry as a constraint in bundle adjustment to improve the accuracy of an SfM result [8].

The class of duplicate structures originating from 3D rotational symmetries and different identical copies of the same surface in the scene is typically not detectable by purely image-based measures. It is this class of duplicate structures that we target for correction. Next, we discuss several related approaches also aiming at mitigating the effects of this class of duplicate structures.

Zach *et al.* [29] introduce the concept of *missing correspondences*. The main idea is to identify image triplets that have consistent sets of three-view feature observations, while minimizing the number of features observed in only two of the images. The valid triplets are then combined into the correct reconstruction. The intuition is that if a substantial fraction of observations are missing from the third image, then that third image is incorrectly registered. They use a Bayesian framework that has a belief network for image triplets in order to verify their correctness and relation to each other. However, the authors enforce the very conservative assumption that a pair of images deemed to be incorrectly registered cannot exist within the same single reconstruction. This is conservative as the images could be viewing a duplicate instance within a single scene that could later be reconciled. In contrast, our method performs the inference over all cameras in the SfM model, and allows incorrectly matched images to correctly register to different parts of the same single reconstruction.

Roberts *et al.* [21] also utilize the idea of missing correspondences by exploiting them as a metric within an expectation-minimization framework to identify incorrectly registered image pairs. They improve over the original formulation of Zach *et al.* [29] by relying on image timestamps to provide approximate sequence information. Hence, they implicitly assume an association between the temporal and spatial order of the images. This allows their method to function in potentially challenging scenarios, but prevents it being applied to unordered Internet photo collections. Our method, in contrast, does not require any temporal information for the images and does correctly handle Internet photo collections.

Loop constraints were exploited by Zach *et al.* [30] to detect incorrect camera registrations. Their algorithm analyzes loops (cycles) of connected cameras in a graph in which cameras are nodes and pairwise transformations between cameras are edges. When traversing a loop and chaining the transformations between the images, one should achieve the identity transform (with some natural drift) upon matching to the first image in that loop (loop closure). If this criterion is broken, then at least one of the transformations in the loop is assumed to be incorrect. Even if there is no drift, assuming an identity transformation over a loop is not sufficient for detecting all erroneous loops in the graph [12].

Jiang *et al.* [12] minimize the number of missing correspondences across the entire reconstruction instead of triplets [29]. To find the minimum they evaluate a set of possible reconstructions and make the key assumption that the set of images under consideration forms one connected model. This assumption fails when the images are actually from two separate scenes, or when there is insufficient overlap between views of a duplicate structure. Our method overcomes these shortcomings by correctly splitting and maintaining separate partial models of the scene (such as datasets 7–9 in Fig. 7).

Instead of using missing correspondences explicitly, Wilson and Snavely [26] utilize the bipartite local clustering coefficient over the visibility graph of an SfM model. This measure identifies tracks of 3D point observations that are suspected of incorrectly linking separate structures. They require prior knowledge of the desired number of splits as an input. Then, their method removes a large number of erroneous tracks and will split incorrectly generated models. Their primary mode of failure is over-segmentation (even splitting already correct models [26]). They do not propose a conclusive technique to merge the split components as they only use medoid SIFT features, matching, and estimating an alignment via RANSAC to fix oversplitting in one of their datasets. Additionally, the authors state that their method is not well suited for the "laboratory-style" datasets of previous papers (datasets limited to a few hundred images). Our method, in contrast, leverages an automatic merging technique, and circumvents oversplitting by detecting if an SfM model is already correct. Furthermore, we demonstrate successful results on both laboratory and large-scale real-world datasets (Fig. 7).

In summary, missing correspondences (an intuition used by many previous methods) report on structure that was expected. This implicitly assumes the repeatability of the correspondence mechanism, which can fail because of noise, occlusion, or changes in viewpoint [19]. This assumption severely limits the range and type of incorrect registrations that can be detected. Therefore, the remaining unsolved challenges for model correction include robustly handling duplicate instances without oversplitting, while at the same time being able to correctly recover one or more final models (depending on the configuration of the underlying scene). It is this challenge that our paper successfully addresses.

3   Algorithm

We propose using *conflicting observations* to identify the incorrect registrations caused by duplicate structure as a more powerful alternative to using missing

Fig. 3. Method overview: ❶ Input SfM model, ❷ Candidate camera graph splits, ❸ Conflicting observations, and ❹ Model merging

correspondences. Conflicting observations are 3D points that when projected, using the corresponding 3D reconstruction information, into and across pairwise registered images, conflict in their spatial location, i.e. there are observations of alternative structures in the same spatial location in the image plane. For instance, consider two separate views of duplicate structure (like the facades of Big Ben, shown in Fig. 1). Each image contains observations of the duplicate 3D points, but the observations of the disjoint secondary structures in the scene are unique. The unique structure in the first image, when projected into the second, overlaps with the second image's unique structure. It is this unique structure that we analyze for conflict, as it is separate from the duplicate object and provides distinct information about the layout of the scene.

3.1   Overview

Given the difficulty of detecting the duplicate structures during the initial registration, our method is a post-processing step to SfM, i.e. the input to our system is the output of a sparse 3D reconstruction pipeline. The registered cameras and the 3D points define a *camera graph* (CG) where nodes correspond to the cameras, and edges exist between nodes whenever the two cameras view a common set of 3D points. Our method uses a recursive processing procedure whose goal is to determine if there are any errors in the current reconstruction (step ❷ and ❸ in the method outline shown in Fig. 3). During this procedure, step ❷ proposes candidate CG splits, dividing the cameras in the current CG into two subgraphs, which are then evaluated for conflict in step ❸.

For step ❸, each 3D point of the model is assigned to one of three classes: points seen by cameras in both subgraphs (potentially duplicate structure), points seen by only the cameras in the first subgraph (unique structure for this subgraph), and points seen only by the cameras of the second subgraph (unique structure in the second subgraph). Then, the unique structures are used to test for conflict between the two subgraphs by counting the number of conflicting observations between camera pairs where both cameras observe common points but the cameras originate from different subgraphs. The number of conflicting observations for such a camera pair provides a conflict score for the CG split. If there is considerable conflict between the subgraphs, the CG is permanently split and the two subgraphs are independently recursively evaluated for further conflict. If a CG has no considerable conflict it is accepted as valid.

After identifying the separate subgraphs of the model, our method (step ❹) attempts to merge the subgraphs to recover the correct model. It proposes candidate alignments between the split 3D models (subgraphs), and then evaluates the conflict for the merge (leveraging conflicting observations). If an alignment with sufficiently low conflict is found, then the two subgraphs are combined; otherwise, they are output as independent components of the reconstruction.

To review, we propose a conflict measure to detect overlap between structures that should be spatially unique. Applying this measure both to candidate CG splits and merges, we can successfully correct a misregistered SfM model.

3.2   Step ❶: Input Reconstruction

As our method is a post-processing step for SfM, we require as input typical outputs of such a system [2,11,24,27]. In our results we used [27] and [24]. Our method assumes the availability of known 3D camera poses (positions and orientations), the original images (for step ❸ of our method), and the locations of the 3D points and their visibility with respect to each camera. To perform sub-model merging (step ❹), the original feature inliers are required, i.e. which features were verified geometric inliers between a pair of images. In the case that some of the above input information is missing, (e.g. SfM without correspondences [10]) it can always be computed from the images and camera poses.

3.3   Step ❷: Candidate Camera Graph Splits

We wish to generate candidate CG splits, where each split divides the cameras into two distinct subgraphs. These two subgraphs will then be passed to step ❸, which will evaluate the conflict between them.

Naïve potential splits can be proposed by enumerating all possible camera groupings. Given that the CG contains m cameras and is potentially densely connected, there would be at most $2^{m-1} - 1$ possible ways to assign the cameras to two different groups where each is a connected component (subgraph). This is exponential in m and computationally prohibitive for most large-scale models.

Minimum Spanning Tree. To reduce the number of candidate splits, we propose to leverage a minimum spanning tree (MST) representation similar to the one constructed in [12], and illustrated in Fig. 4, step 2. Jiang *et al.* [12] assigned to each edge a weight that was inversely proportional to the number of 3D point observations shared between the two cameras. We adopt a similar idea, but reformulate the edge cost to account for the fact that if duplicate structure is present, many of the images will have a large number of common points. Accordingly, this raw number of points should not be overemphasized, hence our edge cost leverages the following ratio where e_{ij} is the edge cost between cameras i and j, and O_i, O_j are the sets of 3D points that are visible in each camera:

$$e_{ij} = 1 - \frac{|O_i \cap O_j|}{|O_i \cup O_j|} \tag{1}$$

Conceptually, an MST formed using this edge cost tends to link cameras together that share similar content, and in contrast to [12], avoids biasing the results for cameras with relatively few or many point observations.

If two cameras see the same set of 3D points then e_{ij} will be zero. Accordingly, two views seeing the same instance of the duplicate structure and the corresponding surrounding unique structure will have a low edge cost. We denote these edges as *desired edges*. Conversely, two cameras, which see two different instances of the duplicate structure but do not see a common unique structure, will have a significantly higher e_{ij} value and are denoted as *confusing edges*.

Intuitively, the MST prefers utilizing desired edges (low edge cost) to connect cameras seeing the same instance of the duplicate structure and will only retain confusing edges (high edge cost), when necessary, to connect cameras seeing different instances of the duplicate structure. Accordingly, the MST will group cameras together that see the same instance of the duplicate structure and the confusing edges will bridge between these groups. With this observation, we can now limit our CG splits to those that are defined by the MST, as removing a confusing edge creates two separate subgraphs defining a candidate split. Defining the search space of candidate model splits in terms of an MST representation reduces the number of potential candidate splits from one that is exponential in the number of cameras to $m - 1$, the edges in the MST. Refer to Fig. 4, steps 1-3 for an illustration of a split in the MST resulting in two subgraphs.

3.4   Step ❸: Conflicting Observations

After leveraging the MST, the next step evaluates the conflict between the two subgraphs produced by each split of the graph to obtain a reduced set of splits.

Common and Unique Structure. First, our approach classifies each 3D point into one of three categories as defined below:

$$\begin{aligned}
\mathbb{D} &= \{P_k : \ (\exists O_{ik} \in O) \wedge \ (\exists O_{jk} \in O)\} \\
\mathbb{U}_1 &= \{P_k : \ (\exists O_{ik} \in O) \wedge \neg(\exists O_{jk} \in O)\} \\
\mathbb{U}_2 &= \{P_k : \neg(\exists O_{ik} \in O) \wedge \ (\exists O_{jk} \in O)\}
\end{aligned} \tag{2}$$

where $\{P\}$ is the set of 3D points, P_k is the k-th point in $\{P\}$, O represents the visibility of points in the cameras ($O_{ik} \in O$ if P_k is visible in camera i, otherwise it is false), and i, j referring to camera i in the first set of cameras and the j-th camera in the second set of cameras. The common points (the candidate duplicate structure) between the two camera groups are denoted by $\mathbb{D}$, with $\mathbb{U}_1, \mathbb{U}_2$ denoting the unique points to each subgraph.

To improve our robustness to noisy scene geometry we enforce a minimum number of observations for each 3D point, where i is any arbitrary camera:

$$P = \{P_k : |\{i : O_{ik} \in O\}| \geq \rho\} \tag{3}$$

By setting $\rho = 3$ (as we did in all of our experiments), we maintain only those 3D points that are more likely to be stable and properly triangulated.

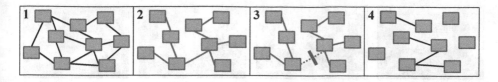

Fig. 4. 1. Full camera graph, 2. Minimum spanning tree, 3. Candidate minimum spanning tree split defining two camera groups, 4. Camera pairs from the full camera graph that were assigned to different groups

Split Camera Pairs. To evaluate the conflict of a candidate split, we analyze the image pairs from the full CG that had originally matched but are now split due to the images being assigned to different subgraphs. For an example of such pairs, refer to Fig. 4, step 4. We require a minimum number γ of 3D points that the cameras of a pair must observe in common in order to avoid images that are weakly connected as they do not represent a reliable measure of conflict.

Next, we project the unique points observed in each image to the other image in the pair, and test for conflicting observations. To mitigate the effects of occlusion or large viewpoint change, only cameras observing the same points from a similar surface incidence angle are considered. The difference in surface incidence angle β between the cameras i and j with their centers (C_i, C_j) and the centroid of their common 3D points $\bar{p}$, where $\bar{p} = \texttt{mean}(\{P_k : (\exists O_{ik} \in O) \wedge (\exists O_{jk} \in O)\})$ (also by construction, $\{P_k\} \subseteq \mathbb{D}$) is defined as:

$$\beta = \texttt{arccos}\left(\texttt{dot}\left(\frac{C_i - \bar{p}}{||C_i - \bar{p}||}, \frac{C_j - \bar{p}}{||C_j - \bar{p}||}\right)\right) \tag{4}$$

Given the limitations in matching over large viewpoint changes, our method disregards camera pairs with a difference in surface incidence angle β greater than a predefined threshold θ. The threshold θ is chosen according to the robustness of the SfM system's features with respect to viewpoint changes (for example, around 20° for SIFT features in our experiments).

Splitting at each of the $m - 1$ MST edges leads to a cubic complexity of the evaluated splits given that there is potentially a quadratic number of pairs of cameras (for a fully connected graph) for a given split. To boost efficiency, instead of evaluating all split camera pairs, we propose to inspect only those pairs with the smallest surface incidence angles β, which still allows us to detect the conflict. Specifically, we can inspect the s smallest pairs, giving quadratic overall complexity when s is a function of m, or a fixed number of smallest pairs (e.g. $s = 100$) to achieve a linear overall complexity. In our experiments, we have found both strategies to be valid, and thus opt for the linear time approach.

As opposed to using an MST to determine the locations to evaluate conflict, one could imagine that we could instead use a clustering or graph-cutting approach on the full CG. We avoided these as they would necessitate computing conflict (t from the next step) between all (or a very large fraction) of the camera pairs which could quickly become computationally prohibitive for larger CGs.

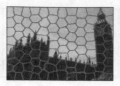

Fig. 5. Example SLICO [1] superpixel segmentations

Conflict Measure. Our conflict measure leverages the unique points in the scene by projecting them into the other image of the camera pair, and expecting that they should not overlap with the unique points of that image. If there is substantial overlap, then we have reason to believe that there is an error in the current reconstruction (refer to Fig. 1 for an example). How does one measure overlap in two projected sparse point sets? Ideally, spatially nearby (in the image) unique points on the same structural surface should conflict, whereas nearby points on separate surfaces that lie at different depths should not conflict.

To establish the surface association of the sparse points, we leverage SLICO superpixels [1], whose only parameter is the desired number of superpixels. SLICO will automatically adapt to the texture in the image in order to maintain regular-sized superpixels (examples of which are shown in Fig. 5). To guard against arbitrary superpixel divisions along the same structural surface, we perform multiple (eight in our experiments) different segmentations of each image by providing mirrored and rotated versions of an image to SLICO. This proved to generate a different segmentation for each (there are only eight different combinations of 90° rotations and mirror operations). With these segmentations, we now define two points to be nearby if their projections lie within the same superpixel in any of the candidate segmentations.

By leveraging the current potential duplicate ($\mathbb{D}$) and unique point sets ($\mathbb{U}_1$, $\mathbb{U}_2$) for every single camera pair, we can evaluate the subsets of these points that are currently visible in the camera pair to identify the conflicting observations.

While we focus on conflicting unique points, the locations of the common points ($\mathbb{D}$) also provide useful information. Both [21] and [29] emphasized the usefulness of considering the spatial location of these observations. For instance, the presence of a matched point between two images would down-weigh the contribution of any nearby missing correspondences. Utilizing this concept, we obtain reduced sets (U_1, U_2) by ignoring unique points (from $\mathbb{U}_1$, $\mathbb{U}_2$) that occupy the same superpixel as a common point (from $\mathbb{D}$) in any of the segmentations.

For a given pair of images, we define the conflict t between them to be the minimum number of points from U_1 or U_2 that conflict in both images. If $\mathtt{proj}(U_1)$ is the projection of the points U_1 into the second image, and $\mathtt{proj}(U_2)$ is the projection into the first, then the conflict t is defined as:

$$N = \mathtt{near}\big(U_1, \mathtt{proj}(U_2)\big) \cap \mathtt{near}\big(U_2, \mathtt{proj}(U_1)\big) \tag{5}$$

$$t = \mathtt{min}\Big(\big|\{u_1 : u_1 \in U_1 \wedge u_1 \in N\}\big|, \big|\{u_2 : u_2 \in U_2 \wedge u_2 \in N\}\big|\Big) \tag{6}$$

where **near**() returns the points that are nearby as defined by the superpixel segmentations. To provide further intuition, consider the case where one unique point from U_1 conflicts with many from U_2. This single point from U_1 could be an extraneous structure, and should not count as significant conflict even though it conflicts with many points from U_2. Therefore, we leverage the minimum of the two set sizes, as this enforces a stronger indication of the presence of conflict.

Given the conflict t for a single split camera pair, the conflict over the split CG is the average of the conflicts from all split camera pairs between the two subgraphs (step 4 in Fig. 4). This average is then independently computed for each split in the MST. If the MST split with the highest conflict is above a predefined threshold τ, we remove the corresponding edge from the MST to generate two separate subgraphs. Each of these subgraphs is then processed by reapplying steps ❷ through ❹ with the exception of not recomputing the MST. This is recursively repeated until we are left with a set of subgraphs that are free from conflicting observations, i.e. their conflict is below our threshold τ.

3.5 Step ❹: Model Merging

Once we have a set of camera subgraphs that are free from significant conflict, we now seek to merge them together and recover a correct reconstruction (if one is possible, as the images may come from entirely separate scenes).

The key concept that we leverage here is the idea of *disconnected inliers*. Disconnected inliers are pairs of 3D points whose 2D features had been identified as inliers during the two-view geometric verification of an image pair in the SfM processing. However, due to the duplicate structure in the scene (or potentially other factors, such as feature mismatches) the inlier ended up being triangulated as two separate 3D points. Therefore, to recover candidate merges, we estimate 3D similarities that would align and reconnect the disconnected inlier points.

To estimate the similarity between the split subgraphs (and their associated disconnected inliers), we leverage a RANSAC technique, once again enforcing that a candidate solution should be made up of at least γ points in order to be considered further. Note that when generating candidate similarities, we ignore any common points that are shared between two or more subgraphs (a union of the final $\mathbb{D}$ sets from each of the split subgraphs, which we denote $\mathbb{D}_{Final}$). These points are the final duplicate structure, and as such, are not reliable for merging as they define the duplicate structure within the scene. However, once a candidate similarity has been proposed, we recompute the similarity inlier set using all disconnected inliers (even including duplicate points).

For each candidate solution, we transform the camera poses using the similarity T and update the unique 3D point structure of the subgraph. The points shared between subgraphs (the duplicate structure) are duplicated and transformed using T to correctly represent the duplicate scene structure. Then, the conflict between the two merged subgraphs is computed. In order to compute this conflict, inliers to T are identified as common structure $\mathbb{D}$. Furthermore, we load any existing 2D inliers for an image pair (from two-view geometric verification) and mark superpixels containing the 2D inlier locations as common

Table 1. Statistics showing the number of cameras and points in the dataset, the time required for our method, and the software used to generate the initial reconstruction

	Dataset Name	# Cams	# Points	Time	SfM
1	Big Ben (using iconics)	13590	167375	20.5 m	[27]
2	Berliner Dom	1618	245079	9.8 h	[27]
3	Sacre Coeur [26]	1112	378882	4.4 h	[24]
4	Notre Dame [26] (iconics)	885	176099	1.8 h	[24]
5	Alexander Nevsky Cathedral	448	92948	16.6 m	[27]
6	Arc de Triomphe	434	93452	16.3 m	[27]
7	Radcliffe Camera	282	71107	31.9 m	[27]
8	Church on Spilled Blood	277	76582	1.4 h	[27]
9	Brandenburg Gate	175	23933	3.0 m	[27]
10	Indoor [12]	152	69632	3.1 m	[27]
11	Cereal [21]	25	12194	36 s	[27]
12	Street [21]	19	7607	39 s	[27]

structure. We do the latter to recover correspondences that would otherwise not have existed because the SfM algorithm ended up placing the cameras at separate locations within the scene (and choosing not to incorporate the relative pose initially computed between the images).

If the conflict is less than τ, the merge is considered correct. Otherwise, we ignore the points that were inliers to T, and attempt to estimate a different similarity. This continues until either a correct merge is found, or no solution can be computed with γ or more inliers. By repeating this process between all split camera groups, we merge all subgraphs that have valid overlapping geometry and recover a more complete and correct representation of the scene.

Now that we have correctly identified the duplicate structure within the scene ($\mathbb{D}_{Final}$), this information can be used to allow additional images to be registered to the reconstruction. For instance, when registering a new image, the image should not be allowed to register only to points contained within $\mathbb{D}_{Final}$, but should instead incorporate unique points not in $\mathbb{D}_{Final}$. In this manner, new images will not be incorrectly registered to the duplicate structure. Furthermore, this process could be embedded into an incremental SfM pipeline, so that disambiguation would occur at certain intervals to detect and mark as confusing any duplicate structure that is found. This would successfully addresses the source of the problem (the behavior of incremental SfM) as described in Section 1.

4   Results

In order to evaluate our method, we applied it to a wide variety of datasets (see Table 1 for a detailed overview of the datasets that led to misregistered models, not including those in Fig. 6 that were already correct). First, we evaluated our method on datasets from previous papers [12,21,26], using their qualitative evaluation metric for the correct camera and model arrangement. Fig. 7 (models

3, 4, 10–12) illustrates the output of our method on these existing benchmark datasets. Upon close inspection, we perform equally well or better than previous methods on their datasets as we split their models correctly (avoiding oversplits) and merge the ones that are mergeable (datasets 10–12). For instance, in dataset 4, we avoid oversplitting the front from the back of Notre Dame, as in [26], though our method did output a small nighttime model, as there were day and nighttime versions of local image features that corresponded to the same geometry, and thus generated conflict. We did leverage iconic selection [11] for this dataset, and for dataset 3, we used the set of images that viewed Sacre Coeur in the covering subgraph from [26]. In addition, we also ran our method on the Seville Cathedral and Louvre datasets from [26]. For the Seville Cathedral, our method split the model into three main components, whereas [26] had oversplit into four. For the Louvre, we had to set $\tau = 2.0$, and were able to split it into two main sub-models. As a note, [26] split the Louvre into three sub-models, the difference being that their method split two components that were correctly oriented with respect to each other but reconstructed at different scales.

To validate that our method only alters misregistered models, we tested it on reconstructions that were already correct (eight of which are shown in Fig. 6). In these cases, our method correctly identified them as having negligible conflict and did not attempt further processing.

Beyond benchmark comparisons, we evaluated our approach on seven novel datasets downloaded from Flickr (Fig. 7, models 1, 2, 5 9). These datasets contain several duplicate structures, and are common examples of the types of ambiguities found in urban scenes. They also represent the originally targeted (and previously unsolved) challenge of robustly disambiguating duplicate structure without making a priori assumptions on the number of correct final models to output. For datasets 1, 2, 5, 6, our method correctly split and merged the reconstructions into a single large model. It even handled the difficult challenge of Big Ben (dataset 1) where there were three split subgraphs in the reconstruction. For dataset 6, our method did output a small nighttime model. The remaining three novel datasets (7–9) successfully split and then remained as separate models, as we manually verified that there were insufficient overlapping views to support a merge. The primary reason for this lack of overlapping views is the layout of the scene itself, where photographers are limited in the number of accessible vantage points from which a desirable photo can be taken.

For further comparison, we ran the code from [26] on our novel datasets. For Big Ben, [26] split it into only two sub-models, failing to distinguish the front and back of the tower. The Berliner Dom split into five models, two of which failed to split the front of the building from the side. Alexander Nevsky Cathedral failed to split at all, but the Arc de Triomphe was correctly split into two components. Radcliffe Camera was oversplit into three models. The Church on Spilled Blood was split into two correct models, but the third smallest camera group was discarded as it was not included in the covering subgraph. Additionally, the Brandenburg Gate remained as one model, but all cameras from the back side of the structure had been discarded. Note that in the generation of these results,

Fig. 6. Example error-free reconstructions correctly identified by our method. From left to right: Trevi Fountain, Sistine Chapel Ceiling, Harmandir Sahib, Colosseum, Notre Dame Facade, Stonehenge, Statue of Liberty, and CAB [8].

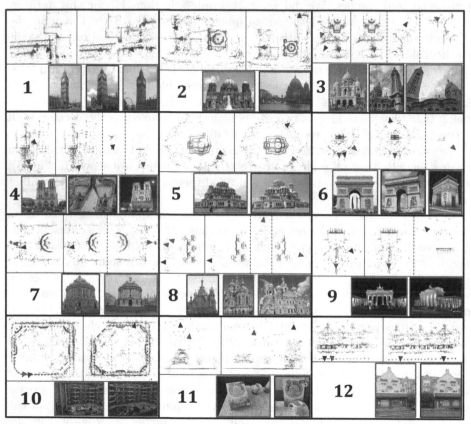

Fig. 7. Example results from our system. Within each dataset cell: top-left is the original reconstruction, top-right is the final merged or split result (split results are separated by a vertical dashed line), and the bottom shows example images from the different split camera subgraphs. Dataset ordering (1-12) corresponds to Table 1.

we extracted 2D tracks (the required input to [26]) from already triangulated 3D points. This should be a benefit to the system, as they are already cleaner than the tracks typically used as input in [26].

While our method exercises approximately linear computational complexity, for large datasets the corresponding overhead can still be reduced by leveraging the idea of iconic view selection from Frahm *et al.* [11]. Please note this reduction is not required but provides computational savings. For the Big Ben dataset (13,590 images) we extracted 402 iconics in approximately linear time. Then, we split and merged a reconstruction built from only iconic images and registered the remaining cluster images to the reconstruction by attaching them to their iconic, along with other nearby images of the same camera subgraph. By only registering to images within the same subgraph, we ignore the effect of multiple instances of duplicate structure in the scene and only register to the instance viewed in the current subgraph. Leveraging the iconics yields the desired corrected 3D model while boosting efficiency due to the significantly reduced number of images considered in the splitting and merging.

While our method performed well on the datasets that we tested, the key assumption enabling our method is the existence of unique structure. If, for instance, the set of images or resulting reconstruction consists only of duplicate structure, our method cannot identify that the images may have come from different instances of the duplicate structure. However, this is rarely the case for real-world datasets, thus making our approach a viable option for general use.

For all experiments (except where previously noted) the same set of parameters ($\gamma = 8$, $\theta = 20°$, 100 superpixels per image, $s = 100$, and $\tau = 7.0$) was used, underlining the robustness of our method. Execution times are from our MATLAB implementation on a 3.3 GHz Xeon processor with 48 GB of RAM.

5 Conclusion

We have presented a novel post-processing method to detect and resolve reconstruction errors caused by duplicate structure (a common occurrence in urban environments). Our method is based on the strong and informative measure of conflicting observations. Our data-driven recursive formulation allows us to not only split an incorrect reconstruction, but to merge it back together (if possible) to recover an error-free result without making assumptions on the final number or configuration of distinct scene elements. In this regard, our experiments confirm that we outperform existing state-of-the-art methods.

Acknowledgments. This material is based upon work supported by the National Science Foundation under Grant No. IIS-1252921 and No. IIS-1349074.

References

1. Achanta, R., Shaji, A., Smith, K., Lucchi, A., Fua, P., Süsstrunk, S.: SLIC Superpixels Compared to State-of-the-Art Superpixel Methods. TPAMI 34(11) (2012)
2. Agarwal, S., Furukawa, Y., Snavely, N., Simon, I., Curless, B., Seitz, S., Szeliski, R.: Building Rome in a Day. Comm. ACM (2011)
3. Bansal, M., Daniilidis, K., Sawhney, H.: Ultra-wide baseline facade matching for geo-localization. In: Fusiello, A., Murino, V., Cucchiara, R. (eds.) ECCV 2012 Ws/Demos, Part I. LNCS, vol. 7583, pp. 175–186. Springer, Heidelberg (2012)

4. Cao, S., Snavely, N.: Graph-based discriminative learning for location recognition. In: CVPR (2013)
5. Cho, M., Lee, K.M.: Bilateral Symmetry Detection via Symmetry-Growing. In: BMVC (2009)
6. Cho, M., Shin, Y.M., Lee, K.M.: Unsupervised Detection and Segmentation of Identical Objects. In: CVPR (2010)
7. Chum, O., Mikulík, A., Perdoch, M., Matas, J.: Total recall II: Query expansion revisited. In: CVPR (2011)
8. Cohen, A., Zach, C., Sinha, S.N., Pollefeys, M.: Discovering and Exploiting 3D Symmetries in Structure from Motion. In: CVPR (2012)
9. Crandall, D., Owens, A., Snavely, N., Huttenlocher, D.: Discrete-Continuous Optimization for Large-Scale Structure from Motion. In: CVPR (2011)
10. Dellaert, F., Seitz, S., Thorpe, C., Thrun, S.: Structure from Motion without Correspondence. In: CVPR (2000)
11. Frahm, J.-M., et al.: Building rome on a cloudless day. In: Daniilidis, K., Maragos, P., Paragios, N. (eds.) ECCV 2010, Part IV. LNCS, vol. 6314, pp. 368–381. Springer, Heidelberg (2010)
12. Jiang, N., Tan, P., Cheong, L.F.: Seeing Double Without Confusion: Structure-from-Motion in Highly Ambiguous Scenes. In: CVPR (2012)
13. Jiang, N., Tan, P., Cheong, L.: Multi-view Repetitive Structure Detection. In: ICCV (2011)
14. Köser, K., Zach, C., Pollefeys, M.: Dense 3D Reconstruction of Symmetric Scenes from a Single Image. In: Mester, R., Felsberg, M. (eds.) DAGM 2011. LNCS, vol. 6835, pp. 266–275. Springer, Heidelberg (2011)
15. Lee, S., Liu, Y.: Curved Glide-Reflection Symmetry Detection. TPAMI 34(2) (2012)
16. Liu, J., Liu, Y.: GRASP Recurring Patterns from a Single View. In: CVPR (2013)
17. Liu, Y., Hel-Or, H., Kaplan, C.S., Gool, L.V.: Computational Symmetry in Computer Vision and Computer Graphics. Foundations and Trends in Computer Graphics and Vision 5(1-2) (2010)
18. Lou, Y., Snavely, N., Gehrke, J.: Matchminer: Efficiently mining spanning structures in large image collections. In: Fitzgibbon, A., Lazebnik, S., Perona, P., Sato, Y., Schmid, C. (eds.) ECCV 2012, Part II. LNCS, vol. 7573, pp. 45–58. Springer, Heidelberg (2012)
19. Mikolajczyk, K., Schmid, C.: A performance evaluation of local descriptors. TPAMI 27(10) (2005)
20. Raguram, R., Tighe, J., Frahm, J.: Improved geometric verification for large scale landmark image collections. In: BMVC (2012)
21. Roberts, R., Sinha, S.N., Szeliski, R., Steedly, D.: Structure from motion for scenes with large duplicate structures. In: CVPR (2011)
22. Schindler, G., Krishnamurthy, P., Lublinerman, R., Liu, Y., Dellaert, F.: Detecting and Matching Repeated Patterns for Automatic Geo-tagging in Urban Environments. In: CVPR (2008)
23. Sinha, S.N., Ramnath, K., Szeliski, R.: Detecting and Reconstructing 3D Mirror Symmetric Objects. In: Fitzgibbon, A., Lazebnik, S., Perona, P., Sato, Y., Schmid, C. (eds.) ECCV 2012, Part II. LNCS, vol. 7573, pp. 586–600. Springer, Heidelberg (2012)
24. Snavely, N., Seitz, S., Szeliski, R.: Photo Tourism: Exploring image collections in 3D. In: SIGGRAPH (2006)
25. Torii, A., Sivic, J., Pajdla, T., Okutomi, M.: Visual Place Recognition with Repetitive Structures. In: CVPR (2013)

26. Wilson, K., Snavely, N.: Network principles for sfm: Disambiguating repeated structures with local context. In: ICCV (2013)
27. Wu, C.: VisualSFM: A Visual Structure from Motion System (2011), http://ccwu.me/vsfm/
28. Wu, C., Frahm, J., Pollefeys, M.: Repetition-based Dense Single-View Reconstruction. In: CVPR (2011)
29. Zach, C., Irschara, A., Bischof, H.: What Can Missing Correspondences Tell Us About 3D Structure and Motion. In: CVPR (2008)
30. Zach, C., Klopschitz, M., Pollefeys, M.: Disambiguating Visual Relations Using Loop Constraints. In: CVPR (2010)
31. Zhao, P., Quan, L.: Translation Symmetry Detection in a Fronto-Parallel View. In: CVPR (2011)
32. Zhao, P., Yang, L., Zhang, H., Quan, L.: Per-Pixel Translational Symmetry Detection, Optimization, and Segmentation. In: CVPR (2012)

Total Moving Face Reconstruction

Supasorn Suwajanakorn, Ira Kemelmacher-Shlizerman, and Steven M. Seitz

University of Washington, USA

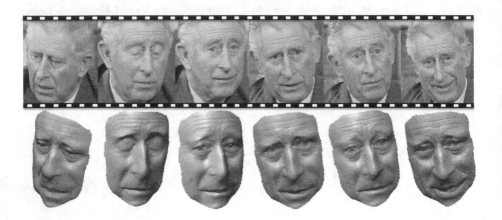

Fig. 1. Given a YouTube video of a person's face our method estimates high detail geometry (full 3D flow and pose) in each video frame completely automatically

Abstract. We present an approach that takes a single video of a person's face and reconstructs a high detail 3D shape for each video frame. We target videos taken under uncontrolled and uncalibrated imaging conditions, such as youtube videos of celebrities. In the heart of this work is a new dense 3D flow estimation method coupled with shape from shading. Unlike related works we do not assume availability of a blend shape model, nor require the person to participate in a training/capturing process. Instead we leverage the large amounts of photos that are available per individual in personal or internet photo collections. We show results for a variety of video sequences that include various lighting conditions, head poses, and facial expressions.

Keywords: 3D reconstruction, faces, non-rigid reconstruction.

1 Introduction

Reconstructing the time-varying geometry of a person's face from a video is extremely challenging. Indeed, the highly nonrigid nature of the human face, coupled with our ability to discern even minute facial details and geometry flaws,

D. Fleet et al. (Eds.): ECCV 2014, Part IV, LNCS 8692, pp. 796–812, 2014.
© Springer International Publishing Switzerland 2014

make it very difficult to achieve high quality results. Operating on free-form video captured "in the wild" adds another level of complexity; only a handful of such results have been reported in the literature [14,13,23,20,17].

Rather than reconstruct the input video in isolation, suppose that we had access to a large collection of other photos of the same person captured at different times, with varying pose, expression and lighting. Indeed, most people are captured in numerous photos and videos over their lifetimes; we propose to leverage the *total corpus of available imagery* of the same person to help reconstruct his/her face in an input video. We call this problem *total* moving face reconstruction.

Virtually all modern 3D face tracking and video reconstruction approaches leverage an assumption that the human face is well represented by a linear combination of *blend shapes*, e.g., Morphable models [9,10,41], AAMs [22,19], and Nonrigid Sfm [14,13,23,20]. The advantage of the blend-shape model is that it makes the problem more constrained, as the number of parameters (blend shapes and/or coefficients) is less than the number of measurements (pixels in the video). The main disadvantage is the low-rank model limits expressiveness and the ability to capture fine details.

Instead, our approach is based on deriving a person-specific face model (from all available imagery), and fitting it to each image in the video using a novel 3D optical flow approach coupled with shading cues. The combination of flow and shading enables capturing even minute shape variations (e.g., dimples, wrinkles, pimples, etc.) over the sequence.

We leverage the corpus of images to compute a person-specific face model that captures both the average 3D shape and the illumination-dependent appearance subspace. One key property of this model is that it enables appearance matching of any new image, and solving for dense correspondence via a 3D optical flow approach, yielding more precise alignment and robust 3D tracking than are possible by matching sparse fiducials, e.g., [17]. Another key property is that our use of previously captured photos enables accurate reconstruction even under degenerate motions (e.g., no head rotation) that foil nonrigid structure-from-motion methods [14,13,23,20]. Finally, we incorporate shading cues to obtain higher resolution details than are possible to capture with any other method.

2   Related Work

High quality time-varying 3D face geometry capture is extremely challenging due to highly non rigid nature of the human face–ultimately we would like to capture wrinkles, eye and muscle movement, dimples, detailed mouth expressions, eye lid details, and so forth. All these together form our perception of a person's face and are highly important for further face analysis.

Early methods in 3D facial performance capture use marker-based motion capture systems, e.g., [26], that track a sparse set of markers on a person's face. This requires the person to spend hours in a lab, and tracks only a sparse set of points. In contrast, modern high detail reconstruction methods use multi-view stereo approaches on input coming from multiple high resolution synchronized cameras which does not require markers but assumes calibration of the cameras and controlled lighting [7,8,11] or uncontrolled lighting[42]. Structured light [45] and light stages [16,2,3,25] provide the ability to use multiple synchronized and calibrated lights for reconstruction.

Recently, RGBD cameras were proven to be extremely successful in face and expression tracking [10,41,33]. The idea is to fit raw depth camera output to a deformable facial expression model (blend shapes) created by an artist for facial expression retargeting, puppeteering, and high quality face tracking. Similarly, [17] showed that it is possible to achieve high quality tracking via 3D regression and fitting to a blend shape model extracted from large number of face shapes captured via kinect fusion method [18]. These methods achieve very impressive face tracking results, however 1) require the person to participate in the training stage or be present in front of a depth camera, and 2) assume that face shapes can be represented by a linear combination of blend shapes. Representing face shapes using linear combinations of laser scans of other people's faces and artist created blend shapes goes back to the classical work by Blanz and Vetter [9] as well as more recent works by [21,40]. These however only enable capture of large scale deformations and tend to miss the fine details (wrinkles, dimples, etc.) that distinguish individuals.

Non-rigid structure from motion methods enable reconstruction from a single video by creating a linear basis for the non rigid motion that appears in the particular video; correspondence between the frames is typically given [14,13,20] or estimated via optical flow [23]. The major drawback of these methods is that the basis is extracted from the video itself which not only limits the ability to capture fine details, but also requires head pose to change significantly throughout the video to enable basis reconstruction.

Most related to our work are single view methods, particularly [30,28,27,29]. These methods can produce detailed reconstructions, but do not estimate how the scene deforms over time. Similar to scene flow methods [39], we reconstruct a dense 3D flow field; key differences include our illumination invariance model, and that we compute 3D to 2D correspondence rather than 3D to 3D. Furthermore, recent scene flow methods either assume availability of a stereo pair of photos taken in the same rigid configuration (e.g., same expression) [37,38] or rigid motion throughout the video [4]. The most relevant to our work is [24], who also operate on monocular video and leverage motion and shading cues to reconstruct a moving face model. However, whereas we simply fit a rigid 3D model independently to each frame, their technical approach involves several additional steps including blend-shape coefficient fitting, keyframe selection, feature-point refinement, multi frame optical flow, and temporal shape filtering (we filter only pose, not shape or flow). We believe the success of our much simpler approach stems from our 3D flow model ([24] move mesh vertices only parallel to the image plane), and our use of *all available imagery* to build an illumination-invariant appearance model. Most importantly, their approach requires a prior, lab-captured model of each actor (requiring a stereo rig and manual work), and hence is *not* applicable to videos of celebrities or other content in personal photo and video collections.

In this paper we target high detail reconstruction from a single video captured *in the wild*, i.e., under uncontrolled imaging conditions. Instead of requiring the person to be scanned in the lab or participate in the reconstruction process (as many other methods require [24,18,10,41,33]), we leverage whatever existing imagery is available online or in personal photo collections. This enables applying our approach on YouTube videos of celebrities (e.g., video of Prince Charles[1] as in Figure 1), for which we produce arguably the best reconstructions to date.

3   Overview of the Method

Given a video of a person, we seek to reconstruct a moving 3D model of his/her face that captures apparent motion and fine-scale shape details as well as possible. Specifically, we compute a 3D reconstruction that optimally fits both the *image motion* and *shading* in each frame. Because the problem is not fully constrained (we have only one view of the deforming face at each time instant), we leverage *all available imagery* of the person's face (e.g., photos on the Internet or in personal collections) to compute a reference model of that person (Section 4), capturing both their average shape and appearance under a subspace of illuminations. The reference model is used to constrain the gross shape of the sought reconstruction.

To compute the 3D facial deformation in each frame, we formulate a novel 3D optical flow problem (Section 5.1) that computes dense correspondence between the 3D model and each video frame, and optimally deform the reference mesh to fit. Similarly, to capture wrinkles and other high frequency structures, we introduce a novel approach to deform the reference mesh so that, when rendered, the mesh shading fits the image shading as accurately as possible.

We note that our method does not guarantee an accurate fit to ground-truth geometry, as the shape of the face may change in each frame and single-image cues are not sufficient for this purpose. Rather, we seek to produce a reasonably convincing model (leveraging all available imagery) which optimally fits the image information in each frame.

4   Average Shape and Appearance from All Available Imagery

While a person's face shape may be slightly different at each time instant, their rough shape (e.g., distance between eyes, nose length, overall geometry), tends to be consistent over time. Hence, we leverage all available imagery (photos and/or video frames) to reconstruct a shape and appearance model of the person that captures their average shape and appearance under a subspace of illuminations.

---

[1] http://www.youtube.com/watch?v=s89KEI2AfBU

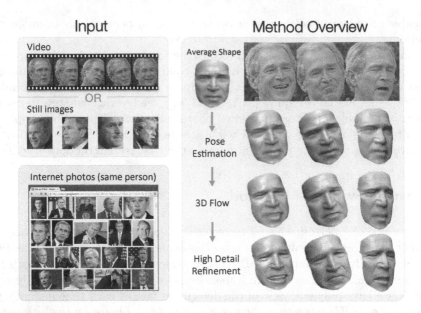

Fig. 2. Overview of our method. Given a video sequence we estimate 3D pose (average shape is rotated to the input pose for each of the 3 examples), followed by estimate of dense 3D flow of the average model to fit the input expression, and final refinement using shading cues (note the appearance of teeth, details in eyes, and so forth.)

In principle, this shape could be acquired in a number of different ways, e.g., a laser scan, kinect fusion model, stereo reconstruction, ohotometric stereo, etc. Given registered or rendered imagery of the same person under many different illuminations, we can construct an illumination subspace by projecting onto the first four singular vectors [5].

In practice, such 3D data with registered imagery is seldom available. Hence, we leverage Kemelmacher et al's Face Reconstruction in the Wild approach [31] to obtain an average shape and appearance model (rank-4 linear basis of the aligned image set). In practice, we find that aligning the images using Collection Flow [32] prior to reconstruction yields slightly sharper reconstructions. We will assume that as a result of this process we have obtained an average shape of the person v_{avg}, texture basis I_{avg}, and initial 3D pose estimate P_0.

5   Total Moving Reconstruction

We now describe our approach for reconstructing a moving 3D face shape by deforming an average model to fit the motion and shading cues in each video frame. The face in any given frame may have unknown and possibly changing lighting conditions, arbitrary facial expressions, and varying head orientation (even profile or other highly non-frontal poses are supported–see supplementary video).

Key to our approach is a metric based on *photo consistency*, i.e., comparing mesh renderings with input video frames. This capability depends critically on being able to match the illumination and shading in each input frame to that of the rendered mesh, a property achieved by our appearance subspace representation (Section 4).

We recover shape in two steps: first, we deform the average shape to fit the image motion, and second, we deform the resulting shape to fit the shading cues in each frame. We now formulate each problem in turn.

5.1   3D Flow Objective

Given an average shape, we seek a 3D flow field mapping it to the reconstructed shape in a given input image (video frame). Denote by $\mathbf{v} := (x, y, z)^\top$ a vertex on the average mesh we wish to deform, and $\boldsymbol{f}(\mathbf{v}) \in \mathbb{R}^3$ is the desired per vertex 3D flow (3D displacement to the reconstruction). As the average shape is provided as a depth map $d(u, v)$, vertices are connected to form triangle meshes over 4 neighbor pixels in a regular 4-connected grid of the depth map and flow $\boldsymbol{f}(\mathbf{v})$ can also be parametrized on 2D image plane as $\boldsymbol{f}(u, v) = \boldsymbol{f}(u, v, d(u, v))$. $I(u, v)$ gives the input image intensity at pixel (u, v), and denote $C(\mathbf{v})$ to be the intensity of vertex $\mathbf{v}$ in the rendering of the average shape from the viewpoint of the input image. Define the camera function as $\mathbb{P} : \mathbb{R}^3 \to \mathbb{R}^2$ which takes a vertex as input and applies a rigid transformation and weak-perspective projection to produce 2D point on the image plane. We therefore cast 3D flow as an optimization problem with the following objective:

$$E_{flow3d}(\boldsymbol{f}) = \sum_{\mathbf{v}} |I(\mathbb{P}(\mathbf{v} + \boldsymbol{f}(\mathbf{v}))) - C(\mathbf{v})|^2 + \alpha \left(|\nabla \boldsymbol{f}_x|^2 + |\nabla \boldsymbol{f}_y|^2 + |\nabla \boldsymbol{f}_z|^2\right)$$

$$(1)$$

where $|\nabla \boldsymbol{f}_x|^2 = \left(\frac{\partial \boldsymbol{f}_x}{\partial u}\right)^2 + \left(\frac{\partial \boldsymbol{f}_x}{\partial v}\right)^2$ is the gradient magnitude of the x component of flow parametrized on 2D image plane and $|\nabla \boldsymbol{f}_y|^2, |\nabla \boldsymbol{f}_z|^2$ along y and z and are defined similarly. $\alpha > 0$ is the smoothness weight that serves as a regularization parameter. We will describe how to optimize this function shortly.

5.2   Shape-from-Shading Objective

Applying the estimated 3D flow field $\boldsymbol{f}$ yields a new mesh $\mathbf{v}' = \mathbf{v} + \boldsymbol{f}$ that deforms the average shape to match the input image. While the resulting reconstruction captures dense nonrigid correspondence, it does not model the impact of the deformation on surface normals and their resulting shading effects. Hence, we introduce a second step to optimize the reconstruction to best fit the *shading* of the input image, by iteratively deforming the mesh vertices and re-rendering.

Specifically, we optimize for new z-coordinate $z(\mathbf{v}')$ of each vertex $\mathbf{v}'$ by minimizing the sum of photometric and position error terms:

$$E_{shading}(z) = \sum_{\mathbf{v}'} |I(\mathbb{P}(\mathbf{v}')) - \boldsymbol{l}^\top \boldsymbol{h}_{\mathbf{v}'}(z(\mathbf{v}'))|^2 + \beta |z(\mathbf{v}') - \mathbf{v}'_z|^2 \qquad (2)$$

$\mathbf{v}'_z$ is the original z-coordinate of $\mathbf{v}'$ after 3D flow, $\boldsymbol{h}_{\mathbf{v}'}$ is a 4D spherical harmonics approximation to surface reflectance at new vertex mesh $(\mathbf{v}'_x, \mathbf{v}'_y, z(\mathbf{v}'))$ and l is a 4D vector of spherical harmonics coefficients. β is a regularization weight for the second position error term that constrains final z to be close to the original shape. We describe in detail each of the optimization steps in the following subsections.

6   Optimization

We now describe our optimization approach for computing 3D flow and shading-based mesh refinement. Our approach requires an initial estimate of 3D head pose and lighting (described in Section 6.3).

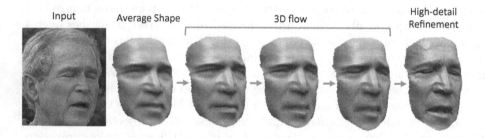

Fig. 3. 3D flow convergence example. The optimization starts from an average model of Bush with closed mouth, the mouth opens with 3D flow estimation iterations and gets refined at the shading step. This computation is done independently for each single frame in the video (temporal constraint is applied only at the rigid pose estimation step).

6.1   3D Flow Estimation

Minimizing Eq. 1 is a non-linear optimization task even if we assume weak-perspective projection with L2 norm because $I\left(\mathbb{P}(\mathbf{v} + \boldsymbol{f}(\mathbf{v}))\right)$ is generally non-linear in the image coordinate. To optimize this objective, we use Levenberg-Marquardt (LM) implemented in the Ceres Solver [1]. This requires a calculation of the Jacobian matrix in which the variables are x, y, and z for each flow value. To compute the derivatives of $I\left(\mathbb{P}(\mathbf{v} + \boldsymbol{f}(\mathbf{v}))\right)$ with respect to each flow component x, y and z, let us denote $\mathbb{P}(\mathbf{v} + \boldsymbol{f}(\mathbf{v})) = (u, v)^{\top}$ and $\boldsymbol{f}(\mathbf{v}) = (x, y, z)^{\top}$. By applying the chain rule with respect to x we get:

$$\frac{\partial}{\partial x} I\left(\mathbb{P}(\mathbf{v} + \boldsymbol{f}(\mathbf{v}))\right) = I_u \frac{\partial u}{\partial x} + I_v \frac{\partial v}{\partial x} \qquad (3)$$

where I_u and I_v denote image derivatives along the horizontal and vertical axis and are computed using the 5-point derivative filter $\frac{1}{12}[-1\ 8\ 0\ -8\ 1]$. Let us further define the camera function as

$$\mathbb{P}(q) = \pi(\mathbf{R}_{3\times3}q + \mathbf{T}_{3\times1}) \tag{4}$$

$$\pi(r) = (f \cdot r_x/\bar{z}, f \cdot r_y/\bar{z})^\top \tag{5}$$

where $\mathbf{R}_{3\times3}$ is a rotation matrix and $\mathbf{T}_{3\times1}$ is a translation vector. π is a weak-perspective projection with $\bar{z}$ being the constant average of vertex z-coordinate; $\frac{\partial u}{\partial x}$ and $\frac{\partial u}{\partial y}$ are evaluated using automatic differentiation. This provides a derivative with respect to x, derivatives with respect to y and z are computed similarly.

To differentiate the smoothness term, we approximate the partial derivatives of $\nabla f_x, \nabla f_y, \nabla f_z$ by forward differences (i.e., re-parametrize flow on 2D image plane $\frac{\partial f_x}{\partial u} = f_x(u+1,v) - f_x(u,v), \frac{\partial f_x}{\partial v} = f_x(u,v+1) - f_x(u,v))$, and then take the derivatives. Similar computation is done for y and z components.

We implement this in a coarse-to-fine multi-resolution scheme [15] to deal with large flow displacements, i.e., we construct a Gaussian pyramid of the input image with down sampling rate of 0.75, and use the output flow in a coarser level as an initialization for the next finer level.

6.2 Shading-Based Refinement

We deform the average mesh to fit the input face according to the estimated 3D flow and use this new mesh as initialization to shading based mesh refinement. The idea is to capture high frequency details, e.g., wrinkles, folds, etc. We assume Lambertian reflectance and use the 1st order spherical harmonics (SH) approximation to Lambertian reflectance [6] to model the relationship between surface normals and image intensities. From Eq. 2, we define the SH approximation to surface reflectance at each new vertex $\mathbf{w} = (v'_x, v'_y, z)$ as

$$h_{\mathbf{v}'} = \left(1, \frac{(\mathbf{w}_u - \mathbf{w}) \times (\mathbf{w}_v - \mathbf{w})}{\|(\mathbf{w}_u - \mathbf{w}) \times (\mathbf{w}_v - \mathbf{w})\|}\right)^\top \tag{6}$$

where $\mathbf{w}_u$ and $\mathbf{w}_v$ are vertices adjacent to $\mathbf{w}$ in the mesh structure along the positive horizontal and vertical directions. We estimate the SH coefficients l by finding the best coefficients that fit the deformed mesh after 3D flow to the input via:

$$\min_l \sum_{\mathbf{v}'} |I\left(\mathbb{P}(\mathbf{v}')\right) - l^\top h_{\mathbf{v}'}\left(v'_z\right)|^2. \tag{7}$$

To finally optimize Eq. 2, we pre-compute $I\left(\mathbb{P}(\mathbf{v}')\right)$ and further linearize by precomputing the normalizing factor $\|(\mathbf{w}_u - \mathbf{w}) \times (\mathbf{w}_v - \mathbf{w})\|$ as suggested in [30] using the deformed mesh. The resulting formulation becomes linear in z and solved efficiently using linear least squares optimization.

6.3 Pose and Lighting

Faces in input frames/photos may appear in an arbitrary 3D pose, and often in highly non-frontal poses, e.g., 90 degrees out of plane rotation. To estimate 3D

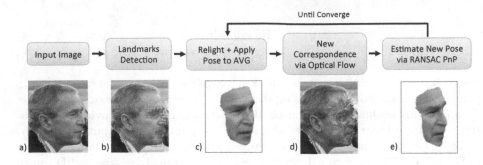

Fig. 4. Pose refinement algorithm. (a) non-frontal photo–challenging for current methods, (b) landmarks detection and (c) pose estimation using landmarks (slightly off) which is used to initialize our refinement. (d) optical flow matching between an average model rendering in the initial pose and input image. (e) final pose estimation result using PnP on dense point sets chosen via RANSAC.

flow we first need to compute the 3D rigid transformation $P = [\mathbf{R} \mid \mathbf{T}]$ that takes the average mesh v and transforms it to the position of the face in the image. While we obtain an initial estimate from the warping process in Section 4, it is performed using a 3D reference model of a different individual (see [31] for more details), thus pose estimation error increases with larger angles of rotation, e.g., due to difference in nose shape across people. We propose the following process (Alg. 1) to recover accurate face pose in a single photo, and we further show how to leverage temporal information in videos to achieve accurate pose estimates. We solve the Perspective-n-Point problem (PnP) using OpenCV's implementa-

---

Data: $P_0 = P_{ref}$ initialize pose from Sec. 4;
I: input image;
A_P^L: rendering of an average shape v_{avg} with texture in pose P and lighting L;
$i = 0$;
Result: 3D pose P
while *until convergence* **do**
  estimate lighting L_i of input I using process described in Sec. 4;
  render v_{avg} in pose P_i and input lighting L_i;
  run 2D optical flow between $A_{P_i}^{L_i}$ and I;
  generate 3D-to-2D correspondences from v_{avg} to I through 2D flow ;
  solve PnP using RANSAC on subset of correspondences:;
  solve PnP on all inliers to compute new estimate of pose P_{i+1};
end

  Algorithm 1. Out of plane pose estimation in a single photo.

---

tion of Levenberg-Marquardt [12]. Following the optimization in Alg. 1 we get high quality pose estimates for challenging poses. To achieve temporal coherence across the video, we refine the individual pose estimates using nearby frames.

Specifically, we use each frame's 12 neighbors and their corresponding poses for refinement, as follows. We compute bi-directional 2D optical flow between every consecutive pair of frames, then we concatenate them to produce flows between frame j and all its neighbors. Once these flows are available, we project 3D points of v_{avg} onto the image plane using pose estimate of frame $j + 1$ then follow 2D flow from frame $j + 1$ to j to produce dense 3D-to-2D correspondences between v_{avg} and the image pixels of frame j. Then we solve RANSAC PnP problem as in Alg. 1 to get another pose estimate for frame j. Performing this for all its neighbors will produce 12 additional estimates for frame j which are averaged together using quarternion average for rotations and linear average for translations. While we did not rigorously evaluate our method in comparison to state of the art [44,46,36], we have found that our pose estimation is comparable to these methods and gives temporally smooth, drift-free pose estimates, as can be observed from the accompanying videos. This process is completely automatic and the same for all video sequences.

7   Results

We evaluate the performance of our approach on a variety of videos downloaded from the Internet. Figure 7 shows example frames from four different videos (Tom Hanks, George Bush, Arnold Schwarzenegger, and Thaksin Shinawatra) downloaded from YouTube.com[2] and the corresponding per-frame 3D shape reconstructions obtained using our algorithm. On the left of Figure 7, we also present the average shapes (that are used to initialize the 3D flow estimation) for each person; these were obtained using [31]. The level of detail in the reconstructions is remarkable; the algorithm succeeds in capturing very fine details such as wrinkles and subtle expressions. Note the change in facial expression (compared to the average shape) in each frame, e.g., mouth opening, eyes close and open, wrinkles appear and disappear, detail in eye region, and so forth. The approach is robust to very large changes in pose, providing high quality results even for profile views (e.g., supplementary video of Tom Hanks). The stability of our results without any temporal smoothing other than pose filtering is evidence for the strength of the photo-based illumination subspace approach. Specifically, the illumination matching process makes the flow more accurate and thus stable. We strongly encourage the readers to watch the accompanying videos where we show per frame reconstructions for full length videos. Specifically, the lengths are: Tom Hanks: 20s (591 frames), George Bush 20s (610 frames), Arnold Schwarzenegger 24s (719frames), and Thaksin Shinawatra 20s (600 frames). Note that unlike non-rigid SfM methods [23], our reconstruction quality is independent of input video length (we can produce good results from

---

[2] URLs of input videos:
Hanks: https://www.youtube.com/watch?v=emLpj38huDA
Bush: https://www.youtube.com/watch?v=BJbUXw87jOA
Schwarzenegger: https://www.youtube.com/watch?v=wH8VtPG-okI
Shinawatra: https://www.youtube.com/watch?v=dZdhr1WcYEM

even a single frame). And since we estimate pose independently in each frame (and then average) by matching to an illumination-matched reference, the approach is not susceptible to drift problems that plague many tracking methods. We show long and short sequences to illustrate the quality of the reconstruction under a large variety of imaging conditions, non rigid motion, pose and lighting.

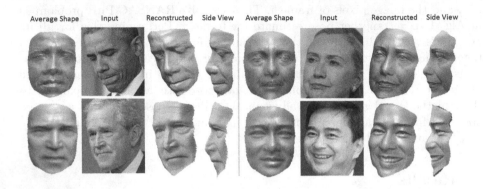

Fig. 5. Example results on still images in non-frontal views. Single view methods typically fail on such extreme poses.

In addition to handling videos, we can also estimate 3D shapes from single still images, and we show a number of results in Figure 5. We chose to show photos of faces that appear in highly non-frontal poses, these are typically the hardest cases for any state of the art single view method. The algorithm's ability to handle such extreme poses stems from our use of a person-specific template and appearance model that can be relit to match the input photo. In contrast, most other face tracking methods use generic face models which produce less reliable pose estimates, particularly for non-frontal poses.

Implementation Details. We use the Ceres solver [1] for optimization in the 3D flow estimation stage with $\alpha = 0.03$. For pose refinement we used the 2D optical flow code of [34] with the following parameters: α=0.02, ratio=0.75, nOuterF-PIterations=4, nSORIterations=40. The regularization weight in shading-based refinement step is $\beta = 2$ for all videos. The running times are 35s for pose estimation (incl. 15s for temporal refinement), 70s for 3D flow, and 0.1s for shading, for a 350×350 frame size (face size 220×260 pixels).

Limitations. While we found our method to be extremely robust to a variety of lighting conditions, individuals and poses, there are a number of limitations that we would like to discuss. The first are due to the use of spherical harmonics approximation to reflectance modeling, and the Lambertian assumption. In Figure 6 we present a number of frames where (a) the person rotates the head and specularities appear on the forehead, and (b) cast shadows appear around the nose area. These are not covered by our reflectance model and therefore the algorithm will produce slightly erroneous results in the specular and shadow vertices.

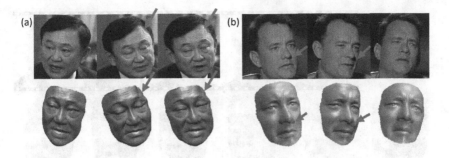

Fig. 6. Limitations of our reconstruction due to (a) specular highlight (b) cast shadows. We show a few frames from a video where the method introduces artifacts on the forehead in case of specularities or near the nose in case of cast shadows. This is due to violations of the Lambertian assumption. The full video and per frame reconstruction is shown in the accompanying video at 30fps.

Comparisons. We provide qualitative comparisons to calibrated results captured in the lab using range sensing and multi view stereo. We run our algorithm on data from [8] and compare their capture with our reconstruction in Figure 8, note the resemblance to the model captured by [8] (acquired by stereo setup) and our single view reconstruction. The base shape was acquired using the method described in Sec. 4 on 100 renders under different random lightings of frame 390 (neutral expression). The input photos are renderings of frames 80 and 340 in the dataset provided by [8]. We have also compared with Kinect Fusion [35] and present the results in Figure 9. The input to our reconstruction is a single frame; to obtain the Kinect Fusion result the person had to stay still while the depth camera captures him from a number of different viewpoints. To preserve consistency we ran our method on the direct RGB stream of kinect camera (lower in resolution than typical videos). We also compare to single view reconstruction methods, see results in the supp. material. The comparisons are qualitative since our method currently does not **guarantee** an accurate fit to ground-truth geometry due to gauge and bas-relief ambiguities. Any monocular uncalibrated approach will have this limitation, unless they assume a 3D model of the person a priori, e.g., [8,10,17,24,41] or sufficient 3D head rotation [23]. Rather, we seek to produce a reasonably accurate model (leveraging all available imagery) which optimally fits the image information in each frame. It is our future work to conduct a quantitative evaluation once time-varying 3D datasets exist with the level of detail we are attempting to capture and extend our work to handle shadows and specularities, and account for non-uniform albedo as introduced by earlier work [43].

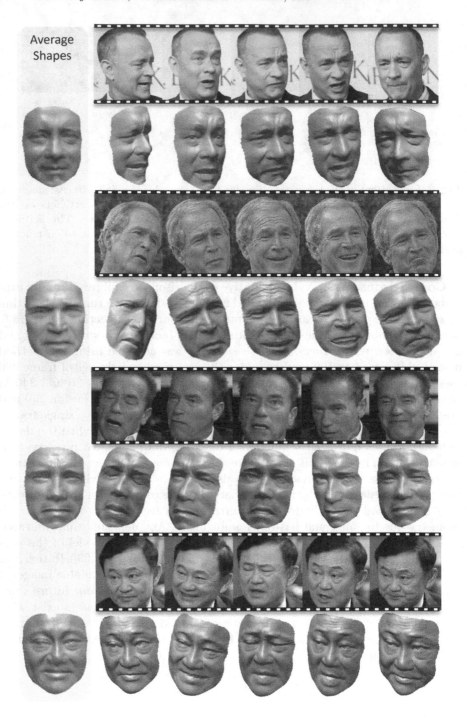

Fig. 7. Results of our reconstruction on four video sequences. Average shape per individual are presented on the left. The video reconstruction results illustrate variety in facial expressions, head pose, appearance of wrinkles, eye detail, and even partial teeth. Take a look at the full videos in the supplementary material for the full experience!

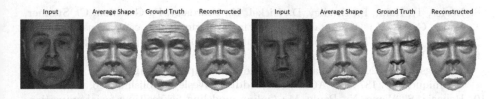

Fig. 8. Comparison to ground truth meshes [8]. Given the input photo (left) we show our reconstruction and the original shape captured by [8] for this particlar expression.

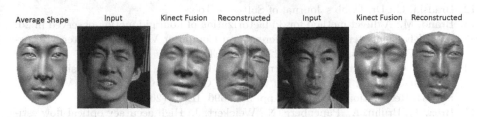

Fig. 9. Comparison to KinectFusion [35]. Two input photos, our reconstructions and results obtained using Kinect Fusion. The input photos are of lower quality than typical video sequences (taken from RGB kinect stream).

Acknowledgements. We thank Google and Intel for supporting this research.

All the examples are viewed best as videos, so we strongly encourage you to watch the supplementary video!

References

1. Agarwal, S., Mierle, K., et al.: Ceres solver,
   https://code.google.com/p/ceres-solver/
2. Alexander, O., Fyffe, G., Busch, J., Yu, X., Ichikari, R., Jones, A., Debevec, P., Jimenez, J., Danvoye, E., Antionazzi, B., et al.: Digital ira: Creating a real-time photoreal digital actor. In: ACM SIGGRAPH 2013 Posters, p. 1. ACM (2013)
3. Alexander, O., Rogers, M., Lambeth, W., Chiang, M., Debevec, P.: The digital emily project: photoreal facial modeling and animation. In: ACM SIGGRAPH 2009 Courses, p. 12. ACM (2009)
4. Basha, T., Moses, Y., Kiryati, N.: Multi-view scene flow estimation: A view centered variational approach. International Journal of Computer Vision 101(1), 6–21 (2013)
5. Basri, R., Jacobs, D., Kemelmacher, I.: Photometric stereo with general, unknown lighting. International Journal of Computer Vision 72(3), 239–257 (2007)
6. Basri, R., Jacobs, D.W.: W Jacobs. Lambertian reflectance and linear subspaces. IEEE Transactions on Pattern Analysis and Machine Intelligence 25(2), 218–233 (2003)
7. Beeler, T., Bickel, B., Beardsley, P., Sumner, B., Gross, M.: High-quality single-shot capture of facial geometry. ACM Transactions on Graphics (TOG) 29(4), 40 (2010)

8. Beeler, T., Hahn, F., Bradley, D., Bickel, B., Beardsley, P., Gotsman, C., Sumner, R.W., Gross, M.: High-quality passive facial performance capture using anchor frames. In: ACM Transactions on Graphics (TOG), vol. 30, p. 75. ACM (2011)

9. Blanz, V., Vetter, T.: A morphable model for the synthesis of 3d faces. In: Proceedings of the 26th Annual Conference on Computer Graphics and Interactive Techniques, pp. 187–194. ACM Press/Addison-Wesley Publishing Co. (1999)

10. Bouaziz, S., Wang, Y., Pauly, M.: Online modeling for realtime facial animation. ACM Transactions on Graphics (TOG) 32(4), 40 (2013)

11. Bradley, D., Heidrich, W., Popa, T., Sheffer, A.: High resolution passive facial performance capture. ACM Transactions on Graphics (TOG) 29(4), 41 (2010)

12. Bradski, G.: Dr. Dobb's Journal of Software Tools

13. Brand, M.: A direct method for 3d factorization of nonrigid motion observed in 2d. In: IEEE Computer Society Conference on Computer Vision and Pattern Recognition, CVPR 2005, vol. 2, pp. 122–128. IEEE (2005)

14. Bregler, C., Hertzmann, A., Biermann, H.: Recovering non-rigid 3d shape from image streams. In: Proceedings of the IEEE Conference on Computer Vision and Pattern Recognition 2000, vol. 2, pp. 690–696. IEEE (2000)

15. Brox, T., Bruhn, A., Papenberg, N., Weickert, J.: High accuracy optical flow estimation based on a theory for warping. In: Pajdla, T., Matas, J. (eds.) ECCV 2004. LNCS, vol. 3024, pp. 25–36. Springer, Heidelberg (2004)

16. Alexander, O., Fyffe, G., Busch, J., Yu, X., Ichikari, R., Jones, A., Debevec, P., Jimenez, J., Danvoye, E., Antionazzi, B.: Digital ira: Creating a real-time photoreal digital actor

17. Cao, C., Weng, Y., Lin, S.: andK. Zhou. 3d shape regression for real-time facial animation. ACM TOG (Proc. SIGGRAPH) 32(4), 41 (2013)

18. Cao, C., Weng, Y., Zhou, S., Tong, Y., Zhou, K.: Facewarehouse: A 3d facial expression database for visual computing (2013)

19. Cootes, T.F., Edwards, G.J., Taylor, C.J.: Active appearance models. In: Burkhardt, H., Neumann, B. (eds.) ECCV 1998. LNCS, vol. 1407, pp. 484–498. Springer, Heidelberg (1998)

20. Dai, Y., Li, H., He, M.: A simple prior-free method for non-rigid structure-from-motion factorization. In: 2012 IEEE Conference on Computer Vision and Pattern Recognition (CVPR), pp. 2018–2025. IEEE (2012)

21. Dale, K., Sunkavalli, K., Johnson, M.K., Vlasic, D., Matusik, W., Pfister, H.: Video face replacement. In: ACM Transactions on Graphics (TOG), vol. 30, p. 130. ACM (2011)

22. Ezzat, T., Poggio, T.: Facial analysis and synthesis using image-based models. In: Proceedings of the Second International Conference on Automatic Face and Gesture Recognition, 1996, pp. 116–121. IEEE (1996)

23. Garg, R., Roussos, A., Agapito, L.: Dense variational reconstruction of non-rigid surfaces from monocular video. In: 2013 IEEE Conference on Computer Vision and Pattern Recognition (CVPR), pp. 1272–1279. IEEE (2013)

24. Garrido, P., Valgaerts, L., Wu, C., Theobalt, C.: Reconstructing detailed dynamic face geometry from monocular video. ACM Transactions on Graphics (TOG) 32(6), 158 (2013)

25. Ghosh, A., Fyffe, G., Tunwattanapong, B., Busch, J., Yu, X., Debevec, P.: Multi-view face capture using polarized spherical gradient illumination. ACM Transactions on Graphics (TOG) 30(6), 129 (2011)

26. Guenter, B., Grimm, C., Wood, D., Malvar, H., Pighin, F.: Making faces. In: Proceedings of the 25th Annual Conference on Computer Graphics and Interactive Techniques, pp. 55–66. ACM (1998)

27. Hassner, T.: Viewing real-world faces in 3d. In: ICCV (2013)

28. Hassner, T., Basri, R.: Example based 3d reconstruction from single 2d images. In: Conference on Computer Vision and Pattern Recognition Workshop, CVPRW 2006, pp. 15–15. IEEE (2006)

29. Kemelmacher-Shlizerman, I.: Internet based morphable model. In: International Conference on Computer Vision, ICCV (2013)

30. Kemelmacher-Shlizerman, I., Basri, R.: face reconstruction from a single image using a single reference face shape. IEEE Transactions on Pattern Analysis and Machine Intelligence 33(2), 394–405 (2011)

31. Kemelmacher-Shlizerman, I., Seitz, S.M.: Face reconstruction in the wild. In: 2011 IEEE International Conference on Computer Vision (ICCV), pp. 1746–1753. IEEE (2011)

32. Kemelmacher-Shlizerman, I., Seitz, S.M.: Collection flow. In: 2012 IEEE Conference on Computer Vision and Pattern Recognition (CVPR), pp. 1792–1799. IEEE (2012)

33. Li, H., Weise, T., Pauly, M.: Example-based facial rigging. ACM Transactions on Graphics (TOG) 29(4), 32 (2010)

34. Liu, C.: Beyond Pixels: Exploring New Representations and Applications for Motion Analysis. PhD thesis. MIT (2009)

35. Newcombe, R.A., Davison, A.J., Izadi, S., Kohli, P., Hilliges, O., Shotton, J., Molyneaux, D., Hodges, S., Kim, D., Fitzgibbon, A.: Kinectfusion: Real-time dense surface mapping and tracking. In: 10th IEEE International Symposium on Mixed and Augmented Reality, ISMAR 2011, pp. 127–136. IEEE (2011)

36. Saragih, J.M., Lucey, S., Cohn, J.F.: Face alignment through subspace constrained mean-shifts. In: 2009 IEEE 12th International Conference on Computer Vision, pp. 1034–1041. IEEE (2009)

37. Valgaerts, L., Bruhn, A., Zimmer, H., Weickert, J., Stoll, C., Theobalt, C.: Joint estimation of motion, structure and geometry from stereo sequences. In: Daniilidis, K., Maragos, P., Paragios, N. (eds.) ECCV 2010, Part IV. LNCS, vol. 6314, pp. 568–581. Springer, Heidelberg (2010)

38. Valgaerts, L., Wu, C., Bruhn, A., Seidel, H.-P., Theobalt, C.: Lightweight binocular facial performance capture under uncontrolled lighting. ACM Trans. Graph. 31(6), 187 (2012)

39. Vedula, S., Baker, S., Rander, P., Collins, R., Kanade, T.: Three-dimensional scene flow. In: The Proceedings of the Seventh IEEE International Conference on Computer Vision 1999, vol. 2, pp. 722–729. IEEE (1999)

40. Vlasic, D., Brand, M., Pfister, H., Popović, J.: Face transfer with multilinear models. In: ACM Transactions on Graphics (TOG), vol. 24, pp. 426–433. ACM (2005)

41. Weise, T., Bouaziz, S., Li, H., Pauly, M.: Realtime performance-based facial animation. ACM Transactions on Graphics (TOG) 30(4), 77 (2011)

42. Wu, C., Stoll, C., Valgaerts, L., Theobalt, C.: On-set performance capture of multiple actors with a stereo camera. ACM Transactions on Graphics (TOG) 32(6) (2013)

43. Wu, C., Varanasi, K., Liu, Y., Seidel, H.-P., Theobalt, C.: Shading-based dynamic shape refinement from multi-view video under general illumination. In: International Conference on Computer Vision ICCV (2011)

44. Xiong, X., De la Torre, F.: Supervised descent method and its applications to face alignment. In: 2013 IEEE Conference on Computer Vision and Pattern Recognition (CVPR), pp. 532–539. IEEE (2013)
45. Zhang, L., Snavely, N., Curless, B., Seitz, S.M.: Spacetime faces: High-resolution capture for˜ modeling and animation. In: Data-Driven 3D Facial Animation, pp. 248–276. Springer, Heidelberg (2007)
46. Zhu, X., Ramanan, D.: Face detection, pose estimation, and landmark localization in the wild. In: 2012 IEEE Conference on Computer Vision and Pattern Recognition (CVPR), pp. 2879–2886. IEEE (2012)

Automatic Single-View Calibration
and Rectification from Parallel Planar Curves

Eduardo R. Corral-Soto and James H. Elder

Centre for Vision Research, York University, Toronto, Canada

Abstract. Typical methods for camera calibration and image rectification from a single view assume the existence of straight parallel lines from which vanishing points can be computed, or orthogonal structure known to exist in the scene. However, there are practical situations where these assumptions do not apply. Moreover, from a single family of parallel lines on the ground plane there is insufficient information to recover a complete rectification. Here we study a generalization of these methods to scenes known to contain parallel curves. Our method is based on establishing an association between pairs of corresponding points lying on the image projection of these curves. We show how this method can be used to compute a least-squares estimate of the focal length and the camera pose from the tangent lines of the associated points, allowing complete rectification of the image. We evaluate the method on highway and sports track imagery, and demonstrate its accuracy relative to a state-of-the-art vanishing point method.

Keywords: camera calibration, projective rectification, contour grouping, traffic surveillance.

1 Introduction

Automatic rectification of imagery to a dominant scene plane is an important subproblem in many applications, including surveillance, geodatabases, autonomous navigation, driving assistance systems, and sports videography. Single-view methods typically rely upon prior knowledge of the features lying on these planar surfaces, such as straight lines or orthogonal structure (e.g., [1,2]). However these methods fail when orthogonal structure is not dominant in the image or when there are no straight lines from which to extract vanishing points. Here we make the observation that it is not the linearity of the visible features used in vanishing point methods that affords information about the surface attitude, but rather their parallelism. This is important because there are many practical cases where the features are parallel curved lines, e.g., highways, racetracks, railway tracks, industrial conveyer belts etc. In this paper we introduce a technique to perform automatic image rectification in such cases. As a target application, we focus on the problem of rectifying highway images taken from pole-mounted cameras. Rectification in this application is an important step toward accurate estimation of vehicle speed.

D. Fleet et al. (Eds.): ECCV 2014, Part IV, LNCS 8692, pp. 813–827, 2014.

Traffic surveillance is one of the main applications for automatic camera rectification [3,2]. Some methods [4,5] use vehicle trajectories in the image to estimate the ground plane orientation, however these have the disadvantage that recalibration after a PTZ shift may take considerable time if traffic is sparse. The majority of static methods assume that straight lines or rectangular patterns or textures are available for vanishing point estimation [2,6].

Prior work has explored concentric circle calibration rigs for multi-view camera calibration [7]. For roadway analysis, Masoud & Papanikolopolous [8] have reported an interactive method for recovering camera parameters that includes the modelling of concentric curves bounding traffic circles. While their work demonstrates the potential for using curves to rectify roadway imagery, their approach was largely manual: the number of curves was assumed known, and control points for each of the curves were provided to the algorithm, sidestepping the difficult problems of feature detection and grouping.

In this paper we present a much more general and fully-automatic, non-parametric single-image approach to projective rectification of planar scenes containing a system of parallel curves, as arise commonly in highway traffic and sports track video. In spirit our approach is related to prior work on *elations*, which are projections of (normally rectilinear) coplanar features related by translation in the plane, from which vanishing points and lines can be inferred [9,10,11]. In our case, however, the features are not rectilinear but curved, and they are related not by translation but by systems of dilations (see below).

To train and evaluate our method we construct a human-labelled dataset of highway camera images in which the parallel curves in the image projecting from lane dividers and highway markers in the scene are identified. Our algorithm proceeds in three stages:

1) *Local feature detection.* Orientation features are detected using local eigenvector analysis, and a classifier is trained to distinguish features lying on curvilinear roadway boundaries from other local features in the scene. 2) *Feature grouping.* A set of probabilistic grouping cues are learned to infer extended curves as connected components of these local orientation features. 3) *Rectification and outlier removal.* Extracted curves are assumed to comprise a subset of inliers that are mutually parallel when back-projected, as well as a subset of non-parallel outliers. To estimate the camera parameters, we form an objective function based upon the average deviation from parallelism between all pairs of inlier curves. Rectification then consists of minimization of this objective, alternating with adjustments in the inlier/outlier assignments.

In summary, the primary contributions of our paper are: 1) A probabilistic method for extracting useful curvilinear features from highways and sports tracks. 2) A novel, effective and fully automatic calibration and rectification algorithm that applies to planar surfaces featuring general parallel curves. 3) Demonstration that the method generalizes, without relearning, to a completely different application domain (a running track).

2 Geometry

We consider the problem of rectifying to a ground plane where the visible features consist of smooth parallel curves. We assume a partially normalized pan-tilt-zoom (PTZ) camera, where all internal camera parameters except for the focal length are assumed to be approximately fixed, and therefore can be estimated using standard pre-calibration procedures [12] and normalized out of the projection matrix [11]. In particular, we assume zero skew and square pixels, and we locate the origin of our image coordinate system at the principal point, which we assume to be at the centre of the image.

We assume a planar ground surface and adopt a right-handed world coordinate system $[X, Y, Z]$ where the Z-axis is in the upward normal direction (Fig. 1). We also assume that the camera has negligible roll, so that the x-axis of the camera is parallel with the ground surface. This assumption is reasonable, since in many applications such as highway surveillance camera roll is minimized at installation, and if there is residual roll it is constant and can be calibrated out. In the unusual case that roll varies with pan/tilt, our method could easily be generalized to estimate roll as well, as it implicitly estimates the horizon line.

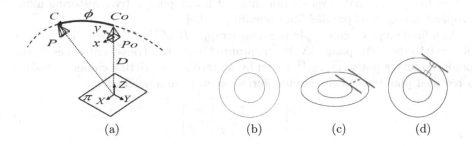

Fig. 1. (a) Camera setup - see text for details. (b) Parallel curves in the scene plane. (c) Compression in the y-dimension preserves the 1:1 mapping of parallel tangent lines but breaks the constraint that the tangents be orthogonal to the line connecting the points. (d) Only rectification with the correct tilt angle ϕ and the correct focal length α will fully restore parallelism.

Without loss of generality, we identify the X-axis of the world coordinate system with the x-axis of the camera, so that the y-axis of the camera is the projection of the Y-axis of the world coordinate system. Under these conditions, points $[X, Y]^T$ on the ground plane project to points $[x, y]^T$ on the image plane according to $\lambda[x, y, 1]^T = H[X, Y, 1]^T$ [11], where λ is a scaling factor, and the homography H is given by

$$H = \begin{bmatrix} \alpha & 0 & 0 \\ 0 & \alpha \cos\phi & 0 \\ 0 & \sin\phi & D \end{bmatrix}. \tag{1}$$

Here α is the focal length in pixels, D is the distance of the optical centre of the camera from the ground plane along the optic axis, and ϕ is the tilt angle of the camera relative to the ground plane: $\phi = 0$ when the camera points straight down at the ground surface and increases to $\pi/2$ as the camera tilts up toward the horizon. Conversely, points in the image can be backprojected to the ground plane using the inverse of this homography, $[X, Y, 1]^T = \lambda H^{-1}[x, y, 1]^T$, where

$$H^{-1} = \begin{bmatrix} \alpha^{-1} & 0 & 0 \\ 0 & (\alpha \cos \phi)^{-1} & 0 \\ 0 & -(\alpha D)^{-1} \tan \phi & \frac{1}{D} \end{bmatrix}. \tag{2}$$

Substituting, in Euclidean coordinates this backprojection becomes:

$$\begin{bmatrix} X \\ Y \end{bmatrix} = \frac{f_s}{1 - f_p y} \begin{bmatrix} x \\ f_e y \end{bmatrix}, \tag{3}$$

where $f_s = \alpha^{-1} D$, $f_p = \alpha^{-1} \tan \phi$ and $f_e = 1/\cos \phi$. Here, f_s is a *scaling factor* that determines the isotropic scaling of the backprojection into metric scene coordinates. f_e is the affine *vertical expansion factor* that determines the extent to which the image is vertically stretched to undo the foreshortening. f_p is the *perspective factor* that reverses the effect of linear perspective, restoring affine properties, e.g., that parallel lines remain parallel.

As a final step, we can apply the homography H of Eqn. (1) with a tilt angle of $\phi = 0$ to the scene points $[X, Y]^T$ computed using (3), transferring these scene points to image points $[x_r, y_r]^T$ taken by a "bird's eye" virtual camera, yielding a rectified plan view of the ground surface seen from a height D:

$$\begin{bmatrix} x_r \\ y_r \end{bmatrix} = \frac{1}{1 - f_p y} \begin{bmatrix} x \\ f_e y \end{bmatrix}. \tag{4}$$

This rectification equation can alternatively be expressed in terms of a homography: $\lambda[x_r, y_r, 1]^T = H_r[x, y, 1]^T$, where

$$H_r = \begin{bmatrix} 1 & 0 & 0 \\ 0 & \frac{1}{\cos\phi} & 0 \\ 0 & -\alpha^{-1} \tan \phi & 1 \end{bmatrix}. \tag{5}$$

To understand how projection will transform parallel curves visible on the ground surface, we appeal to the definition typically attributed to Leibniz (1692-4) [13]: two curves are considered parallel if one is a constant distance d along the normal from the other. In the language of mathematical morphology, one curve is the erosion or the dilation of the other. (Note that the curves are not related by a translation, and hence the theory of elations [9,10,11] does not directly apply.) This means that for every point on the first curve, there is a corresponding point on the second curve such that 1) the line connecting the two points is normal to both curves and 2) the tangent lines through the two points are parallel [14]. Understanding the projection of smooth parallel curves thus entails understanding the projection of these pairs of parallel tangent lines.

A tangent line $\mathbf{L}$ on the ground plane can be represented by the normalized homogeneous vector $\mathbf{L} = [A, B, 1]^T$. The projection $\mathbf{l} = [a, b, 1]^T$ of this line to the image is given by [11] $1/\lambda = H^{-T}\mathbf{L} \rightarrow \lambda\mathbf{L} = H^T\mathbf{l}$. Substituting (1) into this equation allows us to express the tangent line $[A, B, 1]^T$ on the ground plane in terms of its projection $(a, b, 1)^T$ on the image plane:

$$\lambda \begin{bmatrix} A \\ B \\ 1 \end{bmatrix} = \begin{bmatrix} a\alpha \\ b\alpha\cos\phi + \sin\phi \\ D \end{bmatrix}. \tag{6}$$

Now consider two tangent lines $\mathbf{L}$ and $\mathbf{L}'$ from corresponding points on two parallel curves. To be parallel, the coordinates of the two lines must satisfy the relation $A'/A = B'/B$. Substituting from (6), we have:

$$\frac{a'}{a} = \frac{b'\alpha\cos\phi + \sin\phi}{b\alpha\cos\phi + \sin\phi}, \tag{7}$$

and rearranging, we obtain:

$$f_p = \alpha^{-1}\tan\phi = \frac{ab' - a'b}{a' - a}. \tag{8}$$

Thus we observe that the perspective factor f_p can be computed directly from the image coordinates of the two tangent lines projecting from corresponding points on the parallel ground plane curves. From Eqn. (3) it can be seen that this is sufficient information to restore the scene curves to their parallel state. However, on its own, Eqn. (8) is insufficient to uniquely determine the tilt angle ϕ and focal length α. In particular, there remains a one-dimensional family of solutions corresponding to the unknown vertical expansion factor f_e.

In principle it is possible to estimate the internal parameters of a pan-tilt camera, including the focal length α, using point correspondences from a set of images taken with different pan-tilt settings [15]. However for applications such as traffic surveillance, requiring a series of large pan-tilt shifts to recalibrate every time the focal length changes is undesirable, as it may interrupt the normal control protocol and real-time video analytics.

Fortunately, if the curves are not straight we have not exhausted the information available from a single image. Recall that for the curves to be parallel, not only must the corresponding tangent lines be parallel, they must also be orthogonal to the line connecting the corresponding points (Fig. 1). In particular, letting $(X, Y)^T$ and $(X', Y')^T$ be the Euclidean representation of the two corresponding tangent points, we must have $[X' - X, Y' - Y][B, -A]^T = 0$. Substituting from Eqns (3) and (6), and simplifying, we obtain:

$$\cos^2\phi = \frac{\delta_y a}{\delta_x(b + f_p)}, \tag{9}$$

where $\delta_x = w'x' - wx$, $\delta_y = w'y' - wy$, $w = (1 - f_p y)^{-1}$ and $w' = (1 - f_p y')^{-1}$. With the constraint that $0 \leq \phi \leq \pi/2$ (Fig. 1), Eqn. 9 uniquely determines the tilt angle ϕ, allowing the focal length α to be computed directly from Eqn. (8).

An example may make this computation clearer. Suppose that the two curves are concentric (parallel) circles in the scene plane (Fig. 1(a)). On projection, these circles appear as ellipses compressed along the y axis in the image, and these ellipses are *not* parallel (Fig. 1(b)), since the lines connecting pairs of points with parallel tangents are not normal to the curves. The curves will remain non-parallel ellipses even after correction for the perspective factor f_p, due to the uncorrected expansion factor f_e. The only solution to the rectification problem that will make all tangent pairs parallel and orthogonal to the line connecting them must use the correct tilt angle ϕ and the correct focal length α to correct for both perspective f_p and expansion f_e. In general the parallel curves may be much more complex, but the same principle applies.

Thus the presence of parallel curvature on the ground plane represents an opportunity for more complete rectification. The flip side is that as the curvature decreases and the curves become straight, the problem becomes ill-posed and, although the image can still be rectified up to the vertical compression factor, the estimates for focal length $\hat{\alpha}$ and tilt $\hat{\phi}$ will generally be unreliable.

Without some metric knowledge, the scaling factor f_s must remain unknown. However, for many applications (e.g., highway surveillance), camera height is known, so that given both tilt angle ϕ and focal length α, knowledge of the sensor dimensions (pixel pitch) will in principle suffice for metric estimation on the ground plane. We leave this as future work.

Due to noise a single pair of corresponding tangents will in practice be insufficient to render an accurate rectification. Instead, we seek a least-squares solution over a large number of corresponding tangent pairs over multiple parallel curves. We turn to this problem now.

3   Algorithm

Given a single image I and a scene plane containing parallel curves, we wish to estimate the camera parameters ϕ and α in order to rectify the image data by means of the homography H_r from Eqn.(5). This estimate will be based on maximizing the parallelism of rectified image curves. To compute this objective we need to detect and group local features into extended curves, and associate pairs of curves hypothesized to be parallel.

For the sake of concreteness, we will focus here on highway imagery. To optimize accuracy and make our assumptions explicit, we adopted a probabilistic supervised learning approach, randomly partitioning 20 640 × 480 highway videos captured by various highway cameras into training and test datasets of 10 videos each. From each video we extracted and hand-labeled 10 images, sampled sparsely in time. A risk here is that we will over-learn the statistics specific to this dataset. To assess this, we will also apply the method, without relearning, to a completely different application domain (sports videography).

Our automatic rectification algorithm has two main stages: 1) curve extraction, and 2) rectification.

3.1   Curve Extraction

Curve extraction consists of local feature detection and grouping. The parameters for both stages are learned from manually labeled lane marks and lane dividers in our highway dataset.

Local Feature Detection. We use a standard corner detector [16] to extract image features. At each image location i, we construct the 2×2 matrix C_i and compute its eigenvectors $\mathbf{e}_i^1$ and $\mathbf{e}_i^2$ and associated eigenvalues λ_i^1 and λ_i^2. For a smooth curve, the eigenvectors $\mathbf{e}_i^1$ and $\mathbf{e}_i^2$ encode the normal and tangent vectors, respectively. We define an appearance vector $\mathbf{d}_i = [\eta_i, \lambda_i^1, b_i]^T$ where $\eta_i = \lambda_i^2/\lambda_i^1$ is the ratio of the eigenvalues and b_i is the pixel brightness.

We wish to use this appearance vector to determine whether a feature lies on ($\omega_i = 1$) or off ($\omega_i = 0$) a smooth curve on the scene plane. Assuming conditional independence of the appearance features, the likelihoods are approximated as the product of the marginals (Fig. 2), and the likelihood ratio L can be written as

$$L_i = \frac{p(\lambda_i^1|\omega_i = 1)p(b_i|\omega_i = 1)p(\eta_i|\omega_i = 1)}{p(\lambda_i^1|\omega_i = 0)p(b_i|\omega_i = 0)p(\eta_i|\omega_i = 0)}. \tag{10}$$

After discarding features for which $\log L_i < 0$, we thin the features using non-maximum suppression in the $\mathbf{e}_i^1$ direction, normal to the curve. The result is a sparse set of local features (Fig. 3 (a)).

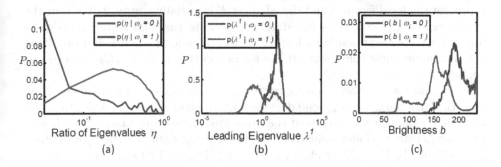

Fig. 2. Likelihood distributions for local features

Feature Grouping. In spirit, our rectification method is local, as it relies only upon pairs of local tangent vectors. In practice, however, grouping the local features into global curves is important, for two reasons. First, for some applications, the local features are not aligned. For example, in the highway imagery shown in Fig. 3(c-d), the lane marks are offset, so that a normal from one will not necessarily intersect another. If we first group these lane marks into curves, these intersections can be determined by interpolation.

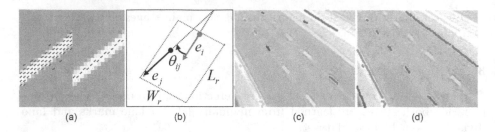

Fig. 3. Curve extraction. (a) Local features before and after thinning. Each vector indicates the direction of the leading eigenvector. (b) Processing window used in the curve segmentation process, (c) First-level segmentation, (d) Second-level segmentation. Each color represents a subset of grouped feature vectors.

A second benefit of grouping lies in outlier removal. In practice, only some of the local features will lie on parallel curves from the dominant scene plane, and identifying outliers is an important part of making the method work. Outlier identification is greatly facilitated by first grouping the local features into curves, as normally a curve will be either wholly an inlier or wholly an outlier.

We found that a simple grouping method was sufficient for this application. From the training dataset, we learn the minimum-area $L \times W$ rectangular search window that, when based at each ON curve feature is guaranteed to include at least one other feature from the same curve, and determined the maximum angle θ_0 between the leading eigenvectors of these two features. (Learned parameters: $L = 10$ pixels, $W = 5$ pixels, $\theta_0 = 39$ deg.) The grouping algorithm then proceeds in three stages: 1) A graph $G(V, E)$ is instantiated, where vertices V represent the local features and the edge set E is initially empty. 2) We tour the graph, searching the window based at each local feature and adding an edge to any other vertex representing a feature within the search window and satisfying the maximum angle constraint. 3) We extract curves $\mathbf{C} = \{C_1, C_2, \ldots, C_M\}$ as connected components of G.

Figure 3(c) shows the resulting curves for an example highway image. Note that the lane marks are segmented as individual, short curves. In order to group these into global curves, we repeat the same procedure using a larger search window, again learned (independently) from the training data (Learned parameters: $L = 145$ pixels, $W = 25$ pixels, $\theta_0 = 20$ deg.). Figure 3(d) shows the resulting global curves for the same highway image.

3.2 Rectification

The input to our rectification algorithm is a set $\mathbf{C}$ of curves, each consisting of a set of local features $f_i = (\mathbf{r}_i, \mathbf{l}_i)$ represented by their location $\mathbf{r}_i = (x_i, y_i, 1)^T$ in the image and tangent line $\mathbf{l}_i = (a_i, b_i, 1)^T$, in homogeneous form. Our goal is to estimate the camera parameters ϕ and α, and therefore the homography H_r, which can be used to rectify the input image (Eqn.(5)). Each iteration t of the algorithm consists of four main steps: 1) Transformation of local features using the current estimate H_{rt} of the homography, 2) Pairwise association of local features on parallel curves, 3) Re-estimation of the homography, and 4) Outlier removal. The steps are interdependent: feature association and outlier removal depend upon the estimated homography, and the estimated homography depends upon feature association and outlier removal. In this sense, our rectification algorithm can be considered a generalization of the iterative closest point method [17,18].

Transformation. The current estimate of the homography H_{rt} is applied to the local feature map to yield approximately rectified features: $\mathbf{p}_i^* = H_{rt}\mathbf{p}_i$, $\mathbf{l}_i^* = H_{rt}^{-T}\mathbf{l}_i$.

Association. The goal of this step is to associate each local feature f_{im} on a curve C_i with one other local feature f_{jn} on each of the other curves $C_j, j \neq i$ in the image. Roughly speaking, we wish to select the feature f_{jn} that lies nearest the normal line for f_{im} (Fig. 4 (a)). In practice, we measure this distance along the tangent line for f_{jn}, which takes into account the curvature of C_j. If no feature on C_j lies within an association tolerance of $T_a = 41$ pixels (learned from training images) of the normal line for f_{im}, no association is made. The outcome of this process is, for each pair of curves $(C_i, C_j), j \neq i$ in the image, a bipartite matching between a number K_{ij} of local features on the two curves. The critical property of each match is the angular deviation $\theta_{ijk}, k \in [1, \ldots, K_{ij}]$ between the associated tangent lines.

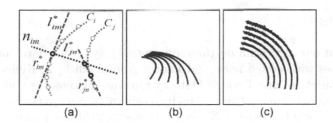

Fig. 4. (a): Association of feature vectors from different curves - see text for details. (b): Example synthetic input with localization noise $\sigma_r = 1$ pixel and no angle noise. (c): Rectified output. Note the noise amplification along the rectified curves.

Re-estimation. Were the homography H_{rt} correct, and in the absence of noise, all of the associated features would be parallel. Thus to estimate the focal length α and tilt angle ϕ we minimize the sum of squared angular deviations θ_{ijk} over all corresponding tangent lines and all pairs of curves in the image using a standard iterative nonlinear optimization method. To initialize the optimization we evaluated two methods: 1) Coarse grid search and 2) Using the mean of the parameters estimated from the training set ($\bar{\phi} = 70$ deg, $\bar{\alpha} = 788$ pixels). Both methods proved equally accurate, but of course using a single, well-chosen initial estimate is faster.

Outlier Removal. The re-estimation process can fail if there are many outlier curves. In this paper an outlier curve is a curve that is not approximately parallel to the rest of the curves in the image. To detect and remove outliers, we define a measure of total deviation ϵ_i for each of the M curves C_i in the image:

$$\epsilon_i = \frac{1}{M-1} \sum_{j \neq i} \frac{1}{K_{ij}} \sum_{k=1}^{K_{ij}} |\theta_{ijk}| . \tag{11}$$

Curves C_i for which ϵ_i exceeds a threshold of 30 deg are discarded, and the total deviation ϵ_i is recomputed for the remaining curves. This process is repeated until all curves lie within the threshold (Fig. 5).

(a)   (b)

Fig. 5. Example highway feature vectors before (a) and after (b) outlier removal

4 Results

We evaluated our algorithm on three datasets: 1) Synthetic data consisting of parallel curves with added noise and known ground truth, 2) Highway images taken by a variety of uncalibrated highway cameras (unknown α and ϕ), and 3) Images of a curved running track taken by a calibrated camera (known α and ϕ). Dataset 3 was acquired with a Nikon D90 camera, calibrated using a standard method [12]: the focal length was estimated at $\alpha = 812$ pixels. We used this camera model when generating the synthetic Dataset 1.

4.1 Experiment 1. Synthetic Data

For our first experiment, we assumed a viewing distance $D = 40$m and a 640×480 pixel image, and simulated 6 concentric circular arcs centred at the origin of the scene plane, with equally-spaced radii ranging from 30 to 55 m, and angular subtense of 90 deg. The rotation of the arcs around the origin of the scene plane was randomized over samples. Each of these arcs was projected analytically to the image using our camera model, and then represented by a field of feature vectors localized to sub-pixel accuracy with an arc length spacing of 1 pixel. We used this dataset to verify the method and assess sensitivity to additive Gaussian iid noise in in both the position and angle of the local features, as a function of tilt angle. Fig.4 (b-c) shows an example stimulus before and after rectification.

Fig. 6 shows results. For low noise (Figs. 6a-b) and larger tilts (Figs. 6c-d) the method produced estimates of tilt angle $\hat{\phi}$ and focal length $\hat{\alpha}$ that are unbiased

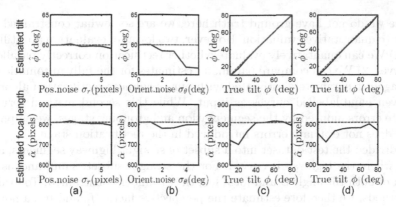

Fig. 6. Experiment 1 Results. Top plots show estimated tilt angle $\hat{\phi}$, bottom plots show estimated focal length $\hat{\alpha}$. Red dashed curves indicate ground truth values, blue curves indicate estimated values. (a) Variation with std. dev. of position noise σ_r. (b) Variation with std. dev. of angle noise σ_θ. (c) Variation with tilt angle ϕ for position noise of $\sigma_r = 1$ pixel. (d) Variation with tilt angle ϕ for angle noise of $\sigma_\theta = 3$ deg.

and accurate. However, with high levels of noise and/or small tilt angles, the method becomes biased: both tilt angle and focal length are underestimated.

We believe that this bias is due to amplification of noise in the objective function induced by rectification. From Eqn. 4, one can see that the perspective factor f_p will cause noise to be attenuated or amplified depending upon the sign of y. However, noise in the rectified y coordinate y_r will increase monotonically with the vertical expansion factor f_e, inducing a bias to smaller values, and hence smaller tilt angles ϕ. Since tilt angle and focal length α are inversely coupled through the perspective factor $f_p = \alpha^{-1}\tan\phi$, this induces a compensating decrease in the estimate of focal length α. This effect becomes more pronounced for smaller tilt angles, where the perspective distortion does not impose as strong a constraint on the rectification. In future work we hope to correct for this high-noise bias by explicitly modelling the propagation of noise across rectification.

4.2 Experiment 2. Highways

For our second experiment, we applied our algorithm to the highway test dataset, which is quite challenging: 1) The images are originally analog, then digitized and compressed, 2) pan, tilt and zoom vary widely, 3) quality of the road markings varies widely, 4) weather and light conditions vary widely. This dataset thus forms a realistic test of the algorithm's potential.

We compare our curvilinear method against a state-of-the-art method for linear vanishing point extraction [1]. This method extracts the vanishing points from the detected families of imaged parallel lines assumed to lie on the ground plane and the resulting horizon line, which can be used to estimate the projective factor f_p. We emphasize that while the linear method should work well for straight highways, it is not expected to work well for curved highways.

Since we do not have ground truth here, we are somewhat constrained with respect to quantitative evaluation. However, two forms of evaluation are still possible. 1) We can qualitatively evaluate whether rectification correctly parallelizes the curves. 2) We can compare parameter estimates for the fully automatic algorithm against parameters estimated with our curvilinear rectification algorithm but given hand-labelled curves as input. While this second method serves to estimate errors induced by the segmentation and grouping stages, we emphasize that it does not evaluate errors introduced in the rectification stage.

We divided the test dataset into a subset of straight highway segments, and a subset where the highway is curved. For the straight subset, simultaneous estimation of both tilt angle ϕ and focal length α is under-constrained. To evaluate the methods, we therefore estimate the perspective factor f_p and use a nominal value for the vertical expansion factor of $f_e = 1$ in Eqns. 3 and 4 in order to rectify the imagery.

Fig. 7(a-b) shows example rectifications for linear and curvilinear methods. While results appear satisfactory in both cases, a paired t-test comparing the error in the estimated perspective factor f_p for 30 different images reveals that the curvilinear method is significantly more accurate, $t(69) = 4.4, p = .00004$.

(a)   (b)   (c)   (d)

Fig. 7. Highway rectification examples. Top row: estimated features, bottom row: resulting rectified image. (a-b) Linear [1] and proposed curvilinear method applied to straight road. Both methods perform well. (c-d) Linear [1] and proposed curvilinear method applied to curved road. While the linear method fails completely, the curvilinear method computes a reasonable rectification.

Fig. 7(c-d) shows example rectifications of a curved highway for both linear and curvilinear methods. In this case the linear method fails catastrophically, while the curvilinear method succeeds in computing a reasonable rectification. Quantitatively over the curved roads in our dataset, the curvilinear method again performs significantly better, $t(29) = 2.5, p = .02$, (Fig. 8). Mean accuracy of the estimated parameters for the curvilinear method applied to curved highways in

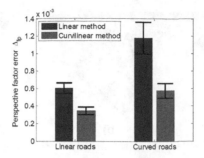

Fig. 8. Experiment 2 results (highway images): comparison of error in the estimated perspective factor f_p using the linear and curvilinear methods. Errors were computed with respect to ground-truth estimated with hand-labeled data.

Table 1. Mean abs. errors for estimated tilt and focal length for curvilinear method. Road results are for curved highways only and are relative to *estimated* ground truth, using our rectification algorithm on hand-segmented data. Track results are based on actual ground truth.

	Mean tilt err Δ_ϕ		Mean focal length err Δ_α	
	deg	%	pixels	%
Roads	2.8	4.0	13.7	1.7
Track	1.2	1.8	14.4	1.8

our test dataset is shown in Table 1. We emphasize that these errors are relative to *estimated* ground truth, computed using our rectification algorithm on hand-labeled data. Average running time of our non-optimized Matlab implementation on a standard dual-core laptop computer was 15.3 sec for curve extraction, and 41.1 seconds for rectification (30 iterations). We expect run time could easily be improved by an order of magnitude with some optimization.

4.3   Experiment 3. Running Track

For our final experiment, we used a calibrated camera to acquire 7 images of a running track. These images were taken from a variety of locations in the stadium stands, at tilt angles of 60, 65 and 70 deg. We applied the same algorithm used for the highway images in Experiment 2, except for omitting the second grouping step, since the curves of the running track are continuous. Importantly, we did not relearn the statistical parameters for feature detection and grouping. Given the substantial differences in the quality of the imagery and the application domain, Experiment 3 provides a good test of how well the method generalizes.

An example result is shown in Fig. 9, where (a) shows the results of curve segmentation, and (b) and (c) show the results after outlier removal and rectification. Here we have ground truth tilt and focal length, allowing us to evaluate the accuracy of the method in absolute terms. Table 1 shows these results. Mean absolute tilt angle error Δ_ϕ was 1.2 deg (1.8%) and mean absolute focal length

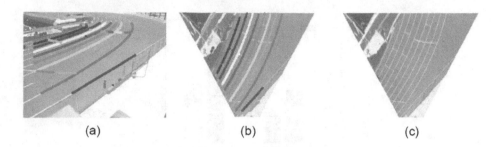

(a)   (b)   (c)

Fig. 9. Experiment 3 results. (a) Output from curve segmentation stage prior to outlier removal. (b) Rectified image with inlier curves. (c) Rectified image.

error Δ_α was 14.4 pixels (1.8%). We believe that the improved accuracy relative to the highway dataset is primarily due to the superior image quality.

5   Conclusions

Methods for single-view calibration and rectification generally assume systems of parallel lines or orthogonal structure in the scene. In this study we have introduced a method that applies to scene planes that may not contain linear structure, but do contain parallel curves, and have shown that these curves provide sufficient information for the estimation of both focal length and tilt angle. Our experiments have demonstrated the efficacy of the method, particularly in situations where conventional methods fail.

Although highway surveillance is our main target application, we have shown that the method generalizes well to sports tracks without relearning. Other potential application domains include autonomous navigation systems, curved conveyer systems for industrial automation and non-contact fingerprint analysis.

Future work may address 1) the analysis of small biases induced by nonlinear propagations of error, 2) estimation of additional camera parameters (e.g., camera roll), 3) estimation of metric properties based upon prior knowledge of sensor placement or object size and 4) generalizations to scenes with multiple systems of parallel curves, e.g., highway interchanges.

Acknowledgements. This work was supported by CIVDDD, NSERC, OCE and the Ministry of Transportation Ontario.

References

1. Barinova, O., Lempitsky, V., Tretiak, E., Kohli, P.: Geometric Image Parsing in Man-Made Environments. In: Daniilidis, K., Maragos, P., Paragios, N. (eds.) ECCV 2010, Part II. LNCS, vol. 6312, pp. 57–70. Springer, Heidelberg (2010)
2. Kanhere, N.K., Birchfield, S.T.: A Taxonomy and Analysis of Camera Calibration Methods for Traffic Monitoring Applications. IEEE Transactions on Intelligent Transportation Systems 11(2), 441–452 (2010)

3. Song, K.T., Tai, J.C.: Dynamic Calibration of Pan-Tilt-Zoom Cameras for Traffic Monitoring. IEEE Transactions on Systems Man and Cybernetics 36(5), 1091–1103 (2006)
4. Schoepflin, T.N., Dailey, D.J.: Dynamic Camera Calibration of Roadside Traffic Management Cameras for Vehicle Speed Estimation. IEEE Transactions on Intelligent Transportation Systems 4(2), 90–98 (2003)
5. Zhang, Z., Li, M., Huang, K., Tan, T.: Robust Automated Ground Plane Rectification Based on Moving Vehicles for Traffic Scene Surveillance. In: 15th IEEE International Conference on Image Processing, pp. 1364–1367 (2008)
6. Ribeiro, E., Hancock, E.R.: Estimating the 3D Orientation of Texture Planes using Local Spectral Analysis. Image and Vision Computing 18(8), 619–631 (2000)
7. Kim, J., Gurdjos, P., Kweon, I.: Geometric and Algebraic Constraints of Projected Concentric Circles and Their Applications to Camera Calibration. IEEE Transactions on Pattern Analysis and Machine Intelligence 27(4), 637–642 (2005)
8. Masoud, O., Papanikolopoulos, N.: Using Geometric Primitives to Calibrate Traffic Scenes. IEEE/RSJ International Conference on Intelligent Robots and Systems (IROS 2004) 2, 1878–1883 (2004)
9. Schaffalitzky, F., Zisserman, A.: Geometric Grouping of Repeated Elements within Images. In: Forsyth, D., Mundy, J.L., Di Gesú, V., Cipolla, R. (eds.) Shape, Contour, and Grouping 1999. LNCS, vol. 1681, pp. 165–181. Springer, Heidelberg (1999)
10. Schaffalitzky, F., Zisserman, A.: Planar Grouping for Automatic Detection of Vanishing Lines and Points. Image and Vision Computing 18, 647–658 (2000)
11. Hartley, R., Zisserman, A.: Multiple View Geometry in Computer Vision, 2nd edn. Cambridge University Press (2004)
12. Zhang, Z.: Flexible Camera Calibration By Viewing a Plane From Unknown Orientations. In: Proceedings of the Seventh IEEE International Conference on Computer Vision, vol. 1, pp. 666–673 (1999)
13. Yates, R.C.: A Handbook on Curves and their Properties. J.W. Edwards, Ann Arbor (1952)
14. Gray, A., Abbena, E., Salamon, S.: Modern Differential Geometry of Curves and Surfaces with Mathematica, 3rd edn. CRC Press, Boca Raton (2006)
15. Hartley, R.I.: Self-Calibration from Multiple Views with a Rotating Camera. In: Eklundh, J.-O. (ed.) ECCV 1994. LNCS, vol. 800, pp. 471–478. Springer, Heidelberg (1994)
16. Harris, C., Stephens, M.: A Combined Corner and Edge Detector. In: Proceedings of the 4th Alvey Vision Conference, pp. 147–151 (1988)
17. Besl, P.J., McKay, N.D.: A Method for Registration of 3-D Shapes. IEEE Transactions on Pattern Analysis and Machine Intelligence 14(2), 239–256 (1992)
18. Fisher, R.B.: Projective ICP and Stabilizing Architectural Augmented Reality Overlays. In: Proceedings of the International Symposium on Virtual and Augmented Architecture (VAA 2001), pp. 69–80. Springer, London (2001)

On Sampling Focal Length Values
to Solve the Absolute Pose Problem

Torsten Sattler[1], Chris Sweeney[2,*], and Marc Pollefeys[1]

[1] Department of Computer Science, ETH Zürich, Zürich, Switzerland
[2] University of California Santa Barbara, Santa Barbara, USA

Abstract. Estimating the absolute pose of a camera relative to a 3D representation of a scene is a fundamental step in many geometric Computer Vision applications. When the camera is calibrated, the pose can be computed very efficiently. If the calibration is unknown, the problem becomes much harder, resulting in slower solvers or solvers requiring more samples and thus significantly longer run-times for RANSAC. In this paper, we challenge the notion that using minimal solvers is always optimal and propose to compute the pose for a camera with unknown focal length by randomly sampling a focal length value and using an efficient pose solver for the now calibrated camera. Our main contribution is a novel sampling scheme that enables us to guide the sampling process towards promising focal length values and avoids considering all possible values once a good pose is found. The resulting RANSAC variant is significantly faster than current state-of-the-art pose solvers, especially for low inlier ratios, while achieving a similar or better pose accuracy.

Keywords: RANSAC, n-point-pose (PnP), camera pose estimation.

1 Introduction

Estimating the absolute camera pose from a set of 2D-3D correspondences, also known as the n-point pose (PnP) problem, is an important step in many Computer Vision applications such as Structure-from-Motion (SfM) [23,25] and image-based localization [12,18,19,21]. Especially for SfM, photo-community collections such as Flickr or Panoramio represent a vast and easily accessible source of data and truly enable large-scale 3D reconstructions [9]. Unfortunately, the EXIF data required to obtain the intrinsic camera calibration of the images is often missing for images obtained from photo sharing websites or is incorrect due to image editing operations applied before uploading the photos [3]. Thus, it is important to estimate both the camera pose and its internal calibration. For the latter, it is often sufficient to estimate only the focal length [2,24].

Computing the camera pose for a calibrated camera is a well-understood problem that has been studied extensively [8,10,14,17]. Given three correspondences between features in an image and points in the 3D model, the camera pose relative to the model can be computed very efficiently by solving a fourth degree

---

* The first and second author contributed equally to this work.

D. Fleet et al. (Eds.): ECCV 2014, Part IV, LNCS 8692, pp. 828–843, 2014.

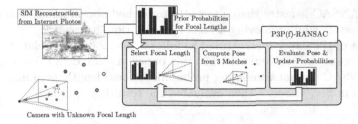

Fig. 1. Illustration of the pose estimation strategy proposed in this paper

polynomial [8,14], resulting in 3-point pose (P3P) solvers that require only about $2\mu s$ on a modern computer [14]. However, estimating the focal length together with the pose is a significantly harder problem. While special configurations such as planar scenes can be handled efficiently [1], computing both quantities generally requires solving a system of multivariate polynomials obtained from four or more 2D-3D correspondences [2,24]. The bottleneck of such approaches is usually the Eigenvalue decomposition of the so-called action matrix and the resulting pose solvers require $46\mu s$ or more for a single instance [4]. Consequently, using such methods inside a RANSAC-loop [8] results in prohibitively long run-times for all but high inlier ratios. In practice, it is thus common to employ pose solvers that achieve similar run-times as P3P [14] but require five or more 2D-3D correspondences [11,16]. As the number of RANSAC iterations grows with both the percentage of false matches and the number of matches required to compute a pose, using such approaches results in significantly longer run-times for low inlier ratios compared to pose solvers using only three or four matches.

In this paper, we consider the problem of estimating the camera pose for a camera with an unknown focal length. Inspired by the brute-force approach of Irschara *et al.* [12], we propose to estimate the focal length by sampling from a discrete set of possible values, followed by computing the pose using the selected focal length instead of simultaneously estimating both quantities. As our main contribution, we propose a novel RANSAC variant, called P3P(f)-RANSAC, that in each iteration randomly selects the focal length value based on the probability of finding a better model for it (*c.f.* Fig. 1). In contrast to [12], which iteratively tests all possible focal length values, we re-estimate the probabilities of each possible focal length value after each RANSAC step using a recursive Bayesian filter. This enables our algorithm to quickly converge toward the focal length closest to the correct value. Consequently, our approach does not necessarily need to evaluate all focal length values, resulting in an average speed-up of more than one order of magnitude compared to [12]. We observe a distribution of focal lengths from photos obtained from photo-sharing websites that allow us to estimate the prior probabilities of the different focal length values, enabling our approach to use importance sampling to find a good pose more quickly. Through experiments on both large-scale SfM datasets and image-based localization tasks, we show that our proposed approach is significantly faster than the state-of-the-art minimal solver [2] while achieving a similar pose accuracy. At the same time,

P3P(f)-RANSAC is faster than a recently published non-minimal solver [16] for low inlier ratios while achieving a higher localization accuracy[1].

The rest of the paper is structured as follows. Sec. 2 reviews related work and Sec. 3 discusses the problem solved in this paper in more detail. We present our novel RANSAC variant combining probabilistic focal length sampling and pose estimation in Sec. 4. Sec. 5 then evaluates the resulting approach.

2   Related Work

Estimating the camera pose from n 2D-3D matches is commonly known as the n-point-pose (PnP) problem and algorithms solving this problem are consequently called pose solvers. In case that the camera is calibrated, three correspondences are sufficient to estimate the pose and P3P solvers usually proceed by first estimating the position of the three points in the local coordinate system of the camera before estimating the transformation from the global into the local system from these positions [10]. Recently, Kneip et al. proposed a method that directly estimates the camera pose in the global coordinate frame [14]. Similar to [8], their method needs to solve a 4th degree univariate polynomial, which can be done in closed form, resulting in run-times of around $2\mu s$. If the gravity direction is known, the pose estimation problem can be simplified such that only two matches are required [15]. While these pose solvers are used inside a RANSAC-loop to robustly handle outliers, it is common to afterwards use the inlier matches to refine the pose through a general PnP algorithm [17].

In the case that the camera calibration is unknown, the classic 6-point direct linear transform algorithm estimates both the full internal and the external calibration of the camera from six 2D-3D matches by computing the SVD of a 12×12 matrix [11]. Triggs generalized this approach to incorporate prior knowledge about some calibration parameters, resulting in 4-point and 5-point solvers [24]. Similar to the 6-point solver, they cannot handle planar point configurations. Handling general configuration usually results in system of multivariate polynomials [2,3,5,13,24]. Bujnak et al. proposed such an approach for the case that only the focal length is unknown [2]. Using four 2D-3D matches, their method needs to perform Gauss-Jordan elimination on a 154×180 matrix followed by computing the Eigenvalues of a 10×10 action matrix, resulting in run-times of $100\mu s$ or more. A faster solver can be obtained using an automatically generated elimination template together with a more efficient way to compute the Eigenvalues, reducing the run-time to $46\mu s$ [4]. [13] show that four correspondences are enough to estimate both the focal length and a radial distortion parameter for general point configurations. However, handling planar and non-planar scenes seperately results in significantly faster run-times [3]. While such minimal solvers still require about $260\mu s$ or more, Kukelova et al. recently proposed a non-minimal 5-point solver that only relies on linear algebra and is thus orders of magnitude faster while still recovering the focal length and up to three radial distortion parameters [16].

---

[1] We make our source code available at http://people.inf.ethz.ch/sattlert

Similar to the approach proposed in this paper, Irschara *et al.* [12] repeatedly apply RANSAC with a P3P solver to each focal length in a set of focal length values to obtain the pose for an uncalibrated camera rather than estimating the focal length directly. The focal length value that produces the best pose is then chosen as the focal length for the camera. However, we show that our probabilistic formulation is much more efficient than the brute-force method proposed by [12]. The key idea of our RANSAC variant is to randomly sample the focal length in each iteration according to a given probability distribution. [22] use a similar RANSAC algorithm to calibrate a network of cameras from silhouettes extracted from video. In each iteration, they randomly select two directions in two images to obtain a hypothesis for the epipoles, which is used to recover the full fundamental matrix. This enables them to recover the epipolar geometry even though they cannot establish reliable point correspondences between the silhouettes detected in different images. While [22] sample according to a fixed distribution, we re-estimate the probabilities after each RANSAC iteration to incorporate information from previous rounds.

3   Problem Formulation

In this paper, we want to solve the problem of estimating the pose for a camera with an unknown focal length from a given set $\mathcal{M} = \{(\mathbf{x}, \mathbf{X}) \mid \mathbf{x} \in \mathbb{R}^2, \mathbf{X} \in \mathbb{R}^3\}$ of 2D–3D matches. Assuming that the principal point coincides with the center of the image, we are thus trying to determine the focal length $f \in \mathbb{R}$ and the rotation $\mathbf{R} \in \mathbb{R}^{3 \times 3}$ and translation $\mathbf{t} \in \mathbb{R}^3$ such that

$$\alpha \cdot \begin{pmatrix} \mathbf{x} \\ 1 \end{pmatrix} = \begin{bmatrix} f & 0 & 0 \\ 0 & f & 0 \\ 0 & 0 & 1 \end{bmatrix} [\mathbf{R}|\mathbf{t}] \cdot \begin{pmatrix} \mathbf{X} \\ 1 \end{pmatrix} \quad \text{for some scalar } \alpha > 0 \qquad (1)$$

holds for all matches $(\mathbf{x}, \mathbf{X}) \in \mathcal{M}$, *i.e.*, that each 3D point $\mathbf{X}$ is projected onto its corresponding image position $\mathbf{x}$. In practice, some of the matches will be wrong due to imperfections in the matching process. The most common strategy to robustly handle wrong matches is to apply a PnP solver that computes the pose from n matches inside a RANSAC-loop [8]. RANSAC iteratively selects a random subset of size n from the given matches and uses it to estimate the camera pose. The pose is then evaluated on all matches, where a match is considered as an *inlier* to the pose if the reprojection error is below a given threshold and as an *outlier* otherwise. The model with the highest number of inliers is considered as the current best estimate of the correct camera pose. RANSAC terminates once the probability of having missed the correct pose falls below the desired failure probability η. Assuming that each all-inlier sample allows us to estimate the correct pose, this probability may be expressed as

$$(1 - \varepsilon^{*n})^k < \eta , \qquad (2)$$

where k is the number of samples generated so far and ε^* is the *inlier ratio*, *i.e.*, the ratio of inliers among all matches, for the current best model. Thus, the maximal number of iterations required for a given inlier ratio ε is

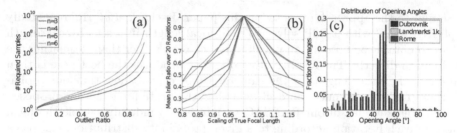

Fig. 2. (a) The number of RANSAC iterations required to ensure that the correct model is found with 99% probability for different PnP solvers. (b) The focal length accuracy required to recover most of the inliers strongly varies between different cameras. Yet, the inlier ratio decreases monotonically on both sides of the optimal focal length value. (c) Histograms of opening angles from images in the Dubrovnik [18], Landmarks 1k [19], and Rome [18] datasets.

$$k_{\max} = \log \eta / \log \left(1 - \varepsilon^n \right) . \tag{3}$$

The probability of selecting an all-inlier sample is maximized by minimizing n. However, the minimal 4-point solver (P4Pf) [4] for the problem of estimating both the pose and the focal length requires $46\mu s$, which is prohibitively expensive for low inlier ratios where many RANSAC iterations are required. Faster pose solvers such as the P5Pfr method [16] that estimates the pose, focal length, and radial distortion of the camera from five matches exist. However, using a non-minimal n reduces the probability of selecting an all-inlier sample exponentially, resulting in a significant increase in the number of required iterations for low inlier ratios (*c.f.* Fig. 2(a)). Instead of using a non-minimal solver, we propose to use a 3-point solver that estimates the pose for a given focal length f [14] and select f from a pre-defined set $\mathcal{F}$ of focal length values. This strategy offers the possible advantage of requiring fewer iterations than RANSAC with P4Pf (*c.f.* Fig. 2(a)) and faster pose computation times by using the P3P solver.

Evaluating all focal length values in $\mathcal{F}$ independently from each other as proposed by [12] will require at least $|\mathcal{F}| \cdot k_{\max}(f_{gt})$ iterations in total, where $k_{\max}(f_{gt})$ is the maximum number of iterations required to confidently compute the pose when using the ground truth focal length. Consequently, the approach from [12] will only be more efficient than using RANSAC with P4Pf or P5Pfr if $|\mathcal{F}|$ is smaller than the difference in the pose solver time or the difference in the number of required iterations, respectively. Notice that using quantized focal length values will invariably result in a lower pose accuracy. Regardless, as long as we are able to recover most of the inliers we will be able to obtain a better pose by applying P4Pf on the resulting inliers with only a small run-time overhead as very few sampling steps will be needed. Unfortunately, the sampling density required to guarantee that we can select a focal length value close enough to f_{gt} to recover most of the inliers strongly depends on the depth-variation of the scene observed by the camera. This can be seen in Fig. 2(b), as we observe

---

Algorithm 1 P3P(f)-RANSAC

Given: Set $\mathcal{M}$ of 2D-3D matches, desired failure probability η, **set** $\mathcal{F}$ **of focal length values with prior probabilities** $P_{\text{prior}}(f)$ **for all** $f \in \mathcal{F}$
1: **initialize sampling probability** $P_{\text{sample}}(f) = P_{\text{prior}}(f)$ for all $f \in \mathcal{F}$
2: **while** probability of having missed the correct pose $\geq \eta$ **do**
3:     **randomly select focal length** $f \in \mathcal{F}$ **according to** P_{sample}
4:     draw random sample $s \subset M$ of size 3
5:     estimate pose [R|t] from s with a P3P solver **using** f
6:     evaluate pose hypothesis $\theta = (f, [R|t])$ on $\mathcal{M}$
7:     **if** new best model found **then**
8:         $\theta^* = (f, [R|t])$
9:     **Update probabilities** P_{sample}
10:     Re-estimate probability of having missed the correct pose
Return: θ^*

---

different sensitivities on the focal length accuracy for different cameras. Thus, we need a rather dense sampling in order to handle all types of scenes, resulting in a large set $\mathcal{F}$. In order to maintain fast run-times when using a large set of values, we model the dependencies between the different focal lengths, enabling us to avoid evaluating all focal length values for at least $k_{\max}(\varepsilon_{\text{gt}})$ steps. This can be done by exploiting a *key observation* that can be made from Fig. 2(b): The maximal inlier ratio obtained by RANSAC for each focal length value decreases monotonically with the distance to f_{gt}. Given the focal length used to generate the current best pose with the highest inlier count, f^*, this observation allows us to model the probability of finding a pose with a higher inlier ratio using another focal length f as a function of $|f - f^*|$.

4   Interdependent Probabilistic Focal Length Sampling

The main idea of our novel pose estimation approach is to use focal length sampling and a P3P solver [14] in order to estimate a hypothesis for the camera pose from $n = 3$ 2D-3D correspondences instead of computing the pose and focal length simultaneously from four matches or more. Once we have found a good pose with a high inlier ratio for a focal length f^*, it becomes very unlikely that focal length values f far away from f^* can be used to estimate a better pose (*c.f.* Fig 2(b)). The central idea behind our approach is thus to preferably select focal length values that have a high likelihood of yielding a pose with a larger number of inliers than the current best estimate. This naturally leads to a probabilistic formulation of the problem of selecting good focal length values. This probabilistic formulation in turn enables us to exploit the fact that certain focal length values are much more likely to be correct than others. Alg. 1 outlines the resulting RANSAC variant, where differences to the classical RANSAC algorithm [8] are highlighted. Besides the 2D-3D matches and the failure probability η, our approach requires a set $\mathcal{F}$ of focal length values with associated prior probabilities as an additional input. These priors are then used to initialize the probability distribution that we use for selecting the focal length value f in Line 3 of Alg. 1. After using P3P to generate a pose hypothesis from f and three randomly selected matches, the hypothesis is evaluated on all matches and the current best pose estimate is updated if necessary. Finally, we use a recursive Bayesian filter to re-estimate the probability distribution used for sampling the focal length to reflect the fact that the current iteration might influence the likelihood of finding a better pose for all other focal length values.

In the following, we will refer to our algorithm as P3P(f)-RANSAC, as it uses a P3P solver inside of a RANSAC loop, where the focal length value f is obtained via parameter sampling. Similarly, we will refer to RANSAC-loops using any other PnP solver as PnP-RANSAC.

In Sec. 4.1, we briefly explain how to obtain the prior probabilities for the focal length values from $\mathcal{F}$. As the main contribution of this paper, Sec. 4.2 derives the probability distribution used for sampling the focal length values and our strategy for re-estimating the sampling probabilities. Finally, Sec. 4.3 argues that using early model rejection techniques [6,7] is crucial for our RANSAC variant in order to offer faster run-times than P4Pf and P5Pfr.

4.1 Obtaining the Prior Probabilities

The focal length of a camera mainly depends on the type of camera and the zoom-level used to take the picture. In this paper, we consider pose estimation scenarios in which a large variety of camera types is used, as is the case in large-scale SfM reconstructions from images downloaded from Flickr [23,9]. Since some camera types are much more popular than others[2], not all focal length values are equally likely to occur. The cameras contained in a large-scale SfM reconstruction of community collection photos thus give us an approximation to the probability distribution of focal length values. However, notice that obtaining prior probabilities for focal length values is an ill-posed problem as the focal length depends on the image resolution. In contrast, the maximal opening angle α_{max} of a camera with focal length f, width w, and height h, related by

$$\tan{(\alpha_{max}/2)} = \frac{\max{(w, h)}}{2 \cdot f} \ , \tag{4}$$

is independent of the image resolution. Thus, we predetermine a set of opening angle values from cameras contained in large-scale SfM reconstructions of unordered image collections [18,19]. We transform the opening angles to focal length values via Eqn. 4 (based on the resolution of the image being localized) before applying P3P(f)-RANSAC. Fig. 2(c) shows the distribution of opening angles for three such datasets, Dubronik (6k images) [18], Rome (15k images) [18], and the Landmarks 1k dataset (205k images) [19]. The distribution of opening angles is consistent across all datasets, indicating that the resulting distributions are a good representation of images taken in the real world. Still, we will show in Sec. 5.2 that the choice of priors is not a crucial parameter.

---

[2] https://www.flickr.com/cameras

4.2 Obtaining and Re-estimating the Sampling Probabilities

Ideally, the probability $P_{\text{sample}}(f)$ of selecting a focal length f should be proportional to the likelihood of obtaining a pose estimate with an inlier ratio $\varepsilon(f)$ that is larger than the inlier ratio ε^* of the current best pose estimate θ^* obtained for focal length f^*. Consequently, we model the sampling probability as

$$P_{\text{sampling}}(f) = \frac{P(\varepsilon(f) > \varepsilon^* \mid f) \cdot P_{\text{prior}}(f)}{\sum_{f' \in \mathcal{F}} P(\varepsilon(f') > \varepsilon^* \mid f') \cdot P_{\text{prior}}(f')} , \tag{5}$$

where $P(\varepsilon(f) > \varepsilon^* \mid f)$ is the probability of finding a better model using the focal length f. As is common in practice, we assume that we can obtain an inlier ratio of at least ε_0 in order to limit the maximal number of RANSAC iterations, i.e., we assume $\varepsilon^* = \varepsilon_0$ until we find a pose with an inlier ratio $> \varepsilon_0$.

In the following, we first derive $P(\varepsilon(f) > \varepsilon_0 \mid f)$ for the case that all models found so far have an inlier ratio of at most ε_0. In this case, we have not yet found a good model and thus have to treat all focal length values independently. We then show that the case of having found a good model with $\varepsilon^* > \varepsilon_0$, in which case $P(\varepsilon(f) > \varepsilon^* \mid f)$ depends on the current best pose θ^*, seamlessly integrates into our definition of the probabilities.

Case 1: $\varepsilon^* = \varepsilon_0$. Using the termination criterion from Eqn. 2, we express the maximal inlier ratio $\varepsilon_{\max}(f)$ that we have missed with probability $\geq \eta$ in terms of the number of random samples $k(f)$ generated so far for focal length f:

$$\varepsilon_{\max}(f) = \sqrt[3]{1 - \sqrt[k(f)]{\eta}} . \tag{6}$$

Since we are only required to compute the correct pose with probability $\geq \eta$, the probability $P(\varepsilon(f) > \varepsilon_0 \mid f)$ of finding a model with a higher inlier ratio is directly related to the probability that the number of correct matches in $\mathcal{M}$ is in the range $(\varepsilon_0 \cdot |\mathcal{M}|, \varepsilon_{\max}(f) \cdot |\mathcal{M}|]$. Notice that the probability of finding a wrong match only depends on the matching algorithm and the structure of the 3D model [21], and *not* on the pose estimation strategy itself. Since this probability can be estimated empirically from training data, we can assume without loss of generality that we know the cumulative distribution function $\text{cdf}(\varepsilon)$ over the inlier ratios for the given matching algorithm and 3D model. Thus, we can express the probability of finding a better model for f as

$$P(\varepsilon(f) > \varepsilon_0 \mid f) = \text{cdf}(\max(\varepsilon_{\max}(f), \varepsilon_0)) - \text{cdf}(\varepsilon_0) . \tag{7}$$

Under the reasonable assumption that $\text{cdf}(\varepsilon)$ is strictly increasing, i.e., that all inlier ratios occur with a non-zero probability, we have $P(\varepsilon(f) > \varepsilon_0 \mid f) = 0$ only if $\varepsilon_{\max}(f)) \leq \varepsilon_0$. Consequently, P3P(f)-RANSAC will terminate after $|\mathcal{F}| \cdot k_{\max}(\varepsilon_0)$ iterations, i.e., if no pose with inlier ratio greater than ε_0 can be found with a probability of at least η.

Case 2: $\varepsilon^* > \varepsilon_0$. Note that $P(\varepsilon(f) > \varepsilon^* \mid f)$ not only depends on the inlier ratio ε^* but also on the value of the focal length f^* used to compute the current best hypothesis θ^*. If f^* is close to the correct focal length f_{gt}, then focal length values far away from f^* are much less likely to result in better pose hypotheses than values close to f^*. This behavior can also be observed in Fig. 2(b), which shows that the inlier ratio decreases monotonically with the distance to the correct focal length when applying RANSAC on correct matches only. While outlier matches might cause local maxima, we found that this relation is still a very good model in practice. Since a similar behavior has been observed for other estimation problems [20], we thus use the following simplifying assumption to derive the sampling probabilities.

Assumption 1. *Let $\varepsilon(f)$ be the maximal inlier ratio that can be obtained for focal length f and let f_{gt} be the correct focal length. For focal length values f and f' with $|f_{gt} - f'| < |f_{gt} - f|$, $\varepsilon(f) \leq \varepsilon(f') \leq \varepsilon(f_{gt})$ should hold.*

Without loss of generality, consider the focal length $f < f^*$. If f is closer to f_{gt} than f^*, Assumption 1 implies that we should be able to find an inlier ratio of at least ε^* for all $f' \in \mathcal{F} \cap [f, f^*)$. Let $\mathcal{F}(f, f^*) = \mathcal{F} \cap [f, f^*)$ be the set of corresponding focal length values and let $P(\varepsilon(\mathcal{F}(f, f^*)) > \varepsilon^* \mid f)$ denote the probability of finding a better pose in the range $[f, f^*)$, then we have

$$P(\varepsilon(f) > \varepsilon^* \mid f) \quad \leq \quad P(\varepsilon(\mathcal{F}(f, f^*)) > \varepsilon^* \mid f) \ . \tag{8}$$

The maximal inlier ratio in this range of focal lengths that we have missed with a probability of at least η is again given by

$$\varepsilon_{\max}(\mathcal{F}(f, f^*)) = \sqrt[3]{1 - \sqrt[k(\mathcal{F}(f, f^*))]{\eta}} \ , \tag{9}$$

where $k(\mathcal{F}(f, f^*)) = \sum_{f' \in \mathcal{F}(f, f^*)} k(f')$ is the sum over all samples generated for the focal lengths from the considered range. As in Case 1, we thus obtain

$$P(\varepsilon(f) > \varepsilon^* \mid f) = \mathrm{cdf}(\max(\varepsilon_{\max}(\mathcal{F}(f, f^*)), \varepsilon^*)) - \mathrm{cdf}(\varepsilon^*) \ . \tag{10}$$

This predict-and-update strategy is a recursive Bayesian filter. Note that we again have $P(\varepsilon(f) > \varepsilon^* \mid f) = 0$ only if the probability of finding a better pose for f drops above the confidence threshold η, *i.e.*, P3P(f)-RANSAC essentially uses the same termination criterion as original RANSAC, offering the same guarantees on the quality of the pose.

Behavior of the Proposed Sampling Strategy. As long as no pose with an inlier ratio above ε_0 is found (Case 1), P3P(f)-RANSAC essentially uses importance sampling to select promising focal length values. As soon as a good model with inlier ratio above ε_0 is found (Case 2), P3P(f)-RANSAC is able to model the dependencies between focal length values, allowing it to quickly focus on a smaller range of focal length values that are most likely to be correct. This behavior is illustrated in Fig. 3. At the same time, our sampling strategy is able to escape local maxima since all focal length values that could lead to a better pose have a non-zero probability of being selected.

Implementation Details. Each focal length value is used for at most $k_{\max}(\varepsilon_0)$ samples. Since both Eqn. 6 and Eqn. 9 only depend on the number of iterations

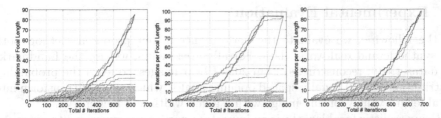

Fig. 3. The number of iterations in which each of the 100 focal length values is selected, plotted over the iterations of P3P(f)-RANSAC for three cameras from the Dubrovnik dataset and an outlier ratio of 50%. The focal length value closest to the true focal length of each camera is highlighted in red. As can be seen, P3P(f)-RANSAC is able to quickly identify a subset of promising focal lengths while ignoring all other values.

and not on ε^*, we can use a lookup table to determine the maximal inlier ratio. We represent the (empirically determined) cumulative distribution function $\text{cdf}(\varepsilon)$ as a discrete set of values. For any inlier ratio ε', we use linear interpolation to compute $\text{cdf}(\varepsilon')$ to guarantee that our discrete representation is still strictly increasing, which prevents P3P(f)-RANSAC from terminating too early.

4.3   Integrating Early Model Rejection

The P3P solver can compute the pose from three 2D-3D matches in $2\mu s$ [14] while the fastest P4Pf solver takes $46\mu s$ [4]. Consequently, P3P(f)-RANSAC should be able to perform 23 times more sampling steps while still being faster than P4Pf-RANSAC. However, evaluating the computed pose on the set of matches also has a significant impact on the run-time of a single RANSAC iteration. Since evaluating a pose takes around $20 - 50\mu s$ (or more for images with a large number of matches), P3P(f)-RANSAC can be at most $2 - 3$ times faster than P4Pf-RANSAC when evaluating each pose on all matches. Obviously, we do not need to fully evaluate poses generated from non-all-inlier samples or with a wrong focal length value. We can thus use approaches that terminate the pose evaluation once it becomes likely that the current pose will not have an inlier ratio higher than ε^* [6,7]. We chose to use the simple $T_{d,d}$ test, which evaluates a pose on all matches only if d randomly selected matches are inlier to the pose, with $d = 1$ as proposed in [6]. As a result of applying this $T_{1,1}$ test, we need to draw $n = 4$ matches in each iteration of P3P(f)-RANSAC, increasing the number of required iterations (*c.f.* Eqn. 3). At the same time, it becomes rather unlikely that any pose estimated from a focal length far away from the correct value, even if it was estimated only from correct matches, is evaluated on all correspondences since significantly fewer correct matches are inliers to such poses (*c.f.* Fig. 2(b)). As a consequence, only a small fraction of all generated poses need to be fully estimated, resulting in a significant speed-up.

5   Experimental Evaluation

In the following, we evaluate the performance of our proposed method both on synthetic and real-world data. For all experiments, we use the Landmarks 1k dataset [19], reconstructed from 205k Flickr images, to learn the probability distribution for 100 equally spaced opening angles, which we then transform into focal length values for any image with a given width and height.

Using realistic focal lengths is an important part of our experiments, since our algorithm utilizes the distribution of likely focal lengths to inform our RANSAC scheme. In order to obtain realistic focal length values, and realistic 2D-3D matches, for our synthetic experiments, we use two large-scale SfM reconstructions and generate pixel-perfect 2D-3D correspondences by reprojecting the 3D points into the images in which they were observed. The Rome model [18] consists of 15k database images and ∼4M points, while ∼1.9M points were reconstructed from 6k images to create the Dubrovnik model [18]. The scale for the latter model is known, allowing us to measure the localization accuracy on the Dubrovnik dataset in meters. Both datasets form a standard benchmark for image-based localization tasks [18,19,21] and we thus evaluate the performance on real-world data of our approach in this application scenario. For both datasets we use a cdf learned from inlier ratios observed on the Dubrovnik dataset.

For our experiments, we used the publicly available implementations of P3P [14] and P4Pf [2] and our own implementation of the P5Pfr solver [16].

5.1   Experiments with Synthetic Data

We conducted two synthetic experiments to measure the performance of our algorithm under increased levels of image noise and outlier ratios.

Image Noise. We measured our algorithm's robustness against image noise by adding increasing levels of Gaussian pixel noise to the 2D positions of the perfect 2D-3D correspondences obtained by reprojecting the 3D points. We tested image noise levels of 0, 0.1, 0.5, 1.0, and 2.0 pixels. Fig. 4 compares the performance of our approach with P4Pf-RANSAC. For all levels of image noise, P4Pf achieves slightly lower rotation, translation, and focal length errors, though the errors are comparable. This indicates that our algorithm is able to estimate the pose and focal length with high precision and is thus robust to noise, which is important for real-world data.

Outlier Ratio. The key idea of our approach is to use the faster P3P solver to estimate camera poses more efficiently while avoiding a brute-force search through all possible focal length values through our novel sampling scheme. In this experiment, we evaluate the robustness of our approach to high outlier ratios. We again use the perfect matches from the Dubrovnik dataset, with 1 pixel of Gaussian noise added to the reprojected points, and create outliers by adding new image points with correspondences to 3D points that were not observed in the image until the desired outlier ratio is achieved.

Fig. 5 shows the performance of our P3P(f) approach and P4Pf-RANSAC for increasing levels of outlier ratios. We plot the median position errors, inlier

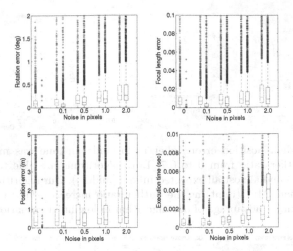

Fig. 4. Performance of our algorithm (red) and P4Pf [2] (blue) are compared for increased levels of image noise. Our algorithm has comparable performance to P4Pf for rotation, position, and focal length errors for all levels of noise. Despite requiring more iterations, our algorithm has a lower run-time than P4Pf as the image noise increases.

ratios, and execution times. As can be seen, our algorithm is able to handle low-inlier scenarios and still produce results that are nearly as accurate as P4Pf while being several orders of magnitude faster. These results demonstrate that Assumption 1 holds well enough even in the presence of outliers. For tasks such as image-based localization, being able to handle low-inlier scenarios accurately and efficiently is extremely important.

5.2 Experiments on Real Data

As a final experiment, we compare the performance of our algorithm to P3P, P4Pf, and P5Pfr in an image-based localization task [18,19,21]. We use two versions of our algorithm: One with focal length priors obtained from the Landmarks 1K dataset, and one with no learned priors (*i.e.* uniform priors). We use the efficient, publicly available localization method of [21] to obtain 2D-3D matches for the 800 and 1000 query images available for the Dubrovnik and Rome datasets, respectively. All query images were obtained by removing cameras from larger SfM reconstructions, providing ground truth positions for the query images. Notice that we do not use perfect correspondences in these experiments.

The results for the Rome dataset are shown in Fig. 6. Algorithms that computed focal length in addition to pose are able to recover noticeably more inliers than the P3P method that was used with ground truth focal lengths values as we did not account for radial distortion. As expected, all of the algorithms are slower than P3P. Our algorithm performed much faster than P4Pf in all cases.

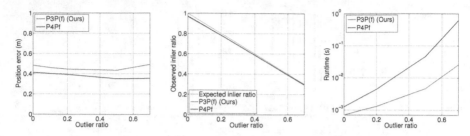

Fig. 5. The median position error, inlier ratio, and run-time was measured while increasing the outlier ratio from 0 to 0.7. Both algorithms are able to recover high quality poses (left) and almost all expected inliers (middle). Our algorithm has a much lower run-time than P4Pf (right) as the outlier ratio increases due to using a faster solver. This is a major advantage of our algorithm in low-inlier scenarios.

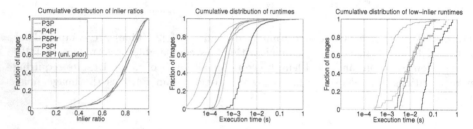

Fig. 6. Localization results from the Rome dataset [18] are shown. Our P3P(f)-RANSAC algorithm is able to recover more inliers than P3P used with ground truth focal lengths from Bundler, and a comparable amount to P4Pf and P5Pfr (left). Our algorithm has an execution time that is nearly one order of magnitude faster than P4Pf (center), despite running for more iterations. In low-inlier cases (inlier ratio ≤ 0.5), our algorithm is significantly faster than alternative algorithms (right).

As shown in Fig. 6, our approach is faster than P5Pfr for most low-inlier cases as it requires fewer matches per sample and thus fewer iterations per focal length.

Tab. 1 shows the position errors of each method on the Dubrovnik dataset, where we can measure distances in meters. The median position error of each camera was recorded over 100 trials for each of the methods. All methods are able to localize almost all images, and our method gives position errors that are comparable to or only slightly higher than P4Pf, which has the lowest errors of all algorithms. P3P(f) achieves better localization accuracy than P5Pfr. As can be also seen in Tab. 1, our method is on average over an order of magnitude faster than P4Pf. At the same time, P3P(f) is consistently faster than P4Pf on all quantiles while being faster than P5Pfr for images with lower inlier ratios. Notice that our P4Pf implementation requires $115\mu s$ compared to the $46\mu s$ required by [4]. Yet, our approach is on average more than 7 times faster than when using the solver from [4] and still achieves faster quantile run-times. On average, P3P(f) is only 1.39 times slower than P3P, even though it requires no knowledge about the focal length, making it well suited for SfM and localization applications.

Table 1. The position errors and localization times measured on the Dubrovnik dataset for an image-based localization task. Besides the results obtained by our approach using the learnt priors for the focal lengths, we also include results for an uniform prior.

Solver	# loc. images	Localization Accuracy [m]					Localization Times [ms]			
		Mean [m]	25%	Quantiles [m] 50%	75%	90%	Mean [ms]	50%	Quantiles [ms] 75%	90%
P3P (exact focal)	792	40.3	1.0	7.6	26.4	111.8	**1.21**	**0.20**	**1.00**	3.01
P4Pf	795	38.7	**0.4**	**1.3**	**4.7**	**20.1**	32.09	4.84	10.78	28.73
P5Pfr	**796**	227.2	0.5	2.0	31.3	200.9	6.02	0.54	3.07	16.44
P3P(f) (Ours)	795	**20.8**	**0.4**	1.6	5.4	27.6	1.68	0.68	1.27	**2.72**
P3P(f) uniform prior	795	28.1	0.5	1.7	5.9	24.3	1.89	0.85	1.46	3.08

Tab. 1 and Fig. 6 also show results obtained using a uniform prior on the focal lengths. As can be seen, our method benefits from using a good prior but performs only slightly worse otherwise. This demonstrates that our novel sampling scheme is the main reason for why P3P(f)-RANSAC succeeds.

6   Conclusion

In this paper, we have proposed a novel approach, termed P3P(f)-RANSAC, for efficiently estimating the pose of a camera with unknown focal length inside a RANSAC loop. Instead of computing the focal length using a minimal solver, our approach samples focal length values according to a probability distribution and then uses the significantly faster P3P solver to estimate the pose of the now calibrated camera. As the main contribution, we have proposed a novel sampling scheme that is able to model the probability of finding a pose better than the current best estimate for all focal length values. As a consequence, our approach is able to avoid evaluating all values and focus on the more promising candidates while offering the same guarantees as RANSAC in the presence of outliers. We have shown that our algorithm achieves a similar pose accuracy as previous pose solvers while achieving significantly faster run-times. These results challenge the notion that using minimal solvers is always an optimal strategy. While this paper focusses on the absolute pose problem, we plan to explore the use of our framework for other pose estimation problems in future work.

Acknowledgements.   This work was supported in part by NSF Grant IIS-1219261, NSF Graduate Research Fellowship Grant DGE-1144085, the CTI Switzerland grant #13086.1 PFES-ES 4DSites, and the European Union's Seventh Framework Programme (FP6/2007-2013) under grant #269916 (V-Charge).

References

1. Abidi, M.A., Chandra, T.: A New Efficient and Direct Solution for Pose Estimation using Quadrangular Targets: Algorithm and Evaluation. PAMI 17(5), 534–538 (1995)

2. Bujnak, M., Kukelova, Z., Pajdla, T.: A General Solution To The P4P Problem for Camera With Unknown Focal Length. In: CVPR (2008)
3. Bujnak, M., Kukelova, Z., Pajdla, T.: Robust Focal Length Estimation by Voting in Multi-view Scene Reconstruction. In: Zha, H., Taniguchi, R.-i., Maybank, S. (eds.) ACCV 2009, Part I. LNCS, vol. 5994, pp. 13–24. Springer, Heidelberg (2010)
4. Bujnak, M., Kukelova, Z., Pajdla, T.: New efficient solution to the absolute pose problem for camera with unknown focal length and radial distortion. In: Kimmel, R., Klette, R., Sugimoto, A. (eds.) ACCV 2010, Part I. LNCS, vol. 6492, pp. 11–24. Springer, Heidelberg (2011)
5. Bujnak, M., Kukelova, Z., Pajdla, T.: Making Minimal Solvers Fast. In: CVPR (2012)
6. Chum, O., Matas, J.: Randomized RANSAC with T(d,d) test. In: BMVC (2002)
7. Chum, O., Matas, J.: Optimal Randomized RANSAC. PAMI 30(8), 1472–1482 (2008)
8. Fischler, M., Bolles, R.: Random sample consensus: A paradigm for model fitting with applications to image analysis and automated cartography. Comm. ACM 24(6), 381–395 (1981)
9. Frahm, J.-M., et al.: Building rome on a cloudless day. In: Daniilidis, K., Maragos, P., Paragios, N. (eds.) ECCV 2010, Part IV. LNCS, vol. 6314, pp. 368–381. Springer, Heidelberg (2010)
10. Haralick, R., Lee, C.N., Ottenberg, K., Nölle, M.: Review and analysis of solutions of the three point perspective pose estimation problem. IJCV 13(3), 331–356 (1994)
11. Hartley, R.I., Zisserman, A.: Multiple View Geometry in Computer Vision, 2nd edn. Cambridge Univ. Press (2004)
12. Irschara, A., Zach, C., Frahm, J.M., Bischof, H.: From Structure-from-Motion Point Clouds to Fast Location Recognition. In: CVPR (2009)
13. Josephson, K., Byröd, M.: Pose Estimation with Radial Distortion and Unknown Focal Length. In: CVPR (2009)
14. Kneip, L., Scaramuzza, D., Siegwart, R.: A Novel Parametrization of the Perspective-Three-Point Problem for a Direct Computation of Absolute Camera Position and Orientation. In: CVPR (2011)
15. Kukelova, Z., Bujnak, M., Pajdla, T.: Closed-form solutions to the minimal absolute pose problems with known vertical direction. In: Kimmel, R., Klette, R., Sugimoto, A. (eds.) ACCV 2010, Part II. LNCS, vol. 6493, pp. 216–229. Springer, Heidelberg (2011)
16. Kukelova, Z., Bujnak, M., Pajdla, T.: Real-Time Solution to the Absolute Pose Problem with Unknown Radial Distortion and Focal Length. In: ICCV (2013)
17. Lepetit, V., Moreno-Noguer, F., Fua, P.: EPnP: An Accurate O(n) Solution to the PnP Problem. IJCV 81(2), 155–166 (2009)
18. Li, Y., Snavely, N., Huttenlocher, D.P.: Location Recognition using Prioritized Feature Matching. In: Daniilidis, K., Maragos, P., Paragios, N. (eds.) ECCV 2010, Part II. LNCS, vol. 6312, pp. 791–804. Springer, Heidelberg (2010)
19. Li, Y., Snavely, N., Huttenlocher, D., Fua, P.: Worldwide Pose Estimation Using 3D Point Clouds. In: Fitzgibbon, A., Lazebnik, S., Perona, P., Sato, Y., Schmid, C. (eds.) ECCV 2012, Part I. LNCS, vol. 7572, pp. 15–29. Springer, Heidelberg (2012)
20. Nister, D.: An Efficient Solution to the Five-Point Relative Pose Problem. PAMI 26(6), 756–770 (2004)

21. Sattler, T., Leibe, B., Kobbelt, L.: Improving Image-Based Localization by Active Correspondence Search. In: Fitzgibbon, A., Lazebnik, S., Perona, P., Sato, Y., Schmid, C. (eds.) ECCV 2012, Part I. LNCS, vol. 7572, pp. 752–765. Springer, Heidelberg (2012)
22. Sinha, S.N., Pollefeys, M.: Camera Network Calibration and Synchronization from Silhouettes in Archived Video. IJCV 87(3), 266–283 (2010)
23. Snavely, N., Seitz, S.M., Szeliski, R.: Photo tourism: Exploring photo collections in 3D. In: SIGGRAPH (2006)
24. Triggs, B.: Camera Pose and Calibration from 4 or 5 Known 3D Points. In: ICCV (1999)
25. Wu, C.: Towards Linear-Time Incremental Structure from Motion. In: 3DV (2013)

Author Index